THE SYNOPTIC GOSPELS

BIBLIOTHECA EPHEMERIDUM THEOLOGICARUM LOVANIENSIUM

CX

THE SYNOPTIC GOSPELS

SOURCE CRITICISM AND THE NEW LITERARY CRITICISM

EDITED BY

CAMILLE FOCANT

LEUVEN
UNIVERSITY PRESS

UITGEVERIJ PEETERS
LEUVEN

1993

CIP KONINKLIJKE BIBLIOTHEEK ALBERT I, BRUSSEL

ISBN 90 6186 543 3 (Leuven University Press)
D/1993/1869/19

ISBN 90 6831 493 9 (Uitgeverij Peeters)
D/1993/0602/46

ISBN 2-87723-064-3

© 1993 Leuven University Press/Presses Universitaires de Louvain
Universitaire Pers Leuven
Krakenstraat 3, B-3000 Leuven-Louvain (Belgium)

Uitgeverij Peeters, Bondgenotenlaan 153, B-3000 Leuven (Belgium)

PREFACE

The 41st session of the *Colloquium Biblicum Lovaniense* took place in August 18-20, 1992. Some 150 New Testament scholars, coming from the five continents, gathered in Leuven to scrutinize the Synoptic Gospels. It was not the first time that the Colloquium took interest in the Synoptic Gospels. In the late 1960s and the early 1970s sessions had been devoted to each of the four Gospels individually: the Synoptic Gospels (1965), Luke (1968), Matthew (1970), Mark (1971), John (1975). The question of the relations between John and the Synoptics was treated in 1990. At that meeting it became clear that more and more scholars think that John knew the Synoptics and even was literarily dependent on one or more of them. One of the conclusions was that the study of "John and the Synoptics" inevitably refers to the Synoptic problem. Therefore, it was decided to examine anew the Synoptic question. But another problem grafted itself on the first one and covered it partially, namely the confrontation of classic source-critical and redactional studies with the methods of the new literary criticism.

The meeting in 1992 coincided with the retirement of Professor Frans Neirynck, New Testament scholar in the University of Leuven and pillar of the *Colloquium Biblicum Lovaniense*. On August 18, during the homage session in the Promotion Hall of the University, F. Neirynck delivered his farewell lecture as opening lecture of the Colloquium.

The Colloquium was sponsored by the Faculties of Theology of Leuven and Louvain-la-Neuve and by the National Fund for Scientific Research (FNRS/NFWO, Brussels). As usual, we enjoyed the well appreciated hospitality of the Pope Adriaan VI College. May the volume retain something of the studious and friendly atmosphere which once again characterized the Colloquium Biblicum Lovaniense.

Special acknowledgements are due to Rita Corstjens and Yvette Nissen for preparing the manuscript of this volume.

Louvain-la-Neuve, November 15, 1992.   Camille FOCANT

CONTENTS

HOMAGE FRANS NEIRYNCK

THE SYNOPTIC GOSPELS

I
MAIN PAPERS

II
OFFERED PAPERS

INDEXES

HOMAGE FRANS NEIRYNCK

The 1992 Colloquium Biblicum Lovaniense began with the homage session for Frans Neirynck in the Promotion Hall of the University on August 18. This ceremony of homage was honoured by the presence of a number of special guests, including Cardinal G. Danneels and the bishops of the Flemish dioceses, Brugge, Antwerpen, Gent, Hasselt, as well as that of many of the collaborators to the Festschrift for F. Neirynck. The farewell lecture by Professor F. Neirynck was conceived as the opening lecture of the Colloquium: *Literary Criticism, Old and New*. J. DELOBEL, dean of the Faculty of Theology, lauded him, recalling the milestones of his academic career (*Professor F. Neirynck: 1960-1992*). The Festschrift was presented by two of the editors, F. VAN SEGBROECK (*Het Jubileumnummer BETL 100*) and C.M. TUCKETT (*The Four Gospels 1992. Festschrift for Professor F. Neirynck*).

Ce fut un honneur pour moi que la tâche m'ait été confiée, en tant que Président des Journées, d'introduire cette séance d'hommage. Le professeur F. Neirynck a été un travailleur infatigable et une des colonnes de base des Journées bibliques depuis le milieu des années 60. Il y est intervenu lors de pratiquement chacune des sessions consacrées au N.T. depuis 1965, comme on peut le voir dans la liste ci-dessous:

1965   La rédaction matthéenne et la structure du premier évangile.
1968   La matière marcienne dans l'évangile de Luc.
1970   The Gospel of Matthew and Literary Criticism.
1971   Duality in Mark: Duplicate Expressions in the Gospel of Mark.
—   Urmarcus redivivus? Examen critique de l'hypothèse des insertions matthéennes dans Marc.
1973   Jesus and the Sabbath: Some Observations on Mark II,27.
1975   John and the Synoptics.
1977   The Miracle Stories in the Acts of the Apostles.
1979   Marc 13: Examen critique de l'interprétation de R. Pesch.
1981   Recent Developments in the Study of Q.
1984   Paul and the Sayings of Jesus.
1986   The Apocryphal Gospels and the Gospel of Mark.
1990   John and the Synoptics: 1975-1990.

Comme on peut le constater, il y a surtout traité des Synoptiques ou de questions en rapport avec les Synoptiques, avec une prédominance dans son attention pour l'évangile de Marc. Aussi bien est-ce un témoignage de notre reconnaissance pour le labeur accompli que d'avoir choisi les évangiles synoptiques comme thème de nos débats à cette occasion.

Le texte de la leçon d'ouverture du professeur F. Neirynck est repris en tête du volume. Il a été dépouillé des mots de circonstance qui l'accompagnaient et qu'on pourra lire ici à la fin de son *Dankwoord*.

C. FOCANT

PROFESSOR F. NEIRYNCK: 1960-1992

Professor Frans Neirynck, die we vandaag huldigen bij gelegenheid van zijn emeritaat, staat sinds meer dan drie decennia in dienst van de Katholieke Universiteit te Leuven. Grondig wetenschappelijk onderzoek, hoogstaand academisch onderwijs, creatieve organisatie en krachtige leiding hebben zijn carrière gekenmerkt. Als decaan van de Faculteit der Godgeleerdheid wil ik het in mijn hulde vooral hebben over zijn bijdrage tot de uitbouw van de Faculteit en tot de promotie van de Katholieke Universiteit in een cruciale fase van hun geschiedenis. Ook zijn wetenschappelijk werk zal ik kort belichten, maar op dat punt zal ik straks aangevuld worden door de Professoren Van Segbroeck en Tuckett.

Aangezien deze hulde plaatsvindt in het kader van de opening van een internationaal congres, zult u mij toestaan het grootste deel van mijn toespraak in het Engels te houden, maar laat ik eerst nog wat in mijn moedertaal verdergaan, want zelfs Professor Neirynck is nationaal begonnen, regionaal zelfs, meer bepaald te Wingene in West-Vlaanderen. Hij werd er geboren op 15 mei 1927, en liep college te Tielt, een instelling die nog andere illustere figuren onder haar oudleerlingen telt. Na zijn priesterstudies te Brugge behaalde hij het doctoraat in de Godgeleerdheid te Leuven. Bij de verdediging van zijn proefschrift op 27 juni 1957 over *De Kindsheidsgeschiedenis in het evangelie van Lukas* behaalde hij de grootste onderscheiding. Het werk werd in 1959 bekroond door de Koninklijke Akademie, waarvan hij later zelf lid zou worden. Het was duidelijk dat hij in de exegese van het Nieuw Testament zijn ware roeping gevonden had. Een kort maar opgemerkt professoraat aan het Grootseminarie te Brugge vormde de overgang en in december 1960 volgde zijn benoeming tot titularis van de leerstoel Nieuw Testament aan de Theologische Faculteit als opvolger van Mgr. Albert Descamps. Leuven, waar zijn hart al was achtergebleven, werd nu voorgoed zijn nieuwe thuis. Het schijnt dat Westvlamingen noeste werkers zijn. Ik zou dat niet durven veralgemenen, maar niemand kan betwisten dat collega Neirynck die faam te volle verdient, zoals uit het vervolg van mijn verhaal zal blijken.

*

Today, Professor Frans Neirynck can look back on a career of more than thirty years as a professor in our Faculty of Theology. Upon his arrival in Leuven in 1960, several of his former professors became his colleagues: Coppens, Philips, Thils, Aubert and Van Roey. In addition to his task of teaching New Testament Exegesis at the Theological Faculty, the young professor was appointed as the secretary of the *Hoger Instituut voor Godsdienstwetenschappen* (Higher Institute of Religious Sciences), which prepares lay-students for the Licentiate in Religious Studies and most often for a function as teachers of religion. In those days, the job of secretary was slightly different from the present situation: no computers, no printers, no photocopiers, no female secretaries, but pure "handicraft" by one man: the professor-secretary who was responsible for the *Acta* of the Faculty, correspondence, study programs and examination results. When he became the academic secretary of the Faculty of Theology in 1965, the dean was Msgr. Joseph Coppens. This collaboration with Coppens was the continuation of a long personal contact as well as the basis for a continuing cooperation until Coppens' death in 1981. The job of an academic secretary is not always exciting but it is an excellent preparation for a more responsible task in the Faculty. One could expect that, sooner or later, he would be entrusted with the direction of the Faculty, but exceptional events hastened his election as dean.

1968 is a "magical" date in the history of Western Universities, and so it was for our Faculty as well, though for peculiar reasons. Already in 1966, the split of the University into two independent entities had been completed juridically: the "Katholieke Universiteit Leuven" and the "Université Catholique de Louvain". The French-speaking university decided to leave Leuven and to build a new campus at Ottignies, later Louvain-la-Neuve. Theology and Canon Law, with their particular status as "ecclesiastical faculties", directly dependent on the Rector Magnificus, and with Latin as the teaching language, were supposed to "transcend" the linguistic quarrels and to stay in Leuven. It was not very realistic, however, to create an "ecclesiastical island", and it was quite understandable that the French-speaking colleagues did not want to be cut off from the other faculties of their University. Their somewhat abrupt decision to renounce the special status and to join the U.C.L. forced the Flemish colleagues to an analogous decision. Frans Neirynck was elected as the first dean of the Dutch-speaking theological Faculty, a chance and a challenge at a crucial moment of our history.

The new dean was confronted with several basic and urgent questions. How to quickly find competent professors to replace the famous scholars who suddenly left? Where to find students to make up the decreasing numbers after the split of the Faculty? How to assure the international tradition of the Faculty at the moment that the foreign students thought of leaving Leuven? How to provide a scientific theological library after the absurd division of the world-famous University Library? Quite a job for the new dean, the academic secretary Professor M. Sabbe and their colleagues and collaborators. Important and risky decisions had to be made quickly. They were made, indeed, and we owe our lasting gratitude to the late rector Piet De Somer and the former administrator Guido Declercq for their active collaboration: both of them had a clear vision of the importance of the Theological Faculty in the heart of the Catholic University.

The following revolutionary solutions were given to the basic problems just mentioned. The integration of the *Hoger Instituut voor Godsdienstwetenschappen* and the *Centrum voor Kerkelijke Studies* (the Theological Institute for the religious orders) provided some eminent senior professors, a series of part-time lecturers and an impressive number of new students. For the first time, lay students were fully integrated into the Faculty, which opened for them the way to further study including the doctorate. For years now, the Faculty is culling the fruits of this '68 decision, in the form of excellent doctoral dissertations presented by young laymen and -women, a promising new generation for the church in this country and abroad.

The academic authorities understood the necessity of a theological library and approved an agreement with the Flemish province of the Jesuits. Their valuable collection of books from the modern and contemporary period was integrated and completed by the rich collection of ancient books from the Major Seminary of Malines. The marvellous new building – our theological laboratory, as we call it – was ready in 1974, and, at the present day, it offers more than 700.000 volumes and more than 1000 current periodicals in all the areas of theology and in several related fields. Whenever we enjoy working in "one of the most important theological libraries in the world" – to quote the appreciation of many scholars coming from abroad – we should never forget that the initial and basic decisions for this success-story have been taken and worked out by the "tandem" Neirynck-Sabbe.

And what about the international tradition of the Faculty, endangered by the possible departure of foreign students in '68? The American College, for more than a century the center for the pastoral formation of North-American seminarians who studied theology at the Faculty, was somewhat shaken by the split of the University. What would their future be, they wondered? They were happy to accept the suggestion of dean Neirynck to collaborate in the creation of a Theology Program in English which offered to their students a full theological formation including the doctoral degree. This unusual initiative, fully backed by the academic authorities, has been an example for most other Faculties who started offering English programs in some form. By this daring intitiative Frans Neirynck has proven that he had a vision for the future of the Faculty and the University. The program continues to florish after more than a quarter of a century and hundreds of students, priests, religious people, laymen and -women from all possible

English-speaking countries have obtained a Louvain degree. Numerous theological institutions and dioceses all over the world count alumni of the Faculty among their leading staff members. The collaboration with North America has been reinforced, but at the same time, the Faculty has become a house for third-world students, especially form Asia and Africa, to the benefit of the Christian communities in developing countries.

When I recall these events of the late sixties in some detail, it is not only to inform today's visitors, but also to refresh our own memory as Faculty members. Indeed, by forgetting the past, even the recent past, one can be very unfair towards those who have built it up. From this short survey of Neirynck's four year period as a dean, you will have understood that he gave to the new Faculty its own face and that he passed on to his successors a strong heritage as a safe basis for further construction. It is amazing that, despite all this time-consuming management, his scientific research has never been interrupted. Thanks to his strong health, his deeply rooted interest for exegesis and the full-time collaboration of his assistants, the end of his period as acting dean was immediately followed by a period of intensified scientific work.

Professor Frans Neirynck's teaching in our Faculty was characterized by exhaustiveness of documentation, clarity of orientation and speed of presentation. These characteristics, together with his familiarity with the Synopsis and the strictness of his methodology, made his teaching of New Testament Exegesis and Biblical Greek a breath-taking but enriching experience. As a promotor, he has been even more demanding, but to quote his last promovendus who defended his doctoral dissertation successfully a few weeks ago: "It has been a great honor and privilege to work with him". I am convinced that all his former thesis students, about seventy including myself, would agree with this deep appreciation.

In his exegesis, Neirynck has always been in line with the Louvain method of historical-critical analysis, but at the same time, his working hypothesis and results were clearly different from those of his own masters, Cerfaux and Descamps. The Gospels became his favoured field of study, and gradually, by the numerous articles he published, the working instruments he produced and the conference-papers he delivered, he became a worldwide known and respected defender of a strict but strongly argued two-source theory to explain agreements and differences between Matthew, Mark and Luke. Every one who attempts to promote or reanimate an alternative hypothesis (proto-Mark; proto-Luke; proto-Matthew; deutero-Mark; Markan posteriority; multiple-source theories) meets Neirynck on his or her way with a refutation which is based on an overall view on all the aspects of the problem, an overall knowledge of the literature concerning the topic and a strong argumentation for Markan priority and Q. His detailed studies of the classical *cruces* for the two-source theory, the duality in Mark and the minor agreements between Matthew and Luke against Mark, have resulted in doctoral dissertations under his guidance and the publication of comprehensive working instruments which no student of the synoptics can ignore.

The horizon was broadened when the Fourth Gospel was integrated in the research in a more systematic way. In Neirynck's view the Gospel of John is too often set apart from the synoptics and explained on the basis of an unknown peculiar tradition. When however the Fourth Gospel is carefully compared with the Synoptics, their close relationship becomes obvious, so that some form of literary dependence is probable. It has become a feature of the Louvain approach to defend John's dependence upon the Synoptics, a heavily debated hypothesis. Once again, Frans Neirynck produced his own exegesis in a scholarly debate with exegetes all over the world. I leave it to my colleagues to mention names and places.

The study of all these topics is being continued in a major research project under his direction, which involves several collaborators. If there has been in recent decades a "Louvain School" in the field of New Testament exegesis which enjoys international esteem, Neirynck is certainly its father, not only by his teaching and publishing, but also by his constant care for the yearly *Colloquium Biblicum Lovaniense*, a tradition founded in 1949, the *Ephemerides Theologicae Lovanienses* and the *Bibliotheca Ephemeridum Theologicarum Lovaniensium*, three Louvain "institutions" which are closely related with his name and his career. His international recognition was sealed by his election as the President for 1989 of the *Studiorum Novi Testamenti Societas*, the prestigious international organisation for exegetes of the New Testament, to which he belongs as a longtime and faithful member.

Since 1972, when his period as acting dean came to an end, Frans Neirynck continued to devote himself in many other ways to the Faculty and the University. Because of his scientific work, it was obvious that he should become a member of the *Onderzoeksraad* of the University. For several years, he also directed the *Commissie voor Publikaties* of the University: a logical appointment taking into account the 274 entries in his own publication list. Together with professors Peremans, Verbeke and Van Roey, he founded the Center for Hellenism and Christianity, which became the editor of the *Series Graeca* of the *Corpus Christianorum*. But he has also been our ambassador for the scientific relations *ad extra*. In 1972, at his initiative and with the support of the Rector, the *Nationaal Fonds voor Wetenschappelijk Onderzoek* (National Fund for Scientific Research) started a special *Committee for Theology and Religious Sciences*. He continuously acted as a member since and, thanks to that committee, young scholars in the field of theology have obtained equal chances to receive a scholarship for scientific research. In 1980, he was appointed as a corresponding member of the *Koninklijke Akademie voor Wetenschappen, Letteren en Schone Kunsten* (the Royal Academy of Sciences, Letters and Fine Arts). In 1988 he became a "working member" and in 1992 Vice-chairman of the Class of Letters.

This brief survey of a Louvain career of over 30 years may have illustrated that Frans Neirynck has not only been a scholar with an impressive scientific production, as my colleagues will show in more detail, but also a manager and a leader who has laid the foundation of the Flemish-English Faculty of Theology and contributed in many ways to the national and international reputation of the Catholic University. We, his students and his colleagues, owe him our deepest gratitude.

J. DELOBEL

HET JUBILEUMNUMMER BETL 100

Het is voor mij een eer u namens de editors van de Feestbundel die op het einde van deze huldezitting aan professor Frans Neirynck zal aangeboden worden, te mogen begroeten. Over de inhoud, de hoofdlijnen en het belang van de bijdragen in het driedelig werk zal co-editor professor Christopher Tuckett zo dadelijk handelen. Sta me toe dat ik iets zeg over de genese van het Festschrift en zijn plaats in de prestigieuze reeks "Bibliotheca Ephemeridum Theologicarum Lovaniensium", waarvan het het 100ste deel is, een waardig jubileumnummer.

*

In the spring of 1990 an idea that had slumbered for some time in the backs of our minds took definite shape: the publication of a Festschrift on the occasion of Professor Neirynck's elevation to the status of *emeritus*, as a token of esteem for his great scientific contribution to gospel studies and in recognition of a professorship of more than thirty years. A conversation on the subject with the Jubilarian made it clear that he was not adverse to giving the undertaking a wider significance: a broad international discussion by specialists on the present state of affairs in gospel studies. Thus was the title born: *The Four Gospels 1992*. Undoubtedly, this might evoke thoughts of Streeter's *The Four Gospels* (1924), a work that has been so influential for the study of the gospels. "1992" in the title is intended to anchor the Festschrift in its time, with an eye to the Europe of 1992. From this perspective colleagues were informed about the project and requested to participate. One hundred twenty-five scholars from home and abroad signaled their agreement without hesitation and with great enthusiasm, and went on to mention how honored they were to be able to contribute to this "homage" for (and I quote a few) "den hoch geschätzten Kollegen", "whose scholarship is simply without parallel", "der so Grundlegendes für die Evangelienforschung geleistet hat", "who has made a very important contribution to the ongoing discussion of the Synoptic Gospels". Or, as a voice from South Africa put it so splendidly in that bewitchingly exotic Afrikaans: "Ek sou graag wou deelneem aangezien ek hoë agting het vir ons kollega". Those invited who, for one reason or another, were not able to contribute to the publication, did not neglect to express their esteem and appreciation for the initiative with even more impressive terms. And, I should like to give special mention to two deceased colleagues: Professor Barnabas Lindars, who died shortly after sending us his contribution for the Festschrift, and Professor Robert Guelich, whose sudden entry into heaven in 1991 super-seded his promised study on "Jesus' Entry into Jerusalem".

Thus the Festschrift – originally conceived as a two-volume work – grew into a rather hefty three volumes that can deservedly be called a panorama of present-day gospel studies. Of the 125 articles, 65 are in English, 35 in German, and 25 in French. The field of participants displays a multifarious and variegated cohort. To expressly consolidate this international stamp, our colleague Christopher Tuckett, of the University of Manchester and secretary of the "Studiorum Novi Testamenti Societas", was invited and found to be quite willing to join the board of editors. I thank him sincerely for the preparedness and wisdom with which he so readily rendered his collaboration.

*

Het leek de editors vanzelfsprekend dat het Festschrift F. Neirynck zou verschijnen in de door hem geleide reeks van de "Bibliotheca Ephemeridum Theologicarum Lovaniensium". Was het toeval, samen-loop van omstandigheden – of, zoals men het vroeger graag uitdrukte, de voorzienigheid? – dat het geplande Festschrift het honderdste num-mer zou worden, een jubileumnummer, hoogtepunt van een reeks die sinds lang een verdiende faam geniet tot ver buiten de landsgrenzen.

Editorship is een veeleisende, tijdrovende, verborgen activiteit waar-mee meestal niet veel eer te behalen valt. De taak is zo bescheiden dat onze Nederlandse taal er zelfs geen eigen woord voor heeft. Voor professor Neirynck is editorship een belangrijk deel van zijn activiteiten van de laatste jaren geweest sinds hij in 1972 het redactiesecretariaat van de BETL-reeks overnam van Mgr. Joseph Coppens. Deze had de reeks in 1947 gestart als een bibliotheek waarin voornamelijk separate herdrukken verschenen van artikelen uit de *Ephemerides Theologicae Lovanienses*. In die reeks verschenen enkele Festschriften (A. Bittre-mieux, A. Jansen, G. Ryckmans), recueils met vroegere artikelen (L. Cerfaux), en monografieën. Uitzonderlijk werden er ook de referaten in ondergebracht van het jaarlijkse Colloquium Biblicum: *Sacra Pagina*, van het jaar van de wereldtentoonstelling te Brussel in 1958, en de drie delen met de referaten van 1967, 1968 en 1969, die samen het etiket "Hommage J. Coppens" meekregen als huldeblijk aan de medestichter van de Bijbelse Studiedagen.

Toen F. Neirynck in 1972 Coppens opvolgde, kreeg de reeks een nieuwe impuls. De Bibliotheca werd van dan af de vaste thuishaven van de jaarlijkse verslagboeken van de Bijbelse Studiedagen, verslagboeken die intussen uitgegroeid zijn tot het vlaggeschip van een hele vloot. Net zoals de Studiedagen zelf werden de verslagboeken op een hoger technisch niveau gebracht, en door het gebruik van internationale talen, Engels, Frans en Duits, voor een ruimer publiek van buiten de landsgrenzen toegankelijk gemaakt. Het *Colloquium Biblicum Lovaniense* en de verslagboeken in de BETL-reeks zijn intussen een begrip en een kwaliteitslabel in de exegetische wereld geworden. De talrijke recensenten van de elkaar in bewonderenswaardige regelmaat opvolgende delen aarzelen niet om te spreken van "un modello di rigore e precizione scientifica". En dat is voor het grootste deel te danken aan de nooit aflatende zorg waarmee de "general editor" elk nieuw manuscript ter hand – of mag ik zeggen: onder handen – neemt. Wat hijzelf in 1981 schreef over zijn voorganger, geldt in nog hogere mate voor hemzelf: "Tout en reconnaissant le travail des rédacteurs des différents volumes, je crois pouvoir dire que J. Coppens fut véritablement l'éditeur de la série". We hoeven enkel de naam J. Coppens te vervangen door die van F. Neirynck. Door de recensenten wordt haast zonder uitzondering met grote lof onder meer melding gemaakt van de overvloedige en betrouwbare indices die de toegankelijkheid van de publikaties in niet geringe mate verhogen.

Tijdens de twintig jaren van Neiryncks editorship werden in de Series Secunda zeventig boekdelen gepubliceerd: 18 verslagboeken van de Bijbelse Studiedagen, 7 Festschriften, 11 recueils met de verzamelde studies van binnen- en buitenlandse eminente collega's, zoals Mgr. A. Descamps, Dom J. Dupont, Professor G.D. Kilpatrick, om er slechts enkele te noemen. En ten slotte nog 27 monografieën waarvan 12 in het Engels, 14 in het Frans en 1 in het Nederlands. Dertien titelpagina's vermelden de naam F. Neirynck als auteur, co-auteur, editor of inleider, wat voldoende de eigen inbreng van de jubilaris in de reeks illustreert. Zijn eigen werken nemen in de BETL-reeks een vooraanstaande plaats in. De Series Secunda werd in 1972 geopend met *Duality in Mark*, een werk waarvan het fundamenteel belang voor de studie van het Marcusevangelie onmiddellijk werd erkend en geprezen, en dat intussen reeds een tweede oplage kende. Twee jaar later verscheen *The Minor Agreements of Matthew and Luke against Mark* (1974), gewijd aan de overeenkomsten tussen Matteüs en Lucas tegen Marcus, een werk dat ontegenzeggelijk aan de basis ligt van de actuele vernieuwde aandacht voor dit probleem. *Jean et les Synoptiques* (1979), in kritische dialoog met de pas verschenen Johannescommentaar van M.-É. Boismard, verdedigde de stelling dat de synoptische evangeliën aan de basis liggen van het vierde evangelie. Ook dit werd de aanzet tot een vernieuwde beschouwing van dit probleem en zelfs tot een groeiende consensus rond de door Neirynck verdedigde stelling. *New Testament Vocabulary* (1984) is een werkinstrument, onmisbaar als aanvulling bij de gebruikelijke Concordantie voor de studie van het synoptisch vocabulaire. In deze opsomming kan men natuurlijk niet voorbijgaan aan de bundels *Evangelica I* (1982) en *Evangelica II* (1991), de nummers 60 en 99 in de BETL-reeks, waarin de wetenschappelijke produktie van de jaren 1960 tot 1990, neergelegd in opmerkelijke artikelen, in twee volumineuze banden werd bijeengebracht. *Evangelica I* en *II* hebben de faam van de Leuvense nieuwtestamenticus voorgoed gevestigd, voor zover dat al niet veel vroeger gebeurd was.

The Four Gospels 1992 is een waardig jubileumnummer, een hoogtepunt in de BETL-reeks, maar het is geen eindpunt. Drie delen van de Series Tertia zijn intussen reeds verschenen (nrs. 101, 102, 103), waaronder een indrukwekkende bibliografie op het Marcusevangelie over de jaren 1950 tot 1990, terwijl een tiental andere in voorbereiding zijn.

Bij de huldiging van de algemene editor, en bij het memoreren van het honderdste nummer van de reeks, past een bijzonder woord van waardering en dank voor de publishers van de BETL-reeks, Leuven University Press, die we hier begroeten in de persoon van de voorzitter, professor H. Van der Wee, de Éditions Duculot die de reeks verzorgden tot 1979, en de Uitgeverij Peeters (Drukkerij Orientaliste) die vanaf 1980 met gerenommeerd vakmanschap instond voor druk, uitgave en distributie. Sta me toe in dit verband een buitenlandse, dus objectieve, stem te laten horen: "Bei der heutigen Krise der Buchkultur kann man nur hoffen, dass die Bände der Colloquia Lovaniensia weiterhin ihre graphisch und drucktechnisch ansprechende Gestalt behalten". Die hoop werd uitgesproken in 1980, bij het verschijnen van nr. 48. Ik meen dat de meer dan 50 delen die intussen verschenen zijn die verwachting voldoende hebben waargemaakt. Ik wil de Heer en Mevrouw Peeters en hun bekwame medewerkers hiervoor uitdrukkelijk feliciteren, en ook danken voor de vlotte en aangename samenwerking gedurende de voorbije maanden.

Dank ook aan de gewaardeerde medewerkers aan *The Four Gospels 1992*. Het was aangenaam samenwerken met zo'n groot aantal eminente collega's die voorbeeldig de gegeven richtlijnen volgden en zonder protest de editoriële ingrepen accepteerden. Is er wellicht niet altijd orthodoxie in de exegetische wereld, discipline is er des te meer.

Een woord van erkentelijkheid ook voor de co-editors, voor professor C.M. Tuckett en voor Gilbert Van Belle en Jos Verheyden, die de uitgave hielpen voorbereiden en de vele honderden bladzijden drukproeven vaak en accuraat hebben doorgenomen en met grote zorg de indices hebben helpen samenstellen, en voor Rita Corstjens en Marc van Rooij, die met deskundigheid de vaak weerbarstige teksten op de computerschijven wisten te persen.

En U, Professor Neirynck, dank ik voor de stimulerende aandacht die u voor *The Four Gospels 1992* hebt gehad. Indien het waar is – en het is waar – dat er u op het gebied van de evangeliestudie, waar ook ter wereld, niet veel ontsnapt, hoe zou dan deze onderneming hier in uw eigen Faculteit voor u verborgen hebben kunnen blijven? Maar die aandacht is zeer vruchtbaar gebleken en heeft ons meer dan eens geholpen. Moge *The Four Gospels 1992* een waardige bekroning zijn voor uw jarenlange inzet voor de evangeliestudie en voor de door u zo voortreffelijk geleide BETL-reeks.

F. Van Segbroeck

THE FOUR GOSPELS 1992
FESTSCHRIFT FOR PROFESSOR F. NEIRYNCK

In introducing this Festschrift to be presented to Professor Frans Neirynck*, I must first of all pay tribute to my fellow editors – Professors Van Segbroeck, Van Belle and Verheyden – since it is they who have shouldered all the hard grind of editorial work to prepare these three volumes to be ready today. The size of this Festschrift is quite enormous: 125 articles spread over more than 2500 pages. The deadline for authors' contributions was January of this year (and NT scholars do not always meet their deadlines!). The editorial task of sub-editing all these essays for publication, of checking and re-checking, reading and re-reading all the proofs, preparing indices, bibliographies etc., would be an enormous undertaking at any time. To complete the whole process within eight months represents a quite outstanding achievement.

We are however here today to celebrate a different achievement, namely, the climax (in one sense) of Professor Neirynck's career as a NT scholar as he becomes Emeritus Professor in this University of Leuven. The publication of a Festschrift to mark such an event is not an unheard-of occurrence; but I am not aware of many Festschriften of this size that have been assembled. I have already mentioned the extent of this three-volume Festschrift: 125 articles covering over 2500 printed pages. The very size of the whole project, the number of scholars from all over the world who wished to contribute to the Festschrift, and the extent of each individual contribution, are all tribute far more eloquent than anything I can say to the esteem and and honour which is accorded to Professor Frans Neirynck by the world of international New Testament scholarship.

In surveying this Festschrift briefly today, it is of course quite impossible to mention every single contribution or author. I can only point to a few of the essays, and I have chosen to try to refer to some of those which relate more directly to Professor Neirynck's own work. But all the contributions are, I believe, worthy tributes to Professor Neirynck's scholarship. The title of the Festschrift is *The Four Gospels 1992*, reflecting Professor Neirynck's scholarly concern throughout his academic career which has been to focus primarily (though by no

---

* The Festschrift was presented to Professor F. Neirynck on August 18, 1992, at the opening session of the 41st Colloquium Biblicum Lovaniense, in the Promotion Hall of the University.

means exclusively) on the gospels of the New Testament and the critical problems which they evoke.

Within synoptic studies, Frans Neirynck's name is always associated with his work on the Synoptic Problem and related topics. He has been a staunch defender of the Two-Source Theory, arguing rigorously and powerfully for the theory of Markan priority and the existence of a Q source. Many of his most valuable contributions have been detailed critical analyses of alternative source theories[1]. Within the broad parameters of the Two-Source Theory, Professor Neirynck has consistently maintained what I might call a strictly "economic" explanation of the pattern of synoptic agreements, by showing that so much of the evidence can be adequately and satisfactorily explained by the redactional activity of the evangelists. His programmatic studies on *Duality in Mark* and *The Minor Agreements of Matthew and Luke against Mark*[2] have become classic statements of the theories that (a) "duality" is a feature of Mark's own style and needs no theory of overlapping pre-Markan sources to explain it; and (b) the problematic minor agreements between Matthew and Luke can all be satisfactorily explained as due to Matthean and Lukan redaction of Mark. This overall interest in the Synoptic Problem and its related problems is reflected in many of the contributions in the Festschrift with essays on the Synoptic Problem and its potential repercussions and/or background by J.S. Kloppenborg and W.R. Farmer, on the Synoptic Problem itself and the problems of Markan priority and Q (J.D.G. Dunn, R.H. Gundry, T.A. Friedrichsen, M.-É. Boismard), on some of the minor agreements including the troublesome Mark 14,65 and parallels (on which Neirynck himself has made such an important contribution[3]) (M.E. Boring, on the Beelzebul pericope; T.A. Friedrichsen, on the parable of the mustard seed; A. Vanhoye, on Lk 22,60-65). So too Neirynck's work on duality in Mark, which has been so decisive in shifting attention away from the possible existence of overlapping pre-Markan traditions to focusing on Mark's own redactional concerns, is reflected in essays here (C. Focant, on the feeding narratives; J. Delorme, on the healing of the epileptic). Indeed the enormous interest in the Gospel of Mark as a whole is striking. Professor E. Best starts his own essay here with the sentence: "From the amount of material he has written on the Gospel of Mark I take it that Mark is

---

1. See for example many of his articles in his two volumes of collected essays *Evangelica* (BETL, 60), Leuven, 1982, and *Evangelica II* (BETL, 99), Leuven, 1991.

2. *Duality in Mark. Contributions to the Study of Markan Redaction* (BETL, 31), Leuven, 1972; revised edition with supplementary notes, Leuven, 1988; *The Minor Agreements of Matthew and Luke against Mark* (with T. Hansen and F. Van Segbroeck) (BETL, 37), Leuven, 1974.

3. ΤΙΣ ΕΣΤΙΝ Ο ΠΑΙΣΑΣ ΣΕ: *Mt 26,68 / Lk 22,64 (diff. Mk 14,65)*, in *ETL* 63 (1987) 5-47; = *Evangelica II*, 95-138.

Frans Neirynck's favourite Gospel as it is mine" (p. 839). The presence of 25 essays in this Festschrift covering an enormous variety of aspects of Markan study reflects that interest.

It would however be totally misleading to suggest that Professor Neirynck has been narrow in his interests. His doctoral dissertation in 1957 was on the Lukan infancy narratives and he published a number of studies on this topic[4]. The interest is reflected here too in the contributions of B. Koet (on Simeon's words) and M. Wilcox (on the significance of Anna in Luke's story). Professor Neirynck has also always taken a keen interest in literary-critical problems as well as the older-style Literarkritik. One of his earliest published essays was on Matthew's redaction and the structure of the Gospel of Matthew (1967)[5], which was followed by other studies including in 1988 another long article of the problems of the structure of Matthew and the possible significance of the phrase ἀπὸ τότε ἤρξατο, about which much has been written[6]. Such concerns are reflected in this Festschrift too with 13 essays devoted to the Gospel of Matthew and at least four of these attempting to deal in some way or other with the issue of the structure of Matthew's Gospel as well as its literary genre (see the contributions of G.N. Stanton, D.C. Allison, B. Standaert, D. Dormeyer).

Professor Neirynck's work on the Synoptic Problem has inevitably led him into the area of Q studies. He has published a number of studies on the origins of the name of the so-called "Q" source, on various individual Q texts (or possible Q texts!) and a valuable *Q-Synopsis* (1988)[7]. Perhaps his most important contribution has been his comprehensive survey article "Recent Developments in the Study of Q", delivered to the 1981 Leuven Colloquium[8]. For those working

---

4. *De kindsheidgeschiedenis in het Lukasevangelie*, diss. Leuven, 1957.

5. *La rédaction matthéenne et la structure du premier Évangile*, in I. DE LA POTTERIE (ed.), *De Jésus aux évangiles. Tradition et rédaction dans les évangiles synoptiques. Donum natalicium J. Coppens II* (BETL, 25), Gembloux, 1967, 41-73; = *Evangelica*, 3-35.

6. ΑΠΟ ΤΟΤΕ ΗΡΞΑΤΟ *and the Structure of Matthew*, in *ETL* 64 (1988) 21-59; = *Evangelica II*, 141-182.

7. Cf. *The Symbol Q (= Quelle)*, in *ETL* 54 (1978) 119-125; = *Evangelica*, 683-689; *Once More: The Symbol Q*, in *ETL* 55 (1979) 382-383; = *Evangelica*, 689-690; *Note on the Siglum Q*, in *Evangelica II*, 474. Among other articles, cf. *Mt 12,25a / Lk 11,17a et la rédaction des évangiles*, in *ETL* 62 (1986) 122-133; = *Evangelica II*, 481-492; *A Synopsis of Q*, in *ETL* 64 (1988) 441-449; = *Evangelica II*, 465-474; *Q^Mt and Q^Lk and the Reconstruction of Q*, in *ETL* 66 (1990) 385-390; = *Evangelica II*, 475-480; *Luke 14,1-6: Lukan Composition and Q Saying*, in C. BUSSMANN - W. RADL (eds.), *Der Treue Gottes trauen. Beiträge zum Werk des Lukas für Gerhard Schneider*, Freiburg, 1991, 243-263; = *Evangelica II*, 183-203. Also *Q-Synopsis. The Double Tradition Passages in Greek* (SNTA, 13), Leuven, 1988.

8. *Recent Developments in the Study of Q*, in J. DELOBEL (ed.), *Logia. Les Paroles de Jésus – The Sayings of Jesus* (BETL, 59), Leuven, 1982, 29-75; = *Evangelica II*, 409-464.

within the parameters of the Two-Source Theory, Q studies have of course mushroomed in recent years, with much attention focused on the possible tradition history of the Q tradition itself, on the problem of the genre of Q, on the specific theological and Christological characteristics of the Q tradition, on the possible Sitz im Leben of a Q "community" which may have been responsible for the preservation of Q, etc. A whole section of the Festschrift, with 15 essays, is devoted to the Sayings Source Q with many of the essays having these concerns very much in mind (e.g., J.M. Robinson; D. Zeller, on the genre of Q; A.D. Jacobson, on apocalyptic in Q; P. Hoffmann, on Son of Man in Q) as well as analyzing individual pericopes in Q (C.M. Tuckett, on the temptation story; D.R. Catchpole, on the centurion's servant; H. Schürmann, on the material in Q 11,14-36). It is often said that such work represents the height of folly, building hypothesis upon hypothesis in a totally unverifiable way. It is perhaps due to the solid exegetical work of scholars such as Frans Neirynck that those of us engaged in such work can feel assured that the basis of this work, the belief in the existence of some sort of Q source, is not simply a hypothetical invention of modern scholarship.

One other feature of Neirynck's work which should also be mentioned here is his work on textual criticism. A series of articles over a number of years has provided the scholarly world with vast amounts of information enabling others to see, for example, precisely where editions of the Greek New Testament and/or Synopses of the Gospels differ from each other and what effect this might have on theories of source relationships, etc.[9]. Not unrelated has been his work analyzing concordances, as well as the publication of his own *New Testament Vocabulary*[10]. Textual criticism is represented in this Festschrift in articles by B. Aland (on early papyri) and J.K. Elliott (on the influence of the text in various printed Synopses on the Synoptic Problem).

A feature of Professor Neirynck's work in his earlier period was an interest in the gospels' accounts of the empty tomb and resurrection narratives. His first main paper to the international Society for New Testament Studies (Professor Neirynck is almost unique in having been invited to deliver no less than four papers to the Society over the years, including an address as President of the Society in 1989) was on the

---

9. See, for example, *The Synoptic Gospels according to the New Textus Receptus*, in *ETL* 52 (1976) 364-379; = *Evangelica*, 883-898; *The New Nestle-Aland: The Text of Mark in N²⁶*, in *ETL* 55 (1979) 331-356; = *Evangelica*, 899-924; *Greeven's Text of the Synoptic Gospels*, in *ETL* 58 (1982) 123-134; = *Evangelica II*, 377-388; *Le texte des évangiles dans la Synopse de Boismard-Lamouille*, in *ETL* 63 (1987) 119-135; = *Evangelica II*, 389-405.

10. *New Testament Vocabulary. A Companion Volume to the Concordance* (with F. Van Segbroeck) (BETL, 65), Leuven, 1984. Other articles include *La nouvelle Concordance du Nouveau Testament*, in *ETL* 52 (1976) 134-142 and 323-345; = *Evangelica*, 955-1002.

Matthean story of the women at the tomb, and indeed a whole section of his first volume of collected essays *Evangelica* (1982) was entitled "The Empty Tomb Stories" (pp. 181-488) covering over 300 pages and containing 13 important articles. So too here in this Festschrift, we have a contribution from Professor Neirynck's former pupil, D. Senior, on Matthew's account of the burial of Jesus.

However, this focus on the empty tomb narratives has a far wider significance in Professor Neirynck's work. The vast bulk of Neirynck's essays are concerned with the relationship between the empty tomb / resurrection narratives in John and their parallels in the synoptics. It is here that Professor Neirynck has perhaps made his most significant contribution alongside his work on the Synoptic Problem and synoptic redaction by arguing that John's gospel is dependent on the synoptics. This has involved publication of a large number of individual studies (especially on the empty tomb narratives) as well as a full-length monograph *Jean et les Synoptiques*, which takes the form of a critical conversation with the work of M.-É. Boismard. Neirynck and Boismard having been (very friendly!) sparring partners on a number of occasions and over a number of years on this topic[11]. The section of his articles in *Evangelica* entitled "The Empty Tomb Stories" is (appropriately!) sub-titled "John and the Synoptics", and several articles in his second collection *Evangelica II* continue the theme. Professor Neirynck has influenced many, and indeed one now sometimes talks of a "Leuven school" on this topic. The subject was the theme of the 1990 Leuven Colloquium, devoted to study of the question "John and the Synoptics", at which Professor Neirynck's own survey of the whole question was characteristically masterful and showed clearly how much scholarly opinion has shifted over the last 15-20 years in favour of the view of John's dependence on the synoptics[12]. It is then not surprising that a large number of contributions to this Festschrift have taken up this topic in various ways, inspired by Neirynck's work. The section on the Gospel of John contains 25 essays, no less than 11 of which deal in some way or other with the problem of the relationship between John and the Synoptics. It is perhaps fair to say that not all have "seen the light" and accepted the theory of Johannine dependence on the synoptics. (Some indeed of the contributors to this Festschrift remain "here-

---

11. *Jean et les Synoptiques. Examen critique de l'exégèse de M.-É. Boismard* (with J. Delobel, T. Snoy, G. Van Belle, F. Van Segbroeck) (BETL, 49), Leuven, 1979. Among his many detailed studies on the topic, one may refer to the two volumes of collected essays, noting especially his *John and the Synoptics*, in M. DE JONGE (ed.), *L'évangile de Jean. Sources, rédaction, théologie* (BETL, 44), Leuven, 1977, 73-106; = *Evangelica*, 365-400; *John and the Synoptics: The Empty Tomb Stories*, in *NTS* (1984) 161-187; = *Evangelica II*, 571-599, and his SNTS Presidential Address *John 21*, in *NTS* 36 (1990) 321-336; = *Evangelica II*, 601-616.

12. *John and the Synoptics: 1975-1990*, in A. DENAUX (ed.), *John and the Synoptics* (BETL, 101), Leuven, 1992, 3-62.

tics"!). Nevertheless the sea-change which has taken place over this whole question in recent years is due above all to Professor Neirynck's work and the work of many associated with him and with this University of Leuven.

I would like to mention two other areas in which Professor Neirynck's work has been influential and which are represented in this Festschrift. At the 1984 Leuven Colloquium, Professor Neirynck gave a magisterial paper on "Paul and the Sayings of Jesus"[13]. The problem of the relationship between Jesus tradition reflected in the Pauline letters and possible parallels in the synoptic tradition has been a perennial one, bearing in mind the fact that the Pauline evidence gives us a window into the development of the tradition prior to the redactional activity of the synoptic evangelists. As with the Synoptic Problem, Professor Neirynck offers a strictly "economic" solution, refusing to see conscious use of Jesus traditions in several alleged allusions in Paul, and being somewhat sceptical about whether the Pauline evidence witnesses to the existence of pre-synoptic sources. Others in this Festschrift have taken up aspects of the problem, for example C. März, C. Breytenbach and W. Schenk, and Professor Neirynck's influence can be clearly seen here.

The other area that should be mentioned concerns the Reception of the Gospels, an area which is covered by a whole section of this Festschrift. Professor Neirynck's work in this area is represented primarily by another magisterial Colloquium paper, "The Apocryphal Gospels and the Gospel of Mark", delivered at the 1986 Colloquium[14]. The view that virtually all the apocryphal gospel literature does indeed represent reception of our canonical gospels, and is not witness to independent gospel traditions, or to pre-redactional stages of the tradition, has been a strong feature of Leuven scholarship for many years. This view was propounded in classic form by É. Massaux (whose famous study on the influence of the Gospel of Matthew on later Christian literature was reissued with a Foreword by Professor Neirynck in 1986)[15], and one may think of a "Leuven school" in relation to this issue, just as in the area of John and the Synoptics. In this Festschrift, I would refer especially to the essays of D. Lührmann on Papyrus Egerton 2 and and B. Dehandschutter on the Gospel of

13. *Paul and the Sayings of Jesus*, in A. VANHOYE (ed.), *L'Apôtre Paul. Personnalité, style, et conception du ministère* (BETL, 73), Leuven, 1986, 265-321; = *Evangelica II*, 511-568.

14. *The Apocryphal Gospels and the Gospel of Mark*, in J.M. SEVRIN (ed.), *The New Testament in Early Christianity* (BETL, 86), Leuven, 1989, 123-175; = *Evangelica II*, 715-772.

15. É. MASSAUX, *Influence de l'évangile de saint Matthieu sur la littérature chrétienne avant saint Irénée*, reissued with Foreword by F. Neirynck (BETL, 75), Leuven, 1986.

Thomas as continuing in this same tradition; however, the section in the Festschrift on the Reception of the Gospels contains 18 essays in all, ranging very widely in their coverage and not all can be mentioned here.

As others have already mentioned, Frans Neirynck's name is renowned for his breadth of scholarship, for his massive knowledge and mastery of secondary literature on almost every topic in NT studies, and for his brilliant analytic mind. His enthusiasm for his subject never seems to wane and there is little that escapes his critical eye. His responses to published works are at times also extremely fast.

All will be aware of the fact that in current New Testament scholarship there is no such thing as a universally agreed theory. Frans Neirynck's critical analyses of differing theories is clear testimony to that. I have already hinted at the fact that not every contribution to this Festschrift is quite in line with the Neirynck view. If the past is anything to go by, we may look forward to incisive responses to these – probably in the very near future! Yet it is surely a mark of greatness within the world of Biblical scholarship that one's views are taken seriously, seriously enough at times to involve detailed discussion and perhaps different conclusions. Without that critical debate with each other, our discipline will die, and Frans Neirynck himself has been one of the leading figures in this respect who has ensured that our discipline remains alive and well. Yet that dialogue has always to take place in an atmosphere of friendship and mutual respect. Frans Neirynck's own person and indeed the existence of this series of Leuven Colloquia to which he has contributed so much by way of inspiration and leadership as well as classic lectures/articles, have ensured that that atmosphere has always been maintained here.

We hope that this three-volume collection of essays will provide Professor Neirynck with some enjoyable reading. As I said, I am sure it will provide the basis for at least five articles in response! We offer it to him in grateful recognition of his many rich contributions to the world of New Testament scholarship over many years, with thanks for the inspiration he has given to us all. We wish him a long and happy retirement and we look forward with anticipation to the many and varied fruits which I am sure will emerge from the greater freedom he will now enjoy as Emeritus Professor of the University of Leuven.

C.M. TUCKETT

F. Van Segbroeck - C.M. Tuckett - G. Van Belle - J. Verheyden (eds.)
The Four Gospels 1992. Festschrift Frans Neirynck (BETL, 100).
Leuven, University Press - Uitgeverij Peeters, 1992.

Volume I: xviii, 1-690 p. – Preliminary Part (1-89).

Part I, *The Gospel(s)*: B. Aland, K. Berger, R. Bieringer, B.D. Chilton, A.B. du Toit, J.K. Elliott, B. Gerhardsson, M.D. Hooker, J.S. Kloppenborg, S. Légasse, W. Schmithals, G. Strecker, A. Suhl, F. Vouga (91-357).

Part II, *The Sayings Source Q*: M.E. Boring, D. Catchpole, J.A. Fitzmyer, H. Fleddermann, T.A. Friedrichsen, P. Hoffmann, A.D. Jacobson, A. Lindemann, C.-P. März, J.M. Robinson, J. Schlosser, H. Schürmann, C.M. Tuckett, N. Walter, D. Zeller (359-688).

Volume II: x, 691-1719 p.

Part III, *The Gospel of Mark*: E. Best, M.-É. Boismard, C. Breytenbach, A.Y. Collins, G. Dautzenberg, J. Delorme, J.R. Donahue, E.E. Ellis, C. Focant, C.H. Giblin, M.D. Goulder, K. Hanhart, W. Kirchschläger, H. Merklein, C. Minette de Tillesse, B. Orchard, N.R. Petersen, V.K. Robbins, P. Rolland, W. Schenk, E. Schweizer, W.R. Telford, B.M.F. van Iersel, G. Van Oyen, J. Verheyden (691-1183)

Part IV, *The Gospel of Matthew*: D.C. Allison, T. Baarda, I. Broer, C.E. Carlston, R.F. Collins, D. Dormeyer, J.D.G. Dunn, R.A. Edwards, D.J. Harrington, R. Pesch, D. Senior, B. Standaert, G.N. Stanton (1185-1448)

Part V, *The Gospel of Luke*: C.K. Barrett, A. Dauer, J. Delobel, V. Fusco, M. Gourgues, R.H. Gundry, L. Hartman, J.D. Kingsbury, B. Koet, D.P. Moessner, R.A. Piper, H. Räisänen, R.C. Tannehill, A. Vanhoye, M. Wilcox (1449-1716)

Volume III: x, 1721-2668 p. – Indexes (2543-2668).

Part VI, *The Gospel of John*: G.R. Beasley-Murray, P. Borgen, U. Busse, M. de Jonge, G.D. Fee, E.D. Freed, S. Freyne, P.J. Judge, D.-A. Koch, J. Kremer, B. Lindars, M.J.J. Menken, J. Painter, E. Ruckstuhl, M. Sabbe, R. Schnakkenburg, G. Schneider, U. Schnelle, D.M. Smith, J. Smit Sibinga, H. Thyen, É. Trocmé, G. Van Belle, W.S. Vorster, J. Zumstein (1721-2221).

Part VII, *The Reception of the Gospels*: E. Brito, M. Carrez, A. de Halleux, B. Dehandschutter, H.J. de Jonge, J. Étienne, W.R. Farmer, A. Haquin, J. Helderman, R. Kieffer, H.-J. Klauck, L. Leloir, D. Lührmann, G. Sanders, C. Steel, G. Thils, J.-M. van Cangh, R. Wielockx (2223-2535).

DANKWOORD

U zal begrijpen: dit is voor mij een moment van intense ontroering. De ontroering van het ogenblik helpt ons soms om de passende woorden te vinden. Maar bij mij is het meestal zo dat ik slechts achteraf goed besef wat ik had moeten zeggen. Het is natuurlijk niet zo dat dit moment mij overvalt „als een dief in de nacht". Van de inrichters kreeg ik zelfs, zoals wellicht u allemaal, een *Table of Contents* toegestuurd op mijn adres, met de uitnodiging om hier op 18 augustus aanwezig te zijn. Het treft me dus niet helemaal onvoorbereid: vandaar ook dit papier.

Ik denk dat ik kan zeggen dat de opzet van het Festschrift in eerste instantie is uitgegaan van twee bijzonder genereuze medewerkers, Jos Verheyden en Gilbert Van Belle, dat Frans Van Segbroeck zich terstond ingezet heeft voor de uitvoering en coördinatie, en ook collega Christopher Tuckett heeft aangezocht om aan het team van *editors* zijn internationale dimensie te geven. De operatie is gestart in juli 1990 en precies twee jaar later kwam het *opus triplex* van de pers. Nu weten we wel dat in de Drukkerij Orientaliste de machines gesmeerd lopen, maar toch was het vooruitzicht niet denkbeeldig dat wij vandaag een „promotie op drukproeven" zouden kennen. Dat dit niet het geval is, danken wij allereerst aan de inzet, week na week, van het Leuvense trio, Van Segbroeck - Van Belle - Verheyden, maar in niet geringe mate ook aan de efficiënte medewerking die hen geboden werd door Marc van Rooij en Rita Corstjens. Zij zitten hier nu alle vijf verdoken op de zijkant: het lijkt mij passend dat niet de Jubilaris maar allereerst deze stille werkers vandaag een applaus krijgen.

Diezelfde groep, aangevuld met Geert Van Oyen, bracht in diezelfde jaren ook de Marcusbibliografie tot voltooiing, *The Gospel of Mark, 1950-1990*, die verschenen is op 11 juli 1992. En, „omne trinum perfectum", op diezelfde 11 juli verscheen ook *John and the Synoptics*, het verslagboek van het Colloquium van 1990, waarmee meteen de Series Tertia van BETL ingezet werd.

Amerikaanse exegeten zijn niet gauw verlegen in het uitdenken van theorieën. Onlangs vond ik in een Festschrift van 1991 een „theorie van het Festschrift", onder de titel: „Festschriften are not for everyone". De auteur somt drie condities op: vooreerst, *seniority* („there must be an occasion"); ten tweede, *productivity* (de produktie van de scholar moet aan de medewerkers onderwerpen aanreiken, „subjects to which to direct their attention in constructive criticism and in commendation"); en er is een derde voorwaarde: „*the willingness to learn*" (een bereidheid „to take instruction ... in such things as the pages of a

Festschrift"). Het komt me voor dat de editors van dit Festschrift vooral gedacht hebben aan „willingness *to read*". Zij hebben een Festschrift aangekondigd van 2.800 bladzijden, maar blijkbaar is er dan toch enige twijfel gerezen omtrent mijn bereidheid om zovele bladzijden te *lezen*: zij hebben het „beperkt" gehouden. Als ik de *Table of Contents* correct lees, beslaan de 125 bijdragen samen, zonder het uitvoerige voorwerk en de Indices, „slechts" 2.300 bladzijden.

*

I would like to address a special word of thanks to Christopher Tuckett, who agreed to join the Leuven people as co-editor of the Festschrift. My dear Chris, in the course of the last ten years I have met you regularly here in Leuven and elsewhere. At the Jerusalem Conference on the Interrelations of the Gospels in 1984, we formed a solid team, united in the defense and in the attack. Your first year as secretary of the Society for New Testament Studies was my year as president of the Society, in Dublin 1989. Here in Leuven we had the privilege to publish your work in ETL and BETL, and in most cases, when I read you, I say to myself: this is what I would like to say, but it is better said.

The vast majority of contributors are members of SNTS and, in a broad sense, they are people of my generation. A few others are not yet on the SNTS membership list but they are worthy candidates for joining very soon the guild of NT scholarship. It was most touching for me that also the still active generation of scholars who were my predecessors and my masters is represented in these volumes: I mention C.K. Barrett, Marie-Émile Boismard, Eugen Ruckstuhl (all three present at our Colloquium); Rudolf Schnackenburg, Heinz Schürmann, Eduard Schweizer.

*

Je me réjouis particulièrement du fait que Mgr G. Thils, mon ancien professeur et ancien collègue à la Faculté de Théologie, a clôturé l'ensemble des articles par une interrogation bien à lui: „Annoncer Jésus-Christ: mais quel Jésus-Christ?". Quatre collègues de Louvain-la-Neuve, co-rédacteurs des *Ephemerides*, se sont joints à lui et donnent à la section sur la réception des évangiles un éclairage spécial du point de vue de la patrologie, la dogmatique, la morale, et la liturgie. – Ik stel het ook ten zeerste op prijs, in diezelfde sectie, twee bijdragen aan te treffen, over Hieronymus en over Maximus Confessor, van de hand van confraters van de Klasse der Letteren van de Koninklijke Academie.

*

Tenslotte wil ik u allen danken voor uw aanwezigheid op deze zitting, en allereerst u, mijnheer de Kardinaal, die erop stond ook in het Festschrift present te zijn. Mijn oudste herinnering aan u gaat terug op 1945: ik was laatstejaarsstudent op de humaniora toen u aan de zesde Latijnse begon. Later, in het Seminarie van Brugge, hebt u de colleges van sacramentologie van mij overgenomen. Naderhand bent u, met wekelijkse intermezzo's, mij ook gevolgd op de weg naar Leuven. Nadien is het anders geworden; het kan verkeren: de laatsten zullen de eersten zijn.

Ik dank ook u, Heren Bisschoppen, voor uw aanwezigheid. Toen ik in de vijftiger jaren voor het eerst deelnam aan de Bijbelse Studiedagen was het een vaste traditie dat Mgr. Charue, als bisschop-exegeet, op de openingszitting aanwezig was. Bij het Vlaams episcopaat is er nu wel geen gebrek aan exegeten. Paul Schreurs was mijn mede-student NT bij Descamps; Paul Van den Berghe was doctoraatsstudent OT (en in feite al volleerd) toen ik hier als professor begon; Roger Vangheluwe, nu mijn bisschop, behaalde zijn licentiaat onder mijn leiding met een verhandeling over Johannes en de Synoptici. Misschien mag ik alvast voorstellen dat uw adressen aan de *mailing list* van het Colloquium toegevoegd worden?

Mijnheer de vertegenwoordiger van de rector, als afscheidnemend voorzitter van de Afdeling Bijbelwetenschap heb ik het geruststellend vooruitzicht dat niet minder dan vijf collega's van het zelfstandig academisch personeel met een onderwijsopdracht Nieuw Testament belast werden: decaan Delobel, Raymond Collins, Frans Van Segbroeck, verbonden aan de Faculteit sinds 1969; en meer recent: Reimund Bieringer en Adelbert Denaux, die nu ook voltijds hoofddocent geworden is.

Nu ik ook als voorzitter van de Commissie voor Publikaties afscheid neem, wil ik de rector danken voor de steun die hij steeds verleend heeft aan die Commissie (in feite, een van de diensten van het rectoraat). Toch moet ik zeggen dat, in deze tijden van bezuiniging, de leden van de Commissie enige reden tot bezorgdheid menen te hebben. Indien ik, meer algemeen, een boodschap aan het beleid mag formuleren, dan is het een vraag die leeft bij een aantal mensen van Humane Wetenschappen: onze universiteit beschikt over een goed-functionerende onderzoeksraad; het is echter de vraag of de zorg voor de bekendmaking van onderzoeksresultaten in publikaties niet, in een of andere vorm, aan die onderzoeksraad dient gekoppeld te worden.

Heel speciaal wil ik de Heer en Mevrouw Peeters danken, uiteraard vandaag voor deze schitterende bibliofiele uitvoering van het Festschrift die u mij laat aanbieden, maar ook en vooral voor de jarenlange samenwerking. Ik kan me moeilijk indenken hoe anders het zou zijn

geweest zonder die vele manuscripten en de stapels drukproeven die ik
in de laatste 20 jaar te verwerken kreeg. Ik heb er vele avondlijke en
nachtelijke uren en verlengde weekends aan besteed. Mijn persoonlijke
exegetische produktiviteit heeft er wellicht onder geleden, maar de
talrijke contacten met auteurs binnen en buiten de Faculteit en vooral
het intense verkeer tussen editor en publisher hebben aan mijn leven een
aparte inhoud gegeven. Het is mijn hoop dat dit nog even mag
doorgaan.

Op 26 februari van dit jaar kreeg ik van de rector het bericht dat ik
vanaf 1 oktober de titel mag voeren van *emeritus*. Dat deed me toen
niet zoveel: het leven ging zijn gewone gang verder. Maar op de dag dat
men zijn afscheidscollege houdt (en de decaan in vriendelijke woorden
komt zeggen dat het ,,voorbij'' is), dan wordt het menens. Des te groter
is daarom mijn dankbaarheid voor de vele collega's en vrienden die hier
vandaag dit moment met mij hebben willen meemaken.

Nogmaals dank ik de vele medewerkers van het Festschrift, de
publishers: Leuven University Press en Uitgeverij Peeters (en de
staf van de Drukkerij Orientaliste): het Jubileumnummer ,,The Four
Gospels 1992'' zal mij een vreugde zijn in lengte van dagen.

F. NEIRYNCK

FAREWELL LECTURE – CONCLUSION

I thank the President of this session and the members of the Organizing Committee for inviting me to deliver the opening paper at this Conference on the Synoptic Gospels. I thank the Dean of our Faculty of Theology who has decided to give to this paper, in the midst of our summer vacation, the décor of a university farewell lecture. Patriarchs and prophets in the Bible have their "last words": it should give comfort to a retiring professor that his last lecture has been scheduled as an opening lecture.

*

Het zal de toehoorders niet ontgaan dat onder exegeten enige diversiteit van opvatting bestaat omtrent de synoptische evangeliën. Ik kan ze alleen maar verzekeren dat de variaties talrijker en de tegenstellingen nog groter zijn dan uit mijn Inleiding al moge blijken. Toch wil ik er ook op wijzen dat over de tegengestelde systemen en theorieën heen vormen van overeenstemming kunnen bestaan. Zo kan, om bij mijn voorbeeld te blijven, een doublet in Marcus uitdrukking zijn van de originele stijl van de evangelist ofwel het resultaat van de combinatie van twee bronnen, maar in beide gevallen wordt de dubbeluitdrukking gerekend tot de stijlkarakteristieken van Marcus. Er is discussie over de relatie van Marcus tot Quelle, maar dezelfde trek in Marcus kan gezien worden als secundair ten opzichte van een meer oorspronkelijke versie, of die nu te vinden is in de eindredactie van de hypothetische Q-bron of in een parallelle traditie. Zo kunnen onze tegenstellingen ten dele gerelativeerd worden.

Maar toch kan ik me voorstellen dat bij de toehoorders vragen rijzen omtrent dit gemis aan consensus bij de studie van de evangeliën. Die vragen leven ook bij mij. Zo is er, om bij het essentiële te blijven, de gangbare opvatting van de Marcusprioriteit (Marcus, bron van Matteüs en Lucas). Ik heb er moeite mee dat exegeten zonder enige vorm van argumentatie daar kunnen van afstappen en zonder meer verklaren dat de afhankelijkheid ten opzichte van Marcus niet relevant is voor de studie van Matteüs en Lucas. Misschien is er toch nood aan een zekere orthopraxie onder exegeten. Met synchronische benaderingen loopt het pas verkeerd wanneer ze beoefend worden met een claim van exclusiviteit. Het is mijn overtuiging dat de positieve inbreng van de "new literary criticism" geïntegreerd kan worden in een globale methode van evangeliestudie.

*

J'ai dû expliquer maintes fois à des collègues étrangers que notre dualité universitaire, Leuven/Louvain et Louvain-la-Neuve, signifie encore autre chose qu'une opération de séparation d'une bibliothèque. Les dix premières années de mon professorat se sont déroulées dans le cadre de la Faculté unitaire, et j'en ai gardé un très vif souvenir personnel et des amitiés durables. Les Journées Bibliques de Louvain, les Ephemerides Theologicae Lovanienses et la Bibliotheca (la BETL) font partie de notre héritage commun, et je suis heureux de constater aujourd'hui que notre collaboration a pu être continuée, et qu'elle s'est même intensifiée, entre autres choses grâce au support des cinq doyens qui, depuis le grand distancement, se sont succédés à nos deux Facultés. S'il est vrai que nos réunions de travail avec les collègues de Louvain-la-Neuve n'ont pas toujours eu lieu au cœur même de la Faculté, ni même au centre de la ville, elles se tenaient régulièrement à une adresse que d'aucuns ont appelée une extension de la Faculté. C'est donc de grand cœur, cher collègue Focant, que je vous salue comme président du Colloque 1992. Vous l'avez remarquablement bien préparé, par correspondance et par de nombreux contacts personnels, et je suis sûr qu'avec vous la présidence du Colloque (1992) est en bonnes mains; son succès est assuré, et je vous en félicite d'avance.

F.N.

THE SYNOPTIC GOSPELS

INTRODUCTION

The 41st session of the *Colloquium Biblicum Lovaniense* took place in August 18-20, 1992. At the meeting on John and the Synoptics (1990) it was clear that, even if the question remains to be discussed, more and more scholars think that John knew the Synoptics and was even literarily dependent on one or more of them. One of the conclusions was that the study of «John and the Synoptics» inevitably refers to the Synoptic problem. Therefore, it was decided to examine anew the Synoptic question. But another problem grafted itself on the first one and covered it partially, namely the confrontation of classic source-critical and redactional studies with the methods of the new literary criticism and the study of the Gospels in a way which is no longer diachronic but synchronic. Thirteen scholars were invited to deliver main papers or to conduct seminars. No less than sixteen short papers were offered.

In his state of the art lecture, *Literary Criticism: Old and New*, F. NEIRYNCK (Leuven) reviewed the principal problems raised in the study of the Synoptic Gospels. He indicated that in his understanding redaction criticism implies composition criticism. He demonstrated the importance of Marcan priority to the interpretation of Matthew and Luke. He also recalled that the minor agreements are a post-Marcan phenomenon and that, in his opinion, they can be explained well if due consideration is given to the Matthean and Lucan redactions. Contrary to some recent suggestions, he does not believe that the final document Q was used by Mk. For the sources of Mk the hypothesis of a primitive gospel in any form (a primitive Matthew, Urmarkus, Q gospel, an extensive passion story, pre-Marcan collections) seems problematic. The acceptance of isolated units remains a more secure starting point, without excluding the possibility that some pericopes have been created by Mk.

In my presidential address, *Mc 7,24-31 par. Mt 15,21-29: critique des sources et/ou étude narrative*, I successively developed a historical-critical exegesis, then a semiotic and narrative analysis of the story of the Syrophoenician woman. The first approach allowed the gathering of many interesting elements, especially with regard to the final redaction, by comparing the texts of Mt and Mk. The semiotic analysis, applied to the text of Mk and particularly through analysis of the figurative level, enables a clearer view that in this micro-narrative the transformation operates on the cognitive level, i.e. a redefinition of the values implicated in the programme of Jesus. The mechanism of this transformation clearly appears in an accurate comparison of Mk 7,27b and 28b.

Regarding the pre-evangelical sources, a first theme to be treated was the pre-Marcan sources. The seminar led by C. BREYTENBACH (Berlin), *Das Markusevangelium als traditionsgebundene Erzählung? Anfragen an die Markusforschung der achtziger Jahre*, raised the following three principal questions: What are we allowed to say with sufficient evidence about the pre-Marcan tradition? If a text appears to be the written living tradition of a religious community, what consequences should we draw to achieve its correct interpretation? Eventually, how should we, men and women of the 20th century, rightly interpret an ancient text that «literarises» a former tradition? These three problems were not only theoretically discussed, but also concretely examined in a diachronic and synchronic analysis of Mk 6,1-6a and 9,9-13. The seminar led by V.K. ROBBINS (Atlanta, GA), *Progymnastic Rhetorical Composition and Pre-Gospel Traditions: A New Approach*, treated the question of the pre-evangelical traditions by illustrating it with the Mediterranean rhetorical culture in which those traditions were transmitted. One of the major characteristics of this culture is that the rhetoric (the argumentative method) conditions both oral and written performances. The progymnastic rhetorical composition of Aelius Theon of Alexandria can help to understand how, to transmit data in such a culture, we have the elaboration of a tradition toward the form of an essay or speech that presents a complete argument. The seminar tried to see how the rhetorical approach offers a method for analysing the tradition anew and discerning many different cultural subgroups in early Christianity, subgroups which belonged to different subcultures and countercultures. The reports on these seminars were given at the plenary session by A. Lindemann and J. Painter respectively.

Two lectures dealt with the relations between Q and one of the Synoptic Gospels. Concerning *Mark and Q*, C.M. TUCKETT (Manchester) examined the famous overlap passages and more particularly Q 11,29-30 / Mk 8,11-12; Q 7,27 / Mk 1,2; Q 3,16 / Mk 1,7-8; Q 13,18-19 / Mk 4,30-32. Some scholars have argued that in these cases the Marcan text could be understood as a Marcan redaction of Q. But that is not sufficient. Methodologically, to assert that Mk depended on Q, evidence must still be given that he reflects elements of Q redaction. But this is not the case in any of the passages he scrutinized. He then drew the conclusion that the view that Mark and Q represent independent versions of common traditions remains the most convincing in the passages considered here. C.P. MÄRZ (Erfurt), *Zur Q-Rezeption in Lk 12,35–13,35 (14,1-24). Die Q-Hypothese und ihre Bedeutung für die Interpretation des lukanischen Reiseberichtes*, elucidated the great eschatological composition of Q which is dissimulated behind Lk 12,35–13,35 (14,1-24). Source criticism allowed him to draw a distinction between three blocks (12,35-46.49-59; 13,24-29) which are perfectly coordinated and thematically attuned. The whole functions as a kind of first discourse about the end of time. When Lk took over the set, he de-eschatologised it to some extent and stressed the punitive aspect for Israel, without adding the perspective of a general rejection of the people, however.

Each of the three Synoptic Gospels was analysed in its final state from either a diachronic or synchronic outlook, or sometimes from both points of view. For Mk, H. MERKLEIN (Bonn), *Mk 16,1-8 als Epilog des Markusevangeliums*, proceeded in two steps. A synchronic analysis allowed him first to determine the narrative function of each part of the text from its place in and connection with the context. In this way, he emphasized the narrative strategy of the text in the semantic field of the narrative (narrative conception) as well as in the pragmatic effect on the reader (narrative intention). This analysis showed two distinct narrative threads, the first being connected with a visit to the tomb, the other with the anointing of Jesus' body in the tomb. On the diachronic level, the first narrative thread would correspond with the *Vorlage* of Mk (15,42-47, followed by 16,2ab.4ab.8ab) while the second would be connected with the redactional work of Mk. The latter would have added the other elements in order to let the kerygma resound in the very place of the empty tomb sealed by a stone which appeared as the sign of the end of the story of Jesus. The pericope of the empty tomb would have become the convenient epilog of a work intended to present the beginning and the founding of the Gospel of Jesus Christ, Son of God.

For the Gospels of Matthew and Mark, it is precisely the reader's position that was treated by D. MARGUERAT (Lausanne), *La construction du lecteur par le texte (Marc et Matthieu)*. The rereading of Mk by Mt implied an important modification in the image of the reader built by the text. After allowing his reader to be ahead, as far as christological knowledge is concerned (1,1), Mk uses literary devices that immediately strip him of the understanding he thinks he has acquired. The evangelist seems to be engaged in a strategy of destabilisation of the theological knowledge of his community. On the other hand, Mt is anxious to foster the theological gains of his reader introduced by assimilation with the disciple in an ideal of comprehension and faithfulness. His strategy aims at strengthening the appropriation of a theological knowledge.

When considering the Gospel of Matthew as a narrative or, more accurately, as the story of a conflict, J.D. KINGSBURY (Richmond, VA), attempted to stress *The Significance of the Cross within the Plot of Matthew's Gospel*. After tracing the unfolding of the plot of Matthew's story of Jesus, he displayed the crucial role played within the story's plot by the pericope of Jesus on the cross (27,38-54). It is not only the place where the entire Gospel-story reaches its culmination, but it is also the pericope where Matthew links the two key themes of salvation and of Jesus as the Son of God. For his part, H. FRANKEMÖLLE (Paderborn), *Das Matthäusevangelium als heilige Schrift und die heilige Schrift des früheren Bundes. Von der Zwei-Quellen- zur Drei-Quellen-Theorie*, focuses his attention on the estimated first task of the exegete, namely the quest for the original meaning of the text, i.e. the significance really meant by Mt which his first historical readers managed to discover. The latter situated their reading of Mt, not within the context of a comparison with Mk and Q, but rather with reference to their knowledge of Holy Scripture. The diachronic analysis remains important for Mt's text which was composed by skillfully gathering so many elements of the tradition: on the one hand, from the primitive Christian tradition (Mk and Q), and on the other hand, from Scripture's tradition (the first Testament). Mt is not satisfied with the simple reedition of Mk and Q with slight modifications, but he also places them in another perspective, that of biblically oriented history: hence, the plea by Frankemölle for an exegesis of Mt which, from a literary as well as a theological point of view, bases itself not only on the Two-Source Theory but on a Three-Source Theory (Holy Scripture, Mk and Q).

The redaction of the Gospel of Luke has been much discussed. Faithful to the Two-Source Hypothesis, V. FUSCO (Napoli), *Le discours eschatologique lucanien: «rédaction» et «composition» (Lc 21,5-36 et Mc 13,1-37)*, demonstrated that the main features of Luke's work are clarity and good style, from the literary point of view, and interest in the problem of Israel put into the perspective of an imminent parousia, from the theological point of view. As for methodology, he stressed that *Redaktionsgeschichte* has to carefully study composition procedures, structures, literary models, in one word, style to its fullest extent. The Dutch-speaking seminar discussed a paper presented by A. DENAUX (Leuven), on *The Delineation of the Lucan Travel Narrative within the Overall Structure of the Gospel of Luke*. A separation of different solutions revealed how much each delineation had immediate consequences, both for determination of the global structure of the Gospel and for articulation of Lucan theology. Moreover, the importance of a good understanding of Lk's intention requires a study of the Gospel that goes beyond a merely diachronic analysis to a synchronic and narrative reading. In the seminar led by F. BOVON (Genève), *Le récit lucanien de la passion de Jésus (Lc 22-23)*, different aspects of the Lucan writing were pinpointed: the firm but not brittle composition, the space and time construction, the forms of character interaction, the circulation of objects. Regarding the sources of the Lucan passion narrative, the alternation of different blocks of material raised the much questioned hypothesis that Lk would have followed alternatively Mk and a special source. The whole seminar stressed the writing and compositional power of an extremely skilled author. The reports on these seminars were given at the plenary session by H.J. de Jonge and J.-M. Sevrin respectively.

Sixteen short papers were offered at the Colloquium. Three of them treated the Synoptic Theories: T.A. FRIEDRICHSEN (Sioux City, MA), *Alternative Synoptic Theories on Mk 4,30-32*; P. ROLLAND (Reims), *Lecture par couches rédactionnelles de l'épisode de l'épileptique (Mc 9,14-29 et parallèles)*; H.B. GREEN (Mirfield), *Matthew 11,7-15: Redaction or Self-Redaction*? Two were devoted to Q: E. BAMMEL (Cambridge), *Der Anfang des Spruchbuchs*; W. SCHENK (Dudweiler), *Die Verwünschung der Küstenorte Q 10,13-15: Zur Funktion der konkreten Ortsangaben und zur Lokalisierung von Q*. No less than seven dealt with Mk (and par.): W.R. TELFORD (Newcastle), *Mark and the Historical-Critical Method: The Challenge of Recent Literary Approaches to the Gospel*; H. KLEIN (Sibiu), *Zur Methode der Erforschung vormarkinischer Quellen*; B. ORCHARD (London), *The Publication of Mark's Gospel*; B.M.F. VAN IERSEL (Nijmegen), *Concentric Structures in Mk 2,1-3,6 and 3,7-4,1: A Case Study*; J. DELORME (Annecy), *Signification d'un récit et comparaison synoptique (Marc 9,14-29 et parallèles)*; C.B. AMPHOUX (Montpellier), *La «finale longue de Marc»: un épilogue des quatre évangiles*; R. KÜHSCHELM (Wien), *Angelophanie - Christophanie in den synoptischen Grabesgeschichten Mk 16,1-8 par. (unter Berücksichtigung von Joh 20,11-18)*. Three treated the comparison and relations with later literature: J.-M. VAN CANGH (Louvain-la-Neuve), *Évolution du motif de la foi dans les miracles synoptiques, johanniques et apocryphes*; D. LÜHRMANN (Marburg), *Ein neues Fragment des Petrusevangeliums*; T. BAARDA (Amsterdam), *Clement of Alexandria and the Parable of the Fisherman: Mt 13,47-48 or an Independent Tradition*? And a last short paper dealt with the history of research on the Synoptic Gospels: M.H. DE LANG (Leiden), *Gospel Synopses from the 16th to the 18th Centuries and the Rise of Literary Criticism of the Gospels*.

One can draw at least three main conclusions. First, whatever marked preference each scholar might have for a particular method or another, rare are those still claiming exclusive rights for one method, at least theoretically speaking. In fact, practically speaking, it is less clear. Attempts to combine both diachronic and synchronic approaches in concrete studies will probably be more and more frequent. And it could bear fruits which we can hardly imagine at this moment. A second point emerges: everybody wishes to contribute to the understanding of the final text, whatever means and methods are used. On the one hand, redaction critics who refuse to allow the evangelists' redaction to be reduced to editing and altering recognizable sources emphasize that they also investigate the final work of the evangelist as a whole. On the other hand, the new literary criticism does not necessarily view the final documents as isolated from the cultural and historical world in which they were produced. Moreover, have not many «new literary criticism» studies been marked by previous redactional studies? It is not impossible that the genesis of texts could gain new importance in the eyes of scholars who investigate narrative techniques or meaning-lines in a work's organisation or who attempt to discern how different texts can form different readers. And, thirdly, it does not seem unimportant to note that the scholars present at the 41st session of the Colloquium Biblicum Lovaniense revealed themselves to be open to the epistemological questions underlying the methods they use and the literary theories on which they depend.

Camille Focant

I
MAIN PAPERS

LITERARY CRITICISM, OLD AND NEW

The previous Colloquium on the New Testament in 1990 was devoted to the Gospel of John and its relationship to the Synoptic Gospels, and on that occasion I had the opportunity to present a survey of the studies on John and the Synoptics. I could observe that this issue had become again a lively debated question and that Johannine dependence is no longer the provocative and isolated thesis it might have seemed to be in 1975[1]. Although the phrase: "How my mind has changed" is now a fashionable title for retrospective essays, such a title would have been inappropriate with regard to the problem of John's relation to the Synoptics. But, and this is my question today, is that also the case regarding the study of the Synoptic Gospels themselves?

I begin with a personal recollection. There is a great variety of scholarly opinion in introductory questions such as the date and the place of origin of each of the Synoptic Gospels, and therefore I am delighted that I can start my own story with a precise date and location: my personal interest in the Synoptic Gospels and the Synoptic Problem began in the year 1953-54 when, as one of the STB students, I attended for the first time Professor L. Cerfaux's course on the Synoptics. With the galley proofs of L. Vaganay's *Le problème synoptique* on his desk, Cerfaux initiated his audience in the primitive-gospel hypothesis, a Proto-Matthew, source of Matthew, Mark and Luke, and much closer to canonical Matthew than Vaganay's *Matthieu grec*. The effect of Cerfaux's course was double. On the one hand, I found his exemplary analytical work of synoptic comparison most stimulating. On the other hand, although like other Cerfaux students at that time I may have professed lip service to Proto-Matthew, I found myself much more attracted to the alternative theory of Markan priority, and I retained the strong conviction that there was some need of refinement in the current argument. The year 1954 was also important for another reason: Hans Conzelmann's *Die Mitte der Zeit* made a great impression. It meant for me the introduction into Synoptic redaction criticism. My subsequent doctoral work on Luke, under A. Descamps, was partially written in dialogue with Conzelmann (1957). And all my later

---

1. *John and the Synoptics: 1975-1990*, in A. DENAUX (ed.), *John and the Synoptics* (BETL, 101), Leuven, 1992, pp. 3-62. Compare my *John and the Synoptics*, lecture delivered at the Colloquium on John in 1975 (in *Evangelica*, pp. 365-400).

For more complete bibliographical data, up to August 1992, I refer to the Bibliography compiled by G. Van Belle in *The Four Gospels 1992. Festschrift Frans Neirynck* (BETL, 100), Leuven, 1992, pp. 3-24. The two volumes of Collected Essays published in 1982 (BETL, 60) and in 1991 (BETL, 99) are here referred to as *Evangelica* and *Evangelica II*.

research and publications on the Synoptics can be characterized in general as redaction-critical.

Redaction criticism and the study of the Synoptic Problem are interconnected, and it is our custom to use the term "literary criticism" in a broad sense, combining the source-critical and redaction-critical dimensions. Thus, I was not unhappy to observe that also in the Old Testament field the pendulum is now swinging back[2]. On the other hand, we all know that in recent years the methods and the name of secular "literary criticism" have won acceptance in biblical studies[3]. The author of a recent Dictionary article on "Literary Criticism" simply dismisses a scholarship that is "interested in questions of history, reaching behind the texts to their sources, and the events which gave rise to them. This type of scholarship has often been referred to as 'literary criticism', but is more appropriately described as 'source criticism', and will not be further discussed here"[4]. Such a narrow circumscription, degrading the *old* literary criticism to historical criticism in contrast to the interpretation of the Bible as literature in the *new* literary criticism needs correction. It also raises a terminological problem: "Literary Criticism" is no longer the translation of "Literarkritik"[5]. My personal practical solution is to use more specific descriptions, such as narrative criticism, rhetorical criticism, the study of "narrative rhetoric", and to maintain the comprehensive term *Literarkritik* in its traditional acceptance.

Practitioners of the new literary criticism already made the announcement that the age of redaction criticism has come to its end[6]. In redaction criticism, they say, the evangelists were treated as redactors, editors of traditional texts, and not really as the authors of the gospels.

2. Cf. L. SCHMIDT, *Literarkritik, I. Altes Testament*, in *TRE* 21 (1991) 211-222: "Eine Trennung von Literarkritik und Redaktionsgeschichte ist (aber) schon forschungsgeschichtlich problematisch. ... Zudem läßt sich sachlich nur schwer zwischen Literarkritik und Redaktionsgeschichte differenzieren. ... M.E. (sind) Analyse und Synthese Gegenstand der Literarkritik" (p. 211).

3. M.A. POWELL, *The Bible and Modern Literary Criticism. A Critical Assessment and Annotated Bibliography* (Bibliographies and Indexes in Religious Studies, 22), New York - Westport, CT - London, 1992, esp. pp. 257-338: "The Gospels" (nos. 1054-1428); M. MINOR, *Literary-Critical Approaches to the Bible. An Annotated Bibliography*, West Cornwall, CT, 1992, esp. pp. 348-450: "The Gospels" (nos. 1565-2035). Cf. my review in *ETL* 68 (1992) 432-433. See also S.D. MOORE, *Literary Criticism and the Gospels. The Theoretical Challenge*, New Haven, CT - London, 1989.

4. M. DAVIES, *Literary Criticism*, in R.J. COGGINS & J.L. HOULDEN (eds.), *A Dictionary of Biblical Interpretation*, London - Philadelphia, PA, 1990, pp. 402-405, esp. 402.

5. The theme of this Colloquium "Source Criticism and the New Literary Criticism" was first announced as: "Literarkritik" and/or Literary Criticism.

6. The title is used by J.B. Muddiman in a review article: *The End of Markan Redaction Criticism?*, in *ExpT* 101 (1989-90) 307-309. Compare the title of Chapter Two in G.N. STANTON, *A Gospel for a New People. Studies in Matthew*, Edinburgh, 1992: "Redaction Criticism: The End of an Era?" (p. 23).

Interpreters now move to holistic readings, to the study of each gospel as a whole; and what they call an excessive allegiance to diachrony is now being replaced by the primacy of synchrony. The shortcomings of the redaction-critical method are listed, and its first weakness is "reliance on the two-source hypothesis"[7]: "with a requestioning of the priority of Mark, the Markan anchor of control for the distinctive divergences of both Matthew and Luke has become precarious. ... The whole edifice of redaction criticism may be resting on a cracked foundation"[8]. Many more quotations of this sort can be given: the two-source theory is "at an impasse", and one of the advantages of the new discipline of literary criticism is its focus on the final form of the gospel text.

At this point, two observations can be made. My first remark concerns the description of the redaction-critical method. The distinction between redaction and tradition is an important aspect, of course, but it is hardly acceptable that the redaction criticism of the past three decades be reduced to a study of "the redactors' alterations of their sources". For most scholars, redaction criticism and composition criticism are synonymous, and their redactional investigations are not exclusive of respect for the final work of the evangelist as a whole. My second remark regards the recommendation of literary criticism because of the lack of source-critical consensus. This reminds me of a recommendation of form-critical study I could hear here in Leuven in the 1950's: "essayer de contourner le problème synoptique", avoid discussion of the synoptic problem by concentrating directly upon individual sayings and small gospel units. The proposal is now to focus on the final gospel text irrespective of the problem of sources. I agree, this can be a refuge for gospel students who are irremediably skeptical in the question of sources. Those who are not (and I am one of them) should have the right to ask what can be gained by not taking into consideration part of the evidence.

I. MATTHEW AND MARK

In the discussion of the synoptic problem, the central issue is, in one form or another, the question of originality of Matthew or priority of Mark. The data of agreement and disagreement in the relative order of pericopes is rightly seen as essential, in particular the divergences

---

7. E.P. SANDERS & M. DAVIES, *Studying the Synoptic Gospels*, London - Philadelphia, PA, 1989, pp. 201-223, esp. 221.

8. D.P. MOESSNER, *Lord of the Banquet. The Literary and Theological Significance of the Lukan Travel Narrative*, Minneapolis, MN, 1989, p. 5.

between Mk 1,21–6,13 and the parallel sections in Matthew (at 4,22 / 14,1). This was the main topic of my contribution to the 1965 Colloquium[9]. It was a special satisfaction to me that, following this paper, Cerfaux in his old age decided to rethink his synoptic solution. The effect of the paper was not only immediate and local. In his 1992 book on Matthew, G.N. Stanton has a section on Markan priority[10]:

> in the second half [of Mt] Mark's order is followed most carefully, but in the first half of the gospel Matthew alters the Marcan order very considerably. Is it possible to offer a plausible explanation of Matthew's inconsistency? If not, Matthew's dependence on Mark would seem to be called in question. F. Neirynck [1967] has faced the problem squarely and has examined carefully Matthew's rearrangements of Mark's order. He shows that it is only in Matt. 4.12–11.1 that a problem is posed by a departure from Mark; ... Within the section 4.23–11.1 Matthew's liberty of order is only relative, for Mark's order can still frequently be traced; where the Marcan order is changed by Matthew, he can be shown to have been inspired by his sources. In short, on the hypothesis of Matthean use of Mark, the evangelist's changes to Mark's order are not arbitrary but consistent and coherent.

I came back to this question at the conclusion of a more recent article on the structure of Matthew[11], with the observation that in "literary-critical" studies no distinction is made "between the original Matthean composition in 4,23–11,1 and the other parts of the Gospel where Matthew faithfully follows the story line of Mk 1,1-20 and 6,14–16,8. The whole extant text is, of course, in all its parts the text of the author of the Gospel, but we can learn from redaction criticism that some parts of this text are more Matthean than some other parts. A 'holistic' approach, when separated from redaction criticism, is unable to tell us the whole truth of the Gospel text"[12].

One can only express approval when it is said that "three questions (are) essential to the literary critical analysis of Matthew's Gospel: (1) the role of the narrator in telling the story; (2) the content of the story (i.e., the characters, plot, and setting); and (3) the effect of the narra-

---

9. *La rédaction matthéenne et la structure du premier évangile*, in *ETL* 43 (1967) 41-73; = *Evangelica*, pp. 3-36. See also *ibid.*, 691-723, 729-736, and more recently, *Matthew 4:23–5:1 and the Matthean Composition of 4:23–11:1*, in D.L. DUNGAN (ed.), *The Interrelations of the Gospels* (BETL, 95), Leuven, 1992, pp. 23-46; *Synoptic Problem*, in *NJBC*, 1990, pp. 587-595.

10. *A Gospel for a New People* (n. 6 above), p. 31.

11. ΑΠΟ ΤΟΤΕ ΗΡΞΑΤΟ *and the Structure of Matthew*, in *ETL* 64 (1988) 21-59; = *Evangelica II*, pp. 141-179.

12. *Ibid.*, p. 179. In *Das Matthäus-Evangelium* (Erträge der Forschung, 275), Darmstadt, 1991, A. Sand quotes this conclusion: "Damit ist Neirynck recht zu geben" (p. 42); curiously enough, the phrase "a 'holistic' approach" is translated in German as "eine 'polemische' Behandlung"!

tive, or in other words, that which the implied author communicates to the implied reader"; and in addition, that the passage under examination should be treated as "one piece of a larger whole, one single segment within the 'sequential composite' of events which constitutes Matthew's overall narrative"[13]. But can the writer of a dissertation on Matthew's Missionary Discourse assume "the storyteller's freedom to tell his story in whatever way and by whatever means he chooses"[14] without even mentioning the question of Matthew's sources? And can he/she propose an outline of Matthew's Gospel without considering its possible basis in Mark[15]?

An extreme example of "narrative-critical reading" is J.P. Heil's essay on Mt 26–28[16]. He divides the text into three major sections

13. D.J. WEAVER, *Matthew's Missionary Discourse. A Literary Critical Analysis* (JSNT SS, 38), Sheffield, 1990, p. 28.

14. *Ibid.*, p. 35.

15. Some literary critics, with reference to J.D. Kingsbury, prefer a tripartite structure of Matthew, with the superscription at 1,1; 4,17; 16,21. Cf. U. LUZ, *Matthäus*, vol. II, 1990, p. 485: "das heute am verbreitesten 'narrative' Gliederungsmodell des Mt-Ev". But the argumentation developed by Kingsbury is, if I may say, a pre-'literary' one (1973). The division at 4,17 and 16,21 is much older (cf. Westcott-Hort). In my view, it is based on a misunderstanding of the phrase ἀπὸ τότε ἤρξατο and its relation to the preceding 4,12-16, resp. 16,13-20. Here, too, Matthew's division at 4,12 and 16,13 is parallel to (and dependent upon) Mk 1,14 and 8,27. Cf. *Evangelica II*, pp. 141-179 (n. 11 above), with additional note, pp. 180-182; see already *Evangelica*, pp. 18-20 (n. 9 above). See also B. STANDAERT, *L'évangile selon Matthieu. Composition et genre littéraire*, in *The Four Gospels 1992*, pp. 1223-1250, esp. 1240-1245 ("Les trois ἀπὸ τότε").

The additional note in *Evangelica II* (on D.R. Bauer 1988, U. Luz 1990, *et al.*) can be supplemented with a reference to J.D. Kingsbury's response, in the new Preface to his *Matthew: Structure, Christology, Kingdom*, Minneapolis, MN, ²1989, pp. IX-XXIV, esp. XV-XX. Kingsbury restates his position: "Asyndetic *apo tote* signals that 4:17 and 16:21 stand apart from the preceding pericopes 4:12-16 and 16:13-20" (p. XX). Contrast A. SAND, *Das Matthäus-Evangelium* (n. 12 above), 1991, pp. 41-42 (on *apo tote* in 4,17 and 16,21): "Daß sie sich auch auf das unmittelbar Vorausgehende beziehen, ist unbestritten (im Sinne von: 'nach diesem Geschehen')" (p. 42, cf. *Evangelica II*, p. 178, n. 203; less consistently, he maintains the caesurae at 4,17 and 16,21). Kingsbury concludes: "The only basis [sic] for Neirynck's assertion of linkage instead of separation as regards 4:17 and 16:21 is his contention that one must revert to Mark if one is to ascertain the structure of Matthew. Since I disagree with this contention, I see no reason to change my position" (p. XX). See, however, also his note 36: "Neirynck establishes the unity of this pericope [16,13-23] not only by reading Matthew in terms of Mark..." (p. XIX). His reply to my observations on the contrast *in Matthew* between the blessing of Peter in 16,17 and the rebuke in 16,23 is rather brief and evasive (*ibid.*). Kingsbury regards it as "one of the great strengths" of his approach not to introduce "all the uncertainties of the synoptic problem into the already complex task of ascertaining the structure of Matthew" (p. XVII, n. 26). But when the literary critic reading the Gospel "in terms of Matthew" finds three key summary-passages in 4,[12-]17–11,1 and three passion-predictions in 16,[13-]21–20,34 (pp. X-XI), can it be indifferent for him to know that the three passion predictions are adopted from the parallel text in Mk 8,27–10,52, whereas the three summaries are the product of a specific Matthean arrangement (Mt 4,23–11,1)?

16. J.P. HEIL, *The Death and Resurrection of Jesus. A Narrative-Critical Reading of Matthew 26–28*, Minneapolis, MN, 1991. See also *The Narrative Structure of Matthew*

(26,1-56; 26,57-27,54; 27,55-28,20), "each composed of nine scenes that function together as a dynamic progression of seven narrative intercalations or 'sandwiches'"[17]. There is not even one mention of Mark in Heil's book on Matthew. But the same author separately published, the year before, an article on the "narrative structure" of Mk 14,1-52, of which Mt 26,1-56 appears to be the perfect replica[18]. I hope, you will understand when I say that the reading of this sort of literary criticism makes me nostalgic: I remember the good time I had in the early 1970's when D.P. Senior was preparing here his doctoral work, a "redactional" study of the passion narrative according to Matthew[19].

II. THE MINOR AGREEMENTS AND LUKAN REDACTION

Literary critics proclaim freedom from priority assumptions as an advantage of their method "given the uncertainties surrounding competing hypotheses in gospel studies today"[20]. In the current situation, however, if we set aside the neo-Griesbachians and their allies, almost all competing theories are variations of the same basic assumption of Markan priority. The priority of Mark can be mitigated by the acceptance of some form of Proto-Mark, Deutero-Mark, or Deutero-Markan recension; or by subsidiary hypotheses, the influence of tradition variants, or dependence of Luke upon Matthew. There is one main stumbling-block at the origin of all these hypotheses: the phenomenon of the minor agreements of Matthew and Luke against Mark in the triple tradition.

Ten years before W.R. Farmer's book on *The Synoptic Problem* we were faced with this phenomenon in Vaganay's *Le problème synoptique*[21], and it is undeniable that his argument, if not convincing, was not devoid of some force of seduction, as can be seen for instance from a late witness by F. Bovon[22]. The minor agreements were studied here

27:55–28:20, in *JBL* 110 (1991) 419-438 (compare *The Death*, pp. 91-110). On this last essay, cf. D.P. SENIOR, *Matthew's Account* (n. 36), pp. 1435-1437.

17. *The Death*, p. 2.

18. *Mark 14,1-52: Narrative Structure and Reader-Response*, in *Biblica* 71 (1990) 305-332.

19. Cf. below, n. 36.

20. D.B. HOWELL, *Matthew's Inclusive Story. A Study in the Narrative Rhetoric of the First Gospel* (JSNT SS, 42), Sheffield, 1990, p. 35.

21. L. VAGANAY, *Le problème synoptique*, Tournai, 1954, pp. 69-74 (esp. the negative agreements diff. Mk 6,31-44; 4,35-41) and 405-425 (Excursus on the negative agreements diff. Mk 9,14-29).

22. F. BOVON, *L'Évangile selon saint Luc (1,1–9,50)* (CNT, IIIa), Genève, 1991, p. 495, n. 18 (regarding Lk 9,37-43a, diff. Mk 9,14-29): "j'admire son analyse conduite de main

in doctoral dissertations by S. McLoughlin[23] and T. Hansen[24], in our volume published in 1974[25] and in a number of special studies[26], and now recently in the dissertation of T.A. Friedrichsen who surveys and evaluates new developments of the discussion in the years 1974-1991[27]. The minor agreements now receive much consideration in two alternative theories, Deutero-Mark[28] and Lukan dependence on Matthew[29]. It is not unimportant to observe that on three points they agree with our redactional approach. First, the minor agreements are post-Markan in nature; second, at least some of the minor agreements can be explained by independent (Matthean and Lukan) redaction; third, in some other instances, Matthean redaction is likely and, in their opinion, the problem is on the side of Luke.

The question to be debated mainly concerns Lukan redaction, and it is not by abstract speculation on the acceptable number of agreements that this question can be solved. Neither is it enough, as indicated in

de maître"; in the German edition, *Das Evangelium nach Lukas (Lk 1,1-9,50)* (EKK 3/1), Zürich - Neukirchen-Vluyn, 1989, p. 508, n. 18: "dessen meisterhafte Analyse (mich) überzeugt (hat)".

23. S. McLOUGHLIN, *The Synoptic Theory of Xavier Léon-Dufour. An Analysis and Evaluation*, 1965, esp. pp. 236-291, 507-510; *Les accords mineurs Mt-Lc contre Mc et le problème synoptique. Vers la théorie des deux sources*, in *ETL* 63 (1967) 17-40 (= BETL, 25).

24. T. HANSEN, *De overeenkomsten Mattheus-Lucas tegen Marcus in de drievoudige traditie*, 1969. Cf. n. 25 below.

25. F. NEIRYNCK, *The Minor Agreements of Matthew and Luke against Mark. With a Cumulative List* (BETL, 37), Leuven, 1974 (with the collaboration of T. Hansen and F. Van Segbroeck). Cf. n. 30 below.

26. *Evangelica*, esp. pp. 637-680 (Mk 2,27); 737-768 (order); 769-780 (Dmk); 781-796 (Mk 2,1-4); 797-809 (Mk 9,2-10); 809-810; *Evangelica II*, pp. 3-42 (cf. n. 30 below); 43-48 (Mk 8,31); 49-58 (πάλιν in Mk); 59-73 (Proto-Mk); 75-94 (Mk 6,30-34); 95-138 (Mk 14,65); 187-190 (Mk 3,1-6); 293-320 (duplicate expressions); 321-322 (Mk 1,12-13a); 481-492 (Mt 12,25a / Lc 11,17a); 773-784 (Mk 1,40-45).

27. T.A. FRIEDRICHSEN, *The Matthew-Luke Agreements against Mark: 1974-1991*, 1992. Cf. *'Minor' and 'Major' Matthew-Luke Agreements against Mk 4,30-32*, in *The Four Gospels 1992*, pp. 649-676; *Alternative Synoptic Theories on Mk 4,30-32*, in this volume, pp. 427-450. See also his 1974-1989 survey in F. NEIRYNCK (ed.), *L'Évangile de Luc - The Gospel of Luke* (BETL, 32), Leuven, ²1989, pp. 335-392; and his critical reviews in *ETL* 65 (1989) 390-394 (M.D. Goulder), 395-408 (R.B. Vinson); 66 (1990) 410-413 (H. Riley); 67 (1991) 373-394 (A. Ennulat, J. Rauscher).

28. In its radical form propounded by A. Fuchs and his school, or in the mitigated form of a Deutero-Markan recension (U. Luz, A. Ennulat).

29. With rejection of the Q source (M.D. Goulder) or in combination with Luke's use of Q (R.H. Gundry). Cf. R.H. GUNDRY, *Matthean Foreign Bodies in Agreements of Luke with Matthew against Mark Evidence that Luke Used Matthew*, in *The Four Gospels 1992* (n. 1), pp. 1467-1495, including on pp. 1475-1479 a reply to my "Note on Lk 9,22" (cf. p. 1468, n. 4: with thanks to Goulder for corrections and suggestions). The instances of agreement with Matthew discussed by Gundry are: Lk 6,13.14; 8,10.12.20.25; 9,1.3.11.22. 27.47; 10,25; 11,17; 18,22.31; 20,3.14.18; 22,41-42.70; 23,47.52; 24,5.6.9. On Lk 24,9, cf. below n. 38.

my paper at the Göttingen Conference (1991)[30], to list the verbal agreements with Matthew. When each agreement is carefully examined in its specific context, and in relation to the parallel text in Mark, similarities *and* dissimilarities may appear, and what at first is supposed to be un-Lukan may become quite acceptable Lukan redaction once it is seen in the macro-context of the entire Lukan work. The conclusion I wrote last year can be repeated here[31]:

> In theory I can have no objection against some influence of oral-tradition variants, some occasional dependence on a revised text of Mark, or some subsidiary Lukan dependence on Matthew. But a modification of the Markan hypothesis suggested on the basis of the minor agreements can only be a minor modification, and it is my impression that no such modification is needed after serious examination of the Matthean *and* *Lukan* redactions.
>
> There is still one dimension of the study of the minor agreements which should be mentioned. Many times the minor agreement works like a signal: the coincidence of Matthew and Luke draws attention to Matthean and Lukan non-coincidental parallels, and without those cases of agreement some aspects of Matthean and Lukan usage would have remained partially unexplored. The minor agreements force us again and again to study each passage in light of the whole Gospel, and this has been, it seems to me, most profitable to our comprehension of the three Synoptic Gospels.

Special mention should be made of the two famous minor agreements in the passion narrative. The suggestion of a textual solution in the case of Lk 22,62 (diff. Mk 14,72) and in the more difficult case of Mt 26,68 (diff. Mk 14,65) gave rise to theoretical discussion about conjectural emendation[32]. The debate is not closed, but I see a growing number of scholars for whom an exceptional instance of conjectural reading is no longer methodologically unacceptable[33].

---

30. *The Minor Agreements and the Two-Source Theory*, in *Evangelica II*, pp. 3-42 (including examination of significant agreements diff. Mk 5,27; 9,19; 4,11; 14,65; 6,30-34; 9,2-10). Cf. *ETL* 67 (1991) 361-372: *A Symposium on the Minor Agreements*. An adaptation of the Cumulative List (1974, pp. 49-195) has been prepared for the Göttingen Conference: *The Minor Agreements in a Horizontal-line Synopsis* (SNTA, 15), Leuven, 1991.

31. *Evangelica II*, p. 41.

32. ΤΙΣ ΕΣΤΙΝ Ο ΠΑΙΣΑΣ ΣΕ, in *ETL* 63 (1987) 5-47; = *Evangelica II*, pp. 95-137 (with additional note, p. 138); see also pp. 27-28. Cf. C.M. Tuckett, *Reading the New Testament. Methods of Interpretation*, London, 1987, p. 34; *The Minor Agreements and Textual Criticism* (unpublished paper, Göttingen, 1991).

33. B. Aland mentions the case of Mt 26,68 as "eine seltene Ausnahme ... möglicherweise" (n. 1), and rightly urges: "Beantwortet kann [die Frage nach den Konjekturen] stets nur aufgrund genauer Erörterung der einzelnen Stelle in ihrem Kontext werden". Cf. *Das Zeugnis der frühen Papyri für den Text der Evangelien diskutiert am Matthäus-evangelium*, in *The Four Gospels 1992*, pp. 326-335, esp. 326. Cf. A. Vanhoye, *L'intérêt de Luc pour la prophétie en Lc 1,76; 4,16-30 et 22,60-65, ibid.*, pp. 1529-1548, esp. 1544-1547

III. The Passion and Resurrection Narratives

D.P. Senior presented in 1972 his dissertation on the passion narrative in Matthew, at the conclusion of four years of research in Leuven. His work is a verse by verse examination of Mt 26,1–27,56 "comparing every single word to Mark's account to see how much one can explain in terms of Matthean use and adaptation of Mark". I quote R.E. Brown: "This dissertation, written under Neirynck's direction in 1972, comes as close as one can to giving a coup-de-grace to any theory positing a major independent source for the Matthean passion narrative"[34]. Similar observations were made by other reviewers[35]. It is Senior's contention that the Matthean *Sondergut* passages, firmly embedded in the Markan context, can be explained as the result of Matthew's theological and literary reflection on his Markan source[36]. My own essay on Mt 28,1-10, first presented in 1967, and in particular

---

(Lk 22,62) and 1547-1548 (Mt 26,68): "L'hypothèse du Prof. F. Neirynck trouve donc là un appui très ferme" (p. 1548).

See also, in *The Four Gospels 1992*, further discussion of the minor agreements by T.A. Friedrichsen (n. 27), R.H. Gundry (n. 29), and M.E. Boring, *The Synoptic Problem, "Minor" Agreements and the Beelzebul Pericope*, pp. 587-619: extensive treatment of Mt/ Lk diff. Mk 3,22-30, with evaluation of the major theories (Griesbach, Farrer-Goulder, Deutero-Mark, and the classical two-source hypothesis); conclusion: "Matthew and Luke used canonical Mark, probably in a slightly revised form, and Q, which contained an independent version of this story" (p. 619).

34. R.E. Brown's review in *CBQ* 38 (1976) 259-260, p. 259. See there also the retraction of his earlier statement (in treating the passion narrative in *John* II, 1970, p. 790) that "The French and the Belgians think that Matthew had a more primitive source than Mark".

35. See, e.g., G. Sellin, in *TLZ* 102 (1977) 437-439: "Es ist das Hauptverdienst dieser Arbeit, daß die Abweichungen von Mk überzeugend als durchgehende matthäische Redaktion erklärt werden können. Dabei vertritt Senior in lobenswerter methodischer Strenge den asketischen Standpunkt konsequenter redaktionsgeschichtlicher Exegese, wie er in Leuven (F. Neirynck) praktiziert wird, und steht damit auf solidem methodischen Fundament in einer Zeit, wo neutestamentliche Forschung wieder ins Stadium des Wagnisses hypothetischer Rekonstruktionen von Quellen und Traditionen zu treten scheint" (col. 438). "Die Hypothese vom Fehlen jeglicher Sonderquellen und -traditionen in der matthäischen Passionsgeschichte ist damit ein gutes Stück weiter bewiesen" (col. 439).

36. D.P. Senior, *The Passion Narrative according to Matthew. A Redactional Study* (BETL, 39), Leuven, 1975 (diss. 1972, with additional notes on recent studies); ²1982. Other publications on Matthew's special material (in chronological order): *The Fate of the Betrayer. A Redactional Study of Matthew XXVII,3-10*, in *ETL* 48 (1972) 372-426 (= 1975, pp. 343-397); *The Death of Jesus and the Resurrection of the Holy Ones, Matthew 27:51-53*, in *CBQ* 38 (1976) 312-329; *Matthew's Special Material in the Passion Story: Implications for the Evangelist's Redactional Technique and Theological Perspective*, in *ETL* 63 (1987) 272-294 (updating his dissertation, with special attention to Mt 27,3-10.24-25.51b-53); *Matthew's Account of the Burial of Jesus: Mt 27,57-61*, in *The Four Gospels 1992* (n. 1), pp. 1433-1448. See also *The Passion of Jesus in the Gospel of Matthew* (Passion Series, 1), Wilmington, DE, 1985.

the redactional interpretation of 28,9-10, has played a noticeable role in the debate on John and the Synoptics[37]. The direction of the argument is well sketched by D.M. Smith[38]:

In an earlier article, Neirynck had shown how Matthew 28:9-10, the story of Jesus' encounter with the women outside the tomb, can be understood as a Matthean editorial composition. The principal argument against this view always refers to the existence of John 20:11-18, the appearance to Mary Magdalene, said to be based on a similar and related tradition. Now Neirynck seeks to show that the Johannine account can be read more intelligibly as an elaboration and retelling of the Matthean story. The logic of his argument is impeccable: if Matthew composed 28:9-10 on no traditional basis, and if John can best be understood against that background, John must have known Matthew's Gospel, and other putative sources become superfluous. John has carried forward what was already occurring in Matthew, the displacement of the angelophany (John 20:11-13) by the appearance of Jesus himself. ... Essential elements of Matthew's brief narrative recur in that of John, albeit mostly in different forms. It is, of course, scarcely possible that Matthew redacted and compressed John; on the other hand, that John created his dramatic narrative and gave to Mary Magdalene the central role is easily imaginable.

It is now widely accepted, even by J.B. Green, that "no reason exists to postulate a second, non-Markan, written narrative source for Matthew's passion narrative"[39]. But Green directly adds that the source-

37. F. NEIRYNCK, *Les femmes au tombeau. Étude de la rédaction matthéenne (Matt. XXVIII.1-10)*, in *NTS* 15 (1968-69) 168-190 (paper read at the SNTS meeting in Gwatt, 1967), reprinted in *Evangelica*, 1982, pp. 273-295 (with additional note, p. 296); updated and supplemented in *John and the Synoptics* (BETL 44, 1977), in *Evangelica*, pp. 365-398 (388-390: "Mt 28,9-10"); *John and the Synoptics: The Empty Tomb Stories* (*NTS* 30, 1984), in *Evangelica II*, pp. 571-600 (579-588: "Jn 20,11-18 and Mt 28,9-10"; with additional note, p. 600); *John and the Synoptics: 1975-1990* (n. 1 above), 1992, pp. 16-35: "John and Matthew" (esp. pp. 33-35, on Mt 28,9-10).

38. D.M. SMITH, *John among the Gospels. The Relationship in Twentieth-Century Research*, Minneapolis, MN, 1992, p. 157 (with reference to *NTS* 1969 and 1984). Some critics continue to envisage the possibility that "Matt 28:9-10 is a compression of the appearance to Mary Magdalene in John 20:11-18" (D.J. HARRINGTON, *The Gospel of Matthew*, Collegeville, MN, 1991, p. 411) or imagine that Mt 28,9-10.16-20 is Matthew's editing of the lost ending of Mark (R.H. GUNDRY, *Mark. A Commentary on His Apology for the Cross*, 1993 [cf. below, n. 138], p. 1021), but no new arguments are brought forward. The same can be said of R. Kühschelm's short paper at this Conference. It is not the formulation of ten questions (which are not unanswerable!) which allows to conclude that "die Annahme einer alten Tradition ... gewichtige Gründe auf ihrer Seite hat" (p. 563; italics mine). Cf. *Angelophanie - Christophanie in den synoptischen Grabesgeschichten. Mk 16,1-8par unter Berücksichtigung von Joh 20,11-18*, in this volume, pp. 556-565. Kühschelm recognizes in Mt 28,9-10 "viel Matthäisches in Sprache und Konzeption", "redaktionelle Gestaltung", "redaktionelle Formung" (*ibid.*). See also GUNDRY, *Matthew*, 1982, p. 591. On the Mt/Lk agreement ἀπαγγέλλειν (*Mark*, p. 1021), cf. *Evangelica*, pp. 261-263.

39. J.B. GREEN, *The Death of Jesus. Tradition and Interpretation in the Passion Narrative* (WUNT, 2/33), Tübingen, 1988 (Diss. Aberdeen, 1985, under I.H. Marshall), p. 23 (at the conclusion of his brief treatment of Matthew, pp. 20-23). Cf. below, n. 43.

critical problem is more complex with regard to the Lukan passion story. In 1968, when I had to deliver a presidential address for the Colloquium on the Gospel of Luke, I chose to treat the question of Luke's use of Mark, in the form of a critical evaluation of T. Schramm's dissertation on this topic (1966). I was confronted there with the theory that "die Sonderquelle in Lk 22,14ff die Grundlage des Berichtes bildet und Primärquelle ist..."[40]. I replied to this thesis with an examination of the transpositions in Luke[41]:

> C'est sur l'argument des transpositions que beaucoup d'auteurs se décident pour une source non-marcienne en Lc 22–24. ... Il me semble plutôt que l'évangile de Marc n'est pas abandonné en Lc 22,14 (ou 15), mais qu'il continue de guider l'évangéliste jusqu'en 24,12. Je le sais, je ne puis me contenter d'exprimer cette opinion: elle est contestée et doit donc devenir un programme d'études ultérieures[42].

J.B. Green's book on *The Death of Jesus*[43] and now also the Seminar at

---

40. T. SCHRAMM, *Der Markus-Stoff bei Lukas. Eine literarkritische und redaktionsgeschichtliche Untersuchung* (SNTS MS, 14), Cambridge, 1971 (diss. Hamburg, 1966), pp. 50-51, esp. 51 (diss., pp. 36-37, esp. 37).

41. *La matière marcienne dans l'évangile de Luc*, in F. NEIRYNCK (ed.), *L'Évangile de Luc. Problèmes littéraires et théologiques. Mémorial L. Cerfaux* (BETL, 32), Gembloux, 1973, pp. 157-201, esp. 195-199 (= *Evangelica*, pp. 37-81, esp. 75-79); reprinted in ID. (ed.), *L'Évangile de Luc - The Gospel of Luke*, Leuven, ²1989, pp. 67-111, esp. 105-109. See also *The Argument from Order and St. Luke's Transpositions*, in *ETL* 49 (1973) 784-815, esp. pp. 804-814: "The Transpositions in Luke"; = *Evangelica*, pp. 737-768, esp. 757-767, on Lk 6,17-19 and 8,19-21 (on the passion narrative: pp. 759-761).

Cf. J.A. FITZMYER, *The Gospel according to Luke*, vol. I (AB, 28), Garden City, NY, 1981, p. 71 (with reference to my analysis of the transpositions): "I am basically in agreement with his approach both to the transpositions and the Lucan passion narrative". Contrast J.B. GREEN, *The Death of Jesus* (n. 39), pp. 29-30: "Neirynck's essay has not dealt the death-blow to the 'argument from transposition' that he (and Fitzmyer) might have us think" (p. 30).

42. *La matière marcienne*, p. 199 (*Evangelica*, p. 79; ²1989, p. 109). "Zu derselben Meinung sind wir für Lk 23,26-49 aufgrund der literarkritischen Untersuchungen gelangt": F.G. UNTERGASSMAIR, *Kreuzweg und Kreuzigung. Ein Beitrag zur lukanischen Redaktionsgeschichte und zur Frage nach der lukanischen "Kreuzestheologie"* (Paderborner Theologische Studien, 10), Paderborn, 1980, p. 112. Cf. p. 154: "Die innerlukanische Verankerung des nicht-markinischen Passionsstoffes macht es schwer, wenn nicht unmöglich, für die Lk-Passion eine von Mk unabhängige und dem Endverfasser des Lk vorgegebene schriftliche Passions-Sonderquelle zu vermuten. [n. 172:] Auch gegen T. Schramm".

43. Cf. n. 39 above. At the end of his analysis of Lk 22–23, par. Mk (pp. 24-104), he concludes that "we can reasonably propose that Luke knew a second, unified narrative" (p. 104; with a reference to "the programmatic statement by Schramm", n. 365). In Appendix (pp. 324-330) the following verses are marked as Lukan redaction of *Sonderquelle* probable (bold), possible (normal print), conflated with Mk (italic): Lk 22,**3a**.b.14-15a.**15b**.16-18.**19-20**.*21-23*.**24-27**.**28-30**.**31-33**.**35-38**.*39-42*.**43-44**.*45*.**48**.**50c**.**51**.52b.**53b**.*54b-62*.**63-64**.66.**67-68**.69.**70-71**; 23,**2**.**4-5**.**6-12**.**13-16**.*18-23*.*24-25*.26c.**27-31**.**34ab**.35.37.**39-43**.**46b**.48.

this Colloquium conducted by F. Bovon[44] call to mind that this question is still controversial. In the 1960s, when Schramm wrote his dissertation, he could rely on the works of Taylor, Schürmann, Jeremias and Rehkopf[45], but it is not in that direction that the study of Luke's passion narrative has developed in the last 25 years. It may be instructive to study the evolution in the position of a Lukan scholar like G. Schneider[46], or to compare the Anchor Bible commentary of J.A. Fitzmyer (1985) with the commentary on John in the same series by R.E. Brown (1970)[47]. The latest commentary on Luke has only one sentence on this question: "Attempts to locate a separate written Lukan source for the passion have not proven successful"[48].

Fitzmyer retains nevertheless a long list of L passages in Lk 22–23.

44. F. BOVON, Le récit lucanien de la passion de Jésus (Lc 22–23), in this volume, pp. 393-423, esp. 406-421: Markan sections (Lk 22,1-14; 22,47–23,5; 23,44–24,11) alternate with sections from the Lukan source: Lk 22,15-46 and 23,6-43.

45. Der Markus-Stoff, p. 50, n. 2; in the text: "Durch umfangreiche, gründliche Arbeiten ist, so scheint es, mit ziemlicher Sicherheit erwiesen..." (sic). In the published text of La matière marcienne (²1989, pp. 105, 304) I could include two posthumous publications: V. TAYLOR, The Passion Narrative in Luke, 1972, and J. JEREMIAS, Die Sprache des Lukasevangeliums, 1980.

46. G. SCHNEIDER, Verleugnung, Verspottung und Verhör Jesu nach Lukas 22,54-71 (SANT, 22), München, 1969, p. 139: "Als Hauptvorlage von Lk 22,54-71 hat der Evangelist die nicht-mk Quelle benutzt"; p. 143: "eine nicht-mk Langform der P, die Luk neben Mk benutzt hat", "die mit dem Einzug Jesu in Jerusalem beginnt", and "die auch Ostergeschichten enthielt". Compare, Das Verfahren gegen Jesus in der Sicht des dritten Evangeliums (Lk 22,54–23,25). Redaktionskritik und historische Rückfrage, in K. KERTELGE (ed.), Der Prozess gegen Jesus (QD, 112), Freiburg, 1988, pp. 111-130, esp. 113: "[in Die Passion Jesu, 1973] kam ich zu der Auffassung, daß Lukas in seinem Kapitel 23 keine Nicht-Mk-Quelle der Passion benutzte, sondern die Mk-Passion bearbeitete und mit Sonderüberlieferungen auffüllte. Dies gilt entsprechend auch für die Inhaftierungsperikope". See also Das Evangelium nach Lukas (ÖTK, 3), Gütersloh-Würzburg, 1977, pp. 28; 435-437; 444: Lk 22,15-18 (ctr. Verleugnung, p. 149); 469-470: Lk 22,69 (ctr. Verleugnung, pp. 118-120). On Lk 22,67-68, cf. below, n. 54.

47. BROWN, John II, p. 790: "we think that a solid defense can be made for the thesis that Luke drew on a truly independent, non-Marcan source". Cf. FITZMYER, Luke II, pp. 1365-1368 ("The Lucan Passion Narrative"), p. 1366: "Luke has only modified the passion narrative in 'Mk' by adding separate stories or sayings from 'L' (or in one instance from 'Q'), by redacting 'Mk' and by freely composing some material... This seems to me to be the better solution. The heavy use of 'L' material in the passion narrative does not argue immediately for a connected written source independent of 'Mk'". See also, e.g., F.J. MATERA, Passion Narratives and Gospel Theologies, New York - Mahwah, NJ, 1986, p. 155 (and p. 239, n. 7, with reference to Fitzmyer); M.L. SOARDS, The Passion according to Luke. The Special Material of Luke 22 (JSNT SS, 14), Sheffield, 1987, pp. 120-123 (and p. 126, on Lk 23); R.J. KARRIS, The Gospel according to Luke, in NJBC, 1990, p. 714.

48. L.T. JOHNSON, The Gospel of Luke (Sacra Pagina, 3), Collegeville, MN, 1991, p. 334. Cf. G.W.E. NICKELSBURG, Passion Narratives, in ABD, 1992, V, 174-175: "While Luke's narrative may well retain unique traditional material, most of the differences from Mark are understandable as expressions of Luke's literary and theological interests, and an independent passion narrative seems an unnecessary hypothesis".

One of the texts he ascribes to L is 22,63-65.66-71, the mistreatment and the interrogation of Jesus by the Jewish authorities[49]. For both episodes I can refer to more recent studies, my own analysis of the Lukan redaction in 22,63-65 (1987)[50] and the essays on the "trial" by W. Radl (1988)[51], F.J. Matera (1989)[52] and A. Dauer (1992)[53]. With regard to the special problem of 22,67-68 (cf. Jn 10,24-26) the point I made in a 1972 book review seems to have found its way: "G. Schneider a sans doute raison de rapprocher 22,67d-68b et 20,1-8. Mais il me semble que ce rapprochement devrait permettre d'expliquer le logion comme une création rédactionnelle de Luc"[54].

Fitzmyer's other instances of L passages in Lk 22 are vv. 15-18.19c-20.27.31-32.33.35-38[55] (all in the S^{Lk} block delineated by Bovon: 22,15-46)[56]. M.L. Soards, more attentive to Lukan redaction and composi-

---

49. *Luke* I, p. 84, with question mark; but see II, p. 1458: "almost certainly". Compare M.L. SOARDS, *The Passion* (n. 47), p. 103: "Verse 64d comes from oral tradition" (cf. Mt); p. 105: "Luke knew an independent oral tradition that lies behind 64a-e" (cf. Jn 10,24-26).

50. ΤΙΣ ΕΣΤΙΝ (n. 32), esp. pp. 14-28 (= *Evangelica II*, pp. 104-118, with additional note, p. 138, on M.L. Soards and J.B. Green).

51. *Sonderüberlieferungen bei Lukas? Traditionsgeschichtliche Fragen zu Lk 22,67f; 23,2 und 23,6-12*, in *Der Prozess gegen Jesus* (n. 46), pp. 131-147, esp. 140-147 (reply to G. Schneider 1969, D.R. Catchpole 1971, A. Strobel 1980).

52. *Luke 22,66-71: Jesus before the* ΠΡΕΣΒΥΤΕΡΙΟΝ?, in *ETL* 65 (1989) 43-59; reprinted in F. NEIRYNCK (ed.), *L'Évangile de Luc - The Gospel of Luke* (n. 41), pp. 517-533: "Luke's version ... does not preserve an independent tradition" (p. 532).

53. *Spuren der (synoptischen) Synedriumsverhandlung im 4. Evangelium. Das Verhältnis zu den Synoptikern*, in A. DENAUX (ed.), *John and the Synoptics* (n. 1), pp. 307-339, esp. 320-336 ("Lk 22,54a.66-71"): "dürfte im wesentlichen auf Mk zurückgehen, die Änderungen gegenüber Mk sind wohl durchweg redaktionell" (p. 336).

54. *ETL* 48 (1972) 570-573 (review of G. Schneider, *Verleugnung*), esp. p. 572. Cf. R. PESCH, *Das Markusevangelium* II, 1977, p. 408; RADL (n. 51), pp. 146-147; MATERA (n. 52), p. 152 (= 526); DAUER (n. 53), pp. 332-333. The remarkable similarity between Jn 10,24-26 and Lk 22,67-68 can be explained by Johannine dependence on Luke's redactional text, indirectly through a pre-Johannine source (Dauer) or, more likely, by John's use of Luke. See, e.g., M. SABBE, *John 10 and Its Relationship to the Synoptic Gospels*, in J. BEUTLER - R.T. FORTNA (eds.), *The Shepherd Discourse of John 10 and Its Context* (SNTS MS, 67), Cambridge, 1991, pp. 75-93, esp. 75-85 ("A Trial of Jesus by the Jews: John 10,22-39"); = M. SABBE, *Studia Neotestamentica. Collected Essays* (BETL, 98), Leuven, 1991, pp. 443-466, esp. 443-455: "the hypothesis of a direct dependence ... is also valid for this pericope" (p. 455).

55. Fitzmyer's list (I, p. 84), corrected in accordance with the commentary in vol. II (pp. 1386, 1412, 1421, 1429).

56. And, of course, ascribed to the *Sonderquelle* by Green (n. 43 above). For Lk 22,43-44 (pp. 56-57: Sonderquelle probable), the textual authenticity is rejected by Fitzmyer (II, pp. 1443-1444). On Lukan authorship, cf. G. SCHNEIDER, *Engel und Blutschweiß (Lk 22,43-44)*, in *BZ* 20 (1976) 112-116 (ctr. *Verleugnung*, p. 159: Sonderquelle). See now also R.E. BROWN, *The Lukan Authorship of Luke 22:43-44*, in *SBL Seminar Papers 1992*, pp. 154-164. Brown convincingly argues for the authenticity. His thesis on the existence of a pre-Gospel tradition "associating an angelic response with the prayer that Jesus made to the Father concerning the hour/cup" (p. 160, cf. 155) is more questionable. Mt 26,53: "the

tion, has reduced this list to Lk 22,19-20, a tradition similar to that
found in 1 Cor 11,23-25, and an independent saying of Jesus incorporated in 22,36[57]. In Lk 23 the following passages are ascribed to L:
vv. 6-12.13-16.27-32.35a.36-37.39b-43[58]. The reader of Fitzmyer's notes
on tradition history in Lk 23 (with bibliographical references up to
1982) may get the impression that this chapter of the commentary needs
updating. With regard to 23,27-31, and the entire section 23,26-49,
F.G. Untergassmair's careful analysis (1980) should be considered[59].
G. Schneider can no longer be cited among those who ascribe to L the
episode of the appearance of Jesus before Herod (23,6-12)[60]. Personally
I would agree with the position that "all the differences between Luke
and Mark in 23,1-25 should be attributed to Luke's redactional acti-

immediate source of the phrase can best be sought within Matthew's own gospel"
(Senior). Jn 12,(28-)29: possibly a recollection of Lk 22,43 (Barrett, Boismard). Justin,
Dial. 103,8: "Justin reprend l'expression bien caractéristique de *Lc.*: ἱδρὼς ὡσεὶ θρόμβοι"
(Massaux). *Historia passionis Domini:* "Sequitur Luc. 22. Apparuit autem ei angelus de
celo confortans eum. Qualiter autem angelus Christum in agonia sue oracionis conforta-
verit dicitur in Evangelio Nazareorum". This is hardly a witness for a pre-Lukan
tradition. If it has any value, it seems to refer to an apocryphal expansion of Lk 22,43 in
which words of the angel were quoted.

    57. *The Passion* (n. 47), p. 54.
    58. *Luke* I, p. 84; II, pp. 1479, 1483, 1494, 1500, 1507 (all in Bovon's second S[Lk]
block). For Fitzmyer the only L elements in Lk 23,44–24,11 (cf. Bovon: Markan block)
are 23,53c (pp. 1523, 1525: cf. Jn 19,41), 56a (pp. 1523, 1526), 56b (p. 1541). Contrast
GREEN, *The Death of Jesus*, pp. 101-102 (Lk 23,50-56a is "best explained as a redaction of
his Markan source"). On 23,56a.b, cf. *Evangelica*, pp. 299-301. In Fitzmyer's list (I, p. 84),
delete 23,46.47b-49 (p. 1513).
    59. *Kreuzweg und Kreuzigung* (n. 42). See now also his essay, *Der Spruch vom "grünen
und dürren Holz" (Lk 23,31)*, in *SNTU* 16 (1991) 55-87. Cf. J.H. NEYREY, *Jesus' Address
to the Women of Jerusalem (Lk. 23.27-31) - A Prophetic Judgment Oracle*, in *NTS* 29
(1983) 74-86; reprinted in his *The Passion according to Luke. A Redaction Study of Luke
Soteriology*, New York - Mahwah, NJ, 1985, pp. 108-121 (p. 121: "... the creation of
Luke himself and does not come from the pre-Luke source"; 1983, p. 84: "does not come
from a pre-Lucan passage, tradition or source"); C.H. GIBLIN, *The Destruction of
Jerusalem according to Luke's Gospel: A Historical-Typological Moral* (AnBib, 107),
Rome, 1985, pp. 93-104 (with reference to Neyrey). In the new interpretation of 23,31
suggested by Untergassmair (1991) "the green wood" refers to the judgment of Jerusalem
and "the dry wood" to the *Endgericht*.
    60. Cf. G. SCHNEIDER, *Das Verfahren* (n. 46), pp. 126-128; and, in the same volume,
W. RADL, *Sonderüberlieferungen* (n. 51), pp. 134-140: "Jesus vor Herodes (23,6-12)". Cf.
K. MÜLLER, *Jesus vor Herodes. Eine redaktionsgeschichtliche Untersuchung zu Lk 23,6-12*,
in G. DAUTZENBERG, et al. (eds.), *Zur Geschichte des Urchristentums* (QD, 87), Freiburg,
1979, pp. 111-141, p. 141: "ohne Abstriche eine Komposition des Lukas" (not mentioned
by Fitzmyer); M.L. SOARDS, *Tradition, Composition, and Theology in Luke's Account of
Jesus before Herodes Antipas*, in *Bib* 66 (1985) 344-364 (p. 358: a Lukan composition, but
a tradition seems to underlie vv. 9a, 12b, and perhaps 7b and 11c); F.J. MATERA, *Luke
23,1-25* (n. 61 below), pp. 541-546.
    Fitzmyer rightly observes that 23,13-16 is "a logical sequence to vv. 6-12 and difficult
to separate from them" (p. 1484). Cf. SCHNEIDER, *Lukas*, p. 476: "Es dürfte insgesamt eine
lukanische Bildung sein, nicht zuletzt auch deswegen, weil es zur Barabbasszene (23,18-25)
überleitet".

vity"[61]. Fitzmyer draws attention to the striking resemblance between Lk 23,4b and Jn 18,38c and suggests that "Luke may well have derived from 'L' the tradition of Pilate's triple declaration of Jesus' innocence" (Lk 23,4.14-15.22; cf. Jn 18,38; 19,4.6)[62]. In his commentary the possibility of Lukan redaction and Johannine dependence on Luke is not really taken into consideration[63]. The most famous contacts with John are found in the resurrection narratives: Lk 24,12 (cf. Jn 20,3-10)[64] and Lk 24,36b.40 (cf. Jn 20,19-20)[65]. The common-tradition hypothesis may seem to provide here a ready answer to the radical thesis of post-Lukan interpolation. Closer examination, however, led me to conclude that in these cases a more creative Lukan intervention is involved[66].

Some more general trends in the study of the gospels may seem to influence exegetical positions regarding the Sondergut in Luke: Lukan redaction or pre-Lukan tradition. The re-evaluation of the apocryphal gospels is now on the program in some schools, and the Gospel of Peter, for instance, is supposed to preserve a pre-canonical passion and resurrection narrative. Thus, for J.D. Crossan, the mourning in Lk

61. F.J. MATERA, *Luke 23,1-25: Jesus before Pilate, Herod, and Israel*, in F. NEIRYNCK (ed.), *L'Évangile de Luc - The Gospel of Luke* (n. 41), pp. 535-551, esp. p. 535. By the same author: *Luke 22,66-71* (n. 52); *Passion Narratives* (n. 47); *The Death of Jesus according to Luke. A Question of Sources*, in *CBQ* 47 (1985) 469-485.

62. *Luke* II, pp. 1471-1472, 1488 (cf. I, p. 88).

63. See my *John and the Synoptics: 1975-1990* (n. 1), pp. 35-46: "John and Luke", where I noted this lacuna in Fitzmyer's commentary (p. 38). On Lk 23,4.14.22, cf. A. DAUER, *Die Passionsgeschichte im Johannesevangelium* (SANT, 30), München, 1972, pp. 156, 158, 160 (Lukan redaction); M. SABBE, *The Trial of Jesus before Pilate in John and Its Relation to the Synoptic Gospels*, in A. DENAUX (ed.), *John and the Synoptics* (n. 1), pp. 341-385, esp. 356 (and n. 28); = *Studia Neotestamentica* (n. 54), pp. 467-513, esp. 483.

64. See my contributions on Lk 24,12 in *Evangelica*, pp. 297-455, esp. 329-334 (*ETL* 1972), 390-396 (*BETL* 45); *Evangelica II*, pp. 588-596 (*NTS* 1984); *John and the Synoptics: 1975-1990*, pp. 42-44. For exposition and evaluation of this approach, cf. H. THYEN, *Johannes und die Synoptiker. Auf der Suche nach einem neuen Paradigma zur Beschreibung ihrer Beziehungen anhand von Beobachtungen an Passions- und Ostererzählungen*, in A. DENAUX (ed.), *John and the Synoptics* (n. 1), pp. 81-107, esp. 105-106.

65. On Lk 24,36b.40, cf. *Jean et les Synoptiques* (BETL, 49), 1979, pp. 126-136; *Evangelica II*, pp. 205-226 (*Luc 24,36-43: Un récit lucanien*, in FS J. Dupont, 1985); *John and the Synoptics: 1975-1990*, pp. 41-42, 44-45.

66. For criticism, cf. W.L. CRAIG, *The Disciples' Inspection of the Empty Tomb (Lk 24,12.24; Jn 20,2-10)*, in A. DENAUX (ed.), *John and the Synoptics* (n. 1), pp. 614-619; A. DAUER, *Lk 24,12 - Ein Produkt lukanischer Redaktion?*, in *The Four Gospels 1992*, pp. 1697-1716. Dauer formulates nine critical observations. Since Dauer himself holds the now exceptional thesis of textual inauthenticity (see my *John and the Synoptics: 1975-1990*, pp. 42-44), one should perhaps not give too much weight to his last difficulty: "widerspricht der Ansicht der meisten Exegeten" (p. 1712). There is no space here for a detailed rejoinder. I just mention his "grundsätzliches Bedenken" against editorial composition of Lk 24,12 (after 24,1-9): Luke's *Dublettenscheu* (pp. 1707-1708: with reference to the omission of Mk 8,1-9 and 14,3-9; see also p. 1709). It would be more to the point to refer to the key passage for my interpretation: Lk 24,22-24, with a different kind of "doublet" in vv. 22-23 (cf. 24,1-9) and v. 24 (cf. 24,12).

23,48, unique to Luke, is "Luke's acceptance of *Gospel of Peter* 7:25 and 8:28"; the story of the two criminals in Lk 23,39-43 is Luke's redactional creation, "but based on elements of the *Cross Gospel*" (GP 4:10.13-14); the "process" before Herod in Lk 23,6-12 is "an attempt to integrate the tradition about Antipas from the *Cross Gospel*" (in GP 1:1-2; 2:5b Herod is in charge of the proceedings)[67]. In each case I agree that there is a certain relationship but I would argue for the inverted direction of influence[68]. M.L. Soards suggests that Lk 23,26-32 is a Lukan composition (vv. 28.32, cf. Mk 15,21.27), but the comparison with the Gospel of Thomas brings him to conclude that Luke (11,27-28; 23,29) and Thomas (logion 79) independently preserve the same tradition[69]. However, the original unity of Lk 11,27-28 and 23,29 (already suggested by R. McL. Wilson in 1960[70]) is much less likely than a secondary combination in Th 79[71]. In his study of the Lukan redaction in 23,27-31 Soards apparently neglects the link of v. 29 with Lk 21,23a (Mk 13,17)[72].

67. J.D. CROSSAN, *The Cross that Spoke. The Origins of the Passion Narrative*, San Francisco, 1988, pp. 260, 169-174, 43-45. Crossan's view is, of course, quite different from the classic hypothesis of a pre-Lukan passion source (cf. Bovon): Lk 23,6-12 is "a pure Lukan creation"; the comment on the friendship of Herod and Pilate in v. 12 is the only possibly pre-Lukan element in the entire incident (p. 44; cf. p. 64).

68. With regard to the episode of the two thieves ("a magnificent tableau" in Lk), Crossan cannot accept that the influence goes from Lk to the Gospel of Peter: "I can see no reason for such textual dismemberment" (p. 173). Note, however, that the same Crossan can accept that "Mark had deliberately dismembered the story of the resurrected youth in the *Secret Gospel* and scattered its literary debris throughout his own Gospel" (p. 283). See my *The Apocryphal Gospels and the Gospel of Mark* (1989), in *Evangelica II*, pp. 715-767 (with additional note, pp. 768-772).

69. M.L. SOARDS, *Tradition, Composition, and Theology in Jesus' Speech to the "Daughters of Jerusalem" (Luke 23,26-32)*, in *Bib* 68 (1987) 221-244, esp. pp. 232-237.

70. *Studies in the Gospel of Thomas*, London, 1960, p. 81. In *Ancient Christian Gospels* (London - Philadelphia, PA, 1990) H. Koester compares Th 79a with Lk 11,27-28 (which he ascribes to Q: pp. 88, 141, 144) and Th 79b with Mk 13,17 (p. 108). Although he notices the contrast with Mk 13,17 (n. 2: "formulated as a woe over those who are pregnant and nursing. Thomas, however, is formulated as a beatitude for those who have not conceived and the breasts which have not given milk"), there is no mention of the much closer parallel in Lk 23,29.

71. Compare the reply to Wilson by H.E.W. TURNER, in ID. – H. MONTEFIORE, *Thomas and the Evangelists* (SBT, 35), London, 1962, pp. 35, 38, 96; H. SCHÜRMANN, *Das Thomasevangelium und das lukanische Sondergut*, in *BZ* 7 (1963) 236-260; = *Traditionsgeschichtliche Untersuchungen zu den synoptischen Evangelien*, Düsseldorf, 1968, pp. 228-247; and independently, W. SCHRAGE, *Das Verhältnis des Thomas-Evangeliums zur synoptischen Tradition und zu den koptischen Evangelienübersetzungen* (BZNW, 29), Berlin, 1964, pp. 164-168. Cf. G. SCHNEIDER, *Lukas*, p. 268; J.A. FITZMYER, *Luke*, p. 1494; and now also M. FIEGER, *Das Thomasevangelium. Einleitung, Kommentar und Systematik* (NeutAbh, NF 22), Münster, 1991, pp. 218-219.

72. On another "tradition" related to Lukan Sondergut (24,39), see my *Luc 24,36-43: un récit lucanien* (1985), in *Evangelica II*, esp. pp. 219-223 ("Le témoignage d'Ignace d'Antioche").

In the opposite sense, the new literary-critical approaches emphasize the literary unity of Luke-Acts and this appears to be beneficial for the redactional interpretation of Luke's special material[73].

IV. The Sayings Source Q

In an assessment of the studies on Q at the 1981 Colloquium[74] I could note to my satisfaction:

> Although there is some hesitation about one or another isolated saying, a rather general tendency can be observed to include [in the reconstruction of Q] only passages attested by both Matthew and Luke and to include all of them[75].

If I had to rewrite my survey in 1992, I would mention that some scholars now tend to include again minor agreements (from the triple tradition)[76] and Sondergut passages[77]. On the other hand, M. Sato (in

73. Cf. D. Senior, *The Passion of Jesus in the Gospel of Luke* (The Passion Series, 3), Wilmington, DE, 1989, p. 8 (see the references to recent studies, nn. 2-5). Cf. p. 10: "my own opinion is that the special character of Luke's Passion narrative is due to his creative reinterpretation of Mark's account".

74. *Recent Developments in the Study of Q*, in J. Delobel (ed.), *Logia. Les paroles de Jésus - The Sayings of Jesus* (BETL, 59), Leuven, 1982, pp. 29-75; = *Evangelica II*, pp. 409-455 (Supplement, pp. 456-464), esp. pp. 415-421 ("The Reconstruction of Q").

75. *Ibid.*, p. 417. The text continues: "The possibility that a *Sondergut* passage may stem from Q is not denied but it is seen as too uncertain to be reckoned with". See the Table on p. 416. – For a more precise and slightly corrected description (12,54-56 is included), cf. my *Q-Synopsis. The Double Tradition Passages in Greek* (SNTA, 13), Leuven, 1988: bold face type is used for words and parts of words that are identical in Mt and Lk; special signs indicate omissions, inversions, synonyms and substitutes.

76. See my *The Minor Agreements and Q*, in R.A. Piper (ed.), *Studies in Q* (forthcoming). Conclusion: "Q 3,2-4; 3,21-22; 6,12-16; 10,25-28; 12,1b; 17,2; 17,31 are proposed in some recent studies as candidates for inclusion in the double-tradition source Q. In none of them, however, the Matthew-Luke agreements against Mark seem to provide conclusive evidence". See especially Section II, on "The Beginning of Q", with reference to D. Catchpole (n. 93 below), J. Lambrecht (n. 91 below), and J.S. Kloppenborg, *City and Wasteland: Narrative World and the Beginning of the Sayings Gospel (Q)*, in *Semeia* 52 (1991) 145-160. On Ναζαρά (Mt 4,13 / Lk 4,16) in the Q source, see now J.M. Robinson, *The Sayings Gospel Q*, in *The Four Gospels 1992*, pp. 361-388, esp. 373-380.

The misuse of the minor agreements by scholars who change the nature of Q by including narratives such as the feeding story (E. Bammel; cf. E.E. Ellis: "a dozen triple-tradition episodes") is not considered here. On the minor agreements as argument against the Q hypothesis (M.D. Goulder), cf. *Evangelica II*, pp. 413-414 (and 463).

77. Cf. J.S. Kloppenborg, *Q Parallels. Synopsis, Critical Notes & Concordance*, Sonoma, CA, 1988. In this handbook for the study of Q (cf. *Evangelica II*, pp. 465-473), the generally accepted extent of Q is printed as unbracketed text, and a number of Sondergut passages appear in parentheses as "probable" extent of Q: Mt 5,41; 7,2a; 11,23b-24; Lk 6,24-26; 6,34-35b; 6,37c-38b; 7,3-5; 7,20; 9,61-62*; 11,21-22*; 11,27-28; 11,36; 12,13-14.16-21*; 12,49*; 13,25(*); 15,8-10; 17,28-29*. The name H. Schürmann (cf.

the line of his adviser, U. Luz) and D. Kosch reckon with the possibility of an intermediate stage of pre-Matthean and pre-Lukan recensions of Q^{78}, in parallel to the Deutero-Markan intermediate between Mark and the Gospels of Matthew and Luke[79].

Sato's Q^{Mt} includes the following Sondergut: Mt 5,5.7-9[K]; 6,34; (7,2a); 7,6; 10,5b-6(Q?); 10,23(Q?); 11,28-30; (23,15-19); (23,24); 25,1-12[80]; Q^{Lk} includes Lk 3,10-14[K]; (4,16-30); 6,24-26[K]; 6,37b-38b[K]; 7,3-6a[K]; 7,29-30 (not in Q); 9,61-62[K]; 10,18-19; 11,5-8[K]; 11,36; 12,16-21[K]; 12,32; 12,35-38; 12,47-48; (12,54-56: not in Q); (13,1-5); (13,6-9); 17,28-29; (18,2-8)[81]. In addition to the passages marked with K, Kosch ascribes to Q^{Lk} the parable of the rich man and the poor Lazarus (16,19-31)[82]. He disagrees with Sato regarding the scattered double-

---

Evangelica II, pp. 418-419) occurs without fail in the critical notes. Only in a few instances, marked here with an asterisk, Kloppenborg refers to his own *The Formation of Q*, Philadelphia, PA, 1987. See his comment on Lk 9,61-62: "Of all the Lukan *Sondergut* this has the strongest probability of deriving from Q" (p. 64), but on the other hand Lk 13,25 is "not in Q" (p. 154). Contrast my *Q-Synopsis*, pp. 11 (9,61-62 in small print) and 49 (13,25, cf. Mt 25,10-12). Cf. below, n. 88.

Other Sondergut passages (cf. Schürmann) are printed in square brackets as "Q origin unlikely", e.g. Mt 10,5b-6.23 (Sato 1984: possibly in Q); Lk 11,5-8 (D.R. Catchpole 1983); Lk 12,35-38 (C.-P. März 1985). On 12,35-38, see now C.-P. MÄRZ, *Zur Vorgeschichte von Lk 12,35-48. Beobachtungen zur Komposition der Logientradition in der Redequelle*, in K. KERTELGE – T. HOLTZ – C.P. MÄRZ (eds.), *Christus bezeugen. FS W. Trilling* (Erfurter Theologische Studien, 59), Leipzig, 1989, pp. 166-178; = C.P. MÄRZ, *"... laßt eure Lampen brennen!" Studien zur Q-Vorlage von Lk 12,35–14,24* (Erfurter Theologische Schriften, 20), Leipzig, 1991, pp. 58-71. See also ID., *Das Gleichnis vom Dieb. Überlegungen zur Verbindung von Lk 12,39 par Mt 24,43 und 1 Thess 5,2-4*, in *The Four Gospels 1992*, pp. 633-648, esp. 639-644; and in this volume, pp. 177-208.

78. See my *Q^{Mt} and Q^{Lk} and the Reconstruction of Q*, in *ETL* 66 (1990) 385-390; = *Evangelica II*, pp. 475-480. Cf. M. SATO, *Q und Prophetie. Studien zur Gattungs- und Theologiegeschichte der Quelle Q* (WUNT, 2/29), Tübingen, 1988 (diss. Bern, 1984); D. KOSCH, *Die eschatologische Tora des Menschensohnes. Untersuchungen zur Rezeption der Stellung Jesu zur Tora in Q* (NTOA, 12), Freiburg/Schw-Göttingen, 1989 (diss. Freiburg/Schw, 1988).

79. Cf. D. KOSCH, *Q: Rekonstruktion und Interpretation. Eine methodenkritische Hinführung mit einem Exkurs zur Q-Vorlage des Lk*, in *FZPT* 36 (1989) 409-425: see the diagram on p. 414 (and n. 18). Compare also U. LUZ, *Das Evangelium nach Matthäus*. I. *Mt 1-7*; II. *Mt 8-17* (EKK, I/1-2), Zürich - Neukirchen-Vluyn, 1985, 1990; vol. I, p. 29 (with reference to Sato): "QMt ist eine nur unwesentlich veränderte und erweiterte Fassung von Q", in contrast to "die vermutlich wesentlich erweiterte Fassung der Logienquelle, die Lukas benutzte"; p. 30: "M.E. benutzten Mt und Lk eine Mk-Rezension, die an manchen Punkten gegenüber unserem Mk sekundär ist" (and vol. II, passim, with reference to A. Ennulat). See my review in *ETL* 63 (1987) 410-413; 67 (1991) 169-171; and *Evangelica II*, pp. 477-480 (and pp. 7-8, on DtMk).

80. *Q* (n. 78), pp. 18-19 (Table), 47-50 (Mt 5,3-12), 51-52 (Q^{Mt}). The parentheses indicate some hesitation: "Unsichere Stellen". See also p. 53: 5,19 and 18,16-17.18 possibly Q^{Mt}.

81. *Q*, pp. 54-59. See also p. 60: 14,28-33; 15,8-10; 17,7-10 possibly Q^{Lk}.

82. *Q: Rekonstruktion* (n. 79), pp. 416-420 ("Zum Profil von Q^{Lk}"), esp. p. 417: the theme of reversal of social conditions. See also pp. 418-419: Q^{Lk} 6,27c-28a; 6,27-28/29-30.31 (inversion); 6,29c.d (inversion).

tradition sayings in Lk 14,26–17,6[83], and the reconstruction of Q he proposes contains all double-tradition passages, in the Lukan order[84], with a number of uncertain texts in parentheses[85].

In contrast to the new "literary" approach in gospel studies, with its concentration on the gospel as a whole and the typical "literary-critical" aversion to distinctions between tradition and redaction, source criticism and redaction criticism are flourishing in the study of Q. The International Q Project[86] has done intensive research on the reconstruction of the Q text. Phrase by phrase, word by word, the options for the source or for the evangelists' redaction were inventoried with pro's and contra's. The establishment of a critical text of Q is in progress[87] and will be completed in 1994. Here too we can observe

83. SATO, Q, pp. 23-24, 52-53, 59-60: the Q origin is doubtful for Lk 14,26.27.34-35; 15,4-7; 16,16.17.18; 17,1.3-4.6 (and the parables 14,16-24; 19,12-27); possibly Q[Lk] and Q[Mt]. Kosch has opted for a "Proto-Lukan" fusion of Q and Sondergut: thus, Q 16,13.16-18; S 16,19-26(31); Q 17,1.3-4.6 was one pre-Lukan block of sayings material (Q: Rekonstruktion, pp. 415, 417).

84. See, most recently, KOSCH, Q und Jesus, in BZ 36 (1992) 30-58, esp. pp. 33-34. The only dislocations are Lk 11,16 (at 11,29) and 17,33 (after 14,26-27); cf. Q Parallels. On the placement of Lk 16,16 / Mt 11,12-13 and Lk 13,34-35 / Mt 23,37-39, see Q Parallels, S18 and S52. On Lk 16,13 / Mt 6,24, cf. SATO, Q, p. 24: the location of the saying is uncertain ("ganz unsicher") but the Q context in Mt indicates its Q origin. See R.A. PIPER, Wisdom in the Q-Tradition. The Aphoristic Teaching of Jesus (SNTS MS, 61), Cambridge, 1988, pp. 86-99: Lk 16,13 is part of a previously existent collection, vv. 9-13, probably known to Matthew (p. 96).

85. They are listed here in a comparative table with Kloppenborg (Q Parallels) and Sato (1988, pp. 18-19):

3,2-4	[Kl]	(S)	7,29-30	[Kl]	[S]	14,16-24	Kl	[S]
3,21-22	[Kl]	(S)	12,1	[Kl]	–	14,34-35	Kl	[S]
4,16	–	(S)	12,49-50	(Kl)	(S)	19,12-27	Kl	[S]
6,20a	<Kl>	(S)	12,54-56	Kl	[S]	Not in Q:		
7,1a	<Kl>	–	14,5	[Kl]	[S]	14,11/18,14b	Kl	[S]

Note: Lk 12,1 and 49-50 have no parallel in Mt. In Kosch's reconstruction Q12,1 includes ἤρξατο λέγειν τοῖς μαθηταῖς αὐτοῦ, cf. Lk v. 1a πρὸς ... (Tora, p. 83). Kloppenborg rightly distinguishes between Lk 12,(49) and [50].

86. The project on "Q: A Lost Collection of Jesus' Sayings" was launched in October 1983 at the Institute for Antiquity and Christianity in Claremont, CA (director: J.M. Robinson), in coordination with the Society of Biblical Literature (Annual Meeting, 1983-1985: Consultation; 1985-1989: Q Seminar); from 1989 on: The International Q Project. Reports of the work sessions (and lists of the participants) are published regularly by J.M. Robinson in JBL: see 109 (1990) 499-501; 110 (1991) 494-498; 111 (1992) 500-508.

On the more issue-oriented work of the Q Seminar, cf. J.S. KLOPPENBORG – L.E. VAAGE (eds.), Early Christianity, Q and Jesus (Semeia, 55), 1992. The Seminar considered a series of topics: orality, textuality and the generation of sayings collections (1983), wisdom materials in Q (1984), Mark and Q (1985), apocalypticism and the Son of man (1986), redactional stratigraphy (1987), the social history of the Q people (1988), early pre-Q collections and their settings (1989). See Preface, p. VII. Continuation in Q Section, J.S. Kloppenborg presiding, 1990-1992.

87. The reconstructions of the Q text are published in the annual reports. See the cumulative list of the decisions 1989-1991 in JBL 111 (1992), p. 508. A few observations

a certain shift of attention from double-tradition texts towards the periphery of Q in minor agreements and Sondergut[88]. The reconstructions already published of Q 11,16; 13,18; 17,2 show that in these cases no serious consideration has been given to the influence of Mark on the Lukan redaction[89].

In Section III of my 1981 survey I treated the problem of "Mark and Q"[90]. Now, in the course of the current year, there seems to be a reemergence of the thesis of Mark's use of Q. New contributions by the old protagonists have been announced, by J. Lambrecht on Mk 1,1-15[91] and by W. Schenk on Mk 6,6b-13[92], and more significantly, D.R. Catchpole, well known and appreciated researcher on Q, has adopted this thesis in two essays on the same sections: The Beginning of Q and

can be made regarding the extent of Q. After examination, some verses are excluded from Q; other sayings are accepted as belonging to Q with a probability of only C and included 〚 〛: 3,1-4, v. 2 Ἰωάννη (cf. Mt -ς, Lk -v), v. 3 πᾶσα . . η . . περίχωρο . . τοῦ Ἰορδάνου (excluded: vv. 1 and 4), but see n. 76 above; 4,16 〚Ναζαρά〛, cf. above, n. 76; — 11,〚16〛 "does belong between Q 11:15 and Q 11:17" (p. 503), but see *Evangelica II*, p. 489 (conclusion: "c'est bien Luc le responsable de la rédaction de Lc 11,16 et sans doute aussi de la place donnée au verset dans l'ensemble de Lc 11,14-36"). — 11,〚36〛: text cannot be reconstructed. — 14,〚5〛: cf. *Evangelica II*, pp. 186, 193-203. — 14,〚16-23〛: vv. 18-20 cannot be reconstructed, vv. 15.22.24 are excluded from Q. — 17,2 Q = Lk, but see n. 76 above. — 17,24.37.26-27.30.34-35 (vv. 28-29 excluded from Q).

88. The 1992 Meeting Program includes among the passages submitted for approval: Q 3,21-22; 9,61-62; 11,27-28; and among the texts ready to be discussed: Lk 9,1 and 10,1; Mt 10,5b-6.23 (pp. 36-38). This acceptance of minor agreements of Mt/Lk against Mk (Lk 3,21-22; 9,1; cf. n. 87 above: Lk 3,3) and Sondergut passages shows some development in the Project. The original proposal concentrated on "the minimal text of Q to emphasize the strict divergence of the method of our reconstruction of Q from earlier reconstructions which could be characterized as 'only what you make it'" (L.E. VAAGE, "The Reconstruction of Q", Seminar paper 1986, p. 11). On Lk 9,61-62, cf. L.E. VAAGE, *The Son of Man Sayings in Q: Stratigraphical Location and Significance*, in *Semeia* 55 (1992) 103-129, p. 114: "It is, however, hardly certain that 9:61-62 ever belonged to Q, at least not if the total absence of any parallel to it in Matthew is taken as significant" (ctr. J.S. Kloppenborg, M.S. Steinhauser); H.T. FLEDDERMANN, *The Demands of Discipleship. Matt 8,19-22 par. Luke 9,57-62*, in *The Four Gospels 1992*, pp. 540-561, esp. 548-552: "both the theme and the vocabulary of Luke 9,61-62 point to Lucan redaction. Q contained only the first two dialogues (Q 9,57-60)" (p. 552).

89. See the references above, n. 76 (Lk 17,2) and n. 87 (Lk 11,16). On Lk 13,18, cf. T.A. Friedrichsen's essay in *The Four Gospels 1992* (n. 27), pp. 662-675 ("The Double Question: Mk 4,30 / Lk 13,18".

90. *Recent Developments* (n. 74), pp. 41-53; = *Evangelica II*, pp. 421-433. See also Additional Notes (*ibid.*, p. 464), with references to J. Schüling 1987 (= 1991), R.A. Piper 1988, D. Lührmann 1989, H. Koester 1990.

91. J. LAMBRECHT, *John the Baptist and Jesus in Mark 1.1-15: Markan Redaction of Q?*, in *NTS* 38 (1992) 357-384. On his earlier work, see my *Recent Developments*, esp. pp. 43-45 (= 423-425).

92. W. SCHENK, *Mk 6,6b-13(30) und sein Verhältnis zu Q*, Seminar paper, SNTS Meeting 1992 (as yet unpublished). On his essay, *Der Einfluss der Logienquelle auf das Markusevangelium*, in *ZNW* 70 (1979) 141-165, see my *Recent Developments*, pp. 42-43 (= 422-423).

The Mission Charge[93]. The Mark/Q overlaps, which in passages such as Q 10,2-12 are used by others as evidence of an earlier pre-Q tradition, are here proposed as Markan redaction of the Q text.

Q 10,2-16 and Mark

In his reconstruction of the Q text behind Lk 10,2-16 Catchpole can attribute to Luke a number of editorial additions[94]. He accepts that Q probably contained the prohibition of greetings on the way, singly attested in Lk 10,4b[95]. He also argues that Q contained, along with other prohibitions, the Gentiles/Samaritans saying (Mt 10,5b)[96], and he assumes that the prohibition of carrying a staff was part of the equipment rule (Q 10,4a)[97]. Catchpole then isolates the original pre-Q tradition consisting of the sheep/wolves saying, the equipment rule, and the instructions on conduct in houses and in towns: Q 10,3.4.5-7.8-12. Internal analysis suggests that one single stratum was later superimposed upon it: Q 10,2.13-15.16 (and Mt 10,5b)[98].

The most problematic verses in this repartition between tradition and redaction are the two conclusions, vv. 12 and 16. The "sending" saying, Q 10,16: "As a saying located at the end of this mission charge it is particularly fitting. It matches the recurrent pattern of positive and negative elements in Q 10:5-7,8-12. It overlaps with the explicit 'sending' saying, Q 10:3, at the start of the pre-Q tradition"[99]. All that is

---

93. D.R. CATCHPOLE, *The Beginning of Q: A Proposal*, in *NTS* 38 (1992) 205-221; *The Mission Charge in Q*, in *Semeia* 55 (1992) 147-174. See also his book, *The Quest for Q*, Edinburgh (forthcoming).

94. *The Mission Charge*, passim, esp. pp. 151, 156, 163, 164-166, 170-171: Lk 10,7d μὴ μεταβαίνετε ἐξ οἰκίας εἰς οἰκίαν, 8a καὶ δέχωνται ὑμᾶς, 8b ἐσθίετε τὰ παρατιθέμενα ὑμῖν, 9b ἐφ' ὑμᾶς, 10a εἰς ἣν δ' ἂν πόλιν εἰσέλθητε, 10b εἰς τὰς πλατείας αὐτῆς, 11b πλὴν τοῦτο γινώσκετε ὅτι ἤγγικεν ἡ βασιλεία τοῦ θεοῦ.

95. *Ibid.*, pp. 151, 168.

96. *Ibid.*, pp. 157-161, esp. 160: "There are very good reasons for thinking that Matt 10:5b could fit into Q and that it would be dropped by Luke". Mt 10,6 (and 15,24) is MtR; cf. 9,36: "very probably dependent upon the same source, namely Mark 6:34" (p. 159).

97. Mt 10,10; cf. Lk 9,3: one of the "LukeR reminiscences of Q even when Mark is the primary source" (p. 151).

98. *Ibid.*, pp. 152-156 (Q 10,2); 162-163 (Q 10,13-15); 166-167 (Q 10,16). On Mt 10,5b, cf. n. 96 above. Schürmann *et al.* who assign Mt 10,5b-6 to Q take vv. 5b and 6 as the two halves of one traditional logion. See, e.g., W.D. DAVIES – D.C. ALLISON, *Matthew*, II, 1991, pp. 164, 169; M. SATO, *Q*, 1988, p. 26 (possibly Q, or Q^Mt); U. LUZ, *Matthäus*, II, 1990, p. 88 (Sondergut or Q^Mt); cf. D.J. HARRINGTON, *Matthew*, 1991, p. 141 (special tradition M). Catchpole's proposal, v. 5b Q and v. 6 MtR, is a reversal and correction of the two stages suggested by M. Trautmann (pp. 159-160). However, Catchpole recognizes that Mt 10,5b-6 exhibits "a nicely balanced symmetry" and he knows "Matthew's fondness for creating antithetical sayings" (*ibid.*). Is it then possible to treat v. 5b "by itself and in its own right"? On "The evangelist's hand" in Mt 10,5b-6, see G.N. STANTON, *A Gospel for a New People* (n. 6 above), pp. 330-391 (cf. 139-140).

99. From *The Mission Charge*, pp. 166-167 (in inverted order).

true, and it seems to suggest that Q 10,16 is well fitting at the conclusion of the pre-Q tradition 10,3-11a. The Sodom saying, Q 10,12: "the latter has often been regarded as a Q-redactional anticipation of the woes on the towns (Q 10:13-15). On this very attractive hypothesis, the pre-editorial tradition ended with the dust-shaking (10:11), while the Sodom saying echoes the Tyre and Sidon saying (10:14) with which it is 'astonishingly parallel'"[100]. But Catchpole concludes his discussion of 10,12 by noting that "it seems fair to register *some hesitation* about the assessment of Q 10:12 as redactional", and in the general conclusion he repeats his suggestion without hesitation[101]. One can agree with a description of 10,12 as the continuation of vv. 10-11a, but is it therefore "*more* a natural development of what precedes it than an anticipation of what follows it"[102]? And is it fair to discuss the radicalism of the saying without further mention of the "parallel" in 10,14? It is not my intention here to contest the value of Catchpole's observations on the traditional mission charge and the superimposition of a single redactional stratum. I simply suggest to correct the repartition of tradition (10,3.4.5-7.8-11a.**16**)[103] and redaction (10,2.**12**.13-15)[104] in the composition of Q 10,2-16.

With regard to the question of Mark's dependence upon Q (the initial suggestion in Catchpole's essay) I may recall the canon I formulated in 1981[105]:

> How do we prove Mark's dependence on Q, and not on a traditional saying or on some pre-Q collection of sayings? This can only be done by

---

100. *Ibid.*, p. 163. See my *Recent Developments*, p. 65 (= 445): "Lk 10,12 has a compositional function in Q as the conclusion of 10,2-12 and the linkage with 10,13-15. Λέγω ὑμῖν replaces here, in a redactional adaptation, the introductory πλήν of the traditional saying in 10,14"; p. 54 (= 434), on 10,12 as one of "the few verses which were accepted as redactional by D. Lührmann" (with references to P. Hoffmann 1972; R. Laufen 1980; W. Schenk 1981; A.D. Jacobson 1982). New references can be added: J.S. Kloppenborg 1987 (*Formation*, p. 196); M. Sato 1988 (*Q*, p. 38); U. Luz 1990 (*Matthäus*, II, p. 89). Apart from Catchpole's dissenting opinion one could speak of a growing consensus on the Q-redaction of this one verse – at least among those who adopt the Lukan order in their reconstruction of Q 10,12.13-15.16. Contrast W.D. Davies – D.C. Allison (p. 164: placement of 10,13-15 LkR or Q^{Lk}); D. Zeller (in *Logia*, p. 404: 10,12 secondary but not Q-redaction).

101. *Ibid*, pp. 164 (my emphasis) and 167.

102. *Ibid*, p. 164 (my emphasis).

103. Cf. A.D. JACOBSON, *The Literary Unity of Q. Lc 10,2-16 and Parallels as a Test Case*, in J. DELOBEL (ed.), *Logia* (n. 74), 1982, pp. 419-423. See also J.S. KLOPPENBORG, *Formation*, pp. 192-197; M. SATO, *Q*, pp. 309-313 (Q 10,3-11a); on 10,16 as *Schlußwort* before the insertion of 10,13-15, see pp. 38, 77.

104. The ἐργάτης saying in v. 7b (cf. v. 2) probably belongs to this same stage of redaction: cf. Catchpole (p. 153), *et al.*; in *Logia*: pp. 404 (D. Zeller) en 421 (A.D. Jacobson).

105. *Recent Developments*, p. 45 (= 425).

showing a specific dependence on the redaction of Q, dependence on sayings of which the creation or at least the formulation can be attributed to the Q redactor, or dependence on the order of the sayings as found in a redactional Q arrangement. It is not enough to observe that Mark's version of the saying is secondary.

Thus, the less rigorous Mk 6,8-9 may be secondary vis-à-vis the equipment rule in Q 10,4a[106], but this is not necessarily evidence of Mark's use of the Q document. If, with Catchpole, we accept traditional pre-Q material in Q 10,3-11, there may be some correspondence between its fourfold division and the contents of Mk 6,7-11: sending (7), equipment (8-9), acceptance (10), rejection (11), but this cannot be used as evidence of Mark's dependence on Q. On the other hand, because Q 10,2.12 are without parallel in Mk 6, one could argue that this Q-redactional frame was unknown to Mark. For Catchpole, Q 10,10-11a is incomplete without v. 12 (judgment theme) and he conjectures that "a sense of this incompleteness underlies the MarkR addition of εἰς μαρτύριον αὐτοῖς"[107]. But Mk 6,11 is scarcely more "complete" than the direct speech in Q 10,11a ending with ὑμῖν = "against you"[108]. The evidence Catchpole adduces against Markan independence of Q finally goes not beyond W. Schenk's 1979 argument[109], particularly the dubious reminiscences of Q 10,13-15 in Mk 6,1-6a[110].

For further discussion of "Mark and Q" I can refer to the contribution by C.M. Tuckett[111]. As a two-source theorist, I am used to

106. Note, however, that the inclusion of "no staff" in the text of Q 10,4a (Catchpole, p. 169; cf. F. Bovon, et al.) is far from certain. Μηδὲ/μήτε ῥάβδον in Mt 10,10 and Lk 9,3 (for Mk 6,8 εἰ μὴ ῥάβδον μόνον) can be the result of assimilation to the other prohibitions. The text of Lk 10,4a (and 22,35) remains a more secure basis for the reconstruction of Q (Polag, Laufen, et al.). – For R.H. Gundry (1982, 1992) and M. Goulder (1989) Lk 9,3 is influenced by Mt 10,10 (Matthean rigorism). More specific reasons for LkR are suggested in the commentaries on Luke by H. Schürmann (p. 501, n. 19; p. 502, n. 24); J.A. Fitzmyer (p. 754), W. Wiefel (p. 170).

107. The Mission Charge, p. 173, n. 29.

108. RSV: "against you"; Fitzmyer: "in protest against you". On the direct speech in 10,11a (compare λέγετε in 10,5 and 9): "Die direkte Rede in V 11 ist ursprünglicher als die bloße Anweisung bei Mk/Mt" (SCHULZ, Q, p. 407; cf. MARSHALL, Luke, p. 423). – The possibility that 10,11a was followed by 10,16 (cf. above) is not taken into consideration by Catchpole (cf. p. 163: "only a weak climax without v. 12, unless v. 16 be drawn in to provide a final comment on the implications of rejection").

109. Cf. above, n. 92.

110. The Mission Charge, pp. 150-151: Mk 6,1 his πατρίς = Capernaum (sic), cf. Q 10,15; Mk 6,2 αἱ δυνάμεις ... γινόμεναι, cf. Q 10,13; Mk 6,3.6 their unbelief and being scandalized, cf. the woes pronounced in Q 10,13-15. Other "Q-reminiscences" noted by Catchpole are: kingdom + repentance in Mk 1,14-15, cf. Q 10,9.13; the Eliah-type call associated with kingdom-centered mission in Mk 1,16-20 and 1,14-15, cf. Q 9,57-60 before 10,2-16; μηδὲ ἀκούσωσιν ὑμῶν in Mk 6,11, cf. Q 10,16.

111. In this volume, pp. 149-175. Less helpful is B.L. MACK, Q and the Gospel of Mark: Revising Christian Origins, in Semeia 55 (1992) 15-39, esp. pp. 25-30: "Mark and Q: An Intertextual Hypothesis". Mack's distinction between the documentary hypothesis

recalling that our first hypothesis is the priority of Mark. The Q source is a second and in fact secondary hypothesis, designed to explain the Matthew-Luke agreements in the double-tradition passages. Personally I am not inclined to exclude from Q dispersed sayings common to Matthew and Luke[112]. On the other hand, I recommend much prudence and reserve with regard to singly attested sayings[113] and, of course, to minor agreements in the triple tradition. In this last case it is not enough to count the Mt-Lk agreements, and no conclusion can be drawn without having seriously examined the possibility of Matthean and Lukan redaction.

J.S. Kloppenborg's work on *The Formation of Q* (1987)[114] has drawn attention to the genre of Q and the history of its composition. Kloppenborg proposes three stages in the development of Q: a first stratum of sapiential instructions, a secondary expansion with interpolated sayings and chriae collections, and a final stage in the direction of a biography (the temptation story)[115]. For F.G. Downing, Q resembles the bios of a Cynic philosopher[116]. In his dissertation, *Q und Prophetie*, M. Sato suggests an alternative proposal and compares the Q source with the prophetic books. The exclusive, eschatological position of *the* prophet makes it different from the Old Testament books: "Mithin scheint Q letzten Endes eine einmalige Grösse zu sein"[117]. In 1976 I used the

and his intertextual model is confusing. Does it mean that creative borrowing and resignification is excluded in a documentary relation? Mack presupposes that Mark used Q. I quote his view on the selection of Q material: "Since Mark was not at all interested in depicting Jesus as a teacher whose teachings were understood and accepted by those who heard him, he 'deleted' the Q[1] material [6,20-21.27-49; 11,2-4.9-13; 12,13-31.33-34.57-59; 16,13]. From Q[2] the material deleted is similar [3,7-9; 7,1-10.18-35; 10,12-15.16; 13,23-24; 14,16-24; 15,4-7; 16,17; 17,3-4; 19,12-13.15-26]" (p. 26). "As for the mission instructions, Mark deleted the references to 'laborers in the harvest,' the message about the kingdom of God being near, and the peace greeting resting on the children of peace who receive those sent" (p. 28).

112. See, e.g., my *Luke 14,1-6. Lukan Composition and Q Saying* (1991, in *FS G. Schneider*, n. 120 below), in *Evangelica II*, pp. 183-203, esp. 202: Q 14,5 among "those sayings whose position in Q cannot be determined with certainty".

113. Cf. above, n. 98, on Mt 10,5b-6.

114. Cf. above, n. 77: *The Formation of Q. Trajectories in Ancient Wisdom Collections.* Compare the original title of Kloppenborg's dissertation: *The Literary Genre of the Synoptic Sayings Source* (Toronto, 1984, under H.O. Guenther).

115. Cf. B.L. MACK, in *Semeia* 55 (1992), p. 16: "Kloppenborg's demonstration [his identification of three major layers in Q's composition] has become the working hypothesis for the [SBL] Q Seminar". For critical remarks, see C.M. TUCKETT, *On the Stratification of Q. A Response*, in the same volume, pp. 213-222; ID., *The Temptation Story in Q*, in *The Four Gospels 1992*, pp. 479-507.

116. F.G. DOWNING, *Quite Like Q. A Genre for 'Q': The 'Lives' of Cynic Philosophers*, in *Bib* 69 (1988) 196-225. But see C.M. TUCKETT, *A Cynic Q?*, in *Bib* 70 (1989) 349-376.

117. *Q und Prophetie* (cf. above, n. 78), p. 95 (1984, p. 110: "In diesem Sinne..."). See also p. 77: "eine Analogie zum Prophetenbuch", but "Gerade diese *exklusive* Position hat kein Prophetenbuch für sich in Anspruch genommen. Hierdurch scheint die Q-Quelle die

phrase "a genre *sui generis*"[118]. It was resumed by Schürmann in 1981: "eine eigene literarische Gattung"[119] and is now corrected and reformulated: "In ihrer Art ist diese Schrift wohl analogielos"[120]. For Kloppenborg, however, Q in each of its compositional stages can be located within the context of ancient sayings collections. The stratigraphy proposed by Kloppenborg and in particular the separation of a collection of "wisdom speeches" as the formative element in Q will remain on the agenda of our Q-research in the 1990's[121].

V. THE GOSPEL OF MARK

The reorientation of Markan studies from redaction criticism to "literary criticism" began in the early 1970's with the work of N. Perrin[122]. Perrin was present at our Colloquium on Mark in 1971 when I gave my lecture on "Duality in Mark and the Limits of Source Criticism". After an analysis of the so-called duplicate expressions and the double-step progression I could make the observation that "there is a sort of homogeneity in Mark, from the wording of sentences to the

Gattung 'Prophetenbuch' zu sprengen"; p. 411: "Die Q-Prophetie ... in der bisherigen Geschichte der Prophetie ... ein Unikum".

118. Art. *Q*, in *IDBSup*, 1976, 715-716, p. 716: "The Q source may represent a primitive Christian genre *sui generis*". See below, n. 121 (D. Zeller).

119. H. SCHÜRMANN, *Das Zeugnis der Redenquelle für die Basileia-Verkündigung Jesu*, in J. DELOBEL (ed.), *Logia*, 1982, pp. 121-200, esp. 121, n. 2; see also p. 131: "eine spezifische, neuartig redigierende Gattung"; = *Gottes Reich – Jesu Geschick*, Freiburg, 1983, pp. 65-152, esp. 65 (n. 1!), 77.

120. ID., *Zur Kompositionsgeschichte der Redenquelle. Beobachtungen an der lukanischen Q-Vorlage*, in C. BUSSMANN – W. RADL, *Der Treue Gottes trauen. FS G. Schneider*, Freiburg, 1991, pp. 325-342, esp. 328 (in answer to Sato's critique; cf. *Q*, pp. 1-2).

121. With regard to the role that has been given to the Gospel of Thomas in this discussion, I can refer to C.M. TUCKETT, *Q and Thomas: Evidence of a Primitive "Wisdom Gospel"? A Response to H. Koester*, in *ETL* 67 (1991) 346-360. See now also D. ZELLER, *Eine weisheitliche Grundschrift in der Logienquelle?*, in *The Four Gospels 1992*, pp. 389-401. I quote his conclusion on the composition of Q: "Das so entstandene Gemisch ist formgeschichtlich ein Unicum, wie F. Neirynck gesehen hat, und nur schwer mit Schriften der Umwelt zu vergleichen. Man kann sich höchstens auf einen sehr allgemeinen Nenner 'Sammlung von Worten eines bedeutenden Mannes mit Nachwirkung' verständigen, wobei in Q zu den Worten Jesu noch die des Täufers kommen, ein Indiz dafür, daß nicht formale Maßstäbe, sondern inhaltliche bei der Komposition leitend waren. Jesus als Weisheitslehrer – das ist in der Logienquelle nur ein Aspekt. Als ganze betrachtet stellt sie fast noch eindrucksvoller seine eschatologische Rolle heraus. Unter diesen Vorzeichen wollen auch die weisheitlichen Teile gelesen werden".

122. Cf. F. NEIRYNCK – J. VERHEYDEN – F. VAN SEGBROECK – G. VAN OYEN – R. CORSTJENS, *The Gospel of Mark. A Cumulative Bibliography 1950-1990* (BETL, 102), Leuven, 1992 (esp. pp. 387-389: N. Perrin's works in chronological order); G. VAN OYEN, *De studie van de Marcusredactie in de twintigste eeuw* (SNTA, 18), Leuven; (Verhandelingen Kon. Academie), Brussels, 1993, Chapter XIII.

composition of the gospel. After the study of these data one has a
strong impression of the unity of the gospel of Mark"[123]. Through
Perrin my work on *Duality* became immediately known in Chicago, and
appreciated, as can be seen from this hyperbolic statement by W.H.
Kelber: "After Neirynck, all source and decomposition theories have to
pass the test of his studies"[124]. The book *Duality in Mark* was
published with the subtitle: "Contributions to the Study of the Markan
Redaction" and in later writings I continued to use the term "redaction-critical" for this kind of study.

Redaction criticism of the Gospel of Mark has been surveyed and
evaluated in a dissertation by C. Clifton Black (1989)[125]. The title of
the book, "The Disciples according to Mark" is somewhat misleading.
The theme of "the disciples" serves as a test case for the confrontation
of three types of redaction criticism[126]. His real topic is the redaction-
critical method. At the end of the book, Black briefly sketches his own
"synthetic" model of interpretation, and there he acknowledges "the
many virtues of the redaction-critical perspective"[127]. The core of the
book is a severe critique of the redaction-critical method applied to
Mark. Black heavily stresses the lack of consensus. His main objection
is "the inherent circularity of Markan redaction criticism": "the rationale and procedure ... is fundamentally circular", "the circularity of the
method (is) embarrassing, (and) vicious"; "redaction criticism does not
work when applied to the Second Gospel"[128]. In fact, if redaction is
understood as the editing of recognizable sources, there is, in contrast
to Matthew and Luke, an inherent difficulty in that we have no access
to the sources of Mark. In this sense Black may be right: "when dealing
with a Synoptic whose priority is assumed, I see no way of escaping this
hermeneutical circle"[129]. But is it necessarily a vicious circle? And is he

---

123. *ETL* 48 (1972), p. 174; in *Duality in Mark* (BETL, 31), Leuven, 1972, ²1988,
p. 37. On "The Acceptance of 'Duality in Mark'", see the Supplementary Notes, in
Duality, ²1988, pp. 217-252.

124. W.H. KELBER (ed.), *The Passion in Mark. Studies on Mark 14–16*, Philadelphia,
PA, 1976, p. 42, n. 3. Cf. *ibid.*, p. 15 (J.R. Donahue). See also W.H. KELBER, *The Oral and
the Written Gospel*, Philadelphia, PA, 1983, pp. 66-67, with my reaction in *Duality*, ²1988,
pp. 226-227.

125. C.C. BLACK, *The Disciples according to Mark. Markan Redaction in Current
Debate* (JSNT SS, 27), Sheffield, 1989 (Diss. Duke University, 1986, under D.M. Smith).
Cf. *The Gospel of Mark* (n. 122), p. 43 (with list of reviews).

126. *Ibid.*, pp. 39-181: R.P. MEYE, *Jesus and the Twelve*, 1968 (the 'conservative'
position); E. BEST, *Following Jesus*, 1981 (the 'mediate' position); T.J. WEEDEN, *Mark –
Traditions in Conflict*, 1971 (the 'liberal' position).

127. *Ibid.*, pp. 223-248 ("Method in Markan Study"), esp. p. 247: "its emphasis on
authors as theological thinkers, its desire to read texts holistically, and its recognition of
the importance of interpreting texts in traditio-historical context". See also, with some
variation, p. 237, including emphasis on "the Evangelists as creative authors in their own
right" and concern for "the literary character of the Gospels".

128. *Ibid.*, pp. 119, 222, 249.

129. *Ibid.*, p. 119.

not arguing with a too narrow definition of redaction criticism, as others are doing in defense of a "literary" approach[130]?

The sources of Mark remains a hotly debated question. The mirage of the primitive-gospel hypothesis comes back again and again, in the form of an original Matthew, Urmarkus, the gospel Q, an extended passion narrative, or in the more attractive form of pre-Markan collections. With regard to all of them, I tried to exorcise where I could[131]. In my opinion, the form-critical supposition of discrete units remains a more secure starting point in our study of the pre-Markan tradition. P. Dschulnigg has confirmed my conclusion on the unity of style in Mark: "Das ganze Evangelium ist von ihm [dem Verfasser] sprachlich mitgeprägt und zwar bis in die einzelnen Perikopen hinein"[132]. This does not mean that seams, insertions, summaries, and other formal categories of R.H. Stein's methodology[133] become simply useless, but it should definitely prevent us of producing the printout of pre-Markan traditions. Nor should we deny the possibility that some pericopae may be Mark's own composition. And without making Mark dependent on the Q document, we can learn from the parallels in Q how sayings material has developed in the Markan redaction[134].

For a more general review and evaluation of recent literary ap-

---

130. Cf. N.R. PETERSEN, *Literary Criticism for New Testament Critics*, Philadelphia, PA, 1978, pp. 18-19: "redaction critics assume that our texts are composed out of sources", "their method (is based) on the distinction between redaction and tradition"; and thus "redaction criticism cannot answer the questions it has raised without becoming something else, namely literary criticism". Cf. ID., *"Literarkritik", the New Literary Criticism and the Gospel according to Mark*, in *The Four Gospels 1992*, pp. 935-948.

131. Bibliographical references in *The Gospel of Mark* (n. 122), pp. 360-366. See also W.R. TELFORD, *The Pre-Markan Tradition* (n. 136 below), passim.

132. P. DSCHULNIGG, *Sprache, Redaktion und Intention des Markus-Evangeliums* (SBB, 11), Stuttgart, 1984, ²1986, p. 269; cf. p. 297.

133. *Duality*, p. 13, n. 2. Cf. R.H. STEIN, *Gospels and Tradition. Studies on Redaction Criticism of the Synoptic Gospels*, Grand Rapids, MI, 1991 (reprinted articles). See my review in *ETL* 68 (1992) 435-436.

134. Cf. C. BREYTENBACH, *Vormarkinische Logientradition. Parallelen in der urchristlichen Briefliteratur*, in *The Four Gospels 1992*, pp. 725-749. This paper was first presented at the SNTS Seminar on Pre-Synoptic Tradition (1991). It is the first part of a larger project that will include the comparative study of all Mark-Q parallels (cf. pp. 726 n. 8, 746, 748). His first list of sayings already includes three Q-parallels: Mk 2,16-17a; 2,17b; 4,9.23; 4,24c (Q 6,38c); 7,15; 9,42 (Q 17,1b-2); 9,50c; 10,11-12 (Q 16,18); 12,17; 14,21; 14,22-24. – On Lk 17,2 (pp. 743-745), see my *The Minor Agreements and Q* (n. 76): the use of Mk 9,42 can explain both Mt 18,6 and Lk 17,2 (not in Q). The combination of Mk 14,21 and 9,42 (Mt 18,6; Lk 17,2) in 1 Clem 46,8 is scarcely an independent oral-tradition variant. Cf. A. LINDEMANN, *Die Clemensbriefe* (HNT, 17/1), Tübingen, 1992, p. 137: the possibility that "er [der Verfasser] die Logien frei zitiert und dabei die Kombination selbst hergestellt hat [ist] m.E. wahrscheinlicher". More references in W.-D. KÖHLER, *Die Rezeption des Matthäusevangeliums in der Zeit vor Irenäus* (WUNT, 2/24), Tübingen, 1987, pp. 63-64.

proaches to the Gospel of Mark, I can now refer to the critical surveys by C. Breytenbach[135] and W.R. Telford[136] and several other papers presented at the Colloquium[137] and in *The Four Gospels 1992*[138].

Tiensevest 27   Frans NEIRYNCK
B-3010 Leuven

135. C. BREYTENBACH, *Das Markusevangelium als traditionsgebundene Erzählung? Anfragen an die Markusforschung der achtziger Jahre*, in this volume, pp. 77-110; ID., *Vormarkinische Logientradition* (n. 134 above).

136. W.R. TELFORD, *The Pre-Markan Tradition in Recent Research (1980-1990)*, in *The Four Gospels 1992*, pp. 693-723; ID., *Mark and the Historical-Critical Method: The Challenge of Recent Literary Approaches to the Gospels*, in this volume, pp. 491-502.

137. Partially in continuation of the 1991 and 1992 sessions of the SNTS Seminar on Pre-Synoptic Tradition (C. Breytenbach, H. Klein, V.K. Robbins, W.R. Telford).

138. Vol. II, pp. 691-1183: "The Gospel of Mark" (25 essays). Two major books on Mark were brought to my attention in the course of this year. Robert M. Fowler, leading scholar of the reader-response criticism applied to the Gospel of Mark, could announce, after a long gestation, the appearance of his *Let the Reader Understand. Reader-Response Criticism and the Gospel of Mark*, Minneapolis, MN, Augsburg Fortress, 1991, XIII-279 p. More recently, in July 1992, Robert H. Gundry graciously offered me an advance copy of his massive commentary, *Mark: A Commentary on His Apology for the Cross*, Grand Rapids, MI, Eerdmans, 1993, LV-1069 p. For a presentation and evaluation of both I may refer the reader to my book reviews in *ETL* 69 (1993) 181-183 (Fowler) and 183-186 (Gundry).

MC 7,24-31 PAR. MT 15,21-29
CRITIQUE DES SOURCES ET/OU ÉTUDE NARRATIVE

En fonction du sous-titre donné au titre général de ces Journées bibliques, la plupart des conférenciers ou présidents de séminaire, à l'exception du Prof. H. Merklein, ont choisi de prendre en considération un corpus textuel assez large. Cela m'a déterminé à confronter la critique des sources et l'analyse narrative sur un corpus très étroit, celui d'une péricope. Mon but est de vérifier la pertinence, les avantages et les limites de ces deux types de démarche quand elles sont appliquées à une péricope isolée. Le champ d'application choisi est celui du seul exorcisme à distance raconté dans les évangiles.

I. L'EXÉGÈSE HISTORICO-CRITIQUE

En vue de se représenter au mieux la genèse de cette péricope, il s'agit d'y distinguer le plus précisément possible tradition et rédaction. Auparavant il convient de traiter la question synoptique et de voir si une des deux versions évangéliques peut être source de l'autre[1].

1. La question synoptique

Quelques auteurs sont impressionnés par la difficulté d'expliquer un des deux textes évangéliques seulement à partir de l'autre. Ils soulignent l'indépendance littéraire des évangélistes pour cette péricope[2]. Mais, si les deux récits diffèrent, la parenté est grande pour le dialogue central. Cela conduit certains à suggérer plus ou moins fermement l'hypothèse d'une source commune[3]. Dans ce sens, on invoque souvent comme

---

1. Pour un état de la question plus complet, voir A. DERMIENCE, *La péricope de la Cananéenne: Matth. 15,21-28. Sources - rédaction - théologie* (diss. dactylographiée), Louvain-la-Neuve, 1981, pp. 14-52.

2. A. JÜLICHER, *Die Gleichnisreden Jesu*, II, Tübingen, 1899, pp. 258-259; E. LOHMEYER, *Das Evangelium des Matthäus*, hrsg. W. Schmauch (KEK, Sonderband), ²1958, p. 252.

3. A. JÜLICHER, *Die Gleichnisreden*, II (n. 2), p. 258, accepte une source commune, mais uniquement pour le dialogue de Mc 7,27-28 par. accompagné peut-être d'une brève introduction. Dans le même sens, voir M. DIBELIUS, *Die Formgeschichte des Evangeliums*, Tübingen, ³1959, p. 261, n. 3. Pour l'ensemble de la péricope, L. VAGANAY, *Le problème synoptique. Une hypothèse de travail*, Tournai, 1954, pp. 321-322, estime que Mc peut bien avoir écourté le Mg mieux suivi par Mt, notamment en 15,23-24. Une possibilité du même type est suggérée par L. CERFAUX, *La section des pains (Mc VI,31–VIII,26; Mt XIV,13–XVI,12)*, in J. SCHMID et al. (ed.), *Synoptische Studien. FS A. Wikenhauser*, München, 1953, pp. 64-77; = *Recueil L. Cerfaux*, I, Gembloux, 1954, pp. 471-485. X. LÉON-

argument la parenté du récit matthéen de la Cananéenne avec son récit de guérison du fils du centurion (Mt 8, 5-13). Car, «si Mc ne peut être pour rien à propos du centurion, Mt n'en dépend pas non plus à propos de la Cananéenne»[4]. Malheureusement, s'il est vrai que ces deux récits, comme tous ceux du premier évangile, sont marqués par le style de leur rédacteur final, rien ne prouve leur caractère indissociable. Il est hasardeux de se baser sur un rapprochement vague entre ces deux guérisons à distance, les seules de la tradition évangélique, pour en déduire qu'elles ont été écrites par la même personne. La comparaison littéraire des deux récits ne prouve certes pas la nécessité d'une telle conclusion[5].

Dans l'hypothèse d'une dépendance littéraire entre les récits matthéen et marcien, on peut hésiter sur l'orientation à lui donner[6]. Les partisans de la priorité matthéenne croient pouvoir assurer le bien-fondé de leur théorie en soulignant l'archaïsme du texte matthéen. Selon eux, Mc aurait adapté à une Église pagano-chrétienne le texte de Mt où s'exprime un particularisme exclusiviste (v. 24), qui devait mal sonner à des oreilles païennes[7]. Le texte le plus particulariste doit être considéré

DUFOUR, *Études d'Évangile* (Parole de Dieu), Paris, 1965, p. 234, affirme plus nettement que Mc et Mt dépendent pour la section des pains, et donc notamment pour la péricope de la Cananéenne, d'un schéma catéchétique présynoptique formé sur base d'associations verbales. En ce qui concerne notre péricope, M.-É. BOISMARD, *Synopse des quatre évangiles en français*, t. II, *Commentaire*, Paris, 1972, p. 236, est perplexe au point de ne pas savoir s'il doit en attribuer l'origine à son document C ou à un hypothétique recueil de miracles. Enfin, dans l'hypothèse de P. ROLLAND, *Les premiers évangiles. Un nouveau regard sur le problème synoptique* (LD, 116), Paris, 1984, surtout pp. 138 et 149-151, Mt et Mc dépendent ici de l'évangile «helléniste», intermédiaire entre l'évangile primitif de Jérusalem et notre Mt grec. Le milieu d'origine du récit de la Cananéenne se rattache au groupe des Sept (Ac 6,1-5), d'orientation universaliste. Durant le colloque, P. Rolland m'a précisé oralement que, selon lui, Mt 15,21-29 et Mc 7,24-31 comportent tous deux des traits secondaires, dus à leur rédaction (par exemple, Mc 7,27a), mais que Mt lui semble plus proche que Mc de la forme primitive de la tradition.

4. M.-J. LAGRANGE, *Évangile selon saint Matthieu* (Études bibliques), Paris, ⁵1941, p. 310, qui ajoute: «pas plus d'ailleurs que Mc ne dépend de Mt».

5. Même si la parenté est grande entre les conclusions des deux récits, où on retrouve les mêmes types d'expression: (Mt 8,13: ὡς ἐπίστευσας γενηθήτω σοι. καὶ ἰάθη ὁ παῖς (αὐτοῦ) ἐν τῇ ὥρᾳ ἐκείνῃ. Mt 15,28: γενηθήτω σοι ὡς θέλεις. καὶ ἰάθη ἡ θυγάτηρ αὐτῆς ἀπὸ τῆς ὥρας ἐκείνης.

6. Après avoir comparé critiquement les deux versions, E.A. RUSSELL, *The Canaanite Woman and the Gospels (Mt 15,21-28; cf. Mk 7,24-30)*, in E.A. LIVINGSTONE (ed.), *Studia Biblica 1978*, II, *Papers on the Gospels* (JSNT, Suppl. Series, 2), Sheffield, 1980, pp. 263-300, conclut (p. 282) que Mt a introduit dans les vv. 22-24 une tradition des disciples et que son v. 24 peut avoir appartenu à une tradition flottante. À ses yeux, «the problem of the literary and traditional relations between Matthew and Mark is not by any means solved and should call into serious question any too confident assumption that Matthew uses Mark as we have it».

7. Ainsi, B.C. BUTLER, *The Originality of St Matthew. A Critique of the Two-Document Hypothesis*, Cambridge, 1951, pp. 130-131; L. CERFAUX, *Recueil*, I (n. 3), p. 475; G. DEHN, *Le Fils de Dieu. Commentaire sur l'évangile de Marc*, Genève, 1957, p. 111;

comme le plus ancien et source de l'autre. On aurait un autre indice d'archaïsme dans la désignation de la demanderesse comme Χαναναία (Mt, 15,22), qui rappelle l'expression biblique classique pour opposer Israël et Canaan[8]. Avec Συροφοινίκισσα (Mc 7,26), Mc aurait éclairé l'expression archaïque de Mt en se référant à des divisions politico-territoriales plus récentes[9].

Les opposants à cette théorie font valoir que le particularisme théologique n'est pas automatiquement un indice d'ancienneté. D'une part, certaines communautés et certaines personnalités ont pu se cantonner dans une telle perspective beaucoup plus longtemps que d'autres. Il peut simplement s'agir de l'option d'un milieu plus conservateur en la matière[10]. D'autre part, en tant qu'il est lié à la vie historique de Jésus (voir aussi Mt 10,5-6) et opposé à un universalisme futur (Mt 24,14; 28,19), ce particularisme de la mission peut bien correspondre aux intentions théologiques de Mt. Ainsi par exemple, selon H. Frankemölle[11], Mt, conformément à une vue de l'histoire inspirée de Dt et Chr, voit Jésus et ses disciples comme envoyés à Israël exclusivement (10,5-6; 15,24)[12]. Mais l'attitude négative de ce dernier envers l'alliance et l'envoyé de Dieu va entraîner son rejet (8,11-12) et son remplacement par des païens accueillis sur base de leur foi en Jésus et sa mission (8,28-34; 15,21-28). Ainsi la foi devient décisive pour l'entrée dans le

---

D. MERLI, *Fiducia e fede nei miracoli evangelici* (Quaderni di «Bibbia e Oriente», 5), Genova, 1973, pp. 115-121. R.A. HARRISVILLE, *The Woman of Canaan. A Chapter in the History of Exegesis*, in *Interpretation* 20 (1966) 274-287, montre combien, critiquement, il est difficile de clore le débat entre partisans de la priorité marcienne ou de la priorité matthéenne (p. 277). S'il semble plutôt favorable à cette dernière, c'est pour des raisons théologiques, parce que Mt insiste sur le salut par la foi seule. On peut aussi citer pour mémoire l'opinion de G. GANDER, *L'évangile de l'Église. Commentaire de l'évangile selon Matthieu*, I, Genève, 1968, p. 189, qui, frappé par le ton de «conversation araméenne populaire», voit dans le récit «la pure et simple copie qu'a dû en rédiger l'apôtre Matthieu vers 38-40 (M)».

8. Ainsi B.C. BUTLER, *The Originality* (n. 7), p. 130; J.B. ORCHARD – H. RILEY, *The Order of the Synoptics. Why Three Synoptic Gospels?*, Macon, GA, 1987, p. 44.

9. Cependant, déjà M.-J. LAGRANGE, *Matthieu* (n. 4), p. 308, faisait remarquer que la différence de termes pouvait bien renvoyer à une différence de perspectives selon les évangélistes et que le terme utilisé par Mt ne fait pas partie de la terminologie courante à cette époque. Selon H. FRANKEMÖLLE, *Jahwebund und Kirche Christi. Studien zur Form- und Traditionsgeschichte des «Evangeliums» nach Matthäus* (NTA, NF, 10), Münster, 1974, p. 136, la mention Χαναναία (v. 22) opposée à οἴκου Ἰσραήλ (v. 24), tout comme l'ajout de Sidon à Tyr (v. 21), cadre bien avec la théologie de Mt opposant volontairement à l'aide de termes bibliques anciens Israël et les païens.

10. Ainsi K. GATZWEILER, *Un pas vers l'universalisme: la Cananéenne (Mt 15)*, in *AsSeign* 51 (1972) 15-24, voir p. 17.

11. H. FRANKEMÖLLE, *Jahwebund* (n. 9), pp. 261-262. Nous reviendrons plus en détail sur cette opinion et d'autres du même type dans l'étude de la rédaction matthéenne.

12. H. FRANKEMÖLLE, *Jahwebund* (n. 9), p. 115, fait remarquer que, dans le cadre de cette théologie matthéenne, le πρῶτον de Mc 7,27 est inacceptable et doit être remplacé par Mt 15,24, créé par Mt.

Royaume des Cieux, ce qui ouvre sur une mission universaliste future (24,14; 28,19). S'il en est ainsi, c'est le principal argument opposé à l'hypothèse de la priorité marcienne[13] qui disparaît. Par ailleurs, le texte de Mt reflète la tendance souvent jugée plus tardive à souligner l'attitude respectueuse des interlocuteurs de Jésus. En l'occurrence, dans chacune de ses trois phrases à Jésus (Mt 15,22.25.27), la Cananéenne l'appelle κύριε. Et si un texte améliore stylistiquement l'autre, il faut bien dire que Mt améliore Mc et non le contraire[14]. Enfin, Mt reste fidèle à son habitude d'abréger les traits novellistiques de sa source (Mc 7,24b.25a.30), tout en développant l'élément dialogue[15].

Cette péricope est sans doute trop brève pour qu'on puisse trancher à partir d'elle la question synoptique. Il m'importait seulement de mettre les argumentations en présence. Comme dans cette première partie je vise à mettre en valeur les résultats auxquels ont mené les recherches de type historico-critique, j'adopterai pour la suite l'hypothèse de la priorité marcienne, car c'est elle qui a servi de base à presque toutes les recherches de type *formgeschichtlich* ou *redaktionsgeschichtlich*. Par ailleurs, l'analyse ultérieure de la rédaction matthéenne confortera le bien-fondé de cette option.

2. *Tradition et rédaction*

1. Distinction entre tradition et rédaction en Mc 7,24-31

Du point de vue *formgeschichtlich*, on repère immédiatement dans notre récit un mélange des genres entre un récit d'exorcisme (Mc 7, 25-26.29-30) et une controverse ou un dialogue pédagogique[16] sur des questions de nourriture plus ou moins réservée (vv. 27-28). À partir de

---

13. Hypothèse tenue par la très grande majorité des exégètes historico-critiques actuellement. Il serait fastidieux d'essayer d'en donner la liste.

14. Par exemple, τὰ κυνάρια ἐσθίει (Mt 15,27) est plus correct que τὰ κυνάρια ... ἐσθίουσιν (Mc 7,28). Dans le même verset, la description matthéenne des miettes qui tombent de la table est aussi beaucoup plus correcte que celle de Mc. Par ailleurs, en 15,22, Mt ne reprend pas l'expression ἧς εἶχεν τὸ θυγάτριον αὐτῆς (Mc 7,25), que M. BLACK, *An Aramaic Approach to the Gospels and Acts*, Oxford, ³1967, pp. 100-101, relève comme le seul passage dans les évangiles où l'on rencontre ailleurs que dans un dialogue ou un discours direct «the characteristic Semitic construction of a relative completed by a personal pronoun» (p. 100). Ceci correspond bien à une tendance générale de Mt relevée par J.P. MEIER, *Law and History in Matthew's Gospel* (AnBib, 71), Roma, 1976, p. 20: «Mt's general tendency is to improve the highly Semitic Greek of Mk in the direction of more acceptable Greek usage».

15. Ainsi H.J. HELD, *Matthäus als Interpret der Wundergeschichten*, in G. BORNKAMM – G. BARTH – H.J. HELD, *Überlieferung und Auslegung im Matthäusevangelium* (WMANT, 1), Neukirchen-Vluyn, 1960, pp. 155-287, voir p. 187.

16. R. BULTMANN, *Die Geschichte der synoptischen Tradition* (FRLANT, 29), Göttingen, ²1931, p. 38, le range parmi les apophtegmes, bien que la pointe ne soit pas une sentence de Jésus, mais plutôt un dialogue de controverse où Jésus pour une fois est vaincu, sans que pour autant le récit projette une ombre sur lui.

là, si on laisse momentanément de côté les versets d'introduction et de conclusion, trois positions peuvent être théoriquement tenues et l'ont été quant à la construction de la péricope.

a. Le récit de miracle est premier et constitue la base à partir de laquelle la péricope a été créée.

Du fait que les vv. 27-28 contiennent plusieurs éléments qui paraissent étrangers au récit de miracle proprement dit, B. Van Iersel[17] déduit que le récit actuel de Mc a été construit en plusieurs phases. À son avis, les vv. 27-28 ont été reliés à un récit de guérison qui existait antérieurement par l'intermédiaire d'une suture rédactionnelle au v. 29. Dans le récit primitif de guérison, le v. 26 était suivi du v. 29 où on lisait: καὶ εἶπεν αὐτῇ ὕπαγε... Lorsqu'il a introduit dans ce cadre les vv. 27-28, Mc les y a reliés en ajoutant avant ὕπαγε les mots διὰ τοῦτον τὸν λόγον[18]. En même temps, Mc a ajouté aux vv. 27b-28 le v. 27a qui correspond à une thématique répandue dans la communauté primitive (voir Ac 3,26; 13,46; Rm 1,16; 2,9-10) et qui convient bien pour éclairer les deux multiplications des pains avec lesquelles il a en commun le mot χορτασθῆναι.

K. Kertelge[19] suit globalement l'analyse précédente, mais limite l'intervention de Mc à l'ajout au v. 27a d'un *theologoumenon* paulinien[20]. Quant à la fusion des vv. 27b-28 avec le récit de miracle, elle a été opérée dans la tradition prémarcienne. Ce dialogue, où le débat est plutôt fictif et pédagogique, n'a pas existé à l'état indépendant. Il a été forgé dans la communauté directement pour être intégré au récit de miracle dont il a modifié le sens. Le *Sitz im Leben* de la péricope ainsi élargie est à chercher dans les débats de la communauté postpascale. Celle-ci y trouvait, selon K. Kertelge, une parole de Jésus fondant de manière assurée l'ouverture de la mission vers les païens. On peut

---

17. B. VAN IERSEL, *Die wunderbare Speisung und das Abendmahl in der synoptischen Tradition (Mk VI,35-44 par., VIII,1-10 par.)*, in NT 7 (1964) 167-194, voir pp. 188-189. M.-É. BOISMARD, *Synopse*, II (n. 3), p. 235, considère, pour sa part, que le dialogue venant de la tradition a été ajouté à un récit de guérison de style tout à fait classique par le Mc-intermédiaire.

18. B. VAN IERSEL, *Die wunderbare Speisung* (n. 17), pp. 188-189, n. 4, montre en détail qu'un tel emploi de ὕπαγε est unique, si on compare avec les 37 autres emplois de cet impératif dans le N.T.

19. K. KERTELGE, *Die Wunder Jesu im Markusevangelium. Eine redaktionsgeschicht-liche Untersuchung* (SANT, 23), München, 1970, pp. 151-156.

20. Pour R. BULTMANN, *Die Geschichte* (n. 16), p. 38, suivi par H.J. HELD, *Matthäus* (n. 15), p. 187, le v. 27a aurait été ajouté plus tard encore par un remanieur du texte. Cela permet d'expliquer le texte de Mt qui dépend de Mc, mais n'a pas cette phrase dans son exemplaire de Mc. Plus radicalement encore, W. BUSSMANN, *Synoptische Studien*, I, *Zur Geschichtsquelle*, Halle, 1925, pp. 49-52, construit l'hypothèse, restée marginale, que dans l'*Urmarkus* la péricope tout entière faisait défaut. Elle n'aurait été ajoutée que plus tard par un remanieur. Il entend expliquer ainsi l'omission de cette péricope par Luc.

cependant faire remarquer que, dans notre récit, une telle ouverture est fondée plutôt sur une parole de la femme païenne et se demander s'il est vraisemblable d'y voir une création de la communauté postpascale.

L'objection principale à cette hypothèse vient de la difficulté d'imaginer quel intérêt pouvait avoir le récit d'exorcisme sans le dialogue des vv. 27-28. C'est d'autant plus vrai que dans les récits de guérison à distance il y a toujours un dialogue important qui en constitue la pointe[21]. Par ailleurs, on ne voit pas très bien l'intérêt du dialogue des vv. 27-28, lorsque ceux-ci sont isolés. Quant à en attribuer la création à la communauté sur simple base du récit de miracle, c'est étrange, car aucun élément du dialogue n'est suggéré par le récit[22].

b. Le dialogue est premier et constitue la base à partir duquel la péricope a été créée.

Frappés de ce que le dialogue est la seule partie vraiment commune à Mt et Mc, certains estiment qu'on y trouve l'élément ferme et stable de la tradition. Originellement, l'appel à l'aide que Mt 16,25 (κύριε βοήθει μοι) a mieux conservé dans sa teneur primitive en style direct pourrait avoir eu une portée générale et relever d'une misère religieuse, comme c'est le cas, par exemple, en Mc 9,24 ou Ac 16,9-10, aussi bien que d'une misère corporelle[23]. Du point de vue des formes littéraires, ce dialogue serait à classer parmi les paroles de Jésus et aurait été conservé dans le contexte de l'annonce de l'Evangile en terre païenne[24]. Plus tard enfin, il aurait été uni au récit de guérison de manière à constituer un paradigme. Une telle hypothèse est difficile. Car, à supposer que la portée primitive du dialogue ait été d'ordre kérygmatique, comment expliquer qu'on se soit éloigné du souci missionnaire si caractéristique des communautés chrétiennes primitives et qu'on ait eu l'idée d'encadrer par un récit de miracle un tel dialogue, où rien pourtant n'évoque une guérison?

T.A. Burkill a tenté de reconstituer en détail la constitution progressive de l'épisode de la Syrophénicienne tel que nous pouvons le lire en

21. À propos de Mc 7,24-30 et Mt 8,5-13, G. THEISSEN, *Urchristliche Wundergeschichten. Ein Beitrag zur formgeschichtlichen Erforschung der synoptischen Evangelien* (SNT, 8), Gütersloh, 1974, p. 120, écrit: «Die Exposition ist hier zur selbständigen Erzählung geworden. Die Mitte (zentrale Motive) fehlt völlig».

22. Ainsi A. DERMIENCE, *La péricope de la Syrophénicienne. Contribution à l'exégèse de Marc 7,24-30* (mémoire dactylographié), Louvain-la-Neuve, 1976, p. 127.

23. Ainsi E. LOHMEYER, *Das Evangelium des Markus* (KEK, I,2), Göttingen, [17]1967, p. 145. Pour sa part, A. JÜLICHER, *Die Gleichnisreden*, II (n. 2), p. 259, suggère que les deux paroles de Mc 7,27-28 sont des paroles de Jésus transformées en un dialogue par les évangélistes et unies à un récit de miracle quand leur contexte originel de prise de position sur le rapport entre Juifs et païens fut perdu de vue.

24. Ainsi E. LOHMEYER, *Markus* (n. 23), p. 145. M. DIBELIUS, *Die Formgeschichte* (n. 3), p. 261, n. 3, souligne sa portée juridique «für eine grundlegende Auseinandersetzung mit dem Heidenproblem».

Mc[25]. Il est, selon lui, le résultat d'une évolution comportant 4 étapes[26].

Étape 1. Face à des païens manifestant leur intérêt pour l'appel de Jésus à la conversion, les premiers prédicateurs chrétiens ont voulu signifier que, seuls, les Juifs étaient invités à faire partie de la communauté chrétienne. Pour ce faire, ils ont eu recours à un logion judéochrétien attribué à Jésus (Mc 7,27b), une sorte de proverbe équivalent au proverbe français: «Charité bien ordonnée commence par soi-même». Ceux qui ont rapporté ce proverbe ont dramatisé la situation en le proposant comme réponse à la demande d'une femme pour sa fille possédée (vv. 25-26). Il apparaissait ainsi clairement que la venue du Messie ne mettait pas fin à l'élection d'Israël quoi qu'il en coûte.

Étape 2. Certains judéo-chrétiens, parvenus à la conviction que la foi en la messianité de Jésus suffisait pour entrer dans la communauté chrétienne, ont modifié le sens du noyau de départ (v. 27b) en y ajoutant la réplique de la Syrophénicienne (v. 28), dont la valeur était confirmée par une parole de Jésus et la guérison de la petite fille (vv. 29-30). L'anecdote ainsi composée mettait fin au privilège exclusif d'Israël, tout en faisant des concessions au camp opposé: les païens ne sont pas encore à table et la guérison ne se fait qu'à distance. De cette façon on présente le Jésus historique comme préfigurant la mission apostolique vers les païens, mais de manière limitée. Cette limite renvoie au fait que cette mission ne s'est effectivement développée qu'après la passion-résurrection du Seigneur.

Étape 3. Mc reçoit de la tradition les vv. 25-30, sans doute sans le v. 27a qu'il ajoute alors lui-même pour mieux souligner que le tour des païens de prendre place à table ne viendra qu'après le rejet de Jésus par le peuple élu. Par ailleurs, Mc ajoute les vv. 24 et 31 pour fournir à l'anecdote de la Syrophénicienne un cadre topographique et la relier au contexte et aussi pour montrer que la réputation de Jésus dépasse les frontières de Palestine, ce qui donne à notre récit une coloration missionnaire[27].

Étape 4. Mt 15,21-28 est rédigé sur base de Mc 7,24-31, mais adapté à l'aide d'autres traditions: la tradition Q sur la guérison du serviteur du centurion (Mt 8,5-13 par. Lc 7,1-10), la tradition matthéenne de Mt 10,6, les traditions marciennes de Mc 2,15-17 et 10,46-52[28].

---

25. T.A. BURKILL, *The Syrophoenician Woman: The Congruence of Mark 7,24-31*, in *ZNW* 57 (1966) 23-37; ID., *The Historical Development of the Story of the Syrophoenician Woman (Mark VII,24-31)*, in *NT* 9 (1967) 161-177. Les pp. 172-177 de cet article sont reprises dans ID., *The Syrophoenician Woman: Mark 7,24-31*, in *Studia Evangelica* 4 (TU, 102), Berlin, 1968, pp. 165-170.

26. T.A. BURKILL, *Historical Development* (n. 25), pp. 175-177.

27. Ce dernier point est loin d'être évident pour un texte où on ne parle pas de prédication ou d'annonce pourtant capitales pour la mission.

28. Dans son étude sur les étapes de la tradition (voir n. 26), T.A. Burkill n'apporte

Cette reconstitution de l'histoire de la tradition n'a guère eu de succès. Ceci n'est sans doute pas dû seulement à son caractère hautement hypothétique, sans véritable appui littéraire[29]. Il faut relever en outre l'invraisemblance de sa deuxième étape. On imagine difficilement qu'un groupe judéo-chrétien même progressiste aurait confié à une femme païenne le soin d'inverser le sens d'un proverbe (v. 27b) défendant les privilèges du peuple élu.

c. Le récit de guérison et le dialogue n'ont jamais existé indépendamment l'un de l'autre.

Ils formaient d'emblée un bloc uni dès la tradition préévangélique et cette source n'a subi que peu de transformations lors de son insertion dans le second évangile. Selon les auteurs défendant cette opinion de loin majoritaire dans l'exégèse[30], seul le v. 27a est pensable comme logion isolé. Par contre, les vv. 27b-28 sont d'emblée coulés dans la forme d'un dialogue. Et celui-ci postule nécessairement un contexte pour qu'on puisse en déterminer le sens. D'une part, sans le récit de guérison, le dialogue n'a pas de sens concret. D'autre part, si on retire le dialogue du récit, il ne subsiste plus que des fragments de récit de miracle, et il est difficile d'imaginer que ceux-ci aient pu exister tels quels à l'état autonome. Les guérisons à distance présentent d'ailleurs chaque fois un dialogue visant à vaincre toute espèce de réticence supposée ou réelle de la part du thérapeute (voir Mt 8,5-13 par. Lc 7,1-10; Jn 4,46b-54).

Si l'on excepte A. Dermience, selon laquelle Mc 7,24-31 aurait été

---

pas plus de précisions quant à la rédaction matthéenne. Par contre, ID., *The Syrophoenician Woman: The Congruence* (n. 25), p. 26, suggère que Mt a introduit le logion de 15,24 en s'inspirant de 10,6 et qu'en conséquence il a supprimé le v. 27a de Mc. Son v. 24 implique que, pour Mt, Jésus n'a pas quitté la Galilée, ce qui est compatible avec son v. 21 si on comprend εἰς au sens de «en direction de» et si on tient compte de ce qu'au v. 22 la Cananéenne sort (ἐξελθοῦσα) de son territoire.

29. Ainsi, S. LÉGASSE, *L'épisode de la Cananéenne d'après Mt 15,21-28*, in *Bulletin de littérature ecclésiastique* 73 (1972) 21-40, p. 22: «En réalité, cette rétrospective manque de tout appui littéraire, bien plus elle s'oppose à la structure du dialogue où tout se tient sans suggérer la moindre manipulation».

30. R. BULTMANN, *Die Geschichte* (n. 16), p. 38; F. HAHN, *Das Verständnis der Mission im Neuen Testament* (WMANT, 13), Neukirchen-Vluyn, ²1965, pp. 24-25; B. FLAMMER, *Die Syrophoenizerin*, in *TQ* 148 (1968) 463-478, voir pp. 463-464; S. LÉGASSE, *L'épisode* (n. 29), p. 21; L. SCHENKE, *Die Wundererzählungen des Markusevangeliums* (SBS, 5), Stuttgart, 1974, pp. 259-261; D.-A. KOCH, *Die Bedeutung der Wundererzählungen für die Christologie des Markusevangeliums* (BZNW, 42), Berlin, 1975, pp. 86-87; H.J. KLAUCK, *Allegorie und Allegorese in synoptischen Gleichnistexten* (NTA, 13), Münster, 1978, p. 274; J. GNILKA, *Das Evangelium nach Markus*, I, *Mk 1-8,26* (EKK, II/1), Zürich-Einsiedeln-Köln-Neukirchen-Vluyn, 1978, pp. 289-290; R. PESCH, *Das Markusevangelium*, I, *Einleitung und Kommentar zu Kap. 1,1-8,26* (HTKNT, II/1), Freiburg-Basel-Wien, 1976, pp. 385-386; D. LÜHRMANN, *Das Markusevangelium* (HNT, 3), Tübingen, 1987, p. 130.

entièrement créé par l'évangéliste Mc[31], la plupart des auteurs estiment qu'on a affaire à un récit traditionnel très légèrement retouché par le rédacteur. Mais, bien que légères, ces interventions rédactionnelles sont assez nombreuses.

Développant les thèmes bien marciens de la «maison» et de la volonté de secret, qui peuvent tous deux être reliés à la célèbre théorie du secret messianique, le v. 24bc est tenu pour rédactionnel[32], même si λανθάνειν est un hapax en Mc[33]. Seul, R. Pesch[34] s'oppose à cette vue. Selon lui, le v. 24bc fait partie du récit primitif parce qu'il est indispensable en fonction de la pointe essentielle du récit, à savoir que Jésus est, malgré lui, tiré du secret où il voulait se retirer. Le v. 24bc montre que son intention n'était ni de prêcher, ni de guérir, mais qu'il a été amené à transgresser celle-ci sous l'influence de la parole de la Syrophénicienne. Bref, l'opposition οὐκ ... ἀλλά des vv. 24c-25 relèverait du récit primitif, car elle est essentielle au récit. Certes cette opposition est importante dans le texte de Mc, mais rien ne dit qu'elle était essentielle au récit primitif. D'ailleurs, Mt en a si peu senti la nécessité pour l'épisode de la Cananéenne qu'il a omis cette partie de Mc. Le caractère rédactionnel ou non du v. 24a est plus discuté. En faveur de son caractère marcien, on évoque sa parenté très grande avec Mc 10,1 (καὶ ἐκεῖθεν ἀναστὰς ἔρχεται εἰς τὰ ὅρια τῆς Ἰουδαίας)[35]. Et Mc aurait introduit d'entrée de jeu la localisation précise τὰ ὅρια Τύρου[36], peut-

---

31. A. DERMIENCE, Syrophénicienne (n. 22), p. 116, pense que «ce récit, anormalement schématique, dépouillé au maximum de notations concrètes révèle une élaboration très poussée, dont la tradition n'est pas coutumière». ID., Tradition et rédaction dans la péricope de la Syrophénicienne: Marc 7,24-30, in RTL 8 (1977) 15-29, voir p. 28, estime que «les versets narratifs de la péricope présentent deux types de composantes: des éléments traditionnels, empruntés apparemment à la péricope composite 'fille de Jaïre-hémorroïsse' et retravaillés par l'écrivain, d'autre part des formules étrangères aux récits de la tradition et qui pourraient être rédactionnelles. Comme l'évangéliste semble être intervenu dans le choix de ces divers éléments, n'a-t-il pas composé ce récit anormalement dépouillé, un peu à la manière des sommaires, en s'inspirant de la tradition»? Voir aussi ID., La péricope de la Cananéenne (Mt 15,21-28). Rédaction et théologie, in ETL 58 (1982) 25-49, voir p. 26, n. 5. Toutes ces monographies ont l'avantage d'avoir souligné le style marcien de notre péricope ou encore que tout le texte porte la trace de son auteur final. Cela n'exclut cependant pas que Mc ait pour l'essentiel repris une péricope à la tradition antérieure. Ainsi S. LÉGASSE, L'épisode (n. 29), p. 21.

32. Ainsi S. LÉGASSE, L'épisode (n. 29), p. 21; L. SCHENKE, Die Wundererzählungen (n. 30), p. 254; D.-A. KOCH, Die Bedeutung (n. 30), p. 91; H.J. KLAUCK, Allegorie (n. 30), p. 273; D. LÜHRMANN, Das Markusevangelium (n. 30), p. 130.

33. Sur 6 emplois dans le NT, ce verbe présente pour les évangiles et les Actes la statistique suivante: 0/1/1/0/1.

34. R. PESCH, Das Markusevangelium, I (n. 30), p. 387.

35. S. LÉGASSE, L'épisode (n. 29), p. 21, n. 1, qui évoque aussi Mc 6,1; D.-A. KOCH, Die Bedeutung (n. 30), p. 89.

36. Il me semble préférable de lire τὰ ὅρια Τύρου avec D L W Δ Θ 28 565 it sy[s.pal] et de considérer τὰ ὅρια Τύρου καὶ Σιδῶνος (א A B f[1.13] 𝔐 lat sy[p.h] sa bo) comme une

être en la déduisant de la mention Συροφοινίκισσα τῷ γένει au v. 26[37].
À l'autre bout du récit, le v. 31 a aussi été composé par Mc[38], qui
fournit de cette façon un cadre topographique à l'histoire de la Syrophénicienne. Ce verset ramène Jésus dans un environnement plus
habituel. Grâce à ses versets d'introduction (v. 24) et de conclusion
(v. 31), Mc crée ainsi un bref voyage au Nord de la Galilée[39].

Au v. 25, l'expression ἀλλ' εὐθύς est tenue pour une transition due à
Mc[40], dont on sait combien il utilise volontiers εὐθύς[41]. Le récit
primitif aurait donc commencé avec ἀκούσασα. Il est possible que
l'expression πνεῦμα ἀκάθαρτον doive également être attribuée à Mc[42]
qui utilise fréquemment le mot ἀκάθαρτος[43], alors que dans les versets
traditionnels (vv. 26.29.30) on a δαιμόνιον.

Alors que G. Theissen[44] pense que la double désignation de la
femme (Ἑλληνίς et Συροφοινίκισσα τῷ γένει) vient de la tradition,
D.-A. Koch[45] estime qu'au v. 26 une de ces deux désignations a été
ajoutée au récit primitif. Mais il ne précise pas laquelle est secondaire,

harmonisation avec Mt 15,21. En sens inverse, cependant, L. SCHENKE, *Die Wundererzählungen* (n. 30), p. 254, n. 772, considère l'abandon de καὶ Σιδῶνος comme une
harmonisation avec Mc 7,31.

37. Ainsi R. BULTMANN, *Die Geschichte* (n. 16), p. 68; E. KLOSTERMANN, *Das Markusevangelium* (HNT, 3), Tübingen, [4]1950, p. 71; K. KERTELGE, *Die Wunder* (n. 19), p. 151;
D.-A. KOCH, *Die Bedeutung* (n. 30), p. 89. Cependant L. SCHENKE, *Die Wundererzählungen*
(n. 30), p. 254, utilise le même argument en sens inverse. Après avoir souligné que ἐκεῖθεν
δὲ ἀναστάς constitue le lien rédactionnel avec ce qui précède, il ajoute: «Dagegen geht das
ἀπῆλθεν εἰς τὰ ὅρια Τύρου καὶ Σιδῶνος wahrscheinlich auf Tradition zurück (vgl. 5,1).
Dieser Ortsangabe entspricht dann auch die Kennzeichnung der Frau als einer Συροφοινίκισσα τῷ γένει (v. 26)». La question de l'origine traditionnelle ou rédactionnelle de la
localisation précise (Tyr) au v. 24 est très difficile à trancher.

38. Ainsi R. BULTMANN, *Die Geschichte* (n. 16), p. 38; S. LÉGASSE, *L'épisode* (n. 29),
p. 21; D.-A. KOCH, *Die Bedeutung* (n. 30), p. 89; D. LÜHRMANN, *Das Markusevangelium*
(n. 30), p. 130. Pour sa part, K.L. SCHMIDT, *Der Rahmen der Geschichte Jesu*, Darmstadt,
1919, pp. 200-201, pense que le v. 31 faisait traditionnellement la transition entre la
guérison de la fille de la Syrophénicienne et celle du sourd-muet, mais a peut-être été
transformé par Mc.

39. Plusieurs auteurs ne traitent pas de ce v. 31 à propos de la péricope de la
Syrophénicienne, car ils le considèrent plutôt comme l'introduction de la péricope
suivante. Mais cela ne met pas en valeur le côté exceptionnel de ce bref épisode de voyage
dans le Nord.

40. Ainsi notamment L. SCHENKE, *Die Wundererzählungen* (n. 30), p. 255; H.J. KLAUCK,
Allegorie (n. 30), p. 273.

41. Évangiles: 7/42/1/3 (total NT: 54).

42. Ainsi H.J. KLAUCK, *Allegorie* (n. 30), p. 273.

43. Évangiles: 2/11/6/0 (total NT: 31).

44. G. THEISSEN, *Lokal- und Sozialkolorit in der Geschichte von der syrophönikischen
Frau (Mk 7,24-30)*, in *ZNW* 75 (1984) 202-225, voir pp. 209-210. Son argument est qu'on
trouve de telles doubles désignations chez Flavius Josèphe (*Vie*, 427; *Contre Apion* I, 179-
180) et chez Philon (*De Abrahamo*, 251). Dans le même sens, R. PESCH, *Das Markusevangelium*, I (n. 30), p. 388.

45. D.-A. KOCH, *Die Bedeutung* (n. 30), p. 87.

ni par qui elle a été ajoutée. Selon L. Schenke[46], c'est le mot Ἑλληνίς qui aurait été ajouté rédactionnellement pour clarifier l'autre expression qui vient de la tradition et dont le sens est difficile à préciser. En ajoutant ce mot et en reliant notre péricope avec la controverse de 7,1-23, Mc accentue l'opposition Juifs-païens (v. 3 οἱ Ἰουδαῖοι; v. 26 Ἑλληνίς). Selon A. Dermience, c'est, au contraire, l'expression Συρο-φοινίκισσα τῷ γένει qui aurait été introduite a posteriori «pour accentuer la portée théologique de la péricope: l'ouverture aux païens de la communauté à laquelle il destinait son évangile»[47].

Le v. 27a est assez généralement considéré comme créé par Mc pour relier la péricope de la Syrophénicienne aux deux récits de multiplication, qui sont les deux seuls autres récits de Mc où se retrouve le terme χορτασθῆναι (Mc 6,42; 8,4.8)[48]. Ou à tout le moins on lui attribue l'insertion de πρῶτον[49]. Le but serait d'atténuer quelque peu la dureté

46. L. SCHENKE, Die Wundererzählungen (n. 30), pp. 255-256. Selon lui, Mc aurait déplacé la précision sur l'origine de la femme qui, primitivement venait en tête du récit. Celui-ci aurait dès lors commencé comme suit: καὶ γυνή, Συροφοινίκισσα τῷ γένει, ἧς εἶχεν τὸ θυγάτριον αὐτῆς πνεῦμα ἀκάθαρτον, ἀκούσασα περὶ αὐτοῦ (Ἰησοῦ), ἐλθοῦσα... (p. 256). H.J. KLAUCK, Allegorie (n. 30), p. 274, considère aussi Συροφοινίκισσα comme primitif, mais la raison invoquée est curieuse: «Die letztere Angabe wird die ältere sein, da sie gleichzeitig Nationalität und Religion zum Ausdruck bringt, während Ἑλληνίς allein auch von einer Diasporajüdin sein könnte».

47. A. DERMIENCE, Tradition (n. 31), pp. 28-29. On ne voit pas très bien en quoi l'usage du terme Συροφοινίκισσα met l'accent sur l'ouverture aux païens. Aux pp. 21-23, A. Dermience souligne le caractère étrange de ce vocable ethnique, dont l'usage au féminin est un hapax dans la langue grecque. Au masculin, on ne le retrouve en grec que dans un dialogue comique de Lucien (Deor. Conc. 4) et en latin deux fois dans des satires de Lucilius (Satires, fgmt 496-497) et de Juvénal (Satires 8,158-162). D'où elle déduit: «D'après ces emplois, les seuls à notre connaissance, le mot composé pourrait bien être une création des Romains, qui exprimaient par là leur mépris pour les ressortissants du Proche-Orient; ils unissaient deux peuples distincts dans une dénomination péjorative, synonyme de trafiquant ou d'exploitant de cabaret. Étant donné le genre d'activités auquel cette dénomination 'ethnique' était associée, on peut en déduire que le féminin évoquait une femme peu recommandable, voire une prostituée» (pp. 22-23). Il convient de remarquer que cette déduction repose sur très peu d'éléments, d'autant plus que, d'après certains manuscrits, on retrouve «Syrophoenix» encore chez Pline l'Ancien (Hist. nat. VII, 201) où le mot n'a pas de sens péjoratif. Mais il est vraisemblable que cette dénomination rare ait été forgée à Rome, sans doute par l'évangéliste qui y a séjourné (ibid., p. 23). G. THEISSEN, Lokal- und Sozialkolorit (n. 44), pp. 221-223, pour sa part, l'attribue à un Palestinien séjournant soit à Rome, soit en Syrie.

48. Ainsi H.J. HOLTZMANN, Die Synoptiker (HNT, 1,1), Tübingen, ³1901, p. 144; F. HAHN, Das Verständnis (n. 30), p. 24; T.A. BURKILL, Historical Development (n. 25), p. 177; K. KERTELGE, Die Wunder (n. 19), p. 153; S. LÉGASSE, L'épisode (n. 29), pp. 21 et 33; H.J. KLAUCK, Allegorie (n. 30), p. 273; J. GNILKA, Markus, I (n. 30), p. 290, n. 30. Par contre R. PESCH, Das Markusevangelium, I (n. 30), p. 388, estime que le v. 27a fait partie du récit primitif. D'autres encore le considèrent comme ajouté par un rédacteur postmarcien (voir ci-dessus, n. 20).

49. B. WEISS, Die Evangelien des Markus und Lukas (KEK, I,2), Göttingen, 1892, p. 127 («Offenbare Milderung des ursprünglichen Wortes Jesu [Matth. 15,24] nach Röm.

du v. 27b à des oreilles pagano-chrétiennes. Tout en reconnaissant cette portée au v. 27a, L. Schenke[50] estime que l'addition ne vient pas de Mc, mais d'une intervention rédactionnelle prémarcienne. À son avis, le contexte antérieur (7,1-23, particulièrement les vv. 6-7) est profondément anti-juif et ne permet guère d'attribuer à Mc l'idée d'une préséance des Juifs qui s'exprimerait par un πρῶτον. Le v. 27a, sans πρῶτον, faisait partie du récit traditionnel[51] où il renforçait le v. 27b. Et la réponse du v. 28 correspondait bien au v. 27 sans πρῶτον. Le lien entre les vv. 27a et b est encore renforcé par γάρ au v. 27b qui suppose une phrase antérieure. Mais ce γάρ pourrait tout aussi bien avoir été ajouté par Mc en même temps que le v. 27a. Sans πρῶτον, ce dernier ne serait qu'un doublet inutile du v. 27b. À notre avis, cette sentence du v. 27a qui n'est pas indispensable au récit et n'a pas d'existence indépendante vraisemblable doit être attribuée à Mc. Celui-ci l'ajoute à l'intention de pagano-chrétiens qui n'appréciaient sans doute guère le logion suivant, mais pouvaient accepter une conception paulinienne de l'histoire du salut qui leur donne une place après les Juifs (Rm 1,16; 2,9-10).

2. *Sitz im Leben* du texte primitif

Tous s'accordent à reconnaître l'importance du dialogue dans notre récit que M. Dibelius[52] classe littérairement parmi les paradigmes et R. Bultmann[53] parmi les apophtegmes, même si la pointe n'en est pas une sentence de Jésus. J. Gnilka pense qu'il ne s'agit même pas d'un apophtegme ou d'un récit de miracle, mais bien d'une controverse d'un

---

1,16»); J. WEISS, *Die Schriften des Neuen Testaments, I, Die drei älteren Evangelien. Die Apostelgeschichte*, Göttingen, ²1907, p. 139; E. KLOSTERMANN, *Das Markusevangelium* (n. 37), p. 72 («Vielleicht ist aber das πρῶτον Abschwächung der Redaktion, wenn auch nicht gleich der ganze v. 27a»); E. SCHWEIZER, *Das Evangelium nach Markus* (NTD, 1), Göttingen, 1968, p. 86; G. BARBAGLIO, *Gesù e i non Ebrei: la Sirofenicia (Mc 7,24-30)*, in *Parola, Spirito e Vita* 16 (1987) 101-114, voir p. 106 («contrassegno della rielaborazione di Marco o anche della sua fonte»).

50. L. SCHENKE, *Die Wundererzählungen* (n. 30), pp. 256-257. Voir aussi J. JEREMIAS, *Jésus et les païens* (CahThéol, 39), Neuchâtel-Paris, 1956, p. 25.

51. Ainsi aussi V. TAYLOR, *The Gospel According to St Mark*, London, 1952, p. 350, qui considère l'entiéreté du v. 27a comme traditionnel parce qu'il lui paraît indispensable pour encourager la Syrophénicienne et permettre sa réplique du v. 28. Il est suivi par B. BUETUBELA, *La Syrophénicienne: Mc 7,24-30. Étude littéraire et exégétique*, in *Revue Africaine de Théologie* 2 (1978) 245-256, voir p. 251.

52. M. DIBELIUS, *Die Formgeschichte* (n. 3), p. 53, n.1, pour qui, cependant, cette péricope ne faisait pas partie primitivement des paradigmes. M.A. BEAVIS, *Women as Models of Faith in Mark*, in *BTB* 18 (1988) 3-9, voir p. 5, souligne que ce récit relève du genre de la *chreia* et que Mc multiplie curieusement les *chreiai* («saying-*chreia*» et «action-*chreia*») attribuées à des femmes (5,24-34; 7,24-30; 12,41-44; 14,3-9), alors que d'habitude dans la littérature évangélique elles sont plutôt attribuées à Jésus.

53. R. BULTMANN, *Die Geschichte* (n. 16), p. 38, qui ajoute: «Und zwar liegt eine Art Streitgespräch vor, in dem diesmal aber Jesus – ohne daß dies einen Schatten auf ihn würfe – der Überwundene ist».

type particulier, un débat pédagogique[54]. Quant aux problèmes communautaires reflétés par ce texte, on pense le plus souvent à celui du particularisme juif ou judéo-chrétien prétendant à une exclusivité du salut. Ce qui ne manque pas de provoquer bien des questions sur le salut des païens et la mission qu'on peut engager chez eux[55]. Le v. 27 révèle la connaissance par la communauté de ce que Jésus se considérait comme envoyé seulement aux brebis perdues d'Israël[56], ce qui marque au moins la préséance d'Israël. Celle-ci aurait pu provoquer le rejet sans plus de toute mission tournée vers les païens. Mais la réponse de la femme manifeste la possibilité que tous, Juifs et païens, puissent se nourrir autour de la même table, sans qu'Israël soit volé. Bref, la surabondance du salut apparu avec Jésus permet de rassasier aussi les païens, sans que la prééminence d'Israël soit niée[57]. Certains croient pouvoir préciser le lieu de formation possible d'un tel récit et pensent à une communauté à la frontière de la Galilée et de la Syrie[58], où la région de Tyr était perçue comme un territoire de mission[59].

54. J. GNILKA, *Markus*, I (n. 30), p. 291, parle de «Lehrgespräch».

55. R. BULTMANN, *Die Geschichte* (n. 16), p. 176 (à propos de Mt 15,24); B. FLAMMER, *Die Syrophoenizerin* (n. 30), p. 468; D.-A. KOCH, *Die Bedeutung* (n. 30), p. 87; H.J. KLAUCK, *Allegorie* (n. 30), pp. 277-278; R. PESCH, *Das Markusevangelium*, I (n. 30), pp. 390-391; J. GNILKA, *Markus*, I (n. 30), p. 290; D. LÜHRMANN, *Das Markusevangelium* (n. 30), p. 131.

56. J. JEREMIAS, *Jésus et les païens* (n. 50), pp. 21-30, estime qu'historiquement Jésus n'a jamais pris l'initiative d'une activité missionnaire tournée vers les païens et qu'il a borné son activité strictement à Israël. Par contre, F. HAHN, *Das Verständnis* (n. 30), pp. 22-23, tout en admettant que l'activité de Jésus a été dirigée en priorité vers Israël, considère comme probable que Jésus ait occasionnellement séjourné en territoire païen et que des non-Juifs lui aient demandé de l'aide. Sans doute la *Formgeschichte* et la *Redaktionsgeschichte* ont-elles montré qu'il n'y a pas eu de «voyage vers le Nord» en bonne et due forme. Mais les noms de lieux liés à certains morceaux traditionnels lui semblent primitifs et non liés à une tradition tardive ou à une activité rédactionnelle.

57. L. SCHENKE, *Die Wundererzählungen* (n. 30), pp. 261-264, estime qu'au premier stade de sa constitution, le texte primitif (sans πρῶτον juxtaposait la réception du salut par les Juifs, d'une part, par les païens, d'autre part. Mais à un second stade on serait passé de cette juxtaposition à une succession du point de vue de l'histoire du salut: «Als später hellenistisch-judenchristliche Missionsgemeinden die Erzählung übernahmen, interpretieren sie diese im Sinne ihrer eigenen Missionstheorie und -praxis durch Einfügung des πρῶτον neu. Das aus der überfülle des von Gott in Jesus Christus geschenkten Heils ermöglichte *Nebeneinander* des Heilsempfangs von Juden und Heiden wird hier in ein heilsgeschichtliches *Nacheinander* verändert» (pp. 263-264). G. SCHILLE, *Die urchristliche Wundertradition. Ein Beitrag zur Frage nach dem irdischen Jesus* (Arbeiten zur Theologie, I/29), Stuttgart, 1967, pp.26-27, n. 64, range notre texte parmi les «Missionslegenden», conçues comme des récits exemplaires pour la mission, «welche die apostolische Gründung einer bestimmten urchristlichen Gemeinde zu legitimieren suchen, indem sie die Existenz eines besonders großen und zudringlichen Glaubens in besagter Stadt (Gemeindegründungstradition) oder im anvisierten Gebiet (Gebietslegende) am Beispiel eines Erstlings oder am Beispiel einer Wundergewährung durch den Kyrios schildern».

58. Ainsi J. GNILKA, *Markus*, I (n. 30), p. 290. L. SCHENKE, *Die Wundererzählungen* (n. 30), p. 262, va dans le même sens, mais émet en outre une hypothèse encore plus précise: «Ob die Erzählung in galiläisch-syrischen Kreisen der Stephanusleute entstanden und überliefert wurde, kann nur vermutet werden». (p. 263).

59. Ainsi R. PESCH, *Das Markusevangelium*, I (n. 30), p. 391.

3. Sens du récit dans la rédaction marcienne

L'analyse antérieure nous a permis de mieux discerner les retouches apportées par Mc au récit primitif lorsqu'il l'a intégré dans son évangile. Il reste à synthétiser les orientations nouvelles qu'il lui a ainsi imprimées. Elles sont de trois ordres.

D'abord, par le v. 24bc Mc suggère que la guérison a été extorquée à Jésus qui voulait rester caché. Ceci relève de sa théorie générale du secret messianique. Mais, en l'occurrence, celui-ci a une coloration particulière du fait que la scène se passse en territoire païen. Faut-il comprendre que, par ce moyen, Mc nous signale discrètement qu'il n'y a pas eu, selon lui, de mission de Jésus en territoire païen et que, même si celui-ci légitime une telle mission (Mc 13,10), il ne l'a jamais pratiquée lui-même[60]? Mais notre texte semble au contraire suggérer de la part de la femme une compréhension profonde de Jésus qui contraste avec l'opposition des pharisiens et des scribes et l'incompréhension des disciples[61]. Une telle compréhension lui permet d'ailleurs d'obtenir pour sa fille la libération de la possession démoniaque, ce qui est une œuvre du Royaume de Dieu (Mc 3,11-12.22-24). Elle reconnaît en Jésus le Messie, en qui le Royaume se fait proche. Par le v. 24bc, Mc insiste sur le fait que, méconnu chez les siens à qui il voulait révéler le Royaume, Jésus est reconnu aussitôt par une païenne, alors même qu'il n'avait pas l'intention de se donner à connaître en dehors d'Israël. De ce fait, l'appellation κύριε (v. 28), qui n'avait peut-être qu'un sens profane dans le récit primitif, doit en tout cas être comprise dans un sens religieux fort dans le texte final de Mc, dont le v. 24bc met toute la péricope sous le registre du secret messianique[62].

Ensuite, en créant un voyage vers le Nord par le biais des indications topographiques des vv. 24 et 31, Mc, à la différence de ce que fera Mt, donne l'impression d'une incursion de Jésus en territoire païen de Tyr et Sidon. Il crée une opposition géographique entre ces territoires où l'esprit impur est mis à mal grâce à la rencontre avec Jésus et ceux du judaïsme dont la conception du pur et de l'impur est critiquée par Jésus (7,1-23). Le contraste est souligné par la précision en 7,1 que les

---

60. Ainsi D.-A. KOCH, *Die Bedeutung* (n. 30), pp. 91-92. Plus nuancé, R. PESCH, *Das Markusevangelium*, I (n. 30), p. 391, précise que, selon Mc, en terre païenne Jésus n'est pas prédicateur, mais exorciste et guérisseur, ce qui est déjà une forme de «mission».

61. Voir à ce sujet C. FOCANT, *La fonction des doublets dans la section des pains*, in *The Four Gospels 1992. FS F. Neirynck* (BETL, 100), Leuven, 1992, pp. 1039-1063.

62. Ainsi B. FLAMMER, *Die Syrophoenizerin* (n. 30), pp. 474-475, sans distinguer toutefois deux étapes de notre récit. Voir aussi G. BARBAGLIO, *La Sirofenicia* (n. 49), p. 109, qui souligne que Mc n'emploie nulle part ailleurs κύριε dans un récit de guérison. Par contre, F. HAHN, *Christologische Hoheitstitel. Ihre Geschichte im frühen Christentum* (FRLANT, 83), Göttingen, ³1966, p. 82, pense que le titre κύριε n'aurait ici qu'un sens profane. Nous estimons pour notre part que c'est possible au stade primitif du récit, mais peu probable dans l'état final de la rédaction marcienne.

pharisiens et les scribes viennent de Jérusalem, centre du judaïsme, alors que la Syrophénicienne est rencontrée en territoire de Tyr. Il est encore renforcé par l'opposition entre πάντες οἱ Ἰουδαῖοι (v. 3) et Ἑλληνίς (v. 26)[63]. Le Jésus de Mc abolit ainsi l'exclusivité des biens messianiques pour le seul peuple soi-disant pur et se laisse arracher une ouverture vers les païens qui prépare la seconde multiplication des pains à leur profit (8,1-10)[64].

Enfin, si Mc abolit l'exclusivité de l'activité messianique au profit d'Israël, il maintient cependant en sa faveur une priorité acceptable pour ses lecteurs pagano-chrétiens, en ajoutant le v. 27a et son fameux πρῶτον qui rappelle les conceptions pauliniennes en la matière (Rm 1,16; 2,9-10). Aussi paraît-il difficile d'attribuer à Mc, comme le fait L. Schenke, l'idée que les Juifs sont les vrais impurs alors que les païens seraient déclarés purs du seul fait que Jésus se tourne vers eux[65].

4. Sens du récit dans la rédaction matthéenne (Mt 15,21-29)

Certes, à la première lecture, il appert que l'opposition entre Juifs et païens est plus dure dans le récit matthéen de la Cananéenne, où la question des relations entre les deux groupes devient pratiquement le thème unique[66]. On ne peut en déduire rapidement que Mt ferait des concessions à un judéo-christianisme étroit[67], alors qu'en fait, c'est toute une autre théologie qui est mise en œuvre dans ce texte et qui se révèle à travers de multiples transformations du texte de Mc. Parmi

---

63. Ainsi L. SCHENKE, *Die Wundererzählungen* (n. 30), p. 265. W. MUNRO, *Women Disciples in Mark?*, in *CBQ* 44 (1982) 225-241, voir p. 227, souligne, à juste titre, qu'en Mc la Syrophénicienne est la seule femme avec qui Jésus entre en dialogue et que, à la différence des autorités juives avec lesquelles le contexte la met en contraste, elle l'emporte en faisant changer Jésus de position.

64. Les colorations johannique et eucharistique que B. FLAMMER, *Die Syrophoenizerin* (n. 30), pp. 475-476, croit avoir discernées dans notre texte ne nous paraissent vraiment pas évidentes.

65. L. SCHENKE, *Die Wundererzählungen* (n. 30), p. 265: «Die Juden sind eigentlich die 'Unreinen' (vgl. vv. 20ff), während die Heiden durch die Zuwendung Jesu zu ihnen für 'rein' erklärt werden». Selon lui, le πρῶτον du v. 27a relève déjà du passé pour Mc: «Das Ziel seiner Interpretation ist vielmehr die Zurückweisung aktueller Tendenzen, die jüdischen Überlieferungen und reinheitsvorschriften als auch für die christliche Gemeinde verbindlich einzuführen. Darauf könnte gleichfalls die eindringliche, zumindest redaktionell erweiterte Jüngerbelehrung (7,17-23) hinweisen, in der sich die Jünger den Tadel gefallen lassen müssen, auch in der Frage nach 'Rein' und 'Unrein' unverständig zu sein. Wie immer beim Vorwurf des Jüngerunverständnis will Markus nämlich auch hier in erste Linie die verkehrte Haltung seiner Gemeinde treffen» (p. 266).

66. H.J. KLAUCK, *Allegorie* (n. 30), p. 280: «Wir können für Mt 15,26f. jede Brotsymbolik ausschließen und bleiben von der Metaphorik her auf das Problem von Juden und Heiden in der christlichen Gemeinde verwiesen. Mt hat durch seine Bearbeitung der mk Vorlage die Frontstellung zwischen beiden Gruppen wieder verschärft».

67. Contre H.J. HELD, *Matthäus* (n. 15), p. 189, justement critiqué par S. LÉGASSE, *L'épisode* (n. 29), p. 38, et H. FRANKEMÖLLE, *Jahwebund* (n. 9), pp. 114-115, n. 165.

celles-ci je ne relèverai, dans le contexte de cet article, que celles qui font sens, en négligeant les nombreuses améliorations stylistiques qui sont pourtant une part importante du travail de Mt[68].

D'entrée, Mt transforme les données topographiques de Mc. Si Jésus se dirige bien vers la région de Tyr et Sidon, rien ne dit qu'il y arrive et encore moins qu'il y entre dans une maison. Au contraire, le fait que la femme sorte de cette région (v. 22 : ἀπὸ τῶν ὁρίων ἐκείνων ἐξελθοῦσα) et vienne à sa rencontre suggère que lui-même n'est pas sorti du territoire de Galilée[69]. Que tel soit bien le sens des vv. 21-22 est confirmé par le v. 29, où en lieu et place de πάλιν ἐξελθὼν ἐκ τῶν ὁρίων Τύρου (Mc 7,31), Mt écrit simplement μεταβὰς ἐκεῖθεν. Jésus n'a pas, comme chez Mc, à quitter un territoire païen où il n'est pas entré. Du coup, Mt fait disparaître la construction marcienne d'un voyage de Jésus vers le Nord en territoire païen. Aussi est-il logique que le récit matthéen commence par καί et non par δέ, comme celui de Mc probablement[70]. En effet, il ne faut pas marquer une opposition avec le contexte précédent puisque, pour lui, Jésus ne quitte pas le territoire d'Israël[71]. L'insistance porte moins en Mt 15,21 sur εἰς à comprendre au sens de «en direction de» que sur ἀνεχώρησεν, verbe typique de Mt[72]. Il s'agit moins, pour Mt, de passer une frontière que de s'écarter

---

68. Ces améliorations stylistiques ont bien été mises en valeur par S. LÉGASSE, *L'épisode* (n. 29), passim, et A. DERMIENCE, *La péricope* (n. 31), passim.

69. M.-J. LAGRANGE, *Matthieu* (n. 4), p. 431; J. SCHMID, *Markus und der aramäische Matthäus*, in ID. et al. (ed), *Synoptische Studien. FS A. Wikenhauser*, München, 1953, p. 174-175; R.A. HARRISVILLE, *The Woman* (n. 7), p. 280; T.A. BURKILL, *The Syrophoenician Woman: The Congruence* (n. 25), p. 26; T. LOVISON, *La Pericopa della Cananea Mt. 15,21-28*, in *RivBib* 19 (1971) 273-305, voir p. 280. En sens inverse, U. LUZ, *Das Evangelium nach Matthäus, II, Mt 8-17* (EKK, I/2), Zürich-Braunschweig-Neukirchen-Vluyn, 1990, p. 433, pour qui «ἀπὸ τῶν ὁρίων ἐκείνων ist fast sicher auf γυνή und nicht auf ἐξελθοῦσα zu beziehen». C'est loin d'être si sûr et A. DERMIENCE, *La péricope* (n. 31), p. 31, après avoir souligné que les deux tournures syntaxiques se retrouvent chez Mt, a bien montré que la structure chiastique des vv. 21a et 22a (καὶ ἐξελθὼν ἐκεῖθεν ὁ Ἰησοῦς // καὶ ἰδοὺ γυνὴ Χαναναία ἀπὸ τῶν ὁρίων ἐκείνων ἐξελθοῦσα) suggère plutôt une mise en parallèle des démarches corrélatives de Jésus et de la Cananéenne. D'où elle conclut à juste titre: «Comme l'adverbe ἐκεῖθεν et le complément ἀπὸ τῶν ὁρίων ἐκείνων occupent la même place centrale, ne serait-ce pas l'indice qu'ils ont une fonction analogue et, par conséquent, dépendent tous deux du participe»? Je ne comprends pas bien ce qui permet à J.H. NEYREY, *Decision Making in the Early Church. The Case of the Canaanite Woman (Mt 15,21-28)*, in *ScEs* 33 (1981) 373-377, voir p. 374, d'attribuer à la rédaction matthéenne une «special emphasis on the gentile location of the episode». En tout cas, cela ne ressort pas de la comparaison avec Mc.

70. Ceci reste vrai, même si on ne peut pas être sûr que le texte original de Mc comportait δέ, puisqu'une partie non négligeable des manuscrits de Mc a καί, au point que M. THRALL, *Greek Particles in the New Testament. Linguistic and Exegetical Studies*, Leiden, 1962, p. 66, penche pour καί. Cependant, à juste titre, les éditions critiques (N[26], Legg) ont opté pour δέ, considérant sans doute καί comme une harmonisation avec le texte de Mt. K.L. SCHMIDT, *Der Rahmen* (n. 38), p. 198, pense, avec raison, que καί résulte d'une harmonisation avec Mt 15,21.

71. S. LÉGASSE, *L'épisode* (n. 29), pp. 24-25.

72. 10/1/0/1.

d'un peuple d'aveugles guidés par des aveugles (15,14). C'est le second de trois retraits successifs (14,13; 15,21; 16,4) chaque fois précédés d'occasions défavorables à Jésus et où s'illustre la séparation entre ce dernier et un Israël mal guidé[73].

Plus nettement qu'en Mc, dès lors, c'est le monde païen qui vient vers Jésus sous la figure d'une femme que Mt caractérise d'emblée comme Cananéenne, alors que, chez Mc, la spécification de la femme ne viendra qu'un verset plus tard. Or, ce terme qui constitue un hapax néotestamentaire[74], s'il peut être une autre dénomination pour «Phénicien», est aussi souvent utilisé dans l'AT pour marquer la distinction entre Israël et ses voisins idolâtres. L'opposition entre Israël et le monde païen est ainsi mise en valeur par la reprise de la vieille opposition biblique entre Israël (v. 24) et Canaan (v. 22)[75]. Sans doute faut-il interpréter dans même sens l'ajout par Mt de Sidon à Tyr. Il reconstitue ainsi le couple biblique «Tyr et Sidon» qui symbolise le monde païen[76].

Mt a la réputation d'être plus bref que Mc, alors que pour cette péricope il est nettement plus long. À ce sujet, il importe de remarquer que la tendance de Mt à abréger se vérifie surtout pour les éléments narratifs, tandis qu'il s'attarde volontiers sur les parties plus discursives. De la supplication en style indirect de Mc on passe d'emblée au style direct en Mt, ce qui donne à son texte la tournure particulière d'un dialogue où s'exprime la foi[77]. La triple formulation de sa demande par

---

73. Ceci a été mis en valeur par X. Léon-Dufour, *Études d'évangile* (n. 3), p. 249, qui parle de «trois 'retraites' de Jésus, en réaction à la triple provocation d'Hérode, des pharisiens et des scribes, des pharisiens et des sadducéens». Voir aussi J.D. Kingsbury, *Matthew: Structure, Christology, Kingdom*, London, 1976, p. 19. D. Good, *The Verb ANAXΩPEΩ in Matthew's Gospel*, in *NT* 32 (1990) 1-12, pense que ce motif du retrait «is part of a three-fold pattern of hostility/withdrawal/prophetic fulfilment Matthew seems to have created» (p. 1). On trouve sept exemples de cette structure, qui aurait été construite de cette manière pour que «the reader understands the withdrawal of Jesus as Wisdom to be part of the larger pattern of God's design. After all, those who oppose Jesus participate in salvation-history. So it is not *retreat from* hostility but rather *withdrawal for* the fulfilment of prophecy that demonstrates Matthew's intention in his creation of this pattern» (p. 12). Dans le dialogue de la Cananéenne avec Jésus on peut voir l'accomplissement des prophéties de Mt 12,18.21, même si le texte ne reproduit pas spécifiquement la formule matthéenne de l'accomplissement (*ibid.*, p. 4).

74. On trouve cependant le terme Canaan en Ac 7,11; 13,19, mais pas pour désigner une réalité contemporaine. Il s'agit dans les deux cas d'évocations de l'histoire biblique.

75. S. Légasse, *L'épisode* (n. 29), p. 26; K. Gatzweiler, *Un pas* (n. 10), p. 18, n. 6; R.A. Harrisville, *The Woman* (n. 7), pp. 280-281; T. Lovison, *La Pericopa* (n. 69), p. 290.

76. M.-J. Lagrange, *Matthieu* (n. 4), p. 308; K. Gatzweiler, *Un pas* (n. 10), p. 18, n. 4; H. Frankemölle, *Jahwebund* (n. 9), p. 136; A. Dermience, *La péricope* (n. 31), pp. 27-28.

77. H. Frankemölle, *Jahwebund* (n. 9), p. 137: «Wie des öfteren gestaltet der Redaktor das Traditionsgut dialogisch und macht aus der Wundergeschichte ein Glaubensgespräch».

la païenne comporte chaque fois le titre κύριε (vv. 22.25.27) et sa première version au v. 22 est particulièrement solennelle, liturgique même. Cette formule qui rappelle Mt 9,27 et 20,30.31 est typiquement matthéenne dans la formulation, Mt étant d'ailleurs le seul évangéliste à combiner les titres κύριε et υἱὸς Δαυίδ dans une adresse à Jésus[78]. Le vocatif κύριε revient 19 fois chez Mt, dans la bouche de disciples et de suppliants, où il a une portée confessionnelle importante[79]. Mt a une prédilection pour le titre υἱὸς Δαυίδ[80], mais c'est la seule fois qu'il le met dans la bouche d'une païenne. Celle-ci s'adresse à Jésus en utilisant à la fois un titre de portée plutôt universaliste et relevant du monde hellénistique et un titre renvoyant au messianisme royal du monde juif. Cette utilisation curieuse[81] des deux titres annonce déjà secrètement ce qui va suivre: la païenne sera exaucée à cause de sa foi, sa capacité à reconnaître le Messie d'Israël méconnu et rejeté par son peuple[82]. Peut-être même faut-il préciser que, dans la construction matthéenne, appeler

78. A. DERMIENCE, La péricope (n. 31), p. 34, n. 68. G. SCHILLE, Anfänge der Kirche. Erwägungen zur apostolischen Frühgeschichte (BEvT, 43), München, 1966, p. 70, souligne le caractère secondaire par rapport au texte de Mc de l'usage d'une telle titulature.

79. J.D. KINGSBURY, The Title «Kyrios» in Matthew's Gospel, in JBL 94 (1975) 246-255, voir pp. 248-249: «But if, as applied to Jesus, kyrios in the First Gospel is both 'relational' and 'confessional', then we can state provisionally at the outset that the purpose for which Matthew employs it is to attribute authority and an exalted status to Jesus. And since in Matthew's view the authority that Jesus wields and the exalted station that is his are derived from God himself (21,23-27; 28,18; cf. 11,27), we may rephrase our statement: Matthew employs kyrios in order to attribue an exalted station to Jesus and an authority that is specifically divine». On a une confirmation de cette vue dans la remarque faite par G. BORNKAMM, Enderwartung und Kirche im Matthäusevangelium, in G. BORNKAMM – G. BARTH – H.J. HELD, Überlieferung (n. 15), pp. 13-53, voir p. 38: «Sehr bezeichnend wird von da aus die Tatsache, daß Matth. zwar den Titel διδάσκαλος bzw ῥαββί reichlich verwendet, aber niemals als Anrede aus dem Munde seiner Jünger, mit einer Ausnahme - Judas Ischariot. Διδάσκαλε nennen ihn die Pharisäer und Fremde. Seiner Jünger nennen ihn κύριε». Le fait que Mt puisse aussi utiliser κύριε dans le sens banal de «Monsieur» (27,63) n'infirme en rien les observations faites sur le sens prégnant de κύριε adressé à Jésus.

80. 10/3/3/0.

81. Contre S. LÉGASSE, L'épisode (n. 29), selon qui la requête de la femme «est foncièrement banale» (p. 26, n. 23) et «offre à Jésus un hommage qui reconnaît en lui le Fils de Dieu qu'adorent les chrétiens». L'usage d'un titre messianique juif par une païenne peut difficilement être tenu pour banal, eu égard du moins à la théologie matthéenne sous-jacente. J.D. KINGSBURY, «Kyrios» (n. 79), p. 253, ne relève cependant pas non plus cet élément étrange, mais souligne seulement qu'ici, comme en 9,27 et 20,30-31, l'intention de Mt est «to attribute to Jesus the Son of David a high station and dominical authority (in these cases, to heal)».

82. H. FRANKEMÖLLE, Jahwebund (n. 9), p. 136, n. 261: «In der Zuordnung der beiden Titel ist bereits der Skopus der Perikope in nuce geliefert». Et J.D. KINGSBURY, Matthew (n. 73), pp. 100-101, note: «But, continues Matthew, Israel not only does not receive Jesus as the Son of David, it does not even recognize him to be such. In this regard Israel, contends Matthew, is without excuse. For one thing, the 'blind', a 'dumb' man, the 'children', and even a Gentile 'woman' are able to 'see' and 'confess' what Israel does not (cf. 9,27; 12,22; 15,22; 21,15 with 13,13; 15,14; 23,16-17.19.24.26)».

Jésus «Fils de David» est une nécessité pour la Cananéenne qui reconnaît ainsi d'avance que Jésus n'est envoyé que pour le peuple d'Israël (v. 24). Ce qui est fait pour elle ne pourra donc être qu'une exception[83].

Le travail opéré par Mt sur la tradition marcienne lui a permis de mettre en évidence trois réponses de Jésus (vv. 24.26.28) chaque fois introduites par ἀποκριθεὶς εἶπεν[84]. La première (v. 24) n'a pas de parallèle chez Mc. Il est difficile de trancher si Mt reprend en ce cas un logion ancien transmis de façon indépendante[85] ou s'il a composé lui-même ce verset[86]. En toute hypothèse, cette parole de Jésus manifeste, on ne peut plus nettement, que toute l'activité messianique de Jésus est réservée au peuple d'Israël[87]. Cohérent avec cette vision, Mt supprime dans la seconde réponse de Jésus la suggestion qu'on trouve dans le parallèle, Mc 7, 27, qu'il y aurait seulement préséance (πρῶτον) d'Israël. Alors que chez Mc l'accent portait sur une restriction temporelle, un délai relié au principe général par γάρ, Mt 15,26 ne présente plus que ce même principe général affirmé de manière absolue[88]. Avant de considérer la troisième réponse de Jésus, il convient de regarder la réplique de la femme qui la précède. Elle n'est pas non plus identique

83. Ainsi, G. STRECKER, *Der Weg der Gerechtigkeit. Untersuchungen zur Theologie des Matthäus* (FRLANT, 82), Göttingen, ³1971, p. 119. Voir aussi U. LUZ, *Matthäus*, II (n. 69), p. 434.

84. H. FRANKEMÖLLE, *Jahwebund* (n. 9), pp. 136-137.

85. R. BULTMANN, *Die Geschichte* (n. 16), p. 38. Dans le même sens, G. STRECKER, *Der Weg* (n. 83), p. 107, pour qui 10,6 est un doublet secondaire de 15,24. J. JEREMIAS, *Jésus et les païens* (n. 50), pp. 21-23, pour sa part, tient les deux expressions pour très anciennes et authentiques paroles de Jésus. Quant à R. HUMMEL, *Die Auseinandersetzung zwischen Kirche und Judentum im Matthäusevangelium* (BEvT, 33), München, 1966, p. 138, il pense que Mt a reçu les deux expressions, mais ne tranche pas si elles lui viennent de Jésus ou de cercles judéo-chrétiens.

86. Selon E. VON DOBSCHÜTZ, *Matthäus als Rabbi und Katechet*, in *ZNW* 27 (1928) 338-348, voir p. 339; W. TRILLING, *Das wahre Israel. Studien zur Theologie des Matthäus-Evangeliums* (SANT, 10), München, ³1964, pp. 100-105; W. GRUNDMANN, *Das Evangelium nach Matthäus* (THKNT, 1), Berlin, 1968, p. 375; U. LUZ, *Matthäus*, II (n. 69), p. 430, Mt aurait composé 15,24 en s'inspirant de 10,6 pour l'appliquer non plus aux disciples, mais à Jésus lui-même. Pour H. FRANKEMÖLLE, *Jahwebund* (n. 9), p. 137, Mt a composé lui-même toutes les paroles particularistes (10,5-6.23; 15,24), sans qu'aucune ait servi de modèle. A. DERMIENCE, *La péricope* (n. 31), pp. 36-39 et 46, tient 15,24 pour matthéen. En sens inverse, selon S. LÉGASSE, *L'épisode* (n. 29), pp. 28-32, ni 10,5-6, ni 15,24 ne peuvent avoir été composés par Mt; il s'agit de sentences nées en milieu judéo-chrétiens particularistes, la seconde radicalisant la première, et que Mt a simplement intégrées dans son évangile.

87. L'expression τὰ πρόβατα τὰ ἀπολωλότα οἴκου Ἰσραήλ ne désigne sans doute pas une catégorie particulière en Israël, mais bien tout le peuple. Le génitif est épexégétique, «maison d'Israël» et «brebis perdues» étant synonymes. On retrouve d'ailleurs la même expression en 10,5b-6 où la catégorie opposée, ce ne sont pas des justes, mais bien les païens et les Samaritains. Cette expression pourrait bien renvoyer à celle de Jr 50 (27 LXX),6: πρόβατα ἀπολωλότα ἐγενήθη ὁ λαός μου.

88. A. DERMIENCE, *La péricope* (n. 31), p. 41.

chez Mc et Mt. Ce dernier modifie et améliore la présentation. Au lieu
de dire que les petits chiens sont sous la table et qu'ils y mangent les
miettes des enfants, Mt 15,27 affirme plus correctement que les petits
chiens mangent les miettes qui tombent de la table de leurs maîtres.
Remplacer παιδίων par κυρίων n'est sans doute pas anodin en l'occurrence. Du coup, en effet, ce n'est pas d'Israël (παιδίων) que les païens
(κυνάρια) reçoivent les biens du salut (ψιχίων), mais de Dieu et du
Christ (κυρίων)[89]. De plus, en ajoutant simplement γάρ, Mt enlève à la
phrase le sens de répartie ou de controverse qu'elle pouvait avoir chez
Mc: «[Oui][90] Seigneur, tout de même les chiens sous la table mangent
les miettes des enfants». Au contraire, chez Mt, elle reprend à son
compte la réponse de Jésus, pour en tirer parti avec humour: «Oui,
Seigneur (sous-entendu, tu as raison: les chiens ne mangent pas ce qui
revient aux enfants); en effet, les chiens mangent (seulement) des
miettes qui tombent de la table de leurs maîtres»[91]. Sur cet arrière-
fond, la troisième et dernière réponse de Jésus met en valeur la foi de
cette païenne, foi qui justifie la guérison instantanée. Alors que Mc
introduisait emphatiquement la réplique de la femme et laconiquement
la réponse de Jésus, Mt, au contraire, solennise cette dernière tandis que
la réplique de la femme est introduite par une formule très brève. Alors
que pour Mc la réplique de la femme était de première importance
comme le souligne διὰ τοῦτον τὸν λόγον (Mc 7,29), pour Mt c'est la
dernière réponse de Jésus et son insistance sur la foi qui constitue le
sommet de la péricope[92]. Quant à la guérison instantanée, elle illustre
la force de la parole de Jésus (et non de la femme) et elle est formulée
dans des termes typiquement matthéens, puisqu'on retrouve la même
formule presque mot à mot en 8,13; 9,22; 17,18[93]. Par contre, dans le

89. S. LÉGASSE, L'épisode (n. 29), p. 38, qui fait remarquer que «rien, chez Matthieu ne
correspond à l'idée, exposée dans la première partie des Actes, d'une médiation du
judaïsme converti» (n. 84). Voir aussi H.J. KLAUCK, Allegorie (n. 30), p. 280, n. 94: «Die
Kinder (d. h. Israel) essen nicht am Tisch des Herrn, weil sie nicht wollen». Remarquons
cependant que l'incitation à interpréter ce trait allégoriquement aurait été plus forte si on
avait eu le singulier τοῦ κυρίου. Pour sa part, A. DERMIENCE, La péricope (n. 31), p. 42,
attribue le changement de terme à une simple préférence de Mt pour un langage plus
juridique: au terme familier «petits enfants» (παιδίων) il préférerait «enfants-maîtres»
(κυρίων).
90. Le mot ναί, qui est un hapax en Mc, manque dans de bons manuscrits anciens. Il
n'est pas repris dans N[26]. Selon B.M. METZGER, A Textual Commentary on the Greek
New Testament, London-New York, 1971, p. 95: «Apparently the word ναί (which occurs
eight times in Matthew, four times in Luke, and nowhere else in Mark) was introduced
here from the parallel passage in Mt 15,27».
91. Nous empruntons cette traduction-interprétation de Mc 7, 28 et Mt 15,27 à
S. LÉGASSE, L'épisode (n. 29), pp. 36-37. On trouvera une compréhension semblable chez
T. LOVISON, La Pericopa (n. 69), pp. 300-301.
92. Ce point a été bien mis en lumière par A. DERMIENCE, La péricope (n. 31), pp. 42-
43.
93. La chose est d'autant plus frappante qu'à chaque fois dans les parallèles synoptiques on ne trouve aucune mention de «cette heure».

récit de Mc, c'est la parole de la femme qui justifie la guérison et celle-ci n'apparaît que lors du retour de la femme à la maison.

Le type de communauté à laquelle est destiné le premier évangile et le type de perspective qui y est dominante restent des problèmes fort discutés[94]. Sans vouloir les trancher, il est possible de dégager de Mt 15,21-29 une perspective théologique cohérente avec le reste de l'évangile. La comparaison a permis de dégager que, si Mc a centré son récit sur la Syrophénicienne, dont la parole constitue la pointe de la péricope[95], Mt a restructuré le récit en un dialogue où s'exprime la foi de la Cananéenne, dont les invocations ont d'ailleurs un ton plus hiératique. Chez lui, c'est la parole de Jésus louant la foi de la Cananéenne qui devient la pointe de la péricope. Cette foi la sauve, alors même que pourtant les biens messianiques sont réservés à la maison d'Israël. Ainsi se dégage la théologie propre à Mt. On aurait tort de lire Mt 15,24 comme une concession à un judéo-christianisme étroit. En fait, selon Mt, Jésus assure la continuité de l'histoire du salut. Aussi le ministère de Jésus et de ses disciples est-il inscrit dans une perspective juive classique, particulièrement celle du Dt et de Chr: ils sont restés fidèles aux promesses du Dieu de l'alliance et ne sont envoyés qu'aux Juifs exclusivement (10,5-6; 15,24)[96]. Mt exclut la perspective marcienne, où on attribue à Jésus l'idée d'étapes successives de l'histoire du salut d'abord ouverte aux Juifs, puis ensuite aux païens (Mc 7,27a). Jésus a été envoyé exclusivement à Israël. Mais l'attitude de ce dernier envers l'alliance et son rejet du Messie qui ira jusqu'à sa mise à mort va entraîner le rejet dans les ténèbres extérieures des υἱοὶ τῆς βασιλείας, chez qui ne se rencontre pas la foi qu'on pourra trouver chez les païens qui viendront ἀπὸ ἀνατολῶν καὶ δυσμῶν (Mt 8,10-12) pour prendre part au festin du Royaume des cieux[97]. Certes le mouvement reste centripète. En 15,21-29, c'est la femme qui sort de son territoire pour venir vers Jésus aux confins de la Galilée. Mais, tout en respectant le principe de l'exclusivité des biens messianiques pour Israël, elle peut cependant y avoir part, bien que païenne, à cause de sa grande foi. Dans la conception théologique de Mt, cette foi est décisive pour l'appartenance à la βασιλεία τῶν οὐρανῶν. Sans doute, dans la communauté de Mt dans le dernier quart du 1er siècle, se demandait-on comment concilier l'essor de la mission chrétienne tournée aussi bien

---

94. Bref état de la question dans A. DERMIENCE, La péricope (n. 31), pp. 46-47.

95. A. DERMIENCE, La péricope (n. 31), p. 44.

96. H. FRANKEMÖLLE, Jahwebund (n. 9), p. 261. Voir dans la même ligne la façon dont Mt retravaille l'épisode de Gadara. Comme le fait remarquer S. LÉGASSE, L'épisode (n. 29), p. 39, n. 91: «On notera qu'à la fin de l'épisode des possédés de Gadara (6,23-27), Matthieu élimine la note missionnaire de Mc 5,19-20 (Lc 8,38-39), où l'on assiste à une préévangélisation des païens».

97. H. FRANKEMÖLLE, Jahwebund (n. 9), p. 261. S. LÉGASSE, L'épisode (n. 29), p. 39, nous semble bien rendre le point de vue de Mt en soulignant que ces attitudes opposées d'Israël et des païens ont fait «basculer l'ordre divin au profit des Gentils».

vers les païens que vers les Juifs avec la fidélité aux promesses de Yahweh à son peuple. Mt veut montrer à la fois que Jésus est resté fidèle à ces promesses tout au long de son ministère, mais aussi que l'accomplissement de celles-ci, loin d'être automatique, est lié à la foi et à l'accueil du messie. Cet accueil et la grande foi rencontrés chez les païens constituent le fondement théologique de l'universalisme[98]. En 15,21-29, ce dernier reste encore embryonnaire et centripète, mais le mouvement s'inversera vers une très large ouverture lors de l'envoi en mission final (Mt 28,19)[99].

II. L'ANALYSE NARRATIVE

Liée lors de sa naissance à la domination du romantisme dans les études littéraires, l'étude historico-critique est partie de l'intérêt porté à de grandes personnalités dont on cherchait à rejoindre l'intention à travers leur œuvre littéraire. On s'y intéresse particulièrement à la genèse historique des textes pour rejoindre les intentions de leur(s) auteur(s). La nouvelle critique ou l'analyse narrative, sous les multiples formes qu'on lui connaît, est née dans le contexte de l'avènement du réalisme en littérature[100]. S'inscrivant dans une perspective non plus diachronique, mais synchronique, cette nouvelle critique insiste sur l'autonomie du texte littéraire à étudier, à la limite, indépendamment de son auteur, de ses conditions de production et de son lecteur[101]. Les

98. H. FRANKEMÖLLE, *Jahwebund* (n. 9), pp. 115 et 261-262; S. LÉGASSE, *L'épisode* (n. 29), pp. 39-40; A. DERMIENCE, *La péricope* (n. 31), p. 49. Tentant de comprendre en quoi consiste cette grande foi qui permet de passer outre à une volonté de Dieu clairement exprimée au v. 24, J.H. NEYREY, *Decision Making* (n. 69), p. 375, écrit: «I suggest that this 'faith' is not great pelagian triumph on her part nor the result of a primitive feminist initiative, but represents Matthew's way of stating that God was working through her, leading her to Jesus, i.e. divine election (see Mt 8,11-12). (...) Jesus' last word, therefore, *acknowledges* divine activity in the gentile woman which clearly seems to be in tension with God's command in v. 24 to avoid gentiles».

99. A. DERMIENCE, *La péricope* (n. 31), pp. 48-49.

100. Pour une comparaison plus détaillée, on peut voir J.-L. SKA, *La «nouvelle critique» et l'exégèse anglo-saxonne*, in *RSR* 80 (1992) 29-53, voir pp. 29-39.

101. On entend ici l'auteur réel, concret et les divers lecteurs concrets et non l'auteur et le lecteur implicites auxquels la nouvelle critique accorde beaucoup d'importance. Avec J.-L. SKA, *«Our Fathers Have Told Us». Introduction to the Analysis of Hebrew Narratives* (Subsidia biblica, 13), Roma, 1990, p. 107, je traduis ainsi les expressions «author implied» et «reader implied». Pour la distinction entre auteur réel et auteur implicite, voir *ibid.*, p. 41. L'auteur implicite est celui qu'on peut reconstituer à partir de son texte seulement, sans s'intéresser à d'éventuels renseignements historiques. Pour la distinction entre lecteur réel et lecteur implicite, voir *ibid.*, pp. 42-43. Le lecteur réel peut être appelé implicite lorsqu'il adhère au contrat proposé par l'auteur implicite, autrement dit, lorsqu'il entre dans ses vues. «In other words, the 'implied reader' is less a person than a role that every concrete reader is invited to perform in the act of reading. Every narration contains an invitation to share a certain experience, to imagine and recreate a universe, to get in

manières de traiter le texte, de l'analyser sont fort différentes. Pour ne prendre qu'un exemple, alors que les anomalies ou bizarreries d'un texte sont automatiquement vues dans la première perspective comme des cicatrices, des «blessures de guerre» renvoyant à une histoire qu'on peut reconstruire, dans la seconde perspective on les lira plutôt comme des signaux envoyés au lecteur implicite pour qu'il construise une lecture intelligente et ne s'arrête pas à une lecture au premier degré. Les évangiles y sont considérés comme des œuvres littéraires à étudier comme produits finis.

L'analyse littéraire s'intéresse d'abord à la forme de l'œuvre. De ce point de vue, il importe cependant de distinguer la forme de l'expression et la forme du contenu [102], tout comme dans l'analyse du signe en linguistique on distingue classiquement signifiant et signifié. Certaines écoles pensent que l'étude de l'organisation de l'expression (mots ou groupes de mots récurrents, inclusions...) fournira la clé du contenu. C'est dans cette optique que se sont développées les analyses compositionnelles encore appelées «analyses rhétoriques» [103], qui, certes, ne manquent pas d'intérêt. Une autre école dite «sémiotique» veut se pencher sur l'organisation même du contenu considérée comme spécifique, c'est-à-dire non identique à l'organisation de l'expression. Ce faisant, elle s'intéresse aux couches profondes de la signification, à la forme du contenu ou encore aux structures du contenu. Pari plus difficile, mais peut-être plus prometteur et que je voudrais mettre en œuvre sur notre petit texte, en m'inspirant, du moins pour l'analyse de la péricope (Mc 7,24-31) [104] isolée de son contexte, de l'école greimassienne de sémiotique [105], tout en limitant le plus possible le recours à un

touch with certain values, feelings, decisions, and world-views. Such participation is another way to describe the 'part' of the implied reader. It does not mean that every 'real reader' will accept the values of the narration that he reads» (*ibid.*, p. 43). Ou encore, dans les termes de D. RHOADS – D. MICHIE, *Mark as a Story*, Philadelphia, 1982, p. 137: «The implied reader is properly an extension of the narrative, a reader that the author creates (by implication) in telling the story. By reconstructing the hypothetical implied reader from the responses suggested throughout the narrative of Mark's Gospel, we can identify some of the overarching effects this story might have on the reader».

102. J'emprunte cette distinction, proposée par F. de Saussure et L. Hjelmslev, à J.-N. ALETTI, *L'art de raconter Jésus Christ. L'écriture narrative de l'évangile de Luc* (Parole de Dieu), Paris, 1989, pp. 8-10.

103. On trouve un exemple assez typique de cette approche notamment dans le commentaire de R. MEYNET, *Quelle est donc cette parole? Lecture «rhétorique» de l'évangile de Luc (1-9; 22-24)* (LD, 99 A et B), 2 vol., Paris, 1979. Pour ma part, j'aurai recours brièvement à cette méthode ci-dessous comme un des critères pour délimiter le texte.

104. Dans les limites de cet article, je m'en tiens au texte de Mc. Pour une analyse semblable du texte parallèle en Mt, on pourra consulter J.-Y. THÉRIAULT, *Le maître maîtrisé! Matthieu 15,21-28*, in *De Jésus et des femmes. Lectures sémiotiques* (Recherches, n.s., 14), Montréal-Paris, 1987, pp. 19-34.

105. Cette école surtout connue dans l'aire francophone s'inspire des travaux de

vocabulaire trop spécifique et nécessitant de trop nombreuses explications, et sans oublier que «l'exégèse est un *art* où il faut jouer avec tous les instruments mis à notre disposition»[106]. Avant d'entreprendre l'analyse proprement dite, il convient de préciser les limites du petit texte et les conditions de son extraction. Après l'analyse de ce passage, je tenterai de le resituer dans son contexte et de préciser quelle est sa fonction narrative dans l'évangile de Mc.

1. *Extraction*

Extraire une scène hors de son contexte narratif en vue de l'analyser n'est pas une opération neutre, ni aisée. En effet, la façon de délimiter le corpus étudié n'est pas sans incidence sur l'interprétation[107]. C'est pourquoi elle ne peut se faire au hasard, sans recourir à des critères. Ceux-ci sont principalement de deux ordres.

Si on s'en tient d'abord aux critères d'ordre sémantique[108], c'est-à-dire les changements de lieu, de temps, de personnages ou d'action, on voit aussitôt qu'entre deux déplacements de Jésus (vv. 24 et 31) apparaît un nouveau personnage (une femme, Syrophénicienne) qui reste en scène du v. 25 au v. 30. Faut-il dès lors, comme dans la plupart des bibles, isoler les vv. 24-30 ou vaut-il mieux inclure aussi le v. 31?

La deuxième catégorie de critères, les critères littéraires ou stylistiques peuvent nous aider à trancher la question. Ceux-ci relèvent de ce que nous avons appelé la forme de l'expression et donc de l'analyse compositionnelle. Si nous tenons compte des symétries existantes, nous découvrons l'architecture suivante:

24 Jésus sort de Galilée (ἐκεῖθεν = Gennésaret selon 6,53)
  24 Jésus vient dans la région de Tyr (εἰς τὰ ὅρια Τύρου) et entre (εἰσελθών)
    dans une maison
    25 Une femme dont la fille a un esprit impur
      25 vient (ἐλθοῦσα) (dans cette maison)
        25 tombe aux pieds de Jésus
          26 et demande que le démon (τὸ δαιμόνιον) soit expulsé de sa fille
            (ἐκ τῆς θυγατρὸς αὐτῆς)

A.J. Greimas. Ce n'est évidemment pas la seule école pour l'analyse de la forme du contenu. J'ai choisi cette voie parmi d'autres possibles en fonction de son intérêt, mais aussi parce que la façon de procéder de la nouvelle critique littéraire américaine est présentée dans ce volume notamment par J.D. Kingsbury.

106. J.-N. ALETTI, *L'art* (n. 102), p. 10.

107. Comme le souligne bien J. DELORME, *L'intégration des petites unités littéraires dans l'évangile de Marc du point de vue de la sémiotique structurale*, in *NTS* 25 (1978-79) 469-491, voir p. 480: «La signification change quand on élargit l'espace textuel de la lecture». Il en va de même quand on le restreint.

108. C'est la dénomination utilisée par J.-N. ALETTI, *L'art* (n. 102), p.17. Dans la critique anglo-saxonne, on parle de «dramatic criteria». Selon ce premier critère, l'extraction se fait à partir d'une première observation des figures (acteurs, espaces, temps).

27 Métaphore des enfants (τέκνων) et des petits chiens (κυναρίοις) selon Jésus
28 Métaphore des enfants (παιδίων) et des petits chiens (κυνάρια) selon la femme
29 Jésus dit à la femme qu'à cause de sa parole le démon (τὸ
δαιμόνιον) est parti de sa fille (ἐκ τῆς θυγατρός σου)
29 La femme reçoit l'ordre de partir (ὕπαγε)
30 La femme repart (ἀπελθοῦσα) dans sa maison
30 et trouve son enfant délivrée du démon
31 Jésus sort (ἐξελθών) de la région de Tyr (ἐκ τῶν ὁρίων Τύρου)
31 Jésus va vers le lac de Galilée (εἰς τὴν θάλασσαν τῆς Γαλιλαίας)

Ce tableau montre bien qu'il y a inclusion entre les vv. 24 et 31 et
qu'il convient d'intégrer ce dernier dans l'analyse de la péricope[109]. Par
ailleurs, on peut remarquer d'emblée le caractère central des deux
métaphores des vv. 27-28 comme axe autour duquel s'articulent les
deux versants de ce bref récit.

2. Analyse sémiotique de Mc 7, 24-31 [110]

Considéré comme un univers de signification en soi, ce texte est censé
avoir son organisation propre que l'on peut découvrir sans recourir à
des informations hors-texte. L'objet de cette analyse, c'est donc de
décrire les articulations constitutives de ce micro-univers sémantique.
Dans la lecture ordinaire, si on peut se faire d'emblée une idée du
contenu du texte sans recourir à des informations extérieures, c'est qu'il
est possible de construire une compréhension du texte rien qu'en
articulant les éléments de son contenu. Par l'analyse sémiotique on vise
à faire cette démarche spontanée de façon plus méthodique, à l'aide de
procédures rigoureuses.
Pour rendre compte rigoureusement de l'articulation du contenu, on
part du postulat que l'effet de sens est produit par un effet de différence.
Aussi on recherche les différences entre les éléments de la signification
(par exemple, malade > < guéri, dedans > < dehors) qu'on peut

109. C'est aussi l'opinion de J.-P. MICHAUD – P.T. DAVIAU, *Jésus au-delà des frontières
de Tyr. Marc 7,24-31*, in *De Jésus et des femmes* (n. 104), pp. 35-57.voir pp. 37-40, qui
donnent également un tableau, mais moins détaillé, de la composition de ce texte. Dans le
même sens, W. KLAMER, *Het verhaal van een exorcisme: Marcus 7,24-31*, in *TvT* 30 (1990)
117-145, voir p. 120, selon qui l'aspect inclusif du v. 31 est encore mis en évidence par
πάλιν. Par contre, en sens inverse, voir B. BUETUBELA, *La Syrophénicienne* (n. 51),
pp. 246-248, qui propose une autre structure littéraire du texte, difficile à accepter parce
qu'elle ne tient pas compte des personnages sujets des différentes actions. Par ailleurs, on
peut se demander pourquoi l'inclusion ἀπῆλθεν εἰς τὰ ὅρια Τύρου (7,24), καὶ πάλιν
ἐξελθὼν ἐκ τῶν ὁρίων Τύρου (7,31) ne figure pas dans la liste des inclusions dressée par
F. NEIRYNCK, *Duality in Mark. Contributions to the Study of the Markan Redaction*
(BETL, 31), Leuven, ²1988, pp. 131-133.
110. Cette analyse doit beaucoup à celle de J.-P. MICHAUD – P.T. DAVIAU, *Jésus au-
delà des frontières de Tyr* (n. 109).

percevoir dans un texte. Mais il ne suffit pas d'en faire un simple relevé. Il faut surtout voir comment elles s'articulent. En effet, un élément de signification n'acquiert sa valeur propre que dans la relation à un terme comparable et différent, fût-ce un terme sous-entendu. Il importe dès lors de voir sur quoi porte la différence entre les termes, autrement dit ce qui est sélectionné comme valeur des éléments différenciés. C'est ainsi que l'on dégage progressivement la structure du contenu. Selon la théorie sémiotique l'organisation du texte fonctionne et, donc, peut être décrite à deux niveaux principaux, le niveau discursif et le niveau narratif[111].

1. Le niveau discursif ou figuratif[112]

Il s'agit de repérer dans le texte les figures et de les classer. Ce repérage peut se faire autour de trois pôles: les acteurs, les temps, les lieux. Il importe surtout de découvrir des relations (différences, oppositions...) entre ces figures. Cela doit permettre de voir sur quelles relations entre quelles figures travaille la signification. En effet, les figures sont disposées en parcours figuratifs et le texte étudié utilise et développe un parcours parmi les multiples parcours possibles pour une figure[113]. Enfin, à partir de la façon dont le texte articule les parcours figuratifs, on peut discerner des valeurs thématiques sous-jacentes.

a. Repérage des figures au fil du texte

En Mc 7,24-31, on est frappé par le grand nombre de figures spatiales, ethniques et géographiques. Tout commence par un déplacement (ἐκεῖθεν) qui renvoie dans le contexte antécédent à une maison où Jésus enseigne ses disciples (7,17) à Gennésaret (6,53). Passant du monde juif, où il vient d'avoir une controverse sur le pur et l'impur, au monde non-juif, Jésus passe aussitôt du dehors au dedans en entrant dans une maison, passage caractérisé comme passage du manifeste au

---

111. Dans le cadre de cet article, je laisse de côté un troisième niveau appelé logico-sémantique. Il s'agit d'une étape plus théorique où on classe les parcours discursifs et narratifs et où on réfléchit sur leur organisation à l'aide d'un modèle logico-sémantique appelé carré sémiotique.

112. J.-C. GIROUD – L. PANIER, Sémiotique. Une pratique de lecture et d'analyse des textes bibliques, in Cahiers Évangile, n° 59 (1987), p. 48, en donne la définition suivante: «À ce niveau le contenu du texte se présente comme un agencement de figures disposées en parcours (parcours figuratifs) dont l'articulation spécifique détermine des valeurs thématiques».

113. Si on prend, par exemple, la figure «porte», elle peut fonctionner sur le parcours figuratif de la barrière faisant obstacle au héros ou au contraire de celle qui s'ouvre à la fin pour accueillir le héros. Quant à la valeur thématique que peut prendre cette figure dans le texte, ce peut être, par exemple, la «séparation» ou la «communication». Les valeurs thématiques sont toujours plus difficiles à découvrir car elles n'apparaissent pas dans l'expression du texte. On doit les construire abstraitement à partir de ce qu'on a observé des figures et des parcours figuratifs.

secret (οὐδένα ἤθελεν γνῶναι), mais qui échoue. Tout ceci concerne le premier acteur du récit, Jésus, sur le plan spatial.

Intervient aussitôt un deuxième acteur, une femme reliée au premier acteur par ce qu'elle a entendu à son sujet et que le récit présente d'emblée en déplacement, elle aussi: elle vient aux pieds de Jésus, c'est-à-dire dans la maison où il voulait rester incognito. Une subordonnée lie deux autres acteurs à cette femme: elle a une petite fille qui a un esprit impur au-dedans d'elle. Mais ce n'est pas tout ce qu'on sait d'elle. Le texte s'arrête encore pour une parenthèse sur son origine précisée doublement. Si le texte s'arrête ainsi pour une telle parenthèse redondante, c'est qu'elle a quelque enjeu. Dans la relation à Jésus, les deux précisions soulignent le caractère étranger de cette femme: au plan ethnico-religieux, elle est Ἑλληνίς, ce qui bibliquement par opposition à Ἰουδαῖα signifie païenne; au plan géographique, elle est Syrophénicienne non par adoption, mais de naissance. Le texte ne donne guère que des indications géographiques sur cette femme, comme si l'essentiel était de caractériser cette femme «géographique» comme on ne peut plus étrangère et liée à l'impur. Bref, jusqu'ici le texte a surtout spatialisé les acteurs en mettant en scène une étrangère en relation avec Jésus qui est lui-même incognito dans une maison à l'étranger. Quant à la demande de la femme formulée en style indirect au v. 26, elle est aussi d'ordre spatial, à savoir que le démon soit expulsé hors de sa fille[114].

Le dialogue des vv. 27-28 fait passer à d'autres figures, celles de la vie domestique: une maison où il y a des enfants et des petits chiens. Le dialogue recourt à la métaphore, c'est-à-dire qu'on y reflète en d'autres termes ce qui se passe au niveau du récit primaire[115]. Jésus tente d'éclairer la situation en évoquant une économie, une loi domestique. Il se réfère comme critère de son action à une loi d'ordre esthétique (καλόν) qui ne vient pas de lui. Derrière la figure du «beau» apparaît en filigrane le destinateur[116] de l'action de Jésus. Cette loi énonce une priorité dans l'ordre temporel: le pain d'abord aux enfants. La femme commence par marquer son accord avec l'économie rappelée par Jésus, mais elle la reformule à sa manière, selon son point de vue. À première vue, les termes de comparaison restent les mêmes. Et pourtant une lecture attentive fait voir qu'entre la parole de Jésus et celle de la femme

---

114. Ceci relève d'une conception de l'humain comme habité par un esprit dont W. KLAMER, *Het verhaal* (n. 109), pp. 121-124, a bien rendu compte. J'y reviendrai à propos de la fonction narrative de Mc 7,24-31 dans son contexte.

115. Les acteurs du récit primaire (Jésus, la femme et sa fille, l'esprit impur) ne sont pas mentionnés dans les métaphores où n'apparaissent pas non plus les figures de l'espace étranger, ni du dedans-dehors.

116. Le mot «destinateur» recouvre le rôle actantiel de celui qui fait faire, qui fait agir le sujet opérateur par ordre, séduction, menace... Il est le garant des valeurs mises en œuvre sur le programme du sujet opérateur. Quand il intervient au niveau de la sanction pour l'évaluation des valeurs susdites, on l'appelle «destinateur épistémique».

un seul terme est rigoureusement commun, à savoir τὰ κυνάρια, comme l'illustre le tableau suivant des éléments métaphoriques des vv. 27b et 28b[117]:

Jésus	Syrophénicienne
λαβεῖν καὶ βαλεῖν	ἐσθίουσιν
τὸν ἄρτον	ἀπὸ τῶν ψιχίων
τῶν τέκνων	τῶν παιδίων
τοῖς κυναρίοις	τὰ κυνάρια
	ὑποκάτω τῆς τραπέζης

Non seulement la femme introduit un terme nouveau (ὑποκάτω τῆς τραπέζης), mais au lieu d'un seul diminutif (κυναρίοις) on en a trois (ψιχίων, παιδίων, κυνάρια)[118]. Et, dans le cadre d'une telle cascade de diminutifs, le changement de τέκνων en παιδίων est sans doute moins anodin qu'il ne paraît[119]. En effet, si le terme παιδίον caractérise d'abord la taille ou l'âge, le terme τέκνον, bien qu'il puisse aussi caractériser la taille ou l'âge, est surtout un terme de parenté[120], celle du sang ou encore la parenté sociale ou spirituelle. Dans ce dernier sens, on pourra parler, par exemple, de τέκνα τοῦ Ἀβραάμ, ce terme incluant bien évidemment des adultes. La comparaison des termes utilisés fait mieux ressortir la différence des points de vue entre Jésus et la Syrophénicienne. Dans la loi domestique telle que l'énonce Jésus, tout est vu du point de vue du maître, qui, de sa table, ne juge pas «beau» de jeter le pain des enfants, c'est-à-dire de la famille, aux petits chiens, du moins aussi longtemps que les enfants ne sont pas d'abord rassasiés. La Syrophénicienne reprend le seul diminutif utilisé par Jésus pour proposer un changement de point de vue. Certes, tout comme κύων, le terme κυνάριον, quand il est utilisé métaphoriquement pour

117. Les mots interviennent aussi dans un ordre fort différent selon les deux métaphores. Pour la présentation j'ai bien dû opter et j'ai suivi l'ordre du v. 27.

118. À ce sujet on peut voir la nette différence de points de vue entre la *Redaktionsgeschichte* et l'analyse narrative. Dans la ligne de la première, on souligne toujours le goût particulier du rédacteur Marc pour les diminutifs, mais sans relever leur valeur argumentative particulière. Dans la ligne de la seconde au contraire, cette cascade de diminutifs est vue comme une stratégie mise par le narrateur au service d'une progression dans le récit par voie argumentative. Ces deux points de vue ne sont d'ailleurs pas contradictoires. C'est encore un autre point de vue que représente R. Pesch, *Das Markusevangelium*, I (n. 30), p. 389, lorsqu'il écrit: «Die Häufung von Diminutivformen im Text (θυγάτριον, κυνάριον, παιδίον, ψιχίον) zeigt Nähe zur volkstümlichen Umgangssprache an».

119. Ceci a été bien mis en évidence par W. Klamer, *Het verhaal* (n. 109), p. 135. B. Buetubela, *La Syrophénicienne* (n. 51), p. 253, fait la même observation, mais sans en tirer parti dans son interprétation.

120. Voir A. Oepke, *ΠΑΙΣ κτλ*, in *TWNT*, V, 1954, pp. 636-653, voir pp. 636-638; Bauer – Aland, *Wörterbuch*, [6]1988, ad loc. Même si le sens parental est évidemment possible pour παιδίον, il n'est pas premier alors qu'il l'est pour τέκνον, ne fût-ce qu'étymologiquement. La juxtaposition des deux termes dans deux phrases opposées par δέ et où il y a une contre-argumentation ne peut pas être banalisée.

désigner un groupe de personnes a un sens péjoratif. Cependant, ce dernier est atténué par le diminutif, qui sert à qualifier un animal favori plutôt qu'un animal méprisé[121]. Se mettant à la place des petits chiens, la Syrophénicienne invite en quelque sorte à considérer la situation à partir d'en-dessous de la table et du point de vue des petits, ce qu'indique la multiplication des diminutifs. Du coup, elle manifeste «l'irrelevance» de la distinction selon le régime de parenté que Jésus avait proposée et qui confortait une distinction ehtnico-religieuse. Pour la Syrophénicienne, il ne s'agit pas de privilégier le rassasiement des uns, mais plutôt que tous puissent manger. Tout en paraissant approuver le point de vue de Jésus[122], par les choix linguistiques opérés (multiplication des diminutifs et παιδίον préféré à τέκνον), la Syrophénicienne argumente et persuade Jésus de la non pertinence des distinctions de parenté religieuse, qui fondent son refus de lui venir en aide[123]. S'il y a encore priorité pour les petits enfants, elle n'entraîne pas un retard dans le nourrissement des petits chiens, car la distinction ne joue plus dans l'ordre temporel, mais dans l'ordre spatial. Si chacun reste à sa place, il n'y a aucun danger que le pain soit enlevé aux enfants. Dès lors, petits enfants et petits chiens peuvent se nourrir simultanément.

Après ce dialogue, une parole de Jésus annonce l'exaucement de la demande de départ: le démon est parti de la petite fille. Ce passage du dedans au dehors, qui met fin au mélange impur de départ, n'est pas raconté, mais seulement constaté dans la parole de Jésus se référant à celle de la femme.

Au v. 31, enfin, le récit revient aux figures spatiales. Mais le déplacement évoqué ne l'est pas dans des termes très clairs. On a souvent relevé la bizarrerie de l'itinéraire proposé et de l'expression εἰς τὴν θάλασσαν τῆς Γαλιλαίας ἀνὰ μέσον τῶν ὁρίων Δεκαπόλεως[124]. Tout se passe comme si ces mentions géographiques indiquaient moins un itinéraire de déplacement que la coexistence des territoires juifs et païens. Sur le chemin du retour au pays des enfants, Jésus gratifie les petits chiens des miettes des enfants (guérison du sourd qui parle difficilement et seconde multiplication des pains) jusqu'au rassasiement (8,8: ἔφαγον καὶ ἐχορτάσθησαν...).

---

121. Pour plus de détails, voir, par exemple, V. TAYLOR, St Mark (n. 51), p. 350; S. LÉGASSE, L'épisode (n. 29), pp. 35-36; W. KLAMER, Het verhaal (n. 109), pp. 134-135.

122. Si du moins il faut lire ναί au v. 28. Sur l'hésitation textuelle à ce propos, voir ci-dessus, note 90.

123. Ce qui fait le caractère curieux de ce récit, car d'habitude dans les récits évangéliques c'est plutôt Jésus qui persuade ses interlocuteurs que les surdéterminations religieuses ou autres ne peuvent empêcher l'aide. Ceci apparaît très clairement en Lc 10,25-37 et a été bien mis en valeur par GROUPE D'ENTREVERNES, Signes et paraboles. Sémiotique et texte évangélique, Paris, 1977, pp. 17-52.

124. Voir à ce sujet les remarques de J.-M. VAN CANGH, La Galilée dans l'évangile de Marc: un lieu théologique?, in RB 79 (1972) 59-76, voir pp. 70-71.

b. Les parcours figuratifs

Les figures découvertes peuvent se regrouper autour de deux parcours figuratifs principaux.

D'un bout à l'autre du récit, nous retrouvons l'opposition dedans-dehors liée à la question de l'espace étranger ou de la personne étrangère. Jésus sort vers le territoire étranger (Tyr) pour y entrer dans une maison en secret. Une femme, sur le caractère étranger de laquelle le texte insiste, y fait irruption, de sorte que Jésus ne peut rester caché. Enfin, il y a la petite fille habitée d'un indésirable esprit impur. Cette mention fait affleurer dans ce petit texte une figure importante dans le contexte antécédent[125] et dans le monde culturel de ce récit, où une séparation rigoureuse s'impose entre Juifs et païens pour éviter l'impureté. La parole de la femme où les païens mangent les miettes des Juifs en même temps qu'eux subvertit cette désignation de l'étranger, du païen comme l'impur. Elle trouve sa sanction positive dans le fait que l'esprit impur est expulsé de sa fille païenne διὰ τοῦτον τὸν λόγον.

Au niveau des paroles de Jésus et de la Syrophénicienne (vv. 27-28) joue un autre parcours figuratif, celui de la vie domestique, incluant pain, enfants, table, petits chiens. Le reste du récit est dominé par le parcours de «l'étranger» posé d'abord négativement (déplacement secret à l'étranger pour Jésus, possession par l'esprit impur pour la petite fille de l'étrangère), puis positivement en finale: le démon est expulsé de la petite fille et Jésus se déplace ouvertement en territoire païen. Ce qui permet le passage, le retournement, c'est justement le recours au parcours de la vie domestique, où la femme introduit la compatibilité dans la simultanéité au plan temporel grâce au maintien de la distinction au plan spatial.

Bref, dans ce texte, tout se passe comme si, au début, personne n'était où il devrait être. Le texte fonctionne un peu comme une remise en place:

– Le démon intrus dans la petite fille en est exclu.

– La femme intruse dans la maison où Jésus se trouvait incognito retourne dans la sienne, mais après avoir conquis sa place par rapport à ce que Jésus peut donner.

– En ne voulant pas qu'on le sache dans une maison en territoire païen, Jésus semblait estimer qu'il n'était pas où il devait. Finalement au contraire il se déplace à découvert en territoire païen.

– La géographie en finale ne fonctionne plus comme élément de séparation religieuse entre les gens comme au début.

---

125. J'y reviendrai plus loin à propos de la fonction narrative du petit récit dans le récit global.

2. Le niveau narratif

À ce niveau plus abstrait, le texte est conçu comme une succession organisées d'états et de transformations de ces états. L'analyse vise dès lors à découvrir les relations qui articulent entre eux des énoncés d'état qui concernent l'être (sujet conjoint ou disjoint d'un objet-valeur) et les énoncés d'opération qui relèvent du faire et permettent le passage d'un état à un autre.

Pour mener cette analyse, je me réfère au schéma narratif fonctionnel de A.J. Greimas[126]. Ce schéma organise la suite des énoncés et leur enchaînement en quatre phases logiquement liées entre elles[127]. Sur base d'un manque de départ (situation initiale), les quatre phases sont autant d'éléments qui peuvent intervenir pour permettre de le combler (situation finale)[128]. Ce sont les suivantes:

– La manipulation ou le faire-faire: Pour que la transformation exigée par le manque initial puisse avoir lieu, il faudra qu'un sujet opérateur réalise le programme nécessaire. Avant même que ce sujet n'entre en action, il faut le mettre en route, le convaincre de réaliser le programme. On appelle destinateur le rôle actantiel de celui qui fait faire quelque chose à un autre actant, que ce soit par ordre, persuasion, menace...

– La compétence ou les conditions du faire: Pour que le sujet opérateur puisse réaliser le programme, il y a des conditions à remplir, qui relèvent essentiellement du savoir-faire et du pouvoir-faire.

– La performance ou la transformation: Il s'agit de rendre compte du faire du sujet qui opère une transformation. Cette dernière porte sur une relation entre un sujet d'état et un objet-valeur auquel il est conjoint ou disjoint. L'objet-valeur est à entendre comme ce dont l'acquisition ou la perte est l'enjeu de tout le récit.

– La sanction ou évaluation positive ou négative de la transformation et du sujet qui l'a prise en charge. Cette évaluation est le fait du destinateur qu'on retrouve en finale. On l'appelle parfois destinateur épistémique pour souligner qu'il représente les valeurs en jeu qui président à l'évaluation.

---

126. Je préfère ce modèle ou schéma fonctionnel hérité des travaux de V. Propp et organisé de manière plus systématique par A.J. Greimas au schéma actantiel dérivant des travaux de R. Barthes.

127. Pour ceci, je reprends la présentation de J.-C. GIROUD – L. PANIER, *Sémiotique* (n. 112), pp. 50-53.

128. Comme l'écrit P. BEAUCHAMP, *Le récit, la lettre et le corps. Essais bibliques* (Cogitatio Fidei, 114), Paris, 1982, p. 187: «Le ressort du récit est le rapport au bien en tant qu'il est absent. Hélène a été enlevée et c'est *l'Iliade*; Ulysse a perdu son Ithaque et c'est *l'Odyssée*. Abraham n'a plus de terre et pas encore de fils: c'est la Genèse. Par contre, dès les amants réunis et le voyageur à bon port, on ne peut plus 'faire d'histoires' et le récit s'arrête.»

Les deux phases centrales axées toutes deux sur la transformation se situent au plan du faire ou plan pragmatique. Par contre, la manipulation et la sanction se situent au plan cognitif. Dans la manipulation, le savoir en question est d'ordre persuasif: pour susciter le désir, la manipulation met en perspective les valeurs à atteindre. Elle ne les donne pas (c'est le rôle de la performance), mais elle donne à connaître ce qu'elles sont censées valoir. Dans la sanction, le savoir est d'ordre interprétatif: la sanction vérifie la conformité des valeurs finalement atteintes avec celles qui sont définies dans la manipulation. Le schéma narratif présenté donne les grandes phases d'un récit classique, mais n'est pas à appliquer mécaniquement aux textes. Dans les textes concrets des choix narratifs divers sont opérés. Mais le schéma est un instrument heuristique permettant notamment de découvrir les choix narratifs. En l'occurrence, il nous permettra de voir que le récit de Mc 7,24-31 est surtout centré sur le plan cognitif, le pragmatique restant dans l'ombre.

Dans le récit de la Syrophénicienne, le manque à combler le plus évident est constitué par la possession dont est victime sa petite fille. Le récit fait aussitôt percevoir Jésus comme sujet opérateur plausible pour un exorcisme. Ce que la femme a entendu de cet homme lui donne à penser qu'il est compétent. Elle reconnaît son pouvoir faire et porte la situation à sa connaissance. Pour le persuader (manipulation), elle tombe à ses pieds et le prie. Jésus répond par une parole impersonnelle derrière laquelle se profile un destinateur qui n'est pas autrement précisé. Cette parole justifie son souci d'incognito en terre païenne et manifeste une limite de sa compétence à une catégorie dont la femme est exclue. Celle-ci marque son accord avec la parole de Jésus, mais la réinterprète dans un sens inclusif. Pour cela elle change le sens de πρῶτον qui ne signifie plus un retard dans le temps. Mais elle respecte la hiérarchie qu'indique l'adverbe, car le fait de manger les miettes se passe sous la table et n'ôte rien au pain des enfants[129]. Autrement dit, elle souligne qu'il n'est pas incompatible avec l'économie domestique introduite par Jésus de nourrir les deux en même temps, étant entendu que chacun reste à sa place. La manipulation opérée par la Syrophénicienne réussit puisque, à cause de sa parole, le démon est expulsé.

L'expulsion proprement dite n'est pas racontée, ce qui est étonnant dans un tel récit. Spontanément les commentateurs suppléent en affirmant que Jésus a chassé le démon. Mais le texte ne le dit pas; il ne mentionne ni un geste de Jésus, ni une force sortie de lui. On a simplement une parole de constat exprimée au parfait passif (v. 29 ἐξελήλυθεν; voir aussi au v. 30 ἐξεληλυθός). La parole manifeste que

---

129. Il ne s'agit effectivement pas de distribuer du pain en miettes, mais de consommer les miettes des petits enfants.

c'est déjà accompli. Tout se passe comme si on restait tout le temps au plan cognitif. De la manipulation sur la compétence on passe directement à la sanction. Et, en finale, Jésus apparaît moins comme sujet opérateur de transformation que comme sanctionnant le programme réalisé. Il se situe plutôt du côté du destinateur épistémique non autrement manifesté que par ce qui arrive et qui n'était pas prévu. La transformation est rattachée par Jésus à la parole de la femme qui apparaît comme une force capable de transformer la situation. Est-ce elle qui a réalisé la transformation? On ne peut en être sûr. C'eût été clair si au v. 29 Jésus avait dit: «À cause de cette parole, va, tu as chassé...» Au lieu de quoi le texte constate simplement que le démon est sorti. Il n'attribue l'expulsion directement à personne, ni à la femme, ni à Jésus. Il dit simplement que l'expulsion est liée à la parole de la femme en réponse à celle de Jésus. Il fait partie de ces textes curieux où Jésus attribue à quelque chose (action ou parole) venant du bénéficiaire ce qui lui était demandé à lui[130]. Il agit ainsi en finale comme interprète du destinateur épistémique[131], c'est-à-dire celui qui représente les valeurs en jeu.

Or, Jésus a fait référence antérieurement aux valeurs de ce destinateur, en disant οὐ γάρ ἐστιν καλόν (v. 27). Rien ne semble indiquer un changement de destinateur. Pourtant la sanction (le démon est expulsé) est liée à la parole de la femme et manifeste que sa compréhension des valeurs placées par le destinateur sur le programme de Jésus[132] est bonne, vraie. Or, elle n'est pas en accord avec la compréhension qu'en avait Jésus (v. 27). Elle les a plutôt redéfinies (v. 28). Et Jésus, en tant qu'interprète du destinateur, sanctionne positivement son interprétation contre la sienne propre. Bref, dans son rôle d'interprète du destinateur, il est transformé[133]. On s'aperçoit ainsi que la performance interpréta-

---

130. J. DELORME, Le salut dans l'évangile de Marc, in LTP 41 (1985) 79-108, voir p. 88, dit à propos de tels textes que «Jésus n'intervient pas comme opérateur de salut, mais comme interprète autorisé du destinateur du salut». Voir aussi J. DELORME, Le salut dans les évangiles synoptiques et les Actes des Apôtres, in DBS 11 (1988), 584-689, voir col. 602-603.

131. Pour une définition de ce terme, voir n. 116. C'est ce que J. DELORME, Le salut (n. 130), p. 87, n. 17, appelle le destinateur de la sanction. Jésus apparaît dans ce type de récit comme le destinateur délégué des valeurs au nom desquelles la sanction intervient.

132. On appelle «programme de Jésus» l'objectif principal pour la réalisation duquel celui-ci a été instauré comme sujet héros du récit évangélique global. Les objets-valeurs, enjeu de ce programme principal, sont évalués différemment dans notre petit récit par Jésus et par la Syrophénicienne.

133. C'est ce que nie J. CAMERY-HOGGATT, Irony in Mark's Gospel. Text and Subtext (SNTS MS, 72), Cambridge, 1992, pp. 150-151, en prétendant qu'il faut donner à la déclaration de Jésus au v. 27 un sens ironique: «Mark would hardly have placed this story here if he understood its meaning as a banal assertion of Jesus' need of rest, or even as an assertion that her faith must be purified of superstition, as Lane goes on to say. This comment represents a challenge as well to the notion that the saying is to be taken at face value. Mark could hardly have included it here if that were the case.(...) The point of this discussion is that the saying is ironic. To read only what lies 'on the surface of it' is to

tive de la femme n'a pas des effets seulement au plan pragmatique avec l'expulsion du démon, mais aussi au plan cognitif dans une redéfinition des valeurs engagées sur le programme de Jésus. Jésus le reconnaît lui-même au plan cognitif au v. 29. Quant à la sanction pragmatique elle transparaît au v. 31 dans le fait que la Galilée devient compatible avec le territoire païen où Jésus circule ouvertement (en contraste avec le souci d'incognito du v. 24), et où il guérit et nourrit. Autrement dit, il accorde son comportement, sa mission à la réinterprétation des valeurs opérée par la femme étrangère et dont il a reconnu la vérité.

3. *Fonction narrative*

J'esquisse seulement cette question qui nécessiterait un parcours qui, par cercles concentriques, de proche en proche s'élargirait à tout l'évangile. Mc est généralement reconnu comme l'évangile qui, proportionnellement, comporte le plus grand nombre d'exorcismes. En fait, on y lit quatre récits d'exorcismes (1,21-28; 5,1-20; 7,24-31; 9,14-29), auxquels il convient d'ajouter quelques mentions rapides dans des sommaires (1,32-34.39; 3,11-12)[134]. Du point de vue narratif, on peut considérer que, normalement, la place où ces exorcismes sont situés dans le récit global n'est pas anodine.

L'exorcisme de Mc 7,24-31 prend place au beau milieu de ce qu'on a coutume d'appeler la «section des pains». Du point de vue de sa fonction dans son contexte, le récit de la Syrophénicienne a souvent été considéré comme illustration ou application pratique de ce dont le principe théorique avait été acquis dans la péricope précédente des

---

misread it. It is instead to be read as a bit of tongue-in-cheek» (p. 150). Cette proposition semble bien motivée par le souci de ne pas attribuer à Jésus ce que le texte de Mc semble lui attribuer. Quelques lignes plus haut, en effet, le même auteur écrit: «The irony in this story is often misunderstood, and for that reason, v. 27 is taken as an undisguised indication that Jesus is racist, or in some way hesitant about including Gentiles in his mission» (p. 150). L'interprétation de J. Camery-Hoggatt ne trahit-elle pas plutôt une méconnaissance du ressort narratif du récit? Les motifs qui l'ont inspirée pourraient bien être du même type que ceux qui, du point de vue historico-critique, ont amené notamment A. JÜLICHER, *Die Gleichnisreden*, II (n. 2), pp. 258-259 à attribuer la réplique du v. 28 à Jésus pour la refuser à une pauvre païenne: «So hohe Gewandtheit nimmt bei einem armen phönizischen Weibe allerdings Wunder. (...) Wenn vir uns aber hinsichtlich des Rahmens für unsere παραβολή in solcher Ungewissheit befinden, darf man (...) bezweifeln, dass Jesus sich von dieser Frau in so fundamentaler Weise seine Grundsätze korrigieren lassen musste. (...) Was Mc und Mt als Gespräch geben, dürfte eine ganz und gar Jesu zukommende Rede sein: vor allem der zweite Satz ein Erzeugnis seines Geistes».

134. À cette liste on peut ajouter la discussion avec les scribes en 3,22-30 et la discussion sur le pouvoir de chasser les démons au nom de Jésus sans être son disciple en 9,38-41. Par ailleurs, on trouve des mentions du pouvoir que les disciples ont de pratiquer des exorcismes en 3,15; 6,7-13 (sans oublier 16,17 dans la finale inauthentique de Mc; on y trouve aussi en 16,9 l'évocation de Marie de Magdala dont Jésus avait chassé sept démons).

discussions sur le pur et l'impur (7,1-23)[135]. Il n'apporterait donc rien de bien neuf. Il ne semble pas que tel soit le cas, du moins si on se place d'un point de vue narratif.

De ce point de vue, en effet, les discussions sur le pur et l'impur de 7,1-23 ne consacrent pas de fait une ouverture vers les païens. Elles marquent plutôt de la part de Jésus la volonté de mettre un point d'arrêt à une extension toujours plus grande des règles de pureté et de ce qui est concerné par ces règles. L'impureté se contracte par le contact et plus encore par la consommation d'aliments impurs (κοινός). Plus la zone du sacré est étendue dans le peuple et touche des activités aussi modestes que manger du pain, plus la distinction avec les païens deviendra forte. On empêche ainsi le consommateur juif de tomber dans la sphère d'influence des païens. Ces interdits vont donc de pair avec un sentiment anti-païen. La prise de position de Jésus va à l'encontre des vues pharisiennes, mais ne peut encore être conçue comme une prise de position en faveur des païens. Cependant sa façon de voir empêche que ne soit effectivement restreint davantage encore l'espace où Juifs et païens peuvent se rencontrer[136]. Du coup, la possibilité que Jésus puisse rencontrer une Syrophénicienne est moins inimaginable, sans qu'il soit question d'une ouverture de principe aux païens.

La rencontre de Jésus avec la mère d'une petite fille possédée d'un esprit impur (ἀκάθαρτος) s'inscrit dans la série des exorcismes de cet évangile où se dessine une conception de la sanctification opposée à celle des pharisiens et des scribes. Habité de l'Esprit de Dieu (1,10), poussé par lui au désert où il vainc Satan (1,12-13), Jésus est reconnu d'emblée comme «Saint de Dieu» par l'esprit impur (ἀκάθαρτος) qui, à la synagogue de Capharnaüm le perçoit comme une menace pour lui et ses semblables (1,21-28). Par rapport aux impurs, la stratégie des pharisiens et des scribes est plutôt passive et défensive: on étend le champ des interdits mettant à l'abri du contact. Par contre, celle de Jésus est plutôt offensive (1,21-28; 5,1-20)[137]. Il ne se met pas à l'abri

---

135. T.A. BURKILL, *The Syrophoenician Woman: The Congruence* (n. 25), pp. 28-29, considère Mc 7,24-31 comme illustration de ce qui précède, traduction en action de la théorie enseignée antérieurement. R. PESCH, *Das Markusevangelium*, I (n. 30), p. 385, parlera plutôt d'une application et W. SCHMITHALS, *Das Evangelium nach Markus* (ÖTK, 2/1), Gütersloh, 1979, p. 355, d'une répétition aux païens de ce qui a été dit aux Juifs. Selon d'autres enfin, Mc 7,24-31 fait apparaître le côté positif de ce dont auparavant on a souligné l'aspect négatif. En ce sens, K. KERTELGE, *Die Wunder* (n. 19), p. 155; L. SCHENKE, *Die Wundererzählungen* (n. 30), pp. 265-267; J. GNILKA, *Markus*, I (n. 30), p. 294.

136. Ainsi W. KLAMER, *Het verhaal* (n. 109), pp. 138-140.

137. L'affrontement combatif de Jésus à l'impureté se manifeste aussi dans la guérison du lépreux (1,40-45) et celle de l'hémorroïsse (5,25-34). Cette différence des stratégies est mise en valeur par J.H. NEYREY, *The Idea of Purity in Mark's Gospel*, in *Semeia* 35 (1986) 91-128, voir p. 111-113. Celle de Jésus est qualifiée de «offensive Reinheit/Heiligkeit» par K. BERGER, *Jesus als Pharisäer und frühe Christen als Pharisäer*, in *NT* 30 (1988) 231-262, voir p. 240.

de l'impureté, il va de l'avant et purifie. Partout il chasse l'impureté, les esprits impurs ou démons.

Mais n'y a-t-il pas des frontières à une telle puissance de sanctification-purification? L'exorcisme de la fille de la Syrophénicienne survient à un moment critique dans l'évangile. La distinction du sacré et du profane, du pur et de l'impur est importante pour l'ordonnancement social, pour que chacun et chaque chose restent à leur place. À Tyr, Jésus franchit des barrières à un triple point de vue: social (une femme), géographique (une étrangère), religieux (une païenne). Le petit récit fait apparaître (v. 27) les implications funestes que le système de sainteté lié à la parenté peut avoir sur les rapports entre un maître juif et une païenne en détresse. Le franchissement de la limite est rendu possible par la femme elle-même, qui, comme nous l'avons vu[138], redéfinit par le fait même les valeurs engagées sur le programme de Jésus et libère sa puissance sanctificatrice pour les païens. C'est cela que le récit met en œuvre dans le contexte subséquent (Mc 7,31-8,10) au grand dam des pharisiens (8,11-13)[139].

La fonction narrative de Mc 7,24-31 est donc de permettre le franchissement des barrières qui faisaient obstacle à la sanctification aussi des païens. Cela se fait symboliquement par un recul imposé à l'esprit impur qui laisse le champ libre au Saint de Dieu. L'espace où l'Esprit de Dieu peut œuvrer en repoussant l'esprit impur en est miraculeusement élargi.

CONCLUSION

Si on compare les deux grands types de méthodes utilisées ci-dessus, l'analyse narrative est fort éloignée des préoccupations de recherches des sources ou de la *Formgeschichte*. Par contre, elle paraît plus proche des préoccupations de la *Redaktionsgeschichte*, puisque dans les deux cas on s'intéresse à l'état final du texte. Pourrait-on la concevoir comme une partie de la *Redaktionsgeschichte*? Elle peut certainement lui être utile et enrichir ses résultats. Mais elle gardera toujours son originalité par rapport à la *Redaktionsgeschichte*, du fait que son approche est marquée par la théorie de l'autonomie du texte par rapport à son auteur.

De ce point de vue, on peut affiner la réflexion en tenant compte de certaines distinctions parmi les différentes approches narratives. Sen-

138. Voir ci-dessus, pp. 71-72.
139. Quant aux disciples, dont il n'est fait aucune mention de 7,24 à 8,1 (moment où Jésus les convoque), leur absence les prive des éléments fournis par la rencontre avec la Syrophénicienne, alors que le lecteur en dispose. Or, ces éléments ne sont pas sans importance pour la compréhension de la seconde multiplication des pains.

sible à la recherche de l'intrigue et à ce que veut l'auteur implicite, le *Literary Criticism* me semble à première vue assez difficilement conciliable, du moins en théorie, avec la perspective de la *Redaktionsgeschichte* liée à la critique des sources. En effet, à chacun des deux modèles théoriques correspond une conception différente de ce qu'on appelle d'ailleurs d'un mot différent soit «auteur», soit «rédacteur». Et ces conceptions paraissent assez contradictoires. D'un côté, on a affaire à un écrivain disposant de sources et les retravaillant en fonction de soucis stylistiques et surtout théologiques. De l'autre, on a affaire à un écrivain sur les sources duquel on ne s'interroge pas, mais le moindre détail de son écriture est relié à tel ou tel procédé littéraire.

Par contre, la sémiotique qui ne parle pas de l'auteur, mais seulement du texte, est plus aisément conciliable avec les recherches diachroniques. Pour elle, quoi qu'il en soit des intentions conscientes ou inconscientes de l'auteur, il s'agit d'analyser l'héritage qu'il nous a laissé de manière à faire percevoir les multiples effets de sens qu'on peut y déceler. Dès lors on peut pratiquer successivement analyse sémiotique et analyse rédactionnelle, sans pour autant opposer deux conceptions de l'auteur et de son travail. Du coup et du moins en théorie toujours, il me semble que l'approche sémiotique peut plus aisément que la narratologie ou le *Literary Criticism*, être perçue comme compatible avec une analyse rédactionnelle classique. Et rien n'empêche que les deux puissent être complémentaires. La *Redaktionsgeschichte*, qui travaille notamment par comparaison synoptique, insiste surtout sur les constantes stylistiques et théologiques de l'auteur et sur ce qui différencie le texte final de ses sources. L'analyse sémiotique, quant à elle, insiste sur l'organisation interne du texte. Considérant le texte du point de vue de son auteur ou rédacteur, la première fait mieux percevoir le texte comme aboutissement de toute une histoire dont il porte les cicatrices. Voyant le texte comme un testament mis à la disposition du lecteur, la seconde met mieux en valeur ce qu'il peut produire dans le travail de la lecture. Chacune des deux méthodes repose sur une épistémologie différente et produit des fruits différents. À mes yeux, il est de l'intérêt de l'exégèse contemporaine de les mettre en œuvre toutes deux et de les faire entrer en dialogue le plus possible. C'est un tel travail de confrontation que nous nous sommes fixé et que nous allons poursuivre tout au long de ce Colloque.

Rue de Fernelmont 37   Camille FOCANT
B-5020 Champion

DAS MARKUSEVANGELIUM ALS TRADITIONSGEBUNDENE ERZÄHLUNG?

ANFRAGEN AN DIE MARKUSFORSCHUNG DER ACHTZIGER JAHRE

In diesem Beitrag soll zunächst ein kritischer Überblick über die Methoden der neueren Markusforschung gegeben werden (I). Anschließend werden unter Aufnahme der neueren Forschung sowie eigener Beiträge[1] Vorschläge zum methodischen Verfahren in der Markusexegese gemacht (II). Abschließend werden einige derzeitige Methodenprobleme exemplarisch an zwei Texten verdeutlicht (III).

I. ZUR NEUEREN METHODIK DER ERFORSCHUNG DER MARKINISCHEN ERZÄHLUNG

1. Zur Orientierung

Wer die Methoden der derzeitigen Markusforschung skizziert, hat einzugrenzen. Es geht hier nicht darum, mit den Mosaiksteinen kleinerer Forschungsbeiträge zu bestimmten Themen[2] ein detailliertes Bild zu erstellen. Vielmehr sollen mit einigen markanten Strichen die Umrisse der gegenwärtigen narrativen Markusforschung in den USA und des konventionelleren Ansatzes, besonders im deutsch-sprachigen Raum, skizziert werden[3]. Da die Tagung aber unter dem Thema »Literarkritik und/oder literary criticism« steht, wird die Forschung unter diesem Blickwinkel betrachtet. Inwieweit werden in der neueren Mar-

---

1. Vgl. C. BREYTENBACH, *Nachfolge und Zukunftserwartung nach Markus. Eine methodenkritische Studie* (ATANT, 71), Zürich, 1984; ID., *Das Markusevangelium als episodische Erzählung*, in F. HAHN (ed.), *Der Erzähler des Evangeliums. Methodische Neuansätze in der Markusforschung* (SBS, 118/119), Stuttgart, 1985, pp. 137-169; ID., *Das Problem des Übergangs von mündlicher zu schriftlicher Überlieferung*, in Neot 20 (1986) 47-58; ID., MNHMONEYEIN. *Das Erinnern in der urchristlichen Tradition*, in A. DENAUX (ed.), *John and the Synoptics* (BETL, 101), Leuven, 1992, pp. 548-557; ID., *Vormarkinische Logientradition. Parallelen in der urchristlichen Briefliteratur*, in The Four Gospels 1992. FS F. Neirynck (BETL, 100), Leuven, 1992, pp. 725-749.

2. Zur mkn. Christologie vgl. C. BREYTENBACH, *Die debat rondom die Markaanse Christologie. Die laaste tien jaar*, in Skrif en Kerk 12 (1991) 135-172.

3. Freilich wird das Bild erst dann Farbe und Nuance bekommen, wenn wichtige Beiträge von britischen und niederländischen Forschern und Studien aus dem romanischen Sprachraum hinzugezogen werden, vgl. z.B. B. STANDAERT, *L'Évangile selon Marc, composition et genre littéraire*, Zevenkerken-Brugge, 1978, und den Beitrag von V. ROBBINS im vorliegenden Band.

kusforschung synchrone und diachrone Perspektive aufeinander bezogen?

Dem neueren amerikanischen Forschungszweig, der den »literary criticism« betreibt, wird dabei zuerst unsere Aufmerksamkeit gewidmet. Die Einstufung des Markusevangeliums als Erzähltext und das Aufkommen des »literary criticism« in der Markusforschung führte bei einigen – vor allem jüngeren – Exegeten, auch aus dem deutschen Sprachraum, zu einer Neubestimmung der üblichen historisch-kritischen Methodenpalette. Daher werden nach einem Blick auf den »literary criticism« vor allem in methodischer Hinsicht innovative neuere Beiträge zur Markusforschung zum Zuge kommen[4].

Die Suche nach neuen Methoden in der Markusforschung wurde durch vor allem drei Faktoren gefördert. Hat anfänglich Norman Perrins Forderung nach dem Entwurf einer umfassenden Kompositionskritik die Forschung angeregt, so waren es doch vor allem die divergierenden Ergebnisse der Redaktionskritik, die in den USA und in Europa zu einer Neuorientierung nötigten. Schließlich bestimmten Entwicklungen in der Sprach- und Literaturwissenschaft, in welche Richtungen die Neuorientierung erfolgte. Im vorliegenden Zusammenhang werde ich weder die Anfänge dieser Neuorientierung seit Perrin[5] noch das Scheitern der Redaktionskritik vorführen. Dazu gibt es ausführliche Studien[6]. Es bleibt aber aufzuzeigen, in welche Richtung(en) die Neuorientierung erfolgte.

2. Das Aufblühen des »literary criticism«

Die Beiträge, die das Markusevangelium unter literaturwissenschaftlicher Perspektive untersuchen, können in zwei Gruppen unterteilt werden.

Zunächst denkt man an die anfänglichen Aufsätze von Norman Petersen[7] und Robert Tannehill[8], die Ende der siebziger und Anfang

---

4. Da ich mich andernorts ausführlich mit den Methoden der Markusforschung bis Anfang der achtziger Jahre beschäftigt habe, wird den neueren Beiträgen hier Vorrang eingeräumt; vgl. BREYTENBACH, Nachfolge, pp. 16-68; ID., Gesamtdarstellungen zum Markusevangelium, in VF 36 (2/1991) 50-55. Gleichzeitig ist hinzuweisen auf das hervorragende Buch von Moore, das die »literary critical« Analyse der Evangelien sehr kenntnisreich darstellt und kritisch würdigt; vgl. S.D. MOORE, Literary Criticism and the Gospels. The Theoretical Challenge, New Haven, CT, 1989.

5. Vgl. BREYTENBACH, Nachfolge, pp. 50-65.

6. Vgl. MOORE, Criticism (Anm. 4); C.C. BLACK II, The Disciples in Mark. Markan Redaction in Current Debate (JSNT SS, 27), Sheffield, 1989. Für Reaktionen der Rezensenten dieses Werkes vgl. die magistrale Bibliographie von F. NEIRYNCK, et al., The Gospel of Mark. A Cumulative Bibliography 1950-1990 (BETL, 102), Leuven, 1992, p. 43.

7. N.R. PETERSEN, Die »Perspektive« in der Erzählung des Markusevangeliums, in HAHN (ed.), Erzähler (Anm. 1), pp. 67-91 (englisches Original: N.R. PETERSEN, Point of View in Mark's Narrative, in Semeia 12 [1978] 97-121).

8. R.C. TANNEHILL, The Gospel of Mark as Narrative Christology, in Semeia 16 (1976)

der achtziger Jahre den »narrative criticism« zum Markusevangelium auf den Weg brachten. Diese Bewegung in der Markusforschung, die zunehmend von dem Buche *Story and Discourse.*

Narrative Structure in Fiction and Film des amerikanischen Literaturtheoretikers Seymour Chatman[9] geprägt wurde, lieferte uns die allgemein verständlichen narrativen Auslegungen der Markuserzählung von Werner Kelber[10] und Jack Kingsbury[11] sowie das Buch von David Rhoads und Donald Michie[12], das als Einführung in die narrative Analyse des Markusevangeliums angesehen werden kann. In diesen Beiträgen und kleineren Studien wurden wichtige Aspekte wie Erzählgerüst (plot), Erzählstandpunkt (point of view)[13] und die Darstellung von Erzählfiguren (characterization)[14] zum ersten Mal in der Markusforschung untersucht. Mit zumindest zwei nennenswerten Monographien förderte diese Bewegung das Verständnis der Theologie des Markusevangeliums: Jack Kingsburys *The Christology of Mark's Gospel*[15] und Christopher Marshalls *Faith as a Theme in Mark's Narrative*[16]. Weder von den theoretischen Grundlagen dieser Forschung noch von der Intention ihrer Verfasser her war zu erwarten, daß diachrone Fragen der Textentstehung hier angesprochen oder bei der Interpretation des Textes verwertet werden würden. So analysiert Willem Vorster z.B. Petrus als Erzählfigur innerhalb der Markuserzählung, ohne theoretisch die Frage aufzuwerfen, wie solch eine Erzählung und die urchristliche Petrustradition sich bei der Abfassung und der damaligen Lektüre bzw. dem Anhören der Erzäh-

---

57-95; ID., *Die Jünger im Markusevangelium – die Funktion einer Erzählfigur*, in HAHN (ed.), *Erzähler* (Anm. 1), pp. 37-66 (englisches Original: *The Disciples in Mark. The Function of a Narrative Role*, in *JR* 57 [1977] 386-405).

9. Vgl. dazu MOORE, *Criticism* (Anm. 4), pp. 43-55.

10. Vgl. W. KELBER, *Mark's Story of Jesus*, Philadelphia, PA, 1979.

11. Vgl. J.D. KINGSBURY, *Conflict in Mark*, Minneapolis, MN, 1989. Für Rez. dazu vgl. NEIRYNCK, *Mark*, p. 261.

12. Vgl. D. RHOADS – D. MICHIE, *Mark as Story. An Introduction to the Narrative of a Gospel*, Philadelphia, PA, 1982. Für Rez. dazu vgl. NEIRYNCK, *Mark*, p. 411.

13. Vgl. PETERSEN, *»Perspektive«* (Anm. 7); J. DEWEY, *Point of View and the Disciples in Mark*, in *SBL 1982 Seminar Papers*, pp. 97-106; C.W. HEDRICK, *Narrator and Story in the Gospel of Mark. Hermeneia and Paradosis*, in *Perspectives in Religious Studies* 14 (1987) 239-258.

14. Vgl. TANNEHILL, *Jünger* (Anm. 8); H.-J. KLAUCK, *Die erzählerische Rolle der Jünger im Markusevangelium* (1982), in ID., *Gemeinde - Amt - Sakrament. Neutestamentliche Perspektiven*, Würzburg, 1989, pp. 137-159; KINGSBURY, *Conflict* (Anm. 11), passim; E.S. MALBON, *Disciples/Crowds/Whoever. Markan Characters and Readers*, in *NT* 28 (1968) 104-130; ID., *Fallible Followers. Women and Men in the Gospel of Mark*, in *Semeia* 28 (1983) 29-48; ID., *The Jewish Leaders in the Gospel of Mark. A Literary Study of Markan Characterization*, in *JBL* 108 (1989) 259-281; W.S. VORSTER, *Characterization of Peter in the Gospel of Mark*, in *Neot* 21 (1987) 57-76.

15. Vgl. J.D. KINGSBURY, *The Christology of Mark's Gospel*, Philadelphia, PA, 1983. Für Rez. dazu vgl. NEIRYNCK, *Mark*, p. 260.

16. C.D. MARSHALL, *Faith as a Theme in Mark's Narrative* (SNTS MS, 64), Cambridge, 1989. Für Rez. dazu vgl. NEIRYNCK, *Mark*, p. 320.

lung in den Gemeinden gegenseitig bedingten[17]. Elizabeth Malbon ihrerseits grenzt ihre »literary« Untersuchung über die jüdischen Führer im Markusevangelium bewußt von dem historisierenden Versuch ab, hinter den jeweiligen Gegnern eine historische Gruppe zu erkennen. Sie konzentriert sich auf das Verhältnis zwischen den verschiedenen Gruppen auf der literarischen Ebene der einheitlichen Markuserzählung[18].

Seit Mitte der achtziger Jahre geriet die narrative Markusforschung zunehmend unter den Einfluß der Rezeptionsästhetik[19], die vor allem von Wolfgang Iser[20] angeregt wurde. Auch wenn Robert Tannehill[21] hier schon früh die ersten Schritte getan hat, war es namentlich Robert Fowler[22], der den zweiten Zweig der literaturwissenschaftlich – orientierten Markusforschung auf den Weg brachte. Neben etlichen kleineren, oft theoretischen Studien über den Lesertyp des Markusevangeliums[23], trieb der »reader response« – Ansatz erste Früchte in den Monographien von Robert Fowler[24] und Bas van Iersel[25]. Diese Beiträge konzentrieren sich zunächst sehr auf den Leser in dem Text und widmen sich meistens nicht der Frage nach den historischen Lesern und der Rolle, die die Bekanntschaft mit vormarkinischer Tradition bei der Lektüre des Textes spielen könnte.

Die 1989 erschienene Monographie von Mary Ann Tolbert, *Sowing the Gospel*, trägt den vielversprechenden Untertitel: *Mark's World in Literary-Historical Perspective*[26]. Tolbert fordert, das Markusevangelium als literarischen Text in den Rahmen der »literary conventions of its own day« zu stellen, damit der Text so verstanden werden kann, »as its author hoped the original audience would be able to do«[27]. Um dies

---

17. Vgl. VORSTER, *Peter* (Anm. 14).

18. Vgl. MALBON, *Leaders* (Anm. 14), pp. 261, 275.

19. Vgl. hierzu MOORE, *Criticism* (Anm. 4), pp. 73-107.

20. Vgl. W. ISER, *Der implizite Leser* (UTB, 163), München, 1972; ID., *Der Akt des Lesens – Theorie ästhetischer Wirkung* (UTB, 636), München, 1976.

21. Vgl. TANNEHILL, *Jünger* (Anm. 8).

22. Vgl. R.M. FOWLER, *Loaves and Fishes. The Function of the Feeding Stories in the Gospel of Mark* (SBL DS, 54), Chico, CA, 1981 [Für Rez. dazu vgl. NEIRYNCK, *Mark*, pp. 168-169]; ID., *Who is »the Reader« of Mark's Gospel*, in *SBL 1983 Seminar Papers*, pp. 31-53. Vgl. auch J.M. BASSLER, *The Parable of the Loaves*, in *JR* 66 (1986) 157-172.

23. Vgl. W.S. VORSTER, *The Reader in the Text. Narrative Material*, in *Semeia* 48 (1989) 21-39; B.M.F. VAN IERSEL, *The Reader of Mark as Operator of a System of Connotations*, in *Semeia* 48 (1989) 83-114; R.M. FOWLER, *The Rhetoric of Direction in the Gospel of Mark*, in *Semeia* 48 (1989) 115-134.

24. R.M. FOWLER, *Let the Reader Understand. Reader-Response Criticism and the Gospel of Mark*, Philadelphia, PA, 1991.

25. Vgl. B.M.F. VAN IERSEL, *Reading Mark*, Edinburgh, 1989. Für Rez. dazu vgl. NEIRYNCK, *Mark*, p. 523.

26. M.A. TOLBERT, *Sowing the Gospel. Mark's World in Literary-Historical Perspective*, Minneapolis, MN, 1989. Für Rez. dazu vgl. NEIRYNCK, *Mark*, p. 507 sowie C.C. BLACK II, in *CBQ* 54 (1992) 382-364.

27. *Ibid.*, p. xii.

zu erreichen, versucht sie, einen literaturgeschichtlichen Kontext zu rekonstruieren. Es überrascht dann doch, daß traditionsgeschichtliche Fragen ausgeklammert werden[28] und auf eine literaturgeschichtliche Einordnung der Teilgattungen im Markusevangelium verzichtet wird[29] – um so mehr als dies geschieht, während versucht wird, die fiktive markinische Gesamterzählung im Kontext der hellenistischen »popular prose« verständlich zu machen. Mit einem Vergleich zwischen dem Markusevangelium und dem hellenistischen Liebesroman (vor allem Chariton von Aphrodisias' »Chareia und Kallirrhoe« und Xenophon von Ephesus' »Ephesiaka«) wird man kaum die Gattung des Evangeliums so bestimmen, daß sich von dieser literaturgeschichtlichen Einordnung her »the authorial audience«[30] des Markusevangeliums in den Griff bekommen ließe. Zu begrüßen ist allerdings, daß Tolbert sich bemüht, das Markusevangelium vor dem Hintergrund zeitgenössischer Erzählungen zu lesen.

Mary Ann Beavis wirft dem rezeptionsästhetischen Ansatz von Fowler »an ahistorical view of the reader of Mark« vor und stellt die Frage nach *Mark's audience*[31]. Ihr Buch steht in der Tradition der Kompositionskritik, die das Evangelium als einheitliches theologisches und literarisches Werk und den Evangelisten als kreativen Autor und Theologen versteht[32]. Die Verfasserin nimmt zwar bewußt Anregungen aus der rezeptionsästhetischen Untersuchung des Markusevangeliums auf, sie will aber zu den historischen Lesern vorstoßen und versucht, der Tatsache, daß es sich beim Markusevangelium um einen hellenistischen literarischen Text handelt, dadurch gerecht zu werden, daß sie das Evangelium im Kontext der griechisch-römischen Lesepraxis und den Evangelisten vor dem Hintergrund der griechischen Schulbildung der Kaiserzeit betrachtet. Es handelt sich um eine Untersuchung des literarischen und sozialen Milieus, dem das Evangelium, der Evangelist und die Zuhörer entstammen. Die Frage nach dem literarischen Aspekt des Evangeliums führt zur Berücksichtigung der historisch möglichen Lesebedingungen. Die Frage nach seinem »social setting« zielt darauf, die Art der Verwendung des Evangeliums in der markinischen Gemeinde zu klären[33], damit »the interpretive community« des Markusevangeliums beschrieben werden kann[34]. Für die Beantwortung dieser Fragen

---

28. *Ibid.*, pp. 21-23.
29. *Ibid.*, pp. 25-26.
30. *Ibid.*, pp. 53, 57.
31. Vgl. M.A. BEAVIS, *Mark's Audience. The Literary and Social Setting of Mark 4.11-12* (JSNT SS, 33), Sheffield, 1989. Für Rez. dazu vgl. NEIRYNCK, *Mark*, p. 31 sowie E.V. GALLAGHER, in *CBQ* 53 (1991) 692-693.
32. »On this approach, tradition is redaction in that the traditional materials are viewed as the result of conscious selection, and as not immune to authorial reworking and supplementation«; *ibid.*, p. 9.
33. *Ibid.*, p. 10.
34. *Ibid.*, p. 16.

verzichtet Beavis in ihrer Untersuchung von Mk 4 auf die Scheidung
von Redaktion und Tradition. Dies sei ein zu unsicheres Instrument.
Unabhängig von seiner Vorgeschichte wird der vorliegende Text als
neue Komposition des Verfassers betrachtet, die Querverbindungen zu
den übrigen Teilen des Evangeliums aufweist[35]. Auch wenn man erhebliche Vorbehalte gegenüber Beavis' Zuordnung des Markusevangliums
zu zeitgenössischen Literaturformen, wie dem Drama, und gegenüber
ihrer Konstruktion der möglichen Schulbildung des Evangelisten hat,
bleibt es hilfreich, daß sie die rezeptionsästhetische Frage nach den
Zuhörern (»audience«) von einer historischen Perspektive aus stellt.
Wie bei Tolbert überrascht es aber, daß Kenntnis und Unkenntnis, die
die Hörer des Evangeliums von der vormarkinischen Tradition hatten,
in diesem Modell unberücksichtigt bleiben.

Meines Erachtens ließen sich bestimmte Varianten einer Lesetheorie,
wie etwa Umberto Ecos Konzeption um den »Modelleser«[36], in der Tat
so auswerten, daß der Einfluß des dem Markusevangelium vorangegangenen Traditionsprozesses auf den historischen Leser nicht aus dem
Blick gerät. Dabei ist es wichtig, darauf zu achten, daß das Markusevangelium zum lauten Vorlesen abgefaßt wurde und daß der Leser als
Vorleser Zuhörer hatte. Wie Thomas Boomershine bereits 1987 unter-
strich, war privates Lesen in der Antike weniger verbreitet und leises
Lesen unüblich[37]. Lesetheorien dürfen nicht anachronistisch auf die
Evangelien angewendet werden.

Im allgemeinen zeigen die mir vertrauten Beiträge aus dem »literary
criticism«, daß sie sich als Alternative zu »Literarkritik« und »Redaktionskritik« verstehen. Nur in Ausnahmefällen, wie etwa bei Norman
Petersen[38] und Joanna Dewey[39], werden traditionelle Fragestellungen
des Werdens des Textes wieder aufgegriffen und in kritische Beziehung
zu den Einsichten des »literary criticism« gebracht. Die Vertreter des
»literary critisicm« meinen, daß die Erforschung der vormarkinischen
Tradition kaum möglich sei und ohnehin keine Bedeutung für das
Verständnis der markinischen Erzählung habe.

Die Wende zur synchronen Analyse des vorliegenden Textes ist aber

---

35. *Ibid.*, pp. 132-133.

36. Vgl. U. Eco, *The Role of the Reader. Explorations in the Semiotics of Texts*,
Bloomington, 1979.

37. Vgl. T.E. BOOMERSHINE, *Peters Denial as Polemic or Confession. The Implications
of Media Criticism for Biblical Hermeneutics*, in *Semeia* 38 (1987) 47-68. Vgl. auch
M.A. BEAVIS, *The Trial before the Sanhedrin (Mark 14:53-65). Reader Response and
Greco-Roman Readers*, in *CBQ* 49 (1987) 581-596. Vgl. auch MOORE, *Criticism* (Anm. 4),
pp. 84-88.

38. Vgl. N.R. PETERSEN, *The Composition of Mark 4:1–8:26*, in *HTR* 73 (1988) 183-
217; ID., *The Reader in the Gospel*, in *Neot* 18 (1984) 38-51.

39. Vgl. J. DEWEY, *Oral Methods of Structuring Narrative in Mark*, in *Int* 53 (1989) 32-
44; ID., *Mark as Interwoven Tapestry. Forecasts and Echoes for a Listening Audience*, in
CBQ 53 (1991) 221-236.

auch an der herkömmlichen Exegese nicht vorbeigegangen. Wie werden diachrone Fragen neuerdings hier angesprochen?

3. *Die Synchronie vor der Diachronie in der neueren Methodenlehre*

Die Scheidung von Tradition und Redaktion als heuristisches Verfahren wurde in der anglo-amerikanischen Forschung weitgehend aufgegeben. Die durch die amerikanische Forschung geprägten Beiträge suchen bewußt Anschluß an literaturwissenschaftliche Methoden und wandeln dabei solche Methoden zum Teil für die besondere Fragestellung der Exegese ab. Gleichzeitig wird die Frage nach dem Werden des Textes mit Hinweis auf ihre Unbeantwortbarkeit weitgehend aufgegeben. Innerhalb der deutsch-sprachigen *Markus*forschung haben ebenfalls etliche Exegeten die Trennung von Redaktion und Tradition als interpretatives Verfahren aufgegeben. Stattdessen wird synchrone Analyse großgeschrieben.

Ein Blick in neuere *Methodenlehrbücher* zeigt, daß man Literarkritik als Methode der Quellenscheidung sowie Redaktionskritik der synchronen Untersuchung der Textkohärenz nachordnet[40]. Die Redaktionskritik wird bei Klaus Berger unter rezeptionskritischem Gesichtspunkt zu einer Methode, die die innovative Abänderung verarbeiteter Tradition untersucht. Der Redaktor selektiert und kombiniert überlieferte Traditionen zu einem neuen Ganzen[41]. Wichtiger als die Scheidung von Tradition und Redaktion ist die Frage, »wie der Gesamtstoff organisiert worden ist, welche Gesichtspunkte der Komposition und Gliederung sich ermitteln lassen und welche Funktion die einzelnen Abschnitte darin haben«[42]. Nach Wilhelm Egger befaßt sich die Redaktionskritik mit der Entstehung des Textes und versucht, den Vorgang der Redaktion und die Rolle des Redaktors zu rekonstruieren[43]. Sowohl Berger als auch Egger setzen aber bei der Redaktionskritik voraus, daß erstens eine synchrone Interpretation des Textes vorliegt und zweitens die Tradition, die redigiert worden ist, feststellbar ist. Beide, Berger und Egger, haben dabei zunächst auf textlinguistischer Grundlage Analyseverfahren vorgeschlagen, wie Texte synchron gelesen werden können. Anders geht Andreas Lindemann vor. Er beruft sich zwar nicht auf die Textlinguistik als heuristische Methode, da er sich aber der Schwierigkeit bewußt ist, die Markus vorliegenden Traditionen zu bestimmen, schlägt er folgendes interpretatives Verfahren zur Bestimmung des redaktionellen Konzeptes des Markus vor: »Grundsätz-

---

40. Vgl. W. EGGER, *Methodenlehre zum Neuen Testament. Einführung in linguistische und historisch-kritische Methoden*, Freiburg/Br, 1987, pp. 162-170; K. BERGER, *Exegese des Neuen Testaments* (UTB, 685), Heidelberg, ³1991, pp. 30-32.
41. Vgl. BERGER, *Exegese* (Anm. 40), p. 202.
42. *Ibid.*, p. 206.
43. Vgl. EGGER, *Methodenlehre*, p. 183.

lich gilt, daß nach den tragenden theologischen Begriffen gefragt werden muß, nach Stichworten, die den Gesamttext strukturieren und
den Leser auf wichtige Aspekte des Handlungsfortgangs aufmerksam
machen, und schließlich nach Kriterien, die die Abfolge der einzelnen
Erzählungen in der gegebenen Reihenfolge plausibel machen«[44]. Auch
Dieter Lührmann sucht die theologische Konzeption des Markusevangeliums »nicht so sehr aus der Redaktion von Tradition (deren Umfang
und Charakter ja ungewiß ist) zu erheben ..., sondern aus ihrem
eigenen inneren Zusammenhang«[45]. Georg Strecker hält zwar die historische Rückfrage für die Rekonstruktion und das Verständnis der
Redaktion für unerläßlich, stellt sie aber neben die Erhebung des
synchronen Aussagegehalts, denn Gegenstand der Methode ist für ihn
nicht die Redaktion, sondern eine theologische Konzeption, die aus
einem Textganzen erschlossen werden soll[46].

Es zeigt sich, daß die Redaktionskritik, ursprünglich Methode zur
Beschreibung der Redigierung von Tradition, neu definiert wird als
Methode entweder zur Untersuchung des Werdens des markinischen
Textes (Egger) oder zur Klärung der vorliegenden Komposition[47],
sogar unter Aufgabe der Unterscheidung von Tradition und Redaktion
(Lührmann).

Bei einigen Arbeiten, die *Einzelperikopen des Markusevangeliums*
untersuchen, wird ebenfalls ein synchrones Analyseverfahren der diachronen Analyse vorangestellt[48]. Solche synchronen Analysen, die
auf sehr unterschiedlichen linguistischen Grundlagen aufbauen, untersuchen den Text zunächst sprachlich, in einigen Fällen nacheinander
unter syntaktischer, semantischer und pragmatischer Perspektive[49].

Die Untersuchung von Otto Schwankl zur Sadduzäerperikope Mk
12,18-27 kann als Beispiel herangezogen werden[50]. Er stellt der Literarkritik eine synchrone Untersuchung voran und fragt zunächst nach der
semantischen Kohärenz. Der Text wird als Einheit verstanden, bis das

---

44. H. CONZELMANN – A. LINDEMANN, *Arbeitsbuch zum Neuen Testament. 10., über-
arbeitete und erweiterte Auflage* (UTB, 52), Tübingen, 1991, pp. 110-111.

45. D. LÜHRMANN, *Auslegung des Neuen Testaments*, Zürich, 1984, p. 98. Vgl. auch
ID., *Das Markusevangelium* (HNT, 3), Tübingen, 1987, p. 14. Für Rez. dazu vgl.
NEIRYNCK, *Mark*, p. 308.

46. Vgl. G. STRECKER, *Neues Testament*, in ID. – J. MAIER, *Neues Testament – Antikes
Judentum*, Stuttgart, 1989, pp. 58-65.

47. Vgl. C.M. TUCKETT, *Reading the New Testament. Methods of Interpretation*,
London, 1987, pp. 122-126.

48. Vgl. z.B. die bereits 1980 abgeschlossene Untersuchung von R. KÜHSCHELM,
*Jüngerverfolgung und Geschick Jesu. Eine exegetisch-bibeltheologische Untersuchung der
synoptischen Verfolgungsankündigungen Mk 13,9-13 par und Mt 23,29-36 par* (ÖBS, 5),
Klosterneuburg, 1983. Für Rez. dazu vgl. NEIRYNCK, *Mark* (Anm. 6), p. 273.

49. Vgl. KÜHSCHELM, *Jüngerverfolgung* (Anm. 48).

50. Vgl. O. SCHWANKL, *Die Sadduzäerfrage (Mk. 12,18-27 parr). Eine exegetisch-
theologische Studie zur Auferstehungserwartung* (BBB, 66), Bonn, 1987, pp. 68-141. Für
Rez. dazu vgl. NEIRYNCK, *Mark*, p. 460.

Gegenteil nachgewiesen ist. »Erst wenn sich der Text als aus disparaten Teilen und Elementen zusammengesetzt erwiesen hat, wird der gewöhnlich vorgesehene zweite Teilschritt der literarkritischen Arbeit fällig, der die ermittelten Teileinheiten und Zusätze in ein chronologisches Verhältnis bringen ... soll«[51]. Markus habe den Text minimal redigiert[52]. Das Sadduzäergespräch gewinne seine Bedeutung erst »durch die Einbindung in den Makrotext des Evangeliums«[53].

Sosehr man auch Schwankls Forderung, literarkritische Erwägungen durch eine synchrone Analyse der Textkohärenz zu kontrollieren, unterstützen mag, es geht nicht an, die auf der synchronen Ebene festgestellte Kohärenz für den vormarkinischen Erzähler in Anspruch zu nehmen – es sei denn, man setzt voraus, Markus redigiere einen schriftlichen Text, was Schwankl aber nicht tut. Genau hier liegt das Problem. Man darf sich die Aufnahme mündlicher Tradition in einen literarischen Text nicht so vorstellen, wie die literarische Bearbeitung der schriftlichen Markusvorlage durch das Matthäus- und Lukasevangelium. Will man bei einer Theorie über die Abfassungsmethoden des Markusevangeliums mit der Aufnahme vormarkinischer Tradition rechnen, ist es entscheidend, ob mündliche Erzählungen literarisch neu erzählt werden oder ob etwa Schriftzitate aus der LXX angeführt werden. Schwankls Verfahren ist nur um den Preis möglich, daß Markus ein Sammler schriftlicher Einzelerzählungen aus der Jesusüberlieferung war[54]. Bei Schwankls synchroner Analyse handelt es sich um ein Verfahren, das seine theoretischen Grundlagen einem weiten Bereich der strukturalen- oder Textlinguistik entlehnt, aber ohne daß es zu einer Integration von synchronen und diachronen Schritte gekommen wäre[55].

Bei Ansätzen, die das *Gesamtevangelium* im Blick haben, kann man nur in Ausnahmefällen von einer eigenständigen Rezeption literaturwissenschaftlicher Ansätze sprechen[56]. In der Regel bleiben die Autoren von der Vermittlung solcher Zugänge durch den amerikanischen »literary criticism« abhängig[57]. Im Gegensatz zur amerikanischen

51. *Ibid.*, p. 302.

52. Schwankl vermutet nur im Begründungssatz in V. 23d eine redaktionelle Ergänzung. Unter literarkritischer Perspektive sei es nicht erforderlich, bei den Wiederholungen in VV. 23a und 25a mit einer Bearbeitung des Textes zu rechnen. Am ehesten rechnet Schwankl mit einem redaktionellen Zusatz in V. 23d, denn auch VV. 18b und 27b lassen »sich gut aus der bewußten und umsichtigen Gestaltung durch den Verfasser erklären«, *ibid.*, pp. 420-421. Er meint damit aber den vormarkinischen Verfasser.

53. *Idem.*

54. Cf. *ibid.*, p. 579.

55. Vgl. auch Egger, *Methodenlehre* (Anm. 40).

56. Vgl. Klauck, *Rolle* (Anm. 14). Vgl. auch R. Zwick, *Montage im Markusevangelium. Studien zur narrativen Organisation der ältesten Jesuserzählungen* (SBS, 18), Stuttgart, 1989. Für Rez. dazu vgl. Neirynck, *Mark*, p. 561.

57. Vgl. dazu die Sammlung von Übersetzungen von in der amerikanischen Forschung einflußreichen Aufsätzen, Hahn (ed.), *Erzähler* (Anm. 1).

Markusforschung bestehen also, von wenigen Ausnahmen abgesehen, im deutschen Sprachraum keine konsequenten Versuche, sprach- und literaturwissenschaftliche Ansätze für die Markusexegese fruchtbar zu machen. Man kann höchstens sagen, daß Markusinterpreten wie Dieter Lührmann[58] und Ludger Schenke[59] die Anregungen, die aus dem amerikanischen »literary criticism« hervorgegangen sind, positiv aufgenommen haben, ohne sie jedoch in ein stringentes methodisches Verfahren umzusetzen. Sie geben dabei aber keinesfalls alle traditionellen historischen und redaktionskritischen Fragestellungen auf[60]. Lührmann interessierte sich schon vor dem Aufkommen des »narrative criticism« in der amerikanischen Exegese für solche Fragestellungen, ohne dabei auf historisch-kritische Gepflogenheiten zu verzichten. Seine spätere literarische Analyse der Rolle der Pharisäer und Schriftgelehrten im vorliegenden Text wird z.B. so verwertet, daß er die historische Frage zu klären versucht, »wie sich gegenwärtige Auseinandersetzung mit jüdischen Gruppen zur Zeit des Mk spiegelt in den Geschichten, die von Begegnungen zwischen Jesus und seinen Jüngern mit Pharisäern und Schriftgelehrten damals in Galiläa und Jerusalem erzählen«[61]. Die Differenz zu Elizabeth Malbons »literary« Ansatz ist deutlich erkennbar. Schenke seinerseits rekonstruiert z.B. den Kontext des Autors und seiner historischen Leser im Rahmen der Geschichte des Urchristentums. Er tut dies aber aus der vorliegenden Gesamterzählung heraus, unter Verzicht auf die Unterscheidung von Tradition und Redaktion[62].

4. Ursachen für die Wende zur synchronen Analyse

Ein Blick in die neueren Monographien zum Markusevangelium zeigt die unverkennbare Tendenz, der synchronen Analyse auf der vorliegen-

---

58. Vgl. LÜHRMANN, *Markusevangelium* (Anm. 45), pp. 20-24; ID., *Das Markusevangelium als Erzählung*, in *Der Evangelische Erzieher* 41 (1989) 212-222.

59. Vgl. L. SCHENKE, *Das Markusevangelium*, Stuttgart, 1988, pp. 52-53. Für Rez. dazu vgl. NEIRYNCK, *Mark*, p. 442.

60. Nicht überall kann man von einer gelungenen Aufnahme des »narrative criticism« durch die deutsch-sprachige Exegese reden. Besonders problematisch ist die Studie von K. SCHOLTISSEK, *Die Vollmacht Jesu. Traditions- und redaktionsgeschichtliche Analysen zu einem zentralen Leitmotiv markinischer Christologie* (NTAbh, 25), Münster, 1992, die m.E. gegenüber der Arbeit von SÖDING, *Glaube* (s.u., Anm. 65), einen deutlichen methodischen Rückschritt signalisiert. Der Vf. geht, trotz aller Würdigung der mkn. Gesamterzählung und deren narrativen Charakters, stets von einer wortwörtlich formulierten und scheinbar rekonstruierbaren vormkn. Tradition aus. Eine solche ausformulierte Tradition ist aber vor allem bei den »Wundererzählungen« weder mit stilistischen Mitteln nachzuweisen noch aus überlieferungstechnischen Gründen vorauszusetzen. Zum Problem vgl. BREYTENBACH, *Problem des Übergangs*; ID., MNHMONEYEIN; ID., *Logientradition*.

61. D. LÜHRMANN, *Die Pharisäer und Schriftgelehrten im Markusevangelium*, in *ZNW* 78 (1987) 169-185, Zitat p. 177.

62. Vgl. SCHENKE, *Markusevangelium* (Anm. 59), pp. 52-53.

den Textebene Vorrang vor der Untersuchung des diachronen Werdens des Textes einzuräumen. In mehreren Fällen führt das Primat der Synchronie vor der Diachronie zu einer Aufgabe der in der Markusexegese der sechziger und siebziger Jahre üblichen Trennung von Redaktion und Tradition als Interpretationsinstrument. Diese Neuorientierung hat mehrere Ursachen, von denen hier nur vier hervorzuheben sind.

Erstens ist das seit der Arbeit von Johannes Schreiber[63] und Theodore Weeden[64] so einflußreiche Konfliktmodell, in dem der Evangelist als Kritiker und Korrektor seiner Tradition gegenübergestellt wurde, nicht nur in der deutschen, sondern auch in der amerikanischen Exegese weitgehend aufgegeben worden. Indem man aber davon ausgeht, daß Markus Tradition rezipiert, um sie bestätigend theologisch zu interpretieren, wird es immer weniger sinnvoll, im vorliegenden Text zwischen Tradition und Redaktion zu trennen. Man nimmt stattdessen den ganzen Text in den Blick. Unter dieser Perspektive ist es einerseits unangemessen, einen Keil zwischen ihn und die vormarkinische Tradition zu treiben, und andererseits legitim, die rezipierte Tradition als Teil der traditionsgebundenen markinischen Erzählung zu untersuchen[65].

Zweitens haben einige stilistische Untersuchungen gezeigt, daß das Markusevangelium von einem relativ einheitlichen Stil geprägt ist[66]. Es ist zwar möglich, den markinischen Stil von dem Stil der anderen Evangelisten zu unterscheiden; die Annahme aber, daß das Markusevangelium grundsätzlich in den verschiedenen Stilen vormarkinischer Tradition geschrieben sei und daß man nun anhand spezifischer markinischer Eigentümlichkeiten die markinischen redaktionellen Zusätze und Verbindungen von jener vormarkinischen Traditionsmasse unterscheiden könne, hat sich als nicht tragfähig erwiesen. Es dürfte nur in Ausnahmefällen möglich sein, aufgrund von Stilkriterien vormarkinische Tradition zu postulieren[67].

Drittens hat die Betonung der Tatsache, daß vormarkinische mündliche Tradition, wie bei mündlicher Tradition anzunehmen, kaum im Sinne von Texteinheiten mit rekonstruierbarem Stil zu denken ist, vor allem in der amerikanischen Forschung dazu geführt, daß man es nicht für sinnvoll hält, die vormarkinische Tradition rekonstruieren zu wollen. Hierbei ist der Einfluß des Buches »The Oral and the Written

---

63. J. SCHREIBER, *Die Christologie des Markusevangeliums. Beobachtungen zur Theologie und Komposition des zweiten Evangeliums*, in *ZTK* 58 (1961) 154-183.

64. T.J. WEEDEN, *Mark – Traditions in Conflict*, Philadelphia, PA, 1971. Für Rez. dazu vgl. NEIRYNCK, *Mark*, p. 542.

65. Vgl. BREYTENBACH, *Nachfolge*, pp. 69-70; T. SÖDING, *Glaube bei Markus* (SBB, 12), Stuttgart, 1985, pp. 101-103. Für Rez. dazu vgl. NEIRYNCK, *Mark*, p. 478.

66. Vgl. P. DSCHULNIGG, *Sprache, Redaktion und Intention des Markus-Evangeliums. Eigentümlichkeiten der Sprache des Markus-Evangeliums und ihre Bedeutung für die Redaktionskritik* (SBB, 11), Stuttgart, 1984. Für Rez. dazu vgl. NEIRYNCK, *Mark*, p. 136.

67. So zu Recht, LÜHRMANN, *Markusevangelium* (Anm. 45), p. 14.

Gospel« von Werner Kelber[68] nicht zu übersehen. In einem klassischen »understatement« formuliert Andreas Lindemann in der 10. Auflage des bekannten »Arbeitsbuches zum Neuen Testament«: »Richtig dürfte sein, daß der genaue *Wortlaut* der dem Evangelisten überkommenen Tradition nicht sicher rekonstruierbar ist«[69] und, daß »... das redaktionelle Konzept des Mk besonders schwer zu analysieren (ist), weil die Mk vorliegenden Traditionen oder 'Quellen' ja nur vermutungsweise bestimmt werden können«[70].

Viertens wirkten die Forschungsergebnisse der sechziger und siebziger Jahre, während derer die Markusexegese versucht hatte, markinische Redaktion von vormarkinischer Tradition zu unterscheiden, abschreckend auf die Forschung der achtziger Jahre[71]. Es gab weder bei der Rekonstruktion einer vormarkinischen Passionsgeschichte noch bei der Feststellung vormarkinischer Sammlungen noch bei der Bestimmung des Umfangs der vormarkinischen Tradition bei Einzelperikopen Anzeichen der Ausbildung eines Konsenses. Neuerdings hielt z.B. Lindemann die Rekonstruktion vormarkinischer Tradition bei den »Machttaten« Jesu in Mk 4,35-6,6a für unmöglich. Für die vorliegende literarische Gestalt der einzelnen Wundererzählungen sei jeweils der Evangelist selbst verantwortlich[72].

Seit den achtziger Jahren zeigt sich die Tendenz, die Gesamterzählung in den Blick zu nehmen und dabei der synchronen Analyse der Einzelperikopen einen gewissen Vorrang vor einer diachronen Untersuchung einzuräumen[73]. Eine interessante Frage ist nun, inwieweit die diachrone Untersuchung überhaupt noch eine Rolle bei der Interpretation spielt. Damit wir diese Frage klären können, ist ein kurzer Blick auf einige neuere Markusarbeiten notwendig.

---

68. W. KELBER, *The Oral and the Written Gospel. The Hermeneutics of Speaking and Writing in the Synoptic Tradition, Mark, Paul, and Q*, Philadelphia, PA, 1976. Für Rez. dazu vgl. NEIRYNCK, *Mark*, p. 254.

69. CONZELMANN–LINDEMANN, *Arbeitsbuch* (Anm. 44), p. 81.

70. *Ibid.*, p. 110.

71. Vgl. z.B. SCHENKE, *Markusevangelium* (Anm. 59), p. 52: »Die vorgelegten Ergebnisse solcher Exegese aber führen in die Verzweiflung«.

72. A. LINDEMANN, *Die Erzählung der Machttaten Jesu in Markus 4,35–6,6a*, in C. BREYTENBACH – H. PAULSEN (eds.), *Anfänge der Christologie. FS F. Hahn*, Göttingen, 1991, pp. 185-207, vgl. pp. 190-191, 196, 203-205.

73. Einige deutsch schreibende Verfasser neuerer exegetischer Studien zum Markusevangelium zeigen sich indessen unbeeindruckt von allem, was sich jenseits des Atlantik tut, und legen das älteste Evangelium mit genau den Methoden aus, wie schon ihre Väter dies taten. Dies gilt auch für Verfasserinnen, vgl. z.B. M. FANDER, *Die Stellung der Frau im Markusevangelium* (Münsteraner Theologische Abhandlungen, 8), Altenberge, 1989 [Für Rez. dazu vgl. NEIRYNCK, *Mark*, p. 154 sowie J. TOPLE, in *CBQ* 54 (1992) 149-151]; vgl. ferner H. SARIOLA, *Markus und das Gesetz. Eine redaktionskritische Untersuchung*, Helsinki, 1990.

5. Die Rolle der vormarkinischen Tradition bei der Interpretation der markinischen Erzählung: Beispiele aus der jüngsten Forschung

Für unsere Fragestellung bietet sich ein Blick in die folgenden drei unabhängig voneinander geschriebenen Arbeiten an, die sich mit dem Glaubensthema und Mk 11,22-25 beschäftigen.

Die Münsteraner Dissertation von Thomas Söding, *Glaube bei Markus*[74], wählt einen synchronen Untersuchungsansatz. Söding will den Text als Ganzes untersuchen: »An erster Stelle der Textanalyse stehen nicht literarkritische Unterscheidungen von Tradition und Redaktion, sondern Analysen des Kontextes und der Struktur einer Einheit-methodische Schritte, die vom vorliegenden Text des Markusevangeliums ausgehen, so wie er in letzter Hand vom Evangelisten gestaltet worden ist«[75]. Nacheinander unterzieht Söding den Kontext des Textes und die Laut-, Wort-, Satz- und Textebene einer Analyse. Er nennt seine Schritte Kontextanalyse und Strukturanalyse[76]. Den synchronen Schritten will Söding literar- und motivkritische Untersuchungen nachordnen, denn er bestreitet die Bedeutung diachronischer Untersuchungen für die Erarbeitung der markinischen Theologie nicht[77]. Betrachtet man entsprechend im Hauptteil C über »Gebetsglaube« die Analyse von Mk 11,22-25, zeigt sich, daß auf die diachrone Analyse nicht verzichtet wurde. Gleichwohl ist aber zu sagen, daß der Vergleich mit den Q-Parallelen zu den Logien in Mk 11,22-25 am Rande bleibt und keine wichtige Rolle in der Interpretation spielt. Für die Auslegung von Mk 6,1-6a gilt, daß das Problem von vormarkinischer Tradition und markinischer Redaktion zwar besprochen wird; die Interpretation der Perikope geschieht aber unabhängig von diesen Erörterungen, bei denen vieles offengelassen wird[78].

Die Emory Dissertation, die Sharyn Dowd 1988 unter dem Titel *Prayer, Power, and the Problem of Suffering. Mark 11:22-25 in the Context of Markan Theology*[79] veröffentlichte, trennt sich ebenfalls von Literar- und Redaktionskritik. Wie Söding erkennt die Verfasserin scharfsinnig, daß eine Konzentration allein auf die Redaktion eine Opposition zwischen Evangelist und Tradition voraussetzt, und widmet sich dem ganzen Text. In der Tradition des amerikanischen »compositional criticism« schließt sie sich vor allem Norman Perrin und John

---

74. Vgl. SÖDING, *Glaube* (Anm. 65).
75. *Ibid.*, pp. 126-127.
76. Cf. *ibid.*, p. 127.
77. Cf. *ibid.*, pp. 7, 128-129.
78. Cf. *ibid.*, pp. 434-436.
79. S.E. DOWD, *Prayer, Power, and the Problem of Suffering. Mark 11:22-25 in the Context of Markan Theology* (SBL DS, 105), Atlanta, GA, 1988. Für Rez. dazu vgl. NEIRYNCK, *Mark*, p. 134.

Donahue an[80] und konzentriert sich auf die vorliegende Erzählung. Vormarkinische Tradition, die sich aus einem Vergleich mit den Q-Parallelen zu der Stelle erheben ließe, spielt, soweit ich sehe, bei ihrer Untersuchung keine Rolle.

Der Neuseeländer Christopher Marshall veröffentlichte 1989 seine Londoner Dissertation unter dem Titel *Faith as a Theme in Mark's Narrative*[81]. Nach einer lesenswerten Kritik an der herkömmlichen Redaktionskritik[82] nimmt Marshall Anregungen aus dem amerikanischen »narrative criticism« auf. In Anschluß an Werner Kelber meint Marshall aber, Markus sei eher ein Erzähler (Redner) als ein Schriftsteller. Das Evangelium wurde zum öffentlichen Vortragen abgefaßt, dies sei noch am Stil zu erkennen. »Repetition and duality, so characteristic of Mark, are also essential strategies in oral communication«[83]. Marshall nimmt dabei an, daß Markus beim Schreiben des Evangeliums auf vormarkinische Tradition zurückgreift, die er kreativ verwertet. Er lehnt es daher unter Rückgriff auf die Redaktionskritik ab, Markus als freischaffenden Autor zu verstehen. Wichtig sei es, zu erkennen, wie Markus aus den verschiedenen Einzelerzählungen eine Erzählung mit kohärentem »plot« geschaffen habe und wie er durch verschiedene stilistische, literarische und kompositionelle Techniken ein Netz von Verbindungen zwischen den einzelnen Perikopen herstelle[84]. Damit dies erreicht werden kann, ist der gesamte markinische Erzähltext in den Blick zu nehmen. Gerade dazu sind in Anlehnung an die Literaturwissenschaft die Rolle des Erzählers, der Handlungsablauf (plot), die Darstellung der Erzählfiguren und der Stil zu beachten. Marshall grenzt sich aber deutlich von der gängigen Position des »narrative criticism« ab, das Evangelium als auto-semantische Sprachform zu verstehen. Das Evangelium verwendet Traditionen, die in historischen Ereignissen verwurzelt sind, und der Autor zeigt uns nicht, daß er nicht davon ausgeht, daß das Erzählte auch geschehen ist. Eine angemessene Interpretation des Evangeliums wird daher nicht nur den geschriebenen Text zu beachten haben, sondern auch den kulturellen und konzeptionellen Horizont der Hörer[85]. Nach alledem ist man überrascht, daß die synoptischen Parallelen zu Mk 11,22-25 bei der Interpretation dieser Stelle kaum berücksichtigt werden[86]. Auch bei der Auslegung von Mk 6,1-6a wird die Frage nach der hier aufgenommenen Tradition zugunsten der Interpretation des »final format« beiseite gelassen[87].

---

80. Vgl. dazu BREYTENBACH, *Nachfolge*, pp. 33-34.
81. Vgl. MARSHALL, *Faith* (Anm. 16).
82. Cf. *ibid.*, pp. 9-14.
83. *Ibid.*, p. 19.
84. Cf. *ibid.*, p. 20.
85. Cf. *ibid.*, pp. 27-28.
86. Cf. *ibid.*, pp. 163-172.
87. Cf. *ibid.*, p. 190.

Es wird also zunehmend davon Abstand genommen, die literarkritische *Scheidung von Tradition und Redaktion* zum Ausgangspunkt der Untersuchung zu machen. Stattdessen wird angestrebt, den Text als ganzen und seine vom Verfasser geschaffene Einheit ernstzunehmen[88]. Die Frage ist aber, was an Stelle der herkömmlichen Redaktionskritik als interpretatives Verfahren geboten wird. Während beim »literary criticism« der Anschluß an Methoden der modernen Literaturwissenschaft zu einem klaren, wenn auch in Einzelfällen unterschiedlich gehandhabten methodischen Verfahren geführt hat, läßt die deutschsprachige Exegese keine eindeutige Orientierung erkennen. Trotz mancher Gemeinsamkeiten zwischen den Arbeiten von Söding und Marshall ist erkennbar, daß sich Marshall über die Entwicklungen in der Literaturwissenschaft kundig gemacht hat und von diesen methodischen Voraussetzungen her über das Markusevangelium schreibt, während Södings synchrones Analyseverfahren mehr oder weniger auf dem »gesunden Menschenverstand« beruht. Die Zurückhaltung, sich selbständig über die Grundlagen der Text- und Literaturtheorie kundig zu machen, scheint die deutschsprachigen Markusarbeiten auszuzeichnen[89]. Sieht man von den wenigen Versuchen ab, die synchrone Analyse auf eine texttheoretische Basis zu stellen, scheint sich eine gefährliche Methodenlosigkeit breit zu machen.

II. Die Rezeption einer traditionsgebundenen Erzählung

1. *Zur synchronen Analyse des Textes*

Die Vorordnung der synchronen Analyse der vorliegenden Textebene vor die diachrone Frage nach dem Werden des Textes ist inzwischen weitgehend akzeptiert. Es bleibt aber die Frage, wie bei der synchronen Analyse vorzugehen ist. Es handelt sich dabei um ein heuristisches Problem. Wie ist es einem Leser möglich, von der graphischen Ausdrucksebene zu einem intersubjektiv mitteilbaren und nachvollziehbaren Verständnis der Buchstabenreihe zu kommen?

Eine Interpretation der markinischen Gesamterzählung lediglich auf der Grundlage einer »*Commonsense-Lektüre*« des Gesamttextes, ohne eine kritische Reflexion darüber, was sich beim Lesen abspielt bzw. wie verfahren wird, genügt wissenschaftlichen Ansprüchen nicht. Auch wenn man dem »literary criticism« vorwerfen kann, daß die Zeitbedingtheit moderner literaturwissenschaftlicher Ansätze zu wenig bedacht wird, hat er recht in seiner Forderung, daß das gewählte Analyse-

---

88 Vgl. Söding, *Glaube* (Anm. 65), pp. 14-15, 126-129.
89. Vgl. aber den avantgardistischen Ansatz von Zwick, *Montage* (Anm. 56).

verfahren sich im Rahmen der allgemeinen Literaturwissenschaft zu behaupten hat.

Dem »literary criticism« gegenüber ist aber darauf zu achten, daß die Exegese sich seit den frühesten Anfängen in philologischer Akribie um die Auslegung des einzelnen Ausdrucks, um das Verstehen der Satzkonstruktion, um die Erfassung des inhaltlichen Zusammenhanges zwischen Sätzen und um die Interpretation der Einzelperikope bemüht hat. Ein methodischer Zugang, der sich vorrangig mit der Gesamterzählung beschäftigt, kann sich kaum um die Mikro-Ebene des Textes kümmern. Gerade aus diesem Grund ist die Forderung nach einem textwissenschaftlichen Ansatz[90], in dem textlinguistische und literaturwissenschaftliche Theorien verwertet werden, nachdrücklich zu wiederholen. Eine detaillierte Auslegung des Makro-Textes verlangt Einsicht in die grammatischen, inhaltlichen und funktionalen Zusammenhänge zwischen den Aussagen jeder Einzelperikope[91]. Für die Beschreibung solcher Zusammenhänge lassen sich texttheoretische Erkenntnisse textsyntaktischer, textsemantischer[92] und textpragmatischer[93] Art in einem Analyseverfahren[94] anwenden. Literaturwissenschaftliche Ansätze sollten um des Details der Auslegung willen in eine breitere Konzeption der sich neuerdings in der Textwissenschaft ausbildenden Textanalyse (Discourse Analysis) aufgenommen werden[95].

Die neuere Entwicklung, auch in Kreisen des »literary criticism«, den Markustext wieder literaturgeschichtlich einzuordnen (Tolbert) und nach den historisch denkbaren Rezeptionsbedingungen zu fragen (Beavis), knüpft an traditionelle Fragen der historischen Kritik an und scheint mir grundsätzlich begrüßenswert.

Selbstverständlich ist auch die Frage nach der Gattung des Markusevangeliums zu stellen, und zwar auf texttheoretischer Ebene als Frage nach der globalen Ebene des Texttypus und in literaturgeschichtlicher Perspektive als Frage nach der Zuordnung des Textes zu zeitgenössischen Gattungen. Texttypologisch besteht ein gewisser Konsens, das Markusevangelium als Erzählung anzusehen. Welcher der zeitgenössischen Erzählgattungen diese Markuserzählung zuzuordnen ist, wird allerdings immer noch kontrovers diskutiert[96]. Für die Beantwortung

---

90. Zur Textwissenschaft vgl. T.A. VAN DIJK, Textwissenschaft. Eine interdisziplinäre Einführung, München, 1980.

91. Vgl. T.A. VAN DIJK, Episodes as Units of Discourse Analysis, in D. TANNEN (ed.), Analyzing Discourse. Text and Talk, Georgetown, 1982.

92. Vgl. T.A. VAN DIJK, Semantic Discourse Analysis, in ID. (ed.), Handbook of Discourse Analysis. Vol. II, New York, 1985, pp. 103-135.

93. Vgl. A. FERRARO, Pragmatics, in VAN DIJK, Handbook. Vol. II, pp. 139-157.

94. Vgl. BREYTENBACH, Nachfolge.

95. Vgl. T.A. VAN DIJK (ed.), Handbook of Discourse Analysis. Volumes 1-4, New York, 1985; W. HEINEMANN – D. VIEHWEGER, Textlinguistik. Eine Einführung, Tübingen, 1991.

96. Mit D. DORMEYER, Evangelium als literarische und theologische Gattung (Erträge

dieser Frage ist es nicht unerheblich, daß das Markusevangelium eine Erzählung ist, die aus kleineren Episoden aufgebaut ist. Die Tatsache, daß Matthäus und Lukas Einzelepisoden aus Markus übernommen und an anderer Stelle wieder als Einzelerzählungen verwendet haben sowie das Faktum, daß Parallelen zu einigen markinischen Erzählungen als Sammlung von Einzelerzählungen im Egerton Papyrus aufgenommen wurden, beweisen, daß in der urchristlichen Überlieferung des synoptischen Stoffes die Einzelepisode und nicht die Gesamterzählung im Zentrum der Rezipienten stand. Unabhängig davon, wie man das Verhältnis des Thomasevangeliums zu den synoptischen Evangelien bestimmt, kann nicht geleugnet werden, daß das Thomasevangelium einzelne Gleichnisse und Logien aus der Jesustradition aufgenommen hat und eben nicht Gesamttexte in narrativem Zusammenhang.

Diese Beobachtungen nötigen zu zwei methodischen Forderungen. Erstens ist es unangemessen, wie Tolbert bei der Frage nach der Gattung des Gesamtevangeliums nur auf die Makro-Erzählung zu achten und auszublenden, daß die Gesamterzählung erst unter Aufnahme von Einzelerzählungen und Spruchgruppen entstanden ist. Zweitens ist es für die Rekonstruktion des Hörerkreises, dem das Markusevangelium vorgelesen wurde, entscheidend, ob er die Einzelepisoden oder Sprüche schon kannte oder nicht. Wer um die Jesusgeschichten und die Episoden aus dem Leben des Petrus wußte, hörte den Text anders[97]. Man kann nicht wie Beavis einfach die diachronen Fragen ausklammern.

Die Bestimmung der Einzelgattungen und der Makrogattung erfordert selbstverständlich den Vergleich mit anderen zeitgenössischen Texten. Sowohl der Vergleich als auch die Klassifizierung von Gattungen bedürfen aber ebenfalls texttheoretischer Grundlegung[98]. Die Zuordnung zu den grundlegenden Texttypen ist nicht nur für die Gattungsbestimmung, sondern auch für die Auslegung wichtig. Wenn der Hörer weiß, daß es sich texttypologisch um eine Erzählung handelt, rezipiert er den Text anders, als wenn er ihn als Argument einstuft. Methoden

der Forschung, 263), Darmstadt, 1989, p. 152, und G. STRECKER, *Literaturgeschichte des Neuen Testaments* (UTB, 1682), Göttingen, 1992, p. 133, ist zu unterstreichen, daß eine Einstufung des MkEv als Erzähltext die Frage der Zuordnung des Evangeliums zu einer der zeitgenössischen Erzählgattungen nicht ausschließt, sondern gerade aufruft; vgl. BREYTENBACH, *Erzählung*, p. 141. Die Einstufung des Markusevangeliums als Erzähltext hat dazu geführt, daß der Gesamttext und dessen Eigenschaften als Erzählung beachtliche Berücksichtigung fanden.

97. Dies zu unterstreichen, ist ein Verdienst des Buches von H.C. WAETJEN, *A Reordering of Power. A Socio-Political Reading of Mark's Gospel*, Philadelphia, PA, 1989, pp. 4, 19-20. Für Rez. dazu vgl. NEIRYNCK, *Mark*, p. 536.

98. Vgl. W. RAIBLE, *Was sind Gattungen?*, in *Poetica* 12 (1980) 320-349; E. GÜLICH, *Textsorten in der Kommunikationspraxis*, in W. KALLMEYER (Hg.), *Kommunikationstypologie (Jahrbuch des Institutes für deutsche Sprache)*, Düsseldorf, 1986, pp. 15-46.

zur Analyse von Erzähltexten haben mittlerweile ihren festen Platz in der Auslegung der synoptischen Evangelien. Es darf dabei aber nicht vergessen werden, daß sich innerhalb der Makro-Erzählung und zwischen den Einzelerzählungen auch andere Texttypen befinden. Bei der Erforschung der Auslegung metaphorischer Texte, wie Gleichnisse und Bildworte, sind große Fortschritte gemacht worden. Die Beantwortung der Frage, wie Argumente gattungsgemäß zu analysieren sind, steckt noch in den Anfängen. Auch hier können textwissenschaftliche Überlegungen nützlich sein[99].

Wenn sich die diachronen Fragen nach dem Werden des Textes weder bei der Gattungsbestimmung noch bei der Rekonstruktion des »Hörerkreises« und der Beschreibung seiner Rezeptionsweise ausblenden lassen, ergibt sich das Problem, auf welche Weise die diachronen Fragen im Falle des Markusevangeliums zu stellen und gegebenenfalls zu beantworten sind.

2. *Auf der Suche nach der vormarkinischen Tradition*

Die weitverbreitete Skepsis gegenüber Stiluntersuchungen als Mittel zur Trennung von Redaktion und Tradition bei Markus ist wohl berechtigt. Geht man zudem davon aus, daß der durch das ganze Evangelium hindurch einheitliche Stil darauf zurückzuführen ist, daß der Evangelist dort, wo er Tradition rezipiert, diese in seinen eigenen Stil faßt, dann erübrigt sich die Frage ohnehin. Die Gesamterzählung liegt in markinischem Stil vor. Stilargumente können nur in Ausnahmefällen dazu verwendet werden, den Rezeptionsprozeß, in dem vormarkinische Tradition literarisiert wurde, klären zu helfen. Dabei wird aber vorausgesetzt, man wisse durch das Vorliegen literarisch unabhängiger Überlieferung, daß der Evangelist Tradition aufgreift. An anderer Stelle habe ich aufzuzeigen versucht, daß vormarkinische Logientradition hinter Mk 2,16-17; 4,9.23.24c; 7,15; 9,42.50e; 10,11-12; 12,17; 14,21.22-24.38 sich durchaus im Vergleich mit den Parallelen in der urchristlichen Briefliteratur (manchmal mit Q-Parallele) nachweisen, aber kaum rekonstruieren läßt[100]. Falls man in solchen Logien Stilmerkmale findet, die immer nur bei der markinischen Variante vorliegen, kann man den Stil des Evangelisten von dem der anderen Tradenten unterscheiden. Von einem Stil der vormarkinischen Tradition aber kann man nur dann reden, wenn Sprachmerkmale in den in Markus aufgenommenen traditionellen Logien auftauchen, die sonst im Evangelium fehlen[101].

---

99. Vgl. J. KOPPERSCHMIDT, *Methodik der Argumentationsanalyse* (Problemata, 119), Stuttgart, 1989; HEINEMANN – VIEHWEGER, *Textlinguistik* (Anm. 95), pp. 249-251.

100. Vgl. BREYTENBACH, *Logientradition* (Anm. 1).

101. Vgl. BREYTENBACH, *Logientradition*, p. 748.

Ein gangbarer Weg zur Erhebung vormarkinischer Tradition ist es, *mit dem Markusevangelium parallele Überlieferung*, die aber literarisch unabhängig vom Text des Evangeliums überliefert wurde, mit dem Markustext zu vergleichen. Ich habe bereits auf die Parallelen zwischen einigen Logien im Markusevangelium und einigen wenigen Stellen in der urchristlichen Briefliteratur aufmerksam gemacht[102]. Darüber hinaus ist auf die dreifach belegte Überlieferung zu achten, die dem Markusevangelium, der Redenquelle und dem Thomasevangelium gemeinsam ist[103]. Sodann ist auf die zweifache Überlieferung zu achten, die das Markusevangelium mit der Redenquelle oder mit dem Thomasevangelium gemeinsam hat[104]. Nimmt man in diesem Zusammenhang an, daß Q dem zweiten Evangelisten nicht literarisch vorlag und daß das Thomasevangelium, wie neuerdings vermehrt angenommen, doch teils sehr alte Überlieferung enthält[105], können folgende Beobachtungen gemacht werden – vorausgesetzt, daß man dabei immer die gesamte Evangelienüberlieferung im Auge behält.

Erstens fällt auf, daß mehrmals die gleichen Sentenzen[106], Bildworte und Gleichnisse bei Markus und Q, Markus und Thomas oder sogar bei allen dreien belegt sind. Dagegen hat Q keine »Wundererzählungen« im strengen Sinn[107], und im Thomasevangelium fehlt jede Wundergeschichte, ebenso in der matthäischen Sondertradition[108]. Sie häufen

---

102. Cf. *ibid.*

103. Bildworte aus Mk, Q und ThEv: Mk 3,22.24-27 // Q 11,15.17-18.21-22/12,24-26.29 // ThEv 21.35 (Die Beelzebulgleichnisse); Mk 4,21 // Q 11,33/5,15 // ThEv 33 (vom Licht auf dem Leuchter). Gleichnisse aus Mk, Q und ThEv: Mk 4,30-32 // Q 13,18-19/13,31-32 // ThEv 20 (Senfkorn); Mk 13,35 // Q 12,39-40/24,43-44 // ThEv 21 (vom Dieb – vgl. 1 Thess 5,1-2; 2 Petr 3,10).

104. Bildworte: (a) aus Mk und ThEv: Mk 2,19-20 // ThEv 104 (Fasten in der Anwesenheit des Bräutigams); Mk 2,21-22 // ThEv 47 (Neuer Wein in alten Schläuchen); (b) aus Mk und Q: Mk 9,50a-d // Q 14,34-35/5,13 (Vom Salz). Gleichnisse: (a) aus Mk und ThEv: Mk 4,3-8 // ThEv 9 (Ausgestreute Saat); Mk 12,1-8 // ThEv 65 (Gleichnis vom Winzer); (b) Mk und Lk: Mk 13,34-37 // Lk 12,35-38 (Von der Wiederkehr des Hausherrn; vgl. Didache 16,1a).

105. Zur Diskussion vgl. F.T. FALLON – R. CAMERON, *The Gospel of Thomas. A Forschungsbericht and Analysis*, in *ANRW* II 25.6 (1988) 4195-4251, dort pp. 4213-4224. H. KOESTER, *Ancient Christian Gospels. Their History and their Development*, London, 1990, pp. 85-86, und B. BLATZ, *Das koptische Thomasevangelium*, in W. SCHNEEMELCHER (ed.), *Neutestamentliche Apokryphen in deutscher Übersetzung. I. Band. Evangelien*, Tübingen, ⁶1990, pp. 93-113, dort p. 96, rechnen mit frühen Formen des synoptischen Stoffes im ThEv.

106. Vgl. BREYTENBACH, *Logientradition* (Anm. 1); D.E. AUNE, *Oral Tradition and the Aphorisms of Jesus*, in H. WANSBROUGH (ed.), *Jesus and the Oral Gospel Tradition* (JSNT SS, 64), Sheffield, 1991, pp. 211-265.

107. Q 7,1-10/8,5-13 (Knecht des Hauptmanns zu Kafarnaum) // Joh 4,46-54 (Apophthegma); Q 11,14-15/12,22-24 (geistbesessener Stummer) (Apophthegma).

108. Mt verkürzt die mkn. Wundererzählungen, fügt aber 9,27-31.32-34 (Heilung eines Blinden und eines Stummen) redaktionell hinzu.

sich aber bei Markus[109] und werden ausgebreitet im lukanischen Doppelwerk[110]. Die Wundererzählung war anscheinend keine beliebte Gattung im Bereich der Tradentenkreise, denen wir die Sprüche und Gleichnisse Jesu verdanken. Man kann auch nicht unwidersprochen auf das Johannesevangelium verweisen, um eine von Markus unabhängige vormarkinische Wundertradition zu belegen[111]. Im Vergleich zu Logien und Gleichnissen hat das Postulat einer vormarkinischen Wundertradition wenig Rückhalt in der Evangelienüberlieferung. Die Wundergeschichten sind uns über das Markusevangelium, über das Sondergut des lukanischen Doppelwerkes und über das Johannesevangelium überliefert worden.

Eine zweite interessante Beobachtung: Die Apophthegmen Bultmanns sind fast alle entweder dem Markusevangelium oder dem lukanischen Sondergut entnommen[112]. Die Frage stellt sich, wie es zu erklären ist, daß die Chrien sich hier konzentrieren und in Q oder im Sondergut des Matthäus so spärlich vorkommen. Das Thomasevangelium sammelt Sprüche im Apophthegmen-Stil. In der Regel wird nur knapp mit *peje Iêsous* (Jesus sagte) eingeführt. Einleitende Fragen der Jünger mit einer anschließenden Antwort Jesu kommen zwar gelegentlich vor[113], Situationsschilderungen gehen aber nur in Ausnahmefällen Sprüchen voran[114]. Hinzu kommt, daß die Chrien in der jüdischen Literatur des Zeitalters des zweiten Tempels ebenfalls nur gelegentlich

109. Heilungen in Mk: 1,29-31 (Schwiegermutter des Simon); 2,1-12 (Gelähmter in Kafarnaum); 3,1-6 (Heilung der verdorrten Hand am Sabbat) und 10,46-52 (Der Blinde von Jericho) (Paradigmen); 1,40-45 (Aussätziger); 5,21c.24b-34 (Blutflüssige Frau); 7,32-37 (Taubstummer); 8,22-26 (Blindenheilung) (Novellen). Exorzismen bei Mk: 1,21-28 (Synagoge in Kafarnaum) (Paradigma); 5,1-20 (Der Besessene von Gerasa); 9,14-29 (Heilung eines besessenen Jungen) (Novellen). Totenerweckungen bei Mk: 5,22-24a.35-43 (Tochter des Jairus) (Novelle). Rettungswunder bei Mk: 4,35-41; Mk 6,45-52 (Stillung des Sturms – Jesus wandelt auf dem Wasser // Joh 6,16-21) (Novellen). Geschenkwunder bei Mk: 6,35-44 // Joh 6,1-15 (Speisung der Fünftausend).

110. Lk läßt Mk 7,24-30.31-37; 8,1-8.22-26 aus, er ergänzt aber 13,10-17; 14,1-6 (Heilung einer Frau am Sabbat) (Apophthegmen) und 7,11-17 (Jüngling zu Nain) (Novelle). Beachte auch die Wundererzählungen in der Apg: (a) Heilungen: 3,1-10; 9,32-35; 14,8-14. (b) Exorzismus: 16,16-18. (c) Totenauferweckung: 9,36-42; 20,7-12. (d) Bestrafungen: 5,1-11; 19,11-20. (e) Türeröffnungswunder: 16,23-40; 12,1-19. (f) Sonstiges: 28,1-6.

111. Joh 4,46-65 // Q 7,1-10/8,5-13 [Heilung des Sohnes des königlichen Beamten] hat eine Parallele in Q. Joh 5,1-9a [Die Heilung am Teich vom Betesda]; 9,1-12 [Heilung eines Blindgeborenen]; 11,1-44 (Lazarus); Joh 2,1-11 (Hochzeit zu Kana); Lk 5,1-11 (Fischzug des Petrus) // Joh 21,1-14 bilden Sondertraditionen, die anderen jhn. Semeia haben Parallelen bei Mk.

112. Ausnahmen: Mk 3,22-30 // Q 11,14-23/12,22-37 (Beelzebulstreit); Q 7,18-35/11,2-19 (Täuferfrage); Q 9,57-62/8,19-22 (Nachfolgeworte); Q 19,39-40/21,15-16 (Jubelruf). Vgl auch SMt 17,24-27 (Tempelsteuer).

113. Vgl. ThEv 12; 18; 20-21; 22; 24; 37; 43; 51-53; 113-114. S. auch 61.

114. Vgl. ThEv 22; 72; 79; 100; 104. S. auch 13 und 60.

(Philo) auftauchen[115]. Die starke Aufnahme von Chrien bei Markus und im lukanischen Sondergut weist wahrscheinlich auf Tradenten-kreise, die die Jesusüberlieferung mit Hilfe hellenistischer Gattungen gestalten. Vergleicht man nun die Chrien bei Markus mit denen, die uns von hellenistischen Schriftstellern überliefert wurden und mit den Sprü-chen des Thomasevangeliums, fällt sofort auf, daß die Situationsschil-derung bei Markus viel breiter ausfällt. Dies hatte wahrscheinlich den Zweck, die Chrien in den vorliegenden literarischen Kontext einzubin-den. Dann hätten sie ihre ausgebreitete Form erst im Rahmen der Literarisierung bekommen, d.h. wir hätten uns die vormarkinische Chrienüberlieferung als viel knappere Einheiten vorzustellen.

Eine dritte Beobachtung: Die Überlieferungstechniken, die bei der Logienquelle zu beobachten sind[116], lassen sich in einigen der kleinen Spruchgruppen[117] im Markusevangelium ebenfalls nachweisen. Interes-santerweise weisen sich mehrere der Sprüche in diesen Gruppen durch Parallen mit Q als traditionell aus. So kann man beobachten, daß ursprünglich isolierte Sprüche wie Mk 8,34 // Q 14,27/10,38 als *Grund-worte* andere Sprüche wie Mk 8,35 // Q 17,33/10,39 als *Kommentar-worte* quasi angezogen haben. Daß dieser Zusammenhang vormarki-nisch ist, zeigt die Q-Verbindung (vgl. Mt) und auch die Parallele in Joh 12,25-26[118]. Mit dem Stichwort ψυχή wurden dann Mk 8,36 und Mk 8,37 angeschlossen.

Zusammenfassend kann gesagt werden, daß die vormarkinische Tra-dition sich nur im Vergleich mit der gesamten Jesus-Überlieferung untersuchen läßt. Wer die Frage nach vormarkinischer Tradition stellt, hat bei den Sentenzen, Mahnworten, Bildworten und den Gleichnissen mehr Boden unter den Füßen als bei Chrien, Wundererzählungen und Erzählungen wie der Verklärungserzählung in Mk 9,2-8.

Es gibt vielleicht doch einen schmalen Weg in die dunkle Welt der vormarkinischen Erzähltradition. Geht man von der m.E. berechtigten Annahme aus, daß die synoptische Überlieferung in Einzeltraditionen, seien es nun Logien, Gleichnisse oder Erzählungen, tradiert wurde,

---

115. Vgl. L. GREENSPOON, *The Pronouncement Story in Philo and Josephus*, in *Semeia* 20 (1981) 73-80. S. auch G.G. PORTON, *The Pronouncement Story in Tannaitic Literature. A Review of Bultmann's Theory*, in *Semeia* 20 (1981) 81-99.

116. Vgl. H. SCHÜRMANN, *Zur Kompositionsgeschichte der Redenquelle*, in C. BUSS-MANN – W. RADL (eds.), *Der Treue Gottes trauen. Beiträge zum Werk des Lukas. FS G. Schneider*, Freiburg, 1991, pp. 325-342.

117. Im Markusevangelium können wir noch mehrere Spruchreihen erkennen. Vgl. die Spruchgruppen zur Martyriumsparänese in Mk 13,9.11 (12) 13 und zum Gebet in 11,23-25. Weitere Spruchgruppen finden sich in Mk 8,34-37 (38?), wo es um die Bestimmungen der Nachfolge geht, sowie in der nach Stichworten zusammengestellten Reihe Mk 9,37.41.42-43.45.47-50 und bei der Auseinandersetzung über Jesu Vollmacht, die Dämo-nen auszutreiben in Mk 3,22-29.

118. Ein weiteres Beispiel wäre Mk 2,18a.19a (Grundwort) 2,21-22 (Kommentar), Mk 4,21b // Q 12,3/10,26 (Grundwort) Mk 4,22 // Q 12,3/10,27 (Kommentar).

kann man unter *überlieferungstechnischem* Gesichtspunkt folgendes fragen: Welche Teile des vorliegenden Markustextes ließen sich als kleine, in sich geschlossene Erzählungen unabhängig vom literarischen Kontext überliefern? Dies trifft z.B. für Mk 4,3-8 zu. Eine solche Fragestellung setzt selbstverständlich eine synchrone Analyse der vorliegenden Textebene voraus. Dies gilt ebenfalls für die komplementäre Frage: Welche Partien des vorliegenden Markustextes erstellen den vorliegenden literarischen Zusammenhang und haben unabhängig vom Erzählzusammenhang keinen geschlossenen Charakter? Dies trifft z.B. auf Mk 4,1-2 zu. Bei Texten, die als Einzelerzählungen überlieferbar sind, ist es sinnvoll, nach vormarkinischer Tradition zu suchen. Da der Evangelist, wie z.B. in Mk 6,1-6a und 8,14-21, aber auch selbst in sich geschlossene Episoden abfaßte, muß man mit anderen Mitteln, wie mit dem Vergleich mit Q beim Senfkorngleichnis, nachweisen, daß der Evangelist eine traditionelle Erzählung rezipiert.

Es gibt aber noch eine andere Form von Tradition bei Markus. Faßt man den Begriff »vormarkinische Tradition« weit, so ist es möglich, die intertextuellen *Beziehungen zwischen dem Markustext und der LXX*, besonders dem Jesajabuch, dem Danielbuch und den Leidenspsalmen, auf der synchronen Ebene im Rahmen einer Theorie der Intertextualität[119] zu betrachten. Aber auch die diachronen Fragen bedürfen einer Klärung. Verwendet Markus die LXX überall mit der gleichen Intention oder lassen sich mehrere Arten der Schriftverwendung erkennen? Wie steht es mit Anspielungen? Sind die Anspielungen auf die Leidenspsalmen auf Teile der Passionsgeschichte beschränkt, während Anspielungen auf das Jesaja- und das Danielbuch sich im ersten Teil des Evangeliums häufen? Es ist ein Desiderat, die Verwendung von Schriftzitaten und Anspielungen im zweiten Evangelium systematisch unter Vergleich der Verwendungen in den Einzelperikopen zu untersuchen. Konkrete Ergebnisse in diesem Zusammenhang werden helfen, die Frage zu beantworten, ob Perikopen wie z.B. Mk 10,2-9 und 12,18-27 sich in der Schriftverwendung ähneln oder nicht und sich für die Frage nach der Herkunft der Perikopen auswerten lassen.

3. *Die Analyse der markinischen Komposition*

Wenn der Text auf synchroner Ebene analysiert worden ist und es durch das Vergleichsverfahren sowie unter überlieferungstechnischem Gesichtspunkt gelungen ist, die Textpartien im Markusevangelium, die auf Tradition zurückgreifen, zu identifizieren, ist die Frage nach den Kompositionstechniken, mit denen Markus die Tradition zu einem

---

119. Vgl. W.S. VORSTER, *Intertextuality and Redaktionsgeschichte*, in S. DRAISMA (ed.), *Intertextuality in Biblical Writings. Essays in honour of Bas van Iersel*, Kampen, 1989, pp. 15-26.

einheitlichen Werk integriert hat, zu stellen. Auf solche markinischen Kompositionstechniken, die in der Forschung bekannt sind, habe ich bereits andernorts aufmerksam gemacht[120], so daß hier lediglich resümiert wird. Die sich im Evangelium ständig wiederholenden Techniken, einzelne Episoden miteinander zu verbinden, und die typischen Schemata für die Anordnung von Einzelperikopen wie Dreieranordnung, Kontrastierung, Verschachtelung und Parallelisierung sind gut bekannt. Solche Techniken, die Auskunft über die Kompositionsarbeit des Evangelisten geben, verdienen im Vergleich mit der zeitgenössischen Literatur untersucht zu werden. Die Techniken, derer sich Markus bei der Verwendung der LXX bedient, bedürfen einer kompositionskritischen Untersuchung.

Einsicht in das Werden der markinischen Komposition, d.h. Einsicht in die Weise, wie der Evangelist seinen Text »gemacht« hat, vertieft das Verständnis für das Evangelium. In der Komposition des Markusevangeliums wird Tradition rezipiert. Nach der Feststellung, daß Tradition vorliegt, muß man die Frage aufwerfen, mit welchen Mitteln der Evangelist diese Tradition in sein Werk integriert hat. Es empfiehlt sich, hier zwischen redaktionellen und kompositionellen Mitteln zu unterscheiden, wobei es bei redaktionellen Mitteln hauptsächlich um die Ergänzung und Verbindung von literarischen Vorlagen wie LXX-Zitaten geht, während kompositionelle Mittel den Entwurf eines größeren Abschnittes durch die Anordnung, Verschachtelung und Plazierung von Traditionseinheiten betreffen.

Darüber hinaus bleibt es wichtig, die unterschiedlichen Zielsetzungen der synchronen Textanalyse und der Analyse der Rekonstruktion der vormarkinischen Tradition zu unterscheiden.

Die Bedeutung eines Textes wird nicht durch seine Entstehungsgeschichte konstituiert, sondern durch die Beziehungen, die der Leser zwischen den Teilen des vorliegenden Textes herstellt[121]. Die Rekonstruktion der Entstehungsgeschichte zeichnet zwar den redaktionellen und kompositionellen Vorgang, der zu dem vermuteten Sinn und den postulierten Funktionszusammenhängen zwischen den Teilen des nun »fertigen« Textes geführt hat, nach, sie kann jene Bedeutungszusammenhänge selbst aber nicht beschreiben. Darum setzt die Redaktionskritik als historisch nach der redaktionellen und kompositionellen Tätigkeit des Evangelisten fragende Methode eine inhaltliche Bestimmung der Traditionsvorlage sowie eine textwissenschaftlich vertretbare Analyse der unter Aufnahme von Traditionen komponierten episodischen Erzählung und der darin enthaltenen Teilepisoden voraus. Da diese dem Exegeten nur als »fertiger« Text vorliegt, setzt die diachrone

---

120. Vgl. BREYTENBACH, *Nachfolge*, pp. 23-26; ID., *Erzählung*, pp. 157-168.
121. Beachte: die vorliegende Textbasis ist die Voraussetzung für eine solche Herstellung der Beziehungen; s.u.

Analyse eine Beschreibung der Bedeutungs- und Funktionszusammenhänge aufgrund des vorliegenden Markustextes voraus. Der Redak-
tions- bzw. Kompositionskritik als Methode, die den Vorgang nach-
zeichnet, wie urchristliche Tradition in der Markuskomposition rezipiert worden ist, muß also eine synchrone textsemantische Analyse
vorausgehen. Hiermit ist ein Grundsatz für das Verhältnis von inhalt-
licher Analyse und Rekonstruktion der geschichtlichen Entstehung
eines Textes formuliert.

Die vorliegende Komposition ist das Ergebnis des redaktionellen und
kompositionellen Vorgehens des Evangelisten, während das Vorgehen
der Weg zu dieser Komposition ist. Unter diesem Gesichtspunkt ist es
notwendig, die Ergebnisse der diachronen Redaktionskritik auf die ihr
vorangegangenen Ergebnisse der synchronen Kompositionsanalyse zu-
rückzubeziehen, um so die traditionskritisch gewonnenen Ergebnisse
und die textwissenschaftlich begründete Analyse der Bedeutungs- und
Funktionszusammenhänge im Text einander bereichern zu lassen.

Allein wenn man die Bedeutung und die Intention des vorliegenden
Markustextes gewonnen hat, zeigen sich Sinn und Zweck der redaktionellen und kompositionellen Tätigkeit des Evangelisten. Wie gelangt
aber der Exeget als Leser zur Intention des Textes? Mit Umberto Eco
ist zu unterscheiden zwischen semantischer und kritischer Interpretation. »Die semantische ... Interpretation ist Resultat des Prozesses,
durch den der Adressat, angesichts der linearen Manifestation des
Textes, diesen mit Sinn erfüllt. Die kritische ... Interpretation hingegen
ist diejenige, mittels derer man zu erklären versucht, aufgrund welcher
Strukturmerkmale der Text diese (oder andere) semantische Interpretationen hervorbringen kann«[122]. Der *Exeget* hat kritisch zu interpretieren; die kritische Interpretation ist eine metalinguistische Aktivität. Es
sollte doch darum gehen, einen Text kritisch zu interpretieren, d.h. die
Möglichkeiten aufzuzeigen, in denen sich der Text verstehen läßt. Dazu
muß der Text selbst als Parameter seiner Interpretation verwendet
werden, denn ein Text kontrolliert und selektiert seine Interpretationen
und Fehlinterpretationen. Mit Eco ist weiterhin bei der semantischen
Interpretation am Literalsinn des Textes festzuhalten; nennen wir dies
die Intention *des Textes.* Wir müssen also zwischen der Intention des
Textes und der Intention *des Lesers* unterscheiden. Wie ist aber jene zu
fassen, wenn wir von dieser ausgehen? Die Initiative des Lesens besteht
im Aufstellen einer Vermutung über die *intentio operis.* Die Richtigkeit
einer Vermutung bezüglich der Intention des Werkes kann aber am
Text als einem kohärenten Ganzen überprüft werden. Die anvisierte
Textkohärenz kontrolliert somit die Antriebe des Lesers[123]. Vermutun-

---

122. U. Eco, *Die Grenzen der Interpretation*, München, 1992, p. 43.
123. Cf. *ibid.*, pp. 49-50.

gen über die Intention des Textes, die sich nicht am Textganzen bestätigen lassen, können keinen Anspruch auf Textgemäßheit erheben. Im Sinne von Popper könnte man sagen, daß es zwar keine Regeln gibt, die uns sagen könnten, welche Interpretation die beste ist, wohl aber daß es Regeln gibt, die uns zeigen können, welche Interpretation dem Text unangemessen ist. Fehlinterpretationen sind u.a daran zu erkennen, daß sie an der Kohärenz des Textes scheitern[124]. Vor diesem Hintergrund wird der Kategorie der Textkohärenz eine zentrale Rolle in der Exegese zugebilligt. Um auf kritischer Ebene von der Kohärenz des Textes her argumentieren zu können, müssen Exegeten und Exegetinnen wissen, wie Kohärenz zwischen den Aussagen in Sätzen bzw. zwischen Sprechakten zu beschreiben ist. Es ist unangemessen, hier Texttheoretisches zu wiederholen[125]. Es empfiehlt sich vielmehr, die im ersten Beispiel vorliegenden semantischen Interpretationen metalinguistisch zu beleuchten.

III. BEISPIELE

Es ist in dem hier gesteckten Rahmen nicht möglich, eine systematische Interpretation der zwei Beispieltexte vorzunehmen. Es genügt, wenn einige relevante methodische Probleme unterstrichen werden[126].

---

124. Cf. *ibid.*, pp. 51-52.

125. Vgl. neben VAN DIJK, *Semantics* (Anm. 92), FERRARO, *Pragmatics* (Anm. 93), und HEINEMANN – VIEHWEGER, *Textlinguistik* (Anm. 95), auch T.A. VAN DIJK – W. KINTSCH, *Strategies of Discourse Comprehension*, New York, 1983, und die exegetische Umsetzung bei BREYTENBACH, *Nachfolge* (dort weitere Lit.).

126. Ich verweise dabei auf meine Gliederung des Textes Mk 9,9-11:

9a Καὶ καταβαινόντων αὐτῶν ἐκ τοῦ ὄρους

9b διεστείλατο αὐτοῖς

9c ἵνα μηδενὶ ἃ εἶδον διηγήσωνται,

9d εἰ μὴ ὅταν ὁ υἱὸς τοῦ ἀνθρώπου ἐκ νεκρῶν ἀναστῇ.

10a καὶ τὸν λόγον ἐκράτησαν πρὸς ἑαυτοὺς συζητοῦντες

10b τί ἐστιν τὸ ἐκ νεκρῶν ἀναστῆναι.

11a καὶ ἐπηρώτων αὐτὸν λέγοντες·

11b ὅτι λέγουσιν οἱ γραμματεῖς ὅτι

11c Ἠλίαν δεῖ ἐλθεῖν πρῶτον;

12a ὁ δὲ ἔφη αὐτοῖς·

12b Ἠλίας μὲν ἐλθὼν πρῶτον ἀποκαθιστάνει πάντα·[;]

12c καὶ πῶς γέγραπται ἐπὶ τὸν υἱὸν τοῦ ἀνθρώπου

12d ἵνα πολλὰ πάθῃ καὶ ἐξουδενηθῇ;

13a ἀλλὰ λέγω ὑμῖν ὅτι

13b καὶ Ἠλίας ἐλήλυθεν,

13c καὶ ἐποίησαν αὐτῷ ὅσα ἤθελον,

13d καθὼς γέγραπται ἐπ' αὐτόν.

1. *Elia und der Menschensohn: Markus 9,9-11*

a. Widerstreit der Meinungen

Auf der *synchronen Ebene* gibt es verschiedene Probleme: Handelt es sich überhaupt um einen kohärent interpretierbaren Text[127]? Nach Bultmann stört V. 12c + d den Zusammenhang. Dies sei eine Interpolation[128]. Auch Lohmeyer betrachtet V. 12c + d als Interpolation. Er erkannte ein zweites inhaltliches Problem der vorliegenden Perikope, als er die Frage der Jünger in V. 10b gegen den Wortlaut des Markus nicht als Frage nach der Auferstehung überhaupt, sondern als Frage nach der Auferstehung des Menschensohnes verstand. Diese Frage sei nun nicht weitergeführt worden. In V. 11b + c werde eine andere, neue Frage nach dem Kommen des Elia an Jesus gestellt[129]. Schweizer benennt ein drittes synchrones Problem in der Perikope. Nach ihm sei der Zusammenhang sehr unklar, sogar unlogisch, und die Verbindung von VV. 9-10 zu VV. 1-13, »wo ja nicht von der Auferstehung die Rede ist, ist ganz lose«[130]. Lohmeyer unterläßt es, nach einem Zusammenhang zwischen den beiden Fragen zu suchen und kommentiert sie ohne gegenseitigen Bezug[131], während Schweizer VV. 11-13 von 8,31 her deutet.

b. Lösungen?

Im Folgenden besprechen wir zwei neuere Auslegungen der Perikope. Sie zeigen deutlich auf, daß es nicht möglich ist, dem Text ein kohärentes Verständnis abzugewinnen, wenn der Leser nicht gleichzeitig selbst einiges zu dem, was »geschrieben steht«, ergänzt. Textkohärenz liegt nicht im Text, sie wird anhand des Textes unter Heranziehung textexterner Informationen von den Lesern bzw. Hörern erstellt.

Nach Gnilka verdanken wir VV. 9-11a der markinischen Redaktion. Das so angeschlossene traditionelle Gespräch in VV. 11b-13 entstammt der Gemeindekatechese bzw. der Auseinandersetzung zwischen Gemeinde und Judentum. Es geht dabei – unter Beibehaltung des traditionellen V. 12c + d[132] – um das Verhältnis zwischen der wiederherstellenden Aufgabe des Elia und dem Leidensschicksal des Menschensohnes. Auch wenn er VV. 11-13 von der Verklärungserzählung und von Mk 8,31 her in den Kontext einbindet, versucht Gnilka doch, die drei genannten synchronen Probleme (s.o.) zu überwinden. Die Frage in V. 10b bezieht er auf die Auferstehung Jesu. Auch wenn das Gespräch

---

127. Zu Textkohärenz vgl. BREYTENBACH, *Nachfolge*, pp. 145-176.

128. Vgl. R. BULTMANN, *Die Geschichte der synoptischen Tradition* (FRLANT, 29), Göttingen, ²1931, pp. 131-132.

129. Vgl. E. LOHMEYER, *Das Evangelium des Markus* (KEK, I/2), Göttingen, ¹⁷1967, p. 181.

130. E. SCHWEIZER, *Das Evangelium nach Markus* (NTD, 1), Göttingen, ¹⁷1989, p. 104.

131. Cf. *ibid.*, pp. 182-183.

132. Nimmt Bezug auf Ps 118,22. Vgl. Mk 8,31; 12,10; Apg 4,11.

im jetzigen Kontext über VV. 9-10 hinaus zurück auf die Verklärungserzählung und Mk 8,31 verweist, gestattet die Auffassung, daß die
Auferstehung und somit die Auferstehung des Menschensohnes Jesus
zu den Endzeitereignissen gehört, einen Übergang von VV. 9-10 zu VV.
11b-13. Den Widerspruch zwischen VV. 12b und 12c+d versucht
Gnilka dadurch zu lösen, daß er jene als Frage[133] und diese als
Gegenthese auffaßt. Jesus stellt in Frage, ob Elia denn wirklich alles
wiederhergestellt habe. »Hätte es eine allgemeine Versöhnung gegeben
und wäre ein bereites Volk geschaffen worden, wäre eine Verachtung
des Menschensohnes nicht denkbar«[134].

Versuchen wir, Gnilkas Lektüre des Textes kritisch zu reflektieren.
Sie beruht auf einer wortsemantischen, einer textsemantischen und zwei
textpragmatischen Entscheidungen sowie der Konstruktion einer argumentativen Superstruktur des Textes. *Wortsemantisch*: Die Referenz
von τὸ ἐκ νεκρῶν ἀναστῆναι. Hiermit werde über den Kontext hinaus
auf die Auferstehung Jesu bzw. des Menschensohnes Bezug genommen[135]. *Textsemantisch*: Die Ko-referenz von ὅταν ὁ υἱὸς τοῦ ἀνθρώπου ἐκ νεκρῶν ἀναστῇ (9d), τὸ ἐκ νεκρῶν ἀναστῆναι (10b) und
Ἠλίαν δεῖ ἐλθεῖν πρῶτον. Diese drei Aussage bezögen sich alle auf
Endzeitereignisse. »Die Auferstehung ist ihnen (sc. den Jüngern) ein
Ereignis der Endzeit«[136]. *Textpragmatisch*: Der Sprechakt in V. 12b sei
als Frage und der in V. 12c+d als Gegenthese zu dieser Frage
aufzufassen[137]. Der Exeget Gnilka und die Herausgeber von Nestle-
Aland[26] konstruieren somit verschiedene Texte. Ein Exeget tut aber
noch mehr. Es gehört auch zu seiner Aufgabe, den Text in einen
Kommunikationszusammenhang hineinzustellen. Historisch lesende Exegeten versuchen, den Kommunikationszusammenhang, aus dem der
Text hervorgegangen ist, zu rekonstruieren. Gnilkas Rekonstruktion
des dem Text zugrundeliegenden Problems kann so gefaßt werden: Wie
läßt sich im Rahmen der Endereignisse die Auferstehung des Menschensohnes mit der Rolle des wiederherstellenden Elia verbinden?
Semantisch gefaßt: Worauf bezieht sich das πρῶτον in V. 11c? Im
Rahmen der Endzeitvorstellung, die im Text zwar nicht ausformuliert
wurde, die Gnilka aber bei den Jüngern voraussetzt, geht das Kommen
des wiederherstellenden Elias der Auferstehung der Toten und somit
der Auferstehung Jesu voraus. Da Elia noch nicht alles wieder hergestellt habe, könnten die Jünger die Auferstehung nicht einordnen. Die

---

133. Mit J. WELLHAUSEN, *Das Evangelium Marci*, Berlin, 1903, pp. 76-77.
134. J. GNILKA, *Das Evangelium nach Markus*. 2. Teilband. *Mk 8,27–16,20* (EKK, II/
2), Neukirchen-Zürich, 1979, pp. 41-42.
135. Vgl. GNILKA, *Evangelium* II, p. 41.
136. *Ibid.*
137. Vgl. GNILKA, *Evangelium* II, pp. 41-42.

Frage ist, so Gnilka: »Bestätigt Jesus diese Eliaerwartung?«[138]. Jesus
löst die Spannung zwischen der Frage in V. 12b und der Gegenthese in
V. 12c+d damit, daß er in V. 13 die Lösung anbietet: »Elia ist bereits
gekommen, in der Gestalt Johannes des Täufers«[139].

Nach Lührmann geht VV. 9-10 auf den Evangelisten zurück. Er
vermutet hinter VV. 11-13 ein Streitgespräch[140]. Auch er rekonstruiert
eine Streitfrage hinter dem vorliegenden Markustext, jedoch anders als
Gnilka. Die Elia-Erwartung der Schriftgelehrten werde gegen die
Erwartung des Menschensohnes Jesu gestellt. Die Schriftgelehrten
meinten, nicht der Menschensohn, sondern Elia komme vor dem Tag
des Herrn. Jesus wiederhole erst diese Meinung und entkräfte sie dann
durch einen gleichwertigen Schriftverweis in V. 12c+d. Unter Aufnahme von 8,31 sei das Gegenargument in V. 12c+d geäußert, daß
auch das Leiden des Menschensohnes in der Schrift vorausgesagt sei. In
V. 13 werde dann in einem zweiten Schritt der Beweis geliefert, daß Elia
bereits als Johannes der Täufer gekommen sei und der Einwand der
Schriftgelehrten insofern unberechtigt sei[141].

Die Interpretationen von Gnilka und Lührmann setzen beide eine
gewisse Endzeiterwartung bei den Lesern voraus. Darüber hinaus wird
erwartet, daß der Leser beim Lesen über das δεῖ in V. 11c die
Anspielung auf die Schrifttradition in Mal 3,23-24 und ggf. Sir 48,10
erkennen wird und diese Schriftaussage mit der Schrifterwartung über
den Menschensohn, die in Mk 8,31 ebenfalls mit einem δεῖ angesprochen wurde und nach Gnilka auf Ps 118,22 zurückgreift, in Verbindung
bringt. Hinter V. 13c erkennt Gnilka 1 Kön 19,2.10.14 (die Verfol-
gung Elias durch Isebel). In solchen Fällen geht es um Intertextualität.
Aus diesem Beispiel wird deutlich, daß *syn*chrone Interpretation keine
*a*chrone, textimmanente Interpretation sein kann, sondern eine Konstruktion der zeitgenössischen Endzeiterwartung und Schriftauslegungs-
tradition, die im Umfeld der Hörer des Textes gegenwärtig war, voraussetzt, bevor man überhaupt von einem kohärenten Text sprechen kann.
Die Kohärenz liegt nicht im Text – es ist die Interpretationsstrategie der
Exegeten Gnilka und Lührmann, die mit Hilfe des Textes eine kohärente Lektüre hervorbringt. Bultmanns, Lohmeyers und Schweizers
Lesestrategien ermöglichten dies nicht. Für sie ist der Text unzusam-
menhängend. Ist er das? Es hängt davon ab, in welchen argumentativen
Kontext wir den Text beim Lesen hineinstellen. Es kann aber nicht
jeder beliebige Kontext sein, sondern – da wir voraussetzen, der Autor
wollte Zusammenhängendes vermitteln – nur einer, der ein kohärentes
Verständnis ermöglicht.

---

138. *Ibid.*
139. *Ibid.*, p. 42.
140. Vgl. LÜHRMANN, *Markusevangelium* (Anm. 45), p. 157.
141. Vgl. LÜHRMANN, *Markusevangelium*, p. 158.

Genauso wichtig ist es aber, daß die Leser bzw. die Hörer des Textes den Text als Argument erkennen, d.h. der Text wird nicht nur in einen argumentativen Kontext hineingestellt, sondern auch in einen texttypologischen. Joel Marcus hat vor kurzem die Interpretation Gnilkas weiter ausgebaut und den Text Mk 9,11-13 einer später belegten jüdischen Gattung zugeordnet, die zum argumentativen Textypus zu rechnen ist[142]. Diese argumentative Gattung finde in Qumran und der Mekhilta (Rabbi Jischmael zugeschrieben) Verwendung und habe die Funktion, anscheinend widersprüchliche Textaussagen miteinander zu versöhnen. Bei der Interpretation von Mk 9,11-13 ist nach Marcus von V.11, dem Grundvers aus der Schrift (Mal 3,22 LXX), auszugehen. In V. 12b wird durch eine Frage die Wiederherstellungsfunktion des Elia problematisiert. In V. 12c + d wird eine kontrastierende Schriftinterpretation dem Grundsatz von V. 11 gegenübergestellt. In V. 13 wird der Grundvers von V. 11 angesichts der damit kontrastierenden Schriftinterpretation in V. 12c+d so ausgelegt, daß der Widerspruch sich auflöst. Weil die Folgerung in V. 13 Resultat der gemeinsamen Interpretation von VV. 11 und 12b ist, kann es mit καθὼς γέγραπται ἐπ' αὐτόν abgeschlossen werden, auch wenn eine Bibelstelle für das Leiden Elias fehlt. In diesem Vers wird impliziert, daß, weil Jesus der leidende Menschensohn ist, sein Vorläufer der leidende Elia sein muß[143]. Leider geht Marcus nicht auf VV. 9-10 ein.

c. Fazit

Dieses Beispiel zeigt m.E., daß es unsachgemäß ist zu meinen, man könne lediglich den vorliegenden Text samt seinem literarischen Ko-Text analysieren. Eine synchrone Lektüre setzt bereits voraus, daß wir unter Berücksichtigung der Entstehungsbedingungen und Ausdrucksebene des Textes einen argumentativen und texttypologischen Kontext um den Text herum und auf ihn hin konstruieren, damit wir ihm einen kohärenten Sinn abgewinnen können. Das zweite Besipiel soll sich mit dem Problem des Textwerdens beschäftigen.

2. *Die Verwerfung Jesu in Nazareth in Mk 6,1-6a*

a. Widerstreit der Meinungen

Bei der diachron zu beschreibenden Entstehung dieser Perikope gibt es zwei deutlich auseinandergehende Positionen. Da die wichtige diachrone Analyse der Perikope mit den Anfängen der Formgeschichte zusammenfällt, widmen wir uns zunächst der Analyse Bultmanns.

Für Rudolf Bultmann ist Mk 6,1-6a ein Musterbeispiel, »wie aus einem freien Logion eine ideale Szene komponiert ist«[144]. Das Logion

142. Vgl. J. MARCUS, *Mark 9,11-13: »As It Has Been Written«*, in ZNW 80 (1989) 42-63.
143. Cf. *ibid.*, pp. 54-55.
144. BULTMANN, *Geschichte* (Anm. 128), p. 30.

in P.Oxy. 1,30-35 sei Mk 6,4-5 gegenüber ursprünglicher und Mk 6,1-6a sei aus jenem Logion entstanden, wobei die zweite Hälfte des Logions in Erzählung umgesetzt wurde. Bultmann erwägt zudem, ob nicht VV. 2-3 und 5 auf eine traditionelle Erzählung über Jesu Erfolg zurückgehen können. Dann wäre der vorliegende Text – ein biographisches Apophthegma – aus zwei Elementen entstanden, dem Logion und der Szene des Erfolges Jesu. Die Erfolgsszene wäre dann (von Mk?) unter dem Eindruck der späteren Erfahrungen in das Gegenteil umgebogen worden[145].

In seiner 1937 zuerst erschienenen Bearbeitung des Markusevangeliums im Meyer'schen Kommentarwerk meint Ernst Lohmeyer, daß Mk 6,1-6a aus verschiedenen, nicht zusammenstimmenden Bruchstücken diverser Überlieferung zusammengesetzt worden sei: Das Logion in 6,4 (Vgl. P.Oxy. 1,30-35), Nachrichten über Jesu Verwandte und Haus, ein Bericht über die Ablehnung Jesu in Nazareth[146].

Nach der Entdeckung der Nag-Hammadi Schriften 1947 konnte man P.Oxy. 1,30-35 mit ThEv 31 identifizieren. Gegen Bultmann versucht Ernst Haenchen geltend zu machen, daß das ThEv nicht nur in Spruch 31 bzw. P.Oxy. 1,30-35[147] einen Doppelspruch überliefere, sondern, wie andere Sprüche, etwa 27 und 47, zeigten, »Einzelsprüche durch die Hinzufügung von Parallelen erweitert«[148].

Die Überlieferung von Doppelsprüchen ist aber kein Spezifikum des ThEv. Sie findet sich bereits bei Mk (Vgl. Mk 2,17 mit P.Oxy. 1224) und in der sehr frühen, vom MkEv und der Redenquelle aufgenommenen Überlieferungschicht (Vgl. Mk 8,34.35//MtQ 10,38.39). Gewichtiger ist das Argument von Wolfgang Schrage, daß P.Oxy. wie Lk δεκτός und nicht das ἄτιμος von Mk bzw. Mt habe. Da das δεκτός in Lk 4,24 auf den Einfluß des LXX-Zitates von Jes in Lk 4,19 zurückzuführen ist[149], könnte das δεκτός in P.Oxy. 1,31 Berührung mit der redaktionellen Ebene des LkEv verraten[150]. Das außerhalb der LXX und der urchristlichen Literatur seltene Verbaladjektiv wird jeweils im Sinne von »willkommen« verwendet[151].

145. *Ibid.*, pp. 30-31.
146. Vgl. Lohmeyer, *Evangelium* (Anm. 129), pp. 110-111.
147. Text nach H. Atteridge in B. Layton (ed.), *The Coptic Gnostic Library. Nag Hammadi Codex II,2-7* (NHS, 20), Leiden, 1989.
148. Vgl. E. Haenchen, *Historie und Verkündigung bei Markus und Lukas*, in Id., *Die Bibel und Wir. Gesammelte Aufsätze.* Zweiter Band, Tübingen, 1968, p. 160.
149. Nach den Belegen bei LSJM ein seltenes Wort. Pape verweist nur auf das Vorkommen im NT. In gPAT nur im anonymen jüdischen Fragment in Barn 5,18 und in einem Callisthenes-Zitat in 24,12. In der LXX aber öfters, auch als Übersetzung von רָצוֹן Lukas und Paulus übernehmen die Übersetzung der LXX von Jes in den Zitaten in Lk 4,19 und 2 Kor 6,2. In Lk 4,24, Apg 10,35 und Phil 4,18 wirkt die LXX-Sprache nach. Das Vorkommen bei den Apostolischen Vätern in Barn 3,2;14,9 (15,8) und in HerSim (passim; z.B. 51,1-2; 52,3; 53,1-4; 67,3-4) verdient eine Untersuchung.
150. So W. Schrage, *Das Verhältnis des Thomas-Evangeliums zur synoptischen Tradition und zu den koptischen Evangelien Übersetzungen* (BZNW, 29), Berlin, pp. 75-76.
151. Vgl. BAA, s.v.; LN, 34.54.

Nimmt man den Einfluß von Lk 2,24 auf P.Oxy. 1,30-33 und ThEv 31,1 an, bleibt das Problem, wie P.Oxy 1,33-35 bzw. ThEv 31,2 enstanden ist. Daß das zweite Glied des Doppellogions in ThEv 31,2 bzw. P.Oxy. 1,33-35 »eine sekundäre Weiterbildung in Analogie zu der eingliedrigen Form des Maschal der Synoptiker« sei, die die Synoptiker voraussetzt, wie Michael Fieger vor kurzem im Anschluß an Schrage meinte[152], ist kaum zutreffend. Der Vorgang, daß aus Erzählungen Logien entstehen, wäre ungewöhnlich. Wahrscheinlich transformierte Mk einen Doppelspruch in eine Erzählung, wie schon Bultmann meinte. Dann ist die »wilkommene« Übereinstimmung zwischen dem Papyrus bzw. ThEv 31 und Lk 4,24 nicht so hoch zu bewerten wie bei Schrage und Fieger.

Es gibt ohnehin noch ein zweites Problem, das ensteht, wenn man ThEv 31,1 vorschnell als Rezeption von Lk 2,24 einstuft. Es gibt drei logische Varianten des Spruches. Es handelt sich dabei um drei »performanical variations« desselben Logions:

(a) Die negative Prädikation eines undeterminierten Propheten in Joh 4,44 (Ein Prophet hat in seiner eigenen Heimatstadt keine Ehre) und in P.Oxy. 1,30-33 (Ein Prophet ist in seiner Heimatstadt nicht willkommen).

(b) Die eingeschränkt positive Prädikation eines undeterminierten Propheten in Mk 6,4 bzw. Mt 13,57b (Ein Prophet ist nicht ehrenlos, außer in seiner Heimat).

(c) Die positive Prädikation mit Verneinung des Subjekts in Lk 4,24 (Kein Prophet ist willkommen in seiner Heimat).

Der Papyrus benützt zwar wie Mk 6,4 οὐκ ἔστιν ... προφήτης ..., es handelt sich aber um eine negative Aussage mit undeterminiertem Subjekt. Wäre das negative ἄτιμος in einer positiven Prädikation verwendet worden, wäre die komplizierte, für Mk typische Formulierung mit Ausnahmesatz nötig, damit die Aussage noch logisch stimmt. Es gibt gute Gründe, mit Joseph Fitzmyer über P.Oxy. 1,30-35 zu urteilen: »The first part of this saying should be considered as authentic as the canonical parallels«[153].

Erich Gräßer hat sich aber von Haenchens Ablehnung eines selbständigen Wertes des Doppellogions im ThEv 31 überzeugen lassen. Er bemüht sich daher, aufzuzeigen, daß Mk aus der Tradition lediglich bekannt war, daß Jesus in seiner Heimatstadt ohne Erfolg predigte (V. 5a). Alles andere in der Perikope schreibt er der mkn. Redaktion zu. Für ihn handelt es sich bei Mk 6,1-6a um einen stark redaktionell geformten Text[154].

Eduard Schweizer versucht nun, im Rahmen der seinerzeit aufkommenden Redaktionskritik konsequent zwischen Redaktion und Tradi-

---

152. Vgl. M. Fieger, Das Thomasevangelium. Einleitung, Kommentar und Systematik (NTAbh, 22), Münster, 1991, pp. 117-118.

153. J.A. Fitzmyer, The Oxyrhynchus Logoi of Jesus and the Coptic Gospel according to Thomas (1959), in Id., Essays on the Semitic Background of the New Testament, London, 1971, pp. 355-433, Zitat p. 402.

154. Vgl. E. Grässer, Jesus in Nazareth (Mc 6,1-6a). Bemerkungen zur Redaktion und Theologie des Markus, in Id., et al., Jesus in Nazareth (BZNW, 40), Berlin, 1972, pp. 1-37, dort pp. 13, 27-28.

tion zu unterscheiden[155]. Er erkennt in Mk 6,1.2a + b mkn. Redaktion. »V. 2 erinnert genau an 1,21.27a«. V. 5b korrigiere V. 5a und sei somit redaktionell. »Zur (mündlichen?) Tradition dürften also VV. 3.4 (bis 'Vaterstadt'...) und V. 5a gehören«. Nach Schweizer habe Mk durch seine redaktionellen Wendungen (VV. 1-2.5b) aus der Erkennung des Propheten die Verwerfung dessen, der mehr als ein Prophet ist, gemacht. Hieraus folgen verschiedene redaktionskritische Hypothesen.

Konservativ schätzt Rudolf Pesch die redaktionelle Tätigkeit des Mk ein. Die biographisch-apophthegmatische Erzählung von der Verwerfung Jesu in seiner Vaterstadt ist von Mk durch V. 1a redaktionell mit dem vorhergehenden Kontext verbunden und im Blick auf die nachfolgende Missionserzählung durch V. 1c erweitert worden. V. 5b ist eine einschränkende Interpolation, sonst habe der Evangelist nur noch in V. 2e τοιαῦται in die traditionelle Erzählung eingefügt[156]. Pesch geht davon aus, daß die »in Parataxe gereiht(e), durch zweifache direkte Rede ausgezeichnet(e)«[157] vormkn. Erzählung in VV. 1b.2-5a.6a Mk ausformuliert vorlag.

In seinem einflußreichen Markuskommentar versucht Joachim Gnilka, die mkn. Vorlage zu rekonstruieren. Wie Pesch sieht er den ursprünglichen Perikopenanfang in καὶ ἔρχεται ὁ Ἰησοῦς εἰς Ναζαρέτ. Der jetzige erste Satz sowie die Erwähnung der Jünger in V. 1b gehe auf das Konto des Evangelisten, der auch den Auftritt in der Synagoge (V. 2a) in Anlehnung an 1,21-22 formuliert habe. Erst Mk habe den Prophetenspruch in V. 4 in die Tradition eingefügt und in einem zweiten Teil um die Verwandten und das Haus ergänzt. Verse 2b und 3 seien traditionell. Dies sei u.a. daran zu erkennen, daß Mk sonst nie von der Weisheit spräche. Die zwei Verse bildeten mit VV. 5a und 6a eine traditionelle Erzählung, die keiner bekannten Erzählform zuzuordnen sei. Als Apophthegma lasse die »sui generis« Erzählung sich nicht beschreiben. Zwischen den traditionellen Versen 5a und 6a habe der Evangelist noch den Nachsatz V. 5b eingefügt[158].

Auch Robert Guelich folgt in seinem Kommentar der Tendenz, die Einleitung in VV. 1-2a, V. 4b + c als Erweiterung und V. 5b als Einfügung dem Evangelisten zuzuschreiben[159].

Dietrich-Alex Koch, der zurückhaltender bei der Trennung von Tradition und Redaktion ist, setzt stärker überlieferungskritisch an. Seiner Meinung nach ist »(d)er Ausgangspunkt der Traditionsbildung

---

155. Vgl. zum Folgenden E. SCHWEIZER, *Markus*, [17]1989, pp. 64-65.

156. Vgl. R. PESCH, *Das Markusevangelium*. I. Teil (HTK, II/1), Freiburg/Br, [2]1977, pp. 315 und 322.

157. *Ibid.*, p. 316.

158. Vgl. J. GNILKA, *Das Evangelium nach Markus*. 1. Teilband. *Mk 1,1–8,26* (EKK, II/1), Neukirchen-Zürich, 1978, pp. 228-229.

159. Vgl. R. GUELICH, *Mark 1–8:28* (Word Biblical Commentary, 34A), Dallas, TX, 1989, pp. 306-307.

von Mk 6,1ff. ... das Logion von V. 4 (ohne die nachträgliche Erweiterung um die συγγενεῖς und die οἰκία, die in eine entsprechende Szene gefaßt wurde.) Diese sei zumindest noch in V. 3 erkennbar«[160]. Bereits vormkn. sei die Tradition von VV. 3-4. um das Thema vom Zusammenhang zwischen Glauben und Wunder in VV. 5a und 6a erweitert worden und mit einer Einleitung – hinter dem jetzigen V. 2 – versehen worden. Die mkn. Redaktion von Mk 6,1-6a sei begrenzt. Es handele sich nicht um eine neue Interpretation, sondern um eine Akzentuierung der Tradition. Der Evangelist habe V. 1 gebildet, V. 2a überarbeitet, V. 4b (καὶ ἐν τοῖς συγγενεῦσιν κτλ.) ergänzt und V. 5b eingeschoben[161].

Für Dieter Lührmann[162] dagegen ist nur V. 4 im Kern eindeutig traditionell, »wie die von Mk unabhängige Parallele Joh 4,44 zeigt«. Mk hat das Logion wegen des Kontextes erweitert. Alles andere, d.h. VV. 1-3.5-6, »entspricht so sehr der markinischen Redaktion, daß eine weitergehende Scheidung von Tradition und Redaktion nicht mehr möglich erscheint«. Lührmann hält V. 1 für redaktionell. »2a zeigt das für Mk typische Motiv des Lehrens Jesu und erinnert den Leser an Jesu Auftreten in Kapharnaum (1,21-28), ebenso zunächst die Reaktion der Hörer in 2b...«. Auch die Erwähnung der Wunder am Schluß von V. 2 gehe auf Mk zurück.

Angesichts dieses Aufgebotes, das sich für diese Perikope durch zusätzliche Alternativen ergänzen läßt, und der Tatsache, daß es bei anderen Perikopen nicht anders aussieht, verwundert es nicht, daß man zunehmend davon absieht, die Trennung von Redaktion und Tradition zum Ausgangspunkt der Interpretation des Markustextes zu machen.

b. Ein Vorschlag

Hiermit stellt sich für uns die Frage, ob sich vormarkinische Tradition hier anders als unter überlieferungskritischem Gesichtspunkt postulieren läßt. Wir wissen, daß die Tradition, nach der Jesus aus Nazareth stammt, Markus bekannt war (Vgl. Mk 1,9.24; 10,47; 14,67; 16,6). Weiterhin war Markus bekannt, daß Jesus ein Handwerker war, daß seine Mutter namens Maria noch lebte (3,21.31-32)[163], daß sie und seine Brüder in Nazareth bekannt waren und daß seine Schwestern in Nazareth lebten (6,3). Ein Vergleich der VV. 4-5 mit dem Doppelspruch ThEv 31 / P.Oxy. 1,30-35 und die formkritische Einstufung des traditio-

---

160. Vgl. D.-A. KOCH, *Die Bedeutung der Wundererzählungen für die Christologie des Markusevangeliums* (BZNW, 42), Berlin, 1975, p. 150.
161. *Ibid.*, pp. 151-152.
162. Zum Folgenden vgl. LÜHRMANN, *Markusevangelium* (Anm. 45), p. 106.
163. Ob Maria, die Mutter von Jesus, Jakobus und Justus (Mk 6,3), mit Maria, der Mutter des kleinen Jakobus und des Justus (Mk 15,40) identisch ist, läßt der Text offen. Dem Leser steht es frei, ob er diese Kombination vornimmt.

nellen Spruches zeigten[164], daß Markus hier auf ein bekanntes Spruchpaar zurückgreift. Er hat die ganze Perikope unter Aufnahme einiger biographischer Informationen über Jesus und seine Familie um den Spruch herum komponiert. Dabei übernahm er nicht den Wortlaut des Spruches, sondern formulierte in der für ihn typischen doppelten Ausdrucksweise, erst negativ und dann postiv[165]. Die zweite Hälfte des Doppelspruches, keine Heilung von Bekannten durch den Arzt, wurde in V. 5 erzählerisch verwendet, aber ebenfalls in der doppelten Formulierungsweise des Evangelisten. Möglich wäre, daß zusätzlich eine Tradition über die Ablehnung Jesu in Nazareth bei der Abfassung der Perikope nachwirkte. Insgesamt gesehen ist aber mit Ausnahme von Jesu Beruf, den Namen seiner Familienangehörigen und dem Inhalt von 6,4a und 5a die jetzige Komposition eine freie Formulierung des Markus. Um einen Doppelspruch herum, den er selbst neu formulierte, schuf er eine Erzählung. Parallelen zu diesem Verfahren finden sich auch in Mk 8,14-21 und 8,12-13[166].

Angesichts dieser Beobachtungen und Möglichkeiten scheint es mir doch voreilig, die Frage nach der vormarkinischen Tradition und ihrer Bedeutung für den vorliegenden Text ad acta zu legen. Bei den Erzählungen muß man in der Tat vorsichtig sein. Eine systematische Auswertung der Beziehungen zwischen Q und Markus sowie Thomas und Markus kann uns helfen, Umrisse und Motive von Teilen der von Markus literarisierten Überlieferung zu rekonstruieren und das Geflecht der vorsynoptischen Überlieferung ein wenig zu entzerren.

Kirchliche Hochschule Berlin   Cilliers BREYTENBACH
Teltower Damm 120-122
D-1000 Berlin 37

---

164. Schon BULTMANN, *Geschichte* (Anm. 128), p. 30, weist auf Parallelen bei Wetstein.
165. Vgl. hierzu F. NEIRYNCK, *Duality in Mark. Contributions to the Study of Markan Redaction* (BETL, 31), Leuven, ²1988, p. 89.
166. Zu Mk 8,14-21 vgl. BREYTENBACH, *Nachfolge*, pp. 191-206.

PROGYMNASTIC RHETORICAL COMPOSITION
AND PRE-GOSPEL TRADITIONS
A NEW APPROACH

During the last decade, a number of NT interpreters have rein-
troduced Hellenistic-Roman rhetorical treatises into the context of
interpretation of the gospels, and some of this work is opening a
remarkably new interpretational approach[1]. For various reasons,
however, the inner workings of this new approach have not become
generally known and understood. The goal of this essay is to explain
the potential of this kind of rhetorical criticism for analysis of pre-
gospel traditions. Since it is impossible to explain the potential of the
method with any success unless the reader understands the data in the
ancient rhetorical treatises that provide the insights for the analysis, this
essay attempts to perform two tasks.

First, this essay correlates key passages in Aelius Theon's *Progymnasmata* (Preliminary Exercises), the *Rhetorica ad Herennium*, and
Hermogenes' *Progymnasmata* with passages in the gospels to exhibit the
rationale for using insights from these documents in interpretation of
New Testament gospels. Since the *ad Herennium* was written ca. 84
B.C.E., Theon's *Progymnasmata* 50-100 C.E., the gospels ca. 65-100 C.E.,
and Hermogenes' *Progymnasmata* late second century C.E.[2], all of these
documents show us primary culture-transmitting activities in Mediterranean society prior to and during the beginnings of Christianity.
Theon's *Progymnasmata*, written in Greek and directly contemporary
with the gospels, is a central document for our new understanding. It is
truly remarkable that a critical edition and English translation of this
document has been made only recently and still is not readily available
to interpreters of the gospels[3].

Second, the essay uses insights from these rhetorical treatises to

---

1. See D.F. WATSON, *The New Testament and Greco-Roman Rhetoric: A Bibliography*,
in *JETS* 31/4 (1988) 465-472, pp. 469-470; *The New Testament and Greco-Roman
Rhetoric: A Bibliographical Update*, in *JETS* 33/4 (1990) 513-524, pp. 517-520.

2. For the dates of Theon and Hermogenes, see R.F. HOCK – E.N. O'NEIL, *The Chreia
in Ancient Rhetoric*. Volume I. *The Progymnasmata*, Atlanta, GA, Scholars, 1986, pp. 64,
156. For the date of the *Rhetorica ad Herennium*, see G.A. KENNEDY, *New Testament
Interpretation through Rhetorical Criticism*, Chapel Hill, University of North Carolina
Press, 1984, p. 12.

3. Available in J. BUTTS, *The "Progymnasmata" of Theon: A New Text with Transla-
tion and Commentary*, Ann Arbor, MI, University Microfilms International, 1987.
Chapter 3 of Theon's treatise, on the Chreia, is available in HOCK–O'NEIL, *The Chreia in
Ancient Rhetoric* (n. 2), pp. 61-112.

probe pre-gospel traditions. Perhaps it comes as a surprise to the reader
that rhetorical criticism would have any goal other than interpretation
of the final form of a text. The subject that occupies the *Progymnasmata*, however, is the "re-performance" of well-known traditions in
Mediterranean society and culture[4]. While some of the traditions come
from "well-known", that is orally transmitted, stories and sayings in
the culture; others have been gleaned from specific authors and documents Theon cites. The topic of discussion and the examples the author
has composed in the *Progymnasmata*, then, are based on written and
oral sources, and this makes the treatise a gold mine for the interpreter
of the New Testament gospels. Rhetorical critics who limit their
analysis to "literary rhetoric", that is, rhetoric "restrained" by literary
boundaries[5], often have little or no interest in documents like this from
antiquity. They bring social and cultural values and meanings to the
gospel traditions intuitively and unconsciously from their own modern
environment without programmatically investigating first century Mediterranean values and meanings. Rhetorical critics who are influenced by
both ancient and modern rhetorical treatises and theories, in contrast,
consciously "revalue" restrained literary rhetoric by exploring multiple
dimensions of social and cultural meanings in the context in which the
traditions were initially composed and recomposed. It is no surprise,
then, that some recent rhetorical critics have gleaned insights from the
Progymnasmata contemporary with the gospels to analyze pre-gospel
traditions[6]. In turn, these treatises provide the basis for this author's
willingness to address, at the *Colloquium Biblicum Lovaniense* honoring
Frans Neirynck (18-20 August 1992), the potential of rhetorical criticism for analysis of pre-gospel traditions.

The twofold undertaking in this essay unfolds in four sections. The
first section explains the place of analysis of pre-gospel traditions and
sources in the context of modern rhetorical analysis. The second section
explains how a rhetorical understanding of gospel traditions differs
decisively from an approach that juxtaposes oral culture with scribal
culture, as literary-historical critics traditionally have done and still do.
The third section describes the rhetorical nature of culture-transmitting
tradition in three steps: (a) the inner rhetorical nature of traditional
forms; (b) abbreviation, expansion, and addition to traditional forms;

---

4. See chapters I and II of Theon's *Progymnasmata*.

5. See B. VICKERS, *Introduction*, in ID. (ed.), *Rhetoric Revalued* (Medieval & Renais-
sance Texts and Studies, 19), Binghamton, NY, Center for Medieval & Renaissance
Studies, 1982, pp. 13-39; cited by W. WUELLNER, *Where Is Rhetorical Criticism Taking
Us?*, in *CBQ* 49 (1987) 448-463, p. 453.

6. B.L. MACK, *A Myth of Innocence: Mark and Christian Origins*, Philadelphia, PA,
Fortress, 1988; B.L. MACK – V.K. ROBBINS, *Patterns of Persuasion in the Gospels*,
Sonoma, CA, Polebridge Press, 1989; and B.L. MACK, *Rhetoric and the New Testament*,
Minneapolis, MN, Fortress, 1990.

and (c) elaboration of traditional forms. The fourth section presents guidelines for analysis of pre-gospel traditions based on insights gleaned from the discussions and displays of progymnastic rhetorical composition in Hellenistic-Roman rhetorical treatises from late Mediterranean antiquity.

I. ANALYSIS OF PRE-GOSPEL TRADITIONS AND SOURCES AS INTERTEXTUAL ANALYSIS

The desire of interpreters to use rhetorical criticism to analyze pre-gospel traditions arises out of the confrontation between the literary-historical paradigm, which dominated the last half of the nineteenth century and the first two-thirds of the twentieth century, and the socio-rhetorical paradigm, which is grounded in modern sociolinguistics and cultural anthropology. The confrontation results from the privileging of sequential effect (diachrony) by the literary-historical paradigm versus the privileging of social and cultural interrelation (synchrony) by the socio-rhetorical paradigm. Each paradigm has an interest in the phenomena privileged by the other, but each paradigm embeds the privileged data of the other in the context of its own privileged data. To analyze pre-gospel traditions, literary-historical criticism engages first in source analysis; then it approaches the final text with a system of evaluation the interpreter develops in the context of a distinction between words that were reproduced from sources and words that were newly written to produce the final text. Socio-rhetorical criticism, in contrast, explores first the social and cultural argumentation in the final form of the text; then it approaches source analysis and sequential effect with a system of evaluation the interpreter develops in the context of the social and cultural meanings at work in the argumentation.

A socio-rhetorical critic approaches a text very much like a cultural anthropologist like Clifford Geertz approaches the interpretation of a village. The approach presupposes that a text, like culture, has "thickness" that results from complex webs of signification[7]. What one sees at first, or even later, is only part of the deeply-textured networks of signification that constitute that village or text. Another presupposition of the approach comes from sociolinguists like M.A.K. Halladay and Roger Fowler who perceive language to be a social product and tool[8]. Language functions in a context of utterance, a context of culture, and

7. C. GEERTZ, *The Interpretation of Cultures*, New York, Basic Books, 1973; *Local Knowledge: Further Essays in Interpretive Anthropology*, New York, Basic Books, 1983.

8. M.A.K. HALLADAY, *Language as Social Semiotic: The Social Interpretation of Language and Meaning*, University Park Press, 1978; R.M. FOWLER, *Literature as Social Discourse: the Practice of Linguistic Criticism*, Bloomington, Indiana University Press, 1981; R. HODGE – G. KRESS, *Social Semiotics*, Ithaca, NY, Cornell University Press, 1988.

a context of reference[9]. This means that words are always actively in dialogue with one another[10]. To restrain words to their "context of utterance", as traditional literary critics do, is an arbitrary restraint for particular ideological purposes. In contrast, socio-rhetorical critics "revalue" the words through multidimensional explorations of meanings and values in the context of their composition and transmission.

The metaphor of texture informs the socio-rhetorical critic as he or she pursues the "thickness" of texts. This metaphor guides the interpreter to four arenas of texture in texts: (a) inner texture; (b) intertexture; (c) social and cultural texture; and (d) ideological and theological texture[11]. New Testament interpreters who have used modern literary criticism during the 1970's and 80's have focussed primarily on the inner texture of texts[12]. In the same environment, however, new vitality has surged into the investigation of "intertexture" in texts[13], and this pursuit has been supported by the turn of secular literary criticism to a "new historicism" informed by anthropological conceptions of literature[14]. From the perspective of postmodern literary criticism, source analysis is a form of intertextual analysis[15]. The

9. R.M. FOWLER, *Linguistic Criticism*, Oxford - New York, Oxford University Press, 1986, pp. 85-101.

10. See V.K. ROBBINS, *The Reversed Contextualization of Psalm 22 in the Markan Crucifixion: A Socio-Rhetorical Analysis*, in *The Four Gospels 1992. FS Frans Neirynck*, 2 (BETL, 100), Leuven, University Press, 1992, pp. 1191-1183, esp. 1181-1183.

11. V.K. ROBBINS, *Jesus the Teacher: A Socio-Rhetorical Interpretation of Mark*, Paperback edition with a new introduction, Minneapolis, MN, Fortress, 1992, pp. XXVII-XXXVIII.

12. V.K. ROBBINS, *Jesus the Teacher* (n. 11), pp. XXIX-XXXVIII. See D.O. VIA, Jr., *The Parables: Their Literary and Existential Dimension*, Philadelphia, PA, Fortress, 1967; N. PERRIN, *What is Redaction Criticism?*, Philadelphia, PA, Fortress, 1969; W.A. BEARDSLEE, *Literary Criticism of the New Testament*, Philadelphia, PA, Fortress, 1970; R.C. TANNE-HILL, *The Sword of His Mouth* (SBL Semeia Supplements, 1), Philadelphia, PA, Fortress - Missoula, MT, Scholars, 1975; N.R. PETERSEN, Jr., *Literary Criticism for New Testament Critics*, Philadelphia, PA, Fortress, 1978; D. RHOADS - D. MICHIE, *Mark as Story: An Introduction to the Narrative of a Gospel*, Philadelphia, PA, Fortress, 1982; R.A. CULPEPPER, *Anatomy of the Fourth Gospel: A Study in Literary Design*, Philadelphia, PA, Fortress, 1983; S.D. MOORE, *Literary Criticism and the Gospels: The Theoretical Challenge*, New Haven, CT - London, Yale University Press, 1989; M.A. POWELL, *What Is Narrative Criticism?*, Minneapolis, MN, Fortress, 1990.

13. E.g., H. KOESTER - J.M. ROBINSON, *Trajectories through Early Christianity*, Philadelphia, PA, Fortress, 1971; J.S. KLOPPENBORG, *The Formation of Q: Trajectories in Ancient Wisdom Collections*, Philadelphia, PA, Fortress, 1987; B.L. MACK, *A Myth of Innocence: Mark and Christian Origins*, Philadelphia, PA, Fortress, 1988; J.D. CROSSAN, *The Cross that Spoke: The Origins of the Passion Narrative*, San Francisco, CA, Harper & Row, 1988.

14. L. PATTERSON, *"Literary History"*, in F. LENTRICCHIA - T. MCLAUGHLIN (eds.), *Critical Terms for Literary Study*, Chicago, IL - London, University of Chicago Press, 1987, pp. 250-262; D. SIMPSON, *Literary Criticism and the Return to 'History'*, in *Critical Inquiry* 14 (1988).

15. S. DRAISMA (ed.), *Intertextuality in Biblical Writings. Essays in honour of Bas van Iersel*, Kampen, Kok, 1989.

intertexture of the source analyst is restrained by the inner texture of the text itself and by texts that exist by dint of historical accident. Source critics may restrict their comparison to other extant texts to establish genetic relationships among them, or they may create source "intertexts" on the basis of boundaries they create in the inner texture of the text. Form and redaction critics expand this kind of analysis by creating more nuanced source boundaries, distinguishing certain wording in the text from other wording to create "written or oral" sources[16]. In both instances, a certain kind of "intertext" is created by the analyst and brought into the context of interpretation of the final text.

The socio-rhetorical critic not only expands the boundaries of intertextual analysis of the text but also programmatically investigates the social, cultural, and ideological texture of the text. The result is that, in a context where some New Testament critics perform "restrained" rhetorical analysis in the form of "New Critical" and formalist literary critical approaches[17], socio-rhetorical critics are using culturally oriented approaches that are informed by postmodern literary criticism and "revalued" rhetorical criticism[18]. A socio-rhetorical critic programmatically brings social, cultural, and ideological meanings and issues into an environment of inner textual and intertextual analysis. The approach privileges the arguments in the final form (inner texture) of the text by going to them first; then the approach programmatically "revalues" the rhetoric through various kinds of intertextual, social, cultural and ideological forms of analysis.

The task in this essay, then, is to turn to pre-gospel traditions with insights from culturally informed literary and rhetorical approaches. We begin with matters of inner texture, in order to understand the context of utterance for the words in the text. Then we turn to intertexture, where the issue is the context of reference – those things to which the words purport to refer in relation to other people's referential use of the words. Literary-historical criticism contributes especially to the exploration of intertexture, but its boundaries are intentionally limited by "genetic" presuppositions. Socio-rhetorical criticism expands the boundaries to include texts that present meanings, values, and uses

16. See an excellent recent example in J. LAMBRECHT, *John and Jesus in Mark 1,1-15. Markan Redaction of Q?*, in *NTS* 38 (1992) 337-356.

17. E.g., R.C. TANNEHILL, *The Narrative Unity of Luke-Acts. A Literary Interpretation.* Vol. 1: *The Gospel according to Luke*, Philadelphia, PA, Fortress, 1986; N.R. PETERSEN, Jr., *Rediscovering Paul: Philemon and the Sociology of Paul's Narrative World*, Philadelphia, PA, Fortress, 1985; M.A. TOLBERT, *Sowing the Gospel: Mark's World in Literary-Historical Perspective*, Minneapolis, MN, Fortress, 1989.

18. E.g., MACK, *A Myth of Innocence* (n. 6); C. MYERS, *Binding the Strong Man: A Political Reading of Mark's Story of Jesus*, Maryknoll, NY, Orbis, 1988; B.B. SCOTT, *Hear Then the Parable: A Commentary on the Parables of Jesus*, Minneapolis, MN, Fortress, 1989.

of words in the cultural environment without proof of a genetic relation to the foregrounded text. The intertextual use of words opens the issue of the context of culture; thus the analysis moves next to the social and cultural texture of the text. To these contexts, which have been the special domain of sociolinguists, socio-rhetorical criticism adds the ideological texture of the text. In this context, approaches that emphasize socio-ideological perspectives in the text, in interpretation, and in the present interpreter – approaches that use terms like ideology, liberation, feminist, or African-American – contribute greatly to the exploration of the ideological texture of the text[19].

II. RHETORICAL CULTURE

As an interpreter approaches a New Testament text, a foremost issue is the kind of "writing" culture the interpreter creates as a context for understanding the words in the document. Literary-historical criticism presupposes a polarity between oral culture and scribal cultural for its context of analysis. In contrast, socio-rhetorical criticism presupposes that rhetorical culture dominated Mediterranean society during the first part of the common era and rhetorical culture provided the environment in which early Christians produced their first literature. One of the primary characteristics of a rhetorical culture is lively interaction between oral and written composition[20]. Only during the last half of the second century did a scribal culture that resisted rhetorical composition as it reperformed the gospel traditions begin to dominate the transmission of early Christian literature[21]. For this stage of transmission the prevailing literary-historical methods of analysis are highly informative. To impose such a scribal environment on the context in which the New Testament gospels initially were written and re-written is a fundamental error.

Source analysis in New Testament texts has been guided, and for the most part still is guided, by textual criticism that imagines a rhetorically disengaged scribal culture as the context for the production of the New Testament gospels. Such a scribal culture expects scribes to move their eyes back and forth from manuscript to manuscript as they copy word for word, intentionally modifying wording only for editorial purposes; or to write down what they hear as another person reads from a manuscript or performs a speech. This approach envisions the relation of texts to one another and to non-extant sources in an environment of

---

19. ROBBINS, *Jesus the Teacher* (n. 11), pp. XXIII-XXXVIII.

20. T.M. LENTZ, *Orality and Literacy in Hellenic Greece*, Carbondale – Edwardsville, Southern Illinois University Press, 1989.

21. H. KOESTER, *Synoptische Überlieferung bei den apostolischen Vätern* (TU, 65), Berlin, Akademie-Verlag, 1957; *Ancient Christian Gospels: Their History and Development*, Philadelphia, PA, Trinity Press International, 1990, pp. 31-43.

accurate copying of texts, and this is the context of culture imagined by literary-historical critics. This image of the context of writing has informed text, source, form, and redaction critics alike. Frans Neirynck, who is being honored in the context of the Colloquium for which this essay is being written, has contributed majestically from this point of view, and his contributions are so comprehensive that they are helping us to open a new era in Gospel analysis and interpretation[22].

Wittingly or unwittingly, literary-historical criticism during the twentieth century has been based on a "printing press" mentality, a way of thinking about texts that presupposes a stability in their wording that emerges only when it is possible to produce a significant number of texts with the same exact wording. While Werner Kelber made this point almost a decade ago, the responses to his observations have been less than satisfactory, and he himself has not had a model to lead him out of this conceptuality as he has performed his own analysis[23]. John Dominic Crossan has approached source criticism creatively during the last decade, combining "deconstructive" criticism with a postmodern "game" approach. His production of "text fragments"[24] and his reversal of genetic relationships between canonical and extracanonical gospels[25] have helped us to see deep weaknesses in traditional source analyses and to have glimpses of another mode of analysis[26]. But his approach is not guided by a "pre-printing press" approach. Rather, it is guided by experiences in a technologically driven "information culture". People in this kind of culture are in a context of "information saturation". In an environment characterized by "the more information the better", individuals and teams begin to play with information, juxtaposing fragments – "sound bites" – in a gamelike manner that makes rules from day to day that befit their socio-ideological location. This kind of cultural setting does share much in common with the rhetorical nature of first and second century Mediterranean society, but

22. See esp. F. NEIRYNCK, *Duality in Mark. Contributions to the Study of the Markan Redaction* (BETL, 31), Leuven, University Press, 1972, ²1988 (revised edition, with Supplementary Notes, pp. 215-252); ID., in collaboration with T. HANSEN and F. VAN SEGBROECK, *The Minor Agreements of Matthew and Luke against Mark with a Cumulative List* (BETL, 37), Leuven, University Press, 1974; *Evangelica Gospel Studies – Études d'évangile. Collected Essays* (BETL, 60), Leuven, University Press - Peeters, 1982; *Evangelica II. 1982-1991. Collected Essays* (BETL, 99), Leuven, University Press - Peeters, 1991.

23. W.H. KELBER, *The Oral and the Written Gospel*, Philadelphia, PA, Fortress, 1983.

24. J.D. CROSSAN, *In Fragments. The Aphorisms of Jesus*, San Francisco, CA, Harper & Row, 1983.

25. J.D. CROSSAN, *The Cross that Spoke: The Origins of the Passion Narrative*, San Francisco, CA, Harper & Row, 1988.

26. V.K. ROBBINS, *Picking Up the Fragments: From Crossan's Analysis to Rhetorical Analysis*, in *Forum* 1/2 (1985) 31-64.

there also are significant differences that must be incorporated into our approach to the New Testament gospels.

As Kelber has addressed Crossan's work, he has succumbed to Elizabeth Eisenstein's presupposition that our challenge is to grasp the intellectual and conceptual apparatus of the kind of scribal activity that intentionally refrains from rhetorical composition[27]. Eisenstein's image emerges from medieval culture, not the Hellenistic-Roman period of late antiquity. Both Kelber and Crossan consider our task to be to understand the relation of oral culture to scribal culture. But this is not correct. Our challenge is to understand the kind of scribal activity that does not refrain from progymnastic rhetorical composition, that is, the level of rhetorical composition that reperforms written and oral sources and traditions in the manner we see in the *Progymnasmata*.

For our purposes, then, it is important to distinguish between an oral culture, a rhetorical culture, and a scribal culture. The differences are as follows: (a) an oral culture has no written literature in view; (b) a rhetorical culture is aware of written documents, uses written and oral language interactively, and composes both orally and scribally in a rhetorical manner[28]; (c) a scribal culture focuses on "copying" and "editing" either oral statements or written texts[29]. Our task is to interpret the composition and recomposition of the gospels in a rhetorical culture prior to the advent of the scribal culture in which they were transmitted from the third century onward.

III. PROGYMNASTIC RHETORICAL COMPOSITION

The purpose of this section is to introduce a new way of envisioning the relation of gospel accounts to one another. The rhetorical manuscripts entitled *Progymnasmata* (Preliminary Exercises), the first of which comes from the first century of our era, and the *Rhetorica ad Herennium*, which comes from the first quarter of the first century B.C.E., are the most important ancient documents for helping us to develop this new approach[30]. The rhetorical perspective of Aelius Theon of Alexandria, which comes from our earliest extant *Progymnasmata*, reveals three basic aspects of culture-transmitting tradition: (a) its inner rhetorical nature; (b) rhetorical recitation, expansion, and addition; and (c) rhetorical elaboration. Theon's discussion of the chreia reveals these aspects most vividly.

27. E. EISENSTEIN, *The Printing Press as an Agent of Change*, Cambridge, University Press, 1979; W.H. KELBER, *From Aphorism to Sayings Gospel and from Parable to Narrative Gospel*, in *Forum* 1/1 (1985) 23-30.

28. LENTZ, *Orality and Literacy in Hellenic Greece* (n. 20).

29. V.K. ROBBINS, *Writing as a Rhetorical Act in Plutarch and the Gospels*, in D.F. WATSON (ed.), *Persuasive Artistry: Studies in New Testament Rhetoric in Honor of George A. Kennedy*, Sheffield, JSOT, 1991, pp. 142-168.

30. HOCK–O'NEIL, *The Chreia in Ancient Rhetoric* (n. 2).

1. *The Inner Rhetorical Nature of Culture-Transmitting Tradition*

The chapter on the chreia (speech or action attributed to a specific personage) in the *Progymnasmata* of Aelius Theon of Alexandria gives special insight into the rhetorical nature of culture-transmitting tradition. First, culture-transmitting tradition uses specific personages for its context of communication. Oral and written recital of action and speech attributed to specific persons in the situations of their daily lives is a central medium for transmitting the data, values, attitudes, and concepts of Mediterranean culture. The widespread presence of this medium in extant early Christian literature shows that significant sectors of early Christianity transmitted Christian traditions in the forms of the public rhetorical media. Sectors of early Christianity that generated idiosyncratic forms of tradition – forms disconnected from attributed action and speech – found it difficult to get their traditions into "public" discourse. These traditions were "esoteric" rather than "public". The kinds of Christian traditions that "lived on" in the culture were attributed to important personages or linked to speech and action so attributed.

A second primary characteristic of culture-transmitting tradition was its argumentative nature. Theon discusses the argumentative qualities of the chreia, the fable (μῦθος), and the narrative (διήγημα) in three individual chapters after his discussion of introductory matters. Incidentally, there is no chapter on the maxim (γνώμη) in Theon's *Progymnasmata*. This is an error that persists among some New Testament interpreters, probably as a result of emphases in the works of Martin Dibelius and Rudolf Bultmann. Since Theon placed the chapter on the chreia first, he exhibited the argumentative nature of culture-transmitting tradition most fully in the chapter on the chreia and referred back to this chapter in the later chapters. For this reason, the chapter on the chreia has been given pride of place among New Testament interpreters who have been developing an approach to early Christian literature that uses insights from its discussions[31].

From Theon's rhetorical perspective, argumentative aspects of culture-transmitting tradition are apparent from its manner of presentation. Chreiai, for example, can be expressed in the manner of: (a) a maxim; (b) an explanation; (c) a witty remark; (d) a syllogism; (e) an enthymeme; (f) an example; (g) a wish; (h) a symbol; (i) an ambiguous statement; (j) a change of subject; (k) or a combination of these. Since all of these are topics of discussion among ancient rhetoricians, the reader begins to see that even the smallest units of popular tradition are argumentative and the arguments cover a spectrum from the most basic

---

31. See the account and the bibliography in MACK, *Rhetoric and the New Testament* (n. 6).

aspects of life to the most cognitive aspects of reflective thinking. Since these inner attributes of chreiai are pervasive in the gospels, Theon's discussion of the inner rhetorical nature of the chreia is highly important for analysis of the gospels and of pre-gospel traditions. The evidence for this has been produced at length in other contexts and is readily available[32], so it will not be exhibited here.

2. Recitation, Internal Composition, and Addition to Culture-Transmitting Tradition

Another phenomenon Theon exhibits in his discussion of the chreia is the freedom, in fact the encouragement, in a rhetorical culture to use one's own wording when transmitting speech and action attributed to specific personages in the culture. Theon's first exercise with the chreia – the recitation (ἀπαγγελία) – reveals the manner in which a rhetorical environment presupposes that writing is thoroughly interactive with speaking. When a grammateus had gleaned attributed action or speech from written or oral tradition, he performed it orally as a chreia for his students and they wrote it "clearly in the same words or in others as well"[33]. In this initial exercise, writers are encouraged to be comfortable transmitting as much or as little verbatim wording as they wish. The requirement is clarity, not verbatim repetition. This exercise exhibits an approach to tradition that is different from a "copying" environment. When writers have learned this exercise, they move their eyes and ears freely away from a "source" as they "compose the tradition anew" with as much or as little verbatim replication as they wish. The extensive word variation in our gospels, in a context of extensive verbatim replication, is to be explained by this approach in the culture[34].

A presupposition that culture-transmitting traditions invite, in fact require, continual reformulation, just like speaking does, guides the exercises with the chreia. Theon reveals this in his statement that "not any of the good elements of rhetoric are at all useful unless each one practises writing every day for himself"[35]. The presupposition behind this is that people engage in oral argumentation each day. This argumentation contains significant repetition of previous statements in a context of significant variation. In order to learn to argue well, Theon says, a person should not only speak each day but also write each day. Performing oral and scribal activity in this way creates a rhetorical

32. V.K. ROBBINS, *The Chreia*, in D.E. AUNE (ed.), *Greco-Roman Literature and the New Testament: Selected Forms and Genres* (SBL Sources in Biblical Study, 21), Atlanta, GA, Scholars, 1988, pp. 13-16; MACK–ROBBINS, *Patterns of Persuasion in the Gospels* (n. 6); MACK, *Rhetoric and the New Testament* (n. 6).
33. HOCK–O'NEIL, *The Chreia in Ancient Rhetoric* (n. 2), p. 95.
34. ROBBINS, *Writing as a Rhetorical Act in Plutarch and the Gospels* (n. 29).
35. BUTTS, *The "Progymnasmata" of Theon* (n. 3), p. 107.

culture – one in which speech is influenced by writing and writing is influenced by speaking. Recitation, then, is the base of a rhetorical culture. People know that certain traditions exist in writing. They also know that all traditions, whether oral or written, need to be composed anew to meet the needs of the day. Each day as they spoke, they were interacting with written traditions; whenever they wrote, they were interacting with oral traditions. This interaction characterized their thinking, their speaking, and their writing.

After the recitation exercise, Theon presents exercises designed to cultivate skills for internal composition of the chreia and for addition of brief comments after the chreia. These exercises feature different inflections (cases and numbers), addition of comment, addition of objection, expansion, and abbreviation. These activities exhibit the manner in which a rhetorical culture can work creatively with the beginnings and endings of culture-transmitting traditions. The beginning may be modified to fit any context of speech, linking a tradition to subject, possessor, object, indirect object, person addressed, singular, dual, or plural (the inflection exercise). The ending may be extended by adding a comment after it that supports or objects to the argument in the chreia (the commentary and objection exercises). Then, the internal length of the chreia may be shortened as much as possible or expanded by amplifying the questions, responses, acts, and experiences in it (the abbreviation and expansion exercises)[36]. These exercises introduce, cultivate, and nurture a consciousness of and a facility with the internal argumentative potential of culture-transmitting traditions and the effect of brief comments after them.

3. *Elaboration of Culture-Transmitting Tradition*

Theon reveals yet another possibility with culture-transmitting traditions – their rhetorical elaboration (ἐργασία). Elaboration "works" a tradition toward the form of an essay or speech that presents a complete argument. Theon's seventh and eighth exercises discuss a first level of elaboration that emerges closely out of the environment of internal composition and addition of a comment. This level of composition amplifies the comment after the chreia by providing arguments for each part of the chreia, using topics, amplifications, digressions, and character delineations as the opportunity arises. This approach to chreia elaboration expands the statement in the chreia without adding significantly new rhetorical figures to its argumentation.

An example of first-level elaboration exists in Mk 7,14-23. The key verses for understanding the nature of the elaboration are as follows:

36. ROBBINS, *The Chreia* (n. 32).

Setting
Introduction: 14 And he [Jesus] called the people to him again, and said to them, "Hear me, all of you, and understand:
Chreia: 15 there is nothing outside a man which by going into him can defile him; but the things which come out of a man are what defile him".
Quaestio: 17 And when he had entered the house, and left the people, his disciples asked him about the parable.
  Argument for First Part of the Chreia
Character delineation: 18 And he said to them, "Then are you also without understanding? Do you not see that
Restatement of first part: whatever goes into a man from outside cannot defile him,
Rationale using a contrary: 19 since it enters, not his heart but his stomach, and so passes on?"
Parenthetical comment (minor digression): Thus he declared all foods clean.
  Argument for Second Part of the Chreia
Restatement of second part: 20 And he said, "What comes out of a man is what defiles a man.
Rationale using amplification: 21 For from within, out of the heart of man, come evil thoughts, fornication, theft, murder, adultery, 22 coveting, wickedness, deceit, licentiousness, evil eye, slander, pride, foolishness.
  Conclusion
23 All these evil things come from within, and they defile a man (RSV).

The progression of the elaboration from "each part of the chreia" and its use of "amplifications, digressions, and character delineations" reveal that this sequence is an instance of first-level elaboration. There is an initial recital of a chreia in 7,14-15. Then there is a restatement of the first part of the chreia in 7,18, followed by a rationale based on a contrary and a parenthetical comment in 7,19. After this, there is a restatement of the second part of the chreia in 7,20, followed by a rationale that uses amplification in 7,22 and a conclusion in 7,23. On the one hand, the comments after the initial chreia "rework" the chreia. On the other hand, elaboration does not add significantly new rhetorical figures to the initial chreia. The elaboration adds character delineations, rationales, a contrary, a brief digression, and an amplified list. All of this restates the thought in the initial abbreviated chreia in a mode closely related to the expansion of a chreia[37]. The form elaborates the chreia rather than simply expanding it, however, since a chreia is stated initially, then the thought in the chreia is worked into a speech that contains a sequence of argumentative steps and a conclusion. An expanded chreia, in contrast, delays the completion of the chreia statement to the end, so that the statements between the beginning and the ending all are part of the expanded chreia statement. In Mk 7,23,

37. HOCK–O'NEIL, *The Chreia in Ancient Rhetoric* (n. 2), pp. 100-103.

the conclusion restates the final part of the initial chreia, much like a speech concludes a topic that has been introduced at the beginning and developed in the body of the speech. The elaboration has added to the chreia by amplifying the initial assertions in a context of rationale and restatement.

There is a second level of elaboration that does not limit itself to expansion but introduces artistic and inartistic arguments that support the initial statement. Burton Mack has discussed this second level of rhetorical elaboration in great detail, and this form was especially directive for the analyses throughout *Patterns of Persuasion in the Gospel*[38]. In this instance the elaboration develops the meaning of the chreia with distinctly additional rhetorical figures that move the reasoning toward a complete argument.

The *Rhetorica ad Herennium* contains two discussions and exhibitions of argumentation that present the procedure and goal of second-level elaboration exceptionally well. Since these texts appear not to be readily available to most New Testament interpreters, the texts are displayed here, both in Latin and English translation. The presence of these texts also will allow us to refer to aspects of rhetorical composition that otherwise are unfamiliar to interpreters trained in the disciplines of form and redaction criticism. The first selection displays the basic constituents of a complete argument. This means, an argument that is perceived by members of Hellenistic-Roman society to be persuasive because it gives an experience of having moved satisfactorily from a particular beginning point to a conclusion. There are specialized forms of argumentation in subcultures and minicultures; when the requirements for that kind of argumentation have been reached, the hearer considers the argument to have hit its target. If the arguments in the gospels have a significant relation to complete arguments as defined by Hellenistic-Roman rhetoricians, then the gospels were not functioning in an environment of specialized ethnic rhetoric, but in a wider cultural environment that included significant aspects of more generalized Hellenistic-Roman forms of argumentation. The text that presents the nature of the complete argument in the *Rhetorica ad Herennium* is as follows:

28 Ergo absolutissima et perfectissima est argumentatio ea quae in quinque partes est distributa: propositionem, rationem, rationis confirmationem, exornationem, conplexionem. Propositio est per quam ostendimus summatim quid sit quod probari volumus. Ratio est quae causam demonstrat verum esse id quod intendimus, brevi subiectione. Rationis confirmatio est ea quae pluribus argumentis corroborat breviter expositam rationem. Exornatio est qua utimur rei honestandae et conlocupletandae causa,

---

38. MACK–ROBBINS, *Patterns of Persuasion in the Gospels* (n. 6). Also see MACK, *Rhetoric and the New Testament* (n. 6).

confirmata argumentatione. Conplexio est quae concludit breviter, colligens partes argumentationis.

Hisce igitur quinque partibus ut absolutissime utamur, hoc modo tractabimus argumentationem:

XIX. "Causam ostendemus Ulixi fuisse quare interfecerit Aiacem.

"Inimicum enim acerrimum de medio tollere volebat, a quo sibi non iniuria summum periculum metuebat.

"Videbat illo incolumi se incolumem non futurum; sperabat illius morte se salutem sibi conparare; consueverat, si iure non potuerat, iniuria quavis inimico exitium machinari, cui rei mors indigna Palamedis testimonium dat. Ergo et metus periculi hortabatur eum interimere a quo supplicium verebatur, et consuetudo peccandi maleficii suscipiendi removebat dubitationem.

"Omnes enim cum minima peccata cum causa suscipiunt, tum vero illa quae multo maxima sunt maleficia aliquo certo emolumento inducti suscipere conantur. Si multos induxit in peccatum pecuniae spes, si conplures scelere se contaminarunt imperii cupiditate, si multi leve conpendium fraude maxima commutarunt, cui mirum videbitur istum a maleficio propter acerrimam formidinem non temperasse? Virum fortissimum, integerrimum, inimicitiarum persequentissimum, iniuria lacessitum, ira exsuscitatum homo timidus, nocens, conscius sui peccati, insidiosus voluit interimere; acerrimum homo perfidiosus inimicum incolumem esse noluit. Cui tandem hoc mirum videbitur? Nam cum feras bestias videamus alacres et erectas vadere ut alteri bestiae noceant, non est incredibile putandum istius quoque animum ferum, crudelem atque inhumanum cupide ad inimici perniciem profectum, praesertim cum in bestiis nullam neque bonam neque malam rationem videamus, in isto plurimas et pessumas rationes semper fuisse intellegamus.

"Si ergo pollicitus sum me daturum causam qua inductus Ulixes accesserit ad maleficium, et si inimicitiarum acerrimam rationem et periculi metum intercessisse demonstravi, non est dubium quin confiteatur causam maleficii fuisse". (*Rhet ad Her*, II.xviii.28–xix.30).

The most complete and perfect argument, then, is that which is comprised of five parts: the Proposition, the Reason, the Proof of the Reason, the Embellishment, and the Résumé. Through the Proposition we set forth summarily what we intend to prove. The Reason, by means of a brief explanation subjoined, sets forth the causal basis for the Proposition, establishing the truth of what we are urging. The Proof of the Reason corroborates, by means of additional arguments, the briefly presented Reason. Embellishment we use in order to adorn and enrich the argument, after the Proof has been established. The Résumé is a brief conclusion, drawing together the parts of the argument.

Hence, to make the most complete use of these five parts, we shall develop an argument as follows:

PROPOSITION

XIX "We shall show that Ulysses had a motive in killing Ajax.

RATIONALE

"Indeed he wished to rid himself of his bitterest enemy, from whom, with good cause, he feared extreme danger to himself.

CONFIRMATION OF THE RATIONALE

"He saw that, with Ajax alive, his own life would be unsafe; he hoped by the death of Ajax to secure his own safety; it was his habit to plan an enemy's destruction by whatsoever wrongful means, when he could not by rightful, as the undeserved death of Palamedes bears witness. Thus the fear of danger encouraged him to slay the man from whom he dreaded vengeance, and, in addition, the habit of wrong-doing robbed him of his scruples at undertaking the evil deed.

EMBELLISHMENT

29 "Now not only do all men have a motive even in their least peccadillos, but certainly they are attracted by some sure reward when they enter upon crimes which are by far the most heinous. If the hope of gaining money has led many a man to wrongdoing, if from greed for power not a few have tainted themselves with crime, if numerous men have trafficked for a paltry profit with arrant deceit, who will find it strange that Ulysses, when under stress of acute terror, did not refrain from crime? A hero most brave, most upright, most implacable against his foes, harassed by a wrong, roused to anger – him the frightened, malevolent, guilt-conscious, guileful man wished to destroy; the treacherous man did not wish his bitter enemy to stay alive. To whom, pray, will this seem strange? For when we see wild beasts rush eagerly and resolutely to attack one another, we must not think it incredible that this creature, too – a wild, cruel, inhuman spirit – set out passionately to destroy his enemy; especially since in beasts we see no reasoning, good or bad, while he, we know, always had designs, ever so many, and ever so base.

RÉSUMÉ

30 "If, then, I have promised to give the motive which impelled Ulysses to enter upon the crime, and if I have shown that the reckoning of a bitter enmity and the fear of danger were the factors, it must unquestionably be acknowledged that he had a motive for his crime. (*Rhet ad Her*, II.xviii.28–xix.30)[39].

A proposition plus a rationale presents an enthymeme (a syllogism with a premise). Therefore, the most complete and perfect argument, according to the *ad Herennium*, begins with enthymematic reasoning. The confirmation of the reason begins with a restatement of the rationale, presents an argument from the example of Palamedes, and ends with a conclusion. This makes the confirmation a complex rhetorical unit in and of itself. Without analyzing the embellishment in detail, we should notice that the final sentence in the unit introduces an argument from the analogy of wild beasts who rush eagerly and resolutely to attack one another. A concluding sentence then ends the argument.

39. [Cicero], *Ad C. Herennium* (LCL, 403), Cambridge, MA, Harvard University Press, 1954, pp. 106-113.

In addition to the way in which the argument proceeds, it is important to notice the comments immediately following the quotation. The author indicates that "there is a time when the Résumé should be dispensed with", "there is a situation, too, in which the Embellishment should be omitted", and "if the argument is brief and the matter also slight or insignificant, then both the Embellishment and the Résumé should be left out" (*Rhet ad Her*, II.xix.30). This means that a complete argument should have an enthymematic argument with some kind of confirmation of the rationale. If it seems appropriate, an embellishment and/or a conclusion may be added to the argument.

The *Rhetorica ad Herennium* also presents an elaboration of a theme in seven parts. It soon becomes clear that this elaboration exhibits additional figures that may be present in a complete argument:

> Hoc modo igitur septem partibus tractabitur – ut ab eiusdem sententiae non recedamus exemplo, ut scire possis quam facile praeceptione rhetoricae res simplex multiplici ratione tractetur:
>
> "Sapiens nullum pro re publica periculum vitabit ideo quod saepe, cum pro re publica perire noluerit, necesse erit cum re publica pereat; et quoniam omnia sunt commoda a patria accepta, nullum incommodum pro patria grave putandum est.
>
> "Ergo qui fugiunt id periculum quod pro re publica subeundum est stulte faciunt; nam neque effugere incommoda possunt et ingrati in civitatem reperiuntur. At qui patriae pericula suo periculo expetunt, hi sapientes putandi sunt, cum et eum quem debent honorem rei publicae reddunt, et pro multis perire malunt quam cum multis. Etenim vehementer est iniquum vitam, quam a natura acceptam propter patriam conservaris, naturae cum cogat reddere, patriae cum roget non dare; et cum possis cum summa virtute et honore pro patria interire, malle per dedecus et ignaviam vivere; et cum pro amicis et parentibus et ceteris necesariis adire periculum velis, pro re publica, in qua et haec et illud sanctissimum patriae nomen continetur, nolle in discrimen venire.
>
> "Ita uti contemnendus est qui in navigio non navem quam se mavult incolumem, item vituperandus qui in rei publicae discrimine suae plus quam communi saluti consulit. Navi enim fracta multi incolumes evaserunt; ex naufragio patriae salvus nemo potest enatare.
>
> "Quod mihi bene videtur Decius intellexisse, qui se devovisse dicitur et pro legionibus in hostes immisisse medios. Amisit vitam, at non perdidit. Re enim vilissima certam et parva maximam redemit. Vitam dedit, accepit patriam; amisit animam, potitus est gloriam, quae cum summa laude prodita vetustate cotidie magis enitescit.
>
> "Quodsi pro re publica decere accedere periculum et ratione demonstratum est et exemplo conprobatum, ii sapientes sunt existimandi qui nullum pro salute patriae periculum vitant". (*Rhet ad Her*, IV.xliii.56–xliv.57).

The following, then, will illustrate a treatment in seven parts – to continue the use of the same theme for my example, in order that you may know how easily, by the precepts of rhetoric, a simple idea is developed in a multiple manner:

THEME

"The wise man will, on the republic's behalf, shun no peril,

RATIONALES

"because it may often happen that if a man has been loath to perish for his country it will be necessary for him to perish with her. Further, since it is from our country that we receive all our advantages, no disadvantage incurred on her behalf is to be regarded as severe.

RESTATEMENT OF THEME WITH RATIONALE

"I say, then, that they who flee from the peril to be undergone on behalf of the republic act foolishly, for they cannot avoid the disadvantages, and are found guilty of ingratitude towards the state.

CONTRARY

"But on the other hand they who, with peril to themselves, confront the perils of the fatherland, are to be considered wise, since they render to their country the homage due her, and prefer to die for many of their fellow citizens instead of with them. For it is extremely unjust to give back to nature, when she compels, the life you have received from nature, and not to give to your country, when she calls for it, the life you have preserved thanks to your country and when you can die for fatherland with the greatest manliness and honour, to prefer to live in disgrace and cowardice; and when you are willing to face danger for friends and parents and your other kin, to refuse to run the risk for the republic, which embraces all these and that most holy name of fatherland as well.

ANALOGY

"He who in a voyage prefers his own to his vessel's security, deserves contempt. No less blameworthy is he who in a crisis of the republic consults his own in preference to the common safety. For from the wreck of a ship many of those on board escape unharmed, but from the wreck of the fatherland no one can swim to safety.

EXAMPLE AND TESTIMONY OF ANTIQUITY

"It is this that, in my opinion, Decius well understood, who is said to have devoted himself to death, and, in order to save his legions, to have plunged into the midst of the enemy. He gave up his life, but did not throw it away; for at the cost of a very cheap good he redeemed a sure good, of a small good the greatest good. He gave his life, and received his country in exchange. He lost his life, and gained glory, which, transmitted with highest praise, shines more and more every day as time goes on.

CONCLUSION

"But if reason has shown and illustration confirmed that it is fitting to confront danger in defence of the republic, they are to be esteemed wise who do not shrink from any peril when the security of the fatherland is at stake". (*Rhet ad Her*, IV.xliii.56–xliv.57)[40].

In addition to the basic parts of the complete argument, this sequence

40. *Ibid.*, pp. 370-375.

explicitly adds arguments from the contrary, from analogy, and from example. As indicated in the notes to the text in the LCL, the argument from example serves also as a testimony from antiquity[41]. An interpreter becomes aware very soon, then, that a unit may serve more than one rhetorical function at a time.

Hermogenes' *Progymnasmata* adapts the elaboration of the theme to an elaboration of a chreia that approximates a complete argument[42]. This adaptation produces a kind of argumentation that is of great interest and importance to the interpreter of the gospels, since it begins with a saying attributed to a specific person. The text is as follows:

Ἀλλὰ νῦν ἐπὶ τὸ συνέχον χωρῶμεν, τοῦτο δέ ἐστιν ἡ ἐργασία. ἐργασία τοίνυν οὕτως ἔστω· (1) πρῶτον ἐγκώμιον διὰ βραχέων τοῦ εἰπόντος ἢ πράξαντος, εἶτα (2) αὐτῆς τῆς χρείας παράφρασις, εἶτα (3) ἡ αἰτία.

Οἷον "'Ισοκράτης ἔφησε τῆς παιδείας τὴν μὲν ῥίζαν εἶναι πικράν, τὸν δὲ καρπὸν γλυκύν".

(1) Ἔπαινος· "'Ισοκράτης σοφὸς ἦν", καὶ πλατυνεῖς ἠρέμα τὸ χωρίον.

(2) Εἶθ' ἡ χρεία· "εἶπε τόδε", καὶ οὐ θήσεις αὐτὴν ψιλὴν ἀλλὰ πλατύνων τὴν ἑρμηνείαν.

(3) Εἶτα ἡ αἰτία· "τὰ γὰρ μέγιστα τῶν πραγμάτων ἐκ πόνων φιλεῖ κατορθοῦσθαι, κατορθωθέντα δὲ τὴν ἡδονὴν φέρει".

(4) Εἶτα κατὰ τὸ ἐναντίον· "τὰ μὲν γὰρ τυχόντα τῶν πραγμάτων οὐ δεῖτα πόνων καὶ τὸ τέλος ἀηδέστατον ἔχει, τὰ σπουδαῖα δὲ τοὐναντίον".

(5) Εἶτα ἐκ παραβολῆς· "ὥσπερ γὰρ τοὺς γεωργοὺς δεῖ πονήσαντας περὶ τὴν γῆν κομίζεσθαι τοὺς καρπούς, οὕτω καὶ περὶ τοὺς λόγους".

(6) Εἶτα ἐκ παραδείγματος· "Δημοσθένης καθείρξας ἑαυτὸν ἐν οἰκήματι καὶ πολλὰ μοχθήσας ὕστερον ἐκομίζετο τοὺς καρπούς, στεφάνους καὶ ἀναρρήσεις".

(7) Ἔστι δὲ καὶ ἐκ κρίσεως ἐπιχειρῆσαι, οἷον "'Ησίοδος μὲν γὰρ ἔφη (Op. 289)

τῆς δ'ἀρετῆς ἱδρῶτα θεοὶ προπάροιθεν ἔθηκαν,

ἄλλος δὲ ποιητής φησι (Epicharmus, Fr. 287 Kaibel)

τῶν πόνων πωλοῦσιν ἡμῖν πάντα τἀγάθ' οἱ θεοί".

(8) Ἐν δὲ τῷ τέλει παράκλησιν προσθήσεις, ὅτι χρὴ πείθεσθαι τῷ εἰρηκότι ἢ πεποιηκότι.

Τοσαῦτα πρὸς τὸ παρόν· τὴν δὲ τελεωτέραν διδασκαλίαν ὕστερον εἴσῃ.

(Hermogenes, *Progymnasmata* 1,10–8,14 [Rabe])

But now let us move on to the chief matter, and this is the elaboration. Accordingly, let the elaboration be as follows: (1) First, an encomium, in a few words, for the one who spoke or acted. Then (2) a paraphrase of the chreia itself; then (3) the rationale.

For example "Isocrates said that education's root is bitter, its fruit is sweet".

---

41. *Ibid.*, p. 373.
42. MACK-ROBBINS, *Patterns of Persuasion in the Gospels* (n. 6), pp. 51-52.

(1) Praise: "Isocrates was wise", and you amplify the subject moderately.

(2) Then the chreia: "He said thus and so", and you are not to express it simply but rather by amplifying the presentation.

(3) Then the rationale: "For the most important affairs generally succeed because of toil, and once they have succeeded, they bring pleasure".

(4) Then the statement from the opposite: "For ordinary affairs do not need toil, and they have an outcome that is entirely without pleasure; but serious affairs have the opposite outcome".

(5) Then the statement from analogy: "For just as it is the lot of farmers to reap their fruits after working with the land, so also is it for those working with words".

(6) Then the statement from example: "Demosthenes, after locking himself in a room and toiling long, later reaped his fruits: wreaths and public acclamations".

(7) It is also possible to argue from the statement by an authority. For example, Hesiod said (Op. 289):

In front of virtue gods have ordained sweat.

And another poet says (Epicharmus, Fr. 287 Kaibel):

At the price of toil do the gods sell every good to us.

(8) At the end you are to add an exhortation to the effect that it is necessary to heed the one who has spoken or acted.

So much for the present; you will learn the more advanced instruction later[43].

After praising the originator of the chreia and introducing the chreia, the speaker or writer provides a rationale and contrary for the chreia. These rhetorical constituents produce an enthymematic beginning and clarify the argument through an initial articulation of what the thesis is and is not, and why. After this, the elaboration supports the statement in the chreia with arguments from analogy, paradigm, and authoritative testimony. These arguments add new rhetorical figures to the argumentative components in the chreia itself, in the manner in which a speech supports its initial thesis with artistic and inartistic data the speaker has created or gathered for this purpose. This level of elaboration may end with a brief exhortative conclusion, since its argumentation has been so carefully and thoroughly developed and reiterated along the way.

It is important for this essay to observe that virtually every unit in the elaboration is a reperformance of tradition. The saying attributed to Isocrates is a striking, succinct formulation that encapsulates the gist of Isocrates, *Ad Demonicum* 45-47[44]. The rationale and the contrary have been formulated in a similar manner. The remaining arguments that are

43. HOCK–O'NEIL, *The Chreia in Ancient Rhetoric* (n. 2), pp. 176-177.

44. *Isocrates* I (LCL, 209), Cambridge, MA, Harvard University Press, 1980, pp. 30-33; cf. *Diogenes Laertius* 5.18, see additional references in HOCK–O'NEIL, *The Chreia in Ancient Rhetoric* (n. 2), pp. 325-326.

based on farmers, Demosthenes, and quotations from Hesiod and Epicharmus come from outside the language field of the topic itself, and each is a reperformance of tradition generally known in Mediterranean society. This kind of writing has close analogies in the synoptic gospels.

An intriguing example of second-level elaboration exists in the account of Jesus' teaching in parables in Mark 4. An abbreviated display, based on Mack's analysis, looks as follows:

(1) *Introduction* (4,1-2a): Jesus, the crowd, the sea, the boat
(2) *Chreia or Fable* (4,2b-9): Parable of the Sower
(3) *Rationale* (ἡ αἰτία)
    Request for Rationale (4,10)
    Rationale given as Direct Statement (4,11-12)
    Rationale given as Paraphrase of the Parable (4,13-20)
(4) *Contrary* (κατὰ τὸ ἐναντίον: 4,21-23)
    And he said to them, "Is a lamp brought in to be put under a bushel, or under a bed, and not on a stand?
    For there is nothing hid, except to be made manifest; nor is anything secret, except to come to light.
    If anyone has ears to hear, let him hear".
(5) *Authoritative Judgment* (ἐκ κρίσεως: 4,24-25)
    And he said to them, "Take heed what you hear. The measure you give will be the measure you get, and still more will be given to you.
    For to him who has will more be given; and from him who has not, even what he has will be taken away".
(6) *Example* (ἐκ παραδείγματος: 4,26-29)
    And he said, "The kingdom of God is as if a man should scatter seed upon the ground, and should sleep and rise night and day, and the seed should sprout and grow, he knows not how. The earth produces of itself, first the blade, then the ear, then the full grain in the ear. But when the grain is ripe, at once he puts in the sickle, because the harvest has come".
(7) *Analogy* (ἐκ παραβολῆς: 4,30-32)
    And he said, "With what can we compare the kingdom of God, or what parable shall we use for it? It is like a grain of mustard seed, which, when sown upon the ground, is the smallest of all the seeds on earth; yet when it is sown it grows up and becomes the greatest of all shrubs, and puts forth large branches, so that the birds of the air can make nests in its shade".
(8) *Conclusion* (4,33-34)
    With many such parables he spoke the word to them, as they were able to hear it; he did not speak to them without a parable, but privately to his own disciples he explained everything[45].

The elaboration develops an argument with a series of independent

45. Based on MACK-ROBBINS, *Patterns of Persuasion in the Gospels* (n. 6), pp. 152-154.

rhetorical figures that secure meanings for the initial chreia that would not have been easy for hearers or readers to attain by themselves. While Mack refers to the recitation of the parable as a "chreia", it is possible that it would be better to refer to it as a "fable"[46]. Instead of abbreviating the topic into a single saying, as Hermogenes' elaboration abbreviates Isocrates, *Ad Demonicum* 45-49, Mk 4,1-12 presents the topic and its rationale in the form of a parable (fable), a request for a rationale (4,10), and Jesus' statement of the rationale (4,11-12). After this, Mk 4,13-20 presents a paraphrase of the parable, which follows a pattern of restatement of the theme and its rationale as it appears in the elaboration in *Rhet ad Her*, IV.xliii.57 (quoted above). After establishing the theme and rationale through statement and restatement, Mk 4,21-23 presents a contrary argument with its own rationale. The presence of the rationale with the contrary reminds one of the contrary in *Rhet ad Her*, IV.xliii.57, which also has a rationale (quoted above). The contrary and its rationale clarify and position the theme of mystery and inside/outside in the parable and its rationale. This argument also introduces a new analogical arena, namely the household, which supplements the arena of the field where people sow seeds. The authoritative judgment in Mk 4,24-25 also has a rationale to support it. The example and analogy, of course, do not have rationales. The conclusion reformulates the language about parables, speaking the word, being able to hear, and the privileged place of the disciples, providing a résumé of the argumentation in the elaboration. Mk 4,1-34, then, is a remarkable instance of second-level elaboration in the synoptic gospels.

In addition to the rhetorical treatises that aid the interpreter with the gospels, excellent contemporary literature exists where interpreters can see the kinds of procedures actually practiced by contemporaries of our New Testament writers. Plutarch's *Lives* and *Moralia* contain multiple accounts of anecdotal traditions, similar to the multiple accounts in the gospels[47]. Also, some of these accounts exist in the writings of Dio Chrysostom, Arrian, the Cynic Epistles, and other literature. Using these literary *corpora*, an interpreter begins to see that gospel traditions were transmitted in a manner highly similar to the transmission of anecdotal traditions in Mediterranean culture[48].

46. Various members of the Seminar at the Colloquium Biblicum Lovaniense (19-20 August 1992) pressed for this modification of the analysis. Since the same exercises were performed with the chreia, fable, and narrative, this could be an appropriate modification.
47. ROBBINS, *Writing as a Rhetorical Act in Plutarch and the Gospels* (n. 29). Also see ID., *Pronouncement Stories in Plutarch's Lives of Alexander and Julius Caesar*, in *SBL 1978 Seminar Papers*, pp. 31-38; *Laudation Stories in the Gospel of Luke and Plutarch's Alexander*, in *SBL 1981 Seminar Papers*, pp. 293-308; *Classifying Pronouncement Stories in Plutarch's Parallel Lives*, in *Semeia* 20 (1981) 29-52; *A Rhetorical Typology for Classifying and Analyzing Pronouncement Stories*, in *SBL 1984 Seminar Papers*, pp. 93-122; *Pronouncement Stories from a Rhetorical Perspective*, in *Forum* 4/2 (1988) 3-32.
48. V.K. ROBBINS, *Ancient Quotes and Anecdotes: From Crib to Crypt*, Sonoma, CA,

IV. Guidelines for Rhetorical Analysis of Pre-Gospel Traditions

Application of insights from the progymnastic rhetorical treatises has opened a new door for interpretation of New Testament literature. If culture-transmitting tradition is argumentative, then individual traditions will be expanded and elaborated to make stronger, more explicit arguments. Certain traditions will be brought into the argumentation of other traditions as rationales, analogies, or authoritative statements to strengthen the argumentation. Actions and situations with various potential meanings will be focused in particular ways, and contextual statements which could be understood in different ways will be positioned with questions, rationales, and contraries. One of the major contributions is to help the interpreter exhibit the nature of argumentation in sections that have been considered to be patchwork compilations. Another aspect of its contribution applies to pre-gospel traditions. Since this essay is concerned with pre-gospel traditions, it will now turn to a number of New Testament passages in a context of principles that have arisen through analysis informed by progymnastic rhetorical procedures.

The quotations above from the *Rhetorica ad Herennium* and Hermogenes' *Progymnasmata* exhibit the rhetorical components and figures that appear again and again in culture-transmitting tradition. As is clear from the discussion in the *ad Herennium*, it is not necessary for an elaboration to contain all of the argumentative components that any rhetorician has produced as an example. Rather, culture-transmitting tradition has this range of components and figures at its disposal, and it selects and uses them in ways that the prior form of the tradition allows and invites. In and of itself, previous tradition in its social and cultural context exercises certain restraints on the use of certain components and figures at the same time that it invites other components and figures. Contexts of utterance, reference, and culture are the environment in which the selection and formulation occurs. The interpreter can expect, therefore, that a selection of components and figures will work together in the tradition in a manner that makes stronger and stronger "Christian" arguments.

This next section builds on the insights gained thus far in this essay on the nature of culture-transmitting tradition. The section works sequentially through the sequence of Hermogenes' elaboration, beginning with the presentation of settings, actions, and sayings that create the social and cultural context for sayings that lead to argumentation. The section continues with discussions of typical developments in the domain of propositions, rationales, and contraries in the gospels.

Polebridge, 1989 is a beginning place for exploring multiple accounts of traditions in Mediterranean culture, including the gospels.

The reader will soon become aware that the rhetorical critic analyzes features that many form critics have discussed, but that the analysis is concerned with the inner nature of the argumentation in a manner that form critics did not explicitly acknowledge and programmatically investigate. Perhaps the most unexpected aspect will be the analysis of "contexts of culture" in the arguments. The brevity of the discussion is likely to leave the reader dissatisfied, and perhaps unconvinced. The purpose of the discussion is not to convince but to provide insights into the nature of pre-gospel and gospel argumentation for those who are interested in looking for such things.

As the section works sequentially through the rhetorical components that appear in Hermogenes' elaboration, a threefold taxonomy of "contexts of culture" emerges: (a) social culture; (b) ideological culture; and (c) scriptural culture. This taxonomy provides an initial framework for analyzing cultural developments in early Christianity, and with its use a distinction begins to emerge between Christian "subcultures" and Christian "countercultures". For the purpose of this essay, a subculture is a subordinate culture that a group develops to sustain itself and nurture its well being in the context of another culture. A counterculture is a subculture that develops aggressive strategies to understand itself as an authentic alternative to a dominant culture, verbalizing attacks on various types of people in an alternative subculture or in the dominant culture.

In this section especially, then, the reader sees the import of the shift from a literary-historical to a socio-rhetorical paradigm of analysis. The goal in sight is a nuanced discussion of social and cultural interaction and developments in early Christianity, not a discussion of literary and historical influences on New Testament texts.

The first step in each section in this part of the essay will be to introduce a title that somehow relates to rhetorical components and figures in culture-transmitting tradition as we see it from discussions of the chreia in Hellenistic-Roman rhetorical treatises. Underneath the title appears one or more principles that emerge from analyses that rhetorical critics have performed thus far on early Christian gospel traditions. After a brief discussion and exhibition of some data from these analyses, the discussion moves to another heading and presentation. Again, the goal simply is to draw together some rhetorical analyses that have been discussing pre-gospel traditions in a manner that focuses on social and cultural dimensions of first century Christianity.

1. *Situations and Actions*

A. Analysis of gospels informed by progymnastic rhetorical procedures reveals that situations, actions, and speech developed interactively in early Christian tradition.

B. In other words, situations and actions are as important as speech in the tradition.

C. The privileging of speech over action and situation in pre-gospel tradition is an ideological bias of traditional interpretation that must be revised.

With the work of Rudolf Bultmann, situations and actions became secondary[49]. The view arose that sayings were primary, and situations and actions were created out of and for sayings, to create a narrative context for them. In this form, such a presupposition is erroneous. A simple test of one's memory of an episode from the past will raise questions about such a procedure. Regularly, one's memory of a situation and of action in that situation is more precise than one's memory of words that were spoken. One of the reasons for this is that many different things may have been said, and the sequence of statements is often as important as the statements themselves. It is not difficult, of course, to create appropriate speech for a situation, as Thucydides knew very well. But appropriate speech is interpretive speech, and interpretation is always ideologically located and focused. Whenever a storyteller creates appropriate speech, the socio-ideological location of the storyteller contributes significantly to the selection and formulation of the topics in the speech. There are, to be sure, special circumstances when a person said something that was striking, like "Ask not what your country can do for you; ask what you can do for your country". This is the circumstance on which both Bultmann and Dibelius had their eye. But situations and actions are as important as speech for characterizing Jesus in early Christian tradition, and New Testament interpreters must develop a method that gives equal voice to all three in the tradition.

Reference to action as well as speech in chreiai is a primary clue to the interactive nature of action, speech, and situation in first century culture-transmitting tradition. The interactive nature of situations, actions, and speech is well exhibited in the tradition of Jesus and the children. A socio-rhetorical analysis of all of the accounts in the gospels reveals two basic synoptic traditions: (a) one in which Jesus places a child before a group of people to make a point; and (b) one in which Jesus insists that children be allowed to be brought to him[50]. The common synoptic wording in the two traditions is as follows:

49. R. BULTMANN, *The History of the Synoptic Tradition*, New York, Harper & Row, ²1968 [from German ⁴1958]. Also, with some variations, M. DIBELIUS, *From Tradition to Gospel*, New York, Charles Scribner's Sons, ²1935; see MACK–ROBBINS, *Patterns of Persuasion in the Gospels* (n. 6), pp. 1-29.

50. This discussion is informed by V.K. ROBBINS, *Pronouncement Stories and Jesus' Blessing of the Children*, in *Semeia* 29 (1984) 43-74.

(1) Mt 18,1-5; Mk 9,33-37; Lk 9,46-48

τίς μείζων;	Who is greatest?
παιδίον	child
ἔστησεν αὐτὸ (ἐν μέσῳ/παρ' ἑαυτῷ)	he set it (in the midst/alongside himself)
καὶ εἶπεν	and he said
ὃς [ ]ἀν δέξηται το[ ]ουτ[ ] παιδί(ο/ω)ν	Who ever receives (this/such a)
ἐπὶ τῷ ὀνόματί μου	child in my name
ἐμὲ δέχεται.	receives me.

(2) Mt 19,13-15; Mk 10,13-16; Lk 18,15-17

προσ(έφερον/ηνέχθησαν) αὐτῷ	They were bringing to him
ἵνα (αὐτῶν ἅ[ψ/πτ]ηται/τὰς χεῖρας ἐπιθῇ αὐτοῖς)	in order that he might (touch/lay his hands on) them
οἱ δὲ μαθηταὶ ἐπετίμησεν αὐτοῖς.	but the disciples rebuked them.
ὁ δὲ 'Ιησοῦς (εἶπεν/λέγων)	But Jesus said,
ἄφετε τὰ παιδία (ἔρχεσθαι/ἐλθεῖν)	Let the children come
πρός με,	to me,
μὴ κωλύετε αὐτά·	do not forbid them;
τῶν γὰρ τοιούτων ἐστὶν ἡ βασιλεία (τοῦ θεοῦ/τῶν οὐρανῶν).	for to such belongs the kingdom of (God/the heavens).

It is clear from these accounts that "pre-gospel" tradition featured Jesus bringing children close to him for some purpose in a "public" setting. Jesus' action with children presents the "context of social culture" and the topoi in Jesus' speech present the "context of ideological culture" in this tradition. New Testament interpreters have shown more interest in ideological culture than social culture – a privileging of word over action and situation, of mind over body, of cognitive issues over practical issues. But both aspects are present, and both are being dealt with creatively and interactively in recitation.

There is significant social and ideological energy at work around Jesus' action with children. The social energy emerges in the recitation of various situations and actions. Concerning action, Jesus: (a) sets a child in their midst, (b) sets a child beside him, (c) holds a child in his arms, (d) insists that children be allowed to come to him, and/or (e) points to a child being suckled by its mother (GospThomas 22). The nurturing of ideological culture occurs in the various sayings that recitation generates. Concerning speech, Jesus discusses: (a) being great, (b) his own acceptance by people, (c) people's acceptance of the kingdom, and/or (d) entering the kingdom.

2. *Propositions, Rationales, and Contraries*

A. Early traditions nurture contextual statements into propositions by adding rationales and contraries that focus their meaning potential in a particular direction.

B. Transmitters of traditions generate explicit rationales for statements that previously were based on implicit, unstated rationales. The explicit articulation of a rationale is a form of expansion or elaboration of the culture-transmitting tradition, nurturing it into an explicit enthymematic or syllogistic argument.

C. The social/ideological/biblical culture nurtured by the initial propositions, rationales, and contraries creates an environment in which people generate new propositions with their own rationales and contraries.

D. Amplification of contraries is a natural way to nurture countercultural strategies in a subcultural environment.

Mk 9,33-37par. and 10,13-16 par.

In Mk 9,33-37 par., Jesus' setting of a child in the midst of a group of people is likely to be the earliest part of the tradition. Whatever Jesus may have intended it to mean, it invited a variety of meanings for early Christians. Transmitters developed these meanings by introducing questions and nurturing contextual statements into propositions with the aid of rationales and contraries. In the Markan version, a particular meaning is nurtured by introducing the question "Who is greatest?" Then the meaning is nurtured by a rationale – "Whoever receives one such child in my name receives me" – and by a contrary – "and whoever receives me, receives not me but him who sent me". The question, rationale, and contrary are part of the cultural transmission of the action by Jesus. In other words, storytellers have created "appropriate speech" as a way of giving focus to the meaning potential of Jesus' action.

In Mk 10,13-16 par., Jesus' action with children is focused by introducing a "contrary action" by the disciples: they rebuke people who try to bring children to Jesus. Again, Jesus' acceptance of children, including occasionally picking them up, is primary in this tradition. And Jesus' reason for this action may well have been unstated by the earliest tradition. Christian storytellers, however, have focused its meaning by introducing the contrary action of the disciples, which nurtures Jesus' act into a thesis: "Let the children come to me". This thesis is further positioned and clarified by the contrary: "Do not forbid them". Then, a rationale nurtures an ideological culture for the action: "For to such belongs the kingdom of (God/the heavens)".

The traditional approach during the last fifty years has been to consider the rationale about the kingdom of God to be primary, because it has been decided, through other arguments, that "kingdom of God" was central to Jesus' teaching. The presupposition has been that various stories were created as contexts for sayings about the kingdom of God. It is certainly true that kingdom of.God ideology is ubiquitous in synoptic gospel tradition. The question is where it came into various pre-gospel traditions and how pervasive it is. A rhetorical

approach presents a method for analyzing the tradition anew, if interpreters have the will to do it. The primary dimension in this tradition is
Jesus' acknowledgment of children in public. The earliest features are
an action and a saying:
  (a) setting a child (in the midst/alongside himself) to make a point;
  (b) saying, "Let the children come to me".
This phenomenon has not been considered to be a very important part
of pre-gospel tradition, presumably because it is not ideological enough.
But this is an item that created a context of social and ideological
culture in pre-gospel tradition. In many Mediterranean traditions about
important people, children do not appear or they appear as troublema-
kers to be disciplined. This social phenomenon in pre-gospel traditions
should be investigated in Mediterranean literature and its significance
should be included in discussions of pre-gospel tradition.

Mt 5,3-12 and Lk 6,20-23
  Using the beatitudes as another example, it is possible to exhibit the
interaction of propositions, rationales, and contraries further[51]. The
common wording between Mt 5,3-12 and Lk 6,20-23 contains propositions and rationales that exhibit energetic development of social, ideological, and scriptural culture:

(a) μακάριοι οἱ πτωχοί
ὅτι (αὐτῶν/ὑμετέρα) ἐστιν ἡ βασιλεία τοῦ θεοῦ.
(b) μακάριοι οἱ πεινῶντες
ὅτι χορτασθήσ(ονται/εσθε).
(c) μακάριοί ἐστε ὅταν ὀνειδίσωσιν (ὑμᾶς/τὸ ὄνομα ὑμῶν)
καὶ (εἴπωσιν/ἐκβάλωσιν) ... πονηρὸν ἕνεκα (ἐμοῦ/τοῦ υἱοῦ τοῦ ἀνθρώπου).
(d) (χαίρετε/χάρητε) καὶ (ἀγαλλιᾶσθε/σκιρτήσατε)
(ὅτι/γὰρ) ὁ μισθὸς ὑμῶν πολὺς ἐν τ(οῖς/ῷ) οὐραν(οῖς/ῷ)·
(οὕτως/κατὰ τὰ αὐτὰ) γὰρ (ἐδίωξαν/ἐποίουν) το(ὺς/ῖς) προφήτ(α/αι)ς (τοὺς
πρὸ ὑμῶν/οἱ πατέρες αὐτῶν).

  The first two units contain a proposition with a social cultural focus
followed by a rationale with an ideological statement (a) those who are
poor/possess the kingdom of God; and (b) those who are hungry/shall
be satisfied. The third unit contains a proposition that thoroughly
intermingles social culture and ideological culture: (c) blessed are you
when people revile (you/your name) and speak evil against (me/the Son
of man). The fourth unit moves away from social culture into an
ideological statement grounded in a scriptural cultural statement: (d)
Rejoice and be glad, because your reward is great in heaven; for they
likewise (persecuted/did to) the prophets.

51. This discussion is informed by V.K. ROBBINS, *Pragmatic Relations as a Criterion
for Authentic Sayings,* in *Forum* 1/3 (1985) 35-63; cf. CROSSAN, *In Fragments* (n. 24),
pp. 168-174.

A rhetorical approach recognizes that explicit rationales regularly emerge in the tradition after strong assertions. The propositions in (a) and (b) emerge from widespread Mediterranean social culture (poverty and hunger). Unit (c) concerns a social culture that has been created by a particular ideological culture within Mediterranean society. Perhaps an earlier stage of this tradition could have existed that referred to people who were despised simply because they were not indigenous to a particular geographical area or had become the targets of a group who had moved into the area. Unit (d), in contrast to the others, contains a rationale for its rationale. *The Rhet ad Her*, II.xviii.28–xix.28 refers to the second rationale as the confirmation of the rationale (*confirmatio rationis*). This confirmation comes from scriptural culture. In the common wording in Matthew and Luke, social culture appears in the "blessing" statements in (a) and (b); ideological culture appears in the rationales in units (a) and (b) and throughout (c). Scriptural culture appears explicitly in the confirmation of the ideological rationale in (d).

Using insights from rhetorical expansion and elaboration, then, it would appear that three theses grounded in widespread social culture stand earliest in the tradition:

(a) Blessed are the poor;

(b) Blessed are those who hunger;

(c) Blessed are those who are despised.

The third unit contains a transition to ideological culture. The consciousness here has a focus on people who are being singled out for special reasons, reasons that suggest a stigma, a peculiarity. While the peculiarity may have begun as a natural social phenomenon with the presence of different kinds of people with one another, it soon nurtured an ideological culture that interacted with it, perhaps intensifying the social stigma.

An early step appears to have been the nurturing of ideological rationales to support a special posture toward the widespread social phenomena of poverty and hunger in Mediterranean society:

(a) because (they/you) possess the kingdom of God;

(b) because (they/you) shall be satisfied.

Then, a more specific ideological culture began to come to expression:

(c) because you have a special name and express a life related to the Son of man;

(d) because your reward is great in heaven.

In turn, a rationale from scriptural culture was brought in to confirm the ideological rationales:

(d) because they likewise (persecuted/did to) the prophets.

In the culture that nurtured the Matthean version of the sayings, ideological and scriptural culture brings about an amplification of the theses and the creation of additional theses and rationales.

Mt 5,4-11

3 (μακάριοι οἱ πτωχοὶ) τῷ πνεύματι...
4 μακάριοι οἱ πενθοῦντες, ὅτι αὐτοὶ παρακληθήσονται
5 μακάριοι οἱ πραεῖς, ὅτι αὐτοὶ κληρονομήσουσιν τὴν γῆν.
6 (μακάριοι οἱ πεινῶντες) καὶ διψῶντες τὴν δικαιοσύνην...
7 μακάριοι οἱ ἐλεήμονες, ὅτι αὐτοὶ ἐλεηθήσονται.
8 μακάριοι οἱ καθαροὶ τῇ καρδίᾳ, ὅτι αὐτοὶ τὸν θεὸν ὄψονται.
9 μακάριοι οἱ εἰρηνοποιοί, ὅτι αὐτοὶ υἱοὶ θεοῦ κληθήσονται.
10 μακάριοι οἱ δεδιωγμένοι ἕνεκεν δικαιοσύνης, ὅτι αὐτῶν ἐστιν ἡ βασιλεία τῶν οὐρανῶν.
11 ... καὶ διώξωσιν ...

3 (Blessed are the poor) in spirit ...
4 Blessed are those who mourn, for they shall be comforted.
5 Blessed are the meek, for they shall inherit the earth.
6 (Blessed are those who hunger) and thirst for righteousness ...
7 Blessed are the merciful, for they shall obtain mercy.
8 Blessed are the pure in heart, for they shall see God.
9 Blessed are the peacemakers, for they shall be called sons of God.
10 Blessed are those who are persecuted for righteousness' sake, for theirs is the kingdom of heaven.
11 ... and persecuted...

Perhaps most interesting among these are the propositions that exhibit a social role or action supported by a culture that has been nurtured and cultivated ideologically and scripturally. Those who are merciful, peacemakers, and persecuted for righteousness' sake appear to point to a social subculture generated out of the ideological and scriptural culture that appeared in the earliest rationales. In other words, initial propositions and rationales nurture a social/ideological/scriptural culture that gives rise to additional propositions with their rationales and confirmations. Part of the skill of analysis of pre-gospel traditions is to detect the cultural environment in which the propositions themselves were generated, since they can appear in any stage of the development.

The Lukan beatitudes, in contrast to those in Matthew, exhibit an intensification of the social posture by means of contraries. This reveals the strengthening of subcultural thinking into countercultural thinking:

Lk 6,20-26
22 ὅταν μισήσωσιν ὑμᾶς οἱ ἄνθρωποι,
καὶ ὅταν ἀφορίσωσιν ὑμᾶς
καὶ ἐκβάλωσιν τὸ ὄνομα ὑμῶν ὡς πονηρὸν ἕνεκα τοῦ υἱοῦ τοῦ ἀνθρώπου.
24 πλὴν οὐαὶ ὑμῖν τοῖς πλουσίοις, ὅτι ἀπέχετε τὴν παράκλησιν ὑμῶν.
25 οὐαὶ ὑμῖν, οἱ ἐμπεπλησμένοι νῦν, ὅτι πεινάσετε.
οὐαί, οἱ γελῶντες νῦν, ὅτι πενθήσετε καὶ κλαύσετε.
26 οὐαὶ ὅταν ὑμᾶς καλῶς εἴπωσιν πάντες οἱ ἄνθρωποι· κατὰ τὰ αὐτὰ γὰρ ἐποίουν τοῖς ψευδοπροφήταις οἱ πατέρες αὐτῶν.

22 when men hate you
and when men exclude you
and cast out your name as evil for the sake of the Son of man.
24 But woe to you that are rich, for you have received your consolation.
25 Woe to you that are full now, for you shall hunger.
Woe to you that laugh now, for you shall mourn and weep.
26 Woe to you, when all men speak well of you, for so their fathers did to the false prophets.

In 6,22, the social culture is described in aggressive, negative terms. Social differentiation is articulated in terms of hatred, exclusion, and being cast out. This intensification of the social differentiation is accompanied by countercultural language in 6,24-26 based on the rhetorical figure of the contrary. Language that exhibits subcultural thinking in the common wording has been nurtured into language that functions as a counterattack. The language is countercultural in posture, adopting the form of a curse. Yet the language does not identify specific opponents. It is pitted in confrontational terms against wealthy, well-fed, and honored people. The curses are supported by ideological and scriptural rationales, but there has been no energetic gleaning of additional items from scripture to function as rationales or confirmations of rationales. The rationales are simply intensifications of earlier ideological and scriptural rationales through the rhetorical figure of the contrary. The Lukan version of the beatitudes nurtures countercultural thinking as it equips Jesus with aggressive social language. The Lukan version does not reveal a subculture that adds new, intricate scriptural resources as rationales. The rationales simply intensify the social aggressiveness of previously generated scriptural rationales.

In summary, the common wording in the beatitudes suggests an early social cultural posture: (a) Blessed are the poor; (b) Blessed are those who hunger; and (c) Blessed are those who are despised. At the earliest stage, whatever rationale existed for this social posture remained implicit, unstated. As transmitters recited these traditions in a culture-forming environment, they generated ideological rationales in support of the social posture, and they martialled scriptural rationales to support (confirm) the ideological rationales. The Matthean version of the beatitudes exhibits an amplification of the beatitudes in the context of an ideological culture that is receiving energetic support from a well-nurtured scriptural culture. In contrast, the Lukan version exhibits a cultural development that was not receiving significantly new energy from an active scriptural culture, but was nurturing a subcultural tradition into a countercultural tradition.

3. Contraries and Analogies

A. The early function of a contrary is to clarify negative or positive implications or propositions.

B. When a contrary is present, the positive is present by implication.

C. Elaboration of a contrary regularly adds a rationale, creating an enthymeme containing complex reasoning.

D. Amplification of a contrary may nurture the positive implication into a proposition.

E. Amplification of a contrary regularly generates additional contraries and/or contrary language.

F. Analogies have a close relation to paradigms. Therefore, transmitters may generate both generalized and specific paradigms out of analogies.

Interpreters regularly have not given careful enough attention to whether statements are contrary or positive statements. Positive statements (propositions) provide a rich environment for the generation of rationales and contraries, as we have seen in the two sub-sections above. Contraries, saying that something is "not" something, have their own ways of being amplified and elaborated which are related to positives but require their own attention. Jesus' statement about a lamp which is not brought in to be put under a bushel or bed but to be put on a lampstand illustrates this kind of tradition well[52].

The common synoptic wording in Mt 5,15; Mk 4,21-25; Lk 8,16 is as follows:

(οὐδε[ ]μήτι) λύχνο(ν/ς) τ[ ]θ[ ] ὑπό
ἐπὶ λυχνίας
no lamp (to be put) under (something)
(but) on a lampstand

The earliest form of this tradition is a contrary statement: a statement that argues that since something is not the case, something else obviously is the case. Bultmann and Jeremias were correct in their observation that we cannot know the initial context for this tradition[53]. Someone, very possibly Jesus himself, used the analogy in a context in which something was said or suggested that the speaker considered to be inappropriate. This contrary has lived on in the tradition, because it uses an analogy to make its point. In other words, the earliest form of

---

52. This discussion is informed by V.K. ROBBINS, *Rhetorical Argument about Lamps and Light in Early Christian Gospels*, in P.W. BÖCKMAN – R.E. KRISTIANSEN (eds.), *Context, Festskrift til Peder Johan Borgen* (Relieff, 24), Universitet i Trondheim, Tapir, 1987, pp. 177-195.

53. BULTMANN, *The History of the Synoptic Tradition* (n. 49), p. 98; J. JEREMIAS, *The Parables of Jesus*, New York, Charles Scribner's Sons, 1963, p. 120.

this tradition merges a contrary rhetorical argument with an argument from analogy.

On the one hand, a contrary argument invites a rationale. Mk 4,22/ Lk 8,17 contains such a rationale. The Markan version reads as follows:

οὐ γάρ ἐστίν τι κρυπτόν, ἐὰν μὴ ἵνα φανερωθῇ· οὐδὲ ἐγένετο ἀπόκρυφον, ἀλλ' ἵνα ἔλθῃ εἰς φανερόν
For there is nothing hid, except to be made manifest; nor is anything secret, except to come to light.

Here we notice that the rationale is formulated in negative terms, just like the contrary argument it supports. The rationale takes the argument into an environment of contrary syllogistic reasoning, which has its own form of complexity. The rationale introduces reasoning from some kind of ideological culture that cared about secret information and insisted that such information was not meant to remain hidden. It would be interesting to know if there are variations of a saying like this in circulation in Mediterranean culture. Its language has not been influenced by the Markan discourse concerning "the mystery of the kingdom" in 4,11, and its reasoning goes beyond the reasoning in that earlier verse. Perhaps the saying reveals subcultural Jewish reasoning that all knowledge now hidden from view will at an appropriate time be revealed to all. It would be informative to know if such reasoning were more widespread in the culture.

Whenever a contrary argument is present, an opposite to the contrary also is present. Thus, the common tradition asserts that a lamp is not brought in to be put under something but "on a lamp-stand". This language reflects the context of social culture for the tradition: people commonly used lamps, and a lamp regularly benefitted more that one person at a time. The presence of an explicit or implicit opposite in a contrary analogy creates a potential for amplification and elaboration of the positive. Amplification of the positive is present in Lk 8,16: "that those who enter may see the light", and in GThom 33: "so that everyone who enters and leaves may see the light".

Mt 5,15 also amplifies the positive dimension of the saying, but instead of keeping the light in a passive position to be seen by others, it emphasizes the active shining forth of the lamp: "and it gives light to all in the house". The Matthean amplification occurs in a context where a transmitter has personalized the active aspect of the positive analogy: "You are the light of the world" (5,14). This is, then, an additional step in the generation of culture-transmitting tradition: the nurturing of analogies into generalized paradigms. A specific paradigm, which is the normal use of the term παράδειγμα, refers to a specific person who embodies a certain attribute, like: Demosthenes, after locking himself in a room and toiling long, later reaped his fruits: wreaths and public acclamations[54]. But rhetoricians were well aware of the close relation between analogies and paradigms. A transmitter of tradition could change the Demosthenes paradigm into a generalized paradigm simply by changing it to "he who locks himself in a room and toils long with speech will later reap his fruits: wreaths and public acclamations".

In early Christian tradition, the development was not from specific to generalized paradigms, but the other way: from analogy, to generalized paradigm, to specific paradigm. The contrary analogy with the lamp generated the context for a positive analogy about light. The positive analogy generated a generalized paradigm in the context of discipleship. Also the positive analogy generated specific paradigms in relation to John the Baptist and Jesus:

> Jn 5,35 He [John] was a burning and shining lamp, and you were willing to rejoice for a while in his light;
> Jn 1,9 The true light [Jesus] that enlightens everyone was coming into the world;
> Jn 8,12; 9,5; cf. 12,46 I [Jesus] am the light of the world.

In the context where transmitters generated the paradigms from the analogy, biblical culture was playing a significant role. In Matthew, Jesus' dwelling in Capernaum, in the territory of Zebulun and Naphtali, is considered to fulfill Isaiah's statement: the people who sat in darkness have seen a great light, and for those who sat in the region and shadow of death light has dawned (Mt 4,13-16). In the Gospel of John, the biblical creation account, where God creates light with his word, has played an influential role, both for the application to John the Baptist and Jesus (Jn 1,5-9; 5,35; 8,12; 12,46).

There is yet one more phenomenon to address. The negative formulation of a contrary analogy may not only influence the formulation of a negative rationale but may also generate a series of negative statements. The persistence of negatives in traditions generated out of the lamp/light analogy is noticeable:

> Jn 1,5 The light shines in the darkness, and the darkness has not overcome it.
> Jn 1,8 He [John] was not the light, but came to bear witness to the light.
> Jn 8,12 Again Jesus spoke to them, saying, "I am the light of the world; he who follows me will not walk in darkness, but will have the light of life".
> Jn 12,46 I have come as light into the world, that whoever believes in me may not remain in darkness.

Once negatives begin to be used like this, they generate other

54. HOCK–O'NEIL, *The Chreia in Ancient Rhetoric* (n. 2), p. 177.

negatives in the context. It would appear that one of the sources of this negative technique in the Fourth Gospel is the tradition concerning light, which appears to have begun as a contrary analogy in the earliest tradition.

4. *Second-level Elaboration that Creates the Boundaries of a Story*

A. Situations and actions may remain primary even when they are a social embarrassment.

B. Transmitters of early tradition elaborate embarrassing social situations by turning the argumentation to topics which they have significant resources to support.

The accounts of a woman's anointing of Jesus in the gospel tradition is an excellent example of the manner in which situations and actions are tenacious in the tradition. In this instance, the situation is socially problematic, and transmitters had to find a way to deal with it. Rhetorical elaboration is the natural tool for this kind of circumstance.

The common wording in synoptic Christian tradition about the woman who anointed Jesus is as follows:

μύρου
οἶκ[ ]
γυνή
ἀλάβαστρον μύρου
τῆς κεφαλῆς
Σίμων[ ]

This wording features an alabaster of ointment, a house, a woman, action on Jesus' head, and Simon (either a healed leper or the disciple). The Markan and Matthean accounts are close recitational variations of one another. The variation between them is precisely of the kind described earlier: they replicate a significant amount of verbatim wording in an environment where they freely use words they prefer. The Lukan account exhibits a significantly different kind of elaboration to deal with the social situation. The Gospel of John has a story that features Mary anointing Jesus' feet with costly ointment, and wiping his feet with her hair (12,1-8). Judas' complaint that the ointment could have been sold for three hundred denarii and given to the poor, and Jesus' response that they would always have the poor with them but they would not always have him, shows that the story is a variant of the Markan and Matthean accounts. The Johannine account exhibits a way of dealing with the situation by attributing it to a person with status in the tradition.

In all the accounts, the situation and action of a woman with Jesus are primary. The beginning of the tradition lies in social culture – interaction between two people in a setting where others look on. It appears that this social culture is problematic: the woman's presence and her specific action require a "Christian" response; otherwise, the context could evoke meanings associated with sexual actions in the environment of a symposium. In order to give a response to this situation and action, more than amplification is necessary. The tradition needs to use elaboration, a procedure that adds significantly new rhetorical figures to the context of social culture. The new rhetorical figures, naturally, will nurture an ideological culture. It is good, however, if the figures can engage another aspect of social culture that can successfully divert the hearers and readers away from the dynamics of the social culture that more naturally call forth a response.

Burton Mack has analyzed both the Markan and the Lukan accounts, but for the purposes of this essay, only Mk 14,3-9 will be exhibited and discussed[55]:

Introduction
 Setting: 3 And while he was at Bethany in the house of Simon the leper, as he sat at table, a woman came with an alabaster jar of ointment of pure nard, very costly, and she broke the jar and poured it over his head.
 Challenge
  Thesis: 4 But there were some who said to themselves indignantly, "Why was the ointment thus wasted?
  Rationale: 5 For this ointment might have been sold for more than three hundred denarii, and given to the poor". And they reproached her.
Response
 Redirection of the question: 6 But Jesus said, "Let her alone; why do you trouble her?"
 Alternative thesis: "She has done a beautiful thing for me".
 Alternative rationale: 7 "For you always have the poor with you",
 Implied analogy: "and whenever you will, you can do good to them";
 Contrary: "but you will not always have me".
 Paradigm: 8 "She has done what she could; she has anointed my body beforehand for burying".
 Authoritative judgment (as encomiastic period): 9 "And truly I say to you, wherever the gospel is preached in the whole world, what she has done will be told in memory of her"[56].

Second-level elaboration begins in the articulation of the challenge to Jesus. By introducing the topic of wasting the ointment when it could be sold and given to the poor, an alternative social culture can direct attention away from the presence of the woman anointing Jesus' body

---

55. Mack–Robbins, *Patterns of Persuasion in the Gospels* (n. 6), pp. 85-106.
56. *Ibid.*, p. 93, with slight variations.

while he reclines at dinner. The initial social culture smacks of symposium activity during Jesus' life and in early Christian circles; the alternative social issue evokes an ideological culture in which Christians are engaged in almsgiving, which is an honorable Mediterranean tradition. Once the transmitter has introduced this topic, abundant argumentative resources lie at hand to deal with this issue.

Jesus turns the topic back towards social culture, but in a manner that bypasses the initial social culture in this tradition. The topic comes from that kind of Christian ideological culture that focused on the death of Jesus. Can anyone fault the woman for anointing Jesus for burial, when people "in the know" are aware that Jesus was hastily buried and his body was gone on the morning after the sabbath when women came to anoint his body? Therefore, a new thesis is at hand: "She has done a beautiful thing to me". A rationale also is ready at hand, "For you always have the poor with you"; with an implied analogy, "and whenever you will you can do good to them"; and a contrary, "But you will not always have me". Thus, the woman is a paradigm of action, and Jesus articulates this argument: "She has done what she could; she has anointed my body beforehand for burying". This creates an environment for an authoritative encomiastic saying at the end: "And truly I say to you, whenever the gospel is preached in the whole world, what she has done will be told in memory of her".

In this instance, then, second-level elaboration creates the final boundary of the story. Expansion of the story introduces a series of new rhetorical figures that approximate a complete argument according to the definition of the rhetoricians. This kind of argumentation nurtures a subculture both socially and ideologically. They know the kinds of subcultural social commitments they need to have (preaching the gospel to the whole world rather than almsgiving), and they have an ideological culture to support them (memory of paradigmatic action toward Jesus, Jesus' defense of that action, and Jesus' death and burial)[57].

CONCLUSION

Socio-rhetorical analysis proceeds in a significantly different manner from literary-historical analysis. The eye and ear of the socio-rhetorical critic is on argumentation and its social and cultural meanings in the context in which it emerged. Exploration of the contexts of utterance, reference, and culture of the argumentation in the gospels begins to

---

57. See V.K. ROBBINS, *Using a Socio-Rhetorical Poetics to Develop a Unified Method: The Woman who Anointed Jesus as a Test Case*, in *SBL 1992 Seminar Papers*, pp. 302-319.

exhibit various kinds of subcultural and countercultural movements in early Christian tradition. Burton Mack's analysis of Mark probes five different cultural subgroups in early Christianity[58]. Each subgroup exhibits a distinctive use of language, a preference for a particular form of tradition, special social strategies, and a significant ideology. His proposal needs to be tested, refined, and expanded in the context of detailed socially and culturally oriented rhetorical analysis. This essay has not started such an analysis, but it has displayed a significant number of the features of culture-transmitting tradition that are the targets of analysis in such an investigation. The purpose has been to start a discussion. An earlier version of this essay was successful, in fact, in initiating a vigorous and fruitful discussion in the Seminar at the Colloquium Biblicum Lovaniense that honored Frans Neirynck. I am grateful for that discussion and look forward to the additional discussion this form of the essay may elicit.

Emory University   Vernon K. Robbins
Department of Religion
Atlanta, GA 30322
U.S.A.

---

58. Mack, *A Myth of Innocence* (n. 6).

MARK AND Q

The problem of the relationship between Mark and Q has been a perennial one for those working within the parameters of the Two Source Theory (2ST). The history of research in the topic has been surveyed often enough in recent years[1], and no attempt will be made here to duplicate such surveys. The question was perhaps a burning one in the early days of the 2ST, though with the rise of form-criticism etc., interest in the problem has somewhat faded[2]. In part this is due to the different ways in which one approaches the gospels in a post-form-critical era[3]. In such a climate of scholarly activity, problems of direct literary dependence seem less relevant and less important as one works more readily with a model of developing tradition-histories. Nevertheless the issue of a possible literary relationship between Mark and Q has continued to be debated, either in terms of explicit discussion of the issue, or implicitly by means of other theories which, as we shall see, are not unrelated to the problem.

The most widely held view today, amongst those who accept some form of the 2ST, is that Mark and Q are not in a relationship of direct literary dependence. There are a number of instances where Mark and Q each appear to have a version of what is ultimately the same tradition; but the two versions are not directly related to each other and represent independent versions of a common tradition[4]. Nevertheless there have always been some scholars who have defended the view that there may be a direct literary relationship involved, a theory which is almost always proposed today in the form that Mark used Q, rather than vice versa[5]. (Hence in the present paper I shall confine

---

1. See M. DEVISCH, *La relation entre l'évangile de Marc et le document Q*, in M. SABBE (ed.), *L'Évangile selon Marc. Tradition et rédaction* (BETL, 34), Leuven - Gembloux, University Press - Duculot, 1974, pp. 59-91, esp. 69-83; R. LAUFEN, *Die Doppelüberlieferungen der Logienquelle und des Markusevangeliums* (BBB, 54), Bonn, Hanstein, 1980, pp. 59-77; J. SCHÜLING, *Studien zum Verhältnis von Logienquelle und Markusevangelium* (FzB, 65), Würzburg, Echter, 1991.

2. Cf. LAUFEN, *Doppelüberlieferungen* (n. 1), p. 76, comparing the amount of space devoted to the topic in older *Introductions* with the situation in more recent publications where the issue often receives only passing mention.

3. Cf. D. LÜHRMANN, *Die Redaktion der Logienquelle* (WMANT, 33), Neukirchen-Vluyn, Neukirchener, 1969, p. 20f.; LAUFEN, *Doppelüberlieferungen* (n. 1), p. 77.

4. For the many advocates of this, see the bibliographical references in DEVISCH, *Marc et le document Q* (n. 1), pp. 79f.; LAUFEN, *Doppelüberlieferungen* (n. 1), pp. 75f., as well as the works of Devisch and Laufen themselves.

5. The theory that Q used Mark was proposed by J. Wellhausen (*Einleitung in die drei ersten Evangelien*, Berlin, Reimer, 1905, pp. 73-89) in the early part of the this century, but

attention to the possibility that Mark used Q, rather than vice versa.) Thus in recent years the possibility that Mark used Q has been suggested (with varying degrees of certainty and in varying degrees of complexity of the overall solution) by J. Lambrecht, W. Schmithals, W. Schenk, H. Fleddermann, B. Mack and D. Catchpole[6]. We may also note that study of Q (and Mark) individually has developed very considerably in recent years, and these developments may affect the way in which one approaches the whole problem of the relationship between Mark and Q, as well as affecting some key results. Hence a survey, and reassessment, of the problem of the relationship between Mark and Q may be in order.

At one level the problem might be thought to be somewhat esoteric, of interest only to source-critics, and moreover only to source-critics working within the presuppositions of the 2ST[7]. However, the problem has a large number of potential repercussions. Even within the parameters of the 2ST, the problem has enormous potential significance. For example, the theory that Mark was dependent on Q could lead to a number of corollaries. On the side of Q studies, the issue would be of considerable importance, since the theory could mean that Q was of considerably larger compass than is usually thought: all the triple

---

has rarely (at least in that explicit form) been defended since. Cf. DEVISCH, *Marc et le document Q* (n. 1), p. 72. However, cf. below for other theories which may in effect approximate to this.

6. See a number of articles and studies by J. LAMBRECHT, including *Die Logia-Quellen von Markus 13*, in *Biblica* 47 (1966) 321-360; *Die Redaktion der Markus-Apokalypse* (AnBib, 28), Rome, Pontifical Biblical Institute, 1967; *Redaction and Theology in Mk. IV*, in M. SABBE (ed.), *L'Évangile selon Marc* (n. 1), pp. 269-307; *Q Influence on Mark 8,34–9,1*, in J. DELOBEL (ed.), *Logia. Les Paroles de Jésus - The Sayings of Jesus* (BETL, 59), Leuven, University Press - Peeters, 1982, pp. 277-304; *John and Jesus in Mark 1.1-15. Markan Redaction of Q?*, in *NTS* 38 (1992) 337-356. W. SCHMITHALS, *Das Evangelium nach Markus* (ÖTK, 2/1-2), Gütersloh, Mohn, 1979; also *Die Worte vom leidenden Menschensohn*, in C. ANDRESEN – G. KLEIN (eds.), *Theologia Crucis - Signum Crucis. FS E. Dinkler*, Tübingen, Mohr, 1979, pp. 417-455, esp. pp. 435-445; also his *Einleitung in die drei ersten Evangelien*, Berlin, de Gruyter, 1985. W. SCHENK, *Der Einfluss der Logienquelle auf das Markusevangelium*, in *ZNW* 70 (1979) 141-165. [In fact both Schmithals and Schenk propose somewhat complicated theories involving prior sources as well. For Schenk, Mark is dependent on an earlier "Prae-Markus" as well as on Q, even in overlap passages. For Schmithals, Mark depends on an earlier *Grundschrift* and an early form of Q, a "Q¹". Cf. the survey by F. NEIRYNCK, *Recent Developments in the Study of Q*, in J. DELOBEL (ed.), *Logia*, 1982, pp. 29-75, on pp. 42f.; = *Evangelica II* (BETL, 99), Leuven, University Press - Peeters, 1991, pp. 422f.] H. FLEDDERMANN, *The Discipleship Discourse (Mark 9:33-50)*, in *CBQ* 43 (1981) 57-75; also *The Mustard Seed and the Leaven in Q, the Synoptics and Thomas*, in *SBL 1989 Seminar Papers*, pp. 216-236; B. MACK, *Q and the Gospel of Mark: Revising Christian Origins*, in *Semeia* 55 (1991) 15-39; D.R. CATCHPOLE, *The Mission Charge in Q*, in *Semeia* 55 (1991) 147-174; and *The Beginning of Q: A Proposal*, in *NTS* 38 (1992) 205-221.

7. Cf. M. DEVISCH, *Marc et le document Q* (n. 1), p. 60: "le problème de la relation entre Mc et Q est un problème de la théorie des deux sources".

tradition material, usually not ascribed to Q, would be potentially Q material which Mark has taken over from Q[8]. On the side of Markan study, such a theory would also involve a drastic re-evaluation of Mark's redaction, since the theory would imply that Mark made a conscious decision not to include a vast amount of teaching material in his gospel. The issue can be developed and used in other directions too. Thus, for example, a recent writer, discussing H.E. Tödt's well-known claim that the Q Christians were the first to identify Jesus with the coming Son of Man, said:

> This must have been in the tradition before Q already, for in Mark it is also clear that the Son of Man about whom Jesus is speaking is no one else than Jesus himself[9].

The main criterion for the claim that any identification of Jesus with the Son of Man must pre-date Q is thus the assumed independence of the Markan tradition. If Mark were dependent on Q such an argument would collapse.

We may also note the extent to which a number of other source-critical theories about the synoptic gospels are closely related to (at times older) theories about the relationship between Mark and Q. For example, theories of the existence of a Deutero-Markan edition of Mark[10], and M.D. Goulder's theory which denies the existence of Q[11], insofar as they seek to explain the pattern of agreements between the gospels in the "overlap" passages, are both not far removed from Wellhausen's theory that Q was dependent on Mark in these passages. In the Deutero-Markus theory, Q is replaced by Deutero-Markus; in Goulder's theory Q is replaced by Matthew. But all these theories claim that the Markan version is more original, that there is a secondary re-writing of Mark by a later editor (for Wellhausen Q, for Fuchs Deutero-Markus, for Goulder Matthew), and it is this secondary

---

8. See M. DEVISCH, *Marc et le document Q* (n. 1), pp. 63f. Cf. too D.R. CATCHPOLE, *Beginning* (n. 6), pp. 216-218, who explicitly exploits the theory of Markan dependence on Q to reconstruct the possible opening of Q from Mk 1,2-5.

9. D. LÜHRMANN, *The Gospel of Mark and the Sayings Collection Q*, in *JBL* 108 (1989) 51-71, on p. 64.

10. See especially the work of A. FUCHS, including his *Die Entwicklung der Beelzebul-kontroverse bei den Synoptikern* (SNTU/B, 5), Linz, Plöchl, 1980; *Die Überschneidungen von Mk und 'Q' nach B.H.Streeter und E.P. Sanders und ihre wahre Bedeutung (Mk 1,1-8 par.)*, in W. HAUBECK – M. BACHMANN (eds.), *Wort in der Zeit. Neutestamentliche Studien. FS K. Rengstorf*, Leiden, Brill, 1980, pp. 28-81; *Durchbruch in der Synoptischen Frage und ihre Konsequenzen*, in *SNTU* 8 (1983) 5-17; *Versuchung Jesu*, in *SNTU* 9 (1984) 95-159. F. KOGLER, *Das Doppelgleichnis vom Senfkorn und vom Sauerteig in seiner traditionsgeschichtlichen Entwicklung* (FzB, 59), Würzburg, Echter, 1988. Other proponents of such a theory are perhaps slightly different: see n. 15 below.

11. See M.D. GOULDER, *On Putting Q to the Test*, in *NTS* 24 (1978) 218-234; also his *Luke - A New Paradigm* (JSNT SS, 20), Sheffield, Sheffield Academic Press, 1989.

version which is the cause of the subsequent Matthew-Luke agreements. Similarly the Griesbach hypothesis (GH) is very close to the converse theory that Mark used Q in the overlap passages: both theories postulate that Mark's version is secondary to, and dependent on, the version which explains the Matthew-Luke agreements (for the 2ST Q, for the GH Matthew). Thus the problem of a possible relationship between Mark and Q is closely connected with much broader issues of synoptic source studies, and indeed of synoptic studies in general.

Further, the "overlap" passages are quite crucial for many synoptic source theories. In his 1971 Leuven paper devoted to the topic of the relationship between Mark and Q, M. Devisch claimed that:

> Pour ceux qui défendent d'autres solutions du problème synoptique, les textes que, dans la théorie des deux sources, on appelle généralement 'les passages qui se recouvrent', ne font aucun problème. Ils constituent, au contraire, les examples les plus probants pour confirmer ces autres théories[12].

Such a claim would however be hard to defend today. The overlap passages in fact remain at times extremely difficult to explain on theories other than the 2ST. In a number of recent studies, F.G. Downing has mounted a powerful attack against the views of Goulder, and against the modern defenders of the GH, on the grounds that, precisely in the overlap passages, those theories have to postulate a procedure on the part of the third evangelist (Luke for Goulder, Mark for the GH) which is quite unparalleled amongst contemporary writers in terms of the complexity of the procedure required: the third writer would have had to "unpick" all the work of one of his sources from his second source (whether Luke unpicking Mark from Matthew, or Mark unpicking Luke from Matthew) in order to retain only the residue. Such a procedure is inherently implausible, as well as being contrary to all that we can see of the way in which writers at the time used sources, so that it must throw an enormous question mark against the overall source theory being proposed[13]. Similarly, I have tried elsewhere to show that, for the GH, the overlap passages must have involved Mark in a redactional procedure which is diametrically opposite to that postulated elsewhere in the tradition: elsewhere a Griesbachian Mark appears as one anxious to preserve what is common to both his alleged sources, whereas in these passages Mark must have adopted a quite different procedure of deliberately avoiding what was common to his

12. M. Devisch, *Marc et le document Q* (n. 1), p. 60.
13. See F.G. Downing, *Compositional Conventions and the Synoptic Problem*, in *JBL* 107 (1988) 69-85; *A Paradigm Perplex: Luke, Matthew and Mark*, in *NTS* 38 (1992) 15-36; also his earlier *Towards the Rehabilitation of Q*, in *NTS* 11 (1964-65) 169-181.

two sources in order to reproduce only what appeared in just one
source[14]. Thus although at one level the problem of the relationship
between Mark and Q is by its nature one that can only be of concern to
those who presuppose the existence of Q, i.e. those who accept a form
of the 2ST, nevertheless the passages which give rise to the problem, i.e.
the "overlap" passages, are equally crucial for other source theories[15].

For those working within the presuppositions of the 2ST, the existence of possible "overlap" passages in Mark and Q has long been
recognised (even if there is debate about precisely which passages are to
be explained in this way). Given then the existence of such an overlap,
there must have been a link between the two streams of the tradition at
some stage and the question is: at what stage? A theory of literary
dependence between Mark and Q suggests that it is at the stage of the
final forms of the tradition in the development of both "texts".

One must say initially that any attempt to argue for direct dependence between Mark and Q will have to involve a highly sophisticated
form of argumentation. P. Wernle pointed out long ago that, in relation
to doublets in the tradition, such a theory is very forced: the existence
of doublets in the tradition has often been taken as a powerful
argument in favour of the view that there are two streams of tradition
here; but a theory of a direct relationship between those streams
suggests per contra that there is only one basic tradition (with a
secondary development)[16]. A theory of direct dependence of Mark on
Q would thus appear to demolish one of the strongest arguments in
favour of the very existence of Q in the first place. One can reply to
this, with Devisch, by pointing out that the existence of doublets in
Matthew and/or Luke relates to the state of the tradition in the later

14. C.M. TUCKETT, *The Revival of the Griesbach Hypothesis* (SNTSMS, 44), Cambridge, University Press, 1983, ch. 8, pp. 76-93.
15. The Deutero-Markus theory is perhaps slightly different in this respect. Defenders
of such a theory by no means agree amongst themselves about the relative significance of
the "overlap" passages. Whilst these texts form the primary evidence for Fuchs and
Kogler, others such as H. Aichinger and C. Niemand have sought to defend the theory in
relation to texts not usually regarded as "Mark-Q overlaps": cf. H. AICHINGER, *Quellen-
kritische Untersuchung der Perikope vom Ährenraufen am Sabbat*, in *SNTU* 1 (1976) 110-
153; *Zur Traditionsgeschichte der Epileptiker-Perikope Mk 9,14-29 par Mt 17,14-21 par Lk
9,37-43a*, in *SNTU* 3 (1978) 114-143; C. NIEMAND, *Studien zu den Minor Agreements der
synoptischen Verklärungsperikopen* (Europäische Hochschulschriften, XXIII/352), Frankfurt - Bern - New York - Paris, Lang, 1989. More recently A. Ennulat and U. Luz have
explicitly shunned the use of such overlap passages to defend the theory of the existence of
a Deutero-Markan editor: see A. ENNULAT, *Die "Minor Agreements" - Ein Diskussionsbeitrag zur Erklärung einer offenen Frage des synoptischen Problems* (Diss. Bern, 1989;
Tübingen, Mohr, forthcoming); U. LUZ, *Das Evangelium nach Matthäus* (EKK, I/1-2),
Zürich - Neukirchen-Vluyn, Benziger - Neukirchener, 1985 - 1990.
16. P. WERNLE, *Die synoptische Frage*, Leipzig, Mohr, 1899, pp. 209f.

period, *after* Mark and Q, whereas the theory of a possible relationship between Mark and Q themselves relates to an earlier stage in the history of the tradition. Hence one cannot necessarily expect Matthew and Luke to have known the pre-history of Mark's (or Q's) tradition[17].

Nevertheless, this debate does show, in more general terms, that arguments for the existence of Q may by their very nature tell against any theory of a relationship between Mark and Q. The point can perhaps be put in a slightly different way. One usually only postulates the existence of a Mark-Q overlap if there is relatively *little* verbal agreement between Mark and Matthew/Luke. A greater degree of agreement between all three gospels would lead more naturally (assuming Markan priority) to the theory that Matthew and Luke are directly dependent on Mark alone. Thus any overlap theory must assume a level of verbal agreement between Mark and the other two gospels that is sufficiently low to preclude the theory that Matthew and Luke are simply dependent on Mark at this point in the tradition. But then the low level of agreement between Mark and Matthew/Luke (= Q) makes it correspondingly harder to plead for any direct literary relationship between Mark and Q, which of necessity has to be based on a relatively *high* level of verbal agreement between Mark and Q (= Matthew/ Luke). A priori, therefore, the evidence which suggests the existence of a Mark-Q overlap is by its very nature less likely to be conducive to a further theory of direct dependence between Mark and Q.

Part of this difficulty might be met if one could show that, where Mark and Q differ, Mark's version is regularly MkR[18]. This is above all the approach adopted in the many articles of J. Lambrecht and in the work of H. Fleddermann and B. Mack[19]: these scholars seek to show at many points that Mark's version is Markan, especially where Mark appears to differ from the Q version. Yet whilst such a method is necessary to show Mark's dependence on Q, it is by no means sufficient. For although such an approach may throw much light on Mark's own interests and concerns, it does not necessarily tell us anything about the precise nature of the pre-Markan tradition. In particular, it cannot tell us in the case of overlap passages whether Mark is redacting Q itself, or a pre-Q stage in the tradition, or a pre-Markan stage which is independent of the Q trajectory[20].

17. M. DEVISCH, *Marc et le document Q* (n. 1), p. 68.
18. Cf. above at n. 5: I am assuming throughout this paper that any possible dependency relationship is with Mark being dependent on Q, not vice versa.
19. See n. 6 above.
20. Very much the same applies to the theories of Fuchs and Kogler who seek to explain the "Q" version as due to a secondary "redaction" or "editing" (*Bearbeitung* is the German word often used) by a Deutero-Markan editor. Whilst their arguments show how the "Q" (or Deutero-Markan) version *might* have been derived, they do not show that it *must* have been derived in this way. Given too the willingness of both scholars to

The methodological problem here has been noted by several scholars before. Hence many have urged that dependence of Mark on Q can only be shown if Mark can be seen to reflect elements of Q's redaction: simply showing that Mark's version might be explained as MkR is not enough[21]. The insistence of the importance of Q's redaction means that the problem of "Mark and Q" is in the first instance a problem of Q studies rather than of Markan studies[22]. Certainly the tremendous interest shown in Q from a "redaction"-critical perspective, seeking to identify redactional features and characteristic elements in the Q tradition, has made it possible to think more meaningfully of the existence of Q's "redaction". However, the whole question of Q's redaction is complicated by the growing number of theories that "Q" underwent a series of stages in its history of development - Q^1, Q^2, Q^3 etc. With this in mind, it is particularly important for the problem of the relationship between Mark and "Q" that one specifies what one is talking about in referring to "Q" in this context: is it Q^3? or Q^2? or even Q^1? I would suggest that, in order to preserve clarity, and also consistency with other areas of NT study, one should perhaps reserve the siglum "Q" for Q in something like its "final" form, i.e. the latest stage in the development of the tradition common to Matthew and Luke insofar as we can trace that development[23]. In the terminology of some, this means that "Q" would mean "Q^3". Q^1, Q^2 etc. are all then stages in the *"pre-'Q'"* development of the tradition and any possible links between Mark and "Q^1", say, would not tell us anything about a relationship between Mark and "Q" as such[24].

concede in principle that the Deutero-Markan editor might have used independent traditions in supplementing and re-writing Mark (cf. FUCHS, *Versuchung* [n. 10], p. 113, on the temptation narrative; KOGLER, *Doppelgleichnis* [n. 10], p. 185, on the parable of the leaven), it becomes at times hard to see why Matthew and Luke must have known such independent traditions *only* as mediated through the hands of the Deutero-Markan editor and not independently (from something like "Q"). The Deutero-Markan theory can thus slide into a position not far removed from the more traditional Mark-Q overlap theory.

21. Cf. NEIRYNCK, *Recent Developments* (n. 6), p. 45 (= *Evangelica II*, p. 425); SCHENK, *Einfluss* (n. 6), p. 145f.; SCHÜLING, *Studien* (n. 1), p. 182. In relation to the Deutero-Mark theory, one should perhaps correspondingly demand that Deutero-Mark (as seen in Matthew and Luke) show evidence of Mark's redaction. However, this would show relatively little since dependence of Matthew and Luke on Mark, and hence the appearance of MkR elements in Matthew and Luke, is not controversial. The precise equivalent demand would be to seek to show MkR elements in either Q or Deutero-Mark itself - but sadly neither is available for us to check!

22. Cf. F. NEIRYNCK, *John and the Synoptics*, in M. DE JONGE (ed.), *L'Évangile de Jean. Sources, rédaction, théologie* (BETL, 44), Leuven - Gembloux, University Press - Duculot, 1977, p. 87; = ID., *Evangelica* (BETL, 60), Leuven, University Press - Peeters, 1982, p. 379, in relation to John and the Synoptics.

23. This is not to preclude the possibility of a development after this stage in the tradition available to only one of Matthew or Luke, i.e. a Q^{Mt} or a Q^{Lk}.

24. Thus, strictly speaking on this definition, the theory of Schmithals (see n. 6 above) is not quite relevant here since Schmithals postulates a relationship involving Mark and an earlier stage in Q's development, viz. Q^1, not the "final" form of Q.

I would however question whether it is indeed justifiable to think in terms of such a complex, *and* identifiable, development in the literary history of Q. Whilst such a complex development is indeed possible, it seems to me very doubtful whether such complexity will ever be clearly identifiable, given the state of our existing evidence. The prime candidate for inclusion in a final "Q³" stage is very often regarded as the Q temptation narrative. I have tried to argue elsewhere that this story can be seen as cohering very closely with other parts of Q, and hence the need to postulate a further, later stage in the development of Q to accommodate this story is to a certain extent obviated[25]. At most then one perhaps can justify a Q¹ + Q² model. Yet even here it may be best to use terminology carefully. To speak of "Q¹" and "Q²" suggests that both were well-defined, unitary "texts". Whilst the evidence of the gospels of Matthew and Luke has suggested to many that it is indeed entirely appropriate to think of the "final" stage of Q in this way as a literary text with a well-defined order, it is much more debatable whether any earlier stage in Q should be conceived of in the same way. There is not the time or space to argue the point in detail here[26]; perhaps though it may be safer to speak in more general terms of Q-tradition and Q-redaction without making further assumptions about the nature of the former, especially in relation to its possible unity, but recognising its potential complexity. These observations are in no way intended to preclude the possibility, or even the necessity, of postulating a multi-stage development in the individual traditions of Q. Indeed I shall argue below that some secondary elements which are visible in Q traditions may be pre-redactional in Q. All I am saying is that we cannot necessarily assume that the whole of Q's tradition in its pre-redactional form existed as a unified literary text prior to its existence in the "final" form of Q.

How then can one identify elements in Q that are Q-redactional / editorial? Clearly it would be quite inappropriate to lay down abstract rules in advance which one can then apply mechanistically to the Q material concerned. Further, one must be wary of assuming that the interests of the Q-redactor, or editor, can be discerned solely on the basis of redactional *changes* made to an underlying tradition. The choice and overall content of material is equally significant in this context[27]. Clearly one needs the sensitive application of a number of criteria and factors. For example, the existence of aporia, or seams, in the tradition may suggest the presence of redactional additions; but also the order and literary structure of the composition as a whole may

25. See my article *The Temptation Narrative in Q*, in *The Four Gospels 1992. FS F. Neirynck* (BETL, 100), Leuven, University Press - Peeters, 1992, pp. 479-507.

26. I hope to try to discuss this further in a forthcoming monograph on Q. See also my *On the Stratification of Q*, in *Semeia* 55 (1991) 213-222.

27. See my *Reading the New Testament*, London, SPCK, 1987, pp. 122f.

be an important indicator of the views of the final editor. In other
words one needs approaches to Q which utilize what have been called
"Literarkritik" *and* "literary criticism". In the present context, however, in the investigation of a possible relation between Mark and Q,
one must beware of applying criteria which implicitly determine the
solution to the problem under discussion in advance. In particular this
applies to those who would argue that an element in Q cannot be Q-
redactional if it appears in Mark as well[28]. Such a criterion will
inevitably mean, almost by definition, that elements of Q-redaction do
not recur in Mark. It will thus be necessary to try to determine what is
Q-redactional independently of the possible Markan parallels and only
then to compare Mark and Q to see if Mark reflects Q-redaction (or,
conceivably, vice versa).

As a starting point, I take the widely held agreement that the theme
of Q's polemic against "this generation", employing ideas associated
with Wisdom and the Deuteronomistic theme of the violence suffered
by the prophets, is a dominant one in the present form of Q; and hence
elements associated with it and which emphasize different aspects of it
are likely to be due, at least in the present arrangement of Q, to the
work of the Q editor (though without necessarily assuming that all such
elements have been created de novo by Q)[29]. Other possible elements of
Q's redaction will have to be analyzed as they occur in the course of the
investigation[30].

In what follows, I take a few passages from amongst the so-called
"overlap" texts to see what light they may throw on our problem. No
pretence can be made here to claim any degree of comprehensive
coverage of the relevant material. And it may well be that, although no

---

28. Cf. Lührmann above (n. 9) on Son of Man in Q; also J.S. KLOPPENBORG, *The
Formation of Q*, Philadelphia, Fortress, 1987, p. 104; S. SCHULZ, *Q - Die Spruchquelle der
Evangelisten*, Zürich, Theologischer, 1972, p. 230. (On both the latter, see below.)

29. LÜHRMANN, *Mark and Q* (n. 9), p. 59, refers to the themes of Wisdom, and polemic
against "this generation", as widely agreed within contemporary Q research as representing the views of Q's redaction. Note however D.R. CATCHPOLE, *Temple Traditions in
Q*, in W. HORBURY (ed.), *Templum Amicitiae. FS E. Bammel* (JSNT SS, 48), Sheffield,
Sheffield Academic Press, 1991, pp. 305-329, who warns against the mistake of assuming
that if something is of close concern to the Q redactor, it cannot be traced back prior to Q
(possibly even to Jesus).

30. One of the most recent treatments of the relationship between Mark and Q, that of
Schüling (n. 1 above), suffers from an unwillingness to ascribe almost anything to Q-
redaction. Schüling correctly sees the importance of the possible appearance of Q-
redactional elements in Mark (cf. n. 21 above), but simply denies that Q-redaction is
responsible for anything except possibly the link statements in Q 10,12; 11,30. His
arguments are however weak and circular. He frequently claims that Q redaction would
have been more active if anything were redactional; but the alleged inactivity is as often as
not simply assumed or asserted. Further, the possible significance of the literary arrangement of the Q material is generally ignored.

links between Mark and Q-redaction appear in these texts, such links might appear in other sets of parallels. Nevertheless it is to be hoped that the analyses presented here may make some contribution to the continuing discussion[31].

Q 11,29-30 / Mk 8,11-12: Request for a Sign

The pericope concerning the request for a sign by Jesus constitutes one of the classic overlap passages within the 2ST[32]. Further it seems clear from the parallels between Matthew and Luke that the Q version of the pericope in Q 11,29-30 is part of a wider literary context within Q containing the account of the Beelzebul controversy (Q 11,14-22), the saying on neutrality (Q 11,23), the mini-parable of the return of the unclean spirits (Q 11,24-26) and the double saying about the Queen of the South and Jonah (Q 11,31-32). The fact that all these pericopes occur in the same contexts in Matthew and Luke testifies to the presence of a Q sequence containing these traditions[33]. Further, *if* (as is often assumed) Luke has generally preserved the order of the Q material more accurately that Matthew, this complex of traditions may well have been closely followed in Q by the series of woes against the scribes/lawyers and Pharisees (Q 11,37-51). Certainly we may note that the climax of the series of woes seems to be the doom oracle in Q 11,49-51 directed against "this generation", and this correlates closely with the Sign pericope and Jesus' complaint about the iniquities of "this generation", and also with the double saying in Q 11,31-32 warning of the coming condemnation of "this generation" for its refusal to respond to what is taking place in the present.

The Q version of the Sign pericope raises an enormous number of wide-ranging and far-reaching questions (e.g. the references to "Jonah", the "Son of Man", the nature of the "sign" etc.). There is not enough time or space to deal with these in any detail here. The rather limited purpose of this paper is simply to consider the problem of the relationship between the Markan version, where a sign is flatly refused, and the Q version, where the general refusal is qualified by some kind of

31. In accordance with what is becoming standard convention, I give the references to Q in terms of the Lukan chapter and verse numbers.

32. Cf. LAUFEN, *Doppelüberlieferungen* (n. 1), p. 85: "allgemein als Doppelüberlieferung anerkannt". I do not attempt a precise reconstruction of the Q version down to the last preposition. I assume, with almost all those working with the Q hypothesis, that in Q the refusal to respond to the request for a sign is qualified in some way by the phrase εἰ μὴ τὸ σημεῖον Ἰωνᾶ. This is in turn then clarified by a Son of Man saying in Q 11,30 and, again following almost all commentators, I take the Lukan version of the saying here in Lk 11,30 to be more original than Matthew's parallel in Mt 12,40. This however will not be discussed in detail here and does not affect the argument above.

33. The precise order in Q is however not certain: cf. the varying position of the parable of the unclean spirits which comes before the Sign pericope in Luke, after in Matthew. However, the issue does not affect the argument here.

exceptive clause "except the sign of Jonah" which in turn is "clarified" by a Son of Man saying in Q 11,30. Could then the Markan version be plausibly seen as dependent on Q?

At one level, the evidence is clearly ambiguous. The argument about whether the more original form of the tradition contained the exceptive clause referring to Jonah, or whether the original tradition gave simply an outright refusal, can go, and has gone, either way: either the Jonah reference can be seen as a secondary addition, or its non-appearance in Mark could be seen as a secondary (Markan?) deletion due perhaps to its unintelligibility or to Mark's own desire to stress the sufficiency of the witness of Jesus' own activity and/or the messianic secret[34].

We may however make more progress by considering the wider Q context. In Q the qualified refusal of a sign in 11,29 is followed by an explanation of the qualification in v. 30 in the Son of Man saying, and by the double saying about the Queen of the South and Jonah in vv. 31-32[35]. Moreover it seems clear that we have here two originally separate traditions: the present link of the double saying and the Sign pericope serves to focus attention almost exclusively on the figure of Jonah (and his counterpart in the Son of Man). The reference to the Queen of the South and Solomon seems rather otiose. This is best explained if the double saying in 11,31-32 was originally a separate tradition, and the present Q sequence linking the double saying and the Sign pericope is secondary[36]. Moreover a clear thematic link between 11,29-30 and

34. For Mark as more original, cf. D. LÜHRMANN, *Das Markusevangelium* (HNT, 3), Tübingen, Mohr, 1987, p. 137; *Redaktion* (n. 3), pp. 34-43; R. PESCH, *Das Markusevangelium* I (HTKNT, II/1), Freiburg-Basel-Wien, Herder, 1976, p. 409; R.A. EDWARDS, *The Sign of Jonah*, London, SCM, 1971, pp. 83-87. For Mark as secondarily deleting the reference to Jonah, see A. VÖGTLE, *Der Spruch vom Jonaszeichen*, in J. SCHMID – A. VÖGTLE (eds.), *Synoptische Studien. FS A. Wikenhauser*, München, Zink, 1953, pp. 230-277, on p. 274; J. GNILKA, *Das Evangelium nach Markus* I (EKK, II/1), Neukirchen-Vluyn, Neukirchener, 1979, p. 305; KLOPPENBORG, *Formation* (n. 28), p. 130. Cf. the survey in R.A. GUELICH, *Mark 1–8:26* (WBC, 34A), Dallas, Word Books, 1989, p. 411, and also KLOPPENBORG, *Formation* (n. 28), p. 129: "The absence of the phrase in Mark is not ultimately decisive".

35. The common sequence in both Matthew and Luke clearly attests to the sequence in Q here.

36. Cf. KLOPPENBORG, *Formation* (n. 28), p. 128; D.R. CATCHPOLE, *The Law and the Prophets in Q*, in G.F. HAWTHORNE – O. BETZ (eds.), *Tradition and Interpretation in the New Testament. FS E.E. Ellis*, Grand Rapids - Tübingen, Eerdmans - Mohr, 1987, pp. 95-109, on pp. 100f. This must then tell against those who would see the whole sequence as a traditio-historical unit, possibly going back to Jesus (so A.J.B. HIGGINS, *The Son of Man in the Teaching of Jesus* (SNTS MS, 39), Cambridge, University Press, 1980, pp. 90ff.; H.F. BAYER, *Jesus' Predictions of Vindication and Resurrection* (WUNT 2.Reihe, 20), Tübingen, Mohr, 1986, esp. pp. 128f.) It must also tell against the view that 11,31-32 is a Q creation (so A.D. JACOBSON, *Wisdom Christology in Q*, Diss. Claremont, 1978, pp. 166-171, cf. his *The Literary Unity of Q*, in *JBL* 101 [1982] 365-389, on p. 382): the fact that the reference to the Queen of the South and Solomon fit so badly in the present context

11,31-32 is the negative attitude shown by, and to, "this generation". In 11,29-30 "this generation" is castigated as evil for demanding a sign; in 11,31-32 it is threatened with eschatological condemnation for its refusal to respond to the great events of the present. Such a negative attitude to "this generation" is thoroughly characteristic of Q-redaction (cf. above). It seems therefore highly likely that the linking of 11,29-30 and 11,31-32 is also due to the Q-redactional layer in the tradition.

It has been argued forcefully by many that Q 11,30 itself is also due to Q's redaction, or at least is a comment secondarily appended to v. 29[37]. This seems quite convincing and indeed there seems little reason to deny this to the Q-redactional stage and to ascribe it to an earlier stage in Q's development. Schürmann does argue for this latter theory, but his main reason for doing so is the alleged discrepancy between what he takes to be the proper interpretation of v. 30 on its own, where the Son of Man is an eschatological figure returning in judgement, and the interpretation of v. 30 demanded by the present broader Q context with v. 32, where the parallel between the Son of Man and Jonah implies that the Son of Man is a present preacher of repentance. Such a decision about the interpretation of v. 30 on its own is however perhaps premature. If one makes no such pre-judgements, then there is no clear need to postulate multi-stage developments in Q: the Son of Man in v. 30 can quite easily be the present Jesus preaching to this generation, and the whole coheres together well at the Q-redactional level[38]. However, even though there may be little justification for postulating several stages in the history of the development of Q at this point, there does seem to be good reason for regarding the present Q version as composite in the sense of reflecting a traditional and a redactional layer[39].

suggests strongly that this half of the saying cannot have been created for the present context.

37. Opinions differ on whether the exceptive clause in v. 29c ("except the sign of Jonah") is also Q-redactional. For vv. 29c + 30 as Q-redaction, cf. LÜHRMANN, *Redaktion* (n. 3), pp. 41f.; EDWARDS, *Sign* (n. 34), pp. 84f.; W. SCHENK, *Synopse zur Redequelle der Evangelien*, Düsseldorf, Patmos, 1981, p. 71; CATCHPOLE, *Law and Prophets* (n. 36), pp. 100f. For v. 30 as Q-redactional, cf. P. HOFFMANN, *Studien zur Theologie der Logienquelle* (NTA, 8), Münster, Aschendorff, 1972, p. 181; D. ZELLER, *Entrückung zur Ankunft als Menschensohn (Lk 13,34f.; 11,29f.)*, in *À cause de l'Évangile. FS J. Dupont* (LD, 123), Paris, Cerf, 1985, pp. 513-530, on p. 526. For v. 30 as a secondary comment added earlier in the tradition-history prior to the final redaction, cf. H. SCHÜRMANN, *Beobachtungen zum Menschensohntitel in der Redequelle*, in R. PESCH – R. SCHNACKEN-BURG (eds.), *Jesus und der Menschensohn. FS A. Vögtle*, Freiburg, Herder, 1975, pp. 124-147, on pp. 133f.; also JACOBSON, *Wisdom Christology* (n. 36), pp. 166-171.

38. Ironically, Kloppenborg adopts Schürmann's reconstruction of the development of the tradition, which is based almost entirely on Schürmann's interpretation of the meaning of "Son of Man" in v. 30, and yet adopts the interpretation of "Son of Man" given here: see his *Formation* (n. 28), pp. 128ff.

39. SCHENK, *Einfluss*, p. 154: "Am sekundären Charakter des Ausnahmesatzes und seiner Erläuterung kann kein Zweifel bestehen, ganz abgesehen vom Markustext".

What is striking for the present purposes is now that Mark betrays no knowledge at all of these features of Q's editorial activity in the wider literary context[40]. Mark exhibits no parallel to the explanatory verse Q 11,30; also Mark shows no awareness of the editorial linking of the Sign pericope with the double saying in Q 11,31-32. We may also note that, if one casts the net wider still in Q's literary context, Mark again shows no awareness of the apparent literary arrangement of Q. Mark does have a version of the Beelzebul controversy (Mk 3,20-30), but it is *not* connected with the Sign pericope in Mark. Mark also has a parallel to the neutrality saying of Q 11,23 in Mk 9,40, but again in a totally different context. Mark has no parallel at all to the parable of the evil sprits. And Mark has no parallel to the series of woes in Q 11,37-51. (The one similar warning against scribes in Mk 12,38-40 has no substantive parallel in the Q series of woes.) Thus Mark seems to show no awareness at all of the literary structuring of Q, insofar as this can be determined. The editorial activity of the Q redactor in bringing together different traditions (evidenced at least in the conjunction of 11,29-30 and 11,31-32) seems to have left no trace in Mark.

What of the detailed wording of Mark? Could Mk 8,11-12 be explained as MkR of the Q version of Q 11,29-30? This seems highly unlikely, especially in view of the well-known unusual elements of the Markan version which are often explained as reflecting Semitic features and which have appeared to many as evidence of a pre-Markan tradition used by Mark. This applies possibly to the τί construction, to the apparent oath formula using εἰ, the ἀμήν formulation, the divine passive etc.[41]. The cumulative force of this evidence makes it very hard to see Mark's version as due to MkR of Q.

Schenk has tried to argue in detail otherwise[42]. He refers to the fact that the τί construction could be standard Koine Greek rather than reflecting Aramaic idiom, that the εἰ construction is equally rare in Aramaic as in Greek, and that the present Markan version is fully in line with Mark's overall tendency in this passage to stress the negative elements in the story and to heighten the motif of the rejection of the

---

40. In the discussion after the paper at the Colloquium, it was suggested that the use of the phrase "this generation" in Mark might itself be evidence of Mark's use of a Q-redactional feature. This is possible; however, one cannot assume that all Q's redactional interests reflect and relate to redactional creations de novo: see above at n. 29 and also CATCHPOLE, *Temple Traditions* (n. 29), pp. 325f., who argues that the polemic against "this generation" is of concern to Q but also pre-dates Q. In any case, the other Markan references to "this generation", in Mk 8,38; 13,30, cannot easily be explained as due to Q influence. *If* Mark were dependent on Q, the reference to "this generation" in Mk 8,38 would be a MkR addition (presumably to Q 12,9); and Mk 13,30 has no obvious Q parallel.

41. See VÖGTLE, *Jonaszeichen* (n. 34), p. 239; PESCH, *Markusevangelium* I (n. 34), p. 409; GUELICH, *Mark* (n. 34), p. 411.

42. *Einfluss* (n. 6), p. 154.

questioners. Schenk's case is not however compelling. The τί construction may well be ambiguous in the present context. The precise force of the τί is uncertain: M. Black has claimed that the usage here reflects a Semitic exclamatory usage, though this has been disputed as an unnecessary explanation since the word can be adequately and satisfactorily translated as simply "why?" here[43]. Possibly similar usages in Mk 2,7.8.24; 4.40 etc., also then make it uncertain if such a usage of τί is MkR or not. The apparent oath formula is however harder to explain in this way. Such a use of εἰ may also be unusual in Aramaic and in Greek; but either way it occurs nowhere else in Mark and hence is hard to credit to MkR[44]. Further, the Markan version of the pericope does not necessarily heighten the negative elements in the story since Mark does not mention the explicit assertion by Jesus that this generation is "evil", a feature which is present in Matthew and Luke and hence almost certainly in Q[45]. Thus, rather than stressing the negative elements, Mark here might appear to give a slightly less polemical edge to the story.

The conclusion here is that Mark may well be dependent on a tradition for his version of the story here: the unusual (possibly Semitic) features in Mark's Greek may indicate that. It *may* also be that Mark's tradition included the exceptive clause referring to the sign of Jonah (though I myself am very doubtful). However, even if that were the case, the analysis here gives no support at all to the claim that Mark's tradition was Q: Mark seems to show no awareness at all of Q's redactional features or Q's editorial activity, insofar as these can be identified. Any links between Mark and Q seem to lie further back in the (probably complex) tradition-history of this passage.

Q 7,27 / Mk 1,2

The second passage to be considered here concerns the citation of Mal 3,1 and Exod 23,20 to be found in Q 7,27 and Mk 1,2[46]. As in the

43. M. BLACK, *An Aramaic Approach to the Gospels and Acts*, Oxford, University Press, ³1967, p. 123. See however the discussion in E.C. MALONEY, *Semitic Interference in Marcan Syntax*, Chico, CA, Scholars Press, 1981, pp. 142-144.

44. Schenk refers to "eine der von Markus bevorzugten elliptischen Redeweisen", with reference to W. LARFELD, *Die neutestamentliche Evangelien nach ihre Eigenart und Abhängigkeit*, Gütersloh, 1925, p. 269. But it remains the case that this particular "elliptische Redeweise" is still unevidenced elsewhere in Mark.

45. Cf. SCHULZ, *Q* (n. 28), p. 254 n. 535, listing the differences between Mark and Q, notes that "Q qualifiziert 'dieses Geschlecht' *betont negativ*" (my italics).

46. The verbatim agreement between Mt 11,10 and Lk 7,27 (apart from an extra ἐγώ in Matthew) allows us to reconstruct the Q version without difficulty as the wording common to Matthew and Luke. (The extra ἐγώ is probably immaterial here.) Elsewhere in this section, there is again widespread verbal agreement between Matthew and Luke which I will assume then reflects the Q version. The small variations in wording are not relevant to the discussion here and will not be discussed.

case of the Sign pericope, the overlap in question involves a relatively small amount of text. Yet, as before, this one verse occurs within what is in Q clearly a larger literary unit: Mt 11,2-19 / Lk 7,18-35 represents a long sequence of Q material in the same order in the two gospels, and hence clearly implies the existence of an extended literary unit in Q. Is there any evidence to suggest that Q 7,27 may be Q-redactional? Several have effectively argued that it is, though without necessarily always drawing any of the consequences in relation to the Mark-Q problem.

The whole unit in Q 7,18-35 is clearly composite, made up of a number of different units of tradition and probably involving a number of separate layers. However, a precise delineation of those layers is by no means straightforward. Within the wider unit, Q 7,24-28 is clearly a significant sub-unit. Further, within this sub-unit, many have argued that vv. 24-26 constitute the base tradition to which are added two (or more) interpretative comments in v. 27 and v. 28[47]. What though is the relative age of these interpretative comments?

A. Jacobson has argued that v. 28 is the most recent addition, and indeed more recent than the stage in Q which supplies the bulk of the rest of the unit in Q: the rest is part of the "compositional" stage concerned with polemic against "this generation"; v. 28 betrays an element of anti-Baptist polemic which is later than the tendency to view John and Jesus as (equal) partners (as in vv. 33-34). Hence v. 28 is to be ascribed to a later "intermediate" stage in the development of Q[48]. This is however hard to envisage: Jacobson's theory involves a later redactor seeking to modify the clear message of the rest of the pericope by making a relatively small insertion in the middle of the unit. Yet the section which presents Jesus and John as partners in parallel (i.e. vv. 31-35) is left unaltered and, in literary terms, forms the climax of the whole section. This latter consideration in particular makes it very unlikely that the view of a later redactor is different from that of the person responsible for these verses. On these grounds, therefore, Jacobson's theory seems unconvincing.

For similar reasons, the theory advocated by Kloppenborg seems equally unlikely. Kloppenborg argues that vv. 27 and 31-35 constitute the contributions of the "final" redactor[49]. V. 28 constitutes a first

47. Cf. R. BULTMANN, *The History of the Synoptic Tradition*, E.T., Oxford, Blackwell, 1963, p. 165; HOFFMANN, *Studien* (n. 37), p. 215; D. ZELLER, *Redaktionsprozesse und wechselnder "Sitz im Leben" beim Q-Material*, in J. DELOBEL (ed.), *Logia* (n. 6), 1982, pp. 395-409, on p. 403; LUZ, *Matthäus* II (n. 15), p. 173; KLOPPENBORG, *Formation* (n. 28), pp. 108f. See the survey of opinion in J. ERNST, *Johannes der Täufer* (BZNW, 53), Berlin, de Gruyter, 1989, pp. 61f.

48. JACOBSON, *Wisdom Christology* (n. 36), pp. 94-98.

49. Though for Kloppenborg the final stage of the development of Q is only reached with the addition of the temptation narrative (together with a few elements of a strongly nomistic nature as well, e.g. Q 16,17: cf. his *Nomos and Ethos in Q*, in J.E. GOEHRING, ET

comment on vv. 24-26, which has the effect of slightly mitigating the high estimate of John implied in 7,26b. By contrast, vv. 27 and 31-35 serve to rehabilitate John, to show that he belongs alongside Jesus as a precursor, a friend of the kingdom, and - with Jesus - one of the messengers of Wisdom[50]. However, whilst some of this may be appropriate to vv. 31-35, it does not explain v. 27 very well. For if v. 27 is seeking in any way to counter the possible negative implications of v. 28, it is very surprising that the comment precedes the saying it is allegedly commenting on[51]. Further, vv. 27 and 31-35 are rather different in the way they treat John, especially in relation to Jesus, and they cannot simply be subsumed under the heading of "treating John as a friend of the kingdom"[52]. V. 27 gives a high place to John as the forerunner predicted in Mal 3; but it is clearly as a forerunner *of Jesus*[53]. Hence already v. 27 itself is distinguishing to a certain extent between John and Jesus[54]. V. 27 thus provides an emphatically positive statement about John's status, coupled with an implied corollary that John's significance is only to be seen in relation to that of Jesus himself. The high regard for John is wholly dependent on the even higher regard which it is presumed is appropriate for Jesus. Vv. 31-35 on the other hand seem to assume that Jesus and John are of equal status: as messengers of Wisdom they confront "this generation" and in turn are rejected. It may be that there is a hint of some difference between Jesus and John in that Jesus is called "Son of Man" in v. 34, and of course they clearly exhibit different life-styles. Yet despite these differences the emphasis is entirely on what the two share in common as messengers of Wisdom who experience hostility and rejection from this generation. Vv. 27 and 31-35 therefore seem to be working with rather different presuppositions and it is not easy to ascribe them to the same redactional stratum.

Some of the same observations relating to the theories of Jacobson and Kloppenborg apply also to the theory recently advanced by Catchpole. Catchpole argues that vv. 27 + 28b are editorial additions to an earlier tradition in vv. 24-26 + 28a. These serve to change the nature of John's expectation from looking forward to the coming of God himself to an expectation of a figure other than God, i.e. Jesus for Q, and to clarify the status of Jesus in relation to John by stressing

AL. (eds.), *Gospel Origins and Christian Beginnings. FS J.M. Robinson*, Sonoma, CA, Polebridge, 1990, pp. 35-48.

50. KLOPPENBORG, *Formation* (n. 28), pp. 110, 117.

51. Cf. A.D. JACOBSON, *The History of the Composition of the Synoptic Sayings Source, Q*, in *SBL 1987 Seminar Papers*, pp. 285-294, on p. 292.

52. KLOPPENBORG, *Formation* (n. 28), p. 117.

53. Cf. the well-known changes to the citation, altering some of the first person pronouns to second person.

54. HOFFMANN, *Studien* (n. 37), pp. 218f.

John's inferiority[55]. Once again, however, there is the problem of why 7,31-35 is left as the climax of the section, since here Jesus and John appear in tandem with no real indication of the inferiority of John[56]. As I argued above in relation to Kloppenborg, Catchpole may well be right in seeing v. 27 as implying that John's status is only to be seen in relation to that of Jesus. But v. 27 scarcely gives any indication of John's *inferiority*. This is clearer in v. 28b and so it is not quite so easy to see v. 28b as coming from the same stratum as v. 27[57].

I argued above that v. 27 is unlikely to be a later modification of v. 28, if only because it comes first, and a secondary comment is more likely to follow the tradition it is seeking to modify and comment on. This makes it most likely that v. 27 is the earlier comment on vv. 24-26, to which v. 28 is added as a later addition. In fact a strong case could be made out for v. 27 being the original conclusion to vv. 24-26. Vv. 24-26 alone seem to be almost a torso and to cry out for some clarification and conclusion[58]. V. 26 ends with the double claim that it is indeed appropriate to think of John as a prophet, but that John is also more than a prophet. To the question "Is John a prophet?", the answer seems to be yes and no: he is a prophet, but he is also more. At the very least, one could say that such a claim is enigmatic! What does it mean to say that John is both a prophet and more? At one level Q 7,27 provides a perfect answer. John is described as an Elijah redivivus figure. He is then a prophetic figure in that he is an Elijah-figure; but he is also more than just any prophet: for he is the inaugurator of the new age forecast by Malachi. Thus v. 27 provides a very good conclusion to

---

55. *Beginning* (n. 6), pp. 207-213.

56. Unless it be in the reference to Jesus as "Son of man" in v. 34 (cf. above), though this would be a very veiled indication of Jesus' superiority *to John*. The stress is much more on the difference between (John and) Jesus and this generation. Catchpole refers briefly to 7,31-35 and "its secondary Christological expansion focused on him who 'has come', the Son of man" (*Beginning* [n. 6], p. 213). But the "expansion" involves vv. 33 *and* 34 together (on most reconstructions of the tradition history of the passage) and perhaps v. 35; and in both cases Jesus is clearly associated *with* John.

57. Catchpole claims that vv.27 and 28b belong together in "exhibit[ing] a unity of Christological and future-eschatological concern" (*Beginning* [n. 6], p. 213). In part this depends on his interpretation of v.28b as referring to Jesus alone, and moreover to Jesus' role in the future. This is possible (though not easy) for v. 28b, but much harder for v. 27, at least in relation to the alleged future aspect: *is* v. 27 about Jesus' role in the future for Q? It is of course future for the scriptural voice quoted; but for Q it is almost certainly regarded as fulfilled in the ministry of Jesus in the present/past (i.e. present in the narrative, past for the readers). John's role is as the forerunner of Jesus' *present* ministry (cf. Q 7,22), not solely of a future role.

58. Cf. H. SCHÜRMANN, *Das Lukasevangelium* (HTKNT, III/1), Freiburg, Herder, 1969, p. 417: "V. 26b verlangt nach einer eigenen Kommentierung"; also KLOPPENBORG, *Formation* (n. 28), p. 109: "Q 7:26b invites further explication"; CATCHPOLE, *Beginning* (n. 6), p. 208: the end of v. 26b "is forceful but lacks the definition which is necessary to conclude a unit of tradition".

vv. 24-26 and there is no need to drive too much of a wedge between
the two [59].

There does however seem to be a seam between v. 27 and v. 28. The
repeated λέγω ὑμῖν of Q 7,28 (cf. v. 26) makes it unlikely that v. 28
belongs with vv. 24-27 originally [60]. It would appear to be a secondary
comment. Whether it is itself a unity, or whether (as some have argued)
v. 28b (with its possible implied critique of John) is a secondary
addition to a more original v. 28a, is also not entirely certain. However,
the tightly structured form of the verse as it now stands, with its clear
antithetic parallelism, suggests that the verse may be a unity and should
not be split up [61]. Whether the verse implies a down-grading of John is
also not clear. This *may* be the case, though equally the verse can be
taken rather as saying something supremely positive about the status of
those in the kingdom [62]: the latter are greater than even John whose
greatness is emphatically affirmed in vv. 24-27 as the prophetic messen-
ger foretold in scripture.

However, it seems clear that any hint of a downgrading of John is
swept aside in vv. 31-35. Clearly this section itself may well be composite and there is no time to discuss those issues here. As they stand,
however, vv. 31-35 clearly present Jesus and John as equal partners,
messengers of Wisdom in a hostile environment. The implied polemic
against this generation, and the use of Wisdom motifs, makes it likely
that Q's redaction is responsible for providing this as the climax of
the wider literary unit [63]. But then the slightly different emphases on
the relative positions of Jesus and John in vv. 27 and 28 compared with
vv. 31-35 suggests that, if vv. 31-35 represent the view of the final

59. For v. 27 as linked to vv. 24-26 very early, cf. SCHÜRMANN, *Lukasevangelium*
(n. 58), p. 417; ZELLER, *Redaktionsprozesse* (n. 47), p. 403; ERNST, *Johannes* (n. 47),
pp. 61f.; SCHÜLING, *Studien* (n. 1), p. 66. Catchpole's claim that form-critically v. 28a "is
the *only* element in vv. 27, 28 which will define and complete v. 26" (*Beginning* [n. 6],
p. 209 - my emphasis) seems too extreme. V. 27 furnishes at least as good a conclusion as
v. 28a (Catchpole's theory) does.

60. We need not discuss whether Q 7,28 contained an ἀμήν (so Matthew but not
Luke) as well. Catchpole, *Beginning* (n. 6), p. 209, argues that the λέγω ὑμῖν of v. 28a
could be a redactional resumption of v. 26, "so that, although the editor regards v. 27 as
important, the remarkable implications of vv. 26b, 28a should not be lost". This however
seems to imply a somewhat ambivalent attitude to v. 27 on the part of the editor: vv. 27
and 28b are added editorially to stress John's inferiority to Jesus, but then v. 28a has to be
emphasized to stress the thoroughly positive picture of John emerging from vv. 26 and
28a. I would argue that things are rather simpler if v. 28 is regarded as a unity and
secondary to vv. 24-27.

61. See SCHÜRMANN, *Lukasevangelium* (n. 58), p. 419; LÜHRMANN, *Redaktion* (n. 3),
p. 27; LUZ, *Matthäus* II (n. 15), p. 173; SCHÜLING, *Studien* (n. 1), p. 83. *Pace* CATCHPOLE,
Beginning (n. 6), p. 208.

62. Or conceivably of Jesus if Jesus is ὁ μικρότερος (so HOFFMANN, *Studien* [n. 37],
p. 221; CATCHPOLE, *Beginning* [n. 6], pp. 208f., and some others).

63. See LÜHRMANN, *Redaktion* (n. 3), p. 31; ZELLER, *Redaktionsprozesse* (n. 47), p. 403.

redactor of Q, vv. 27 + 28 give the view of an earlier stage in the tradition. Thus vv. 27 + 28 are probably *pre*-redactional in Q[64].

Some have tried to argue that v. 27 must be a later element within Q on the grounds that it is an OT citation, and indeed the only explicit OT citation in Q apart from the temptation narrative which is itself widely regarded as a relative late-comer in the tradition history of Q[65]. However, such a view of the place of the temptation narrative in Q's development may be unnecessary (cf. n. 25 above). Jesus appears there supremely as the one who is obedient to scripture; hence the idea that the events of the gospel tradition are in accordance with scripture is not alien to Q. Nevertheless the fact remains that Q 7,27 is one of the very rare places in Q where the OT is explicitly cited. Given the problems from a literary point of view in assigning v. 27 to a very late stage in the development of Q, it is perhaps easiest to see the verse as a traditional element willingly accepted by Q, rather than as a later addition alien to the rest of Q. It coheres well with Q, but the explicit nature of the citation makes it unlikely to have been created redactionally by the Q editor. Q 7,27 thus seems to be a *pre*-redactional element in Q.

On the Markan side, there is very little to say. Once again Mark appears to show no awareness of Q-redactional elements in the Q unit. The only link between Mark and Q is the parallel to Q 7,27. Mark gives no hint that he knew the wider literary context in which Q 7,27 is now embedded. All elements of literary structuring of the Q pericope are thus missing from Mark. In relation to the single verse Q 7,27 itself, there is nothing to determine whether Mark could or could not have used Q for this verse: the "redaction" by Mark would have involved straight copying of the text (simply omitting ἔμπροσθέν σου) so one cannot (as with Mk 8,11-12) produce arguments to the effect that the Markan version is unlikely to be due to MkR. Further, the Markan parallel has its own problems by virtue of the fact that the citation in Mk 1,2b is at first sight a little intrusive: the introduction in v. 2a suggests that the quotation given will be from Isaiah, and yet a quotation from Isaiah only comes in v. 3. Hence some have argued that the verse is a secondary insertion into the text of Mark[66]. Yet whatever

64. For a very similar view about the tradition-history of the whole passage, see ZELLER, *Redaktionsprozesse* (n. 47), p. 403. SCHULZ, *Q* (n. 28), p. 230, also takes vv. 27 + 28 as additions to an earlier tradition, but at a pre-redactional stage in Q: however, his only reason appears to be that these verses are part of the "Q-Doppelüberlieferungen" (though only v. 27 is!). See above for the circularity here.

65. Cf. A. POLAG, *Die Christologie der Logienquelle* (WMANT, 45), Neukirchen-Vluyn, Neukirchener, 1977, pp. 158f.; LUZ, *Matthäus* II (n. 15), p. 173; M. SATO, *Q und Prophetie* (WUNT, 2.Reihe, 29), Tübingen, Mohr, 1988, p. 35.

66. Cf. M.-J. LAGRANGE, *Évangile selon saint Marc*, Paris, Gabalda, 1929, p. 4; T.W. MANSON, *The Sayings of Jesus*, London, SCM, 1949, p. 69; V. TAYLOR, *The Gospel according to St Mark*, London, Macmillan, 1952, p. 153. Catchpole points to the aporia in the Markan text as indicating the possibility of a redactional addition to an earlier

one makes of the Markan context, it remains the case that the verse is not redactional in Q. Hence if Mark got it from a source, that source cannot be shown to have been Q. There is thus no evidence here for concluding that Mark was dependent on Q.

Mk 1,7-8 / Q 3,16

A further overlap passage which may be significant in the present context is the report of the preaching of John the Baptist in Mk 1,7-8 / Q 3,16 about a future "baptism" by a "stronger one" who will baptise with holy spirit and (in Matthew and Luke) with fire. Both Mark and Q (on the 2ST) record this saying[67]. As always in such cases, the reconstruction of the Q version is complicated by the Markan parallel, and indeed the reconstruction could be significantly affected by one's theories about the relationship between Mark and Q. The two versions appear to differ at a number of points: Q probably brings together two sayings – one about the contrast between the present and the future baptisms, and one about John's unworthiness to carry/untie the sandals of the coming figure – into a single, chiastically constructed unity, whereas Marks keeps the two sayings separate; Q has John refer to his baptism in the present ($\beta\alpha\pi\tau\iota\zeta\omega$) whereas Mark has John refer to this as past ($\dot{\epsilon}\beta\dot{\alpha}\pi\tau\iota\sigma\alpha$); famously Q has John predict a coming baptism which will be in/with fire as well as (probably) holy spirit, whereas Mark as no reference to the fire; and Q appends the saying about the threshing floor, which has no parallel in Mark. I leave aside discussion of many of these features here: apart from the fact that these details highlight the differences between the Markan and Matthew/Luke ver-

tradition (*Beginning* [n. 6], p. 214); but he offers no explanation of the reason why Mark should have added the citation at this point to produce such a disjointed text.

The awkward nature of the Markan text here is also the basis for the argument of FUCHS, *Überschneidungen* (n. 10), pp. 60ff., who claims that Matthew's and Luke's alterations to Mark (which include, as well as the transfer of Mk 1,2, the inversion of the Isaiah quotation and the description of John in Mk 1,3f.) are only intelligible as secondary developments of the Markan text. Yet Fuchs is not explicit about where the rest of the unit in Mt 11 / Lk 7 has come from: is this too part of the Deutero-Markan expansion? But then the "editing" presupposed here would be qualitatively different from that postulated elsewhere, involving here a wholesale transfer of one verse to a new context and the massive creation of a very large unit to introduce it. The other changes made by Matthew and Luke may well be secondary changes of Mark - but they could just as easily be changes made independently by Matthew and Luke.

GOULDER, *Luke* (n. 11), pp. 391-393, appears to ascribe the whole of Mt 11,7-10 to MtR of Mark alone. But the examples he cites of possible parallels to Matthean "lead-in's" to Markan statements are not convincing (e.g. Mt 10,37a + 37b leading to v. 38: but 10,37 is more an independent bipartite saying, and v. 38 is parallel in structure to v. 39). Goulder's main argument is that Matthew and Mark agree in the very unusual form of the OT "citation". But this only shows MtR of Mark if a pre-Markan form of the citation is excluded a priori.

67. This is widely accepted: cf. LAUFEN, *Doppelüberlieferungen* (n. 1), pp. 93f.; ERNST, *Johannes* (n. 47), pp. 48ff.

sions, most do not clearly point to the priority of one version over against the other. For example, the problem of the most original form of the prediction of the coming baptism (spirit, fire, spirit/wind + fire) has been much debated with no clear unanimity[68]. Further, the question of whether the literary separation of the two sayings is an original or a secondary feature can be, and has been, answered both ways[69].

More important for the present context may be not so much the question of the literary *form* of the double saying (as separate or as integrated) but rather that of the substance and origin of the two sayings. Few would deny that the prediction of a future baptism with spirit and/or fire is a very primitive tradition. However, many have argued that the other saying (about the "sandals") is a later Christian addition[70]. Further, several scholars have argued that this addition is due to Q's redaction[71]. The presence of the saying in Mark as well then raises acutely the problem of the relationship between Mark and Q: do we have here an element of Q's redaction reappearing in Mark, thus implying Mark's knowledge of Q?

One of the few scholars to realise the implications of the problem in relationship to the Mark-Q problem is Kloppenborg. Kloppenborg accepts that the saying about the sandals is a secondary addition in Q, but points to the presence of the saying in Mark and in John and Acts (Jn 1,27; Ac 13,25) and argues that these factors indicate that it is "a very early addition to the saying [about the two baptisms]. To credit it to Q redaction would raise more problems that it would solve". Hence Kloppenborg assigns the addition to "the early pre-history, not to the Q redaction, of this saying [about baptism]"[72]. However, this simply highlights the problem under discussion here. The presence of a parallel in John[73] says little about the pre-redactional state of the synoptic tradition unless one assumes the independence of John from the synoptics. I myself am inclined to such a view, but this can no longer be

---

68. Cf. LAUFEN, *Doppelüberlieferungen* (n. 1), pp. 100f. for a survey of the different possibilities.

69. Cf. LAUFEN, *Doppelüberlieferungen* (n. 1), pp. 97f. For the sayings as originally not intertwined, cf. M. DIBELIUS, *Die urchristliche Überlieferung von Johannes der Täufer*, Göttingen, Vandenhoeck & Ruprecht, 1911, p. 54; also Laufen himself. For the converse, cf. SCHULZ, *Q* (n. 28), p. 370; HOFFMANN, *Studien* (n. 37), p. 21.

70. For this as secondary, cf. BULTMANN, *History* (n. 47), p. 246; DIBELIUS, *Täufer* (n. 69), p. 54.

71. HOFFMANN, *Studien* (n. 37), p. 31 ("Das in Q eingeschobene Interpretament", cf. p. 28: "Q-Zusatz"); H. MERKLEIN, *Die Umkehrpredigt bei Johannes dem Täufer und Jesus von Nazaret*, in *BZ* 25 (1981) 29-46, on p. 32; SCHENK, *Synopse* (n. 37), p. 19; CATCHPOLE, *Beginning* (n. 6), p. 215; JACOBSON, *Wisdom Christology* (n. 36), pp. 33-35 ascribes to his "intermediate" stage of redaction.

72. KLOPPENBORG, *Formation* (n. 28), pp. 104f.

73. This is also referred to by LAUFEN, *Doppelüberlieferungen* (n. 1), p. 98, as evidence for the independence of the two sayings.

assumed as self-evident[74]. So too elements in the speeches in Acts may be simply due to Luke's own knowledge of Mark's gospel. Kloppenborg's ascription of the saying to a pre-redactional stage in Q's development seems to be almost entirely based on presuppositions about the independence of Q and Mark, of John and the synoptics, and perhaps about the nature of some of the speeches in Acts[75]. Nevertheless other arguments may well be relevant here.

Bultmann's original claim – that the saying about the stronger one is a Christian addition to an earlier saying about the future baptism – seems persuasive. Other arguments to the contrary do not always convince. Laufen's plea for the existence of two originally independent sayings[76] seems unconvincing, if only because the "sandals" saying scarcely makes sense without something additional to say what precisely the figure whose sandals John is unworthy to untie/carry will do. Two recent studies of John the Baptist also seek to trace the saying back to the historical John. Ernst seeks to delete any hint of a "Christian" interpretation by taking the reference to the "stronger one" as Yahweh. However he has to delete the μοῦ from the phrase ἰσχυρότερός μου, and take the comparative ἰσχυρότερος as a superlative, to make his case[77]. Webb argues (to my mind convincingly) against this general interpretation, pointing in particular to the problem of the reference to "sandals" if the figure concerned is God (as well as the lack of evidence for the deletion of the μοῦ)[78]. Further, it seems highly unlikely that, at least for Q, the coming figure is regarded as anyone other than Jesus, whatever may have been the case in any pre-Q tradition. The question of John the Baptist in Q 7,19 clearly picks up the words of John's prediction in 3,16; and Jesus' answer in Q 7,22-23 can scarcely be taken as anything other than a positive response to the question whether he himself is the "coming one", i.e. the one predicted by John. Webb himself simply takes the combined evidence of Mark

74. Cf. many of the papers delivered at the 1990 Leuven Colloquium published in A. DENAUX (ed.), *John and the Synoptics* (BETL, 101), Leuven, University Press - Peeters, 1992. See too F. NEIRYNCK, *John and the Synoptics* (n. 22); also his *Jean et les Synoptiques* (BETL, 49), Leuven, University Press, 1979.

75. Cf. too CATCHPOLE, *Beginning* (n. 6), p. 215.

76. LAUFEN, *Doppelüberlieferungen* (n. 1), pp. 116f.

77. ERNST, *Johannes* (n. 47), p. 50; cf. too J.H. HUGHES, *John the Baptist: The Forerunner of God Himself*, in *NT* 14 (1972) 191-218.

78. R.L. WEBB, *John the Baptizer and Prophet* (JSNT SS, 62), Sheffield, Sheffield Academic Press, 1991, pp. 284f. The problem is met only with great difficulty if the image is a completely hypothetical metaphor. Thus Webb says: "John's statement is *not* simply a descriptive statement concerning what the figure is wearing, ... nor is it a description of what the figure does with his own sandals ... Rather, John's words form an evaluative statement of his own unworthiness to perform an action with respect to this figure's sandals ... The evaluation of John's unworthiness to perform such an action loses some of its significance if it is an action which it is impossible for him to actually do".

and Q as sufficient basis for reconstructing the historical Baptist and does not consider the possibility of secondary, pre-Q developments in the tradition, apart from some rather general considerations about the unlikelihood of the existence of secondary creations here at all[79]. However, the clear qualitative distinction drawn between John and the coming figure in the "sandals" saying does seem rather extraneous in the context of John, and perhaps fits better within a context of later rivalry between (followers of) Jesus and John.

Nevertheless it is very hard to see such rivalry playing any role at the level of Q's redaction. In some respects the saying in Q 3,16b is similar to Q 7,28, with a possible tendency to downgrade John[80]. However, I argued earlier that any such tendencies in Q 7 are superseded by the redactional stage in Q which is thoroughly positive about John and which places John alongside Jesus as one of the messengers of Wisdom rejected by this generation. Further, the thrust of Q as a whole is to be totally positive about John. Q (probably) opens with a substantial section giving John's preaching (Q 3,7-9 + 16-17); it is followed fairly closely by an extended section in Q 7,18-35 about the relationship between John and Jesus, where, for all but one possible small exception (Q 7,28b), Q's Jesus is outspokenly positive about John, and, as we have seen, the literary unit climaxes in the verses (7,31-35) placing Jesus and John alongside each other in parallel. John's preaching in Q of imminent judgement (Q 3,7-9) is paralleled by the preaching of Jesus later in Q (Q 12,39-46; 17,22-37); so too his prediction of a "coming one"[81] is picked up again in Q 7,18-19 and implicitly affirmed in Q 7,22-23 by Jesus and probably echoed again in the reference to ὁ ἐρχόμενος in Q 13,35[82]. Further, the prediction of the coming "fire", which runs as a leitmotif through Q's account of John's preaching (Q 3,9.16.17), is echoed again in Lk 12,49 which may well be Q material[83]. Thus in terms of the overall structure and contents of Q, insofar as these can be determined, the general impression given by Q is clear: John's preaching is adopted and emphatically affirmed by Q, both by being explicitly given in full measure in its own right and by being taken up by Jesus is a totally positive way.

---

79. WEBB, *John the Baptizer* (n. 78), p. 268.

80. On the basis of this similarity, Jacobson ascribes both sayings to his later postulated "intermediate" redaction; similarly, Catchpole ascribes both to the Q-redactional level.

81. I am persuaded that Matthew's ὁ ἐρχόμενος is probably closer to the Q wording, with Luke assimilating to Mark, even if the term is not a title: cf. on the latter point WEBB, *John the Baptizer* (n. 78), pp. 270f.

82. Cf. HOFFMANN, *Studien* (n. 37), p. 177.

83. See KLOPPENBORG, *Formation* (n. 28), p. 151 and others noted there; also C.P. MÄRZ, *"Feuer auf die Erde zu werfen bin ich gekommen ..."*. *Zum Verständnis und zur Entstehung von Lk 12,49*, in *À cause de l'Évangile* (n. 37), 1985, pp. 479-511.

All this suggests that, if Q 3,16b is a secondary addition reflecting an element of reserve about John, this reserve has nothing to do with Q's redactional concerns. This would then suggest some support for Kloppenborg's view that the saying is a *pre*-redactional element in Q. It seems hard to deny that, taken on its own, the saying does reflect an element of negativity about John. But when the saying is taken up and used by Q, it can only be in a thoroughly positive way, perhaps to highlight the importance and significance of Jesus though without wishing to downgrade John. If this is the case, then the best solution seems to be that the saying is an early addition in the tradition, taken over by Q subsequently. To see it as a later addition seems to create more problems than it solves: if it is a Q addition then it does not correlate with Q's overall presentation and literary structure; and if it is later still (e.g. as in Jacobson's theory, part of a later stage of Q editing subsequent to the "compositional" stage which has left its mark on the vast bulk of this part of Q), then it is hard to see why reserve about John should be expressed in what is, in literary terms, such an insignificant way, leaving the positive view about John dominating in the rest of the Q material.

The conclusion of this section must be that the "stronger one" saying may be a secondary addition to the tradition, but it is pre-Q and not due to Q redaction. Hence the presence of the saying in Mark as well does not necessarily show any awareness of a Q-redactional feature and hence we cannot deduce that Mark is dependent on Q[84].

Q 13,18-19 / Mk 4,30-32

As a final example I consider briefly the parable of the mustard seed which, within the presuppositions of the 2ST, is usually regarded as a classic "overlap" passage. I have examined this parable elsewhere and so will not repeat that discussion again here[85]; moreover many of the source-critical problems have been discussed afresh recently and in great detail by T. Friedrichsen[86]. For those who accept the 2ST in some form, the Lukan version in Lk 13,18f is usually regarded as preserving Q most accurately (though obviously with debate about

---

84. As before, alternative solutions are not persuasive. Fuchs, *Überschneidungen* (n. 10), pp. 67ff., seeks to show how the texts of Matthew and Luke might be due to a Deutero-Markan editing of Mark; but there is really nothing here to demand such a theory. The well-known phenomenon of the appended saying in Q 3,17, very closely linked to v. 16 grammatically, is no problem for the 2ST provided that one can accept the possibility of an overlap between Mark and Q with the grammar of the Q version very close to that of Mark.

85. See my *Revival* (n. 14), pp. 78-85.

86. T.A. FRIEDRICHSEN, *"Minor" and "Major" Matthew-Luke Agreements against Mark 4,30-32*, in *The Four Gospels 1992* (n. 25), 1992, pp. 649-676; also his *Alternative Synoptic Theories in Mk 4,30-32*, in this volume, pp. 427-450.

individual details). What is then striking is that, in the parable itself, "Mark and Luke have virtually nothing in common beyond the barest essentials necessary for telling a parable comparing the Kingdom of God to a mustard seed"[87]. Attempts to explain all the differences between Mark and Q/Luke as MkR by Lambrecht (and more recently Fleddermann) seem unconvincing[88].

The passage is also examined in some detail by Schenk in his article seeking to show Markan dependence on Q[89]. At first Schenk says that the parable is a "Beispiel für die Markus-Priorität", claiming that the Markan contrast parable, told in the present tense, is more original. Q then converts the parable into one focusing on growth and assurance of the end-result: hence the contrast elements disappear, the narrative changes from the present to the aorist, the "shrub" becomes a "tree" which as a mustard tree is not particularly big, and the seed is "sown" in a "garden", thereby revealing a non-Palestinian milieu since mustard was not sown[90]. But then the two temporal clauses in Mark which refer to the "sowing" of the seed, which in any case are disruptive and hence probably secondary and due to MkR, are most easily explained as due to influence from the Q version. Mark also adds the OT allusion at the end of v. 32 as an allegorizing feature. Matthew and Luke then independently take over this redacted version of Mark's, both rewriting the allegorizing conclusion. Thus "Markan priority" (i.e. in relation to Q) is really only a priority of the Markan Vorlage:

> Markus-Priorität liegt Q gegenüber dann vor, wenn ein Stoff schon der vormarkinischen Überlieferung angehörte. Die Markus-Priorität ist also genauer eine Priorität des Prae-Markus. Q-Priorität liegt dagegen dort vor, wo erst die markinische Redaktion Q-Material übernommen hat[91].

Schenk's analysis is however not easy to accept. The claim that Mark's double ὅταν σπαρῇ can only derive from the Q version rests on some dubious criteria. *Pace* Schenk (and perhaps Dalman), mustard was sown – albeit in fields if not (legally) in gardens[92]. (Presumably the long discussion in *Kil.* 2,8-9 was only necessary precisely because it was

---

87. See my *Revival* (n. 14), p. 81. I leave aside the question of the introduction to the parable which is more disputed: see FRIEDRICHSEN, *"Minor" and "Major" Agreements* (n. 86), pp. 662-675, arguing for LkR of Mark in the opening questions of Lk 13,18.

88. See the works cited in n. 6 above. In my earlier study (n. 85 above) I tried to respond to the work of Lambrecht; this is now developed further, taking note too of Fleddermann's work, in FRIEDRICHSEN, *"Minor" and "Major" Agreements* (n. 86), pp. 653-662.

89. *Einfluss* (n. 6), pp. 144f.

90. Schenk refers to G. DALMAN, *Arbeit und Sitte in Palästina* I/2, Gütersloh, 1928, pp. 369f.

91. *Einfluss* (n. 6), pp. 145f.

92. In fact all that Dalman said was that he had not seen one particular type of mustard as a cultivated crop in Palestine.

sown.) And in any case, given two versions (Mark and Q) which both (allegedly) reflect a "non-Palestinian" milieu, it is almost impossible to say which is logically prior. All that the evidence allows us to say is that the "sowing" of the seed is firmly present in the earliest form of the tradition to which we now have access. It is thus by no means clear that the reference to the seed being "sown" is due to a Q-redactional addition to the tradition, and hence not easy to see the common references to sowing as evidence of Mark's dependence on Q. In any case, as noted earlier, the two versions have very little in common and so any theory of a literary relationship between Mark and Q is particularly difficult here.

Schenk's explanation of the end of the parable is also problematic. He argues that the expansion of the reference to the tree took place independently in Matthew and Luke. However, the identical expansion in both gospels, which also involves changing the OT allusion (from Ezek 17,23 to Dan 4,21), seems far easier to ascribe to the Q layer in the tradition. Schenk's theory depends on a rather arbitrary assumption that all OT allusions in parables are (a) secondary, and (b) exclusively Markan (cf. Mk 4,29; 12,10) and hence cannot have been present in Q. The use of OT allusions elsewhere in Q material (cf. Q 4,1-13; 7,27; 10,13-15; 11,31-32; 13,35; 17,26-30, even if these are not strictly "parables") should make one at least pause before denying the possibility of an OT allusion in Q here too. Hence it seems easier to take the common ending in Matthew and Luke as evidence of the Q version and to see the (different) OT allusions as yet another indication of the independence of Q from Mark. As before a theory of Markan independence from Q seems to be the most satisfactory way of explaining the evidence[93].

---

93. Kogler's detailed defence of the Deutero-Markan theory in relation to this parable (see his monograph as in n. 10 above) scarcely provides much convincing evidence for those who are not otherwise persuaded by the overall theory. He goes through the text of Mark in minute detail, showing how a Deutero-Markan editor *might* have proceeded; but there is very little — if anything — in his analysis to show that the development must have taken place in this way. Indeed the effect of Kogler's analysis is to reduce the redactional activity of Matthew and Luke to virtual vanishing point. However, the process also involves a number of coincidences. Luke must have (by chance?) deleted almost all the specifically Markan elements from Deutero-Mark to leave only the Deutero-Markan additions; he must also have changed all the verbs into the aorist (except ἔβαλεν which was already there in Deutero-Mark) so as to create a neat parallel to the parable appended by Deutero-Mark, viz. the leaven. Yet it is surely easier to see the leaven as constructed in parallel with a version of the mustard seed from the start. For further critique of the Deutero-Markus theory here, see F. FENDLER, Studien zum Markusevangelium (GTA, 49), Göttingen, Vandenhoeck & Ruprecht, 1991, pp. 175-180; also FRIEDRICHSEN, Alternative Synoptic Theories (n. 86), pp. 430-440.

Conclusion

The main conclusion of this paper is that the view that Mark and Q represent independent versions of common traditions remains the most convincing in the passages considered here. Clearly such a theory in relation to all the Mark-Q overlaps cannot be established definitively on the basis of examining only a few passages in the tradition. As noted at the start of this paper, it might be that Mark's dependence on Q could be shown more easily at other points in the tradition not examined here. Nevertheless the importance of the whole question of the relationship between Mark and Q is such that the issue needs to be constantly re-examined in the light of our developing understandings of the very varied nature of early Christianity.

Department of Religions and Theology   Christopher M. TUCKETT
University of Manchester
Manchester M13 9PL, England

ZUR Q-REZEPTION IN LK 12,35–13,35 (14,1-24)

DIE Q-HYPOTHESE UND IHRE BEDEUTUNG
FÜR DIE INTERPRETATION DES LUKANISCHEN REISEBERICHTES

Lk 12–13 gehört in verschiedenster Hinsicht zu den besonders aufschlußreichen Passagen des lukanischen Reiseberichtes. Der Abschnitt läßt den differenzierenden Umgang des Lukas mit der Eschatologie seiner Vorlagen erkennen. Er bündelt entscheidende theologische Linien, besonders Lk 13,31-35 wird nicht selten geradezu als »Herzstück« des Reiseberichtes angesehen. Weiter stellt sich mit diesem Textbereich die Frage nach der übergreifenden Struktur des Reiseberichtes[1]. Schließlich ist Lk 13 auch für die Rezeption der Redequelle durch den Evangelisten von besonderer Bedeutung, weil die Q-Akoluthie von 12,53 an nicht mehr so deutlich in Erscheinung tritt wie zuvor und manche Autoren deshalb fragen, ob Lukas nicht schon hier den Faden der Q-Akoluthie, dem er von 9,51 an weitgehend gefolgt ist, mehr und mehr verläßt[2].

Unsere Überlegungen setzen zwar nur beim letzten der genannten Punkte an und fragen speziell nach der Q-Rezeption in Lk 12,35–13,35; sie haben aber dabei durchaus die Gesamtproblematik des Textbereichs im Auge. Denn gerade im ersten Teil des lukanischen Reisebericht, wo Lukas sich relativ eng an seine Vorlage hält, dürfte die Erhellung der Q-Rezeption auch Aufschlüsse über den lukanischen Kompositionswillen und das Verständnis einzelner Abschnitte geben.

Wir gehen bei unserer Untersuchung – heuristisch – von der Beobachtung aus, daß in Lk 12,35–13,35 (und 14,1-24) gerade jene Texte, die mit mehr oder weniger großer Wahrscheinlichkeit für Q reklamiert werden können, in ähnlicher Weise eschatologisch geprägt sind und untereinander Verbindungen erkennen lassen, die nicht erst auf die Lukasredaktion zurückgeführt werden können. Die Vermutung legt sich nahe, daß hinter 12,35–13,35 (und möglicherweise 14,1-24) schon in Q eine eschatologisch geprägte Textabfolge stand, auf die der

---

* Literaturverzeichnis, s. pp. 205-208.

1. Vgl. zusammenfassend die Übersicht bei H.L. EGELKRAUT, *Mission*, pp. 204-209.

2. Vgl. etwa K. DORN, *Gleichnisse*, p. 186: »Kap 13 stellt nach Ansicht vieler Exegeten innerhalb des lk Reiseberichts eine Besonderheit dar. Einerseits markiert es den Beginn eines stärkeren Hervortretens der Sondergutanteile im Reisebericht überhaupt, andererseits ist von einer 'mehr zufälligen Akkumulation zusammengewürfelter Tradition' die Rede«.

Evangelist zurückgegriffen hat und die er seiner Gesamtkonzeption dienstbar gemacht hat[3].

I. Lk 12,35–13,35: Komposition, Aussage und Zusammenhang bei Lukas

Unsere Überlegungen setzen mit der Frage nach dem lukanischen Verständnis der eschatologischen Texte in Lk 12,35–13,35 ein. Dabei wird es notwendig sein, zunächst generell die lukanische Komposition in Lk 12–13 zu erfassen und dann die Funktion der einzelnen Texte in 12,35–13,35 in diesem Horizont zu klären.

1. Mit den meisten neueren Autoren gehen wir davon aus, daß Lukas mit 12,1 eine Redekomposition einleitet, die sich bis 13,9 erstreckt und durch den Adressatenwechsel 12,54a in zwei unterschiedliche Teile aufgegliedert wird: Der erste Teil – 12,1-53 – spricht in den »Innenraum« der Jüngergemeinde, der zweite Teil – 12,54–13,9 – erscheint als Bußpredigt Jesu an das Volk[4]. Schwierigkeiten ergeben sich allerdings bei der Zuordnung der auf 13,9 folgenden Abschnitte. Einerseits nämlich findet sich sowohl in 13,10 als auch in 13,22 jeweils eine als »situationsverändernd«[5] einzustufende Einleitung; 13,22 wird dabei zumeist als übergreifendes Gliederungssignal und Einleitung des zweiten Teiles des Reiseberichtes bewertet[6]. Andererseits aber schließen die Texte in 13,10–13,35 thematisch so eng an 12,54–13,9 an, daß man eher auf einen von 12,54 bis 13,35 weitergetragenen Zusammenhang schließen möchte. Dafür spricht auch die Beobachtung, daß Lukas mit 13,31-35 einen gewichtigen Abschluß setzt, der keineswegs nur 13,22-30 im Blick hat, sondern auch auf 12,54-13,21 ausgreift[7]. Es wird deshalb

---

3. Die hier vorgelegten Überlegungen basieren auf unseren Untersuchungen zur Q-Vorlage von Lk 12,35–14,24 (C.-P. MÄRZ, Lampen, passim), die wir hier – an einigen Stellen modifizierend – aufnehmen und auf die redaktionsgeschichtliche Problematik hin weiterführen. Für nähere Begründungen sei generell auf diesen Sammelband verwiesen, wo sich auch über den hier bewußt schmal gehaltenen Bezug auf die Fachliteratur hinaus ausführliche Hinweise und Belege finden.

4. Vgl. etwa J. ERNST, Lk, pp. 350ff., 415; W. SCHMITHALS, Lk, pp. 142, 150; G. SCHNEIDER, Lk, p. 380.

5. Vgl. G. SELLIN, Reisebericht, pp. 107ff.

6. So etwa G. SCHNEIDER, Lk, pp. 304-305; W. WIEFEL, Lk, p. 259. R. BULTMANN, Geschichte, p. 387, sieht einen Einschnitt zwischen 13,30 und 13,31, K.L. SCHMIDT, Rahmen, pp. 270-271, zwischen 13,17 und 13,18. Vgl. generell die Übersichten bei A. DENAUX, Reisverhaal, passim.

7. Vgl. die entsprechenden Bezüge der Motive in 13,31-35: Das Heilswirken Jesu an Israel zielt auf 13,10-17 (vgl. 12,54b-56); die Nichtannahme dieses Mühens auf 12,54b-57; 13,10-17; 13,26-27, die Zerstörung Jerusalems auf 13,1-9. Deutliche Verbindungen lassen sich auch zwischen Lk 12,49-53, dem Abschluß der Jüngerrede, und 13,31-35 ausmachen (Hinweis auf den Tod Jesu, aus dem sich innergeschichtliche Konsequenzen für die jeweils angesprochene Gruppe ableiten; christologische Selbstaussagen). Vgl. R. SCHNACKEN-

sinnvoll sein, die Situationsangaben in 13,10 und 13,22 nochmals genauer auf ihre literarische Funktion im Zusammenhang von 12,54–13,35 hin zu befragen.

Für 13,10 scheint diese relativ deutlich: Die Heilung der gekrümmten Frau Lk 13,10-17 fungiert im Anschluß an 12,54–13,9 als »Exempel für das« 13,8-9 angesprochene »Mühen Jesu um Israel«[8]. Die Einleitung führt in diesem Sinne knapp »ohne nähere örtliche und zeitliche Bestimmung«[9] eine neue Situation ein und beläßt den neuen Abschnitt sachlich in enger Verbindung mit der vorausgegangenen Bußpredigt an das Volk. Bemerkenswert ist freilich, daß 13,10 sich dabei einer »nach Lukas für das öffentliche Wirken Jesu typischen (vgl. Lk 4,16.31-32) Notiz«[10] bedient und mit dieser offenbar das Heilswirken Jesu insgesamt in Erinnerung rufen möchte. U. Busse konstatiert zu Recht: »Der redaktionellen Intention, rechtes Verhalten angesichts der gegenwärtigen Gottesherrschaft und des in ihr angebrochenen Heils (vgl. Lk 13,18-21) an typischen Begebenheiten auf dem Wege Jesu nach Jerusalem paränetisch zu veranschaulichen, kommt ... auch die Episode der verkrüppelten Frau entgegen«[11]. 13,10 sucht insofern nicht eine geschlossene Handlungslinie zu konstituieren, sondern zielt eher darauf, die Wundergeschichte vom Kontext abzuheben, um ihre exemplarische Bedeutung herauszuarbeiten[12].

Größere Probleme bereitet die entsprechende Zuordnung von 13,22. Schon K.L. Schmidt hat den »Sammelberichtscharakter«[13] von 13,22 hervorgehoben. Er charakterisiert den Vers als eine vom Evangelisten der folgenden Perikope vorangestellte Einleitung, die den Leser wieder daran erinnern soll, daß Jesus auf dem Weg nach Jerusalem sei. Um freilich die literarischen Funktion dieser »Sammelnotiz« näher zu erfas-

---

BURG, *Lk 13, 31-33*, pp. 239-240, der folgende lukanischen Akzente für 13,31-33 herausarbeitet: eine Theologie des Weges, die Bedeutung Jerusalems und der Tod Jesu.

8. W. WIEFEL, *Lk*, p. 255.

9. F. HAUCK, *Lk*, p. 181.

10. U. BUSSE, *Wunder*, p. 291.

11. *Ibid.*

12. U. BUSSE, *Wunder*, p. 456, verweist darauf, daß Lukas die »Mehrzahl seiner Wundergeschichten vom Kontext« isoliert und erörtert dabei besonders die periphrastische Konjugation: »Ein weiters literarisches Mittel, eine Episode von ihrem Kontext abzuheben, ist die constructio periphrastica. Lukas schildert mit ihr eine allgemeine Ausgangslage, auf deren Hintergrund und unter deren Voraussetzung sich eine spezielle Handlung entwickelt (vgl Lk 4,31; 11,14; 13,10)«. Vgl. die weiteren Hinweise, pp. 456-457: »Ebenso generalisiert und typisiert er einzelne Wundererzählungen durch plurale Erzählschlüsse oder Überleitungen (vgl Lk 5,26; 7,18; 9,43b; 13,17) oder unterstreicht ihren lehrhaften Charakter durch fiktive Dialoge (Lk 11,15.16; 13,14ff.) und Verallgemeinerungen«. Vgl. zur periphrastischen Konjugation G. BJÖRK, ἦν διδάσκων, p. 96: Besonders ein im Präsens verwandtes Partizip gibt den durchhaltenden Hintergrund für die dann folgende Handlung an.

13. K. L. SCHMIDT, *Rahmen*, p. 261, sieht 13,22 allerdings im Zusammenhang mit 9,51; 17,11; 19,11.

sen, gilt es, deren Bezüge zum näheren Kontext zu beachten. Dabei fällt zunächst ins Auge, daß 13,22 mit διδάσκων an 13,10 anknüpft und offensichtlich zunächst einmal die dort gegebene allgemeine Einleitung aufnimmt, auch wenn – wie in 13,10 – keine direkte Weiterführung der Handlungslinie, sondern mehr ein sachlicher Zusammenhang ausgedrückt ist[14]. Der Hinweis scheint zugleich v. 26 vorzubereiten, wo jene, die beim Gericht abgewiesen werden, sich auf Jesu Lehrtätigkeit auf ihren »öffentlichen Plätzen« berufen. Zudem scheint er – in Verbindung mit 13,10 – den szenischen Hintergrund für das Rätselwort 13,33 anzuzeigen[15]. Der nachgestellte Hinweis καὶ πορείαν ποιούμενος εἰς Ἱεροσόλυμα verdichtet die Sammelnotiz auf die Vorstellung der Reise nach Jerusalem hin und dient so als Einleitung zu 13,31-33 und 13,34-35. Zu beachten ist, daß dem Leser bereits in 13,1-5 (und hintergründig auch in 13,6-9) Jerusalem wieder in den Blick gebracht worden ist, der Hinweis in 13,22b also im Zusammenhang einer thematischen Linie zu sehen ist, die mit 13,1-5 einsetzt und bis 13,31-35 reicht. Damit aber ist nicht nur die Reisenotiz 13,22, sondern der gesamte Abschnitt, insbesondere aber der Schluß Lk 13,31-35 an den Anfang des Reiseberichts zurückgebunden[16].

Das bedeutet: 13,22 leitet zwar den Abschnitt 13,22-35 ein, – wahrt aber auch die Verbindung zum Vorhergehenden. Die Sammelnotiz muß somit nicht zwangsläufig als übergreifender Neuansatz verstanden werden, sondern läßt sich angemessener als disponierendes Gliederungs-

14. Vgl. hilfreich noch immer B. WEISS, *Lk*, p. 509: Mit 13,22 »ist nicht ein neuer Akt der Weiterreise indiziert..., da ja keinerlei Stationen angegeben sind, oder gar eine neue Reise, sondern nur daran erinnert, dass Jesus sich noch auf der 9,51 begonnenen Reise befand. Diese Erinnerung ist aber nicht sowohl durch die Unterbrechungen 11,37. 13,10 ... nötig geworden, sondern dadurch, daß das Folgende nicht mehr in der Synagoge (V. 10) spielt«. In diesem Sinne spricht E. KLOSTERMANN, *Lk*, p. 146, von einer »vagen lukanischen Einleitung«. Beachtenswert ist im Hinblick auf die Imperfektform des tragenden Verbs in 13,22 (διεπορεύετο) vielleicht auch der Hinweis von U. BUSSE, *Wunder*, p. 455: Es ist eine »luk. Eigenart, für den Leser wichtige Hintergrundinformationen, ohne deren Kenntnis das Verstehen des Textes erschwert wäre, in imperfektivischen Sätzen (vgl u.a. Lk 8,29; 18,39), d.h. in mit der Haupterzählung (im Aorist) korrespondierenden Aspekt, in die Schilderung einfließen zu lassen«.

15. Die exemplarisch berichtete Heilungsgeschichte anläßlich des »Lehrens« in der Synagoge dürfte auch das Verständnis von διδάσκων in 13,22 mit prägen.

16. H.L. EGELKRAUT, *Mission*, p. 13, hat mit Recht darauf hingewiesen, daß die Reisenotizen fast durchweg in speziellen Zusammenhängen erscheinen: »The journey references are arranged in clusters because the redactor, Luke, spun them out of pericopae which implied that Jesus was travelling or going up to Jerusalem. Because of this, their effect on the reader is less conspicious than if they were evenly spread over the entire passage«. Egelkraut nennt folgende »cluster«: 9,51-10,1 (9,51.53.57; 10,1); 13,31-35 (13, 22.33); 18,31ff. (18,31; 19,11.28; 19,41.45) – isolierte Notizen sieht er in 10,38; 17,11. Zum Verhältnis von 9,51-52 und Lk 13,31-35 zu Recht: »In terms of journey material proper Luke had only two pericopae available: The rejection at the Samaritan village, 9,52-56, and the warning against Herod; 13,31-35« (p. 14). Zu 13,22: »Lk 13,22 anticipates already 13,31ff. and is probably derived from there« (p. 14).

element im Rahmen eines sich auch thematisch als Sacheinheit empfeh-
lenden Abschnitts 12,54–13,35 verstehen. Lukas hat also – wie zuvor in
9,51–10,42 und 11,1-54[17] – auch hier einen größeren Erzählkomplex
geschaffen, der über die eigentliche Rede in 12,1–13,9 hinaus bis 13,35
reicht. Diesen gliedert er durch den Adressatenwechsel in 12,54a in
einen an die Jünger (12,2-53) und einen an das Volk (12,54–13,35)
gerichteten Teil[18]. Der erste Teil ist dabei zwar durch den Wechsel der
Adressaten in 12,12.22.41 strukturiert, bleibt aber ansonsten im Rahmen der in 12,1 eingeführten Szenerie. Inhaltlich ist er bestimmt von
der Stellung der Jünger bzw. der Kirche in dieser Weltzeit[19]. Der zweite
Teil – 12,54–13,35 – setzt bei dem an das Volk gerichteten Abschluß
dieser mit 12,1 begonnenen Rede ein, leitet dann aber stufenweise in
neue Situationen über. Folgt man den Einleitungen, dann lassen sich
fünf Szenen ausmachen, in denen jeweils zwei Texte miteinander verbunden sind (12,54-59; 13,1-9; 13,10-21; 13,22-30; 13,31-35). Gewichtet
man die »situationsverändernden« Angaben in 13,10 und 13,22 stärker,
dann ergeben sich drei Teile (12,54–13,9; 13,10-21; 13,22-35), die auch
thematisch jeweils besondere Akzente setzen: 12,54–13,9 beinhaltet die
eigentliche Bußpredigt; 13,10-21 erzählt das Heilswirken Jesu und seine
unterschiedliche Resonanz; 13,22-35 nennt die Konsequenzen der Verschlossenheit gegenüber dem in Jesu Tun eröffneten Kairos[20]. Der
Evangelist versteht diese Abfolge offenbar exemplarisch: Wie in einem
»Zeitraffer« verdichtet wird hier in einem Handlungszusammenhang die
Bußpredigt Jesu vor Israel in ihren verschiedenen Aspekten und Ent-
wicklungsstadien zur Sprache gebracht. Der Abschnitt bildet so einen
angemessenen Abschluß des ersten Teiles des lukanischen Reiseberichtes; er bezieht sich auf den Sammlungsimpuls an dessen Anfang zurück
und wird nicht zufällig in 19,41-44 rekapituliert.

2. Fragen wir nach dem lukanischen Verständnis der eschatologischen Texte in Lk 12,35–13,35, dann hat dies auf dem Hintergrund
der lukanischen Komposition in Lk 12–13 zu geschehen. Dies gilt nicht
nur für die unterschiedliche Funktion der eschatologischen Aussagen
im ersten und zweiten Teil des Erzählkomplexes, sondern mehr noch
für das spezifische Gewicht und die Zuordnung der einzelnen Texte im
besonders nachdrücklich strukturierten zweiten Teil.

Im *ersten Teil*, der nach der Intention des Lukas zugleich die blei-

17. Vgl. etwa J. BRUTSCHEK, *Maria-Marta*, pp. 62-64.
18. So schon F. HAUCK, *Lk*, pp. 164-187: 12,1-53 sind »Jüngermahnungen«, 12,54-
13,35 »Bußworte an das Volk«.
19. Vgl. W. GRUNDMANN, *Lk*, p. 251.
20. A. POLAG, *Umfang*, p. 26, vermutet als Strukturmuster für Lk 13 das »heilsgeschichtliche Schema: Heilsangebot-Ablehnung-Verwerfung/Übergang zu den Völkern«.

bende Mahnung an die Kirche zur Sprache bringen soll, bilden die direkten eschatologischen Aussagen in Lk 12,35-48.49-53 zwar den Abschluß und haben wohl auch als Hintergrund der übrigen Paränese zu gelten, sie sind aber nicht besonders hervorgehoben. Das Gleichnis von den wachenden Knechten Lk 12,35-40 mahnt zur Stetsbereitschaft, weil die Stunde der Wiederkunft ungewiß ist, und betont den großen Lohn, den der gute Knecht am Ende von seinem Herrn empfangen wird. Das sich anschließende Gleichnis vom guten und vom bösen Knecht Lk 12,42-46 ist durch die Frage des Petrus 12,41 hintergründig als Paränese an die Amtsträger markiert und durch die nachfolgenden VV. 47-48 nunmehr auf deren größere Verantwortlichkeit ausgerichtet[21].

Kräftige eschatologische Akzente begegnen in dem kleinen Summarium 12,49-53 am Ende der Rede an die Jünger. Der Feuerspruch 12,49 zeigt Jesus selbst in drängender Erwartung des Gerichtes, 12,51-53 läßt mit Mich 6,7 immerhin einen gängigen eschatologischen Topos anklingen. Doch diese Aussagen sind durch den Zusammenhang gebunden: Der Feuerspruch wird durch den Hinweis auf den Tod Jesu ergänzt, 12,51-53 knüpft mit der Zeitangabe ἀπὸ τοῦ νῦν an diese Aussage an und zeichnet »die Gegenwart als Zeit der bedrängten Kirche«[22].

Anders liegen die Dinge im *zweiten Teil* des Erzählkomplexes, wo Lukas »historisierend« die eschatologische Predigt Jesu vor Israel zur Sprache bringt. Besondere Aufmerksamkeit verdient dabei die deutende Zuordnung der einzelnen Abschnitte im Rahmen der lukanischen Komposition.

Der erste Abschnitt – 12,54-13,9 – muß aus der Verbindung zweier unterschiedlich geprägter Szenen verstanden werden: Während 12,54-59 allgemein und generell davor warnt, sich dem Kairos zu verschließen, und zum Handeln in letzter Stunde mahnt, bringt 13,1-9 eine sehr spezifische Konkretisierung. Die Niedermetzelung der Galiläer und der Einsturz des Turmes von Schiloah werden als Vorzeichen eines Strafgerichtes gewertet, das das Volk (vgl. πάντες in 13,3.6), wenn es sich nicht bekehrt, treffen wird. Auch wenn dieses Strafgericht nicht näher beschrieben ist, so wird der Leser doch hintergründig auf die Zerstörung Jerusalems gewiesen[23]. Die eng zusammengezogene Frist der Bekehrung (vgl. 12,58-59, auch 19,41-44), die Konzentration der Beispiele auf Jerusalem, der Vergleich mit konkreten geschichtlichen Geschehnissen

---

21. Vgl. bes. die ausführliche Darstellung bei F. PRAST, *Presbyter*, pp. 228-248.
22. H. KLEIN, *Prüfung*, p. 374. Vgl. auch C.-P. MÄRZ, *Feuer*, pp. 26-31.
23. Vgl. etwa J. ERNST, *Lk*, p. 420; E. SCHWEIZER, *Lk*, p. 145. K. DORN, *Gleichnisse*, p. 192: »Daß sich diese Drohung in streng verbalem Sinne für Jerusalem erfüllt hat bzw. erfüllen wird, läßt Lk ... in 19,41-44 und 21,20-24 in kaum zu überbietender Deutlichkeit verlauten«.

(vgl. »*genauso* umkommen...« in 13,4.6) jedenfalls können in der Rückschau von der lukanischen Position nach dem Jahre 70 kaum anders verstanden werden, denn als Ansage des Jüdischen Krieges und der Zerstörung Jerusalems und des Tempels (vgl. Lk 19,41.48; 21,12-18) als innergeschichtliches Strafgericht über die von Israel verweigerten Bekehrung. Von diesen Vorgaben her muß das Feigenbaumgleichnis als Hinweis auf das Heilswirken Jesu als letzte Chance für Israel[24] in einer bereits auf die Eskalation hintreibenden Situation gedeutet werden[25]. Damit ist eine spezifische Akzentuierung der allgemeinen Aussage in 12,54-59 vorgenommen und zugleich ein Spannungsbogen zu 13,31-35 aufgerichtet: Das, was hier noch als bedrohliche Möglichkeit ins Spiel gebracht wird, ist dort bereits als kommende Wirklichkeit angesagt.

Der zweite Abschnitt – 13,10-21 – steht ganz in diesem Spannungsbogen zwischen 13,1-9 und 13,31-35. Er führt dem Leser das in 13,8-9 zunächst nur angedeutete Heilstun Jesu an Israel vor Augen. Dabei geht die Heilungsgeschichte in 13,14 in ein Streitgespräch über, das auf dem Hintergrund von 13,1-9 besondere Schärfe erhält. Auch wenn das Volk sich am Ende über die Taten Jesu freut, bleibt die Reaktion gespalten. Lukas gebraucht nicht zufällig in 13,15 (wie in 12,56) die Anrede ὑποκρίται und akzentuiert damit eher die Ablehnung[26].

Das der Heilungsgeschichte angefügte Doppelgleichnis verweist mit dem Stichwort βασιλεία auf 13,28-29 und scheint auch mit den »Vögeln des Himmel, die in den Zweigen des Baumes wohnen« (13,19), auf jene, die nach 13,29 von allen Himmelsrichtungen kommen und in die Basileia einziehen, Bezug zu nehmen, bringt also den Horizont der weltweiten Mission in den Blick[27]. Die beiden Gleichnisse verdeutlichen somit im lukanischen Zusammenhang, daß das Gottesreich, das im Heilstun Jesu nur verborgen zur Wirkung kommt und Ablehnung erfährt, doch eine herrliche eschatologische Vollendungsgestalt finden wird, die sich auch gegen den Widerstand Israels hinweg und über den Rahmen dieses Volkes hinaus durchsetzen wird. Beachtet man den mit 13,1-9 eingeführten Hintergrund der Zerstörung Jerusalems, dann wird der Blick auch über dieses angedrohte Strafgericht hinaus auf die Sammlung des neuen Gottesvolkes und dessen eschatologische Vollendung in der Basileia geführt.

---

24. Nach M. DORN, *Gleichnisse*, p. 192, erscheint die gewährte Frist angesichts der vorausgegangenen Fruchtlosigkeit »als außerordentlicher Gnadenerweis... Die angekündigten Bemühungen des Gärtners unterstreichen das ungewöhnliche an dieser Frist nur noch«.

25. Lukas versteht die Zeit Jesu offenbar als bereits von den Vorzeichen des jüdischen Krieges durchzogene und damit auf die Zerstörung Jerusalems hintreibende Situation.

26. Vgl. etwa die Analyse von U. BUSSE, *Wunder*, pp. 289-304.

27. Vgl. für viele P. ZINGG, *Wachsen*, p. 107: »Der Zusammenhang zwischen V. 19 und V. 29 verweist auf die weltweite Mission. Die Kirchensituation des Luk. wird sichtbar«.

Der dritte Abschnitt – 13,22-35 – konstituiert sich wie der erste[28] aus zwei aufeinander bezogenen Szenen, die durch die Einleitung in 13,22 und die Überleitung in 13,31 zusammengehalten sind und deshalb auch in Zuordnung zueinander gelesen werden müssen[29].

Die erste Szene – 13,24-30 – erscheint zwar durch die Einleitung in V. 24 als Mahnrede, ist aber durch die einleitende Frage und den Zusammenhang auf die Möglichkeit des Ausschlüsses aus der Basileia orientiert und fungiert fast im Sinne einer Gerichtsankündigung über die, die sich dem Kairos des Heilswirkens Jesu verschließen. 13,26-27 stellt in diesem Sinne fest, daß bei der Parusie nicht der wie auch immer geartete Kontakt mit Jesus, sondern die Bekehrung alleiniges Kriterium des Eintritts in die Basileia sein wird. Dabei ist an dieser Stelle keineswegs ein genereller Ausschluß Israels verfügt, wohl aber ist ausgesprochen, daß auch Juden, wenn sie sich dem Wort Jesu verschließen, ausgeschlossen werden und ihr Platz im Reich Gottes von anderen – Heiden, die das Wort Jesu angenommen haben – eingenommen wird[30].

Die zweite Szene – 13,31-35 – liegt insofern auf der gleichen Linie wie 13,24-30, als es auch hier um die Ablehnung des Heilswirkens Jesu und das daraus resultierende Strafgericht geht. Abgehoben wird 13,31-35 vom Vorhergehenden freilich dadurch, daß Anklage und Gerichtsansage auf Jerusalem konzentriert und nicht mehr konditioniert sind, sondern definitiv zugesprochen werden (vgl. 19,41-44; 20,9-19; 21,20-24). Durch 13,31-33 verbindet Lukas diese Gerichtsansage mit dem Gedanken der Reise nach Jerusalem: »Reise, Passion, Schuld der Juden und (von da zu verstehen) Geschick der Stadt bilden einen festen Komplex«[31]. Von daher wird auch verständlich, daß Jerusalem bereits auf dem Wege direkt angesprochen und das Heilswirken Jesu um Israel als Bemühen um Jerusalem verstanden wird (so auch 19,41-44). Letztlich steht die Stadt, die die »Stunde ihrer Heimsuchung nicht erkannt hat« und deshalb dem Gericht verfällt, für den Unglauben, der Jesus in Israel entgegengebracht wird und »der sich schließlich in Jerusalem

28. Auffällig ist, daß sowohl in 13,1 als auch in 13,31 die Szene durch »Hinzutretende« geöffnet wird.
29. Vgl. H.L. EGELKRAUT zu 13,31-35: »It is linking to the preceding pericope in a number of ways: (1) by means of the journey reference 13,22 which is spun out of 13,31ff.; (2) by means of the Lukan phrase 'ἐν αὐτῇ τῇ ὥρᾳ' which moves this episode in closest proximity with the foregoing parable, and (3) by means of stating the reason for Israel's exclusion which was the topic of the preceding passage«.
30. Vgl. zur Auslegung zusammenfassend C.-P. MÄRZ, Q-Vorlage, pp. 98-101.
31. H. CONZELMANN, Mitte, p. 125. Vgl. zusammenfassend etwa auch W. WIEFEL, Lk, p. 22: »Wie kein anderer Evangelist verbindet er [=Lukas] das Schicksal der Stadt Jerusalem und den Weg des Kreuzes. Er würde das nicht tun, wenn er nicht unter dem auch ihn erschütternden Eindruck des Jüdischen Krieges stehen würde. In Aufnahme der ihm gegebenen Tradition läßt er sichtbar werden, wie Jesusweg und Jerusalemschicksal miteinander verknüpft sind (13,1-9.31-34; 19,39-46; 20,9-19; 21,10-14; 23,26-31)«.

vollendet«[32]. Damit scheint die in 13,24-30 ausgesprochene Bedrohung Israels mit dem eschatologischen Gericht aktualisierend durch den Gedanken der Zerstörung Jerusalems kommentiert zu sein. In diesem Sinne erscheint 13,31-35 dann in der Tat wie die abschließende Verknüpfung der den Abschnitt 12,54-13,35 zusammenhaltenden »Sinnlinien«. Bezeichnend ist aber, daß der Urteilsspruch nicht direkt dem Volk, sondern den schon in Kapitel 11 mit den Weherufen behafteten Pharisäern gesagt wird. Lukas will zwar die Scheidung in Israel verdeutlichen, nicht aber von einem generellen Ausschluß des Volkes reden.

II. Literarkritische Orientierung

Unsere knappe Skizze zum lukanischen Verständnis der eschatologischen Texte in Lk 12,35–13,35 hat das nachhaltige kompositorische Bemühen des Evangelisten gerade in diesem Abschnitt deutlich gemacht. Sie zeigte freilich auch dessen Interesse an der Kommentierung einzelner Textzusammenhänge, die möglicherweise auf Q zurückgehen (12,54-56; 13,22-30). Wir fragen deshalb literarkritisch: nach der Stellung der Q-Texte im Rahmen der lukanischen Komposition und suchen mögliche vorlukanische Verbindungen zu erheben. Dabei bemühen wir uns zunächst um eine generelle literarkritische Einschätzung des Abschnitts Lk 12,35–13,35 und versuchen dann, die Q-Vorlage wenigstens in ihrem Grundbestand herauszuarbeiten. Bei diesen Überlegungen beziehen wir die in ihrer Herkunft aus Q umstrittenen Texte 12,35-38; 12,49 und 12,54b-56 für die Frage nach dem Textbestand der Quelle ausdrücklich mit ein, weil sie aufgrund der Diskussionslage als mögliche Elemente einer vormaligen Q-Abfolge mit in Betracht gezogen werden müssen[33].

32. H. GLÖCKNER, Heilsverkündigung, p. 85.
33. Weil immer auch mit möglichen Auslassungen einzelner Q-Texte durch Matthäus oder Lukas gerechnet werden muß, ist es methodisch problematisch, beider Rekonstruktion der Quelle nur von den sogenannten »sicheren«, d.h. den durch beide synoptischen Seitenreferenten eindeutig für Q bezeugten Einzeltexten auszugehen. Da Q nicht vornehmlich isolierte Einzeltexte, sondern Spruchkompositionen überliefert (Vgl. zusammenfassend etwa H. SCHÜRMANN, Kompositionsgeschichte, passim), kann eine solche Einschränkung aufs Ganze gesehen zu erheblichen Fehlurteilen gerade hinsichtlich der literarischen Struktur und damit dann doch hinsichtlich der Aussage der Einzeltexte in der Quelle führen. Die Frage nach möglichen vorlukanischen Kompositionen muß deshalb den synoptischen Vergleich methodisch ergänzen. Besondere Probleme ergeben sich u.E. mit der Annahme, Q habe Mt und Lk in unterschiedlichen Rezensionen – QMt und QLk – vorgelegen. Auch wenn diese Möglichkeit nicht von vornherein in Abrede gestellt werden kann, erscheint es problematisch, wenn sie faktisch als »Lösung« für die in der Zugehörigkeit zu Q unsicheren Texte eingesetzt wird (vgl. grundsätzlich zur Annahme von QMt und QLk: F. NEIRYNCK, Q Mt and Q Lk, passim). Wenig hilfreich erscheint deshalb für unseren Textbereich die Einschätzung von M. SATO, Q, pp. 57-58, Lk 12,35-38; 12,54-56 seien

1. Literarkritisch betrachtet präsentiert sich der Abschnitt Lk 12,35–13,35 im wesentlichen als eine Kombination von Texten aus der Redequelle und dem lukanischen Sondergut; direkte Rezeption von Markus-Texten findet sich nicht. Betrachtet man dabei die Sonderguttexte – Lk 12,47-48[34]; 13,1-5[35]; 13,6-9[36]; 13,10-17[37]; 13,31-33[38] –, dann zeigt sich, daß diese sich fast durchgängig deutend auf Zusammenhänge hinordnen, die aus Q-Texten gebildet sind: Lk 12,47-48 schließt an 12,42-46 an; 13,1-5.6-9 führt 12,54-59 weiter; 13,31-33 leitet 13,34-35 ein; eine besonderes Problem stellt lediglich 13,10-17 dar. Wir werden deshalb zunächst einmal grundsätzlich davon ausgehen dürfen, daß auch für unseren Abschnitt die Q-Akoluthie die Basis der lukanischen Darstellung bildet – auch wenn der Evangelist stärker als zuvor Sonderguttexte einfließen läßt.

Überblickt man die in Lk 12,35–13,35 für Q reklamierten Texte, so fällt zunächst auf, daß die meisten von ihnen in drei Blöcken – 12,35-46; 12,49-59; 13,24-30 – beieinander stehen. Die Texte sind dabei teilweise fest miteinander verbunden und weisen thematische Verbindungen auch über lukanische Absätze hinweg auf. Da Lukas auch sonst dahin tendiert, seine Vorlagen »blockweise« aufzunehmen, liegt die

möglicherweise erst in QLk – in den Zusammenhang eingefügt worden. Sato versucht so zwar der deutlichen – offensichtlich vorlukanischen – Bindung der genannten Texte an den jeweiligen Kontext Rechnung zu tragen, möchte aber wegen der fehlenden formellen Mt-Parallele eine direkte Zugehörigkeit zu Q nicht in Betracht ziehen – obwohl sich im ersten Fall Hinweise auf eine matthäische Auslassung beibringen lassen und im zweiten Fall die Probleme mit den Unsicherheiten in der Textbezeugung von Mt 16,2b-3 zusammenhängen. Grundsätzlich steht die Frage, ob die von Sato vermuteten Rezensionen QLk und QMt nicht doch eher als Vorstufen etc im Horizont der Redaktion des jeweiligen Evangelisten anzusiedeln sind.

34. Vgl. etwa A. WEISER, *Knechtsgleichnisse*, pp. 222-223; F. PRAST, *Presbyter*, pp. 245ff. – anders etwa W. SCHMITHALS, *Lk*, p. 148: »Vermutlich eine redaktionelle Bildung«; M. SATO, *Q*, p. 57, erwägt Herkunft aus QLk (s.o. vorige Anm.).

35. Wenig überzeugend die Annahme von K. DORN, *Gleichnisse*, p. 188, Lk 13,1-5 gehe weitgehend – zumindest aber in der Umkehrforderung – auf Lukas zurück. M. SATO, *Q*, pp. 58-59, hält Einfügung in QLk für möglich.

36. Wenig überzeugend K. DORN, *Gleichnisse*, pp. 189ff.: Wegen der thematischen Nähe zu Q-Aussagen (Lk 3,7ffQ) und einem ähnlichen Bildfeld wie 13,18-21 könne für 13,6-9 Herkunft aus Q vermutet werden (in VV. 6a und 7a ließen sich Spuren der Redaktion erkennen). M. SATO, *Q*, p. 59, erwägt Einfügung durch QLk.

37. Vgl. etwa die Analyse von U. BUSSE, *Wunder*, pp. 289-304, der auf eine Sondertradition schließt, anders W. SCHMITHALS, *Lk*, p. 152: »13,10-17 ... ist eine relativ formlose, sekundäre – vermutlich erst lukanische – Parallele zu 6,6-11«.

38. Lk 13,31-33 ist schwer einzuschätzen – vgl. etwa J.A. FITZMYER, *Lk*, p. 1028: Lk 13,31-33 stammt aus der Quelle »L«; R. SCHNACKENBURG, *Lk 13,31-33*, zusammenfassend p. 237: »Die Szene 13,31 mit dem anschließenden Wort Jesu V. 32 geht auf eine lukanische Sonderquelle zurück, während V. 33 aus lukanischen Tendenzen vom Evangelisten redaktionell gebildet ist, um zugleich zu dem Q-Logion V. 34-35 überzuleiten«; M. RESE, *Überlegungen*, zusammenfassend p. 224: »Lukas scheint das Stück Lk XIII,31-33 selbst verfaßt zu haben«; ähnlich A. DENAUX, *L'hypocrisie*, passim; SCHMITHALS, *Lk*, p. 156: »am ehesten als redaktionelle Bindung (sic!) des Lukas verständlich«.

Vermutung nahe, daß wir in den genannten Abschnitten auf bereits in Q vorgeprägte Zusammenhänge treffen. Abgehoben von den eben erwähnten miteinander verbundenen Q-Texten finden sich in unserem Zusammenhang nur zwei Texte, die wegen eindeutiger Mt-Parallelen auf Q zurückgeführt werden können: Das Doppelgleichnis vom Senfkorn und vom Sauerteig Lk 13,18-21 und der Gerichtsspruch über Jerusalem Lk 13,34-35; hinzuweisen ist auch auf das in der nächsten Szene erscheinende Gleichnis vom großen Gastmahl Lk 14,16-24, das thematisch mit Lk 13,28-29 verbunden zu sein scheint.

Das Doppelgleichnis Lk 13,18-21 leitet bei Lukas von der Heilung der verkrümmten Frau (13,10-17) zur Bildrede über das Gericht (13,24-30) über und steht so im Dienst der lukanischen Komposition. Es ist deshalb wohl erst vom Evangelisten in den Zusammenhang eingebracht worden, seine Stellung in Q ist nicht mehr auszumachen[39]. Auch der Gerichtsspruch gegen Jerusalem (13,34-35) dürfte nach dem bisher Gesagten erst durch Lukas in den Zusammenhang eingebracht worden sein[40]. Dafür spricht schon, daß er redaktionell mit einer – wohl auf Sondergut basierenden – Einleitung versehen wird und so zusammen mit 13,31-33 geradezu als Schlüsseltext der lukanischen Komposition in Lk 12,54-13,35 erscheint. Auch die differenzierende Adressatenangabe in 13,31 spricht eher dafür, daß Lukas hier zwar einen Text neu in den Zusammenhang einbringt, diesen aber auch in gewisser Weise vom vorausgehenden Zusammenhang abzusetzen sucht. Gute Gründe sprechen zudem dafür, daß die durch Matthäus bezeugte Position des Spruchs im Anschluß an Mt 23,34-36 par. Lk 11,49-51 als Abschluß der Weherede gegen Pharisäer und Schriftgelehrte auf Q zurückgehen dürfte. Schon D. Lührmann hat auf die inhaltliche Nähe beider Texte hingewiesen und führt aus, es sei »am wahrscheinlichsten, daß Lk 13,34-35/Mt 13,37-39 in Q auf das Gerichtswort (= Mt 23,34-36 par. Lk 11,49-51) folgte«, da es »verwunderlich wäre, wenn zwei nach Charakter und Inhalt so ähnliche Worte getrennt voneinander gestanden hätten«[41]. H. Schürmann hat darauf abgehoben, daß auch aus

---

39. Vgl. etwa P. Hoffmann, *Studien*, p. 5; C.-P. März, *Feuer*, p. 14; Ders., *Lk 12,45b-56*, pp. 32ff.; J.S. Kloppenborg, *Formation*, p. 23; anders etwa W. Schmitkals, *Lk*, p. 152: »In der Spruchquelle Q schlossen die vorliegenden Gleichnisse an die apokalyptische Rede (12,35-39) passend an«.

40. Vgl. etwa H. Schürmann, *Redekomposition*, p. 58: »Daß diese Kontextualisierung das Werk des Lukas ist, kann schwerlich bestritten werden«.

41. *Redaktion*, p. 48. Ähnlich urteilen etwa J. Ernst, *Lk*, p. 431; G. Schneider, *Lk*, p. 309; W. Schenk, *Synopse*, pp. 80-81; W. Schmithals, *Lk*, p. 155; J. Freudenberg, *Weherede*, pp. 44-46, 88-89; H. Schürmann, *Redekomposition*, p. 58: »Es läßt sich in Q nur schwerlich eine geeignetere Position finden«. Die Gegenposition – der Jerusalem-Spruch sei in Q nach Lk 13,24-29(30)Q plaziert gewesen – wird argumentativ v.a. von D.E. Garland, *Intention*, pp. 187-197; M. Sato, *Q*, pp. 42-43; J.S. Kloppenborg, *Formation*, pp. 227ff.; D. Kosch, *Tora*, pp. 101-104 (vgl. dort die ausführlichen Hinweise zu den Vertretern der jeweiligen Position) vertreten. Garland, der die wichtigsten Ansätze zusammenfaßt, argumentiert gegen eine vormalige Verbindung von Lk 11,49-51 par. Mt

traditionskritischen Überlegungen heraus eine vormalige Verbindung beider Worte wahrscheinlich ist. Anhand der verbindenden Elemente beider Logien arbeitet er heraus, daß der zweite Spruch – also Lk 13,34-35 – »an das vorstehende Logion« – also an Lk 11,49-51 – bereits vorlukanisch angeglichen worden ist, was die Annahme einer vormaligen Verbindung unumgänglich macht[42]. Bemerkenswert ist weiter, daß auch Lukas den Spruch durch die Situationsangabe 13,31 den Pharisäern zuordnet und so auch redaktionell die Verbindungen zur Pharisäerrede anklingen läßt (s. IV.2).

Anders liegen die Dinge beim Gastmahlsgleichnis Lk 14,16-24, das thematisch besonders an 13,28-29 anschließt und im Q gut an einen Lk 13,24-30 entsprechenden Zusammenhang angeschlossen haben könnte. Der Zusammenhang, in dem das Gleichnis im dritten Evangelium steht, geht ohne Zweifel auf den Evangelisten zurück. Es empfiehlt sich deshalb Lk 14,16-24 im Zusammenhang von Lk 13,24-30 mit zu bedenken[43].

2. Für unsere Frage nach der direkten Q-Vorlage von Lk 12,35-13,35 sind wir somit in der Tat auf die drei Abschnitte 12,35-48; 12,49-59 und 13,24-30 mit 14,16-24 verwiesen und haben nach deren Vorgaben in der Redequelle zu fragen. Dabei bedarf es im Rahmen dieser übergreifenden Untersuchung nicht einer detaillierten Rekonstruktion der Q-Vorlage, sondern lediglich einer Ermittlung des vorlukanischen Grundbestandes und der entsprechenden Zusammenhänge[44].

23,34-36 mit Lk 13,34-35 par. Mt 23,37-39 v.a. mit der Feststellung, daß beide Sprüche formkritisch betrachtet keine ursprüngliche Einheit seien, eine Kombination schon auf der Ebene von Q deshalb nicht zwingend sei, zumal sie mit der Schwierigkeit operieren müsse, daß Lukas eine an sich sinnvolle Verbindung zweier Logien aufgelöst habe. Für den lukanischen Zusammenhang stellt er heraus, daß Lk 13,34-35 durchaus als sinnvoller Abschluß von 13,23-30 zu gelten habe; als Fremdkörper erweise sich freilich Lk 13,31-33, wodurch der in Q vorgegebene Zusammenhang 13,23-30.34-35 offensichtlich dem Konzept der Reise eingepaßt werden solle. – Die Einschätzung Garlands beruht – und die weiteren Überlegungen werden dies deutlich machen – auf einer ungenügenden Klärung sowohl des lukanischen Redaktionsanliegens in Lk 12,54-13,35 wie des thematischen Zusammenhanges der Q-Vorlage.

42. H. SCHÜRMANN, Redekomposition, pp. 58-59.

43. Auch Lk 14,5 (par. Mt 12,11) und Lk 14,11 (par. Mt 23,12) werden bisweilen als Elemente der Lk 12,35-14,24 zugrunde liegenden Q-Vorlage gewertet. Doch sind beide Texte so fest mit dem jeweiligen Zusammenhang verbunden, daß zumindest ihre lukanische Stellung auf den Evangelisten zurückgeführt werden muß. Zu 14,5 vgl. etwa F. NEIRYNCK, Lk 14,1-6, p. 259: Er zählt Lk 14,5 zu »those sayings whose position in Q cannot be determined with certainty. ... Luke appended the saying to the healing story composed in dependence on Mk 3,1-6«.

44. Unser Rekonstruktionsversuch des Q-Wortlauts, der in den verschiedenen Beiträgen in C.-P. MÄRZ, Lampen, näher begründet wird, ist als Anhang diesem Aufsatz beigegeben (pp. 203-205). Lk 12,57 und ὑποκρίται (Lk 12,56) führen wir hier – anders als im unserem Sammelband – auf den Evangelisten zurück.

Lk 12,35-48 erscheint auf den ersten Blick als formal und inhaltlich in sich geschlossener Abschnitt: Thematisch zusammengehalten durch die Metapher von den Knechten und die Gegenüberstellung von Lohn und Strafe, formal abgegrenzt durch die gewichtige Einleitung in 12,35 und den Neuansatz in 12,49. Als Basisstruktur läßt sich die Verbindung der beiden Knechtsgleichnisse Lk 12,35-38 und Lk 12,42-46 ausmachen[45]. Deutlich erkennbar ist dabei das Bemühen, 12,36-40 an 12,42-46 anzugleichen und beide Texte auch durch das gewichtige Mahnwort 12,35 zu einer in sich geschlossenen Einheit zu verbinden[46]. Diese prägende Grundanlage des Abschnitts scheint freilich bei Lukas durch eine speziell auf Lk 12,42-46 bezogene Deutung überlagert zu sein, die v.a. in der Anfrage des Petrus V. 41, die dem Gleichnis angeschlossenen VV. 47-48, aber auch in der sparsamen lukanischen Bearbeitung des Gleichnisses selbst sichtbar wird: V. 41 engt den Kreis der Adressaten auf die Zwölf ein und läßt 12,42-46 so hintergründig als Mahnung an die kirchlichen Amtsträger erscheinen[47]. In V. 42 spricht Lukas – diff. Mt! – nicht vom »Knecht«, sondern vom »Hausverwalter«, womit wohl »die übergeordnete Stellung und besondere Verantwortung des Gemeindeleiters angedeutet werden soll«[48]. Auch die dem Gleichnis beigefügten VV. 47-48 liegen inhaltlich auf der Linie dieser offensichtlich nachträglichen Interpretation und erscheinen zusammen mit V. 41 als thematische Rahmung von 12,42-46[49]. Stufen wir mit der neueren Forschung diese Deutung als lukanisch ein, dann liegt in der Tat die Vermutung nahe, daß die Verbindung von Lk 12,35-40 und Lk 12,42-46 im Grundbestand bereits auf die Quelle zurückgeht[50].

45. Vgl. grundsätzlich C.-P. MÄRZ, *Vorgeschichte*, pp. 61-62, 65-68.

46. Siehe u. pp. 193-194.

47. Die Frage des Petrus zielt auf eine Näherbestimmung der Adressaten. »Nun bezieht sich der sachliche Gehalt nicht auf etwas, was zum Proprium des lk Theologoumenons vom Zwölfer-Apostolat gehört…, sondern visiert die ganze Zeit der Kirche zwischen Himmelfahrt und Parusie an. So legt sich die Annahme nahe, daß die Frage in V. 41 auf die Unterscheidung Gemeinde – Amtsträger generell abhebt und daß die Apostel hier lediglich die Funktion paradigmatischer Transparenzfiguren übernehmen« (F. PRAST, *Presbyter*, p. 235). Vgl. grundsätzlich die ausführliche Analyse von V. 41 bei A. WEISER, *Knechtsgleichnisse*, pp. 216-222, der v.a. auch den redaktionellen Charakter des Verses nachweist.

48. F. PRAST, *Presbyter*, p. 242.

49. Vgl. etwa A. WEISER, *Knechtsgleichnisse*, pp. 222-225, zusammenfassend p. 225: VV. 47-48 »sind nur der abschließende Ausdruck der Intention, in der Luk dem Gleichnis vom treuen und untreuen Knecht den Stempel seines Verständnisses aufgeprägt hat: die Amtsträger zu treuem und selbstlosem Dienst vor ihrem Herrn und gegenüber den ihnen anvertrauten Christen aufzurufen«. – Vgl. auch F. PRAST, *Presbyter*, pp. 245-247.

50. Vgl. etwa zusammenfassend F. PRAST, *Presbyter*, p. 247: »Luk hat« das Gleichnis vom guten und bösen Knecht »durch verschiedene Eingriffe und einen Rahmen zu einer Mahnung für Amtsträger umfunktioniert… Doch bleibt das Gleichnis eingebunden in einen engeren, bereits von Q überlieferten (Lk 12,35-46) … Kontext«. Vgl. weiter C.-P. MÄRZ, *Lk 12,35-48*, pp. 58-59; DERS., *Gleichnis*, pp. 639-644.

Diese Vorstellung läßt sich auch vom synoptischen Vergleich her rechtfertigen: Lk 12,39-40.42-46 wird durch die direkte Mt-Parallele (Mt 24,43-44.45-51a) als Q-Bestand ausgewiesen. Für Lk 12,35-38 ist zwar keine direkte Mt-Parallele auszumachen, eine Reihe von Beobachtungen legt freilich die Vermutung nahe, daß Mt diesen Text im Zusammenhang mit Lk 12,39-40.42-46 gelesen, aber zugunsten des eindrücklicheren Jungfrauengleichnisses ausgelassen hat[51]: Verwiesen sei besonders auf mögliche Reminiszenzen von Lk 12,35-38 in Mt 24,43 (φυλακή, γρηγορεῖν)[52], die ausgleichende Funktion des redaktionellen Verses Mt 24,42[53] und die allem Anschein nach bereits traditionelle Verbindung von Lk 12,40 mit Lk 12,35-38[54]. Wir können deshalb in der Tat davon ausgehen, daß die Verbindung Lk 12,35-38.39-40.42-46 im Grundbestand bereits in Q vorgegeben war.

Lk 12,49-59 gibt insofern besondere Probleme auf, als hier von der Akoluthie her zumindest drei meist für Q reklamierte Texteinheiten – Lk 12,51-53; 12,54b-56; 12,58-59 – beieinanderstehen, die aber durch die redaktionelle Adressatenangabe in 12,54a voneinander abgehoben sind. Auffällig ist auch, daß Lk 12,49 mit dem Gewicht einer entscheidenden theologischen These einsetzt, dieses thematische Potential aber in dem schmalen heilsgeschichtlichen Summarium Lk 12,50.51-53 nicht wirklich eingelöst wird. Es scheint, daß dieser drängende Gerichtsspruch auf Lk 12,58-59 ausgreift, obwohl dieser Text bei Lukas einen anderen Abschnitt der Rede zugeordnet ist. Ähnliche Verbindungslinien über den Absatz 12,54a hinweg lassen sich auch zwischen 12,51-53 und 12,54b-56 ausmachen: Lk 12,51-53 deutet konkrete Erfahrungen der

---

51. Als im Grundbestand auf Q zurückgehend beurteilen Lk 12,35-38 mit unterschiedlicher Begründung etwa: J. SCHMID, *Mt und Lk*, p. 340; E. HIRSCH, *Frühgeschichte*, II, p. 120; H. SCHÜRMANN, *Reminiszenzen*, p. 124; A. WEISER, *Knechtsgleichnisse*, p. 236; G. SCHNEIDER, *Parusiegleichnisse*, pp. 30-36; F. PRAST, *Presbyter*, pp. 223-248; H.-J. KLAUCK, *Allegorie*, pp. 326-339; M. DORN, *Gleichnisse*, pp. 197-204 – zusammenfassend C.-P. MÄRZ, *Lk 12,35-48*, pp. 58-59; DERS., *Gleichnis*, pp. 639-644 – gg. J.S. KLOPPENBORG, *Formation*, p. 148, n. 202: »There are no verbatim agreements between Matt 25,1-13 and Luke 12,35-38, and despite the common image of a wedding feast, the narrative logic is quite different. An argument for inclusion might be made on the grounds of coherence with other Q sayings: admonitions to watchfulness are found elsewhere in Q. But the description of the eschatological banquet as a wedding feast and that of the Son of Man serving at a banquet are unattested in Q«.

52. Vgl. etwa C.H. DODD, *Parables*, p. 167, nn. 1-2; H. SCHÜRMANN, *Reminiszenzen*, p. 124; C.-P. MÄRZ, *Gleichnis*, p. 640.

53. Vgl. E. HIRSCH, *Frühgeschichte*, II, p. 120: Mt 24,43 »ist kein Anfang, sondern eine Anknüpfung. Es muß also in Q etwas motivisch ungefähr Passendes vorhergegangen sein«.

54. Für die vormalige Verbindung von Lk 12,40 mit 12,35-38 spricht neben thematischen Verbindungen v.a. der Vergleich mit Mk 13,33-37 – vgl. C.-P. MÄRZ, *Gleichnis*, pp. 641-643 – gg. S. SCHULZ, *Q*, p. 258; M. DORN, *Gleichnis*, p. 203: »... vorluk. Einschub der VV. 39f«.

frühen Kirche auf dem Hintergrund von Mich 6,7 als Zeichen der Endzeit; Lk 12,54b-56 mahnt zur Wahrnehmung der »Zeichen der Zeit«.

Auch hier scheinen sich also unterschiedliche Ebenen der Komposition abzuzeichnen: Auf Lukas dürfte die durch 12,54a bewirkte differenzierende Zuweisung der Texte an unterschiedliche Adressatengruppen zurückgehen, die Verbindungen zwischen den Texten dagegen scheinen bereits vorlukanisch angelegt zu sein und eine Spruchgruppe anzuzeigen, die mit 12,49 einsetzte und bis 12,59 reichte[55].

Der synoptische Vergleich bringt zwar zunächst einige offene Fragen zu Tage, scheint aber bei genauerer Nachfrage diese Vermutung zu stützen: Wichtig ist dabei zunächst, daß der einleitende »Feuerspruch« (Lk 12,49) – obwohl eine direkte Mt-Parallele fehlt – besonders wegen der Nachklänge in Mt 10,34 auf Q zurückgeführt werden kann[56]. Die Parallelität mit 12,51 macht zugleich deutlich, daß auch die Verbindung von Lk 12,49 mit 12,51-53 auf die Quelle zurückgeht, Lk 12,50 aber wohl erst durch den Evangelisten eingebracht worden ist[57]. Größere Probleme ergeben sich für 12,54b-56[58]: Da die Mt-Parallele unseres Textes – Mt 16,2b-3 – von wichtigen Handschriften (B ℵ syr^{sc}) nicht bezeugt wird, rechnen viele Autoren mit einer sekundären Einfügung von Mt 16,2b-3 zwischen Mt 16,1-2a.4[59]. Gegen diese Annahme freilich spricht, daß sich eine solche nachträgliche Einfügung nur schwer begründen läßt, wohingegen eine nachträgliche Streichung von Mt 16,2b.3 gut als Angleichung an Mt 12,38-39 (vgl. Mk 8,11-12) verständlich gemacht werden kann[60]. Der Vergleich von Lk 12,54b-56 und Mt 16,2b-3 läßt zudem erkennen, daß zwischen beiden Texten mit literarischer Abhängigkeit gerechnet werden muß. Die sinnvollste Erklärung ist deshalb, beide Texte auf eine gemeinsame Quelle zurückzuführen. Als direkter Hinweis darauf, daß Matthäus den Text im Zusammenhang einer mit dem Feuerspruch beginnenden Spruchgruppe gelesen hat, kann dabei der zweimalige Gebrauch des seltenen Wortes πυρράζει in Mt 16,2-3 gewertet werden, in denen offensichtlich das πῦρ aus Lk 12,49 nachklingt. Damit dürfte nicht nur Mt 16,2b-3 als ursprünglicher Matthäustext, sondern auch die durch Q vorgegebene Verbin-

---

55. Vgl. zusammenfassend C.-P. MÄRZ, *Lk 12,49-59*, passim, bes. pp. 49-56

56. Vgl. etwa J. SCHMID, *Mt und Lk*, pp. 276-277; E. Hirsch, *Frühgeschichte*, II, p. 122; A. POLAG, *Christologie*, p. 164; H. SCHÜRMANN, *Reminiszenzen*, pp. 234-235; E. ARENS, *Sayings*, pp. 68-69. Zusammenfassend C.-P. MÄRZ, *Feuer*, passim.

57. Vgl. E. ARENS, *Sayings*, p. 77; C.-P. MÄRZ, *Feuer*, pp. 10-11.

58. Vgl. grundsätzlich auch C.-P. MÄRZ, *Lk 12,54b-56*, passim.

59. Vgl. etwa E. KLOSTERMANN, *Lk*, p. 141; F. HAUCK, *Lk*, p. 177; K. und B. ALAND, *Text*, p. 309.

60. Vgl. schon das Urteil von B. WEISS, *Mt*, p. 387: »Da V. 2.3 wegen der großen Verschiedenheit von Lc 12,54-56 keine Eintragung von dorther sein können, so müssen sie in den ältesten Codd ausgefallen sein; doch eher in Reminiszenz an Matth 12,39 als Mc 8,12«. Aufschlußreich die Hinweise von J.S. KOPPENBORG, *Formation*, p. 152, bes. Anm. 219.

dung eines entsprechenden Textes mit einer mit 12,49 beginnenden Spruchgruppe aufgewiesen zu sein.

Schwieriger ist die vorlukanische Verbindung von Lk 12,58-59 mit 12,49.51-53.54a-56 aus dem synoptischen Vergleich zu begründen, da Mt den Spruch in deutlich abweichender Form, in anderem Kontext und ohne den verbindenden V. 57 bietet. Da dieser Zwischenvers aber doch wohl als lukanische Ausweitung von 12,56 oder doch zumindest als stark lukanisch überarbeitet zu gelten hat[61], weisen Lk 12,58-59, vor allem die lukanische Position und die thematische Verbindung mit 12,49 der vorlukanischen Spruchgruppe zu.

Lk 13,24-30 präsentiert sich als zwar aus Einzeltexten zusammengewachsene, aber formal wie inhaltlich in sich geschlossene Spruchgruppe, die – wie bereits deutlich wurde – durch 13,22 und 13,31-35 redaktionell umrahmt ist und mit dem Gedanken der Reise nach Jerusalem in Verbindung gebracht wird. Dies läßt auch hier an einander überlagernde Intentionen denken und scheint Lk 13,24-30 als im Grundbestand vorlukanische Komposition auszuweisen[62].

Diese Vorstellung findet durch den synoptischen Vergleich eindrucksvolle Bestätigung: Alle Mt-Parallelen zu den einzelnen in Lk 13,24-30 zusammengestellten Texten – Mt 7,13-14; 7,22-23; 8,11; 25,10, auch 20,16 – lassen sich durchweg als nachträglich in den jeweiligen Zusammenhang eingebrachte Textelemente ausmachen. Drei davon – Mt 7,13-14.22-23; 8,11 – stehen auch bei Mt so eng beieinander, daß sich eine vormalige Verbindung nahelegt[63]. Ganz offensichtlich hat der erste Evangelist zwei in Q vorgegebene Zusammenhänge interpretierend ineinander geschoben bzw. die Lk 13,24-30 entsprechende Textabfolge aufgelöst und die einzelnen Textelemente mit dem Schluß der Bergpredigt verbunden. Angeregt worden dürfte die Verbindung durch den sowohl in Lk 13,25-27Q als auch in Lk 6,46Q (vgl. par. Mt 7,21) berichteten Kyrie-Ruf. Den bei der Verbindung ausgefallenen Vers Lk 13,25Q trägt Mt dann als Schluß des Jungfrauengleichnisses nach[64]. Keine Klarheit läßt sich bezüglich des abschließenden Verses Lk 13,30 gewinnen. Immerhin spricht die Stellung bei Lukas wie der thematische Zusammenhang mit Lk 13,24-29 dafür, daß der Vers die vorlukanische Spruchgruppe abschloß[65].

61. Bezüglich der literarkritischen Einschätzung von 12,57 rechneten wir in C.-P. MÄRZ, *Lk 12,49-59*, p. 48; DERS., *Lk 12,54b-56*, pp. 40-41, wohl doch zu optimistisch noch generell mit vorlukanischem Bestand. Vgl. etwa D. ZELLER, *Mahnsprüche*, p. 64.

62. Als vorlukanische Spruchgruppe beurteilen Lk 13,24-29(30) etwa J. SCHMID, *Mt und Lk*, pp. 254ff.; E. HIRSCH, *Frühgeschichte*, II, pp. 88, 129-130; G. SELLIN, *Reisebericht*, p. 129; W. SCHENK, *Synopse*, pp. 102-105; vgl. zusammenfassend C.-P. MÄRZ, *Q-Vorlage*, pp. 72-77.

63. Vgl. MÄRZ, *Q-Vorlage*, pp. 73-77.

64. Vgl. bes. die Argumentation von W. SCHENK, *Auferstehung*, pp. 283-286.

65. Vgl. C.-P. MÄRZ, *Q-Vorlage*, pp. 88-89, 101.

Darf man in der Tat davon ausgehen, daß der Abschnitt 13,31-33.34-35 erst durch Lukas an diese Stelle gesetzt worden ist, dann legt sich von den Gegebenheiten bei Lukas her durchaus eine vormalige direkte Verbindung von Lk 14,16-24 und Lk 13,24-29(30) nahe[66]. Denn das Gastmahlsgleichnis, das man trotz der stark abweichenden Matthäusparallele auf Q wird zurückführen müssen[67], knüpft thematisch an Lk 13,28-29 an und ist auch durch die Gestalt des οἰκοδεσπότης (14,21) mit 13,25 verbunden. Da aber Lukas an dieser Verbindung offenbar nicht sonderlich interessiert ist und das Gleichnis in einen speziellen szenischen Rahmen (14,1-24) einbindet, werden wir die Berührungen zwischen Lk 13,25.28-29 und 14,16-24 als vorlukanisch bewerten dürfen[68]. Der synoptische Vergleich trägt, da Mt das Gleichnis in einem völlig anderen Zusammenhang bietet für dessen Stellung in Q nicht allzu viel aus. Auffällig ist immerhin, daß im ersten Evangelium in der zweifellos redaktionellen Einleitung des Gleichnisses – Mt 22,2 – wie in Lk 13,28-29 und 14,15 ausdrücklich auf die Basileia Bezug genommen ist und dieser Beleg als das einzige sicher redaktionelle Vorkommen von βασιλεία τοῦ θεοῦ im ersten Evangelium bewertet werden kann[69].

III. STRUKTUR, BEDEUTUNG UND ZUSAMMENHANG DER Q-VORLAGE

Die Rekonstruktion der Q-Vorlage von Lk 12,35–14,24 hat – wenn unsere Überlegungen richtig sind – drei unterschiedlich geartete, aber aufeinander bezogene Spruchgruppen zu Tage gebracht: Lk 12,35-46Q; Lk 12,49-59Q und Lk 13,24-30Q mit den Anschluß von 14,16-24Q. Es wird für die weitere Arbeit wichtig sein, die Struktur und Bedeutung der einzelnen Abschnitte, aber auch die Art ihrer Verbindung sowie ihre Stellung im Zusammenhang der Quelle wenigstens im Umriß zu erfassen und zu bewerten.

1. Die erste Spruchgruppe – *Lk 12,35-46Q* – läßt sich unschwer als eine aus drei vormals eigenständigen Texten – 12,35-38.40; 12,39; 12,42-46 – zusammengewachsene Texteinheit ausmachen[70]. Als Basisstruktur der kleinen Komposition erscheint die Verbindung des Gleichnisses von den wachenden Knechten (12,35-40) mit dem Gleichnis vom

---

66. Vgl. in diesem Sinne etwa G. *Sellin, Reisebericht*, p. 130; den ausführlichen Nachweis bei C.-P. MÄRZ, *Q-Vorlage*, pp. 77-78.

67. Vgl. zusammenfassend C.-P. MÄRZ, *Q-Vorlage*, pp. 89-95.

68. Schon F. MUSSNER, *Gleichnis*, p. 120, hat mit viel Berechtigung auf die Verbindung von Lk 13,24-30 und Lk 14,16-24 hingewiesen, diese aber der Lukasredaktion in Rechnung gestellt. Zu beachten sind auch bemerkenswerte Verbindungen von Lk 14,16-24 mit 12,35-46 – dazu C.-P. MÄRZ, *Q-Vorlage*, pp. 102ff.

69. Vgl. näherhin C.-P. MÄRZ, *Q-Vorlage*, pp. 77ff.

70. Zur Komposition C.-P. MÄRZ, *Lk 12,35-48*, pp. 61-64, 65-68.

guten und bösen Knecht (12,42-46). Deutlich erkennbar ist dabei das Bemühen, das Gleichnis von den wachenden Knechten in der Struktur an das Gleichnis vom guten und bösen Knecht anzugleichen und so eine in etwa symmetrisch geformte Spruchgruppe zu schaffen: 12,37a (vgl. 12,38b) nimmt fast wörtlich 12,43 auf, 12,37b klingt an 12,44 an und 12,40 berührt sich mit 12,45; auch die für 12,42-46 bestimmende Zweiteilung in einen positiven und negativen Teil ist durch die Einfügung des kleinen Diebesgleichnisses (12,39) zwischen 12,38 und 12,40 zumindest angedeutet[71]. Lk 12,35-40.42-46Q präsentiert sich somit von der Form her als Spruchgruppe, an der ein weit über die bloße Verbindung dreier vormals eigenständiger Texte hinausgehender Gestaltungswille deutlich wird: Durch ein feierliches, von alttestamentlicher Metaphorik geprägtes Mahnwort (12,35) eingeleitet entfaltet sich die Komposition in zwei aufeinander bezogenen Abschnitten, in denen jeweils unter dem Hinweis auf Lohn und Strafe zu eschatologischer Wachsamkeit aufgerufen wird. Thematisch hat dabei das Gleichnis von den wachenden Knechten mehr die Wachsamkeit für das Kommen des Herrn als eschatologische Grundhaltung im Blick, während Lk 12,42-46Q mehr »auf die treue Erfüllung ihrer übertragenen Aufgabe während der Abwesenheit des Herrn«[72] abzielt. Die Zusammenführung beider Texte scheint von der Intention bewegt, beide Aspekte miteinander zu verbinden und die generelle Mahnung zur eschatologischen Wachsamkeit als Aufruf zu ethischer Bewährung in der Zeit zwischen Ostern und der Parusie auszulegen. Darauf orientiert auch das einleitende Mahnwort, das man wohl als Nachklang von Spr 31,17 und damit als Aufforderung zu tätigem Einsatz verstehen darf[73]. Dieses Mahnwort in seiner Orientierung auf weissungsgemäße Dienstbereitschaft sowie die Knechtsmetaphorik und deren spezifische Ausformnung[74] lassen die kleine Komposition als spezielle Jüngerparänese erscheinen und ordnen sie dem Innenraum der Gemeinde zu.

Die zweite Spruchgruppe – *Lk 12,49.51-59Q* – besteht im Kern aus drei Texten zwischen denen sich unschwer ein thematisches Gefälle ausmachen läßt: 12,51-53 nennt konkrete Erfahrungen bei der Annahme der Jesusbotschaft und deutet sie im Lichte von Mich 6,7 als Anzeichen der beginnenden Endzeit; 12,54b-56 verdeutlicht mit dem Hinweis auf die Praxis der Wetterbeobachtung die Notwendigkeit der

---

71. Vgl. dazu C.-P. MÄRZ, *Gleichnis*, pp. 639-644.
72. A. WEISER, *Knechtsgleichnisse*, p. 179. In diesem Sinne vgl. auch W. SCHENK, *Synopse*, p. 95, der in Lk 12,42b-46 »Die Auftragstreue der wartenden Gemeinde«, in 12,39-40 (12,35-38 rechnet er nicht Q zu) »Die Stetserwartung der Gemeinde Jesu« angesprochen sieht.
73. Vgl. näherhin C.-P. MÄRZ, *Lk 12,35-48*, pp. 61-62.
74. Vgl. A. WEISER, *Knechtsgleichnisse*, pp. 175, 203-204.

Erkenntnis solcher eschatologischer »Zeichen der Zeit«; 12,58-59 fordert zu entsprechendem Handeln in einer derart eschatologisch geprägten Situation auf[75]. Ein Textverbund scheint auf, der zur Wahrnehmung der Gegenwart als Endzeit und zu entsprechender Reaktion in letzter Minute aufruft. Die kleine Komposition erinnert so an die die Quelle einleitende Täuferpredigt. An diese scheint v.a. auch der einleitende »Feuerspruch« (12,49) anzuknüpfen, der der Spruchgruppe wie eine Eingangsthese vorangestellt ist und sinnvoll nur von der thematischen Verbindung mit der Ankündigung des kommenden »Feuertäufers« durch Johannes (Lk 3,16 par. Mt 3,11) verständlich gemacht werden kann: Jesus bringt sich selbst als den zum Gericht kommenden Feuertäufer zur Sprache. Der Spruch zeichnet dabei ihn selbst hintergründig als in drängender Erwartung des kommenden Gerichtes stehend. Die Spruchgruppe Lk 12,49-59Q bringt so nach der mehr auf ethische Bewährung orientierten Komposition Lk 12,35-40.42-46Q einen neuen Akzent ins Spiel und läßt vor allem die Naherwartung als bleibenden Horizont der eschatologischen Paränese aufscheinen. Die Verbindungen mit der Täuferpredigt lassen die Einheit mehr als Mahnung an Israel bzw. als generelle eschatologische Paränese denn als Mahnung an die Jüngergemeinde erscheinen.

Die dritte Spruchgruppe – *Lk 13,24-30Q* – ist wesentlich durch den einleitenden prophetischen Mahnspruch Lk 13,24Q bestimmt, der das Bemühen um den Eintritt in die Basileia in der Gegenwart als Bedingung für den tatsächlichen Eintritt beim Gericht einfordert[76]. Durch diesen »Einlaßspruch« ist der sich anschließenden Texteinheit insgesamt der Charakter einer Mahnrede aufgeprägt[77]. Lk 13,25-29(30)Q nimmt in diesem Sinne die eschatologische Begründung des Mahnspruchs (V.24b) auf und stellt den Angeredeten in einer prophetisch-fiktiven Gerichtsszene die Möglichkeit ihres eigenen Ausschlusses warnend vor Augen. VV. 25-27 zeigen in einem kleinen »Gerichtsdialog« ihre Abweisung[78]. Der Versuch der vergeblich Anklopfenden, sich mit der auf ihren Straßen geschehenen Verkündigung Jesu[79] zu empfehlen, verdeutlicht hintergründig das Wort Jesu als Gerichtsmaßstab: Sie werden abgewiesen, weil sie nur auf die vor ihnen geschehene Verkündigung, nicht aber auf ihre Annahme dieser Verkündigung verweisen können.

---

75. Vgl zur Komposition C.-P. März, *Lk 12,49-59*, pp. 47-56.
76. Vgl. zur Gattung der prophetischen Mahnsprüche D. Zeller, *Mahnsprüche*, pp. 15-48; H. Windisch, *Sprüche*, passim, zählt Lk 13,24 zu den »Einlaßsprüchen«; A. Polag, *Christologie*, p. 87, zu den »Drohworten, die eine Umkehr nicht ausschließen«.
77. Vgl. zusammenfassend C.-P. März, *Q-Vorlage*, pp. 96-102, 104-113.
78. Zur Gattung des »Gerichtsdialogs« vgl. E. Brandenburger, *Recht*, pp. 96ff.
79. Die Phrase ἐφάγομεν ἐνώπιόν σου καὶ ἐπίομεν Lk 13,26 dürfte von Lukas eingefügt sein, um die Verbindung zu den Pharisäermahlzeiten in 11,37-12,53 und 14,1-24 zu verdeutlichen – vgl. genauer C.-P. März, *Q-Vorlage*, pp. 86-87.

Das Bemühen um den Eintritt in die Basileia, von dem V. 24 spricht, ist somit gleichbedeutend mit der Annahme des Wortes Jesu (vgl. Lk 12,8-9Q). In VV. 28-29 erscheinen die vom Hausvater Abgewiesenen als die definitiv vom Festmahl der Basileia Ausgeschlossenen, deren Plätze von anderen eingenommen werden. Sind die Angesprochenen in 13,25ff. als Zeitgenossen Jesu erkenntlich, so werden sie 13,28-29 im Hinblick auf ihre Zugehörigkeit zu Israel bestimmt. Das heißt: Israeliten werden abgewiesen, weil sie das Wort Jesu nicht angenommen haben; an ihre Stelle treten andere – Heiden! – für die dann freilich dasselbe Kriterium Geltung haben muß[80]. Hat V. 30 in Q die Spruchgruppe abgeschlossen, dann hat er in diesem Sinn zusammengefaßt. Das Gastmahlsgleichnis kann im Zusammenhang mit dieser Spruchgruppe nur als Verschärfung der israel-kritischen Akzente verstanden werden[81].

2. Die kurze Analyse der drei für Q ermittelten Texteinheiten hat deren thematische Verbindungen, aber auch ihre unterschiedliche Prägung deutlich werden lassen. Besonders ins Auge fällt die Differenz zwischen der ersten Spruchgruppe auf der einen und der zweiten und dritten auf der anderen Seite. Die von der Knechtsmetaphorik bestimmte erste Spruchgruppe hebt deutlich auf den innergemeindlichen Bereich ab, läßt das Problem der sich verziehenden Parusie erkennen und mahnt zur Stetsbereitschaft als Dienstbereitschaft in der Zeit zwischen Ostern und der Parusie. Die zweite Spruchgruppe zielt dagegen im Anschluß an die Täuferpredigt auf eine generelle Gerichtspredigt ab und akzentuiert nachdrücklich die Nähe des Gerichts. Die dritte Spruchgruppe schließlich versteht sich als Mahnrede an jüdische Zeitgenossen Jesu, akzentuiert aber mit Nachdruck gerade auch die israel-kritischen Aussagen. Das sich in der Quelle wahrscheinlich an Lk 13,24-29(30) Q anfügende Gastmahlsgleichnis liegt auch auf dieser Linie und schließt den Gedankengang mit dem Gerichtsspruch an die Ersteingeladenen, die dem Ruf des Hausvaters nicht gefolgt sind, ab[82].

80. In Lk 13,29-30 ist nicht einfach das Motiv der Heidenwallfahrt aufgenommen, sondern aus der Sicht von Q die eschatologische Konsequenz der beginnenden Heidenmission beschrieben.

81. Vgl. C.-P. MÄRZ, Q-Vorlage, pp. 77-78, 98, 101-102, 111-113.

82. Vgl. zur speziellen Orientierung der Q-Texte etwa M. SATO, Q, p. 4: »Die meisten Q-Sprüche zeigen bestimmte Adressaten: Z.B. sind die Spruchsammlungen Lk 6,20-49 par bzw. Lk 12,2-31 par oder die Spruchgruppe Lk 11,2-13 par – zumindest in der jetzigen Form – an die Gläubigen adressiert, während Lk 11,29-32 par; 11,39-52 par; 13,28f.34f par die feindlichen Israeliten als spezifische Adressaten im Auge haben. Dies zeichnet Q gegenüber weisheitlichen Spruchsammlungen aus«. Für die von uns untersuchten Texte vgl. etwa D. ZELLER, Q, p. 81: In 12,39-46 (12,35-38 zählt er nicht zu Q!) »setzen sich die Mahnungen Jesu, als deren Hörer seit 12,2 die Jünger zu denken sind, ... fort«. Zu 13,34-35; 13,28-29; 14,16-24 – von Zeller im Anschluß an Lk 12,39-46 unter der Überschrift »Gericht über das ungläubige Israel« behandelt vgl. p. 85: »Im Schlußteil der Logienquelle nehmen einige – bei Lk ziemlich eng zusammenstehende – Fragmente noch einmal

Diese Differenzen treten noch deutlicher in Erscheinung, wenn wir den Kontext dieser eschatologischen geprägten Textfolge im Rahmen der Quelle beachten. Lk 12,35-40.42-46Q erscheint dabei formal wie inhaltlich eng mit den wohl schon in Q zusammenstehenden Jüngersprüchen Lk 12,2-12.22-34Q verbunden: Die beiden Mahnsprüche Lk 12,35.40Q nehmen die die vorangehenden Texte prägende Serie von Imperativen (Lk 12,22.24.27.29.31.33Q) auf und ordnen Lk 12,35-40.42-46Q der voranstehenden Textabfolge zu; Lk 12,33-34Q und Lk 12,39Q sind durch die gleichen Motive und entsprechenden Sprachgebrauch miteinander verknüpft[83]. Anders liegen die Dinge bei Lk 12,49-59Q und Lk 13,24-29(30)Q mit 14,16-24Q: Beide Spruchgruppen schließen zwar thematisch durchaus an Lk 12,35-40.42-46Q an[84], können aber nicht in gleicher Weise mit der Jüngerrede in Verbindung gebracht werden. Die Vorstellung legt sich nahe, daß Lk 12,35-40.42-46Q in der Quelle den eschatologischen Abschluß der Jüngerrede Lk 12,2-12.22-34Q bildete. Lk 12,49-59Q und Lk 13,24-29(30)Q mit Lk 14,16-24Q knüpfen zwar an die in Lk 12,35-40.42-46 herausgestellte Gerichtsthematik an, bilden aber doch einen eigenen thematischen Zusammenhang. Ein Neuansatz scheint schon durch den gewichtigen »Feuerspruch« Lk 12,49Q angezeigt zu sein, der auch den anschließende Textzusammenhang mit der scharfen Gerichtspredigt des Täufers in Verbindung bringt. Durch Lk 13,24-29(30)Q und 14,16-24Q erhält die Komposition dann wie Lk 3,7-9.16-17Q ausdrücklich den Charakter einer Gerichtspredigt an Israel[85]. Damit dürfte aber gerade dieser

---

das Thema auf, das schon in der Täuferpredigt ... und in den Reden wider dieses Geschlecht sowie die Schriftgelehrten und Pharisäer ... anklang: die Kritik am Unglauben Israels«.

83. Vgl. als Erklärungsmöglichkeit unsere traditionsgeschichtlichen Überlegungen in C.-P. MÄRZ, *Lk 12,35-48*, pp. 68-71

84. Nicht zufällig folgt in der Quelle der Feuerspruch im Anschluß an die Strafandrohung gegen den bösen Knecht in 12,46Q.

85. Im oben dargelegten Sinn sind unsere Aussagen in C.-P. MÄRZ, *Q-Vorlage*, pp. 102-104, wo zwar die Verbindungslinien angemessen bewertet, die drei Q-Spruchgruppe aber noch im Sinne einer eschatologischen Redeeinheit verstanden wurden, zu modifizieren. Anders J. S. KLOPPENBORG, *Formation*, pp. 148-149, der Lk 12,22-34Q und 12,39-59Q als thematisch unterschiedlich geprägte Textblöcke auseinanderhält:»Whereas 12,22-34 is hortatory in character and sapiential in its idiom and mode of argumentation, 12,39-59 is aggressive and threatening in tone, and marked by warnings of judgement«. Problematisch an diesem Urteil wie an Kloppenborgs These insgesamt ist die im einzelnen doch sehr formale Argumentation im Hinblick auf weisheitlich geprägte Zusammenhänge. (Vgl. jetzt die Kritik von D. ZELLER, *Grundschrift*, passim, speziell etwa p. 391: »Die angeblichen 'sapiental instructions' erweisen sich bei näherer Betrachtung doch nicht als so weisheitlich. Entweder sind sie mit prophetischen Mikrogattungen durchsetzt ... oder sie bestehen im wesentlichen aus Elementen anderer Gattungen. ... Die weisheitliche Eigenart von Passagen erschöpft sich bei Kloppenborg manchmal darin, daß sie Forderungen enthalten bzw. mahnend auf die Gemeinde ausgericht sind«.) Von Bedeutung ist auch, daß Kloppenborg 12,35-38 nicht auf Q zurückführt, weshalb er 12,39-40 besonders

kleinen »Rede« im Zusammenhang der Quelle beachtliches Gewicht zugekommen sein. Im Anschluß an W. Schenk, der freilich den Text-bestand etwas anders faßt, wird man von der »ersten Endzeitrede« im Zusammenhang von Q sprechen dürfen[86].

Beachtet man die Kompositionsgeschichte der einzelnen Texteinhei-ten, dann spricht viel dafür, daß Lk 12,35-40.42-46 schon auf einer der Q-Redaktion vorausliegenden Kompositionsebene zumindest mit Lk 12,22-31(32ff?) verbunden war und Lk 12,49-59Q; Lk 13,24-29(30)Q und Lk 14,16-24Q erst durch die Q-Redaktion angefügt worden sind[87]. Dies würde die Bedeutung, die diesem Textblock im Rahmen der Quelle zukommt, noch unterstreichen.

IV. Die Q-Rezeption in Lk 12,35–14,24

Die Eruierung der Q-Vorlage von Lk 12,35–13,35 erlaubt nun im Vergleich mit der lukanischen Kompositionen des Abschnitts die Inten-tion des Evangelisten näher zu bestimmen und sein Redaktionsverfah-ren genauer herauszuarbeiten. In diesem Sinne sollen zunächst noch einmal die einzelnen Elemente der lukanischen Q-Rezeption in Lk

gewichten kann: »The theme of the unforeseen nature of the judgement occurs program-matically in 12,39-40. Q12,42-46 continues this motif and paints the judgment in strikingly ominous tones (12,46). Then the compiler incorporates two sayings expressing Q's charakteristic notion that the signs of the end are already evident to all who wish to see (12,51-52.54-56; cf. 3,7-9; 11,20; 11,30.31-32). This adds a note of urgency to the concluding apocalyptic warning and exhortation to make amends quickly before the judgment comes (12,57-59)« (*ibid.*, pp. 153-154). Bemerkenswert ist immerhin der Hinweis auf eine Abstufung in dieser Adressierung: »The former [= 12,22-34] is presumably addressed to the community itself; the latter [= 12,39-59] looks beyond the bounds of the community, threatening all with judgment«. Als weitere unserem Textbereich berührenden Q-Block bestimmt Kloppenborg Lk 13,24-30.34-35; 14,16-24.25-27; 17,33; 14,34-35 (*ibid.*, pp. 223-237). Diese Redekomposition, in der sich weisheitliche Ermahnung und prophe-tische Ankündigungen miteinander verbinden, basiert nach Kloppenborg auf einer weis-heitlich geprägten Basisformation: 13,24; 14,26.27; 17,33; 14,34-35. Diese sei nachträglich »expanded by polemical sayings directed not against adherents of Q's preaching, but against those who rejected it« (p. 237). Vgl. die berechtigte Kritik von D. ZELLER, *Grundschrift*, p. 391: »12,24 ist nur in der mt Gestalt ein weisheitliches Mahnwort – und die ist in ihrer Ursprünglichkeit schwer festzumachen. Für die Nachfolgeworte 9,57-62; 13,26-27 kann Kloppenborg nur auf kynische und stoische Analogien verweisen; sie passen nicht ins weisheitliche Ethos und sind wegen ihrer starken Bindung an das einzige 'Ich' Jesu ... auch formal nicht als Weisheitslogien zu betrachten«. »Nichts beweist, daß der Aufruf 13,24 und die Nachfolgebedingungen 14,26s einmal aufeinander folgten« (*ibid.*, pp. 390-391).

86. W. SCHENK, *Synopse*, pp. 94-101, faßt Lk 12,2-12.22-31.33-34Q als »Gemeinde-rede«; Lk 12,39-40.42-46.51-53.58-59; 13,18-21Q als »Erste Endzeitrede«; 13,24-30; 14,5.11.16-24.26-27. 17,33; 14,34-35; 15,4-7; 16,13.17-18; 17,1.3-4.6 als »Zwei-Wege-Rede«.

87. Vgl. die traditionsgeschichtlichen Überlegungen in C.-P. MÄRZ, *Feuer*, pp. 20-26; DERS., *Lk 12,49-59*, pp. 49-56; DERS., *Lk 12,35-48*, pp. 64-71; DERS., *Q-Vorlage*, pp. 104-113. – Anders wird die Traditionsgeschichte etwa von M. SATO, *Q*, p. 41, problematisiert.

12,35–13,35 gesammelt und dann auf ihre Bedeutung für das Verständnis von Lk 12,35-13,35 hin bedacht werden.

1. Betrachten wir die Komposition von Lk 12–13 und näherhin das lukanische Verständnis der eschatologischen Texte in Lk 12,35–13,35 auf dem Hintergrund der entsprechenden Q-Vorgaben, dann fällt zunächst ins Auge, daß Lukas sich auch in diesem Abschnitt eng an die Akoluthie der Quelle hält. Er nimmt nicht nur die drei von Q her vorgegebenen Spruchgruppen in ihrem Textbestand und weitgehend auch in ihrer Struktur auf, sondern folgt ebenso – freilich interpretierend – den in Q vorgezeichneten thematischen Linien. Bedeutsam ist dabei die Tatsache, daß der Evangelist die unterschiedliche Ausrichtung von Lk 12,35-40.42-46Q (Abschluß der Jüngerrede) und von Lk 12,49-59Q; 13,24-29(30)Q; [14,16-24Q] (Gerichtspredigt an Israel) rezipiert und ihr in der Zweiteilung der Erzähleinheit 12,1–13,35 Ausdruck verleiht.

Darf man aber davon ausgehen, daß sich Lukas auch in 12,35–13,35 – wie er dies im Reisebericht von 9,51 an praktiziert – an der Abfolge der Redequelle orientiert, dann gewinnen gerade die Abweichungen von der Q-Akoluthie besonderes Gewicht. Dies gilt zunächst für das szenische Arrangement, mit dem Lukas die in der Quelle ohne Situationsangaben gebotenen Redetexte in dem Erzählrahmen des Reiseberichtes einordnet; dies gilt noch mehr für die Textanteile, die den Q-Texten interpretierend beigefügt sind, und dies gilt in besonderer Weise für Umstellungen der Abfolge in der Quelle selbst[88].

Die erste Spruchgruppe – Lk 12,35-40.42-46Q – übernimmt Lukas ohne gravierende sachliche Änderungen: Er verstärkt lediglich durch die Ein- bzw. Anfügung der VV. 41.47-48 und die redaktionellen Änderungen in VV. 42-46 den Bezug auf die nachösterliche Gemeinde.

Deutlichere Akzente setzt Lukas in Bezug auf die zweite in Q vorgegebene Spruchgruppe – Lk 12,49.51-53.54b-56.58-59Q. Dies wird daran sichtbar, daß er zwar die Texte beieinander stehen läßt, durch den Adressatenwechsel in 12,54a aber unterschiedlichen Abschnitten zuordnet und zudem noch nachhaltig interpretiert. Das durch 12,54a abgetrennte und der Jüngerrede zugewiesene Textsegment Lk 12,49.51-53Q gestaltet er zu einem heilsgeschichtlichen Summarium aus. Der redaktionelle Zwischenvers Lk 12,50 ergänzt dabei die Gerichtsaussage 12,49 durch den Hinweis auf Jesu Tod. Eine lukanische Neuakzentuierung macht sich freilich auch für Lk 12,54b-56.58-59Q geltend. Während in Q von der Erkenntnis der »Zeichen der Zeit« die Rede war, spricht Lukas vom Erkennen »der Zeit«[89]. Damit sagt sich nicht mehr

---

88. Das lukanische Vorgehen ist besonders im Hinblick auf Mk zu erheben. Vgl. etwa J. ERNST, *Lk*, p. 24: »Bei der Genauigkeit und Treue des Lk gegenüber seinem Überlieferungsstoff fallen einige Perikopenumstellungen besonders ins Gewicht«.

89. Vgl. C.-P. MÄRZ, *Lk 12,54b-56*, pp. 38-40.

– wie in Q! – die letzte Möglichkeit des Menschen zur Umkehr vor dem unmittelbar bevorstehenden Gericht an, sondern die Zeit Jesu als letzte Chance für das empirische Israel wirklich Israel zu bleiben. Diese Intention des Lukas wird deutlicher an den redaktionell in den Zusammenhang eingebrachten Sonderguttexten Lk 13,1-5 und 13,6-9, die die eschatologische Paränese hintergründig auf die Androhung der Zerstörung Jerusalems hin aktualisieren.

Besondere Beachtung verdient im Hinblick auf die Q-Rezeption der Abschnitt Lk 13,10-17.18-21. Während sich nämlich die übrigen redaktionellen Einfügungen – Lk 12,41.47-48.50.(57?); 13,1-9.22-23.33-35 – jeweils kommentierend bestimmten von Q herkommenden Text-Vorgaben zuordnen, fügt Lukas hier einen Abschnitt ein, der in dieser Form in der Vorlage der Quelle keine Basis hatte. Mit Lk 13,18-21 ist dabei offensichtlich eine Spruchgruppe, deren Situierung in der Quelle freilich nicht mehr erhoben werden kann, aus ihrem vorgegebenen Zusammenhang herausgelöst und an dieser Stelle eingefügt worden.

Die lukanische Rezeption der dritten Spruchgruppe ist entscheidend durch den redaktionell gestalteten Abschluß des Abschnitts Lk 13,31-35 bestimmt, der das Gastmahlsgleichnis aus seiner Funktion als Abschluß der Gerichtsrede an Israel verdrängt hat. Dies bekommt auch dadurch besonderes Gewicht, als Lukas auch im Falle des Jerusalemspruchs eine Umstellung der durch die Quelle vorgegebenen Akoluthie vornimmt und diesen durch die Einleitung mit 13,31-33 zu einem Abschluß ausformt, der den gesamten Abschnitt 12,54-13,35 thematisch bündelt. Durch die redaktionelle Einleitung 13,22-23 werden 13,24-30 und 13,31-35 zu einem Abschnitt zusammengefaßt, mit dem vorhergehenden Zusammenhang verbunden, zugleich wird die für die Aussagen von 13,31-33 nötige Situierung angedeutet.

2. Schon die Auflistung der redaktionellen Akzente in Lk 12,35–13,35 läßt das spezifische Interesse des Lukas an dem an das Volk gerichteten Abschnitt Lk 12,54–13,35 erkennen; sie bringt zugleich das Bemühen des Evangelisten um eine entsprechende Deutung der in Q vorgegebenen eschatologischen Texte in den Blick. Für Lukas, der den Reisebericht auch im Hinblick auf einen Prozeß fortschreitender »Scheidung in Israel« hin formte, bot offenbar gerade die in der Quelle an die Jüngersprüche Lk 12,2-12.22-46Q anschließende Gerichtspredigt an Israel die Möglichkeit, im Rahmen dieser Entwicklung eine gewichtige Zäsur zu setzen und einen gewissen Abschluß des Werbens Jesu um das empirische Israel zu markieren. Dabei wird den in Q vorgegebenen eschatologischen Texten sehr nachhaltig das lukanische Verständnis der eschatologischen Predigt Jesu aufgeprägt: Die in Q zumindest Lk 12,49.51-53Q anklingende Ankündigung des baldigen Gerichtes wird neutralisiert, die der Predigt Jesu innewohnende Naherwartung auf die

Zerstörung Jerusalems »umorientiert«, wobei das Endgericht als der große und allgemeine eschatologische Rahmen mit im Spiel bleibt. Beide Aspekte – die heilsgeschichtliche Zäsur im Werben Jesu um Israel und die Neuinterpretation eschatologischer Aussagen – werden dabei wesentlich durch den Abschluß des Abschnitts Lk 13,31-35 bestimmt und durch den Jerusalem-Spruch hintergründig reguliert.

Schon O.H. Steck[90] und D. Lührmann[91] haben darauf verwiesen, daß erst Lukas diesen Gerichtsspruch in den Zusammenhang eingebracht und so zum »Höhepunkt« seines Reiseberichtes gemacht habe. Dies läßt sich auf dem Hintergrund unserer Überlegungen weiter verdeutlichen. Es hat sich nämlich erwiesen, daß der Evangelist nicht nur Lk 13,34-35 in einen neuen Kontext »umgesetzt« hat, sondern von diesem Gerichtsspruch her auch die beiden Spruchgruppen Lk 12,49-59Q und 13,24-30; 14,16-24Q redigierte und so den gesamten Abschnitt Lk 12,54-13,35 konzipierte.

Wichtig ist dabei zunächst, daß Lukas den Spruch gegen Jerusalem mit einer im Kern wohl auf Sondergut basierenden Einleitung – 13,31-35 – versieht. Denn »durch die Vorschaltung von 13,31-33« bezieht Lukas »das (in 13,34-35 angesprochene) Prophetenschicksal direkt auf Jesus und hebt somit den Zusammenhang der Zerstörung Jerusalems mit dem Tod Jesu deutlich hervor. Gerade die Vorschaltung von VV. 31-33, in denen Lukas Jesus in V. 33 sich selbst als Propheten bezeichnen läßt, artikuliert das spezielle lukanische Interesse, die Zerstörung Jerusalems als Strafe für die Ablehnung des Propheten Jesu zu sehen«[92]. Die Spruchgruppe Lk 13,24-29(30) wird durch die Sammelnotiz 13,22 mit 13,31-35 szenisch zusammengeschlossen. Es bleibt so zwar der Ausblick der Bildrede 13,24-30 auf die Parusie und die Aufforderung, sich nun um den Eintritt in die Basileia zu mühen, bestehen. Sie erfährt aber durch die Ansage des innergeschichtlichen Strafgerichts in der Zerstörung Jerusalems eine im Rückblick des Lukas unmittelbar verifizierbare Aktualisierung. Ganz in dieser Linie liegt auch die spezifische Rezeption der zweiten Spruchgruppe Lk 12,49.51-59. Lukas trennt durch den Adressatenwechsel die Eröffnung 12,29.51-53, die direkt auf das kommende Gericht Bezug nimmt, von 12,54-56.58-59 und ergänzt diesen Textabschnitt, der vom Erkennen der Zeichen der Zeit und von entsprechender Reaktion in letzter Minute spricht, durch 13,1-5.6-9.

Bedeutsam für das lukanische Verständnis der Umstellung des Jerusalem-Spruches sind dabei auch die thematischen Verbindungslinien, die der Evangelist von der Rede gegen Pharisäer und Schriftgelehrte (11,37-54) bis hin zum Spruch gegen Jerusalem zieht. Die Weherufe

---

90. *Israel*, pp. 40ff.
91. *Redaktion*, p. 45.
92. M. HOFFMANN, *Heil*, pp. 80-81.

gegen Schriftgelehrte und Pharisäer werden von Lukas in 11,57-58 mit
dem Hinweis abgeschlossen, daß sie Jesus weiterhin »belauern, um
etwas aus seinem Munde zu erjagen«. Nicht zufällig begegnet das
Motiv nochmals bei der Einladung zum Mahl bei einem Führer der
Pharisäer in 14,1. Gerade die Pharisäer sollen offenbar wegen der an
ihnen exemplifizierten Haltung der Verschlossenheit gegenüber der Verkündigung Jesu in 12,1–13,35 hintergründig präsent bleiben. In diesem
Sinn wird die Jüngergemeinde gleich zu Beginn der Rede in 12,1 vor der
ὑπόκρισις der Pharisäer gewarnt. Auch der Beginn der Bußpredigt an
das Volk ist durch das Motiv der ὑπόκρισις markiert, insofern Lukas
in 12,56 das Volk direkt als ὑποκρίται ansprechen läßt. Freilich steht
die Anrede nicht isoliert, sondern im Hinblick auf die Unfähigkeit, den
Kairos zu erkennen, und orientiert sich deshalb mehr an der genannten
Haltung. In gleicher Weise werden in 13,15 wohl v.a. die sich um den
Synagogenvorsteher sammelnden Widersacher Jesu als ὑποκρίται angesprochen, denn an ihnen zeigt sich jene an den Pharisäern exempli-
fizierte Haltung der Verschlossenheit. Deutlich ist auch der Rückbezug
in 13,26, wo mit dem merkwürdigen ἐφάγομεν ἐνώπιόν σου καὶ
ἐπίομεν, wohl auf die Mahlzeiten Jesu mit Pharisäern in 11,37-54 und
14,1-24 Bezug genommen ist: Formale Nähe zu Jesus – wie Zeitgenos-
senschaft oder persönliche Kontakte und gemeinsam Mahlzeiten – ohne
wirkliche Bekehrung wird nicht vor dem Ausschluß aus dem Reiche
Gottes bewahren. Auf diesem Hintergrund ist deutlich, warum der
Evangelist die Pharisäer in 13,31 als Adressaten des Gerichtsspruchs
wider Jerusalem einführt: Das Urteil resultiert aus der Ablehnung Jesu
und wird denen gesagt, an denen die Verschlossenheit zuvor festge-
macht worden ist. Das Volk erscheint an dieser Stelle noch durchaus
offen für Jesu Werben. Die Orientierung auf die Pharisäer in 13,31
verdeutlicht somit, daß es in 13,31-35 nicht um die Verwerfung Israels
geht, sondern um die Scheidung *in* Israel, die freilich an dieser Stelle
bereits soweit fortgeschritten ist, daß der Urteilsspruch über Jerusalem
ausgesprochen werden kann.

Diesem differenzierten Einsatz des Jerusalem-Spruches durch Lukas
entspricht auf ihre Weise die Einfügung des Abschnitts 13,10-21 zwischen 12,54–13,9 und 13,22-35. Nach Lk 13,6-9 erscheint der Text
geradezu als Probe, ob Israel die Chance des Heilswirkens Jesu nutzt.
Zweierlei wird dabei deutlich: Die Heilungsgeschichte selbst geht faktisch in ein Streitgespräch über und zeigt zumindest auf Seiten des
Synagogenvorstehers und seines Anhangs, also auf Seiten der offiziellen
Vertreter Israels, unverhohlene Ablehnung[93]. Das Volk aber freut sich
und bleibt deshalb – auch über 13,34-35 hinaus – als »offene« Größe im
Spiel[94]. Die Zäsur in 13,34-35 erscheint somit in der Tat nicht als

---

93. Vgl. etwa U. BUSSE, *Wunder*, pp. 298-301.
94. Vgl. ähnlich etwa M. DORN, *Gleichnisse*, p. 193: »Lk differenziert nicht nur

genereller Ausschluß des Volkes in seiner Gesamtheit[95], wohl aber drückt sich in der Zerstörung Jerusalems aus, daß sich das empirische Israel in seiner offiziellen Verfassung und seinem Anspruch als Heilsvolk durch Verstockung um die Chance gebracht hat, das wirkliche und wahre Israel zu bleiben. Auch wenn das Volk weiterhin als missionarisches Potential gesehen wird, sagt sich in der Ankündigung der Zerstörung Jerusalem und noch mehr des Tempels eine heilsgeschichtliche Wende an. Noch deutlicher wird dieses Anliegen des Lukas durch die Anfügung des Doppelgleichnisses vom Senfkorn und vom Sauerteig. Auch hier nimmt der Evangelist offenbar eine Umstellung der für ihn bislang maßgeblichen Q-Akoluthie in Kauf, was die Bedeutung, die er diesem Text im Zusammenhang von 12,54–13,25 zumißt, nachhaltig unterstreicht.

Das Doppelgleichnis, das im vorliegenden Zusammenhang ohne Zweifel hintergründig die Heidenmission ins Spiel bringt, öffnet die Szene auf einen Prozeß hin, der über die Absage des empirischen Israel und die Zerstörung Jerusalem hinausreicht. Damit kommt bereits an dieser Stelle die Sammlung des neuen Gottesvolkes in den Blick, die der Evangelist bereits ab 14,1 anfanghaft beschreibt und die schließlich in die weltweite Mission der Kirche münden wird[96]. »Lukas verliert also trotz gewisser Tendenzen, die kommenden Ereignisse zugespitzt auf Jerusalem zu sehen, den größeren Rahmen der über Israel hinausgreifenden Mission nicht aus den Augen«[97].

APPENDIX

Rekonstruktion der Q-Vorlage von Lk 12,35-14,24
(vgl. C.P. MÄRZ, Lampen, pp. 44ff., 58-61, 81-95)

1. Lk 12,35-38.39-40.42-46 Q

35 ἔστωσαν ὑμῶν ὀσφύες περιεζωσμέναι καὶ οἱ λύχνοι καιόμενοι,

bezüglich der Schuldzuweisung für Jesu Tod zwischen Führern und Jerusalem auf den einen und dem Volk auf der anderen Seite, sondern auch schon in Fragen der Reaktion auf die Botschaft Jesu, weshalb das in 13,1-9 angekündigte Vernichtungsgericht trotz der relativ bescheidenen Misssionserfolge unter den Juden nach Ostern nicht Israel, sondern letztlich nur Jerusalem trifft«.

95. Vgl. etwa H.L. EGELKRAUT, Mission, p. 268; A. GEORGE, Israël, passim.
96. Vgl. M. DORN, Gleichnisse, p. 193: »Die Fortführung des Kontextes durch die beiden Wachstumsgleichnisse kann Lk konsequent für seine Aussagen nutzen. Den 'Heuchlern' der jüdischen Obrigkeit kann er damit aufzeigen, daß sich das im Wirken Jesu bereits angebrochene Reich trotz ihres Widerstandes ausbreiten wird, wofür die Offenheit des Volkes ein erster Hinweis ist. ... Dieses Reich, das jetzt die menschlichen Grenzen und Begrenzungen (Satan und Sabbat) übersteigt, wird auch die Grenzen Israels durchbrechen und die Heiden, die Vögel des Himmels, mit einbeziehen«.
97. M. DORN, Gleichnisse, p. 193.

36 καὶ ὑμεῖς ὅμοιοι ἀνθρώποις (προσδεχομένοις) τὸν κύριον ἑαυτῶν
    πότε ἀναλύσῃ ἐκ τῶν γάμων,
    ἵνα ἐλθόντος καὶ κρούσαντος εὐθέως ἀνοίξωσιν αὐτῷ.
37 μακάριοι οἱ δοῦλοι ἐκεῖνοι,
    οὓς ἐλθὼν ὁ κύριος εὑρήσας γρηγοροῦντας.
    ἀμὴν λέγω ὑμῖν ὅτι περιζώσεται καὶ ἀνακλινεῖ αὐτούς.
38 κἂν ἐν τῇ δευτέρᾳ, κἂν ἐν τῇ τρίτῃ φυλακῇ ἔλθῃ καὶ εὕρῃ οὕτως,
    μακάριοί εἰσιν ἐκεῖνοι.
39 τοῦτο δὲ γινώσκετε ὅτι εἰ ᾔδει ὁ οἰκοδεσπότης ποίᾳ ὥρᾳ ὁ κλέπτης
    ἔρχεται,
    οὐκ ἂν ἀφῆκεν διορυχθῆναι τὸν οἶκον αὐτοῦ.
40 καὶ ὑμεῖς γίνεσθε ἕτοιμοι, ὅτι ᾗ ὥρᾳ οὐ δοκεῖτε ὁ υἱὸς τοῦ ἀνθρώπου
    ἔρχεται.
42 τίς ἄρα ἐστὶν ὁ πιστὸς δοῦλος καὶ φρόνιμος,
    ὃν κατέστησεν ὁ κύριος ἐπὶ (οἰκετείας) αὐτοῦ
    τοῦ δοῦναι αὐτοῖς τὴν (τροφὴν) ἐν καιρῷ;
43 μακάριος ὁ δοῦλος ἐκεῖνος ὃν ἐλθὼν ὁ κύριος αὐτοῦ εὑρήσει οὕτως
    ποιοῦντα.
44 ἀμὴν λέγω ὑμῖν ὅτι ἐπὶ πᾶσιν τοῖς ὑπάρχουσιν αὐτοῦ καταστήσει αὐτόν.
45 ἐὰν δὲ εἴπῃ ὁ δοῦλος ἐκεῖνος ἐν τῇ καρδίᾳ αὐτοῦ· χρονίζει μου ὁ κύριός,
    καὶ ἄρξηται τύπτειν τοὺς συνδούλους αὐτοῦ,
    ἐσθίῃ δὲ καὶ πίνῃ μετὰ τῶν μεθυόντων,
46 ἥξει ὁ κύριος τοῦ δούλου ἐκείνου
    ἐν ἡμέρᾳ ᾗ οὐ προσδοκᾷ καὶ ἐν ὥρᾳ ᾗ οὐ γινώσκει,
    καὶ διχοτομήσει αὐτὸν καὶ τὸ μέρος αὐτοῦ μετὰ τῶν ἀπίστων θήσει.

2. Lk 12,49.51-53.54b-56.(57).58-59 Q

49 πῦρ ἦλθον βαλεῖν ἐπὶ τὴν γῆν
    καὶ τί θέλω εἰ ἤδη ἀνήφθη.
51 (δοκεῖτε) ὅτι ἦλθον εἰρήνην βαλεῖν ἐπὶ τὴν γῆν·
    οὐκ (εἰρήνην) ἀλλὰ μάχαιρα.
53 ἦλθον γὰρ διχάσαι ἄνθρωπον κατὰ τοῦ πατρὸς αὐτοῦ
    καὶ θυγατέρα κατὰ τῆς μητρὸς αὐτῆς
    καὶ νύμφην κατὰ τῆς πενθερᾶς αὐτῆς
    καὶ ἐχθροὶ τοῦ ἀνθρώπου οἱ οἰκιακοὶ αὐτοῦ.
54b ὅταν ἴδητε νεφέλην ἀνατέλλουσαν ἐπὶ δυσμῶν
    λέγετε ὅτι ὄμβρος ἔρχεται
    καὶ γίνεται οὕτως.
55 καὶ ὅταν νότον πνέοντα
    λέγετε ὅτι καύσων ἔσται,
    καὶ γίνεται.
56 τὸ πρόσωπον τοῦ οὐρανοῦ οἴδατε διακρίνειν
    τὰ σημεῖα τοῦ καιροῦ πῶς οὐ δύνασθε;
[57 τί ἀφ' ἑαυτῶν οὐ (κρίνετε) τὸ δίκαιον;]
58 (ὡς) γὰρ ὑπάγεις μετὰ τοῦ ἀντιδίκου σου ἐπ' ἄρχοντα
    ἐν τῇ ὁδῷ δὸς ἐργασίαν ἀπηλλάχθαι ἀπ' αὐτοῦ,
    μήποτε (κατασύρῃ) σε πρὸς τὸν κριτήν,
    καὶ ὁ κριτής σε παραδώσει τῷ ὑπηρέτῃ,
    καὶ εἰς φυλακὴν βληθήσῃ.

59 λέγω σοι, οὐ μὴ ἐξέλθῃς ἐκεῖθεν
    ἕως (ἂν) ἀποδῷς τὸν ἔσχατον κοδράντην.

3. Lk 13,24-29(30); 14,16-24 Q

24 (ἀγωνίζεσθε) εἰσελθεῖν διὰ τῆς στενῆς θύρας,
    ὅτι πολλοὶ ζητήσουσιν εἰσελθεῖν (δι' αὐτῆς)
    καὶ ὀλίγοι εὑρήσουσιν αὐτήν.
25 (ἀφ' οὗ ἂν) ἐγερθῇ ὁ οἰκοδεσπότης καὶ ἀποκλείσῃ τὴν θύραν,
    καὶ ἄρξησθε ἔξω ἑστάναι καὶ κρούειν τὴν θύραν
    λέγοντες· κύριε, ἄνοιξον ἡμῖν,
    καὶ ἀποκριθεὶς ἐρεῖ ὑμῖν· οὐκ οἶδα ὑμᾶς πόθεν ἐστέ.
26 τότε ἄρξεσθε λέγειν· ... ἐν ταῖς πλατείαις ἡμῶν ἐδίδαξας.
27 καὶ ἐρεῖ λέγων ὑμῖν· οὐκ οἶδα πόθεν ἐστέ·
    ἀπόστητε ἀπ' ἐμοῦ πάντες οἱ ἐργαζόμενοι τὴν ἀνομίαν.
28 ἐκεῖ ἔσται ὁ κλαυθμὸς καὶ ὁ βρυγμὸς τῶν ὀδόντων,
    ὅταν ὄψεσθε Ἀβραὰμ καὶ Ἰσαὰκ καὶ Ἰακὼβ
    ἐν τῇ βασιλείᾳ τοῦ θεοῦ,
    ὑμᾶς δὲ ἐκβαλλομένους ἔξω.
29 καὶ ἥξουσιν ἀπὸ ἀνατολῶν καὶ δυσμῶν
    καὶ ἀνακλιθήσονται ἐν τῇ βασιλείᾳ τοῦ θεοῦ.
30 (καὶ ἰδοὺ) εἰσὶν ἔσχατοι οἳ ἔσονται πρῶτοι,
    καὶ εἰσὶν πρῶτοι οἳ ἔσονται ἔσχατοι.

16 ἄνθρωπός (τις) ἐποίει δεῖπνον μέγα, καὶ ἐκάλεσεν πολλούς,
17 καὶ ἀπέστειλεν τὸν δοῦλον αὐτοῦ τῇ ὥρᾳ τοῦ δείπνου εἰπεῖν τοῖς κεκλη-
    μένοις·
    ἔρχεσθε, ὅτι ἤδη ἕτοιμά ἐστιν.
18 (καὶ ἤρξαντο ἀπὸ μιᾶς πάντες παραιτεῖσθαι.
    ὁ πρῶτος εἶπεν αὐτῷ· ἀγρὸν ἠγόρασα, καὶ ἔχω ἀνάγκην ἐξελθὼν ἰδεῖν
    αὐτόν·
    ἐρωτῶ σε, ἔχε με παρῃτημένον.
19 καὶ ἕτερος εἶπεν· ζεύγη βοῶν ἠγόρασα πέντε, καὶ πορεύομαι δοκιμάσαι
    αὐτά·
    ἐρωτῶ σε, ἔχε με παρῃτημένον.
20 καὶ ἕτερος εἶπεν· γυναῖκα ἔγημα καὶ διὰ τοῦτο οὐ δύναμαι ἐλθεῖν.)
21 καὶ παραγενόμενος ὁ δοῦλος ἀπήγγειλεν τῷ κυρίῳ αὐτοῦ ταῦτα.
    τότε ὀργισθεὶς ὁ οἰκοδεσπότης εἶπεν τῷ δούλῳ αὐτοῦ·
23 ἔξελθε εἰς τὰς ὁδοὺς (τῆς πόλεως), καὶ ὅσον ἐὰν εὕρῃς εἰσάγαγε ὧδε,
    ἵνα γεμισθῇ μου ὁ οἶκος.
24 λέγω γὰρ ὑμῖν ὅτι οὐδεὶς τῶν κεκλημένων (γεύσεταί) μου τοῦ δείπνου.

LITERATURVERZEICHNIS

K. und B. ALAND, *Der Text des Neuen Testaments*, Stuttgart, 1982.
E. ARENS, *The ἦλθον-Sayings in the Synoptic Tradition* (OBO, 10), Freiburg/
    Schw.-Göttingen, 1976.

G. Björk, *ἦν διδάσκων. Die periphrastische Konstruktion im Griechischen*, Uppsala, 1940.

E. Brandenburger, *Das Recht des Weltrichters. Untersuchungen zu Mt 25,31-46* (SBS, 99), Stuttgart, 1980.

R. Bultmann, *Die Geschichte der synoptischen Tradition* (FRLANT, 29), Göttingen, 1961.

U. Busse, *Die Wunder des Propheten Jesus* (FzB, 24), Würzburg, 1979.

H. Conzelmann, *Die Mitte der Zeit. Studien zur Theologie des Lukas*, Tübingen, ⁵1964.

A. Denaux, *L'hypocrisie des Pharisiens et le dessein de Dieu. Analyse de Lc., XIII,31-33*, in F. Neirynck (ed.), *L'Évangile de Luc* (BETL, 32), Gembloux, 1973, pp. 243-285; ²1989, pp. 155-195 (Notes additionnelles: 316-323).

Ders., *Het Lucaanse reisverhaal (Lc. 9,51-19,44)*, in *Collationes Brugenses et Gandavenses* 14 (1968) 214-242.

C.H. Dodd, *The Parables of the Kingdom*, London, 1953.

M. Dorn, *Die Gleichnisse des lukanischen Reiseberichtes aus Sondergut und Logienquelle*, Diss. theol., Würzburg, 1988.

H.L. Egelkraut, *Jesus' Mission to Jerusalem. A Redaction Critical Study of the Travel Narrative in the Gospel of Luke, Lk 9,51-19,48* (EHS, 23/80), Frankfurt/M, 1976.

J. Ernst, *Das Evangelium nach Lukas* (RNT), Regensburg, 1977.

J.A. Fitzmyer, *The Gospel According to Luke II* (AB, 28A), Garden City, NY, 1985.

J. Freudenberg, *Die synoptische Weherede: Tradition und Redaktion in Mt 25 par*, Diss. masch., Münster, 1973.

D.E. Garland, *The Intention of Matthew 23* (SNT, 12), Leiden, 1979.

A. George, *Israël*, in Ders., *Études sur l'œuvre de Luc*, Paris, 1978, pp. 87-125.

R. Glöckner, *Die Verkündigung des Heils beim Evangelisten Lukas*, Mainz, 1975.

W. Grundmann, *Das Evangelium nach Lukas* (THKNT, 3), Berlin, ⁶1971.

F. Hauck, *Das Evangelium des Lukas* (THKNT, 3), Leipzig, 1934.

E. Hirsch, *Die Frühgeschichte des Evangeliums. II. Die Vorlagen des Lukas und das Sondergut des Matthäus*, Tübingen, 1941.

M. Hoffmann, *Das eschatologische Heil Israels nach den lukanischen Schriften*, Diss. theol., Heidelberg, 1988.

P. Hoffmann, *Studien zur Theologie der Logienquelle* (NTAbh, 8), Münster, ²1975.

H.-J. Klauck, *Allegorie und Allegorese in synoptischen Gleichnistexten* (NTAbh, 13), Münster, ²1986.

G. Klein, *Die Prüfung der Zeit (Lukas 12,54-56)*, in *ZTK* 61 (1964) 373-390.

J.S. Kloppenborg, *The Formation of Q. Trajectories in Ancient Wisdom Collections* (Studien in Antiquity and Christianity, 2), Philadelphia, PA, 1986.

E. Klostermann, *Das Lukasevangelium* (HNT, 5), Tübingen, ³1975.

D. Kosch, *Die eschatologische Tora des Menschensohnes. Untersuchungen zur Rezeption der Stellung Jesu zur Tora in Q* (NTOA, 12), Freiburg/Schw.-Göttingen 1989.

D. Lührmann, *Die Redaktion der Logienquelle* (WMANT, 33), Neukirchen-Vluyn, 1969.

C.-P. März, »... laßt eure Lampen brennen!« Studien zur Q-Vorlage von Lk 12,35-14,24 (ErfTS, 20), Leipzig, 1991.

Ders., »Feuer auf die Erde zu werfen, bin ich gekommen...«. Zum Verständnis und zur Entstehung von Lk 12,49, in Ders., Lampen, pp. 9-31.

Ders., Lk 12,54b-56 par Mt 16,2b.3 und die Akoluthie der Redequelle, ebd., pp. 32-43.

Ders., Zur Vorgeschichte von Lk 12,49-59, ebd., pp. 44-57.

Ders., Zur Vorgeschichte von Lk 12,35-48, ebd., pp. 58-71.

Ders., Zur Q-Vorlage von Lk 13,22-14,24, ebd., pp. 72-113.

Ders., Das Gleichnis vom Dieb. Überlegungen zur Verbindung von Lk 12,39 par Mt 24,43 und 1 Thes 5,2.4, in The Four Gospels 1992. FS F. Neirynck (BETL, 100), Leuven, 1992, pp. 633-648.

F. Mussner, Das »Gleichnis« vom gestrengen Mahlherrn (Lk 13,22-30), in Ders., Praesentia Salutis, Düsseldorf, 1967, pp. 113-124.

F. Neirynck, Luke 14,1-6. Lukan Composition and Q Saying, in Ders., Evangelica II, Leuven, 1991, pp. 183-203.

Ders., Q^{Mt} and Q^{Lk} and the Reconstruction of Q, in Ders., Evangelica II, pp. 475-480.

A. Polag, Der Umfang der Logienquelle, Lizenziatsarbeit masch., Trier, 1966.

Ders., Die Christologie der Logienquelle (WMANT, 45), Neukirchen-Vluyn, 1977.

F. Prast, Presbyter und Evangelium in nachapostolischer Zeit (FzB, 29), Stuttgart, 1979.

M. Rese, Einige Überlegungen zu Lukas XIII,31-33, in J. Dupont (ed.), Jésus aux origines de la christologie (BETL, 40), Leuven-Gembloux, 1975 ([2]1989), pp. 201-225.

M. Sato, Q und die Prophetie (WUNT, II/29), Tübingen, 1988.

W. Schenk, Auferweckung von den Toten oder Gericht nach den Werken. Tradition und Redaktion in Matthäus 25,1-13, in NT 20 (1978) 278-299.

Ders., Synopse zur Redequelle der Evangelien, Düsseldorf, 1981.

J. Schmid, Matthäus und Lukas. Eine Untersuchung des Verhältnisses ihrer Evangelien (Biblische Studien. Freiburg, 23,2-4), Freiburg i. Br., 1930.

K.L. Schmidt, Der Rahmen der Geschichte Jesu, Darmstadt, 1969.

W. Schmithals, Das Evangelium nach Lukas (ZBKNT, 3,1), Zürich, 1980.

R. Schnackenburg, Lk 13,31-33. Eine Studie zur lukanischen Redaktion und Theologie, in Der Treue Gottes trauen. FS G. Schneider, Freiburg-Basel-Wien, 1991, pp. 229-241.

G. Schneider, Parusiegleichnisse im Lukas-Evangelium (SBS, 74), Stuttgart, 1975.

Ders., Das Evangelium nach Lukas, I/II (ÖTK 3), Gütersloh-Würzburg, 1977.

H. Schürmann, Sprachliche Reminiszenzen an abgeänderte Bestandteile der Redequelle im Lukas- und Matthäusevangelium, in Ders., Traditionsgeschichtliche Untersuchungen, Düsseldorf, 1968, pp. 111-125.

Ders., Die Redekomposition wider »dieses Geschlecht« und seine Führung in der Redequelle (vgl. Mt 23,1-39 par Lk 11,37-54). Bestand - Akoluthie - Kompositionsformen, in SNTU 11 (1986) 33-81.

Ders., Zur Kompositionsgeschichte der Redequelle. Beobachtungen an der lukanischen Q-Vorlage, in Der Treue Gottes trauen. FS G. Schneider, Freiburg-Basel-Wien, 1991, pp. 335-342.

S. SCHULZ, *Q. Die Spruchquelle der Evangelien*, Zürich, 1972.

E. SCHWEIZER, *Das Evangelium nach Lukas* (NTD, 3), Göttingen, 1982.

G. SELLIN, *Komposition, Quellen und Tradition des lukanischen Reiseberichtes (Lk* IX,51–XIX,28), in *NT* 20 (1978) 100-135.

O.H. STECK, *Israel und das gewaltsame Geschick der Propheten* (WMANT, 23), Neukirchen-Vluyn, 1967.

A. WEISER, *Die Knechtsgleichnisse der synoptischen Evangelien* (SANT, 29), München, 1971.

B. WEISS, *Die Evangelien des Markus und Lukas* (KEK, 1/2), Göttingen, 1901.

W. WIEFEL, *Das Evangelium nach Lukas* (THKNT, 3), Berlin, 1987.

H. WINDISCH, *Die Sprüche vom Eingehen in das Reich Gottes*, in *ZNW* 27 (1928) 163-192.

D. ZELLER, *Die weisheitlichen Mahnsprüche bei den Synoptikern* (FzB, 17), Würzburg, 1977.

DERS., *Kommentar zur Logienquelle* (SKK NT, 21), Stuttgart, 1984.

DERS., *Eine weisheitliche Grundschrift in der Logienquelle?*, in *The Four Gospels 1992. FS F. Neirynck* (BETL, 100), Leuven, 1992, pp. 389-401.

P. ZINGG, *Das Wachsen der Kirche* (OBO, 3) Freiburg/Schw.-Göttingen 1974.

Arndstraße 2   Claus-Peter MÄRZ
D-O-5071 Erfurt

MK 16,1-8 ALS EPILOG DES MARKUSEVANGELIUMS

Die klassische Literarkritik, die sich als Quellenscheidung versteht, tut sich mit dem Markusevangelium besonders schwer. Die zu Gebote stehenden Kriterien sind bescheiden. Die Stilkritik ist schon aufgrund des relativ geringen Umfangs des Evangeliums problematisch. Sofern sie – wie es häufig geschieht – als bloße Stilstatistik betrieben wird, ist sie methodisch ohnehin kaum brauchbar[1]. Die immer wieder angeführten »Brüche«, »Sprünge«, »Widersprüche«, »Doppelungen« etc. können gewiß weiterhelfen. Ihre Beurteilung hängt jedoch stark vom subjektiven Ermessen ab. Zudem besteht die Gefahr, daß derartige Beobachtungen – als Instrument diachroner Fragestellung – zu schnell auf die Zerlegung des Textes abzielen, wo es diesen zunächst einmal zu verstehen gälte.

Im folgenden wird versucht, die zur möglichen Quellenscheidung führenden Beobachtungen aus einer vorgängigen synchronen, näherhin narrativen Analyse zu gewinnen[2]. Ausgegangen wird von den einzelnen

---

1. Zur Kritik: T. KAUT, *Befreier und befreites Volk. Traditions- und redaktionsgeschichtliche Untersuchung zu Magnifikat und Benediktus im Kontext der vorlukanischen Kindheitsgeschichte* (BBB, 77), Frankfurt am Main, 1990, pp. 15-31; S. DECK, *Wortstatistik – ein immer beliebter werdendes exegetisches Handwerkszeug auf dem (mathematischen) Prüfstand*, in *BN* 60 (1991) 7-12. Vgl. auch die Ausführungen von F. MUSSNER u.a., *Methodologie der Frage nach dem historischen Jesus*, in K. KERTELGE (ed.), *Rückfrage nach Jesus. Zur Methodik und Bedeutung der Frage nach dem historischen Jesus* (QD, 63), Freiburg-Basel-Wien, 1974, pp. 118-147, spec. pp. 130-131, und die Kritik von M. REISER in *BZ NF* 30 (1986) 132-134 an P. DSCHULNIGG, *Sprache, Redaktion und Intention des Markus-Evangeliums und ihre Bedeutung für die Redaktionskritik* (SBB, 11), Stuttgart, 1984.

2. Aus der umfangreichen Literatur können hier nur einige wenige Titel aufgeführt werden. Zur Theorie narrativer Analyse: V.J. PROPP, *Morphologie des Märchens*, München, 1972; A.J. GREIMAS, *Sémantique structurale. Recherche de méthode*, Paris, 1966; C. BRÉMOND, *Logique de récit*, Paris, 1973; E. GÜTTGEMANNS, *Einleitende Bemerkungen zur strukturalen Erzählforschung*, in *LB* 23/24 (1973) 2-47; DERS., *Narrative Analyse synoptischer Texte*, in *LB* 25/26 (1973) 50-73; R. BARTHES, *Introduction à l'analyse structurale des récits*, in *Communications* 8 (1966) 1-27. Hilfreich ist m.E. auch: W. ISER, *Der Akt des Lesens. Theorie ästhetischer Wirkung* (UTB, 636), München, 1976. Einführungen in die Diskussionsstand finden sich bei: E. GUELICH – W. RAIBLE, *Linguistische Textmodelle. Grundlagen und Möglichkeiten* (UTB, 130), München, 1977, pp. 192-314; D. MARGUERAT, *Strukturale Textlektüren des Evangeliums*, in *Theologische Berichte* 13, Zürich-Einsiedeln-Köln, 1985, pp. 41-86; W. EGGER, *Nachfolge als Weg zum Leben. Chancen neuerer exegetischer Methoden, dargelegt an Mk 10,17-31* (ÖBS, 1), Klosterneuburg, 1979, pp. 6-48; DERS., *Methodenlehre zum Neuen Testament. Einführung in linguistische und historisch-kritische Methoden*, Freiburg-Basel-Wien, 1987, pp. 119-129. Beispiele für die Anwendung narrativer Analysen auf neutestamentliche Texte: W. EGGER, *Nachfolge* (s.o.); J. HINTZEN, *Verkündigung und Wahrnehmung. Über das*

Segmenten des Textes. Deren narrative Funktion ergibt sich nicht nur aus ihrem Inhalt, sondern mehr noch aus ihrer Sequenz und ihrer textuellen und kontextuellen Verzahnung. Zu erschließen ist die narrative Strategie des Textes sowohl auf der (semantischen) Ebene der Erzählung selbst (narrative Konzeption) als auch im Blick auf deren (pragmatische) Wirkung beim Leser (narrative Intention). Eine derartige Untersuchung zielt von ihrem Ansatz her natürlich nicht auf literarkritische Quellenscheidung. Sie will im Gegenteil die vorliegende Geschichte zunächst einmal als in sich kohärente Erzählung verständlich machen. Dies schließt aber nicht aus, daß die Geschichte unterschiedliche (unter Umständen auch in Spannung stehende) Erzählfäden enthält, die sich möglicherweise sogar zu unterscheidbaren Isotopien zusammenordnen lassen. In diesem Fall besteht eine gute Chance für Rückschlüsse auf die Textgenese, insbesondere dann, wenn die Isotopien mit sukzessiven narrativen Konzepten in Verbindung gebracht werden können.

I. NARRATIVE ANALYSE VON MK 16,1-8

In der Sequenz des Textes lassen sich 33 Segmente (= S) unterscheiden (1. Spalte: Verszahl; 2. Spalte: Segment-Nummer)[3]:

Mk 16,1-8

1	1	Καὶ διαγενομένου τοῦ σαββάτου
	2	Μαρία ἡ Μαγδαληνὴ καὶ Μαρία ἡ τοῦ Ἰακώβου καὶ Σαλώμη
	3	ἠγόρασαν ἀρώματα
	4	ἵνα ἐλθοῦσαι ἀλείψωσιν αὐτόν.
2	5	καὶ λίαν πρωῒ τῇ μιᾷ τῶν σαββάτων
	6	ἔρχονται ἐπὶ τὸ μνημεῖον
	7	ἀνατείλαντος τοῦ ἡλίου.
3	8	καὶ ἔλεγον πρὸς ἑαυτάς·
	9	τίς ἀποκυλίσει ἡμῖν τὸν λίθον ἐκ τῆς θύρας τοῦ μνημείου;

Verhältnis von Evangelium und Leser am Beispiel Lk 16,19-31 im Rahmen des lukanischen Doppelwerkes (BBB, 81), Frankfurt am Main, 1991; speziell zu Mk 16,1-8: E. GÜTTGE-MANNS, *Linguistische Analyse* (s. Literaturhinweise); L. MARIN, *Frauen* (s. Literaturhinweise). Die hier vorgelegte Analyse ist keinem bestimmten Verfahren verpflichtet, sondern stellt einen eigenständigen Versuch dar, der allerdings auf Elemente anderer Verfahren (bes. C. BRÉMOND, W. ISER) zurückgreift.

3. Zur Unterscheidung von der herkömmlichen Einteilung (in Kapitel und Vers) werden im folgenden die (durchnumerierten) Segmente durch vorangestelltes »S« gekennzeichnet. Soweit (in der herkömmlichen Weise) Stellen aus dem Markusevangelium angeführt werden, geschieht dies in der Regel ohne Angabe von »Mk« (also z.B. nur: 15,42).

4 10 καὶ ἀναβλέψασαι θεωροῦσιν
   11 ὅτι ἀποκεκύλισται ὁ λίθος·
   12 ἦν γὰρ μέγας σφόδρα.
5 13 Καὶ εἰσελθοῦσαι εἰς τὸ μνημεῖον
   14 εἶδον νεανίσκον
   15 καθήμενον ἐν τοῖς δεξιοῖς
   16 περιβεβλημένον στολὴν λευκήν,
   17 καὶ ἐξεθαμβήθησαν.
6 18 ὁ δὲ λέγει αὐταῖς·
   19 μὴ ἐκθαμβεῖσθε·
   20 Ἰησοῦν ζητεῖτε τὸν Ναζαρηνὸν τὸν ἐσταυρωμένον·
   21 ἠγέρθη,
   22 οὐκ ἔστιν ὧδε·
   23 ἴδε ὁ τόπος
   24 ὅπου ἔθηκαν αὐτόν.
7 25 ἀλλὰ ὑπάγετε
   26 εἴπατε τοῖς μαθηταῖς αὐτοῦ καὶ τῷ Πέτρῳ
   27 ὅτι προάγει ὑμᾶς εἰς τὴν Γαλιλαίαν·
   28 ἐκεῖ αὐτὸν ὄψεσθε,
   29 καθὼς εἶπεν ὑμῖν.
8 30 Καὶ ἐξελθοῦσαι ἔφυγον ἀπὸ τοῦ μνημείου,
   31 εἶχεν γὰρ αὐτὰς τρόμος καὶ ἔκστασις·
   32 καὶ οὐδενὶ οὐδὲν εἶπαν·
   33 ἐφοβοῦντο γάρ.

Segment 1: S 1 verweist zurück auf die Szene von 15,42-47, die am
»Rüsttag« (παρασκευή) spielte, der als »Vortag des Sabbat« (προσάββατον) erläutert wurde (V. 42). Eben dieser in 15,42-47 noch bevor-
stehende Sabbat ist nun vorüber.

Segment 2: Die Frauenliste verweist zurück auf 15,47. Übereinstim-
mend wird beide Male Μαρία ἡ Μαγδαληνή genannt. Über 15,40, wo
Μαρία ἡ Ἰακώβου τοῦ μικροῦ zugleich als Ἰωσῆτος μήτηρ bezeichnet
wird, ergibt sich zudem, daß auch die Μαρία ἡ (τοῦ) Ἰακώβου von
16,1 identisch ist mit der Μαρία ἡ Ἰωσῆτος von 15,47. In 15,40 findet
sich auch die in 15,47 nicht genannte Σαλώμη, so daß die Frauenliste
von 16,1 insgesamt auf die in 15,40-41 namentlich genannten Frauen
zurückweist.

Während jedoch aus 15,40-41 noch kein Vorverweis auf 16,1-8 zu
erkennen ist, eröffnet 15,47 mit ἐθεώρουν ποῦ τέθειται eine Perspektive,
die eine erzählerische Konstellation von Frauen und Grab – etwa einen
Besuch der Frauen am Grab – erwarten läßt.

Segmente 3 und 4: S 3 und S 4 gehören zusammen, sofern das Kaufen
der ἀρώματα die Voraussetzung für die Verwirklichung der in S 4
genannten Salbungsabsicht ist. Vor dem Hintergrund von 15,42-47 sind
S 3/4 für den Leser überraschend, da dort durch nichts angedeutet war,
daß das Begräbnis – etwa aus Zeitmangel – überstürzt abgewickelt und

der Leichnam Jesu noch nicht abschließend für die letzte Ruhe präpariert worden wäre. Josef von Arimathäa hatte noch Zeit, um ein Leinentuch zu kaufen (15,46). Die Frauen hingegen blieben untätig und schauten nur zu (15,47).

Ist die Salbungsabsicht im Rückblick auch überraschend, so wird vorausschauend damit dem Leser signalisiert, daß im weiteren Fortgang der Geschichte die Frauen nicht nur – wie von 15,47 her zu erwarten – zum Grab gehen werden (um es zu besuchen), sondern auch in dieses hineingehen wollen bzw. werden. Insofern weist ἐλθοῦσαι ἀλείψωσιν über S 6 hinaus auf S 13 und indirekt sogar auf S 30. Die partizipiale Formulierung ἐλθοῦσαι ἀλείψωσιν ist offensichtlich bewußt auf εἰσελθοῦσαι und ἐξ-ελθοῦσαι in S 13 bzw. 30 hin gestaltet. So wird durch S 3/4 die durch 15,47 vorgegebene narrative Perspektive eines möglichen Grabbesuchs überlagert bzw. ergänzt durch die Perspektive eines zu erwartenden Hineingehens in das Grab.

Vom Thema her erinnern S 3/4 an die Salbung Jesu durch die (ungenannte) Frau in 14,3-9. Aus der dort gemachten Bemerkung προέλαβεν μυρίσαι τὸ σῶμά μου εἰς τὸν ἐνταφιασμόν (V. 8) darf kein Widerspruch zu S 3/4 konstruiert werden, als ob nach 14,3-9 eine Salbung des Leichnams Jesu überflüssig sei. Der Leser ist durchaus in der Lage, die Salbung von 14,3-9 als symbolische Vorwegnahme der nun in S 3/4 angekündigten Salbung des nun tatsächlich toten Jesus zu verstehen. Einen Vorverweis auf eine tatsächlich zu erwartende Salbung des Leichnams stellt 14,8 allerdings nicht dar. Umgekehrt gewinnt die zunächst überraschende Salbungsabsicht von S 3/4 durch 14,3-9 für den Leser zumindest ein gewisses Maß an Plausibilität, und zwar unabhängig davon, ob er von der Ungebräuchlichkeit von Totensalbungen im Judentum wußte oder nicht[4].

Segment 6: Daß die Frauen zum Grab »kommen«, entspricht der Erwartung, die der Leser seit 15,47 hegt. Von 15,47 her war ein Gang zum Grab allerdings nur für Maria Magdalena und für die Maria des Joses abzusehen. Erst über S 2 ist dem Leser klar, daß nicht nur sie, sondern alle in 15,40 genannten Beobachterinnen der Kreuzigung Jesu zum Grab gehen werden. Erst S 3/4 setzen den Leser zudem in die Lage, das ἔρχεσθαι ἐπὶ τὸ μνημεῖον von S 6, das im Lichte von 15,47

---

4. Das Salben von Toten wird in der rabbinischen Tradition nur beiläufig erwähnt; vgl. Str-B II 52-53 (bes. Schab 23,5). Die Salbung eines bereits bestatteten Leichnams ist nicht belegt (vgl. R. PESCH, *Mk II* [s. Literaturhinweise], pp. 529-530). Die Salbung von Gebeinen (vgl. N. HAAS, *Anthropological Observations on the Skeletal Remains from Givᶜat ha-Mivtar*, in *IEJ* 20 [1970] 38-59, spec. pp. 40-49.59) ist ein mit Mk 16,1 nicht vergleichbarer Vorgang (vgl. H.-W. KUHN, *Der Gekreuzigte von Givᶜat ha-Mivtar. Bilanz einer Entdeckung*, in C. ANDRESEN – G. KLEIN [ed.], *Theologia crucis, signum crucis. FS E. Dinkler*, Tübingen, 1979, pp. 303-334, spec. p. 328). Ein gewisses Problem stellt der Begriff der ἀρώματα dar, der eigentlich Gewürze bzw. Würzkräuter bezeichnet (LSJ, s.v.). Man wird wohl an »pflanzliche Essenzen« zu denken haben (so: J. GNILKA, *Mk II* [s. Literaturhinweise], p. 340).

auf einen Besuch am Grab hindeutet, als bloße Voraussetzung für ein nachfolgendes εἰσέρχεσθαι εἰς τὸ μνημεῖον (S 13) wahrzunehmen.

Insofern bestätigt S 6 den Befund einer Verquickung bzw. Überlagerung von zwei unterscheidbaren narrativen Perspektiven, deren eine von 15,47 ausgeht, während die andere erst durch S 3/4 eingeführt wird und auf die tatsächliche Fortsetzung der Geschichte in S 13-30 hinzielt.

Segmente 5 und 7: Durch die Zeitangaben erscheinen die Tätigkeiten von S 3 und S 6 als unterbrochene, wenngleich in sich zusammenhängende Handlungsfolge. Während das Kaufen der ἀρώματα aufgrund von S 1 nach Sonnenuntergang anzusetzen ist, soll durch λίαν πρωΐ in S 5 der ganz frühe Morgen des folgenden Tages angezeigt werden. Dazwischen liegt also die Nacht, in der das in S 4 intendierte Handeln offenbar nicht möglich war. Vor dem Hintergrund der in S 1 – 4 aufgebauten Handlung fällt der Zeitangabe in S 5 die Aufgabe zu, die Intention von S 4 so früh wie möglich in die Tat umsetzen zu lassen. Eine nähere Terminierung der Zeitangabe λίαν πρωΐ ist über das Lexem πρωΐ nicht möglich[5]. Vom Erzählduktus her ist man am ehesten geneigt, an die Morgendämmerung zu denken, weil sie den frühestmöglichen Zeitpunkt darstellt, der einen Gang zum Grab erlaubt.

Syntaktisch wie erzählerisch nachklappend wird dann allerdings in S 7 erklärt, daß der sehr frühe Zeitpunkt mit dem Sonnenaufgang zusammenfällt. Doch dürfte es dem Leser kaum Schwierigkeiten bereiten, die beiden Zeitangaben zu kombinieren[6]. Er wird sich das erzählte Geschehen wohl so vorstellen, daß die Frauen beim ersten Morgengrauen aufgebrochen und bei Sonnenaufgang beim Grab angelangt sind.

Bemerkenswert ist vielleicht noch, daß die Zeitangaben in proportionaler Kohärenz zu den beiden bereits erwähnten Erzählperspektiven stehen. Unter der Perspektive, daß die Frauen *zum Grab* gehen wollen, ist die erste Morgendämmerung der gegebene Zeitpunkt (was nicht ausschließt, daß dann auch die Sonne aufgeht). Unter der Perspektive, daß die Frauen *in das Grab* hineingehen wollen (um den Leichnam zu salben), ist der Sonnenaufgang der angemessene Zeitpunkt (was wiederum nicht ausschließt, daß die Frauen schon bei der ersten Morgendämmerung aufgebrochen sind)[7]. Denn die Salbung in einem nur durch die Eingangsöffnung

5. Aus 13,35 läßt sich nicht ableiten, daß πρωΐ generell die vierte Nachtwache bedeute. λίαν πρωΐ gibt einfach einen sehr frühen Zeitpunkt an, der sowohl noch in der letzten Phase der Nacht (so 1,35; vgl. Joh 20,1) als auch bereits in der ersten Phase des Tages (so wohl 11,20; 15,1) liegen kann.

6. Erleichtert wird dies durch ἔρχεσθαι (S 6), das semantisch den Verlauf des Hingehens voraussetzt bzw. assoziieren läßt.

7. Diese Abfolge von Aufbruch bei Morgendämmerung und Ankunft am Grabe bei Sonnenaufgang wird allerdings erst durch die Rezeption des Lesers hergestellt. Folgt man strikt der grammatischen Syntax des Textes, erscheinen S 5 und S 7 als gleichzeitige Akte.

erhellten Felsengrab benötigt, sofern man nicht künstliches Licht voraussetzen will (was in der Geschichte aber überhaupt nicht bedacht wird und daher auszuscheiden ist), wohl doch die Helligkeit des Tagesgestirns, welches das Innere des Grabes wenigstens mit Dämmerlicht erfüllt.

Die Tagesangabe τῇ μιᾷ τῶν σαββάτων stellt inhaltlich sicher, daß der Gang zum Grab am Tag unmittelbar nach dem in 15,42-47 bevorstehenden und in S 1 zu Ende gegangenen Sabbat stattfindet. Doch war dies auch aus der Perspektive von 15,47 oder S 1 kaum anders zu erwarten.

Auffällig ist die Formulierung τῇ μιᾷ τῶν σαββάτων, die einen Hebraismus darstellt[8]. Da dieser jedoch schon bald in die christliche Eigensprache eingegangen ist (vgl. 1 Kor 16,2; Apg 20,7), dürfte ihn der Leser nicht als fremdartig empfunden haben. Ob er damit zugleich an die christliche Sonntagsfeier erinnert wurde (bzw. werden sollte), läßt sich aus der Geschichte heraus nicht entscheiden und bedürfte genauerer traditionsgeschichtlicher Recherchen. Unter dieser Rücksicht dürfte es nicht uninteressant sein, daß die gleiche Formulierung – abgesehen von den synoptischen Parallelstellen (Lk 24,1; vgl. Mt 28,1) – auch in Joh 20,1 auftaucht, noch dazu in einer vergleichbaren syntagmatischen Verbindung (siehe dazu unten II,1).

Segmente 8 und 9: Die bisher nur handelnden Frauen beginnen nun, zueinander zu sprechen (S 8)[9]. Die Frage in S 9 stellt das genaue Widerlager zu 15,46 dar. Die Frauen überlegen, wer ihnen eben *den* (τόν) Stein, den Josef von Arimathäa *an* die Tür (ἐπὶ τὴν θύραν) des Grabes *her*angewälzt hat (προσεκύλισεν) wieder *von* der Tür (ἐκ τῆς θύρας) *weg*wälzen wird (ἀποκυλίσει).

Sofern es sich bei dem Stein um einen der in Palästina gebräuchlichen Rollsteine handelt, erscheint die in S 9 geäußerte Frage als unbegründet. Ein Rollstein soll ein Grab vor wilden Tieren schützen, ist aber von Menschenhand relativ leicht zu betätigen. Man wird also voraussetzen müssen, daß der Erzähler derartige Realien nicht kannte bzw. auch bei seinen Lesern nicht als bekannt voraussetzte. Dennoch – auch vor dem Hintergrund des bisherigen Erzählduktus – kommt die Frage für den Leser einigermaßen überraschend. Denn sofern die Frauen den Leichnam Jesu *salben* wollten (S 4), hätten sie das Problem von S 9 schon vor ihrem Aufbruch zum Grab bedenken können bzw. müssen.

Daß die Frage von S 9 erst jetzt gestellt wird, zeigt allerdings auch, daß sie erzählstrategisch gar nicht die Funktion hat, das technische Problem der Graböffnung einer Lösung näher zu bringen. Die Proble-

---

8. Zum philologischen Befund vgl. E. LOHSE, σάββατον κτλ., in *TWNT* 7 (1964) 1-35, spec. pp. 6-8.
9. Es ist, wie sich zeigen wird, die einzige Sprechhandlung, die von den Frauen berichtet wird.

matisierung des Steins dient vielmehr dazu, den Leser auf eine neue, bisher nicht absehbare Entwicklung der Geschichte vorzubereiten, die in irgendeiner Weise mit dem Stein zusammenhängen muß. Insofern haben S 8/9 präludierende (auf S 11 verweisende), nicht eigentlich, wie oft gesagt wird, retardierende Funktion.

Segmente 10 bis 12: Rückblickend hat S 10 zunächst die Funktion, wenigstens nachträglich den für die Rede von S 8/9 nötigen erzählerischen Spielraum zu schaffen. Der Leser könnte sich sonst fragen, warum die Frauen – in S 6 am Grabe angekommen – noch die Frage von S 9 stellen, obwohl doch – wie aus S 11 gleich zu erfahren ist – der Stein weggewälzt ist. Durch S 10 wird die Vorstellung vermittelt, daß die Frauen erst einmal das Problem des Steins diskutieren, bevor sie das Grab selbst in Augenschein nehmen. Es bleibt allerdings festzuhalten, daß diese narrativ epexegetische Funktion von S 10 ausschließlich an ἀναβλέψαι, präzise sogar an dem ἀνα-βλέπειν, und nicht an θεωροῦσιν oder dem Sehen als solchem hängt. Dieses ist für die Wahrnehmung des folgenden S 11 unerläßlich.

Auf erzählsemantischer Ebene zeigt S 11, daß die in S 9 anklingende Sorge der Frauen überflüssig war. Für den Leser schafft S 11 eine völlig neue Situation. Sie war durch keine der bisherigen Erzählperspektiven angedeutet, stellt diese im Gegenteil sogar in Frage. Wie die Geschichte sich weiterentwickeln wird, ist für den Leser an dieser Stelle nicht absehbar. Insofern markiert S 11 einen potentiellen Wendepunkt: Werden die Frauen Besuchs- und Salbungsabsicht – von Furcht gepackt – vergessen und fliehen? Oder werden sie – für die wunderbare Fügung der Graböffnung dankend – um so eifriger zur Verwirklichung ihrer ursprünglichen Absicht schreiten? Vielleicht – so mag der Leser erwarten – gibt ihm die emotionale Reaktion der Frauen eine erste Tendenzanzeige. Diese Erwartung wird allerdings enttäuscht, sofern die Frauen – wie gleich aus S 13 zu erfahren ist – einfach in das Grab hineingehen, ohne den weggewälzten Stein emotional auch nur zu registrieren.

Die erzählerische Härte, die sich aus einer unmittelbaren Sequenz von S 11 und S 13 ergeben würde, wird allerdings durch S 12 abgemildert. Semantisch weist S 12 zurück auf die Frage von S 9 und erklärt nachträglich deren (überraschenden) Inhalt. Unter dieser Rücksicht wäre es allerdings effektiver gewesen, S 12 unmittelbar nach S 9 zu plazieren bzw. direkt in die Rede der Frauen und damit in das Handlungsgefüge selbst einzubauen. Daß dies nicht geschehen ist, zeigt, daß die tatsächliche Funktion von S 12 über die (semantische) Ebene des narrativen Konzeptes hinausgeht. Der Erzählsequenz zufolge beansprucht S 12, Begründung (γάρ) für S 11 zu sein. Auch dies macht auf rein semantischer Ebene nur wenig Sinn. Die Funktion von S 12 ist offensichtlich pragmatischer Art, d. h., der Befund von S 11 soll dem *Leser* begründet bzw. ergründet werden. Ihm wird signalisiert, daß das

Wegwälzen des Steins, der jetzt anders als noch in 15,46 als μέγας σφόδρα bezeichnet wird, auch »überaus große« Kräfte verlangt. Der Leser beginnt zu ahnen, daß hier übermenschliche Mächte am Werk sind. Indirekt wird in ihm jener heilige Schauer geweckt, der narrativ eigentlich bei den Frauen zu erwarten gewesen wäre. Dies ist auch der Grund, daß der Leser den narrativ relativ harten Übergang von S 11 nach S 13 nicht so stark empfindet. Er ist auf ein außergewöhnliches Widerfahrnis vorbereitet und folgt insofern gespannt den scheinbar emotionslos agierenden Frauen ins Grab.

Segment 13: Wenn das ἔρχεσθαι der Frauen das Ziel haben soll, den Leichnam Jesu zu salben (S 4), dann muß das ἔρχεσθαι ἐπὶ τὸ μνημεῖον (S 6) in ein εἰσέρχεσθαι εἰς τὸ μνημεῖον überführt werden. Eben dies geschieht in S 13. An der Salbungsabsicht der Frauen hat sich durch den erstaunlichen Befund von S 11 offenbar nichts geändert. Den weggewälzten Stein scheinen sie lediglich als Möglichkeit wahrzunehmen, ins Grab zu gelangen.

Es wird deutlich, daß der Erzähler an der Realisierung der sich in S 11 potentiell anbahnenden Wende nicht interessiert ist und die mit S 4 eröffnete Erzählperspektive, die in das Grab weist, aufrechterhalten will.

Segmente 14 bis 16: Zwar ist der Leser durch S 11/12 auf ein außergewöhnliches Ereignis vorbereitet. In der Konkretion aber trifft er genauso unvermutet auf den Jüngling wie die Frauen.

Einen Rückverweis auf den νεανίσκος von 14,51 wird der Leser – trotz vergleichbarer Konstruktion (jeweils verbunden mit περιβεβλημένος und Akkusativ) – nicht erkennen. Daß der dort nackt fliehende, unbestimmte (τις) Jüngling nun im Grab sitzen soll, ist durch nichts in der narrativen Struktur der Geschichte vorbereitet.

Aufgrund seines weißen Gewandes (S 16) ist der Jüngling als Wesen aus der himmlischen Welt zu agnostizieren. Auf diese Assoziation, die dem antiken Menschen ohnehin geläufig sein dürfte[10], ist der Leser des Markusevangeliums zudem durch die Verklärungsgeschichte 9,2-10 vorbereitet. Die himmlische Welt, in die Jesus dort u. a. durch seine strahlend weißen Kleider eingetaucht erschien (9,3), leuchtet jetzt in Gestalt des weiß gekleideten Jünglings den Frauen entgegen.

Den Jüngling mit Jesus selbst zu identifizieren kommt dem Leser allerdings nicht in den Sinn. Die Übereinstimmung mit 14,62, wo der Menschensohn als ἐκ δεξιῶν καθήμενος τῆς δυνάμεως (!) gekennzeichnet ist, bleibt auf der rein lexematischen bzw. (teilweise) syntaktischen Ebene und berührt

---

10. Vgl. Joh 20,12; Apg 1,20, und vor allem die mit weißen Gewändern bekleideten Erwählten in Offb 4,4; 6,11; 7,9.13.

nicht die (durch den Kontext völlig anders definierte) begriffliche und narrative Semantik.

Die »rechte« Seite (S 15) ist hier wohl als die Glück verheißende Seite zu verstehen[11], so daß Frauen und Leser Gutes von dem so sitzenden Jüngling erwarten dürfen.

Segment 17: Trotz dieser prinzipiell positiven Perspektive ist die Reaktion der Frauen stilgemäß (Angelophanie). Ἐκθαμβέομαι heißt wie das Simplex θαμβέομαι »erschreckt werden, (sich) erschrecken« (vgl. 9,15; 14,33; 1,27; 10,24.32). Eine technische Bedeutung im Sinne des heiligen Schauers ist nicht vorauszusetzen. Doch ist es sachgemäß, daß das »Erschrecken« sich gerade in der Begegnung mit dem Heiligen einstellt (vgl. bes. 1,27 mit 1,25). Vergleichbare Reaktionen kennt der Leser aus Wundererzählungen (2,12; 4,41; 5,33.42; 6,51), nicht zuletzt von der Verklärung (9,6).

Daß die Reaktion der Frauen, die man ähnlich schon nach S 11 hätte erwarten können, erst jetzt erfolgt, ist für die Erzählstruktur der Geschichte aufschlußreich. Es bestätigt sich (siehe zu S 13), daß der Erzähler den potentiellen Wendepunkt in S 11 nur als Vorspiel für die eigentliche – nun im Grab zu erwartende – Wende verstanden wissen will.

Segmente 18 und 19: Mit μὴ ἐκθαμβεῖσθε im Munde des himmlischen Boten wird die erzählte Welt (die Reaktion der Frauen in S 17) zur besprochenen Welt. Eben dadurch soll das Erschrecken überwunden werden. Im übrigen gehört S 19 als Redeeinleitung (wie vorher schon S 17) zum Stil von Angelophanien. Frauen und Leser sind darauf eingestimmt, daß ihnen eine wichtige, menschlich unerfindliche Botschaft zuteil wird.

Segmente 20 bis 24: Bevor der Jüngling seine eigentliche Botschaft ausrichtet, spricht er in S 20 – wie vorher schon in S 19 – noch einmal direkt die Frauen an[12]. Ἰησοῦν ζητεῖτε verweist zurück: nicht nur auf das »Zum-Grab-Kommen« der Frauen in S 6, sondern dezidiert auf deren Salbungsabsicht in S 4. Von den beiden Appositionen zu »Jesus« ist ὁ Ναζαρηνός dem Leser bereits aus der bisherigen Darstellung des Evangeliums geläufig (1,24; 10,47; 14,67). Von Bedeutung ist, daß mit ὁ Ναζαρηνός bis auf den Anfang der im Markusevangelium erzählten Geschichte Jesu zurückverwiesen wird, die damit begonnen hat, daß »in jenen Tagen Jesus ἀπὸ Ναζαρὲτ τῆς Γαλιλαίας gekommen und von

---

11. Vgl. Str-B I 980-981; W. GRUNDMANN, δεξιός in *TWNT* 2 (1935) 37-39, spec. p. 37.

12. S 20 gibt ihn – seiner himmlischen Herkunft entsprechend – als Wissenden zu erkennen.

Johannes im Jordan getauft worden ist« (1,9)[13]. Die zweite Beifügung ὁ ἐσταυρωμένος erinnert an die Passionsgeschichte, vor allem an Mk 15, wo die an Jesus vollzogenen Handlungen im »Kreuzigen« gipfeln (15,13.14.15.20.24.25.27; vgl. 15,21.30.32). Ein Bezug auf kerygmatische Formulierungen ist wenig wahrscheinlich[14]. Die Botschaft, die der Jüngling ausrichtet: ἠγέρθη (S 21), kommt narrativ nicht gänzlich unvorbereitet. Unmittelbar verweist sie zurück auf 14,28: μετὰ τὸ ἐγερθῆναί με προάξω ὑμᾶς εἰς τὴν Γαλιλαίαν. Dieser Rückbezug wird in S 27 dann auch ausdrücklich thematisiert. Sachlich ist an die Leidensansagen zu erinnern, die durchweg die Auferstehungsaussage einschließen (8,31; 9,31; 10,34). Allerdings scheinen die Jünger diese Aussage nicht verstanden zu haben (9,10.32; vgl. 8,32). Das gilt auch für die Frauen, wie nicht zuletzt ihre Salbungsabsicht bestätigt. Bemerkenswert ist allerdings, daß die Begrifflichkeit der Leidensansagen in Mk 16 nicht aufgegriffen wird[15]. Ἐσταυρωμένος verweist auf den narrativen Kontext von Mk 15, ἠγέρθη dagegen erinnert an kerygmatische Formulierungen, näherhin an die sogenannte Auferweckungsformel (ὁ θεὸς Ἰησοῦν ἤγειρεν ἐκ νεκρῶν bzw. ὁ ἐγείρας [τὸν] Ἰησοῦν ἐκ νεκρῶν)[16], die teilweise auch passivisch begegnet (ἠγέρθη: Röm 4,25)[17]. Insofern ist S 21 für den Leser nichts Neues. Neu ist lediglich, daß er die aus dem Kerygma bekannte Botschaft *im (leeren) Grab* hört. Was soll damit zum Ausdruck gebracht werden?

Mit Blick auf S 20 und 22 könnte man daran denken, daß die Auferweckung als Entrückung interpretiert werden soll. Tatsächlich gehören die Motive von der Suche und der Unauffindbarkeit des Leichnams – zumindest teilweise – zur Topik von Entrückungen[18]. Offen bleibt freilich die

---

13. Vielleicht darf man in Ναζαρηνός auch einen Vorverweis auf Γαλιλαία in S 27 sehen, so daß sich auch von hier noch einmal der Bogen zu 1,9 spannen würde.

14. Vergleichbare Wendungen in 1 Kor 1,23; 2,2; Gal 3,1 sind spezifisch paulinische Ausdrücke, die nicht als allgemein geläufiger kerygmatischer Standard vorausgesetzt werden können. Auch die Rede von Jesus, ὃν ὑμεῖς ἐσταυρώσατε, in Apg 2,26 und 4,10 ist keine kerygmatische Formulierung, sondern geht auf das Konto der *lukanischen* Predigt vor Israel.

15. Statt vom »Töten« (ἀποκτείνειν: 8,31; 9,31; 10,34) spricht S 20 vom »Kreuzigen« (σταυροῦν), und an die Stelle des »Auferstehens« (ἀνίστημι: 8,31; 9,9.10.31; 10,34) tritt in S 21 das »Auferwecken« (ἐγείρειν).

16. Vgl. dazu: K. WENGST, *Christologische Formeln und Lieder des Urchristentums* (StNT, 7), Gütersloh, 1972, pp. 27-48, spec. p. 33.

17. Vgl. Röm 6,4.9; 7,4; 8,34; ἐγήγερται: 1 Kor 15,4; vgl. 1 Kor 15,12.13.14.16.17.20. Siehe auch: 1 Thess 1,10; Apg 4,10; 2 Kor 5,14; 2 Tim 2,8.

18. Dies gilt vor allem für den griechisch-römischen Traditionsbereich, vgl. dazu: P. HOFFMANN, *Auferstehung II. Auferstehung Jesu Christi 1. Neues Testament*, in TRE 4 (1979) 478-513, spec. p. 499. Zum gesamten Material siehe G. LOHFINK, *Die Himmelfahrt Jesu. Untersuchungen zu den Himmelfahrts- und Erhöhungstexten bei Lukas* (StANT, 26), München, 1971, pp. 32-74. Auf den Zusammenhang mit antiken Entrückungen verwies zuerst E. BICKERMANN, *Das leere Grab* (s. Literaturhinweise).

Frage, ob mit einer derartigen Würdigung die spezifische Funktion von
S 20 und 22 bzw. von S 20-24 getroffen ist. Darüber kann letztlich nicht
die Topik der Gattung, sondern nur die konkrete narrative Struktur der
Geschichte selbst Auskunft geben.

Folgt man dem narrativen Konzept der Geschichte, so ist für die
Funktionsbestimmung von S 21 zunächst S 20 als vorgegebener Hintergrund zu beachten. S 20 aber ruft mit Ἰησοῦν ζητεῖτε S 4 in Erinnerung. Die Salbungsabsicht von S 4 bleibt auch der Horizont, vor dem
S 21 in den folgenden Segmenten weiter erläutert wird: Er ist nicht hier
(S 22); der »Platz« (τόπος), wo man ihn hingelegt hat, ist – wie die
Frauen sehen können – leer (S 23-24). Damit stößt die Salbungsabsicht
von S 4 genau an dem »Platz«, wo die Frauen meinten, sie verwirk-
lichen zu können, im wahrsten Sinn des Wortes ins Leere. Die Hand-
lungsstrategie, die die Geschichte bisher beherrscht hat (Salbungsabsicht – zum Grab kommen – ins Grab hineingehen – salben), bricht
zusammen, weil ihr das intendierte Ziel entzogen und das sie leitende
Motiv ad absurdum geführt ist. Insofern markieren S 20-24 eine scharfe
Zäsur gegenüber dem bisherigen Handlungsgefüge der Geschichte.
Zugleich wird deutlich, daß die mit der Salbungsabsicht eröffnete
Erzählperspektive nur den Sinn hatte, die Frauen ins Grab zu bringen,
damit ihnen *dort* das Kerygmá verkündet wird.

Um die Tragweite dieses demnach bewußt inszenierten Geschehens
abzuschätzen, ist noch einmal auf S 20 zurückzukommen. Nicht ohne
Absicht ist dort nicht nur »Jesus« genannt, sondern dezidiert »Jesus,
der Nazarener, der Gekreuzigte«. Aufgerufen ist damit die Geschichte
Jesu, und zwar in ihrem vollen Umfang, wie sie im Markusevangelium
dargestellt ist: als Geschichte, die von Nazareth ausgeht (1,9) und am
Kreuz endet (15,33-41). Das Grab ist die letzte Konsequenz dieser nun
beendeten Geschichte, und dem Erzähler liegt offensichtlich daran, die
Geschichte Jesu bis zu dieser Konsequenz in das Grab hinein zu
verfolgen. Unter dieser Rücksicht kommt der Verweis auf den τόπος
ὅπου ἔθηκαν αὐτόν in S 23/24 nicht von ungefähr. Die Formulierung
erinnert einerseits an Josef von Arimathäa, der ἔθηκεν αὐτὸν ἐν
μνημείῳ (15,46), und andererseits an die Frauen, die sahen, ποῦ
τέθειται (15,47).

> Im Unterschied zu 15,47, wo ποῦ τέθειται das *Grab als solches* bezeichnet
> hat, bezieht sich der τόπος ὅπου ἔθηκαν αὐτόν in S 23/24 allerdings
> präzise auf den *Platz im Grab*, wo die Salbung hätte stattfinden sollen.
> Dies unterstreicht, daß S 23/24 fest mit der Perspektive der Salbung
> verbunden ist, während zur narrativen Ausgestaltung von 15,47 ein Besuch
> *am Grab* genügen würde.

Der Platz im Grab, wo man ihn hingelegt hat, ist die letzte Station des
Gekreuzigten (S 20) und damit zugleich der Ort, wo die gesamte im

Markusevangelium dargestellte Geschichte des Nazareners ihren – nach herkömmlichen Maßstäben – unwiderruflichen Endpunkt gefunden hat. Die von den Frauen beabsichtigte Salbung ist der adäquate letzte Dienst, der eine abgeschlossene Geschichte endgültig besiegelt. Damit wird aber auch deutlich, warum der Leser an diesen Ort geführt wird und an diesem Ort des letzten Endes die Auferweckungsbotschaft hören soll: nicht nur, um festzustellen, daß die Salbungsabsicht der Frauen vergeblich war, sondern um zu lernen, daß die durch diesen Ort scheinbar unwiderruflich festgelegte Wirklichkeit am Kerygma zerbricht. Gerade die *im Grab* verkündete Auferstehungsbotschaft macht eine abschließende Retrospektive auf die Geschichte Jesu unmöglich und lehrt, diese aus der fortdauernden und zukunftweisenden Perspektive des Kerygmas zu lesen. Die *im Grab* verkündete Auferstehungsbotschaft läßt die Geschichte des Nazareners in einem völlig neuen Licht erscheinen. Die abgeschlossene Geschichte wird neu aufgebrochen, sie wird neu qualifiziert, beziehungsweise, die Geschichte Jesu gewinnt ihre eigentliche Qualität im Sinne definitiven Ursprungs. Durch die Botschaft im Grab wird die beendete Geschichte zur ἀρχή, zum Anfang und zur Grundlegung des Evangeliums Jesu Christi, des Sohnes Gottes (1,1)[19]. Insofern ist die Grabesgeschichte nicht Epilog im Sinne eines Nachwortes oder Ausklangs, sondern Epilog im Sinne einer abschließenden Verifikation der bereits im ersten Vers des Markusevangeliums angekündigten und dem gesamten literarischen Unternehmen zugrundeliegenden Programmatik.

Schon aus der Abfolge von S 21 zu S 22-24 wird man schließen dürfen, daß dem Erzähler nicht daran gelegen ist, das leere Grab als Beweis für die Auferweckung in Szene zu setzen. Eher gewinnt man den Eindruck, daß das Leersein des Grabes aus der (kerygmatischen) Auferweckungsaussage erschlossen ist. Doch läßt sich auch nicht übersehen, daß die narrative Verquickung von Kerygma und leerem Grab das Leserinteresse in besonderer Weise auf das leere Grab lenkt. Insofern darf man gespannt sein, wie der Erzähler mit der einmal hergestellten Konfiguration von Auferweckungsbotschaft und leerem Grab im weiteren Verlauf der Geschichte umgeht.

Segmente 25 bis 29: S 25 bis 29 gehören – als Teil der Rede des Jünglings – engstens mit S 19 bzw. 20 bis 24 zusammen. Allerdings ändert sich jetzt die Blickrichtung. Eine neue Erzählperspektive wird aufgebaut. Ging es der Geschichte bisher darum, die Frauen *in das Grab hinein* zu bringen (um sie *dort* das Kerygma hören zu lassen), so sollen die Frauen jetzt *aus dem Grab heraus* zu Botinnen für die Jünger werden.

---

19. Zu diesem Verständnis von ἀρχή vgl. besonders R. PESCH, *Das Markusevangelium I* (HThK, II,1), Freiburg-Basel-Wien, 1976, p. 75-76.

Der Inhalt der Botschaft, den die Frauen den Jüngern vermitteln sollen, ist diesen im Prinzip allerdings bereits bekannt. S 27 ist eine fast wörtliche (jetzt präsentisch formulierte) Wiederholung von 14,28. S 29 stellt sogar ausdrücklich sicher, daß diese Botschaft bereits vorhergesagt ist. Man könnte höchstens vermuten, daß die Jünger die Vorhersage von 14,28 – ähnlich wie die Ankündigung der Auferstehung in den Leidensansagen – vor Ostern nicht verstanden haben. So mag es auf der narrativen Ebene vielleicht noch sinnvoll erscheinen, 14,28 den Jüngern nach der Auferweckung noch einmal ins Gedächtnis zu rufen. Dies ändert jedoch nichts daran, daß der Leser aus dem Auftrag an die Jünger nichts erfährt, was ihm vorher nicht schon bekannt war. Zumindest er, der Leser, hat 14,28 verstanden. Zudem weiß er aus dem Glaubensbekenntnis, daß Jesus »erschienen« ist, sofern man Bekenntnisformulierungen wie zum Beispiel 1 Kor 15,3b-5 als bekannt voraussetzen darf: ... καὶ ὅτι ὤφθη Κηφᾷ εἶτα τοῖς δώδεκα (V. 5; vgl. 1 Kor 15,6.7.8; Lk 24,34)[20]. Von daher wird der Leser auch nicht allzusehr erstaunt sein, wenn aus dem Kreis der Jünger Petrus eigens hervorgehoben wird[21]. So bringt die Botschaft, die den Frauen aufgetragen wird, dem Leser *inhaltlich* keinen Erkenntniszuwachs. Sie komplettiert im wesentlichen – insbesondere durch S 28 – das in S 21 gehörte Kerygma im Sinne des geläufigen Glaubensbekenntnisses.

Was der Leser an Neuem wahrnimmt, bewegt sich – mit der bereits angesprochenen Öffnung einer neuen Erzählperspektive – auf der *narrativen* Ebene. Was mit dieser neuen, aus dem Grab herausführenden Sinnrichtung an pragmatischer Intention verbunden ist, wird der Leser am Ende von S 25 -29 noch kaum abschätzen können. Soll ihm das aus dem Glaubensbekenntnis Bekannte aus der Perspektive des leeren Grabes bestätigt werden? Soll das Osterkerygma aus dem leeren Grab heraus zusätzlich begründet werden? Oder soll gar das an das leere Grab gebundene Kerygma den hermeneutischen Schlüssel für das Verständnis des gesamten Evangeliums bereitstellen? Die Fragen sind letztlich müßig. Was für den Leser in jedem Fall feststeht, ist, daß die Geschichte aufgrund der neuen Sinnrichtung zunächst einmal weitergeht.

20. Bemerkenswert ist die Formulierung von Lk 24,34: ὄντως ἠγέρθη ὁ κύριος καὶ ὤφθη Σίμωνι. Sie stimmt mit unserer Geschichte in S 21 (ἠγέρθη), S 26 (Σίμωνι - τῷ Πέτρῳ) und S 28 (ὤφθη - ὄψεσθε) überein. Zitiert Lk 24,34 eine Formel, die auch hinter Mk 16,6-7 steht, oder bringt Lk 24,34 lediglich auf den Nenner, was in Mk 16,6-7 virtuell (aus dem Kerygma erschlossen) angelegt ist?

21. Daß der Gemeinte nicht als »Kephas« (wie in der traditionellen Formel), sondern als »Petrus« bezeichnet wird, erklärt sich aus dem narrativen Kontext des Evangeliums, das nie »Kephas«, sondern fast immer »Petrus« verwendet. Von »Simon« ist in 1,16.29-30.36 und 3,16 die Rede. Von 3,16 an, wo Jesus dem »Simon« den Namen »Petrus« (gräzisierte Form des aramäischen »Kephas«) gibt, wird mit einer Ausnahme (14,37) nur noch von »Petrus« gesprochen (5,37; 8,29.32-33; 9,2.5; 10,28; 11,21; 13,3; 14,29.33.37.54.66-67.70.72; 16,7).

Wenigstens am Rande sei darauf aufmerksam gemacht, daß der Auftrag, den die Frauen erhalten (S 26), seinerseits nicht auf einen *Auftrag*, sondern nur auf eine *Mitteilung* an die Jünger abzielt (S 27-29). Zumindest werden diese *nicht aufgefordert, nach Galiläa zu gehen, damit* sie den Auferstandenen dort sehen. Der Gang nach Galiläa wird vielmehr als nahezu selbstverständlich vorausgesetzt, wenn festgestellt wird, daß Jesus *voraus*gehen wird, was dann wiederum nur die Voraussetzung ist für das (im Grunde schon feststehende) Sehen des Auferstandenen. Im übrigen fällt auf, daß die Frauen *nicht beauftragt werden, das eigentliche Kerygma des ἠγέρθη (S 21) zu bezeugen*[22]. Ob freilich der Leser die hier sensibel registrierten Leerstellen an dieser Stelle der Erzählung bewußt wahrnimmt, kann man füglich bezweifeln. Wahrscheinlich hat er das nicht direkt Gesagte aus einer positiven Erwartungshaltung heraus ergänzt bzw. als selbstverständlich vorausgesetzt. Der weitere Fortgang der Geschichte wird allerdings zeigen, daß die beobachteten Leerstellen nicht zufällig auftauchen, sondern im Duktus und im Dienste des noch zu explizierenden (überraschenden) Erzählverlaufs stehen.

Segmente 30 bis 33: Mit ἐξελθοῦσαι in S 30 wird εἰσελθοῦσαι von S 13 rückgängig gemacht und die Szene im Grab endgültig abgeschlossen. Die weitere (vom Hauptverb markierte) Bewegung der Frauen beginnt ἀπό (nicht ἐκ!) τοῦ μνημείου, also dort, wo die Frauen nach S 6 hingekommen waren: ἐπὶ τὸ μνημεῖον. Allerdings ist die (nun umgekehrte) Bewegung gegenüber S 6 intensiviert. Dem ἔρχεσθαι korrespondiert nicht ein ἀπ-έρχεσθαι, sondern ein φεύγειν. Als Motiv wird in S 31 angegeben, daß die Frauen »Zittern und Entsetzen« erfaßt hatte. Vor dem Hintergrund, daß die Frauen den Anblick des Jünglings eine ganze Weile ausgehalten und seine Botschaft bis zum Ende angehört haben, wird der Leser über die plötzliche Flucht und ihre Motivation überrascht sein.

Immerhin bietet ihm die Vergangenheitsform εἶχεν die Möglichkeit, die emotionale Reaktion von S 31 mit der von S 17 zusammenzusehen und das Zittern und Entsetzen als Explikation und Weiterführung des schon beim Anblick des Jünglings die Frauen befallenden Erschreckens zu werten. Das Erschrecken von S 17 war von vornherein allerdings überhaupt nicht auf eine (dem Leser) absehbare Flucht angelegt. Es gehörte vielmehr zur Topik der (in S 14-16 narrativ aufgebauten) Angelophanie, die ihrerseits wiederum auf die Übermittlung einer Botschaft abzielte (S 20-29). Im Rahmen dieser Angelophanie hatte das Erschrecken von S 17 in der Besprechung des Jünglings in S 19 seinen narrativen Widerpart gefunden,

---

22. In der matthäischen Rezeption wird diesem »Desiderat« Rechnung getragen. Die Mitteilung wird zum Auftrag ὅτι ἠγέρθη ἀπὸ τῶν νεκρῶν (Mt 28,7). Daß dadurch die gesamte Erzählstrategie verändert wird, sieht man vor allem daran, daß die Frauen sich dann auch sofort aufmachen, die Botschaft auszurichten (Mt 28,8). Vgl. auch – im Rahmen der sofort stattfindenden Erscheinung Jesu (Mt 28,9) – die relecture von S 25-28 (par Mt 28,7) in Mt 28,10: ὑπάγετε ἀπαγγείλατε τοῖς ἀδελφοῖς μου ἵνα ἀπέλθωσιν εἰς τὴν Γαλιλαίαν, κἀκεῖ με ὄψονται.

so daß die von S 17 geweckte Lesererwartung eigentlich bereits gesättigt war. Daß das μὴ ἐκθαμβεῖσθε – wie sich nun in S 31 herausstellt – nur die Funktion haben sollte, die Frauen für die Dauer der Botschaft im Grabe festzuhalten, bevor deren sich stauendes Zittern und Entsetzen in eine Fluchtbewegung ausbricht, war von vornherein zumindest nicht absehbar. Eine vom Duktus der Geschichte her einsichtige, mit S 31 identische oder vergleichbare Reaktion hätte man bestenfalls nach S 11 erwarten können. Dort hatte die Geschichte einen potentiellen Wendepunkt erreicht, der aber – unter Unterdrückung jeder emotionalen Reaktion der Frauen (!) – nicht realisiert wurde.

So wird trotz der (im Nachhinein sich ergebenden) Möglichkeit, S 31 mit S 17 zu kombinieren, in S 30-31 doch eine gewisse (semantische) Konstruiertheit der Geschichte deutlich. Ob der Leser diese Konstruiertheit in den hier analysierten Einzelheiten erkennt, ist eine andere Frage. Doch zeigt die Analyse immerhin, daß die Überraschung, mit der der Leser die Flucht der Frauen (S 30) einschließlich ihrer Motivation (S 31) registriert, nicht von ungefähr kommt, sondern in der Semantik des Textes angelegt ist.

Erzählpragmatisch hat die so erzeugte Überraschung des Lesers eine (im Rahmen der Leserlenkung) durchaus beabsichtigte Funktion. Gerade weil der Leser in S 30-31 eine andere Reaktion vorfindet, als er aufgrund von S 25-29 meinte voraussehen zu können, ist er gewarnt, sich vorschnell auf einen bestimmten Ausgang der Geschichte festzulegen. Die Möglichkeit, daß die Geschichte auch ganz anders ausgehen könnte als mit der Ausführung des Auftrags von S 25-26, ist zumindest offengehalten. Insofern ist S 30-31 Hinführung zu dem ungewöhnlichen Abschluß der Geschichte in S 32-33. Die Frauen sagen niemandem etwas (οὐδενὶ οὐδέν) (S 32). Als Motiv wird Furcht angegeben (S 33). Im durativen Imperfekt (ἐφοβοῦντο) formuliert, ist sie wohl als die Fortdauer der Haltung zu verstehen, die am Grab in emotionaler Reaktion hervorbrach (S 31). Entsprechend ist dann das »Niemandemetwas-Sagen« die bleibend gültige Feststellung (εἶπαν: komplexiver Aorist) der schon hinter der Fluchtbewegung von S 30 stehenden Reaktion auf das leere Grab. Welche Funktion hat diese Wendung der Geschichte, die zugleich deren Ende darstellt?

Im Zusammenhang mit S 32 wird meist auf die sogenannten *Schweigegebote* verwiesen, die in der Tat eine vergleichbare Formulierung aufweisen[23]. Häufig sieht man in S 32 eine Art Inversion: Während die Schweigegebote zu Lebzeiten Jesu zum Teil ausdrücklich übertreten worden seien, werde jetzt – nach der Auferweckung, wo das gebotene

---

23. 1,44 καὶ λέγει αὐτῷ· ὅρα μηδενὶ μηδὲν εἴπῃς. 5,43 καὶ διεστείλατο αὐτοῖς πολλὰ ἵνα μηδεὶς γνοῖ τοῦτο. 7,36 καὶ διεστείλατο αὐτοῖς ἵνα μηδενὶ λέγωσιν. 8,30 καὶ ἐπετίμησεν αὐτοῖς ἵνα μηδενὶ λέγωσιν περὶ αὐτοῦ. 9,9 καὶ ... διεστείλατο αὐτοῖς ἵνα μηδενὶ ἃ εἶδον διηγήσωνται.

Schweigen nach Mk 9,9 nicht mehr gilt – tatsächlich geschwiegen. Gerade dadurch solle der Leser in das Evangelium zurückverwiesen werden; ihm solle signalisiert werden, daß das Verständnis der Osterbotschaft nur in der Nachfolge zum Kreuz gewonnen werden könne. So sehr diese Wertung ganz ohne Zweifel der Gesamtkonzeption des Markusevangeliums entspricht, so wenig vermag es zu überzeugen, daß eben dieses Anliegen durch S 32-33 zum Ausdruck gebracht werden soll.

> Die These von der Inversion fällt dahin, sobald man die sogenannten Schweigegebote in der angemessenen Weise differenziert. Soweit Schweigegebote durchbrochen werden, beziehen sie sich auf Wundertaten (1,44-45; 7,36), deren Größe sie dadurch unterstreichen sollen. Die eigentlichen Schweigegebote hingegen, die an die Adresse der Dämonen (1,34; 3,12) oder der Jünger (8,30; 9,9) gerichtet sind und sich auf das Geheimnis der Person Jesu beziehen, werden nie durchbrochen. Nur mit diesen Schweigegeboten könnte das Schweigen der Frauen verglichen werden, das dann aber keine Inversion zu diesen darstellen, sondern deren fortdauernde Gültigkeit (nun sogar gegen den anderslautenden Auftrag von S 25-29) zum Ausdruck bringen würde. Dies aber macht, nachdem die in 9,9 genannte Bedingung für die Beendigung des Schweigens durch S 21 eindeutig erfüllt ist, keinen Sinn.

Einen Rückverweis auf den Kreuzweg und eine Einweisung des Lesers in die für das Verstehen der Osterbotschaft nötige Nachfolge stellen S 32-33 nicht dar. Denn weder brechen die schweigenden Frauen zur Nachfolge auf, so daß sie dem Leser zum »Vorbild« werden könnten[24], noch kann umgekehrt vorausgesetzt werden, daß die Frauen in unangemessener, durch die eigene Praxis der Kreuzesnachfolge nicht abgedeckter Weise die Osterbotschaft verkündet hätten, wenn sie nicht geschwiegen hätten. Immerhin waren es gerade die Frauen, die Jesus bis unter das Kreuz nachgefolgt sind (15,40-41). So wird sich mit Hilfe der Schweigegebote das Rätsel von S 32-33 nicht lösen lassen.

Weiterhelfen kann auch hier nur eine Besinnung auf die *narrative Funktion* von S 32-33 im Rahmen der Gesamtstrategie der Geschichte. Es zeigt sich, daß nach dem Scheitern der in das Grab hineinführenden Erzählperspektive auch die aus dem Grab herausführende Erzählperspektive (S 25-29) nicht zum intendierten Ziel führt. *Semantisch* gesehen, stellt sich also die gesamte Geschichte als mißglückte Geschichte dar, in der auch das Kerygma, um dessentwillen die Frauen in das Grab geführt wurden, sich im Schweigen der Frauen zu verlieren scheint. Gänzlich anders stellt sich allerdings die Sache dar, sobald man die *Pragmatik* der Geschichte mitberücksichtigt. Kein (christlicher) Leser wird nämlich befürchten, daß aufgrund des nicht ausgeführten Auftrags

---

24. Gegen: J. GNILKA, *Mk II* (s. Literaturhinweise), p. 344.

der Frauen die Jünger nicht nach Galiläa gehen (vgl. S 27) und
demzufolge dann auch den Auferstandenen nicht sehen (vgl. S 28) bzw.
die Botschaft von der Auferweckung (vgl. S 21) überhaupt nicht erfahren werden. Von Auferweckung und Erscheinung weiß der Leser bereits
aus dem Kerygma, und wahrscheinlich ist ihm auch Galiläa als Ort der
Erscheinung aus der Überlieferung bekannt.

Aus dem Blickwinkel dieser pragmatischen Betrachtensweise bestätigt sich
nun auch, daß die oben beobachteten semantischen Leerstellen – das
Fehlen eines direkten Auftrags an die Jünger und das Fehlen eines
Auftrags zur Bezeugung des Kerygmas (siehe zu S 25-29) – mit Bedacht
gewählt waren.

Die Botschaft von Auferweckung (und Erscheinung) ist also durch das
Scheitern der in S 25-29 aufgebauten Erzählperspektive nicht gefährdet.
Im Gegenteil! Wie die erste, in S 3-4 aufgebaute Erzählperspektive um
des Kerygmas willen scheitern mußte, so lenkt gerade das Scheitern der
zweiten Erzählperspektive wieder zum Kerygma zurück. Was dem
Leser nach der Geschichte bleibt, ist das Kerygma. Dennoch ist die
Geschichte mehr als nur schmückendes oder gar verzichtbares Beiwerk.
Denn gerade das *im leeren Grab* ertönende Kerygma ist es, welches das
in 1,1 vorgestellte Programm abschließend verifiziert und die Geschichte Jesu als Anfang und Grundlage des Evangeliums Jesu Christi
begreifen läßt. Eben dieser hermeneutische Zusammenhang dürfte aber
auch Grund dafür sein, daß der Erzähler sich genötigt fühlt, die
narrativ hergestellte Verquickung wieder zu lösen und somit das Kerygma aus einer möglichen hermeneutischen Umklammerung des leeren
Grabes zu befreien. Die Konfiguration von leerem Grab und Kerygma,
die, sofern sie das Grab als Ende der Geschichte Jesu ad absurdum
führte, zur adäquaten Interpretation der Geschichte Jesu im Sinne der
markinischen Konzeption (als ἀρχὴ τοῦ εὐαγγελίου Ἰησοῦ Χριστοῦ)
nötig war, wird reduziert auf das schon die Konfiguration strukturie-
rende und hermeneutisch bestimmende Element des Kerygmas. Das
endgültige Mißlingen der Geschichte auf der narrativen Ebene (S 30-33)
hat also pragmatisch eben das zum Ziel, was das Mißlingen der ersten
Erzählperspektive (S 20-24) auf der semantischen Ebene bezweckt hat:
Die Bindung der Geschichte Jesu an das Kerygma, die dort hergestellt
wurde, um diese Geschichte als Anfang und Grundlage des Evangeliums Jesu Christi wahrzunehmen, wird nun als *bleibender hermeneu-
tischer Schlüssel* einer so zu lesenden Geschichte Jesu festgehalten.

Was sich aus der Sicht des Lesers im Schweigen der Frauen verliert,
ist nicht das Kerygma. Dieses kennt er, und dieses wird ihm in der
Geschichte sogar noch einmal ausdrücklich mitgeteilt. Was im Schweigen der Frauen zum Verstummen gebracht wird, ist der potentielle
(d. h. durch die Geschichte selbst erst möglich gemachte) Wunsch des
Lesers, nun seinerseits – wie die Frauen in der Geschichte – den Ort zu

suchen, wohin man Jesus gelegt hat, um im leeren Grab sich des Kerygmas zu versichern und sich dort die Motivation für seine Verkündigung zu holen. Das leere Grab steht ganz im Dienste des Kerygmas bzw. im Dienste der theologischen Zielsetzung der narrativen Konzeption des gesamten Markusevangeliums und ist insofern auch konstitutiv. Eine selbständige, davon ablösbare Bedeutung kommt ihm aber nicht zu. Eine für das reale Interesse des Lesers oder die sachliche Begründung des Glaubens bedeutsame Funktionalisierung wird durch das Schweigen der Frauen verhindert. Nicht die »Evidenz« des leeren Grabes, sondern der Glaube an das Kerygma ist der tragende Grund christlicher Existenz. Der Leser wird daher nicht in das leere Grab, sondern insofern tatsächlich auf den Kreuzweg verwiesen.

II. LITERARKRITISCHE FOLGERUNGEN (DIACHRONIE)

Setzt man die gewonnenen Einsichten gemäß des eingangs aufgestellten methodischen Postulats um, so kommt man zu einem relativ klaren Ergebnis.

1. Rekonstruktion und Gehalt der Vorlage

Die vorliegende Geschichte ist von einem übergreifenden narrativen Konzept bestimmt. Entscheidend für seine Verwirklichung ist, daß die Frauen *in das Grab hinein*gehen, wenngleich das damit verbundene Handlungsziel dort zerbricht, wie umgekehrt auch das dort aufgebaute neue Handlungsziel sich im Schweigen der Frauen verliert. Beides steht im Dienste des Kerygmas, das als der entscheidende und bleibende Schlüssel für das Verstehen der Geschichte Jesu herausgestellt wird.

Unter dieser Rücksicht des in das Grab hineinführenden Erzählfadens stellen S 3-4, S 8-9, S 13-29 und S 32-33 einen festen Handlungszusammenhang dar, der der gleichen narrativen Isotopie angehört. Vor allem das im Grab stattfindende Geschehen (S 13-29), das durch εἰσελθοῦσαι (S 13) und ἐξελθοῦσαι (S 30) wie durch Klammern zusammengehalten wird, bildet ein kaum zu trennendes Handlungsgeflecht.

Nun hat die Analyse gezeigt, daß der in das Grab hineinführende Erzählfaden einen anderen, zwar untergeordneten, aber doch unterscheidbaren Erzählfaden überlagert. Er findet sich gerade in den eben nicht genannten Segmenten der Geschichte. Grundlegend für die Entfaltung seines narrativen Programms ist das *Kommen zum Grab* bzw. der *Besuch am Grab*. Daß wir es hier mit einem ursprünglich selbständigen Handlungszusammenhang zu tun haben, bestätigt vor allem der Befund, daß die Frauen in der jetzigen Geschichte die – an sich aufregende – Entdeckung des weggewälzten Steins (S 11) völlig reaktionslos registrieren. Die potentielle narrative Wende wird nicht realisiert bzw. sie wird unterdrückt, um die Frauen ohne Umschweife in das Grab gelangen zu lassen. Löst man die durch εἰσελθοῦσαι und ἐξελ-θοῦσαι inkludierte Szene im Grab (S 13-29) heraus, so folgt in S 30-31 genau jene Reaktion, die für den Befund von S 11 narrativ adäquat ist. Dazu paßt im übrigen auch die Formulierung von S 30. Das Fliehen ἀπὸ τοῦ μνημείου ist die genaue Umkehrung der für den Besuch am Grab konstitutiven Bewegung des Kommens ἐπὶ τὸ μνημεῖον.

Die Isolierbarkeit und ursprüngliche Selbständigkeit eines vom Kommen zum Grab bestimmten Erzählfadens finden ihre Bestätigung in der vorausgehenden Geschichte (15,42-47), die allein über diesen Erzählfaden mit 16,1-8 verknüpft ist. Auf die semantische Differenz zwischen dem Ort ποῦ τέθειται (= das Grab als solches) in 15,47 und dem τόπος (im Grab) ὅπου ἔθηκαν αὐτόν in S 23-24 wurde bereits hingewiesen (siehe oben zu S 23-24)[25]. Dabei ist der Ort im Grab (S 23-24) nur von der Salbungsabsicht in S 4 her zu erklären, nicht aber – wie übrigens auch die Salbungsabsicht selbst nicht – von 15,42-47 abzuleiten. Auch darauf wurde bereits hingewiesen (siehe oben zu S 3/4). 15,46-47 läßt einen *Besuch der Frauen am Grab* erwarten, nicht aber ein Betreten der Grabkammer zum Zwecke der Salbung.

Umgekehrt gewährleistet der vom Besuch am Grab bestimmte Erzählfaden in 16,1-8 eine narrativ ausreichende und befriedigende Sättigung der in 15,47 noch unabgeschlossenen Geschichte von 15,42-47. Welche Elemente von 16,1-8 zu diesem Erzählfaden im einzelnen dazugehören, ist nun zu prüfen. Dabei kommt es weniger auf eine Rekonstruktion des Wortlautes an, wenngleich dieser hier – wie sich zeigen wird – noch relativ sicher zu greifen ist. Setzt man einen 15,42-47 weiterführenden Erzählduktus voraus, so ist nicht zu erwarten, daß die in 15,47 genannten Frauen gleich noch einmal genannt werden. Desgleichen ist nicht damit zu rechnen, daß der Kreis der zum Grab gehenden Frauen erweitert wird. Unter dieser Voraussetzung ist die Frauenliste in S 2 als Eintrag des an der Salbung interessierten Erzählers zu begreifen, der über die in 15,47 genannten Frauen hinaus auch die in 15,40 erwähnte Salome beteiligen will. Daß er die zweite Maria nicht als Μαρία ἡ Ἰωσῆτος wie in 15,47 oder in der vollen Bezeichnung von 15,40 als Μαρία ἡ Ἰακώβου τοῦ μικροῦ καὶ Ἰωσῆτος μήτηρ einführt, erklärt sich wohl aus dem bewußten Rückgriff auf 15,40 (vgl. Salome!) unter dem gleichzeitigen Bestreben der Vereinfachung.

Die gleiche vereinfachende Tendenz ist in 15,47 anzutreffen, wo ansonsten ja auch die vorhandene Bezeichnung Μαρία ἡ Ἰωσῆτος durch Ἰακώβου τοῦ μικροῦ καὶ ... μήτηρ von 15,40 hätte ergänzt werden müssen. Viel-

---

25. Eine semantische Differenz ergibt sich auch bezüglich des Plurals ἔθηκαν, der von einer Beteiligung mehrerer ausgeht, während 15,46 nur Josef von Arimathäa handeln läßt.

leicht stellt aber schon 15,40 eine unter dem Zwang der Vereinheitlichung stehende Kombination einer Μαρία ἡ Ἰωσῆτος (15,47) und einer ursprünglich nur als ἡ Ἰακώβου τοῦ μικροῦ bezeichneten Μαρία in 15,40 dar. Die ursprünglich als Frauen bzw. als Töchter des Jakobus und des Joses zu unterscheidenden Marien werden dann zu der *einen* Maria, die als *Mutter* sowohl »die des Jakobus« als auch »die des Joses« sein kann[26].

Ist aber neben S 3-4 auch S 2 aus der auf den Besuch am Grabe abzielenden Geschichte auszuscheiden, dann gilt das auch für S 1. Als Genitivus absolutus ist S 1 grammatisch und syntaktisch fest mit der Hauptaussage von S 3 verbunden. Diese bereitet es auch inhaltlich vor, indem es im Nachhinein das späte Handeln der Frauen zumindest indirekt mit dem Sabbat rechtfertigt[27].

Die narrativ ungezwungene Fortsetzung von 15,47 findet sich in S 5 und S 6. Auch S 7 ist narrativ mit S 5 vereinbar, wenngleich es wohl eher dem in das Grab hineinführenden Handlungsfaden zuzuordnen ist (siehe oben zu S 7). Zu diesem zählen dann auch S 8 und S 9, während S 10 (evtl. ohne ἀνα-βλέψασαι bzw. mit dem Hauptverb βλέπουσιν [vgl. oben zu S 10]) und S 11 wieder zur Grabbesuchsgeschichte zu rechnen sind und deren narrativen Wendepunkt darstellen, der dann die Reaktion von S 30-31 hervorruft.

Insgesamt läßt sich so aus 16,1-8 eine Geschichte herauslösen, die – als Fortsetzung von 15,42-47 – ein einheitliches narratives Konzept aufweist. Sieht man einmal davon ab, daß der Bearbeiter möglicherweise auch in die Formulierung eingegriffen hat, dann hat sie folgendermaßen gelautet:

15,42ff*   ......
15,47   ἡ δὲ Μαρία ἡ Μαγδαληνὴ καὶ Μαρία ἡ Ἰωσῆτος ἐθεώρουν ποῦ τέθειται.
16,2*   καὶ λίαν πρωῒ τῇ μιᾷ τῶν σαββάτων (S 5) ἔρχονται ἐπὶ τὸ μνημεῖον (S 6) .
16,4*   καὶ (ἀναβλέψασαι) θεωροῦσιν (bzw. βλέπουσιν) (S 10) ὅτι ἀποκεκύλισται ὁ λίθος (S 11).
16,8*   καὶ ἔφυγον ἀπὸ τοῦ μνημείου (S 30*). εἶχεν γὰρ αὐτὰς τρόμος καὶ ἔκστασις (S 31).

Bemerkenswert ist, daß das rekonstruierte Erzählstück inhaltlich (und teilweise auch wörtlich) das enthält, worin Mk 16,1-8 mit Joh 20,1-10 übereinstimmt:

---

26. Jedenfalls erklärt die (aus der narrativen Analyse resultierende!) Annahme, daß die Liste von 16,1 aus 15,40 und 15,47 erschlossen sei, das Nebeneinander der drei Listen besser als die häufig vertretene These, daß 15,40 die redaktionelle Kombination von 15,47 und 16,1 sei (so schon: J. WELLHAUSEN, *Mk* [s. Literaturhinweise], pp. 133-135). Vor allem die Hinzufügung von Jakobus in 15,40 bliebe dann nur schwer erklärlich.
27. Unter derselben Tendenz steht wohl auch καὶ ἤδη ὀψίας γενομένης in 15,42, evtl. auch der interpretierende Zusatz ὅ ἐστιν προσάββατον zu παρασκευή.

Joh 20,1-2   Τῇ δὲ μιᾷ τῶν σαββάτων
              Μαρία ἡ Μαγδαληνὴ
              ἔρχεται
              πρωῒ σκοτίας ἔτι οὔσης
              εἰς τὸ μνημεῖον
              καὶ βλέπει τὸν λίθον ἠρμένον ἐκ τοῦ μνημείου.
              τρέχει οὖν καὶ ἔρχεται πρὸς Σίμωνα Πέτρον ...

Möglicherweise ist dies ein Indiz dafür, daß beide Texte auf eine gemeinsame Tradition zurückgehen. Unter dieser Prämisse könnte man weiter fragen, ob die (zumindest als Auftrag erteilte) Sendung zu den Jüngern und speziell zu Petrus in S 26 nicht eine Reminiszenz bzw. eine Modifikation eines bei Joh 20,2 noch ursprünglich erhaltenen Laufs der Frau(en) zu Petrus ist. Das ist denkbar. Allerdings läßt sich S 26 auch ohne Zuhilfenahme dieser traditionsgeschichtlichen Hypothese erklären (siehe oben). Im übrigen ist die weitere Ausgestaltung der Geschichten bei Mk und Joh so unterschiedlich, daß sich methodisch einigermaßen Gesichertes kaum mehr sagen läßt.

Erst recht kann man mit Verweis auf die beiden Engel, die Maria Magdalena nach Joh 20,12 im Grabe sitzen sieht, m. E. nicht behaupten, daß mit dem Gang zum Grab bereits ursprünglich eine irgendwie geartete Inspektion des Grabesinneren verbunden gewesen sein müsse. Das Nebeneinander von Joh 20,1-2.3-10 und 20,11-18 unterstreicht im Gegenteil, daß hier zwei unterschiedliche narrative Konzepte vorliegen.

Nun könnte man gegen die oben dargebotene Rekonstruktion den sachlichen Einwand erheben, daß die Tradierung einer Geschichte ohne jeden Verkündigungsinhalt (der in S 13-29 enthalten ist) in der christlichen Gemeinde nicht vorstellbar sei[28]. Dies ist allerdings schon methodisch ein fragwürdiges Argument, sofern ein theologisches Postulat zum Kriterium literarischer Rekonstruktion gemacht wird. Doch ist der Einwand auch inhaltlich nicht stichhaltig.

Dabei ist die Feststellung nicht unwichtig, daß der rekonstruierte Text 16,2*.4*.8a (= S 5-6.10-11.30*.31) keine selbständige Geschichte darstellt (die schon wegen ihrer Kürze merkwürdig wäre), sondern den Abschluß der sogenannten Grablegungsgeschichte 15,42-47 bildet. Der Sinn von 16,2*.4*.8a läßt sich daher nicht unabhängig von 15,42-47 erheben, wie umgekehrt auch 15,42-47 seinen (ursprünglichen) Sinn nur im Kontext mit 16,2*.4*.8a freigibt. Beide Texte sind Teil eines kohärenten narrativen Programms, das den Sinn der Einzelaussagen bestimmt. Was ergibt sich daraus für das Verständnis der Erzählung? Mit 15,46 scheint die Geschichte Jesu abgeschlossen zu sein. Der Stein, der

---

28. So: K.M. Fischer, *Ostergeschehen* (s. Literaturhinweise), p. 59; L. Oberlinner, *Die Verkündigung der Auferweckung Jesu* (s. Literaturhinweise), p. 177.

das Grab verschließt, ist ausdrucksstarkes Signum dafür. Die narrative Perspektive, die sich mit 15,47 eröffnet, ist allerdings nur scheinbar neu. Sie bleibt jedenfalls begrenzt, da sie – vor dem Hintergrund von 15,46 – zunächst nicht weiter reicht als bis zur Erwartung eines Besuchs am Grab, der seinem Charakter entsprechend das in 15,46 festgestellte Ergebnis einer abgeschlossenen Geschichte wiederum nur memorieren und insofern bestätigen würde. In diese Richtung weist auch der tatsächliche Fortgang der Erzählung. Die Frauen gehen am ersten Tag der Woche in aller Frühe zum Grab (S 5-6). Was immer an Handlung am Grabe von ihnen hätte erwartet werden können, wird durch S 10-11 als nicht mehr realisierbar beiseite geschoben. S 10-11 stellen den narrativen Wendepunkt der gesamten (in 15,42 begonnenen) Geschichte dar. Das bislang verfolgte und (scheinbar) evidente narrative Konzept, das auf das Begräbnis Jesu, das Zu-Ende-Bringen seiner Geschichte und bestenfalls noch auf das Bewahren seines Gedächtnisses ausgerichtet war, wird ad absurdum geführt. Das trotz sorgfältiger Verschließung nun geöffnete Grab gibt dem Leser zu erkennen, daß die Geschichte Jesu mit der Grablegung eben nicht abgeschlossen ist, sondern weitergeht, ja gerade an den Grenzen menschlicher Möglichkeiten erst ihre entgrenzende und grenzüberschreitende Wirkung entfaltet.

Ob das Grab leer ist, wird, wenngleich es vom Erzähler wohl vorausgesetzt wird, von den Frauen nicht festgestellt. Insofern ist es narrativ richtig beobachtet, daß »der Stein ... nicht *für* die Frauen ... weggewälzt worden« ist[29]. Ob man im Umkehrverfahren daraus schließen darf, daß das Grab »für den aus dem Grab Befreiten, den auferstandenen Jesus«, geöffnet wurde[30], bleibt jedoch fraglich. Die Geschichte ist nicht daran interessiert, das Wie der Auferstehung zu erklären (es geht also nicht um eine narrative Entfaltung der Auferstehungsbotschaft). Die Erzählung vom Grabbesuch der Frauen und ihrer Entdeckung des geöffneten Grabes darf nicht für sich interpretiert werden. Sie ist der Abschluß und das narrative Widerlager der vorher erzählten Grablegung, deren (vordergründiges) Handlungsziel sie destruieren will. Dies zum Ausdruck zu bringen ist die Funktion des weggewälzten Steins. Die Frauen, die zitternd und entsetzt vom Grab fliehen, haben die damit intendierte Botschaft durchaus richtig verstanden: als erfahrungsweltlich nicht mehr erklärbares Zeichen, welches das menschliche Urteil einer abgeschlossenen Geschichte Jesu radikal durchkreuzt und aufhebt. Gerade so schafft die Erzählung den (imaginativen) Spielraum, der den rezipierenden Leser die vorausgehende Grablegung und überhaupt die gesamte Passionsgeschichte im Sinne einer gottgewirkten Geschichte lesen läßt, die gerade am vermeintlichen

---

29. R. PESCH, *Mk II* (s. Literaturhinweise), p. 531.
30. *Loc. cit.*

Ende neue Zukunft eröffnet. Eine unmittelbare Verlautbarung des Kerygmas muß damit nicht verbunden sein, wenngleich dieses die selbstverständliche Voraussetzung dafür ist, daß der Leser das (an sich mehrdeutige) Motiv des weggewälzten Steins so aufnimmt, daß er die Geschichte in dem von ihr selbst intendierten Sinn wahrnehmen kann.

2. Zur Redaktionsgeschichte von Mk 16,1-8

Redaktionsgeschichtlich gesehen, besteht die literarische Leistung des »Erzählers« von 16,1-8 darin, daß er aus der ursprünglich zu 15,42-47 gehörigen Handlungssequenz von 16,2*.4*.8a (= S 5-6.11-12.30-31) eine Geschichte macht, die jetzt eine eigenständige Perikope darstellt, wiewohl sie sequentiell auch weiterhin an die (nun ebenfalls selbständige) Grablegungsgeschichte von 15,42-47 gebunden bleibt. Da die Intention der jetzt vorliegenden Geschichte auf der Isotopie des Gesamtwerkes liegt (s. o. zu S 20-24.25-29.32-33), ist der »Erzähler« dieser Geschichte redaktionsgeschichtlich als Evangelist zu bezeichnen.

Hinter der Gestaltung von 16,1-8 steht das Anliegen des Evangelisten, seinem Werk einen adäquaten, der Intention dieses Werkes selbst entsprechenden Abschluß zu schaffen, der in Analogie zum »Prolog« (1,1-13 bzw. 1,1-8)[31] dann als »Epilog« des Evangeliums zu verstehen ist. Wenn es die Absicht des Evangelisten war, die Geschichte Jesu von der Taufe des Johannes bis zum Tod Jesu am Kreuz als Anfang und Grundlage des Evangeliums Jesu Christi, des Sohnes Gottes, darzustellen (1,1), dann gab es keinen geeigneteren Ort als das Grab, um die dort (an und für sich) abgeschlossene Geschichte Jesu durch die Verkündigung der Auferstehungsbotschaft neu aufzubrechen und im Sinne von 1,1 bleibend in Gang zu setzen. Den Ansatz für diese Abzweckung der Geschichte fand der Evangelist bereits in der Vorlage, die – wie wir gesehen haben – ja ebenfalls den »Abschluß« der Geschichte Jesu negieren wollte. Die konkrete Durchführung seines Anliegens bewerkstelligt der Evangelist mit Hilfe der Auferweckungsbotschaft, die er im leeren Grab verlautbaren läßt. Doch auch hierfür findet er in der Vorlage insofern einen Anhaltspunkt, als bereits diese das Kerygma als Verstehenshorizont voraussetzte. So gesehen, macht der Evangelist die latente Hermeneutik der Vorlage zum narrativen Programm seiner Geschichte. Tatsächlich bedarf es zur traditionsgeschichtlichen Erklärung der Szene im Grab (S 13-29) keiner weiteren Tradition als des Kerygmas, etwa in Form von 1 Kor 15,3b-5.

---

31. Narrativ ist eine Ausdehnung des Prologs auf 1,1-15 jedenfalls nicht haltbar, da spätestens mit VV. 14-15 eine neue Szene (Zeit - und Ortswechsel!) beginnt, die bereits zum Corpus des Evangeliums gehört. Aufgrund von S 20 ist sogar zu überlegen, ob der »Prolog« nicht auf 1,1-8 zu begrenzen ist. Dies würde auch den markanten Neueinsatz mit καὶ ἐγένετο ἐν ἐκείναις ταῖς ἡμέραις in 1,9 gut erklären.

Die Einführung des Jünglings als Verkündiger der Botschaft erklärt sich hinlänglich als Motivübernahme aus der Gattung der Angelophanie. Die konkrete Ausgestaltung der Botschaft des Jünglings versteht sich als Explikation des Kerygmas im Sinne des Anliegens des Evangelisten. Dabei faßt S 20 die vergangene Geschichte des Nazareners ins Auge, deren Abgeschlossenheit durch die Osterbotschaft von S 21 negiert wird (vgl. S 22-24). So kann der Jüngling die baldigen Erscheinungen Jesu in Galiläa ankündigen (S 27-28). Auf diese Perspektive hatte der Evangelist Jünger und Leser bereits durch 14,28 vorbereitet, was angesichts des realen Scheiterns des Auftrags an die Frauen zumindest im Blick auf die Leser narrativ auch erforderlich war.

Unter der Voraussetzung, daß der Evangelist sein Anliegen mit Hilfe des im (nun leeren) Grab verkündeten Kerygmas verwirklichen will, verbleiben noch zwei Probleme. Das eine ist literarischer Art und relativ leicht zu lösen. Im Unterschied zur Vorlage, der zufolge die Frauen zum Grab kommen und vom Grab weg fliehen, müssen diese nun in das Grab gebracht werden. Der Evangelist bewerkstelligt dies mit dem Vorhaben einer Salbung (S 3-4), die er als zum Begräbnis gehörig aus 14,8 kennt. Für die weiteren Einzelheiten, mit denen der Evangelist den Gang der Frauen in das Grab inszeniert, kann auf die narrative Analyse verwiesen werden. Das zweite Problem ist theologischer Art. Auch hier ist das Wesentliche bereits im Rahmen der narrativen Analyse gesagt worden. So wichtig die Verbindung von Kerygma und leerem Grab ist, um die Geschichte Jesu im Sinne von 1,1 als Anfang und Grundlage des Evangeliums verständlich zu machen, so nachteilig könnte sie sich auswirken, wenn dadurch das Interesse der Leser auf das leere Grab konzentriert würde, so daß dieses geradezu als Bestätigung des Kerygmas erscheinen könnte. Damit geriete der Evangelist auch in Widerspruch zu seiner Vorlage, die mit dem Motiv vom geöffneten Grab nicht Interesse für dieses wecken, sondern gerade vom Grab weg auf die durch das Grab nicht beendete Geschichte Jesu hinlenken wollte. Dieser Intention bleibt der Evangelist treu. Zu diesem Zwecke läßt er den Auftrag, mit dem die Frauen betraut sind, in deren Flucht und Schweigen scheitern. Bei dieser Deutung wird ihm entgegengekommen sein, daß auch die Vorlage nichts von einer Nachricht von seiten der Frauen wußte, sondern lediglich deren Flucht unter Schrecken und Entsetzen festhielt. Diese, dem mysterium tremendum des geöffneten Grabes korrespondierende, *sprachlose* Reaktion wird dann, als der weggewälzte Stein nur mehr die Funktion hat, den Weg in das Grab hinein freizumachen, wo die entscheidende Botschaft ertönt, zur Reaktion des *Schweigens*, das in (gegenläufiger) Korrespondenz zu dem ausdrücklich erteilten Auftrag eben diesen unterdrückt.

So ist der merkwürdig erscheinende Schluß in S 32-33 durchaus auch aus der Genese der Geschichte zu verstehen und in der Vorgabe der verarbeiteten Tradition angelegt. In der jetzigen Geschichte ist das Schweigen der Frauen zudem das literarische Mittel, mit dessen Hilfe der Evangelist sich und seinen Lesern verständlich machen kann, warum die von ihm durch theologische Reflexion elaborierte Geschichte auf dem Wege historischer Traditionsübermittlung bislang noch nicht bekannt wurde. Sachlich entläßt der Evangelist mit dem Schweigen der Frauen die Leser aus der Bindung an das leere Grab und führt sie unmittelbar zurück zum Kerygma. Eben dieses Kerygma ist es, das die Perikope vom leeren Grab zum angemessenen Epilog eines Werkes macht, das den Anfang und die Grundlage des Evangeliums von Jesus Christus, dem Sohn Gottes, darlegen will.

LITERATURHINWEISE ZU MK 16,1-8

1. *Kommentare*

J. ERNST, *Das Evangelium nach Markus* (RNT), Regensburg, 1981.

J. GNILKA, *Das Evangelium nach Markus II* (EKK, II/2), Zürich - Einsiedeln - Köln - Neukirchen-Vluyn, 1979.

W. GRUNDMANN, *Das Evangelium nach Markus* (THKNT, 2), Berlin, [4]1968.

E. HAENCHEN, *Der Weg Jesu. Eine Erklärung des Markus-Evangeliums und der kanonischen Parallelen* (GLB), Berlin, [2]1968.

E. KLOSTERMANN, *Das Markusevangelium* (HNT, 3), Tübingen, [5]1971.

E. LOHMEYER, *Das Evangelium des Markus* (KEK, I/2), Göttingen, [7]1963.

D. LÜHRMANN, *Das Markusevangelium* (HNT, 3), Tübingen, 1987.

R. PESCH, *Das Markusevangelium II* (HTKNT, II/2), Freiburg-Basel-Wien, 1977.

A. SCHLATTER, *Markus. Der Evangelist für die Griechen*, Stuttgart, 1935.

J. SCHMID, *Das Evangelium nach Markus* (RNT, 2), Regensburg, [4]1958.

W. SCHMITHALS, *Das Evangelium nach Markus II* (ÖTK, II/2), Gütersloh-Würzburg, 1979.

R. SCHNACKENBURG, *Das Evangelium nach Markus II* (Geistliche Schriftlesung, II/2), Düsseldorf, 1971.

J. SCHNIEWIND, *Das Evangelium nach Markus* (NTD, 1), Göttingen, [10]1963.

E. SCHWEIZER, *Das Evangelium nach Markus* (NTD, 1), Göttingen, [2]1968.

V. TAYLOR, *The Gospel According to St. Mark*, London, 1955.

J. WELLHAUSEN, *Das Evangelium Marci*, Berlin, [2]1909.

2. *Abhandlungen und Aufsätze*

K. ALAND, *Der Schluß des Markusevangeliums*, in DERS., *Neutestamentliche Entwürfe* (TB, 63), München, 1979, pp. 246-283.

K. BACKHAUS, *»Dort werdet ihr ihn sehen« (Mk 16,7). Die redaktionelle Schlußnotiz des zweiten Evangeliums als dessen christologische Summe*, in *TGl* 76 (1986) 277-294.

H.-W. BARTSCH, *Der Schluß des Markusevangeliums*, in *TZ* 27 (1971) 241-254.

DERS., *Der ursprüngliche Schluß der Leidensgeschichte. Überlieferungsgeschichtliche Studien zum Markus-Schluß*, in M. SABBE (ed.), *L'Évangile selon Marc. Tradition et rédaction* (BETL, 34), Gembloux-Leuven, 1974, pp. 411-433.

DERS., *Inhalt und Funktion des urchristlichen Osterglaubens*, in *ANRW* II.25.1 (Berlin - New York, 1982) pp. 794-843, mit einer Bibliographie von H. RUMPELTES, pp. 844-890.

P. BENOIT, *Marie-Madeleine et les disciples au tombeau selon Joh 20,1-18*, in W. ELTESTER (ed.), *Judentum - Urchristentum - Kirche. FS J. Jeremias* (BZNW, 26), Berlin, 1960, pp. 141-152, jetzt auch in dt. Übersetzung: *Maria Magdalena und die Jünger am Grabe nach Joh 20,1-18*, in P. HOFFMANN (ed.), *Überlieferung* (s.u.), pp. 360-376.

E. BICKERMANN, *Das leere Grab*, in *ZNW* 23 (1924) 281-292, jetzt auch in P. HOFFMANN (ed.), *Überlieferung* (s.u.), pp. 271-284.

J. BLINZLER, *Die Brüder und Schwestern Jesu* (SBS, 21), Stuttgart, 1967.

E.L. BODE, *The First Easter Morning. The Gospel Accounts of the Women's Visit to the Tomb of Jesus* (AnBib, 45), Rome, 1970.

T.E. BOOMERSHINE, *Mark 16:8 and the Apostolic Commission*, in *JBL* 100 (1981) 225-239.

DERS. – G.L. BARTHOLOMEW, *The Narrative Technique of Mark 16:8*, in *JBL* 100 (1981) 213-223.

I. BROER, *Das leere Grab. Ein Versuch*, in *Liturgie und Mönchtum* 42 (1968) 42-51.

DERS., *Zur heutigen Diskussion der Grabesgeschichte*, in *BibLeb* 10 (1969) 40-52.

DERS., *Die Urgemeinde und das Grab Jesu, Eine Analyse der Grablegungsgeschichte im Neuen Testament* (StANT, 31), München, 1972.

DERS., *»Seid stets bereit, jedem Rede und Antwort zu stehen, der nach der Hoffnung fragt, die euch erfüllt« (1 Petr 3,15). Das leere Grab und die Erscheinungen Jesu im Lichte der historischen Kritik*, in DERS. – J. WERBICK (ed.), *»Der Herr ist wahrhaft auferstanden« (Lk 24,34). Biblische und systematische Beiträge zur Entstehung des Osterglaubens* (SBS, 134), Stuttgart, 1988, pp. 29-61.

L. BRUN, *Bemerkungen zum Markusschluß*, in *TSK* 84 (1911) 157-180.

DERS., *Der Auferstehungsbericht des Markusevangeliums*, in *TSK* 87 (1914) 346-388.

DERS., *Die Auferstehung Christi in der urchristlichen Überlieferung*, Oslo-Gießen, 1925, spec. pp. 9-31.

R. BULTMANN, *Die Geschichte der synoptischen Tradition* (FRLANT, 29), Göttingen, ⁶1964, spec. pp. 308-312.

H.J. CADBURY, *Mark 16,8*, in *JBL* 46 (1927) 344-345.

H. VON CAMPENHAUSEN, *Der Ablauf der Ostereignisse und das leere Grab* (Sitzungsberichte der Heidelberger Akademie der Wissenschaften, Philosophisch-historische Klasse, 1952, 4. Abhandlung), Heidelberg, ³1966.

J.-M. VAN CANGH, *La Galilée dans l'Évangile de Marc: un lieu théologique?*, in *RB* 79 (1972) 59-76.

W.L. CRAIG, *The Empty Tomb of Jesus*, in R.T. FRANCE – D. WENHAM (ed.), *Gospel Perspectives. Studies of History and Tradition in the Four Gospels II*, Sheffield, 1981, pp. 173-200.

DERS., *The Historicity of the Empty Tomb of Jesus*, in *NTS* 31 (1985) 39-67.

J.D. CROSSAN, *Mark and the Relatives of Jesus*, in *NT* 15 (1973) 81-113.

DERS., *Empty Tomb and Absent Lord (Mark 16:1-8)*, in W.H. KELBER (ed.), *The Passion in Mark. Studies on Mark 14–16*, Philadelphia, 1976, pp. 135-152.

M. DIBELIUS, *Die Formgeschichte des Evangeliums*, Tübingen, ⁵1966, spec. pp. 182.190-192.

D. DIETZFELBINGER, *Markus 16,1-8*, in H. SCHNELL (ed.), *Kranzbacher Gespräch der Lutherischen Bischofskonferenz zur Auseinandersetzung um die Bibel*, Berlin-Hamburg, 1967, pp. 9-22.

J.R. DONAHUE, *Introduction: From Passion Traditions to Passion Narrative*, in W.H. KELBER (ed.), *The Passion in Mark. Studies on Mark 14–16*, Philadelphia, 1976, pp. 1-20.

D. DORMEYER, *Die Passion Jesu als Verhaltensmodell. Literarische und theologische Analyse der Traditions- und Redaktionsgeschichte der Markuspassion* (NTAbh NS, 11), Münster, 1974, spec. pp. 221-237.

M.S. ENSLIN, ἐφοβοῦντο γάρ, *MARK 16,8*, in *JBL* 46 (1927) 62-68.

C.F. EVANS, *I will go before you into Galilee*, in *JTS* NS 5 (1954) 3-18.

K.M. FISCHER, *Das Ostergeschehen*, Göttingen, ²1980, spec. pp. 55-62.

R.H. FULLER, *The Formation of the Resurrection Narratives*, London, 1972, spec. pp. 50-70.

G. GHIBERTI, *La risurrezione di Gesù*, Brescia, 1982, spec. pp. 145-168.

H. GIESEN, *Der Auferstandene und seine Gemeinde. Zum Inhalt und zur Funktion des ursprünglichen Markusschlusses (Mk 16,1-8)*, in *SNTU/A* 12 (1987) 99-139.

M. GOGUEL, *La foi à la résurrection de Jésus dans le Christianisme primitif. Étude d'histoire et de psychologie religieuses* (Bibliothèque de l'École des Hautes Études. Sciences religieuses, 47), Paris, 1933, spec. pp. 173-233.

H. GRASS, *Ostergeschehen und Osterberichte*, Göttingen, ⁴1970, spec. pp. 15-23.

E. GÜTTGEMANNS, *Linguistische Analyse von Mk 16,1-8*, in *LB* 11 /12 (1972) 13-53.

H.-P. HASENFRATZ, *Die Rede von der Auferstehung Jesu Christi. Ein methodologischer Versuch* (Forum Theologiae Linguisticae, 10), Bonn, 1975, spec. pp. 87-131.

M. HENGEL, *Maria Magdalena und die Frauen als Zeugen*, in O. BETZ – M. HENGEL – P. SCHMIDT (ed.), *Abraham unser Vater. Juden und Christen im Gespräch über die Bibel. FS O. Michel*, Leiden-Köln, 1963, pp. 243-256.

P. HOFFMANN, *Auferstehung Jesu Christi 1. Neues Testament* in *TRE* 4 (1979) 478-513, spec. pp. 498-500.

DERS. (ed.), *Zur neutestamentlichen Überlieferung von der Auferstehung Jesu* (WdF, 522), Darmstadt, 1988.

P.W. VAN DER HORST, *Can a Book End with ΓΑΡ? A Note on Mark XVI.8*, in *JTS* NS 23 (1972) 121-124.

M. HORSTMANN, *Studien zur markinischen Christologie. Mk 8,27-9,13 als Zugang zum Christusbild des zweiten Evangelisten* (NTAbh NS, 6), Münster, 1969, spec. pp. 128-134.

B.M.F. VAN IERSEL, *»To Galilee« or »in Galilee« in Mark 14,28 and 16,7?*, in *ETL* 58 (1982) 365-370.

H. KESSLER, *Sucht den Lebenden nicht bei den Toten. Die Auferstehung Jesu*

Christi in biblischer, fundamentaltheologischer und systematischer Sicht, Düsseldorf, 1985, spec. pp. 118-125.

J. KREMER, *Zur Diskussion über »das leere Grab«. Ein Beitrag zum Verständnis der biblischen Überlieferung von der Entdeckung des geöffneten, leeren Grabes*, in É. DHANIS (ed.), *Resurrexit. Actes du Symposium International sur la résurrection de Jésus (Rome 1970)*, Città del Vaticano, 1974, pp. 137-159.

DERS., *Die Osterevangelien. Geschichten um Geschichte*, Stuttgart-Klosterneuburg, 1977, spec. pp. 30-54.

DERS., *Die Auferstehung Jesu Christi*, in W. KERN – H.J. POTTMEYER – M. SECKLER (ed.), *Handbuch der Fundamentaltheologie 2. Traktat Offenbarung*, Freiburg-Basel-Wien, 1985, pp. 175-196.

X. LÉON-DUFOUR, *Résurrection de Jésus et message pascal*, Paris, 1971, spec. pp. 149-186.

A.T. LINCOLN, *The Promise and the Failure: Mark 16:7,8*, in *JBL* 108 (1989) 283-300.

A. LINDEMANN, *Die Osterbotschaft des Markus. Zur theologischen Interpretation von Mk 16.1-8*, in *NTS* 26 (1980) 298-317.

G. LOHFINK, *Der Ablauf der Ostereignisse und die Anfänge der Urgemeinde*, in *TQ* 160 (1980) 162-176.

J. LUZARRAGA, *Retraducción semítica de φοβέομαι en Mc 16,8*, in *Bib* 50 (1969) 497-510.

L. MARIN, *Die Frauen am Grabe. Versuch einer Strukturanalyse an einem Text des Evangeliums*, in C. CHABROL – L. MARIN (ed.), *Erzählende Semiotik nach Berichten der Bibel*, München, 1973, pp. 67-85.

Ch. MASSON, *Le tombeau vide. Essai sur la formation d'une tradition*, in *RTP NS* 32 (1944) 161-174.

T.A. MOHR, *Markus- und Johannespassion. Redaktions- und traditionsgeschichtliche Untersuchung der Markinischen und Johanneischen Passionstradition* (ATANT, 70), Zürich, 1982, spec. pp. 365-403.

W. MUNRO, *Women Disciples in Mark?*, in *CBQ* 44 (1982) 225-241.

F. MUSSNER, *Die Auferstehung Jesu* (Biblische Handbibliothek, 7), München, 1969, spec. pp. 128-135.

W. NAUCK, *Die Bedeutung des leeren Grabes für den Glauben an den Auferstandenen*, in *ZNW* 47 (1956) 243-267.

F. NEIRYNCK, *Marc 16,1-8. Tradition et rédaction*, in *ETL* 56 (1980) 56-88.

DERS., *The Empty Tomb Stories*, in *NTS* 30 (1984) 161-187.

DERS., *ΑΝΑΤΕΙΛΑΝΤΟΣ ΤΟΥ ΗΛΙΟΥ (Mc 16,2)*, in *ETL* 54 (1978) 70-103.

F.-J. NIEMANN, *Die Erzählung vom leeren Grab bei Markus*, in *ZKT* 101 (1979) 188-199.

L. OBERLINNER, *Die Verkündigung der Auferweckung Jesu im geöffneten und leeren Grab. Zu einem vernachlässigten Aspekt in der Diskussion um das Grab Jesu*, in *ZNW* 73 (1982) 159-182.

DERS., *Zwei Auslegungen: Die Taufperikope (Mk 1,9-11 parr) und die Grabeserzählung (Mk 16,1-8 parr)*, in A. RAFFELT (ed.), *Begegnung mit Jesus? Was die historisch-kritische Methode leistet* (Freiburger Akademieschriften, 1), Düsseldorf, 1991, pp. 42-66.

R. OPPERMANN, *Eine Beobachtung in bezug auf das Problem des Markusschlusses*, in *BN* 40 (1987) 24-29.

G.R. OSBORNE, *The Resurrection Narratives. A Redactional Study*, Grand Rapids, MI, 1984, spec. pp. 43-72.195-219.

H. PAULSEN, *Mk XVI 1-8*, in *NT* 22 (1980) 138-175, jetzt auch in P. HOFFMANN (ed.), *Überlieferung* (s.o.), pp. 377-415.

R. PESCH, *Zur Entstehung des Glaubens an die Auferstehung Jesu. Ein Vorschlag zur Diskussion*, in *TQ* 153 (1973) 201-228.

DERS., *Der Schluß der vormarkinischen Passionsgeschichte und des Markusevangeliums: Mk 15,42–16,8*, in M. SABBE (ed.), *L'Évangile selon Marc. Tradition et rédaction* (BETL, 34), Gembloux-Leuven, 1974, pp. 365-409.

DERS., *Das »leere Grab« und der Glaube an Jesu Auferstehung*, in *Internationale katholische Zeitschrift »Communio«* 11 (1982) 6-10.

DERS., *Zur Entstehung des Glaubens an die Auferstehung Jesu*, in *FZPT* 30 (1983) 73-98.

B. RIGAUX, *Dieu l'a ressuscité. Exégèse et théologie biblique* (SBFLA, 4), Gembloux, 1973, spec. pp. 184-222.

H. RITT, *Die Frauen und die Osterbotschaft. Synopse der Grabesgeschichten (Mk 16,1-8; Mt 27,62–28,15; Lk 24,1-12; Joh 20,1-18)*, in G. DAUTZENBERG – H. MERKLEIN – K. MÜLLER (ed.), *Die Frau im Urchristentum* (QD, 95), Freiburg-Basel-Wien, 1983, pp. 117-133.

W. SCHENK, *Der Passionsbericht nach Markus. Untersuchungen zur Überlieferungsgeschichte der Passionstraditionen*, Gütersloh, 1974, spec. pp. 259-271.

L. SCHENKE, *Auferstehungsverkündigung und leeres Grab. Eine traditionsgeschichtliche Untersuchung von Mk 16,1-8* (SBS, 33), Stuttgart, 1968.

J. SCHMITT, *Résurrection de Jésus dans le Kérygme, la Tradition, la Catéchèse*, in *DBS* 10 (1985) 487-582, spec. pp. 532-542.557-560.

G. SCHNEIDER, *Die Passion Jesu nach den drei älteren Evangelien*, München, 1973, spec. pp. 143-153.

E.L. SCHNELLBÄCHER, *Das Rätsel des νεανίσκος bei Markus*, in *ZNW* 73 (1982) 127-135.

K. SCHUBERT, *»Auferstehung Jesu« im Lichte der Religionsgeschichte des Judentums*, in É. DHANIS (ed.), *Resurrexit. Actes du Symposium International sur la résurrection de Jésus (Rome 1970)*, Città del Vaticano, 1974, pp. 207-224.

Ph. SEIDENSTICKER, *Die Auferstehung Jesu in der Botschaft der Evangelisten. Ein traditionsgeschichtlicher Versuch zum Problem der Sicherung der Osterbotschaft in der apostolischen Zeit* (SBS, 26), Stuttgart, 1967.

R.H. STEIN, *A Short Note on Mark XIV.28 and XVI.7*, in *NTS* 20 (1974) 445-452.

B. STEINSEIFER, *Der Ort der Erscheinungen des Auferstandenen. Zur Frage alter galiläischer Ostertraditionen*, in *ZNW* 62 (1971) 232-265.

A. VÖGTLE, *Was heißt »Auslegung der Schrift«? Exegetische Aspekte*, in W. JOEST – F. MUSSNER – L. SCHEFFCZYK – A. VÖGTLE – U. WILCKENS, *Was heißt Auslegung der Heiligen Schrift?*, Regensburg, 1966, pp. 29-83, spec. pp. 61-67.

DERS. – R. PESCH, *Wie kam es zum Osterglauben?*, Düsseldorf, 1975, spec. pp. 85-98.

U. WILCKENS, *Auferstehung. Das biblische Auferstehungszeugnis historisch untersucht und erklärt* (Themen der Theologie, 4), Stuttgart-Berlin, 1970, spec. pp. 43-64.

238 H. MERKLEIN

H.-W. WINDEN, *Wie kam und wie kommt es zum Osterglauben? Darstellung, Beurteilung und Weiterführung der durch Rudolf Pesch ausgelösten Diskussion* (Disputationes Theologicae, 12), Frankfurt a. M. - Bern, 1982, spec. pp. 35-47.

Regina-Pacis-Weg 1a   Helmut MERKLEIN
D-5300 Bonn

LA CONSTRUCTION DU LECTEUR PAR LE TEXTE
(MARC ET MATTHIEU)

La problématique que les Journées Bibliques de Louvain ont décidé d'aborder nous précipite dans le conflit des méthodes de lecture: *Source Criticism and the New Literary Criticism*. Le modèle méthodologique que représente la critique historique, après avoir dominé sans partage l'exégèse académique durant deux siècles, se trouve défié par de nouveaux modèles inspirés de la critique littéraire contemporaine. Dans cette nouvelle querelle des Anciens et des Modernes, des chapelles se sont fondées; elles signalent d'un côté l'effervescence des phénomènes de mode ou organisent d'un autre côté le repli frileux sur un intégrisme historico-critique. Mais au-delà de ces cristallisations de combat, le monde de l'exégèse ne peut esquiver la question des modifications induites par l'émergence de la nouvelle critique littéraire dans l'épistémologie de la lecture.

Le conflit des méthodes a poussé les exégètes à vérifier la pertinence de leur appareil de lecture ou à le compléter, à titre combinatoire, par l'emprunt de procédures nouvelles[1]. Mais l'enjeu est plus fondamental: ce conflit interroge sur le statut reconnu au texte dans chacune des lectures. À ce titre, il me paraît fécond d'examiner quels déplacements introduit, dans le rapport au texte, le changement de paradigme qu'instaure la «nouvelle critique littéraire» face à la classique *Literarkritik*[2]. Cet examen permettra de fixer la problématique à laquelle s'attache ma contribution.

---

1. À consulter dans ce sens: K. BERGER, *Exegese des Neuen Testaments* (UTB, 658), Heidelberg, 1977; C. BUSSMANN – D. VAN DER SLUIS, *Die Bibel studieren. Einführung in die Methoden der Exegese*, München, 1982; G. STRECKER – U. SCHNELLE, *Einführung in die neutestamentliche Exegese* (UTB, 1253), Göttingen, 1983; C.M. TUCKETT, *Reading the New Testament. Methods of Interpretation*, London, 1987.
2. Les déplacements herméneutiques induits par la nouvelle critique littéraire face à la critique historique ont été signalés à maintes reprises. On consultera, du point de vue de la sémiotique française: J. DELORME, *Incidences des sciences du langage sur l'exégèse et la théologie*, in B. LAURET – F. REFOULÉ (éd.), *Initiation à la pratique de la théologie*, tome I, Paris, 1982, pp. 299-311; du point de vue de la narratologie: W.S. KURZ, *Narrative Approaches to Luke-Acts*, in *Bib* 68 (1987) 195-220; du point de vue de la critique historique: J. ZUMSTEIN, *Critique historique et critique littéraire*, in ID., *Miettes exégétiques* (Le Monde de la Bible, 25), Genève, 1991, pp. 51-62.

I. L'AVÈNEMENT DU LECTEUR

1. Les déplacements introduits par ce nouveau paradigme qu'est la «nouvelle critique littéraire» sont multiples, comme sont variées les composantes de la nébuleuse *New literary criticism*[3]. Je crois cependant possible, pour faire court, de les rassembler autour de deux axes.

Premier axe: avec la nouvelle critique littéraire, l'intérêt se déplace de la généalogie du texte au texte fini. L'engendrement n'intéresse plus, mais l'enfant, appelé à grandir dans la lecture et par la lecture. L'enfant, c'est le texte pris en lui-même, le texte rencontré comme une totalité organisée, le texte structuré par une argumentation de nature à agir sur tout lecteur potentiel. Ce passage, bien connu en méthodologie, de la diachronie à la synchronie s'appuie sur un autre déplacement, plus fondamental celui-là – et c'est le changement de paradigme: le passage d'une herméneutique centrée sur l'histoire à une herméneutique centrée sur le texte[4]. Ce n'est plus du hors-texte que représente l'histoire que l'interprète requiert les clefs de la lecture, mais de la totalité signifiante que constitue le texte.

Second axe: avec la nouvelle critique littéraire, l'intérêt se transfère du pôle de l'auteur au pôle du lecteur. Ce n'est pas seulement dire qu'identifier le sens du texte avec l'intention de son auteur, comme le faisait un peu naïvement la critique littéraire classique, nous est devenu interdit; de ce point de vue, il sera prudent de passer de l'*intentio auctoris* à l'*intentio operis*[5], ou pour emprunter les catégories de la

---

3. Le manuel de M.A. POWELL, *What is Narrative Criticism?*, Minneapolis, MN, 1990, présente une typologie différenciant quatre courants, les uns de type synchronique (structuralisme et narratologie), les autres empruntant à la pragmatique de la communication (critique rhétorique et *reader-response criticism*); cf. pp. 11-21. On ajoutera à cet inventaire l'esthétique de la réception et le post-structuralisme guidé par les travaux de J. Derrida.

4. Voir J. ZUMSTEIN, *Critique historique* (n. 2), pp. 51-52 et 61-62.

5. Dans une étude de 1985, «'*Intentio lectoris*'. *Notes sur la sémiotique de la réception*» (in *Les limites de l'interprétation*, Paris, 1992, pp. 19-47), Umberto Eco se prononce sur les trois types d'intention que l'interprétation d'un texte peut se donner comme objectif de rechercher: l'*intentio auctoris*, l'*intentio operis* et l'*intentio lectoris*. La quête de l'*intentio auctoris* définit une herméneutique générative, dont l'ambition est de reconstituer la signification investie dans le texte par son auteur; on reconnaît ici la quête du sens historique qui anime la démarche historico-critique. La quête de l'*intentio operis* cherche «dans le texte ce qu'il dit en référence à sa propre cohérence contextuelle et à la situation des systèmes de signification auxquels il se réfère», tandis que viser l'*intentio lectoris* revient à «chercher dans le texte ce que le destinataire y trouve en référence à ses propres systèmes de signification et/ou en référence à ses propres désirs, pulsions, volontés» (*ibid.*, pp. 29-30). Eco critique avec raison cette dernière démarche herméneutique, qui cède à l'infinitude du sens chère à Derrida, mais où le texte devient un pur prétexte à la dérive interprétative, pour privilégier la quête de l'*intentio operis*, dans laquelle le texte demeure à la fois l'objet de l'analyse *et* le paramètre de l'interprétation qu'il permet de construire. La reconnaissance de la pluralité des sens du texte, jointe au constat que la potentialité sémantique du texte dépasse infiniment la visée consciente de son auteur, permettra sans

narratologie, de passer de l'auteur concret à l'auteur implicite[6]. Mais ce n'est pas de cette recomposition de la notion d'auteur que je veux parler. Umberto Eco, le sémioticien, a synthétisé les déplacements critiques intervenus dans les théories de la lecture cette dernière décennie, en disant qu'est advenue «l'heure du lecteur». Il énonce ainsi cette conviction commune: «Le fonctionnement d'un texte (même non verbal) s'explique en prenant en considération, en sus ou au lieu du moment génératif, le rôle joué par le destinataire dans sa compréhension, son actualisation, son interprétation, ainsi que la façon dont le texte lui-même prévoit sa participation»[7]. L'accent s'est donc déplacé de l'activité de l'auteur à celle, programmée, du lecteur. Je prétends que si cet axe de recherche est actuel, il n'est pas nouveau, et qu'il suffit de penser à la rhétorique gréco-romaine ou à la pragmatique des sophistes pour en être convaincu. Néanmoins, Eco a bien discerné le point de focalisation où peuvent se reconnaître des courants aussi divers que la sémiotique française, la narratologie, la pragmatique du *reader-response criticism*, la nouvelle rhétorique, la théorie du «Lecteur Modèle» ou l'esthétique de la réception[8]. Nous assistons au retour, mais avec une

effort à la critique historique de redéfinir à partir de l'*intentio operis* le sens historique qu'elle a pour vocation de reconstituer.

6. Wayne BOOTH (*The Rhetoric of Fiction*, Chicago, IL, 1961) a été le premier à parler explicitement de «implied author (carrying the reader with him)», pour distinguer l'auteur concret (une figure historique à reconstituer en dehors de son œuvre) de l'auteur implicite, intrinsèquement présent à son œuvre par ses choix d'écriture (une figure littéraire à reconstruire par l'analyse de sa stratégie textuelle).

7. *Les limites de l'interprétation* (n. 5), p. 22. Ce changement de paradigme dans les études littéraires avait été annoncé par H.R. JAUSS en 1969 (*Paradigmawechsel in der Literaturwissenschaft*, in *Linguistische Berichte* 3, 1969). Du point de vue de l'histoire des idées, il est intéressant de noter que l'essor des théories de la réception dès la fin des années 60 réagissait contre le durcissement objectivant du structuralisme et contre le formalisme anglo-saxon. Ces théories ont reçu leur instrumentation des travaux de Maria CORTI (*Principi della communicazione letteraria*, Milan, 1976), Seymour CHATMAN (*Story and Discourse*, Ithaca, 1978) et Wolfgang ISER (*Der implizite Leser*, München, 1972; *Der Akt des Lesens*, München, 1976). L'attention dévolue désormais à la réception du texte a généré ce que Eco qualifie d'«insistance quasi obsessionnelle sur le moment de la lecture, de l'interprétation, de la collaboration ou coopération du récepteur» (*Les limites de l'interprétation*, p. 24), face à laquelle, sans dénier qu'un texte prévoit son propre lecteur et qu'il en porte les traces, le sémioticien italien réhabilite aujourd'hui la résistance que présente l'œuvre elle-même à l'infinitude du désir interprétatif du lecteur.

8. Pour évaluer les résultats de la sémiotique fançaise, on consultera l'ouvrage devenu classique du GROUPE D'ENTREVERNES, *Signes et paraboles. Sémiotique et texte évangélique*, Paris, 1977 ou le récent livre de Jean DELORME, *Au risque de la parole*, Paris, 1991. Le *narrative criticism* a trouvé sa réalisation exemplaire dans l'étude de R.A. CULPEPPER, *Anatomy of the Fourth Gospel. A Study in Literary Design*, Philadelphia, PA, 1983; en français, voir J.-N. ALETTI, *L'art de raconter Jésus-Christ*, Paris, 1989. La théorie du *reader-response criticism* est présentée dans: J. TOMPKINS (éd.), *Reader-Response Criticism: From Formalism to Post-Structuralism*, Baltimore-London, 1980; une belle illustration en est fournie par R.M. FOWLER, *Let the Reader Understand. Reader-Response Criticism and the Gospel of Mark*, Minneapolis, MN, 1991. Le panorama des études rhétoriques a été dressé par B.L. MACK, *Rhetoric and the New Testament*, Minneapolis, MN, 1990. Quant à

instrumentation rénovée, d'une antique question: quel effet exerce intrinsèquement le discours sur son destinataire?

2. Selon moi, le paradigme de lecture introduit par la nouvelle critique littéraire peut donc se définir par ces deux axes: d'une part l'on passe d'une herméneutique de l'histoire à une herméneutique du texte, d'autre part l'on quitte une fascination de l'auteur pour se déporter vers le pôle de la lecture. Je ne m'attarderai pas sur le premier point, sinon pour me distancier d'alternatives trop simples pour être sérieuses: si l'exégèse historico-critique doit impérativement redécouvrir la dimension du texte comme tel, il est tout aussi vrai que la nature même de la littérature biblique, et sa référence constitutive à l'histoire, ne rendent pas obsolète le mandat de la critique historique[9]. L'oubli de la référence historique du texte, et de son contexte originel d'énonciation, n'est pas à terme une entreprise recommandable. L'attention portée à la communication entre l'auteur et le lecteur requiert forcément que l'on s'intéresse au contexte où s'est déroulé cet échange, et ce contexte a sa place dans un milieu et une culture historiquement situés[10].

Mon intention est de me concentrer sur le second déplacement, en me laissant guider par le questionnement renouvelé sur le poste du lecteur. Mais qui est le lecteur? On sait que la dissociation opérée entre le lecteur empirique ou historique (auquel était destiné l'écrit) et le lecteur impliqué par le texte a suscité un tel foisonnement de définitions que chacun est requis de préciser de quel lecteur il parle[11]. Je ne recourrai pas à l'appellation «lecteur implicite» *(implied reader)*, pour éviter la coupure, inhérente à la narratologie, entre le texte et son contexte historique d'énonciation[12]. Je désigne par «lecteur» moins une per-

---

la théorie du «Lecteur Modèle» et à l'esthétique de la réception, elles découlent la première des travaux de Umberto Eco (*Lector in fabula*, Paris, 1985), la seconde des réflexions de Jacques DERRIDA (*De la grammatologie*, Paris, 1967).

9. Je me suis expliqué là-dessus dans mon article: *À quoi sert l'exégèse? Finalité et méthodes dans la lecture du Nouveau Testament*, in RThPh 119 (1987) 149-169.

10. Il n'est pas inutile de rappeler ce qu'écrivait le linguiste Roman JAKOBSON en 1961 (!): «Les essais qui ont été tentés de construire un modèle du langage sans relation aucune au locuteur ou à l'auditeur, et qui hypostasient ainsi un code détaché de la communication effective, risquent de réduire le langage à une fiction scolastique» (in *Essais de linguistique générale*, Paris, 1963, p. 95).

11. L'inflation des appellations (lecteur empirique, lecteur historique, lecteur réel, lecteur implicite, lecteur idéal, lecteur modèle, lecteur hypothétique, énonciataire, narrataire, lecteur compétent,...) devra trouver prochainement une stabilisation. La notion de lecteur est problématisée par N.R. PETERSEN, *The Reader in the Gospel*, in *Neotestamentica* 18 (1984) 38-51; R.M. FOWLER, *Who is 'the Reader' in Reader-Response Criticism?*, in *Semeia* 31 (1985) 5-23; J.D. KINGSBURY, *Reflections on 'the Reader' of Matthew's Gospel*, in *NTS* 34 (1988) 442-460.

12. Je me fie ici à l'affirmation de M.A. POWELL, dans son manuel *What is Narrative Criticism?*, Minneapolis, MN, 1990: The «implied reader is distinct from any real, historical reader in the same way that the implied author is distinct from the real,

sonne qu'un rôle, que tout lecteur est appelé à endosser dans l'accomplissement de l'acte de lecture. L'élaboration de ce rôle comporte aussi bien une dimension historique (elle est conditionnée par le groupe lecteur que l'auteur concret avait en vue) qu'une dimension hypothétique (ce rôle est une figure idéale, cumulant tous les effets du texte prévus ou non prévus par l'auteur)[13].

Il est certain qu'une étude socio-historique permettrait de cerner le profil du groupe lecteur originel auquel l'auteur destinait son œuvre, mais ce n'est pas ici le propos. Je m'intéresse au lecteur à qui le texte se destine jadis et aujourd'hui, le lecteur dont le texte a programmé l'active participation dans l'acte de lecture, bref, le lecteur sur lequel le texte exerce son effet[14]. Partant du principe qu'écrire, c'est construire avec le texte sa propre conception du lecteur, je souhaite observer à l'intérieur du texte la figure du lecteur en construction[15].

3. Je formule ainsi ma question: quel lecteur le texte évangélique cherche-t-il à promouvoir? De quel sujet lecteur le récit d'évangile vise-t-il l'avènement?

L'enquête se concentrera sur l'évangile de Marc; mais dans le but de faire saillir les différences entre deux figures de lecteur, les modifications apportées par l'évangile de Matthieu seront mises en évidence; dans

historical author... Unlike rhetorical criticism, narrative criticism does not interpret works from the perspective of the text's actual, original audience; it is not necessary to know everything they knew in order to understand the text aright» (pp. 19-20).

13. Je rejoins dans cette acception la définition de Jean-Louis SKA: «... the 'implied reader' is less a person than a role that every concrete reader is invited to perform in the act of reading. Every narration contains an invitation to share a certain experience, to imagine and recreate a universe, to get in touch with certain values, feelings, decisions, and worldviews» («*Our Fathers Have Told Us*». *Introduction to the Analysis of Hebrew Narratives* [Subsidia biblica, 13], Roma, 1990, p. 107). La nature heuristique du concept de lecteur est bien soulignée par R.M. FOWLER, qui distingue trois facettes: le lecteur ... «has an individual persona (mine), a communal persona (the abstracted total experience of my critical community), and a textual persona (the reader implied in the text at hand)» (*Let the Reader* [n. 8], p. 40).

14. R.C. TANNEHILL a bien décrit comment l'auteur inscrit en creux dans le texte le profil de lecteur qu'il se souhaite: «... the author has a view of his readers and anticipates how they will respond to his story. Therefore, not only the standpoint of the author but also the standpoint of the reader (in the view of the author) may find indirect expression in the story» (*The Disciples in Mark: The Function of a Narrative Role*, in *JR* 57, 1977, 386-405, citation p. 390). De son point de vue de sémioticien, Jean DELORME adopte une manière moins causale et plus incitative pour décrire la génération du lecteur par le texte: «Le récit a sa manière de faire advenir un sujet pour l'écouter. Il dépayse l'auditeur ou le lecteur, occupe son imagination, profite de son désir de savoir le déroulement et la fin de l'histoire. Sans s'adresser à lui, il capte ses facultés et les met en action» (*Au risque* [n. 8], p. 157).

15. C. COMBET-GALLAND a entrepris une démarche similaire sur le chapitre 16 de l'évangile de Marc: *Qui roulera la peur? Finales d'évangile et figures de lecteur*, in *ETR* 65 (1990) 171-189.

cette comparaison, il sera postulé que Matthieu est une relecture de Marc.

L'intérêt de cette recherche me paraît double. Premièrement, sur une question pointée par la nouvelle critique littéraire, il s'agit de combiner les instruments neufs avec les outils éprouvés de la critique des sources. Deuxièmement, l'image du lecteur façonnée par le texte présente un intérêt théologique et historique certain: théologique si l'on veut mieux percevoir le projet pastoral de chaque évangéliste, et historique si l'on veut comparer cette image avec les effets du texte dans l'histoire (sa *Wirkungsgeschichte*). Chaque évangile se crée son public, se crée sa communauté de lecture, se crée son église, et il n'est pas indifférent de se demander quel profil de croyant se dessine en creux dans la stratégie narrative de chaque évangéliste.

Mais comment percevoir la figure du lecteur en construction dans le texte? À quels indices aperçoit-on la stratégie de l'évangéliste envers son lecteur? Je pose l'hypothèse que la façon dont se nouent les rapports entre les personnages, au niveau du récit évangélique, a une pertinence sur l'effet que le texte entend exercer sur le lecteur. Autrement dit: la construction du réseau de personnages interne au récit vise un effet pragmatique sur le lecteur. Or, au centre du réseau des personnages figure le héros du récit, Jésus, qui n'est autre que le Seigneur que le lecteur est appelé à confesser[16]. L'hypothèse posée à titre heuristique consiste donc à dire qu'il y a homologie entre les rapports qui relient Jésus aux personnages, au plan du récit, et d'autre part les rapports appelés à se nouer entre le lecteur et le Seigneur confessé, au plan de l'existence.

Deux observations liminaires sont à faire encore pour ouvrir le champ de la recherche.

La première observation est que l'homologie postulée entre la configuration des personnages au plan du récit et l'action sur le lecteur ne se réduit en aucun cas à une formule simple, qui serait par exemple l'identification du lecteur avec la figure du disciple, comme si le lecteur était appelé à se reconnaître sans autre dans ce qu'éprouvent les disciples de l'évangile[17]. Analyser la construction du lecteur par le texte

16. R.A. CULPEPPER a bien montré que dans la narration évangélique, les personnages ne disposent pas d'autonomie, mais tirent leur rôle narratif du lien qui s'établit avec Jésus; du point de vue pragmatique, chaque personnage présente au lecteur une attitude possible à l'égard du Maître (*Anatomy* [n. 8], pp. 101-148). Ses conclusions sur l'évangile de Jean peuvent être sans difficulté étendues à l'ensemble des évangiles.

17. W. ISER souligne dans *The Implied Reader*, Baltimore-London, 1974, p. 291, que le procédé d'identification narrative du lecteur à un personnage n'est pas un but en soi, mais un stratagème dont use le narrateur, et par lequel il cherche à provoquer des réactions chez le lecteur. Il faut donc éviter de travailler avec une notion trop statique du processus d'identification, comme si l'évangéliste distribuait au fil du texte à l'intention de son lecteur des modèles positifs (à adopter) et des modèles négatifs (à rejeter). Dans un essai consacré à Jn 20, C. COMBET-GALLAND dresse l'hypothèse que le savoir sur la résurrection

évangélique, que ce soit chez Marc ou chez Matthieu, ne saurait donc se résoudre par une étude de la condition du disciple. La seule narration de l'événement de la Passion, auquel n'assistent pas les compagnons de Jésus, signale que le lecteur se trouve dans une position épistémologique différente de celle des disciples de l'évangile. Le savoir que la narration évangélique communique au lecteur dépasse largement celui des disciples du récit. Mais comment, ou plutôt de quoi se bâtit le savoir du lecteur?

Cette question nous fait passer à une seconde observation. La narratologie nous enseigne que dans la constitution du savoir du lecteur, l'apport est multiple. Son savoir naît de l'accumulation des savoirs partiels, attribués dans l'énoncé aux différents acteurs; mais il intègre aussi les données que lui communique le narrateur, lorsqu'il commente l'action. Le narrateur peut aussi jouer d'un savoir préacquis chez le lecteur, pour créer l'ambivalence constitutive du procédé d'ironie[18]. En conclusion, on peut dire que le savoir du lecteur est le fruit d'un cumul de savoirs disséminés au fil du récit.

Nous tenterons de saisir la construction de la figure du lecteur en explorant successivement trois domaines: la christologie, la sotériologie et l'éthique. Nous abordons le premier, la christologie, en nous intéressant à la présentation narrative de Jésus.

II. LA CHRISTOLOGIE

1. Le récit de Marc, comme on sait, se présente sous la forme d'une succession de fragments dont l'unité se fait dans la lecture, moins par continuité thématique que par un effet de contiguïté narrative; le récit avance d'une péricope à l'autre par un jeu récurrent d'écarts, de déplacements, de progression brisée. La *Formgeschichte* nous a appris à identifier, dans cette succession de fragments, les unités formelles conçues originellement au sein de la tradition orale. La construction narrative de Matthieu va profondément transformer l'agencement du récit marcien, par l'aménagement de larges séquences narratives ou discursives (les grands discours matthéens).

Cette progression brisée, qu'agence la narration de Marc, est nettement perceptible à sa gestion de l'espace: Jésus ne cesse de se déplacer

de Jésus se construit au travers du parcours offert au lecteur d'une scène à l'autre, si bien que chaque personnage (Marie, Pierre et son compagnon, les disciples, Thomas) constitue à chaque fois, sur le registre du savoir, un modèle offert au dépassement par le personnage suivant (*L'aube encore obscure*, in *Cahier biblique 26, Foi et Vie*, Paris, 1987, pp. 17-25).

18. Le commentaire de l'auteur peut être explicite, ou alors implicite et c'est alors que le texte s'ouvre à une lecture symbolique ou développe un effet rhétorique d'ironie; dans ce cas, l'auteur joue d'une connivence non déclarée avec le lecteur, comme l'a bien montré R.A. CULPEPPER à propos de l'évangile de Jean (*Anatomy* [n. 8], pp. 151-202).

dans ce récit, passant des lieux déserts à la maison, du chemin à la synagogue, du rivage à la montagne. Le lecteur est entraîné par le récit d'un micro-épisode à l'autre, chacun se déroulant en un lieu différent. Ce constat n'est pas seulement vrai de la fameuse séquence du chemin (8,27-10,52), qui relie la Galilée à Jérusalem[19]. Le ton est donné dès les premiers versets de l'évangile, où l'on passe du désert (1,4) au Jourdain (1,5), du Jourdain au désert (1,12), du désert en Galilée (1,14), de la Galilée au bord de la mer (1,16), du bord de la mer à Capharnaüm (1,21), et ainsi de suite. Durant les dix premiers chapitres de Marc, on dénombre pour Jésus pas moins de 54 changements de lieu[20], alors que pour la période équivalente, Matthieu compte vingt chapitres et ramène à 47 le nombre de déplacements[21]. *Cum grano salis*, on peut dire qu'avant le récit de la Passion chez Marc, la mobilité de Jésus est une marque plus importante du personnage que la perspective de la souffrance. Quels types de lecteurs construisent deux gestions aussi différentes de l'espace que celles de Marc et Matthieu?

2. Commençons par jeter un regard sur la première manifestation publique du Jésus de Marc, la journée à Capharnaüm (Mc 1), dont on connaît la fonction programmatique au sein de l'évangile.

La journée s'ouvre par un exorcisme à la synagogue (1,21-28); elle se poursuit par une guérison dans la maison de Simon et d'André (1,29-32) et s'achève après le coucher du soleil à la porte de la ville (1,32-34). Ces trois lieux sont symboliques chez Marc: la synagogue est lieu de l'autorité libératrice de Jésus, la maison symbolise la proximité avec les disciples, l'espace ouvert symbolise l'affluence de la foule[22]. Or, au

19. La formule ἐν τῇ ὁδῷ scande la séquence: 8,27; 9,33; 9,34; 10,17 (εἰς ὁδόν); 10,32; 10,46 (παρὰ τὴν ὁδόν); 10,52.

20. De Nazareth au bord du Jourdain (1,9); désert (1,12); Galilée (1,14); bord de la mer (1,16); Capharnaüm, synagogue (1,21); maison de Simon et André (1,29); porte (1,33); lieu désert (1,35); toute la Galilée (1,39); lieux déserts (1,45); Capharnaüm, maison (2,1); bord de la mer (2,13); bureau des taxes (2,14); maison de Lévi (2,15); champs de blé (2,23); synagogue (3,1); vers la mer (3,7); sur la montagne (3,13); à la maison (3,20); bord de la mer (4,1a); dans la barque (4,1b); à l'écart (4,10); dans la barque (4,35); au pays des Géraséniens (5,1); bord de la mer (5,21); en chemin (5,24); maison du chef de synagogue (5,38); synagogue (6,1); villages alentour (6,6); lieu désert (6,31); dans la barque (6,45); vers la montagne (6,46); sur la mer (6,48); Gennésareth (6,53); villages, villes et hameaux (6,56); territoire de Tyr (7,24); Décapole (7,31); Sidon (7,31); à l'écart (7,33); lieu désert (8,1); région de Dalmanoutha (8,11); dans la barque (8,14); Bethsaïda (8,22); villages voisins de Césarée de Philippe (8,27a); en chemin (8,27b); haute montagne (9,2); pied de la montagne (9,14); au travers de la Galilée (9,31); Capharnaüm, la maison (9,33); au-delà du Jourdain (10,1); à la maison (10,10); en chemin (10,17; 10,32); Jéricho (10,46); sur le chemin (10,52). Sur l'itinérance de Jésus dans le second évangile, voir la thèse de D. MABONGO, *Le nomadisme de Jésus dans l'évangile de Marc*, Strasbourg, 1991.

21. Mt 3,13; 4,1.5.8.12.13.18.23; 5,1; 8,1.5.14.23.28; 9,1a.1b.7.9.10.19.23.28.32.35; 12,1. 9.15; 13,1.54; 14,13.22.23.25.35; 15,21.29.32.39; 16,13; 17,1.14.22.24; 19,1.15; 20,17.28.

22. Sur la symbolisation marcienne de l'espace, voir par exemple J. SCHREIBER, *Theologie des Vertrauens. Eine redaktionsgeschichtliche Untersuchung des Markusevangeliums*, Hamburg, 1967, pp. 162-170, surtout pp. 162-164 et 168-169.

moment précis où l'évangéliste vient de noter l'affluence des malades autour de Jésus, qui «ne laissait pas parler les démons parce qu'ils le connaissaient» (1,34), prend place un curieux épisode que Matthieu n'a pas retenu. C'est la scène de la fuite de Jésus dans un lieu désert, où Simon et ses compagnons finissent par le retrouver (1,35-38). «Ils le trouvèrent et lui disent: tous te cherchent. Et il leur dit: allons ailleurs, dans les bourgades voisines, afin que là aussi je proclame; c'est pour cela en effet que je suis sorti» (1,37-38). L'absence de Jésus est dramatisée par la redondance ἐξῆλθεν καὶ ἀπῆλθεν (1,35) marquant la séparation, par le verbe καταδιώκειν indiquant l'intensité de la poursuite, et par l'expression πάντες ζητοῦσίν σε (1,37) qui signale l'universalité de la recherche. Visiblement, la scène a dérangé Matthieu, d'abord par la dureté du verbe de la recherche (καταδιώκειν), ensuite parce que l'image d'un Jésus s'enfuyant à la dérobée contrevient à sa vision du Messie à disposition des foules; l'épisode choquait sa christologie[23].

Quoi qu'il en soit, la scène a valeur programmatique chez Mc, et il est à regretter que les commentateurs si souvent la détachent de la journée à Capharnaüm[24]. Elle a valeur programmatique: elle ajoute aux trois premiers lieux symboliques (la synagogue, la maison, le lieu ouvert) un quatrième, l'endroit désert, si important dans la topologie du deuxième évangile[25]. La scène organise la fuite de Jésus et la battue des disciples pour le retrouver, et dès lors la question centrale posée par la journée à Capharnaüm n'est pas «qui est Jésus?». Qui il est, l'esprit impur l'a déclaré d'entrée («Je sais qui tu es: le saint de Dieu» 1,24), et les démons le savent (1,34). La question n'est pas «qui est Jésus?», mais «où est Jésus?». On peut le dire autrement: à peine l'identité de Jésus est-elle déclarée que l'intéressé disparaît. Nous tenons là une structure

---

23. L'embarras christologique de Matthieu se mesure à la gêne qu'a provoqué l'épisode chez Luc: la poursuite se mue en recherche (ἐπεζήτουν Lc 4,42) et les reproches en tentative de la foule de garder Jésus avec soi (4,42); en outre, le Jésus de Luc légitime son départ par sa vocation messianique (4,43: ἀπεστάλην). Le seul élément subsistant chez Matthieu de ce tableau, Mc 1,39, a été inséré dans le sommaire rédactionnel 4,23 et valorisé dans le sens d'une christologie de la disponibilité à toutes les souffrances (θεραπεύων πᾶσαν νόσον καὶ πᾶσαν μαλακίαν ἐν τῷ λαῷ). Dans la perspective matthéenne, cette activité de prédication et de guérison accomplit la mission du serviteur de Dieu (Mt 8,14-17) et concrétise la miséricorde divine. Cf. U. LUZ, *Das Evangelium nach Matthäus I* (EKK, I/1), Zürich-Neukirchen, 1985, pp. 179-180; W.D. DAVIES – D.C. ALLISON, *The Gospel According to Saint Matthew I* (ICC), Edinburgh, 1988, pp. 613-615.

24. Ainsi R. PESCH (*Das Markusevangelium* [HTK, II/1], Freiburg, 1976, pp. 116-117 et 137), J. GNILKA (*Das Evangelium nach Markus I* [EKK, II/1], Zürich-Neukirchen, 1978, pp. 87-89) et W.L. LANE (*The Gospel according to Mark* [NICNT], Grand Rapids, MI, 1974, pp. 70-71 et 80), qui limitent la journée à Capharnaüm à 1,21-34. Par contre, J. ERNST étend la séquence jusqu'au verset 39 (*Das Evangelium nach Markus* [RNT], Regensburg, 1981, p. 61).

25. Voir J. SCHREIBER, *Theologie des Vertrauens* (n. 22), pp. 168-169.

propre à Marc, et cette structure va se répercuter tout au long de la chaîne du récit.

3. La multiplication des départs de Jésus, cultivée par le narrateur jusqu'à l'excès entre le chapitre 1 et le chapitre 10, place le lecteur en face d'un Christ qui s'en va, d'un Christ qui devance, d'un Christ constamment hors d'atteinte. Toute réponse sur l'identité de Jésus est remise en jeu par son départ. Mon hypothèse de lecture est que Jésus n'échappe pas seulement aux disciples; il échappe continuellement au lecteur, glissant d'un lieu à l'autre, en sorte que la question de son identité se réouvre dès qu'on la croit close.

Deux observations classiques faites sur la géographie de Marc viennent à l'appui de cette thèse. La première est que la topographie palestinienne est parfaitement déficiente dans cet évangile[26]; l'intérêt aux voyages de Jésus n'est donc pas documentaire et l'évangéliste s'avère moins préoccupé d'assurer à sa narration une cohérence topographique qu'une logique dans la symbolisation de l'espace[27]. La seconde observation est que les tentatives d'identifier dans l'évangile un lieu privilégié gouvernant la structure du récit, en dehors de la polarisation Galilée-Jérusalem, ont échoué[28]. On est confirmé dans l'idée que la logique narrative de Mc n'est pas commandée par une géographie, fût-elle palestinienne, ou par un lieu précis, fût-il la maison. La logique réside dans le déplacement. La logique *est* le déplacement[29]. Précisons: le déplacement de Jésus, car après 1,38, il faudra attendre 4,35 pour voir le Maître accompagner les disciples – mais quel accompagnement, puisque dans la barque secouée par la tempête, Jésus aussitôt s'absente par le sommeil!

Matthieu a pris le parti inverse. Dans sa narration, la mobilité de Jésus n'est pas seulement freinée par les longues stations où la parole du Maître est offerte aux disciples et aux foules. Il faut bien voir que

---

26. W. MARXSEN, *Der Evangelist Markus. Studien zur Redaktionsgeschichte des Evangeliums* (FRLANT, 67), Göttingen, 1959, pp. 33-61.

27. Avec D. MABONGO, *Le nomadisme de Jésus* (n. 20), p. 75.

28. Hormis les séquences reconnues 8,27–10,52 (en chemin) et 11,1–16,8 (à Jérusalem), la structuration interne de 1,1–8,26 échappe au critère géographique; le constat négatif est posé par D.-A. KOCH, *Inhaltliche Gliederung und geographischer Aufriss im Markusevangelium*, in *NTS* 29 (1983) 145-166, surtout pp. 150-154. C. BREYTENBACH reconnaît une structuration épisodique à l'évangile de Marc, mais renonce également à chercher une logique topographique au scénario narratif (*Das Markusevangelium als episodische Erzählung*, in F. HAHN [éd.], *Der Erzähler des Evangeliums. Methodische Neuansätze in der Markusforschung* [SBS, 118/119], Stuttgart, 1985, pp. 137-169, surtout pp. 162-169).

29. Citons ici l'heureuse expression d'É. TROCMÉ, *La formation de l'Évangile selon Marc* (EHPR), Strasbourg, 1963, p. 61, note 238: «La confusion topographique qui résulte de la multiplication de ces départs < i.e. de Jésus > aux chapitres 3 à 10 lui importe assez peu, puisqu'elle sert *son désir de montrer un Jésus qui s'en va*» (c'est moi qui souligne).

Matthieu a élu le terme de la suivance, ἀκολουθεῖν, pour décrire la condition du croyant[30]. Le lecteur de Matthieu est convié à se retrouver dans la figure du disciple que le maître appelle dans la suivance[31], une condition qui se concrétise dans l'écoute de l'enseignement, dans une communauté de destin avec Jésus et dans la rupture avec le monde[32]. La différence est nette: là où Matthieu insiste sur la suivance du disciple, Marc pointe sur le Seigneur qui s'en va. Le lecteur de Matthieu est orienté sur la difficulté de suivre; le lecteur de Marc est désorienté par un Seigneur insaisissable. Le lecteur de Matthieu voit sa place tracée aux pieds du Maître; le lecteur de Marc voit le Maître s'en aller dès qu'il s'est installé.

4. Une dernière observation sur le vocabulaire du mouvement nous permettra de saisir avec quelle cohérence Marc et Matthieu, chacun dans leur sens, ont fixé narrativement la position de Jésus face à son entourage, induisant du même coup la position du lecteur face à lui; c'est l'usage du vocabulaire de la précédence (προάγειν, προέρχεσθαι)[33]. Marc utilise à trois reprises προάγειν pour parler de Jésus qui devance les disciples: sur le chemin de Jérusalem en 10,32 (les disciples ont peur, ils sont effrayés de suivre celui qui monte à la mort; Matthieu a biffé cette notation négative de la suivance) ou alors pour marquer la précédence du Ressuscité en Galilée (14,28; 16,7: Matthieu a affaibli la portée de cette annonce[34]). Plus nettement que le premier évangile, le récit de Marc considère la précédence de Jésus à l'égard des disciples comme le rapport adéquat qui doit s'établir entre le Maître et les siens. À la découverte du tombeau vide, l'annonce qu'«il vous précède en Galilée» (16,7), qui orchestre la rencontre entre le monde du récit et le

30. La fonction typologique de l'ἀκολουθεῖν chez Matthieu a été explicitement formulée en premier lieu par G. BARTH, *Das Gesetzesverständnis des Evangelisten Matthäus*, in G. BORNKAMM – G. BARTH – H.J. HELD, *Ueberlieferung und Auslegung im Matthäusevangelium* (WMANT, 1), Neukirchen, [5]1968, pp. 94-96. Pour une étude synthétique: J.D. KINGSBURY, *The Verb Akolouthein («to follow») as an Index of Matthew's View of his Community*, in *JBL* 97 (1978) 56-73. Cette compréhension éthique de la suivance, qui va de pair avec la transparence du concept μαθητής, ne constitue pas une création matthéenne, mais la radicalisation d'une donnée de ses sources.

31. L'étude de J.D. KINGSBURY conclut avec raison que le lecteur implicite de l'évangile de Matthieu ne saurait être confondu avec avec la figure du disciple (*Reflections on 'the Reader'* [n. 11], pp. 442-460, voir pp. 457-458); mais ce constat, contrairement à ce qu'affirme Kingsbury, ne supprime pas la transparence du concept μαθητής chez Matthieu, ou plutôt son ambivalence, μαθητής désignant à la fois le compagnon du Jésus historique et la condition exemplaire du croyant.

32. Je reprends ici une formulation de J. ZUMSTEIN, basée sur l'étude de Mt 4,18-22; 9,9; 8,18-22; 10,37-39: *La condition du croyant dans l'évangile selon Matthieu* (OBO, 16), Fribourg-Göttingen, 1977, pp. 215-232.

33. Προάγειν: Mc 6,45 (Mt 14,22); 10,32; 11,9 (Mt 21,9); 14,28 (Mt 26,32); 16,7 (Mt 28,7). Προέρχεσθαι: Mc 6,33; 14,35 (leçon variante: προσέρχεσθαι) (Mt 26,39).

34. Mt 28,7 affaiblit la portée de προάγει ὑμᾶς εἰς τὴν Γαλιλαίαν en faisant précéder cette clause d'une autre annonce: ἠγέρθη ἀπὸ τῶν νεκρῶν.

monde du lecteur, n'est pas à comprendre comme un rendez-vous, mais comme l'annonce qu'à jamais l'identité du Christ échappe à la saisie des siens.

Cette observation se trouve confirmée par une autre série de textes où, à l'inverse, Jésus est devancé par les disciples ou par les foules. C'est le cas à trois reprises chez Marc, mais à chaque fois l'évangéliste note l'anomalie. En 6,33, la foule occupe le rivage avant que Jésus et les siens abordent (προῆλθον αὐτούς); mais elle est aussitôt taxée de «brebis n'ayant pas de berger» (6,34; Mt a biffé). En 11,9, un cortège précède Jésus (οἱ προάγοντες) à son entrée à Jérusalem et pousse l'acclamation messianique; mais on connaît par le récit de la Passion comment évolueront les sentiments de la foule à l'égard de celui qu'elle célèbre! Dans la stratégie narrative de Marc, précéder le Christ équivaut à prendre possession de lui; l'évangéliste inflige à cette tentative le déni le plus vif. La réplique de Jésus à Pierre qui s'insurge devant la souffrance du Fils de l'homme, ὕπαγε ὀπίσω μου, σατανᾶ (8,33), s'inscrit dans la même perspective, puisqu'elle reconduit avec force le disciple derrière le maître. Le texte le plus significatif à cet égard est 6,45, où Jésus force ses disciples à traverser le lac et à le précéder vers Bethsaïda (προάγειν εἰς τὸ πέραν); devant leur peine, il les rejoint en marchant sur l'eau et s'apprête à «passer le long d'eux» (παρελθεῖν αὐτούς 6,48), ce qui déclenche leur effroi. Cette curieuse trajectoire, que Matthieu a supprimée, joue avec le sens théologique que reçoit παρέρχεσθαι dans la LXX, pour exprimer la théophanie du Dieu qui se révèle mais ne se livre pas (Ex 33,19.22; I R 19,11)[35]. Cet épisode marcien rapproche donc deux thèmes qui sont apparus dans les textes précédents: Jésus à la fois se manifeste et échappe aux siens, et d'autre part le παρελθεῖν rétablit la position adéquate de Jésus qui précède les siens. L'effroi des disciples (6,49-52) fait surgir un troisième motif vers lequel nous allons maintenant nous tourner: le motif de l'incompréhension, lié à la christologie marcienne du secret messianique.

5. L'itinérance de Jésus dans le second évangile trouve son corrélat dans la mise en place systématique des *consignes de silence*; l'une et l'autre tiennent d'une christologie du secret. Que ce soit après les guérisons (1,44; 5,43; 7,36; 8,26), après les exorcismes (1,25.34; 3,12) ou après les confessions de foi (8,30; cf 9,9), la foule se voit refuser un accès immédiat à l'identité de Jésus. Or, si nous le rapprochons de ce

35. Les multiples hypothèses avancées pour l'interprétation de cet obscur passage de Marc ont été recensées critiquement par T. SNOY, *Marc 6,48: «... et il voulait les dépasser». Proposition pour la solution d'une énigme*, in M. SABBE (éd.), *L'Évangile selon Marc. Tradition et rédaction* (BETL, 34), Leuven-Gembloux, 1974, pp. 347-363. La lecture qu'il suggère, assez proche finalement de l'interprétation proposée naguère par Lohmeyer, joue sur le sens théophanique de παρελθεῖν, mais en l'intégrant à la théorie marcienne du secret messianique. Il est vrai que l'alternance de révélation et d'incognito dans un même texte est une structure récurrente chez Marc (1,40-45; 7,24; 7,36; 9,30; etc).

qui vient d'être dit, nous constatons que les consignes de silence exercent le même effet, mais sur le registre du discours, que le motif de la précédence de Jésus. Plus généralement, l'itinérance de Jésus dans l'évangile de Marc offre à la christologie du secret sa configuration narrative, car elle aussi soustrait constamment Jésus à l'appréhension des personnages du récit. Deux textes permettront de le vérifier: 1,23-27 et 9,1-13.

Mc 1,25 constitue la première consigne de silence signifiée par Jésus dans l'évangile. Or, quand surgit-elle? Elle apparaît lors du premier acte public de Jésus à Capharnaüm (1,23-27), et par cet exorcisme qui inaugure le ministère de Jésus, Marc pose d'emblée à l'intention du lecteur le pouvoir du Fils sur le monde des esprits. Ce pouvoir est libérateur. Mais on notera qu'en même temps, dans ce geste inaugural à valeur programmatique, Marc – et voilà qui est intéressant – dénonce au lecteur comme démoniaque l'appropriation du savoir sur le Christ. «Je sais qui tu es: le Saint de Dieu. Jésus le menaça en disant: Tais-toi et sors de cet homme» (1,24b-25a). Se croire détenteur du mystère christologique est dénoncé comme un fait démoniaque. Le motif de la fuite de Jésus tôt le lendemain, dont nous avons parlé plus haut[36], porte la même signature théologique.

Le second texte (Mc 9,1-13) est celui de la transfiguration. Son emplacement stratégique, après la confession de Pierre à Césarée et la première annonce de la Passion, a souvent été relevé; de même, sa fonction dans le scénario évangélique: par la transfiguration, l'attestation messianique trouve son apogée et en même temps la souffrance du Fils de l'homme s'annonce irrémédiablement[37]. La narration de Marc atteint ici son sommet, peut-être même son centre[38], et Matthieu n'a rien retiré à cette intensité christologique. Cependant, le traitement de ce colloque de l'histoire du salut s'avère bien différent chez Marc et chez Matthieu du point de vue qui nous intéresse, c'est-à-dire l'effet sur les disciples. À la voix céleste qui proclame «Celui-ci est mon fils bien-aimé, en qui j'ai pris plaisir; écoutez-le» (Mt 17,5), les disciples mat-théens réagissent par une prosternation tremblante, dont ils sont relevés par Jésus; puis, dans un dialogue privé avec le maître, l'objection des scribes à propos d'Élie est levée par l'affirmation qu'Élie est déjà venu, «alors les disciples comprirent qu'il leur parlait de Jean le Baptiste» (Mt 17,13). La tradition de la transfiguration est travaillée chez Mat-thieu par une christologie du dévoilement. Les disciples de Marc, eux,

---

36. Voir p. 247.

37. Avec netteté: B. STANDAERT, *L'évangile selon Marc. Composition et genre littéraire*, Brugge, 1978, pp. 41-108.

38. B. STANDAERT voit coïncider en 8,27–9,13 le sommet de l'argumentation et l'apogée de la construction dramatique du second évangile (*L'évangile selon Marc* [n. 37], pp. 89-96, 571-579); il n'est pas certain que la narration marcienne se prête à un tel schématisme concentrique.

n'ont rien: ni prosternation, ni relèvement par le maître, ni compréhension. Le potentiel de sens que représente la vision du Christ glorifié en conversation avec Élie et Moïse est aussitôt réprimé par une consigne de silence, dont la validité est limitée (fait unique chez Marc) à la résurrection du Fils de l'homme (9,9); mais les disciples ne comprennent pas «ce que veut dire ressusciter des morts» (9,10). Au travers de la remarque, le lecteur est questionné pour savoir s'il comprend mieux qu'eux: non pas l'idée générale de résurrection, qui va de soi, mais la résurrection de Jésus, qui laissera les femmes au tombeau dans le même état de consternation[39]. On perçoit ici à quel point le motif de l'incompréhension des disciples chez Marc ne répond pas à un intérêt historique, mais vise le lecteur et interpelle le lecteur sur son propre entendement.

6. Je conclus ce premier chapitre consacré à la christologie. Quels profils de lecteur voit-on se construire à travers deux présentations aussi différenciées de Jésus que celles de Marc et de Matthieu?

La narration de Marc fonctionne sur un mode de progression brisée, dont la trame et le rythme sont fournis par l'itinéraire de Jésus. Or, il est apparu que sa mobilité est l'expansion narrative d'une christologie du secret: le héros du récit, échappant sans cesse, affirmant son droit de précédence, refusant de se laisser cerner dans une image de thaumaturge ou de controversiste, remet en cause toute déclaration identitaire à son sujet (1,24-25; 1,35-38; 6,45-52; 10,32; 16,7)[40]. Cette clôture constamment différée de la confession de foi christologique trouve dans le motif de l'incompréhension son corrélat anthropologique (8,30-33; 9,9-10; 11,9).

Le lecteur de Matthieu se trouve face à un scénario biographique réorganisé: l'idéal de la suivance lui est proposé, assorti d'une promesse de compréhension. Le Messie délivre son aide miséricordieuse à la foule des souffrants (Mt 4,23-25) et offre la force thérapeutique de sa parole aux disciples-lecteurs. Assurément, insécurité et hostilité ne seront pas épargnées au lecteur de Matthieu; mais pour assumer les douleurs de la suivance, il peut s'adosser au savoir acquis auprès du maître de la

39. Bien vu par C. SENFT, qui commente ainsi la consigne de silence limitée à la résurrection du Fils de l'homme: «L'évangéliste *oppose* à la vision glorieuse de la transfiguration une autre manifestation de la gloire de Jésus: celle de Pâques. La vision sur la Montagne est certes une révélation authentique du Fils de Dieu (v. 7). Mais elle suscite l'image illusoire et le désir d'un Christ sans contestation et sans croix (9,5-6)» (*L'évangile selon Marc* [Essais bibliques, 19], Genève, 1991, p. 75).

40. D. MABONGO interprète l'itinérance du Jésus de Marc dans des catégories éthiques: sa mobilité serait un modèle à suivre pour les missionnaires de la chrétienté marcienne et l'indice de son amour envers l'humanité (*Le nomadisme de Jésus* [n. 20], pp. 123-125 et 158-160). Mais cette lecture ne rend pas compte du lien entre établi par le récit entre la mobilité et les consignes de silence; en outre, le motif du retrait de Jésus (1,35-38; 6,30-31) n'est pas justifié par le service des foules.

Torah et à sa promesse d'assistance «jusqu'à la fin des temps» (Mt 28,20).

La conclusion que je viens d'énoncer engage déjà l'idée que les scénarios biographiques de Marc et de Matthieu sont homogènes avec leur conception du croire et du comprendre. En d'autres termes, un récit qui constamment met en route Jésus et fait partir ses personnages ou un récit qui au contraire organise leur rencontre configurent chacun une interprétation différente du croire et du comprendre. Il nous faut maintenant préciser cette idée; c'est l'objet du chapitre suivant.

III. Croire et comprendre

1. Quelle conception l'évangéliste Marc se fait-il du croire et du comprendre? William Wrede, le premier, a désigné le chapitre 4, et la fameuse «théorie des paraboles» (4,11-12), comme le lieu où se cristallise cette réflexion dans l'évangile[41]. Or, ce chapitre 4 de Marc risque d'être faussement lu à partir de Matthieu, c'est-à-dire lu comme un enseignement sur le Royaume, dont les paraboles énigmatiques font le partage entre les disciples qui comprennent et l'Israël qui refuse[42].

En effet, l'interrogation des disciples matthéens porte sur l'usage des paraboles à l'égard des foules («Pourquoi *leur* parles-tu en paraboles?» 13,10). La réponse de Jésus chez Matthieu isole hermétiquement deux groupes: aux disciples, Dieu donne à connaître les μυστήρια τῆς βασιλείας τῶν οὐρανῶν (13,11); aux autres, la connaissance est refusée parce qu'ils refusent d'entendre (13,13-15 cite Es 6,9-10)[43]. Le rédacteur du premier évangile a relu le dialogue de Mc 4 à partir de l'expérience historique du refus d'Israël, et de l'isolement auquel se trouvent acculés les chrétiens éjectés de la Synagogue. L'Eglise matthéenne, traumatisée par cette récente expulsion, se trouve dans un état d'extrême fragilité (nous reviendrons plus bas sur cette situation). Ce qu'on perçoit, en tous les cas, c'est la ferme volonté du rédacteur d'accentuer ce que les

---

41. W. Wrede, *Das Messiasgeheimnis in den Evangelien* (1901), Göttingen, ²1913, pp. 51-65.

42. Par exemple W.L. Lane: «Mark appears to have selected these parables and placed them at this point in his presentation to illustrate the character of the Kingdom of God». «Mark 4:11-12 is properly understood only in the context of the contemporaneous situation set forth in Ch. 3, where unbelief and opposition to Jesus is blatant... It is against this background that in Ch. 4: 11-12 Jesus makes a sharp distinction between the disciples (to whom God entrusts the mystery of the Kingdom) and the unbelieving multitude (from whom the truth is concealed)» (*The Gospel of Mark* [n. 24], citations pp. 149 et 157).

43. Pour la justification de ce qui suit, je renvoie à l'exégèse de Mt 13,10-17 dans D. Marguerat, *Le jugement dans l'Évangile de Matthieu* (Le Monde de la Bible, 6), Genève, 1981, pp. 415-423.

croyants ont, et ce qu'ils ont pour l'avoir reçu de Dieu (13,11-12). Le discours peut alors s'allonger de quelques paraboles complétant la catéchèse (13,24-30.33.36-50). Et le bonheur des disciples peut être célébré, puisqu'ils voient et qu'ils entendent ce à quoi prophètes et justes ont aspiré en vain (macarisme de 13,16-17). Le premier évangile ne cessera dès lors de magnifier la condition des disciples-lecteurs, gratifiés de la bénédiction de comprendre.

Qu'en est-il de Marc? Comment parle au lecteur le récit de Marc? On se trouve, on l'a dit, dans une tout autre constellation théologique[44]. Je vois trois différences.

Première différence: Marc ne s'interroge pas sur la coupure entre l'Eglise et Israël, mais sur la parabole comme mode de communication de la parole[45]. L'intérêt de Marc n'est pas de collecter un enseignement sur la βασιλεία, mais de réfléchir à la façon dont la parole se communique et dont le Christ se donne à connaître; la parabole du semeur (4,3b-9), à laquelle une relecture ecclésiale avait déjà accolé avant lui une réflexion sur l'échec et le succès de la parole (4,14-20), lui en a fourni l'occasion. C'est le processus de communication de l'Évangile qui intéresse ici Marc.

Deuxième différence: Ce qui est donné à connaître de Jésus n'est pas un contenu d'enseignement (les μυστήρια de Mt 13,11), mais le fait qu'en Jésus se manifeste et se cache le μυστήριον du Royaume de Dieu (4,11). Marc discerne dans la parabole la forme obligée de toute communication du kérygme, appropriée à son objet qu'elle doit dévoiler et cacher en même temps[46]. C'est à la forme parabolique du *logos* que réfléchit Marc lorsqu'il groupe, autour des trois paraboles que fournit sa tradition, quelques logia sur le thème du caché et du révélé (4,21-25)[47]. L'explication de la parabole du semeur (4,14-20) fait de la

---

44. Les thèses développées ici l'ont été en premier lieu dans D. MARGUERAT, *La parabole, de Jésus aux évangiles*, in *ACFEB, Les paraboles évangéliques. Perspectives nouvelles* (LD, 135), Paris, 1989, pp. 61-88, surtout pp. 80-82. Pour l'étude de Mc 4, voir: V. FUSCO, *Parola e regno. La sezione delle parabole (Mc 4,1-34) nella prospettiva marciana*, Brescia, 1980; C.M. TUCKETT, *Mark's Concerns in the Parables Chapter (Mark 4,1-34)*, in *Bib* 69 (1988) 1-26; É. CUVILLIER, *Parabolè dans la tradition synoptique*, in *ETR* 66 (1991) 25-44; C. SENFT, *L'évangile selon Marc* (n. 39), pp. 43-57.

45. La preuve en est fournie par la récurrence du vocable λόγος tout au long du discours (4,14.15a.15b.16.17.18.19.20.33), ainsi que par l'abondance du vocabulaire de la communication et de la connaissance: διδάσκειν/διδαχή (vv. 1-2), ἀκούειν (vv. 3.9.12.15. 16.18.20.23.24.33), ἐρωτᾶν (v. 10), μυστήριον (v. 11), βλέπειν (vv. 12.24), ὁρᾶν (v. 12), συνιέναι (v. 12), εἰδέναι (vv. 13.27), γινώσκειν (v. 13), κρυπτός (v. 22), φανεροῦν (v. 22), ἐπιλύειν (v. 34).

46. Sur le thème de la parole-parabole, qui révèle en se voilant, cf C. SENFT, *L'évangile selon Marc* (n. 39), p. 52.

47. L'*opinio communis* des commentateurs reconstitue l'histoire de la tradition de Mc 4 en trois stades: a) une collection indépendante de paraboles (vv. 3-9 et 26-32); b) une relecture ecclésiale avec adjonction de l'explication (vv. 14-20) et d'un cadre; c) ajout de logia retouchés rédactionnellement (vv. 10-13 et 21-25) et mise en contexte narratif par le

diffusion de la parole un événement large et public, mais en même temps, elle fait de l'échec de sa communication un facteur inhérent au μυστήριον du Royaume. Les logia agglutinés aux vv. 21-25 affirment tout d'abord l'irrépressible dévoilement de ce qui est caché: la parole/parabole n'est pas destinée à se cacher, mais à être découverte (vv. 21-22); le v. 23 formule ensuite la condition obligée pour que soit manifestée cette révélation à l'homme: écouter. La révélation christologique n'est donc pas ésotérique: il y a tension, mais non contradiction, entre recevoir le mystère (4,11) et la nécessité d'écouter pour qu'il soit accessible[48]. Les deux paraboles finales, la semence qui pousse toute seule (4,26-29) et la graine de moutarde (4,30-32), se retrouvent autour de l'idée que dans le caché se prépare une éclatante révélation.

Troisième différence: la déclaration de Jésus chez Marc (4,11) crée une division entre deux groupes: les disciples, posés comme initiés à qui le μυστήριον a été donné, et les autres, ceux du dehors (οἱ ἔξω), pour qui tout reste obscur. Mais l'invitation est large: au seuil du discours, le Jésus de Marc a déclaré que «quiconque fait la volonté de Dieu, voilà mon frère, ma sœur, ma mère» (3,35). Non seulement les Douze, mais «ceux qui l'entourent» (4,10) peuvent se considérer parmi les bénéficiaires du μυστήριον[49]. Cependant l'évangéliste crée aussitôt le paradoxe dont Matthieu ne veut pas: le don du μυστήριον n'équivaut pas au don de la compréhension. Les disciples de Marc trébuchent déjà sur la parabole du semeur; «vous ne comprenez pas cette parabole, dit Jésus, alors comment comprendrez-vous toutes les paraboles?» (4,13). Nous voici au cœur de notre question. Quel lecteur construit le récit de Marc, lorsqu'il installe au chapitre 4 la division entre initiés et gens du dehors? Sans risque de se tromper, on peut affirmer que le texte induit une identification du lecteur avec le groupe d'initiés. Jusque là, le récit de l'évangile a tout fait pour favoriser cette identification (1,16-20; 3,13-19; 3,35)[50].

2. Or, que nous expose le second évangile? Quel scénario déroule la narration marcienne? J'ose dire: la narration de Marc déroule l'inverse du scénario matthéen. L'évangéliste organise en effet une inexorable

---

rédacteur (vv. 1-2 et 33-34). Cf. à titre représentatif J. GNILKA, *Das Evangelium nach Markus* (n. 24), pp. 156-192. Discussion chez C.M. TUCKETT, *Mark's Concerns* (n. 44).

48. C. SENFT tente d'articuler théologiquement les deux pôles dans une heureuse formule: «La parole est en quelque sorte portée à la rencontre de l'homme, offerte à son attention, appelant ses questions, prête à se découvrir. Cela étant, l'attention et l'écoute de l'homme ne sont pas son initiative autonome, mais *sa réponse devenue possible dans l'espace de liberté créé par la parole...*» (*L'évangile selon Marc* [n. 39], p. 53).

49. C.M. TUCKETT (*Mark's Concerns* [n. 44], p. 44) et É. CUVILLIER (*Parabolè* [n. 44], p. 32) insistent sur l'imprécision voulue dans laquelle Marc laisse les contours du groupe bénéficiaire du μυστήριον.

50. Voir l'analyse de R.C. TANNEHILL, *The Disciples in Mark* [n. 14], pp. 392-396.

déconstruction du statut d'initié qu'il vient d'établir[51]. Les signes surabondent. Sitôt après le discours en paraboles, l'échec de la confiance des disciples est dramatisé dans l'histoire de la tempête (4,35-51). Sitôt de retour de mission, les disciples échouent face à la demande de nourrir la foule affamée (6,37); puis la traversée de la mer leur fait prendre le Seigneur pour un fantôme (6,45-51). Par deux fois, l'incompréhension où les laisse le miracle des pains est exposée (6,52; 8,14-21), et la seconde fois, leur incompréhension est alignée sur celle des pharisiens avec les termes même d'Esaïe 6,9-10 (8,18). Au moment où Jésus révèle ouvertement sa passion (8,31-32), Pierre par son refus révèle qu'il n'est pas dedans, mais dehors. Quant à la transfiguration, prise pour l'épiphanie du Fils mais en occultant la croix, elle débouche sur une consigne de silence observée sans comprendre (9,10). La fuite des disciples loin de la croix et leur absence au tombeau vide feront le reste[52].

Le récit a systématiquement déconstruit le statut d'initié posé au chapitre 4. Transformant le groupe d'initiés en non-initiés, l'*insider* en *outsider*, il a anéanti la notion de privilège lié à une information confidentielle[53]. L'évangile de Marc n'est pas l'évangile gnostique de Thomas; il ne protège pas un secret, mais narrativise sa dissolution. À l'inverse de ce scénario, le lecteur de Matthieu, si l'on peut dire, est progressivement structuré par le déploiement discursif dans l'évangile des «mystères du Royaume des cieux» qu'il lui est donné de connaître; ce sont les six grands discours du Christ matthéen (Mt 5-7; 10; 13; 18; 23; 24-25). Le récit de Marc, lui, tour à tour désoriente et réoriente le lecteur, lui apprenant la vulnérabilité de toute connaissance par la dramatisation narrative de l'échec des disciples[54].

51. Ce thème a été pensé par Werner H. KELBER dans un article remarquable: *Récit et révélation: voiler, dévoiler et revoiler*, in *RHPhR* 69 (1989) 389-410. Les propos qui suivent s'inspirent largement de cette étude.

52. Le processus de dissociation progressive qu'opère l'auteur entre le lecteur et la figure des disciples, à partir du chapitre 4, a été finement observé par R.C. TANNEHILL, *The Disciples in Mark* (n. 14), pp. 399-404.

53. Selon W.H. KELBER, trois facteurs conditionnent le secret ésotérique: a) il sert à défendre et à renforcer l'identité d'un groupe restreint; b) il est étroitement lié à la possession de connaissance spéciales; c) il est garant d'une autorité dévolue à ceux qui le détiennent. Or, Marc se sert du schéma ésotérique pour le subvertir (*Récit et révélation* [n. 51], pp. 395-398). La thèse de l'ésotérisme subverti que défend Kelber a de quoi s'appuyer: 1) sur les logia du dévoilement en 4,21-22; 2) sur la définition floue du groupe bénéficiaire du μυστήριον en 4,10; 3) sur la dissolution progressive du prestige des initiés au cours du récit.

54. Un autre procédé littéraire de Marc peut être rangé sous le même dessein narratif: la propension de l'évangéliste à composer des structures brisées. Un exemple: 8,22-33. L'étrange procédure en deux temps dans la restauration de la vue de l'aveugle (8,23-24.25) prend tout son sens dans le dialogue qui suit à Césarée de Philippe, où aux réponses insatisfaisantes des ἄνθρωποι (8,28) succède la confession adéquate de Pierre (8,29); mais la symétrie est aussitôt brisée par les reproches de Pierre et le *retro Satanas* (8,31-33). B. STANDAERT pense à tort que Pierre est renvoyé à la transfiguration pour recevoir la

Ce n'est pourtant pas le dernier mot théologique de l'évangile de Marc. Car tout en planifiant la déconstruction du statut d'initié, le récit raconte comment s'opère malgré tout l'expansion du mystère; il renvoie le lecteur en quête d'exemplarité à des figures volontairement marginales: une femme syro-phénicienne (7,24-30), une foule affamée de parole (6,34; 8,2), un père qui confesse l'incroyance dans la foi (9,24). Sous la croix, ce sera le tour du centurion romain (15,39). Mieux encore: ce sont les disciples faillis que le Ressuscité précède en Galilée. Au long du scénario d'échec court le fil de la grâce.

3. Marc, à n'en pas douter, joue avec le lecteur un jeu plus subtil que Matthieu. Mais où conduit ce jeu de déconstruction des modèles? Quelle conscience veut-il susciter chez le lecteur? Quelle compréhension de l'existence chrétienne est induite par une telle séquence de chutes et de recommencements?

Pour avancer une réponse, il faut se souvenir ici d'une observation faite au début de notre étude: le savoir du lecteur ne s'identifie pas à celui d'une figure du récit, mais résulte d'un cumul de savoirs disséminés au fil du récit. En l'occurrence, et sur le point qui nous intéresse, le lecteur assiste au long du récit à l'effondrement des initiés-disciples. Mais il assiste simultanément à l'incompréhensible fidélité de Jésus à leur égard, le dernier repas à Jérusalem constituant le pinacle de cette fidélité (Mc 14,17-25). Le lecteur n'en reste toutefois pas à cette mise en crise de la connaissance, car à la différence des disciples, il ne s'absente pas de la Passion! Il est fait témoin du spectacle que les disciples ont fui: l'arrestation du maître, son procès injuste, les outrages qui lui sont infligés, sa mort. Comme le dit justement Werner H. Kelber: «En observant ainsi non seulement ce que les disciples pouvaient observer, mais aussi ce qui était hors de leur portée, les lecteurs prennent progressivement le rôle réservé aux disciples. Cela fait passer les lecteurs (...) au rang des nouveaux initiés»[55].

Faut-il en conclure que le lecteur de Marc, convié par le récit à assister à la débâcle des initiés-disciples, se voit doter d'un savoir hiérarchiquement supérieur? Faut-il penser que le lecteur de Marc est fait témoin de l'échec des disciples pour mieux être installé dans un statut de certitude théologique? Nullement. Car le lecteur n'a pas été

révélation christologique définitive (9,4), mais c'est compter sans le retour du motif de l'incompréhension en 9,5.10 (*L'évangile selon Marc* [n. 37], pp. 112-118). Autre exemple: 10,46–11,11. De nombreuses identités verbales rapprochent 10,46-52 de 11,1-11: le chemin (10,46.52; 11,8), μαθηταί (10,46) / δώδεκα (11,11); ἐκάθητο (10,46) / ἐκάθισεν (11,7), κράζειν (10,47.48; 11,9) l'acclamation davidique (10,47-48; 11,10), ἱμάτιον (10,50; 11,8), etc. Or cette structure parallèle, qui culmine dans l'acclamation messianique de 11,10, se solde par une sortie de la ville (11,11) et par la malédiction du figuier (11,12-14). De tels procédés trahissent la volonté du narrateur de différer la clôture du savoir du lecteur.

55. W.H. KELBER, *Récit et révélation* (n. 51), p. 407.

préparé à ce qu'il lui est donné d'assister[56]. C'est une chose que Jésus meure de mort brutale, livré aux mains des Romains, conformément à ce qui avait été prédit (Mc 8,31); c'en est une autre qu'il éprouve en cette mort l'absence de Dieu (Mc 15,34); l'événement déborde la prédiction. Que le Fils de l'homme après trois jours serait arraché à la mort avait été prédit (Mc 8,31; 9,9), mais non que l'épiphanie du Fils serait reconnue par un militaire romain, au creux même de l'absence de Dieu (Mc 15,39). La résurrection avait été annoncée; mais non cette nouvelle d'un Nazaréen déjà parti en Galilée, chassant de peur les femmes loin du tombeau (Mc 16,8).

On constate donc que si le récit donne aux lecteurs un avantage sur les initiés-disciples, le mécanisme narratif du voilement se réduplique pour eux. Au moment où les disciples s'étant absentés, le récit prend en charge les lecteurs, il leur fait subir le même brouillage du savoir qu'à eux[57]. Les lecteurs sont devenus, par la vertu du récit, les témoins privilégiés de l'épiphanie du Fils de Dieu; mais la comprennent-ils? Ou faut-il répéter à leur propos: «Ils ne comprenaient pas cette parole et craignaient de l'interroger» (9,32)?

4. Concluons cette troisième partie consacrée à la relation du croire et du comprendre. Il était apparu dans le chapitre précédent qu'à la différence de Matthieu, la mobilité de Jésus chez Marc constituait un vecteur de sa christologie, et qu'elle trouvait son corrélat dans l'incompréhension des disciples. L'étude de Mc 4, et la stratégie de déconstruction du statut d'initié qui s'ensuit, ont permis de percevoir comment le motif de l'incompréhension est géré narrativement: les disciples ne sont pas déclarés inaptes d'entrée, mais installés dans un statut d'initiés (4,11), dont la narration s'attache inexorablement à ruiner le prestige. Mais la visée de Marc ne culmine pas dans la négation de toute initiation croyante. Au contraire, il s'agit de reconnaître que c'est en retirant tout privilège et tout prestige au statut de croyant que l'évangile de Marc remplit sa fonction d'initiation[58]; une théologie de la grâce

---

56. Avec W.H. KELBER, *Récit et révélation* (n. 51), pp. 408-409.

57. Je me sépare de la conclusion de R.C. TANNEHILL, qui voit dans la confusion progressive des disciples marciens un appel à la repentance du lecteur (*The Disciples in Mark* [n. 14], p. 393: «This tension between identification and repulsion can lead the sensitive reader beyond a naively positive view of himself to self-criticism and repentance»). Il y va plus fondamentalement d'une déconstruction de tout privilège attaché à la situation de disciple; Marc développe une théologie du paradoxe et de la grâce, et non pas une parénèse du repentir. Dans le même sens, voir maintenant: C. FOCANT, *La fonction narrative des doublets dans la section des pains (Mc 6,6b-8,26)*, in *The Four Gospels 1992*. *FS F. Neirynck* (BETL, 100), Leuven, 1992, tome 2, pp. 1039-1063, surtout pp. 1058-1063.

58. Je dois cette précision à une remarque de B. Standaert. Gerald L. BRUNS a consacré une importante recherche au caractère initiatique de la littérature antique: *Inventions. Writing, Textuality and Understanding in Literary History*, New Haven, CT, 1982, cf. pp. 17-43.

habite et gouverne ici la stratégie narrative de l'auteur. Cette observation met en relief le parti inverse pris par l'évangéliste Matthieu; celui-ci abandonne en effet l'orientation marcienne de déconstruction du savoir croyant; il y substitue l'installation du disciple-lecteur dans une appropriation de la connaissance théologique, à laquelle vont servir les grands discours de son évangile.

On peut déjà en déduire que de part et d'autre, le lecteur construit par le texte n'est pas le même. Ou si l'on préfère: le texte de Matthieu et celui de Marc ne sont pas porteurs d'un même projet et n'engendreront pas le même lecteur. À ce stade se pose alors une question qu'il n'est pas illégitime de vouloir résoudre: comment expliquer deux profils de lecteurs aussi divergents? Faut-il se borner à le constater, ou peut-on identifier les raisons de ces différences? De mon point de vue, la recherche des causes doit faire appel à l'histoire; c'est le milieu historique de production du texte qu'il s'agit de solliciter, pour risquer ne fût-ce qu'une hypothèse sur les motivations et les contraintes avec lesquelles travaille chaque évangéliste. Nous le ferons à propos de l'éthique, à laquelle notre dernier développement est consacré.

IV. LA LECTURE DE LA TORAH ET L'OBÉISSANCE

1. Les positions théologiques clairement dissemblables que nourrissent nos deux évangélistes à l'égard de la Torah ont été maintes fois étudiées[59]. Je rappelle succinctement les résultats de la comparaison.

a) Les récits de controverse chez Marc montrent que l'évangéliste n'est pas intéressé à la Torah comme telle, mais à la christologie (2,1-3,6; 12,13-34). Marc s'attache à montrer que les défis lancés par Jésus à la Loi sont des défis libérateurs de l'homme, qu'ils sont immédiatement ressentis comme scandaleux par les gardiens de la Torah (2,6-7) et qu'ils conduisent le libérateur à la mort (3,6). Matthieu en revanche déploie l'autorité de Jésus sur la Torah (5,17-20); c'est l'autorité du didascale eschatologique, qui restaure la volonté originelle du Créateur en recentrant l'interprétation de la Loi sur l'impératif d'amour (5,21-48; 7,12; 22,34-40; 23,23).

b) Partant de ces positions fondamentales, la recomposition de l'éthique chez les deux évangélistes n'ouvrira pas les mêmes perspectives. L'autorité de la Torah comme telle n'est en cause ni d'un côté ni de l'autre. Mais le désaccord entre Jésus et ses adversaires porte chez Marc

---

59. Récemment: U. Luz, in R. SMEND - U. Luz, Gesetz (Biblische Konfrontationen, 1015), Stuttgart, 1981, pp. 86ss, 116-119 (qui note la difficulté de séparer tradition et rédaction dans les traditions marciennes sur la Torah); F. VOUGA, Jésus et la Loi dans la tradition synoptique (Le Monde de la Bible, 17), Genève, 1988.

sur leur utilisation du commandement pour camoufler leur incrédulité devant la révélation: «La Loi comme tradition religieuse est devenue, pour lui, instrument d'obstruction à la volonté de Dieu»[60]. Chez Matthieu, le désaccord porte sur une lecture erronée de la Loi, à laquelle l'évangile oppose et superpose une herméneutique nouvelle de la Torah. La recomposition matthéenne des controverses sur le sabbat (12,1-14) et la séquence des antithèses (5,21-48) sont symptomatiques d'une volonté de fonder une *halakah* chrétienne, qui vise à codifier le comportement chrétien en fonction d'une lecture rectifiée de la Torah; l'évangile de Matthieu ne développe pas encore de casuistique, à mon sens, mais il en prépare la venue[61]. Qu'en est-il du lecteur de Marc? Ce lecteur n'est assurément pas préparé à recevoir une *halakah*, ni un débat sur la Loi. Quel critère reçoit-il pour décider d'observer ou non le repos sabbatique, sinon que «le sabbat a été fait pour l'homme et non l'homme pour le sabbat» (2,27)? Il s'agit pour lui, sans garantie, de «discerner en chaque situation concrète la volonté concrète et précise de Dieu, en vue de quoi le 4e commandement ne fournit aucune indication ou directive, positive ou négative»[62]. L'évangile de Marc ne vise pas à construire une éthique positive, mais à montrer comment Jésus met fin au jeu sacrilège des scribes avec la parole de Dieu.

2. Cette rapide typologie des programmes éthiques de Matthieu et de Marc ne contredit pas le tableau que nous avons élaboré jusqu'à maintenant; elle s'y intègre même remarquablement. Au demeurant, la fonction différenciée octroyée à la Torah reflète la position respective de ces deux évangiles dans la géographie des christianismes primitifs.

La rédaction de l'évangile de Marc dans les années 60, à Rome ou à Antioche, s'opère à distance du judaïsme; ni proximité, ni conflit[63]. L'auteur s'adresse à une chrétienté forte de son héritage, qui a intégré la tradition judéo-chrétienne dans le patrimoine hellénistique. La rédaction du premier évangile, quinze ans plus tard, s'exerce en de tout autres conditions: la communauté matthéenne vient d'être expulsée de la Synagogue, dans le cadre du repli juif sur l'orthodoxie pharisienne-rabbinique qui suit la disparition du Temple; les rapports christianisme-judaïsme ont tourné à la rivalité de frères ennemis. L'extrême violence à l'encontre d'Israël, qui parcourt cet évangile de part en part, est un

---

60. F. VOUGA, *Jésus et la Loi* (n. 59), p. 175.

61. Cette position a été argumentée, à partir de Mt 5,21-26, dans D. MARGUERAT, *Le jugement dans l'Évangile de Matthieu* (n. 43), pp. 142-167. Autre point de vue: F. VOUGA, *Jésus et la Loi* (n. 59), pp. 191-213.

62. C. SENFT, *L'évangile selon Marc* (n. 39), p. 37.

63. D. LÜHRMANN précise que l'information de Marc sur le judaïsme est bonne lorsque ses sources la lui fournissent; lorsqu'il doit la compléter par des moyens rédactionnels, des lacunes apparaissent, et pas seulement dans les données topographiques (*Das Markus-evangelium* [HNT, 3], Tübingen, 1987, p. 6).

indicateur irréfutable à la fois de l'intensité du conflit et de l'indicible fragilité de la chrétienté matthéenne dans cet affrontement[64].

On ne s'étonnera pas que, de conditions de production aussi dissemblables, soient nés des projets théologiques aussi dissemblables que ceux de Marc et de Matthieu. Le lecteur que Matthieu a à l'esprit appartient à une chrétienté fragilisée, en pleine crise identitaire, expulsée de son héritage vétérotestamentaire, contestée dans son droit à revendiquer la Torah; Matthieu cherche à réhabiliter le lecteur en construisant une identité qui lui assure son droit face à Israël (5,20.48; 21,43). Le lecteur que vise l'évangile de Marc vit d'une tout autre appartenance confessionnelle; il relève d'une chrétienté qui a affiché son Seigneur au panthéon des θεῖοι ἄνδρες[65]; le débat avec le judaïsme sur la messianité de Jésus est dépassé; les gestes libérateurs de Jésus ont anéanti la Loi de pureté (7,14-23); une interprétation libérale de la Torah suffit à guider l'éthique. Marc cherche à déconstruire cette position trop forte, dont la sécurité religieuse lui rappelle celle des pharisiens (cf 4,11-12 et 8,18); il la démantèle à l'aide d'une théologie de la croix et d'une christologie du secret.

V. Conclusion

L'hypothèse posée au départ de la recherche était que la façon dont se nouent les rapports entre personnages au plan du récit évangélique (et spécifiquement les rapports avec Jésus) vise un effet pragmatique sur le lecteur. Une première démarche a permis d'établir une homologie entre l'itinérance de Jésus dans l'évangile de Marc et la christologie du secret: celle-ci trouve dans la mobilité de Jésus sa configuration narrative, dans l'exacte mesure où l'une et l'autre soustraient le Christ à l'emprise de ses interlocuteurs. Une seconde démarche a fait voir comment l'évangéliste Marc, au travers du dispositif des personnages, construit le poste du lecteur: à la différence de Matthieu, la narration marcienne identifie les disciples avec le groupe d'initiés, pour organiser ensuite à l'intention du lecteur la déconstruction du statut d'initié. En troisième lieu, à l'occasion d'une comparaison des programmes éthiques de Marc et de Matthieu, la position respective de chaque évangéliste s'est avérée éclairante pour comprendre quel profil de lecteur chacun entend promouvoir.

---

64. Voir D. MARGUERAT, *Le jugement dans l'Évangile de Matthieu* (n. 43), pp. 378-407; U. LUZ, *L'évangéliste Matthieu: un judéo-chrétien à la croisée des chemins. Réflexions sur le plan narratif du premier évangile*, in D. MARGUERAT – J. ZUMSTEIN (éd.), *La mémoire et le temps. Mélanges offerts à Pierre Bonnard* (Le Monde de la Bible, 23), Genève, 1991, pp. 77-92, surtout pp. 84-88.

65. Voir D.-A. KOCH, *Die Bedeutung der Wundererzählungen für die Christologie des Markusevangeliums* (BZNW, 42), Berlin, 1975.

Le lecteur que construit l'évangile de Marc reçoit au premier verset du livre une primauté de savoir christologique, qui le conditionne à identifier Jésus avec le Fils de Dieu: «Commencement de l'Évangile de Jésus-Christ Fils de Dieu» (1,1). Mais la stratégie narrative de l'auteur fait du récit tout autre chose qu'une quête progressivement assouvie de cette identité; elle problématise tout savoir sur Jésus et déconstruit le modèle auquel le lecteur s'est identifié. La clef est donnée au chapitre 4: la parole ne se laisse saisir que par celui qui remet en cause sa compréhension. Tout se passe comme si, à donner au premier verset la «réponse» sur l'identité de Jésus, l'évangéliste avait besoin de tout son récit pour faire résonner la question: qui est celui-ci? Peut-être faut-il prendre au pied de la lettre le premier mot de l'évangile: ἀρχή (1,1). Le lecteur de Marc apprend que s'installer dans le savoir est le contraire de l'Évangile. Il faut sans cesse se risquer à commencer[66].

L'évangile de Matthieu fait méthodiquement découvrir à son lecteur que le prophète a dit vrai: le Fils est l'Emmanuel, Dieu avec nous (1,23; 28,20); il l'est par le geste et la parole. Pour en bénéficier, il faut s'identifier au μαθητής, dont la condition n'est pas idéalisée (échec, persécution et menaces la frappent); mais la condition du disciple-lecteur est surplombée par l'assistance du Messie d'Israël et par l'enseignement structurant du Maître de la Loi. Le langage est de renforcement.

De part et d'autre, assurément, l'Évangile ne construit pas le même lecteur.

Avenue Dauvel 9   Daniel MARGUERAT
CH-1004 Lausanne

---

66. «Le récit est alors tout entier un lieu de renvoi: le message de résurrection, avec le rendez-vous en Galilée, renvoie au début de l'Évangile, là où Jésus paraît en Galilée et appelle ses disciples à le suivre. Il renvoie à la lecture toujours à recommencer de l'Évangile. Il refait commencer la bonne nouvelle» (C. COMBET-GALLAND, *Qui roulera la peur* [n. 15], p. 188).

THE SIGNIFICANCE OF THE CROSS WITHIN THE PLOT
OF MATTHEW'S GOSPEL

A STUDY IN NARRATIVE CRITICISM

Generically, whatever else Matthew's Gospel may be, it is a narrative with a beginning, middle, and end[1]. This narrative tells the story of Jesus, from conception and birth to death and resurrection. The story of Jesus is one of conflict, so that its plot turns on conflict. At the human level, this conflict is between Jesus and Israel, and especially between Jesus and the religious authorities[2]. The fundamental resolution of this conflict comes at the end of the story, in the pericopes that tell of Jesus' death and resurrection. In point of fact, the "cross" is the place where Matthew's story of Jesus reaches its culmination. The purpose of this article is to trace the unfolding of the plot of Matthew's gospel-story and, in so doing, to show how and to what effect Jesus' conflict with the authorities reaches its resolution in the cross and resurrection and its culmination in the cross.

I

In the beginning of his story (1,1–4,16), Matthew introduces the reader to both Jesus, the protagonist, and the religious authorities, Jesus' antagonists. In the pericopes that tell of Jesus' origin and baptism (1,18-25; 3,13-17), Matthew describes Jesus as the Messiah, the Son of God, whose God-given mission is to save his people from their sins. In describing Jesus as the Messiah, Matthew presents him as the Anointed One, Israel's long awaited King. In describing Jesus as the

---

1. For a discussion of the structure of Matthew's Gospel, cf. J.D. KINGSBURY, *Matthew: Structure, Christology, Kingdom*, Minneapolis, MN, Fortress, ²1989, pp. 1-39. For the most thorough exploration of this topic to date, cf. D.R. BAUER, *The Structure of Matthew's Gospel: A Study in Literary Design* (Bible and Literature Series, 15), Sheffield, Almond Press, 1988. For F. NEIRYNCK's view of the structure of Matthew, cf. *AΠO TOTE HPΞATO and the Structure of Matthew*, in *ETL* 64 (1988) 21-59 (= *Evangelica II*, pp. 141-179, 180-182), and for my response, cf. KINGSBURY, *Matthew: Structure, Christology, Kingdom*, pp. XVI-XX.

2. For an approach to the overall plot of Matthew's gospel-story that views the conflict between God and Satan as constituting the main plot and the conflict between Jesus and the religious authorities as a subplot, cf. M.A. POWELL, *The Plot and Subplots of Matthew's Gospel*, in *NTS* 38 (1992) 198-202. For yet another approach to the plot of Matthew, cf. F.J. MATERA, *The Plot of Matthew's Gospel*, in *CBQ* 49 (1987) 233-253.

Son of God, Matthew ascribes to him a unique filial relationship with God. By virtue of this relationship, Jesus is the wholly obedient, supreme agent of God, whom he designates as Father (4,1-11; 26,39), and God is the one who is authoritatively and decisively at work in Jesus to save (1,23; 3,17).

Without so much as permitting the religious authorities to come into contact with Jesus, Matthew also introduces them in the beginning of his story. Still, in the first pericope in which they appear – in the persons of the chief priests and the scribes of the people (2,1-6) – Matthew invites the reader to distance himself or herself from them by depicting them as standing in the service of wicked King Herod. Herod, eager to know where the Messiah is to be born, calls the chief priests and the scribes together and asks them. In ready reply, they inform Herod that Bethlehem is the place. By thus assisting Herod, the chief priests and the scribes make themselves complicit in Herod's unsuccessful plot to kill Jesus. In so doing, they signal the reader that, later in the story, they will prove themselves to be deadly opponents of Jesus.

It is, however, in the scene in which the religious authorities make their major debut that Matthew reveals unmistakably how he would have them understood in his story. This scene occurs in the pericope on the ministry of John the Baptist (3,7-10), and those representing the religious authorities are the Pharisees and Sadducees (3,7). Seeing the latter coming to him for baptism, John, the forerunner of Jesus, greets them with a scathing epithet: "Brood of vipers!" he calls them (3,7). What "brood of vipers" means becomes clear at a later point in Matthew's story. At 12,34 Jesus, addressing the Pharisees, exclaims, "Brood of vipers! How can you speak good when you are evil?" As Jesus' words indicate, John, in calling the Pharisees and Sadducees a "brood of vipers", describes them – and indeed the religious authorities as a whole[3] – as "evil". In Matthew's purview, "evil" is the "root trait" that characterizes the religious authorities; it is the trait from which such other traits as being "hypocritical"[4], "spiritually blind"[5], and "conspiratorial"[6] spring[7].

From what we have said thus far, it is apparent that Matthew, in introducing Jesus and the religious authorities to the reader, character-

3. On treating the religious authorities as a single character, cf. J.D. KINGSBURY, *Matthew as Story*, Philadelphia, PA, Fortress, ²1988, pp. 17-18.

4. Cf., e.g., Matt 23,13.15.23.25.27.29.

5. Cf., e.g., Matt 15,14; 23,16-22.24.26.

6. Cf., e.g., Matt 12,14; 26,3-4; 27,1.

7. Concerning the way in which Matthew characterizes such persons or groups of persons as Jesus, the disciples, the religious leaders, the crowds, and minor characters, cf. KINGSBURY, *Matthew as Story* (n. 3), pp. 9-28. For an extensive treatment of the religious leaders in Matthew's Gospel, cf. M.A. POWELL, *The Religious Leaders in Matthew's Gospel: A Literary-Critical Approach*, Ph.D. dissertation, Union Theological Seminary in Virginia, 1984.

izes them in starkly contrasting terms. On the one hand, we have Jesus. Jesus stands forth as the Messiah, the Son of God, the one who enjoys a unique filial relationship with God and serves God in perfect obedience. Jesus, therefore, is "righteous" (27,19; also 27,4.24). On the other hand, we have the religious authorities, who are Jesus' antagonists. Through the words of John the Baptist and Jesus, Matthew characterizes them as "evil". As such, they are "like Satan", whom Matthew describes as the "Evil One" (13,38). As is obvious, therefore, Matthew works in *stereotypes*. For him, there is no middle ground: Whereas Jesus is "righteous", the religious authorities are "evil". By so contrasting Jesus and the religious authorities, Matthew leads the reader to anticipate that, sooner or later, Jesus and the authorities will become entangled in bitter conflict.

Jesus first clashes with the religious authorities in the middle of Matthew's story. Still, to understand how the ongoing conflict between Jesus and the authorities evolves, we need to keep ourselves apprised of the movement of the story. Matthew divides the middle (4,17–16,20) into two parts. In the first part (4,17–11,1), he tells of Jesus' proffering salvation to Israel through a ministry of teaching, preaching, and healing (4,23; 9,35; 11,1). In the second part (11,2–16,20), he tells of Israel's response to Jesus' ministry, which is that of repudiation. Because in the first part the motif of Jesus' proffering salvation to Israel is the leitmotif that governs the story, so in this part Matthew subordinates the motif of conflict to the motif of Jesus' proffering salvation. The upshot is that as conflict erupts between Jesus and the authorities in this first part of the middle of Matthew's story (4,17–11,1), such conflict is "preliminary" in nature and foreshadows the more intense conflict that will soon follow.

Chapter 9 is the point at which Jesus and the religious authorities first stand opposite one another. Virtually at once, conflict breaks out and persists through a cycle of four controversies (9,1-8.9-13.14-17.32-34). As was just noted, however, this conflict is "preliminary" in nature, and Matthew signals this, albeit in retrospect, by avoiding all reference in chapter 9 to three features that generally distinguish Jesus' later conflict with the authorities.

The first feature to which Matthew does not refer in chapter 9 is the main one and has to do with the tone on which this cycle of four controversies ends. At the close of the final controversy (9,34), it is striking that Matthew says nary a word to the effect that the religious authorities conspire to destroy Jesus[8]. The absence of such a narrative

8. How different this is in Mark's gospel-story! At the end of Jesus' first cycle of controversies, Mark reports, "The Pharisees when out, and immediately held counsel with the Herodians against him, how to destroy him" (Mark 3,6).

remark reveals that Matthew, in chapter 9, has not yet invited the reader to look upon Jesus' conflict with the authorities as "to the death".

The second feature one does not find in chapter 9 is that none of the controversies proves to be "acutely confrontational" in nature; that is to say, in none of them is Jesus himself challenged because of something that he himself says or does. To illustrate this, consider these controversies. In 9,1-8, some men bring to Jesus a paralytic. Perceiving their faith, Jesus forgives the paralytic his sins. Witnessing this, some scribes standing there take umbrage at Jesus' act and charge him with committing blasphemy against God for having arrogated to himself the divine authority to forgive sins. In raising their charge, however, the scribes do not approach Jesus himself. Instead, they utter their charge "in their hearts", so that Jesus must read their thoughts in order to refute their charge.

In 9,9-13 Jesus, together with his disciples, reclines at table with many toll-collectors and sinners. Observing this, the Pharisees take offense, for in having table fellowship with outcasts such as these, Jesus, in their view, defiles himself. Despite their enormous displeasure, however, the Pharisees do not assail Jesus himself for his behavior. Instead, they go to the disciples and take them to task: "Why does your teacher", they demand to know, "eat with toll-collectors and sinners"?

In 9,14-17, the disciples of John, who on this occasion side with the Pharisees, insist on knowing why the disciples of Jesus do not fast, as custom dictates. In this instance, the disciples of John do indeed approach Jesus and it is to him that they put their question. Regardless, the question they ask pertains not to Jesus, but exclusively to the disciples: "Why ... do your disciples not fast"?

Last, in 9,32-34 the Pharisees, having looked on as Jesus exorcises a demon, charge, either to the crowds[9] or, more likely, merely to themselves[10], that "by the prince of demons he [Jesus] casts out demons". Once again, therefore, Matthew pictures Jesus' opponents as attacking him, but not to his face.

The third feature that is conspicuous by its absence from chapter 9 is that none of the issues that provoke the authorities (or, in one instance, the disciples of John) to take exception to acts of Jesus touches on the Mosaic law as such, to wit: forgiving sins and then demonstrating through the performance of a miracle that God has given him authority to forgive (9,1-8); having table fellowship with toll-collectors and sinners (9,11); temporarily suspending as far as the disciples are concerned the obligation to fast as dictated by prevailing piety (9,14); and

9. Cf. Matt 9,33.
10. Cf. Matt 12,24-25a.

exorcising a demon (9,32-34). Now it is true, of course, that not every matter, to be "utterly serious" within the world of Matthew's story, must have to do with the Mosaic law. After all, for forgiving sins and affirming that he is the Son of God, Jesus incurs the potentially capital charge of blasphemy (9,3; 26,63-66). But this notwithstanding, it is a mark of the enormous importance that Matthew attaches to the Mosaic law that he does not declare that the religious authorities are bent on killing Jesus until the conflict between Jesus and them has shifted to focus on a precept of the Mosaic law, as we shall see in a moment.

Accordingly, if one reviews the four controversies that Jesus has with the religious authorities in chapter 9, one discovers that they are not yet "to the death", that not one of them is "acutely confrontational" in nature, and that their focus is not on Mosaic law. In broader perspective, these insights corroborate the point we made at the outset of this discussion: In chapter 9, the conflict between Jesus and the religious authorities is yet "preliminary" to the more intense conflict still to take place.

This more intense conflict is not long in coming. Specifically, it occurs in the second part of the middle of Matthew's story (11,2–16,20). We recall that in the first part of the middle (4,17–11,1), the leitmotif that controls the action is that of Jesus' proffering salvation to Israel. In line with this, Matthew subordinated the motif of conflict to the leitmotif of Jesus' proffering salvation by depicting the conflict between Jesus and the religious authorities as "preliminary" in nature. Here in the second part of the middle, the leitmotif controlling the story focuses on Israel's response to Jesus' ministry; Israel, in fact, repudiates Jesus[11]. Because in this part the motif of conflict has now become part and parcel of the leitmotif of Israel's repudiating Jesus, Matthew as a matter of course shapes Jesus' conflict with the authorities so that it becomes noticeably more intense.

In chapter 12, Jesus once again clashes with the religious authorities. Unlike earlier conflict, the immediate issue that sparks debate is the Mosaic law itself: breaking the divine command to rest on the sabbath (12,1-8.9-14)[12]. In the two controversies at hand, one discovers that there is clear progression as one moves from the first one to the second in terms of how acutely confrontational each is. In the first controversy (12,1-8), the Pharisees confront Jesus, but the charge they make has to do not with him but with the disciples: "Behold, your disciples are doing what is not lawful to do on the sabbath!" In the second controversy (12,9-14), the Pharisees again confront Jesus. This time, however – and, in fact, for the first time in Matthew's story – the

---

11. On this point, cf. KINGSBURY, *Matthew as Story* (n. 3), pp. 72-74.
12. Cf. Exod 20,8-11; Deut 5,12-15.

accusation they make in the question they raise concerns an act that they anticipate Jesus himself is about to perform: If Jesus heals a man with a withered hand on the sabbath who is not in danger of dying, he will have violated Moses' command that enjoins rest (12,10). In the case of both these controversies, Jesus rebuts the Pharisees by asserting that attending to human need in these instances is not only not unlawful but is necessitated by God's will that mercy be shown or that good be done (12,3-8.11-12). In direct response to Jesus' setting himself against the law of Moses as they interpret it, the Pharisees now do what they hitherto have not done: They go out and take counsel against Jesus, how to destroy him (12,14). With this sharp turn of events, Matthew's story has arrived at that juncture where the conflict between Jesus and the religious authorities has intensified to the point where it has become "mortal". Indeed, it is a mark of Jesus' conflict with the authorities throughout the rest of Matthew's story that this conflict does remain mortal, and the observation that Jesus "withdraws" in the face of the conspiracy to destroy him (12,15) only corroborates this.

Later in chapter 12, Jesus again confronts the religious authorities and again the note that his controversies with them sounds is shrill. In 12,22-37, Jesus exorcises a demon from a man who is blind and dumb so that the man sees and speaks. Whereas Jesus' miracle amazes the crowds and prompts them to wonder whether he could perhaps be the Son of David, the Pharisees, on overhearing the crowds, reiterate to themselves the very charge they earlier leveled against Jesus (9,34): They insist that he casts out demons not on the authority of God but on the authority of Satan (12,24). Discerning their thoughts (12,25), Jesus minces no words in responding to them: He accuses the Pharisees of being agents of Satan (12,27); he contends that their vilification of him is tantamount to committing blasphemy against God (12,30-32); and he asserts that their charge springs from hearts that are evil (12,33-37).

In 12,38-45, the conflict is no less intense. In this controversy, some scribes and Pharisees accost Jesus and demand that he show them a sign. In demanding a sign, the scribes and Pharisees have in mind that Jesus should predict a miracle that God will subsequently perform and thus prove that he acts not on the authority of Satan but on the authority of God. Attacking the scribes and Pharisees, Jesus castigates them as an "evil and adulterous generation" (12,39), that is to say, as persons who are "like Satan" and "faithless to God".

Accordingly, as the second part of the middle of Matthew's story draws to a close (11,2-16,20), the reader is keenly aware that the conflict between Jesus and the religious authorities is beyond reconciliation. Each time Jesus and the authorities meet in controversy, the impression reinforces itself in the mind of the reader that their struggle is henceforth a struggle "to the death".

From the middle of Matthew's story we turn to the end (16,21–28,20). Here Matthew tells of Jesus' journey to Jerusalem and of his suffering, death, and resurrection (16,21). So that the reader knows that Jesus' journey to Jerusalem and his passion do indeed constitute the leitmotif guiding the end of the story, Matthew punctuates the latter with three passion-predictions (16,21; 17,22-23; 20,17-19); moreover, at the outset of the passion narrative Jesus reminds the disciples of these predictions (26,2). Because the motif of conflict is integral to the motif of going up to Jerusalem to suffer and die, the reader can be certain that Jesus' conflict with the authorities in Jerusalem will in no wise diminish in its ferocity.

On his way to Jerusalem, Jesus teaches the disciples. In fact, only once does he clash with religious authorities. In 19,3-12, Pharisees confront Jesus to put him to the test on the matter of divorce. In return, Jesus puts the Pharisees to shame, lecturing them on the attitude toward divorce taught by scripture. Yet, as Matthew reveals in the final verses of this controversy (19,10-12), the purpose the latter serves has relatively little to do with Jesus' larger conflict with the authorities. Instead, Jesus uses this controversy to instruct the disciples on divorce. The upshot is that it is not until after Jesus has arrived in Jerusalem that he has his last great confrontation with the authorities prior to his passion (21,12–22,46).

We recall that Matthew, in the middle of his story (4,17–16,20), depicted the conflict between Jesus and the religious authorities as gradually intensifying: In the first part of the middle (4,17–11,1), this conflict had a "preliminary" quality about it (chap. 9); in the second part of the middle (11,2–16,20), it intensified to the point where it became a struggle "to the death" (chap. 12). Here in the end of the story, Jesus has now entered Jerusalem (21,1-11). Although the conflict he has had with the authorities has already been "to the death", Matthew nonetheless makes use of some five literary devices to indicate that the conflict Jesus has in Jerusalem (21,12–22,46) is of still greater intensity.

The first such device Matthew uses is the setting in which he places all of Jesus' controversies in Jerusalem. This setting is the temple (21,12.23), and the reason it heightens still more the intensity of Jesus' conflict with the authorities is that the temple is both the place of God's presence – God, whom Jesus calls Father – and the seat of the authorities' power. It is from the temple out that the authorities rule the land of the Jews. For Jesus to defeat the authorities in debate in the temple is for him to defeat them at the very center of their power and privilege.

The second device Matthew employs to show that Jesus' conflict in Jerusalem is of still greater intensity is the "acutely confrontational" tone with which he imbues each controversy. In each case, it is none but Jesus whom the authorities attack, and their constant aim is either to call him to account for something that he himself has said or done or simply to get the best of him in debate (21,15.23; 22,16-17.23-28.35-36). In the final controversy, however, Matthew reverses the roles so that Jesus seizes the initiative and puts the Pharisees on the spot (22,41-46).

The third device Matthew uses to heighten still further the intensity of Jesus' conflict in Jerusalem is to arrange for all the controversies between him and the religious authorities to revolve around the critical question of "authority": the authority by which Jesus cleanses the temple (21,23), discharges his ministry (21,23), and interprets scripture and the law (22,17.24.36.43-45). The importance of this issue of authority, of course, is that it underlies the whole of Jesus' conflict with the authorities and goes to the heart of whether Jesus is to be received as the supreme agent of God or repudiated as a fraud and agent of Satan (27,63).

The fourth device by which Matthew intensifies still further the conflict between Jesus and the religious authorities in Jerusalem is his depiction of all the groups that together make up the united front of the authorities as clashing with Jesus over a span of less than two days (21,12-17; 21,23–22,46): the chief priests, the scribes, the elders of the people, the disciples of the Pharisees, the Herodians, the Sadducees, a Pharisaic lawyer, and the Pharisees (21,15.23; 22,16.23.34-35.41). The effect that this parade of opponents over a short span of time has is that it not only enables the reader to look on as the respective groups or combinations of groups take their turn at trying to defeat Jesus in debate, but it also conveys the impression of "unceasing", and therefore highly intense, conflict.

Finally, the fifth device by which Matthew heightens still further the intensity of Jesus' conflict in Jerusalem is his characterization of the atmosphere in which this conflict takes place as being extremely hostile. To illustrate, Matthew reports, following Jesus' narration of the parable of the vineyard (21,33-46), that the chief priests and the Pharisees become so incensed at hearing Jesus' parable that they want to arrest him immediately and only hold back for fear of the crowds (21,45-46). Short of the passion narrative, this is the sole place in Matthew's story where the authorities are actually said to want to seize Jesus.

On what note does Matthew bring this last great confrontation between Jesus and the religious authorities in Jerusalem and prior to the passion to a close? Matthew states this pointedly at 22,46, where he declares: "And no one was able to answer him [Jesus] a word nor from that day did any one dare to ask him any more questions". Jesus reduces all of the authorities to silence. Reduced to silence, the authorities fade from the scene until Matthew has begun the passion narrative.

In the opening verses of the passion narrative (chaps. 26–28), Matthew is at pains to inform the reader that, on the human level, it is the religious authorities who are squarely responsible for Jesus' death (26,3-4). At the palace of the high priest Caiaphas, the chief priests and the elders make their plans to have Jesus arrested and killed by deceit. This strategy on the part of the authorities to act with deceit shows that, during the passion, "being deceptive" is the character trait that they exhibit most.

For our purposes, the scene that is of greatest importance in Matthew's passion narrative is the last scene in which the religious authorities confront the earthly Jesus (27,41-43). In this scene, the members of the Sanhedrin look up at Jesus on the cross and mock him on three counts. They mock him because although he demonstrated such astonishing authority in the course of his ministry to heal and to save others, here on the cross he does not even possess the power to save himself. They mock him as the King of Israel, as the king whose kingship is fraudulent because he cannot even get himself down from the cross. And they mock him as the Son of God, as the one who allegedly enjoys a unique filial relationship with God and yet God, in this, Jesus' greatest hour of need, does nothing to deliver him from death. In other words, as the authorities look up at Jesus on the cross, they see him as a fraud[13] who is stripped of all authority, they see the cross as the sign of his destruction, and they see themselves as having won the victory in their conflict with him.

Ironically, however, what the religious authorities do not perceive is that God and Jesus, too, will the death of Jesus. Jesus wills his own death because he is the perfectly obedient Son of God. God wills Jesus' death because, through it, he will renew his covenant and proffer all humans everywhere the forgiveness of sins and salvation (1,23; 20,28; 26,28). To demonstrate that Jesus' death is in line with his saving purposes, God raises Jesus from the dead on the third day (28,5-6)[14]. In raising Jesus, God both vindicates him and exalts him. The upshot is that this same Jesus whom the religious authorities see as stripped of all authority is, in fact, entrusted by God with all authority in heaven and on earth (28,18). In combination, therefore, the events of the cross and resurrection mark the places in Matthew's story where the principal conflict among humans in this story, that between Jesus and the religious authorities, comes to fundamental "resolution".

True as this is, the cross itself is nevertheless the place where Matthew's story reaches its "culmination". From the standpoint of the religious authorities, the cross attests to Jesus' destruction and their victory. From the standpoint of Matthew and of the reader, however,

13. Cf. Matt 27,63.
14. Cf. also Matt 16,21; 17,23; 20,19.

the cross stands as a sign of the victory Jesus has won. By the twist of irony, therefore, the cross attests, not to the destruction of Jesus, but to the salvation that God henceforth proffers through Jesus to all humankind.

In retrospect, we have now seen how the plot of Matthew's story of Jesus unfolds. This plot is one of conflict, and this conflict, at the human level, is above all between Jesus and the religious authorities. As Matthew's story progresses, Jesus' conflict with the authorities becomes ever more intense until, at the last, it finds its fundamental "resolution" – in favor of Jesus – in his cross and resurrection. By the same token, it is in Jesus' cross that Matthew's story reaches its "culmination", for the cross becomes the place where God in Jesus accomplishes universal salvation. To announce this salvation is one purpose for which Matthew tells his story. In addition, Matthew is concerned to show that despite his conflict with Israel and especially the authorities, Jesus does not turn his back on them. At the close of the story, the risen Jesus commissions the disciples to go and make of all nations his disciples. To be sure, the expression "all nations"[15] includes the gentiles; besides them, however, it also includes the people and the leaders of Israel. Although during his earthly ministry the leaders were Jesus' inveterate enemies and Matthew himself seems doubtful that they will ever turn to Jesus, the risen Jesus would nonetheless also have them become his disciples. It is on this saving note that the reader exits from Matthew's story.

II

Thus far, I have been tracing the unfolding of the plot of Matthew's gospel-story. In so doing, I have made several major assertions three of which, it will be recalled, are the following: I have asserted, respectively, that Matthew presents Jesus as the Messiah Son of God (1,18-25; 3,13-17), that Jesus' mission is to save his people from their sins (1,21), and that the "cross" of Jesus is the place where Matthew's story reaches its culmination. If these three assertions are correct, then we can anticipate that in the pericope of Jesus on the cross (27,38-54), Matthew will deal prominently with the two themes of "salvation" and Jesus as the "Son of God". It is, then, in terms of these two themes that I should now like to examine this pericope.

This pericope may be divided into two parts: 27,38-44; and 27,45-54.

15. For a study of this expression, cf., e.g., J.P. MEIER, *Nations or Gentiles in Matthew 28:19?*, in *CBQ* 39 (1977) 94-102.

Each of these parts contains an introduction and three scenes. In the first part (27,38-44), the introduction tells of Jesus' being crucified between two revolutionaries (or robbers)[16]; and the three scenes depict the acts of mockery perpetrated against Jesus by, respectively, the passers-by, or people[17], the members of the Sanhedrin, who are representative of the religious authorities (27,41-43), and the two revolutionaries who have been crucified with Jesus (27,44). In the second part (27,45-54), the introduction describes the darkness that envelops the entire region from the sixth to the ninth hours (27,45); and the three scenes tell, respectively, of the two cries of Jesus and of his death (27,46-50), of the supernatural portents God causes to occur (27,51-53), and of the confession of Jesus made by the centurion and the Roman soldiers with him (27,54). To repeat, 27,38-54 is made up of two parts, each of which contains an introduction and three scenes.

The theme of "salvation" stands out prominently in both parts of this pericope. In the three scenes of the first part (27,38-44), Jesus is challenged three times to save himself by coming down from the cross: by the passers-by (27,40), the members of the Sanhedrin (27,42), and the revolutionaries[18] crucified with him (27,44). Jesus, in turn, reacts to none of these challenges. The massive clue Matthew provides as to why Jesus does not react can be found in the words of the passers-by: "... save yourself, if you are the Son of God, and come down from the cross!" (27,40). The expression the passers-by use, "... if you are the Son of God", calls the temptation account to mind. Here Satan approaches Jesus and says, for example, "If you are the Son of God, command that these stones become loaves" (4,3). Accordingly, just as Jesus, in the temptation account, is put to the test by Satan, so Jesus, as he hangs on the cross, is put to the test by the passers-by, the members of the Sanhedrin, and the revolutionaries. Whereas the latter groups or individuals put Jesus to the test by challenging him, Jesus resists their challenges, for he is the Son who knows and does the Father's will (4,1-13; 27,38-44). Moreover, in that Jesus resists these challenges, he shows that he keeps his own counsel. At 16,25, Jesus declared to the disciples, "For those who want to save their life will lose it" (NRSV; cf. also

---

16. Cf., e.g., W. BAUER – W.F. ARNDT – F.W. GINGRICH – F.W. DANKER, *A Greek-English Lexicon of the New Testament and Other Early Christian Literature*, Chicago, IL, University of Chicago Press, ²1979, p. 473.

17. That the "passers-by" are representative of the Jewish people can be discerned from the flow of the narrative (cf. 27,39-40 with 27,20.24-25).

18. That the revolutionaries crucified with Jesus do as the others and also challenge Jesus to save himself by coming down from the cross is indicated by the expression τὸ δ' αὐτό ("in the same way"; cf. *A Greek-English Lexicon* [n. 16], p. 123) in 27,44. Accordingly, the revolutionaries crucified with Jesus revile him "in the same way" as the passers-by and the members of the Sanhedrin do, namely, by challenging him to save himself through descent from the cross.

26,39.42). Jesus makes no effort to save his own life. As a result, he demonstrates that, even in his own case, salvation is not of oneself!

The theme of salvation also stands out prominently in the second part of this pericope (27,45-54). At the ninth hour, after darkness has covered the entire region from the sixth hour, Jesus cries out, "Eli, Eli, lema sabachthani?" (27,46). When certain persons standing at the foot of the cross, who apparently are Jews, hear this, they exclaim, "This one calls Elijah!" (27,47). Quickly, one of them runs and gets a sponge, fills it with wine vinegar and places it on a reed, and tries to give Jesus to drink[19] (27,48). The others shout, "Let us see if Elijah comes to save him" (27,49).

The notion that Elijah might come to save Jesus stems from the Old Testament account of Elijah's having been taken up by a whirlwind into heaven (2 Kings 2,11). Because Elijah was said to have been translated into heaven without seeing death, Jewish expectation attached itself to his person. One strand of this expectation was the notion that although Elijah enjoyed the bliss of heaven, he could nevertheless return to earth and, for example, rescue the righteous person who was innocently suffering[20]. It is seemingly with a view to this notion that Matthew reports concerning certain persons at the foot of the cross that they, hearing Jesus utter the words Eli, Eli, understand him to be appealing to Elijah to save him from death[21]. Moreover, upon hearing Jesus' cry, one of these persons hastens to offer Jesus wine vinegar to drink; apparently, his intention is to refresh[22] and strengthen Jesus so that, in the event Elijah reaches Jesus in time, he and his compatriots can perhaps witness a spectacular act of deliverance. One sees, therefore, that despite the fact that wine vinegar was a refreshing drink, the act of offering it to Jesus is nonetheless to be construed as an act of mockery and hostility (Ps 69,21).

As the reader observes these persons beneath the cross waiting to see whether Elijah will come to save Jesus, it is clear from Matthew's story that Elijah will not come. One reason Elijah will not come is that Matthew has already shown that the figure who fulfills the eschatological expectations associated with Elijah is John the Baptist (11,14; 17,13), and John is now dead (14,1-12). And the second reason Elijah will not come is that Jesus, in crying out, "Eli, Eli", was not appealing

19. As is apparent, I take the verb ἐπότιζεν in 27,48 to be a conative imperfect (cf., e.g., H.E. DANA – J.R. MANTEY, *A Manual Grammar of the Greek New Testament*, New York, NY, Macmillan, [14]1966, p. 189.

20. Cf., e.g., J.T. WALSH, *Elijah*, in D.N. FREEDMAN (ed.), *The Anchor Bible Dictionary*, New York, NY, Doubleday, 1992, II, p. 465.

21. *Ibid.*

22 Concerning "wine vinegar", the *Greek-English Lexicon* (n. 16), p. 574, observes that "it relieved thirst more effectively than water and ... was a favorite beverage of the lower ranks of society and of those in moderate circumstances ... esp[ecially] of soldiers".

to Elijah but to God ("My God, my God"; 27,46). In treating the theme of salvation in 27,38-54, therefore, Matthew is at pains to show that just as it is idle for one to look to oneself for salvation, so it is likewise idle for one to look for salvation to a popular figure of deliverance such as Elijah.

If salvation is not of oneself and not of a popular figure of deliverance such as Elijah, of whom, then, is salvation? Matthew informs the reader of this through Jesus' own words from the cross: "'Eli, Eli, lema sabachthani?' that is, 'My God, my God, why have you forsaken me?'" (27,46). These words, of course, constitute Jesus' cry of dereliction and come from Psalm 22. Psalm 22 is a lament. In a lament such as Psalm 22, there are at least two chief emphases[23]. The one emphasis is on the sense of abandonment that the suffering, righteous person experiences ("... why have you forsaken me"; 27,46). And the second emphasis, which sharply contrasts with the first, is on the great trust that the righteous person places in God ("My God, my God"; 27,46)[24]. In other words, the way Matthew would have the reader understand Jesus' cry of dereliction is along lines such as these: My God, my God, even though you abandon me into death, nevertheless will I continue to trust in you. As proof of the correctness of this interpretation, one need only glance at the earlier words uttered by the members of the Sanhedrin. In their mockery of Jesus, these authorities, too, quoted Psalm 22 and declared, "He trusts in God" (27,43). In mockingly declaring this, these authorities unwittingly spoke the truth about Jesus: He perfectly trusts in God. In Matthew's view, therefore, Jesus goes to his death perfectly trusting in God. Does God honor Jesus' trust? We know that he does, in the resurrection (28,6).

In this pericope of Jesus on the cross (27,38-54), therefore, Matthew makes three weighty theological assertions concerning the theme of salvation. He asserts that salvation is not of oneself, not even in the case of Jesus. He asserts that neither is salvation of some popular figure of deliverance, not even if that person be Elijah. No, Matthew asserts, salvation, far from being of this world, is solely of God.

The second theme that stands out prominently in Matthew's pericope of Jesus on the cross (27,38-54) is that of Jesus as the "Son of God". This theme, too, is central to both parts of the pericope. In all three

23. Cf., e.g., H.-J. KRAUS, *Psalmen* (Biblischer Kommentar Altes Testament, XV/1), Neukirchen, Neukirchener Verlag, 1960, p. 176, who describes these two emphases as, respectively, "die Klage" ("the lament") and "Vertrauensäusserungen" ("expressions of trust").

24. In Psalm 22 itself, observe that vv. 2-3 (English vv. 1-2), which stress the element of "forsakenness", are immediately followed by vv. 4-6 (English vv. 3-5), which stress the element of "trust".

scenes of the first part (27,38-44), Jesus is repudiated as the Son of God. In all three scenes of the second part (27,44-54), Jesus is attested to as the Son of God.

In the first part, then, Jesus is repudiated as the Son of God. In the first scene, the passers-by blaspheme him: "... if you are the Son of God[25], then come down from the cross" (27,40). In the second scene, the members of the Sanhedrin mock him: "He trusts in God, let [God] save him now if he wants him; for he said, 'I am the Son of God'"[26] (27,43). And in the third scene, the revolutionaries crucified with Jesus revile him "in the same way" as the passers-by and the members of the Sanhedrin, namely, in his capacity as the Son of God (27,44). Three times, therefore, Jesus is repudiated as the Son of God.

By contrast, in the second part of the pericope Jesus is three times attested to as the Son of God. In the first scene, Jesus attests to himself as the Son of God. As we noted above, the shouts "My God, my God" in Jesus' cry of dereliction are expressions of trust in God (27,46). Jesus, we said, goes to his death perfectly trusting in God. In Matthew's story, however, who is this Jesus who goes to his death perfectly trusting in God? As the members of the Sanhedrin unwittingly testify in 27,43, this Jesus is the Son of God. To repeat, therefore, in this first scene of the second part of the pericope Jesus attests to himself as the Son of God (27,46).

In the second and third scenes of the second part (27,51-53.54), it is God in the one instance and the centurion and the Roman soldiers in the other who attest to Jesus as the Son of God (27,51-52). After Jesus cries aloud a second time from the cross, he relinquishes his spirit and dies (27,50). In response to Jesus' death, God causes a series of supernatural portents to occur: The curtain of the temple is split in two, the earth is shaken, the rocks are split, the tombs are opened, and many saints who had died are raised to life (27,51-52). How would Matthew have the reader construe the overall significance of these supernatural portents? Matthew indicates this, not in this second scene (27,51-53), but in the third scene that tells of the centurion and the Roman soldiers with him (27,54). In the third scene, Matthew reports: "Now the centurion and those with him who were watching Jesus, when they saw the quake and the things which were happening, became exceedingly

25. On the "definiteness" of the expression "Son of God" (= "the Son of God"), cf. the well-known article by E.C. COLWELL, *A Definite Rule for the Use of the Article in the Greek New Testament*, in *JBL* 52 (1933) 12-21.

26. Although Matthew's use of "Son of God" in 27,43 constitutes an exception to Colwell's rule, the members of the Sanhedrin in this verse are making direct reference to the exchange that took place at Jesus' trial between the high priest and Jesus (26,63-64). At Jesus' trial, the high priest commanded him to declare whether he is the Messiah, "the Son of God". In light of this, it is apparent that Matthew would have the reader construe "Son of God" in 27,43 as also being definite (= "the Son of God").

afraid, saying, 'Truly, this man was the Son of God!'" (27,54). The critical thing to observe here is that with this narrative comment, Matthew informs the reader that it is through the supernatural portents God causes to occur ("the quake and things which were happening") that the Roman soldiers are impelled to confess: "Truly, this man [Jesus] was the Son of God!". On the basis of this narrative comment, therefore, it becomes eminently clear that Matthew invites the reader to understand the confession of the Roman soldiers as performing "double duty": On the one hand, it interprets the meaning of the supernatural portents God causes to occur; and on the other hand, it constitutes the Roman soldier's own understanding of Jesus. Accordingly, in the three scenes that make up the second part of the pericope of Jesus on the cross (27,45-54), Matthew leads the reader to regard Jesus as attested to three times as the Son of God: by Jesus himself through the words "My God, my God" (27,46); by God through the supernatural portents he causes to occur (27,51-52); and by the centurion and the Roman soldiers through their confession of Jesus (27,54).

Should it be correct that Jesus, while on the cross, is three times repudiated as the Son of God (by the passers-by, the members of the Sanhedrin, and the two revolutionaries) and three times attested to as the Son of God (by Jesus himself, God, and the Roman soldiers), the question that necessarily arises is this: Why should Matthew be so concerned to have Jesus die on the cross precisely in his capacity as the Son of God? Apparently, the clue Matthew gives the reader in answering this question is to be found in 27,51, where Matthew remarks, "And behold, the curtain of the temple was split in two, from top to bottom...".

Scholars vigorously debate which curtain in the temple Matthew refers to: that before the holy place or that before the holiest place. I prefer to think that Matthew refers to the curtain before the holiest place. Were God to cause this curtain to be torn in two, what would Matthew have this signify? This question, too, is vigorously debated by scholars[27], yet I choose to think that Matthew intends the tearing in two of the curtain before the holiest place to symbolize the destruction of the temple and its cult. Only one person once each year ever went behind the curtain of the holiest place, and this was the high priest on the Day of Atonement[28]. Entering the holiest place, the high priest sprinkled blood on the mercy seat to atone for the sins of the priests and the people. By narrating that God, in immediate response to the

---

27. On this, cf., e.g., T.J. GEDDERT, *Watchwords: Mark 13 in Markan Eschatology* (JSNT SS, 26), Sheffield, JSOT, 1989, pp. 141-143, who cites some thirty-five different ways in which the tearing of the veil of the temple has been interpreted.

28. For an account of the ritual associated with the Day of Atonement (the day of purification, or expiation), cf., e.g., D.P. WRIGHT, *Day of Atonement*, in *The Anchor Bible Dictionary* (n. 20), II, pp. 72-76.

death of Jesus, causes the curtain of the holiest place to be torn in two, Matthew suggests that God sets aside the temple and its cult because Jesus, his perfectly obedient and trusting Son, has now shed his blood once for all for the expiation of sins. Is there any support in Matthew's story for this interpretation? Yes, there is, in two key passages. The one passage supporting this interpretation reports on the words Jesus utters at the last supper: "This is my blood of the covenant which is poured out on behalf of many for the forgiveness of sins" (26,28; cf. also 20,28). The other key passage tells of the words of the angel to Joseph: "... and you shall call his name 'Jesus', for he shall save his people from their sins" (1,21). In sum, therefore, the reason Matthew is so concerned to stress that the Jesus who hangs on the cross and dies is the Son of God is that, to his way of thinking, it is only through the death of God's perfectly obedient and trusting Son that God chooses to reestablish his covenant and to proffer salvation and the forgiveness of sins to all people, Jews and gentiles alike.

In looking back over this pericope of Jesus on the cross (27,38-54), one can see how closely Matthew ties the theme of salvation to the theme of Jesus as the Son of God. In this pericope, Matthew affirms that salvation is not of this world – neither of oneself nor of any popular figure of deliverance even if it be Elijah – but is exclusively of God. Indeed, Matthew affirms that God, through the death of his perfectly obedient and trusting Son, has reestablished his covenant whereby he proffers salvation and the forgiveness of sins to all humans everywhere.

III

It has been the aim of this article to set forth the significance of the "cross" within the plot of Matthew's gospel-story. In the first major section of this article, we traced the unfolding of the plot of Matthew's story of Jesus. In so doing, we saw that the pericope of Jesus on the cross (27,38-54) plays a crucial role within the story's plot in two respects: Together with the pericope on the resurrection (28,1-10; cf. 27,64), it constitutes the place in the story where Jesus' conflict with Israel and especially with the religious authorities comes to fundamental "resolution"; and it also constitutes the place where the entire gospel-story reaches its "culmination". In the second major section of this article, we investigated this pericope of Jesus on the cross in terms of its treatment of the two key themes of salvation and Jesus as the Son of God. On the basis of this investigation, it became apparent that Matthew links these two themes to each other and shows that God, through the death of his Son Jesus, reestablishes his covenant whereby he proffers salvation and the forgiveness of sins to all humankind. In these various ways, therefore, the "cross" proves itself to be of central significance to the gospel-story so skillfully narrated by Matthew.

Union Theological Seminary   Jack Dean KINGSBURY
3401 Brook Road
Richmond, VA 23227
U.S.A.

DAS MATTHÄUSEVANGELIUM ALS HEILIGE SCHRIFT UND DIE HEILIGE SCHRIFT DES FRÜHEREN BUNDES

VON DER ZWEI-QUELLEN- ZUR DREI-QUELLEN-THEORIE

Historische Texte sind historisch auszulegen. Diese Grundregel ist bei Vertretern der historisch-kritischen Bibelauslegung unstrittig, wird aber nicht immer konsequent umgesetzt. Impliziert sie doch, daß früher geschriebene Texte nicht mit der Kenntnis späterer Entwicklungen zu lesen sind. Mag das Vorverständnis des Auslegers fast übermächtig sein, das kritische Bewußtsein hat in Distanz die Eigenart und die Fremdheit des Textes aus seiner je eigenen geschichtlichen Situation bewußt zu machen, damit der Text möglichst in der Intention seines Autors und unter den historischen Bedingungen seiner Zeit geschichtlich gelesen werden kann. Geht es dem Prediger um die Applikation des Textes für den gegenwärtigen Hörer, so ist es vornehmste Aufgabe des Exegeten, »Anwalt des ursprünglichen Textsinnes« zu sein[1]. Daß letzterer dabei von der Auslegungsgeschichte des auszulegenden Textes geprägt ist, gehört zur Kontingenz menschlichen Seins; allerdings ist dieser hermeneutische Zirkel, ist diese Differenz zwischen Textsinn und Auslegung wie Aneignung desselben sich selbst und den Lesern der Auslegung bewußt zu machen. Die bewußten oder unbewußten Motive der Auslegungs- und Rezeptionsgeschichte sind deutlich von der vom Text freigesetzten, immer nur potentiell vorhandenen Wirkungsgeschichte deutlich zu unterscheiden[2].

Daß die angedeuteten Probleme auch mit sprachlichen Vorentscheidungen zu tun haben, sei im folgenden am Begriff »Altes Testament« entfaltet. Parallele Überlegungen ließen sich auch am Begriff »Antithesen« als Überschrift für Mt 5,21-48 anstellen, die zwar aus polemischer

---

1. K. MÜLLER, *Exegese/Bibelwissenschaft*, in P. EICHER (ed.), *Neues Handbuch theologischer Grundbegriffe* 2, München, ²1991, pp. 23-44, ebd. p. 24.
2. Zum inflationären und undifferenziert verwendeten Begriff »Wirkungsgeschichte« vgl. H. FRANKEMÖLLE, *Evangelium und Wirkungsgeschichte. Das Problem der Vermittlung von Methodik und Hermeneutik in neueren Auslegungen zum Matthäusevangelium*, in *Salz der Erde – Licht der Welt. Exegetische Studien zum Matthäusevangelium. FS A. Vögtle*, Stuttgart, 1991, pp. 31-89, ebd. pp. 63-84; vgl. auch H. RÄISÄNEN, *Die Wirkungsgeschichte der Bibel*, in *EvTh* 52 (1992) 337-347. Zu einer kritischen Reflexion der »Vergegenwärtigung eines in der Vergangenheit formulierten Textsinnes« als Aufgabe des Exegeten (MÜLLER, *Exegese* [Anm. 1], p. 24) unter Voraussetzung einer (kontinuierlichen?) »Traditionsgeschichte« (ebd. pp. 38-40) vgl. J. EBACH, *Vergangene Zeit und Jetztzeit. Walter Benjamins Reflexionen als Anfragen an die biblische Exegese und Hermeneutik*, in *EvTh* 52 (1992) 288-309.

Sprechsituation (Auseinandersetzung der mt Kirche mit dem pharisäisch erstarkten, rabbinisch geprägten Judentum) stammen, ihre Bezeichnung aber vom Antijudaisten Markion erhalten haben[3]. Dies spricht für sich, da anzunehmen ist, daß das antijüdische Verständnis, der Gegensatz von Christentum – Judentum in der Regel beim Begriff »Antithesen« bis heute mitschwingt. Die redaktionsgeschichtliche Erkenntnis, daß sich Matthäus inhaltlich »nicht gegen die Tora« richtet, sondern eine »im Rahmen des von der Tora Vorgegebenen bleibende Interpretation der Tora« liefern möchte[4], vermag antijüdische Vorurteile kaum aufheben.

Die negativen Konnotationen, die christlicherseits beim Begriff »Antithesen« mitschwingen, besetzen auch – in der Regel, wie angenommen werden darf – den Begriff »Altes Testament«. »Alt« ist Gegenbegriff zu »neu«, wobei meist impliziert ist, daß »alt« nicht nur als »veraltet/vergangen/unvollständig«, sondern auch als »überholt« verstanden wird, wonach also das Neue das Alte verdrängt und ersetzt. Daß solche Assoziationen weitreichende Folgerungen für das Verständnis des Verhältnisses von Altem Testament – Neuem Testament oder auch Altem Bund – Neuem Bund haben, ist unzweifelhaft[5]. Der Begriff »Altes Testament« ist folglich für Juden unannehmbar, ja diskriminierend[6]. Bei Christen setzt er viele antijüdische Vorurteile frei, was gerade für Leser des »Neuen Testaments« (fast) unausweichlich ist, beachtet man den sonstigen Sprachgebrauch im NT von »alt« und »neu«. Die Rede vom »alten Bund« (2 Kor 3,14) steht durchaus parallel zu Wendungen wie »der alte Mensch«, der mit Christus mitgekreuzigt worden ist,

---

3. Diesen Hinweis verdanke ich K.Wengst unter Verweis auf A. VON HARNACK, *Marcion. Das Evangelium vom fremden Gott*, Darmstadt, 1985 (= Leipzig, [2]1924), pp. 74-92, 280-281*; ebd. p. 74, Anm. 2 verweist Harnack darauf, daß der kecke Titel« Antithesen, dem Hauptwerk Markions, »m.W. in der griechischen Literatur einzigartig« ist; dies kann er als rhetorische Figur nicht verstanden haben, da die Antithese als rhetorische Figur in der gesamten Antike wohlbekannt war; vgl. H. LAUSBERG, *Handbuch der literarischen Rhetorik*, München, 1960, § 495.

4. So etwa I. BROER, *Anmerkungen zum Gesetzesverständnis des Matthäus*, in K. KERTELGE (ed.), *Das Gesetz im Neuen Testament*, Freiburg, 1986, pp. 128-145, ebd. p. 136; der ganze Band belegt einen Paradigmen-Wechsel in der vieldiskutierten Gesetzes-Frage bei katholischen Exegeten. Ähnlich von evangelischer Seite etwa U. LUZ, in P. LAPIDE – DERS., *Der Jude Jesus. Thesen eines Juden, Antworten eines Christen*, Zürich, 1979, p. 164, der diese Meinung allerdings in seinem Kommentar stillschweigend nicht aufrecht hält; vgl. DERS., *Das Evangelium nach Matthäus I*, Zürich-Neukirchen, 1985, pp. 244-250.

5. Zu den durch solche Begriffe freigesetzten Klischees vgl. E. ZENGER, *Das Erste Testament. Die jüdische Bibel und die Christen*, Düsseldorf, 1991, der mit dem Begriff »Erstes Testament« die genannten Schwierigkeiten ausschalten möchte; zu neuen Bezeichnungen, auch der eigenen, und den damit implizierten möglichen Mißverständnissen vgl. ebd. pp. 144-154.

6. Was durch Gänsefüßchen allein wohl kaum vermieden werden kann, wie es J.J. PETUCHOWSKI – C. THOMA, *Bibel*, in *Lexikon der jüdisch-christlichen Begegnung*, Freiburg, 1989, pp. 47-52, ebd. pp. 47-48, versuchen.

während die Christen am »neuen Leben« partizipieren (Röm 6,4.6; Eph 4,22.24). Die Oppositionen »altes – neues Kleid« (Mk 2,21 parr.), vom »jungen Wein in alten Schläuchen« (Mk 2,22 parr.) u.a. bestimmen unweigerlich das christliche Vorverständnis auch beim Begriff »Altes Testament«. »Neu« meint im NT überall »frisch, jung, nie dagewesen« als Gegenbegriff zu »veraltet, überholt«[7].

Selbstverständlich ist es bei Bibeltheologen eine Binsenwahrheit, daß es im 1.Jh. n.Chr. in den urchristlichen Gemeinden ein »Neues Testament« noch nicht gab, entsprechend dazu auch kein »Altes Testament«. Dennoch ist es selbst in der wissenschaftlichen Literatur zum Matthäusevangelium allenthalben üblich, vom »AT-Gebrauch«, von den »alttestamentlichen Zitaten bei Matthäus« u.a. zu sprechen[8]. Man mag solche Wendungen zwar als standardisierte Kürzel in der wissenschaftlichen Literatur erklären oder auch als rein religionswissenschaftlich orientierte moderne Fachtermini bezeichnen; doch die Vermutung liegt nahe, daß diese (unreflektierte) Praxis eine überzogen christologische Lesart des MtEv (wie des NT insgesamt) erheblich beeinflußt. Solche Sprachmuster bieten offensichtlich die Legitimation für ein aus der Alten Kirche stammendes, die Schrift des früheren Bundes überbietendes und ersetzendes Textverständnis. Dagegen ist zu betonen: Eine Beachtung der historischen Situation müßte einen Paradigmen-Wechsel implizieren – derart, daß die heilige Schrift des früheren Bundes unter literarkritischen, form- und gattungskritischen sowie traditionskritischen Aspekten sehr viel stärker beachtet würde, als dies bis heute geschieht. Beachtet man zusätzlich die Perspektive der damaligen Leser, die im Hinblick auf das MtEv wohl z.T. die Schriften des früheren Bundes, jedoch nicht das MkEv und die Logienquelle (setzt man einmal die Zwei-Quellen-Theorie für die Lösung des synoptischen Problems hypothetisch voraus) kannten, gewinnt man schon aus literar- und theologiegeschichtlichen Gründen eine neue, historisch zutreffende Perspektive, die in diesem Beitrag nur angedeutet, aber nicht umfassend eingelöst werden kann.

Zwei Wege bieten sich an, um vertraute Denkschablonen zu überwinden – gemäß dem Tagungsthema »Source Criticism and the New Literary Criticism«. Das zweite Stichwort deutet eine neue Sensibilität gegenüber dem Text als literarischem Werk an. Danach kommt es darauf an, den Text als Text in seiner übergreifenden Gestalteinheit

---

7. Zum angegebenen Wortinhalt und zu dem angedeuteten, antithetischen Wortfeld vgl. etwa J. BAUMGARTEN, καινός neu, in EWNT 2 (1981) 563-571, und G. SCHNEIDER, παλαιός alt, veraltet, in ebd. 3 (1983) 15-17 oder BAUER-ALAND, Wörterbuch, pp. 799-800, 1225-1226.

8. Belege erübrigen sich, da dies eine gängige Fehlleistung ist. Vgl. auch P. MAIBERGER, Bibel, in NBL 1 (1991) 291-292, wonach Flavius Josephus, Ant I 15; VIII 159 »die 'Bücher' des AT« so benennt (ebd., p. 291).

(ihn hörten bzw. lasen die Erstadressaten) zu würdigen. Das erste Stichwort weist auf die bei Exegeten beliebte und jahrzehntelang intensiv betriebene Traditionsgeschichte hin, bei der aber ebenfalls von der Intention der Verfasser neutestamentlicher Schriften und ihrer Adressaten eine neue Sensibilität zu gewinnen ist (unter der Voraussetzung einer glaubensgeschichtlichen Kontinuität der Schrift des früheren Bundes und des eigenen Werkes). Beiden Aspekten soll im Hinblick auf das MtEv im folgenden nachgegangen werden, wobei in einem ersten Abschnitt grundsätzlich das Verhältnis von Quellenkritik und Formkritik, von diachroner und synchroner Betrachtung kurz zu umschreiben ist.

I. »Literarkritik« und/oder »Literary Criticism«?

Daß die Beziehung von herkömmlicher Literarkritik (mit ihrer im traditionellen Sinn verstandenen Aufgabe, vorgegebene schriftliche und verarbeitete Quellen zu eruieren) und Literary Criticism bzw. Formkritik (interessiert allein am synchronen, vorliegenden Text in seiner Gestalteinheit) oft bewußt oder im exegetischen Vollzug unbewußt (ohne die begrenzte Aufgabenstellung anzugeben) als Alternative gesehen wird, braucht nicht ausführlich belegt zu werden. Denn synchrone und diachrone Textbetrachtungen werden nicht nur ständig praktiziert, sondern in ihrem Verhältnis zueinander auch (in Methodenbüchern) vermehrt reflektiert[9]. Dies besagt nicht, daß das Verhältnis geklärt ist.

Gegen alle Ansätze, die Textanalyse auf die synchrone Ebene zu beschränken, vertritt der Verfasser seit Jahren ein offenes Methoden-

---

9. Vgl. etwa K. Berger, *Exegese des Neuen Testaments. Neue Wege vom Text zur Auslegung*, Heidelberg, 1977; Ders., *Einführung in die Formgeschichte*, Tübingen, 1987; H. Schweizer, *Biblische Texte verstehen. Arbeitsbuch zur Hermeneutik und Methodik der Bibelinterpretation*, Stuttgart, 1986; W. Egger, *Methodenlehre zum Neuen Testament. Einführung in linguistische und historisch-kritische Methoden*, Freiburg, 1987; H.K. Berg, *Ein Wort wie Feuer. Wege lebendiger Bibelauslegung*, München-Stuttgart, 1991. Zu kritischen Hinweisen vgl. J. Roloff, *Neutestamentliche Einleitungswissenschaft. Tendenzen und Entwicklungen*, in *TR* 55 (1990) 385-423, ebd. pp. 419-421. Zu Überblicken zu Arbeiten im Kontext des New Literary Criticism vgl. etwa N.R. Petersen, *Literary Criticism for New Testament Critics*, Philadelphia, PA, 1978; Ders., *»Literarkritik«, the New Literary Criticism and the Gospel according to Mark*, in *The Four Gospels 1992. FS F. Neirynck*, Leuven, 1992, II, pp. 935-948; R.A. Spencer (ed.), *Orientation by Disorientation. Studies in Literary Criticism and Biblical Literary Criticism presented in Honor of W.A. Beardslee*, Pittsburgh, 1980, pp. 25-50. Vgl. auch die unverbunden nebeneinander stehenden Beiträge in dem Tagungsband W.O. Walker (ed.), *The Relationships Among the Gospels*, San Antonio, 1978, von G. Kennedy, *Classical and Christian Source Criticism* (ebd., pp. 125-155) und von R.M. Frye, *Literary Criticism and the Gospels* (ebd. pp. 261-302). Zu Matthäus vgl. G. Stanton, *The Origin and Purpose of Matthew's Gospel. Matthean Scholarship from 1945 to 1980*, in *ANRW* II.25.3 (1985) 1889-1951, ebd. pp. 1895-1906, 1930-1934.

ensemble, in dem synchrone und diachrone, handlungsorientierte und rezeptionsorientierte Aspekte einander ergänzen, sofern sie nur zur Sinnerhellung der vorliegenden Texte beitragen[10]. Es bleibt zu hoffen, daß die Antinomie Sychronie – Diachronie, wie sie vielfach in der exegetischen Literatur vorliegt, sich ähnlich gegenstandslos erweist wie in der allgemeinen Sprachwissenschaft. Nach einem jahrzehntelangen Streit unter den Linguisten beendete E. Coseriu dort die Diskussion; er verwies darauf, daß die angebliche Antinomie nicht der Objektebene, sondern der Betrachtungsebene angehört, sie sich nicht auf den Text an sich, sondern auf die Sprachwissenschaft bezieht, es demnach keinen Gegensatz zwischen Zeichensystem und Geschichtlichkeit gibt, vielmehr im Gegenteil die Geschichtlichkeit der Sprache ihre »Systematizität« einschließt[11]. Diese Erkenntnis fand auch Eingang in die linguistischen Standardwerke. »In der Tat hängen Synchronie und Diachronie eng miteinander zusammen, ist doch die Synchronie ein Stellenwert innerhalb des zeitlich-diachronischen Kontinuums und die Diachronie andererseits eine Summe von Synchronien«[12]. Gleiches gilt auch für das Verhältnis von Traditionsgeschichte (näherhin der Frage nach den Quellen) zur synchronen Literar- und Formkritik, zu strukturalen Analysen, zur Aktantentheorie, zu semantischen Wortfelduntersuchungen, zu rhetorischen Analysen usw.[13]. Der vorliegende Text mit seinem synchronen Zeichenangebot ist nichts anderes als gleichsam ein Standfoto aus dem laufenden Film der Sprach- und Traditionsgeschichte, der Textentwicklung.

Dennoch bleibt umstritten, wie das Verhältnis von Synchronie und Diachronie bestimmt werden kann und ob es einen Primat der Synchronie vor der Diachronie gibt: Nicht nur entgegen des bis heute vorherrschenden traditionsgeschichtlichen Ansatzes, verbunden mit einem hermeneutisch oft unreflektierten Interesse an dem vom Text bezeugten historischen Geschehen, gilt es, den Text als Text ernster zu nehmen, als dies in der Vergangenheit oft der Fall war. Darüber hinaus ist die synchrone Betrachtung aber auch deswegen die primäre, weil ohne

---

10. Vgl. FRANKEMÖLLE, *Biblische Handlungsanweisungen. Beispiele pragmatischer Exegese*, Mainz, 1983, bes. pp. 11-49; DERS., *Evangelium und Wirkungsgeschichte* (s. Anm. 2), pp. 38-64 (mit der Unterteilung: Der Text als Text – Text in Traditionen – Texte in Situation – rezeptionsorientierte Aspekte); vgl. auch H. MERKLEIN, *Integrative Bibelauslegung? Methodische und hermeneutische Aspekte*, in BK 44 (1989) 117-123 sowie das gesamte Heft zum Thema »Neuere Zugänge zur Bibel«.

11. E. COSERIU, *Synchronie, Diachronie und Geschichte. Das Problem des Sprachwandelns*, München, 1974, bes. pp. 225, 237.

12. W. WELTE, *Moderne Linguistik: Terminologie/Bibliographie I*, München, 1974, p. 344 (als Zitat von G. Hebig); vgl. auch H. STAMMERJOHANN (ed.), *Handbuch der Linguistik. Allgemeine und angewandte Sprachwissenschaft*, München, 1975, pp. 474-476.

13. Zur eigenen Benennung und Zuordnung in einer Skizze vgl. FRANKEMÖLLE, *Biblische Handlungsanweisungen* (s. Anm. 10), pp. 21-32.

Analyse des vorliegenden Textes die Frage nach Quellen und verarbeiteten Traditionen in der Luft hängt. Und letztlich: Versteht man Texte
als Äußerungen aus einer bestimmten Situation und für eine bestimmte
Situation, als Texte eines bestimmten Autors für bestimmte Adressaten,
auf deren Bewußtsein und deren Verhalten er einwirken will, versteht
man zudem Reden und Schreiben als intentionales Handeln[14] – und
zwar mit dem ganzen Text als Einheit (Mt wollte ja nicht nur etwa
Kap. 16 schreiben), dann ist in der Intention des Autors immer vom
Text als Text in seiner übergreifenden Einheit auszugehen.

Dem synchronen Gestaltungswillen des Autors korrespondiert die
Perspektive des Lesers: Die Adressaten des MtEv lasen eben dieses;
eine Kenntnis des MkEv und der Logienquelle ist wohl kaum anzunehmen. Vorauszusetzen hingegen ist wohl die Kenntnis der heiligen
Schrift des früheren Bundes (s.u.). Weder liest der Adressat einen Text
in verschiedenen Schichten (dies müssen Studenten im exegetischen
Proseminar auch erst lernen), noch intendiert ein Autor eine solche
Lektüre. Diese Bemerkungen richten sich nicht gegen traditionsgesät-
tigte Texte wie z.B. das MtEv. Die dort verarbeiteten Traditionen
würden aber verkannt, würde man sie nur als Traditionen lesen, d.h. als
Texte aus vergangenen historischen Situationen. Autoren, die früher
Gesagtes oder Geschriebenes rezipieren und aktualisieren[15], erinnern
dabei nicht an Vergangenes, sondern an dessen Gültigkeit und an seine
Bedeutung für die Gegenwart. Es geht um die bleibende Gültigkeit der
früheren Verkündigung in neuer geschichtlicher Situation, in der die
alte Botschaft neu verwirklicht werden und zur Geltung kommen soll.
Als Beispiel dafür, wie gläubige Menschen die eigene reale Freiheit in
ganzheitlicher Sicht auf Jahwes gegenwärtiges Wirken zurückführen, sei
an die Aktualisierung der Exodus-Erfahrungen Israels im Deuteronomium erinnert (vgl. Dtn 5,3: »Nicht mit unseren Vätern hat Jahwe
diesen Bund geschlossen, sondern mit uns, die wir heute hier alle am
Leben sind«). Mit diesem »unendlich variierten 'Heute', das der dt
Prediger seinen Hörern einhämmert«, meint er »die Zeit des Mose und
die des Dt in einem«; nicht anders die neutestamentlichen Theologen[16].

---

14. Zum Entwurf und zu Beispielen aus dem MtEv vgl. FRANKEMÖLLE, *Biblische
Handlungsanweisungen* (s. Anm. 10). In einem solchen Konzept geht es nicht um eine
verkürzte Weitergabe ethischer Prinzipien, wie hier und da in Reaktion auf das Buch
vermutet wird.

15. Das gesamte Erste Testament belegt diese ständige Aktualisierung; vgl. dazu etwa
H.W. HERTZBERG, *Die Nachgeschichte alttestamentlicher Texte innerhalb des Alten Testaments*, Berlin, 1936; J. SCHREINER, *Interpretation innerhalb der schriftlichen Überlieferung*,
in J. MAIER – DERS. (eds.), *Literatur und Religion des Frühjudentums*, Würzburg-Gütersloh, 1973, pp. 19-30.

16. Zum Konzept des dtr Geschichtswerkes vgl. G. VON RAD, *Theologie des Alten
Testaments I*, München, 1957, pp. 232-244; zum Zitat ebd., p. 244. Zur Aktualisierung in
der jüdischen Liturgie vgl. den Mischna-Traktat Pessachim 10,5; vgl. auch die Aktualisierung von Ps 95,7 (»Ach, würdet ihr doch heute auf seine Stimme hören!«), in bSanh 98a,

Matthäus steht hier ganz in der Kontinuität der Theologen der heiligen Schrift des früheren Bundes. Die schriftkundigen Adressaten des MtEv (sie hatten – wie wohl schon im Frühjudentum üblich – Lesen und Schreiben mit und an Texten der Tora in der Kinderschule, im Elternhaus und in der Synagoge gelernt[17]) konnten solche traditionsgeschichtlichen Hinweise auf die Schrift des früheren Bundes im MtEv unzweifelhaft erkennen. Für nichtjüdische, heidnische oder auch heutige, nicht unbedingt schriftkundige, christliche Leser fehlt diese Tiefendimension. Von den ersten Adressaten ist jedoch anzunehmen, daß sie das MtEv gleichzeitig synchron und diachron gelesen haben, da sich im langsamen Akt des Hörens und Lesens traditionsgeschichtliche Assoziationen einstellen mußten, was von Mt – gerade in der Vorgeschichte in Kap. 1–2 – sehr bewußt gesteuert wurde. Insofern hat synchrone und diachrone Analyse einander zu ergänzen, wobei die Literarkritik Grundlage und Voraussetzung für die Traditionskritik ist, wie oben begründet wurde[18].

Der vorliegende Beitrag verfolgt eine begrenzte und hypothetische Fragestellung: Inwiefern trägt eine Erarbeitung synchroner und diachroner Textdimensionen tatsächlich zur Sinnerhellung einer biblischen Schrift bei? Anhand der Hypothese »Das Matthäusevangelium als heilige Schrift in Kontinuität zur Schrift des früheren Bundes« soll diese Aufgabenstellung konkretisiert werden. Seine Legitimation gewinnt der Beitrag aus den Ergebnissen und Einsichten, die bei dieser Perspektive gewonnen werden. Er ist selbst nur eine Momentaufnahme im eigenen Erkenntnisprozeß und versucht, ihn auch bei seinen Lesern anzustoßen.

II. Das Matthäusevangelium als »heilige Schrift«

Es ist unbestritten, daß das MtEv in der frühen Kirche des 2. Jh. nicht nur das am meisten gelesene und zitierte Buch im langsamen

---

wonach der Messias »heute« kommt, nämlich »heute, wenn ihr auf meine Stimme hört«. Zum Überblick und zur Literatur zum neutestamentlichen »heute« vgl. M. VÖLKEL, σήμερον, in EWNT 3 (1983) 575-576.

17. Vgl. B. LANG, Schule und Schulunterricht im alten Israel, in DERS., Wie wird man Prophet in Israel? Aufsätze zum Alten Testament, Düsseldorf, 1980, pp. 104-119; historisch informativ, jedoch fast allwissend präsentiert sich R. RIESNER, Jesus als Lehrer, Tübingen, 1981, pp. 97-199. Zur hellenistisch-jüdischen Situation in neutestamentlicher Zeit vgl. K. BERGER, Hellenistische Gattungen im Neuen Testament, in ANRW II.25.2, Berlin, 1984, pp. 1034-1432, ebd. pp. 1296ff. Zu den Synagogen als Unterrichtsort und Lehrhaus vgl. TWNT 7 (1964) 823-824; 9 (1973) 172-175.

18. Vgl. auch W. RICHTER, Exegese als Literaturwissenschaft. Entwurf einer alttestamentlichen Literaturtheorie und Methodologie, Göttingen, 1971, pp. 49-69, 152-165, der bereits Literarkritik nicht als Quellenkritik, sondern synchron versteht.

Prozeß des Werdens eines ntl Schriftkanons[19] wurde[20], es war auch jene ntl Schrift, die aufgrund dieser bevorzugten Rezeptionsgeschichte als erste in ihrer Dignität mit »der Schrift« des früheren Bundes gleichgestellt wurde. Dieser Vorgang kann vor allem formal belegt werden durch die identische Verweis- und Zitierformel γέγραπται, wie sie sich Mitte des 2. Jh. eindeutig bei Justin belegt findet (Dial 49,5; 101,3; 104,1; 111,3)[21]. Doch bereits der Barnabasbrief von ca. 130 n. Chr. bestätigt in 4,14 mit einem Zitat aus Mt 22,14 und der Einleitungswendung »wie geschrieben steht« in Fortführung von Zitaten aus der Schrift des früheren Bundes, daß »in unserem Brief ein bei Matthäus stehendes Herrenwort wie das A.T. als γραφή citiert ist«[22]. Auch der zweite Klemensbrief aus der Zeit zwischen 130-150 n. Chr. führt in 2,4 nach Zitaten aus der früheren Schrift ein Jesuswort aus Mt 9,13b ein mit der Formel »und die zweite Schrift sagt«, womit ebenfalls eindeutig das MtEv als Autorität gleichwertig neben die Schrift des früheren Bundes tritt[23]. Auch jene Stellen in der altkirchlichen Literatur, die von »dem neuen Gesetz unseres Herrn Jesus Christus« (Barn 2,1; vgl. auch Hirt des Hermas, Sim V 6,3-4; Justin, Dial 11 u.a.)[24]

19. Vgl. dazu W.G. KÜMMEL, Einleitung in das Neue Testament, Heidelberg, [19]1978, pp. 420-437 mit seiner These, wonach die ntl Kanonbildung aus der innerkirchlichen Entwicklung »mit innerer Notwendigkeit« (p. 428) sich vollzog, wohingegen er die Bildung des ntl Kanons als Reaktion auf die Schaffung eines Kanons durch Markion bekanntlich nicht als Veranlassung, sondern nur als Förderung sieht. In ihrer Einseitigkeit ist diese These zu Recht umstritten.

20. Vgl. dazu W.D. KÖHLER, Die Rezeption des Matthäusevangeliums in der Zeit vor Irenäus, Tübingen, 1987; zusammenfassend, weniger zurückhaltend: O. KNOCH, Kenntnis und Verwendung des Matthäus-Evangeliums bei den Apostolischen Vätern, in L. SCHENKE (ed.), Studien zum Matthäusevangelium. FS W. Pesch, Stuttgart, 1988, pp. 157-177.

21. Da es Justin nicht um die Autorität der Schrift als Schrift geht, sondern um die Autorität der Worte und Taten Jesu, kennt er daneben auch andere Einleitungsformeln; vgl. KÖHLER, Die Rezeption (s. Anm. 20), pp. 259-260.

22. So schon A. VON HARNACK, Geschichte der altchristlichen Literatur bis Eusebius I, Leipzig, 1904, p. 417; ähnlich KNOCH, Kenntnis und Verwendung (s. Anm. 20), p. 173; zurückhaltender KÖHLER, Die Rezeption (s. Anm. 20), pp. 111-113, 122-123.

23. Vgl. KNOCH, Kenntnis und Verwendung (s. Anm. 20) pp. 174-175; als Stelle, an der eine Matthäus-Abhängigkeit gut möglich, aber nicht sicher ist, wertet KÖHLER, Die Rezeption, pp. 135-136 die Stelle, wobei auch er davon ausgeht, daß 2 Klem 2,4 eine Evangelienschrift zitiert. Insgesamt ist er jedoch der Auffassung: »Explizit als 'Schrift' werden die Evangelien in der Zeit vor Irenäus so gut wie nicht zitiert« (518); bei den oben zitierten Stellen bei Barnabas und Justin vermutet er eine »unbeabsichtigte und unbewußte Prägung durch den Umgang mit dem AT« (ebd.). Für Irenäus betont Köhler jedoch, daß »AT/NT-Mischzitate immerhin 78mal als 'Schrift' bezeichnet« werden (ebd.). Dies spricht gegen seine Vorsicht bei der Wendung »wie geschrieben steht«.

24. Der Versuch von D. ZELLER, Jesus als vollmächtiger Lehrer (Mt 5-7) und der hellenistische Gesetzgeber, in L. SCHENKE (ed.), Studien (s. Anm. 20), pp. 299-317, Berührungen mit hellenistischen Anschauungen über den Gesetzgeber und König nachzuweisen, muß als gescheitert angesehen werden, da traditionsgeschichtliche Verbindungen, die über allgemein verbreitete Strukturparallelen hinausgehen, sich nicht nachweisen lassen und die Kategorie des staatlichen Gesetzgebers und Königs für den mt Jesus unzutreffend ist.

sprechen, bestätigen die Gleichsetzung des MtEv mit der Schrift des früheren Bundes, dem Ersten Testament, unabhängig davon, ob sie im polemischen Kontext stehen, das Gesetz des Moses aufheben oder nicht.

Es bleibt die Frage, ob die damit kurz angedeutete Rezeptionsgeschichte und Wertigkeit des MtEv in Parallelität zur Schrift des früheren Bundes dem Selbstverständnis dieses Evangeliums entspricht. Dies ist in der Tat der Fall:

Knüpft man an den Gedanken des »Gesetzes« an und befragt man das MtEv danach, ob es sich im Kontext der Schrift des früheren Bundes als Tora des Gottes Israels und Jesu Christi versteht (wenn auch nicht als nova lex im Verständnis der Kirchenväter oder der reformatorischen Theologen), so ist dies eindeutig zu bejahen. Als Erläuterung seien einige Aspekte benannt, ohne daß sie hier textuell differenziert begründet werden können. Das Hauptaugenmerk liegt auf der gegenseitigen Ergänzung von synchron-literarkritischer und diachron-traditionsgeschichtlicher Perspektive. In der Intention des Matthäus wie auch in der Erwartungshaltung seiner Adressaten bilden beide Sichtweisen eine Synthese. Dabei ist vorab darauf hinzuweisen, daß das Erste Testament nicht nur eine Frage der literarischen Tradition, sondern der Hermeneutik ist. Die griechisch überlieferte Schrift des früheren Bundes (Septuaginta) ist wie jüdischer Glaube insgesamt nicht »Tradition«, sondern der Lebens- und Denkhorizont schlechthin; das heißt: Man kann den Schrift-Bezug des Mt gar nicht genug betonen[25] (vor allem, solange er in der christlichen Theologie literarisch und thematisch verdrängt wird).

1. »Alles, was ich euch geboten habe« (28,20)

Der kompositorisch und inhaltlich schon immer bewunderte, gattungskritisch bislang nie zufriedenstellend gedeutete Schluß des MtEv (28,16-20) eröffnet nicht nur eine alle Völker und alle Zeiten umspannende, nach vorn hin offene Geschichte (19: »Geht zu allen Völkern, und macht alle Menschen ...«; 20: »alle Tage bis zum Ende der Welt«), Matthäus beendet mit diesen Versen ebenso großartig wie eindeutig eine bereits abgeschlossene Geschichte (18: »Gegeben wurde mir alle Vollmacht im Himmel und auf der Erde«; 20: »Lehret sie alles halten, was ich euch aufgetragen habe«). Daß Matthäus diese vergangene christologische Geschichte nicht als reine Vergangenheit versteht, sie vielmehr zur Basis und zum Ausgangspunkt der neuen Geschichte macht (19: »Darum gehet hin ...«; 20: »Und siehe, ich bin mit euch ...«)

---

25. Gegen G.N. STANTON, *Matthew: ΒΙΒΛΟΣ, ΕΥΑΓΓΕΛΙΟΝ, or ΒΙΟΣ?*, in *The Four Gospels. FS F. Neirynck*, Leuven, 1992, II, pp. 1187-1201, ebd. pp. 1195-1196, Anm. 37. Ist das Dtn kein Evangelium? Ist das mt Evangelium kein »literarisches Werk«?

bestätigt nicht nur seine rhetorischen Fähigkeiten, sondern in erster Linie seine Kraft, theologisch-systematisch zu denken. Christologie und Ekklesiologie stehen nicht nur in unaufhebbarer Interdependenz zueinander, vielmehr empfängt die Ekklesiologie auch ihre (gnadenhafte) Ermöglichung erst durch die Zusage des Mitseins Jesu als Immanuel (1,23)[26].

Diesen traditionsgeschichtlich gesättigten Text hat Matthäus insgesamt redaktionell gebildet[27]. Traditionsgeschichtliche Elemente und Motive stammen aus dem Urchristentum (vgl. 28,7.16 mit Mk 16,7; 28,18 in Aufnahme von 11,27 mit QLk 10,22 in Verarbeitung von Dan 7,13-14[28], dann natürlich vor allem die Kenntnis von Erscheinungen des Auferweckten); traditionsgeschichtliche Elemente und Motive stammen aber auch über die bereits genannte Menschensohn-Vorstellung hinaus aus der Schrift des früheren Bundes (hier ist vor allem der Gedanke des Mitseins Gottes grundlegend[29], dann aber auch der Gedanke der auf ein Ende zulaufenden Geschichte in 28,20b wie auch die gesamte literarische Gattung, mag man sie auf eine Selbstvorstellung Gottes wie in Gen 26,24; 17,1-2; 46,3-4; Ex 3,15.10.12 zurückführen oder auf den Schluß der griechischen jüdischen Bibel in 2 Chr 36,23[30]). Ob der Hinweis auf den Zweifel diesen Topos der Ostergeschichten aufnimmt (vgl. etwa Lk 24,36-43; Joh 20,24-29) oder als redaktionell anzusehen ist, da er sich kontextuell »nicht als gattungsmäßige Reminiszenz an das Motiv in den Erscheinungsgeschichten bagatellisieren«[31] läßt, sei dahingestellt. Primär dürfte es wohl die

26. Zu diesem kategorialen Basissatz der mt Theologie und zu seiner Funktion für den kompositorischen Aufbau des Evangeliums vgl. H. FRANKEMÖLLE, *Jahwe-Bund und Kirche Christi. Studien zur Form- und Traditionsgeschichte des »Evangeliums« nach Matthäus*, Münster, [2]1984, pp. 7-83, 308-331.

27. J. GNILKA, *Das Matthäusevangelium II*, Freiburg, 1988, p. 505, scheint einen solchen Satz als Widerspruch zu empfinden. Für redaktionelle Bildung mit Verarbeitung unterschiedlicher Traditionen plädieren etwa FRANKEMÖLLE, *Jahwe-Bund* (s. Anm. 26), pp. 42-72; J. LANGE, *Das Erscheinen des Auferstandenen im Evangelium nach Matthäus*, Würzburg, 1973, pp. 20, 180-181; J.D. KINGSBURY, *The Composition and Christology of Matt 28: 16-20*, in *JBL* 93 (1974) 573-584, ebd. p. 579. Eine umsichtige Darstellung von Thesen zur Tradition und Redaktion findet sich bei L. OBERLINNER, *»... sie zweifelten aber« (Mt 28,17b). Eine Anmerkung zur matthäischen Ekklesiologie*, in *Salz der Erde – Licht der Welt* (s. Anm. 2), pp. 375-400.

28. Vgl. dazu FRANKEMÖLLE, *Jahwe-Bund* (s. Anm. 26), pp. 61-72; LANGE, *Erscheinen* (s. Anm. 27), pp. 180-181 versteht Mt 11,27 als Basistext, aus dem Mt die Verse 28,16-20 heraus entwickelt hätte.

29. Zu einem Überblick vgl. FRANKEMÖLLE, *Jahwe-Bund* (s. Anm. 26), pp. 72-79.

30. Nach einem Überblick über verschiedene Vorschläge zur Gattung der Verse 28,16-20 plädiert GNILKA, *Das Matthäusevangelium II* (s. Anm. 27), p. 504 für das erstere, während ich weiterhin – vgl. *Jahwe-Bund* (s. Anm. 26), pp. 46-61 – für ein »Bundesformular« plädieren möchte – nicht in sklavischer Übernahme, sondern selbstverständlich so, daß Matthäus für sein »Evangelium« auch Elemente der Gattung variiert oder umstellt.

31. P. HOFFMANN, *Das Zeichen für Israel. Zu einem vernachlässigten Aspekt der matthäischen Ostergeschichte*, in DERS. (ed.), *Zur neutestamentlichen Überlieferung von der*

Intention des Matthäus sein, nach Ostern und trotz Ostern die Ambivalenz christlichen Glaubens in »Zweifel« und »Kleinglauben« darzustellen[32].

Matthäus hat – auch gemäß antiker Regeln – seine Schlußperikope besonders sorgfältig gestaltet und zu einem raffinierten »Meisterstück« der Formulierung und des Inhaltes gemacht[33]. Ihm ist dabei eine vollkommene Synthese nach Form, Gattung und Inhalt sowie von jüdischen und christlichen Glaubensvorstellungen gelungen. Dies sollte an diesen Schlußversen, die seit langem als »Schlüssel des Matthäusevangeliums« angesehen werden[34], etwas ausführlicher dargestellt werden. Nur so zeigt sich das Anliegen des Matthäus, die Kontinuität seiner Botschaft mit Vorstellungen der Schrift in Einklang zu bringen.

Für das Verständnis des gesamten Evangeliums geschieht dies noch mehr durch eine Wendung, die bislang ausgespart wurde. Es handelt sich um die Worte »Alles, was ich euch geboten habe« (28,20). Diese Wendung hat nicht nur kompositionskritische Funktion, indem sie auf das gesamte sprachliche und nichtsprachliche Handeln Jesu, auf seine Lehre und seine Tätigkeit zurückweist – und sie als Einheit versteht –, vielmehr bestätigt sie am Ende noch einmal mit ihrer sprachlichen Formulierung die Kontinuität des mt Werkes mit der Schrift des früheren Bundes. Bereits W. Trilling stellte 1959 – und dies ist bis heute unbestritten – fest: »Das Verbum ἐντέλλεσθαι steht von Jesu Weisung in diesem absoluten, streng religiösen Sinn nur hier im Neuen Testament. Nimmt man (πάντα) ὅσα hinzu, so ergibt sich eine Wendung, die im Alten Testament (= Septuaginta) beheimatet ist. Sie ist dort ein geläufiger Ausdruck für den fordernden, autoritativen Willen Gottes, durchzieht den ganzen Pentateuch und wird besonders lebhaft im Deuteronomium verwendet«[35]. Jesus als der auferweckte Menschen-

---

Auferstehung Jesu, Darmstadt, 1988, pp. 416-452, ebd. p. 442; ausführlich entfaltet diesen Gedanken OBERLINNER, »… *sie zweifelten aber*« (s. Anm. 27) mit der »These: Der Zweifel der Jünger steht nicht im Zusammenhang mit der Auferstehung Jesu, sondern ist die Reaktion auf die Offenbarung Jesu von seiner Vollmacht und die Übertragung der Aufgabe an die Jünger zur Verkündigung« (p. 388). Methodisch läge damit die Figur des Hysteron proteron vor, was bei einem narrativ und rhetorisch versierten Erzähler wie Matthäus erstaunlich wäre.

32. Vgl. HOFFMANN, *Das Zeichen für Israel* (s. Anm. 31), p. 442; FRANKEMÖLLE, *Jahwe-Bund* (s. Anm. 26) pp. 22-23.111-115.152-157.173-174.261-262.

33. So schon A. von Harnack; zum ausführlichen Zitat vgl. FRANKEMÖLLE, *Jahwe-Bund* pp. 48-49.

34. Zu einem Forschungsüberblick vgl. A. SAND, *Das Matthäus-Evangelium* (EdF, 275), Darmstadt, 1991, pp. 136-138.

35. W. TRILLING, *Das wahre Israel. Studien zur Theologie des Matthäus-Evangeliums*, München, ³1964, p. 37; ausführlicher FRANKEMÖLLE, *Jahwe-Bund* (s. Anm. 26), pp. 95-98. Als Zitat aus Dtn 24,1 fand Matthäus das Verbum in Mk 10,4 vor (vgl. Mt 19,7), ebenso in der Logienquelle als Zitat aus Ps 91,11 (vgl. Mt 4,6 mit Lk 4,10); jüngere Handschriften tragen das Verbum auch beim Abstieg vom Berg der Verklärung in 15,4 – durchaus angemessen – beim Zitat aus der Tora ein.

sohn mit kosmisch-universaler Vollmacht (diese Identität des Erhöhten mit dem Irdischen wird durch das zweifache »Jesus« in 28,16.18 als Subjekt betont, das auch in Vers 20 in der Wendung »Was ich euch geboten habe« vorausgesetzt ist) spricht und sprach im Verlauf der evangeliaren Erzählung in der Autorität und als Offenbarer Jahwes, wie durch den Immanuel-Titel (1,23) von Anfang des Evangeliums an betont wird (was in der Literatur zum MtEv viel zu wenig beachtet wird; s.u. II.9). Daher steht der mt Jesus nicht Moses als menschlichem Offenbarungsmittler gegenüber, da er wie Jahwe in der Schrift des früheren Bundes verbindliche Weisungen »gebietet«[36].

Bereits dieser Gedanke der Selbsterschließung Gottes im geschichtlichen Jesus von Nazareth, wonach Jesus die menschliche Daseinsweise Gottes ist, impliziert, daß Jesus nach Matthäus kaum ein »neues Gesetz« verkündet haben dürfte (dies wäre im jüdischen und judenchristlichen Raum blasphemisch und daher undenkbar), vielmehr die ursprüngliche Willensoffenbarung Gottes erneuert.

2. »Dein Wille geschehe« (6,10)

Die Durchsetzung des Willens Gottes ist nach Matthäus universal-kosmologisch, wie die Wendung »wie im Himmel, so auch auf Erden« in 6,10b belegt (was in 28,18 auf Jesus übertragen wird; vgl. auch 5,18). Näherhin geht es um »den Willen des Vaters«, wie nur Matthäus 6mal konkretisiert (6,10; 7,21; 12,50; 18,14; 21,31; 26,42). Vor allem die Anlehnung von 26,42 an 6,9 bestätigt, daß der mt Jesus sein eigenes Geschick – auch in der Passion – ganz dem Willen des Vaters unterstellt. Gottesbild und Christologie sind dadurch gleichermaßen charakterisiert, ebenso auch das Verständnis des mt Jesus von seinem eigenen Lebensweg. Insofern bleibt die redaktionelle Bitte um die Verwirklichung des Gotteswillens in 6,10b, gerade auch als formale Mitte des Herrengebetes und aufgrund fehlender Parallelen in der jüdischen Literatur, für Matthäus charakteristisch[37]. Dem mt Jesus geht es um nichts anderes als um die Verwirklichung des Willens des Vaters.

Was hier theozentrisch formuliert wird, umschreibt Matthäus (ebenfalls redaktionell) auch in anthropologischer Perspektive: »Laß es nur

---

36. Zwar kann auch Moses Subjekt der Wendung »was ich euch geboten habe« sein, doch in den meisten Fällen ist es Jahwe selbst; vgl. G. SCHRENK, ἐντέλλομαι, in TWNT 2 (1935) 541; TRILLING, Israel, pp. 37-38.

37. Vgl. FRANKEMÖLLE, Biblische Handlungsanweisungen (s. Anm. 10), pp. 71-74. Die These von Luz, Matthäus I (s. Anm. 4), p. 335, Matthäus habe die Zusatzbitten »schon vorgefunden«, konterkariert er ebd. mit seiner Beobachtung, »wie sehr der Evangelist in seiner eigenen Diktion die Sprache seiner Gemeinde aufnimmt« (wer will dann noch unterscheiden?). Während Luz, p. 344 jüdische Parallelen ablehnt, verweist J. GNILKA, Das Matthäusevangelium I, Freiburg, 1988, pp. 221 u.a. auf 1 Makk 3,60: »Wie ein Wille im Himmel ist, so soll es geschehen«; hier fehlt der geprägte liturgische Gebetsstil, außerdem stört der kriegerische Kontext den Gedanken einer Vorlage.

geschehen! Denn nur so können wir die ganze Gerechtigkeit erfüllen«
(3,15), das heißt: Von der Taufe (3,13-17) bis zur Passion (26,42) ist
nach Matthäus Jesus wegen dieser absoluten Unterordnung und Akzep-
tanz des Willens des Vaters sein »Sohn«, der von sich sagen kann: »Mir
ist von meinem Vater alles übergeben worden; niemand kennt den
Sohn, nur der Vater, und niemand kennt den Vater, nur der Sohn«
(11,27 par. Lk 10,22). Allerdings: Von den Synoptikern hat allein
Matthäus diese Willenseinheit und Tateinheit im gesamten Evangelium
redaktionell herausgestellt. Dies macht die Normativität der Worte Jesu
aus, aber auch die Normativität des MtEv. In diesem Konzept hat die
Schrift des früheren Bundes eine unaufhebbare Funktion.

3. »Als Jesus alle diese Worte beendet hatte« (26,1)

Während die Schlußwendung in 28,20 »Alles, was ich euch geboten
habe« deutlich 26,1 rekapituliert, faßt die Wendung in 26,1 alle vorhergehenden Worte Jesu in den fünf großen Redekompositionen zusammen, wie die überleitende Formel – ohne das zusammenfassende »alle«
– belegt (7,28; 11,1; 13,53; 19,1)[38]. Akzeptiert man die ungebrochene
Kontinuität der mt Welt- und Wirklichkeitsdeutung im Glauben an das
neue Handeln Gottes in und durch Jesus Christus mit seinem Handeln
in der Geschichte des früheren Bundes und setzt man entsprechend
nicht nur die inhaltliche Normativität, sondern auch die literarische
Bedeutung derjenigen biblischen Schriften, die dieses Handeln bezeugen, für Matthäus voraus (s.u.), dann dürfte die Rezeption von Einlei-
tungs- und Schlußformeln zur Mosesrede im Deuteronomium (1,1;
4,44; 28,69; 31,1.24; 32,44-45; 33,1) nachvollziehbar sein[39].

Die Einheit der fünf großen Redekompositionen im MtEv wird nicht
nur durch den zusammenfassenden Rückverweis in 26,1 und seine
Rekapitulation in 28,20 garantiert, sondern auch – bei aller thematischen Variation – durch den konstanten eschatologischen Ausblick bei
jeder Rede. Dieser Befund erlaubt es, die Kap. 23-25 als Rede über die
eschatologische Dimension für Israel und die Kirche (aus Juden und
Heiden) angesichts des Gerichtes des Menschensohnes[40] als Einheit

---

38. Zur Funktion der Überleitungswendung und zur Funktion der Redekompositionen für die Einheit des MtEv vgl. FRANKEMÖLLE, *Jahwe-Bund* (s. Anm. 26), pp. 333-339.

39. Zu den Stellen und zum Einfluß auf die mt Geschichts-Erzählung vgl. FRANKE-
MÖLLE, ebd., pp. 339-342.

40. Zu Recht führt K.Ch. WONG, *Interkulturelle Theologie und multikulturelle Gemeinde im Matthäusevangelium. Zum Verhältnis von Juden- und Heidenchristen im ersten
Evangelium*, Freiburg-Göttingen, 1992, pp. 125-154 die »judenchristlichen« und »heidenchristlichen« Texte im Evangelium nicht – wie vielfach vertreten – auf die Frage nach
Tradition und Redaktion zurück, sondern auf die Annahme, daß Juden- und Heidenchristen gleichberechtigte Mitglieder in der Gemeinde des Matthäus sind. Zum grundsätzlichen Verhältnis von Traditionen und Redaktion und der Bedeutung der redaktionellen Intention selbst bei nachweisbaren traditionellen Texten vgl. FRANKEMÖLLE, *Jahwe-*

zu verstehen (zum eschatologischen Ausblick vgl. 7,21-22; 10,40ff.;
13,49ff.; 18,35; 25,1-46). Maßstab des Gerichtes ist kein neues »Gesetz«, sondern der ursprüngliche Wille Gottes mit seinem normativen
Anspruch. Ihn will nach Matthäus Jesus wieder zur Geltung bringen.
Auch dieser Gedanke verbürgt die Einheit der heiligen Schrift des
früheren Bundes und des MtEv. Dabei behauptet Matthäus wie seine
biblischen Vorgänger die Einheit von Wort und Tat, von Gottes- und
Nächstenliebe. Nicht weniger als jene klagt er die Verwirklichung des
Gotteswillens im Tun ein.

4. »Wer aber die Gebote hält und halten lehrt, ...« (5,19)

Die Wendung »... und lehret sie alles halten, was ich euch geboten
habe« im Schlußvers des Evangeliums (28,20) greift unmißverständlich
auf 5,19 zurück. Für das Verständnis des Mt ist hier die Abfolge
aufschlußreich: Ihm geht es nicht nur um die Einheit von Hören und
Tun – dies wäre schon wichtig genug (vgl. 7,15-27) –, Matthäus kennt
auch die Problematik des Standes der Lehrer, die zwar die Halacha
verkünden, »Wandel« und »Weg« kennen, der durch die Weisungen
Gottes angegeben ist, ihn aber – im Gegensatz zu Johannes dem Täufer
(vgl. 21,32) – selbst nicht gehen (vgl. bes. 23,1-12). Jesus selbst erfüllt
»die ganze Gerechtigkeit« (3,15). Also kommt es nach Mt auch bei den
Christen (zur Identifizierung mit den Jüngern vgl. 28,19) alles darauf
an, den Willen Gottes in der Interpretation Jesu zu tun und ihn andere
zu lehren. Wie die Orthopraxie der Maßstab für die Gerichtsverfallen-
heit Israels war (aufgrund des falschen Verhaltens zu Jesus; vgl. 3,7-12;
21,28-32.33-46; 22,1-14; 27,25), so ist die Orthopraxie ebenso Maßstab
im Gericht für die Christen (vgl. 22,11-14; 23,1-39[41]; 25,31-46 u.a.)[42].
Daß Reden und Tun, Logien und Erzählungen nach Mt einander
ergänzende Aspekte sind, bestätigt sich am Gesamtaufbau des Evangeliums, was schon immer gesehen wurde. Hinzuweisen ist vor allem auf
die Inklusion von 4,23 und 9,35 zur Bergpredigt und zu den 10
»Wundergeschichten«. Sie ist für die Leser eine unmißverständliche
Deutung, wird aber auch von der Überleitungsformel am Ende aller
Reden (»Und es geschah, als ...«) bestätigt. Sprachliches und nicht-
sprachliches Handeln gehören nach Mt zusammen, wie die Verbindung
der narratio und locutio im Epilog in 28,16-20 bestätigt. Christen sind
bleibend an das sprachliche und nichtsprachliche Handeln des irdischen

---

Bund (s. Anm. 26), näherhin die im Sachregister unter »Traditionen« angegebenen Seiten;
DERS., Biblische Handlungsanweisungen (s. Anm. 10), pp. 21-23, 50-52, 73-76, 198-201,
200-202.
  41. Zur kirchlichen Intention dieses Kapitels als Element des MtEv vgl. FRANKEMÖLLE,
Biblische Handlungsanweisungen (s. Anm. 10), pp. 133-190.
  42. Zu den Stellen, nach denen sowohl Juden wie Christen »einzig nach ihren Werken
gerichtet« werden, vgl. WONG, Interkulturelle Theologie (s. Anm. 40), pp. 125-154.

Jesus gebunden, an seinen Weg – im Glauben an sein »Mitsein« als Immanuel (1,23; 18,20; 26,29; 28,20). In dem, was die Halacha des mt Jesus betrifft, stimmt Mt in der Unbedingtheit der gnädigen Willensoffenbarung Gottes in den Schriften des früheren Bundes und durch Jesus von Nazareth insgesamt und im einzelnen überein[43]. Nicht zuletzt in dieser ungebrochenen Kontinuität des Verständnisses der Tora in ihrer bleibenden Gültigkeit auch für diejenigen, die an Jesus als die menschliche Daseinsweise Gottes glauben, ist das Thema dieses Beitrages begründet. Wenn Matthäus sich in diesem Kontext mit anderen Tora-Deutungen seiner Zeit oder auch mit schriftlich überlieferten Interpretationen auseinandersetzt, so entspricht dies ganz dem durchgehend belegten Toraverständnis aller großen Theologen im Frühjudentum[44].

Unter neuen Lebensbedingungen, auch bei der Adressatengemeinde des Matthäus, geht es darum, daß der Glaube durch das Tun beglaubigt wird: »Ihr sollt auf meine Satzungen und auf meine Vorschriften achten. Wer sie einhält, wird durch sie leben. Ich bin der Herr« (Lev 18,5).

Die Unbedingtheit der bleibenden Gültigkeit der gnädigen Willensoffenbarung Gottes, der Tora, hat wie kein anderer Evangelist Matthäus in den sogenannten Antithesen formuliert, wobei zum Verständnis an die oft einseitig neutestamentliche Auslegungsgeschichte zu erinnern ist. Die Antithesen sind die spezifisch matthäische Form, die Vergangenheit gegenwärtig zu machen und die Tradition lebendig zu erhalten.

5. »Ich aber sage euch ...« (5,22.28.32.34.39.44)

Angesichts der unterschiedlichen Thesen zur Tradition und Redaktion bei den Antithesen[45] sollen hier lediglich Aspekte benannt werden, die für das eigene Thema wichtig sind. So stellt sich grundsätzlich die Frage, ob überhaupt ausreichende Kriterien angegeben werden können, Redaktion und Tradition (soweit sie über den Stoff der Logienquelle

---

43. Zu einer jüdischen Deutung vgl. Ph. SIGAL, *The Halakhah of Jesus of Nazareth According to the Gospel of Matthew*, Lanham, MD, 1986; vgl. auch J.J. PETUCHOWSKI – C. THOMA, *Lexikon der jüdisch-christlichen Begegnung*, Freiburg, 1989, pp. 127-131; R. SMEND – J. ZMIJEWSKI, *Gesetz*, in *NBL* 1 (1991) 825-829.

44. Vgl. K. MÜLLER, *Gesetz und Gesetzeserfüllung im Frühjudentum*, in K. KERTELGE (ed.), *Das Gesetz* (s. Anm. 4), pp. 11-27, und die übrigen Beiträge dieses Sammelbandes, die einen Paradigmenwechsel im christlichen Gesetzes-Verständnis signalisieren – selbst in der paulinischen Deutung. Vgl. auch P. VON DER OSTEN-SACKEN, *Die Heiligkeit der Tora. Studien zum Gesetz bei Paulus*, München, 1989.

45. Vgl. etwa I. BROER, *Anmerkungen zum Gesetzesverständnis des Matthäus*, in K. KERTELGE, *Das Gesetz* (s. Anm. 4), pp. 128-145 (als Zusammenfassung und Weiterführung früherer Arbeiten sowie in Auseinandersetzung mit neuerer Literatur); LUZ, *Matthäus I* (s. Anm. 4), pp. 244-250.

hinausgeht) exakt zu trennen (wichtig vor allem bei der Diskussion um die 1., 2. und 4. Antithese als mt Sondergut). Zu fragen ist auch, ob die vielverhandelte Problematik, inwieweit Mt sich mit der Schrift selbst oder nur mit ihren Auslegungen auseinandersetzt, überhaupt für ihn zutreffend ist. Sollte er als universal orientierter hellenistischer Judenchrist (wie anzunehmen ist) gemäß pharisäischer Überzeugung Schrift und Tradition als gleichberechtigte Offenbarungsquellen ansehen, wäre eine Trennung einzig modern-künstlich und daher seinem Selbstverständnis und dem seiner hellenistisch-judenchristlichen Adressaten unangemessen.

Die Frage ist nicht, ob Mt (wenn er die antithetische Sprachform in 5,21-48 geschaffen hat, was ich annehme[46]) die »Antithesen« mit seinem sonstigen Verständnis, der Erfüllung der Tora durch Jesus, hat vereinbaren können[47], sondern vielmehr: Ist unser, durch Markion geprägtes Verständnis des Begriffs »Antithesen« für Mt zutreffend? Muß man die Frage verneinen, sind alle theologischen Skrupel prinzipiell zu überwinden, zumal die Antithese als geprägte Form nicht den Rahmen jüdischen Sprechens sprengt[48]. Zu beachten bleibt jedoch hier die Besonderheit bei Matthäus, daß Jesus weder seine Weisung aus der Schrift ableitet noch sie nur anderen Auslegungen von Schriftgelehrten entgegensetzt, vielmehr mit der Autorität des offenbarenden Gottes des früheren Bundes parallelisiert (vgl. die Gottesrede »es wurde gesagt«). Nicht die Ethik ist der Maßstab, vielmehr die Christologie.

Wenn aber der irdische Jesus gleichzeitig die menschliche Daseinsweise und Selbsterschließung Gottes ist, Jesus wirklich der Immanuel, der »Gott-mit-uns« (1,23) ist, dann wendet der mt Jesus sich nicht gegen Moses, sondern aktualisiert die von Moses übermittelte Offenbarung und damit den Willen des Gottes selbst (vgl. 5,17-20; 7,12). Dem mt Jesus geht es um den »Willen des Vaters« (6,10; 7,21; 12,50; 18,14; 21,31; 26,42) bzw. um die »Gerechtigkeit« Gottes, wobei letzterer Begriff allein 5mal von Mt in die Bergpredigt eingetragen wurde (5,6.10.20; 6,1.33). Dabei signalisiert dieser Begriff (wie vor allem 5,6

---

46. So vor allem mit dem begründeten Entwurf von I. BROER, *Freiheit vom Gesetz und Radikalisierung des Gesetzes*, Stuttgart, 1980.

47. Diese Überlegung ist der Hauptgrund für LUZ, *Matthäus I* (s. Anm. 4), pp. 245-246, die redaktionelle Herkunft der Antithesen durch Mt abzulehnen.

48. Vgl. die Beispiele bei GNILKA, *Das Matthäusevangelium I* (s. Anm. 37), pp. 151-152; LUZ, *Matthäus I* (s. Anm. 4), p. 247. Die dort behauptete »Besonderheit« Jesu nach Matthäus im Vergleich zu anderen jüdischen Schriftgelehrten und seine angebliche Souveränität kann wohl nicht mehr weiter behauptet werden. Zur Begründung vgl. den in Anm. 44 genannten, weiterführenden Aufsatz von K. MÜLLER, *Beobachtungen zum Verhältnis von Tora und Halacha in frühjüdischen Quellen*, in I. BROER (ed.), *Jesus und das jüdische Gesetz*, Stuttgart, 1992, pp. 105-133. Zur eigenen, weiterführenden Position, vgl. H. FRANKEMÖLLE, *Die sogenannten Antithesen des Matthäus (5,21ff.). Von der Macht der Vorurteile*, in DERS. (ed.), *Das bekannte Buch - das fremde Buch. Die Bibel*, Mainz, 1993 (im Druck).

und 6,33 andeuten) die Einheit von Heilszusage und Heilsbewährung, von »Gerechtigkeit« als Gabe und Forderung[49]. Damit hält Mt an der Intention der Tora des früheren Bundes fest, deren Weisungen er nicht aufheben, sondern deren von Gott herkommende Gültigkeit der mt Jesus verkünden will. Kompositionell dürfte Mt zwischen den sogenannten Antithesen in 5,21-48 und den Versen über die bleibende Gültigkeit der Tora in 5,17-20 keinen Widerspruch gesehen haben, was bei einem (unbestritten anerkannten) »systematischen« und rhetorisch gebildeten Theologen auch nicht zu erwarten ist. Die Radikalisierung – auch in der antithetischen Sprachform – entspricht im übrigen dem mt Denkstil[50]. Gerade aufgrund dieser Ausrichtung wird deutlich, daß Mt sein Werk über alle anderen zeitgenössischen Auslegungen der Tora und der Geschichte vom Handeln Gottes in Jesus (etwa auch im MkEv) gestellt sah. Er sieht sein Werk an der Seite der Schriften des früheren Bundes; dies wird durch weitere Aspekte verstärkt.

6. »Damit erfüllt würde, was der Herr gesagt hat« (1,22)

Daß bei Mt im Verhältnis der Antithesen (vgl. die Wendung »Den Alten wurde gesagt«) zu den sogenannten Erfüllungszitaten[51] Kongruenz besteht, er das Wort Gottes und das durch den jeweiligen Propheten mündlich und schriftlich geoffenbarte Wort Gottes in Identität sieht, bestätigen vor allem jene beiden Erfüllungs-Zitate, in denen es

---

49. Zu »Heilszusage und Heilsbewährung in der mt Theologie« vgl. das so überschriebene Kapitel bei FRANKEMÖLLE, Jahwe-Bund (s. Anm. 26), pp. 257-307; anders G. STRECKER, Der Weg der Gerechtigkeit, Göttingen, ³1971, pp. 157-58; vgl. DERS., Das Gesetz in der Bergpredigt – die Bergpredigt als Gesetz, in T. VEIJOLA (ed.), The Law in the Bible and in Its Environment in the Finnish Exegeticae Society, Helsinki, 1990, pp. 109-125, 124-125.

50. Vgl. I. BROER, Die Antithesen und der Evangelist Matthäus, in BZ 19 (1975) 50-63, 57 unter Hinweis auf 5,17; 10,34; 15,11.17-18.20 und 19,8-9. Antithetisch ist darüberhinaus auch das Verhältnis von Israel und Kirche, der Gedanke von den zwei Wegen, die vielfach variierte Vorstellung vom falschen und richtigen Verhalten usw.

51. Der Begriff »Erfüllungszitate« bzw. »Reflexionszitate« ist in der Literatur umstritten, was eher der Neigung der modernen Autoren zu einer gattungsmäßigen Systematisierung entspricht, aber nicht der Funktion dieser Zitate im MtEv. Matthäus kann seine Perspektive auch narrativ entfalten, wie die Funktion der Schriftgelehrten Israels in Mt 2 für die Kirche Gottes (in Jesus Christus) aus den Völkern belegt. Eine formelhafte »Erfüllungs«-Wendung findet sich in folgenden Zitaten: 1,22-23; 2,15.17-18.23; 4,14-16; 8,17; 12,18-21; 13,35; 21,4-5; 27,9; einzubeziehen wären auch die freieren Zitate mit einer »Erfüllungsformel« bzw. die Reflexionszitate in 2,5-6; 3,3; 13,14; 24,15; 26,31.54.56; 27,9-10.35. Zur eigenen Deutung vgl. FRANKEMÖLLE, Jahwe-Bund (s. Anm. 26), pp. 14-16, 345-346, 357-358, 386-387, 389-390, 392-393; F. VAN SEGBROECK, Les citations d'accomplissement dans l'Évangile selon saint Matthieu d'après trois ouvrages récents, in M. DIDIER (ed.), L'évangile selon Matthieu. Rédaction et théologie (BETL, 29), Gembloux, 1972, pp. 107-130; G.M. SOARES PRABHU, The Formula Quotations in the Infancy Narrative of Matthew, Roma, 1976; zur neueren Diskussion vgl. LUZ, Matthäus I (s. Anm. 4), pp. 134-141; A. SAND, Das Evangelium nach Matthäus, Regensburg, 1986, pp. 76-82.

überhaupt um die Neuschöpfung Jesu Christi (1,22) und um die »Aufhebung« der Exodus-Erfahrung Israels in der Geschichte Jesu (2,15) geht. Diese beiden Zitate werden eigens als »vom Herrn gesagt« charakterisiert. Die dort feststellbare theozentrische Dignität kennzeichnet nach Mt aber alle Schriftzitate. Dem entspricht, daß das Verbum πληρόω exklusiv nur auf die Geschichte Jesu bzw. auf sein Tun bezogen ist, dieses Verbum also christologische Qualität hat[52]. Aus all dem folgt: Nach Mt steht die Geschichte Jesu in ungebrochener Kontinuität zur Geschichte Israels (Diskontinuität gibt es nur auf seiten der Menschen), vor allem ist der eine Gott der Handelnde dieser kontinuierlichen und einheitlichen Geschichte. Dabei sieht Mt die Richtung nicht nur von den Zitaten der Schrift zur Geschichte Jesu hin, sondern auch umgekehrt (wodurch die Bezeichnung »Erfüllungszitate« problematisch wird): »Zitat und Kontext haben sich wechselseitig beeinflußt«[53].

Diese Erkenntnis prägt nicht nur die sogenannten Erfüllungszitate bzw. Reflexionszitate, vielmehr das Verhältnis des Mt zur heiligen Schrift überhaupt. Bislang steht eine Bearbeitung der ca. 110 bis 120 wörtlich rezipierten Stellen aus der heiligen Schrift und der ca. 370 bis 400 Anspielungen und Motivrezeptionen durch den Evangelisten Matthäus leider noch aus[54]. Die nüchterne Kenntnisnahme dieses Faktums der Verwobenheit des mt Evangeliums und des Evangeliums der Schrift des früheren Bundes bestätigt nicht nur Mt als schriftgelehrten Theologen und die Bedeutung der Schrift für ihn, sondern mehr noch: seine Glaubens- und Lebenswelt, seinen halachischen und haggadischen Lebensodem, ohne den Mt nicht atmen könnte und sein Werk nicht hätte schreiben können. Wo wir christliche Exegeten literarische Kenntnisse des »Alten Testaments« nachzuweisen versuchen, ist – dies sollte der Hinweis auf die Vielzahl der rezipierten biblischen Schriftstellen andeuten – gelebter Glaube und Glaubenspraxis vorauszusetzen.

Auch aus diesen Hinweisen folgt: Mt versteht sein Evangelium als Fortsetzung, Bestätigung, Bekräftigung und Besiegelung der Schrift des früheren Bundes (dem entspricht die Semantik beim Verbum »erfüllen« im biblischen Sprachgebrauch, das nur unter markionitischer Perspektive als »überbieten« oder gar »außer Kraft setzen« verstanden werden kann). Die Konsequenz daraus lautet: Schon Mt versteht sein Werk als heilige Schrift – parallel zur heiligen Schrift des früheren Bundes. Die letzte Begründung für ein solches Verständnis liefert das mt Gottesbild in Einheit mit der Christologie, die nicht nur durch die christologischen Hoheitstitel (vor allem durch Immanuel und Menschensohn spezifisch

52. Vgl. Luz, *Matthäus I* (s. Anm. 4), p. 155.
53. Van Segbroeck, *Citations* (s. Anm. 51), p. 129.
54. Die Zahlen variieren je nach Textausgabe; zugrundegelegt wurden die Einheitsübersetzung, die Zürcher Übersetzung, die Elberfelder Bibelübersetzung und Nestle-Aland.

mt geprägt ist), sondern auch durch das gesamte sprachliche und nichtsprachliche Handeln (was wiederum spezifisch mt ist)[55]. All dies hat auch Auswirkungen auf die Gattung des MtEv.

7. »Dieses Evangelium von der Basileia« (24,14)

In Übereinstimmung mit der starken redaktionellen Betonung der Einheit von Wort und Tat, Reden und Tun (s.o. II.4) ist es nicht erstaunlich, daß Mt beim Begriff »Evangelium« nicht nur die heilsvermittelnde Botschaft von der Basileia, sondern auch die heilsvermittelnde Praxis meint, wie 24,14 und vor allem 26,13 belegen. Dies entspricht der Einheit der Theo-logie und Christologie des Mt, so daß die Botschaft des Mt vom eschatologisch handelnden Gott[56] im sprachlichen und nichtsprachlichen Handeln Jesu und in seiner Person die Grundstruktur für sein ganzes Werk wie auch für den Begriff »Evangelium« abgibt. Insofern bleibt zu fragen, ob die bei den Apostolischen Vätern (vgl. bes. Did 8,2; 11,3; 15,3.4; 2 Clem 8,5 und durchgehend bei Justin) sich findende Übertragung des bis dahin als mündliche Predigt verstandenen Begriffs »Evangelium« auf die literarische Gattung »Evangelium«[57] von Mt vorbereitet wird oder sich sogar schon bei ihm findet. Dies dürfte in der Tat der Fall sein, wie schon Dibelius 1919 als »alte Beobachtung« notierte. Danach änderte Mt die mk Wendung »das Evangelium« (13,10; 14,9) in 24,14 und 26,13 in »dieses Evangelium«. Seine Folgerung daraus lautet: »Für Markus ist das Evangelium eine außerhalb des Buches stehende Größe; Matthäus kann mit Recht sagen: 'dies Evangelium, das ich in meinem Buche darbiete'«[58]. Während Mk mit dem Begriff »Evangelium« an der Verkündigung Jesu selbst festhält, dann aber auch damit den Glauben verbindet, daß sich in diesem Jesus der Sohn Gottes, der Messias usw. geoffenbart hat[59], betont nach G.N. Stanton Matthäus als erster

---

55. Zur Christologie im praktischen Vollzug vgl. etwa FRANKEMÖLLE, Die »Praxis Christi« (Mt 11,2) und die handlungsorientierte Exegese, in D.-A. KOCH (ed.), Jesu Rede von Gott und ihre Nachgeschichte im Neuen Testament. FS W. Marxsen, Gütersloh, 1989, pp. 142-164; DERS., Christlich Glauben in ambivalenter Wirklichkeit. Handlungsanweisungen durch Wundergeschichten (am Beispiel von Mt 8–9), in Katechetische Blätter 114 (1989) 419-425 sowie DERS., Biblische Handlungsanweisungen (s. Anm. 10), passim.

56. Diesen Gedanken hat zu Recht und umfassend herausgestellt H. MERKLEIN, Die Gottesherrschaft als Handlungsprinzip. Untersuchung zur Ethik Jesu, Würzburg, ²1981.

57. Zum Forschungsüberblick vgl. H. FRANKEMÖLLE, Evangelium – Begriff und Gattung, Stuttgart, 1988, pp. 33-38; D. DORMEYER, Evangelium als literarische und theologische Gattung, Darmstadt, 1989, pp. 4-16.

58. M. DIBELIUS, Die Formgeschichte des Evangeliums, Tübingen, ⁶1971, p. 264, Anm. 1; aufgenommen von J.D. KINGSBURY, Matthew. Structure, Christology, Kingdom, Philadelphia, PA, 1975, pp. 131, 163; R.H. GUNDRY, Matthew, Grand Rapids, MI, 1981, p. 480; LUZ, Matthäus I (s. Anm. 4), p. 182.

59. Zu Forschungspositionen vgl. FRANKEMÖLLE, Evangelium (s. Anm. 57), pp. 138-149.

»emphatisch, daß sein Werk ʻein Evangelium’ ist«⁶⁰. Ob Mt dies
»emphatisch« tut, sei dahingestellt. Auch wenn eine Identifikation von
»Evangelium« mit dem mt Werk »noch nicht direkt vollzogen« ist, so
kündet sie sich nach U. Luz bereits an, da das durch den Kontext nicht
präzisierte »dieses Evangelium« in 24,14 »nur das im ganzen Mt-Ev
enthaltene Jesus-Evangelium meinen (kann)«⁶¹. Diese Tendenz einer
biographischen Transformierung des Begriffes »Evangelium« trägt auch
zur theologischen Qualifizierung des MtEv als heiliger Schrift ein
wichtiges Mosaiksteinchen bei, identifiziert Mt doch gerade die mündliche mit der schriftlichen Botschaft vom eschatologisch handelnden
Gott im sprachlichen und nichtsprachlichen Handeln Jesu. Sie findet
sich und ist identisch mit dem vorliegenden Evangelium. Im Kontext
der eigenen These, wonach das MtEv bei der Vereinigung von narrativen Texten und Redekompositionen, basierend auf der Kontamination
von MkEv und Q, das deuteronomistische und chronistische Geschichtswerk rezipierte, ist der Hinweis von J.A. Grassi bemerkenswert, daß in
der gesamten früheren Schrift einzig und allein sich im Deuteronomium
die Wendung »alle Worte dieses Gesetzes, die in diesem Buch aufgeschrieben sind« findet (28,58, in Variation auch in 28,61; 29,20.26;
30,10; 31,9.24). Grassi entwickelt aus diesem literarischen Befund die
bedenkenswerte These, daß die mt Wendung »dieses Evangelium von
der Basileia« die deuteronomistische Wendung »dieses Buch dieses
Gesetzes« variiert und daß das MtEv als »Deuteronomium« des zweiten
Testamentes für das Volk Gottes die gleichen Funktionen habe wie
jenes im früheren Bund⁶².

Es bleibt aber die Frage, warum Mt (vor allem bei der Annahme
einer Verarbeitung der vorhin genannten deuteronomistischen Wendung) in Aufnahme von Mk 1,1 die dort vorliegende, wenn auch in
seinem Sinn transformierte Überschrift »Evangelium Jesu Christi ...«
als Überschrift nicht rezipiert hat. Hier dürften synchrone und diachrone Motive eingewirkt haben.

8. »Buch der Geschichte« (1,1)

Ob sich die Wendung »βίβλος γενέσεως: Buch der Geschichte/des
Werdens/der Herkunft« in 1,1 auf den unmittelbar anschließenden

60. G.N. STANTON, *Matthew* (s. Anm. 25), pp. 1187-1201, ebd. p. 1195; da Stanton das
MtEv als »Leben Jesu« interpretiert (s.o.), blendet er den biblischen Einfluß auf das MtEv
in einseitiger und übertriebener Weise aus (vgl. ebd. pp. 1195-1196, Anm. 37).

61. Luz, *Matthäus I* (s. Anm. 4), p. 182; eindeutiger GNILKA, *Das Matthäusevangelium
II* (s. Anm. 27), p. 388 (»Es ist einfach das Evangelium, so wie es Mt erzählt und
verkündigt«); vgl. auch R.H. GUNDRY, *Matthew*, Grand Rapids, MI, 1982, p. 480.

62. J.A. GRASSI, *Matthew as a Second Testament Deuteronomy*, in *BTB* 19 (1989) 23-
30; zur eigenen »deuteronomistischen« Deutung des MtEv vgl. FRANKEMÖLLE, *Jahwe-
Bund* (s. Anm. 26), pp. 382-400; zu einzelnen rezipierten Traditionen aus dem deuteronomistischen und chronistischen Geschichtswerk vgl. die im Sachregister bei »Chronist, chr
Theologie« und »Deuteronomist, dtr Theologie« angegebenen Seiten.

Stammbaum oder auf das gesamte Werk bezieht, wird bis in die jüngste Zeit hinein dezidiert so oder so beantwortet[63]. Unbestritten ist jedoch: Mt verbindet vom ersten Vers seines Werkes an Traditionen der Schrift mit der des Urchristentums.

Wie stark die jüdische Grundstruktur ist, zeigt sich für jeden Leser in der über Q und MkEv hinausgehenden Vorgeschichte des Mt (Kap. 1–2), die – wie bei Prologen in der Antike üblich – formal und inhaltlich sehr bewußt und äußerst sorgfältig gestaltet ist. Sie ist der hermeneutische Schlüssel für das ganze Evangelium. Schon hier erhält der Leser für das richtige Verständnis folgende Leseanleitungen, die Mt im Ansatz bei Mk vorfand, aber entschieden modifiziert und erweitert[64] (vgl. Mk 1,1-3 mit dem christologischen Bekenntnis als Erfüllung der Zitate aus Mal 3,1; Ex 23,20 und Jes 40,3 LXX, wobei Mt parallel zu Lk Mal 3,1 aus Q in 3,3 streicht und erst in 11,10 rezipiert):

Deutlich ist, daß Matthäus – wie Markus – christliche, bibelkundige Leser voraussetzt, für die er den mk »Anfang des Evangeliums Jesu Christi, des Sohnes Gottes« (Mk 1,1) vertiefend reflektiert und zwar in verschiedener Richtung: In Differenz zu Mk betont Mt beim Bekenntnis zu »Jesus Christus« mit »Sohn Davids« zunächst den nationalen, messianisch-christologischen Aspekt der Herkunft aus dem Geschlecht Davids, was durch die Genealogie (1,2-17) konkretisiert wird (1,6.17); hier könnte Mt in der Tat die alte, judenchristliche Zweistufenchristologie adaptieren[65]. Diesem Bekenntnis entspricht im Evangelium die Sendung Jesu und der Jünger »nur« zu Israel (10,6; 15,24). Zugleich aber und anders als Mk betont Mt jedoch nicht nur den Partikularismus in 1,1, sondern mit dem Bekenntnis zu Jesus als dem »Sohn Abrahams« auch den Universalismus[66] in der Vorstellung des Herbeiströmens der Heiden (8,10-13) und der Mission zu »allen Völkern«

---

63. Die erstere These vertritt entschieden etwa STANTON, *Matthew* (s. Anm. 25), pp. 1188, 1196. Im gleichen Band der Festschrift für F. Neirynck impliziert der Titel von D. DORMEYER, *Mt 1,1 als Überschrift zur Gattung und Christologie des Matthäus-Evangeliums*, Leuven, 1992, pp. 1361-1383, die Gegenpostition; er verbindet damit die These einer »Zweistufenchristologie des Matthäus«, womit das Bekenntnis zum Sohn Gottes und zum Immanuel im Prolog jedoch unterbewertet wird. Zur eigenen, zweiten These vgl. FRANKEMÖLLE, *Jahwe-Bund* (s. Anm. 26), pp. 360-365; vgl. auch A. SAND, *Das Evangelium nach Matthäus*, Regensburg, 1986, pp. 40-41.

64. Ohne Zweifel hat Mt den biographischen Rahmen des Lebens Jesu von Mk übernommen, inklusive die Vorbereitung des Wirkens Jesu, letzterer aber wie dem ganzen Werk durch die vorgeschaltete »Kindheitsgeschichte« eine neue Tiefendimension gegeben; zur Struktur des neugestalteten Evangeliums vgl. etwa F. NEIRYNCK, *Evangelica*, Leuven, 1982, pp. 3-36, 691-723, 729-736; *Evangelica II*, 1991. Zum Exordium in Mk 1,1-3 vgl. jetzt R. KAMPLING, *Israel unter dem Anspruch des Messias*, Stuttgart, 1992, pp. 25-46.

65. Vgl. GNILKA, *Das Matthäusevangelium I* (s. Anm. 37), pp. 12-13; DORMEYER *Mt 1,1* (s. Anm. 63), p. 1367 unter Hinweis vor allem auf Röm 1,3-4.

66. Zum Völkersegen an Abraham vgl. Gen 12,1-3; 17,1-14 u.a., rezipiert von Mt etwa auch in 3,9 und 8,11.

(26,13; 28,19). Auch im Prolog ist dieser Gedanke in 1,1 nicht singulär (vgl. in der Genealogie die Rolle der heidnischen Frauen in 1,3.5a.b.6 und die der heidnischen Magier in 2,1-12; auch in der weiteren Vorgeschichte wird dieser Aspekt thematisiert: 3,9; 4,8.15-16.19.24-25). Ein solch starker, für jeden Leser überraschender Akzent ist sehr auffällig (dies wird von uns Heidenchristen allzu schnell unterbewertet). Dabei dürfte der Hinweis auf die heidnischen Frauen im Stammbaum und auf die Magier als Aufhebung ihrer Ausgrenzung verstanden werden, keineswegs jedoch als Auslöschung ihrer heidnischen Identität, vielmehr versteht Matthäus diesen Aspekt der Geschichte als integriertes Element der Geschichte Gottes mit Israel, mit Jesus und mit den »Völkern« (daher »müssen« Heiden in Kap. 1 und 2 auftreten).

Aus dieser Spannung von Partikularismus und Universalismus in 1,1 entwickelt sich die gesamte Dramaturgie des Evangeliums: Mt geht es um das Verhältnis Israels zu dem von Gott exklusiv zu ihm gesandten letzten Boten Jesus, um die Gründe und Folgen seiner Ablehnung, um das Werden und Wachsen der Jüngerschar Jesu, seiner Kirche (16,18) aus Juden und Heiden, woraus sich das spannungsvolle Verhältnis Israel – Kirche entwickelt. Der Vers 1,1 kann somit nur als Überschrift zum gesamten Evangelium verstanden werden. Er enthält zwar nicht sein Resümee, wohl aber den Stoff, den Mt in seinem »Buch« (1,1) erzählen will, das Grundproblem, dessen Lösung der Leser erwarten darf. Dies alles entfaltet Matthäus nicht nur in synchroner, sondern auch in diachroner Perspektive. Da es Matthäus um die Geschichte Gottes mit Israel bis auf Jesus hin geht sowie um die Geschichte Gottes in und durch Jesus bis zu seinem Mitsein mit seiner Kirche bis zum Ende der Zeit, ließ sich diese narrative Ausrichtung als Geschichtserzählung mit einem Begriff versehen, der sich in den Geschichtserzählungen der Schrift anbot und zugleich auch für jeden Leser aus dem pagan-griechischen Bereich verständlich war. Gegen die heute z.T. übliche Deutung von βίβλος in 1,1 als »Urkunde, Dokument«, bezogen nur auf den Stammbaum[67], ist kritisch zu fragen: »Verzichtet Matthäus tatsächlich auf eine Überschrift, wie sie seine Markusvorlage kennt, und fällt ohne Überschrift mit der Tür ins Haus, hier mit einem Stammbaum-Dokument in das Evangelium«[68]? Dagegen ist davon auszugehen, daß nicht nur jeder Leser aus dem pagan-griechischen, sondern auch aus dem jüdischen und christlichen Bereich den Begriff βίβλος in 1,1 im damals üblichen Sinn als »Buch« verstanden haben dürfte[69].

---

67. LUZ, *Matthäus I* (s. Anm. 4), p. 88; GNILKA, *Das Matthäusevangelium I* (s. Anm. 37), p. 7.
68. DORMEYER, *Mt 1,1* (s. Anm. 63), p. 1363.
69. Vgl. BAUER-ALAND, p. 282; *NBL* I, pp. 340-342; SAND, *Matthäus* (s. Anm. 63), p. 39.

Für einen rhetorisch versierten Verfasser, als der Mt sich in seinem gesamten Werk im Kleinen und Großen präsentiert, ist ein Bezug nur auf den Stammbaum kaum anzunehmen. Matthäus will – analog zu Biographien von Philosophen und Staatsführern in der hellenistischen Umwelt sowie von Vorgaben der Schrift (vgl. Tob 1,1; Nah 1,1; Bar 1,1.3; Sir Prol 31), aber in Aufnahme und Veränderung der kerygmatisch-geschichtlichen Erzählung des Mk – ein »Buch der Geschichte/des Werdens« all der oben genannten Probleme vorlegen. Daß das MtEv dabei keine übliche Biographie im hellenistischen Sinn ist, sondern in Weiterführung des MkEv eine biographisch orientierte, theologische Geschichtsdarstellung[70], ist im Ansatz fraglos, im einzelnen jedoch umstritten. Das MtEv in seiner übergreifenden Gestalteinheit enthält die dramatische Erzählung der Geschichte des Volkes Israel mit Jesus und seinen Nachfolgern (5,11-12; 10,17-18; 23,34), aber umgekehrt auch die Geschichte Jesu mit Israel und seiner in der Schrift überlieferten Geschichte (vgl. die Rezeption der Moses-, Israel- und Jakob-Motive in Kap. 2 und die spezifisch mt »Erfüllungszitate«). Das MtEv ist die Ätiologie, die »archäologische« Erzählung (vgl. das Stichwort ἀρχή in Mk 1,1), das »Buch der Geschichte/des Werdens/der Herkunft« dieser dramatischen Entwicklung und jener Situation, in der sich die Leser des MtEv befinden.

Traditionsgeschichtlich knüpft Mt bei der Wendung βίβλος γενέσεως an Gen 2,4 LXX und 5,1 an (vgl. auch Gen 6,9; 11,27; 25,19; 37,2) – beginnend jeweils mit der Lebensgeschichte einer Person und ihrer Familie. Vor allem Gen 5,1 mit der Wendung »Buch der Geschichte der Menschen« könnte Mt die Anregung nicht nur für seine Überschrift, sondern auch für das universalistische Bekenntnis zu Jesus als »Sohn Abrahams« in 1,1 geliefert haben. Indem Mt im eigentlichen Stammbaum die absteigende Linie von Abraham zu Jesus (1,2-16) betont, beginnt er sein Werk in Korrespondenz dazu in 1,1 mit der aufsteigenden Linie, wodurch jene Person an den Anfang und in den Mittelpunkt gestellt wird, um die es Mt geht. Zielt die Genealogie mit dem Periodisierungsschema darauf hin, daß die gesamte Geschichte Israels mit den universalen Heilsverheißungen aufgrund der Treue Gottes auf Jesus Christus hin angelegt war, so signalisiert der Buchtitel des gesamten Werkes, daß Mt die für die Leser gegenwärtige Situation einer zu allen Menschen geöffneten Kirche mit ihrer geschichtlichen Herkunft von Jesus Christus her darstellen will[71].

Inhalt seines (den Lesern vorliegenden) Evangeliums (zu 24,15 und 26,53 s.o. II.7) als »Buch der Geschichte« (1,1) ist das eschatologische Handeln Gottes in und durch Jesus Christus und der dadurch »erzwun-

---

70. Zur Begründung vgl. D. DORMEYER, *Evangelium* (s. Anm. 57), pp. 113-130.
71. Ausführlicher vgl. FRANKEMÖLLE, *Jahwe-Bund* (s. Anm. 26), pp. 308-314, 360-382.

genen«, im Verlauf des Evangeliums erzählten (Kap. 2–28) neuen Geschichte Gottes mit Israel (als Gerichts-Geschichte) und mit dem »Volk Jesu« (vgl. 1,21), mit seiner »Kirche« (16,18), wobei offen bleibt, ob diese Geschichte für die beteiligten Menschen gut ausgeht; hier ist an die mt Gerichtsaussagen am Ende jeder Rede und an die Heilsungewißheit der Adressaten zu erinnern (s.o. II.4).

Mit den bisherigen Hinweisen, den Prolog des MtEv in diachroner Perspektive zu deuten, sollte vor allem die narrative Intention des Evangelisten betont werden. Es bedarf jedoch noch der ergänzenden Ausführungen zur theozentrischen und christologischen Dimension, will man sein Anliegen und sein Werk nicht grundlegend mißverstehen.

9. »Sie werden seinen Namen Immanuel nennen« (1,23)

Mit der bisherigen Beschränkung auf die menschliche Ebene ist die grundlegend theozentrische Ausrichtung des MtEv insgesamt, aber auch der Vorgeschichte noch nicht bewußt gemacht worden. Erst wenn das göttliche dramaturgische Handeln einbezogen wird, erreicht die mt Konzeption Stimmigkeit und Kohärenz zwischen Prolog und Epilog und dem in den Reden und Erzählungen behaupteten Anspruch des irdischen Jesus. Nach Mt ist Jesus nicht erst von Anfang an »dem Fleische nach« Messias, Sohn Abrahams, Prophet, Lehrer, vielmehr »Sohn Gottes« in dezidierter Form (vgl. die Vater/Herr-Sohn-Relation in 1,22; 2,15); dieser Glaube ist die Zielaussage der gesamten mt Vorgeschichte[72]. Dieses Bekenntnis ist die Grundaussage des christlichen Glaubens nach Mt[73]. Nicht nur die Auferweckungs- und Verklärungsgeschichte, nicht nur die Erzählung von der Taufe Jesu, sondern der Prolog erzählt bereits die Ätiologie dieses Glaubens. Die Überschrift zum Evangelium in 1,1 dürfte insofern daran partizipieren, als der Begriff βίβλος γενέσεως eine »Doppelfunktion«[74] im Sinne von »Buch der Geschichte/des Werdens/der Herkunft« als Einleitung zur Genealogie und zum ganzen Evangelium erfüllt. Mt versteht γένεσις in der doppelten Bedeutung des »Werdens«: Vor die Geschichte Jesu und dem von ihm bewirkten Geschehen für Israel und für die Kirche stellt Mt als Voraussetzung die Frage nach der »Herkunft« Jesu (1,2-16) in genealogisch-anthropologischer Hinsicht, aber auch nach dem »Werden Jesu Christi« unter theozentrischer Perspektive (1,18-25): Jesus verdankt seine spezifische Existenz einzig einer Neuschöpfung durch Gottes lebenschaffenden Geist, was Mt – dies belegt das Schriftzitat zur Jungfrauengeburt aus Jes 7,14 LXX – als schriftgemäß versteht.

---

72. Zur Begründung vgl. R. PESCH, *Der Gottessohn im matthäischen Evangelienprolog (Mt 1–2)*, in *Bib* 48 (1967) 395-420.

73. Vgl. KINGSBURY, *Matthew* (s. Anm. 58), pp. 40-83.

74. So P. GAECHTER, *Die literarische Kunst im Matthäus-Evangelium*, Stuttgart, 1965, p. 54; zu anderen Stimmen vgl. FRANKEMÖLLE, *Jahwe-Bund* (s. Anm. 26), p. 360, Anm. 6.

Dieses Zitat ist um so auffälliger, weil Mt hier zum ersten Mal ein »Erfüllungszitat« einführt und ein solches nur hier bei einem Hoheitstitel steht. Insofern kann dieser gar nicht hoch genug bewertet werden für die theologische Konzeption des Mt. Der Gott Israels, der sich in den zweimal vierzehn Geschlechtern der Geschichte Israels als der Handelnde erweist, führt eben diese Geschichte nicht nur auf den Menschen Jesus zu (1,16), sondern bindet nach Mt seine Selbsterschließung an ihn, offenbart sich in ihm und wurde in ihm Mensch: »Immanuel, das heißt übersetzt: Gott (ist) mit uns« (1,23) ist die mt Deutung des mk vielfältig deutbaren und mißdeutbaren Bekenntnisses zum »Sohn Gottes« (Mk 1,1). Für seine biblisch vorgebildeten Leser liefert Mt eine unmißverständliche Interpretation[75] durch den schriftgemäßen Titel »Immanuel«, der in der Übersetzung für die griechischen Leser die theozentrische Basiskategorie des MtEv bildet (neben 28,20 vgl. auch 17,17; 18,20; 26,29.38.40)[76]. Die Übertragung von Gottes-Prädikaten auf Jesus Christus fand Mt bereits bei Mk und in Q vor (zum κύριος-Titel im Prolog vgl. etwa Mk 1,3 par Mt 3,3), jedoch hat Mt den Prozeß der personalen Identifizierung in der Funktion stärker als seine Vorlagen betont und damit zugleich die soteriologische Deutung des Namens »Jesus« (1,21: »denn er wird sein Volk retten von ihren Sünden«) und den ekklesiologischen Gedanken (»mit euch«) verbunden. Alle anderen Hoheitstitel leisten dies nicht.

»Immanuel« garantiert die soteriologische Dignität des für die Leser vielleicht nicht mehr sofort verständlichen Namens »Jesus«, da das theophore Element in »Jesus« (dessen hebräischer Name »Jeschua« bedeutet: »Jahwe erweist sich als Rettung/Heil/Erlösung«) festgehalten wird[77]. Matthäus geht es von Anfang des Evangeliums an mittels biblisch begründeter Deutung des Namens »Jesus« (vgl. Ps 129,8 LXX) darum, daß Gott selbst in Jesus sein Volk erlöst, da Jesus der »Immanuel: der Gott mit uns« ist. »Beide Namen sind im Grunde identisch. Indem das Kind Jesus genannt wird, geht also die Immanuel-Weissagung zwar nicht buchstäblich, aber doch sinngemäß in Erfüllung«[78]. Nach Mt ist der irdische Jesus als Person gleichzeitig Ort

---

75. Dormeyer, *Mt 1,1* (s. Anm. 63), p. 1382 behauptet: »Die Christologie des Matthäus potenziert die assoziative Dunkelheit des Markus, den antiken Stil der obscuritas«; bei seinem Überblick über christologische Titel im Matthäusevangelium kommt — dies ist auffällig — Immanuel als exordialer Titel nicht vor.

76. Zur Begründung Frankemölle, *Jahwe-Bund* (s. Anm. 26), pp. 7-83; vgl. auch Gnilka, *Das Matthäusevangelium II* (s. Anm. 27), pp. 535-536.

77. Vgl. F. Delitzsch, *Der Jesus-Name*, in *Zeitschrift für die gesamte lutherische Theologie und Kirche* 37 (1876) 209-214; vgl. auch G. Schneider, Ἰησοῦς in *EWNT* 2 (1981) 440-452, ebd. pp. 442-443.

78. M. Oberweis, *Beobachtungen zum AT-Gebrauch in der matthäischen Kindheitsgeschichte*, in *NTS* 35 (1989) 131-149, ebd. pp. 140-141; Oberweis weist nach, daß Mt die beiden ersten Kapitel nicht nur von wörtlichen Zitaten, sondern auch nach der Technik impliziter biblischer Zitate gestaltet hat; dieser Ansatz ist für die hier vertretene These bedeutsam und wäre ausführlich in einer Monographie am gesamten MtEv aufzuarbeiten.

der Selbstoffenbarung und des heilsmittlerischen Wirkens Gottes, da
»Jesus« der »Jahwe hilft« ist. Trifft dies zu, dann dürfte das Motiv der
Jungfrauengeburt aus Jes 7,14 wie dort so auch hier für Mt »ein
Zeichen« für Jesus als die menschliche Daseinsweise Gottes auf Erden
sein. Wie die anderen Stellen im Evangelium belegen, ist dies der
Glaubensinhalt der Kirche aus den Völkern, worauf auch die Verände-
rung von der zweiten Person Singular in die dritte Person Plural (»sie
werden seinen Namen Immanuel nennen«, in der Septuaginta ist es die
Frau) hindeutet[79]. »Dies alles ist geschehen« (die von Gott auf Jesus
Christus hin geführte Geschichte Israels, seine Neuschöpfung, seine
soteriologische Funktion), damit und weil er sich so als »Immanuel«
erweist. Mt ist kein Vertreter einer Präexistenz-Christologie, wohl aber
behauptet er glaubend die Identität des Irdischen mit seiner göttlichen
Seinsweise (und schaffte so mit »Immanuel« gleichsam einen titularen
Vorgriff auf die Kompromißformel des Konzils von 451 in Chalcedon,
wonach Jesus Christus »wahrer Gott und wahrer Mensch« ist). Nach
der Auferweckung wird daher seine ihm zustehende Vollmacht universal-kosmologisch (28,18) sowie alle Völker umspannend (25,31-46;
28,19) umschrieben.

Die Theozentrik[80] und die theozentrisch strukturierte und gedachte
Christologie – Mt versteht beide Aspekte als Einheit – sind letzte
Grundlage für alle bisher genannten Punkte und damit für das Verständnis des MtEv als heilige Schrift in der Kontinuität der heiligen
Schrift des früheren Bundes. Diskontinuität gibt es nur auf seiten der
Menschen. Wenn die Treue Gottes und sein Handeln die Konstante in
der bisherigen Geschichte Israels und in der Geschichte Gottes durch
Jesus an Israel ist, dann ist dieser schriftgemäße Denkansatz des Mt
nicht nur thematisch, sondern auch exegetisch-methodisch ernster zu
nehmen, als es bislang geschieht. Dies sei abschließend in Thesen
stichwortartig (Stich-Worte wollen anstacheln) formuliert.

III. Zur Gattung des Matthäusevangeliums

1. Die Alternative von traditionsgeschichtlich orientierter, auf Quellen fixierter »Literarkritik« und synchron verstandener »Literarkritik/
Literary Criticism« ist künstlich und wird von einem traditionsgesättig-
ten Text wie dem MtEv ad absurdum geführt. Mt erweist sich als

---

79. Zur universalen Deutung von 1,21.23 vgl. FRANKEMÖLLE, *Jahwe-Bund* (s. Anm.
26), pp. 12-21, 211-220.
80. Vgl. R.L. MOWERY, *God, Lord and Father. The Theology of the Gospel of Matthew*,
in *BR* 33 (1988) 24-36; DERS., *The Activity of God in the Gospel of Matthew*, in D.J. LULL
(ed.), *SBL 1989 Seminar Papers*, pp. 400-411; zum eigenen Ansatz vgl. FRANKEMÖLLE,
Jahwe-Bund (s. Anm. 26), pp. 159-165.

Meister der Redaktion durch Komposition von Traditionen, wobei sein kompositionell strukturiertes Werk in seiner übergreifenden Gestalteinheit allein durch Strukturanalysen, Formkritik, semantische Wortfeldanalysen, rhetorische Analysen usw. beschreibbar ist[81]. Dennoch ist sein Text als »Gewebe« keinesfalls nur synchron verstehbar zu machen, weder für Mt selbst noch für seine Leser, deren biblisches Glaubenswissen er vom ersten bis zum letzten Vers umfassend voraussetzt. Gleiches gilt auch für urchristliche Traditionen. Mt geht hier von einer thematischen und glaubensgeschichtlichen Einheit aus. Dies wäre hermeneutisch bei der Auslegung stärker zu berücksichtigen (Exegeten sind in der Regel nur an der textlichen Rezeption bestimmter Zitate, Worte u.a. interessiert).

2. Ohne Zweifel ist das MtEv unter christologischer Perspektive als narratio eine Neuausgabe des MkEv, was durch den gesamten Aufriß bestätigt wird; die entscheidenden Einschnitte finden sich parallel zu Mk in 4,17 und 16,21 (ἀπὸ τότε). Auch die Rezeption von Stoffen aus der Logienquelle ist unbestritten (jedenfalls für die, die von der Zweiquellentheorie ausgehen). Das sogenannte Sondergut ist dagegen bekanntlich umstritten, der Anteil von Tradition (gar als Quelle) und Redaktion kann nur in einem synthetischen Verständnis des gesamten MtEv vermutet werden (die gerade in neueren Kommentaren vorgegebene Sicherheit zur Differenzierung von Tradition und Redaktion teile ich nicht; am Beispiel der Hapaxlegomena als angebliches Argument für Traditionen ließe sich das Problem methodisch und hermeneutisch in seiner hypothetischen Fragwürdigkeit leicht darstellen). Sondergut ist etwa ein Viertel des Stoffes, während etwa ein Viertel aus Q stammt und etwa die Hälfte Vorlagen im MkEv hat.

Während letzteres jedoch sowohl in seiner thematischen wie literarischen Bedeutung für das MtEv gesehen wird, gilt Gleiches nicht für die literarische Bedeutung von Q als Gattung – und dies, obwohl die Reden das MtEv erst zu dem machen, was es ist. Ohne Reden wäre es nur eine um die Vorgeschichte erweiterte Neuauflage des MkEv. Dies ist es aber nicht! Die Kontamination von Erzählungen und Reden zeigt sich auch in der doppelten Strukturierung: Neben den deutlichen, im MkEv vorgegebenen Einschnitten in 4,17 und 16,21 ist aufgrund der Gesamtkomposition des MtEv der wichtigste Einschnitt in 16,1 (wegen des Rückbezuges in 28,20 auf 16,1 und der dort sich findenden, alle Reden zusammenfassenden Schlußformel in 16,1; s.o. II.1 und 3). Dies ist keine Notlösung, sondern bestätigt das raffinierte rhetorische Vorgehen des Mt. Dem entspricht auch, daß sich nicht nur in der Abfolge

---

81. Zur in sich stimmigen sprachlichen Gestalt vgl. W. SCHENK, *Die Sprache des Matthäus. Die Text-Konstituenten in ihren makro- und mikrostrukturellen Relationen*, Göttingen, 1987.

der Erzählung eine Dramaturgie mit deutlicher Steigerung (in Anlehnung an Mk) findet, sondern auch eine Dramaturgie mit deutlicher
Steigerung in den Reden (5–7: Die Tora Jesu in Identität mit der Schrift
in Auseinandersetzung mit deren vielgestaltiger, jüdischer Auslegungsgeschichte; 10: Unterweisung für die Boten Jesu; 13 als literarisches
und theologisches Zentrum der Reden: Die Basileia Gottes in Gleichnissen; 18: Über das Miteinander in der christlichen Gemeinde; 23-25:
Die eschatologische Gerichtsperspektive für Israel und die Kirche so
wie für Juden und Heiden). Der eschatologischen Perspektive am Ende
der einzelnen Rede (s.o.) entspricht das vollzogene bzw. drohende
Gericht über Israel und die Kirche, wobei auch Kap. 23 – woran zu
erinnern ist – als Text des Evangeliums ekklesiologisch orientiert ist[82].

Mt hat alle traditionellen Stoffe durch Auslassungen, Umstellungen,
Überarbeitungen und vor allem durch thematisch verdichtende Kompositionen bearbeitet; dies gilt auch für die Stoffe aus Q. Dennoch machen
sie nicht die Vorlage für die Redekompositionen als Gattung im MtEv
aus. Mt selbst macht deutlich (s.o. II.1 und 3), daß das Deuteronomium
mit den Reden von Josua, Samuel, David und vor allem Moses ihm den
entscheidenden redaktionellen Hinweis zur Gestaltung gab (mag auch
allgemein der Brauch antiker Geschichtsschreibung, an den Lk etwa in
der Apostelgeschichte anknüpft, auch Mt bekannt gewesen sein; von
einer Rezeption dieser Tradition ist jedoch nichts zu spüren).

Ist dies zutreffend, dann ist im Sinne des Mt die übliche innerchristliche Zwei-Quellen-Theorie zu einer Drei-Quellen-Theorie (Schrift,
Markus, Q) zu erweitern – und zwar in literarisch formaler wie in
thematisch-theologischer Hinsicht. Wer wollte behaupten, daß unter
dieser Perspektive das MtEv als heilige Schrift und als literarisch
verstandenes »Evangelium« (s.o. II.4) in Kontinuität zur heiligen
Schrift des früheren Bundes genügend gewürdigt worden ist? Es gilt,
eine markionitisch geprägte, christliche Engführung aufzubrechen. Das
Motiv dazu liefert nicht der ökumenische Dialog im christlich-jüdischen
Gespräch[83], sondern das Selbstverständnis des Mt von der eigenen
christlichen Identität. Sie steht einerseits in Kontinuität zur Identität
Israels im früheren Bund, dem literarisch die Einheit von der Schrift des
früheren Bundes und der Schrift der eigenen Gemeinde entspricht,
zugleich aber andererseits in Auseinandersetzung mit der pharisäisch
geprägten, sich normativ verstehenden Theologie seiner Zeit mit der
Folge der Trennung von pharisäischer Synagoge und Kirche, phari-

---

82. Zur Begründung vgl. FRANKEMÖLLE, *Biblische Handlungslanweisungen* (s. Anm.
10), pp. 133-190.
83. Zu Konsequenzen aus einer wirklich monotheistisch gedachten Theologie für den
christlichen Glauben vgl. H. FRANKEMÖLLE, *Jüdisch-christlicher Dialog. Interreligiöse und
innerchristliche Aspekte*, in *Catholica* 46 (1992) 114-139.

säischem Judentum und Christentum[84]. In dieser »Zersetzungs-Geschichte« war das MtEv mit seiner polemisch ausgerichteten »Enterbungs-Theologie« (vgl. vor allem 21,33-46; 27,3-10.24-25 – in Rezeption jüdischer Rechtsvorstellungen!) ein wichtiger Faktor[85], was dem Verständnis des Mt von seiner Theologie als jüdischer Reformtheologie und von seiner Gemeinde als der Gemeinde Gottes in Jesus Christus im Kontext des damaligen Reformjudentums nicht entsprach. An diesem Punkt ist historisch-kritisch Sachkritik an der israelfeindlichen Auslegungsgeschichte des MtEv zu üben, da eine innerjüdische Auseinandersetzung nicht Modell für das Verhältnis von jüdischen Gläubigen und heidenchristlichen Gläubigen sein kann (wie der »Erkenntnisfortschritt« des Paulus vom 1. Thessalonicherbrief zum Römerbrief verdeutlichen kann).

Das heißt: Die Theologie des Mt ist als situative Theologie ernst zu nehmen und sein Text als Text-in-Situation mit einer bestimmten Funktion und Handlungsorientierung zu verstehen. Eine auf synchrone Literarkritik beschränkte Auslegung erfaßt nur einen Aspekt. Nur eine integrative Bibelauslegung, die auch traditionsgeschichtliche Rezeptionen in ihrem redaktionellen Stellenwert beachtet, vermag einem Werk wie dem des Mt gerecht zu werden. Wenn Mt aber sein Werk als heilige Schrift in kontinuierlicher Fortsetzung der heiligen Schrift des früheren Bundes verstand, hat dem die Auslegung zu entsprechen. Die Forschung zum MtEv mit ihrer verengt innerchristlichen Perspektive hat dieses Selbstverständnis des Mt bislang noch nicht wirklich ernst genommen. Die Folgerungen für synchron-literarkritische und diachron-traditionsgeschichtliche Forschungen sind noch einzulösen.

Von seinem Selbstverständnis her ist Mt ein hervorragender Vertreter einer biblischen, die Schrift des früheren und des neuen Bundes umfassenden Theologie mit ihrer jeweils lebendigen Tradititonsgeschichte, so daß also die vieldiskutierte »biblische Theologie« schon im Begriff viel zu kurz greift, da nicht nur das lebendige Frühjudentum ausgeblendet wird, sondern der textfixierte und textimmanente Begriff »biblische Theologie« die jeweils vom Glauben geprägten sozialen Lebensformen der verschiedenen frühjüdischen Gruppen (einschließlich der Jesusbewegung) nicht beachtet.

Matthäus sieht die Verbundenheit der ältesten Jesusbewegung mit ihrem jüdischen Mutterboden nicht nur in der Rezeption von schrift-

---

84. Zu den theologiegeschichtlichen, politischen, sprachlichen, sonstigen kulturellen u.a. Faktoren vgl. H. FRANKEMÖLLE, *Die Entstehung des Christentums aus dem Judentum. Historische, theologische und hermeneutische Aspekte im Kontext von Röm 9–11*, in S. SCHRÖER (ed.), *Christen und Juden. Voraussetzungen für ein erneuertes Verhältnis*, Altenberge, 1992, pp. 34-83.

85. Vgl. etwa R. KAMPLING, *Das Blut Christi und die Juden. Mt 27,25 bei den lateinischsprachigen christlichen Autoren bis zu Leo dem Großen*, Münster, 1984.

lichen Traditionen, von Sprache und Verkündigung, sondern in der Ausdrucksweise, im Denken und in der durch die Praxis be-glaubigten Lebensweise der Christen. Darin dürfte Papias von Hierapolis in der Deutung von Kürzinger recht haben, daß der Verfasser des MtEv sein griechisch geschriebenes Werk nach hebräischem Stil geordnet hat, da der Begriff διάλεκτος als »Fachausdruck der rhetorischen Techne« zu verstehen sei[86]. Mt variiert nicht nur die Logienquelle und das MkEv, er hebt sie auch in seiner evangeliaren, biblisch orientierten Geschichtserzählung auf. Das vorliegende »Buch der Geschichte Jesu Christi« (1,1) in Identität mit seinem »Evangelium« (24,14; 26,13) ist sein Versuch, aller Welt vom sprachlichen und nichtsprachlichen Handeln Jesu als Immanuel, als »Gott mit uns« (1,23), zu verkündigen.

Helmarshauser Weg 2   H. FRANKEMÖLLE
D-4790 Paderborn

---

86. J. KÜRZINGER, *Papias von Hierapolis und die Evangelien des Neuen Testaments*, Regensburg, 1983, p. 21; vgl. auch DORMEYER, *Evangelium* (s. Anm. 57), pp. 7-11.

LE DISCOURS ESCHATOLOGIQUE LUCANIEN
«RÉDACTION» ET «COMPOSITION»
(Lc 21,5-36 et Mc 13,1-37)

I. La question

«Rédaction» et «composition» se recoupent et s'entrelacent de manière tellement forte que, pour la *Redaktionsgeschichte*, on avait proposé au départ le nom de *Kompositionsgeschichte* ou de *Kompositionskritik*[1]. Ici, nous voudrions illustrer ces multiples recoupements moins de manière théorique que de manière concrète en examinant le discours eschatologique de Luc à la lumière de sa source, la version marcienne.

Les deux textes ont en effet une présentation substantiellement parallèle aussi bien dans les grandes lignes que dans chaque section, mais avec des différences notables à expliquer *rédactionnellement* comme modifications intentionnelles de Luc ou bien *littérairement* par l'utilisation d'autres sources. Déjà chez Augustin nous trouvons l'explication rédactionnelle, même si elle est un peu alourdie par des préoccupations apologétiques: «Lucas [...] patefecit quod esse posset incertum, non ad sæculi finem, sed ad expugnationem Jerusalem pertinere [...] dicens apertius de hac eadem re, quæ illi posuerunt obscurius...»[2]. Les

---

1. Cf. E. Haenchen, *Der Weg Jesu. Eine Erklärung des Markus-Evangeliums und der kanonischen Parallelen* (Sammlung Töpelmann, II/6), Berlin, 1966, p. 24; cf. Id., *Die Apostelgeschichte* (KEK, 3), Göttingen, [14]1965, pp. 37-47.93-99. Cf. F. Neirynck, *La rédaction matthéenne et la structure du premier évangile*, in I. de la Potterie (ed.), *De Jésus aux Évangiles. Tradition et rédaction dans les Évangiles synoptiques. Donum natalicium J. Coppens*, II (BETL, 25), Gembloux-Paris, 1967, pp. 41-73, voir p. 48, n. 30 (= Id., *Evangelica* [BETL, 60], Leuven, 1982, pp. 3-36, voir p. 10, n. 30): «Dans sa communication du 2 septembre 1965 à Heidelberg, C.-H. Hunzinger proposa de parler de *Kompositionskritik*. Le terme marquerait mieux l'indépendance vis-à-vis de la *Formgeschichte* et deviendrait facilement international (en anglais: *source criticism, form criticism, composition criticism*)». Le terme *(compositio, dispositio, ordo, structura...)* dérive de la rhétorique ancienne: cf. H. Lausberg, *Handbuch der literarischen Rhetorik*, München, [2]1973, pp. 241-247; A.D. Leeman, *Orationis ratio. Teoria e pratica stilistica degli oratori, storici e filosofi latini*, Bologna, 1974, pp. 151-153, 193-201; B. Mortara Garavelli, *Manuale di retorica*, Milano, 1988, pp. 273-280, voir p. 273: «E' un lavoro ben codificato di 'costruzione', di 'strutturazione', nel senso proprio di sistemazione organica, di coordinamento delle unità che costituiscono insiemi, in modo che questi risultino come totalità internamente organizzate e vicendevolmente disposte secondo equilibri perfetti...».

2. Augustin, *ep. 199*, 9, 29-30 (ed. A. Goldbacher; CSEL 57), Vindobonae-Lipsiae, 1911, pp. 243-292; la citation: nn. 29 et 30, pp. 269,18-19; 270,15-16. Position plus concordiste dans le *De consensu evangelistarum*, l. II, c. LXXVII, nn. 147-151 (ed. F. Weihrich; CSEL, 43), Vindobonae-Lipsiae, 1904, pp. 251-256.

modernes développeront cette explication avec plus de clarté, mettant
en lumière que l'auteur du troisième évangile récrit l'oracle *post eventum*
à partir d'un point de vue différent non seulement chronologiquement
mais encore théologiquement; allaient déjà en ce sens F.C. Baur (qui
considère Matthieu comme source de Luc) et d'autres personnalités de
l'école de Tübingen[3].

Même lorsqu'à la *Tendenzkritik* de Tübingen succéda la *Quellenkritik*, l'explication rédactionnelle continua à être partagée (désormais
dans le cadre de l'hypothèse des deux sources)[4], mais on lui opposa une
explication purement littéraire, à savoir l'hypothèse d'une source supplémentaire différente de Marc[5]. Aujourd'hui, comme J. Verheyden[6] l'a

3. F.C. BAUR, *Kritische Untersuchungen über die kanonischen Evangelien, ihr Verhältnis
zueinander, ihren Charakter und Ursprung*, Tübingen, 1847, pp. 477s.; A. HILGENFELD, *Die
Evangelien nach ihrer Entstehung und geschichtlichen Bedeutung*, Leipzig, 1854, pp. 211-
213, 224s.

4. H.J. HOLTZMANN, *Die synoptischen Evangelien. Ihr Ursprung und geschichtlicher
Charakter*, Leipzig, 1863, pp. 235-237, 326s.; J. WELLHAUSEN, *Das Evangelium Lucae*,
Berlin, 1904, pp. 117s.: «Er hat die Weissagung up to date gebracht» [= *Evangelienkom-
mentare*, Berlin - New York, 1987, pp. 575s.]; F.C. BURKITT, *The Use of Mark in the
Gospel according to Luke*, in F.J. FOAKES JACKSON – K. LAKE (ed.),*The Beginnings of
Christianity*. I. *The Acts of the Apostles*, London, 1922, II, pp. 106-120.

5. V. TAYLOR, *A Cry from the Siege: A Suggestion Regarding a Non-Marcan Oracle
Embedded in Lk XXI,20-36*, in *JTS* 26 (1924-25) 136-144 (Proto-Luc: marciens seulement
les vv. 21a.23a.26b-27.29-33); ID., *Behind the Third Gospel. A Study of the Proto-Luke
Hypothesis*, Oxford, 1926, pp. 101-125; T.W. MANSON, *The Sayings of Jesus*, London,
[2]1949, pp. 323-337 (p. 325: «...a solid block of L material...»); W.L. KNOX, *The Sources
of the Synoptic Gospels*, I. *St. Mark*, ed. H. CHADWICK, Cambridge, 1953, pp. 109-112;
P. WINTER, *The Treatment of His Sources by the Third Evangelist in Luke 21-24*, in *ST* 8
(1954) 138-172 (pp. 141-155: «The Apocalyptic Discourse»; marciens seulement les vv.
12-13.16-17.21a.23a.26b-27.29-33); W. BUNDY, *Jesus and the First Three Gospels. An
Introduction to the Synoptic Tradition*, Cambridge, MA, 1955, pp. 458-476; K.H. RENG-
STORF, *Das Evangelium nach Lukas* (NTD, 3), Göttingen, [8]1958, pp. 233-238; L. GASTON,
Sondergut und Markustoff in Luk. 21, in *TZ* 16 (1960) 161-172; ID., *No Stone on Another.
Studies in the Significance of the Fall of Jerusalem in the Synoptic Gospels* (NTSup, 23),
Leiden, 1970, pp. 244-256 (Proto-Luc; avec une longue liste des partisans antérieurs);
H.W. BARTSCH, *Wachet aber zu jeder Zeit! Entwurf einer Auslegung des Lukasevangeliums*,
Hamburg-Bergstedt, 1965, pp. 118-123; E.E. ELLIS, *The Gospel of Luke* (NCB), London,
1966, pp. 240-247; L. HARTMAN, *Prophecy Interpreted. The Formation of Some Jewish
Apocalyptic Texts and of the Eschatological Dicourse Mark 13 Par.* (ConBNT, 1), Lund,
1966, pp. 226-235; T. SCHRAMM, *Der Markus-Stoff bei Lukas. Eine literarkritische und
redaktionsgeschichtliche Untersuchung* (SNTS MS, 14), Cambridge, 1971, pp. 171-182;
A. SALAS, *Discurso escatológico prelucano. Estudio de Lc 21,20-36* (Bibl. de «La Ciudad de
Dios», I/16), El Escorial, 1967, pp. 17-34; E.P. SANDERS, *The Tendencies of the Synoptic
Tradition* (SNTS MS, 9), Cambridge, 1969, p. 292 (vv. 6.12-13.19.20-36); W. GRUND-
MANN, *Das Evangelium nach Lukas* (THKNT, 3), Berlin, [6]1971, p. 378; W. NICOL,
Tradition and Redaction in Luke 21, in *Neotestamentica* 7 (1973) 61-71; I.H. MARSHALL,
The Gospel of Luke (NICNT, 3), Grand Rapids, MI, 1978, pp. 754-757, 770s., 774, 781s.;
E. SCHWEIZER, *Das Evangelium nach Lukas* (NTD, 3), Göttingen, 1982, pp. 206-215;
P. ROLLAND, *Luc, témoin de la forme primitive du discours eschatologique*, in *Bulletin de
liaison sur l'origine des Synoptiques*, n° 2, nov. 1989, pp. 9-11; ID., *La forme primitive du
discours eschatologique*, ibid., n. 11, mai 1992, pp. 10-12.

6. J. VERHEYDEN, *The Source(s) of Luke 21*, in F. NEIRYNCK (ed.), *L'Évangile de Luc -
The Gospel of Luke* (BETL, 32), Leuven, [2]1989, pp. 491-516.

mis en lumière, les divers arguments allégués en sa faveur ont été en grande partie abandonnés, réduisant la source hypothétique à un minimum toujours plus restreint; parfois, on lui attribue uniquement certains éléments épars[7]: plus que d'une «source» proprement dite, une autre version du discours eschatologique, il s'agirait alors seulement d'un oracle sur la chute de Jérusalem[8] ou d'une série de «smaller additions»[9]; mais, dans ce cas, il serait plus correct de les définir comme «rédactionnelles»[10].

Mais notre objectif ici est moins la critique directe de cette hypothèse littéraire[11] que la réflexion méthodologique. Ces explications littéraires, en effet, ont été mises en question avec la *Redaktionsgeschichte*. De fait, comme le notait Conzelmann à propos de cette page lucanienne, elles négligent l'importance particulière que le rédacteur-théologien attribue à *ce* texte précis et qui peut l'avoir stimulé à le réélaborer plus à fond[12].

7. B.H. STREETER, *The Four Gospels. A Study of Origins*, London, 1924, p. 222 (vv. 18.34-36); pour les vv. 20-24, il admet la rédaction lucanienne (pp. 494, 540); F. REHKOPF, *Die lukanische Sonderquelle, ihr Umfang und Sprachgebrauch* (WUNT, 5), Tübingen, 1959 (vv. 34-38); J. JEREMIAS, *Die Sprache des Lukasevangeliums. Redaktion und Tradition im Nicht-Markusstoff des dritten Evangeliums* (KEK, Sonderband), Göttingen, 1980, pp. 283-285 (seulement en partie les vv. 34-38); J.A. FITZMYER, *The Gospel According to Luke II* (AB, 28A), Garden City, NY, 1985, pp. 1323-1330 (vv. 18. 21b.22.24.28.34-36: cependant, «...not an independent form of the whole discourse, but isolated material of the same character...»).

8. L. SABOURIN, *Il Vangelo di Luca*, Roma, 1989, pp. 324s. (vv. 23b-24). Hésitant, G.M. STANO, *La distruzione di Gerusalemme dell'anno 70 e l'esegesi di Dan. 9,24-27 (cf. Mt 24,15; Mc 13,14)*, in *La distruzione di Gerusalemme del 70 nei suoi riflessi storico-letterari*. Atti del V convegno biblico francescano, Roma 22-27.9.1969 (Collectio Assisiensis, 8), Assisi, 1971, pp. 79-110, aux pp. 80s. Cf. les autres auteurs cités sous notre section V, ci-dessous.

9. J.C. HAWKINS, *Horae Synopticae. Contributions to the Study of the Synoptic Problem*, Oxford, ²1909, pp. 194-197: il énumère parmi les «smaller additions» les vv. 12a.18.19.21b.22.25b.26a.34-36; pour le v. 19, il émet l'hypothèse d'une tradition indépendante, et pour les vv. 18 et 34-36, celle de réminiscences pauliniennes (cf. Ac 27,34; 1 Th 5,3-4); les autres versets sont considérés comme rédactionnels.

10. «Certains élements [...] ont une origine étrangère à Marc mais on les appelle justement rédactionnels parce que le même rédacteur semble responsable de leur formulation et de la place qui leur est donnée dans le récit marcien»: F. NEIRYNCK, *La matière marcienne dans l'évangile de Luc*, in ID. (ed.), *L'Évangile de Luc. Problèmes littéraires et théologiques*. Mémorial L. Cerfaux (BETL, 32), Gembloux, 1973, pp. 157-201 (= Leuven, ²1989, pp. 67-111; = ID. *Evangelica* [n. 1], pp. 37-82), voir p. 179.

11. B. RIGAUX, *Témoignage de l'évangile de Luc* (Pour une histoire de Jésus, 4), Bruges-Paris, 1970, pp. 282-294; NEIRYNCK, *La matière marcienne* (n. 10); A. DEL AGUA PÉREZ, *Deráš lucano de Mc 13 a la luz de su «Teología del Reino»: Luc 21,5-36*, in EstBib 39 (1981) 285-313; J.T. CARROLL, *Response to the End of History. Eschatology and Salvation in Luke-Acts* (SBL DS, 92), Atlanta, GA, 1988, pp. 103-119.

12. H. CONZELMANN, *Die Mitte der Zeit. Studien zur Theologie des Lukas* (BHT, 18), Tübingen, ⁵1964, pp. 116-124; ID., *Luke's Place in the Development of Early Christianity*, in L.E. KECK – J.L. MARTYN (ed.), *Studies in Luke-Acts. FS P. Schubert*, London, 1968, pp. 298-316, spécialement pp. 298s. Au même moment aussi W. MARXSEN, *Der Evangelist Markus. Studien zur Redaktionsgeschichte des Evangeliums* (FRLANT, 67 = NF, 49), Göttingen, ²1959 (= ¹1956), pp. 129-135.

Nous sommes loin du temps où il était permis d'attribuer en bloc à une autre tradition tous les éléments différents de Marc[13], ou d'en appeler de manière générique au présupposé que Luc ne modifie pas ses sources aussi fortement[14].

Cependant, le contraire peut également arriver. Comme le notait déjà Cadbury, il n'est pas correct de vouloir expliquer par les sources ce qui doit l'être rédactionnellement; mais il n'est pas plus correct de vouloir expliquer rédactionnellement ce qui doit l'être par les sources[15]. La prétention à vouloir tout expliquer littérairement conduit à une prolifé-ration de sources, strates, rédactions successives, comme dans l'hypo-thèse des stades multiples[16]; mais tout aussi erronée est la prétention à tout expliquer rédactionnellement, en attribuant n'importe quelle diffé-rence à l'activité théologique des évangélistes, y compris d'énormes omissions, déplacements ou modifications dont on ne réussit d'aucune façon à saisir le sens[17]: c'est ce qui arrive à notre avis dans l'hypothèse néo-griesbachienne[18] ou dans celle de la priorité matthéenne[19].

13. Ainsi, A. SCHLATTER, *Das Evangelium des Lukas. Aus seinen Quellen erklärt*, Stuttgart, [2]1960 (= [1]1931), pp. 130-134.

14. Cf. p. ex. G. BEASLEY-MURRAY, *Jesus and the Future. An Examination of the Criticism of the Eschatological Discourse, Mark 13, with Special Reference to the Little Apocalypse Theory*, London, 1956, p. 227: «Luke does not normally edit his sources so drastically».

15. H.J. CADBURY, *The Style and Literary Method of Luke*, II. *The Treatment of Sources in the Gospel* (HTS, 6), Cambridge, 1920, p. 75: «The relation of Luke to Mark is not merely a literary problem. There can be no doubt that some of the changes made by Luke in Mark are due to historical reasons, others are due to the general motives of the author – to his so-called «tendencies» – i.e. for doctrinal reasons [...] On the other hand the discovery of non-literary tendencies in New Testament writers is made entirely too easy in some schools of criticism, and should be attempted only after the literary habits of the writer have been carefully examined. The question may often be raised whether a single detail, or even a repeated phenomenon in Luke, supposed to show some special religious or social interest, may not be merely stylistic or artistic».

16. M.-É. BOISMARD, *La «Two-Gospel Hypothesis»: Le discours eschatologique*, in D.L. DUNGAN (ed.), *The Interrelations of the Gospels. A Symposium led by M.-É. BOISMARD – W.R. FARMER – F. NEIRYNCK*, Jerusalem 1984 (BETL, 95), Leuven, 1990, pp. 265-288; cf. la critique de F. NEIRYNCK, *Response to the Multiple-Stage Hypothesis, III. The Eschatological Discourse*, in *Ibid.*, pp. 108-124.

17. Cf. V. FUSCO, *Consensi e dissensi nella questione sinottica*, in *Cristianesimo nella storia* 8 (1987) 591-608. De façon plus large, dans une *Introduzione generale ai Sinottici* pour la nouvelle série *Corso di studi biblici* (Torino, en cours de publication).

18. W.R. FARMER, *The Synoptic Problem*, Dillsboro, NC, [2]1976, pp. 271-278; ID., *Certain Results Reached by Sir John C. Hawkins and C.F. Burney which make more sense if Luke knew Matthew, and Mark knew Matthew and Luke*, in C.M. TUCKETT (ed.), *Synoptic Studies. The Ampleforth Conferences 1982 and 1983* (JSNT SS, 7), Sheffield, 1984, pp. 75-98, surtout pp. 91-97; A.J. McNICOL, *The Composition of the Synoptic Eschatological Discourse*, in DUNGAN (ed.), *The Interrelations* (n. 16), pp. 157-200. – Pour la critique: C.M. TUCKETT, *Response to the Two-Gospel Hypothesis, II. The Eschatological Discourse*, in *Ibid.*, pp. 63-76; ID.,*The Revival of the Griesbach Hypothesis. An Analysis and Appraisal* (SNTS MS, 44), Cambridge, 1983, pp. 167-185; F. NEIRYNCK, *Note on the Eschatological Dicourse*, in DUNGAN (ed.), *The Interrelations* (n. 16), pp. 77-80; S.E. JOHNSON, *The Griesbach Hypohesis and Redaction Criticism* (SBL MS, 41), Atlanta, GA, 1991.

19. M.D. GOULDER, *Luke. A New Paradigm* (JSNT SS, 20), Sheffield, 1989, pp. 701-

Ainsi donc, le problème de la méthode devient plus aigu. L'explication *redaktionsgeschichtlich*, dans la ligne de Conzelmann[20], est en train de perdre du terrain. Les monographies les plus importantes sur le discours eschatologique[21], même si elles en gardent les thèses de fond, ne réussissent pas à expliquer par là l'ensemble du texte ni à en saisir l'unité; et elles se voient dans l'obligation d'emprunter d'autres chemins qui, pourtant, ne s'avèrent pas plus convaincants. On reconnaît que l'expression «cette génération» (v. 32) ne peut pas être privée de sa valeur temporelle, puisqu'on est justement dans un contexte dominé par la question du «quand?»[22]; ou alors on est forcé d'attribuer une contradiction manifeste à un rédacteur dont on a tant vanté la cohérence théologique[23].

Il reste cependant plausible que Luc écrivant après la chute de Jérusalem et voulant distinguer plus clairement celle-ci de la fin du monde, élimine alors différents restes – conservés encore par Marc[24] –

718; cf. aussi D. WENHAM, *The Rediscovery of Jesus' Eschatological Discourse* (Gospel Perspectives, 4), Sheffield, 1984: discours eschatologique pré-synoptique utilisé par tous les trois et mieux conservé en Mt.

20. Dans une ligne semblable: E. GRÄSSER, *Das Problem der Parusieverzögerung in den synoptischen Evangelien und in der Apostelgeschichte* (BZNW, 22), Berlin, 1957, pp. 152-170; cf.[3]1977, pp. XXVIII-XXXII; W.C. ROBINSON, *Der Weg des Herrn. Studien zur Geschichte und Eschatologie im Lukas-Evangelium* (TF, 36), Hamburg-Bergstedt, 1964; J.-D. KAESTLI, *L'eschatologie dans l'œuvre de Luc. Ses caractéristiques et sa place dans le développement du Christianisme primitif* (Nouvelle série théologique, 22), Genève, 1969, pp. 41-57; S. ZEDDA, *L'escatologia biblica*, I. *Antico Testamento e Vangeli Sinottici* (Esegesi biblica, 6), Brescia, 1972, pp. 347-398; H. HENDRICKX, *The End Will Not Be At Once* (Studies in the Synoptic Gospels, 7), Makati, 1992.

21. J. ZMIJEWSKI, *Die Eschatologiereden des Lukas-Evangeliums. Eine traditions- und redaktionsgeschichtliche Untersuchung zu Lk 21,5-36 und Lk 17,20-37* (BBB, 40), Bonn, 1972; R. GEIGER, *Die lukanische Endzeitreden. Studien zur Eschatologie des Lukas-Evangeliums* (EHS, XXIII/16), Frankfurt/M-Bern, 1976; F. KECK, *Die öffentliche Abschiedsrede Jesu in Lk 20,45-21,36. Eine redaktions- und motivgeschichtliche Untersuchung* (FzB 25), Stuttgart, 1976.

22. J. LAMBRECHT, *Redactio sermonis eschatologici*, in *VD* 43 (1965) 278-287; ID., *Reading and Re-reading Lk 18,31-22,6*, in *À cause de l'Évangile. FS J. Dupont* (LD, 123), Paris, 1985, pp. 585-612; cf. aussi J. DRURY, *Tradition and Design in Luke's Gospel. A Study in Early Christian Historiography*, London, 1976, p. 109: «Mark 13 has been historicized and, in the last verses, moralized. But there is no sign of any reduction of eschatological belief, only that for Luke it is set in history more firmly and distinctly than for Mark». De même BARTSCH, *Wachet* (n. 5), p. 123: Luc historicise le passé, non le futur; GOULDER, *Luke* (n. 19), p. 714.

23. La contradiction est admise par J. DUPONT, *Les épreuves des chrétiens avant la fin du monde*, in *AssSeign* 64 (1969) 77-86; = *Études sur les évangiles synoptiques* (BETL, 70), Leuven, 1985, pp. 1117-1127; ID., *La ruine du temple et la fin des temps dans le discours de Marc 13*, in *Apocalypses et théologie de l'espérance*. Congrès de Toulouse, 1975 (LD, 95), Paris, 1977, pp. 207-269; = *Études*, pp. 368-433; ID., *Les trois apocalypses synoptiques* (LD, 121), Paris, 1985.

24. H. CONZELMANN, *Geschichte und Eschaton nach Mc 13*, in *ZNW* 50 (1959) 210-221; F. HAHN, *Die Rede von der Parusie des Menschensohnes Markus 13*, in R. PESCH – R. SCHNACKENBURG – O. KAISER (ed.), *Jesus und der Menschensohn. FS A. Vögtle*, Freiburg-Basel-Wien, 1975, pp. 240-266.

d'une tradition qui avait lié plus étroitement la fin de Jérusalem à la fin du monde en l'interprétant à l'aide des *topoi* apocalyptiques de la grande tribulation eschatologique, du déchaînement de l'impiété[25]. Il n'a pas pour autant reporté la parousie à un point absolument indéterminé aux extrêmes limites du futur.

Mais cette discussion elle-même, que nous avons abordée dans d'autres études auxquelles nous nous permettons de renvoyer ici[26], nous intéresse surtout à présent sous son profil méthodologique[27]. Doit-on remettre en cause, comme le pensent d'aucuns, la validité de la *Redaktionsgeschichte* comme telle[28], ou plutôt d'une certaine manière de la pratiquer qui a privilégié unilatéralement l'approche diachronique (la «rédaction») au détriment de l'approche synchronique (la «composition»)[29]? Dans les pages de Conzelmann, mais aussi dans d'autres études plus récentes, une réflexion préliminaire sur la structure du discours fait défaut; l'intérêt se porte seulement vers les modifications rédactionnelles[30]. Ces modifications, indubitablement, nous aussi, nous trouvons nécessaire de les analyser et de les expliquer attentivement l'une après l'autre, verset par verset, des plus manifestes aux plus

25. Cf. J. Ernst, *Die eschatologischen Gegenspieler in den Schriften des Neuen Testaments* (BU, 3), Regensburg, 1967, pp. 3-23; R. Stuhlmann, *Das eschatologische Maß im Neuen Testament* (FRLANT, 132), Göttingen, 1983, pp. 53-60; E. Brandenburger, *Markus 13 und die Apokalyptik* (FRLANT, 134), Göttingen, 1984, pp. 43-73.

26. *Lc 21,32 alla luce dell'espressione «questa generazione»*, in *Letture cristiane dell' A.T. FS A. Rolla*; = *Asprenas* 31 (1984) 397-424; *Chiesa e Regno nella prospettiva lucana*, in G. Lorizio – V. Scippa (ed.), *Ecclesiae sacramentum. FS A. Marranzini*, Napoli, 1986, pp. 113-135; *Problemi di struttura nel discorso escatologico lucano (Lc 21,7-36)*, in G. Marconi – G. O'Collins (ed.), *Luca-Atti. FS E. Rasco*, Assisi, 1991, pp. 105-134; *«Point of View» and «Implicit Reader» in two eschatological texts (Lk 19,11-28; Acts 1,6-8)*, in *The Four Gospels 1992. FS F. Neirynck* II (BETL, 100/B), Leuven, 1992, pp. 1677-1696.

27. A.E. Nielsen, *The Purpose of the Lucan Writings with Particular Reference to the Eschatology*, in P. Luomanen (ed.), *Luke-Acts. Scandinavian Perspectives* (Publ. of the Finnish Exeg. Soc., 54), Helsinki-Göttingen, 1991, pp. 76-93; cf. p. 76: «...an example of increasing lack of consensus *in method* and interpretation...» (nous soulignons).

28. Ainsi par exemple, A.L. Moore, *The Parousia in the New Testament* (NTSup, 13), Leiden, 1966, pp. 86-88: «The redactional-critical method appears to encourage exaggerated emphases... Conzelmann finds throughout Lk. 21 a conscious alteration of Mk. 13...».

29. Cf. V. Fusco, *Parola e Regno. La sezione delle parabole (Mc 4,1-34) nella prospettiva marciana* (Aloisiana, 13), Brescia, 1980, pp. 63-66 («*Redaktionsgeschichte*, sincronia, diacronia»); cf. aussi, in *Bib* 72 (1991) 123-127, nos observations sur C.C. Black, *The Disciples According to Mark. Markan Redaction in Current Debate* (JSNT SS, 27), Sheffield, 1989. Plus largement: K. Berger, *Exegese des Neuen Testaments. Neue Wege vom Text zur Auslegung* (UTB, 658), Heidelberg, 1977; W. Egger, *Methodenlehre zum Neuen Testament. Einführung in linguistische und historisch-kritische Methoden*, Freiburg/Br, 1987; avec nos réflexions in *RivBib* 38 (1990) 91-94.

30. Conzelmann, *Die Mitte der Zeit* (n. 12), p. 108: «Wir haben von den Stellen abgesehen, wo Lukas einfach die Tradition weitergibt». Dans l'introduction, toutefois, il parlait de la nécessité de considérer la configuration (*Gestalt*), la «mosaïque» créée par les divers éléments (*Ibid.*, pp. 2-4).

légères, cependant non pas isolément, mais à la lumière de tout le contexte – c'est-à-dire en étudiant la *rédaction*, mais à la lumière de la *composition*.

II. DÉCOR, DESTINATAIRES, QUESTION DE DÉPART
(vv. 5-7; cf. Mc 13,1-4)

1. *Décor et destinataires*

Chez Marc, le dialogue initial avait lieu alors que Jésus sortait du temple (Mc 13,1a), tandis que le discours était prononcé plus tard, «à l'écart», avec les quatre disciples privilégiés sur le Mont des Oliviers (Mc 13,3); chez Luc, en revanche, Jésus reste dans le temple et ne se rendra au Mont des Oliviers que pour y passer la nuit (21,37-38). Peut-être est-ce justement parce qu'il se trouve encore à l'intérieur du temple que Jésus est invité à en admirer la beauté plus que la masse imposante (Mc 13,1b); les interlocuteurs ne sont plus les disciples[31] mais des gens dont on ne précise pas l'identité, τινες, qui interpellent Jésus avec le nom toujours utilisé par les étrangers en Luc, διδάσκαλε[32].

Dans certains textes vétérotestamentaires comme Za 14,4, le Mont des Oliviers est mentionné dans le contexte de la théophanie eschatologique. Aussi a-t-on pensé que c'est là la raison pour laquelle Luc a voulu l'éliminer comme décor du discours[33]. Pourtant, c'est un fait que le discours parle aussi de la Parousie; il y trouve même son point culminant et unifiant. En outre, on observe facilement que, dans d'autres épisodes, non moins chargés de résonances eschatologiques, comme l'entrée triomphale à Jérusalem (19,28-39) ou l'Ascension (Ac 1,9-11) un tel décor a été conservé. Le changement est donc dû à la préférence de Luc pour un décor *public*, et peut-être aussi à l'intention d'éliminer, plutôt, des allusions symboliques négatives par rapport au Judaïsme: comme le fait de prononcer l'oracle tout juste *en sortant du temple*, et ensuite de prononcer le discours sur le Mont, *étant en face du*

---

31. L'usage de διδάσκαλε n'est donc pas une exception, comme l'écrit C.H. TURNER, *Marcan Usage: Notes, Critical and Exegetical, on the Second Gospel, X. Titles used in addressing Christ, etc.*, in *JTS* 29 (1927-28) 346-361, cf. pp. 347-349.

32. Les scribes et les pharisiens (7,40; 10,25; 11,49; 19,39; 20,21.28.39); le père du garçon épileptique (9,38: en Lc il n'est pas un modèle de foi); l'homme qui recourt à Jésus pour le partage de l'héritage (12,13); le riche qui refuse l'appel (18,18). Les disciples l'appellent souvent κύριε, ou au moins ἐπιστάτης (5,5; 8,24.45; 9,33.49), avec une nuance plus forte d'autorité: cf. A. OEPKE, ἐπιστάτης, in *TWNT* 2 (1935) 619s; O. GLOMBITZA, *Die Titel διδάσκαλος und ἐπιστάτης für Jesus bei Lukas*, in *ZNW* 49 (1958) 275-278; ainsi également les dix lépreux (17,13). Dans deux de ces cas, Marc avait διδάσκαλε (cf. Lc 8,24 avec Mc 4,38; Lc 9,49 avec Mc 9,38).

33. CONZELMANN, *Die Mitte der Zeit* (n. 12), p. 116, cf. pp. 68s.

temple[34]. Dans le récit de la passion, Luc présente aussi des omissions similaires (cf. Mc 14,55-61 et Lc 22,66-67; Mc 15,29-30, et Lc 23,35; Mc 15,38-39 et Lc 23,44-47) dictées par son attitude plus positive par rapport à Israël[35].

En plaçant le discours dans le temple, Luc a voulu en faire le point culminant des derniers enseignements de Jésus au peuple[36] à Jérusalem (cf. 19,47-48; 20,1.9.19.26.45; 21,37-38; 22,39)[37]. À la communauté chrétienne, en revanche – d'une manière qui se rapproche un peu du quatrième Évangile – sera dédié une sorte de discours d'adieu sur le modèle des «testaments»[38], discours inséré dans la dernière Cène (Lc 22,21-38)[39]. Cela correspond du reste à toute l'image lucanienne de l'enseignement de Jésus[40]. La mise en situation «à l'écart» est conservée seulement pour le «secret messianique» au sens le plus étroit du terme, quand l'identité de Jésus est en jeu (Lc 9,18; cf. Mc 8,27-30)[41]; elle est systématiquement éliminée dans d'autres cas (cf. Mc 4,10.34 avec Lc 8,9; Mc 9,28-29 avec Lc 9,43; voir aussi Mc 7,14; 10,10-12)[42].

À plus forte raison est-ce le cas ici, puisqu'il s'agit d'un grand discours *prophétique* où tiendra une grande place *le sort de Jérusalem* (vv. 20-24). En effet, ce discours s'ouvre avec la formule prophétique traditionnelle: « Des jours viendront...», caractéristique surtout des

---

34. Cf. G. BIGUZZI, *Io distruggerò questo tempio. Il tempio e il giudaismo nel vangelo di Marco*, Roma, 1987, pp. 89-93.

35. Cf. V. FUSCO, *La morte del Messia (Lc 23,26-49)*, in *Gesù e la sua morte*. Atti della XXVII settimana biblica, Brescia, 1984, pp. 51-73. Interprétation différente chez A. CASALEGNO, *Gesù e il tempio. Studio redazionale su Luca-Atti*, Brescia, 1984, pp. 114-116: les retouches lucaniennes exprimeraient une prise de distance plus forte par rapport au temple qui a rempli sa fonction dans l'histoire du salut.

36. KECK, *Abschiedsrede* (n. 21), pp. 67-69, fait commencer le discours en 20,45 («Et tandis que tout le peuple écoutait, il dit à ses disciples...») et considère que les interlocuteurs anonymes en Lc 21,7 seraient les disciples. Mais on ne voit pas pourquoi la polémique contre les scribes et l'obole de la veuve (20,45–21,4) devrait avoir un lien plus particulier avec l'enseignement eschatologique (21,5-37). Pour Luc, à partir de l'entrée de Jésus à Jérusalem, on a toute une suite d'enseignements dans le temple sur différents thèmes (cf. 19,47-48; 20,1.6.9.19.26.45; 21,37-38).

37. ZMIJEWSKI, *Eschatologiereden* (n. 21), pp. 91s.; KECK, *Abschiedsrede* (n. 21), pp. 64s.

38. Parallèles remarquables avec le discours d'adieu de Paul: V. FUSCO, *L'idea di successione nel discorso di Mileto (At 20,18-35)*, in S. MURATORE – A. ROLLA (ed.), *Una Hostia. FS C. Ursi*, Napoli, 1983, pp. 87-142.

39. Explication différente en H. FLENDER, *Heil und Geschichte in der Theologie des Lukas* (BEvT, 41), München, 1968, pp. 18-20: l'autre discours eschatologique (Lc 17,22-37) serait orienté vers la communauté. Contre le caractère «ésotérique» de ce discours, il y a la présence des pharisiens à qui est attribuée la question de départ (Lc 17,20s).

40. Cf. P.S. MINEAR, *Jesus' Audiences, according to Luke*, in *NT* 16 (1974) 81-109.

41. Nous la trouvons aussi dans un autre dialogue avec les disciples, avec un contenu presque ouvertement messianique (10,23); en revanche, elle joue un rôle essentiellement narratif dans l'introduction de la multiplication des pains (9,10).

42. Cf. FUSCO, *Parola e Regno* (n. 29), pp. 133-135.

oracles de malheur (cf. Jr 7,32; Ez 7,12; Is 39,6 etc.) et utilisée aussi dans d'autres contextes semblables chez Luc (Lc 5,35; 17,22; 19,43; 23,29); il se poursuit avec les verbes au futur et en utilisant d'autres formules prophétiques, comme l'exhortation à la fuite, les *Malheur!*, etc[43]. S'il en est ainsi, comme dans les prophéties vétéro-testamentaires, l'auditoire doit nécessairement comprendre ceux à qui s'adresse l'oracle, à savoir les gens de Jérusalem, le λαός (cf. v. 23).

Pour Luc, cependant, tout l'enseignement pré-pascal de Jésus a la foule pour auditoire, mais en même temps les disciples, et à travers eux, l'Église[44]. Ici aussi, non seulement certaines parties du discours comme celles qui concernent la persécution (vv. 12-19), la Parousie (vv. 25-27), la parénèse conclusive (vv. 34-36), mais aussi la partie sur le sort de Jérusalem (vv. 20-24) intéressent l'Église et pas seulement Israël. Dans toute l'œuvre de Luc, le problème d'Israël ne regarde pas seulement le passé, la préhistoire de l'Église, mais aussi son futur; il se présente toujours lié au problème de la Parousie (cf. Lc 19,11-28; Ac 1,6-8)[45]. Le discours eschatologique en offre également une confirmation très claire.

2. *La question de départ (v. 7)*

Il est pourtant vrai que la question de départ ne mentionne aucunement la Parousie. Mieux: Luc a même laissé tomber ces expressions qui, en Marc, pouvaient faire allusion à d'autres événements en plus de la destruction du temple: συντελεῖσθαι est remplacé par γίνεσθαι[46]. Le πάντα a été omis devant ταῦτα[47]. On a pensé que Luc avait voulu exclure dès le départ toute connexion entre la destruction de Jérusalem

---

43. Cf. G. NEBE, *Prophetische Züge im Bilde Jesu bei Lukas* (BWANT, 127 = VII/7), Stuttgart, 1989, pp. 190-198.

44. Avec J. DUPONT, *Les béatitudes*, III. *Les évangélistes* (EB), Paris, 1973, pp. 21-40; ID., *Renoncer à tous ses biens (Lc 14,33)*, in NRT 93 (1971) 561-582, spécialement pp. 578s.; = *Études sur les évangiles synoptiques* (n. 23), pp. 1076-1097, voir pp. 1092s.; noter la conclusion: «Ces explications permettent de se rendre compte de l'erreur qu'on commettrait en supposant que, chez Luc, un enseignement destiné aux foules ne concerne pas les disciples et ne peut pas trouver son application immédiate pour les lecteurs chrétiens de l'évangile». Cf. aussi G. LOHFINK, *Die Sammlung Israels. Eine Untersuchung zur lukanischen Ekklesiologie* (SANT, 39), München, 1975, pp. 48s., 72-74. Il ne s'agit donc pas d'une contradiction à expliquer par une source supplémentaire, comme le pense par exemple MANSON, *The Sayings of Jesus* (n. 5), p. 324.

45. V. FUSCO, *Progetto storiografico e progetto teologico nell'opera lucana*, in *La storiografia nella Bibbia*. Atti della XXVIII Settimana biblica, Bologna, 1986, pp. 123-152; ID., *«Point of View»* (n. 26).

46. Cf. cependant SCHRAMM, *Markus-Stoff* (n. 5), p. 174: συντελεῖσθαι, pour Luc, n'implique pas nécessairement une allusion eschatologique (cf. Lc 4,2.13; Ac 21,27).

47. ταῦτα πάντα peut avoir une résonnance eschatologique: textes en K. BERGER, *Die Amen-Worte Jesu. Eine Untersuchung zum Problem der Legitimation in apokalyptischer Rede* (BZNW, 39), Berlin, 1970, pp. 68s.

et la Parousie[48]. Mais cette explication laisse perplexe: même dans d'autres cas, on pose à Jésus des questions qui reçoivent une réponse négative (cf. 13,23), et Conzelmann lui-même a souligné à ce propos celles qui portent sur la proximité de l'Eschaton (17,20; 19,11; Ac 1,6)[49]; ici aussi une question en ce sens n'aurait pas empêché la réponse négative; au contraire, elle l'aurait mise davantage en relief.

Pourquoi alors les retouches lucaniennes? Peut-être aussi parce que le rapprochement entre συντελεῖσθαι et μέλλειν sonne mal, car ce second verbe indique que l'événement est encore *in fieri*; en ce sens, γίνεσθαι convient mieux, d'autant qu'il est suggéré par ce qui suit (v. 9; Mc 13,7). Ensuite, une fois éliminé le συντελεῖσθαι, le πάντα seul devenait presque insignifiant. Mais même en laissant tout comme en Marc, l'allusion était si vague qu'elle en devenait presque imperceptible, pratiquement inutile. Matthieu a senti le besoin d'expliciter: πότε ταῦτα ἔσται, καὶ τί τὸ σημεῖον τῆς σῆς παρουσίας καὶ συντελείας τοῦ αἰῶνος (Mt 24,3): de cette façon, cependant, il est tombé dans le piège inverse. Il laisse presque supposer a priori que la destruction du temple (ταῦτα) et la fin du monde devaient coïncider. *Il n'était sûrement pas facile*, en somme, de maintenir la référence à la destruction du temple et en même temps de suggérer l'éventualité d'un lien pressenti, soupçonné, et peut-être souhaité avec l'Eschaton, mais sans le donner pour sûr a priori. *Par ailleurs, ce n'était pas non plus nécessaire*: le fait de ne pas y faire allusion dans la question de départ n'empêchait pas d'en parler dans le discours[50]. En voilà assez, nous semble-t-il, pour justifier aussi cette nouvelle formulation lucanienne.

III. Guerres et autres désastres
(vv. 8-11; cf. Mc 13,5-8)

1. *Jésus commence à répondre (vv. 8-9)*

Le premier élément de réponse (vv. 8-9) a un ton négatif: Jésus annonce d'emblée qu'il y aura de fausses alarmes, des impostures dont

---

48. Ainsi, par exemple, Conzelmann, *Die Mitte der Zeit* (n. 12), p. 117; Grässer, *Problem* (n. 20), pp. 155s.; Kaestli, *Eschatologie* (n. 20), p. 43; N. Walter, *Tempelzerstörung und synoptische Apokalypse*, in *ZNW* 57 (1966) 38-49, voir pp. 48s.; Geiger, *Endzeitreden* (n. 21), p. 168; W. Wiefel, *Das Evangelium nach Lukas* (THKNT, 3), Berlin, 1988, p. 349.

49. Cf. Fusco, «*Point of View*» (n. 26).

50. «Il s'en tient donc provisoirement au sort du Temple, et ne parlera de la fin du monde que quand il pourra montrer clairement qu'elle n'a rien à voir avec les événements de l'an 70»: J. Dupont, *Les épreuves* (n.23), pp. 78s.; = *Études sur les évangiles synoptiques* (n. 23), pp. 118s; Id., *Les trois apocalypses* (n. 23), p. 109. Ce regard sur le contexte nous semble précieux; mais, comme nous le verrons un peu plus loin, dans le contexte, on ne nie pas *tout* lien, mais seulement un lien direct, immédiat (cf. v. 9).

il faudra se garder. Après un premier avertissement plus général (v. 8a: βλέπετε μὴ πλανηθῆτε), cet élément s'articule en deux membres parallèles: une première annonce (v. 8b: πολλοὶ γὰρ ἐλεύσονται ἐπὶ τῷ ὀνόματί μου λέγοντες· ἐγώ εἰμι, καί, ὁ καιρὸς ἤγγικεν) suivie de l'impératif concernant la réaction à adopter (v. 8c: μὴ πορευθῆτε ὀπίσω αὐτῶν); ensuite une seconde annonce (v. 9a: ὅταν δὲ ἀκούσητε πολέμους καὶ ἀκαταστασίας[51]) suivie à son tour d'un impératif (v. 9b: μὴ πτοηθῆτε). Le crescendo est clair: d'abord, on parle de *personnes* qui prêcheront faussement, prématurément, la proximité de la fin (v. 8); puis de *faits* impressionnants qui sembleraient leur donner raison: mais, même alors, il ne faut pas se troubler, et ici on en donne le motif: δεῖ γὰρ ταῦτα γενέσθαι πρῶτον ἀλλ᾽ οὐκ εὐθέως τὸ τέλος (v. 9c). Telle est donc la réponse aux faux prophètes, la position juste à opposer à leurs propos alarmistes[52]. On ne nie pas *tout* rapport avec la fin, mais seulement un rapport de succession immédiate[53]. Mieux: en conservant l'expression δεῖ et en ajoutant l'autre, elle aussi typiquement apocalyptique, πρῶτον, ces événements n'en restent pas moins insérés dans un contexte eschatologique[54]. La petite retouche οὐκ εὐθέως au lieu de οὔπω a été considérée comme une insistance supplémentaire sur le retard[55], sans tenir compte du fait que Luc-Actes n'emploie jamais οὔπω (sauf en Lc 23,53 où, cependant, certains manuscrits lisent οὐδέπω) et, quand il le trouve en Marc, il l'élimine toujours d'une manière ou d'une autre (cf. Mc 4,40 *si vera lectio* avec Lc 8,25; Mc 11,2 avec Lc 19,30).

Dans la bouche des faux prophètes, Luc ajoute aussi ὁ καιρὸς ἤγγικεν, et il insère également le grave avertissement μὴ πορευθῆτε ὀπίσω αὐτῶν (v. 8b); mais c'est une erreur de supposer qu'il l'aurait fait pour inculquer aux lecteurs, aux chrétiens de son temps, l'éloignement de la Parousie[56]: dans ce contexte du discours, nous sommes encore dans la période qui précède la chute de Jérusalem, et c'est *à ce moment-*

---

51. Non pas «guerres et *rumeurs de guerres*», aussi bien pour éviter un anti-climax malheureux et répétitif que pour rappeler plus clairement la situation historique à la veille de la révolte judéenne, avec l'Empire troublé à l'extérieur et à l'intérieur. – KECK, *Abschiedsrede* (n. 21), pp. 79-83, 101-105, sur base du rapport avec les faux-prophètes, pense à des rébellions dans l'Église; mais le rapport se trouve plutôt dans le fait que ces prophètes faisaient appel à ces événements comme à des signes de la fin. Il est erroné de présupposer que tout doit être expliqué en référence à l'actualité.

52. DUPONT, *Les trois apocalypses* (n. 23), p. 107.

53. J. ERNST, *Das Evangelium nach Lukas* (RNT), Regensburg, 1977, p. 556.

54. Aussi, il est difficile que le τέλος se rapporte seulement à la fin de Jérusalem, comme le pense FITZMYER, *Luke* (n. 7), p. 1327.

55. MARXSEN, *Der Evangelist Markus* (n. 12), pp. 129s.

56. CONZELMANN, *Die Mitte der Zeit* (n. 12), pp. 112, 118. GRÄSSER, *Problem* (n. 20), pp. 157s. Une autre explication, à notre avis hors contexte, chez ZMIJEWSKI, *Eschatologiereden* (n. 21), pp. 113-118, 125-128, qui pense à quelque hérésie eschatologico-christologique du temps de Luc.

là, en référence à ces désastres mentionnés dans le contexte, ταῦτα, qu'est exclue la proximité de la Parousie, et non pas *maintenant*, au moment où Luc écrit[57].

La formulation de Marc: βλέπετε μή τις ὑμᾶς πλανήσῃ· πολλοὶ ἐλεύσονται ... καὶ πολλοὺς πλανήσουσιν était malheureuse non seulement en raison de la répétition mais aussi parce qu'elle exprimait la mise en garde seulement en forme indirecte, et en des termes qui pouvaient donner à penser que les faux prophètes réussiraient sûrement à en séduire beaucoup. Luc préfère éliminer une connotation aussi peu encourageante et rendre la mise en garde plus explicite en utilisant l'impératif. Mais pour évaluer les deux ajouts, ὁ καιρὸς ἤγγικεν, et μὴ πορευθῆτε ὀπίσω αὐτῶν, il faut garder à l'esprit non seulement le parallèle immédiat, mais aussi le second texte dans lequel Marc mentionne les faux prophètes au moment du siège de Jérusalem (Mc 13,21-22); Luc préfère en parler seulement ici, soit pour éviter la répétition[58], soit pour éliminer le *topos* apocalyptique du déchaînement final de l'impiété, avec sa connotation si peu encourageante («des prodiges à même de séduire même les élus...»). Nous devons nous demander cependant si Luc n'a pas anticipé ici quelque élément. En effet, l'impératif μὴ πορευθῆτε ὀπίσω αὐτῶν récupère d'une certaine manière le μὴ πιστεύετε de Mc 13,21 en le formulant en termes plus concrets[59]. Mais alors, on pourrait peut-être aussi expliquer de la même manière l'autre ajout ὁ καιρὸς ἤγγικεν: il pourrait avoir la fonction de faire comprendre quel était le message de ces faux prophètes; Marc, en effet, dans l'autre passage omis par Luc, en offrait une «citation»: ἴδε ὧδε ὁ χριστός, ἴδε ἐκεῖ (Mc 13,21); même le contexte (τότε, c'est-à-dire au moment de la grande tribulation) en rendait plus évident l'aspect eschatologique: si Luc, en revanche, avait laissé seulement «c'est moi» (autrement dit, le Christ dont on attend la venue), l'aspect eschatologique serait resté seulement sous-entendu: en ajoutant ὁ καιρὸς ἤγγικεν, Luc n'a rien fait d'autre qu'anticiper dans ce contexte ce qu'il trouvait déjà chez Marc.

2. *Jésus commence à annoncer plus en détail les choses qui doivent arriver (vv. 10-11)*

Le petit mystère de la nouvelle formule introductive qui suit si

---

57. Cf. FUSCO, «*Point of View*» (n. 26).

58. Luc aime concentrer en un point unique ce qui se rapporte à un même sujet: ainsi, dans le récit de la crucifixion, il unifie toutes les dérisions, y compris l'inscription sur la croix et le vinaigre, les deux offres de boire (cf. Lc 23,35-38 avec Mc 15,23.26.31-32.36) et le double cri de Jésus (cf. Lc 23,46 avec Mc 15,34.37): FUSCO, *La morte del Messia* (n. 35). Cf. CADBURY, *Style* (n. 15), pp. 83-90.

59. Avec une certaine analogie avec le «doublet» μὴ ἀπέλθητε μηδὲ διώξητε de Lc 17,23: cf. R. LAUFEN, *Die Doppelüberlieferungen der Logienquelle und des Markusevangeliums* (BBB, 54), Bonn, 1980, pp. 361s.

rapidement la première, τότε ἔλεγεν αὐτοῖς (v. 10a), s'explique de manière assez simple d'un point de vue stylistique. Ici, Marc, bien qu'il s'agisse d'une réponse (cf. v. 3: ἐπηρώτα) ne l'introduit pas comme à son habitude par le *verbum dicendi* à l'aoriste, mais par ὁ δὲ ἤρξατο λέγειν αὐτοῖς: c'est évidemment parce que dans ce cas, la réponse se transforme en un enseignement prolongé[60]. Mais Luc n'aime guère ces tournures avec ἤρξατο: pas moins de douze fois sur quinze, il les élimine[61]; cette fois, tenant compte qu'il s'agit d'une réponse, il la remplace précisément par εἶπεν. Mais il se rend compte lui aussi que tout le discours, même s'il vient en réponse à une question, s'étend ensuite bien au-delà de celle-ci et qu'il serait donc incongru de l'introduire tout entier par ce seul εἶπεν. Ce devrait être la raison pour laquelle il insère, dès que possible, une seconde formule avec le *verbum dicendi* à l'imparfait (v. 10a: τότε ἔλεγεν αὐτοῖς), caractéristique non pas des simples réponses, mais d'enseignements plus longs[62].

Il n'est donc pas fondé de trouver ici la trace d'une autre source[63]; mais il n'est pas plus fondé d'attribuer à cette formule introductive la fonction de séparer nettement le passage qui suit de celui qui précède. Aux vv. 8-9 déjà, on parlait de «guerres et soulèvements»; aux vv. 10-11, on repart précisément de la même réalité, décrite au moyen de réminiscences bibliques comme le soulèvement de «nation contre nation et royaume contre royaume» (Is 19,2; 2 Ch 15,6); ensuite une série de conjonctions (τε ... καί) relie sans solution de continuité à ces événements politiques les autres types de désastres, non seulement les famines et les tremblements de terre déjà mentionnés chez Marc, mais aussi «des pestes[64], des phénomènes terrifiants et de grands signes venant du ciel». Bien qu'il y ait une intensification par rapport à Marc, il s'agit toujours d'événements tragiques et malheureux courants dans l'histoire humaine

---

60. C.H. TURNER, *Marcan Usage: Notes, critical and exegetical, on the second Gospel*, VIII. *Auxiliary and quasi-auxiliary verbs*, in *JTS* 28 (1926-27) 349-362, voir p. 353: «it is a real commencement of new matter, the eschatological discourse». Inhabituel aussi le δέ, peut-être pour souligner l'importance particulière de cet enseignement: M. ZERWICK, *Untersuchungen zum Markus-Stil* (Scripta Pont. Inst. Bibl., 81), Roma, 1937, pp. 10-11. Parallèles en M. REISER, *Syntax und Stil des Markusevangeliums im Licht der hellenistischen Volksliteratur* (WUNT, II/11), Tübingen, 1984, pp. 44s.

61. CADBURY, *Style* (n. 15), pp. 162s; J.W. HUNKIN, «*Pleonastic*» ἄρχομαι *in the New Testament*, in *JTS* 25 (1923-24) 390-402.

62. Non remarqué par TURNER, *loc. cit.*: «... Notwithstanding, both the other Synoptists prefer to treat our Lord's words simply as an answer...».

63. Comme le pensent par exemple SCHRAMM, *Markus-Stoff* (n. 5), pp. 174s.; MARSHALL, *Luke* (n. 5), pp. 764s: «...a redactional motive for the interruption is not discernible».

64. Λιμοὶ καὶ λοιμοί paronomase traditionnelle remontant à Hésiode et Platon: cf. E. NORDEN, *Die antike Kunstprosa von VI. Jahrhundert v. Chr. bis in die Zeit der Renaissance*, I-II, Leipzig-Berlin 1915-1918, II, p. 490.

et mentionnés dans les chroniques de ces années-là[65]. Si Luc force la dose, c'est justement pour souligner que ces événements, même s'ils sont impressionnants, ne marquent pas immédiatement le moment de la fin[66]!

L'élimination de ἀρχὴ ὠδίνων ταῦτα (Mc 13,8b)[67] vise, pour certains, à dés-apocalyptiser complètement ces événements, pour d'autres au contraire, à en faire non plus le *début*, mais le moment culminant du drame eschatologique (vv. 10-11 = vv. 25-26); dans l'un ou l'autre cas, il vise à éliminer toute continuité entre événements de l'histoire et Parousie. Mais l'explication la plus obvie saute aux yeux dans le verset suivant: en insérant πρὸ δὲ τούτων πάντων (v. 12a), au début de la section sur les persécutions, Luc assigne à celles-ci la priorité chronologique: il ne pouvait donc continuer à qualifier d'ἀρχή d'autres événements[68]. Par ailleurs, l'indication (abstraction faite de son caractère éventuellement obscur pour des lecteurs sans familiarité avec le langage apocalyptique) était encore répétitive comparée à celle qui apparaît déjà auparavant en lien avec les mêmes événements: δεῖ γὰρ ταῦτα γενέσθαι πρῶτον ἀλλ᾽ οὐκ εὐθέως τὸ τέλος (v. 9c): l'une et l'autre phrases expriment l'idée d'un lien, mais pas immédiat.

IV. LES PERSÉCUTIONS
(vv. 12-19; cf. Mc 13,9-13)

1. *Articulation du texte*

Des éléments *en plus* par rapport à Marc, comme le v. 18, aussi bien que des éléments *en moins* qu'il est à première vue impossible de justifier comme des omissions puisqu'il s'agit de thèmes chers à Luc, comme l'évangélisation des païens (Mc 13,10) et l'action de l'Esprit saint (Mc 13,11b), ont fourni des arguments à ceux qui soutiennent l'hypothèse de la source non marcienne[69]. Aujourd'hui l'explication rédactionnelle

---

65. Sur cette question, plus largement: FUSCO, *Problemi di struttura* (n. 26), pp. 111-114, 118-124. Cf. maintenant aussi G. THEISSEN, *Lokalkolorit und Zeitgeschichte in den Evangelien. Ein Beitrag zur Geschichte der synoptischen Tradition* (NTOA, 8), Freiburg/Schw-Göttingen, 1989, pp. 289-292.

66. L'affirmation apodictique de SCHRAMM, *Markus-Stoff* (n. 5) p. 175: «V. 11b ... sicher nicht von Lk selbst gebildet ist», est sans fondement.

67. Sur cette image d'origine apocalyptique, cf. G. BERTRAM, ὠδίν κτλ., in *TWNT* 9 (1973) 668-675.

68. Ainsi CONZELMANN, *Die Mitte der Zeit* (n. 12), p. 119; J. SCHMID, *Das Evangelium nach Lukas* (RNT, 3), Regensburg, ³1955, p. 305.

69. Ainsi, par exemple, A. PLUMMER, *The Gospel According to St. Luke* (ICC), Edinburgh, ⁵1922, p. 479: «Would he have omitted this, if either of those documents [Mt, Mc] was before him?»; C.K. BARRETT, *The Holy Spirit and the Gospel Tradition*, London, ⁵1970, pp. 130-132; ELLIS, *Luke* (n. 5), p. 243; SCHWEIZER, *Lukas* (n. 5), p. 210: «hätte Lukas ohne Vorlage so geändert?»; SCHRAMM, *Markus-Stoff* (n. 5), pp. 175-178: «schlech-

prévaut[70], mais avec des divergences telles que la question mérite d'être reprise.

Malgré toutes les différences, la structure générale permet bien de reconnaître le texte marcien comme le point de départ de Luc:

- première annonce: les persécutions, occasion de témoignage (Mc 13,9; Lc 21,12-13)

[parenthèse sur l'évangélisation des païens (Mc 13,10), omise par Luc]

- exhortation et promesse (Mc 13,11; Lc 21,14-15)

- seconde annonce: trahisons, haine universelle, meurtres (Mc 13,12-13a; Lc 21,16-17)

- exhortation et promesse (Mc 13,13b; Lc 21,18-19).

Dans un crescendo dramatique, on annonce d'abord une vague d'arrestations avec interrogatoires, flagellations (vv. 12-13), puis trahisons, haine universelle, meurtres (vv. 16-17). Chacune des deux annonces est suivie d'une exhortation qui comporte également une promesse d'aide: lors des interrogatoires, il ne faut pas se préoccuper des paroles à dire parce qu'elles seront suggérées par le Seigneur (vv. 14-15); dans la haine universelle, même pas un cheveu ne sera touché et par la persévérance on atteindra le salut (vv. 18-19).

Sur la base des modifications lucaniennes, tout le texte change de tonalité: d'avertissement, il devient surtout encouragement[71]. L'annonce des premières interventions hostiles (v. 12) est suivie par ἀποβήσεται ὑμῖν εἰς μαρτύριον (v. 13) qui met en lumière leur issue positive; la description de l'auto-défense en souligne davantage l'efficacité (v. 15); l'annonce des trahisons (v. 16a) est équilibrée d'une certaine manière par la précision «...et ils en tueront certains [seulement] d'entre vous» (v. 16b); enfin, à l'annonce de la haine universelle (v. 17) fait pendant paradoxalement la promesse: «...mais pas même un cheveu de votre tête ne sera perdu» (v. 18). La haine des adversaires, si elle pouvait avoir libre cours, conduirait à l'anéantissement de tous les chrétiens; mais Dieu ne le permet pas. Ici aussi, comme dans la construction impersonnelle avec ἀποβήσεται (v. 13), le sujet sous-entendu est Dieu, avec sa providence. L'intensification de la protection divine va de pair avec l'intensification de l'hostilité.

2. *Cadre chronologique (v. 12a)*

Après l'annonce des guerres et des autres désastres qui marqueront le «commencement des douleurs» (Mc 13,7-8), Marc en venait à parler

---

terdings undenkbar»! Selon M. MAHONEY, *Luke 21,14-15. Editorial Rewriting or Authenticity?*, in *ITQ* 47 (1980) 220-238, nous aurions ici la forme la plus originaire du logion; elle viendrait du Proto-Luc, utilisé par l'évangéliste avant de connaître Mc.

70. VERHEYDEN, *The Source(s)* (n. 6), p. 506: «The tendency among recent proponents to reduce the number of verses attributed to Luke's source ist most clear for vv. 12-19».

71. DUPONT, *Les trois Apocalypses* (n. 23), pp. 114-117.

des persécutions avec un avertissement: βλέπετε δὲ ὑμεῖς αὐτοῖς (Mc 13,9) qui pouvait faire penser à une succession chronologique[72] ou à une simultanéité (c'est ainsi qu'a compris Mt 24,9: τότε). Luc, en revanche, élimine de ces désastres l'indication «le commencement des douleurs» et précise que «avant toutes ces choses» (v. 12a) commenceront les persécutions. Nous devons supposer qu'il élargit l'horizon en embrassant aussi les persécutions déjà advenues dans les premiers temps de l'Église (cf. 1 Th 2,14-16), comme le confirment également divers contacts, thématiques et verbaux, avec Ac 3–7. Dans la tradition prémarcienne, par contre, il est probable qu'on parlait seulement des persécutions qui menaçaient; mais une fois l'oracle placé dans la bouche du Jésus pré-pascal, c'était créer une inconséquence que d'ignorer les persécutions ayant déjà eu lieu dans le passé; peut-être Marc ne s'est-il pas posé la question; Luc, en revanche, l'a fait[73], et il l'a résolue de la manière la plus simple, sans déplacer la section entière mais en se limitant à ajouter d'abord: «Mais avant toutes ces choses»[74].

Bien que la tonalité parénétique soit indéniable[75], il ne s'agit donc pas uniquement des persécutions que les chrétiens endurent à son époque[76]; mais pas non plus *seulement* de celles du passé[77]; Luc ne parlera pas ensuite d'une cessation des persécutions; au contraire, en décrivant la Parousie comme libération, avec l'invitation à «relever la tête» (v. 28), il semble présupposer que les souffrances des croyants prendront fin seulement alors. Ce qui se situe avant toutes les autres choses, à la rigueur, est seulement leur *début*.

3. *La première annonce des persécutions (vv. 12b-13; cf. Mc 13,9)*

À partir d'ici, on trouve différentes retouches qui permettent de mieux coller à la réalité historique[78]. Marc, en effet, décrivait les

---

72. THEISSEN, *Lokalkolorit* (n. 65), pp. 133s., note 3; 144s., 289.

73. MARXSEN, *Der Evangelist Markus* (n. 12), p. 131; BARTSCH, *Wachet* (n. 5), p. 120; R. MADDOX, *The Purpose of Luke-Acts* (FRLANT, 126), Göttingen, 1982, p. 116.

74. Peut-être aussi pour empêcher que le πρῶτον du v. 9 (qui est tel seulement par rapport au τέλος) soit mal compris dans le sens d'antériorité absolue.

75. G. BRAUMANN, *Das Mittel der Zeit. Erwägungen zur Theologie des Lukasevangeliums*, in *ZNW* 54 (1963) 117-145; F. SCHÜTZ, *Der leidende Christus. Die angefochtene Gemeinde und das Christuskerygma der lukanischen Schriften* (BWANT, 89 = NF, 9), Stuttgart, 1969, p. 14; R. KÜHSCHELM, *Jüngerverfolgung und Geschick Jesu. Eine exegetisch-bibeltheologische Untersuchung der synoptischen Verfolgungsankündigungen Mk 13,9-13 par. und Mt 23,29-38 par.* (ÖBS, 5), Klosterneuburg, 1983.

76. Avec F.W. HORN, *Glaube und Handeln in der Theologie des Lukas* (GTA, 26), Göttingen, 1983, pp. 216-220.

77. Ainsi GOULDER, *Luke* (n. 19), p. 709: Luc ici penserait seulement aux persécutions des apôtres qui ne dureront pas au-delà de 70: c'est pour cette raison qu'il omettrait εἰς τέλος (v. 19).

78. H. BAARLINK, *Die Eschatologie der synoptischen Evangelien* (BWANT, 120 = VI/20), Stuttgart, 1986, pp. 158-163.

persécutions de manière concrète et vivante, en évoquant quelques situations caractéristiques comme en une série de tableaux, en les disposant en crescendo: la comparution devant les tribunaux, la flagellation dans les synagogues, la citation devant les gouverneurs et les rois. Luc conserve ces trois tableaux, mais il en complète la série en insérant au début le moment traumatisant de l'arrestation: «ils vous mettront la main dessus»[79]. Cependant, les persécutions ne se concrétisaient pas toujours selon ces modalités; c'est peut-être la raison pour laquelle Luc préfère ne pas parler des coups en général, même si c'est parfois le cas (cf. Ac 5,40; 16,23.27; 22,19)[80]; il ajoute par contre les «prisons» si souvent mentionnées dans les Actes (cf. Ac 5,19.22.25; 8,3; 12,4.5.6. 10.17; 16,23.24.27.37.40; 22,4; 26,10) et insère le verbe plus vague «poursuivre» (διώκειν: 9 fois en Ac; 2 en Lc; 7 en Mt; 1 en Mc; 2 en Jn; cf. aussi διωγμός en Ac 8,1 et 13,50)[81].

D'autres interventions ont un caractère stylistique. La première annonce en Mc 13,9 était formulée en trois propositions coordonnées avec καί, mais qui ne sont pas parfaitement homogènes entre elles puisque la première est à la voix active avec «vous» comme objet (παραδώσουσιν ὑμᾶς εἰς συνέδρια) et les deux autres avec «vous» comme sujet, mais l'une est à la voix passive (καὶ εἰς συναγωγὰς δαρήσεσθε) et l'autre à la voix active (καὶ ἐπὶ ἡγεμόνων καὶ βασιλέων σταθήσεσθε). Luc préfère un phrasé plus compact[82]: une seule proposition principale (ἐπιβαλοῦσιν … καὶ διώξουσιν) qui régit deux propositions subordonnées rendues plus parallèles entre elles (παραδίδοντες … ἀπαγομένους). Puisqu'il a omis aussi bien la flagellation que les «tribunaux»[83], Luc réutilise pour les synagogues le verbe employé par Marc pour les tribunaux, παραδίδωμι[84]; même le second verbe, ἀπαγομένους, récupère des éléments omis par la suite (καὶ ὅταν ἄγωσιν ὑμᾶς: Mc 13,11). Ἕνεκεν τοῦ ὀνόματός μου est préféré à ἕνεκεν ἐμοῦ pour aligner la phrase sur le διὰ τὸ ὄνομά μου qui suit au v. 17 (repris de Mc 13,13); il convient d'ailleurs mieux à un contexte ecclésial[85].

79. Expression traditionnelle (cf. Mc 14,46; Jn 7,30.44) déjà utilisée pour Jésus (Lc 20,19), puis, dans un parallèle significatif, également pour les disciples (Ac 4,3; 5,18; 12,1; 21,27); cf. KÜHSCHELM, *Jüngerverfolgung* (n. 75), p. 288; J.J. KILGALLEN, *La persecuzione negli Atti degli Apostoli*, in MARCONI–O'COLLINS (ed.), *Luca-Atti* (n. 26), pp. 204-233.

80. Peut-être parce que des descriptions trop crues lui répugnent un peu: même la flagellation de Jésus (Mc 15,15), bien qu'elle soit mentionnée dans la dernière annonce de la passion (Lc 18,33), est passée sous silence dans le récit de la passion, de même que le couronnement d'épines et les autres outrages (Mc 15,16-20).

81. Cf. DUPONT, *Les béatitudes,* III (n. 44), p. 333.

82. Cf. CADBURY, *Style* (n. 15), pp. 151s.: «More compact sentences».

83. Pas seulement parce que superflus puisque les synagogues ont déjà été mentionnées, mais aussi parce qu'en Lc-Ac, on parle seulement du Sanhédrin de Jérusalem (Lc 22,66; Ac 4,15; 5,21.27.34.41; 6,12.15; 22,30; 23,1.6.15.20.28; 24,20).

84. À moins qu'en Marc, εἰς συνέδρια soit considéré comme faisant partie de la phrase suivante: C.H. TURNER, *Marcan Usage. III. εἰς and ἐν in St. Mark,* in *JTS* 26 (1924-25) 14-20, voir pp. 19s.

85. Surtout en Ac 3-4, on rencontre un rapport particulier entre le thème du «nom» et

Marc concluait la première annonce par l'expression εἰς μαρτύριον αὐτοῖς, sans verbe; cela donnait l'impression d'une sorte d'appendice après une proposition déjà surchargée. La liaison est gauche: en effet, pour le sens, le pronom devrait se rapporter à tous les persécuteurs mentionnés, juifs et païens; mais formellement, il peut dépendre seulement de la dernière phrase qui a pour sujet les chrétiens (καὶ ἐπὶ ἡγεμόνων καὶ βασιλέων σταθήσεσθε), et non des précédentes qui ont pour sujet les persécuteurs eux-mêmes (παραδώσουσιν ὑμᾶς ...). Il est compréhensible que, pour éliminer ces inconséquences, Luc ait décidé de transformer l'expression en une proposition autonome qui puisse se rapporter plus clairement à toutes les situations décrites auparavant, que ce soit chez les juifs ou chez les païens.

Pour cela, Luc choisit un verbe, ἀποβήσεται, qui permet la construction impersonnelle, étant donné que ce n'est pas la volonté humaine, ni celle des persécuteurs, ni celle des persécutés eux-mêmes, qui détermine ce retournement inattendu; en effet, ἀποβαίνειν au moyen avec εἰς et l'accusatif équivaut à «se transformer en», et se dit en particulier d'une situation négative qui, de manière imprévisible, laisse transparaître un aspect positif (un bon parallèle, même pour le contenu, se trouve en Ph 1,19; voir aussi Jb 13,16 LXX).

Reste la question de savoir si μαρτύριον[86] doit être entendu comme *nomen actionis* (la persécution se transformera pour les chrétiens en une occasion de *rendre témoignage*)[87] ou au sens objectif de quelque chose qui a valeur de preuve, de document (la persécution se transformera pour les chrétiens en un *témoignage en leur faveur* devant Dieu)[88]. En Marc, μαρτύριον avait le sens objectif, sur la base du pronom αὐτοῖς,

le contexte des persécutions provoquées par le témoignage rendu à Jésus; cf. expressions comme «souffrir pour le Nom», ou «pour mon nom» (Ac 5,41; 9,15.16), risquer sa vie pour le nom de Jésus (Ac 15,26), mourir pour le nom du Seigneur Jésus (Ac 21,13). Davantage de détails en ZMIJEWSKI, *Eschatologiereden* (n. 21), pp. 157-161. Monographie: G. BETORI, *Perseguitati a causa del Nome. Strutture dei racconti di persecuzione in Atti 1,12-8,4* (AnBib, 97), Roma, 1981.

86. Une troisième hypothèse chez KECK, *Abschiedsrede* (n. 21), pp. 199-208, qui comprend: la persécution judaïque sera pour les disciples le signe que le jugement sur Jérusalem est désormais menaçant. Mais μαρτύριον n'est pas synonyme de σημεῖον; en outre, si les persécutions commencent dès le début (cf. Ac 3–4), comment peuvent-elles être le signe de la fin de Jérusalem?

87. En ce sens, H. STRATHMANN, μάρτυς κτλ., in *TWNT* 4 (1942) 509s.; T. BAUMEISTER, *Die Anfänge der Theologie des Martyriums* (Münster. Beitr. z. Theol., 45), Münster, 1980, pp. 117s.; KÜHSCHELM, *Jüngerverfolgung* (n. 75), pp. 202-204.

88. Cf. L. HARTMAN, *Testimonium Linguae. Participial Constructions in the Synoptic Gospels. A Linguistic Examination of Luke 21,13* (CNT, 19), Lund, 1963, pp. 57-75. Cf. aussi ZMIJEWSKI, *Eschatologiereden* (n. 21), pp. 161-169; MARSHALL, *Luke* (n. 5), pp. 767s.; J. DUPONT, *La persécution comme situation missionnaire (Mc 13,9-11)*, in R. SCHNACKENBURG – J. ERNST – J. WANKE (ed.), *Die Kirche des Anfangs. FS H. Schürmann* (ErfTS, 38), Leipzig, 1977, pp. 97-114, voir pp. 99s.; = *Études sur les évangiles synoptiques* (n. 23), pp. 456-473, spécialement pp. 458s.

qui exprimait l'idée du témoignage à charge : la prédication repoussée se transforme en une preuve contre les incrédules au jugement dernier (cf. Mc 1,44; 6,11); cependant, le contexte supposait aussi l'action évangélisatrice des disciples : εἰς πάντα τὰ ἔθνη ... κηρυχθῆναι τὸ εὐαγγέλιον. Luc a laissé tomber αὐτοῖς et a inséré ὑμῖν à la place; ce datif d'avantage laisse ouvertes les deux possibilités : en effet, étant donné que le devoir incombe aux chrétiens de témoigner de Jésus (Ac 1,8 : ἔσεσθέ μου μάρτυρες), quand leur est donnée l'occasion de le faire, en un certain sens, c'est une faveur qui leur est faite. Hartman fait remarquer que μαρτύριον dans le N.T. (à la différence de μαρτυρία) ne serait jamais un *nomen actionis*; pourtant, il reconnaît lui-même qu'en Ac 4,33, ἀπεδίδουν τὸ μαρτύριον ne peut pas signifier «ils donnaient la "preuve" de la résurrection», et que, en 1 Co 1,6, le terme est quasiment synonyme de εὐαγγέλιον[89]. Dans ces conditions, le sens actif semble plus adapté au contexte précédent (v. 12b : ἕνεκεν τοῦ ὀνόματός μου) et suivant (vv. 14-15 : ἀπολογηθῆναι, στόμα, σοφία...), et également à la perspective lucanienne dans le livre des Actes, en particulier aux nombreux épisodes où l'arrestation se transforme en témoignage (Ac 23,11; 22,15; cf. aussi 9,15-16).

4. *L'omission de la phrase sur l'évangélisation des païens (Mc 13,10)*

Mc 13,10 donne l'impression d'une parenthèse[90] entre le v. 9 et le v. 11, insérée par association d'idées avec le terme μαρτύριον[91], mais il n'y a aucune raison de supposer que la phrase n'était pas présente dans le texte employé aussi bien par Matthieu (cf. Mt 24,14) que par Luc[92]. On ne peut soutenir que Luc l'ait considérée comme superflue après l'allusion précédente au μαρτύριον[93], qui ne parle pas des païens en général, mais seulement des «rois et gouverneurs», ou à cause de l'insertion par la suite de καιροὶ ἐθνῶν (v. 24)[94], où l'on ne parle pas des païens comme destinataires de l'Évangile, mais comme oppresseurs de Jérusalem. Nous nous trouvons donc bel et bien devant une omission.

---

89. L. HARTMAN, *Testimonium Linguae* (n. 88), p. 69.

90. C.H. TURNER, *Marcan Usage. IV. Parenthetical clauses in Mark*, in *JTS* 26 (1924-25) 145-156, voir pp. 152s.; M. ZERWICK, *Markus-Stil* (n. 60), p. 132. Le καί a une fonction causale-explicative : REISER, *Syntax und Stil* (n. 60), pp. 126-128.

91. J. LAMBRECHT, *Die Redaktion der Markus-Apokalypse* (AnBib, 28), Roma, 1967, pp. 135s.

92. Cf. G. STRECKER, *Literarkritische Überlegungen zum εὐαγγέλιον-Begriff im Markusevangelium*, in H. BALTENSWEILER – B. REICKE (ed.), *Neues Testament und Geschichte. FS O. Cullmann*, Göttingen-Zürich, 1972, pp. 91-104, voir pp. 98-101.

93. MOORE, *The Parousia* (n. 28), pp. 86-88.

94. R.H. HIERS, *The Problem of the Delay of the Parousia in Luke-Acts*, in *NTS* 20 (1973-74) 145-155.

Une difficulté éventuelle par rapport au terme εὐαγγέλιον[95] n'explique pas l'élimination de la phrase entière, étant donné que Luc disposait d'une terminologie très riche pour exprimer l'idée d'une autre manière. Et puisque Luc est extrêmement favorable aussi bien à l'évangélisation des païens[96] qu'au rôle des Douze dans cette évangélisation[97] (cf. Lc 24,47 et Ac 1,6-8), la raison de l'omission devrait être plutôt le contexte dans lequel le thème avait été situé ici par Marc: ou bien le contexte proche, les persécutions (vv. 12-19), ou bien le contexte plus général, le discours eschatologique. Conzelmann considère l'une et l'autre hypothèses: Luc n'a pas voulu mettre ensemble persécution et évangélisation, parce que l'une appartient au passé et l'autre au présent[98]. Toutefois, comme cela a déjà été dit (cf. IV.2), c'est seulement le *début* des persécutions qui appartient au passé, et pour cette raison, même si les premières persécutions sont racontées en Ac 3-4, tandis que les païens sont rejoints seulement en Ac 10-11, à un certain moment les deux expériences seront en cours en même temps.

L'autre hypothèse formulée par Conzelmann[99] est que Luc a voulu éliminer complètement le lien qui, chez Marc encore, reliait l'évangélisation à la Parousie[100]. La difficulté, c'est que déjà le texte de Marc, en interprétant l'évangélisation comme condition préliminaire à la Parousie[101] à travers le πρῶτον de l'histoire du salut[102], soulignait non la

95. KÜHSCHELM, *Jüngerverfolgung* (n. 75), p. 202. Cf. MARXSEN, *Der Evangelist Markus* (n. 12), pp. 95-98.

96. Étrange est l'hypothèse de ERNST, *Lukas* (n. 53), pp. 552s., selon laquelle Luc, en omettant aussi l'expression sur le «salut de toute chair» (Mc 13,20) et sur le rassemblement universel des élus (Mc 13,27), veut corriger un optimisme excessif à propos du salut. Mais Luc a des expressions encore plus fortes, par exemple: «Toute chair verra le salut» (Lc 3,6: cf. Is 40,5).

97. Selon GOULDER, *Luke* (n. 19), p. 708, l'omission est due au fait que ce ne sont pas les Douze, mais Paul qui réalisera la mission chez les païens.

98. CONZELMANN, *Die Mitte der Zeit* (n. 12), p. 119; cf. aussi p. 206, n. 2: «Mc 13,10 widerspricht der lukanischen Auffassung von der Gliederung der Ereignisse». GRÄSSER, *Problem* (n. 20), p. 160.

99. CONZELMANN, *Die Mitte der Zeit* (n. 12), pp. 199s., n. 4; MARXSEN, *Der Evangelist Markus* (n. 12), p. 129.

100. Il semble prouvé que ce πρῶτον se réfère à la Parousie; elle est donc dépassée l'explication selon laquelle Luc aurait omis Mc 13,10 pour ne pas affirmer que l'évangélisation universelle devait se réaliser *avant la destruction de Jérusalem*: M.-J. LAGRANGE, *Évangile selon saint Luc* (EB), Paris, 1921, pp. 525 et 529. Selon A. FEUILLET, *Le discours de Jésus sur la ruine du temple d'après Marc* XIII et Lc XXI 5-36, in *RB* 55 (1948) 481-502; 56 (1949) 61-92, voir pp. 492s., Marc n'avait pas perçu la difficulté parce qu'il se référait à cette première phase de prédication universelle, déjà réalisée et rejetée par Israël (Rm 10,18); Luc, en revanche, l'a omise parce qu'il a pensé à la prédication qui doit encore se prolonger jusqu'à l'arrivée du πλήρωμα τῶν ἐθνῶν (Rm 11,25). Partiellement rectifié en ID., *La signification fondamentale de Marc XIII. Recherches sur l'eschatologie des synopti-ques*, in *RThom* 80 (1980) 181-215, cf. pp. 195s., 207s.

101. Cf. O. CULLMANN, *Le caractère eschatologique du devoir missionnaire et la conscience apostolique de Saint Paul*, in ID., *Des sources de l'évangile à la formation de la théologie chrétienne*, Neuchâtel, 1969, pp. 51-75.

102. Cf. Mc 7,27 par.; 9,11-12 par.; Lc 17,25; 21,9; Ac 3,26; 13,46; Rm 1,16; 2,9.10; 2

proximité de la Parousie, mais bien son retard[103]; pourquoi alors Luc aurait-il dû l'éliminer? D'autant que, selon d'autres, la raison de l'omission serait au contraire l'exigence de ne lier la Parousie à aucune condition préalable, de sorte qu'elle puisse être attendue à tout moment, même avant que l'évangélisation universelle soit terminée[104]; cette supposition est pourtant en désaccord avec la perspective lucanienne exprimée on ne peut plus clairement en Ac 1,6-8.

Développant les remarques de F. Hahn, J. Dupont[105] a observé que les expressions principales de Mc 13,10: εἰς πάντα τὰ ἔθνη ... κηρυχθῆναι, ont été réutilisées en Lc 24,27: κηρυχθῆναι ... εἰς πάντα τὰ ἔθνη; le δεῖ est remplacé par le thème de l'accomplissement des Écritures, tandis que n'apparaît plus le πρῶτον, à savoir l'idée de l'évangélisation comme condition préliminaire à la Parousie; l'intention de Luc aurait donc été de déplacer le thème dans un contexte mieux adapté, mais aussi de le détacher du cadre des événements eschatologiques[106].

L'hypothèse du déplacement se révèle éclairante. En effet, bien que d'habitude il suive ses sources pas à pas, parfois, pour obtenir un ordre

Th 2,3. Ce *theologoumenon* chrétien dérive du thème apocalyptique de la «mesure» qui doit se remplir: cf. D. Rössler, *Gesetz und Geschichte. Untersuchungen zur Theologie der jüdischen Apokalyptik und der pharisäischen Orthodoxie* (WMANT, 3), Neukirchen, 1960, pp. 55-63; W. Harnisch, *Verhängnis und Verheißung der Geschichte. Untersuchungen zum Zeit- und Geschichtsverständnis im 4. Buch Esra und in der Syr. Baruchapokalypse* (FRLANT, 97), Göttingen, 1969, pp. 276-287; Fusco, *Parola e Regno* (n. 29), pp. 356-361; Stuhlmann, *Das eschatologische Maß* (n. 25).

103. Grässer, *Problem* (n. 20), p. 159: «Die Funktion als retardierendes Moment im Ablauf der Heilsereignisse ist offensichtlich»; Conzelmann, *Geschichte und Eschaton nach Mc 13* (n. 24), pp. 218s.; Hahn, *Die Rede* (n. 24), p. 257.

104. Bartsch, *Wachet* (n. 5), pp. 120s.; Geiger, *Endzeitreden* (n. 21), p. 252. Explication opposée chez Kaestli, *Eschatologie* (n. 20), p. 47: comme il s'agit d'une condition que les chrétiens de l'époque pouvaient considérer comme déjà réalisée (cf. Col 1,6.23), il l'aurait éliminée pour empêcher que la Parousie soit conçue comme imminente. La première prémisse est exacte, pas la seconde: cf. Fusco, *«Point of View»* (n. 26).

105. F. Hahn, *Das Verständnis der Mission im Neuen Testament* (WMANT, 13), Neukirchen, ²1965, pp. 111-119; J. Dupont, *La portée christologique de l'évangélisation des nations d'après Luc 24,47*, in J. Gnilka (ed.), *Neues Testament und Kirche. FS R. Schnackenburg*, Freiburg/Br-Basel-Wien, 1974, pp. 125-143, voir pp. 131-134; = *Nouvelles études sur les Actes des Apôtres* (LD, 118), Paris, 1984, pp. 37-57, voir pp. 45-48; Id., *Les trois apocalypses* (n. 23), p. 114; également S.G. Wilson, *The Gentiles and the Gentile Mission in Luke-Acts* (SNTS MS, 23), Cambridge, 1973, pp. 47s.; P. Zingg, *Das Wachsen der Kirche. Beiträge zur Frage der lukanischen Redaktion und Theologie* (OBO, 3), Freiburg/Schw-Göttingen, 1974, p. 254; J. Kremer, *Weltweites Zeugnis für Christus in der Kraft des Geistes. Zur lukanichen Sicht der Mission*, in K. Kertelge (ed.), *Mission im Neuen Testament* (QD, 93), Freiburg/B, 1982, pp. 145-163; B. Prete, *Il testo di Luca 24,47: «Sarà predicata a tutte le genti la conversione per il perdono dei peccati»*, in Id., *L'opera di Luca. Contenuti e prospettive*, Torino, 1986, pp. 328-351, spécialement pp. 334s.; G. Betori, *Lc 24,47: Gerusalemme e gli inizi della predicazione ai pagani negli Atti degli Apostoli*, in Marconi–O'Collins (ed.), *Luca-Atti* (n. 26), pp. 149-177.

106. Dupont, *Les trois apocalypses* (n. 23), pp. 114-115, note qu'une fois éliminé le πρῶτον, le reste de la phrase n'avait plus de sens dans ce contexte.

meilleur, Luc n'hésite pas à opérer des déplacements même dans l'ordre des péricopes et non seulement à l'intérieur de celles-ci[107]. Et quand sont en jeu des thèmes dont la portée théologique est grande, il n'hésite pas à les transférer même dans des contextes assez éloignés mais plus significatifs, et, si c'est nécessaire, même d'un livre à l'autre[108]; un bel exemple est l'importante citation d'Is 6,9-10 sur l'aveuglement du peuple: omise presque complètement dans le parallèle lucanien de l'évangile (Lc 8,10; cf. Mc 4,10-12), elle est utilisée ensuite, et de manière bien plus solennelle, dans la conclusion du second volume de l'œuvre de Luc (Ac 28,26-27)[109]. De même dans notre cas, Luc pouvait difficilement se contenter d'introduire seulement en passant, dans une sorte de parenthèse, un thème aussi important pour lui que la nécessité de l'évangélisation universelle. Cependant, entrent en jeu également des raisons plus positives: dans la perspective de Luc, l'appel des Gentils ne peut avoir lieu si le Messie n'a pas d'abord mené à terme complètement son ministère pour Israël: de là vient cette sorte de réserve ou d'atténuation du thème universaliste que l'on remarque dans le premier volume lucanien[110]; d'autre part, le dessein de salut ne pourra être compris sinon à la lumière des Écritures dont l'intelligence ne sera donnée que par la résurrection (cf. Lc 24,44-49).

Cependant, à notre avis, le déplacement ne se fait pas seulement en Lc 24,47, mais aussi en Ac 1,6-8 (deux textes par ailleurs liés étroitement[111], selon la technique de l'«entremêlement des extrémités»[112]) où

107. CADBURY, *Style* (n. 15), pp. 76-79; Cf. la discussion entre H.F.D. SPARKS, *St. Luke's Transpositions*, in *NTS* 3 (1956-57) 219-223; J. JEREMIAS, *Perikopen-Umstellungen bei Lukas?*, in *NTS* 4 (1957-58) 115-119; H. SCHÜRMANN, *Die Dubletten im Lukasevangelium*, in *ZKT* 75 (1953) 338-345; ID., *Die Dublettenvermeidungen im Lukasevangelium*, in *ZKT* 76 (1954) 83-93; = ID., *Traditionsgeschichtliche Untersuchungen zu den synoptischen Evangelien*, Düsseldorf, 1968, pp. 272-278 et 279-289.

108. Sur la nécessité de tenir compte aussi des Actes dans la comparaison avec Marc, cf. W. ÜBELACHER, *Lukasskrifternas förhållande till Markusevangeliet*, in *SEÅ* 56 (1991) 45-77; aussi en allemand: *Das Verhältnis von Lk/Apg zum Markusevangelium*, in LUOMANEN, *Luke-Acts* (n. 27), pp. 157-194: sur Lc 21, pp. 179-181. Synopse Lc 21 / Actes en CARROLL, *Response* (n. 11), pp. 117-119.

109. J. GNILKA, *Die Verstockung Israels. Isaias 6,9-10 in der Theologie der Synoptiker* (SANT, 3), München, 1961, p. 130: «Hier und nicht im Parabelkapitel erblickt er den passenden Ort für die Prophetie, die an dieser Stelle in ihrer ganzen Tragweite zur Geltung kommt»; J. DUPONT, *Le salut des Gentils et la signification théologique du livre des Actes*, in *NTS* 6 (1959-60) 132-155; = ID., *Études sur les Actes des Apôtres* (LD, 45), Paris, 1967, pp. 393-419; ID., *La parabole du semeur dans la version de Luc*, in *Apophoreta. FS E. Haenchen* (BZNW, 30), Berlin, 1964, pp. 97-108; = ID., *Études sur les Évangiles synoptiques* (n. 23), pp. 1019-1031. Pour la critique à d'autres explications de type littéraire, cf. FUSCO, *Parola e Regno* (n. 29), p. 266, note 178.

110. Cf. FUSCO, *Progetto* (n. 45), pp. 138-140 et la bibliographie citée. Cf. aussi KECK, *Abschiedsrede* (n. 21), pp. 145s.: en Lc 21, c'est plutôt Israël qui est au premier plan.

111. J. DUPONT, *Le salut des Gentils* (n. 109), pp. 139-141; = ID., *Études sur les Actes des Apôtres* (n. 109), pp. 401-404; ID., *La Mission de Paul d'après Actes 26,16-23 et la Mission des Apôtres d'après Luc 24,44-49 et Actes 1,8*, in M.D. HOOKER – S.G. WILSON

Luc a déplacé aussi un autre élément du discours eschatologique, le logion sur l'ignorance du καιρός (Ac 1,7; cf. Mc 13,32)[113]. Ici, en effet, même si le terme πρῶτον n'apparaît pas, le témoignage jusqu'aux extrémités de la terre est de fait considéré comme condition préalable à la Parousie, en réponse à la question des disciples sur la venue du Règne[114]. Plus que d'une omission, il s'agit donc d'un déplacement qui n'est cependant pas dicté par la volonté d'éliminer le rapport entre évangélisation universelle et Parousie.

5. *L'auto-défense des chrétiens soumis à interrogatoire (vv. 14-15; cf. Mc 13,11). L'omission de la référence au Saint-Esprit.*

Puisqu'il a éliminé la parenthèse, Luc n'a pas besoin du raccord marcien qui répétait les verbes déjà utilisés (Mc 13,11a: καὶ ὅταν ἄγωσιν ὑμᾶς παραδιδόντες); avec un simple οὖν il peut introduire directement l'impératif. Mais celui-ci n'est pas répété deux fois comme chez Marc, d'abord négativement («ne vous préoccupez pas de ce que *vous direz*») puis positivement («mais ce qui vous sera donné à ce moment-là, cela, *vous le direz*»); il est unique, mais en compensation, il est renforcé par l'introduction typiquement lucanienne, θέτε οὖν ἐν ταῖς καρδίαις ὑμῶν[115].

D'autres retouches proviennent de l'exigence de remplacer les termes génériques par des termes plus précis: προμεριμνᾶν par προμελετᾶν[116]; λαλεῖν, que Marc répétait trois fois, par ἀπολογηθῆναι; dans la ligne de ce verbe sont introduits aussi les opposants qui ne pourront

---

(ed.), *Paul and Paulinism. FS C.K. Barrett*, London, 1982, pp. 290-301; = *Nouvelles études* (n. 105), pp. 446-456.

112. J. DUPONT, *La question du plan des Actes des Apôtres à la lumière d'un texte de Lucien de Samosate*, in NT 21 (1979) 220-231; = *Nouvelles études* (n. 105), pp. 24-36; à présent, également G. BETORI, *Alla ricerca di un'articolazione per il libro degli Atti*, in *RivBib* 37 (1989) 185-205; ID., *Strutturazione degli Atti e storiografia antica*, in *Cristianesimo nella storia* 12 (1991) 251-263.

113. Reformulé de manière à ne pas attribuer cette ignorance à Jésus, mais encore parfaitement reconnaissable, parce que la connaissance des χρόνοι ἤ καιροί est une prérogative du Père: cf. A. GEORGE, *Jésus fils de Dieu dans l'Évangile selon saint Luc*, in *RB* 72 (1965) 185-209, voir pp. 199s.; = ID., *Études sur l'œuvre de Luc* (SB), Paris, 1978, pp. 215-236, voir pp. 227s.; G. SCHNEIDER, *Parusie-Gleichnisse im Lukas-Evangelium* (SBS, 74), Stuttgart, 1975, pp. 65s.

114. H. CONZELMANN, *Die Apostelgeschichte* (HNT, 7), Tübingen, ²1972, pp. 26s.; cf. FUSCO «*Point of View*» (n. 26). Voir aussi A. BARBI, *La missione negli Atti degli Apostoli*, in G. GHIBERTI (ed.), *La missione nel mondo antico e nella Bibbia*. XXXª Settimana biblica nazionale, Bologna, 1990; = *Ricerche storico bibliche* 2 (1990) n° 1, pp. 127-154.

115. Cf. Lc 1,66: ἔθεντο ... ἐν τῇ καρδίᾳ αὐτῶν; Lc 9,44 (diff. Mc 9,31): θέσθε ὑμεῖς εἰς τὰ ὦτα ὑμῶν τοὺς λόγους τούτους; Ac 5,4; 19,21.

116. Pour le sens de «se préparer un discours», cf. textes d'auteurs grecs en W. BAUER – W.F. ARNDT – F.W. GINGRICH, *A Greek-English Lexicon of the N.T. and Other Early Christian Literature*, Chicago, IL - London ²1979, sub voce.

«résister» ni «contredire». Aussi bien la terminologie que cet intérêt pour l'aspect «apologétique» sont lucaniens; qu'on pense aux nombreuses scènes judiciaires dans les Actes[117]. Dans le N.T., on trouve ἀπολογεῖσθαι deux fois en Luc et six fois dans les Actes, toujours en contexte judiciaire; dans les autres écrits du N.T., on le trouve seulement deux fois chez Paul. Ἀνθίστημι revient en Ac 6,10 pour Étienne (comme ici en lien avec σοφία) et en Ac 13,8 pour Paul; ἀντειπεῖν apparaît en Ac 4,14 pour Pierre, et le terme apparenté ἀντιλέγειν en Lc 2,34; 20,27; Ac 13,45; 28,19.22 (jamais en Mc et Mt); ἀντίκειμαι se trouve en Lc 13,17 au milieu d'autres retouches typiquement lucaniennes comme la joie et la louange du peuple.

La formule de promesse reprend le verbe δίδωμι (cf. Mc 13,11), mais de sorte que le don de Dieu ne soit plus, de façon presque miraculeuse, la parole elle-même, mais la capacité de la formuler: «Je vous donnerai un *langage* et une *sagesse...*» (cf. Ac 6,3.10; 7,10.22; Lc 2,40); dans les Actes aussi, Luc préfère écrire que l'Esprit fortifiait (Ac 1,8), remplissait (Ac 4,8; 6,5; 7,55; 11,24; 13,9); c'est seulement dans le cas de prophéties, impulsions véritablement surnaturelles, que Luc utilise l'expression «l'Esprit saint dit» (Ac 8,29; 11,12; 13,2; 19,1; 20,23; 21,11; 23,9; cf. 16,6.7)[118]. Ici, cependant, le don n'est pas attribué au Saint-Esprit[119], en opposition non seulement au parallèle marcien mais aussi au «doublet» lucanien de Lc 12,11-12, et au livre des Actes qui, justement en contexte de persécutions, décrit les disciples qui parlent «remplis de l'Esprit saint» (cf. Ac 4,8). Comment cela se fait-il?

Le doublet Lc 12,11-12[120] dérive de la *Quelle*[121], comme le con-

---

117. Cf. V. STOLLE, *Der Zeuge als Angeklagter. Untersuchungen zum Paulus-Bild des Lukas* (BWANT, 102), Stuttgart, 1973, pp. 237-241; A.A. TRITES, *The Importance of Legal Scenes and Language in the Book of Acts*, in *NT* 16 (1974) 278-284; E. RICHARD, *Acts 6,1-8,4. The Author's Method of Composition* (SBL DS, 41), Missoula, MT, 1978, pp. 284s.

118. G. BETORI, *Lo Spirito e l'annuncio della Parola negli Atti degli Apostoli*, in *RivBib* 35 (1987) 399-441, surtout pp. 433s.

119. CONZELMANN néglige cette différence, en combinant toujours les deux textes (*Die Mitte der Zeit* [n. 12], p. 119): «Nicht der Geist selbst redet, sondern der Mensch (freilich: es wird ihm gegeben)»; ainsi aussi *Ibid.*, pp. 195s note 2; 211 note 1; 219 note 2; de même G. HAYA-PRATS, *L'Esprit, force de l'Église. Sa nature et son activité d'après les Actes des Apôtres* (LD, 81), Paris, 1975, pp. 26, 77, 101, 141.

120. «Allgemein als Doppelüberlieferung anerkannt»: ainsi le classifie LAUFEN, *Doppelüberlieferungen* (n. 59), p. 90; cf. J. DUPONT, *La persécution* (n. 88); ID., *Les béatitudes*, II. *La bonne nouvelle* (EBib), Paris, 1969, pp. 359-363; NEIRYNCK, *Note* (n. 18), pp. 78s. Moins évidente est l'explication de A. FUCHS, *Sprachliche Untersuchungen zu Matthäus und Lukas. Ein Beitrag zur Quellenkritik* (AnBib, 49), Roma, 1971, pp. 37-44, 171-191, basée sur le *Deutero-Marc* comme source unique et sur la supposition que c'est Luc qui a déplacé le logion au ch. 12. Très difficile aussi pour les griesbachiens, comme McNICOL, *Composition* (n. 18), pp. 188-193, d'expliquer les deux textes de Luc à partir du seul Matthieu.

121. MANSON, *The Sayings of Jesus* (n. 5), pp. 108-110; S. SCHULZ, *Q - Die Spruchquelle der Evangelisten*, Zürich, 1972, pp. 442-444; ID., *Griechisch-deutsche Synopse der Q-*

firme également Mt 10,19-20[122] qui a unifié mais laisse transparaître l'influence des deux sources; une confrontation directe entre les deux textes lucaniens met en évidence des différences sans importance pour le sens et difficilement explicables comme retouches rédactionnelles (εἰσφέρωσιν au lieu de ἄγωσιν; εἴπητε au lieu de λαλήσητε; τὸ ἅγιον πνεῦμα au lieu de το πνεῦμα τὸ ἅγιον) qui font penser à deux versions grecques indépendantes[123]. Luc a conservé le logion dans les deux contextes sans les uniformiser[124]; les uniques contacts (éventuellement rédactionnels dans les deux textes, mais avec des formulations différentes) sont le verbe ἀπολογεῖν, et la construction qui fait en sorte qu'on n'attribue pas les paroles elles-mêmes à l'intervention surnaturelle[125].

Überlieferung, Zürich, 1972, p. 86; D. ZELLER, *Die Weisheitlichen Mahnsprüche bei den Synoptikern* (FB, 17), Würzburg, 1977, p. 83, note 213; p. 191, note 234; A. POLAG, *Fragmenta Q. Textheft zur Logienquelle*, Neukirchen, 1979, p. 60; F. NEIRYNCK, *Recent Developments in the Study of Q*, in J. DELOBEL (ed.), *Logia. Les paroles de Jésus - The Sayings of Jesus* (BETL, 59), Leuven, 1982, pp. 29-75, voir pp. 35-41; = *Evangelica*, II (BETL, 99), Leuven 1991, pp. 409-464, voir pp. 415-421; W. SCHMITHALS, *Einleitung in die drei ersten Evangelien*, Berlin - New York, 1985, pp. 220s., 230s. (admet l'influence de Q sur Mc); J.S. KLOPPENBORG, *The Formation of Q. Trajectories in Ancient Wisdom Collections* (Studies in Antiquity and Christianity), Philadelphia, PA, 1987, pp. 91s., 206-216, 243s.; ID., *Q Parallels. Synopsis, Critical Notes & Concordance*, Sonoma, CA, 1988, p. 126; M. SATO, *Q und Prophetie. Studien zur Gattung und Traditionsgeschichte der Quelle Q* (WUNT, II/29), Tübingen, 1988, pp. 212-214; F. NEIRYNCK, *Q-Synopsis. The Double Tradition Passages in Greek* (SNTA, 13), Leuven, 1988, p. 41.

122. Matthieu l'a transféré, en même temps que d'autres dits sur la persécution, du discours eschatologique au discours missionnaire (cf. Mt 10,17-22 avec Mc 13,9-13): V. TAYLOR, *The Original Order of Q*, in A.J.B. HIGGINS (ed.), *New Testament Essays. FS T.W. Manson*, Manchester, 1959, pp. 246-269; = V. TAYLOR, *New Testament Essays*, London, 1970, pp. 95-118; = A.J. BELLINZONI (ed.), *The Two-Source Hypothesis. A Critical Appraisal*, Macon, GA, 1985, pp. 296-317, à la p. 307; V.K. AGBANOU, *Le discours eschatologique de Matthieu 24–25. Tradition et rédaction* (EB NS, 2), Paris, 1983, pp. 67-80.

123. Ici, la question d'une influence éventuelle de Q sur Mc ne nous concerne pas; c'est l'hypothèse de LAMBRECHT, *Markus-Apokalypse* (n. 91), pp. 115-120; ID., *Die Logia-Quellen von Markus 13*, in *Bib* 47 (1966) 321-360, voir pp. 322-337; ID., *Q-Influence on Mk 8,34-9,1*, in DELOBEL (ed.), *Logia* (n. 121), pp. 277-304, voir pp. 299s.

124. Peut-être par oubli (SCHÜRMANN, *Dubletten* [n. 107], pp. 341, 343; *Dublettenvermeidungen* [n. 107], p. 92 note 78), ou par changement intentionnel: cf. LAGRANGE, *Luc* (n. 100), pp. 524s: «...ayant donné déjà ce passage sous sa forme traditionnelle, il l'a écrit ici d'une façon un peu différente...»; P. HOFFMANN, *Studien zur Theologie der Logienquelle* (NTAbh NF, 8), Münster, ³1982, p. 269; J. KREMER, *Jesu Verheissung des Geistes. Zur Verankerung der Aussage von Joh 16,13 im Leben Jesu*, in *Die Kirche des Anfangs* (n. 88), pp. 247-276, en particulier pp. 262-265; ID., *Weltweites Zeugnis* (n. 105), pp. 145-163, spécialement pp. 152-154. - Sur ce procédé lucanien, cf. H.J. CADBURY, *Four Features of Lucan Style*, in KECK–MARTYN (ed.), *Studies in Luke-Acts* (n.12), pp. 87-102.

125. M.-A. CHEVALLIER, *Souffle de Dieu. Le Saint-Esprit dans le Nouveau Testament*, I. *Ancien Testament, Hellénisme et Judaïsme. La tradition synoptique. L'œuvre de Luc* (Le point théologique, 26), Paris, 1978, pp. 133-136; HAYA-PRATS, *L'Esprit* (n. 119), pp. 73-82; KÜHSCHELM, *Jüngerverfolgung* (n. 75), pp. 226-228.

On n'a aucune raison de postuler des déplacements d'un contexte à l'autre[126].

Le problème alors est de voir si la nouvelle formulation qui, dans le second texte, n'attribue pas une telle intervention à l'Esprit saint peut être rédactionnelle. Pourrait également jouer ici (comme pour l'évangélisation des païens, cf. IV.4) l'exigence de ne pas anticiper des thèmes plus adaptés à un autre contexte: de fait, ici, nous sommes assez proches du moment de la promesse de l'Esprit par le Ressuscité (Lc 24,49; Ac 1,6-8); dès lors, il est possible que la mention de l'Esprit, tolérée dans un autre contexte beaucoup plus distant (Lc 12,11-12), ait été considérée ici comme inopportune[127]. Mais il y a aussi une raison plus positive: ici, c'est Jésus lui-même qui est au premier plan[128]: *pour son nom*, les chrétiens sont arrêtés (v. 12), sont haïs (v. 17); pour son nom, comme le confirme le livre des Actes, ils souffrent, prennent des risques, meurent (5,41; 9,15.16; 15,26; 21,13), au point qu'en eux, en dernière analyse, c'est lui-même qui est persécuté, comme cela sera dit à Saul (Ac 9,4-5). Pour cette raison, c'est lui-même (noter l'emphase: ἐγὼ γάρ[129]) qui aide les disciples à répliquer aux adversaires: «L'esito del processo sarà un trionfo di Cristo stesso»[130].

6. *Annonce de l'intensification des persécutions; exhortation à la persé-vérance (vv. 16-19; cf. Mc 13,12-13)*

Ici, Marc faisait alterner les sujets des verbes. Parfois, ce sont les persécuteurs, parfois les persécutés. Formellement, la phrase «...et ils les mettront à mort», aurait comme sujet et objet, respectivement les enfants et les parents; pour élargir aux chrétiens trahis par d'autres familiers, Marc a dû ajouter: παραδώσει ... εἰς θάνατον; mais de toute manière, une disparité subsiste car la mort est présentée comme un fait pour certains, et pour les autres, seulement comme une intention de la part de ceux qui les trahissent.

126. Curieusement attribués à l'hypothèse des deux sources (qui, en revanche, tient compte du phénomène des doublets et y trouve justement une confirmation) par B. REICKE, *A Test of Synoptic Relationships - Matthew 10,17-23 and 24,9-14 with Parallels*, in W.R. FARMER (ed.), *New Synoptic Studies*. The Cambridge Gospel Conference and Beyond, Macon, GA, 1983, pp. 209-229, cf. p. 213; McNICOL, *Composition* (n. 18), p. 192.

127. Cf. FITZMYER, *Luke* (n. 7), pp. 1327s.: «...it suits in general the Lucan tendency not to mention the holy Spirit in this latter part of the Gospel...».

128. ZMIJEWSKI, *Eschatologiereden* (n. 21), pp. 169-172; KÜHSCHELM, *Jüngerverfolgung* (n. 75), pp. 205s. Forcée est l'explication de E. FRANKLIN, *Christ the Lord. A Study in the Purpose and Theology of Luke-Acts*, London, 1975, pp. 13, 15: «Witness is to the present authority of Jesus rather than to be seen against the background of the return». Un peu générique celle de MARSHALL, *Luke* (n. 5), pp. 768s.: «A Lucan tendency to stress the place of Jesus as the giver of gifts associated with the Spirit could have led to the rewording of the text».

129. PLUMMER, *Luke* (n. 69), p. 479.

130. ZEDDA, *Escatologia* (n. 20), p. 369.

Luc uniformise même la première phrase avec le sujet «vous»[131]; il évite les répétitions (ἀδελφὸς ἀδελφὸν ... πατὴρ τέκνον ... τέκνα ἐπὶ γονεῖς) en mentionnant une seule fois les «parents» et les «frères», et en complétant la liste de manière plus réaliste en mentionnant les «familiers» (terme utilisé seulement par Luc chez les Synoptiques: Lc 1,58; 2,44; 14,12) et les «amis» (quinze fois en Luc, une fois seulement chez les autres: Mt 11,19); il clarifie le sujet de θανατώσουσιν (les persécuteurs) et son objet (les chrétiens en général); mais il sent le besoin de préciser: «(seulement) *certains* d'entre vous» (v. 16). En effet, dans le récit des Actes, des cas comme celui d'Étienne ou de Jacques restent une exception (Ac 7,54-60; 12,1-2; noter à cet endroit l'expression κακῶσαί *τινας* τῶν ἀπὸ τῆς ἐκκλησίας).

L'annonce de la haine universelle (v. 17) est suivie d'un ajout totalement neuf: «... mais pas même un cheveu de votre tête ne sera perdu» (v. 18), une sorte de proverbe (1 Sam 14,45; 2 Sam 14,11; 1 R 1,52, etc) dont l'application dépend beaucoup du contexte et du ton avec lequel il est prononcé; ici, on devrait le comprendre comme une promesse d'intégrité au sens physique (cf. Ac 27,34). Pour certains, il y a là une contradiction à expliquer par la superposition de deux sources différentes[132]; ou bien à éliminer en interprétant le v. 18 comme une allusion au salut éternel[133], ou vice versa en interprétant au sens matériel la promesse conclusive du v. 19[134]. En réalité, ce n'est pas le seul cas où, en s'adressant aux persécutés, la parénèse néo-testamentaire les exhorte à affronter la mort, mais en même temps les encourage à s'en remettre à la providence de Dieu qui peut les en délivrer (Mt 10,28-32 // Lc 12,4-9; Ap 2,10; 13,1). La soi-disant contradiction disparaît: il y aura certainement des gens tués, mais seulement *certains* (v. 16b); pour tous les autres, pour la majorité, même si ce n'est pas la totalité, la promesse d'intégrité formulée de manière plus générale reste valable.

L'exhortation conclusive doit être rapportée au salut eschatologique, même si l'on prend ψυχή non pas au sens grec d'«âme» (cf. Mt 10,28) mais au sens sémitique de «vie», totalité de l'être humain (נֶפֶשׁ: cf. Lc 6,9; 12,22)[135]. Quelle que soit l'issue de l'épreuve, la mort (v. 16b) ou la délivrance (v. 18)[136], le passage se conclut, comme chez Marc, par une

131. Dupont, *Les trois apocalypses* (n. 23), p. 113; Id., *Les béatitudes,* I. *Le problème littéraire* (EB), Paris, 1969, pp. 283-289; cf. Cadbury, *Style* (n. 15), pp. 124s.

132. Schramm, *Markus-Stoff* (n. 5), pp. 177s.: «...ein krasser Fall von (schematischer) Quellenkombination»; Fitzmyer, *Luke* (n. 7), p. 1341.

133. Par exemple, Plummer, *Luke* (n. 69), p. 480; Lagrange, *Luc* (n. 100), pp. 526s.; Marshall, *Luke* (n. 5), pp. 769s.; W. Schmithals, *Das Evangelium nach Lukas* (ZBK NT, III/1), Zürich, 1980, p. 202, pour ne citer que quelques-uns.

134. Ainsi Kühschelm, *Jüngerverfolgung* (n. 75), pp. 211-213, 291s.

135. Avec P. Ortiz Valdivieso, ΥΠΟΜΟΝΗ *en el Nuevo Testamento,* Bogota, 1969, pp. 35s; J.-W. Taeger, *Der Mensch und sein Heil. Studien zum Bild des Menschen und zur Sicht der Bekehrung bei Lukas* (SNT, 14), Gütersloh, 1982, p. 22.

136. Excessif Keck, *Abschiedsrede* (n. 21), pp. 214-219, qui réfère la promesse surtout à qui perd la vie terrestre.

exhortation, qui est en même temps promesse, valable pour tous les croyants qui auront été persévérants.

Mais comment expliquer la reformulation lucanienne? Là où Marc écrivait ὁ δὲ ὑπομείνας εἰς τέλος οὗτος σωθήσεται, Luc formule ainsi son exhortation: ἐν τῇ ὑπομονῇ ὑμῶν κτήσασθε [*var.* κτήσεσθε] τὰς ψυχὰς ὑμῶν (v. 19). Souvent, on s'arrête seulement à l'omission de εἰς τέλος, en l'expliquant, comme d'habitude, par l'intention lucanienne d'exclure l'imminence de la Parousie[137]: mais il faut considérer aussi toutes les autres modifications; la difficulté véritable est de comprendre lesquelles ont été directement voulues par le rédacteur, positivement ou négativement, et lesquelles éventuellement sont seulement dérivées des modifications directement voulues:

- la tonalité générale: en Marc, plus menaçante, avec l'emphase sur οὗτος: «Celui qui aura persévéré jusqu'à la fin, *celui-là* [seulement] sera sauvé!»; plus encourageant chez Luc;
- le substantif ὑπομονή plutôt que le verbe ὑπομένειν;
- la construction non pas en troisième personne, mais avec le «vous», préférée par Luc dans toute la péricope[138];
- la construction κτάομαι τὴν ψυχήν[139], au lieu de σωθῆναι[140]: d'autant plus surprenante que Luc a une prédilection pour le vocabulaire du «salut»[141] et que ne joue pas ici la tendance lucanienne à omettre σῴζειν quand il s'agit du salut au sens purement physique (cf. Lc 8,40-56 et Mc 5,23-28);
- l'actif au lieu du passif;
- l'impératif (si c'est la bonne leçon)[142] de préférence au futur[143]: exhortation plus que promesse?

137. MARXSEN, *Der Evangelist Markus* (n. 12), pp. 131s.

138. DUPONT, *Les béatitudes*, III (n. 44), p. 27.

139. A. GEORGE, *L'emploi chez Luc du vocabulaire de salut*, in *NTS* 23 (1977) 308-320, à la p. 311; = *Études* (n. 113), pp. 307-320, à la p. 310, y reconnaît une «...légère précision, plus positive, sur la nature du salut»; J. ERNST, *Herr der Geschichte. Perspektiven der lukanischen Eschatologie* (SBS, 88), Stuttgart, 1978, pp. 74, 106s., un «...besondere Interesse des Lukas an der Heilssicherheit und am Heilbesitz, der gegen die Gerfährdungen in dieser Zeit zu schützen ist...».

140. Selon MARSHALL, *Luke* (n. 5), p. 770, le but serait d'éliminer l'ambiguïté du σωθήσεται de Marc, mais il nous semble clair qu'il se réfère au salut eschatologique.

141. W.C. VAN UNNIK, *L'usage de ΣΩΖΕΙΝ, «sauver», et de ses dérivés dans les évangiles synoptiques*, in *La formation des Évangiles. Problème synoptique et Formgeschichte* (RechBib, 2), Bruges, 1957, pp. 178-194, voir pp. 186s.; = ID., *Sparsa collecta*, I. *Evangelia - Paulina - Acta* (NTSup, 29), Leiden, 1973, pp. 16-34, voir p. 25: «Chose étonnante: Luc qui, d'habitude, se sert de ce verbe avec une véritable prédilection, *cette fois* ne l'emploie guère». L'A. laisse ouvertes diverses hypothèses: «Aurait-il connu une autre version, où un verbe araméen signifiant «acquérir ou posséder la vie» avait été traduit de la sorte? Ou a-t-il peut-être voulu accentuer l'aspect actif de cette ὑπομονή?»

142. Des textes et des versions d'une autorité notable (A, B, Θ, *f* 13, lat, sy, sa, bo), lisent le futur κτήσεσθε. Cependant, l'impératif κτήσασθε, dans ce contexte de verbes généralement au futur, est la *lectio difficilior*. Dans le contexte de l'exhortation, même le futur équivaudrait à un impératif.

143. En tout cas, le motif de l'élimination de σωθήσεται ne peut pas être que le salut

– la mention de la ψυχή[144].

Il est possible que plusieurs facteurs jouent aussi en même temps. Conzelmann pense aussi bien à l'élimination de εἰς τέλος qu'à un intérêt pour le substantif ὑπομονή (mais, à son avis, c'est toujours dans le cadre de la dés-eschatologisation lucanienne)[145]. Il pourrait cependant y avoir d'autres raisons plus plausibles de préférer le substantif «persévérance» au verbe «persévérer»; dans le verbe, ce qui est au premier plan, c'est l'acte dans son accomplissement, tandis que le substantif souligne davantage l'attitude spirituelle comme telle[146]; en effet, Luc, bien qu'il utilise aussi les composés de μένειν[147], montre son intérêt pour le terme ὑπομονή dans l'explication de la parabole du semeur: καρποφοροῦσιν ἐν ὑπομονῇ (Lc 8,15: noter également la construction identique avec εἰς). Comme Cerfaux[148] l'a mis en lumière, cette retouche lucanienne présuppose un lien étroit entre la ὑπομονή et le πειρασμός (v. 13): la persévérance est l'attitude spirituelle nécessaire au chrétien pour affronter l'épreuve. À plus forte raison donc quand l'épreuve assume la forme violente de la persécution, comme c'est le cas dans notre contexte.

Sans exclure une préférence de Luc pour le substantif ὑπομονή, observons cependant que cette construction peut avoir été choisie également parce que elle seule permettait l'usage du «vous», préféré par Luc dans toute la section, et que cela facilite aussi le ton plus positif, avec l'accent sur «votre»:

ἐν τῇ ὑπομονῇ   ὑμῶν
κτήσασθε τὰς ψυχὰς ὑμῶν

Le salut reste lié à une condition, mais en indiquant cette condition par

est une réalité déjà présente pour Luc (MADDOX, *Purpose* [n. 73], pp. 116-118: qu'il l'ait remplacé par le futur κτήσεσθε ou par l'impératif κτήσασθε, les deux présupposent le «pas encore».

144. Selon SABOURIN, *Luca* (n. 8), p. 323, la modification première aurait été l'introduction de ψυχή, pour montrer clairement qu'il s'agit du salut spirituel.

145. CONZELMANN, *Die Mitte der Zeit* (n. 12), p. 119s., 123s.: mais cf. les critiques de ORTIZ VALDIVIESO, ΥΠΟΜΟΝΗ (n. 135), p. 37. – Également peu convainquante pour nous l'interprétation de S. BROWN, *Apostasy and Perseverance in the Theology of Luke* (AnBib 36), Rome, 1969, pp. 48-50: déplacement de l'eschatologie, non pas vers l'éthique, mais vers l'ecclésiologie. Suivi aussi par J.S. CROATTO, *Persecución y perseverancia en la teología lucana. Un estudio sobre la «hupomoné»*, in *RevistB* 42 (1980) 21-30, et par KÜHSCHELM, *Jüngerverfolgung* (n. 75), pp. 210s.

146. Bien vu par GEIGER, *Endzeitreden* (n. 21), pp. 191s.

147. ἐμμένειν: Ac 14,22; προσμένειν: Ac 11,23; 13,43; ὑπομένειν par contre seulement dans le sens matériel: Lc 2,43; Ac 17,14.

148. L. CERFAUX, *Fructifiez en supportant (l'épreuve), à propos de Luc VIII,15*, in *RB* 64 (1957) 481-491; = *Recueil Cerfaux*, III (BETL, 71), Leuven, 1985, pp. 111-122; J. DUPONT, *La parabole du Semeur*, in *Foi et Vie. Cahiers bibliques* n° 5 (1967) 3-25, voir pp. 18-21; = *Études sur les évangiles synoptiques* (n. 23), pp. 236-258, voir pp. 251-254; ORTIZ VALDIVIESO, ΥΠΟΜΟΝΗ (n. 135), pp. 28-34; C. SPICQ, ὑπομένω, ὑπομονή, in *Notes de lexicographie néo-testamentaire*, III. *Supplément* (OBO, 22/3), Fribourg-Göttingen, 1982, pp. 658-665.

le substantif «persévérance» qualifié par l'adjectif «votre», on considère presque comme un présupposé qu'ils possèdent déjà cette condition et qu'eux-mêmes sont parmi ceux qui se sauveront.

L'omission de εἰς τέλος pourrait être simplement une conséquence de cette nouvelle construction. Εἰς τέλος en effet peut être régi seulement par le verbe: une phrase comme ἐν τῇ ὑπομονῇ ὑμῶν εἰς τέλος, κτήσασθε τὰς ψυχὰς ὑμῶν n'est pas possible. Par ailleurs, il n'est pas du tout évident que εἰς τέλος soit simplement un équivalent de «jusqu'à la Parousie». Τέλος en soi est un terme générique; dans ce contexte, il peut se référer à la fin des temps (cf. v. 9), mais le contexte encore plus immédiat est la persécution à laquelle est soumis l'individu, qui se traduit en tentation d'y échapper par l'apostasie (cf. au v. 16 les allusions aux trahisons entre familiers et amis, c'est-à-dire probablement entre les chrétiens eux-mêmes). Dans ce contexte, «persévérer jusqu'à la fin» signifie simplement persévérer *tant que dure l'épreuve*, par opposition à la tentation de céder, de renoncer à un certain moment. L'épreuve peut ensuite cesser de différentes manières, éventuellement même avec la Parousie, pour ceux qui seront en vie à ce moment; mais pour certains, déjà avant, avec la mort (cf. v. 16b); pour d'autres, avec la mise en liberté, avec la fin de la persécution violente contre eux (v. 18)[149]. Quelle que soit la modalité, il va sans dire qu'il est toujours nécessaire de persévérer «jusqu'à la fin»: si la persévérance ne va que jusqu'à un certain point, elle n'est plus de la persévérance. Luc pourrait donc aussi avoir omis εἰς τέλος simplement *parce qu'il était superflu*. Mais au cas où il aurait compris cette expression dans le sens de «jusqu'à la Parousie»[150], il pourrait l'avoir éliminée parce qu'il est inconséquent de promettre le salut seulement à ceux qui persévéreront «jusqu'à la Parousie», de suite après avoir mentionné aussi les chrétiens martyrisés auparavant (v. 16b). Peut-être aussi l'a-t-il fait pour ne pas avaliser l'idée selon laquelle seule la Parousie aurait pu mettre fin aux épreuves en cours: mais même dans cette hypothèse, on ne peut déduire qu'il ait voulu positivement exclure l'éventualité de son imminence.

Enfin, le choix de la construction ἐν τῇ ὑπομονῇ ὑμῶν peut égale-

---

149. Est donc non fondée l'explication selon laquelle Luc aurait compris εἰς τέλος «jusqu'à la fin *de la persécution*», et l'aurait éliminé parce que, pour lui, les persécutions ne finiront jamais (cf. IV.2): SCHÜTZ, *loc. cit.* (n. 75); ZMIJEWSKI, *Eschatologiereden* (n. 21), pp. 175-177; ou bien parce qu'il pense seulement aux persécutions du passé: GOULDER, *Luke* (n. 19), p. 709.

150. On peut faire l'hypothèse que l'exhortation à résister «jusqu'à la fin» a été formulée, dans la tradition pré-marcienne, dans un climat d'attente de la Parousie imminente (THEISSEN, *Lokalkolorit* [n. 65], p. 143): on avait en vue seulement la tribulation qui menaçait et on supposait qu'elle aurait été la dernière (cf. Mc 13,19); on ne pensait donc pas aux autres manières dont l'épreuve pourrait prendre fin en d'autres circonstances.

ment expliquer la formulation curieuse κτήσασθε τὰς ψυχὰς ὑμῶν[151]. En effet, un verbe à la voix active avec «vous» comme sujet devient nécessaire dans le second membre de phrase; mais dans le langage néo-testamentaire, σῴζω à l'actif appelle Dieu ou Christ[152] comme sujet; de là vient que Luc ait cherché un verbe différent. Dans tout le N.T., κτάομαι, littéralement «se gagner, acheter, acquérir»[153], n'est jamais employé pour parler du salut; il peut avoir été suggéré par l'expression «gagner» sa propre vie (cf. surtout le logion de Lc 17,33 avec le verbe περιποιήσασθαι[154]; mais aussi Ez 13,18-19 LXX; He 10,39: εἰς περιποίησιν ψυχῆς)[155]; il peut avoir été choisi parce qu'il donne l'idée de quelque chose qui s'obtient peu à peu: jour après jour, à travers sa persévérance, le chrétien s'acquiert le salut.

V. LE SORT DE JÉRUSALEM
(vv. 20-24; cf. Mc 13,14-23)

1. Aperçu général

Par rapport à Marc, cette section a un aspect très différent. Jérusalem, qui, chez Marc, n'était pas nommée explicitement, apparaît immédiatement au premier plan (v. 20a) et y reste jusqu'à la fin de la péricope, créant une sorte d'inclusion (v. 24). La dernière indication, ἄχρι οὗ πληρωθῶσιν καιροὶ ἐθνῶν (v. 24c) est décidément théologique: ses termes sont chargés de résonnance d'histoire du salut, comme πληροῦν et καιροί, où le regard se tourne de manière prophétique vers le futur qui, en ce cas, est encore réellement futur même pour l'auteur et les lecteurs. Loin de réduire la ville sainte d'Israël à une réalité «profane» et appartenant désormais seulement au passé[156], le regard se tourne aussi, au-delà de la destruction elle-même, vers toute la période où le sol de la ville sera foulé par les païens (v. 24c), expression où se dit tout le sens de sa sacralité[157]. Ce qui est au premier plan, ce n'est pas le

---

151. Et non vice versa (cf. ci-dessus, notes 139, 140, 144), parce que, s'il l'avait voulu, il aurait pu écrire: ὁ δὲ ὑπομείνας εἰς τέλος, οὗτος κτήσεται τὴν ψυχὴν αὐτοῦ.

152. Si le sujet est l'homme, on utilise le passif, «être sauvé»; très rares, les exceptions sont déterminées par des contextes particuliers: Mc 8,35 par.; 1 Cor 7,16; 9,22; 1 Tm 4,16.

153. Cf. Ac 1,18; 8,20; 22,28; Lc 18,12; cf. κτήματα: Ac 2,45; 5,1; κτήτορες: Ac 4,34.

154. DUPONT, Les béatitudes, III (n. 44), pp. 129s.; ID., Les trois apocalypses (n. 23), pp. 118s.; ID., L'après-mort dans l'œuvre de Luc, in RTL 3 (1972) 3-21, voir p. 18; = Nouvelles études (n. 105), pp. 358-379, voir pp. 374s.

155. Cf. C. SPICQ, περιποιέομαι, περιποίησις, in Notes de lexicographie néo-testamentaire (OBO, 22), II, Fribourg-Göttingen, 1978, pp. 687-689.

156. Ainsi CONZELMANN, Die Mitte der Zeit (n. 12), p. 71.

157. Il ne nous paraît donc pas exact de le compter parmi les passages où Jérusalem est vue de manière négative, comme chez B. CORSANI, Gerusalemme nell'opera lucana, in Gerusalemme. Atti della XXVI Settimana Biblica; = FS C.M. Martini, Brescia, 1982, pp. 13-26. Point de vue différent chez V. FUSCO, Effusione dello Spirito e raduno

sort des chrétiens impliqués dans ces événements tragiques[158], mais le sort de la ville elle-même.

L'hypothèse d'une autre source s'est appuyée sur les différences notables avec Marc. Du point de vue *littéraire* on a trouvé inexplicable que Marc soit parfois suivi à la lettre, puis parfois complètement ignoré; du point de vue *historique*, on a contesté l'idée de la reformulation *post eventum*; du point de vue *théologique*, on a trouvé peu lucanienne, trop «judéo-chrétienne»[159] ou même «peu "chrétienne"»[160], cette perspective centrée à ce point sur Jérusalem. Une fois de plus, la question littéraire et la question exégétique, mais aussi, dans le cas présent, la question historique, se recoupent étroitement. Pour des motifs pratiques, cependant, nous considérons les trois aspects en les distinguant.

2. *Le problème littéraire*

Les *omissions* sont nombreuses, mais toutes peuvent s'expliquer, surtout par l'exigence d'éliminer un lien trop direct avec la fin des temps: l'expression «l'abomination de la dévastation» (cf. Dn 9,27; 11,31; 12,11)[161] a été remplacée en quelque sorte par un renvoi plus global aux Écritures (v. 22b)[162]; la tribulation «comme il n'y en a pas eu depuis le commencement du monde et comme il n'y en aura jamais plus» (et que pourrait-elle être, sinon la tribulation eschatologique?) se trouve réduite à «une grande angoisse sur la terre»; les *topoi* apocalyptiques de l'abrègement des jours à cause des élus (Mc 13,20) et des séductions des faux messies (Mc 13,21-22) ont été simplement omis.

Ces omissions entraînent aussi des *restructurations*. Une fois éliminée l'«abomination de la dévastation», on donne comme signe l'encerclement de la ville, tandis que le terme «dévastation» est déplacé et attribué à l'événement annoncé: de cette manière, l'un comme l'autre deviennent parfaitement clairs: rien n'est dit en langage chiffré; voilà peut-être pourquoi tombe également l'avertissement: «*que le lecteur comprenne…*»[163].

dell'Israele disperso. Gerusalemme nell'episodio di Pentecoste (Atti 2,1-13), in *Ibid.*, pp. 201-218.

158. Tombent aussi pour cette raison: l'insistance sur l'urgence de la fuite (Mc 13,14b-16); l'allusion à l'éventualité que cela arrive en hiver (Mc 13,18: mais omission dictée aussi par la réalité historique); les avertissements à ne pas se laisser séduire (Mc 13,21-23); le terme «tribulation» (θλῖψις) que Luc préfère utiliser pour les souffrances des chrétiens (cf. Ac 11,19; 14,22; 20,23).

159. KNOX, *Sources* (n. 5), I, pp. 110s.

160. Ainsi RENGSTORF, *Lukas* (n. 5), p. 236.

161. Cf. B. RIGAUX, Βδέλυγμα τῆς ἐρημώσεως; *Mc 13,14; Mt 24,15*, in *Bib* 40 (1959) 675-683. - Selon THEISSEN, *Lokalkolorit* (n. 65), pp. 136-139, Luc s'est rendu compte qu'originellement l'expression ne se référait pas, comme dans le contexte de Marc, à la destruction du temple.

162. NEIRYNCK, *La matière marcienne* (n. 10), p. 178.

163. Autre conjecture chez D. DAUBE, *The New Testament and Rabbinic Judaism*,

On trouve également de nombreux *ajouts* dus essentiellement à l'exigence de décrire avec plus de détails historiques le sort de Jérusalem (v. 24a-b) et d'en donner une interprétation théologique (vv. 22.23b. 24c).

Malgré toutes ces modifications, la structure de Marc apparaît clairement comme le point de départ du travail lucanien[164]: *Quand vous verrez...* (v. 20: cf. Mc 13,14a), *alors... qu'ils fuient* (v. 21: cf. Mc 13,14b), *malheur... car il y aura...* (v. 23b: cf. Mc 13,19); noter aussi le terme «jours», bien que sa position soit différente (v. 22; cf. Mc 13,19). Après l'indication du signe (v. 20: *Quand vous verrez...*), nous trouvons deux phrases, parallèles en quelque sorte[165], et avec un certain crescendo

vv. 21-22: - *formule de type prophétique*: invitation à la fuite[166]
　　　　　 - *motivation* (encore générique): *puisque ce sont* des jours de châtiment pour accomplir tout ce qui est écrit
vv. 23-24: - *formule de type prophétique*: «Malheur...»
　　　　　 - *motivation* (plus détaillée): *car ce sera* grande angoisse dans le pays et colère contre ce peuple: ils tomberont au fil de l'épée... Jérusalem sera foulée aux pieds, etc.

Dans l'exhortation à la fuite, Marc soulignait surtout l'urgence de celle-ci avec des images très concrètes:

«Alors
ceux (qui sont) en Judée　　qu'ils fuient sur les montagnes
qui est sur le toit　　　　　qu'il ne descende pas ni ne rentre etc.
qui est à la campagne　　　　qu'il ne retourne pas prendre son manteau».

Dans le «doublet» Lc 17,31, en contexte plus eschatologique, Luc conserve les images de la fuite précipitée du toit ou à travers les champs. Ici, en revanche, tout en maintenant la structure à trois membres[167], il n'en laisse intact que le premier tandis qu'il modifie les deux autres pour souligner non pas tant l'urgence que la direction de la fuite[168]: le plus loin possible de la ville. Normalement, à l'approche des ennemis, les habitants de la campagne cherchent refuge à l'intérieur des murs; à présent, c'est le contraire qu'il faudra faire.

London, 1956, pp. 422-424: «Que le lecteur comprenne» pourrait être non pas une parenthèse, mais l'apodose, et dans ce cas, Luc l'aurait seulement explicitée.

164. Neirynck, *Response* (n. 16), p. 116.

165. Keck, *Abschiedsrede* (n. 21), p. 159.

166. Cf. R. Bach, *Die Aufforderung zur Flucht und zum Kampf im alttestamentlichen Prophetenspruch* (WMANT, 9), Neukirchen, 1962, pp. 15-50.

167. F. Neirynck, ΤΙΣ ΕΣΤΙΝ Ο ΠΑΙΣΑΣ ΣΕ. *Mt 26,68 | Lk 22,64 (diff. Mk 14,65)*, in *ETL* 63 (1987) 5-47, voir p. 18, note 80; = *Evangelica II* (n. 121), pp. 95-138, voir p. 108, note 80.

168. Dupont, *Les trois apocalypses* (n. 23), p. 124.

«Alors

ceux (qui sont) en Judée	qu'ils fuient vers les montagnes
ceux (qui sont) *à l'intérieur d'elle*	qu'ils s'en éloignent
ceux (qui sont) à la campagne	qu'ils n'entrent pas *en elle*».

La construction a quelque chose d'un chiasme qui met au premier plan l'oracle de malheur sur Jérusalem. C'est raisonner de manière trop mécanique que d'affirmer que le pronom «elle» ne peut se rapporter qu'au terme «Judée», et de voir dans cette inconséquence la trace d'une superposition de sources[169]. Bien que le mot «Judée» soit matériellement plus proche (v. 21a), Jérusalem a également été mentionnée peu auparavant (v. 20a) puis rappelée par le pronom αὐτῆς (v. 20b); par ailleurs, des expressions comme «entrer en elle» et «sortir d'elle» n'ont de sens que pour une ville. Οἱ ἐν ταῖς χώραις équivaut justement à «en Judée», et donc εἰς αὐτήν désigne Jérusalem[170].

3. *Le problème historique*

Harnack s'oppose déjà à l'hypothèse d'une réécriture *post eventum* quand il abaisse la datation de Lc-Ac avant 70, soutenant que la description lucanienne, tant ici qu'en 19,41-44, ne présenterait rien de spécial en comparaison de tout ce qui arrivait chaque fois qu'une ville tombait aux mains des ennemis, et en comparaison des modèles déjà offerts par les prophéties vétéro-testamentaires[171]; cette argumentation, illustrée avec plus de détails par Dodd[172], est devenue un des chevaux de bataille pour ceux qui soutiennent une date antérieure à 70[173] et/ou une source différente de Marc.

Bien plus, selon certains, la description serait tellement *différente* des événements de 70 qu'*elle ne peut pas* avoir été écrite après eux[174]. Luc n'aurait jamais osé qualifier les Romains d'«ennemis»; la fuite eut bien lieu, mais avant le siège, et non pas vers les montagnes, mais en

---

169. Ou bien une intention symbolique particulière: fuite «dans les campagnes» = adieu au Judaïsme: ZMIJEWSKI, *Eschatologiereden* (n. 21), pp. 208-212, 222-224; CASALEGNO, *Gesù e il tempio* (n. 35), pp. 119-123; DEL AGUA PÉREZ, *Derás* (n. 11), p. 305.

170. Bien vu par KECK, *Abschiedsrede* (n. 21), p. 151.

171. A. VON HARNACK, *Beiträge zur Einleitung in das NT*, III. *Die Apostelgeschichte*, Leipzig, 1908, p. 220.

172. C.H. DODD, *The Fall of Jerusalem and the «Abomination of Desolation»*, in *JRS* 37 (1947) 47-54; = ID., *More New Testament Studies*, Manchester, 1968, pp. 69-83. Ainsi également F. FLÜCKIGER, *Lk 21,20-24 und die Zerstörung Jerusalems*, in *TZ* 28 (1972) 385-390.

173. J.A.T. ROBINSON, *Redating the New Testament*, London, 1976, pp. 186-197. Pour une mise au point récente: C. FOCANT, *La chute de Jérusalem et la datation des évangiles*, in *RTL* 19 (1988) 17-37.

174. B. REICKE, *Synoptic Prophecies on the Destruction of Jerusalem*, in D.E. AUNE (ed.), *Studies in New Testament and Early Christian Literature. FS A.P. Wikgren* (NTSup, 33), Leiden, 1972, pp. 121-134; ID., *A Test* (n. 126).

Transjordanie, selon la notice d'Eusèbe. Ces arguments ne sont guère convaincants: les Romains ne sont pas appelés «ennemis» du point de vue du narrateur et des lecteurs (19,43: «*tes* ennemis») ni même systématiquement, mais seulement dans ce contexte particulier. De même, pour Luc, la fuite doit évidemment avoir lieu quand l'encerclement n'est pas encore terminé, comme le suggère le participe présent: ὅταν δὲ ἴδετε κυκλουμένην ὑπὸ στρατοπέδων Ἰερουσαλήμ. La fuite à Pella, mis à part les problèmes concernant son historicité[175], est hors de contexte, si l'on tient compte qu'ici on n'a pas affaire à une chronique, mais qu'on parle de la fuite uniquement pour souligner la catastrophe qui atteint la ville.

En positif, il faut constater qu'en Lc 19,41-44 et 21,20-24 divers éléments correspondent à la réalité historique non pas d'un siège *quelconque*[176], mais de *ce* siège-*là*, un événement qui a conclu cette guerre qui mit à rude épreuve la puissance de Rome et qui eut un large retentissement chez les contemporains:

a. «*des campements*» au pluriel (21,20: κυκλουμένην ὑπὸ στρατοπέδων): les Romains en effet firent converger, pour l'encerclement, plusieurs légions de provenances diverses, renforcées par des contingents fournis par les alliés[177];

b. *le terre-plein le long de tout le périmètre de la ville* (19,43; 21,20) n'était pas construit lors de n'importe quel siège; ce fut un choix stratégique précis de Titus parmi les diverses propositions qui lui furent faites[178], choix guidé aussi par la nécessité de ne pas laisser les troupes désœuvrées; celles-ci s'enthousiasmèrent au point de réaliser l'ouvrage en trois jours seulement[179];

---

175. Cf. J. VERHEYDEN, *De vlucht van de christenen naar Pella. Onderzoek van het getuigenis van Eusebius en Epiphanius* (Verhandelingen van de Kon. Acad. voor Wetenschappen, Letteren en Schone Kunsten van België / Kl. d. Letteren, Jaarg. 50; n° 127), Brussels, 1988.

176. Cf. E. SCHÜRER, *The History of the Jewish People in the Age of Jesus Christ (175 B.C.-A.D.. 135)*. A new English Version revised and edited by G. VERMES - F. MILLAR, I, Edinburgh, 1987, pp. 484-513; F.-M. ABEL, *Histoire de la Palestine depuis la conquête d'Alexandre jusqu'à l'invasion arabe* (EB), Paris 1952, II, pp. 22-43; ID., *Topographie du siège de Jérusalem en 70*, in *RB* 56 (1949) 238-258; M. HENGEL, *Entstehungszeit und Situation des Markusevangeliums*, in H. CANCIK (ed.), *Markus-Philologie. Historische, literargeschichtliche und stilistische Untersuchungen zum zweiten Evangelium* (WUNT, 33), Tübingen, 1984, pp. 1-45, voir p. 28: Marc peut-être avant 70, mais certainement pas Luc! H. JAGERSMA, *A History of Israel from Alexander the Great to Bar Kochba*, London, 1985, pp. 138-147; THEISSEN, *Lokalkolorit* (n. 65), pp. 292s.

177. FLAVIUS JOSÈPHE, *de bell.*, V, 1, 6 (ed. G. VITUCCI; Fondaz. Lorenzo Valla: Scrittori greci e latini), Verona, 1978, II, pp. 174-176; TACITE, *hist.* V, 1 (ed. A. ARICI; Classici latini, 5/2), Torino, ²1970, pp. 500-502.

178. TACITE, *hist.*. V, 13 (ed. cit., pp. 524s.).

179. FLAVIUS JOSÈPHE, *de bell.*, V, 12,1-2 (ed. cit., II, pp. 286-290). On calcule qu'il était long de 7,215 km et, par analogie avec les ruines de Massada, haut de 2 à 3 m: ABEL, *Histoire* (n. 176), II, pp. 28s.

c. *les massacres plus atroces que de coutume* (v. 24a; cf. 19,44; 23,27-31) à cause du zèle religieux qui, même après la prise d'assaut, poussa les défenseurs à résister encore, quartier par quartier; et même après la perte de la zone du temple, dans la ville haute; les survivants refusèrent de se rendre parce que leur demande de pouvoir sortir librement ne fut pas accueillie[180];

d. en conséquence, *la destruction quasi complète* du temple et de la ville (19,44; 21,6) tant de la part des défenseurs que des envahisseurs assoiffés de vengeance et sourds désormais aux contrordres des chefs, et à cause des incendies qu'il ne fut plus possible de dompter;

e. même *la déportation* de prisonniers comme esclaves (v. 24b) fut plus forte que d'habitude pour briser définitivement toute velléité ultérieure de rébellion[181];

f. le prolongement de la *présence étrangère sur le sol de la ville sainte* même après la destruction (v. 24c): le territoire de la ville et de la campagne fut en effet réparti entre des colons; Jérusalem fut transformée en ville païenne[182].

Ainsi donc, l'hypothèse de retouches *post eventum* apparaît à l'évidence, non pas à cause d'un préjugé de type rationaliste contre la possibilité des prophéties, mais en raison de la constatation que, de tous ces éléments, on ne trouve aucune trace dans la version marcienne; et par ailleurs, ils correspondent à la conscience historiographique de Luc qui pousse celui-ci à insérer des allusions ponctuelles à l'histoire contemporaine quand il en a la possibilité (cf. Lc 2,1-3; 3,1-2; 23,6-12; Ac 5,36-37, etc.). Ceci n'exclut pas l'influence des modèles vétéro-testamentaires, ce qui serait également dans la tendance de Luc[183]. D'autre part, l'intention de cette réécriture *post eventum* n'est pas simplement historiographique ou apologétique, mais surtout théologique et aussi pastorale: en soulignant plus en détail la pleine réalisation de cette prophétie, l'évangéliste ravive chez les lecteurs la confiance que toutes les autres s'accompliront immanquablement.

180. FLAVIUS JOSÈPHE, *de bell.*, VI, 6, 2-3 (ed. cit., II, pp. 384-394); DION CASSIUS, *Hist. rom.*, LXV, 4-7 (ed. E. CARY; LCL, 176), VIII, London, 1982, pp. 264-271.

181. On calcule que 600.000 personnes auraient été massacrées, un quart de la population; si on ajoute les déportés, la population fut réduite de moitié: cf. J.A. SOGGIN, *Storia d'Israele. Dalle origini a Bar Kochbà* (Biblioteca di cultura religiosa, 44), Brescia, 1985, p. 485.

182. Cf. ABEL, *Histoire* (n. 176), pp. 44-65; B. LIFSHITZ, *Jérusalem sous la domination romaine. Histoire de la ville depuis la conquête de Pompée jusqu'à Constantin (63 a.C. - 325 p.C.)*, in *ANRW* II.8 (1977) 444-489, en particulier pp. 469-473; B. ISAAC, *Judaea after 70*, in *JJS* 35 (1984) 44-50; P. SCHÄFER, *Geschichte der Juden in der Antike. Die Juden Palästinas von Alexander dem Großen bis zur arabischen Eroberung*, Stuttgart-Neukirchen, 1983, pp. 145-147.

183. Plus que de «sémitismes», il s'agit de «septuagintismes»: NEIRYNCK, *La matière marcienne* (n. 10), pp. 179-193.

4. Le problème théologique

N'étant plus directement liée à la fin du monde, la destruction de la ville sainte ne peut plus être interprétée à l'aide des *topoi* apocalyptiques de la tribulation finale[184]. Il ne s'agit cependant pas, comme on l'a souvent affirmé, d'une complète «dés-eschatologisation» et «historicisation».

On ne peut pas non plus soutenir que Luc, ayant repoussé l'interprétation eschatologique de l'événement, offre une autre interprétation, limitée au seul Israël, à travers l'idée de la punition divine (vv. 22a.23b). Certes, Luc rend explicite ce thème déjà présent dans la tradition chrétienne dans la ligne de la théologie deutéronomiste[185], et rappelé aussi par Marc dans un autre contexte (cf. Mc 12,1-12). Mais il ne s'arrête pas à cet aspect négatif, et fait encore moins de cet événement le signe du rejet du judaïsme: le recours au langage vétérotestamentaire[186] et l'interprétation de l'événement comme accomplissement des Écritures (v. 22) le situent précisément dans l'histoire des rapports entre Dieu et son peuple en le mettant à côté d'autres moments où le peuple fut puni, certes, mais jamais rejeté[187]; à cette lumière, même l'allusion mystérieuse à l'accomplissement des καιροὶ τῶν ἐθνῶν (20,24) pourrait renvoyer à un futur de salut pour la ville et pour Israël (cf. Ac 1,6-8)[188].

Il ne s'agit pas d'un fragment étranger aux perspectives lucaniennes, mais d'un point de vue rédactionnel qui affleure aussi ailleurs dans toute l'œuvre de Luc (Lc 13,31-35; Ac 3,17; 13,27); cela ne signifie évidemment pas qu'il ne puisse recourir à des traditions antérieures[189]. Nous pensons surtout à deux épisodes propres à Luc situés de manière quasi symétrique: quand, en arrivant à Jérusalem, Jésus pleure sur la ville (19,41-44), et quand, en en sortant pour le supplice, il invite les

---

184. Peu fondée également l'hypothèse de G. BRAUMANN, *Die lukanische Interpretation der Zerstörung Jerusalems*, in *NT* 6 (1963) 120-127: parce qu'il a lié la Parousie à la souffrance des chrétiens persécutés, Luc ne la lie pas au destin de la Jérusalem persécutrice. On ne voit pas pourquoi elle n'aurait pas pu être liée aux deux: dans la tradition biblique, *dies salutis* et *dies irae* sont comme les deux faces de la même réalité.

185. Cf. O.H. STECK, *Israel und das gewaltsame Geschick der Propheten. Untersuchungen zur Überlieferung des deuteronomistischen Geschichtsbildes im Alten Testament, Spätjudentum und Urchristentum* (WMANT, 23), Neukirchen, 1967, p. 56 avec la note 5.

186. Au v. 22a, allusion à Os 9,72 LXX (ἡμέραι τῆς ἐκδικήσεως); au v. 24, allusion à Za 12,3 LXX: «En ces jours-là, je ferai de Jérusalem une pierre foulée aux pieds par toutes les nations»; Dn 8,13-14 aussi parle d'une période où le sacrifice sera aboli et le sanctuaire foulé aux pieds (cf. Ap 11,2); le thème revient également dans la littérature apocalyptique; cf. KECK, *Abschiedsrede* (n. 21), pp. 224-231.

187. Bien vu par SCHMITHALS, *Lukas* (n. 133), p. 202.

188. FRANKLIN, *Christ the Lord* (n. 128), pp. 13, 130.

189. Cf. S.A. PANIMOLLE, *Il discorso di Pietro all'assemblea apostolica*, II. *Parola, fede e Spirito (At 15,7-9)* (Studi biblici, 2), Bologna, 1977, pp. 52s., qui fait remarquer la rareté d'expressions comme καιροὶ ἐθνῶν, πληροῦν.

femmes à se joindre à ces pleurs (23,28-31)[190]. Les deux textes présentent toute une série de contacts verbaux et thématiques avec notre péricope: l'expression prophétique «des jours viendront» (19,43; 21,22-23; 23,29); les allusions au siège (19,43; 21,20), à la destruction des édifices avec l'expression «ils ne laisseront pas pierre sur pierre» (19,44; cf. 21,6) et aux massacres des habitants (19,44; 21,24; cf. aussi 19,27) avec le «malheur» aux mères (21,23) ou encore - avec un renversement paradoxal - la béatitude des stériles (23,28-31). L'interprétation théologique également est identique: non seulement l'idée d'une culpabilité du peuple (même en 23,28-31 avec l'image du bois vert et du bois sec), mais en même temps l'effort pour la situer dans le dessein de Dieu: l'allusion au καιρός salvifique que Jérusalem n'a pas compris (19,41-44) avec le theologoumenon de l'aveuglement, νῦν δὲ ἐκρύβη ἀπὸ ὀφθαλμῶν σου, une construction qui, par le passif «théologique», renvoie aux desseins inscrutables de Dieu, et qui, par l'insistance sur le νῦν, semble renvoyer à un futur où la cécité sera vaincue.

Ce mystérieux renvoi au futur confirme une fois de plus que le vif intérêt de Luc pour le sort de Jérusalem ne doit pas être opposé à son intérêt tout aussi vif pour la Parousie. Comme on l'a déjà noté, les deux problèmes sont toujours étroitement liés en Luc-Actes. De même ici: le lien avec l'Eschaton n'est pas absent: le discours, en effet, ne s'arrête pas au sort de Jérusalem; il continue immédiatement pour atteindre son point culminant dans l'annonce de la venue du Fils de l'homme (vv. 25-27).

VI. LA PAROUSIE
(vv. 25-27; cf. Mc 13,24-27)

En Marc, le raccord «en ces jours-là, après cette tribulation...» (Mc 13,24a), quoiqu'il distingue les deux événements, n'en précise nullement la distance. Luc, qui a déjà placé entre l'un et l'autre les καιροὶ ἐθνῶν (v. 24b) mais sans en en indiquer la durée non plus, remplace le raccord de Marc (peut-être aussi pour éviter ici le terme «tribulation»[191]) par un simple καί tout aussi vague[192] qui révèle son peu d'intérêt pour la question chronologique[193].

190. J. DUPONT, *Il n'en sera pas laissé pierre sur pierre (Mc 13,2; Lc 19,44)*, in Bib 52 (1971) 301-320, surtout pp. 314-319; = *Études sur les évangiles synoptiques* (n. 23), pp. 434-455, surtout pp. 447-452; C.H. GIBLIN, *The Destruction of Jerusalem according to Luke's Gospel: A Historical-Typological Moral* (AnBib, 107), Roma, 1985.

191. Comme déjà au v. 23; cf. Mc 13,19: cf. V.1.

192. L'affirmation de CONZELMANN, *Die Mitte der Zeit* (n. 12), p. 121: «Zwischen v. 24 und 25 liegt ein scharfer Einschnitt» est injustifiée. Critiquée par FLENDER, *Heil und Geschichte* (n. 39), p. 103s; C. BURCHARD, *Der Dreizehnte Zeuge. Traditions- und kompositionsgeschichtliche Untersuchungen zu Lukas' Darstellung der Frühzeit des Paulus* (FRLANT, 103), Göttingen, 1970, pp. 181s.

193. Bien noté chez ZMIJEWSKI, *Eschatologiereden* (n. 21), pp. 240s.

L'indication plus sommaire: «*Il y aura des signes dans le soleil, dans la lune et les étoiles*» se présente comme une simplification du texte de Marc[194] qui spécifiait ce qu'il advenait de chacun de ces corps célestes; cela reflète une mentalité plus sobre, moins portée au langage apocalyptique. En revanche, il mentionne la réaction des gens sur la terre (vv. 25b-26), signe que Luc s'intéresse davantage au scénario humain, à l'οἰκουμένη, qu'au scénario cosmique[195].

Dans la description de la Parousie elle-même (Mc 13,26), «la nuée» est au singulier et non pas au pluriel, comme aussi lors de la Transfiguration (Lc 9,34) et de l'Ascension (Ac 1,9). Le singulier pourrait rappeler de manière plus générique la nuée des théophanies; le pluriel rappellerait de façon plus spécifique Dn 7,13; la retouche pourrait être analogue à l'omission d'autres éléments de Daniel («l'abomination de la dévastation»); toutefois, même avec le singulier, l'allusion à Daniel n'est pas exclue[196].

L'inversion «puissance et grande gloire», au lieu de «grande puissance et gloire», évite de réduire «gloire» à faire figure d'appendice et donne un ton qui convient mieux à une conclusion. En effet, Luc préfère conclure cette section par l'apparition du Fils de l'homme . Il laisse tomber la note finale où Marc évoque le rassemblement universel des élus (Mc 13,27); il le fait peut-être parce qu'il a peu de sympathie pour ce dernier terme qu'il a déjà éliminé auparavant (cf. Mc 13,20. 22)[197], mais aussi parce que *l'universalité* était déjà exprimée par les termes οἰκουμένη, ἄνθρωποι, ἔθνοι, et parce que *l'aspect salvifique* sera exprimé immédiatement après par les mots «votre libération» (v. 28).

VII. LA RÉPONSE SUR LE SIGNE ET SUR LE MOMENT
(vv. 28-33; cf. Mc 13,28-31)[198]

Les paraboles se réfèrent toujours à un contexte qui précède, à une situation bien précise en vue de laquelle elles sont prononcées. Ici, par

194. C.H. DODD, *According to the Scriptures*, London, 1952, p. 48, y voit une plus grande accentuation de la référence à Joël 2,31 (cf. Ac 2,21).

195. GRUNDMANN, *Lukas* (n. 5), p. 384.

196. G. LOHFINK, *Die Himmelfahrt Jesu. Untersuchungen zu den Himmelfahrts- und Erhöhungstexten bei Lukas* (SANT, 26), München, 1971, pp. 187-193; D.L. BOCK, *Proclamation from Prophecy and Pattern. Lucan Old Testament Christology* (JSNT SS, 12), Sheffield, 1987, pp. 132-137. – Sur l'influence de *Daniel* en Luc-Actes, cf. J. WEHNERT, *Die Wir-Passagen der Apostelgeschichte. Ein lukanisches Stilmittel aus jüdischer Tradition* (GTA, 40), Göttingen, 1989, pp. 170-179.

197. Le terme revient seulement dans la parabole de la veuve et du juge (Lc 18,7), où il semble conserver sa nuance eschatologique; dans les Actes, prévalent d'autres désignations des chrétiens: les saints, les frères, les disciples, les croyants.

198. Cf. J. DUPONT, *La parabole du figuier qui bourgeonne (Mc 13,28-29 par.)*, in *RB* 75 (1968) 526-548, voir pp. 533-536; = *Études sur les évangiles synoptiques* (n. 23), pp. 474-497, voir pp. 481-484.

contre, Marc fait introduire la parabole par Jésus lui-même, un peu *ex abrupto*, avec la formule inhabituelle: Ἀπὸ δὲ τῆς συκῆς μάθετε τὴν παραβολήν. Luc préfère l'introduire lui-même avec la formule plus familière: καὶ εἶπεν παραβολὴν αὐτοῖς (v. 29a)[199]; mais auparavant, il se préoccupe d'indiquer avec davantage de clarté le point que la parabole doit illustrer (v. 28)[200]. Il en résulte une certaine répétition par rapport à l'application qui vient ensuite (v. 31); mais de toute évidence, à un endroit aussi décisif du discours, ce qui a prévalu chez Luc, c'est l'exigence de plus grande clarté et non celle d'éviter des répétitions.

Le nouveau raccord (v. 28) réutilise des éléments déjà présents en Marc[201]: ἀρχομένων δὲ τούτων γίνεσθαι (cf. Mc 13,29: ὅταν ἴδητε ταῦτα γινόμενα), ἐγγίζει (cf. Mc 13,28-29: ἐγγύς ἐστιν). Les autres éléments de la phrase ne font rien d'autre qu'illustrer la réaction positive des croyants: se relever, relever la tête. Tandis que les autres s'épouvantent parce qu'ils ne savent pas ce qui se passe (v. 26), pour les chrétiens, c'est un événement joyeux, le retour de Jésus. Au vu surtout de leurs souffrances, cet événement est présenté comme «libération» (ἀπολύτρωσις), aussi pour introduire de la variété par rapport aux expressions utilisées avant (v. 27: venue du Fils de l'homme) et après (v. 31: règne de Dieu).

Dans la parabole, on note seulement de légères retouches, toutes pour raisons de style ou de clarté; elles ne modifient ni l'image ni l'application[202]. Puisque l'introduction a été changée, Luc doit nommer le sujet (v. 29b: «regardez le figuier et tous les autres arbres»); cette amplification[203] vient peut-être d'une adaptation à des milieux différents de celui de Palestine[204]. Le double verbe, «devient tendre et

199. Conformément aussi à sa tendance constante à ne pas laisser les paraboles sans une introduction qui les désigne explicitement comme telles, surtout les plus brèves dont le caractère parabolique pourrait passer inaperçu (5,36; 6,39; 8,4; 12,16; 13,6; 14,7; 15,3; 18,1.9; 19,11; 20,9): CADBURY, *Style* (n. 15), pp. 106s.; DUPONT, *Les béatitudes,* I (n. 131), pp. 55s., note 3; F. NEIRYNCK, *Luc 24,36-43: un récit lucanien,* in *À cause de l'Évangile* (n. 22), pp. 655-680, voir pp. 269s.; = *Evangelica II* (n. 121), pp. 205-226, voir p. 217. Pour plus de détails: FUSCO, *Problemi di struttura* (n. 26), pp. 110s.

200. Est donc sans fondement l'explication littéraire basée sur la prétendue contradiction entre le v. 28 et le v. 27 (ainsi GASTON, *Sondergut,* [n. 5], pp. 165s.; SCHRAMM, *Markus-Stoff* [n. 5] pp. 180s.; SCHWEIZER, *Lukas* [n. 5], p. 208). Sur la fonction du v. 28, cf. FUSCO, *Problemi di struttura* (n. 26), pp. 114-116.

201. Cf. NEIRYNCK, *La matière marcienne* (n. 10), p. 178: «Au v. 28, Luc s'oriente vers la parabole de Mc., XIII,28-29 et s'en inspire»; DUPONT, *Les trois apocalypses* (n. 23), p. 136: «Tout se passe comme si le v. 28 avait été construit sur le modèle du v. 31, lui-même calqué sur le v. 29 de Marc».

202. Contre ERNST, *Lukas* (n. 53), p. 567, selon lequel l'image de salut deviendrait en Luc une image de jugement.

203. Cas semblables: Lc 3,19 par. Mc 6,18; Lc 19,47 par. Mc 11,18; Lc 23,49 par. Mc 15,40 etc. Cf. CADBURY, *Style* (n. 15), pp. 115-117.

204. On a pensé aussi à une intention symbolique: le figuier pourrait représenter Israël (cf. Lc 13,6-9); pour cette raison, en contexte universaliste, on aurait ajouté les autres

poussent ses feuilles», est remplacé par un seul, «bourgeonnent». L'ajout de ἤδη, «déjà», (v. 30a) complète le parallélisme par rapport à l'application (v. 30b).

Dans l'application, Marc avait: «...est proche, aux portes» (Mc 13,29); Luc élimine cette redondance[205] et, par souci de plus grande clarté, il insère le sujet manquant[206]: «... le Règne de Dieu est proche». En Marc, le sujet sous-entendu était le Fils de l'homme (cf. Mc 13,26); Luc n'a pas l'intention de distinguer la venue du Fils de l'homme (v. 27) de la venue du Règne, mais il veut éviter des répétitions; il n'y a aucune raison de douter que les trois expressions (v. 27: venue du Fils de l'homme; v. 28: libération; v. 31: Règne de Dieu) se réfèrent à la même réalité et doivent être comprises dans le sens le plus rigoureusement eschatologique[207].

Luc conserve sans hésitation, dans toute sa solennité, l'affirmation que toutes les choses annoncées s'accompliront pour «cette génération»[208]. La formulation est quasi identique, excepté le remplacement de μέχρις οὗ par ἕως ἄν[209], conjonction largement préférée en Lc-Ac (vingt cas contre trois). On a voulu attribuer une grande importance (de manières très diverses, d'ailleurs) au fait que Luc ait écrit seulement πάντα plutôt que ταῦτα πάντα[210]: en réalité, ce ταῦτα était superflu

arbres: H.-J. KLAUCK, Allegorie und Allegorese in synoptischen Gleichnistexten (NTAbh NF, 8), Münster, 1978, pp. 324s.

205. Les deux expressions suffisaient même individuellement: cf. Jc 5,9. – Exemples d'omissions semblables en CADBURY, Style (n. 15), pp. 151s.

206. Phénomène très fréquent chez Luc: cf. CADBURY, Style (n. 15), pp. 150s.

207. Avec A. GEORGE, Le Règne de Dieu, in Études (n. 113), pp. 285-306, voir p. 294; ID., L'eschatologie, Ibid., 321-347, voir p. 330; ROBINSON, Der Weg (n. 20), pp. 59-66. En revanche, les interprétations qui attribuent à Luc une espèce d'«eschatologie réalisée» sont hors contexte (fin d'un monde, non du monde, triomphe historique...): cf., par exemple, LAGRANGE, Luc (n. 100), p. 532; FEUILLET, Le discours (n. 100), pp. 83s; ID., La signification (n. 100), p. 209; C.E. CARLSTON, The Parables of the Triple Tradition, Philadelphia, PA, 1975, pp. 81-84; A. SALAS, «Vuestra liberación está cerca» (Lc 21,28). Dimensión liberacionista del acto redentor, in La Ciudad de Dios 189 (1976) 3-22; G. VOSS, Die Christologie der lukanischen Schriften in Grundzügen (StudNeot, 2), Paris-Brugge, 1965, pp. 43s., 114-118, 125; FRANKLIN, Christ the Lord (n. 128), pp. 14s.; ZMIJEWSKI, Eschatologiereden (n. 21), pp. 269-272.

208. Cf. FUSCO, Lc 21,32 (n. 26); à la bibliographie citée à cet endroit, ajouter: E. LÖVESTAM, The ἡ γενεὰ αὕτη Eschatology in Mk 13,30 parr., in J. LAMBRECHT (ed.), L'Apocalypse johannique et l'Apocalyptique dans le Nouveau Testament (BETL, 53), Leuven, 1980, pp. 403-413; précédemment: ID., En problematisk eskatologisk utsaga: Mc 13,30 par., in SEÅ 28-29 (1963-65) 64-80.

209. Trop peu pour rendre plausible l'explication inverse selon laquelle ce serait Marc qui modifierait Luc, comme le pense D. PEABODY, A Pre-Markan Prophetic Sayings Tradition and the Synoptic Problem, in JBL 97 (1978) 391-409, voir p. 399.

210. CONZELMANN, Die Mitte der Zeit (n. 12), p. 122: «Dann bezieht sich die Aussage nicht auf die berichteten Einzelheiten, sondern auf das Ganze der göttlichen Planes»; GRÄSSER, Problem (n. 20), p. 166; SCHNEIDER, Parusie-Gleichnisse (n. 113), pp. 59s.: «...er die Amen-Aussage nicht mit Markus auf die anbrechenden Parusieereignisse (Lk 21,25-27) beziehen wollte». Raisonnement opposé en C.L. HOLMAN, The Idea of an Imminent

étant donné que πάντα a une fonction pronominale[211]. Retenons donc, aussi sur base du contexte, que pour Luc, ce πάντα embrasse tous les événements déjà mentionnés, y compris la Parousie.

VIII. LA CONCLUSION PARÉNÉTIQUE
(vv. 34-36; cf. Mc 13,32-37)

Alors que Marc parsemait tout son discours d'une série d'avertissements avec βλέπετε (Mc 13,5.9.23.33), Luc ne conserve que le premier (v. 8) et préfère concentrer toute la parénèse ici, à la fin: on reconnaît bien là son souci habituel de plus grande cohérence, mais peut-être s'inspire-t-il aussi du modèle des discours hellénistiques qui se terminent par l'appel direct à l'auditeur[212].

Puisqu'il a transféré en Ac 1,7 le logion sur l'ignorance du moment (cf. IV.4), Luc omet aussi la parabole qui l'illustrait, les serviteurs en attente du maître (Mc 13,33-36), parabole qu'il a déjà utilisée ailleurs dans la version de la *Quelle* (Lc 12,35-38)[213]. À la place, Luc présente un passage parénétique complètement neuf, tournant autour des thèmes favoris du troisième évangile tels que le danger des richesses et la nécessité de la prière[214], passage qui n'exige donc pas de source particulière[215]: même les contacts avec les lettres pauliniennes s'expli-

Parousia in the Synoptic Gospels, in *Studia biblica et theologica* 3 (1973) 15-31: le ταῦτα πάντα de Mc 13,30 reprend le ταῦτα de Mc 13,29 qui se référait spécifiquement aux signes: en écrivant seulement πάντα sans ταῦτα, Luc veut inclure aussi la Parousie. Autre explication chez GEIGER, *Endzeitreden* (n. 21), pp. 236s.: Luc omet ταῦτα parce que ces événements appartenaient désormais au passé. Selon VOSS, *Christologie* (n. 207), p. 125: «...das Fehlen des ταῦτα nimmt dem Ausdruck ἕως ἂν πάντα γένεται die Beziehung an die bevorstehenden Bedrängnisse und läßt mehr an die Apg 3,21 erwähnte ἀποκατάστασις πάντων denken».

211. Cf. *Problemi di struttura* (n. 26), pp. 128-133. Cf. aussi FRANKLIN, *Christ the Lord* (n. 128), p. 14: «His omission of *tauta* is probably merely stylistic, for *tauta panta* appears in verse 36, and it therefore has no special significance». Un peu différemment, ERNST, *Herr der Geschichte* (n. 139), pp. 44s.: Luc n'aurait pas saisi la distinction subtile que Marc fait entre les deux expressions.

212. DEL AGUA PÉREZ, *Deráš* (n. 11), p. 309; J. KREMER, *Lukasevangelium* (Die neue Echter Bibel / NT, 3), Würzburg, 1988, pp. 207s.

213. KLAUCK, *Allegorie* (n. 204), pp. 328-331; explication différente chez CARLSTON, *Parables* (n. 207), pp. 84-87 (Lc 12,35-38 dériverait de Mc 13,34-37).

214. W. OTT, *Gebet und Heil. Die Bedeutung des Gebetsparänese in der lukanischen Theologie* (SANT, 12), München, 1965, pp. 73-75; A. GEORGE, *La prière*, in ID., *Études* (n. 113), pp. 395-427, voir p. 415; HORN, *Glaube und Handeln* (n. 76), pp. 222s., 281-283.

215. Comme le pensent par exemple FITZMYER, *Luke* (n. 7), p. 1326; JEREMIAS, *Die Sprache* (n. 7), pp. 283-285 (ce seraient des constructions non lucaniennes: μεριμναί, ἐν παντὶ καιρῷ, δέομαι construit avec ἵνα); L. AEJMELAEUS, *Wachen vor dem Ende. Die traditionsgeschichtlichen Wurzeln von 1. Thess. 5,1-11 und Luk. 21,34-36* (SFEG, 44), Helsinki, 1985; GOULDER, *Luke* (n. 19), pp. 715s. (Luc puiserait chez Matthieu et chez Paul); pour un panorama des autres opinions, cf. F. NEIRYNCK, *Paul and the Sayings of Jesus*, in A. VANHOYE (ed.), *L'Apôtre Paul. Personnalité, style et conception du ministère*

quent par l'influence du langage traditionnel de la parénèse chrétienne[216].

Cependant, dans le nouveau morceau, Luc récupère les éléments
essentiels du parallèle marcien[217], la soudaineté et la nécessité de veiller
en tout temps. Des contacts verbaux précis le confirment également:
l'adjectif αἰφνίδιος, «imprévu» (idée exprimée par Marc avec le synonyme ἐξαίφνης[218] et avec des verbes: Mc 13,32: οὐδεὶς οἶδεν; 13,33.35:
οὐκ οἴδατε); l'expression ἡ ἡμέρα ἐκείνη (cf. Mc 13,32: Περὶ δὲ τῆς
ἡμέρας ἐκείνης); l'impératif ἀγρυπνεῖτε δὲ ἐν παντὶ καιρῷ (cf. Mc 13,33:
βλέπετε, ἀγρυπνεῖτε· οὐκ οἴδατε γὰρ πότε ὁ καιρός ἐστιν). D'autres
éléments dérivent du contexte: le Fils de l'homme (cf. v. 26), l'implication de l'humanité entière (cf. v. 26), l'expression ταῦτα πάντα et la
construction avec μέλλειν γίνεσθαι (cf. vv. 28.31.32).

IX. Conclusion

La conclusion qui ressort de l'analyse des différentes sections est
triple: *exégétique, littéraire* mais surtout *méthodologique*. Du point de
vue exégétique, l'unité du discours se comprend lorsqu'on lit celui-ci
non pas en termes de dés-eschatologisation, mais en restant dans la
perspective de la proximité de la Parousie et en tenant compte de
l'intérêt particulier que Luc manifeste pour le problème d'Israël. Du
point de vue littéraire, il n'est pas nécessaire de recourir à d'autres
sources que l'évangile canonique de Marc. Mais arrêtons-nous surtout
à quelques conclusions de type méthodologique.

Entre l'exégèse des textes et la reconstruction des sources, nous avons
vu s'instaurer une réelle circularité, inévitable et féconde. La question
synoptique elle-même ne peut être posée en termes purement objectifs,
mathématiques, sans qu'on ait à se prononcer sur le sens des textes, sur

(BETL, 73), Leuven, 1986, pp. 265-321, voir pp. 278-281; = *Evangelica II* (n. 121),
pp. 511-568, voir pp. 524-527.

216. «...a composition of Luke based on conventional homiletic of the primitive
Church...» (KNOX, *Sources* [n. 5], I, p. 110). Cf. E. LÖVESTAM, *Spiritual Wakefulness in the
New Testament* (LUÅ. NF, I/55/3), Lund, 1963, pp. 122-132; T. HOLTZ, *Traditionen im 1.
Thessalonicherbrief*, in U. LUZ – H. WEDER (ed.), *Die Mitte des Neuen Testaments. Einheit
und Vielfalt neutestamentlicher Theologie. FS E. Schweizer*, Göttingen, 1983, pp. 55-78,
voir pp. 66-71; = ID., *Geschichte und Theologie des Urchristentums. Gesammelte Aufsätze*,
ed. E. REINMUTH – C. WOLFF (WUNT, 57), Tübingen, 1991, pp. 246-269, voir pp. 262-
268; C.M. TUCKETT, *Synoptic Tradition in I Thessalonians?*, in R.F. COLLINS (ed.), *The
Thessalonian Correspondence* (BETL, 87), Leuven, 1990, pp. 160-182, surtout pp. 173-176.

217. «...une sorte de paraphrase basée sur les éléments les plus caractéristiques du
texte de Marc»: J. DUPONT, *La parabole du maître qui rentre tard dans la nuit (Mc 13,34-
36)*, in A. DESCAMPS – A. DE HALLEUX (ed.), *Mélanges bibliques. FS B. Rigaux*,
Gembloux, 1970, pp. 89-116, voir pp. 93s.; = *Études sur les évangiles synoptiques* (n. 23),
pp. 498-526, voir pp. 502s.

218. SPICQ, αἰφνίδιος, αἰφνιδίως, ἐξαίφνης, in *Notes*, III (n. 148), pp. 8-12.

les intentions des évangélistes. Il ne suffit donc pas de présenter la *Literarkritik* comme «correctif» de la *Redaktionsgeschichte*, selon l'expression de T. Schramm[219]; le contraire est également nécessaire, comme l'a précisé F. Neirynck: une critique littéraire qui attribuerait au rédacteur une attitude servile par rapport à ses sources en viendrait à reposer sur des bases extrêmement fragiles[220]. «Sans doute – écrit Neirynck – une solution *literarkritisch* ne peut être repoussée sans examen sérieux, mais on peut se poser la question si la priorité méthodologique ne revient pas à l'explication rédactionnelle, c.-à.-d. l'intelligence des modifications du texte de Marc à la lumière des tendances littéraires et théologiques de chacun des évangélistes»[221].

Soulignons dans cette citation les deux adjectifs: *littéraires* et *théologiques*. Certes Luc ne manque pas d'affirmer une perspective théologique bien précise; cependant, la prétention, qui a caractérisé une certaine *Redaktionsgeschichte*, de vouloir expliquer théologiquement toutes ses modifications du texte de Marc s'avère peu correcte: un grand nombre de changements sont aussi de caractère stylistique.

Au lieu de conférer un poids excessif à des critères comme la statistique des mots, les répétitions ou les tensions à l'intérieur du texte[222], critères nécessaires eux aussi mais qui, considérés isolément, peuvent s'avérer peu valables ou même trompeurs[223], il importe d'intensifier l'étude des procédés de composition, des structures, des modèles

219. SCHRAMM, *Markus-Stoff* (n. 5), p. 186: «Literarkritik als Korrektiv redaktionsgeschichtlicher Arbeit» (cf. les préliminaires méthodologiques aux pp. 1-4: «Literarkritik - Formgeschichte - Redaktionsgeschichte»); repris parmi les «Regeln der Redaktionskritik» également par BERGER, *Exegese* (n. 29), pp. 216s., mais avec l'exemple peu heureux de Lc 21,10a: τότε ἔλεγεν αὐτοῖς: cf. ci-dessus, III.2.
220. *La matière marcienne* (n. 10), p. 201. Cf. aussi F.G. UNTERGASSMAIR, *Kreuzweg und Kreuzigung Jesu. Ein Beitrag zur lukanischen Redaktionsgeschichte und zur Frage nach der lukanischen «Kreuzestheologie«* (Paderborner theol. St., 10), Paderborn, 1980, pp. 108-112 («Kritik an die bisherigen Literarkritik von Lk 23,26-49»).
221. NEIRYNCK, *La matière marcienne* (n. 10), p. 194; cf. aussi ID., *The Argument from Order and St. Luke's Transpositions*, in *ETL* 49 (1973) 784-815, voir p. 815: «...the phenomenon of order is studied with an undue limitation of the creative activity of the evangelist. Thus the argument of order shows us again how interrelated redactional and source-critical study should be»; = *The Minor Agreements of Matthew and Luke against Mark, with a Cumulative List* (BETL, 37), Leuven, 1974, pp. 291-322, voir p. 322; = *Evangelica* (n. 1), pp. 737-768, voir p. 768.
222. M.É. BOISMARD – A. LAMOUILLE, *La vie des évangiles. Initiation à la critique des textes*, Paris, 1989, pp. 11-31 («Les clefs de la critique littéraire»).
223. P. DSCHULLNIGG, *Sprache, Redaktion und Intention des Markusevangeliums. Eigentümlichkeiten der Sprache des Markusevangeliums und ihre Bedeutung für die Redaktionskritik* (SBB, 11), Stuttgart, 1984, pp. 284-289 («Allgemeine Ueberlegungen zur Problematik der Literarkritik»); C. BREYTENBACH, *Nachfolge und Zukunftserwartung nach Markus. Eine methodenkritische Studie* (ATANT, 71), Zürich, 1984, pp. 344-346 («Probleme der vokabelstatistischen Methode»); J. SCHREIBER, *Der Kreuzigungsbericht des Markusevangeliums, Mk 15,20b-41. Eine traditionsgeschichtliche und methodenkritische Untersuchung nach William Wrede (1859-1906)* (BZNW, 48), Berlin 1986, pp. 77-117, 309-323.

littéraires, du style dans le sens le plus large du terme, la *Stilkritik*, comme Dibelius définissait son programme d'étude sur les Actes et qui a fait de lui un pionnier de la *Redaktionsgeschichte* autant que de la *Formgeschichte*[224].

En ce sens, nous pourrions dire que sans un effort accru de critique «littéraire», *Literary Criticism*, dans le sens des modernes, d'attention soutenue à la facture littéraire du texte, on ne peut pas pratiquer correctement la critique «littéraire», *Literarkritik*, entendue au sens des anciens dans la perspective de la *Quellenkritik*. En conjuguant plus correctement la «rédaction» avec la «composition», l'approche dia-chronique avec l'approche synchronique, l'une et l'autre deviennent plus fructueuses et s'avèrent indispensables pour une pleine compréhen-sion du texte. En ce sens, la *Redaktionsgeschichte* des Synoptiques, loin de devoir être considérée comme épuisée, attend qu'on la relance, et sollicite encore notre travail.

Pontificia Facoltà Teologica   Vittorio Fusco
dell'Italia Meridionale
Via Petrarca 115
I-80122 Napoli

---

224. M. Dibelius, *Stilkritisches zur Apostelgeschichte*, in H. Schmidt (ed.), *Eucharis-terion. H. Gunkel zum 60. Geburtstag* (FRLANT 36 = NF 19), Göttingen, 1923, II, pp. 27-49; = M. Dibelius (ed. H. Greeven), *Aufsätze zur Apostelgeschichte* (FRLANT, 60), Göttingen, 1951, pp. 9-28.

THE DELINEATION OF THE LUKAN TRAVEL NARRATIVE
WITHIN THE OVERALL STRUCTURE
OF THE GOSPEL OF LUKE

In the sixties I had the opportunity of preparing my doctoral dissertation under the competent and stimulating guidance of Professor Frans Neirynck, who trained me thoroughly in the 'Louvain' exegetical methods. My research focused on Lk 13,22-35, an important section of the Lukan travel narrative[1]. One of the questions treated there was the delineation of the Lukan travel narrative: where does it begin and end? Like most scholars, I marked the beginning at Lk 9,51. This verse marks in the most solemn way the moment when Jesus resolves to go up to Jerusalem. But against the majority opinion of that time, I considered verse 19,44 rather than 19,27 or 19,28 as the end-mark of the travel narrative. In a Flemish periodical, bearing the melodious Latin name *Collationes Brugenses et Gandavenses*, in which Frans Neirynck also started publishing the first fruits of his long exegetical career, I published (in 1968-69) the results of my study of the Lukan travel narrative[2]. The Flemish language being much less known than Flemish painting, my article and the arguments adduced there in support of 19,44 as the end of Luke's travel narrative remained unnoticed, with a mere handful of exceptions, one of them being Frans Neirynck, from whose all-seeing eye nothing published in the field of Synoptic research can escape[3]!

In what follows, I should like to take up the discussion again, looking at what has been done since and presenting in a new way the questions and the arguments involved. After a survey of the different opinions regarding the structure of Luke[4], I will argue that Lk 9,51-

---

1. A. DENAUX, *De sectie Lc. XIII,22-35 en haar plaats in het lucaanse reisbericht*, Leuven, 1967 (dactyl.); ID., *L'hypocrisie des Pharisiens et le dessein de Dieu. Analyse de Lc., XIII,31-33*, in F. NEIRYNCK (ed.), *L'évangile de Luc. The Gospel of Luke. Revised and Enlarged Edition of L'évangile de Luc. Problèmes littéraires et théologiques* (1973) (BETL, 32), Leuven, 1989, pp. 155-195.316-323 (note additionnelle).

2. A. DENAUX, *Het lucaanse reisverhaal (Lc. 9,51–19,44)*, in *Collationes Brugenses et Gandavenses* 14 (1968) 214-242; 15 (1969) 464-501.

3. F. NEIRYNCK, *La matière marcienne dans l'Évangile de Luc*, in ID. (ed.), *L'évangile de Luc* (BETL, 32), Gembloux, 1973, pp. 157-201, spec. p. 185, n. 142; revised and enlarged edition (n. 1 above), p. 95, n. 142 (= ID., *Evangelica* [BETL, 60], Leuven, 1982, p. 65, n. 142).

4. A. GEORGE, *Tradition et rédaction chez Luc. La construction du troisième évangile*, in *ETL* 43 (1967) 100-129 (= I. DE LA POTTERIE [ed.], *De Jésus aux Évangiles* [BETL, 25], Gembloux, 1967, pp. 100-129; = *Études sur l'œuvre de Luc* [Sources Bibliques], Paris,

19,44 forms what is usually and rightly called the Lukan travel narrative, and that this text unit does not form the second part of the tripartite Gospel of Luke but rather the first of three subsections within the second main part of the Gospel (9,51–24,53).

I. The Main Divisions of Luke's Gospel

One of the means of understanding and interpreting the Gospels is the study of their general structure. This is especially clear in a time when redaction criticism forms an integral part of the historical critical method: "If form criticism has taught us to locate and relate the separate paragraphs, while source criticism has shown the interplay of the larger sections, redaction criticism has sharpened our perception of the total configuration which Luke designed in bringing his Gospel to completion"[5]. The evangelist reveals his theology by the way in which he organizes, arranges, or structures his gospel. The outline of the Gospel must be examined in order to discover the different motives which guided its author. Therefore critics sometimes distinguish two sides of the redaction-critical method: (1) emendation criticism, i.e. the editor's modification, addition, or elimination of specific words as well as changes in sentence structure, and (2) composition criticism, i.e. the structural and organizational characteristics of the work as a whole[6]. Thus a balanced redaction criticism has always had to do with what is presently referred to as diachronic and synchronic approaches.

1978, pp. 15-41); W. E. HULL, *A Structural Analysis of the Gospel of Luke*, in *RevExp* 64 (1967) 421-425; ID., *A Teaching Outline of the Gospel of Luke*, in *RevExp* 64 (1967) 426-432; A.J. HULTGREN, *Interpreting the Gospel of Luke*, in *Interpretation* 30 (1976) 353-365; S.J. KISTEMAKER, *The Structure of Luke's Gospel*, in *JETS* 25 (1982) 33-39; J. LEAL, *El plan literario del III Evangelio y la geografía*, in *Estudios Eclesiásticos* 29 (1955) 197-215; ID., *La geografía y el plan literario del III Evangelio*, in *XV semana bíblica española (20-25 Sept. 1954)*, Madrid, 1955, pp. 227-246; C.F. NÖSGEN, *Der schriftstellerische Plan des dritten Evangeliums*, in *TSK* 49 (1876) 265-292; F. O'FEARGHAIL, *The Introduction to Luke-Acts. A Study of the Role of Lk 1,1–4,44 in the Composition of Luke's Two-Volume Work* (AnBib, 126), Rome, 1991; B. PRETE, *L'opera di Luca. Contenuti e prospettive*, Torino, 1986, pp. 34-79; P. ROLLAND, *L'organisation du Livre des Actes et de l'ensemble de l'œuvre de Luc*, in *Bib* 65 (1984) 81-86; É. SAMAIN, *L'évangile de Luc et le livre des Actes: éléments de composition et de structure*, in *Foi et Vie* 70 (1971) 3-24 (Cahiers bibl. n° 10); B. STANDAERT, *L'Art de composer dans l'œuvre de Luc*, in *À cause de l'évangile. FS J. Dupont* (LD, 123), Paris, 1985, pp. 323-347; W. WILKENS, *Die Auslassung von Mark. 6,45-8,26 bei Lukas im Licht der Komposition Luk. 9,1-50*, in *TZ* 32 (1976) 193-200; ID., *Die theologische Struktur der Komposition des Lukasevangeliums*, in *TZ* 34 (1978) 1-13; ID., *Die Versuchungsgeschichte Luk. 4,1-13 und die Komposition des Evangeliums*, in *TZ* 30 (1974) 262-272.

5. W.E. HULL, *Structural Analysis* (n. 4), p. 422.
6. R.A. EDWARDS, *The Redaction of Luke*, in *JR* 49 (1969) 392-405, spec. pp. 393-394.

Criteria

Several criteria have been used to define the overall structure of a gospel. Traditionally, chronological and geographical data were given much attention. The classical *Literarkritik* looked rather at Luke's use of different sources, literary criteria and/or the theological-thematic motifs and their influence on the general outline of his Gospel. More recently, with the rise of synchronic methods, still other criteria for detecting the overall structure have been taken into consideration. On the one hand there is the more formal aesthetic approach which looks for structural patterns such as parallellism, chiasmus, and concentric structures. On the other hand there is the narrative reading which concentrates on dramatic criteria, such as changes of place, of time and of *dramatis personae* or "characters" (entering or leaving the "stage"). These changes can be signals of a shift or a progress in the dramatic action, the main divisions (and subdivisions) of a narrative being determined by divisions of this dramatic action. The main criterion for the delimitation of a narrative unit is thus the analysis of the plot or the dramatic action[7].

The distinction between criteria is not always clear. Traditional criteria are sometimes integrated in more recent methods and applied in a different way[8]. The criteria need not be mutually exclusive. The different conclusions at which scholars arrive in determining the structure of Luke depend in great measure on the weight they give to each of them. Dependence on a single norm might lead to subjective opinions. Therefore one should try to discover as many different types of criteria

---

7. For the criteria used in detecting the structure of Luke, see B. RIGAUX, *Témoignage de l'évangile de Luc* (Pour une histoire de Jésus, 4), DDB, 1970, pp. 82-103; C.H. TALBERT, *Literary Patterns, Theological Themes and the Genre of Luke-Acts* (SBL MS, 20), Montana, 1974; P. BOSSUYT – J. RADERMAKERS, *Jésus. Parole de la Grâce selon saint Luc*, Vol. 2, Bruxelles, 1981, pp. 19-23; J.-N. ALETTI, *L'art de raconter Jésus Christ. L'écriture narrative de l'évangile de Luc*, Paris, 1989, pp. 17.112-116. A useful systematic treatment of the question of criteria can be found in G. MLAKUZHYIL, *The Christocentric Literary Structure of the Fourth Gospel* (AnBib, 117), Rome, 1987, pp. 87-135. The latter distinguishes three sets of criteria: (1) *literary criteria*: conclusions, introductions, inclusions, characteristic vocabulary, geographical indications, literary-chronological indications, liturgical feasts, transitions, bridge-passages, hook-words, techniques of repetition, change of literary "genres" (pp. 87-112); (2) *dramatic techniques*: change of scenes, technique of alternating scenes, technique of double-stage action, introduction of *dramatis personae*, change of *dramatis personae*, the law of stage duality, technique of vanishing characters, technique of seven scenes, technique of diptych-scenes, sequence of action-dialogue-discourse, dramatic development, dramatic pattern (pp. 112-121); and (3) *structural patterns*: parallelism, chiasmus, concentric structure, spiral structure (pp. 121-135). See also J.L. SKA, *"Our Fathers Have Told Us". Introduction to the Analysis of Hebrew Narratives* (Subsidia biblica, 13), Rome, 1990, pp. 1-3.

8. E.g. geographical data have in the past played an important role and still do in a narrative approach; literary criteria are used in historical-critical as well as in synchronic approaches.

as possible to detect the structure. Convergence of criteria of diverse natures can guarantee greater objectivity[9].

Chronology, Geography, Sources

From the second century onwards, and until the nineteenth century, Luke, contrary to Mark, was supposed to have written his Gospel following a chronological order. But this view is no longer accepted by modern criticism. Although it was "Luke the historian" himself who probably added the famous synchronisms with profane history in 1,5; 2,1-3 and 3,1-2 to his Markan source, it was generally supposed that he followed the chronological and geographical progression of his predecessor: Galilee, going up to Jerusalem, Jerusalem[10]. In Luke, the second stage is of course more elaborate and was called, according to the emphasis laid upon certain passages, the "Perean"[11] or "Samaritan" section[12]. It is highly probable that this preference for chronological or geographical criteria in delineating the structure of Luke was

9. G. MLAKUZHYIL, *Structure of the Fourth Gospel* (n. 7), p. 137.

10. B. RIGAUX, *Témoignage* (n. 7), pp. 83-85.

11. The qualification "Perean section" is inspired by a tendency to harmonize with Mk 10,1 (πέραν τοῦ ᾿Ιορδάνου). The "other village" of Lk 9,56, it is said, is not a Samaritan village. The pericopes situated around Jericho (Lk 18,35-43; 19,1-10) are more easily associated with a Perean journey than with one through Samaria. In this sense: H.J. HOLTZMANN, *Die Synoptiker* (HNT, I,1), Tübingen-Leipzig, 1901, p. 357; T. ZAHN, *Lucas* (KNT, 3), Leipzig, 1913, p. 402; W. GASSE, *Zum Reisebericht des Lukas*, in *ZNW* 34 (1935) 293-299. The term "Perean section" is preferred in the English-speaking world: C. WEST-WATSON, *The Peraean Ministry*, in *JTS* 11 (1910) 269-274; D.R. WICKES, *The Sources of Luke's Perean Section*, Chicago, IL, 1912; E.D. BURTON, *Some Phases of the Synoptic Problem*, in *JBL* 31 (1912) 95-113; *sed contra*: B.H. STREETER, in W. SANDAY (ed.), *Studies in the Synoptic Gospels*, Oxford, 1911, p. 159: "It is a mistake to call this the 'Peraean' section...", with reference to Lk 9,51-53 and 17,11.

12. J. WELLHAUSEN, *Einleitung in die drei ersten Evangelien*, Berlin, ²1911, p. 52: "Ein neuer Abschnitt beginnt da, wo die unstete Wanderung in die Reise nach Jerusalem übergeht, die bei Lukas nicht durch Peräa, sondern durch Samarien führt. Er reicht von 9,51–18,14 und enthält gar keine Markusstücke und vieles dem Lukas ganz Eigentümliche". Arguments adduced in support of the designation "Samaritan section" are: (i) the fact that, according to Fl. JOSEPHUS, *Ant.*, 20,6,1, § 118; *Bell.*, 2,12,3, § 232; *Vita*, 52, § 269, most pilgrims going up from Galilee to Jerusalem passed through Samaria; (ii) the "other village" of Lk 9,56 is a Samaritan one, because Jesus' reaction at the initial rejection differs favourably from that of the disciples; (iii) the presence of Lk 10,30-37 and 17,11-17, two Samaritan pericopes, within this section. Even scholars who approach the Lukan travel narrative from a literary-theological point of view sometimes prefer to speak of a "Samaritan" section or ministry: the geographical disposition Galilee - Samaria - Judea reveals Luke's theological interest in the universalism of christianity. Cf. F. NICOLARDOT, *Les procédés de rédaction des trois premiers évangiles*, Paris, 1908, p. 119; R. BULTMANN, *Die Geschichte der synoptischen Tradition*, Göttingen, ⁶1964, p. 24: "die Reise durch Samaria ist eine Konstruktion des Lk"; E. KLOSTERMAN, *Das Lukasevangelium* (HNT, 5), Tübingen, ²1929, p. 110: "Samaritanerabschnitt"; B. RIGAUX, *Témoignage* (n. 7), pp. 90-92. A recent plea is that of M.S. ENSLIN, *The Samaritan Ministry and Mission*, in *HUCA* 51 (1980) 29-38.

greatly influenced by an historical-biographical understanding of the Gospel.

The geographical criterion having already pointed to a tripartite division of the Gospel of Luke, this was reinforced by the source-critical approach which dominated the critical research during the nineteenth century and which has continued to exercise its influence till today. Once Markan priority was accepted, it became evident that Luke took the Markan outline as the basis for his own Gospel, except for one section. Whereas Luke follows Mark quite closely in 3,1–9,50 (= Mk 1,1–9,41), 18,15–21,38 (= Mk 10,13–13,37) and 22,1–24,12 (= Mk 14,1–16,8)[13], Lk 9,51–18,14 forms an exception. There Luke is clearly leaving his primary source, whatever may be the provenance of the material collected in it[14]. Defenders of the two-source theory call this non-Markan section the "great interpolation", as distinct from the small interpolation of Lk 6,20–8,3 and the insertion of Lk 19,1-27 within the Markan frame. Others prefer to speak of the "central section", a very current designation nowadays[15]. Although the term "central section" sounds more neutral from a source-critical point of view (defenders of the Proto-Luke theory also use it), it also implies a choice as to the structure of Luke. To use the words of William E. Hull[16]:

13. Up to 9,51, Luke follows quite closely the Markan order, except for the omission of Mk 6,45–8,26, the insertion of non-Markan material in Lk 3,1–4,30 and 6,20–8,3, and five changes of the Markan order (two simple inversions: Lk 6,12-16 par. Mk 3,13-19; Lk 8,19-21 par. Mk 3,31-35; and three thoroughly rewritten pericopes in a completely different context: Lk 4,16-30 par. Mk 6,1-6a; Lk 5,1-11 par. Mk 1,16-20; and Lk 7,36-50 par. Mk 14,3-9). From 18,15 on, Luke again takes up the Markan thread from where he had left it at 9,51 and, except for the insertion of 19,1-27, he follows it very faithfully up to the Passion narrative, where he evidences greater independence with respect to Mark's vocabulary, content and order.

14. See on this question J.C. HAWKINS, *The Disuse of the Markan Source in St. Luke 9,51-18,14*, in W. SANDAY (ed.), *Oxford Studies* (n. 11), pp. 29-59; D.R. WICKES, *Sources* (n. 11); G. SELLIN, *Komposition, Quellen und Funktion des lukanischen Reiseberichtes (Lk. IX 51–XIX 28)*, in *NT* 20 (1978) 100-135, spec. pp. 113-132; J.W. WENHAM, *Synoptic Independence and the Origin of Luke's Travel Narrative*, in *NTS* 27 (1980-81) 507-515.

15. E.g., C.L. BLOMBERG, *Midrash, Chiasmus, and the Outline of Luke's Central Section*, in R.T. FRANCE – D. WENHAM (eds.), *Gospel Perspectives III*, Sheffield, 1983, pp. 217-261; J.H. DAVIES, *The Purpose of the Central Section of St. Luke's Gospel*, in *Studia Evangelica* II (TU, 87), Berlin, 1964, pp. 164-169; C.F. EVANS, *The Central Section of St. Luke's Gospel*, in D.E. NINEHAM (ed.), *Studies in the Gospels. Essays in Memory of R.H. Lighfoot*, Oxford, 1955, pp. 37-53; H.K. FARRELL, *The Structure and Theology of Luke's Central Section*, in *Trinity Journal* 7 (1986) 33-54; C.C. McCOWN, *The Geography of Luke's Central Section*, in *JBL* 57 (1938) 51-66; G. OGG, *The Central Section of the Gospel according to St. Luke*, in *NTS* 18 (1971-72) 39-53; J.L. RESSEGUIE, *Interpretation of Luke's Central Section (Luke 9:51–19:44) since 1856*, in *Studia Biblica et Theologica* 5 (1975) 3-36; ID., *Point of View in the Central Section of Luke (9:51–19:44)*, in *JETS* 25 (1982) 41-48; G.W. TROMPF, *La section médiane de l'évangile de Luc: l'organisation des documents*, in *RHPR* 53 (1973) 141-154.

16. W.E. HULL, *Structural Analysis* (n. 4), p. 423.

Once this 'Central Section' is seen in proper perspective, then the basic form of the entire Gospel may be readily grasped. Whereas Matthew exhibits a five-fold pattern, and Mark and John – in different ways – develop a two-fold scheme, Luke has utilized a three-fold arrangement of his material. As with the other Synoptics, he describes first the ministry of Jesus in Galilee and concludes finally with his passion in Jerusalem. But between these two foci of the gospel ellipse he has inserted his 'Great Interpolation' depicting the journey which lay between these two basic spheres of activity. Whereas the other Synoptics make only passing mention of this transition from the north to the south (Mt 19:1; Mk 10:1), Luke has expanded the last journey 'on the way to the Cross' into his most conspicuous section.

Tripartite and multi-partite divisions of Luke's Gospel

The tripartite division of the Gospel of Luke, or at least of Jesus' public ministry in that Gospel, is very common today, even with more redaction-critical approaches. After the preface or the prologue (1,1-4), and the introductory chapters in which the parallelism of the birth of John the Baptist and Jesus is set out (1,5-2,52), to which the preparation of Jesus' ministry in 3,1-4,13 is sometimes added, the public life of Jesus is divided into three main stages: his mission in Galilee (and Judaea) (3,1 or 4,14-9,50), his going up to Jerusalem (9,51-19,27/28), and his ministry in Jerusalem (19,28/29-24,53). It could be said that this structure actually represents the majority opinion: it is to be found in introductions, commentaries, and special studies. But it is certainly not the only one. Many scholars are inclined to multiply the number of major sections, because they take the introductory chapters as one or more sections (e.g. 1,5-2,52 || 3,1-4,13), or because they divide the third episode into different sections (e.g. 19,28/29-21,38 || 22,1-23,38 || 24,1-53). This is especially the case with commentaries which often divide the Gospel of Luke into five, six, seven, or even eight parts. In most cases, this structure is not the result of a careful analysis of the Gospel itself, i.e. of the various indications given by its redactor, but merely a practical division of the commentary for the reader. In fact, when one compares the caesurae of the multi-partite divisions, it becomes clear that they are very similar to the subsections of the tripartite divisions. Thus the differences between the multi-partite and the tripartite divisions are not as important as one might be led to believe. In an appendix I have compiled a conveniently arranged survey, first of tripartite divisions, and second of multi-partite divisions. The number of commentaries collated is sufficiently high to give a reliable impression of how the Gospel of Luke is usually structured. Composed mostly of twentieth century commentaries, some nineteenth century works have also been included in the Appendix so that a certain evolution in the approach to Luke's structure can be observed.

Delineation of the Central Part of Luke's Gospel

Let us now look more thoroughly at the central part of Luke's Gospel. Our survey shows clearly that the great majority of 20th century scholars take 9,51–19,27/28 as the boundaries of this section. This is the choice of modern criticism. It replaces the former mere source-critical approach which limited the central section to the non-Markan unit 9,51–18,14, an opinion represented in the older commentaries of W.M.L. de Wette (1836), A. Wright (1900), H.J. Holtzmann (1901), J. Wellhausen (1904) and E. Klostermann (1929), and in older 'classics' such as C. Weizsäcker (1901), W. Sanday (1906), J.V. Bartlet (1911), J.C. Hawkins (1911), W.H. Cadman (1923), B.H. Streeter (1924) and W. Larfeld (1925)[17]. Several studies on the Lukan travel narrative, even some more recent ones, accept this delimitation: Schaarschmidt, W. Gasse, L. Girard, X. de Meeüs, E. Lohse, C.F. Evans, I. Fransen, M.S. Enslin, J.W. Wenham, A.J. Tankersley[18]. Others, like the commentaries of C.F. Keil (1879), P. Schanz (1863), Th. Zahn (1920), M.-J. Lagrange (1927), S. Greijdanus (1940), J. Keulers (1951), E.J. Tinsley (1965) and M. Goulder (1989) prefer 18,30 as the end of the central section[19], or even 18,34 (W. Bartelt, 1937, C.L. Blomberg, 1983)[20], because the verses 33-34 are parallel to Mk 10,31-34, verses which relate to Jesus' last journey to Jerusalem.

But, as already noted, most scholars take 19,27, the final verse of the parable of the pounds, as the end of Jesus' journey to Jerusalem,

17. W.L.M. DE WETTE, *Lukas und Markus*, Leipzig, 1836; A. WRIGHT, *Luke*, London, 1900; H.J. HOLTZMANN, *Synoptiker* (n. 11), pp. 18-19; J. WELLHAUSEN, *Das Evangelium Lucae*, Berlin, 1904, p. 45; E. KLOSTERMANN, *Lukas* (n. 12), p. 110; C. WEIZSÄCKER, *Untersuchungen über die evangelische Geschichte*, Tübingen, 1901, p. 83; W. SANDAY, *Outlines of the Life of Christ*, Edinburgh, 1906, p. 130; J.V. BARTLET, *The Sources of St. Luke's Gospel*, in *Oxford Studies* (n. 11), p. 340; J.C. HAWKINS, *Disuse* (n. 14), p. 29; W.H. CADMAN, *The Last Journey of Jesus to Jerusalem*, London-Oxford, 1923, p. 105; B.H. STREETER, *The Four Gospels*, London, 1924, p. 203; W. LARFELD, *Die neutestamentlichen Evangelien*, Gütersloh, 1925, pp. 60f.163.

18. SCHAARSCHMIDT, *Die Einschaltung im Lukasevangelium (9,51 bis 18,14) als Grundlage der biblischen Geschichte von Jesus*, in *TSK* 101 (1929) 357-380; W. GASSE, *Reisebericht* (n. 11); L. GIRARD, *L'Évangile des voyages ou la section Lc. 9,51–18,14 de Saint Luc*, Paris, 1964; X. DE MEEÜS, *La composition de Lc. 9,51–18,14* (Diss. doct. Théol.), Leuven, 1954; E. LOHSE, *Missionarisches Handeln nach dem Evangelium des Lukas*, in *TZ* 10 (1954) 1-13 (= ID., *Die Einheit des Neuen Testaments*, Göttingen, 1973, pp. 165-177); C.F. EVANS, *Central Section* (n. 15); I. FRANSEN, *La montée vers Jérusalem (Lc. 9,51–18,14)*, in *BVC* 11 (1965) 68-87; M.S. ENSLIN, *Samaritan Ministry* (n. 12); J.W. WENHAM, *Synoptic Independence* (n. 14); A.J. TANKERSLEY, *Preaching the Christian Deuteronomy: Luke 9,51–18,14* (Diss. Claremont), 1983.

19. C.F. KEIL, 1879; P. SCHANZ, 1863; T. ZAHN (n. 11); M.-J. LAGRANGE, *Luc*, Paris, 1927; S. GREIJDANUS, *Lucas*, 2 vols., Amsterdam, 1940-41, pp. v-x; J. KEULERS, *De evangeliën volgens Marcus en Lucas* (De Boeken van het Nieuw Testament), Roermond-Maaseik, 1951; E.J. TINSLEY, *Luke*, London, 1965; M. GOULDER, *Luke*, Sheffield, 1989.

20. W. BARTELT, *Lukas*, Freiburg, 1937, pp. XIII-XVI; C.L. BLOMBERG, *Luke's Central Section* (n. 15).

because in their opinion 19,28 begins the pericope of the entry into Jerusalem (Lk 19,28-40 par. Mk 11,1-10). It is unfeasable to enumerate all those who accept this opinion, but a quick look at the appendix will suffice to demonstrate its popularity[21]. A few commentators, like V. Rose (1909), A. Plummer (1922), J. Dean (1935), G.B. Caird (1963), L'Eplattenier (1982) and the studies of J. Leal (1955), A. George (1967), G. Ogg (1971), F. Neirynck (1973), G. Sellin (1978), J.L. Espinel (1980), W.J. Barnard and P. van 't Riet (1984), P. Rolland (1984), and W. Radl (1988) consider 19,28 to be the final verse of the travel narrative[22]. This verse may indeed be considered to be the end of the parable of the pounds and an "inclusion" with its opening verse 19,11[23].

In recent times, however, the opinion that the entry story (Lk 19,28/ 29-40) and the lament over Jerusalem (19,41-44) form an essential part, if not the climax, of the Lukan travel narrative, is finding more approval, as the following list of adherents of this opinion shows: R. Morgenthaler (1949), N. Geldenhuys (1951), A. Denaux (1969), F.V. Filson (1970), D. Gill (1970), P. Von der Osten-Sacken (1973), M. Miyoshi (1974), L. Morris (1974), A.J. Mattill Jr. (1975), J.L. Resseguie (1975; 1982), A.J. Hultgren (1976), A. Büchele (1978), D.R. Miesner (1978), C.H. Talbert (1982), H.K. Farrell (1986), J.B. Tyson (1986), M.C. Parsons (1987), J.N. Aletti (1989), H. Baarlink (1989), J.L. Vesco

21. Cfr. also J.M.S. BALJON, *Lukas*, Utrecht, 1908, p. 234; P.J. BERNADICOU, *Self-Fulfillment According to Luke*, in *BibToday* 56 (1971) 505-512; J. BLINZLER, *Die literarische Eigenart des sogenannten Reiseberichts im Lukasevangelium*, in J. SCHMID, e.a. (eds.), *Synoptische Studien. FS A. Wikenhauser*, München, 1953, pp. 20-53, spec. p. 20, n. 1; H. CONZELMANN, *Die Mitte der Zeit* (BHT, 17), Tübingen, [5]1964, p. 56; C.H. GIBLIN, *The Destruction of Jerusalem According to Luke's Gospel* (AnBib, 107), Rome, 1985, pp. VII.30-31; R. LAPOINTE, *L'espace-temps de Lc 9,51–19,27*, in *Église et Théologie* 1 (1970) 275-290; C.C. MCCOWN, *The Geography of Jesus' Last Journey to Jerusalem*, in *JBL* 51 (1932) 107-129, spec. p. 107; J.T. NIELSEN, *Lucas* I, Nijkerk, 1979, p. 14; K.L. SCHMIDT, *Der Rahmen der Geschichte Jesu*, Berlin, 1919 (= Darmstadt, 1964), pp. 246-273; J. SCHNEIDER, *Zur Analyse des lukanischen Reiseberichtes*, in *FS A. Wikenhauser*, pp. 207-229; F. STAGG, *The Journey Towards Jerusalem in Luke's Gospel. Luke 9:51–19:27*, in *Review and Expositor* 64 (1967) 499-512; G.W. TROMPF, *Section médiane* (n. 15).

22. Commentaries: V. ROSE, *Luc*, Paris, [6]1907; A. PLUMMER, *Luke* (ICC), Edinburgh, [5]1922; J. DEAN, 1935; G.B. CAIRD, *Luke*, Harmondsworth, 1963; C. L'EPLATTENIER, *Luc*, Paris, 1982. Other studies: W.J. BARNARD – P. VAN 'T RIET, *Lukas, de Jood. Een joodse inleiding op het Evangelie van Lukas en de Handelingen der Apostelen*, Kampen, 1984, pp. 103-117; J.L. ESPINEL, *La vida-viaje de Jésus hacia Jerusalén (Lc 9,51–19,28)*, in *Cultura Biblica* [M/AFEBE] 37 (1980) 93-111; A. GEORGE, *Tradition* (n. 4), p. 101, n. 4 and pp. 109-112; J. LEAL, *El plan literario* (n. 4), pp. 198-199.205-207; F. NEIRYNCK, *Matière marcienne* (n. 3), p. 65; G. OGG, *Central Section* (n. 15); W. RADL, *Das Lukas-Evangelium* (EdF, 261), Darmstadt, 1988, pp. 46-48; P. ROLLAND, *Organisation* (n. 4), p. 83; G. SELLIN, *Komposition* (n. 14).

23. I. DE LA POTTERIE, *La parabole du prétendant à la royauté (Lc 19,11-28)*, in *À cause de l'évangile* (n. 4), pp. 613-641, spec. pp. 627-631 discusses the question whether verse 19,27 or 19,28 forms the end of the parable of the pounds, without reference to the travel narrative.

(1989) D.P. Moessner (1989)[24]. Moreover, a number of scholars would even integrate the entry into, and the cleansing of, the temple (Lk 19,45-46) in the travel narrative itself: L. Soubigou (1933), J.H. Davies (1964), P. Kariamadam (1978; 1987), C.H. Talbert (1982), J. Rius-Camps (1983), J. Lambrecht (1985), P.H.M. Welzen (1986), J.M. Dawsey (1987)[25]. And finally, there are some who even include the summary of Jesus' teaching in the temple (Lk 19,47-48): F. Schleiermacher (1817!), J.M. Creed (1930), K.E. Bailey (1976), H.L. Egelkraut (1976) and F. O'Fearghail (1991)[26]. It should be noted that this

24. Commentaries: N. GELDENHUYS, Luke, 1951, p. 46; E.E. ELLIS, Luke, 1966, pp. 32.35-36: accepts the division 9,51–19,44, but refuses to call it a Travel Narrative; L. MORRIS, Luke (Tyndale NT Comm.), Grand Rapids, MI, 1974. Studies in chronological order: R. MORGENTHALER, Die lukanische Geschichtsschreibung, Zürich, Vol. I, 1949, pp. 163.172; A. DENAUX, Reisverhaal (n. 2), pp. 467-475; F.V. FILSON, The Journey Motif in Luke-Acts, in W.W. GASQUE – R.P. MARTIN (eds.), Apostolic History and the Gospel, Exeter, 1970, pp. 68-77; D. GILL, Observations on the Lukan Travel Narrative and Some Related Passages, in HTR 63 (1970) 199-221; P. VON DER OSTEN-SACKEN, Zur Christologie des lukanischen Reiseberichtes, in EvTh 33 (1973) 476-496; M. MIYOSHI, Der Anfang des Reiseberichtes Lk 9,51–10,24 (AnBib, 60), Rome, 1975, p. XI; A.J. MATTILL, Jr., The Jesus-Paul Parallels and the Purpose of Luke-Acts: H.H. Evans Reconsidered, in NT 17 (1975) 15-46, spec. p. 30; J.L. RESSEGUIE, Interpretation (n. 15), p. 3, n. 2; Point of View (n. 15); A.J. HULTGREN, Interpreting (n. 4); A. BÜCHELE, Der Tod Jesu im Lukasevangelium (Frankfurter theologische Studien, 26), Frankfurt/M, 1978, pp. 146-147; D.R. MIESNER, The Missionary Narrative: Patterns and Implications, in C.H. TALBERT (ed.), Perspectives on Luke-Acts, Danville, VA - Edinburgh, 1978, pp. 199-214, spec. p. 199; H.K. FARRELL (n. 15); J.B. TYSON, The Death of Jesus in Luke-Acts, Columbia, SC, 1986, pp. 22.34.52.98; M.C. PARSONS, The Departure of Jesus in Luke-Acts (JSNT SS, 21), 1987, p. 91; J.N. ALETTI, L'art (n. 7), pp. 112-116; H. BAARLINK (red.), Inleiding tot het Nieuwe Testament, Kampen, 1989, pp. 137-142.145-149: 9,43b–19,44; J.L. VESCO, Jérusalem et son prophète. Une lecture de l'Évangile selon saint Luc, Paris, 1988, pp. 43-52; D.P. MOESSNER, Lord of the Banquet: The Literary and Theological Significance of the Lukan Travel Narrative, Minneapolis, MN, 1989.

25. L. SOUBIGOU, Luc, Paris, 1933, pp. 563-568: 9,51–19,46 contains three journeys: 9,51–13,21; 13,22–17,10; 17,11–19,46; J.H. DAVIES (n. 15), pp. 164.166,n.2.168; P. KARIAMADAM, The End of the Travel Narrative (Lk 18,31–19,46), Rome, 1978; Discipleship in the Lucan Narrative (Lk 9,51–19,46), in Jeevadhara 10 (1980) 111-130; The Composition and Meaning of the Lucan Travel Narrative (Lk 9,51–19,46), in Bible Bhashyam 13 (1987) 179-198; C.H. TALBERT, Literary Patterns (n. 7), p. 51; J. RIUS-CAMPS, Qüestions sobre la doble obra lucana IV. Lc 10,25–18,30: une perfecta estructura concèntrica dins la Secció del Viatge (9,51–19,46), in Revista Catalana de Teologia (Barcelona) 8 (1983) 283-357; J. LAMBRECHT, Reading and Rereading Lk 18,31–22,6, in FS J. Dupont (n. 4), p. 593, with hesitation; P.H.M. WELZEN, Lucas, evangelist van gemeenschap. Een onderzoek naar de pragmatische effecten van Lc 15,1–17,10 (Diss. doct. Theol.), Nijmegen, 1986, pp. 47-53; J.M. DAWSEY, Jesus' Pilgrimage to Jerusalem, in PerspRelStud 14 (1987) 217-232, spec. p. 217, n. 2: travel notices from 9,51 till 19,45.

26. F. SCHLEIERMACHER, Über die Schriften des Lukas. Tl. I, 1817, p. 158 (= Sämtliche Werke. I. Abt. Zur Theologie. 2. Bd., Berlin, 1836, p. 116); J.M. CREED, Luke, London, 1930, pp. 139-141; K.E. BAILEY, Poet and Peasant. A Literary cultural Approach to the Parables in Luke, 1976, pp. 79-85; H.L. EGELKRAUT, Jesus' Mission to Jerusalem: A Redaction Critical Study of the Travel Narrative in the Gospel of Luke, Lk 9:51–19:48 (Europäische Hochschulschriften, XXIII,80), Frankfurt/M-Bern, 1976; and F. O'FEARGHAIL, Introduction (n. 4), pp. 48-51.

modern shift from 19,27/28 towards 19,44/46, perceived already by some redaction-critical studies, is now endorsed by nearly all scholars who work with narratological criteria.

The choice between Lk 19,27 and Lk 19,44 is the real problem of the end of the Lukan travel narrative, given the fact that 18,15/30 is not presently defended and that the alternatives 19,27 or 28 and 19,44 or 46 are but smaller disagreements, which nonetheless should also be discussed. In other words, does Lk 19,28/29-44/46 belong to the travel narrative or to the Jerusalem section and why? That seems to be the real issue here.

Does the "Lukan Travel Narrative" exist?

This is the case at least if there exists something like a "Lukan travel narrative". It would be interesting to examine from what moment on commentators began to speak of the central section in these terms. As early as 1742, J.A. Bengel calls Lk 9,51–19,28 "Iter magnum Hierosolymitanum, ad passionem etc.", although it is inserted in a larger section 9,18–19,28[27]. But on the other hand, C.F. Nösgen was able in 1876 to write an article on the structure of Luke without even mentioning the travel narrative[28]. And in his *Einleitung in das Neue Testament* (1900), Th. Zahn manifests a clear-cut opposition to such: "Es ist daher auch als ein blosser Schein zu beurteilen, dass wir 9,51–19,46 den Bericht über eine Reise von Galiläa nach Jerusalem vor uns haben". He concedes that the sequence of the Lukan "travel notices" might possibly reflect in great part the historical reality. But this was not Luke's intention. Zahn gives four reasons for this view: (i) the travel notices, spread over these nine chapters, are not at all interconnected, as is the case with Acts 13–28. (ii) In 9,51–19,46, Luke brings the same kind of asyndetic sequence of pericopes as in the foregoing section, so that the reader does not know where or when the episodes should be situated. (iii) The first solemn announcement of the last journey to Jerusalem (9,51) does not mark a sharp caesura: with respect to the content, what comes before and after this verse is very closely related. A similar observation can be made concerning the other introductions indicating a change of place: they have no connection with the surrounding pericopes. (iv) The more explicit travel indications in 9,51, 13,22 and 17,11 merely constitute a key to a better understanding of the pericope which they introduce, but they do not yield a coherent overall journey scheme[29]. Consequently, 9,51–19,46 plays no role in the structure he

---

27. J.A. BENGEL, *Gnomon Novi Testamenti* (Tübingen, 1742), Tübingen-London, 1855 (ed. J. Steudel), pp. 206-208.

28. C.F. NÖSGEN, *Plan* (n. 4).

29. T. ZAHN, *Einleitung in das Neue Testament*. 2. Bd., Leipzig, 1900, pp. 375-377.

proposes in his commentary on Luke[30]. Zahn is right in affirming that Lk 9,51-19,46 does not afford a reliable account ("Bericht") of the journey the historical Jesus actually made. In that sense I can agree with his first two remarks. But this observation does not exclude the possibility that, on a literary-narrative level, Luke inserted in his Gospel something like a narrative framework of a journey, which would then function as a literary device rather than as a historical description. I do not agree with Zahn's third and fourth remarks. In my opinion, from a narrative-literary point of view, Lk 9,51 marks a clear turning point in the dynamic course of the Gospel narration. Moreover, the travel notices 9,51; 13,22 and 17,11, fulfil a multiple introductory function: they not only introduce the immediately following pericope, but also a subsection.

In his commentary, J. Fitzmyer asserts rather too boldly that "commentators such as A. Schlatter, J. Wellhausen, Schmidt, Ellis think that the Lucan Gospel has no travel account at all", even if he adds immediately: "No little part of the reason for denying it is the implication that the historical Jesus did not say or do all these things on the way to Jerusalem"[31]. One should thus distinguish between the literary and the historical level. Authors like Wellhausen and Schmidt have rightly argued that the Lucan travel narrative should not be seen as a historical account of what actually happened. But that does not mean that on the literary level they do not accept any sense of a *Lukan* "travel narrative". J. Wellhausen introduces his commentary on Lk 9,51-18,14 as follows: "Nach Joa lehrt Jesus das Meiste und Wichtigste in Jerusalem selber, nach Lc (im geringeren Grade schon nach Mc) wenigstens auf der Reise nach Jerusalem, obgleich gar manches garnicht in diese Situation passt"[32]. In his classic, *Der Rahmen der Geschichte Jesus* (1919), K.L. Schmidt simply labels one of his chapters: *"Der lukanische Reisebericht Lk 9,51-19,27"*. In a careful study he argues in a convincing way that the framework ("Rahmenstücke") of this section is mainly redactional. Finally he asserts that the literary and historical value of the Lukan travel narrative is rather limited[33]. One can hardly say then that Schmidt "thinks that Luke has no travel account at all". Schlatter's large Commentary on Luke (1931) had indeed no travel account, but it should be added that he proposed there no structure of the gospel. In his smaller and later commentary on Mark and Luke, Schlatter accepted 9,51-19,27, called *"Die Wanderung von Galiläa nach Jerusalem"*, as one of the seven main divisions of the

---

30. T. ZAHN, *Lucas* (n. 11), pp. V-VII.
31. J.A. FITZMYER, *Luke I-IX* (AB, 28), Garden City, NY, 1981, p. 825.
32. J. WELLHAUSEN, *Lucas* (n. 17), p. 46.
33. K.L. SCHMIDT, *Rahmen* (n. 21), pp. 246-271.

Gospel[34]. According to E.E. Ellis, Luke's primary intention in the central division 9,51-19,44 is "to present a theme not a chronicle, to present Jesus the teacher not Jesus the traveller. Throughout the ministry from 4.42 onwards Jesus is presented always without a home, always on a mission, always on the move. Therefore, it is improper in any case to call Luke's central division 'The Travel Narrative'"[35]. In fact, Ellis' structure of Luke's Gospel is entirely thematic, neither chronological nor geographical. Yet it should be observed that Ellis has rightly delimited 9,51-19,44 as a literary unit, and that, at least in this section, geography can not be totally excluded. Thus the last subsection 18,15-19,44, is entitled "The road to Jerusalem: Discipleship and the rejected king"[36].

Studying the composition and structure of Luke, Étienne Samain concedes that the motif of the "journey to Jerusalem" cannot be overlooked, but also would not limit it to the central section. In Luke's perspective Jesus' going up to Jerusalem neither starts with Lk 9,51 nor ends at the moment he enters the holy city. It begins from Nazareth (Lk 4,29-30). It is re-started forcefully at 9,51 by means of the literary device of the "journey". The journey leads certainly to Jerusalem but does not have a precise conclusion. Luke intends to maintain Jerusalem as the first horizon of the final events of the Saviour's ministry but this remains the stage for the beginning of Acts (cp. Lk 24,47-49 with Acts 1,8, and Lk 24,50-53 with Acts 1,9-12). All through these chapters Jerusalem remains in the center of Luke's preoccupations and this orientation forbids us to accept a break of any kind between Lk 9,51 and Acts 2,1[37]. Samain is certainly right in stressing the importance of the Jerusalem motif throughout the whole Gospel and in the first chapter of Acts. But this does not justify his view that the travel narrative has no end in Luke's Gospel. In my opinion, he also underestimates the structural and narrative importance of Lk 9,51.

Even in recent times there has been some doubt about the existence of anything like a Lukan travel narrative. In the commentary of Bossuyt-Radermakers (1981), the travel narrative does not figure among the five main sections 1,5-4,44||5,1-9,17||9,18-17,10||17,11-21,38||22,1-24,53[38]. Although J. Lambrecht sees the end of the Lukan travel narrative at 19,46, he also has expressed his doubts about it: "The ascent to this city [i.e. Jerusalem] should be seen in function of

---

34. A. SCHLATTER, *Das Evangelium des Lukas*, Stuttgart, 1931; *Die Evangelien nach Markus und Lukas* (Erläuterungen zum NT, 2), Stuttgart, 1962, p. 410.

35. E.E. ELLIS, *Luke* (n. 24), p. 148.

36. *Ibid.*, pp. 30-37.

37. É. SAMAIN, *L'évangile* (n. 4), pp. 6-8; *Le récit lucanien du voyage de Jésus vers Jérusalem. Quelques études récentes*, in *Foi et Vie* 72 (1973) 3-23 (Cahiers bibl. N° 12).

38. P. BOSSUYT - J. RADERMAKERS, *Luc* (n. 7), pp. 29-33.

what will happen there. So it seems less appropriate to look for a formal conclusion of this ascent if one thereby intends to indicate a clear break, the conclusion of a gospel section... Luke mentions Jesus' entering the temple only by means of a participial construction (see 19,45a). For Luke the events which occur during the descent of the Mount of Olives (acclamation, hostile reaction, Jesus' weeping over the city) as well as the cleansing of the temple itself are far more important than the actual entry into it"[39].

Finally we should mention authors like R. Morgenthaler, A.J. Hultgren and W. Radl[40] and commentators like S. Greijdanus, H. Schürmann and G. Schneider[41] who accept an extension of the second main part in Luke's Gospel: it begins at 4,14 or at 5,1, with the result that the structural function of 9,51 is minimized to a certain degree; and according to Hultgren, Radl and Greijdanus it even ends at 21,38 (see Appendix). James L. Resseguie concludes his survey of the "Interpretation of Luke's Central Section (Luke 9:51–19:44) since 1856" in this way: "The content of the central division has been adequately described, and the tension with the form (trip motif) is reduced if we assume that this section is not a travel narrative. But the important problem as to why Luke has gathered this material into the central part of his gospel remains unsolved. Until this problem is solved the enigma of the central section is still with us"[42]. In what follows I will try to expose my own view, in dialogue with the opinions mentioned.

II. THE DELINEATION OF THE LUKAN TRAVEL NARRATIVE
(Lk 9,51–19,44)

1. The Structural Function of Luke 9,51

As we have said above, some scholars like C.F. Nösgen and T. Zahn contest the structural importance of 9,51. Others seem to minimize it to a certain degree, although they recognise the limited structural function of this verse[43]. It is thus necessary to consider the importance and the

---

39. J. LAMBRECHT, Reading (n. 25), p. 593; compare also M. GOULDER, Luke II (n. 19), p. 457, and H. BAARLINK, Die zyklische Struktur von Lukas 9.43b–19.28, in NTS 38 (1992) 481-506, spec. p. 481: "Immer mehr entsteht die Überzeugung, dass diese grosse Einschaltung zu Unrecht eine Reisebericht genannt wird", with reference to Robert-Feuillet and W.C. Robinson.

40. R. MORGENTHALER (n. 24), vol. I, pp. 159-194, spec. pp. 163.168-172.188; A.J. HULTGREN (n. 4); W. RADL (n. 22), pp. 46-48.

41. J.M.S. GREIJDANUS, Lucas I (n. 19), p. v; H. SCHÜRMANN, Das Lukasevangelium. Bd. I (HTKNT, 3/1), Freiburg, 1969; ²1984, pp. 260-261; G. SCHNEIDER, Das Evangelium nach Lukas. Bd. I (ÖTK, 3/1), Gütersloh-Würzburg, 1977, pp. 7-8.120.

42. J.L. RESSEGUIE, Interpretation (n. 15), pp. 35-36.

43. See notes 40 and 41.

place this verse has in the composition of the Third Gospel. It seems to us that in 9,51 Luke consciously marks the beginning of the second main part of the public life of Jesus. There are several indications which support this view.

1. There is a large consensus that Lk 9,51 is a redactional verse, built upon Mk 10,1.32[44]. This has been convincingly argued by G. Lohfink and J. Jeremias and their arguments need not be repeated here[45].

2. Having a solemn and biblical character, Lk 9,51 aptly serves as an introduction to a new section: "Stylistically, therefore, the aim of the writer seems to have been to sound an especially solemn note by an unusually strong concentration of biblical idioms"[46]. Many Lukan characteristics of this verse are in fact Septuagintisms: the threefold formula (i) ἐγένετο δέ ... (ii) ἐν with infinitive... (iii) καὶ αὐτός ... ἐστήρισεν; συμπληροῦσθαι τὰς ἡμέρας; τὸ πρόσωπον στηρίζειν; abundant τοῦ with infinitive after verbs of intention, decision, exhortation, command, etc.; (ἀπέστειλεν ἀγγέλους) πρὸ προσώπου αὐτοῦ.

3. Luke likes to create introductions which open not only one pericope, but two or more. We consider these introductions with double or triple function to be a Lukan device. By this means Luke links isolated pericopes to each other. This seems to be also true for Lk 9,51. We give a short survey of the eight cases in the third gospel:

Lc 5,17 amplifies Mc 2,1-2 and anticipates elements from Mk 2,6 (ἦσαν δὲ τινες τῶν γραμματέων ἐκεῖ καθήμενοι) and Mk 2,13, the introduction of the following pericope. The motif of teaching καὶ αὐτὸς ἦν διδάσκων could be a combination of Mk 2,2 καὶ ἐλάλει αὐτοῖς τὸν λόγον and of Mk 2,13 καὶ ἐδίδασκεν αὐτους. The addition of οἳ ἦσαν ἐληλυθότες ἐκ πάσης κώμης may be inspired by Mk 2,13 καὶ πᾶς ὁ ὄχλος ἤρχετο πρὸς αὐτόν. Moreover the Lukan introduction 5,27, parallel to Mk 2,13, omits from the Markan text what

44. K.L. SCHMIDT, *Rahmen* (n. 21), p. 260: "Es bleiben für die Erörterung noch die genauen Ortsangaben übrig. Bei vier dieser Angaben handelt es sich um Perikopeneinleitungen, die von Lk geschaffen sind. Besonders greifbar ist das gleich bei der ersten Notiz 9,51"; I.H. MARSHALL, *The Gospel of Luke* (NICNT), Exeter, 1978, p. 403: "The opening verse of the pericope sets the theme of the whole 'travel' section, and is probably to be ascribed to Luke himself"; J. FITZMYER, *Luke* I (n. 31), p. 826: "v. 51 is almost certainly Lucan composition, with its characteristic wording and the markedly christological motif of Jesus fixedly facing his Jerusalem destiny, a note that only Luke has".

45. G. LOHFINK, *Die Himmelfahrt Jesu* (SANT, 26), München, 1971, pp. 215-217, enumerates eight Lukan characteristics in Lk 9,51-52a: ἐγένετο δέ; ἐν with substantivised infinitive; συμπληροῦσθαι τὰς ἡμέρας; τὰς ἡμέρας τῆς ἀναλήμψεως; καὶ αὐτός; τὸ πρόσωπον ἐστήρισεν; τοῦ πορεύεσθαι; ἀπέστειλεν ἀγγέλους πρὸ προσώπου αὐτοῦ. J. JEREMIAS, *Die Sprache des Lukasevangeliums* (KEK), Göttingen, 1980, p. 179: has the same characteristics except one: he does not mention τὸ πρόσωπον στηρίζειν, but he adds Ἰερουσαλήμ; in 52a he considers πρὸ προσώπου αὐτοῦ as a redactional expression.

46. C.F. EVANS, *Central Section* (n. 15), p. 38.

has been anticipated in 5,17. Only an expression of time μετὰ ταῦτα is added to connect the episode of the call of Levi to the preceding pericope. This confirms our impression that Lk 5,17 not only introduces Lk 5,17-26, but also Lk 5,27ff. Lk 8,1-3 seems to be a redactional introduction[47] to the whole section 8,1-21. These verses take their place within the Lukan motif of the authentic witnesses who must have accompanied Jesus from Galilee on (cp. Lk 23,5.49.55; 24,6-10.22-24; Acts 13,31). After having introduced the principal witnesses, the disciples (5,1-11), and the Twelve (6,13), Luke now introduces the secondary witnesses, the women (8,1-3). Mk 4,10 οἱ περὶ αὐτὸν σὺν τοῖς δώδεκα could have suggested the place of 8,1-3. Luke seems to take up fragments from Mk 4,1 and 4,10-11, which he combines. He further omits the Markan elements which could interrupt the unity of 8,1-21: compare Mk 4,1 and Lk 8,4; 4,4 and 8,5; 4,10 and 8,9; 4,13 and 8,11; 4,21 and 8,16; 4,24 and 8,18.

Lk 11,15 par. Mt 12,24 (cp. Mk 3,22) together with Lk 11,16 par. Mt 12,38. Luke combines the two introductions in Q (cp. Mt 12,24.38) into one by anticipating the second. Lk 11,15-16 is an introduction with a double function: it introduces the pericopes 11,17-26 and 11,29-32.

Lk 12,1 not only introduces the exhortation to fearless confession (12,2-12), but, by mentioning the multitude and by means of the word πρῶτον, the following pericope (12,13-21) is already announced. The multitude is present from the beginning, but Jesus first addresses his disciples (12,2-12), and then somebody from the crowd intervenes (12,13).

Lk 13,22-23; Lk 13,22 does not introduce only or even primarily the logia of 13,24-30, but announces rather 13,31-35; the introduction proper to 13,24-30 is given in 13,23: the logia of 13,24-30 are presented as Jesus' answer to the question of the anonymous person.

Lk 17,11-12a not only introduces the pericope of the ten lepers (17,12-19), but these verses place the following pericopes in the framework of the journey to Jerusalem, up to the topographic notices of 18,31 (going up to Jerusalem) and 18,35 (Jericho).

Lk 19,11-12a introduces in the first place the parable of the pounds (19,12-28), but at the same time also the final stage of the travel narrative (19,11-44).

This redactional technique seems to have been applied to Lk 9,51 also: this verse fulfils a triple function. First of all it introduces the pericope immediately following (9,51-56): the Samaritans refuse to receive Jesus because he has set his face towards Jerusalem. But Lk 9,51 introduces also the whole narrative of Jesus' journey to Jerusalem (9,51-19,44): for the first time we hear about Jesus' decision to go up to the holy city. This firm decision creates a dramatic tension that reaches its tragic climax when Jesus approaches the city which refuses to receive the heavenly Visitor. Finally, by mentioning the perspective of the "assumption" (ἀνάλημψις), verse 9,51 announces the second main part of the Gospel (9,51-24,53), which also ends with the motif of the

---

47. The redactional terminology of Lk 8,1-3 has been examined by J. DELOBEL, *L'onction par la pécheresse. La composition littéraire de Lc., VII, 36-50*, in *ETL* 42 (1966) 415-475, spec. 445-449.

ascension. Lk 9,51 finds its completion (cf. 13,32) only in the events of the day of ch. 24, notably 24,51 (cf. Acts 1,9-10a). The structural significance of 9,51 is seen undeniably in Acts 1,2.11.22 (ἀναλαμβάνεσ-θαι) and may be said to function as a title of 9,51–24,53 ("Überschrift-funktion")[48].

4. The ἀνάλημψις motif.

The assertion that Lk 9,51 has a triple introductory function, depends much on the interpretation one gives to the word ἀνάλημψις. The ascent of Jesus to Jerusalem, which means his going up to the place of rejection, passion and death, is placed within the perspective of the "ἀνάλημψις". What is the exact meaning of this hapax? Three interpretations have been given. (i) Most scholars give it a very broad meaning: Jesus' ἀνάλημψις refers to the whole chain of events (passion, crucifixion, resurrection) leading up to his ascension[49]. But it seems to me that this is rather the meaning of the whole verse. The idea of Jesus' prophetic death may be implied already in the expression "he steadfastly set his face to go to Jerusalem"[50], and it could be that the plural

48. Many scholars recognise that Lk 9,51 functions as a title of a larger section, but they limit its "Überschrift" function to the "travel narrative": J. SCHMID, Lucas (RNT, 3), Regensburg, ⁴1960, ad loc.; J. SCHNEIDER, Zur Analyse (n. 21), p. 212; G. LOHFINK, Himmelfahrt (n. 45), p. 217; G. SELLIN, Komposition (n. 14), p. 104. In our opinion, Lk 9,51, because of the ἀνάλημψις motif, functions as the title of the second main section of Lk 9,51-24,53.

49. J.L. RESSEGUIE, Interpretation (n. 15), p. 30, n. 156, refers to the commentaries of G.C. Caird, J.M. Creed, N. Geldenhuys, W. Grundmann, E. Klostermann, W. Manson, K.H. Rengstorf, A. Schlatter, M.A. Tolbert, and T. Zahn, and to the studies of J. Dupont, D. Gill, G. Lohfink, I.H. Marshall, E. Kränkl, B. Reicke, K.L. Schmidt, H. Schürmann, P.A. van Stempvoort. But it should be added that P.A. VAN STEMPVOORT, The Interpretation of the Ascension in Luke and Acts, in NTS 5 (1958-59) 30-42, p. 33, does not accept the technical meaning of "Ascension": "Acts i.2 do not speak about the 'ascension' in the developed sense, but about the 'passing away and being taken up' in the sense of Luke ix.51. It distorts the whole meaning of Acts i.2 and Luke ix.51, to interpret them in the later technical terminology of the Church". P.A. van Stempvoort should rather be classified among the defenders of the second interpretation: the normal meaning of ἀνάλη(μ)ψις and ἀναλαμβάνεσθαι in the time of Luke and the first centuries is "to die, to be taken up in the sense of to pass away, removal out of this world". We could add G. SELLIN, Reisebericht (n. 14), p. 134, n. 115: "Für Lk. ix.51 selbst ist die Alternative Tod (so FRIEDRICH) oder Himmelfahrt (so VON DER OSTEN-SACKEN) freilich zu eng: der ganze Weg durch Leiden und Tod bis in den Himmel wird gemeint sein: cp. DAVIES; LOHFINK, 213ff.".

50. According to C.A. EVANS, "He Set His Face": A Note on Luke 9,51, in Bib 63 (1982) 545-548; "He Set His Face": Luke 9,51 Once Again, in Bib 68 (1987) 80-84: the biblical expression "he set his face" certainly means "resolute determination" of "firm resolve" (so most commentators), but may in addition connote the sense of judgment (cf. Ez 21,2-6) and of dispatch: "It is not simply that Jesus has made up his mind to go to Jerusalem, but that he has been sent by God to the city and has been given a message of judgment" (p. 548). That the expression has a polemic undertone is not impossible, as is shown by the usage στηρίζειν τὸ πρόσωπον ἐπί in Ezekiel 6,2; 13,17; 21,2.(7); 25,2; 28,21; 38,2, but the preposition ἐπί is lacking in Lk 9,51 and the idea of "violent death"

ἡμέραι has a broader meaning than the genitive ἀναλήμψεως. This majority interpretation looks rather like a compromise between the two following interpretations which exclude each other. (ii) Critics like J. Schmid, G. Friedrich[51] and even P.A. van Stempvoort believe that ἀνάλημψις refers only to Jesus' death. Their conclusion is partly based on the fact that in pre-New Testament times ἀνάλημψις never meant ascension[52]. But does this suffice to exclude the meaning of ascension in Lk 9,51? When one tries to define the exact meaning of ἀνάλημψις in Lk 9,51, should not more weight be given to the Septuagint which Luke certainly knew and used[53] and above all to the Lukan context itself (i.e. Luke-Acts) rather than to remote non Biblical texts? (iii) Several scholars, however, interpret ἀνάλημψις in the sense of (bodily) "ascension"[54]. It seems to me that this is the only possible meaning here, a meaning which is specific to Luke: he is the only New Testament author who distinguishes Jesus' resurrection-exaltation from his bodily ascension. The arguments which convince are the following:

(a) As we said above, the word group ἀνάλημψις/ἀναλαμβάνεσθαι in Luke is the primary context in which to define the meaning of ἀνάλημψις in Lk 9,51. The hapax ἀνάλημψις should be interpreted first of all in the light of Luke's specific use of the verb ἀναλαμβάνεσθαι in the beginnings of Acts. Luke himself thinks clearly of a bodily, visible ascension of Jesus into heaven at the end of his gospel (24,51: καὶ ἀνεφέρετο εἰς τὸν οὐρανόν) and in the first chapter of Acts (1,9-10a: ἐπήρθη καὶ νεφέλη ὑπέλαβεν αὐτὸν ἀπὸ τῶν ὀφθαλμῶν αὐτῶν.

and thus of prophetic judgment is implied already in the expression "to go up to Jerusalem" (cf. Lk 13,31-35; 18,31-34).

51. J. SCHMID, Lukas (n. 48), p. 176; G. FRIEDRICH, Lk. 9,51 und die Entrückungschristologie des Lukas, in P. HOFFMANN, e.a. (eds.), Orientierung an Jesus. Zur Theologie der Synoptiker. FS J. Schmid, Freiburg, 1973, pp. 48-77. G. LOHFINK, Himmelfahrt (n. 45), p. 212, n. 1 mentions C.H. Weisse, W. Michaelis, K.L. Schmidt and J. Schmid as earlier defenders of this meaning, and concludes on p. 217: "Die ἀνάλημψις von Lk 9,51 meint zunächst und in erster Linie den Tod Jesu. Wie die theologische Programmatik der Reise zeigt, ist der Begriff jedoch auch auf die Himmelfahrt hin geöffnet".

52. G. FRIEDRICH, art. cit., p. 71; W. BAUER, Wörterbuch zum NT, 1988, k. 112, does not exclude this meaning of "Tod, Hinscheiden" in PsSal 4,18, a Christian inscription from Aphrodisias: Byzantion 2,'26.331 and Ps. Clem. Hom. 3,47, although he prefers clearly the meaning of "Ascension" in Lk 9,51. P.A. VAN STEMPVOORT, Ascension (n. 49), p. 32 refers to W. Bauer and adds a series of other texts supporting this meaning.

53. The verb ἀναλαμβάνεσθαι is used in the LXX to describe the "assumption" of Henoch (Sir 49,14) and Elijah (4 Kgs 2,9-11; 1 Macc 2,58; Sir 48,9).

54. For ἀνάλημψις in the sense of "Himmelfahrt", G. LOHFINK, Himmelfahrt (n. 45), p. 212, n. 2 refers to H. OLSHAUSEN, Biblischer Commentar I,585; W.M.L. DE WETTE, Kurze Erklärung, p. 77; A. PLUMMER, Luke, p. 262; and P. SCHUBERT, The Structure and Significance of Luke 24, in Neutestamentliche Studien für R. Bultmann (BZNW, 21), 1954, pp. 165-186, spec. 184: "When the time leading to his ascension was in process of fulfilment". See also P. VON DER OSTEN-SACKEN, Christologie (n. 24), pp. 479-480, esp. n. 21 (refutation of G. Friedrich) and 22 (predecessors); W. BAUER (n. 52); J.G. DAVIES, He Ascended into Heaven, London, 1958, p. 40.

καὶ ὡς ἀτενίζαντες ἦσαν εἰς τὸν οὐρανὸν πορευομένου αὐτοῦ). The verb ἀναλαμβάνεσθαι in Acts 1,11.22 clearly refers back to the description of Acts 1,9-10a and Acts 1,2 should also be interpreted in the same sense[55]. In Lk 24,51 and Acts 1,9-10a Luke himself indicates undoubtedly how he understands the verb. To him it means nothing more than the bodily ascension of Jesus into heaven. Now it seems plausible that when Lukes uses spontaneously the noun ἀνάλημψις in Lk 9,51, the hapax clearly refers to the verb ἀναλαμβάνειν and has therefore the same meaning.

(b) Yet one could object that Acts 1 is a more remote context than the travel narrative and the whole verse 9,51. This is true, but a more thorough look at the structure of Lk 9,51 seems rather to confirm our previous argument. J.H. Davies has remarked that in Luke-Acts several key events are introduced by verses of similar structure: "when the time of X was fulfilled, Y occurred", Y being the action appropriate to X[56]:

Lk 1,57
Τῇ δὲ Ἐλισάβετ   ἐπλήσθη   ὁ χρόνος   τοῦ τεκεῖν αὐτήν,
καὶ ἐγέννησεν υἱόν.

Lk 2,6-7
                  ἐπλήσθησαν   αἱ ἡμέραι   τοῦ τεκεῖν αὐτήν,
καὶ ἔτεκεν τὸν υἱὸν αὐτῆς τὸν πρωτότοκον.

Lk 2,21
Καὶ ὅτε   ἐπλήσθησαν   ἡμέραι ὀκτὼ   τοῦ περιτεμεῖν αὐτόν,
καὶ ἐκλήθη τὸ ὄνομα αὐτοῦ Ἰησοῦς.

Lk 2,22
Καὶ ὅτε   ἐπλήσθησαν   αἱ ἡμέραι   τοῦ καθαρισμοῦ αὐτῶν κτλ.
ἀνήγαγον αὐτὸν εἰς Ἱεροσόλυμα παραστῆσαι τῷ κυρίῳ.

Acts 2,1-4 Καὶ
            ἐν τῷ συμπληροῦσθαι   τὴν ἡμέραν   τῆς πεντηκοστῆς
ἦσαν πάντες ὁμοῦ ἐπὶ τὸ αὐτό. Καὶ ἐγένετο ἄφνω κτλ.

Lk 9,51 Ἐγένετο δὲ
            ἐν τῷ συμπληροῦσθαι τὰς ἡμέρας   τῆς ἀναλήμψεως αὐτοῦ
καὶ αὐτὸς τὸ πρόσωπον ἐστήρισεν τοῦ πορεύεσθαι εἰς Ἰερουσαλήμ.

Davies' division of the structure in two parts, which in itself makes sense, sets him on a false track of interpretation. We prefer to distinguish three elements in the formula. First, there is (i) a time or a period (ἡμέρα[ι]; χρόνος) of fulfilment: the finite aorist tense (ἐπλήσθη[σαν])

55. So rightly J. DUPONT, ΑΝΕΛΗΜΦΘΗ, in *NTS* 8 (1961-62) 154-157, p. 156 (= *Études sur les Actes de Apôtres* [LD, 45], Paris, 1967, pp. 477-480) against P. VAN STEMPVOORT.

56. J.H. DAVIES, *Purpose* (n. 15), p. 165: "In 9,51 X is Jesus' ἀνάλημψις, and Y is his setting his face to journey to Jerusalem. The turning to Jerusalem is his deliberate commencement of the ἀνάλημψις, which comprises the entire movement of Jesus from this world to heaven".

suggests that the period has come to an end, while the two cases with an infinitive in the present tense (συμπληροῦσθαι) suggest rather that the period has arrived or is at least not yet completed. Secondly, there is (ii) the term, a precise moment which forms the purpose and the end of that period. Most commentators understand the genitive completing the notion of time as epexegetic or of quality, and it must be conceded that the cases with a notion of time in the singular (Lk 1,57; Acts 2,1) strongly suggest this. But the parallelism with Lk 2,6 shows that χρόνος in Lk 1,57 can mean a period of several ἡμέραι, which should be distinguished from the moment of bearing which normally does not take several days! Thus in Lk 9,51 the complement should rather be taken as a genitive of direction and purpose, as this is the case in Lk 1,57; 2,6[57]. In Acts 2,1 it is not clear how the pentecostal event, i.e. the pouring out of the Spirit, is understood to be related to the day on which this takes place. So in that case we may indeed have to do with an epexegetic genitive[58]. Finally (iii), we have the element Y being the action appropriate to X. Lk 2,22 is especially illuminating: a period of several days has come to fulfilment, the purpose of which is the purification and the action appropriate to it is the leading of the child to Jerusalem. In light of all this we may interpret Lk 9,51 as follows: Jesus' decision to part towards Jerusalem (Y) initiates a period of fulfilment (αἱ ἡμέραι, including the whole of Jesus' further life: journey, passion, death, resurrection and ascension), of which the ascension is the final purpose (X). A literal translation of Lk 9,51 would give: "And it happened, when the days leading to his ascension were in process of fulfilment (or: had arrived), that he steadfastly set his face to go to Jerusalem".

57. So for Lk 9,51, P. SCHUBERT, *Structure* (n. 54) p. 184, n. 32, with reference to BDF, § 166. The infinitives τοῦ τεκεῖν in Lk 1,57; 2,6 and τοῦ περιτεμεῖν in 2,21 (where the circumcision itself does not last for 8 days!) could also represent a genitive of purpose. This is rightly seen by G. Lohfink (*Himmelfahrt*, p. 214) with regard to Lk 1,57 and esp. 2,6, which he translates "es erfüllten sich die Tage *im Hinblick* auf ihres Gebärens". But unfortunately Lohfink does not reckon with the possibility that Lk 9,51 uses the same kind of genitive. The nearest parallel to Lk 2,6 is Gen 25,24 καὶ ἐπληρώθησαν αἱ ἡμέραι τοῦ τεκεῖν αὐτήν, which renders the Hebrew וַיִּמְלְאוּ יָמֶיהָ לָלֶדֶת. Compare Jer 32,34LXX ὅτι ἐπληρώθησαν αἱ ἡμέραι ὑμῶν εἰς σφαγήν, which renders 25,34MT כִּי־מָלְאוּ יְמֵיכֶם לִטְבוֹחַ, where we have the same preposition *le*. For Lk 2,22, see Lev 12,4.6. The LXX uses for the expression "the days were fulfilled" the verb πληροῦσθαι: cf. Gen 25,24; 29,21; Lev 12,4.(6); Num 6,5.(13); 1 Sam 18,26; 2 Kgs 7,12; 1 Chron 17,11; Tob 8,20; 10,1; (14,5); Jer (25,12); 25,34; Luke has a preference for πλησθῆναι (1,23.57; 2,6.21.22), but in Lk 21,24; Acts 7,23.30; 9,23; 13,25 he uses πληροῦσθαι and in Lk 9,51; Acts 2,1 he has συμπληροῦσθαι.

58. This is more probable if we consider that πεντεκοστή originally meant "the fiftiest (day)". Τῆς πεντεκοστῆς in Acts 2,1 is probably an appositive genitive (BDF, § 167): in that case ἡμέρα τῆς πεντεκοστῆς means literally "the day which is the fiftiest day" or "the day which is the pentecostal day".

(c) Sometimes the parallelism with the term ἔξοδος in Lk 9,31 is invoked to support a broader meaning of ἀνάλημψις in Lk 9,51[59]. No one can deny that the correspondence between those verses is deliberate and close[60]. But that does not justify us in assimilating both concepts to each other. For Luke, ἔξοδος refers to Jesus' death[61] and ἀνάλημψις means his "ascension". The correspondence between Lk 9,51 and 9,31 is complementary not confusing.

(d) Our interpretation of ἀνάλημψις in the sense of "ascension" has consequences for our understanding of the theology as well as of the structure of Luke's Gospel. The mention of the ascension motif right at the opening verse of the travel narrative means that Luke sees Jesus' journey to Jerusalem from the very beginning in the light of the Ascension. The way of the Messiah does not end in Jerusalem, but in heaven. The cluster "journey, passion, guilt and destination of Jerusalem"[62] is complemented by another complex "journey, kingdom of God, resurrection, ascension"[63]. Because of this overall perspective of the ascension, I also think that the second main part of Luke's Gospel covers the whole section 9,51 till 24,53 and that the "classical" tripartite delineation does not do justice to Luke's editorial composition[64]. Of

59. According to G. Lohfink (*Himmelfahrt* [n. 45], pp. 213-214) the principal meaning of both ἔξοδος and ἀνάλημψις is "death", but both words are open concepts and connote the idea of "assumption" ("Entrückung"). A. BÜCHELE, *Der Tod Jesu* (n. 24), p. 149, esp. n. 222, rightly states against Lohfink that 9,51 (1. aspect: exaltation/glorification) complements 9,31 (1. aspect: Jesus' passion and death), but still accepts with Lohfink that both ἔξοδος and ἀνάλημψις refer to a "complex process" which combines the two aspects of Jesus' passion/death and glorification (resurrection and exaltation).

60. P. SCHUBERT, *Structure* (n. 57), pp. 184-185.

61. For a short survey of the discussion about the meaning of ἔξοδος in Lk 9,31, see J. FITZMYER, *Luke* I-IX (n. 31), p. 800.

62. H. CONZELMANN, *Mitte* (n. 21), p. 125: "Reise, Passion, Schuld der Juden und (von da zu verstehen!) Geschick der Stadt bilden einen festen Komplex".

63. So P. VON DER OSTEN-SACKEN, *Christologie* (n. 24), pp. 477-478. C.H. TALBERT, *Literary Patterns* (n. 7), pp. 112-116, points in the right direction stressing the fact that the ascension motif in Lk 9,51 opens a perspective which runs throughout the remaining chapters of Luke, although he also seems to give an overly comprehensive sense to the concept "ascension": "At least from Luke 9:51 everything in the Third Gospel moves toward ascension... This Lucan connection between Jesus' journey to Jerusalem and his ascension means that for the Third Evangelist the journey is the first part of that ascent to heaven which he calls Jesus' ἀνάλημψις. To regard the journey as the first stage of the ascension means that in Luke the death and resurrection of Jesus are viewed in an ascension framework. They are further stages in the ascent. For Luke the ascension motif includes Jesus' death-burial-resurrection. The very structure of the Third Gospel demands such a reading".

64. Accepting an overall dynamic from 9,51 till the end of the Gospel, does justice to the fragment of truth in the views of Samain (see n. 37) and Lambrecht (see n. 39), the Jerusalem motif of course being present also after 19,44; it also meets some remarks on the relation between Lk 9,51 and Acts 2,1 made by Prof. U. Busse during the seminar. But the travel narrative cannot therefore be extended from Lk 9,51 to Acts 2,1. Cf. EGELKRAUT, *Jesus' Mission* (n. 26), p. 10, n. 5.

course, this second main part can be divided into several subsections, of which the "travel narrative" (9,51-19,44) is but one.

5. From a narrative point of view, it must be said that Lk 9,51 evokes a situation very different from the one before. In the first part of the Gospel (Lk 3,1-9,50) it is said that Jesus is always on the way, preaching the Good News, beginning from Galilee, and through the whole of Judaea (4,42-44). He has no precise geographic goal in mind. One may speak of a "tour of preaching" (the programme of 4,42-44 is worked out in 5,1.12.15; 6,1.17; 7,1.11; 8,1). From 9,51 on this changes. Jesus fixes his eyes very consciously on a definite purpose: the city of Jerusalem (cf. the expression στηρίζειν τὸ πρόσωπον). He never loses sight of that goal. The repeated travel notices (13,22; 17,11; 19,11.28) suggest that Jesus carries out the decision he has taken once and for all. Instead of the foregoing "tour of preaching", from 9,51 on we have a "travel situation"[65].

2. The Structural Function of the καὶ ἐγένετο-Formula

The threefold καὶ ἐγένετο-formula with which Lk 9,51 opens the travel narrative is one of the specific characteristics of the Lukan style. It occurs no less than 38 times in his gospel[66] and may be considered a Septuagintism which Luke likes to insert in his narration[67]. Because the expression is found no less than 26 times at the beginning of a pericope, F. Neirynck has stressed the importance of the formula for the struc-

---

65. R. MEYNET, *Luc* II, Paris, 1988, pp. 205-206, who develops a rhetorical approach to Luke, points to other differences between Lk 3,1-9,50 and Lk 9,51-21,38: Lk 3,1-9,50 (642 lines) often brings the couple "to teach/to cure"; the section does have teachings but still more healings or manifestations of power (15x). In 9,51-21,38 (1059 lines) only five healings are mentioned (some of them are very short); the section is constituted mainly by words of Jesus, his teaching being almost always a response or a reaction; the healings and manifestations of power are replaced by the perspective and acceptance of passion and death.

66. The references are: 1,8-9; 1,23; 1,41; 1,59; 2,1; 2,6; 2,15; 2,46 // 3,21-22; 5,1-2; 5,12; 5,17-18; 6,1; 6,6; 6,12; 7,11; 8,1; 8,22; 9,18; 9,28; 9,33; 9,37 // 9,51; 11,1; 11,14b; 11,27; 14,1-2; 16,22; 17,11-12; 17,14b; 18,35; 19,15; 19,29; 20,1; 24,4; 24,15; 24,30; 24,51.

67. Cf. M. JOHANNESSOHN, *Das biblische KAI ΕΓΕΝΕΤΟ und seine Geschichte*, in *Zeitschrift für vergleichende Sprachforschung* 53 (1925) 161-212; K. BEYER, *Semitische Syntax zum neuen Testament*. Band I, *Satzlehre* Teil 1, Göttingen, 1962, pp. 29-62; F. NEIRYNCK, *La matière marcienne dans l'évangile de Luc*, in ID. *L'évangile de Luc* (BETL, 32), Gembloux, 1973, pp. 157-201 (= ID., *Evangelica* [BETL, 60], Leuven, 1982, pp. 37-83, esp. pp. 64-73). These authors distinguish three parts in the formula: (i) introduction (καὶ ἐγένετο or ἐγένετο δέ); (ii) expression of time, and (iii) apodosis. In the light of the observations made above, it would be preferable to give a broader title to the second part of the formula, because it has more connotations than only a temporal one. Neirynck (pp. 191-193, resp. 71-73) also gives a very useful presentation of the Greek text of all the occurrences.

ture of Luke[68]. Leaving aside the introductory stories (1,1-4; 1,5–2,52; 3,1-20), he distinguishes 3 parts in the gospel: 3,21–9,50: Jesus in Galilee; 9,51–19,28: the going up to Jerusalem; 19,29–24,53: Jesus in Jerusalem[69]. Each part begins with the ἐγένετο-formula and, within the three parts, the formula often has a structural function. In the first part: nearly all the larger subsections are marked by ἐγένετο (cp. the references in italics): *3,21–4,44; 5,1–6,11* (and within: *5,1.12.17; 6,1.6*); *6,12-49; 7,1-50; 8,1-21; 8,22-56*; 9,1-17; *9,18-27; 9,28-36; 9,37-45.46-50.* In the second part: the usage is less systematic but the formula still opens several subsections: *11,1-13; 11,14-36* (and *11,27-28); 14,1-35; 17,11-19.* A tripartite division of the central section (9,51ff.; 13,22ff.; 17,11ff.) would even draw more attention to the last usage in 17,11. In Lk 18,35, the beginning of the Marcan story of the healing of the blind man (Mk 10,46-52) becomes the opening of a larger section 18,35–19,28. So the formula stands in a good position there. Finally, in the third part: *19,29-48; 20,1–21,38; 22,1–24,53.* In chapter 24, the articulations of the stories are marked by καὶ ἐγένετο: see v. 4 for 24,1-12; vv. 15 and 30 for 24,13-35; and v. 51 for 24,36-53. One recognises a similar literary function of the formula in the transfiguration story (9,33), and in the healing of the ten lepers (17,14b), in the parable of the pounds (19,15, add. Mt), and in several places of the infancy stories: 1,8.23.41 and 59, and after 2,1 (!) in 2,6.15.46 (cp. the remaining case: 16,22: within the parable, the formula has the same function as in the narratives).

I generally would agree with Neirynck's observation that the ἐγένετο-formula plays an important structuring role in Luke. However, in itself, the ἐγένετο-formula is not sufficient to indicate the beginning of a new pericope, section or part: (a) other factors should be taken into account (content, change of time, place, characters, etc.) to delineate a text unit; and (b) some pericopes, subsections (and maybe also parts) do not have the ἐγένετο-formula. Thus the ἐγένετο-formula should not be the only nor an exclusive criterion of structure; it has but a supplementary cogency. To delineate the divisions of the gospels one should look first for other criteria.

At first sight there seem to be two series of the καὶ ἐγένετο-formula: (i) text units where the ἐγένετο-formula is clearly put at the beginning

---

68. F. NEIRYNCK, *art. cit.*, pp. 64-66, gives (p. 64) the corrected list of Grobel (*Formgeschichte und synoptische Quellenanalyse* [FRLANT, 53], Göttingen, 1937, p. 73): (1) ἐγένετο + καί + verb. fin. (10/12): 5,1.12.27; 8,1.22; 9,28[?].51; 14,1; 17,11; 24,15 (other usages, not at the beginning: 19,15; 24,4) (2) ἐγένετο + verb. fin. (12/21): 1,41; 2,1; 7,11; 9,18.37; 11,1.14.27; 17,35; 18,35; 19,29; 20,1; 24,51 (other usages, not at the beginning: 1,8.23.59; 2,6.15.46; 9,33; 17,14; 24,30) (3) ἐγένετο + infin. (4/5): 3,21 (cfr. Mc); 6,1 (= Mk); 6,6.12 (other usage, not at the beginning: 16,22).

69. Here he depends on A. GEORGE, *Construction* (n. 4), pp. 100-129.

of a pericope, section, or part; (ii) and cases where the ἐγένετο-formula occurs within a text unit. Grobel and Neirynck recognize a non-introductory usage in 1,8.23.59; 2,6.15.46; 9,33; 16,22; 17,14; 19,15; 24,4.30. Their list may be completed with 1,41; 11,14b; 24,15 and 24,51, so that only 22 of the 38 usages serve as an introduction. For the second series Neirynck tries to show that they fulfil at least a structural function *within* the story.

We would like to point to another feature of the καὶ ἐγένετο-formula which arises from a more narrative-critical approach and which has some consequences for the question of structure. In most of the cases belonging to the second series, the ἐγένετο-formula occurs after an introductory part of the text unit, where a general situation is described or, more precisely, where the necessary conditions are given for the narrative action to be possible. The action proper is then introduced by the ἐγένετο-formula. The second part of the formula takes up, often literally, elements of the foregoing general introductory description[70]. The formula indicates the very central point of the narrative. Compare:

1,5-7 (ἱερεύς τις ὀνόματι Ζαχαρίας ἐξ ἐφημερίας ... ἐναντίον τοῦ κυρίου) 8-9 (ἐν τῷ ἱερατεύειν αὐτὸν ἐν τῇ τάξει τῆς ἐφημερίας αὐτοῦ ἔναντι τοῦ θεοῦ)

1,39-40 (Μαριὰμ ἠσπάσατο τὴν Ἐλισάβετ) 41 (ὡς ἤκουσεν τὸν ἀσπασμὸν τῆς Μαρίας ἡ Ἐλισάβετ)

1,57-58 (ἐπλήσθη ὁ χρόνος) 1,59 (ἐν τῇ ἡμέρᾳ τῇ ὀγδόῃ)

2,1-5 (ἀνέβη δὲ καὶ Ἰωσὴφ ἀπὸ τῆς Γαλιλαίας ... εἰς Βηθλέεμ σὺν Μαριὰμ) 6-7 (ἐν τῷ εἶναι αὐτοὺς ἐκεῖ)

2,41-45 (ἡμέρας ὁδὸν ... ὑπέστρεψαν) 46 (μετὰ ἡμέρας τρεῖς)

11,14a (ἦν ἐκβάλλων δαιμόνιον) 14b (τοῦ δαιμονίου ἐξελθόντος)

16,19-21 (πλούσιος ... πτωχὸς ... ἐπιθυμῶν χορτασθῆναι) 22 (ἀποθανεῖν τὸν πτωχόν)

19,12-14 (ἄνθρωπός τις εὐγενὴς ἐπορεύθη εἰς χώραν μακρὰν λαβεῖν ἑαυτῷ βασιλείαν καὶ ὑποστρέψαι) 15 (ἐν τῷ ἐπανελθεῖν αὐτὸν λαβόντα τὴν βασιλείαν)

23,56b-24,3 (v. 55: αἱ γυναῖκες ... ἐθεάσαντο τὸ μνημεῖον καὶ ὡς ἐτέθη τὸ σῶμα αὐτοῦ; v. 3: οὐχ εὗρον τὸ σῶμα τοῦ κυρίου Ἰησοῦ) 4 (ἐν τῷ ἀπορεῖσθαι αὐτὰς περὶ τούτου)

24,13-14 (δύο ἐξ αὐτῶν ... καὶ αὐτοὶ ὡμίλουν πρὸς ἀλλήλους) 15 (ἐν τῷ ὁμιλεῖν αὐτοὺς καὶ συζητεῖν)

24,28-29 (μεῖνον μεθ' ἡμῶν ... καὶ κέκλικεν) 30 (ἐν τῷ κατακλιθῆναι αὐτὸν μετ' αὐτῶν)

24,50 (εὐλόγησεν αὐτούς) 51 (ἐν τῷ εὐλογεῖν αὐτὸν αὐτούς)

Apart from 1,23; 2,15 and 9,33 where the phenomenon does not occur[71], there remain two cases to be considered, which have some

70. Cf. the remark of M. JOHANNESSOHN, *Das biblische ΚΑΙ ΕΓΕΝΕΤΟ* (n. 67), p. 174: "Die Wiederaufnahme von bereits Erzählten mit Hilfe dieser Konstruktionen findet sich verhältnismässig selten"; he refers to 1 Kgs 5,3-4; 4 Kgs 2,8-9; 2 Chr 13,15; 2 Kgs 3,6. So Luke seems to have intensified this usage.

71. Within the Infancy Gospel, the remaining cases are: 1,23 (which announces the conclusion of the narrative) and 2,15 (which introduces a new element of the story), and within 3,1–9,50 the only case is 9,33 (transfiguration story). The phenomenon we observed above does not occur in these three texts. However, 1,23 could be more distantly related to 1,5.8; 2,15 to 2,13; and 9,33 to 9,30.

importance for the minor problems signaled above with respect to the extent of the travel narrative: the alternatives 19,27/28 and 19,44/46/48.

(a) How should we understand the connection of Lk 19,28 and 19,29? Should 19,28, together with 19,29, be taken as the introduction of the entry story? If the observations made above are right, then one would be inclined to say yes. The second part of the ἐγένετο-formula in 19,29 (ὡς ἤγγισεν εἰς Βηθφαγὴ καὶ Βηθανία[ν] πρὸς τὸ ὄρος τὸ καλούμενον Ἐλαιῶν), is in a certain sense a realization of the more general statement of 19,28 ἐπορεύετο ἔμπροσθεν ἀναβαίνων εἰς Ἱερο-σόλυμα. But on the other hand there are several indications that 19,28 forms a conclusion to the parable of the pounds, as I. de la Potterie has shown convincingly[72]. First, the adverb ἔμπροσθεν is a catchword linking vv. 27 and 28. Second, the formula καὶ εἰπὼν ταῦτα refers to what precedes, or even more precisely to the conclusion of the parable, which describes the punishment of the citizens by the king. The formula καὶ τοῦτο (ταῦτα) εἰπών occurs several times with Luke, either with the singular τοῦτο (Lk 23,46; 24,40; Acts 7,60), or with the plural ταῦτα (Acts 1,9; 28,29 var.). We may add: Acts 19,40; 20,36; 23,7 (τοῦτο); 26,30 var. and 27,35. In none of these cases does ταῦτα (τοῦτο) εἶπον mark the beginning of the pericope, and in some cases it forms clearly the conclusion (Acts 19,40) or it announces it (Acts 7,60; 20,36; 26,30 var.; 28,29 var.). One particular feature of Lk 19,29 is the word order καί + verb + demonstr. pron. In all other cases the order is the reverse. Maybe it is due to a parallelisation with 19,11 ἀκουόντων δὲ αὐτῶν ταῦτα. Third, although verse 28 marks the transition from a parable story into a journey story, Jesus' name is not mentioned. This suggests that the action of the king in the parable is continued in that of Jesus, who "goes up to Jerusalem", where he will be proclamed king by his disciples. Fourth, Luke does not use here the biblical name Ἰερουσαλήμ, but the profane term Ἱεροσόλυμα, to indicate the city which is guilty for not having accepted Jesus as the Lord. Fifth, verses 19,11 (διὰ τὸ ἐγγὺς εἶναι Ἰερουσαλὴμ αὐτόν) and 19,28 (ἀναβαίνων εἰς Ἱεροσόλυμα) seem to form an inclusion, the two forms of the name expressing two aspects of the role and the destiny of Jerusalem: as the Holy City and the city which refuses to receive Jesus as King. And finally, the structure of the pericope demands also the presence of v. 28. All this supports the view that vv. 19,28 still belongs to the parable and that the "entry-story" begins with 19,29.

(b) How to judge the combination of Lk 19,45-46.47-48 + 20,1? The cleansing of the temple (vv. 45-46) is the necessary precondition for the temple section 20,1–21,38, and specially the summary about the daily teaching in the temple (vv. 47-48) (καὶ ἦν διδάσκων τὸ καθ᾽ ἡμέραν ἐν τῷ ἱερῷ... ὁ λαὸς γὰρ ἅπας ἐξεκρέματο αὐτοῦ ἀκούων) forms the

---

72. I. DE LA POTTERIE, *Parabole* (n. 23), pp. 627-629.

general framework of the temple section. The second part of the καὶ ἐγένετο-formula in 20,1 (ἐν μιᾷ τῶν ἡμερῶν διδάσκοντος αὐτοῦ τὸν λάον ἐν τῷ ἱερῷ) resumes almost literally the summary in vv. 47-48. Therefore we are invited, in the light of what has been said above, to attach 19,45-46.47-48 to what follows rather than to what precedes. Moreover, the temple-section 19,(45-46).47-48–21,38 is framed by a literary inclusion 19,47-48 and 21,37-38, as has been remarked by several authors[73], and forms therefore a clearly defined text unit.

But other scholars prefer to attach 19,45-46 and 47-48 to the preceding "entry story" rather than to the following temple section. They invoke several reasons. First of all, the goal of the journey is the city. The journey is not ended until Jesus actually enters the city, and indeed, until he enters the temple itself. Lk 19,45a (καὶ εἰσελθὼν εἰς τὸ ἱερόν) represents the final travel notice, marking the end of the journey. But Lk 19,45a is linked grammatically to the notice of the expulsion of the merchants from the temple in 19,45b (εἰσελθὼν ... ἤρξατο ἐκβάλλειν) which is likewise linked to the citation in 19,46. The end of the travel narrative cannot therefore be placed before 19,46. Moreover, the teaching summary of Lk 19,47-48, with its climax of Jesus' rejection and acceptance, provides a more suitable conclusion to the travel narrative than 19,45-46 and has the character of a Lukan conclusion (cf. Lk 4,44; 21,37-38; 24,53). Thus Lk 19,45-48 forms a closely knit unit and it follows that the travel narrative's conclusion should be placed at 19,48. This is confirmed by Lk 20,1 whose wording (cf. its καὶ ἐγένετο-formula) corresponds better to Lk 9,51 than 19,45 or 19,47 and which forms therefore a worthy opening verse of the temple section[74].

Being firmly convinced that Lk 19,45-48 forms a closely knit unit, I cannot accept a sharp caesura between 19,46 and 19,47. So there remain but two possibilities: 19,45-48 is attached either to the preceding context or to the following context. Until now I defended the latter possibility, but I must admit that the arguments for joining this unit to the preceding context are also worth considering. Yet the arguments for joining it to the temple section are not disproved by them and retain their force. Maybe my feelings of perplexity can only be solved by accepting that Luke has here followed the principle of "intertwining" which Lucian of Samosata recommended to historians and which Luke seems to have applied also in the book of Acts[75]. If this be true, then

73. J. LAMBRECHT, Reading (n. 25), p. 589, esp. n.8: Lk 19,47-48: καὶ ἦν διδάσκων τὸ καθ᾽ ἡμέραν ἐν τῷ ἱερῷ [...] [...] ὁ λαὸς γὰρ ἅπας ἐξεκρέματο αὐτοῦ ἀκούων; Lk 21,37-38: ἦν δὲ ... διδάσκων τὰς ἡμέρας ἐν τῷ ἱερῷ [...] καὶ πᾶς ὁ λαὸς ὤρθριζεν πρὸς αὐτὸν ἐν τῷ ἱερῷ ἀκούειν αὐτοῦ.

74. See H.L. EGELKRAUT, Jesus' Mission (n. 26), pp. 7-10; and especially F. O'FEARGHAIL, Introduction (n. 4), pp. 48-51.

75. J. DUPONT, La question du plan des Actes à la lumière d'un texte de Lucien de Samosate, in NT 21 (1979) 220-231 (= ID., Nouvelles études sur les Actes des Apôtres [LD,

Lk 19,45-48 would interlace the travel narrative (Lk 9,51–19,48) and the temple section (Lk 19,45–21,38). But the main problem with which all those who defend Lk 19,44 or 46 or 48 as the end of the travel narrative are commonly confronted, has still to be considered: what is the place and the function of the so called "entry story" within the overall composition of Luke's Gospel? This will be done in our last paragraph (4.), but we must first look more thoroughly at the "travel notices" in general (3.).

3. The Function of the Travel Notices

The well known tension between the content (mainly teaching and discussion) and the framework (the so called "travel notices") of the "Central Section" in Luke cannot be solved by eliminating either the content or the framework. One can easily agree with the view that the framework is a literary device which the redactor of the Third Gospel has imposed upon the material he received from tradition and that therefore the "central section" does not offer an historical account of Jesus' journey to Jerusalem. However this view does not allow us to eliminate the journey framework as something unimportant in Luke's composition. It plays a decisive role in the organisation of the narrative of his Gospel. It also shows both Luke's dependence on Mark and at the same time his independence in composition.

1. Luke's journey motif has indeed been inspired by Mark 10,1-52. Luke shows knowledge of the Markan travel notices 10,1.17a.32a. (33).46a; 11,1a. Although the verses Mk 10,1.17.32a do not have a direct parallel in Luke, Mk 10,1.17 may have influenced Lk 17,11-12a, and Mk 10,32 has an echo in Lk 19,28. Mk 10,33 (ἰδοὺ ἀναβαίνομεν εἰς Ἰεροσόλυμα) finds its direct parallel in Lk 18,31, and the mention of Jesus' passage through Jericho in Mk 10,46 is taken over in Lk 18,35 and 19,1. The motif (ἐγγίζουσιν) εἰς Ἰεροσόλυμα in Mk 11,1 does not figure in the corresponding verse Lk 19,29, but Luke anticipates it in the inclusion framing the parable of the pounds: Lk 19,11 (διὰ τὸ ἐγγὺς

118], Paris, 1984), p. 29: Lucian describes this rule of "intertwining of facts" (ἡ συμπεριπλοκὴ τῶν πραγμάτων) as follows: the historian "fera que tout soit accompli et achevé: après avoir épuisé le premier point, il amènera le second, rattaché au premier et lié à la manière (des anneaux) d'une chaîne, en sorte qu'il n'y ait pas d'interruption (hôs mè diakekophthai) ni plusieurs récits juxtaposés l'un à l'autre (mèdé diègèseis pollas eînai allèlais parakeiménas), mais que toujours le premier point non seulement voisine avec le second, mais communique avec lui et qu'ils soient mêlés par leurs extrémités (all'aei to prôton tôi deutérôi mè geitniân monon, alla kai koinôneîn kai anakekrâsthai kata ta akra)". Note the parallelism between the judgment of the citizens by the king in the parable 19,27 and the judgment of Jerusalem by Jesus in 19,41-44. What is more, the whole parable Lk 19,11-28 and the so called "Entry in Jerusalem" (Lk 19,29-44) elucidate and explain each other. This invites us to attach Lk 19,29-44 rather to what precedes than to what follows.

εἶναι Ἰερουσαλήμ) and Lk 19,28 (καὶ εἰπὼν ταῦτα ἐπορεύετο ἔμπροσ-θεν ἀναβαίνων εἰς Ἱεροσόλυμα). All this clearly shows Luke's depen-dence on Mark.

Many scholars consider Lk 19,29 (or 19,28) as the beginning of a new section because this verse is parallel to Mk 11,1, which in the Second Gospel opens the Jerusalem section[76]. But here R.A. Edwards' distinc-tion between emendation criticism and composition criticism should be called to mind[77]. From the correct source-critical observation that Luke 19,29 is dependent on Mk 11,1 it does not follow automatically that Lk 19,29 has the same structural function in Luke as Mk 11,1 does in Mark. Here we should give more weight to composition criticism, which is also an essential aspect of redaction criticism. And in this sense synchronic readings could enrich and equilibrate a redaction criticism which is too narrowly based on source- or emendation criticism.

Indeed, W.C. Robinson has already observed that the travel notices continue even after 19,27, pointing to verses 28-29, 36-37, 41, and 45[78]. So we have an impressive concentration of travel notices from 18,31 on. They suggest an ongoing movement which comes to rest in the temple section (cp. 19,45). By continuing the travel notices Luke suggests that the "entry story" is part of the travel narrative. The consequences of this for a redactional interpretation of Luke's composition have not always been seen. Many interpreters remain on a too exclusively source-critical level. They interpret Luke from Mark and do not pay enough attention to Luke's overall narrative structure.

2. Here a narrative reading could be helpful. J.-N. Aletti, a representa-tive of this approach, points to an important narrative criterion for defining Luke's structure, namely the indications of place[79]. They authorize us to make a first delineation (the references between brackets have been added by me):

9,51   καὶ αὐτὸς τὸ πρόσωπον ἐστήρισεν τοῦ πορεύεσθαι ΕΙΣ ᾽ΙΕΡΟΥΣΑΛΗΜ
9,53   καὶ οὐκ ἐδέξαντο αὐτόν, ὅτι τὸ πρόσωπον αὐτοῦ ἦν πορευόμενον ΕΙΣ ᾽ΙΕΡΟΥ-ΣΑΛΗΜ
   (9,57   καὶ πορευομένων αὐτῶν ἐν τῇ ὁδῷ)
   (10,38 ἐν δὲ τῷ πορεύεσθαι αὐτοὺς αὐτὸς εἰσῆλθεν εἰς κώμην τινά)
   (11,1   καὶ ἐγένετο ἐν τῷ εἶναι αὐτὸν ἐν τόπῳ τινὶ προσευχόμενον)

76. F. NEIRYNCK, Matière marcienne (n. 3), p. 195(95), n. 142: "Lc., XVIII,35-XIX,28 forme ainsi une unité littéraire et c'est le verset allégé de Mc., XI,1 qui sert de parallèle à Lc., XIX,29".
77. See note 6.
78. W.C. ROBINSON Jr., The Theological Context for Interpreting Luke's Travel Narra-tive, in JBL 79 (1960), p. 21, n. 7.
79. J.-N. ALETTI, L'art (n. 7), pp. 113-114.

13,22   καὶ διεπορεύετο κατὰ πόλεις καὶ κώμας διδάσκων καὶ πορείαν ποιούμενος ΕΙΣ
ΊΕΡΟΣΟΛΥΜΑ
13,33   οὐκ ἐνδέχεται προφήτην ἀπολέσθαι ἔξω ΊΕΡΟΥΣΑΛΗΜ (Jesus)
13,34   ΊΕΡΟΥΣΑΛΗΜ ΊΕΡΟΥΣΑΛΗΜ, ἡ ἀποκτείνουσα τοὺς προφήτας (Jesus)
14,25   συνεπορεύοντο δὲ αὐτῷ ὄχλοι πολλοί
17,11   καὶ ἐγένετο ἐν τῷ πορεύεσθαι ΕΙΣ ΊΕΡΟΥΣΑΛΗΜ

18,31   ἰδοὺ ΆΝΑΒΑΙΝΟΜΕΝ ΕΙΣ ΊΕΡΟΥΣΑΛΗΜ (Jesus to the Twelve)
  18,35   ἐγένετο δὲ ἐν τῷ ἐγγίζειν αὐτὸν εἰς Ἰεριχώ
  19,1   καὶ εἰσελθὼν διήρχετο τὴν Ἰεριχώ.
  19,11   εἶπεν παραβολήν, διὰ τὸ ἐγγὺς εἶναι ΊΕΡΟΥΣΑΛΗΜ αὐτόν
19,28   καὶ εἰπὼν ταῦτα ἐπορεύετο ἔμπροσθεν ΆΝΑΒΑΙΝΩΝ ΕΙΣ ΊΕΡΟΣΟΛΥΜΑ.
19,29   καὶ ἐγένετο ὡς ἤγγισεν εἰς Βηθφαγὴ καὶ Βηθανία πρὸς τὸ ὄρος τὸ καλούμενον
Ἐλαιῶν
  (19,36   πορευομένου δὲ αὐτοῦ)
  (19,37   ἐγγίζοντος δὲ αὐτοῦ ἤδη πρὸς τῇ καταβάσει τοῦ Ὅρους τῶν Ἐλαιῶν)
19,41   καὶ ὡς ἤγγισεν, ἰδὼν ΤΗΝ ΠΟΛΙΝ ἔκλαυσεν ἐπ' αὐτήν, λέγων

19,45   καὶ εἰσελθὼν εἰς τὸ ΊΕΡΟΝ...
19,47   καὶ ἦν διδάσκων τὸ καθ' ἡμέραν ἐν τῷ ΊΕΡΩ
20,1   καὶ ἐγένετο ἐν μιᾷ τῶν ἡμερῶν διδάσκοντος αὐτοῦ τὸν λαὸν ἐν τῷ ΊΕΡΩ
21,5   καί τινων λεγόντων περὶ τοῦ ΊΕΡΟΥ
21,20.24   ὅταν δὲ ἴδητε κυκλουμένην ὑπὸ στρατοπέδων ΊΕΡΟΥΣΑΛΗΜ ...
καὶ ΊΕΡΟΥΣΑΛΗΜ ἔσται πατουμένη ὑπὸ ἐθνῶν (Jesus)
21,37   ἦν δὲ τὰς ἡμέρας ἐν τῷ ΊΕΡΩ διδάσκων,
τὰς δὲ νύκτας ἐξερχόμενος ηὐλίζετο εἰς τὸ ὄρος τὸ καλούμενον Ἐλαιῶν.

The sequence of the verbs, combined with the proper names, shows a
clear progression: in a first movement Jesus goes (πορεύεσθαι) towards
Jerusalem (until Lk 17,11), after this he starts the ascent (ἀναβαίνειν)
(18,31; cp. 19,28) from near Jericho; then he comes near (ἐγγίζω), first
to Bethphage and Bethany (19,29), then to the descent (κατάβασις) of
the Mount of Olives (19,37), and at last to the city itself (19,41), which
comes in view now (ἰδὼν τὴν πόλιν). Finally, he enters the temple
(19,45). On the other hand, from 19,45 till 21,38, the text repeats
several times that Jesus remains in the temple and signals his movements only in 21,37 (a Lukan rewriting of Mk 11,19 and maybe Mk
11,11b; 14,26): by day Jesus remains in the temple to teach there and,
without explicitly exiting or entering into the city, spends the nights on
the Mount of Olives. These indications of place invite us to distinguish
between two sections: the journey to Jerusalem (9,51–19,44, – in
different stages [9,51-13,21; 13,22-17,10; 17,11-18,30, and 18,31-19,44])
–, and the temple section (19,45–21,38)[80].

80. Or Lk 9,51–19,44.45-48 and Lk 19,45-58;20,1–21,38 if we take into account what
has been said on pp. 380-383 above. The unity and coherence of the last section of the travel
narrative would be still more apparent, if R. Meynet (*Initiation à la rhétorique biblique.*
"Qui donc est le plus grand?" Vol. I, Paris, 1982, pp. 85-131) is correct in finding a

In the light of this editorial framework, I find it difficult to accept Fitzmyer's comment on Lk 19,28-40: "With this episode one begins the fifth major part of the Lucan Gospel (19:28-21:38). Jesus' long journey is over, and the Lucan Gospel joins the other three in depicting his entry to Jerusalem"[81]. Is the journey really over in 19,28? What then with the travel notices in 19,28.29.37, and especially 41? How can one say that the journey is over when it is explicitly said in 19,41 that Jesus is still drawing near to Jerusalem (ἤγγισεν), and when Luke suggests that Jesus is looking towards the city from the descent of the Mount of Olives (19,37.41)? In 19,29-38 Luke does in fact join the other three gospels, but it should not be overlooked that he reworks the tradition before him (Mk 11,1-10) in quite a radical way (see 4.).

3. Can this spatial criterion be confirmed by other narrative criteria? According to Aletti, neither the indications of action nor those of time can do: Jesus' teaching activity during the journey does not end with his entry into the temple but is emphasized rather during the temple section. The indications of time remain extremely vague before and after 19,45. Only the criterion of the characters or *dramatis personae* confirms the results to which the indications of place have pointed us. For certain actors disappear after Jesus' entry into the temple: the Pharisees (Φαρισαῖοι), mentioned for the last time in 19,39, and the multitudes (ὄχλοι), are totally absent during the episodes which take place within the temple. Their departure corresponds to the entering into the stage of two kinds of actors: the people (λαός), who literally hang upon Jesus' lips (19,48), and the group of the Chief Priests and the Scribes (ἀρχιερεῖς καὶ γραμματεῖς), who are looking to do away with him (19,47; 20,19; 22,2.4). From 19,45 on, the relation between Jesus and this opponents is deteriorating in a brusque way[82].

4. *The Lukan Version of the Entry-Story (Lk 19,29-44)*

The way in which Luke in 19,29-44 has reworked his Marcan source (Mk 11,1-11), is another indication that he considers this episode to belong to the Travel Narrative. In 19,28.29-38 he does not use a source other than Mark[83], so that the differences from Mk 11,1-10 reveal his

concentric structure in Lk 18,31–19,46 (each part of which is marked by a geographical indication): A: 18,31-34 (v. 31: Jerusalem; vv. 32-33: illtreatment of the Son of Man; v. 34: incomprehension); B: 18,35-43 (Jericho); C: 19,1-10 (Jericho); D: 19,11-28 (Jerusalem: 2x) (center: parable of the pounds); C': 19,29-36 (Mount of Olives); B': 19,37-40 (Mount of Olives); A': 19,41-46 (v. 41: The City/vv.45-46 Temple; v. 43: illtreatment of Jerusalem; vv. 42.44: incomprehension).

81. J. FITZMYER, *Luke X-XXIV* (AB, 28A), Garden City, NY, 1985, p. 1242.

82. J.-N. ALETTI, *L'art* (n. 7), pp. 114-116.

83. C.-P. MÄRZ ("*Siehe, dein König kommt zu dir...*". Eine traditionsgeschichtliche *Untersuchung zur Einzugsperikope* [ErfTS, 43], Leipzig, 1980, pp. 9-18) argues that the

own ideas. The origin of the *Sondergut* passage Lk 19,39-44 is of course more disputed, but "these verses certainly form an integral part of Luke's version of Jesus' approach to the city, and should be intelligible to the reader from the course of the narrative"[84].

By his rewriting of Mk 10,1-11, and by the addition of Lk 19,39-44, Luke reinterprets the Marcan "Entry Story" so that it takes on almost the opposite meaning. Lk 19,29-44 becomes a kind of "Acclamation/ Rejection Story". It presents the climax of the dramatic tension developed from 9,51 on. On his way to Jerusalem Jesus had already predicted the destiny that would await him there: cf. 13,33: οὐκ ἐνδέχεται προφήτην ἀπολέσθαι ἔξω Ἰερουσαλήμ; 13,35: Ἰερουσαλὴμ Ἰερουσαλήμ, ἡ ἀποκτείνοντα τοὺς προφήτας. As a prophet he knew that he would be killed by the city. In a three-fold movement[85], the final episode of the travel narrative now describes the unwillingsness of the city to receive him, which functions as a prelude to his death.

Lk 19,29-36: in the first stage, all happens "just as he (= Jesus) had told them (= disciples)". The word of Jesus is literally realised, thus confirming his identity as a prophet (vv. 29-34). This prophet is King (vv. 35-36): they make him sit down, they enthrone him, they spread their cloaks as a carpet on the road. He must sit on a mount on which no one has yet ridden, because the king must be the first in all things.

Lk 19,37-40: the Marcan entry is amplified by the addition of vv. 39-40. Luke builds a clear contrast between the acclamation of the disciples (vv. 37-38) and the opposition of the Pharisees (v. 39). The city has no part in the reception of Jesus. The inhabitants do not go out to welcome Jesus. The reason is already given in the parable of the pounds 19,14: οἱ δὲ πολῖται αὐτοῦ ἐμίσουν αὐτόν, and οὐ θέλομεν τοῦτον βασιλεῦσαι ἐφ' ἡμᾶς. The πολῖται are the inhabitants of the πόλις.

---

verses Lk 19,29a (καὶ ἐγένετο ὡς).37.38 are not taken from a Proto-Lukan source, but are due to Lukan redaction of Mk 11,1-10. A similar view is taken by R. Jacob, *Les péricopes de l'entrée à Jérusalem et de la préparation de la cène* (EB, 2), Paris, 1973, pp. 53-67; and by M. Trautmann, *Zeichenhafte Handlungen Jesu. Ein Beitrag zur Frage nach dem geschichtlichen Jesus* (FzB, 37), Würzburg, 1980, pp. 359-360.

84. C.H. Giblin, *Destruction* (n. 21), p. 47. He regards these verses as Luke's own composition (cf. Loisy), as does D. Lührmann, *Biographie des Gerechten als Evangelium. Vorstellungen zu einem Markus-Kommentar*, in *Wort und Dienst* 14 (1977) 25-50, esp. pp. 44-46. J. Dupont, *Il n'en sera pas laissé pierre sur pierre (Mc 13,2; Lc 19,44)*, in *Bib* 52 (1971) 301-320 (= Id., *Études sur les Évangiles synoptiques* I [BETL, 70A], Leuven, 1985, pp. 434-455: Lk 19,41.42 and 44b is editorial, Lk 19,33-44a is based on a source.

85. C.H. Giblin, *Destruction* (n. 21), p. 47, distinguishes a three-stage description of Jesus' drawing near (ἐγγίζειν, vv. 29,37,41): "The first stage deals with Jesus' appropriation of a colt, and a kind of enthronement by his disciples (vv. 29-34,35-36). The second stage depicts messianic acclamation by his disciples and Jesus' response to an objection to their conduct voiced by some of the Pharisees from the crowd (vv. 37-38,39-40). The third stage consists of Jesus' poignant weeping over the city as he beholds it (vv. 41-44)".

Would it be too farfetched to think of the Jerusalemites? Αὐτοῦ and τοῦτον refer to ἄνθρωπός τις εὐγενής who should be interpreted christologically. The verb πορεύεσθαι is attributed to the man of noble birth (19,12) and to Jesus (19,28). Only the crowd of the disciples begins to praise God and acclaim Jesus as the coming King (Lk 19,37: τὸ πλῆθος τῶν μαθητῶν instead of Mk 11,9: οἱ προάγοντες καὶ οἱ ἀκολουθοῦντες). In Lk 19,11-12 it is even suggested that the real enthronement of Jesus will take place in heaven (εἰς χώραν μακράν), after his death and departure. The opposition comes from τινες τῶν Φαρισαίων ἀπὸ τοῦ ὄχλου (19,39-40). The "Pharisees" are the well known opponents of the Lukan travel narrative[86]. They exercise their influence on the "crowds". From 19,45 on both groups disappear from the stage.

Lk 19,41-44 is "an anguished, sympathetic, prophetic oracle of judgment ... Jesus' oracle contrasts the city and its inhabitants with his disciples: 'If (only) you knew on this day, you, too (καὶ σύ), the conditions for peace'"[87]! The reason why Jerusalem, in contrast to the disciples who have acknowledged Jesus as the Messianic King bringing heavenly peace (19,38), does not know the conditions for peace is that "it has not known the time of visitation (ἐπισκοπή)". Jesus' coming on earth is God's visitation to his people (cp. Lk 1,78-79; 7,16; 1 Petr 2,12), and his journey of the Holy City forms its climax. Luke knows the motif of the gods walking on earth to visit men (Acts 14,11-13). He also makes use of the motif of the guest. The two are integrated for christological purposes. The last verse of the travel narrative defines Jesus' journey as a failed visitation. His journey to the city is God's last offer of salvation. Jesus, the heavenly guest is refused hospitality by Jerusalem.

From the Marcan phrase καὶ εἰσῆλθεν εἰς Ἱεροσόλυμα εἰς τὸ ἱερόν (Mk 11,11), Luke only takes over καὶ εἰσελθὼν εἰς τὸ ἱερόν (Lk 19,45). So he does not actually say that Jesus enters the city but only that he enters the temple. From this data, H. Conzelmann concluded that Luke separates the temple from the city and that according to him Jesus enters only the temple, not the city[88]. His view has been disputed by several authors[89]. I could agree to a certain degree with their objec-

86. D.P. MOESSNER, Lord of the Banquet (n. 24), pp. 187-206.

87. C.H. GIBLIN, Destruction (n. 21), pp. 55-56.

88. H. CONZELMANN, Mitte (n. 21), pp. 68-71 and 185-186, followed by E. LOHSE, in TWNT 7 (1964) 331; H. FLENDER, Heil und Geschichte in der Theologie des Lukas, München, 1965, p. 86; A. DENAUX, Reisverhaal (n. 2), pp. 468-469.475, esp. n. 25 (my answer to George's criticism of Conzelmann); M. TRAUTMANN, Handlungen (n. 83), p. 358.

89. So J. LAMBRECHT, Reading (n. 25), pp. 585-612, esp. pp. 591-592, referring to DAVIES, Purpose (n. 15), p. 168, n. 3; A. GEORGE, Tradition (n. 4), pp. 112-115; M. BACHMANN, Jesus und der Tempel (BWANT, 109), Stuttgart-Berlin-Köln-Mainz, 1980, pp. 8-10.132-170, and esp. n. 54 on p. 146.

tions: for Luke, city and temple are very closely associated; inasmuch as the temple lies in Jerusalem and is the heart of it, one could say that Jesus enters the city when entering the temple. Yet I cannot set aside the impression that Luke's omission of Mk 11,11 (εἰς Ἱεροσόλυμα) and of Mk 11,15 (καὶ ἔρχονται εἰς Ἱεροσόλυμα) in Lk 19,45, straight after the refusal of the city to welcome him (Lk 19,29-44), is not simply a matter of absent-mindedness, but the result of conscious editing. And when he integrates two motifs of Mk 11,19 in his conclusion to the temple section Lk 21,37[90], he consciously omits the third motif ἔξω τῆς πόλεως. Furthermore, the preceding expression ἦν δὲ τὰς ἡμέρας ἐν τῷ ἱερῷ διδάσκων suggests that the place from which Jesus is ἐξερχόμενος is the temple. And although Luke was a foreigner, he could easily have come to know that the eastern side of the temple, where Jesus would have entered the temple coming from Bethany, coincided with the city wall. So in his mind it was possible for Jesus to avoid the city when entering and leaving the temple. But above all, for Luke Temple and City were theological realities. He makes a clear distinction between the temple, where Jesus acts as a messianic King and Lord giving his teachings (19,45-21,38), and the city Jerusalem, where the unbelieving Jewish leaders are master and where the drama of the Passion will take place (Lk 22–23). Maybe Conzelmann was not completely wrong when he stressed the opposition between city and temple in that context, even though he may have overstated his case.

CONCLUSION

Standing in a tradition of diachronic reading, and thus using the classical methods of source-, form-, and redaction criticism, we would like to characterize our attitude towards synchronic readings with Paul's words πάντα δὲ δοκιμάζετε, τὸ καλὸν κατέχετε (1 Thess 5,21). With respect to the problem of the extent of Luke's travel narrative, our former results of redactional study, which attempted to keep in balance emendation and composition criticism, are now confirmed by narrative-critical observations. The convergence of the results of both approaches strengthens their force. Synchronic reading can well be integrated into a redaction-critical approach. This also shows the openness of diachronic reading to new developments in exegetical research. We fear however that the same could not be said concerning some representatives of a synchronic reading, for it is surely wrong to refuse to apply to biblical texts the fundamental starting-point which

90. Καὶ ὅταν ὀψὲ ἐγένετο corresponds to τὰς δὲ νύκτας, and ἐξεπορεύοντο to ἐξερχόμενος.

underlies all historical research: to understand something (or some-body) one should know where it comes from and how it grew to its actual condition[91].

APPENDIX

THE STRUCTURE OF THE GOSPEL OF LUKE: A SURVEY

In this survey we give for each type of structure, first the introductory chapters (|) and then the main divisions of the corpus (||), and the names of scholars who have proposed them. For commentaries only the author's name is given, followed by the year of publication and the pages where his delimitation is to be found.

Subsections within a main division are also indicated by |. Sometimes authors consider the introductory chapters as a main part, with the consequence that the tripartite division is given up. In that case, we mention it, except when Lk 1,1-4 is taken as part I. Sometimes authors take Lk 24 separately as a conclusion, corresponding with the introduction, but not as a main part. In that case we do not consider it as a main part. Minor divergences between authors within a similar division are each time mentioned after the author's name.

Three main divisions

1,1-4 | 1,5-2,52
3,1-9,50 || 9,51-19,27 || 19,28-24,53
    B. RIGAUX, *Témoignage* (1970) (pp. 100-104); H. CONZELMANN – A. LINDEMANN (1976) (p. 260: 1,1-2,52); X. LÉON-DUFOUR (1976) (p. 113: 1,1-2,52).
    H.J. HOLTZMANN, *Synoptiker*, [3]1901, pp. 18-19: 18,14 || 18,15; E. KLOSTERMANN ([2]1929) (p. VII: 1,1-2,52; 18,14 || 18,15-24,12 | Schluss: 24,13-53).
    C.H. GIBLIN (1985) (pp. 1-9); S.J. KISTEMAKER (1982): 1,1-2,52; 19,28-21,38 | 22,1-24,53: conclusion); C.C. MCCOWN, *Geography*, 1941, p. 29.

1,1-2,52 | 3,1-20
3,21-9,50 || 9,51-19,28 || 19,29-24,53
    A. GEORGE (1967), accepted by F. NEIRYNCK (1973).

1,1-4 | 1,5-3,38

---

91. The recent monograph on Luke's travel narrative of D.P. MOESSNER, *Lord of the Banquet* (n. 24) offers an example of this. It contains many valuable observations, but its conscious limitation to a synchronic reading leads to oversimplifications (e.g. his presentation of the redaction-critical method on pp. 4-6 is a one-sided caricature), to incon-sistancies (Moessner refuses to consider the possibility of Luke's use of sources and traditions but he himself claims that Luke's travel narrative is based on the deutero-nomistic conception of Israel's history and on the Moses-Exodos typology, a claim which supposes also a diachronic approach), and to unproven historical affirmations (e.g. pp. 292ff., on the provenance and the setting of the Journey Motif: "the travel notices do present a believable, historical route", p. 293 [sic!]; and pp. 315ff., on the tradents of the New Exodus Travel Narrative).

4,1–9,50 || 9,51–19,27 || 19,28–24,53

H. CONZELMANN (1953) (pp. 21-86 treats only the main parts; no attention for the structure of the introductory chapters); K.H. RENGSTORF (1975) (p. 12).

C.F. NÖSGEN (1876): 4,1–9,45 || 9,46–18,30 || 18,31–24,53; 1,32 is the key to the structure (pp. 290-291); the travel narrative does not play any role.

1,1-4 | 1,5–2,52 | 3,1–4,13
4,14–9,50 || 9,51–19,27 || 19,28–24,53

A. WIKENHAUSER – J. SCHMID (⁶1973) (pp. 249-254: 1,5–4,13).

F. BOVON (1989) (pp. 14-17); J. ERNST (1977) (pp. 723-728); C.F. EVANS (1990) (pp. v-vi: 1,1–4,13); C. L'EPLATTENIER (1982): 1,5–4,13; 19,28 || 19,29); L. SABOURIN (1985) (p. 13: 1,1–2,52); cp. J. SCHMID (⁴1960) (pp. 7-8.366-367: 1,5–4,13; 19,28–23,56 | 24,1-53: conclusion); L. SOUBIGOU (1933) (pp. 563-568: three journeys: 9,51–13,21 | 13,22–17,10 | 17,11–19,46 || 19,47).

W.E. HULL (1967): 1,5–4,13; 19,28–23,56 | 24,1-53: conclusion); R. MICHIELS (1986) (pp. 79-80: 9,51–18,14 | 18,15–19,27 | 19,28–21,38 || 22,1); P. ROLLAND (1984) (p. 83: 19,28 || 19,29); W. WILKENS, *Versuchungsgeschichte* (n. 4), 1974: the tripartite division of Jesus' public life follows the three temptations 4,3-4; 4,5-8 and 4,9-12; *Struktur* (n. 4), 1978: 1,5–9,50 ||).

1,1-4
1,5–9,50 || 9,51–19,44 || 19,45–24,53

E.E. ELLIS (1963) (pp. 30-37: note the non-geographical tripartition: the Messiahship and mission of Jesus; the teaching of the Messiah; the consummation of Messiah's mission).

Larger second main part, which relativizes the structural importance of 9,51; subsections of the second main part are indicated by a |.

1,1-4
1,5–4,13 || 4,14-9,50 | 9,51-19,44 | 19,45-21,38 || 22,1–24,53

A.J. HULTGREN (n. 4) (1976).

1,1-4
1,5–4,13 || 4,14–9,50 | 9,51–19,44 || 19,45–24,53

R. MORGENTHALER (1949) (pp. I,163.168-172.188; on p. 172 he even speaks of 4 scenes: 1. Jerusalemergeschichten: 1,5–4,13 || 2. Unterwegs (in Galiläa): 4,14–9,50 || 3. Unterwegs (in Samaria) nach Jerusalem: 9,51–19,44 || 4. Jerusalemergeschichten: 19,45–24,53).

1,1-4 | 1,5–2,52
3,1–4,13 || 4,14-44 | 5,1-9,50 | 9,51-19,28 | 19,29–21,38 || 22,1–24,53.

W. RADL (n. 22) (1988) (pp. 46-48: same delineation of the second main part as with Hultgren, but in itself divided in four subsections).

1,1-4 | 1,5–2,52 | 3,1–4,13
4,14-44 || 5,1–9,50 | 9,51–19,27 || 19,28–24,53

G. SCHNEIDER (1977) (pp. 7-9.25); H. SCHÜRMANN, *Lukas* (1969), ²1982, pp. 146. 260-261: 3,1–4,44 ||).

Some authors split up the episodes, especially the third one (Lk 19,27ff), so that in fact they give up the tripartite division of Luke. Or they take the introductory chapters as one or more main parts. So, in fact, the differences in structuration are not as great as may appear from this survey.

Four main divisions

1,5–2,40 || 2,41-52

3,1–4,13 || 4,14–9,17 || 9,18–19,28 || 19,29–24,53

J.A. BENGEL, *Gnomon NT* (1742), ed. 1855, pp. 206-208: I. Initium (1,5–2,40); II. Medium, cum esset annorum XII. et deinceps (2,41-52); III. Cursus ipse. 1. 3,1–4,13: aditus: ubi describitur baptista: baptismus: tentatio || 2. 4,14–9,17: annus acceptus in Galilaea || 3. 9,18–19,28: praeparatio ad passionem etc. || 4. 19,29–24,53: acta Hierosolymitana).

1,1-4 | 1,5–2,52 | 3,1–4,13

4,14–9,50 || 9,51–19,27 || 19,28–21,38 || 22,1–24,53

P. DAUSCH (1918) (pp. XII-XIV: 19,28–23,56 || 24,1-53); J. KEULERS (1951) (pp. 304-307: 1,1–2,52 || 3,1–4,13 ||; but see pp. 109-110: the public life of Jesus: 4,14–9,50 || 9,51–18,30 || 18,31–21,38); K. STAAB (1956); J. WEISS, 1906, pp. 381.382.401. 405.424.462.469).

1,1-4 | 1,5–2,52

3,1–9,50 || 9,51–19,27 || 19,28–21,38 || 22,1–24,53

A. LOISY (1927) (p. 24); A. PLUMMER (⁵1922) (pp. XXXVIII-XI: 19,28 || 19,29).

1,1-4

1,5–4,30 || 4,31–9,50 || 9,51–19,46 || 19,47–24,53

H. BAARLINK (ed.), *Inleiding NT*, 1989, pp. 145-149: overlapping pericopes: 4,14-30; 9,43b-50 and 19,28-44; result: 1,5–4,30 || 4,14–9,50 || 9,43b–19,44 || 19,28–24,53; C.H. TALBERT (1982): 4,15||4,16; 19,44||19,45; P.H. WELZEN (1986): a narrative organisation of the structure.

1,1-4

1,5–4,13 || 4,14–9,50 || 9,51–21,38 || 22,1–24,53

A. BISPING (²1867) (p. 145: 1,1–4,13 ||); J. DILLERSBERGER (1939-1941: 19,28 || 19,29); J. KNABENBAUER (²1926) (pp. 658-660: 19,27 || 19,28); R. MEYNET (1988) (pp. 276-277: rhetorical approach; the first three main parts have 8 subdivisons: for 9,51–21,38: 9,51–10,42 | 11,1-54 | 12,1–13,21 | 13,22–14,35 | 15,1–17,10 | 17,11–18,30 | 18,31–19,46 | 19,47–21,38).

1,1-4

1,5–3,38 || 4,1–9,50 | 9,51–18,30 | 18,31–21,38 || 22,1–23,56 || 24,1-53

S. GREIJDANUS, *Lucas I*, 1940, pp. V-VIII; *Lucas II*, 1941, pp. V-X.

1,1-4

1,5–2,52 || 3,1–9,50 || 9,51–19,27 || 19,28–24,53

S.F.H.J. BERKELBACH VAN DER SPRENKEL (1964): 3,38 || 4,1; J. MOFFATT (1918) (p. 264: 4,13 || 4,14); J. LEAL (1955: 19,28 || 19,29); F. SCHLEIERMACHER (1817) (pp. 18-19.50.158.250: 19,48 || 20,1); E. SCHWEIZER (1984) (pp. XI-XV).

Five main divisions

3,1–4,15 || 4,16–7,50 || 8,1–9,50 || 9,51–18,14 || 18,15–24,53

J. WELLHAUSEN (1904) (pp. 3.8.33.45.100: no comment on the preparatory chapters; source-critical structuration).

1,1-4

1,5–4,13 || 4,14–9,50 || 9,51–19,27 || 19,28–21,38 || 22,1–24,53

A.L. ASH (1972) (p. 21: 23,56 || 24,1); W. BARTELT (²1937) (pp. XIII-XVI: 18,34 ||

18,35); W.G. KÜMMEL (^{18}1973) (pp. 95-97: 9,51–13,30 || 13,31–19,27 || 19,28–24,53);
A. STÖGER (1961) (pp. I,15-19; II,7-10); E.J. TINSLEY (1965) (pp. 24.51.107.170.187:
18,30 || 18,31).

1,1-4

1,5–4,44 || 5,1–9,17 || 9,18–17,10 || 17,11–21,38 || 22,1–24,53
P. BOSSUYT – J. RADERMAKERS (1981) (pp. I,29-33).

Six main divisions (with some exceptions)

1,1-4

1,5–2,52 || 3,1–4,13 || 4,14–9,50 || 9,51–19,27 || 19,28–21,38 || 22,1–24,53
G.B. CAIRD (1963) (pp. 41.45.67.83.137.213: 9,51–19,28 || 19,29–24,53); J.M. CREED
(1930) (pp. LVII-LVIII: 9,51–19,48 || 20,1–24,53): five divisions.
W.M.L. DE WETTE (1836) (9,51–21,38; 9,51–18,14 | 18,15–19,28 | 19,29–21,38 ||
22,1–23,56 || 24,1-53); S.M. GILMOUR (1952) (pp. VIII, 23-26: 19,28–24,12 || 24,13-
53); F. HAUCK (1934) (pp. 8-9); J. KREMER (1988) (pp. 8.24.45.54.113(IV?).186.209);
M.-J. LAGRANGE (^{5}1941) (pp. XXXIV-XXXV: 9,51–18,30 || 18,31–23,56 || 24,1-53); I.H.
MARSHALL (1978) (pp. 7-12: 19,10 || 19,11); B. PRETE, *L'opera di Luca*, 1986, pp. 34-
79: 1,1-4 ||); A. VALENSIN – J. HUBY (^{2}1941) (p. XVII).

Seven main divisions

1,1-4

1,5–2,52 || 3,1–4,13 || 4,14–9,50 || 9,51–19,27 || 19,28–21,38 || 22,1–23,56 || 24,1-
53
F.W. DANKER (1972) (pp. V-X: 3,38 || 4,1); C.A. EVANS (1990) (p. 15); J. FITZMYER,
Luke I, 1981, pp. 136-142: 23,56a || 23,56b); F. GODET (1871) (pp. I,483-484;
II,555); W. GRUNDMANN (1969) (pp. V-IX: 4,30 || 4,31); L. MARCHAL (1935) (pp.
22.53.66.131.228.253.280). E. OSTY (^{2}1953) (pp. 167-174); F. RIENECKER (1976) (pp.
XII-XII: 3,38 || 4,1); V. ROSE (^{6}1907) (pp. XIX-XXIII); A. SCHLATTER (1962) (p. 410);
W. WIEFEL (1988) (pp. VI-IX: 4,30 || 4,31).

1,1-4

1,5–2,52 || 3,1–4,13 || 4,14–7,50 || 8,1–11,13 || 11,14–18,30 || 18,31–21,38 || 22,1–
24,53
T. ZAHN ($^{1-2}$1913) (pp. V-VII) (cf. *Einleitung* Vol. II, 1900, pp. 375-377).

1,1-4

1,5–2,52 || 3,1-20 || 3,21–4,13 || 4,14–9,50 || 9,51–19,44 || 19,45–23,56 || 24,1-53
N. GELDENHUYS (1951) (p. 46).

Eight main divisions

2.5.1: 1,1-4

1,5–2,52 || 3,1-20 || 3,21–4,13 || 4,14–9,50 || 9,51–19,44 || 19,45–21,38 || 22,1–
23,56 || 24,1-53
L. MORRIS (1974) (pp. 61-63).

Tiensestraat 112   Adelbert DENAUX
B-3000 Leuven

LE RÉCIT LUCANIEN DE LA PASSION DE JÉSUS (LC 22-23)

Dans la première partie de cet article, j'aimerais attirer l'attention sur le récit de la Passion selon saint Luc (Lc 22–23) dans une perspective littéraire, synchronique et narrative, sans oser, ni vouloir adopter une terminologie particulière[1]. Dans la seconde, j'examinerai la question des sources suivant une démarche diachronique.

I. Approche synchronique: L'œuvre littéraire de Luc

À relire ces chapitres, il m'a semblé que le regard devait se poser tour à tour sur diverses réalités. Considérer, premièrement, le mouvement du texte à l'intérieur d'une structure (un récit n'est-il pas à la fois fixe dans sa lettre ou sa composition et mobile dans l'invitation au voyage qu'il adresse?). Deuxièmement, découvrir les coordonnées spatiales et temporelles qui servent à la fois de limites et de possibles au récit. Troisièmement, analyser le jeu des personnages, si particulier au récit de la Passion, avec la continuité de l'un, Jésus, et la présence épisodique de tant d'autres, par exemple Judas ou Hérode. Quatrièmement, examiner – ce que l'on néglige souvent – les nombreux objets mentionnés et imaginer leur fonction ou leur circulation. Cinquièmement, détecter la présence de divers schémas que Luc utilise pour articuler la vie et la mort d'un personnage. Sixièmement, définir le nombre et la nature des niveaux auxquels l'œuvre se donne à lire. Septièmement, enfin, passant du récit au narrateur et à son point de vue, repérer la conscience que cette personne peut avoir de la distance entre la voix qu'il prête aux personnages et l'opinion qu'il fait courir sous sa plume.

1. *Une composition ferme et un mouvement souple*

On dit volontiers qu'à la différence du reste de l'évangile, le récit de la Passion est un récit continu. Cette constatation ne représente qu'une demi-vérité, car ce récit suivi est de fait un assemblage d'épisodes distincts, tel un mur qui tire sa beauté de pierres tout à la fois

---

1. Au cours des années, ma réflexion en matière littéraire a été stimulée par les œuvres de Claude Lévi-Strauss, Roland Barthes, Jean Starobinski, Gérard Genette, Frank Kermode, George A. Kennedy, Jean Delorme et Jean-Noël Aletti. Je leur en suis reconnaissant. En matière exégétique, la bibliographie relative à Lc 22–23 que j'ai retenue est citée en annexe (pp. 421-423). Le lecteur y trouvera les indications bibliographiques complètes. Dans les notes, les titres sont signalés en abrégé.

semblables et différentes. Les épisodes, pour leur part, se suffisent à eux-
mêmes, tel le reniement de Pierre ou la comparution devant Hérode,
tout en entrant au service de la grande cause, je veux dire, du récit tout
entier. De plus, certains épisodes se répondent, comme des préparatifs
correspondant au voyage ou des instructions à leur application. Ainsi le
discours d'adieux (22,14-38) introduit-il, selon un usage littéraire qui
prend appui sur une réalité sociale, à la séparation et à la mort
(22,47ss.). Pareillement, le cadre étant judiciaire, la dernière étape d'un
procès ne peut être que l'exécution de la peine, comme le pendant final
de l'agonie est la mise au tombeau. Cette interaction du tout et des
parties peut être interprétée. J'y vois d'abord une marque de la conco-
mitance, dans la vie de Jésus, entre l'histoire du salut et l'histoire
profane. J'y découvre ensuite une solidarité sotériologique entre le sort
du Fils et celui des enfants, du Messie souffrant et de son peuple. J'y
perçois enfin l'embarras dans lequel l'auteur place ici la lectrice et le
lecteur: vont-ils admirer un tel destin certes tragique, mais beau de
l'inexorable grandeur humaine et de la marque divine providentielle?
Ou vont-ils se révolter contre cette parodie de justice, cette erreur
judiciaire, triplement consciente, et cet aveuglement d'un peuple à
reconnaître son chef?

2. *La construction de l'espace et du temps*

C'est l'interaction du temps et de l'espace qui donne à penser, ainsi
que l'addition du sacré et du profane. Commençons par cette dernière
paire: Luc localise à Jérusalem non seulement la passion, ce que la
tradition lui imposait de faire, mais aussi ses préparatifs et son issue
heureuse. Il est conscient du cacactère sacré de la ville. Peut-être
s'inspire-t-il de la prophétie d'Esaïe 2 sur la montagne élevée d'où
descendront la Parole et l'Esprit de Dieu. En même temps, Luc opère
une mutation: à Jérusalem, c'était le Temple qui attestait la présence
protectrice de Dieu. Certes, Jésus y enseigne longuement, mais dès la
Passion c'est à côté du temple que s'établit la sacralité. Dorénavant, le
«lieu dit du Crâne» (23,33) trouve sa place à côté de celui du Temple et
va le supplanter. Selon Luc, pour Jésus, puis pour ses apôtres, le
Temple n'est plus le lieu sacramentel de la présence mystérique, mais le
lieu presque profane où la Parole peut retentir et orienter le regard vers
le lieu du supplice. C'est au calvaire et non au Temple que s'est jouée
l'ultime étape salvifique de portée universelle.

Une remarque analogue peut être faite à propos du temps. Le ch. 22
nous fait entrer dans le temps le plus sacré de la religion hébraïque, la
Pâque. Or l'événement décisif ne coïncide pas avec l'instant le plus sacré
du cérémonial juif. À la Pâque hébraïque, Luc ajoute la résurrection
dominicale. Quant au sabbat mentionné (23,54.56), il est attente
comblée de façon inattendue, donc provocante, le lendemain et non à la

fin des temps (24,1ss.). Pur sa part, la mort de Jésus garde son caractère profane et historique que ne recouvre aucun voile liturgique et que n'affecte aucune typologie pascale.

Si l'on examine la désignation concrète de l'espace et l'énoncé des marques chronologiques, nous découvrons un agencement qui supprime les ennuyeuses coïncidences. Le moment le plus sombre ne se passe pas au milieu de la nuit! L'espace et le temps du récit s'éloignent et se rejoignent, filent en parallèle ou se croisent comme les motifs d'une frise grecque ou les évolutions d'un couple de patineurs.

Les lieux du récit correspondent, en leur première moitié, à la volonté exprimée par Jésus[2] et, en leur seconde, à celle des adversaires. Le passage d'une volonté à l'autre s'opère entre les vv. 46 et 47 du ch. 22. À ce moment, de sujet grammatical, Jésus «tombe» à l'accusatif (la «déclinaison» se dit en grec πτῶσις). Les seules occurrences, où Jésus demeure le sujet de la phrase et de l'action, sont des discours (cf. par exemple, 22,48.51.52). Encore deviennent-elles, elles aussi, plus rares.

De par la volonté de Jésus, le récit introduit le lecteur et la lectrice dans un espace protégé, dans la maison dont le maître a besoin (οἰκία, κατάλυμα, ἀνάγαιον μέγα ἐστρωμένον sont les termes précis pour suggérer cet espace, 22,10-12). C'est l'espace qui est prédisposé à la préparation de la Pâque (on notera l'importance du verbe ἑτοιμάζω aux vv. 8.12 et 13 du ch. 22). Cette Pâque elle-même sert de prolégomène aux dernières dispositions du Maître. L'essentiel du ch. 22, la scène des adieux, se déroule dans cette demeure, mise à disposition, comme le seront plus tard les églises de maison.

De cet intérieur, la volonté du héros – soulignée par les mots «selon son habitude» (22,39) – le dirige lui et ses disciples vers le Mont des Oliviers, un lieu (τόπος, 22,40) extérieur où se déroulent l'ultime tentation (22,39-46; cf. 4,1-13) et la rencontre de l'adversaire (arrestation, 22,47-51). Si Jésus reste, dans ce lieu extérieur, maître de la parole, il perd le contrôle des opérations. C'est dorénavant la volonté pernicieuse des humains qui s'accomplit (23,25: τὸν δὲ Ἰησοῦν παρέδωκεν τῷ θελήματι αὐτῶν). Curieusement, ces actions des autorités juives, conduites par Judas, lui-même envahi par la présence de Satan (22,3), sont également et prioritairement une inflexion historique suivant une autre volonté, celle de Dieu (le mot θέλημα figure au v. 42b).

Dans cet espace extérieur, au moment crucial où s'opère le transfert des volontés, une sentence nous signale la qualité de l'heure qui se vit (22,53: «votre heure», «la puissance des ténèbres»). Dorénavant, le récit se saisit du héros et le déplace en plusieurs lieux de malheur: on l'arrête, le conduit, puis l'introduit (les verbes sont banals, mais parlants dans leur banalité oppressive elle-même) dans l'οἰκία du grand prêtre (22,54). Plus loin, il est dirigé, escorté, dans la salle de réunion du

---

2. Cette volonté s'exprime en terme de désir (22,15) ou d'habitude (22,39).

peuple (συνέδριον 22,66). Puis, troisième étape du procès, le récit pousse Jésus, par multitude interposée, jusque devant Pilate, à l'intérieur donc du prétoire du gouverneur (23,1). Luc, comme l'on sait, ajoute une instance judiciaire: du prétoire romain, l'inculpé est envoyé (ἀνέπεμψεν αὐτόν, 23,7) auprès d'Hérode, dans le palais (le mot n'est pas mentionné) qu'il occupe durant son séjour à Jérusalem (l'expression y est, 23,7).

Enfin, au terme de cette procédure itinérante et cahotique, Jésus est renvoyé auprès de Pilate. En ce lieu, déjà connu, le gouverneur n'impose pas son point de vue, à défaut sa volonté[3]. Il se contente de laisser faire. Le v. 24 exprime une décision, mais c'est celle de ne rien faire ou de laisser faire par d'autres ce qu'il regrette personnellement: καὶ Πιλᾶτος ἐπέκρινεν γενέσθαι τὸ αἴτημα αὐτῶν (23,24).

Dès lors, c'est à l'extérieur que le récit situe de nouveau le cours de l'histoire. Au Mont des Oliviers qui dépendait encore de la volonté de Jésus, répond ici un autre τόπος (23,33), le lieu du Crâne qui permet aux adversaires d'accomplir leur œuvre funeste.

Comme l'*extra muros* du Mont des Oliviers, l'*extra muros* du lieu du Crâne devient un espace d'obscurité[4]. La tentation et l'arrestation d'un côté, la crucifixion et la mort de l'autre appartiennent au monde des ténèbres.

À sa mort, Jésus devient un corps inerte qui suit, lui aussi, son chemin: il va être doublement enclos, enroulé d'abord dans un suaire (23,53), puis placé dans un tombeau (23,53). Le ch. 24 est au contraire un chapitre d'ouverture: ouverture du tombeau, échappée de la mort vers la vie et la gloire, sortie de la ville vers Emmaüs, ouverture des esprits et des Écritures (24,32).

De nouveaux espaces protecteurs se présentent au matin de Pâques, en correspondance avec la chambre haute: la maison où le Ressuscité se met à table avec ses deux disciples (24,30), puis la chambre haute où il apparaît aux Onze réunis (24,36).

En résumé, le texte lucanien évoque des lieux intérieurs et extérieurs et, parmi les intérieurs, des maisons communautaires et protectrices qui font face aux édifices d'un pouvoir contraignant et excessif[5]. Chacun de ces lieux – il faut le préciser – est un lieu de passage, des verbes de mouvement leur étant toujours associés. Des étapes alternent donc avec des stations[6].

Dans ces espaces, l'histoire prend forme. Attentive aux lieux, la

---

3. Cf. 23,20 où est signalée cette volonté velléitaire: θέλων ἀπολῦσαι τὸν Ἰησοῦν.

4. Cf. 24,44: καὶ σκότος ἐγένετο ἐφ' ὅλην τὴν γῆν...

5. Ultime et provisoire demeure, le tombeau (23,53.55) a une valeur neutre et universelle. S'y rejoignent tous les humains, protecteurs ou persécuteurs.

6. F.G. UNTERGASSMAIR, *Kreuzweg und Kreuzigung Jesu*, pp. 42 et 201, suggère à bon escient cette notion liturgique de «station» à propos du récit lucanien de la Passion de Jésus.

narration scande aussi les temps. Le récit débute «au jour des Azymes» (22,7): ce jour, un jeudi, où Luc curieusement situe les préparatifs de la Pâque, prépare aussi la passion de Jésus, plus précisément son dernier repas (22,7). Puis vient l'heure, c'est-à-dire le début de la Pâque, le jeudi soir. De la mention du jour, le récit a donc passé à la précision de «l'heure» (22,14). Cette longue soirée de communion se poursuit jusque tard dans la nuit au Mont des Oliviers où tout bascule. La nuit pascale, moment de fête et de libération, devient alors «votre heure» (et non plus celle de Dieu) et la «puissance des ténèbres» (et non celle de la lumière) (22,53). Jésus est alors arrêté (22,47-53). La nuit se poursuit dans la première maison inhospitalière, celle du grand prêtre. Interrogatoire d'un côté, reniement de l'autre (22,54-62.63-71).

Alors, le jour se lève (καὶ ὡς ἐγένετο ἡμέρα, «et quand il fit jour», 22,66). En fait, ce jour ne répondra pas à sa définition. Il sera un jour de ténèbres, reprise et poursuite de la nuit précédente. Une intense obscurité, une éclipse de soleil (23,45), en supprimera la lumière, de la sixième à la neuvième heure (23,44). Un jour interrompu, un temps brisé. Dans ce demi-jour qui sombrera dans la nuit, le Christ est introduit successivement en trois édifices, construits pour que règne la justice, mais occupés en ce jour de ténèbres, par des êtres qui bafouent et châtient l'innocence. Ces trois lieux: le sanhédrin du peuple, le prétoire du gouverneur et le palais d'Hérode.

Nous avons assisté aux préparatifs de la Pâque; nous voici au jour de la Pâque qui, selon Luc, tombe cette année-là sur un vendredi, «parascève», préparation du sabbat. L'histoire de Jésus en son jour dominical accomplira et la Pâque et le sabbat.

De ce sabbat, on ne nous indique que le début et la fin (23,54.56; 24,1). L'immobilité y règne et marque le temps du sceau de la mort. Rien ne s'y passe que l'attente des femmes (23,54-56). Mais cette attente est merveilleuse: elle atteste, sur le registre de la religion traditionnelle, le respect dû aux morts et l'affection indéracinable des femmes. Elle prépare, sur le registre de la religion nouvelle, le témoignage de la résurrection et du tombeau vide.

De ce sabbat ambivalent, tiraillé entre la fin de l'histoire et le début de l'eschatologie, entre le rite et la foi, le texte nous dit qu'il «pointe», qu'il «commence à luire» (ἐπέφωσκεν, 23,54). Il fait voir sa lumière au moment où la nuit se répand – si le jour commence bien le soir – et où elle maintient son emprise – au sens figuré de la mort dominatrice.

La mélodie du temps et l'accompagnement de l'espace conduisent la lectrice et le lecteur dans un même questionnement: faut-il célébrer ce qui se passe en un hymne à la croix ou se lamenter de la violence des humains?

3. *Le jeu des personnages*

Nous avons déjà rencontré l'enchaînement conflictuel de diverses volontés: celle de Jésus qui planifie sa Pâque, sa double Pâque pourrait-on dire, juive puis chrétienne; celle des adversaires qui devient déterminante dès l'arrestation[7], ne laissant plus à Jésus que l'initiative, la liberté de la parole. Derrière la volonté humaine des autorités juives, Luc a nettement désigné le véritable coupable, Satan entré dans Judas (22,3; le livre des Actes répétera que les Juifs ont certes agi, mais par ignorance, Ac 3,17; 13,27). Pour ne pas laisser cependant échapper l'histoire à sa trajectoire providentielle, Luc a rappelé la volonté des volontés, celle qui prend le risque de ne pas anéantir l'adversaire, mais qui, à ce tournant que constitue le jardin des Oliviers, tient à faire boire la coupe au Fils bien-aimé. Ce dernier, conscient du carrefour historique où il se trouve et où Dieu lui-même s'est placé, exprime son désir humain («éloigne cette coupe de moi!»), mais range – par avance et dans la confiance – sa volonté à celle du Père: πλὴν μὴ τὸ θέλημά μου ἀλλὰ τὸ σὸν γινέσθω, «pourtant, que ce ne soit pas ma volonté mais la tienne qui se réalise!» (22,42). Pour un moment, la volonté de Dieu sera que triomphe la volonté du Diable. Ce renversement dramatique s'opère dans les scènes du Mont des Oliviers et de l'arrestation. Πειρασμός est le mot que dessine alors la plume de l'auteur (22,46). «Épreuve» et «tentation» pour les disciples qui ne comprendront pas ce qui se passe. «Épreuve» et «tentation» surtout pour Jésus qui doit laisser faire, retenir l'énergie divine qu'il a en lui et qu'en d'autres temps (6,19) il a su dispenser pour faire triompher la santé et la vie. Jésus refuse de se défendre: à la question de l'entourage de Jésus, «Seigneur, et si nous frappions par l'épée?» (22,49), la réponse est un non qui se manifeste narrativement par un refus de violence[8] et un geste de guérison (22,51)[9]. La force de vie qui lui reste est destinée aux autres. Il est temps – le Fils aligne ici sa volonté sur celle de son Père – que la mort fasse son travail.

L'unité de l'action est assurée par un personnage. Jésus actif, avons-nous vu, puis consciemment passif, demeure sur le devant de la scène et tient le rôle principal. Les autorités jouent, elles aussi, un rôle déterminant. Elles mettent l'action en branle, mais disparaissent progressivement de la scène, dès lors qu'elles ont obtenu ce qu'elles voulaient. Elles ne sont signalées plus qu'une fois après la condammnation: les chefs, lit-on, se moquent de Jésus crucifié (23,35).

Le rôle du peuple est plus difficile à analyser: au début, il est signalé à

---

7. Cf. 23,51: ἡ βουλὴ καὶ ἡ πρᾶξις αὐτῶν.

8. Ce ne sont pas des légions d'anges qui s'avancent, les armes à la main (cf. Mt 26,53), mais un ange consolateur qui s'approche (22,43).

9. En guérissant l'oreille coupée, Jésus utilise sa force divine pour la dernière fois (22,51).

l'arrière-plan comme favorable à Jésus (22,2: ὁ λαός; 22,6: ὄχλος). Ensuite, on ne doit sans doute l'identifier ni à la foule qui vient arrêter Jésus (22,47: ὄχλος), ni à celle qui le défère au tribunal de Pilate (23,1: τὸ πλῆθος αὐτῶν). En revanche, c'est bien lui, le peuple (λαός), qui est convoqué officiellement par Pilate aux côtés des grands prêtres et des chefs d'Israël (23,13). Luc l'intègre donc à ce qui sera la décision finale. Sans que Luc l'admette explicitement, le peuple s'est laissé entraîner par ses chefs: avec eux, il crie «celui-ci, supprime-le!» (23,18); puis le fameux «crucifie! crucifie-le!» (23,21). Luc souligne ce fait par l'adverbe, rare sous sa plume, παμπληθεί, «en foule» (23,18). C'est encore le peuple, sans mention de ses chefs, qui accompagne Jésus vers son supplice. Il est signalé, cette fois-ci, aux côtés des femmes de Jérusalem en pleurs (23,27). Rien ne dit que le peuple continue à marquer son hostilité. Au contraire, à la croix, «il se tient là» muet, alors que les chefs se moquent d'un crucifié incapable de se sauver lui-même (23,35). Et, finalement, c'est dans une attitude de quasi-repentance que Luc le signale à la mort de Jésus: le peuple s'en retourne, écrit-il, en se frappant la poitrine (23,27). De ce peuple, Luc veut surtout faire un témoin oculaire. Le peuple a constaté, peut-être contemplé, les événements (τὰ γενόμενα, 23,48). L'évangéliste utilise le verbe θεωρῶ avec insistance (23,35 et 23,48, où il recourt aussi au mot θεωρία). En ce dernier passage, le peuple voisine avec les amis et les compagnons du crucifié. Proche de Jésus au début du récit, le peuple se retrouve aux côtés des disciples à la fin, après avoir suivi les autorités, rencontré Pilate, puis accompagné les femmes de la ville. La succession de ces tableaux a une signification. Elle évoque, de façon narrative, une série d'états d'âme et l'évolution d'une attitude.

Si l'on examine chaque épisode de la Passion pour lui-même, on constate que Luc suit un usage que le théâtre et le roman antiques nous ont fait connaître. L'évangéliste n'aime guère faire dialoguer plus de deux personnages à la fois. Même si plusieurs acteurs sont en même temps sur scène, deux seuls s'expriment. Et si plusieurs instances interviennent, elles le font à tour de rôle et non pas simultanément.

Malgré l'omniprésence de Jésus, quelques épisodes se déroulent sans lui. Cette absence s'explique au début et à la fin du drame, lors du complot (22,1-6) et lors des scènes de deuil (23,50-54.55-56). Ils servent de cadre. En deux autres endroits, le narrateur opère une digression pour montrer, dans un cas, un apôtre (et lequel!) qui «craque» (22,54-62) et, dans l'autre, un disciple engagé dans la suivance (23,26).

Dans un autre épisode, Jésus est confronté à trois personnages ou groupes de personnages. Lors de l'arrestation, il dialogue d'abord avec Judas, puis avec ses disciples, enfin avec ceux qui ont mandaté Judas (22,47-53). Cette surabondance est exceptionnelle et Luc en vient à bout par trois dialogues successifs et non par une conversation générale. Si

Jésus est perdant à cet instant, au niveau des faits, il a, face à ces interlocuteurs, chaque fois le *dernier* mot: telle est la conviction de Luc.

Pilate – comme tout juge de l'Antiquité – doit faire face à deux parties. La séquence de la première audience (23,1-7) est dès lors la suivante: les chefs juifs s'adressent à Pilate (Pilate ne leur répond pas aussitôt). Pilate se tourne vers Jésus (Jésus renvoie la question). Pilate parle aux chefs juifs qui n'entrent pas dans ses vues. Les chefs juifs réitèrent leur plainte à Pilate.

Pilate trouve alors une échappatoire: la comparution devant Hérode. Cette solution ayant échoué, une seconde audience s'avère nécessaire. Elle regroupe à nouveau trois personnages, mais se déroule différemment. Jésus n'y intervient plus (23,13-25). Tout se passe entre Pilate et les adversaires de Jésus. Ici, Pilate parle le premier. Le dialogue dure et il est marqué par la redondance de l'épisode de Barabbas. L'enchaînement des répliques y est le suivant: Pilate s'adresse aux chefs juifs (longue explication). Les chefs répondent à Pilate (violente intervention unanime). Pilate leur réplique (courte intervention, mais de même contenu: libération). Eux à Pilate (courte et cinglante réplique: «Crucifie! Crucifie-le!»). Pilate leur répond (nouvelle déclaration d'innocence)[10]. Eux à Pilate (style indirect, à grands cris). Pilate à eux (style indirect, décision).

Dans ces deux scènes devant Pilate, il y a un crescendo: de l'une à l'autre, la violence augmente; de l'une à l'autre, la voix de Jésus est de plus en plus couverte; de l'une à l'autre, Pilate accentue sa certitude d'innocence, donc confirme son opinion inébranlable, mais au moment où l'opposition enfle, sa volonté à lui se dégonfle. À la fin, il «lâche» Jésus. Le passage du discours direct au discours indirect incruste le dire dans une réalité durable et inévitable. Le narrateur et, à travers lui, les lecteurs constatent: voilà ce qu'ils ont voulu, voilà ce qu'il a laissé faire.

J'aimerais attirer encore l'attention sur les scènes les plus nombreuses et, d'une certaine façon, les plus paradoxales. Ce sont les scènes en vis-à-vis, où le projecteur n'éclaire que deux personnages, celles dont la description devient si précise que des noms propres et des titres précis apparaissent. Jésus, lui, est connu; il domine la situation depuis le début. Il n'est donc plus indispensable de formuler son nom. Il est l'αὐτός, «lui», solennel et admiré, ou le οὗτος, «celui-ci», énigmatique ou critiqué. L'attention se déplace vers son interlocuteur. Et c'est là que réside le paradoxe. Car la scène ne devrait être qu'un maillon dans la chaîne, qu'un épisode fonctionnel parmi d'autres. Or, tout en étant cela, elle est aussi, et peut-être d'abord, une scène indépendante, paradigmatique, avec un héros qui n'est pas le Maître, mais le disciple ou

---

10. Selon Luc, Pilate affirme ici l'innocence de Jésus pour la «troisième fois» (23,22). La première fois, ce fut à la fin de la première audience (23,4) et la deuxième au début de la seconde (23,14).

l'adversaire. Le bon brigand, le centurion, Symon de Cyrène, Joseph d'Arimathée, sans parler de Judas, des filles de Jérusalem ou du groupe des femmes en deviennent ainsi, à tour de rôle et l'espace d'un instant, les protagonistes. Cette technique littéraire fort habile nous détourne provisoirement de l'inexorable, ou nous le manifeste sous un autre angle. Elle humanise le drame, le déplace de l'absurde solitude vers une solidarité subséquente. L'art narratif, qui se concentre sur un destin, en montre l'impact sur tous en leur variété bariolée et hésitante.

Finalement, il ne faut pas oublier deux dialogues décisifs, méta-narratifs si l'on peut dire, puisqu'il s'agit des deux prières de Jésus. Dans les deux invocations, Dieu est interpellé comme «Père» (22,42 et 23,34). Dans la première, la prière de Jésus est exaucée, autrement que souhaité, par l'apparition de l'ange bienfaisant (22,43-44). Dans la seconde, il s'agit d'une requête qui reste en suspens. Dieu ne répond pas et ne dit pas s'il va pardonner. Ce silence menaçant du Dieu de Luc demeurera jusqu'à la fin des Actes: il s'explicitera dàns le second livre de Luc, par l'offre du kérygme et l'exigence de la conversion. Cette référence extra-historique à Dieu rappelle efficacement qu'une volonté suprême régit le drame et utilise à bon escient la volonté des personnages.

4. *La circulation des objets*

Il suffit d'avoir rencontré la solitude pour savoir l'importance que peuvent prendre certains objets. Leur valeur varie suivant leur origine, leurs détenteurs et les périodes de la vie que traversent ces derniers. Les objets ont par ailleurs leur fonction. Par exemple, ils peuvent être utiles ou non. Ils ont aussi leur heure. Leur qualité varie enfin selon leur degré de nouveauté et la durée de leur usage. Les objets ont leur vie qu'il s'agit d'appécier dans le concert ou la cacophonie des relations humaines, car ils font partie de l'histoire, quand ils ne font pas, eux-mêmes, l'histoire.

Or, le récit lucanien de la Passion signale bon nombre d'objets[11]. Les uns sont des objets réels à l'intérieur de la narration, par exemple la cruche d'eau qui sert de point de repère (22,10); les autres sont des objets allusifs, mentionnés, parfois comme métaphores, dans les discours des personnages, ainsi le tamis à travers lequel, selon la sentence de Jésus, Simon Pierre va passer (22,31). Cette répartition fait surgir des équivoques sur lesquelles le récit joue parfois: la plus fameuse concerne les épées, tantôt métaphores suggérées par Jésus, tantôt objets tendus par le disciple empressé (22,35-38.49).

---

11. Je laisse de côté, dans le récit lucanien de la Passion, ce qui n'est pas à proprement parler un objet, telle partie du corps, oreille, cheveu, ventre, crâne, main, genou, ou tel végétal, plante ou arbre.

Venons-en aux objets réels du récit. Pour nous, l'argent est devenu abstrait. Pour les anciens, ἀργύριον est une réalité concrète, des pièces qui ont leur poids. Au début du récit de la Passion, il y a de l'argent qui circule (22,5), qui passe des chefs à Judas, en compensation et en échange d'une autre παράδοσις, la livraison de Jésus. La tradition chrétienne a bien fait de méditer ce marchandage, cette offre d'objets en échange d'un sujet si assujetti qu'à la fin il n'est plus qu'un objet inerte, un σῶμα neutre.

Au moment où s'opère cette transaction, Jésus institue une autre circulation d'objets: autour d'une table, explicitement mentionée (22,21), qui anticipe celle du Royaume (22,30), Jésus désigne une coupe qui ouvre sur l'avenir de ce Royaume (22,17-18), puis il distribue du pain qui ne sert pas d'échange, à la différence de l'argent, mais de présence sacramentelle et de référence au passé de Jésus (22,19). Enfin, il fait circuler la coupe qui marque la communion du sacrifice d'alliance.

Deux autres scènes «à objets» se répondent: celles des épées. D'un côté, la question de l'équipement des chrétiens que le texte aborde avec cette attention que Luc porte aux médiations (22,35-38); de l'autre, le pataquès du disciple empressé, impulsif ou zélote (22,49-51). La deuxième scène fournit le sens à attribuer à μάχαιρα dans la première: les épées dont les disciples auront besoin, quand la protection de leur Maître aura disparu, ne sont pas des armes tangibles, mais une force spirituelle, articulant le meilleur de l'être humain et la splendeur du don de Dieu (dans l'école paulinienne où Luc a fait ses classes, on utilisait la métaphore de l'épée pour décrire l'Esprit Saint ou la Parole de Dieu, cf. Ep 6,17 et He 4,12-13; plus généralement, la vie chrétienne était comparée à un service militaire)[12].

L'objet par excellence de la Passion, c'est évidemment la croix. Suggérée dès le cri des chefs et de la foule («crucifie! crucifie-le!» 23,21), elle est mentionnée au début du chemin de croix (23,26). Curieusement elle est alors associée à Simon qui la porte, alors que Jésus n'en aura jamais la charge. C'est elle qui portera Jésus (23,33). Là encore, une réflexion s'impose. Est-ce trop osé de dire que le Christ seul l'affronte dans sa fonction de châtiment capital («là, ils le crucifièrent», 23,33). Le disciple «derrière Jésus» la rencontre de façon moins dramatique. Il est à la croix ce que Joseph d'Arimathée sera au corps de Jésus. Un ami, un disciple, qui partage à sa mesure et soulage comme il peut le sort de son Maître.

L'Écriture (Ps 22,19) impose au récit évangélique de la Passion la distribution des habits par tirage au sort. Sans s'attarder sur ce caractère scripturaire de l'épisode, Luc le signale en passant (23,34). On peut se demander si le texte n'oppose pas les habits du vivant à ceux du

---

12. Je ne prétends pas avoir expliqué ainsi la réponse énigmatique de Jésus: ἱκανόν ἐστιν, «c'est assez» (22,38).

mort, les vêtements répartis au linceul (σινδών) dans lequel le corps du crucifié est enroulé (23,53). N'oublions pas l'importance que les anciens attribuaient au vêtement comme signe d'identité et de situation sociale[13]. Ôter au Christ ses vêtements, c'était précipiter la fin de sa vie; le couvrir d'un linceul, c'était confirmer son trépas. Adversaires qui tirent au sort et partisans qui respectent le rituel de deuil s'accordent pour constater l'issue tragique sur laquelle ils n'ont nulle prise.

Il y aurait encore d'autres réalités matérielles à mentionner, le vinaigre avant la mort (23,36), les aromates et la myrrhe après (24,1), l'écriteau accroché au corps nu du crucifié, trahissant et communiquant son identité royale (23,38). Il faudrait surtout signaler le sort d'un autre objet, la déchirure du voile du Temple qui lui ôte sa raison d'être (23,45). Le texte met en rapport ce prodige avec un autre signe miraculeux, les ténèbres qui plongent la terre entière dans l'obscurité, l'éclipse de soleil (23,44-45). Il ne suffit pas de dire que, dans les récits antiques, des prodiges accompagnaient la naissance ou la mort des héros et des dieux. Ce signe a une fonction particulière qui confirme ce que j'ai suggéré plus haut à propos du Temple: le sanctuaire perd sa fonction d'autrefois. La présence divine est dorénavant ailleurs, dans un lieu ἀχειροποίητος, «non fait de main d'homme» (cf. Ac 7,48).

5. L'entre-jeu de quatre modèles

Une amie me confiait récemment que, malgré sa tristesse, elle était soulagée de la dignité avec laquelle son frère était mort. Cette grandeur contrastait, disait-elle, avec certaines attitudes qu'il avait eues de son vivant.

Autre a été la vie, autre fut la mort. À l'écoute de ce diagnostic, j'ai supposé des schémas très anciens dans notre civilisation. Je pensai aussitôt à la mort des méchants, plus particulièrement des persécuteurs et constatai que Luc, avec le récit de la mort d'Hérode Agrippa (Ac 12,20-23), avait ouvert la voie à Lactance[14]; telle fut sa vie, telle fut sa mort, du péché à son châtiment. Puis je songeai plus précisément aux dires de cette amie: en plus contrasté, Luc les avait anticipés par l'épisode du bon brigand (23,39-43), comme il avait frayé le passage aux légendes des Acta Pilati[15]. A bien fini qui avait mal commencé. Le cas de Judas me vint ensuite en mémoire: c'est la mort misérable de celui qui est bien parti, le disciple renégat (Ac 1,15-20), celui qui préfigure les futurs lapsi du temps de Tertullien puis de Cyprien. Troisième modèle.

---

13. Cf. E. HAULOTTE, Symbolique du vêtement selon la Bible (Théologie, 65), Paris, 1966.

14. Cf. LACTANCE, De la mort des persécuteurs (SC, 39), ed. J. Moreau, 2 vol., Paris, 1954.

15. Cf. Acta Pilati, 26 (= Descensus Christi ad inferos, 10). Il s'agit du récit de l'accès du bon brigand au Paradis; cf. A. DE SANTOS OTERO, Los Evangelios Apócrifos (Biblioteca de Autores Cristianos, 148), Madrid, ⁶1988, pp. 463-464.

Il ne reste qu'une case à remplir de ce carré de possibles: une fin digne d'une belle vie. Celle de Jésus bien sûr qui inaugure – surtout en sa version lucanienne – le genre littéraire des actes de martyre[16] et prépare d'autres textes, liturgiques, homilétiques et théologiques.

Que penser de ces quatre patterns? Existent-ils? Sont-ils aussi archaïques que je le suppose? Sont-ils enracinés en la seule Grèce, en la seule tradition d'Israël ou appartiennent-ils, tels des archétypes, à toute conscience humaine qui réfléchit en société?

Quelles que soient les réponses à ces questions, je puis préciser quelques caractéristiques du quatrième modèle. Dans la correspondance entre la vie et la mort, il faut une prescience de cette issue, une dépréoccupation de soi au profit de son entourage, une raison d'être qui fournira une raison d'accepter la mort; une mission à remplir dont la mort, loin d'obstruer la réalisation, l'accélère au contraire; une jalousie suscitée qui, devant le succès de cette existence, lui tend un funeste piège. On songe à la mort de Socrate à côté de celle de Jésus. On n'oubliera pas celle de Syméon (2,25-35), ni celle d'Étienne (Ac 6,8–8,1).

6. *Les trois niveaux de l'œuvre*

On a beaucoup écrit sur la théologie du récit lucanien de la Passion. Certains y ont repéré des tendances doctrinales (théodicée et histoire du salut; christologie); d'autres, une préoccupation historique (confirmer le credo); d'autres enfin une orientation parénétique (rôle des disciples et du peuple). Le conflit des volontés analysé plus haut a déjà conduit à distinguer deux niveaux de lecture, présents l'un et l'autre chez Luc: a) le niveau narratif, suggestif d'une histoire humaine, d'un drame que Luc, dans le schéma de contraste, résume par ces mots «celui que vous avez crucifié» (Ac 2,36); b) le niveau méta-historique, théologique, qui voit dans l'histoire et ses lignes courbes le dessein salvifique que Dieu achève droitement, celui que Luc confesse dans les Actes en évoquent lors de la Pentecôte «la volonté fixée et la prescience de Dieu» (Ac 2,23). À mon sens, il faut ajouter, à ces niveaux historique et métahistorique, c'est-à-dire narratif et doctrinal, un niveau éthique ou parénétique. Martin Dibelius et Albert Vanhoye ont dit à ce sujet l'essentiel[17]: la figure du Christ que Luc dessine est celle du juste souffrant, du prophète rejeté, du martyr. Le juste faisait partie de son peuple, le

---

16. Cf H. DELEHAYE, *Les passions des martyrs et les genres littéraires* (Subsidia Hagiographica, 13B), Bruxelles, ²1966.

17. Cf. M. DIBELIUS, *Die Formgeschichte des Evangeliums*, pp. 178-218; A. VANHOYE, *La Passion selon les quatre Évangiles*, pp. 18-19.30-33.57-61. Le Père Vanhoye vient de corriger sur un point son interprétation: il ne pense plus pouvoir s'appuyer sur le v. 62 du ch. 22 (les pleurs amers de Pierre après le reniement) dont il admet aujourd'hui l'inauthenticité; cf. A. VANHOYE, *L'intérêt de Luc pour la prophétie en Lc 1,76; 4,16-30 et 22,60-65*.

prophète avait une mission et le martyr communiait avec les siens. Le récit de la Passion, celui de Luc en tout cas, n'a pas été écrit comme une simple page d'histoire, ni comme l'énoncé d'une doctrine de l'expiation ou de la substitution. Sa forme est destinée à des lecteurs appelés, implicitement mais réellement, à partager le sort de Jésus: dans l'émotion de la foi et le sérieux de l'engagement. Les figures des disciples devaient les aider à s'y retrouver, car ils pouvaient s'identifier à Simon de Cyrène ou apprendre à dépasser une existence à la Judas ou à la Simon Pierre. Tant la figure entraînante de Jésus sur le chemin d'une sotériologie subjective (incluant la foi et la vie des croyant-e-s) que l'éclairage des compagnons de Jésus, disciples, femmes ou passants, ont pris chez Luc une coloration parénétique. Dans le tableau que Luc offre à notre méditation, j'ajouterai donc aux niveaux narratif et doctrinal un niveau moral.

7. *Le narrateur*

Le narrateur sait ce qu'il se veut. Il n'hésite jamais. Il n'affiche nulle part son ignorance. Il connaît le déroulement des faits, même les plus confidentiels (22,4) et les plus secrets (23,45). Il est au courant des habitudes des personnages (22,39), de leur état d'esprit (22,5), de leurs projets (22,6), de leur valeur (23,50). Il connaît les agissements de chacun, les plus lâches (22,54-62) comme les plus héroïques (23,34). Il a un projet théologique et littéraire que les pages précédentes ont suggéré.

Or, s'il sait tout cela et veut tout cela, il raconte pourtant son histoire sans s'impliquer lui-même dans le récit, à la différence de ce qu'il fait dans les passages en «nous» ou les prologues en «je». Il ne juge jamais: au pire moment de la trahison de Judas ou du reniement de Pierre, il garde une parfaite réserve.

Il tient à cette attitude, car il veut donner l'impression que les faits parlent d'eux-mêmes et que les personnages expriment le sens qu'ils attribuent aux événements. Il n'utilise jamais lui-même l'Écriture pour légitimer et expliquer le drame qui se déroule. Il signale simplement que le héros a établi cette correspondance (22,37). Il ne ressent pas le besoin de démontrer personnellement que les griefs adressés à Jésus sont faux. Il se contente de rapporter à trois reprises l'avis de Pilate et laisse l'évidence éclairer le lecteur. Le récit, pense-t-il, est plus fort parce que, étant arrangé par ses soins, il a l'air objectif.

Le narrateur n'interrompt pas – il faut l'ajouter – son récit à la mise au tombeau (23,50-54). La narration du ch. 24 constitue l'indispensable sortie du tunnel. Elle lève les ambiguïtés et les paradoxes des ch. 22-23. En particulier et principalement, elle fait percevoir que le laisser-aller de Jésus n'était pas de l'inconscience, que la lucidité du héros n'était pas de l'aveuglement et que sa confiance dans les événements représentait la face visible d'une harmonieuse communion avec celui qui détermine l'histoire. La mise du Juste au rang des injustes (22,37) ne pouvait être que provisoire. En permettant à la volonté de Satan de s'accomplir, le Christ laissait faire plus faible que lui. En se soumettant à la volonté de Dieu, il espérait que celle-ci serait finalement gagnante et qu'il avait eu raison d'y adapter librement la sienne[18].

II. APPROCHE DIACHRONIQUE: LES SOURCES ET LEUR REPRISE PAR LUC

1. État de la question

La question que chaque exégète se pose à un moment ou à un autre est celle de la documentation dont l'évangéliste Luc a bénéficié pour écrire les ch. 22-23 de son premier livre. Diverses raisons en accentuent l'intérêt: la relation à l'évangile de Marc y est d'une autre nature que dans la période galiléenne de Jésus. Dans un récit pourtant suivi, l'ordonnance de Luc diffère de celle de Marc. Pour prendre un seul exemple, à la séquence de Marc (comparution devant le Sanhédrin Mc 14,53-64; moqueries Mc 14,65; reniement Mc 14,66-72, préparé par le v. 54) correspond l'ordre inverse chez Luc (reniement Lc 22,54-62; moqueries Lc 22,63-65; comparution devant le Sanhédrin Lc 22,66-71). Par ailleurs, quand on peut mettre en parallèle telle péricope de Marc et de Luc, la parenté est moins grande ici que dans le reste de l'évangile. Ainsi, dans le récit du procès devant les autorités juives, Luc ignore-t-il la recherche de témoins et le logion sur le Temple, mais il atteste un dédoublement que Marc ignore de la question sur la messianité de Jésus (Lc 22,66-71 // Mc 14,53-64). Enfin, le récit lucanien diverge aussi par le contenu des épisodes qui le constituent: Luc omet l'onction de Béthanie (Mc 14,3-9; cf. Lc 7,36-50), mais transmet une instance judiciaire ignorée des autres évangiles, la comparution devant Hérode (Lc 23,8-12). À ces particularités, il convient d'ajouter une dernière constatation: sans que la parenté reflète une dépendance littéraire, Luc partage avec l'évangéliste Jean certains détails de la Passion (par ex. il n'y a pas chez

---

18. Je remercie les collègues qui, lors des Journées Bibliques, ont réagi à cet exposé. Voici quelques éléments critiques que j'ai notés: a) Ne faut-il pas tenir compte du statut des lecteurs qui, d'entrée de jeu, connaissent l'issue du drame? b) Ai-je assez respecté la stratégie de Luc qui évite de parler d'une condamnation à mort de Jésus? c) Ce que je disais – je l'ai modifié depuis lors – du narrateur implicite, qui se tiendrait sur la réserve, n'était-il pas en contradiction avec les paragraphes antérieurs de mon texte qui insistaient sur l'organisation théologique et littéraire du récit? d) Ne faut-il pas considérer l'œuvre entière pour découvrir des tendances ou des intentions liées à des structures et à des effets de composition? e) L'effacement du narrateur n'est-il pas un effet rhétorique de plus? (J'ai tenu compte de cette suggestion dans la version définitive de mon texte). f) Le récit lucanien – telle est ma conviction – communique une certitude, celle de l'innocence de Jésus le juste.

eux deux réunions du Sanhédrin, mais une seule, Lc 22,66-71 // Jn 18,24, précédée d'une étape dans la maison du grand prêtre, Lc 22,54 // Jn 18,13-14.19-23)[19].

L'importance quantitative et qualitative de ces données explique l'immense littérature qu'elles ont engendrée. Les commentaires récents de Joseph A. Fitzmyer[20] et de Wolfgang Wiefel[21] en présentent les grandes lignes[22]. Chacun admet que Marc n'est pas le créateur du genre littéraire «récit de la Passion» et que son récit est fait à la fois de tradition et de rédaction[23]. Le *Sitz im Leben*, l'enracinement social, dans l'Église, d'un tel récit a dû être liturgique[24]. Ce fut pour commémorer la mort de Jésus que l'on a cherché à se la rappeler, à la raconter et à l'interpréter (en particulier à l'aide de l'Écriture). Si l'on suppose une certaine pluralité de communautés primitives, on doit admettre que divers récits de la Passion ont pu voir le jour. Une telle supposition ne doit cependant pas favoriser l'hypothèse d'une autonomie totale des récits évangéliques de la Passion. La parenté littéraire et même verbale fréquente s'y oppose. Comment alors imaginer et reconstruire cette relation?

a. *Première possibilité*: comme dans le reste de son évangile, Luc, ici encore, suit Marc, mais il s'autorise à le modifier de manière plus drastique qu'ailleurs en raison de traditions dont il a ouï dire ou d'un récit, peut-être oral, que sa communauté lui a transmis. Les divergences par rapport à Marc auraient ainsi une origine *traditionsgeschichtlich*.

b. *Deuxième possibilité*, qui n'est qu'une variante de la première: Luc interviendrait plus vigoureusement qu'ailleurs au niveau rédactionnel. Il ne disposerait guère que de Marc et de son imagination accompagnée de convictions et de références scripturaires. Les écarts par rapport à Marc s'expliqueraient ici de façon *redaktionsgeschichtlich*.

c. *Troisième possibilité*: Luc fait ici faux bond à sa source principale, Marc, et aligne son texte sur un récit, sans doute écrit, auquel il donne la préférence pour des raisons doctrinales ou pratiques, affectives ou raisonnées[25]. Étant donné que l'évangéliste connaît aussi le récit marcien, il se permet d'entrelarder cette narration qui lui est propre de

---

19. Sur les liens entre Jean et Luc, et la littérature qu'ils ont engendrée, cf. F. NEIRYNCK, *John and the Synoptics (1975-1990)*, in A. DENAUX (ed.), *John and the Synoptics* (BETL, 101), Leuven, 1992, pp. 35-46.

20. Cf. J.A. FITZMYER, *The Gospel According to Luke*, II, pp. 1365-1368.

21. Cf. W. WIEFEL, *Das Evangelium nach Lukas*, pp. 12-13 et 357-358.

22. Cf. F. BOVON, *Luc le théologien*, pp. 175-181.

23. Pour l'histoire des traditions et l'élaboration d'un récit suivi, cf. R. BULTMANN, *Die Geschichte der synoptischen Tradition*, Göttingen, ³1957, pp. 297-303; M. DIBELIUS, *Die Formgeschichte des Evangeliums*, pp. 178-218.

24. Cf. É. TROCMÉ, *The Passion as Liturgy*.

25. Il peut s'agir de la suite du bien propre qu'il utilise dans le récit de voyage ou d'une source particulière au récit de la Passion.

matériaux extraits du deuxième évangile. Comme dans la première hypothèse, Luc jouirait donc de deux sources, mais il donnerait sa préférence à la seconde. L'argumentation est ici *literarkritisch* à l'origine, tout en bénéficiant d'arguments *formgeschichtlich* puis *redaktionsgeschichtlich*.

Il n'est pas souhaitable de présenter la liste des partisans de ces diverses hypothèses. Je puis dire que la liste en est longue, qu'elle contient des noms prestigieux et qu'aucune nation n'en a eu le monopole.

Dès avant l'apparition de l'histoire de la rédaction, certains partisans de la *Formgeschichte*, Kendrick Grobel[26] et Jack Finegan[27], maintiennent que Luc n'a disposé d'aucune autre source suivie que celle de Marc. L'originalité et la marge de liberté créatrice accordées à chaque auteur biblique par les tenants de la *Redaktionsgeschichte* n'ont pu qu'inciter les chercheurs à attribuer toujours davantage à l'évangéliste les particularités de son récit[28]. Telle est l'attitude prise par notre jubilaire Franz Neirynck[29], par Martin Rese[30] dans une thèse d'habilitation inédite, par Joseph A. Fitzmyer[31] dans le volume II de son commentaire, par Marion L. Soards[32] dans son analyse de Lc 22, par Franz Georg Untergassmair[33] qui, à partir de Lc 23, attribue l'originalité lucanienne à un «spezifisches Verkündigungsanliegen»[34] et par Donald Senior[35] dans sa présentation récente de tout le récit de la Passion, pour n'en citer que quelques-uns.

Qui fut à l'origine de l'hypothèse inverse, d'un Proto-Luc ou d'un bien propre à l'évangéliste dans le récit de la Passion? Je l'ignore. En Allemagne, dès la fin du siècle dernier, divers auteurs se plurent à l'émettre: Paul Feine[36] et Bernhard Weiss[37]. En cette zone linguistique, l'hypothèse, jamais très populaire[38], n'a pas disparu puisque nous la rencontrons chez d'aussi éminents exégètes qu'Adolph Schlatter[39],

---

26. K. GROBEL, *Formgeschichte und synoptische Quellenanalyse*.
27. J. FINEGAN, *Die Überlieferung der Leidens- und Auferstehungsgeschichte Jesu*.
28. Tout en concédant que Luc a pu disposer de bribes de traditions isolées.
29. F. NEIRYNCK, *La matière marcienne dans l'évangile de Luc*, p. 109.
30. M. RESE, *Die «Stunde» Jesu in Jerusalem*; cf. E. SCHWEIZER, *Zur Frage der Quellenbenutzung durch Lukas*, p. 46, n. 47.
31. J.A. FITZMYER, *The Gospel According to Luke*, II, pp. 1365-1366.
32. M.L. SOARDS, *The Passion According to Luke*, pp. 120-123.
33. F.G. UNTERGASSMAIR, *Kreuzweg und Kreuzigung Jesu*, p. 112.
34. *Ibid.*, p. 1.
35. D. SENIOR, *The Passion of Jesus in the Gospel of Luke*, p. 10.
36. P. FEINE, *Eine vorkanonische Überlieferung des Lukas*, in ID., *Evangelium und Apostelgeschichte*, Gotha, 1891.
37. B. WEISS, *Die Quellen des Lukasevangeliums*, Stuttgart-Berlin, 1907.
38. Dans leurs travaux signalés ci-dessus, p. 407, n. 23, les deux maîtres allemands, R. Bultmann et M. Dibelius, s'opposent à l'hypothèse.
39. A. SCHLATTER, *Das Evangelium des Lukas. Aus seinen Quellen erklärt*, Stuttgart, ²1960.

Joachim Jeremias[40] et Eduard Schweizer[41], sans oublier Friedrich Rehkopf[42] qui la reconstruit à l'aide de S^{Lc} et de Q, et Tim Schramm[43]. L'hypothèse se rencontre aussi, dès le début de ce siècle et sans doute auparavant, en Grande-Bretagne et aux États-Unis chez John C. Hawkins[44], Alfred Morris Perry[45], Burnett Hillman Streeter[46] et surtout Vincent Taylor[47], qui, par son influence personnelle, l'a rendue plus populaire dans son pays qu'en Allemagne. Aujourd'hui, on la retrouve aux États-Unis sous la plume de Joseph B. Tyson[48].

Il existe une dizaine de monographies récentes sur le récit lucanien de la Passion[49]! Ce qui frappe, c'est le désintérêt affiché à l'égard de la question qui nous préoccupe. Certains auteurs en font totalement abstraction, car ils opèrent une lecture littéraire, structurale, rhétorique, narratologique ou théologique. Anton Büchele[50] présente une analyse *redaktionsgeschichtlich* qui recourt moins au contraste entre la tradition et la rédaction qu'à l'analyse des structures, superficielle et profonde, et des motifs[51], le tout accompagné par un effort intertextuel (les autres textes étant le reste de Luc-Actes). Il en va de même pour Robert J. Karris[52]. Cet exégète suppose que le talent artistique de Luc favorise une élaboration théologique qu'il résume par les mots: Dieu fidèle, justice et nourriture. Paru la même année dans la même collection catholique américaine, le livre de Jerome Neyrey[53] est de la même veine. Il envisage Luc comme un auteur à comprendre en lui-même, ce

---

40. Cf. J. JEREMIAS, *Die Sprache des Lukasevangeliums*.

41. E. SCHWEIZER, *Zur Frage der Quellenbenutzung durch Lukas*.

42. F. REHKOPF, *Die lukanische Sonderquelle. Ihr Umfang und Sprachgebrauch* (WUNT, 5), Tübingen, 1959.

43. T. SCHRAMM, *Der Markus-Stoff bei Lukas. Eine literarkritische und redaktionsgeschichtliche Untersuchung* (SNTS MS, 14), Cambridge, 1971.

44. J.C. HAWKINS, *Three Limitations to St. Luke's Use of St. Mark's Gospel*, in W. SANDAY (ed.), *Studies in the Synoptic Problem by Members of the University of Oxford*, Oxford, 1911, pp. 27-94, esp. 76-94.

45. A.M. PERRY, *The Sources of Luke's Passion-Narrative* (Historical and Linguistic Studies in Literature Related to the NT, 2. Ser. IV, 2), Chicago, IL, 1920.

46. B.H. STREETER, *The Four Gospels: A Study of Origins*, London, [4]1930 (j'utilise l'édition originale de 1924, pp. 199-222).

47. V. TAYLOR, *The Passion Narrative of St. Luke*.

48. J.B. TYSON, *The Lukan Version of the Trial of Jesus*, in *NT* 3 (1959) 249-258. Cf. J.B. TYSON, *The Death of Jesus in Luke-Acts*.

49. Je ne suis pas très au courant du succès que ces hypothèses ont remporté en France et dans les pays francophones. Il faudrait se reporter aux travaux de E. Osty, L. Cerfaux, A. George, J. Dupont, X. Léon-Dufour, M.-J. Boismard et A. Vanhoye, dont on trouve les références bibliographiques dans le commentaire de J.A. FITZMYER, *The Gospel According to Luke* (cf. l'index des noms propres dans le vol. II, dès la p. 1603).

50. A. BÜCHELE, *Der Tod Jesu im Lukasevangelium*.

51. Motifs christologique, ecclésiologique et parénétique.

52. R.J. KARRIS, *Luke, Artist and Theologian*.

53. J. NEYREY, *The Passion According to Luke*.

qui le conduit à intégrer, plus que d'autres, les parallèles au récit de la Passion extraits du livre des Actes. Il insiste sur la figure de Jésus en croix comme Sauveur sauvé, nouvel Adam, ἀρχηγός, «guide» conduisant au salut, dont le courage au jardin des Oliviers s'oppose à la λύπη des disciples (intéressante analyse de ce terme) et dont la foi, qui résiste jusqu'à la fin, a une portée salvifique et exemplaire. Les objectifs et les résultats de Marion L. Soards[54], s'ils intègrent, comme je l'ai dit, la recherche des sources, visent principalement la rédaction lucanienne et plus particulièrement l'orientation théologique de l'auteur (tendances christologique, eschatologique et ecclésiologique). Christologie: en Jésus le plan de Dieu se réalise. Eschatologie: dès le dernier repas, l'histoire de Jésus inaugure les temps derniers. Ecclésiologie: les interactions entre Jésus et ses disciples offrent aux lecteurs de Luc des instructions sur leur propre rôle dans le plan de Dieu.

Il n'est pas étonnant que les monographies récentes qui embrassent l'ensemble de Luc ou de Luc-Actes participent, elles aussi, de cette valorisation de la forme littéraire ultime et de l'orientation doctrinale de l'évangéliste au détriment des matériaux, sources et traditions, dont celui-ci a pu disposer. Le constat vaut pour le quintette franco-américain: Charles H. Talbert, Robert C. Tannehill, Charles L'Eplattenier, Jean-Noël Aletti et Roland Meynet[55].

2. *Une hypothèse*

Dans ce climat marqué, d'un côté, par une analyse de la rédaction qui se désintéresse de la tradition et, de l'autre, par des études littéraires ou théologiques, nous nous trouvons dans une situation historico-critique bloquée autour des trois théories signalées dont aucune ne fait la décision. Pour tenter de desserrer l'étau, j'aimerais émettre une hypothèse, résultant de mon contact avec l'évangéliste en d'autres sections de son œuvre[56]. J'ai constaté en effet, aussi bien dans le premier tiers de l'Évangile (période galiléenne du ministère de Jésus) que dans la première moitié des Actes, que Luc pratiquait une méthode simple et même rudimentaire dans le recours à ses sources. Il m'est apparu a) qu'il se contentait le plus souvent d'avoir deux documents à

---

54. M.L. SOARDS, *The Passion According to Luke*.

55. Cf. C.H. TALBERT, *Reading Luke*; R.C. TANNEHILL, *The Narrative Unity of Luke-Acts*; J.-N. ALETTI, *L'art de raconter Jésus-Christ*; C. L'EPLATTENIER, *Lecture de l'Évangile de Luc*; R. MEYNET, *L'Évangile selon saint Luc*.

56. Ma position ressemble un peu à celle de V. TAYLOR, *The Passion Narrative of St. Luke*. Toutefois, l'exégète britannique raisonne toujours avec l'a priori que l'une des sources est dominante. Cf. H.J. CADBURY, *The Style and Literary Method of Luke*, II, *The Treatment of Sources in the Gospel* (HTS, 6), Cambridge, MA, 1920, p. 76: «It is well known that sections of Luke derived from Mark and those of other origin are arranged in continuous blocks and not interspersed as in the Gospel of Matthew».

disposition (par exemple Marc et Q dans Lc 3-9 ou des traditions de Jérusalem et des traditions d'Antioche dans Ac 1-15); b) qu'il n'aimait pas fusionner ses sources dans la même péricope ou la même section: par exemple, dans le Sermon dans la Plaine, il quitte Marc et, dans les récits subséquents, il ignore Q; c) qu'il pratiquait donc une alternance telle qu'elle nous interdit de parler de priorité donnée à une source au détriment d'une autre; d) que Luc, quand il le pouvait, préférait une lente alternance de blocs assez amples à une succession rapide d'épisodes isolés. Comme tout un chacun, Luc ne recherchait ni les embarras, ni les complications. Les conditions pratiques de son travail intellectuel, jusqu'aux dimensions de sa table et au substrat matériel de sa documentation, n'encourageaient pas Luc à multiplier les sources ni ne l'incitaient à les utiliser en même temps[57].

Tout le pousse à s'appuyer, pour le passage qu'il écrit, sur un document et sur un seul qu'il va reprendre, reformuler et adapter avec une grande liberté. Quand il le voudra, il abandonnera cette première source pour se tourner – si nécessaire grâce à une transition – vers la seconde.

Dans une bonne analyse, qui distingue la tradition et la rédaction, Marion L. Soards[58] cite à la suite tous les passages non-marciens du récit de la Passion de Luc et repousse l'hypothèse d'une deuxième source continue à côté de Marc par cet argument qu'il voudrait infaillible: cela ne fait pas un récit suivi. Je réponds: Et pour cause! En auteur lucide, Luc déteste les répétitions et, si les récits sont assez proches (ce qui, pour des raisons d'enracinement ecclésial et liturgique, est assez vraisemblable), il ne reprend en gros que la moitié de chacun d'eux, sacrifiant sans hésitation l'autre moitié. Il préfère perdre tel détail de l'autre version plutôt que de se rendre la tâche difficile en cherchant à l'insérer dans la version présentement utilisée.

À mon avis, l'alternance – solution simple dont la banalité même accentue la vraisemblance – peut se vérifier assez facilement. À juste titre, la ressemblance d'un passage avec sa source – Marc étant la comparaison tangible dans la moitié des cas – ne doit pas être évaluée à l'aide d'un seul critère, par exemple la statistique du vocabulaire. Il faut y ajouter l'argument d'ordre des épisodes et celui des motifs narratifs ou théologiques.

Sans avoir le temps de démontrer toutes les raisons de mes choix, voici comment je répartis la matière des ch. 22-23 de Luc.

---

57. Sur les conditions, matérielles en particulier, du travail intellectuel dans l'Antiquité et l'usage de sources par les auteurs classiques, cf. G. KENNEDY, *Classical and Christian Source Criticism*, in W.O. WALKER (ed.), *The Relationships Among the Gospels: An Interdisciplinary Dialogue*, San Antonio, TX, 1978, pp. 125-155. Et naturellement, H.-I. MARROU, *Histoire de l'éducation dans l'Antiquité* (Points, Histoire, 56), 2 vol., Paris, ⁶1981.

58. M.L. SOARDS, *The Passion According to Luke*, pp. 120-121.

Luc paraît alterner deux sources dans sa deuxième apocalypse. En tout cas, la parabole du figuier (Lc 21,29-33) s'appuie sur Marc (Mc 13,28-31), tandis que l'exhortation finale, sans parallèle marcien, doit prendre pied dans un autre document (Lc 21,34-36). La fin du chapitre (Jésus de jour dans le temple, de nuit sur le mont des Oliviers; le peuple attentif à son enseignement dans le temple dès le petit matin, Lc 21,37-38) est une transition rédactionnelle de Luc.

Pour le début du récit de la Passion, l'évangéliste suit manifestement Marc, moyennant l'omission de l'onction à Béthanie qu'il considère comme un doublet de son récit galiléen (Lc 7,36-50): complot, trahison, préparatifs de la Pâque (Lc 22,1-14 // Mc 14,1-2.10-17).

Dans le récit du dernier repas, Luc bifurque et opte pour son bien propre qui place la désignation du traître après et non, comme Marc, avant l'institution de la Cène (Lc 22,21-23). Lc 22,15-20 est formé de deux parties comme le récit de Marc, mais, ici encore, en ordre inverse: la coupe eschatologique est mentionnée d'entrée de jeu (Lc 22,16-18), alors qu'elle suit l'institution chez Marc (Mc 14,25). La formulation lucanienne de ce premier fragment est, à mon avis, indépendante du deuxième Évangile. Il doit en aller de même – malgré la proximité avec Marc – de l'institution proprement dite (Lc 22,19-20), qui a une allure que j'appellerais «antiochienne» ou «helléniste» (εὐχαριστήσας et non εὐλογήσας; «donné pour vous»[59] après la mention du corps, au lieu d'aucune précision; l'évocation du souvenir, absente de Marc; la coupe eucharistique après le repas; «cette coupe» et non «cela»; «l'alliance dans mon sang» et non «mon sang, celui de l'alliance»; sang répandu «pour vous» et non «pour beaucoup»). C'est cette formulation que Paul connaît lui aussi en 1 Co 11,23-25. Marc et Matthieu reflètent, au contraire, la version que je nommerais «jérusalémite» ou «araméenne» de la Cène. Proches l'une de l'autre, en raison du conservatisme bien connu de la liturgie, les deux versions n'en sont pas moins clairement distinctes.

Sur sa lancée, Luc poursuit la lecture et la réécriture de son bien propre: dans la désignation du traître (Lc 22,21-23) et la querelle sur «le plus grand» (Lc 22,24-30). La proximité avec Marc, dans ce dernier épisode, pourrait pousser l'exégète à se demander: Luc ne se réfère-t-il pas de nouveau à son autre source, Marc, pour un instant, c'est-à-dire pour une péricope? Mais, comme Luc préfère reprendre alternativement des blocs entiers plutôt que des unités isolées, je repousse cette hypothèse. Il en découle, ce qui est important pour l'exégèse, que les particularités lucaniennes de cet épisode, comparées à celles de Marc, ne sont pas toutes rédactionnelles. Une partie, voire la majorité, sont traditionnelles, issues du bien propre. Si le mot emblématique φιλονεικία, «querelle», «dispute» est peut-être rédactionnel, le contraste

---

59. Paul a «celui pour vous» sans le verbe «donner» en 1 Co 11,24.

μείζων-νεώτερος, «le plus âgé» – «le plus jeune», est sans doute traditionnel. Il y a une particularité intéressante dans cet épisode, le fameux «moi, je suis au milieu de vous, comme le servant» (Lc 22,27, parallèle très différent de Mc 10,45). L'indépendance ici de Luc par rapport à Marc se confirme par les derniers versets de la péricope (en particulier à propos des douze trônes, Lc 22,28-30) que Matthieu à notre surprise connaît aussi et situe au même endroit. Les expressions de Matthieu et de Luc sont assez différentes.

Luc poursuit, comme Marc, par l'annonce du reniement de Pierre (Lc 22,31-34 // Mc 14,26-31). Deux arguments nous empêchent toutefois de comprendre la version de Luc comme l'adaptation de celle de Marc: Marc, qui a fait sortir le Maître et ses disciples en chantant et les a déplacés au Mont des Oliviers, situe donc la scène à l'extérieur. Chez Luc, Jésus reste dans la chambre haute où il poursuit son discours. Par ailleurs, les textes sont fort différents: Marc cite l'Écriture et mentionne la dispersion des brebis, tandis que Luc annonce à Pierre l'épreuve du tamis. À la différence du Pierre de Marc, le Pierre de Luc ne réitère pas son engagement à mourir pour son maître (Mc 14,31).

À mon avis, l'incident des deux épées, sans aucun parallèle dans les autres évangiles (Lc 22,35-38), faisait partie, lui aussi, du discours d'adieux propre à la seconde source de Luc. L'évangéliste poursuit la relecture de ce document dans l'épisode du jardin des Oliviers (Lc 22,39-46 // Mc 14,32-42), dont on sait les divergences d'avec son pendant marcien (Gethsémané, le nom du lieu n'est pas mentionné; il n'est pas question d'une mise à part des trois disciples préférés, ni d'une âme désolée; par ailleurs, le texte signale l'apparition, absente de Marc, d'un ange protecteur; la fin de l'épisode est beaucoup plus ramassée chez Luc que chez Marc).

À mon avis, dès l'arrestation, Luc se replace sous la houlette de Marc (Lc 22,47-53 // Mc 14,43-52). Il y a dans ces versets une parenté littérale telle qu'elle ne peut s'expliquer sans une dépendance littéraire. Luc déplace simplement la liste des autorités et leur équipement (Mc 14,43b devient Lc 22,52) et opère deux omissions: l'explicitation du signe convenu, le baiser (Mc 14,44), et la fuite des disciples, dont le jeune homme tout nu (Mc 14,50-52). L'évangéliste reste fidèle à Marc dans l'épisode suivant: le reniement de Pierre qu'il a déplacé, le situant, comme je l'ai dit plus haut, *avant* le récit de la comparution devant le Sanhédrin (Lc 22,54-62 // Mc 14,66-72). C'est à Marc aussi qu'il a emprunté la dérision de Jésus comme prophète (Lc 22,63-65 // Mc 14,65). Chez Marc simplement l'ordre est différent: la scène de dérision suit et non précède l'audience devant le Sanhédrin. C'est à Marc encore qu'il reprend la comparution devant le Sanhédrin (l'introduction Lc 22,66, Luc la reprend à Marc, mais à ce qui, chez Marc, est la deuxième, Mc 15,1, et non la première audience, Mc 14,53.55). Il s'agit de Lc 22,66-71 // Mc 14,53-64, dont on sait que Luc omet une bonne partie (les faux témoins et le logion sur le Temple, Mc 14,56-61a). On le constate, les principales interventions dans le texte de Marc – encore une fois le principe d'économie – sont des coupures et des omissions. Dans le dialogue, il y a aussi des variantes, même si Luc et Marc rappellent tous les deux la question du Sanhédrin sur la messianité et l'allusion au Fils de l'homme dans la réponse de Jésus. Luc refuse – avec Matthieu, *minor agreement*! – la réponse affirmative de Jésus et opère un dédoublement, sans doute exégétique à l'intention des Grecs[60], de la question et de la réponse (chez lui, une fois le titre Messie est mentionné et une fois celui de Fils de Dieu). Par ailleurs, dans le refus explicite des témoins, Lc 22,71, Luc trahit sa connaissance du texte de Marc (et de l'épisode des faux témoins, Mc 14,56-61a).

Corrigeant la chronologie de Marc (chez Marc on parvient au matin, chez Luc on y est déjà, Lc 22,66) et limitant le nombre des audiences du Sanhédrin (Marc: deux, Mc 14,53.55 et 15,1; Luc: une seule, Lc 22,66), Luc reste attaché à Marc dans la scène du procès devant Pilate (Lc 23,1-5 // Mc 15,1-5) quand bien même on pourrait hésiter, en raison des griefs politiques que Luc transmet et que Marc ignore. La péricope est une péricope de transition.

Dès le passage suivant, comparution devant Hérode, Luc alterne sa documentation et suit son bien propre (Lc 23,6-12). Il en poursuit la reprise dans le récit de la deuxième comparution devant Pilate, particularité de Luc, avec les déclarations d'innocence de Jésus de la part du gouverneur, et la présentation de l'échange entre Jésus et Barabbas (Lc 23,13-25)[61]. Comme il a déjà transmis deux scènes de dérision, l'une de Jésus comme prophète (Lc 22,63-65), l'autre, brève, comme roi (Lc 23,11, à la fin de la comparution devant Hérode), Luc n'a pas de raison de renouer ici avec Marc qui, comme l'on sait, place sa seconde scène d'outrages après la condamnation par Pilate (Mc 15,16-20a). Il se peut en revanche que Luc s'inspire de Marc dans la mention de Simon de Cyrène (Lc 23,26 // Mc 15,20b-21).

En tout cas, dans le dialogue avec les femmes qui engagent les rites de deuil, Luc continue à suivre son autre source (Lc 23,27-31). C'est à elle qu'il donne la priorité dans la scène de la crucifixion (Lc 23,32-43),

---

60. On note le même processus dans le Sermon dans la plaine. Là où Matthieu dit simplement «aimez vos ennemis et priez pour ceux qui vous persécutent», Luc paraphrase et par là dédouble chacun de ces impératifs (Mt 5,44 // Lc 6,27-28); cf. F. BOVON, *L'Évangile selon saint Luc (1,1–9,50)* (CNT, 3a), Genève, 1991, pp. 308-310.

61. Voici un indice en faveur de ma répartition de la matière entre les deux sources. En 23,21, Luc écrit σταύρου, σταύρου αὐτόν, là où Marc a σταύρωσον αὐτόν (Mc 15,13). Comme l'impératif aoriste de Marc est correct et que l'impératif présent de Luc ne l'est pas, on doit en conclure que Luc reproduit ici une autre source que Marc. Il a laissé passer la maladresse de sa source. Sinon, on doit imaginer l'invraisemblable: qu'il ait façonné lui-même une formule impropre.

si différente de Marc: «Père, pardonne-leur ...» (Lc 23,34a)[62], présentation à cet endroit du vinaigre (Lc 23,36b), moqueries royales (Lc 23,37), mention ici de l'écriteau (Lc 23,38), dialogue avec les deux larrons (Lc 23,39-43, sans parallèle synoptique).

Pour la fin de la scène, c'est-à-dire pour les derniers instants de Jésus, Luc renoue avec Marc. Il est heureux de mentionner deux signes surnaturels concomittants de la mort de Jésus: l'éclipse de soleil et la déchirure du voile du Temple, qu'il signale en deux versets empruntés presque textuellement à Marc (Lc 23,44-45 // Mc 15,33 et 38). La mort de Jésus est exprimée, elle aussi, en termes marciens (Lc 23,46a.c // Mc 15,37). Luc a pris cependant deux libertés importantes par rapport à Marc: il a biffé tout ce qui a trait au cri de déréliction (Mc 15,34-36) et a ajouté – à la place? – une ultime phrase, confiante, de Jésus («Père je remets mon esprit entre tes mains», Lc 23,46b). Curieuse, ensuite, est évidemment la divergence entre la confession marcienne et lucanienne du centenier au pied de la croix (Lc 23,47 // Mc 15,39). Luc n'a sans doute pas inventé l'expression «un homme juste». Ce doit être une réminiscence – facile à retenir – de l'autre source. Quant à la présence de la foule et des femmes (Lc 23,48-49.55), je la mets au compte de la rédaction lucanienne qui s'appuie partiellement sur Marc (Mc 15,40-41). Je ne m'explique pas le silence de Luc sur l'identité des femmes[63]. En 8,1-3, Luc n'a pas cette discrétion, ni en 24,10!

Dans l'épisode de la mise au tombeau, comme dans celui du tombeau vide, Luc continue à suivre Marc (Lc 23,50-56 // Mc 15,42-47 et Lc 24,1-11 // Mc 16,1-8). En revanche, dans les récits d'apparition (Lc 24,12-49), il s'appuie sur son bien propre vers lequel il se tourne, heureux d'y trouver encore quelque chose, alors que Marc lui fait dorénavant faux bond (Mc 16,8). Quant à la scène d'ascension (Lc 24,50-53), elle est peut-être entièrement rédactionnelle.

En résumé, voici le va-et-vient d'une source à l'autre que Luc opère suivant l'hypothèse ici avancée:

| Parallèle à Mc | S^{Lc} |

21,29-33
Le figuier

                        21,34-36
                        Mise en garde

---

62. Faut-il voir dans 23,34b, le partage des habits, une exception? La proximité est ici grande avec Mc 15,24.

63. Silence qui se poursuit en 23,55 // Mc 15,47.

22,1-14
Complot, préparation Pâque

22,15-46
Dernier repas, discours d'adieu,
Mont des Oliviers

22,47–23,5
Arrestation, reniement,
outrages, Sanhédrin, Pilate

23,6-43
Hérode, Barabbas, condamnation,
chemin vers croix, Crucifixion

23,44–24,11
Derniers instants, centurion,
sépulture, tombeau vide

24,12-53
Apparitions à Pierre, aux disciples
d'Emmaüs, aux Douze, Ascension

3. *Vérifier l'hypothèse*

L'hypothèse que j'ai avancée, celle de l'alternance, présuppose deux sources, dont seule la première, Marc, est connue[64]. Il convient donc d'assurer, si faire se peut, l'existence de la seconde par d'autres arguments que la dissection opérée jusqu'ici. Deux démarches s'offrent à l'esprit. La première consiste à repérer, dans les passages que nous attribuons au bien propre, la présence d'indices stylisitiques et grammaticaux convergents et spécifiques. Je n'ai pas encore accompli cette tâche qui peut bénéficier des résultats de certains travaux[65] et reprendre la méthode appliquée à l'évangile de Jean[66]. La seconde démarche consiste à chercher les traces de ce document propre à Luc en dehors de l'évangile canonique. Il se peut en effet que parmi les plus anciens témoignages patristiques de ces épisodes, certains s'appuient sur la source de Luc et non sur Luc lui-même[67].

64. On peut évidemment se demander quelle forme de Marc Luc a eue sous les yeux.

65. La méthode s'est affinée avec le temps grâce aux travaux sucessifs de J.C. Hawkins, H.J. Cadbury, H. Schürmann, J. Jeremias, F. Rehkopf et T. Schramm. Cf. F. NEIRYNCK, *La matière marcienne dans l'Évangile de Luc*, pp. 70-72; E. SCHWEIZER, *Zur Frage der Quellenbenutzung durch Lukas*.

66. Cf. E. RUCKSTUHL – P. DSCHULNIGG, *Stilkritik und Verfasserfrage im Johannesevangelium. Die johanneischen Sprachmerkmale auf dem Hintergrund des Neuen Testaments und des zeitgenössischen hellenistischen Schrifttums* (NTOA, 17), Fribourg/Suisse-Göttingen, 1991.

67. Mon collègue de Genève Enrico Norelli a fait progresser ma réflexion méthodologique. Il a émis l'hypothèse que l'auteur de l'*Ascension d'Isaïe* dépendait, pour l'évocation de la naissance de Jésus, non de l'Évangile de Matthieu en sa forme canonique, mais des traditions dont le premier évangéliste a pu se servir. Je le remercie de m'avoir permis de prendre connaissance d'une étude à ce sujet qui n'a pas encore paru.

Une particularité lucanienne de la scène du jardin des Oliviers, c'est l'apparition de l'ange et les caillots de sang (Lc 22,43-44). Cet épisode est attesté au IIe s. dans un évangile judéo-chrétien et chez Justin Martyr. L'*Historia passionis domini*, texte médiéval latin, signale que l'épisode du réconfort apporté par l'ange au Christ angoissé est présent dans l'évangile que ce document appelle des Nazaréens[68]. Il se peut que cet évangile soit appuyé sur la source de Luc. Justin, qui signale dans son *Dialogue avec Tryphon*[69], la «sueur comme des caillots de sang», se réfère certainement, lui, à Luc et non à sa source. La manière dont il introduit la référence, avec l'allusion au prologue de l'évangile le prouve indubitablement. Il se peut que l'épître aux Hébreux (He 5,7) avec sa dramatisation des prières et des larmes de Jésus, sans doute au jardin des Oliviers, connaisse la même tradition que Luc.

En plus de l'évangile, les Actes canoniques (Ac 4,27-28) et l'*Évangile de Pierre* (EvPi 1-5)[70] attestent la participation d'Hérode au procès de Jésus (Lc 23,6-12). Ces passages s'appuyent-ils sur l'évangile de Luc ou sur la source dont il a disposé? À les lire, ces deux passages ne paraissent pas dépendre directement de l'évangile de Luc en la forme fixe que nous lui connaissons. Alors? Ont-ils connu la source?

La réplique de Jésus aux pleurs des femmes, propre à Luc (23,28-31), a un parallèle énigmatique dans l'*Évangile de Thomas* (EvTh 79)[71]. En sa première moitié, la sentence 79 de ce texte reprend un autre passage propre à Luc (Lc 11,27-28: la béatitude de la femme hors de la foule et la réplique de Jésus). En sa seconde moitié, elle transmet l'oracle de malheur du récit de la Passion (sans référence à la mort du Christ ni aux pleurs des femmes): «Viendront, en effet, des jours où vous direz: Heureux le ventre qui n'a pas conçu et les seins qui n'ont pas allaité.» Comme il s'agit d'un topos apocalyptique qui a un parallèle en Lc 21,23 et une origine éventuelle dans Es 54,1, il est difficile de préciser d'où l'*Évangile de Thomas* tire son information, et s'il s'appuie sur Luc ou sur l'une de ses sources[72].

---

68. Le texte est cité dans K. ALAND (ed.), *Synopsis quattuor evangeliorum ...*, Stuttgart, ³1965, p. 457. Cf. P. VIELHAUER – G. STRECKER, *Judenchristliche Evangelien*, in W. SCHNEEMELCHER, *Neutestamentliche Apokryphen in deutscher Übersetzung*, 5. Auflage der von E. Hennecke begründeten Sammlung, I, Tübingen, 1987, pp. 127-128 et 137.

69. *Dialogue avec Tryphon*, 103,8; texte cité dans la *Synopsis* (n. 68), p. 457; JUSTIN, *Dialogue avec Tryphon. Texte grec, traduction française, introduction, notes et index* (Textes et Documents pour l'étude historique du christianisme), II, ed. G. ARCHAMBAULT, Paris, 1909, pp. 140-143.

70. Cf. *Synopsis* (n. 68), p. 479; M.G. MARA, *Évangile de Pierre. Introduction, texte critique, traduction, commentaire et index* (SC, 201), Paris, 1973, pp. 40-43.

71. Cf. *Synopsis* (n. 68), pp. 482 et 527. Je cite la traduction de H.C. PUECH, *En quête de la Gnose*, II, *Sur l'Évangile selon Thomas* (Bibliothèque des Sciences Humaines), Paris, 1978, p. 23.

72. Sur EvTh 79, cf. R.McL. WILSON, *Studies in the Gospel of Thomas*, London, 1960, p. 81 (la sentence 79 de l'EvTh est peut-être primitive; Luc l'aurait divisée, plaçant une

Un évangile judéo-chrétien paraît avoir affirmé que la prière de Jésus pour les bourreaux («Père, pardonne-leur...», 23,34) avait provoqué de nombreuses conversions parmi les Juifs présents. Nous le savons par l'*Historia passionis domini*[73], et par un commentaire médiéval d'Esaïe[74], qui renvoient, tous deux, à l'*Évangile des Nazaréens*, et nous en trouvons une trace, faible il est vrai, chez saint Jérôme[75]. Cet évangile partage donc un logion avec Luc et présente en plus un développement légendaire. Mais s'appuyait-il sur Luc ou sur sa source?

L'*Évangile de Pierre*[76], à propos des brigands, en dit un peu plus que Marc et Matthieu et un peu moins que Luc (23,39-43): «L'un de ces malfaiteurs les réprimanda en disant: Nous, c'est à cause des méfaits que nous avons faits que nous souffrons ainsi; tandis que celui-ci, devenu sauveur des humains, en quoi vous a-t-il fait du tort»[77]? L'*Évangile de Pierre* est ici indépendant de l'Évangile de Luc. Son texte paraît même plus archaïque que le texte de Luc. S'il s'appuie sur une traditon antérieure à Luc, connaît-il la source de Luc?

Luc est le seul témoin néotestamentaire à attester l'ultime sentence de Jésus: «Père, je remets mon esprit entre tes mains» (23,46). Ce logion est cité par Justin dans son *Dialogue avec Tryphon*[78]. Cet auteur ajoute, «comme je l'ai appris cette fois encore de leurs Mémoires». Suivant son habitude, il doit se référer aux évangiles en voie de canonisation, ici à Luc, plutôt qu'à sa source.

Le seul fragment grec du Diatessaron[79] qui soit conservé correspond

partie ici, Lc 11,27-28, une autre là, Lc 23,29; sinon, il faut admettre que l'auteur de l'EvTh a regroupé ces sentences par *key-words*); B. GÄRTNER, *The Theology of the Gospel of Thomas*, trad. du suédois par E.J. SHARPE, London, 1961, pp. 252-253; J.É. MÉNARD, *L'Évangile selon Thomas* (NHS, 5), Leiden, 1975, pp. 180-181; M. FIEGER, *Das Thomasevangelium. Einleitung, Kommentar und Systematik* (NTAbh NF, 22), Münster, 1991, pp. 218-221.

73. Cf. *Synopsis* (n. 68), p. 484; P. VIELHAUER – G. STRECKER, *Judenchristliche Evangelien* (n. 68), p. 138.

74. Cf. *Synopsis* (n. 68), p. 484; P. VIELHAUER – G. STRECKER, *Judenchristliche Evangelien* (n. 68), p. 136. Il s'agit du *Commentaire d'Esaïe* ad Es 53,12, édité sous le nom d'HAYMON DE HALBERSTADT dans PL 116, 994. Il faut sans doute attribuer ce commentaire à Haymon d'Auxerre.

75. *Epistula*, 120, 8; cf. *Synopsis* (n. 68), p. 484; SAINT JÉRÔME, *Lettres. Texte établi et traduit* (Collection des Universités de France), VI, ed. J. LABOURT, Paris, 1958, p. 141.

76. *Évangile de Pierre*, 10-16; Cf. *Synopsis* (n. 68), p. 484; M.G. MARA, *Évangile de Pierre* (n. 70), pp. 46-49.

77. *Évangile de Pierre*, 13; la traduction est de ma plume.

78. JUSTIN, *Dialogue avec Tryphon*, 105, 5; cf. *Synopsis* (n. 68), p. 489; JUSTIN, *Dialogue avec Tryphon* (n. 69), II, pp. 148-150.

79. L'attribution de ce fragment au *Diatessaron* a été questionnée, mais elle est très vraisemblable. Ce fragment trouvé à Doura-Europos est accessible en photographie, édition et traduction anglaise dans l'ouvrage de B.M. METZGER, *Manuscripts of the Greek Bible*, Oxford, 1981, pp. 66-67; Sur le *Diatessaron*, cf. W.L. PETERSON, *Tatian's Diatessaron*, in H. KÖSTER, *Ancient Christian Gospels: Their History and Development*, Philadelphia, PA - London, 1990, pp. 403-430, particulièrement pp. 412-413.

à la mention évangélique de la présence des femmes et au début de la scène de la déposition (Lc 23,49 et 55-56). La relation de ce fragment à l'Évangile de Luc est étroite. «De Zébédée» renvoie à Mt 27,56, «Salomé» à Mc 15,40, mais la suite reprend en les fusionnant Lc 23,49 et 55 (présence des femmes), puis Lc 23,54 (date), Mc 15,42 (date), Lc 23,50-51 (présentation de Joseph), Mt 27,57 (disciple de Jésus), Jn 19,38 (action secrète par crainte des Juifs) et Lc 23,51 (cité de Judée; attente du Royaume de Dieu et – ordre inverse de Luc – non-participation au projet des chefs juifs). Si Tatien travaille, à ce qu'il semble, sur nos évangiles canoniques, ce fragment n'atteste pas une connaissance directe de la source de Luc.

Dans le récit propre à Luc de l'apparition aux Douze, si je puis déborder le seul récit de la Passion, le Christ ressuscité incite les disciples à le toucher et à le distinguer ainsi d'un fantôme ou d'un esprit, qui ne saurait avoir ni chair ni os (Lc 24,39). Or une phrase très semblable circule assez largement dans l'Antiquité: elle est attestée par un évangile judéo-chrétien («iuxta Evangelium, quod Hebreaeorum lectitant Nazarei») selon saint Jérôme[80]. Origène[81] la connaît et l'attribue à la *Petri doctrina* qu'il rejette. Enfin, Ignace d'Antioche la cite lui aussi: Λάβετε, ψηλαφήσατέ με καὶ ἴδετε, ὅτι οὐκ εἰμὶ δαιμόνιον ἀσώματον[82]. Ces témoignages sont précieux et pourraient bien se référer à la source que Luc utilise dans son récit d'apparition (24,39).

De cet inventaire, il ressort qu'un évangile judéo-chrétien au moins partage avec Luc diverses connaissances qui leur sont propres. Comme je vois mal un judéo-chrétien puiser à un évangile aussi pagano-chrétien

---

80. JÉRÔME, *Comm. Is.*, XVIII, praef., et *De viris illustribus*, 16, cf. *Synopsis* (n. 68), p. 503.

81. ORIGÈNE, *De principiis*, I, prooemium 8; cf. *Synopsis* (n. 68), p. 503; *Origenes vier Bücher von des Prinzipien, herausgegeben, übersetzt, mit kritischen und erläuternden Anmerkungen versehen* (Texte zur Forschung, 24), ed. H. GÖRGEMANNS et H. KARPP, Darmstadt, 1976, pp. 94-97.

82. IGNACE d'ANTIOCHE, *Smyrn.*, 3,1-3; cf. *Synopsis* (n. 68), p. 503; IGNACE d'ANTIOCHE, *Polycarpe de Smyrne, Lettres. Martyre de Polycarpe. Texte grec, introduction, traduction et notes* (SC, 10), ed. P.T. CAMELOT, Paris, ⁴1969, pp. 134-135. Ce passage, ainsi que les témoignages d'Origène et de Jérôme, ont suscité une abondante littérature; cf. particulièrement H. KÖSTER, *Synoptische Überlieferung bei den Apostolischen Vätern* (TU, 65), Berlin, 1957, pp. 45-56; H. PAULSEN, *Die Briefe des Ignatius von Antiochia und der Brief des Polykarp von Smyrna. Zweite neubearbeitete Auflage der Auslegung von W. BAUER* (HNT. Die Apostolischen Väter, 2), Tübingen, 1985, pp. 92-93; W.R. SCHOEDEL, *Ignatius of Antioch: A Commentary on the Letters of Ignatius of Antioch* (Hermeneia), Philadelphia, PA, 1985, pp. 226-229; A. ORBE, *Cristología Gnóstica. Introducción a la soteriología de los siglos II y III* (Biblioteca de Autores Cristianos, 385), II, Madrid, 1976, pp. 516-517. Cf. PSEUDO-HIPPOLYTE, *In sanctum Pascha*, 30, qui combine Jn 20,27 (avec des éléments de Jn 20,25) et Lc 24,39, un rapprochement que l'on retrouve chez JEAN CHRYSOSTOME, *De cruce et latrone homilia*, 1,4, PG 49, 405; cf. G. VISONÀ, *Pseudo Ippolita, In sanctum Pascha. Studio, edizione, commento* (Studia Patristica Mediolanensia, 15), Milano, 1988, pp. 276 et 403 (je remercie mon ami Enrico Norelli de m'avoir signalé cette référence).

que celui de Luc, j'émets l'hypothèse, certes aventureuse, que cet auteur avait connaissance de la seconde source de Luc. Les autres témoignages sont trop peu nombreux et trop peu explicites pour leur appliquer la même hypothèse. Dans le cas de Justin et de Tatien, il faut même l'exclure. Ces deux auteurs doivent se référer à notre évangile de Luc et non à sa source. Les cas de l'*Évangile de Thomas* et de l'*Évangile de Pierre* restent énigmatiques.

4. *En guise de conclusion provisoire*

Trois tâches supplémentaires attendent celui qui se sera aventuré jusqu'ici.

1. S'il y a bel et bien un document, outre Marc, derrière le récit lucanien de la Passion et s'il s'agit d'un texte continu, faut-il y voir la suite de ce qu'il est convenu d'appeler le bien propre de Luc, le *Sondergut*, dont l'existence durant le récit de voyage, et même dès la Galilée, est certaine? Si l'enracinement liturgique des récits de la Passion semble s'y opposer, une même qualité littéraire, telle la scène du jardin des Oliviers ou celle des disciples d'Emmaüs, paraît au contraire le proposer, voire l'imposer.

2. Si tel est le cas, quel genre littéraire faut-il attribuer à ce document et quelle fonction remplissait-il? Je lui accorderai le genre «évangile» et le rapprocherai donc de Marc. D'un niveau littéraire supérieur, il serait à Luc ce qu'a été Marc à Matthieu. À mon avis, Q n'en faisait pas partie et constituait un document distinct. À quoi servait-il? À l'édification de croyants d'origine helléniste?

3. Pourquoi a-t-il disparu? Parce que Luc l'a éclipsé (comme Matthieu et Luc ont rendu Q inutile)? Parce que Marcion y a recouru? Cette dernière hypothèse[83] devrait être vérifiée à l'aide du livre IV de l'*Adversus Marcionem* de Tertullien. Marcion n'attribuait pas explicitement à Luc l'évangile qu'il reconnaissait (cet écrit, comme l'on sait, ne commençait qu'avec le ministère de Jésus adulte).

4. L'étude de la rédaction lucanienne de cette source devrait permettre aussi de préciser les intentions littéraires et théologiques de l'évangéliste. Dès maintenant, on peut insister sur la conformité du sort de Jésus au dessein de Dieu, sur le rejet du juste souffrant et du prophète

---

83. Sur l'évangile de Marcion, cf. A. HARNACK, *Marcion. Das Evangelium vom fremden Gott. Eine Monographie zur Geschichte der Grundlegung der katholischen Kirche. Neue Studien zu Marcion*, Darmstadt, 1985; R.J. HOFFMANN, *Marcion: On the Restitution of Christianity: An Essay on the Development of Radical Paulinist Theology in the Second Century* (American Academy of Religion, Academy Series), Chico, CA, 1984. Cet auteur estime que Marcion utilisait un *Urlukas* et que l'évangile canonique de Luc est une réaction antimarcionite. Il a été critiqué et doit être lu avec circonspection. Toujours sur Marcion, cf. C.B. AMPHOUX, *Les premières éditions de Luc*, in *ETL* 67 (1991) 312-327, et 68 (1992) 38-48.

authentique, sur la fidélité et la confiance du Fils à l'égard de son Père céleste, sur la valeur rédemptrice de sa vie et de sa mort, qui constituent une seule grande œuvre, sur la fonction exhortative de ce destin pour les disciples et, à leur suite, les croyantes et les croyants. Tous ces thèmes lucaniens, connus par les relectures de Marc et de Q, trouvent leur ultime confirmation dans la réinterprétation de la Source propre au troisième évangile. À condition, il faut l'ajouter, que cette source du récit de la Passion ait bel et bien existé. Ce n'est là qu'une hypothèse, comme reste incertaine aussi la suggestion d'une alternance régulière.

BIBLIOGRAPHIE RELATIVE À LC 22–23

J.-N. ALETTI, L'art de raconter Jésus-Christ. L'écriture narrative de l'évangile de Luc, Paris, 1989, pp. 155-176.

B.E. BECK, Imitatio Christi and the Lucan Passion Narrative, in W. HORBURG – B. MCNEIL (eds.), Suffering and Martyrdom in the New Testament. Mélanges G.M. Styler, Cambridge, 1981, pp. 40-46.

F. BOVON, Luc le théologien. Vingt-cinq ans de recherches (1950-1975), Genève, ²1988, pp. 175-181.

ID., Luc-Actes, in É. CHARPENTIER (ed.), Évangiles synoptiques et Actes des apôtres, Paris, 1981, pp. 224-230.

A. BÜCHELE, Der Tod Jesu im Lukasevangelium. Eine redaktionsgeschichtliche Untersuchung zu Lk 23, Frankfurt/M, 1978.

J.D. BUTIN – A. MAIGNAN – P. SOLER (eds.), L'Évangile selon Luc commenté par les Pères, Paris, 1987.

H. COUSIN, Le prophète assassiné. Histoire des textes évangéliques de la Passion, Paris, 1976.

M. DIBELIUS, Die Formgeschichte des Evangeliums, 3e éd. avec une annexe par G. Bornkamm, Tübingen, 1959, pp. 178-218.

A.J. DROGE – J.D. TABOR, A Noble Death: Suicide and Martyrdom Among Christians and Jews in Antiquity, San Francisco, CA, 1992.

J. FINEGAN, Die Überlieferung der Leidens- und Auferstehungsgeschichte Jesu, Giessen, 1934.

B.S. FINNELL, The Significance of the Passion in Luke (thèse manuscrite), Baylor University, 1983.

J.A. FITZMYER, The Gospel According to Luke, 2 vol., Garden City, NY, 1981-1985.

J. Massyngbaerde FORD, My Enemy is my Guest: Jesus and Violence in Luke, New York, 1984.

J.F. GORMLEY, The Final Passion Prediction: A Study of Luke 22,33-38 (thèse manuscrite), Fordham University, 1974.

J.B. GREEN, The Death of Jesus: Tradition and Interpretation in the Passion Narrative, Tübingen, 1988, esp. pp. 24-104 et 324-330.

K. GROBEL, Formgeschichte und synoptische Quellenanalyse, Göttingen, 1937.

J. JEREMIAS, Die Sprache des Lukasevangeliums. Redaktion und Tradition im Nicht-Markusstoff des dritten Evangeliums, Göttingen, 1980.

R.J. KARRIS, Luke, Artist and Theologian: Luke's Passion Account as Literature, New York, 1985.

F. KECK, Die öffentliche Abschiedsrede Jesu in Lk 20,45–21,36, Stuttgart, 1976.

K. KERTELGE (ed.), Der Tod Jesu. Deutungen im Neuen Testament, Freiburg/B, 1976.

J.S. KLOPPENBORG, Exitus clari viri: The Death of Jesus in Luke, in Toronto Journal of Theology 8 (1992) 106-120.

J. KODELL, Luke's Theology of the Death of Jesus, in D. DURKEN (ed.), Sin, Salvation, and the Spirit, Collegeville, MN, 1979, pp. 221-230.

E. LA VERDIERE, A Discourse at the Last Supper, in The Bible Today 72 (1974) 1540-1548.

X. LÉON-DUFOUR, Passion, in DBS VI (1960), col. 1419-1492.

C. L'EPLATTENIER, Lecture de l'Évangile de Luc, Paris, 1982, pp. 243-286.

M. LIMBECK (ed.), Redaktion und Theologie des Passionsberichts nach den Synoptikern, Darmstadt, 1981.

L. MARIN, Sémiotique de la Passion. Topiques et figures, Paris, 1971.

F.J. MATERA, Passion Narratives and Gospel Theologies: Interpreting the Synoptics through Their Passion Stories, New York, 1986.

R. MEYNET, L'évangile selon saint Luc, analyse rhétorique, 2 vol., Paris, 1988.

ID., Avez-vous lu saint Luc? Guide pour la rencontre, Paris, 1990, pp. 89-139.

Narrativité et théologie dans les récits de la Passion, in RSR 73 (1985) 1-244.

F. NEIRYNCK, La matière marcienne dans l'évangile de Luc, in ID. (ed.), L'Évangile de Luc. Problèmes littéraires et théologiques (Mémorial L. Cerfaux), Gembloux, 1973, pp. 157-201; Leuven, ²1989, pp. 67-111, plus pp. 304-305. Je me réfère à la 2e éd.

J. NEYREY, The Passion According to Luke: A Redaction Study of Luke's Soteriology, New York, 1985.

M. RESE, Die «Stunde» Jesu in Jerusalem [Lk 22,1-53]. Eine Untersuchung zur literarischen und theologischen Eigenart des lukanischen Passionsberichts (thèse d'habilitation manuscrite), Münster, 1970.

G. SCHNEIDER, Das Problem einer vorlukanischen Passionserzählung, in BZ NF 16 (1972) 222-244.

ID., Verleugnung, Verspottung und Verhör Jesu nach Lk 22,54-71, München, 1969.

ID., Die Passion Jesu nach den älteren Evangelien, München, 1973.

H. SCHÜRMANN, Der Paschamahlbericht Lk 22,(7-14) 15-18, I, Münster, 1953.

ID., Der Einsetzungsbericht Lk 22,19-20, II, Münster, 1955.

ID., Jesu Abschiedsrede Lk 22,21-38, III, Münster, 1956.

E. SCHWEIZER, Zur Frage der Quellenbenutzung durch Lukas, in ID., Neues Testament und Christologie im Werden. Aufsätze, Göttingen, 1982, pp. 33-85.

D. SENIOR, The Passion of Jesus in the Gospel of Luke, Wilmington, DE, 1989.

M.L. SOARDS, The Passion According to Luke: The Special Material of Luke 22, Sheffield, 1987.

D.D. SYLVA (ed.), Reimaging the Death of the Lukan Jesus, Frankfurt/M, 1990.

C.H. TALBERT, Reading Luke: A Literary and Theological Commentary on the Third Gospel, New York, 1986, pp. 206-225.

R.C. TANNEHILL, The Narrative Unity of Luke-Acts: A Literary Interpretation, I, Philadelphia, PA, 1986.

V. Taylor, *The Passion Narrative of St. Luke: A Critical and Historical Investigation*, ed. O.E. Evans, Cambridge, 1972.

É. Trocmé, *The Passion as Liturgy: A Study in the Origin of the Passion Narratives in the Four Gospels*, London, 1983.

J.B. Tyson, *The Death of Jesus in Luke-Acts*, Columbia, 1986.

F.G. Untergassmair, *Kreuzweg und Kreuzigung Jesu. Ein Beitrag zur lukanischen Redaktionsgeschichte und zur Frage nach der lukanischen «Kreuzestheologie»*, Paderborn, 1980.

A Vanhoye, et alii, *La Passion selon les quatre Évangiles*, Paris, 1981.

Id., *Structure et théologie des récits de la Passion dans les évangiles synoptiques*, in *NRT* 89 (1967) 137-163.

Id., *L'intérêt de Luc pour la prophétie en Lc 1,76; 4,16-30 et 22,60-65*, in *The Four Gospels 1992. FS F. Neirynck* (BETL, 100), Leuven, 1992, II, pp. 1529-1548.

A. Vööbus, *The Prelude to the Lukan Passion Narrative: Tradition-, Redaction-, Cult-, Motif-Historical and Source-Critical Studies*, Stockholm, 1968.

J. Wanke, *Beobachtungen zum Eucharistieverständnis des Lukas auf Grund der lukanischen Mahlberichte*, Leipzig, 1973.

W. Wiefel, *Das Evangelium nach Lukas*, Berlin, 1988.

P. Winter, *The Treatment of His Sources by the Third Evangelist in Luke XXI-XXIV*, in *SJT* 8 (1955) 138-172.

À leur arrivée, les participants au séminaire francophone des Journées bibliques apprirent avec tristesse la nouvelle du décès tout récent de Dom Louis Leloir (15 août 1992), qui, sans cela, aurait dû être des leurs[84]. Ancien professeur de l'Université de Louvain, ce spécialiste des littératures chrétiennes orientales était aussi un bibliste. Pour moi, il était surtout le collaborateur infatigable et l'ami indéfectible de l'Association pour l'étude de la littérature apocryphe chrétienne (AELAC). J'ai donc proposé d'offrir le travail de notre séminaire à sa mémoire. Que ces pages lui soient, elles aussi, un hommage posthume.

Faculté autonome de Théologie protestante   François Bovon
Université de Genève
CH-1211 Genève 4

---

84. Je me permets de signaler ici sa contribution dans *The Four Gospels 1992. FS F. Neirynck* intitulée *Le Commentaire d'Éphrem sur le Diatessaron. Réflexions et suggestions*, pp. 2358-2367.

II
OFFERED PAPERS

ALTERNATIVE SYNOPTIC THEORIES ON MK 4,30-32

The Parable of the Mustard Seed, Mk 4,30-32 par. Mt 13,31-32 par. Lk 13,18-19, and its twin Parable of the Leaven in Mt 13,33 par. Lk 13,20-21, taken together, would not be the first pericope considered to comprise a real test case of the Two-Source Theory. And yet, in spite of thorough and careful study of this passage from the two-source perspective[1], the recent literature reflects that this passage plays a role in the other major hypotheses on the market: Griesbach, Deuteromarkus, Lucan dependence on Matthew[2]. But does any of them provide a better explanation of the literary phenomena than the standard hypothesis[3]?

I. THE GRIESBACH HYPOTHESIS

A few words about the Griesbach hypothesis can suffice[4]. For the

---

1. See especially the discussion of the earlier literature by R. LAUFEN, *Die Doppelüberlieferungen der Logienquelle und des Markusevangeliums* (BBB, 54), Königstein/Taunus - Bonn, 1980 (1976-77 Diss., Bonn), esp. *ΒΑΣΙΛΕΙΑ und ΕΚΚΛΗΣΙΑ. Eine traditions- und redaktionsgeschichtliche Untersuchung des Gleichnisses vom Senfkorn*, pp. 174-200, with notes on pp. 470-490; = in J. ZMIJEWSKI and E. NELLESSEN (eds.), *Begegnung mit dem Wort. FS H. Zimmermann* (BBB, 53), Bonn, 1980, pp. 105-140. In the Introduction to New Testament methodology by Laufen's director this passage was one of his fundamental examples: cf. H. ZIMMERMANN, *Neutestamentliche Methodenlehre. Darstellung der historisch-kritischen Methode*, Stuttgart, 1967; ²1968, pp. 123-127; ⁶1978, pp. 129-133; neu bearb. Aufl. von K. KLIESCH, ⁷1982, pp. 120-124. – For Neirynck's review of Laufen's dissertation, see *ETL* 57 (1981) 181-185.

2. Cf. T.A. FRIEDRICHSEN, *The Matthew-Luke Agreements against Mark. A Survey of Recent Studies: 1974-1989*, in F. NEIRYNCK (ed.), *L'Évangile de Luc – The Gospel of Luke* (BETL, 32), Leuven, ²1989, pp. 335-392, esp. sections I.5. "Mark: Conflation of Matthew and Luke", pp. 345-350; I.9. "Deuteromarkus", pp. 360-365; I.10. "Luke's Knowledge of Matthew", pp. 365-367; II.A.1. "Luke used Matthew as an 'Overlay' on Mark and Q" (R.H. Gundry), pp. 367-371; and II.A.2. "Luke used Mark and Matthew but no Q source" (M.D. Goulder, *et al.*), pp. 371-384. For *Urmarkus*, cf. below, n. 51.

3. For a discussion of this passage from the two-source perspective, see T.A. FRIEDRICHSEN, *'Minor' and 'Major' Matthew-Luke Agreements against Mk 4,30-32*, in *The Four Gospels 1992. Festschrift Frans Neirynck* (BETL, 100), Leuven, 1992, pp. 649-676. – For a presentation of the 'minor agreements' against Mk 4,30-32, see F. NEIRYNCK, *The Minor Agreements*, 1974, § 29, pp. 94-95, or *The Minor Agreements in a Horizontal-line Synopsis* (SNTA, 15), Leuven, 1991, § 29, p. 35. See, too, the paralleled texts of Matthew and Luke in his *Q-Synopsis. The Double Tradition Passages in Greek* (SNTA, 13), Leuven, 1988, pp. 48-49, and his table of "Mark and Q" in *Recent Developments in the Study of Q*, in J. DELOBEL (ed.), *Logia* (BETL, 59), 1982, pp. 26-75, esp. 53 (= *Evangelica II*, pp. 409-455, esp. 433).

4. The use of "Two-Gospel Hypothesis", I find, is easily confused with Two-Source Hypothesis, especially in what would be the usual abbreviations (2GH and 2SH), and

most part, neo-Griesbachians[5] give little attention to Luke's use of
Matthew in this pericope, except to say summarily that "Luke does not
follow Matthew in adding further parables to that of the Sower"[6].
There is consensus among them that Mark is following Matthew at this
point[7], and to such a degree that Luke falls almost completely out of
the picture[8]. As a result, little concern is shown for the fact that Mark's
"conflation" of Matthew and Luke has woven an entire "web"[9] of

thus, I prefer to avoid it. Moreover, as a description it has come under some fire, for
M.D. Goulder's hypothesis is also a "Two Gospel Hypothesis": Luke used Mark and
Matthew. Cf. F. NEIRYNCK, *A Symposium on the Minor Agreements*, in *ETL* 67 (1991)
361-372, esp. p. 362.

5. Most important for the consideration here are the two recent commentaries on
Mark from this point of view: C.S. MANN, *Mark. A New Translation with Introduction
and Commentary* (AB, 27), Garden City, NY, 1986, pp. 270-272 (cf. *ETL* 63, 1987, 425-
428); H. RILEY, *The Making of Mark: An Exploration*, Macon, GA, 1989, pp. 50-51 (cf.
ETL 66, 1990, 410-413). Cf. too: D.L. DUNGAN, "Response to the Two-Source Hypothesis", in ID. (ed.), *The Interrelations of the Gospels* (BETL, 95), Leuven, 1990, pp. 201-
216, esp. pp. 213-214; and the collaborative work of W.R. FARMER, D.L. DUNGAN,
A.J. MCNICOL, D.B. PEABODY and P.L. SHULER, *Narrative Outline of the Markan
Composition According to the Two Gospel Hypothesis*, in *SBL 1990 Seminar Papers*,
pp. 212-239, esp. 220-221 (referred to as FARMER). – For a most thorough critique of the
Griesbach Hypothesis, see C.M. TUCKETT, *The Revival of the Griesbach Hypothesis.
Analysis and Appraisal* (SNTS MS, 44), Cambridge, 1983 (1979 Diss., Lancaster, dir.
D.R. Catchpole).

6. RILEY, p. 50.

7. MANN, p. 272; RILEY, pp. 50-51; DUNGAN, p. 213: "Mk turns back to Mt for one
more 'seed' parable, making some minor additions in vss. 31,32" (he astoundingly makes
no mention of the positive minor agreements); FARMER, p. 220, has a slightly better
expression: "Mk returns to Mt for another 'seed' parable, making some minor changes in
it (all 'minor agreements', see vss. 31, 32)".

B. ORCHARD, *A Synopsis of the Four Gospels. In Greek. Arranged according to the Two-
Gospel Hypothesis*, Edinburgh, 1983, §§ 106, 149 and 239, appears to indicate that with
respect to order no two Synoptic Gospels have the Mustard Seed in a strictly parallel
context (printed in bold type). With respect to the parable chapter, Lk 8,4-18 is printed as
directly parallel to Mk 4,1-25 (§§ 100-104), but no pericope of Mt 13 is printed in bold
next to its parallel in Mk 4.

8. MANN, p. 271, gives at least passing reference to Mark's knowledge of Luke: "Mark
has the double question, as has Luke...". RILEY, p. 50, refers to the Mustard Seed and the
Leaven as "Matthew's", with no mention of Luke. But, although Mark may have, Riley
has not totally forgotten Luke (p. 51): "Both Lk 13:18 and Mk 4:30 introduce the parable
... with a double question, but the wording is so dissimilar that there is no reason to
suppose either dependent on the other.... It is Matthew's text, not Luke's – which is not
before Mark at this point – that with some expansion is the basis of Mk 4:30-32". In
much the same vein, DUNGAN writes: "Skipping Mt's Parable of the Leaven, Mk finds a
summary passage in Mt 13:34f., and converts it into a conclusion [4,33-34] that looks
back to the opening lines in 4:1" (p. 214). In the pooled effort of FARMER, the same
expression is expanded by "which Mk does not need" (p. 221). – It could at least have
been admitted that Mark 'skipped' the second parable of Matthew *and* Luke. Then,
perhaps, one could expect that a more substantial redactional reason than the one given
for Mark's departure from his "conflating" would be brought forward.

9. Cf., for example, W.R. FARMER, *The Synoptic Problem*, 1964; [2]1976, pp. 132, 137-
138. – Farmer's own image is every bit as much an entanglement for him as it is for the
Two-Source Theory.

positive minor agreements[10]. Moreover, the supposed Marcan omission of so much material is often simply dismissed with generalities of "does not need"[11], of no "interest" to Mark[12], or of all the parables included by Mark are "about seed sown"[13]. It seems fair to say that it is not surprising that many find such explanations less than convincing. If there are pericopae that can provide a coherent and consistent view of Mark as a conflator of Matthew and Luke, the parables of the Mustard Seed and the Leaven are not among them. In addition to Mark's choice of material, "the detailed wording of his version [of the Mustard Seed] ... presents problems for the GH"[14]:

10. Cf. above, n. 7 (on Dungan). MANN, pp. 271-272, mentions δένδρον and ἐν τοῖς κλάδοις αὐτοῦ (against 4,32), noting that "the imagery is that of Dan 4:12 and Ezek 17:23, 31:6", but fails to provide any explanation for Mark's supposed variation of the concurrent testimony of his sources – unless the notation that "the plant has been known to attain a height of twelve feet" is supposed to satisfy. RILEY, p. 51, is even more incredible in his avoidance of the positive minor agreements. First, he does not mention any of them. Second, when he accidentally picks one up, he bobbles the comparison: Having recognized some of the "verbal similarities" between Mk 4,26-29 and 30-32 (καὶ ἔλεγεν, ἡ/τὴν βασιλεία/αν τοῦ θεοῦ, ὡς ἐπὶ τῆς γῆς), he notes that "the similarity might have been even greater if Mark had not been influenced by Matthew's wording in the parable of the Mustard Seed. In the first parable is the phrase *a man should cast* (4:26...), which is similar to that used by Luke in ... 13:18-19, 'a man cast'. But in Mk 4:31 as in the parallel in Mt 13:31 there is no word for 'man' and the seed is 'sown' and not 'cast'". – Of course Mt 13,31 (= Lk 13,18) has ὃν λαβὼν ἄνθρωπος. Thus, both ἄνθρωπος from Matthew *and* Luke and ἔβαλεν from Luke, could easily have been taken over by "Mark the Conflator" (the title of an article by G. MURRAY, in *DownR* 102, 1984, 157-162).

11. FARMER, p. 221 (cf. above, n. 8).

12. MANN, p. 272: "Mark's interest in the deeds of Jesus, and his minimal concern for extended blocks of teaching, has been noted before". This is primarily stated in reference to Mk 4,21-25, but it is in the context of a discussion of the synoptic relationship for Mk 4,26-34. – Mann's difficulty with the Two-Source Theory at this point results mainly from concentrating on only half of the theory. Given the hypothesis that the Mustard Seed and the Leaven comprise a twin parable in Q, and that Matthew is conflating his sources (to wit, more effectively than Mark has done so on the Griesbach hypothesis), it is mistaken to hold that "he put Mark aside at 13:24", and it is not at all difficult to explain why he placed Mk 4,33-34 after the Leaven. Moreover, on the "usual" understanding of "the usual synoptic theory", that the material "parallel" to Mk 4,21-25 "is scattered throughout Matthew" is far from "bizarre". If one is going to object to a theory, it should at least be represented correctly.

13. RILEY, p. 50, goes on to note: "Matthew, it is true, has a further parable about seed – the Wheat and the Tares – which Mark does not include, but like that of the Dragnet, it is interpreted from a different point of view: 'so will it be at the close of the age' (Mt 13:40, 49). Mark's three parables are only concerned with sowing and with the harvest that results. It is the theme that he follows through not only by adding ... the one parable peculiar to his Gospel, but also by including Matthew's ... Mustard Seed without ... the Leaven...". – I see no harvest in Mk 4,30-32. Moreover, Mark could have kept the Wheat and the Tares without the explanation, or altered the explanation to fit his own perspective. Having said that, however, it seems that "the close of the age" is not wholly absent from Mark's parable chapter: εὐθὺς ἀποστέλλει τὸ δρέπανον, ὅτι παρέστηκεν ὁ θερισμός (4,29; cf. Joel 4,13).

14. See TUCKETT, *Revival*, pp. 78-85; quotations are from pp. 79 and 80, respectively. – With respect to the double question in Mark, "presumably inspired by Luke" (p. 79), it is

For the overall picture, if Mark is using Matthew and Luke as his sources, is that Mark has carefully and systematically avoided everything that is common to Matthew and Luke: where they agree, Mark disagrees, and where Matthew disagrees with Luke, Mark follows Matthew closely. Thus Mark appears to have taken an intense dislike to Luke (apart from the form, but not the wording, of the opening double question), and to have gone through Matthew's text, changing it where Matthew and Luke agree, but leaving it alone where they differ. Moreover, the result is, in places, grammatical chaos. This seems such an incoherent redactional procedure ... that it must place a serious question-mark against his [Farmer's] overall theory.

II. DEUTEROMARKUS

For the Two-Source Theory these parables represent one of the consensus Mark-Q overlaps[15], because of 1) the quantity and quality of the Matthew-Luke agreements against Mark, 2) the conflation in Matthew (e.g., the mixing of verbal tenses) of the texts of Mark (present) and Luke = Q (aorist), 3) the Lucan location of the double parable in a non-Marcan context[16], and 4) the paucity of Mark-Luke

interesting to see that Tuckett seems to provide a better presentation of how Mark would have had to have worked on the basis of this hypothesis than even those who propose it (cf. above, n. 8). Cf. too, H. BIGGS, *The Q Debate since 1955*, in *Themelios* 6 (1981) 18-28, p. 23. See now DAVIES and ALLISON, *Matthew* (n. 17), 1991, II, p. 407: "On the Griesbach hypothesis, Mk 4.30-2 is a product of Mt 13.31f. and Lk 13.18f. We think this problematic. The thesis entails that Mark was at some pains to avoid reproducing his sources when they gave concurrent testimony. If his sources were the First and Third Gospels ... Mark has, for seemingly no good reason, neglected the joint agreement of his sources and also gone off on his own to produce a rather awkward sentence [v. 31]. How likely is this? Much more probable ... is the conflation of Mark and Q (= Lk 13.18f.) by Matthew".

15. The Preaching of John the Baptist (Mk 1,7-8), the Temptation (Mk 1,12-13), the Beelzebul Controversy (Mk 3,22-30), the parable of the Mustard Seed (Mk 4,30-32), and the Sending out of the Twelve (Mk 6,6b-13) are generally regarded to be Mark-Q overlaps. Some other passages which find two-source theorists more divided are: the Baptism (Mk 1,9-11), the Nazareth pericope (Mk 6,1-6a), the Great Commandment (Mk 12,28-34). – Cf. my survey (n. 2), pp. 387-389.

16. Cf. the less than accurate presentation in E.P. SANDERS and M. DAVIES, *Studying the Synoptic Gospels*, London - Philadelphia, PA, 1989, p. 79: "The parable of the Mustard Seed exists in basically only one form. There are minor variations from gospel to gospel, but there are not two different forms of the parable. The Mustard Seed and Leaven are both assigned to Q, the Mustard Seed called a Mark-Q overlap, only because there are several minor agreements between Matthew and Luke and, more important, Matthew and Luke agree in putting the Leaven after the Mustard Seed – a major exception to the rule that they do not agree in order against Mark. Putting the Mustard Seed into Q, thus, is only an effort to avoid a difficulty". But cf. p. 215: with respect to the Mustard Seed "there are three versions"! – Sanders continues to press this so-called agreement in order (cf. *NTS* 15, 1968-69, 246-261, p. 257) in spite of, and without reference to, convincing criticism. Cf. F. NEIRYNCK, *The Argument from Order and St. Luke's Transpositions*, in *ETL* 49 (1973) 784-815, pp. 787 and 800 (= *The Minor*

agreements against Matthew[17]. Given these it was rather surprising to read in a recent dissertation by a Marcan priorist that no one has provided "positive arguments" for asserting that the Mustard Seed was found in Q[18]. To support this contention, in the course of his defense of the Deuteromarcan hypothesis[19], F. Kogler provides a list of "several" two-source theorists who see no need to hypothesize a Q-version of the Mustard Seed[20] (in his order): J.C. Hawkins, K.-P. Hertzsch, H.C. Kee, J. Lambrecht and J. Wellhausen. It is evident that Kogler's list neither contains "several" names, nor offers

Agreements, 1974, pp. 291-322, esp. 294 and 307; Evangelica, pp. 737-768 with an additional note on p. 768, esp. 740 and 753; and cf. Evangelica II, p. 803).

17. For these four arguments for a Mark-Q overlap, see TUCKETT, Revival, p. 85, and F. FENDLER, Studien (cf. below, n. 19), p. 179. Cf. major recent commentaries, e.g.: W.D. DAVIES and D.C. ALLISON, Jr., Matthew. II, 1991, p. 416; J. ERNST, Lukas, 1977, p. 424; ID., Markus, 1981, p. 144; J.A. FITZMYER, Luke. II, 1985, p. 1015; J. GNILKA, Markus. I, 1978; ²1986; ³1989, pp. 186-187; ID., Matthäusevangelium. I, 1986, p. 494; R.A. GUELICH, Mark, 1989, p. 247; I.H. MARSHALL, Luke, 1978, p. 560; R. PESCH, Markusevangelium. I, 1976; ⁴1984, p. 260; G. SCHNEIDER, Lukas, 1977; ²1984, pp. 301-302; W. WIEFEL, Lukas, 1988, p. 257.

18. F. KOGLER, Das Doppelgleichnis vom Senfkorn und vom Sauerteig in seiner traditionsgeschichtlichen Entwicklung. Zur Reich-Gottes-Vorstellung Jesu und ihren Aktualisierungen in der Urkirche (FzB, 59), Würzburg, 1988 (1987 Diss., Linz, dir. A. Fuchs), p. 46: "Kein einziger Autor, der das Gleichnis vom Senfkorn Q zuweist, hat dafür auch positive Argumente beigebracht, warum diese Perikope in Q gestanden haben muß. Einzig und allein die agreements 'zwingen' scheinbar die Vertreter der Zweiquellentheorie zu dieser Vermutung". Cf. the review by F. NEIRYNCK in ETL 65 (1989) 440-441. – 'Positive Argumente', in the Deuteromarcan literature, often appears to mean 'theological arguments'. It seems, however, that source-critical solutions are not first and foremost based on the analysis of the implied theology of the gospels.

19. F. KOGLER, maintains that it was Deuteromark who first combined the Mustard Seed and the Leaven (cf. p. 185; see below, n. 34) and replaced Mk 4,26-29 with the Weeds among the Wheat and added its interpretation (Mt 13,24-30.36-43; cf. pp. 201, 207, 209). He is supported by J. RAUSCHER, Vom Messiasgeheimnis zur Lehre der Kirche. Die Entwicklung der sogenannten Parabeltheorie in der synoptischen Tradition (Mk 4,10-12 par. Mt 13,10-17 par. Lk 8,9-10), Diss., Linz, 1990 (cf. ETL 67, 1991, 385-390). An opening for a Deuteromarcan interpretation of Mk 4,30-32 and parallels was already supplied by their director, A. FUCHS, Die Entwicklung der Beelzebulkontroverse bei den Synoptikern. Traditionsgeschichtliche und redaktionsgeschichtliche Untersuchung von Mk 3,22-27 und Parallelen, verbunden mit der Rückfrage nach Jesus (SNTU/B, 5), Linz, 1980 (1977 Habilitationsschrift, Regensburg), p. 110 n. 217.

Those who support a recension of Mark, however, see no need to rely on a Zwischenstufe to explain the Matthew-Luke agreements here: U. LUZ, Matthäus. 2, 1990, p. 327, esp. n. 5, contra Kogler (cf. n. 54); F. FENDLER, Studien zum Markusevangelium (GTA, 49), Göttingen, 1991 (1990 Diss., Göttingen, dir. G. Strecker), esp. his "Eine Auseinandersetzung mit F. Kogler", pp. 175-180; and A. ENNULAT, Die 'Minor Agreements' – ein Diskussionsbeitrag zur Erklärung einer offenen Frage des synoptischen Problems, Diss., Bern, 1989 (dir. U. Luz), pp. 5, 7, 11 and 128-129 (cf. ETL 67, 1991, 373-391, and F. NEIRYNCK in ibid., p. 369). Cf. below, n. 29.

20. F. KOGLER, p. 37: "Mehrere Verfechter der Zweiquellentheorie glauben beim Gleichnis vom Senfkorn keine Q-Form postulieren zu müssen". Cf. his n. 12 for the list of names.

an accurate representation. Hawkins certainly holds that the Q version of the parable of the Mustard Seed might well account for the Matthew-Luke agreements[21]. In his brief study of the Marcan Mustard Seed, Hertzsch neither mentions sources nor Matthew/Luke[22]! That Mt 13,31-32 depends on Mk 4,30-32 is clear for Wellhausen, but an explanation of these agreements and an evident position on Luke's source are found in neither his *Einleitung*[23] nor his commentaries[24].

21. Kogler refers to *Horae Synopticae. Contributions to the Study of the Synoptic Problem*, Oxford, 1899; ²1909 (repr. 1968), p. 109: Hawkins lists "every exclusively Matthaeo-Lucan parallel" (pp. 108-109; 1899, pp. 88-89) and thus does not consider the Mustard Seed here. For Mk 4,30-32 (Tischendorf § 50 = Mk 4,26-34, including 4,30-32, Mt 13,31-33 / Lk 13,18-21), as well as other discourse sections (§§ [14, 15, 17], 47, 50, 56, 75, 111, 134, 139), "it seems reasonable ... to suppose that ... the editors of Matthew and Luke turned to the Matthaean Logia, or some other such document (Q), in search of additional matter which should contain more of the teaching of Jesus than supplied by Mark" (p. 208; 1899, p. 172; cf. *The Minor Agreements*, 1974, p. 25 n. 68). – Cf. too, Hawkins's contribution in W. SANDAY (ed.), *Studies in the Synoptic Problem by Members of the University of Oxford*, Oxford, 1911, pp. 29-138, esp. 50ff. on Lk 13,18.19: "Matthew combined the two sources which are substantially preserved for us in our Mark and Luke" (p. 51).

22. Kogler refers to K.-P. HERTZSCH, *Jésus herméneute. Une étude de Marc 4,30-32*, in *Reconnaissance à Suzanne de Diétrich* (Cahiers bibliques/FoiVie, n° hors série), Paris, 1971, pp. 109-116, p. 109.

23. Kogler provides no bibliographical entry and his footnote supplies only "*Einleitung*, 57ff", with no reference to the edition on which he is depending: *Einleitung in die drei ersten Evangelien*, Berlin, 1905; ²1911 (the second edition is reprinted in ID., *Evangelienkommentare*. Mit einer Einleitung von M. HENGEL, Berlin - New York, 1987). It appears, however, that the reference is to the second edition, "§ 5. Nicht aus Markus Stammendes bei Matthäus und Lukas", pp. 57-64 (cp. 1905, § 7, pp. 65-73). Neither the Mustard Seed nor the Leaven is included in Wellhausen's "Reihenfolge der gemeinsamen Stücke" (pp. 57-58). It is not clear, however, whether or not this is to be considered a complete list, for in 1905 he called it "die Reihenfolge der wichtigeren gemeinsamen Stücke" (1905, p. 66; added in 1911 are Mt 6,9-13; 8,11.12.19-21; 13,16.17; 18,12-14; 19,28 and the Lucan parallels). The only reference to the Mustard Seed that I found in the *Einleitung* noted: "Die zweite Parabel (4,26-29) erscheint in der Tat als bloße Variante der ersten; die dritte (4,30-32) verrät ihr späteres Alter durch den bei Markus sonst in dieser Weise nicht vorkommenden Begriff des Reiches Gottes, der zu Matthäus hinüberleitet" (p. 46; 1905, p. 55). It is interesting to note, however, that in the list of Marcan pericopae taken over by Matthew and Luke, § 23 (Mk 4,30-32) is included in Matthew's list, but not Luke's (respectively, pp. 49 and 52; 1905, pp. 57 and 61). This leaves open the question from where Luke took this parable, and whether that source influenced Matthew's use of Mark. There appears to be no direct mention of the Leaven. – Because Wellhausen's list of 'Q' pericopae may not be complete for him, because he does not appear to attribute the Mustard Seed in Luke to Mark, and because his general position certainly allows for the overlapping of Mark-Q (cf. "§ 6. Markus verglichen mit Q", pp. 64-79; cp. 1905, § 8, pp. 73-89), it may be that, at least with respect to the *Einleitung*, Kogler has read more than Wellhausen has written.

24. Kogler refers the reader to *Das Evangelium Matthaei*, Berlin, ²1914, pp. 67f.; *Das Evangelium Marci*, Berlin, ²1909, p. 35f.; and *Das Evangelium Lucae*, Berlin, 1904, p. 73 (all reprinted in ID., *Evangelienkommentare*, Berlin - New York, 1987). It is clear that Wellhausen considers Mt 13,31-32 to be dependent on Mk 4,30-32 (*Matthaei*, p. 68). For Mk 4,30, he notes: "Das Exordium hat hier die Form semitischer Poesie. Der Parallelis-

Rather than maintaining that the Mustard Seed was not in Q, Kee contends that the Leaven was joined to it in Q[25]. Finally, Lambrecht[26] has plainly stated that the Mustard Seed and Leaven already comprised a "twin-similitude" in Q[27]. Most incredible about the inclusion of him by Kogler is that Lambrecht also defends the position that Mark took the Mustard Seed from Q[28]! Kogler's list, therefore, offers hardly any support for his contention that "many" two-source theorists have held that the Mustard Seed was not in Q. Moreover, there *are* grounds for maintaining that this parable was in Q, and though Kogler may

mus der Glieder findet sich ebenso Lc 7,31. 13,18, fehlt dagegen Lc 13,20 und Mt 11,16. 13,31" (*Marci*, p. 35). At Mk 4,31.32: "ὡς κόκκῳ (4,16.26) wird von Lukas richtig erklärt mit ὁμοία ἐστίν" (*Marci*, pp. 35-36). But in his commentary on Luke (p. 73), again there is no reference to Mk 4,30-32 (§ 23; cf. above, n. 23), as there was in *Matthaei*. Moreover, the only comment is: "Der Anlaß für diese Stellung der beiden auch in Mt. 13,31-33 vereinigten Parabeln scheint in der zweiten Hälfte von 13,17 angegeben zu werden". – I fail to see how Kogler can so certainly exclude the Mustard Seed from Wellhausen's Q.

25. Kogler points to *Jesus in History. An Approach to the Study of the Gospels*, New York - Atlanta, GA, 1970; [2]1977, pp. 86 and 109. Kee provides a list of Q passages (pp. 85-87), in which the Leaven is included but not the Mustard Seed. But Kogler's second page reference to Kee seems to state the opposite of what Kogler is pressing: "To the familiar Parable of the Mustard Seed, Q has appended the Parable of the Leaven, since both make the same point". Also with respect to Kee, Kogler comments parenthetically: "im Gefolge davon auch Perrin-Duling, Testament, p. 102". – In N. PERRIN – D.C. DULING, *The New Testament. An Introduction. Proclamation and Parenesis, Myth and History*, New York, 1974; [2]1982, p. 102. Duling takes over Kee's classifications and list of Q pericopae (pp. 100-102). But this can hardly be pressed, for Duling (and Perrin before him) is not completely precise in his presentation: "The parables of the Mustard Seed and the Leaven (13:31-33 = Mark 4:30-32 = Luke 13:18-21) in Matthew's context ..." (p. 280; 1974, p. 183).

26. It is true that in a list of parables in *Les paraboles dans les synoptiques*, in *NRT* 102 (1980) 672-691, p. 688, Lambrecht includes the Mustard Seed in the Marcan parables without repeating it in the list of Q-parables. It can be doubted, however, whether he intended the list to be taken as literally (or source-critically) as Kogler has.

27. *Parabels in Mc 4*, in *TT* 15 (1975) 26-43, p. 37: "Uit Matt. en Luc. kunnen we konkluderen dat in Q een 'tweelinggelijkenis' overgeleverd is: het Mosterdzaadje en het Zuurdeeg". For much the same expression, cf. *Terwijl Hij tot ons sprak. Parabels van Jezus*, Tielt-Amsterdam, 1976; [3]1980, p. 129 (= *Once More Astonished. The Parables of Jesus*, New York, 1981, p. 99); *Parabels in Mt. 13*, in *TT* 17 (1977) 25-47, p. 27. Cf. now, *Nieuw en oud uit de schat. De parabels in het Matteüsevangelie*, Leuven, 1991, p. 162 (= *Out of the Treasure. The Parables in the Gospel of Matthew* [Louvain Theological & Pastoral Monographs, 10], Louvain, 1992, p. 166). – All of the earlier works are noted in Kogler's bibliography, and employed in his footnotes. In fact, in reference to Lambrecht's *Mt. 13* (p. 37) and *Mc 4* (p. 43), Kogler even correctly (though with an unhappy formulation) notes that Lambrecht holds that Matthew "seine zwei Quellen (Mk und Q) (kontaminiert)" (p. 32 n. 3). In this context, Kogler (p. 33 n. 3) also correctly refers to Lambrecht's *Once More Astonished*, pp. 99-100. Kogler's use of "Les paraboles" to support his contention is at best an eclectic use of sources, at worst, misleading.

28. Most especially in *Redaction and Theology in Mk., IV*, in M. SABBE (ed.), *Marc* (BETL, 34), Leuven-Gembloux, 1974; Leuven, [2]1988 (additional note, pp. 307-308), pp. 269-307, esp. 291-297. Cf. too, *Mc 4*, pp. 36-37. – For a response to *Redaction in Mk IV*, see my article (n. 3), especially the section on "Did Mark know Q?", pp. 653-662.

disagree with them, it would have been better if he had directly argued against them rather than simply dismiss them[29]. From his point of view, given Marcan priority and the independence of Matthew and Luke, it seems that there is at least (only?) one important reason for Kogler to deny Q the Mustard Seed: the need for Deuteromark is thereby greatly increased.

Throughout his study Kogler employs Deuteromark as a working hypothesis[30], rather than demonstrating that the independent redactions of Matthew and Luke on Mark and Q are incapable of explaining the similarities and differences between the synoptic versions of the Mustard Seed and the Leaven[31]. The reconstruction of Deuteromark is rather straightforward: wherever two or more gospels agree, there goes Deuteromark[32]; when all three differ, some other factors play a role in the reconstruction[33]. This results in a very Lucan Deuteromark for Mk

---

29. Cf. the review by A. Puig i Tàrrech, in *Bib* 71 (1990) 134-137, esp. pp. 135-136. – Although G. Strecker and U. Schnelle strongly support the standard position of a Mark-Q overlap for the Mustard Seed in their version of the Deuteromarcan hypothesis (*Einführung in die neutestamentliche Exegese* [UTB, 1253], Göttingen, 1983, pp. 55 and 80-81; ²1985; durchgesehene und ergänzte Auflage, ³1989, pp. 59 and 85-86), they surprisingly do not take Kogler to task on this point in their reviews in *TLZ* 115 (1990) 810-812 and *SNTU* 14 (1989) 277-278, respectively.

30. E.g., *Doppelgleichnis*, p. 218. Fendler, *Studien*, p. 177, notes this as he opens his criticism of Kogler's work: "Die Auseinandersetzung mit den Hauptthesen Koglers wird sich im folgenden eher in genereller Weise als anhand von Detailfragen vollziehen müssen, weil die Entscheidung des Verfassers für die Deuteromarkus-Hypothese (trotz S. 43) schon vor der 'detaillierten Analyse' auf den ersten 76 Seiten seines Buchs fällt und die Detailarbeit schon nicht mehr primär der Begründung dieser Hypothese, sondern der Rekonstruktion der postulierten Quelle und der traditionsgeschichtlichen Entwicklung der einzelnen Abschnitte insgesamt dient".

31. The work of C. Niemand, *Studien zu den Minor Agreements der synoptischen Verklärungsperikopen. Eine Untersuchung der literarkritischen Relevanz der gemeinsamen Abweichungen des Matthäus und Lukas von Markus 9,2-10 für die synoptische Frage* (Europäische Hochschulschriften, Reihe 23, 352), Frankfurt - Bern - New York - Paris, 1989, is the most systematic approach to the establishment of Deuteromarkus as a necessary explanation for the minor agreements. Cf. F. Fendler, *Studien*, pp. 180-184. – Nevertheless, Niemand is too quick to accept this hypothetical stage: see the responses by F. Neirynck in *ETL* 65 (1989) 441-442, and in *Evangelica II*, pp. 34-40.

32. Even to the 'common omission' of πάντων from Mk 4,32: "Diesem negativen agreement darf nicht allzuviel Bedeutung geschenkt werden, weil πάντων erstens inhaltlich (fast) überflüssig ist und weil zweitens eine ausdrückliche Parallele zu Mk 4,32b par. Mt 13,32c bei Lk fehlt. Lediglich im Zusammenhang mit den anderen Übereinstimmungen der Seitenreferenten gegen Mk verdient auch das Fehlen von πάντων Beachtung" (p. 68; cf. too, pp. 71, 138, 141-142). – One exception is καί¹ in Mk 4,32 / Lk 13,19. which is proposed to have been changed to δέ (= Mt 13,32) in Deuteromarkus (cf. below, n. 34).

33. Ascribed to the Deuteromarcan Mustard Seed (cf. below, n. 34) are: καί in Mk 4,30; omit πῶς of Mk 4,30 and οὖν of Lk 13,18; τίνι¹ and καί of Lk 13,18; ὁμοία ἐστίν and ἔβαλεν εἰς κῆπον of Lk 13,19; ὅ, μέν ἐστιν, ἐστίν² of Mt 13,32. This also plays a role when the forms differ. In Deuteromark are ὁμοιώσω of Lk 13,18, αὐτοῦ of Mt 13,31, and αὐξηθῇ and γίνεται of Mt 13,32.

4,30-31a; a Matthean one for 4,31b-32a; and again a Lucan form for 4,32b and the Leaven[34].

It is, of course, difficult to disprove this theory, except to show that it is unnecessary[35] and that the proposed redactional changes of Matthew/Luke on Deuteromark are hard to envisage. Kogler points, as do other Deuteromarcan scholars, to the "relatedness" of the Matthew-Luke agreements to the Marcan text as one of his main arguments[36].

34. KOGLER, pp. 200 and 295, proposes the following as the Deuteromarcan version of *Mt* 13,31-32.33 / **Lk** 8,19-20:

καὶ ἔλεγεν· τίνι ὁμοία ἐστὶν ἡ βασιλεία τοῦ θεοῦ
καὶ τίνι ὁμοιώσω αὐτήν;
ὁμοία ἐστὶν κόκκῳ σινάπεως,
ὃν λαβὼν ἄνθρωπος ἔβαλεν εἰς κῆπον αὐτοῦ,
ὃ μικρότερον μέν ἐστιν πάντων τῶν σπερμάτων,
ὅταν δὲ αὐξηθῇ μεῖζον τῶν λαχάνων ἐστὶν
καὶ γίνεται δένδρον,
ὥστε τὰ πετεινὰ τοῦ οὐρανοῦ κατασκηνοῦν ἐν τοῖς κλάδοις αὐτοῦ. καὶ πάλιν εἶπεν·
τίνι ὁμοιώσω τὴν βασιλείαν τοῦ θεοῦ;
ὁμοία ἐστὶν ζύμῃ,
ἣν λαβοῦσα γυνὴ ἐνέκρυψεν εἰς ἀλεύρου σάτα τρία
ἕως οὗ ἐζυμώθη ὅλον.

On the introductory double question, F. NEIRYNCK comments, in *ETL* 65 (1989), p. 441: "I think the observation is correct that Lk 13,18 is a secondary *Verbesserung* of Mk 4,30, but the corrector can be Luke rather than Dmk (*BETL* 60, 1982, p. 52), and the 'original' double question can be Markan usage (*ETL* 53, 1977, p. 178; = *Evangelica*, p. 516)". For more discussion, cf. the treatment of the double question in my article (n. 3), pp. 662-675.

35. If the two-source theorist can satisfactorily explain the pericope, then the *onus probandi* rests squarely on the shoulders of those who wish to introduce a hypothetical stage in the literary relationship. To assume this hypothetical stage and show that it *could* explain the phenomena, as Kogler does (cf. above, n. 30), is not sufficient.

36. Cf. KOGLER, pp. 65-70, 74, 99, 201, 218 (from his *Sachregister*, p. 291): "Die einzelnen agreements im Gleichnis vom Senfkorn werden nun nicht nur der Reihe nach aufgezählt, vielmehr soll an den augenfälligsten Stellen auch auf die Abhängigkeit der Übereinstimmungen vom Mk-Text (= *Relativität* der agreements zum Mk-Text) hingewiesen werden" (p. 65). For much the same argument by other Deuteromarcan scholars, cf. my survey (n. 2), p. 363 n. 117. – "Relativität" is the new term to indicate the close relationship of the minor agreements to the Marcan text: The minor agreements "sind Mk gegenüber *sekundär*, und sie sind nur in *Abhängigkeit* von diesem Text wirklich zu verstehen (= Relativität)". Cf. A. FUCHS, *Die 'Seesturmperikope' Mk 4,35-41 parr im Wandel der urkirchlichen Verkündigung*, in *SNTU* 15 (1990) 101-133, p. 129, cf. too, p. 125; see further, Fuchs's review of J. KIILUNEN, *Das Doppelgebot der Liebe in synoptischer Sicht*, Helsinki, 1989, in *SNTU* 15 (1990) 163-165, p. 165; C. NIEMAND, *Verklärungsperikopen* (n. 31), p. 273, and *Bemerkungen zur literarkritischen Relevanz der minor agreements. Überlegungen zu einigen Aufgaben und Problemen der agreement-Forschung*, in *SNTU* 14 (1989) 25-38, pp. 35 and 37.

FENDLER, p. 177, makes a general observation which mitigates the significance of the phenomenon of "Relativität": "Für minor agreements allgemein gilt die – nicht in Koglers Schema passende – Regel: je näher sie dem Markustext stehen (hohe Relativität), desto unauffälliger sind sie, desto weniger stellen sie auch im Rahmen der Zweiquellentheorie ein Problem dar; je auffälliger sie aber sind, desto geringer ist per definitionem ihre Relativität zum Markustext" (cf. F. NEIRYNCK, *A Symposium*, p. 371).

But close comparison of the Mustard Seed texts shows very little relationship between the Marcan and Lucan texts[37]. His second main argument is the "ecclesiological background" reflected in the minor agreements[38]. It remains unconvincing, however, that only a special *Zwischenstufe* can answer for this when Matthew's and Luke's own theological concerns and their independent, and quite different, redactions of their sources are able to explain their theological *Umakzentuierungen*[39].

A glance at a few more particular redactional aspects of Kogler's proposal throws further doubt on it. The Matthean redaction of Deuteromark is virtually limited to his stereotyped introduction formula, ἄλλην παραβολὴν παρέθηκεν (ἐλάλησεν) αὐτοῖς (13,31.33), and to his characteristic qualification of the kingdom as τῶν οὐρανῶν (13,31.33). Although he retains the Deuteromarcan aorist indicative against the aorist subjunctive passive of Mk 4,31, Matthew agrees with the Marcan σπείρω against the Deuteromarcan replacement, βάλλω, which Luke maintains in 13,19. Matthew never uses βάλλω for sowing seed, and if his Weeds among the Wheat is his own replacement for Mk 4,26-29, there is evidence of Matthew replacing βάλλω for sowing (Mk 4,26) with σπείρω (Mt 13,24.27). But in Kogler's opinion, Mt 13,24-30 and its explanation (13,36-43) come from the hand of Deuteromark[40], so too then, Deuteromark has substituted σπείρω for βάλλω. With respect to σπείρω and βάλλω, Kogler's Deuteromark is ambidextrous[41].

37. Cf. FENDLER, p. 178: "Besonders der lukanische Text erscheint demgegenüber sowohl inhaltlich als auch formal eigenständig und vom Markustext nahezu unberührt".
38. Cf. KOGLER, pp. 133-136, 187, 203-205, 216-217, 223-224 (from his *Sachregister*, p. 291): "Der aufzeigbare ekklesiologische Hintergrund für die einzelnen dmk Eingriffe in seine Mk-Vorlage ... ist eines der wesentlichsten Argumente für die Dmk-Hypothese" (p. 222).
39. Cf. FENDLER, p. 178: "Auch Koglers zweites Hauptargument ... hat bei näherer Betrachtung keine zwingende Relevanz. ...diese Beobachtungen (lassen sich) mit einer zugrunde liegenden Q-Fassung erklären". "Die Deuteromarkus-Hypothese erweist sich zur Erklärung des synoptischen Sachverhalts dieser Perikope dagegen nicht nur als überflüssig, sondern auch als unwahrscheinlich" (p. 180; for much the same formulation in a general objection to Deuteromark, cf. J. SCHMID, *Einleitung*, Freiburg, ⁶1973, p. 288).
40. Cf. above, n. 19.
41. RAUSCHER, *Messiasgeheimnis* (n. 19), p. 244 n. 22, 'corrects' this in his overall support of Kogler, going, it seems, a bit too far himself: "Gegen *Kogler*, ... der die lk Formulierung ἔβαλεν εἰς κῆπον als dmk veranschlagen möchte[,] ... ist für den Text Dmk par. Mt 13,31/Lk 13,19 eher der Mt Formulierung ἔσπειρεν ἐν τῷ ἀγρῷ αὐτοῦ der Vorzug zu gehen". – This solves the problem of Deuteromark replacing βάλλω with σπείρω at Mk 4,26 and doing just the opposite at Mk 4,31. But two, perhaps even more problematic, difficulties arise with Rauscher's proposal. First, where is there evidence for Luke's preference for βάλλω over σπείρω? Nowhere else does Luke use βάλλω for sowing (cf. below at n. 93); the most similar use is for fertilizing (13,8 βάλω κόπρια). Of course, if Deuteromark had kept Mk 4,26-29, that could have inspired Luke. But alas, Luke did not know this parable. Second, κῆπος is hapax in Luke, so it would be much more likely, on

Luke, on the other hand, is most active in bringing the Deuteromarcan Mustard Seed (esp. Mt 13,32) into more strict parallel with the Deuteromarcan Leaven. Why Deuteromark did not already do this is attributed to rather general and vague ecclesiological concerns[42]. Most surprising, even contradictory, is that Kogler proposes that Deuteromark may have read μικρὰ ζύμη[43] in his Leaven *Vorlage*! In this way not only did Deuteromark not bring the parables into closer parallel, but he made them more dissimilar by maintaining the size contrast in the first and omitting it from the second. More specific to Luke is his rewriting of the Deuteromarcan καὶ γίνεται δένδρον into the *hapax* formulation, καὶ ἐγένετο εἰς δένδρον. For this "Septuagintism"[44], "everything points to Lucan redaction", according to Kogler[45]. But, Ps 117,22 LXX in Mk 12,10 and parallels offers little support since the verb is an aorist passive (deponent) and the context is not that of growth. Lk 4,23, γενόμενα εἰς τὴν Καφαρναούμ, not only in terms of the verb form, but also of context and meaning, is difficult to compare to καὶ ἐγένετο εἰς δένδρον. Since Lk 13,19 is the case at hand, Kogler might have done better not to list it as evidence. Finally, although γινόμαι + εἰς is found "auffällig oft" in Acts, there is nothing comparable to Lk

---

any theory, that Matthew would change κῆπος in his source to ἀγρός, than for Luke to do the opposite (cf. below at nn. 88-92). It begins to look like Deuteromarkus can't help but introduce redactional difficulties that do not even arise in the hypothesis of independent redaction of Matthew and Luke on Mark and Q.

42. Cf., e.g., KOGLER, pp. 126-127: With the Deuteromarcan *Uminterpretation* "(wird) die Aufmerksamkeit vom kleinen Senfkorn auf den Wachstumsprozeß hingelenkt". "In der Zeit (des *Dmk-Ev*) ... bestand sicherlich kein Grund mehr, den Anfang allzusehr in den Mittelpunkt zu rücken, denn da blickte die *Kirche* bereits längere Zeit auf den 'kläglichen' Beginn zurück, und es ging vielmehr um das *Wachsen der Basileia*, die in etwa mit der Kirche identifiziert wurde". "*Mt* übernimmt aus Dmk diese Uminterpretation". "*Lk* führt die dmk Umakzentuierung noch weiter, in dem er auf den unscheinbaren Anfang gar nicht mehr ausdrücklich reflektiert, vielmehr sofort nach der Aussaat vom Wachsen spricht. Gerade darin zeigt sich bei Lk ein noch späteres theologisches (ekklesiologisches) Stadium".

43. Deuteromark brought the two parables together "denn im dmk Gleichnis vom Sauerteig liegt der Akzent deutlich am Vorgang des *Durchsäuerns* der riesigen Mehlmenge. Diese Aussage befindet sich auf der gleichen Ebene wie die Hervorhebung des Wachstumsprozesses im Gleichnis vom Senfkorn *durch Dmk*" (pp. 185-186). – But could not Deuteromark have been more successful with his concentration upon the *Wachstum* if he had eliminated the size contrast from the Mustard Seed? At least it seems that this has to be admitted, especially in light of Kogler's hypothetical non-Marcan, yet pre-Deuteromarcan, source: "...in der Vorlage von Dmk (lag) der Akzent im Gleichnis vom Sauerteig – ähnlich wie beim Gleichnis vom Senfkorn – auf dem Kontrast (und nicht auf dem Wachstum!)". To this he adds a footnote (n. 342): "Über den konkreten Text in der dmk Vorlage können allerdings nur Vermutungen geäußert werden. So wäre die Formulierung μικρὰ ζύμη denkbar".

44. Cf. FITZMYER, *Luke*, p. 1017: "For the Septuagintism ... see Gen 20:12, etc."

45 KOGLER, p. 140: "Auch hier deutet alles auf eine lk Redaktion hin"; cf. n. 211: "Gegen Laufen" (cf. below, n. 47).

13,19[46]. It is not impossible that Luke would have written καὶ ἐγένετο
εἰς δένδρον if he had read καὶ γίνεται δένδρον in his source, but from
the evidence available, very little points to Lucan redaction[47].

Most problematic for the Deuteromarcan hypothesis is the proposed
Lucan transposition of Mt 13,31-32.33 from Lk 8 to 13,18-19.20-21.
Kogler correctly points out that Luke has other transpositions and that
the double parable functions well in the Lucan context[48]. In themselves, these are not explanations of *why* Luke transposed this material[49]. From the perspective of the Two-Source Theory, however, it is
not as surprising that Luke reduces Mark's parable chapter to "nur *ein
einziges* Gleichnis ... samt Deutung"[50]. Luke omits Mk 4,26-29 with its
cryptic reference to Joel 4,13[51], and perhaps his knowledge of the

46. KOGLER, p. 140. Cf. n. 212: "Die Stellen der Apg sind: 4,11; 5,36 (hier sogar der
Aorist wie in Lk 13,19); 20,16; 21,17; 25,15". – Acts 4,11 ὁ γενόμενος εἰς κεφαλὴν
γωνίας is a paraphrase of Ps 117,22 LXX. Acts 5,36 καὶ ἐγένοντο εἰς οὐδέν is formally the
most parallel to Lk 13,19, but even if Luke himself wrote this in reference to the negative
fate of some misguided men, would it be evident that he would redactionally employ the
phrase for the positive growth of a seed? Acts 20,16 γενέσθαι εἰς Ἱεροσόλυμα; 21,17
γενομένων δὲ ἡμῶν εἰς Ἱεροσόλυμα; 25,15 περὶ οὗ γενομένου μου εἰς Ἱεροσόλυμα can
hardly be taken as support for the redactional likelihood of καὶ ἐγένετο εἰς δένδρον in Lk
13,19.
47. Cf. LAUFEN, *ΒΑΣΙΛΕΙΑ und ΕΚΚΛΗΣΙΑ* (n. 1), p. 107, n. 16 (= p. 471, n. 16):
"Daß Lukas die semitisierende Formulierung mit εἰς (von hebr. le) selbst geschaffen hat,
ist nicht anzunehmen".
48. KOGLER, pp. 211-213: "Warum aber versetzt Lk unsere Doppelperikope gerade ins
13. Kapitel? – ... Lk (nimmt) auch eine Reihe anderer Umstellungen von Perikopen vor. –
... Lk (ist) bestrebt 'thematische Einheiten mit dem Zusammenhang zu schaffen, in den er
die einzelnen Gleichnisse einfügt' [O. KNOCH, *Wer Ohren hat, der höre. Die Botschaft der
Gleichnisse Jesu*, Stuttgart, ²1985, pp. 56-57]. ... Lk 13,18-21 ist ... als Kommentar zu
13,10-17, insbesondere zu V. 17b, zu verstehen. – Lk verwendet unser Doppelgleichnis
nicht nur als Kommentar der vorhergehenden Perikope, sondern zugleich auch als
Abschluß einer größeren Einheit, nämlich des ersten Teils des Lk Reiseberichts (9,51–
13,21). ... – Als viertes Argument, das für eine gezielte Einfügung der Gleichnisse vom
Senfkorn und vom Sauerteig in Lk 13,18-21 spricht, kann noch ins Treffen geführt
werden, daß Lk damit nicht nur das Vorhergehende abschließt, sondern auch auf den
nächsten Abschnitt überleitet, der in der EÜ mit 'Von der neuen Ordnung im Reich
Gottes' überschrieben ist. – Abschließend ist noch darauf hinzuweisen, daß Lk außer in
13,10-21 auch sonst gern die Themen 'Heilen' und 'Reich Gottes' eng verbindet: vgl. z.B.
Lk 9,2.6.11 und bes. 10,9". – Although he favors a *deuteromarkinische Rezension*, U. LUZ,
Matthäus. II, p. 327, n. 5 is unconvinced (cf. n. 19).
49. From the perspective of Lucan dependence on Matthew, which is not so different
from Kogler's Deuteromarkus position here, cf. J. DRURY, *Parables* (n. 58), p. 138: "Why
these two parables follow upon the healing of the bent woman is obscure".
50. KOGLER, p. 210.
51. For example: J.D. CROSSAN, *The Seed Parables of Jesus*, in *JBL* 92 (1973) 244-266,
p. 253: "problems [with the tensions created by the allusion to Joel 4,13] may also have
contributed to Matthew's and Luke's decision to omit the parable". S.E. JOHNSON, *St.
Mark* (BNTC), London, 1960 (Harper's New Testament Commentaries, New York, 1961;
³1977; repr. Peabody, MA, 1988), p. 94: "The obscurity of the parable has no doubt led
the other evangelists to omit it, but Matthew seems to have modelled the Parable of the

Mustard Seed and the Leaven in a different context serves as the inspiration for this particular transposition. It seems that Kogler's theory makes Luke's work in chapter 8 most odd, especially if Kogler agrees with J. Rauscher's completion of Deuteromark 4: the Marcan parable chapter is recast into a nine-part apocalypse[52]. Except for the absence of Mt 13,14-15[53].16-17.44-50, and the presence of some Marcan sayings, the Deuteromarcan parable chapter is quite close to the Matthean one: 13,1-9.10-13.18-23; Mk 4,21-25; Mt 13,24-30.31-32.33. 34-35.36-43. With respect to Mt 13,31-32.33 in particular, and the entire chapter in general, Matthew's redaction is nearly an act of

---

Tares on it...". H. WEDER, *Die Gleichnisse Jesu als Metaphern* (FRLANT, 120), Göttingen, 1978; [4]1990, p. 104: "Mt bringt an dessen Stelle das Gleichnis vom Unkraut unter dem Weizen; Lk läßt es aus, weil es schlecht in den Kontext paßt". For a more specific explanation of the possible redactional motives of Matthew and Luke, see J. DUPONT, *La parabole de la semence qui pousse toute seule (Mc 4,26-29)*, in *RSR* 55 (1967) 367-392, esp. pp. 390-391 (= *Études sur les évangiles synoptiques* [BETL, 70], Leuven, 1985, pp. 295-320, esp. 318-319; additional note, p. 320). See too, DAVIES and ALLISON, *Matthew*. II, 1991, pp. 407-408: "One objection made to Markan priority in the section at hand is the common omission ... of Mk 4.26-9.... Matthew probably omitted or replaced Mk 4.26-9 because retention of it would have destroyed the structure of the chapter, which requires three parables and only three parables in 13.24-43. As for Luke, in chapter 13 he has long since left his Markan source, so we can hardly anticipate the parable of the seed growing secretly here. One might expect it, however, in chapter 8.... But Luke does not in fact use any of Mk 4.26-34, for the good and simple reason that it is 'not relevant to his ... purpose [in chapter 8] of presenting Jesus' teaching on the importance of hearing the word of God aright' (Marshall, p. 330)".

Of course, the ghost of *Urmarkus* always threatens to arise to the occasion. For example: H. KOESTER, *Ancient Christian Gospels*, 1990, p. 276: "If Matthew found the parable in his copy of Mark, one must resort to the explanation that he replaced it with the parable of the Tares. However, ...Matthew was eager to expand this chapter. Since Luke also does not reproduce this parable..., it is more likely the original text of Mark did not include it". H.-M. SCHENKE – K.M. FISCHER, *Einleitung*. V. II: *Die Evangelien*, 1979, p. 21: "es (ist) wahrscheinlich, daß dem Markus-Evangelium diese[s] Stück erst hinzugefügt worden [ist], nachdem Mt und Lk es als Quelle benutzt haben". P. VIELHAUER, *Geschichte der urchristlichen Literatur* (de Gruyter Lehrbuch), Berlin - New York, 1975, p. 273: "Das Fehlen ... läßt sich ... nicht als Auslassung motivieren; Mt und Lk scheinen es tatsächlich nicht in ihrem Mk gelesen zu haben; es ist möglicherweise ein nachmarkinischer Zuwachs" (cf. p. 275). – But the significance of this so-called common omission can be questioned: F. NEIRYNCK, *The Two-Source Hypothesis: Introduction*, in D.L. DUNGAN (ed.), *The Interrelations of the Gospels* (BETL, 92), Leuven, 1990, pp. 3-22, esp. 13: "... the common omission of Mk 4:26-29 is cited [as a difficulty], although in Luke the entire section of Mk 4:26-34 has no parallel in chapter 8". U. LUZ, *Matthäus*. II, 1990, p. 322, n. 11: "Die gemeinsame *Auslassung* von Mk 4,26-29 durch Mt/Lk ist sogar ein 'Major Agreement'. Aber Mt bietet einen Ersatz; Lk streicht den ganzen Abschnitt Mk 4,26-34 und ersetzt ihn durch 8,19-21" Cf. too, the comment by Davies and Allison in the preceding paragraph.

52. RAUSCHER, p. 260: "Dmk hat das mk Gleichniskapitel in eine kleine [neunteilige] Apokalypse umgestaltet".

53. RAUSCHER, p. 90: "eine nachträgliche aber sehr frühe Interpolation durch einen späteren Tradenten".

somnabulance and Luke's a *tour de force*. I would prefer the latter for both.

III. LUCAN DEPENDENCE ON MATTHEW

The father of the theory of Lucan dependence on Matthew, E. Simons, believed that for the parables of the Mustard Seed and Leaven Luke followed his second source and that there was no influence of Matthew in this case[54]. R. Morgenthaler, too, held that while Matthew conflated the two forms, Luke passed over the Mustard Seed in its Marcan context with "the intention to reproduce later the Q-form in the midst of a large Q-unit"[55]. In the light of the theory's background and his own proposal of a "broadened Q", including much of the Lukan *Sondergut*, which was either omitted or radically redacted by Matthew, it is quite surprising that R.H. Gundry does not include the parables of the Mustard Seed and Leaven in his Q[56]. For him, Matthew redacts Mk 4,30-32 and Luke is influenced by Matthew in his use of Mark. The picture for the Leaven, however, is different. With respect to Mt 13,33, Gundry writes: "The question in Luke, 'To what should I liken the kingdom of God?' drops out"[57]. Did Matthew know Luke's Leaven from Q?

M.D. Goulder[58] notes that one general argument for Q, which can

54. E. SIMONS, *Hat der dritte Evangelist den kanonischen Matthäus benutzt?*, Bonn, 1880, p. 76: "Das erste Gleichniss findet sich auch bei Mr., im Verfolg der Mr.-Quelle liess es Lc. aus, weil er es nach Λ bringen wollte.... Das Gleichniss stand in beiden vor einander unabhängigen Quellen, und wie Mt. dieselben kombinirt hat (Syn.-Ev. S. 230, Mt.-Ev. S. 349), so werden auch bei Lc. Reminiscenzen an die eine Form in die Wiedergabe der anderen eingeflossen sein. – Eine Abhängigkeit von Mt. ist dabei so wenig zu konstatiren wie in der Zwillingsparabel".

55. "Die einleuchtendste und überzeugendste Erklärung besteht ... in diesem Fall in der Annahme, daß Mt in Kap 13 der Mk-Ordnung der Perikopen folgt und diese (wie in Mt 3; 12; 23; 24) mit der Quelle Q und S erweitert. Da Q auch ein Senfkorngleichnis enthielt, mischt er Mk- und Q-Form. Lk aber hat das Senfkorngleichnis in der direkten Mk-Parallele übergangen, weil er die Absicht hatte, später die Q-Form inmitten von großen Q-Verbänden wiederzugeben" (R. MORGENTHALER, *Statistische Synopse*, Zürich-Stuttgart, 1971, p. 296).

56. R.H. GUNDRY, *Matthew. A Commentary on His Literary and Theological Art*, Grand Rapids, MI, 1982; ²1983, p. xi. On Mt 13,31-32.33, see pp. 265-269 (cf. above, n. 2). See the review by F. NEIRYNCK in *ETL* 63 (1987) 408-410.

57. *Matthew*, p. 268. On the opening of the Leaven: "As in the opening of the parable about the mustard tree ... riddance of the deliberative question and the collapsing of two clauses into one clause result in emphasis on the present magnitude of the kingdom" (*ibid.*).

58. M.D. GOULDER, *Luke. A New Paradigm.* Vol. I: Part I. *The Argument;* Part II. *Commentary: Luke 1.1-9.50;* Vol. II: Part II (cont.). *Commentary: Luke 9.51-24.53* (JSNT SS, 20), Sheffield, 1989, esp. pp. 41-43 ("Conflation"), 566-570 (cf. above, n. 9). For responses to his commentary, see *ETL* 65 (1989) 390-394 (= Appendix II) and 67

be applied here, is "the apparent phenomenon of 'conflation': Mark gives a passage in one context, and Luke in another, while the Matthaean version is in the Marcan context and combines features of both". The "'obvious' explanation" for "*the* classic instance", Mt 13,31-32.33 and Lk 13,18-19.20-21, "would be that Luke has the Q version, which Matthew has conflated with the Marcan one"[59]. But for Goulder, "the appearance of conflation is always deceptive", for "it is possible to explain the Matthaean version as Matthew's own elaboration of Mark, and Luke will then be following the Matthaean form"[60]. With respect to the Mustard Seed and the Leaven, Luke "is in his big Matthaean block, so he turns up Matthew rather than Mark"[61]. From the point of view of his hypothesis that might well be the case, but Goulder also needs to explain why Luke omitted the Mustard Seed

(1991) 434-436. An earlier treatment by Goulder is found in *Midrash and Lection in Matthew*, London, 1974, esp. pp. 369-371. For the same position, Lucan dependence on Matthew and no Q, cf. J. DRURY, *Luke* (J.P. Phillips New Testament Commentaries), London - New York, 1973, and *The Parables in the Gospels. History and Allegory*, London - New York, 1985, esp. pp. 114, 137-138: "The *mustard seed* ... is another conflation by Luke, probably using memory as well as the texts, of Mark and Matthew". – Goulder's approach is taken up and mangled by V.S.-K. YOON, *Did the Evangelist Luke Use the Canonical Gospel of Matthew?*, 1986 Diss., Graduate Theological Union, Berkeley, CA (dir. W.R. Herzog II); UMI, Ann Arbor, MI, 1988; for Mk 4,30-32, cf. pp. 107-109. See the review in *ETL* 67 (1991) 391-394.

59. *Luke*, p. 41 (italics added). Goulder notes that this pericope was "commended to me as a clearer example [than Mk 3,22-30] by Christopher Tuckett". – Nevertheless, for conflation in Matthew, "12,31-32 en 13,31-32 zijn wellicht de duidelijkste voorbeelden". Cf. F. NEIRYNCK, *De overlevering van de Jezuswoorden en Mk. 9,33-50*, in *Concilium* 2, 1966, n° 10, 62-73, p. 68 (= *Evangelica*, pp. 811-820, esp. 817).

60. *Luke*, p. 43. What is also "deceptive" is the manner in which Goulder presents the three texts (pp. 41-42). Because he chooses to do so in English, he has to fudge a bit on the similarities and differences. He uses "capitals where all three are in common", but even with the distinction between "SAID" (Mk/Lk) and "SAYING" (Mt), should these be capitalized? For example, Goulder is more consequent for "NEST" (Mk/Mt) and "NESTed" (Lk). Of course, THE KINGDOM OF is nominative in Mt/Lk, accusative in Mk, which only the most attentive reader of English will discern. "Bold type" indicates Matthew-Luke agreement: although used twice by Luke, when in parallel to Matthew, the two words "is like" are not separated in Luke as is necessary in the English text; "his" is fine, but at least Luke should be translated "his own" (ἑαυτοῦ); although bolding would be difficult, the translation could reflect the minor agreement in word order, "NEST/ed" before "in its branches" rather than after "under its shadow". The "italics where Matthew agrees with Mark" could likewise benefit from some further precision. – The option for the use of translation certainly makes the commentary readable for more people, but it might have been better to insist on the Greek text, at least in combination with its translation, when the argument requires it. Cf. *Note on Luke 9,22*, in *ETL* 65 (1989) 391-392 (= *Luc – Luke* [BETL, 32], 1989, p. 395 and *Evangelica II*, p. 45) and F. NEIRYNCK, *The Minor Agreements and the Two-Source Theory*, in *Evangelica II*, esp. pp. 15-16 and 33.

61. GOULDER, *Luke*, p. 43, cf. too, p. 566: "As usual through the Journey, he opts for the Matthaean version" (cf. *Midrash*, p. 369).

(and Leaven) from the Marcan context in the first place[62], most especially because in his use of Mk 4,1-20, according to Goulder (and also Gundry), Luke has been influenced by Matthew[63]. For Goulder the transposition is a matter of the lectionary needs of the respective communities[64]:

> ...the Lucan church now needs a Tabernacles lesson. ... Tabernacles was primarily the old harvest festival Ingathering, and Mark and Matthew had both provided harvest sermons – Mk 4.1-34 including a number of harvest parables and related matter, and Matthew 13 similarly. The earlier Gospels may have had to cover worship over a series of holy days, as Tabernacles is from 15th to 22nd Tishri; but for so Gentile a community as Luke's, it is unlikely that we should think of more than Sunday worship. If so, we should have a reason for his shorter pericope.

But it is quite difficult to demonstrate convincingly that Matthew 13 was intended to be an eight-part lection corresponding to the eight days of Tabernacles[65]. "If so", however, Luke would have had to have noticed or known of Matthew's intention, not needed it for his own

62. "If Luke was acquainted with Matthew and had read the Mustard Seed in Mt XIII, 31-32, strictly parallel with Mk IV, 30-32, the question remains why Luke omitted the parable, together with the Leaven, in Lk VIII and transferred them to Lk XIII". F. NEIRYNCK, *Luke's Transpositions* (n. 16), p. 800 (= p. 753).

63. "Matthew's familiar wording still echoes repeatedly in Luke's ears" (*Luke*, p. 414; in the following list a comparison with GUNDRY, *Matthew*, will be provided: Mt = Matthean influence, r? = Gundry does not mention the case, thus the agreement may be due to independent redaction): τοῦ σπείρειν/εἶραι against Mk 4,3 (p. 414; *Mt* r?, p. 252); ὁ ἔχων for ὃς ἔχει in 4,9 (p. 414; *Mt*, p. 254); ὁ δὲ ... εἶπεν for καὶ ἔλεγεν, the addition of γνῶναι, the plural τὰ μυστήρια for the singular, and the "advancing of δέδοται to follow ὑμῖν" against 4,11 (*Mt*, p. 255) [these are "clearly more serious" than those against 4,10 (*Mt* r?, p. 254-255)] (p. 415); "Luke agrees with the Matthaean abbreviation" in the omission of καὶ μὴ ἰδῶσιν from 4,12 (p. 416; *Mt*, p. 257); perhaps in τῇ/τῆς καρδίᾳ/ας against 4,15 (p. 416; *Mt*, p. 259); ὁ/τὸ δέ different from 4,18.20; the word order, καλὴν/ἣ before γῆν/γῇ, against 4,20 (p. 416; *Mt* r?, pp. 260-261). In addition, Gundry specifically notes Matthean influence on Luke in the common omissions from Mk 4,2-3 ἐν τῇ διδαχῇ αὐτοῦ· ἀκούετε (p. 252), the omission of ἐγένετο from and addition of αὐτόν to Mk 4,4 (p. 253), the omissions from Mk 4,7 καὶ καρπὸν οὐκ ἔδωκεν and Mk 4,13 καὶ λέγει αὐτοῖς (p. 254).

64. *Luke*, p. 407.

65. *Midrash*, p. 188: The eight lections are Mt 13,3-9.10-17.18-23.24-30.31-35.36-43.44-52.53-58. "The church could have used the eight Matthaean sections in series as they stood, or perhaps longer pieces on the first and last days, and the Saturday". – Cf. the critique by C.F. EVANS, *Goulder and the Gospels*, in *Theology* 82 (1979) 425-432. G. STANTON notes that "with a wave of the lectionary wand, Q is consigned to oblivion", in *The Origin and Purpose of Matthew's Gospel: Matthean Scholarship from 1945 to 1980*, in *ANRW* II/25,3, 1984, 1889-1951, p. 1902 (Stanton must like this statement, for he repeats it *verbatim* on p. 1938). For further critique by Stanton of Goulder's rejection of Q, especially on the basis of the minor agreements, see now, *A Gospel for a New People. Studies in Matthew*, Edinburgh, 1992, esp. pp. 33-34.

purposes, and yet proceeded to keep, more or less, Matthew's first through third lections (13,3-9.10-17.18-23), re-introduce some Marcan sayings (4,21-25) and also keep Matthew's fifth lection (13,31-35) all for his one Sunday lection.

Attention must be turned to a more specific treatment of the texts and especially the Matthew-Luke agreements. One aspect of the "apparent conflation" that the theory of Lucan dependence on Matthew explains by Matthean redaction on Mark and then Lucan redaction on Matthew is the mixture of tenses in Mt 13,31-32. Goulder notes: "The argument has been particularly appealing because Mark has a straight description of nature in the present tense, and Luke a straight story in the aorist, while Matthew starts with 'a man took and sowed' and later veers back to Mark's present. ... Hence the picture of Matthew the conflator..."[66]. But to 'drift back' to or 'relapse' into or 'veer back' to the present tense of Mark implies that Matthew is doing so from somewhere[67]. But is it from Matthean redaction? This is certainly possible, for "all the other parables in Matthew 13 are told as stories", and, as Goulder adds parenthetically, "even the leaven"[68]. It can be asked, how difficult could it have been for Matthew, who so consistently has aorist tenses in his other parables, even the Leaven, to be more consistent with his verb tense in his redaction of Mk 4,30-32[69]? Gundry discerns a theological motivation for at least one of Matthew's changes of tenses: "The shift from the past tense of sowing to the present tense of the mustard's becoming [γίνεται] a tree does not come by accident from a conflation of Mark and Q. It is a deliberate shift due to Jesus' past establishment of the kingdom and the present magnitude of the kingdom"[70]. Although Gundry's theological interpretation may

66. *Luke*, p. 568.

67. *Luke*, pp. 42, 567, and 568, respectively.

68. *Luke*, p. 42.

69. Although cognizant of Mk 4,26-29 in his writing of Mt 13,24-30, Matthew consistently employs the aorist in the narrative of the parable, except for some instances of verbs of speaking, none of which come from Mark.

70. GUNDRY, p. 268; this follows on an earlier comment: "...'a man' refers to Jesus the sower (see v 37). And Matthew's using the indicative mood (ἔσπειρεν instead of Mark's subjunctive σπαρῇ) makes the verb refer to Jesus' establishing the kingdom in past history" (p. 226). – To Mt 13,32 γίνεται compare Mk 4,32 ποιεῖ. Cf., too, GOULDER, *Luke*, p. 569: "in the context γίνεται δένδρον should probably be taken as a historic present 'it became a tree'".

With respect to identifying the ἄνθρωπος with Jesus, the only other support Gundry offers is that "despite his fondness for Mark's 'on the ground' (8,2), Matthew replaces it with 'in his field' to link this parable with the one concerning the tares, where the latter phrase occurs (v 24). This link further confirms the identification of the 'man' with Jesus, since in the explanation of the tares no doubt is left (v 37)". First, Matthew is not so "fond" of ἐπὶ τὴν γῆν for field or ground for sowing, except in the two parallels to Mk 4,8 (εἰς).20, and ἐν τῷ ἀγρῷ could be little more than an avoidance of "the change in meaning from 'ground' to 'world'" (TUCKETT, *Revival*, p. 82). Second, if Gundry is correct in his interpretation, then is not his Matthew mitigating that identification when on his

not be totally incorrect, if the shift has nothing to do with sources and everything to do with theology, is it not at least curious that no comparable shift takes place in any other parable of Matthew 13? Could not one at least expect that Matthew would have written ἕως οὗ ζυμοῦται ὅλον in 13,33? On the other hand, Goulder's more strictly redactional explanation is no more convincing[71]:

> We may notice first the false logic of inferring from Matthew's mixture of aorists and presents the conflation of two sources: Matthew is by common consent rewriting Mark alone in most of the Passion narrative, and constantly shifts between his own preferred aorist and Mark's preferred historic present (e.g. 26.20ff./31, 37/38, 44/45). So Matthew could be developing Mark alone here also; ... retaining the general Marcan presents..., but glossing in his own story line.

Firstly, because the passion narrative and the parable chapter are hardly comparable genres, has not Goulder risked introducing his own "false logic"? Secondly, the Marcan passion narrative is already marked by a mixture of aorists and presents, and the Matthean aorists are not part of Matthew "glossing in his own story line", as Goulder describes the case in Mt 13,31-32. Moreover, in the three examples (Mt 26,31.38.45 all taken over from Mark) the present tense is λέγει before a climactic word of Jesus, which is characteristic of Matthew[72]. Finally, even though Matthew does "constantly" mix verbal tenses in the passion narrative, in the parable chapter, he does so *only* in Mt 13,31-32, while "constantly" employing the aorist in the narrative of the other parables. It looks more and more logical that for 13,31-32.33 Matthew may have been faithful to the tenses of two sources.

With respect to the Matthew-Luke agreements, both Gundry and Goulder attribute ὃν ἄνθρωπος λαβών to Matthew's preference for

---

own he adds λαβών to make "a parallel between the man's taking a mustard seed here and the woman's taking leaven in v 33c", since the γυνή can hardly be Jesus? Inspite of ἄνθρωπος and ἐν τῷ ἀγρῷ, can Mt 13,37 be applied so strongly to the Mustard Seed when it is specifically an interpretation of the Weeds among the Wheat? Finally, "that Luke agrees with Matthew against Mark in writing ὃν λαβὼν ἄνθρωπος suggests Matthean influence, since Luke neither identifies the man with Jesus nor shows a special liking of λαβών" seems a bit overstated. Luke often uses ἄνθρωπος in his parables (cf. below at nn. 79-80), and thus, even on Gundry's hypothesis could have introduced it on his own, perhaps inspired by γυνή. With respect to λαβών, Luke has no dislike for it (cf. below at nn. 75-76) and, like Matthew, reads it in his source (if, as seems to be implied, Matthew and Luke find the Leaven in their second source). All in all, much like in Kogler's Deuteromarcan hypothesis, there seems to be only one reason for Gundry to deny his "broadened Q" the Mustard Seed (cf. at n. 56).

71. *Luke*, p. 569.

72. At 26,45 Matthew also takes over ἔρχεται from Mk 14,41. On λέγει in Matthew, see W. SCHENK, *Das Präsens historicum als makrosyntaktisches Gliederungssignal im Matthäusevangelium*, in *NTS* 22 (1975-76) 464-475. Cf. too, F. NEIRYNCK, *Symposium* (n. 4), p. 369, n. 20.

ἄνθρωπος and for having "people in all his parables", as well as to his redactional use of λαβών[73]. From the perspective of the Two-Source Theory this conclusion may not be so evident. Firstly, Luke also has people in all his parables. In fact, Mk 4,30-32 is the only parable in the synoptic gospels which lacks a personal subject. With respect to ἄνθρωπος, it is found in triple-tradition parables at Mk 12,1; 13,34, in double-tradition parables at Mt 13,31; 18,12; 22,2, and in special Matthean parables at Mt 13,44.45; 18,23; 21,28. Mt 13,24 may find its parallel in Mk 4,26. Moreover, Luke uses ἄνθρωπος in his own parables at 10,30; 15,11; 16,1.19; 18,10 (δύο)[74]. Most important is that Luke never rejects ἄνθρωπος as the subject of a parable when he finds it in Marcan or double-tradition parables. Secondly, besides its first occurrence in Mt 13,31, λαβών occurs ten times in Matthew: 17,27; 25,16.18.20; 27,24 are special to him; 14,19; 26,26.27 are from Mark and 27,48.59 are added to Mark. But it is not exclusively Matthean, for Luke takes over the first two of Matthew's Marcan uses (Lk 9,16; 22,19) and implies the third in his ὡσαύτως (22,20), uses it redactionally at 20,29 (Mk 12,20 ἔλαβεν; Mt 22,25 omit) and twice in his special material (24,30.43)[75]. In addition, why did Matthew write ἔλαβεν for λαβών in Mk 8,36, especially after using λαβών in the first feeding story? Both Matthew and Luke avoid λαβών at Mk 9,36, though it is Luke who maintains the root in his ἐπιλαβόμενος. Finally, with respect to the formulation, relative pronoun – aor. nom. part. – subject – verb, in other parables, Matthew has one in his special material at 13,44 while all the others (13,31.33; 24,46) are paralleled in Luke[76]. Given these considerations, it is very difficult to positively ascribe ὃν λαβὼν

73. GOULDER, p. 42: Matthew has "an ἄνθρωπος ten times (13.24, 31, 44, 45; 18.12, 23; 21.28, 33; 22.2; 25.1[4]) to Mark's three; with ὃν λαβὼν ἄνθρωπος cf. 13.33Q ἦν λαβοῦσα γυνή, 13.44M ὃν εὑρὼν ἄνθρωπος, 24.46Q ὃν εὑρὼν ὁ κύριος. He has λαβών 20/7/8, often Mt R". Cf. too, *Midrash*, pp. 52, 55, 98, 369. GUNDRY, p. 266: "... 'which' never does acquire a verb in Mark. Therefore Matthew eliminates 'when', changes 'is sown' to 'he sowed' in correspondence with the active forms of this verb in vv 3, 4, 18, 24, and makes 'which' the object of the verb. Then, to identify the subject he characteristically adds ἄνθρωπος (35,17). ...λαβών [is] a favorite of his (3,7)". Cf. DRURY, *Parables*, pp. 114-115.

74. It ought to be noted that in all these cases, except 18,10, the expression used is Luke's "standard ἄνθρωπός τις" (GOULDER, p. 609). With respect to Lk 15,11-32 and Mt 21,28-32 Goulder maintains that Luke depends on Matthew (pp. 582, 609); GUNDRY argues that Luke's parable was in the "broadened Q" (p. xi), from which Matthew took it and redacted it into his own version (pp. 5, 422).

75. GOULDER, p. 779, notes on Lk 24,13-35: "Lucan ideas and language are so pervasive that it has proved difficult to isolate clearly any tradition from redaction". Without explicitly stating it, Lk 24,30, including its λαβών, seems to be redactional for Goulder (cf. pp. 783-784 and 788). Lk 24,43 likewise appears to be redactional for Goulder (cf. pp. 790-792). – Perhaps Acts 9,19, καὶ λαβὼν τροφήν (said of Paul) could have been noted in this connection.

76. Cf. GOULDER, p. 569 and above, n. 73.

ἄνθρωπος to Matthean redaction and thus exclude it from Q. With respect to the entire phrase, even if Matthew wrote ὃν εὑρὼν ἄνθρωπος ἔκρυψεν (13,44) wholly on his own, it may well have been inspired by 13,31.33[77].

Of all the supposed Matthean changes from the point of view of this hypothesis, Goulder claims they are all "characteristic of Matthew, with the sole exception of αὐξάνειν"[78]. Both Matthew and Luke avoid the participle at Mk 4,8[79]. Another 'Q' instance is seen in Mt 6,28 and Lk 12,27. Matthew also uses the compound συναυξάνω in 13,30. Other than these uses of plants, Luke is the only synoptist who further employs the verb: of the child Jesus (1,80; 2,40), the word of God or the Lord (Acts 6,7; 12,24; 19,20) and the people of God (Acts 7,17). Gundry believes that one of the "manifold ways further emphasis falls on the magnitude of the kingdom [is] ... in Matthew's substituting 'it has grown' for Mark's second and redundant 'it has been sown'"[80]. By doing so "it also forges a link with 'to grow together' in the parable of the tares (v. 30)"[81]. But even for Gundry, neither αὐξάνω nor its compound συν- is Matthean. This, then, is one case where Gundry may have found his own "broadened Q" helpful: αὐξάνω in 13,32 is from Q and συναυξάνω in 13,30 is a combination of that root and the prefix of Matthew's favorite συναγάγετε of the same verse[82].

According to Goulder, Matthew "likes trees ... and the grand, slightly exaggerated mode is regular to his Gospel"[83]. For Gundry, it is another example of the "magnitude of the kingdom" as well as an additional indication of Matthean influence on Luke "for Luke does not otherwise show special interest in largeness"[84]. Besides here, δένδρον in Mt 3,10bis has its parallel in Luke. Moreover, Mt 7,17bis. 18bis.19 and their "revised" form[85] in 12,33ter have their parallel in Lk

77. Cf. GUNDRY, p. 276: "The use of ἄνθρωπος for a disciple echoes v 25. See also 8:27; 9:8. ... ἔκρυψεν not only comes from Prov 2:1 LXX and Matthew's special vocabulary (4,2). It also reflects v 33. Just as the woman hid leaven, so a man hid the treasure he found". – Because of the formulation, Gundry should not exclude 13,31 from his consideration of ἄνθρωπος here. Moreover, since Gundry does not appear to exclude the Leaven from Q (cf. above at n. 57), it becomes difficult to do so for the Mustard Seed.

78. GOULDER, p. 43. DRURY, *Parables*, p. 138, passes over this difficulty.

79. For GUNDRY, p. 254, "the subtraction causes the emphasis to fall solely on the giving of fruit, a prominent metaphor in Matthew for works". According to GOULDER, Luke is "cutting down the irrelevances" (p. 411).

80. *Matthew*, p. 266.

81. *Ibid.*, p. 267.

82. GUNDRY, p. 265, offers no explanation of συναυξάνω, but notes that "Matthew likes ... συναγάγετε (10,10)". Cf. the "Greek Index", p. 648: of Matthew's 24 uses of συνάγω, Gundry considers ten to be "insertions in paralleled material" and another ten to be "occurrences in passages peculiar to Matthew".

83. *Luke*, pp. 42-43. Cf. *Midrash*, pp. 61, 369.

84. *Matthew*, p. 267.

85. *Ibid.*, p. 239.

6,43bis.44. The only clear redactional use comes in Mt 21,8. For the hapax στιβάδας (ἐκ τῶν ἀγρῶν) in Mk 11,8, Matthew writes κλάδους (ἀπὸ τῶν δένδρων), "a more natural and usual word". "The switch from a layer of straw, grass, and reeds to branches ... dictates a corresponding switch from fields to trees"[86]. Since Luke parallels virtually every use of Matthew in the double-tradition material and has his own redactional use at 21,29, it appears that Luke "likes trees" every bit as much as Matthew – perhaps even more: compare ἴδετε τὴν συκῆν καὶ πάντα τὰ δένδρα (Lk 21,29) with ἀπὸ δὲ τῆς συκῆς μάθετε τὴν παραβολήν (Mt 24,32 = Mk 13,28). The data concerning δένδρον are consistent with its ascription to Q at Mt 13,32 par. Lk 13,19.

Some peculiarities in Lk 13,18-19.20-21 are also problematic for the theory of dependence on Matthew. As discussed above, ἐγένετο εἰς δένδρον is difficult to ascribe to Lucan redaction of γινέται δένδρον, though not impossible[87]. The hapax κῆπος in Lk 13,19 for ἀγρός in Mt 13,31 is attributed to either Luke's ignorance of Jewish law[88] or his knowledge of non-Palestinian farming[89]. Luke takes over ἀγρός from Mk 5,14; 6,36; 13,16; 15,21, uses it in parallel to Matthew at Lk 12,28; 14,18 and in his own material at 15,15.25; 17,7. If, therefore, ἀγρός were in Luke's source, ignorance of Jewish law would not seem to motivate such an unusual change on Luke's part. Moreover, even if the sowing of mustard were allowed in gardens outside Palestine, unless it were *prohibited* to do so in fields there would still be no necessary reason for Luke to change ἀγρός to κῆπος – and there is certainly no corroborating evidence that he would have. On the other hand, if

---

86. *Ibid.*, p. 410.

87. GOULDER, p. 570, lists it amongst the "hapaxes" of Lk 13,19, but offers no explanation, unless "LXX" is meant to be one.

88. GOULDER, pp. 566-567: "Matthew knows that mustard may be sown as a crop, and must be sown in the open field (*m. Kil.* 3.2; cf. 2.8): Luke is not so strong on Jewish law (§ 26), and thinks a single grain of mustard would go more convincingly in the (herb-)garden". Cf. DRURY, *Parables*, p. 138: "A man sows the seed – in his garden according to Luke, and contrary to Jewish law which he does not know as well as Matthew".

89. GUNDRY, p. 268: "Luke makes an adaptation to horticulture outside Palestine by writing 'into his own garden' in place of Mark's general reference to the ground and Matthew's reference to a field". This is also seen as the case for two-source theorists who believe ἀγρός was in Q. For example, I.H. MARSHALL, *Luke*, p. 561: "According to rabbinic sources (Kil. 3:2; SB I, 669), mustard was not cultivated in gardens, but in fields (cf. Mt.); Luke presumably has rewritten the parable in non-Palestinian terms (*pace* Schulz, 299)" (cf. below, n. 91). – With respect to reconstructions of Q, H. ZIMMERMANN, *Methodenlehre* (n. 1), ²1968, p. 127, S. SCHULZ, *Q. Die Spruchquelle der Evangelisten*, Zürich, 1972, p. 299, and W. SCHENK, *Synopse zur Redenquelle der Evangelien*, Düsseldorf, 1981, p. 99, include εἰς κῆπον in their reconstructions. H.K. MCARTHUR, *The Parable of the Mustard Seed*, in *CBQ* 33 (1971) 198-210, p. 201, and A. POLAG, *Fragmenta Q. Textheft zur Logienquelle*, Neukirchen-Vluyn, 1979, ²1982, p. 66, opine that ἐν τῷ ἀγρῷ was in Q (perhaps ἐν should also be in small print in Polag's presentation).

κῆπος were in Matthew's source, he could have been moved both by his knowledge of Jewish law and his preference for ἀγρός[90] to change κῆπος to ἀγρός[91]. B.B. Scott goes, and I believe correctly, even further: "Most likely, the parable begins, like the parable The Leaven, with a metaphor of impurity: the planting of mustard seed in a garden"[92]. The Lucan ἔβαλεν is also difficult for Gundry's and Goul-

90. Cf. GUNDRY, p. 641: Of the seventeen Matthean uses of ἀγρός, Matthew inserts it in paralleled material three times, employs it ten times in material peculiar to him and four times uses it parallel to Mark and/or Luke.

91. Cf. TUCKETT, Revival, p. 84: "...κῆπος is a Lukan hapax. ... Certainly it is unlikely that Luke would have wanted to change an original ἀγρός (9 times in Luke, 1 in Acts); on the other hand, a change by Matthew to ἀγρός if κῆπος had stood in his source is quite intelligible given Matthew's liking for the word (he uses it 16 times, and cf. the use of it in verses 24, 27, 44 of this chapter). Thus again there is evidence of the existence of a pre-Lukan source with Matthew rewriting it in his own idiom". B.B. SCOTT, Hear then a Parable. A Commentary on the Parables of Jesus, Minneapolis, MN, 1989, pp. 375-376, notes that "Schulz argues that because of the rarity of the word 'garden' in the New Testament, Luke is not responsible for the adjustment; rather he found the word in his source". Ἐν τῷ ἀγρῷ "probably represents his [Matthew's] stereotyped phrase". Ἐπὶ τῆς γῆς "appears to be the direct result of [Mark's] performance. In this parable it occurs twice, both times within a Markan insertion". "Both Matthew and Mark are most probably responsible for the particular description of where the mustard seed is planted, but Luke and Thomas ['tilled ground'] have no special reason for their description. ... Though it is possible that Luke is conforming to Roman custom, it is just as likely that he found 'garden' in his inherited tradition and that 'garden' belongs to the parable's originating structure". DAVIES and ALLISON, Matthew. II, p. 418, also ascribe κῆπος to Q (cf. above, n. 89).

92. SCOTT, Hear then a Parable (n. 91), p. 376. Cf. "Reconstruction: Originating Structure", p. 379: "The seed was most likely planted in a garden, because (a) 'garden' is rare in the New Testament; (b) it resembles Thomas's 'tilled ground'; (c) Matthew's 'in the field' and Mark's 'upon the ground' more likely result from their own styles; and (d) 'garden' is the more difficult reading". – With respect to (b), for Scott, Thomas is an "independent source" (p. 5): "The best formal argument for Thomas's independence is that of order" (n. 2). This is not so important for our concern here, but for the dependence of Thomas on the Synoptics, see B. DEHANDSCHUTTER in ETL 47 (1971) 119-129; in F. NEIRYNCK (ed.), Luc – Luke, 1973, pp. 287-297; ²1989, pp. 197-207 (additional note, pp. 324-326); in M. SABBE (ed.), Marc, 1974; ²1988, pp. 203-219 (with additional note, pp. 219-220); in ETL 55 (1979) 242-265; in Studia Evangelica VII (TU, 126), 1982, pp. 157-160; and in J. DELOBEL (ed.), Logia, 1982, pp. 507-515; C.M. TUCKETT, Thomas and the Synoptics, in NT 30 (1988) 132-157; Mark's Concerns in the Parables Chapter (Mark 4,1-34), in Bib 69 (1988) 1-26; F. NEIRYNCK, The Apocryphal Gospels and the Gospel of Mark, in J.-M. SEVRIN (ed.), The New Testament in Early Christianity (BETL, 86), Leuven, 1989, pp. 123-175, esp. pp. 133-140 (= Evangelica II, pp. 715-772, esp. 725-732 and the additional notes on pp. 768-769); and J. LAMBRECHT, Redaction in Mk IV (n. 28), p. 292, n. 98. – Concerning (c), Scott opines that "the notion that Mark knew Q... seems unlikely" (p. 365, n. 12).

Cf. TUCKETT, Revival, p. 84: "It is often noted that this [κῆπος] reflects a non-Palestinian culture, but how this should be interpreted is not clear. Jewish law decreed that mustard seed should not be sown in gardens; but is Luke changing a story which was originally in line with Jewish law, as many have said? This depends on how far one believes that the parable is meant to be describing an everyday occurrence. ... It may be ... that Luke's 'garden' is not a secondary change, but an integral part of the original

der's hypotheses, for although there may be some indication of Matthew using σπείρω for βάλλω (cp. Mt 13,24.27 and Mk 4,26; cf. above), there is no indication that Luke would have done the opposite. Even if "'sowing' is a bit pompous for a single grain" and it is more appropriate that it be "put in the garden"[93], the single seed did not deter Matthew from using σπείρω and it is not *in se* an explanation of Luke's supposed change. It is not impossible that Luke may have been influenced by Mk 4,26, or because the context of the Mustard Seed in Luke is not particularly about sowing that he may have taken over βάλλω (used of manure) from his own 13,8. But neither is mentioned by those who support Lucan dependence on Matthew, perhaps because they are not all that compelling. Again, the direction from Luke (Q) to Matthew seems more likely. Finally, πάλιν is "rare in Luke", and even if "Luke uses it for repetition, not resumption" it is still not so clear that πάλιν in Lk 13,20 is "probably due to similar use in Mt. 13.45,47"[94].

This section can be concluded with a more general observation. Lucan dependence on Matthew 13,31-32.33 and Mk 4,30-32 without the Mustard Seed in Q leads to a rare redactional response of Luke to Mark and Matthew: Luke takes over from Matthew almost all of what disagrees with Mark, "only a few essential phrases"[95] on which Mark

story, the point being that the Kingdom will erupt from the most unexpected beginnings in the most unexpected places".

93. GOULDER, *Luke*, p. 567. – Perhaps B.H. YOUNG, *Jesus and His Jewish Parables. Rediscovering the Roots of Jesus' Teaching* (Theological Inquiries), New York - Mahwah, NJ, 1988, pp. 207-208, throws some doubt on this entire discussion: "The mishnaic tractate, Kilaim, deals with the commandments from the Pentateuch which prohibit the planting together of diverse kinds. Rabban Simeon b. Gamaliel said that it was permitted to cultivate mustard and saffron on the perimeters of a vegetable garden. It was also taught that one may plant a row of mustard in the middle of a field as long as there was sufficient distance between the mustard and other crops. ... Whether these halachic discussions ... are related to Jesus' parable seems improbable. Thus it seems futile to search for some great halachic significance in the differences between the synoptics, as the mishnaic passages and the Jerusalem Talmud permit sowing mustard seed in both a garden (at least on the perimeters) and in a field – under prescribed circumstances". But if these discussions play any role in the parable at all, then εἰς κῆπον is not totally absolved of its problematic nature, whereas παρὰ κῆπον may have been more acceptable. Nevertheless, even if Young is correct in concluding that the "differences are best understood as the work of the evangelists", he seems to go against both his own theory of Lucan priority (cf. below, n. 130) and good redaction criticism when he proposes that "Luke sometimes stylizes his text in Greek and he may have tried to improve his source by adding a more exact term like garden instead of field".

94. GOULDER, *Luke*, p. 570. For the Matthean redactional use of πάλιν "with the referent within the same pericope", see F. NEIRYNCK, *The Minor Agreements: Note on a Test Case. A Response to W.R. Farmer*, in *ETL* 67 (1991) 73-81, p. 78 (= in *Evangelica II*, 1991, pp. 49-58, esp. 55; additional note, p. 58).

95. GOULDER, *Luke*, p. 42. Cf. TUCKETT, *Revival*, p. 81: "Mark and Luke have virtually nothing in common beyond the barest essentials necessary for telling a parable comparing the Kingdom of God to a mustard seed".

and Matthew agree (ἡ/τὴν βασιλεία/ν, κόκκῳ σινάπεως, τὸ πετεινὰ τοῦ οὐρανοῦ, κατεσκήνωσεν / κατασκηνοῦν [Mt = Mk]), and only six small introductory items which agree with Mark against Matthew: a double question, ἔλεγεν, ὁμοιώσω (Mk -σωμεν), τοῦ θεοῦ, τίνι, αὐτήν. Interestingly, this situation is much the same as the Lucan version of *another* classic Mark-Q overlap, Mk 3,22-30 and parallels[96]. The argument, then, is far from "meretricious", for it is only in the Mk-Q pericopae that in Goulder's hypothesis a quite aberrant Luke is met "going through Matthew, and for some reason deliberately leaving out everything that had been in *Mark*, and only including the things which Matthew *added*"[97].

Each of the most important challenges to the majority hypothesis of independent redaction of Matthew and Luke on Mark shows "how the tradition *could* have developed, but there is little which specifically tells against the usual view"[98]. Quite the contrary, each position seems to encounter more difficulty explaining the literary phenomena at Mk 4,30-32 and parallels than does the standard hypothesis. It can be safely said that at least for the parable of the Mustard Seed the Two-Source Theory is in no need of fundamental alteration.

4242 Natalia Way   Timothy A. FRIEDRICHSEN
Sioux City, IA 51106
U.S.A.

96. Even after seeing Goulder's Commentary, *Luke*, pp. 502-509, as directed, I fail to see how the Beelzebul Controversy is an "unfortunate example" of Matthean conflation and the hypothesis of the overlapping of Mark and Q (p. 184 n. 43; in reference to F.G. DOWNING, in *NTS* 11, 1964-65, 169-181). Cf. TUCKETT, *Revival*, pp. 85-89.

97. GOULDER, p. 42. Cf. now F.G. DOWNING, *A Paradigm Perplex: Luke, Matthew and Mark*, in *NTS* 38 (1992) 15-36, pp. 33-34: "...the Beelzebul controversy ... is one of four quite distinctive sequences where a Matthew dependent on Mark has augmented his Markan text in detail. (The other three are the Baptism and Temptation, the Mission Charge, and the Eschatological Discourse.) Each time our imaginary Luke ignores the most common witness where Matthew and Mark largely or entirely agree, further changes what is similar but less extensively so, and picks out for close repetition only the sole witness of Matthew's additions. ... It would be a very strange procedure indeed for Goulder's Luke who is 'no amateur when it comes to reconciling his sources' (410)". – It could even be admitted that, inspite of its other major difficulties, the inverse hypothesis of Matthean dependence on Luke is more descriptive of the Matthean text in the classic Mark-Q overlaps. Cf. R.V. HUGGINS, *Matthean Posteriority: A Preliminary Proposal*, in *NT* 34 (1992), 1-22, who has recently supported this hypothesis. From this point of view, "Mark/Q overlaps disappear behind a curtain only to emerge a moment later as examples of Matthew supplementing Mark with parallel or thematically related Lukan material" (p. 2; for Mk 3,22-30; 4,30-32, cf. his chart on p. 12).

98. Quoted from C.M. TUCKETT's review of Kogler's dissertation in *JSNT* 39 (1990) 119-120, p. 119.

LECTURE PAR COUCHES RÉDACTIONNELLES
DE L'ÉPISODE DE L'ÉPILEPTIQUE
(Mc 9,14-29 ET PARALLÈLES)

L'épisode de l'épileptique est célèbre pour les nombreux accords mineurs entre Mt et Lc contre Mc qu'on y observe. Pour cette raison, il a été choisi par L. Vaganay[1], puis par X. Léon-Dufour[2] comme illustration de la difficulté d'admettre la validité de l'hypothèse des deux sources. Ces accords mineurs ont été inventoriés de manière complète par F. Neirynck[3].

Contre le caractère originel du récit de Marc, on peut aussi faire valoir qu'il présente une étrangeté. Au v. 17, le père de l'enfant déclare qu'il a «porté» son fils à Jésus. Pourtant, au v. 19, Jésus demande aux assistants de le «porter» vers lui, ce qu'ils font aussitôt (v. 20). Le texte de Mc semble donc être le fruit d'une préhistoire complexe.

C'est pourquoi il paraît utile de mettre à l'épreuve sur cette péricope l'hypothèse de travail que nous avons présentée il y a quelques années[4], et qui se résume dans le schéma suivant:

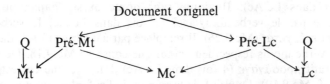

La méthode de recherche des textes sources (Pré-Mt et Pré-Lc) est relativement simple. Les accords de Mt et de Lc contre Mc sont retenus comme des éléments archaïques, reflets du Document Originel et envers de la rédaction marcienne. La comparaison entre Mt et Mc permet d'éliminer de Mt les traits typiquement matthéens et de reconstituer ainsi Pré-Mt. La comparaison entre Lc et Mc permet d'éliminer de Lc les traits typiquement lucaniens et de reconstituer ainsi Pré-Lc. On ne

---

1. L. VAGANAY, *Le problème synoptique*, Paris-Tournai, 1954, pp. 405-425.
2. X. LÉON-DUFOUR, *L'épisode de l'enfant épileptique*, in *Études d'Évangile*, Paris, 1965, pp. 183-227.
3. F. NEIRYNCK, *The Minor Agreements of Matthew and Luke against Mark*, Leuven, 1974, pp. 126-130.
4. P. ROLLAND, *Les premiers évangiles. Un nouveau regard sur le problème synoptique*, Paris, 1984. Voir aussi *La question synoptique demande-t-elle une réponse compliquée?*, in *Bib* 70 (1989) 217-223: réponse aux objections de M.-É. BOISMARD, in *RB* 95 (1988) 97-101.

suppose d'omission chez Mt et chez Lc que si elles sont absolument nécessaires à la cohérence narrative des textes sources.

Les modifications attribuables à la rédaction matthéenne sont assez évidentes: Le geste d'adoration (γονυπετῶν αὐτόν) est une addition; Mt a tendance à multiplier de telles attitudes, car pour lui Jésus est «Dieu-avec-nous» (Mt 1,23). Le verbe σεληνιάζεται n'est attesté ailleurs qu'en Mt 4,24; il doit remplacer ici le verbe plus courant δαιμονίζεται. L'expression ἀπὸ τῆς ὥρας ἐκείνης est une addition typiquement matthéenne (Mt 8,13; 9,22; 15,28). L'adverbe τότε est très fréquent chez Mt; il doit ici se substituer à un simple καί. Le thème de l'ὀλιγοπιστία est très matthéen (Mt 6,30; 8,26; 14,31; 16,8); la source devait parler d'ἀπιστία, comme en Mc 9,24. L'allusion au grain de sénevé (Mt 17,20b) est une addition tirée de Q (cf. Lc 17,6); elle a entraîné un remaniement de la fin du verset: καὶ οὐδὲν ἀδυνατήσει ὑμῖν doit se substituer au proverbe πάντα δυνατὰ τῷ πιστεύοντι, attesté en Mc 9,23.

Les modifications attribuables à la rédaction de Luc sont elles aussi assez nombreuses. Comme d'habitude, Luc substitue ἀνήρ à ἄνθρωπος. Il ajoute le verbe ἐβόησεν (cf. Lc 18,38). Il remplace l'invocation ἐλέησον (cf. Mt 17,15) par une expression plus respectueuse: δέομαί σου ἐπιβλέψαι (deux verbes familiers du langage lucanien). Il ajoute le motif du «fils unique» (cf. Lc 7,12 et 8,42). Il ajoute l'adverbe ἐξαίφνης (4 fois dans Lc-Ac). Il ajoute sans doute aussi l'hapax μόγις. Il remplace par le verbe ἀποχωρεῖ (3 fois dans Lc-Ac) le verbe plus courant ἐξέρχεται (Mc 9,26). Il remplace par ἐδεήθην (15 fois dans Lc-Ac) le verbe moins respectueux εἶπα, que conserve Mc 9,18. De même, l'impératif προσάγαγε (4 fois dans Lc-Ac) doit être une correction de φέρε (cf. Mc 9,19). Le motif de la remise de l'enfant à son père est une addition lucanienne (cf. Lc 7,15). De même, le concert de louanges de Lc 9,43a est une conclusion de type lucanien (cf. Lc 13,17; 18,43; 19,37).

Allégés de ces traits matthéens et lucaniens, les textes sources peuvent ainsi être reconstitués avec vraisemblance:

Pré-Mt	Pré-Lc
καὶ ἐλθόντων πρὸς τὸν ὄχλον	... συνήντησεν αὐτῷ ὄχλος πολύς.
προσῆλθεν αὐτῷ ἄνθρωπος	καὶ ἰδοὺ ἄνθρωπος ἀπὸ τοῦ ὄχλου
λέγων· κύριε,	λέγων· διδάσκαλε,
ἐλέησόν μου τὸν υἱόν,	ἐλέησον μου τὸν υἱόν,
ὅτι δαιμονίζεται	ὅτι πνεῦμα λαμβάνει αὐτὸν
καὶ κακῶς πάσχει·	καὶ κράζει
πολλάκις γὰρ πίπτει εἰς τὸ πῦρ	καὶ σπαράσσει αὐτὸν μετὰ ἀφροῦ
καὶ πολλάκις εἰς τὸ ὕδωρ.	καὶ ἐξέρχεται ἐξ αὐτοῦ
	συντρῖβον αὐτόν.
καὶ προσήνεγκα αὐτὸν	καὶ εἶπα
τοῖς μαθηταῖς σου,	τοῖς μαθηταῖς σου
	ἵνα ἐκβάλωσιν αὐτό,

καὶ οὐκ ἠδυνήθησαν
αὐτὸν θεραπεῦσαι.
ἀποκριθεὶς δὲ ὁ Ἰησοῦς εἶπεν·
ὦ γενεὰ ἄπιστος
καὶ διεστραμμένη,
ἕως πότε μεθ' ὑμῶν ἔσομαι;
ἕως πότε ἀνέξομαι ὑμῶν;
φέρετέ μοι αὐτὸν ὧδε.

καὶ ἐπετίμησεν αὐτῷ ὁ Ἰησοῦς
καὶ ἐξῆλθεν ἀπ' αὐτοῦ
τὸ δαιμόνιον,
καὶ ἐθεραπεύθη ὁ παῖς.

καὶ οὐκ ἠδυνήθησαν.

ἀποκριθεὶς δὲ ὁ Ἰησοῦς εἶπεν·
ὦ γενεὰ ἄπιστος
καὶ διεστραμμένη,
ἕως πότε ἔσομαι πρὸς ὑμᾶς
καὶ ἀνέξομαι ὑμῶν;
φέρε ὧδε τὸν υἱόν σου.
ἔτι δὲ προσερχομένου αὐτοῦ
ἔρρηξεν αὐτὸν τὸ δαιμόνιον
καὶ συνεσπάραξεν·
ἐπετίμησεν δὲ ὁ Ἰησοῦς

τῷ πνεύματι τῷ ἀκαθάρτῳ
καὶ ἰάσατο τὸν παῖδα.

καὶ προσελθόντες οἱ μαθηταὶ τῷ Ἰησοῦ κατ' ἰδίαν εἶπον·
διὰ τί ἡμεῖς οὐκ ἠδυνήθημεν ἐκβαλεῖν αὐτό;
ὁ δὲ λέγει αὐτοῖς·
διὰ τὴν ἀπιστίαν ὑμῶν, πάντα γὰρ δυνατὰ τῷ πιστεύοντι.

Les deux textes pré-matthéen et pré-lucanien ne diffèrent que par un mouvement de foule différent (dû à l'absence chez Lc de la question sur Élie), par une description différente des symptômes de la possession démoniaque, et par l'absence chez Lc de l'entretien particulier entre Jésus et les disciples, qui semble être une addition du Pré-Mt. La reconstitution du Document Originel (DO), dans notre hypothèse, ne peut être que conjecturale. On voit seulement que le Pré-Mt a insisté sur la nécessité de la foi pour obtenir une guérison, tandis que le Pré-Lc s'est appesanti sur la misère de l'enfant guéri par Jésus. On ne peut exclure que le DO n'ait comporté aucune description des symptômes de la maladie, et se soit présenté de la manière suivante:

> Une foule vint à lui.
> Et voici, un homme lui dit:
> «Maître, aie pitié de mon fils,
> parce qu'il est démoniaque
> et se porte mal.
> Et je l'ai apporté à tes disciples,
> et ils n'ont pas pu le guérir».
> Répondant, Jésus dit:
> «O génération incrédule et pervertie,
> jusques à quand serai-je avec vous?
> jusques à quand vous supporterai-je?
> Portez-le moi ici».
> Et Jésus lui enjoignit, et le démon sortit de lui,
> et l'enfant fut guéri.

L'important est de voir comment dans notre hypothèse on peut expliquer la rédaction de Mc à partir du Pré-Mt et du Pré-Lc. Nous le ferons à l'aide d'une synopse en trois parties, car le texte de Mc se délimite de la manière suivante:
1. La question sur l'impuissance des disciples (Mc 9,14-18, avec inclusion entre μαθητάς au v. 14 et μαθηταῖς au v. 18). 2. La réponse théorique sur l'incrédulité (Mc 9,19-24, avec inclusion entre ἄπιστος au v. 19 et ἀπιστία au v. 24). 3. La réponse pratique par l'exorcisme réussi (Mc 9,25-29, avec inclusion entre ἔξελθε au v. 25 et ἐξελθεῖν au v. 29).

1. *La question sur l'impuissance des disciples*

Pré-Mt	Mc	Pré-Lc
καὶ ἐλθόντων	14 καὶ ἐλθόντες	… συνήντησεν αὐτῷ
πρὸς	πρὸς τοὺς μαθητὰς	
	εἶδον ὄχλον πολὺν	ὄχλος πολύς.
	περὶ αὐτοὺς	
	καὶ γραμματεῖς	
	συζητοῦντας	
	πρὸς αὐτούς.	
	15 καὶ εὐθὺς	
τὸν ὄχλον	πᾶς ὁ ὄχλος	
	ἰδόντες αὐτὸν	
	ἐξεθαμβήθησαν	
προσῆλθεν	καὶ προστρέχοντες	
αὐτῷ	ἠσπάζοντο αὐτόν.	
	16 καὶ ἐπηρώτησεν	
	αὐτούς·	
	τί συζητεῖτε	
	πρὸς αὐτούς;	
	17 καὶ ἀπεκρίθη αὐτῷ	καὶ ἰδοὺ
ἄνθρωπος	εἷς	ἄνθρωπος
	ἐκ τοῦ ὄχλου·	ἀπὸ τοῦ ὄχλου
λέγων·		λέγων·
κύριε,	διδάσκαλε,	διδάσκαλε,
ἐλέησόν	ἤνεγκα	ἐλέησόν
μου τὸν υἱόν,	τὸν υἱόν μου	μου τὸν υἱόν,
	πρὸς σέ,	
ὅτι δαιμονίζεται	ἔχοντα πνεῦμα	ὅτι πνεῦμα
	ἄλαλον·	
	18 καὶ ὅπου ἐὰν	
	αὐτὸν καταλάβῃ,	λαμβάνει αὐτόν
καὶ κακῶς πάσχει·		καὶ κράζει
	ῥήσσει αὐτόν,	καὶ σπαράσσει αὐτὸν
	καὶ ἀφρίζει	μετὰ ἀφροῦ
	καὶ τρίζει	
(...)	τοὺς ὀδόντας	(...)
	καὶ ξηραίνεται·	

καὶ προσήνεγκα αὐτὸν	καὶ εἶπα	καὶ εἶπα
τοῖς μαθηταῖς σου,	τοῖς μαθηταῖς σου	τοῖς μαθηταῖς σου
	ἵνα αὐτὸ ἐκβάλωσιν,	ἵνα ἐκβάλωσιν αὐτό,
καὶ οὐκ ἠδυνήθησαν	καὶ οὐκ ἴσχυσαν.	καὶ οὐκ ἠδυνήθησαν.
αὐτὸν θεραπεῦσαι.		

Le vocabulaire de Mc est ici typiquement marcien. Le verbe συζητεῖν se lit 6 fois en Mc (1,27; 8,11; 9,10.14.16; 12,28), et n'est attesté ni par Mt ni par Lc dans les passages parallèles. Le verbe ἐκθαμβεῖσθαι n'est employé que par Mc (9,15; 14,33; 16,5.6). Le verbe προστρέχειν ne se trouve dans les synoptiques qu'en Mc 9,15 et 10,17. Le verbe ἀσπάζεσθαι est attesté également en Mc 15,18. Le verbe ἐπερωτᾶν est particulièrement fréquent chez Mc (8/25/17). L'adjectif ἄλαλος ne se lit que chez Mc (7,37; 9,17.25). L'intervention de la rédaction marcienne à partir de sources plus concises se justifie beaucoup mieux que la suppression simultanée de tous ces termes typiquement marciens par Mt et par Lc.

Les réactions de Mc ont été les suivantes:

a) Il s'est empressé de mettre en scène les disciples, pour souligner leur impuissance lorsque Jésus n'est pas avec eux ou lorsqu'ils n'invoquent pas sa présence par la prière (cf. Mc 9,29). Il les a confrontés aux scribes, devant lesquels ils font piètre figure s'ils se confient à leurs propres forces.

b) Il a relié étroitement l'épisode de l'épileptique à la transfiguration, en montrant la foule «remplie de frayeur» devant Jésus qui descend de la montagne où il a été glorifié.

c) Il a souligné l'importance de l'enseignement sur la foi qui allait suivre, en attribuant à Jésus l'initiative de questionner les disciples, comme en Mc 9,33-34.

d) Il a ménagé une progression dans l'attitude du père, qui ne va pas tout de suite demander à Jésus de «prendre pitié», mais ne le fera que plus tard («aie compassion de nous», v. 22). Au début, le père se contente de dire: «Je t'ai apporté mon fils».

e) Il a introduit le motif de l'esprit «muet». Motif étrange, puisqu'au v. 26 l'esprit «criera». Mais motif symbolique, car l'action de Jésus consiste à «faire parler les muets» (cf. Mc 7,37), conformément à la promesse d'Is 35,5-6.

f) Il a insisté sur la détresse de l'enfant maltraité par l'esprit mauvais, qui le conduit à «grincer des dents et devenir raide».

Par ailleurs, Mc a omis en cet endroit la description pré-matthéenne des symptômes de la maladie, afin d'enrichir le dialogue entre Jésus et le père de l'enfant qu'on lira dans la suite. Il a également omis le motif pré-lucanien de l'esprit qui «brise» l'enfant, car il l'a reporté dans la troisième partie de son récit, où il veut montrer l'enfant «devenu comme mort» (v. 26), que Jésus va ressusciter.

2. La réponse théorique sur l'incrédulité

Pré-Mt	Mc	Pré-Lc
ἀποκριθεὶς δὲ	19 ὁ δὲ ἀποκριθεὶς	ἀποκριθεὶς δὲ
ὁ Ἰησοῦς εἶπεν·	αὐτοῖς λέγει·	ὁ Ἰησοῦς εἶπεν·
ὦ γενεὰ ἄπιστος	ὦ γενεὰ ἄπιστος,	ὦ γενεὰ ἄπιστος
καὶ διεστραμμένη,		καὶ διεστραμμένη,
ἕως πότε	ἕως πότε	ἕως πότε
μεθ' ὑμῶν ἔσομαι;	πρὸς ὑμᾶς ἔσομαι;	ἔσομαι πρὸς ὑμᾶς
ἕως πότε	ἕως πότε	καὶ
ἀνέξομαι ὑμῶν;	ἀνέξομαι ὑμῶν;	ἀνέξομαι ὑμῶν;
φέρετέ μοι αὐτὸν ὧδε.	φέρετε αὐτὸν πρός με.	φέρε ὧδε τὸν υἱόν σου.
	20 καὶ ἤνεγκαν	ἔτι δὲ προσερχομένου
	αὐτὸν πρὸς αὐτόν.	αὐτοῦ
	καὶ ἰδὼν αὐτὸν	ἔρρηξεν αὐτὸν
	τὸ πνεῦμα εὐθὺς	τὸ δαιμόνιον
	συνεσπάραξεν αὐτόν,	καὶ συνεσπάραξεν·
	καὶ πεσὼν ἐπὶ τῆς γῆς	
	ἐκυλίετο ἀφρίζων.	
	21 καὶ ἐπηρώτησεν	
	τὸν πατέρα αὐτοῦ·	
	πόσος χρόνος ἐστὶν	
	ὡς τοῦτο γέγονεν αὐτῷ;	
	ὁ δὲ εἶπεν·	
	ἐκ παιδιόθεν·	
(πολλάκις γὰρ	22 καὶ πολλάκις	
πίπτει εἰς τὸ πῦρ	καὶ εἰς πῦρ	
καὶ πολλάκις	αὐτὸν ἔβαλεν	
εἰς τὸ ὕδωρ)	καὶ εἰς ὕδατα	
	ἵνα ἀπολέσῃ αὐτόν·	
	ἀλλ' εἴ τι δύνῃ,	
(ἐλέησον)	βοήθησον ἡμῖν	
	σπλαγχνισθεὶς ἐφ' ἡμᾶς.	
	23 ὁ δὲ Ἰησοῦς	
	εἶπεν αὐτῷ·	
	τὸ εἰ δύνῃ,	
(πάντα γὰρ δυνατὰ	πάντα δυνατὰ	
τῷ πιστεύοντι)	τῷ πιστεύοντι.	
	24 εὐθὺς κράξας	
	ὁ πατὴρ τοῦ παιδίου	
	ἔλεγεν·	
	πιστεύω· βοήθει	
(διὰ τὴν ἀπιστίαν)	μου τῇ ἀπιστίᾳ.	

Dans l'exclamation initiale de Jésus, Mc a supprimé le mot διεστραμμένη (inspiré de Dt 32,5) pour mettre en relief le mot ἄπιστος, car toute cette section est consacrée à l'incrédulité surmontée par le père. Celui-ci fait partie de la «génération incrédule» dont il est le représentant, car il demandera en son nom que Jésus vienne en aide, non pas à lui, mais à «nous» (v. 22). Sa foi va s'affermir peu à peu, passant d'un espoir incertain à une confiance totale en la parole du Christ. Mc a pris bien soin d'introduire la démarche de foi avant la guérison, car il est fermement persuadé, comme Paul, que l'homme ne peut être sauvé que moyennant une adhésion libre au Christ qui vient nous combler de ses dons (cf. Mc 1,15; 11,23-24). La foi est d'autant plus nécessaire que l'homme est en proie aux attaques du démon qui veut nous mener à la perdition (v. 22). C'est pourquoi le père de l'enfant «crie» pour appeler Jésus à son secours (v. 24). La foi elle-même est un don, qui ne vient pas des forces humaines, mais qui est suscitée par Dieu dans le cœur de celui qui n'y met pas d'obstacle.

3. *La réponse pratique par l'exorcisme réussi*

Pré-Mt	Mc	Pré-Lc
	25 ἰδὼν δὲ ὁ Ἰησοῦς	
	ὅτι ἐπισυντρέχει ὄχλος,	
καὶ ἐπετίμησεν	ἐπετίμησεν	ἐπετίμησεν δὲ
		ὁ Ἰησοῦς
αὐτῷ ὁ Ἰησοῦς,	τῷ πνεύματι	τῷ πνεύματι
	τῷ ἀκαθάρτῳ	τῷ ἀκαθάρτῳ
	λέγων αὐτῷ·	
	τὸ ἄλαλον	
	καὶ κωφὸν πνεῦμα,	
	ἐγὼ ἐπιτάσσω σοι,	
καὶ ἐξῆλθεν ἀπ᾽ αὐτοῦ	ἔξελθε ἐξ αὐτοῦ	
τὸ δαιμόνιον,	καὶ μηκέτι εἰσέλθῃς	
	εἰς αὐτόν.	
	26 καὶ κράξας	(καὶ κράζει
	καὶ πολλὰ σπαράξας	καὶ σπαράσσει (...)
(καὶ ἐξῆλθεν)	ἐξῆλθεν·	καὶ ἐξέρχεται (...)
	καὶ ἐγένετο	
	ὡσεὶ νεκρός,	συντρῖβον αὐτόν)
	ὥστε τοὺς πολλοὺς	
	λέγειν ὅτι ἀπέθανεν.	
	27 ὁ δὲ Ἰησοῦς κρατήσας	
	τῆς χειρὸς αὐτοῦ	
	ἤγειρεν αὐτόν,	
καὶ	καὶ ἀνέστη.	καὶ
ἐθεραπεύθη ὁ παῖς.		ἰάσατο τὸν παῖδα.
καὶ προσελθόντες	28 καὶ εἰσελθόντος	
	αὐτοῦ εἰς οἶκον	
οἱ μαθηταὶ τῷ Ἰησοῦ	οἱ μαθηταὶ αὐτοῦ	
κατ᾽ ἰδίαν	κατ᾽ ἰδίαν	
εἶπον·	ἐπηρώτων αὐτόν·	
διὰ τί ἡμεῖς	ὅτι ἡμεῖς	
οὐκ ἐδυνήθημεν	οὐκ ἐδυνήθημεν	
ἐκβαλεῖν αὐτό;	ἐκβαλεῖν αὐτό;	

ὁ δὲ λέγει αὐτοῖς·   29 καὶ εἶπεν αὐτοῖς·
    (...)   τοῦτο τὸ γένος
                                ἐν οὐδενὶ
                                δύναται ἐξελθεῖν
                                εἰ μὴ ἐν προσευχῇ.

Plusieurs mots sont aimés de Mc: μηκέτι (1,45; 2,2); πολλά (1,45; 3,12; 5,10; 5,38; 5,43; 6,20; 6,34; 9,26; 15,3); γένος (7,26). L'hapax ἐπισυντρέχει rappelle le verbe συντρέχειν en 6,33. Au début de cette séquence, Mc réintroduit la foule, pour qu'elle soit témoin de l'exorcisme. Il rapporte les paroles par lesquelles Jésus intervient, comme en d'autres endroits de Mc (4,39; 5,41; 7,34). Surtout, il transforme la guérison de l'enfant en une résurrection, comme il l'avait déjà fait pour la guérison de la belle-mère de Pierre (Mc 1,31), utilisant le même schéma que pour la résurrection de la fille de Jaïre (Mc 5,41-42). Il s'agit de montrer que la puissance de résurrection du Christ, manifestée dans la transfiguration, est à l'œuvre dans tout son comportement. Enfin, ayant anticipé le thème de la puissance de la foi dans le dialogue entre Jésus et le père, Mc lui substitue celui de la prière, qui est l'expression concrète de la foi (cf. Mc 11,23-24).

L'hypothèse de genèse des synoptiques que nous avons testée sur cet épisode nous dispense de rechercher des explications compliquées pour justifier les accords de Mt et de Lc contre Mc. Mais elle confirme en général, pour Mt et pour Lc, les conclusions élaborées à partir de l'hypothèse des deux sources. Surtout, elle nous permet de bien comprendre l'activité rédactionnelle de Mc et de mettre en valeur le message particulier qu'il a voulu nous transmettre. Elle nous rend sensibles à l'originalité de son texte, qui sans elle est quelquefois négligée[5].

Séminaire Régional   Philippe ROLLAND
6, rue du Lieutenant-Herduin
F-51100 Reims

5. Cet article a été rédigé avec la collaboration de Dominique Hermant.

MATTHEW 11,7-15

REDACTION OR SELF-REDACTION?

The study of the prehistory of this text has hitherto usually proceeded at two levels: the establishment of a basic Q text behind Matthew and Luke, and analysis of the stages by which that reached its putative final form[1]. This insistence on working from a supposedly neutral parent text by definition forecloses, prematurely in my submission, certain options which concentration on the text of Matthew would leave open. The object of this paper is to explore these for what light they can throw on the still unresolved problems of the passage. Should the findings convince, they will raise questions for majority assumptions about Q. I should therefore make clear that the alternative to the Two-Document hypothesis that I favour is not that of Griesbach, but that of James Hardy Ropes and Austin Farrer and Michael Goulder (FGH)[2], for which Matthew had access to Mark, and Luke to them both.

To begin with Matt 11,7-9: there is clear evidence of verse structure

---

1. Significant contributions from this angle include: M. DIBELIUS, *Die urchristliche Überlieferung von Johannes der Täufer untersucht* (FRLANT, 15), Göttingen, Vandenhoeck & Ruprecht, 1911, pp. 7-15, 21-29; C.H. KRAELING, *John the Baptist*, New York - London, Scribner, 1951; W. WINK, *John the Baptist in the Gospel Tradition* (SNTS MS, 7), Cambridge, University Press, 1968, pp. 18-41; H. SCHÜRMANN, *Traditionsgeschichtliche Untersuchungen zu den synoptischen Evangelien*, Düsseldorf, Patmos, 1968, pp. 111-158; D. LÜHRMANN, *Die Redaktion der Logienquelle* (WMANT, 41), Neukirchen, Neukirchener, 1969, pp. 26-29; S. SCHULZ, *Q. Die Spruchquelle der Evangelisten*, Zürich, Theologischer, 1972, pp. 229-236, 261-267; P. HOFFMANN, *Studien zur Theologie der Logienquelle* (NTAbh, NF, 8), Münster, Aschendorff, ²1974, pp. 51-79, 215-224; B.D. CHILTON, *God in Strength* (SNTU, B 1), Freistadt, Plöchl, 1979, pp. 204-230; P.S. CAMERON, *Violence and the Kingdom* (ANTI, 5), Frankfurt, Lang, 1982; J.S. KLOPPENBORG, *The Formation of Q*, Philadelphia, PA, Fortress, 1987, pp. 108-110; R. CAMERON, *"What have you come out to see?": Characterizations of John and Jesus in the Gospels*, in ID. (ed.), *The Apocryphal Jesus and Christian Origins* (Semeia, 49), Atlanta, GA, Scholars, 1990, pp. 35-69; D.R. CATCHPOLE, *The Beginning of Q: A Proposal*, in *NTS* 38 (1992) 205-221, esp. pp. 207-213. Studies from the same starting point confining themselves to the Matthaean material are W. TRILLING, *Die Täufertradition bei Matthäus*, in *BZ* NF 2 (1959) 271-289; J.P. MEIER, *John the Baptist in Matthew's Gospel*, in *JBL* 99 (1980) 383-404.

2. J.H. ROPES, *The Synoptic Gospels*, Cambridge, MA, Harvard University Press, 1934: ²Oxford, Blackwell, 1960, pp. 66-68; A.M. FARRER, *On Dispensing with Q*, in D.E. NINEHAM (ed.), *Studies in the Gospels* (Essays in memory of R.H. Lightfoot), Oxford, Blackwell, 1955, pp. 55-86; M.D. GOULDER, *Luke: A New Paradigm* (JSNT SS, 20), Sheffield, Academic Press, 1989, esp. pp. 3-128. See also J. DRURY, *Tradition and Design in Luke's Gospel*, London, Darton, Longman & Todd, 1976; H.B. GREEN, *The Credibility of Luke's Transformation of Matthew* and *Matthew 12,22-50: An Alternative to Matthaean Conflation*, both in C.M. TUCKETT (ed.), *Synoptic Studies* (JSNT SS, 7), Sheffield, JSOT, 1984, pp. 131-155 and 157-176; E.P. SANDERS - M. DAVIES, *Studying the Synoptic Gospels*, London, SCM, 1989, esp. pp. 112-119.

underlying the present text, but in order to uncover it it is necessary to discount obviously redactional elements: v. 8b (ἰδοὺ ... εἰσιν) is evidently a gloss on the line which precedes it (cf. the gloss at 12,27b, which similarly interrupts the rhythm of that passage), and ναὶ λέγω ὑμῖν in v. 9 is inserted in order to prepare the way for the quotation which follows in v. 10. The elimination of these[3] leaves a stanza of three bicola in 3-3 rhythm, each consisting of a repeated question followed by a fresh answer:

> τί ἐξήλθατε εἰς τὴν ἔρημον θεάσασθαι;
> κάλαμον ὑπὸ ἀνέμου σαλευόμενον;
> ἀλλὰ[4] τί ἐξήλθατε ἰδεῖν;
> ἄνθρωπον ἐν μαλακοῖς ἠμφιεσμένον;
> ἀλλὰ τί ἐξήλθατε ἰδεῖν;[5]
> προφήτην καὶ περισσότερον προφήτου.

However, on the assumption that the redaction is Matthaean, there are indications that the *Vorlage* did not end at this point[6]. Only here does Matthew use ναί to introduce the solemn λέγω ὑμῖν in preference to the more Hebraic ἀμήν[7], and this indicates that he was inhibited from his normal usage by the presence of the saying introduced by ἀμήν in v. 11, which therefore already stood in some form in the text that he was modifying. But in what form? The tension between the unqualified greatness of John in v. 11a and the restriction of it in v. 11b is familiar enough; if the present form of the verse is the product of redaction, v. 11b can only be understood as part of the latter. Yet a solemn saying that consisted of v. 11a alone, as Martin Dibelius[8] proposed, would make a very abrupt and unrhythmical conclusion to the structured stanza[9] outlined above. Does the context in Matthew offer any alternative?

3. DIBELIUS' observation (*Täufer* [n. 1], p. 11) that the second and third answers contained an extra member was, to say the least, metrically imprecise.

4. According to R.H. GUNDRY, *Matthew: A Commentary on his Literary and Theological Art*, Grand Rapids, MI, Eerdmans, 1982, p. 207, ἀλλά has the force of the Aramaic *'ella'*, 'if not'. It is thus more than a conjunction, and can carry a metrical stress.

5. I assume the currently received punctuation as printed in N-A[26]; cf. *TCGNT*, p. 29.

6. So, for other reasons, KLOPPENBORG, *Formation* (n. 1), pp. 108-109; CATCHPOLE, *Beginning* (n. 1), p. 208.

7. 30 times in Matthew, of which 9 come from Mark.

8. *Täufer*, pp. 12-14; R. BULTMANN, *History of the Synoptic Tradition*, Oxford, Blackwell, 1963, pp. 164-165; LÜHRMANN, *Redaktion* (n. 1), p. 27; CATCHPOLE, *Beginning*, pp. 208-209.

9. Cf. R. SCHNACKENBURG, *God's Rule and Kingdom*, New York, Herder - London, Burns Oates, 1963, p. 133. But CATCHPOLE, *Beginning*, p. 208 and n. 14, rightly objects to the use of *GosThom* 46 as evidence for the pre-gospel form of the verse: "direct dependence on the synoptic tradition cannot be excluded". This holds *a fortiori* for *GosThom* 78, where the specific reference to John has evidently been suppressed; *contra* R. CAMERON, *Characterizations*, p. 44.

The contention of this paper is that it is to be found in the supplementary statement of John's importance at Matt 11,13. If Matthew's text here is examined on its own, without reference for the moment to Luke 16,16, it can be seen that the intrusive wording in it is not ἐπροφήτευσαν (which is after all what prophets do), nor πάντες[10], but καὶ ὁ νόμος, which is seemingly superfluous in this context. Matthew has here introduced the law into a statement about the prophets as he has introduced the prophets into statements about the law at 5,17 and 22,40 (the latter clearly redactional, the former arguably so[11]). The particle γάρ does little, in its present context, to clarify the relation of this verse to the preceding one[12]; the prophetic activities of the (former) prophets do not obviously explain the violence currently offered to the kingdom. But if v. 13 is shorn of the intrusive words and detached from its present context, it makes an appropriate complement to v. 11a:

ἀμὴν λέγω ὑμῖν· οὐκ ἐγήγερται ἐν γεννητοῖς γυναικῶν μείζων Ἰωάννου < τοῦ βαπτιστοῦ > [13]· πάντες γὰρ οἱ προφῆται ἕως Ἰωάννου ἐπροφήτευσαν.

It indicates in what sense the poem in its original form understood John's greatness: he is the prophet who is the climax and the conclusion of the (OT) prophetic line.

Luke's omission from this context of the material represented by Matt 11,12-13 reflects his awareness of its dramatic inappropriateness to a situation in John's lifetime (his sensitivity to considerations of this sort is as superior to Matthew's as his organization of sayings material is inferior). The form in which he reproduces it at 16,16 can be explained in terms of another of his redactional habits[14]: where a saying is found in his source in more than one variant, he tends to prefer the version outside the context that he is following to the one within it. An obvious example is Luke 6,43-45, parallel in context to Matt 7,17-20, but much closer in wording to Matt 12,33.35. In the present passage he has noted the parallel to Matt 11,13 at 5,17, and adopted the word order of the latter. This inference is supported by the material which he has added to 16,16: 16,17 is parallel to Matt 5,18

10. HOFFMANN, Studien (n. 1), p. 57, argues on his own assumptions that Matthew read πάντες in his Vorlage, since he would hardly have introduced it redactionally if faced with the text found in Luke 16,16a. Cf. CHILTON, Strength (n. 1), p. 14.

11. SCHÜRMANN, Untersuchungen (n. 1), p. 118, notes the formal correspondence between Matt 5,17 and 10,34 (diff. Luke 12,51).

12. TRILLING, Täufertradition (n. 1), pp. 276-77, argues that the particles δέ and γάρ would function better with the order of 11,12 and 11,13 inverted (cf. Luke 16,16), implying that the present order is due to MattR. But it would be strange for a redactor to go to the trouble of inverting and leave them still untouched.

13. Τοῦ βαπτιστοῦ may be due to the later redaction; see n. 24 below.

14. See GREEN, Matthew 12,22-50 (n. 2), p. 159.

(including the clause which the latter seems to owe to anticipation of Matt 24,35 [par. Mark 13,31]), but reformulated on the model of Matt 19,24 (par. Mark 10,25): εὐκοπώτερόν ἐστιν...[15]; 16,18 conflates Matt 5,32 (shorn of its exceptive clause) with 19,9 (or its source Mark 10,11-12)[16]; and the expression ἀπὸ τότε which distinguishes the time of the kingdom from that of the law and prophets at 16,16b, a hapax in Luke as in the rest of the NT, is characteristic of Matthew and used by him to introduce Jesus' proclamation of the kingdom (after John's arrest) at Matt 4,17[17]. The proximity of these texts to one another in Matthew offers a simpler explanation of the sequence in Luke than any appeal to a presumed original order of Q[18]; though the arrangement has a logic of sorts, the content is due to selection in the first place, and whoever made it included items that betray a knowledge of Mark. The lameness of the result is not unparalleled in Luke's writing[19], especially where he seems to be making stop press additions[20].

Let us now return to the text of the underlying poem. Of the three answers to the repeated question, the first is strikingly onomatopoeic, with its succession of short syllables suggestive of a reed swaying in the breeze. But it is linked to the second by repeated assonance of the letter α and by subtle alliteration of consonants: in particular, those of μαλακοῖς reproduce those of κάλαμον (apart from the inflections) in inverse order. While the inspiration of this is clearly Hebraic[21], the

15. Cf. J.P. MEIER, *The Vision of Matthew*, New York, Paulist, 1979, p. 235.

16. See GOULDER, *Luke* (n. 2), pp. 631-632; cf. p. 634.

17. Mt 4,17; 16,21; 26,16; Luke only here. SCHÜRMANN's suggestion (*Untersuchungen*, p. 117) that Matthew found the expression in Q ignores the incidence of its 'present tense' ἀπ' ἄρτι (Matthew only; cf. 23,39; 26,29.64). Matthew's ἕως ἄρτι at 11,12 may even have influenced Luke's choice of a different, but still Matthaean, expression here.

18. The correspondence is noted by SCHÜRMANN, *Untersuchungen*, pp. 117-118, anticipated by E. RODENBUSCH, *Die Komposition von Lucas 16*, in *ZNW* 4 (1903) 243-254, esp. p. 247; other references in CHILTON, *Strength*, pp. 206-207. But the idea of Matthew having found the contents of Luke 16,16-18 in a single context in his source and distributed them across his gospel is implausible.

19. Comp. Luke 11,33-36; 11,49-51 (on this HOFFMANN, *Studien*, pp. 168-169; KLOPPENBORG, *Formation*, p. 144; H.B. GREEN, *Matthew, Clement and Luke*, in *JTS* NS 40 [1989] 1-25, p. 23).

20. See GREEN, *Credibility* (n. 2), pp. 141-142. The insertion of Luke 16,16-18 breaks into an obvious sequential connection between 16,15b and the parable beginning at 16,19. That does not make it pre-Lucan, as Schürmann and those who follow him suppose. HOFFMANN, *Studien*, p. 54, and CHILTON, *Strength*, pp. 207-208, recognize a thematic connection between Luke 16,1-9 and 16-18, reasserting the validity of the law as a counterweight to the content of Luke 15 (Chilton admits the threat to Q here!). This can account for Luke's insertion at this point, even if its precise location is awkward and possibly hasty.

21. For the incidence of devices of this sort in Hebrew verse, see W.G.E. WATSON, *Classical Hebrew Poetry* (JSOT SS, 26), Sheffield, JSOT, 1984, pp. 225-228; and compare the evidence from the Hebrew text of the Song of Songs presented by F. LANDY in R. ALTER – F. KERMODE (eds.), *The Literary Guide to the Bible*, London, Collins, 1987, pp. 307-308.

composition has as clearly been done in Greek[22]; as a translator's *tour de force* it would have no parallel in the tradition. The final answer is marked by alliteration of the letter π, a feature of the first half of the Matthaean Beatitudes (Matt 5,3-6)[23], the final distich of the Matthaean Lord's Prayer (Matt 6,13), the logion of the Easy Yoke (Matt 11,28-30), the promise to Peter (Matt 16,18), and the final commission (Matt 28,18-20) – all of them generally recognized to be redactional in whole or part.

The concluding comment as I have reconstructed it can be read as a concentric pattern[24]:

a   οὐκ ἐγήγερται
b   ἐν γεννητοῖς γυναικῶν
c   μείζων Ἰωάννου·
d   πάντες γὰρ οἱ προφῆται
e   ἕως Ἰωάννου ἐπροφήτευσαν.

The two inner lines b and d are matched by alliteration of the initial letters γ and π respectively; this is reflected in the internal consonants of the verbs ἐγήγερται and ἐπροφήτευσαν in the outer lines a and e. The pivotal line c focuses on the subject of the whole piece. This form of composition is not unparalleled in Matthew. At 23,38[25] we find:

a   ἀφίεται
b   ὑμῖν
c   ὁ οἶκος
d   ὑμῶν
e   ἔρημος.

And if this is dismissed as an insignificant variation on a Q passage, the same cannot be said of the first half of the Lord's Prayer (Matt 6,9-10):

a   Πάτερ ἡμῶν ὁ ἐν τοῖς οὐρανοῖς,
b   ἁγιασθήτω τὸ ὄνομά σου·
c   ἐλθέτω ἡ βασιλεία σου·
d   γενηθήτω τὸ θέλημά σου,
e   ὡς ἐν οὐρανῷ καὶ ἐπὶ γῆς.

22. For Greek as the original language of the synoptic sayings material, see now H.O. GUENTHER, *Greek: Home of Primitive Christianity*, in *Toronto Journal of Theology* 5 (1989) 247-279; cf. H.D. BETZ, *Wellhausen's Dictum "Jesus was not a Christian but a Jew"* in the Light of Recent Scholarship, in *ST* 45 (1991) 83-110, p. 90. For the Farrer-Goulder Hypothesis, however, its primitiveness is less evidently a *datum*.

23. Noted by C. MICHAELIS, *Die π-Alliteration der Subjektsworte der ersten 4 Seligprei-sen in Mt V, 3-6*, in *NT* 10 (1968) 148-161.

24. See WATSON, *Poetry* (n. 21), pp. 187-188. As the lines as arranged are otherwise in 2-stress rhythm, τοῦ βαπτιστοῦ is best treated as redactional.

25. Matt 23,37-39 (if Q is not assumed) gives the impression, like 11,7-13, of an earlier text that has undergone redaction: there is a change of implied speaker in 23,39, and the use of ἀπ' ἄρτι there corresponds with 26,29.64 (both MattR of Mark). This would make 23,38 the original ending of the logion.

Here b and d are closely matched by terminal and internal rhyming, while the enclosed line c, though syntactically coordinate with them, stands on its own, and contains the central aspiration of the Prayer.

The conclusion to which this evidence from prosody so far points is that the hand which framed the little poem underlying Matt 11,7-13 is the same as that which afterwards composed the whole gospel. Why then should the evangelist have undertaken such a major redaction of his own work?

The answer to this is to be sought, I would argue, in Matthew's discovery and appropriation of the gospel of Mark, and its impact on his Christology. Chronological considerations alone make it improbable that this took place in the opening stages of his personal history as a Christian disciple and communicator, and the seeming ambivalence of his references to John (not fully accountable to sources)[26] needs to be approached diachronically. The original conclusion to the poem as I have reconstructed it attributes a finality to John as prophet which leaves no room for a prophetic component in the function of Jesus himself. The Messiah, fulfiller of prophecy (and authoritative expositor of Torah), is not himself a prophet. Nevertheless, at this stage of the evangelist's thinking, they are still figures of comparable stature, as is confirmed by other texts. Matt 11,18 seems to imply that the prophetic call to repentance (involving fasting) belongs typically to John, and 12,41-42, if detached from its present context (to which it is not integral[27]), can be construed, as Kraeling[28] (and others before him[29]) saw, in the same sense: John is the one greater than Jonah, as Jesus is the one greater than Solomon. Such an account of their relationship was not finally reconcilable with Mark's Son of God Christology, to which John is related in terms of Mal 3,1 (the precursor[30]: see Mark 1,2) and 3,22 (Elijah: see Mark 9,11-13). Both Marcan texts have influenced Matthew's redaction of the present passage:

---

26. WINK, *Baptist* (n. 1), pp. 27-41, esp. his conclusions at pp. 40-41, implies that Matthew's contribution is limited to skilful assimilation of his diverse sources. TRILLING, *Täufertradition*, pp. 287-289, allows him the possibility of a more personal involvement with his material.

27. The two verses clearly form a pair, but the catchword connection with the context involves only that which speaks of Jonah.

28. *John the Baptist* (n. 1), p. 137.

29. J.H. MICHAEL, *The Sign of Jonah*, in *JTS* 21 (1920) 146-159, pp. 149-150; B.W. BACON, *Studies in Matthew*, London, Constable, 1930, p. 383; further references in J. JEREMIAS, '*Ιωνᾶς*, in *TDNT* 3 (1965) 406-410, p. 409, n. 21.

30. Not named as Elijah (even if implied), and thus not unacceptable to Luke (cf. Luke 7,27) as the explicit identification at Matt 11,14 clearly was. (The position of H. CONZELMANN, *The Theology of St Luke*, London, Faber, 1960, pp. 24-25, 101, n. 1, calls for some nuancing here; MEIER, *Baptist* [n. 1], p. 384, goes too far in the other direction.)

a. Mark 1,2, as everyone knows, conflates Ex 23,20 and Mal 3,1, the former in its LXX form (v. 2a), the latter rendered somewhat freely (v. 2b). Matthew and Luke reproduce the Marcan version almost verbatim, except for the addition of ἔμπροσθέν σου, a reminiscence, it would seem, of Gen 24,7LXX, which has a catchword link (ἄγγελον) with the other two texts. Their agreement with Mark includes the substitution of κατασκευάσει for the unhelpful ἐπιβλέψεται of Mal 3,1bLXX. This is unparalleled in any other version and still awaits satisfactory explanation[31]. It is best understood in the total context of Mark 1,2-3, where the first text is followed by a quotation of Isa 40,3LXX. Κατασκευάσει in Mark 1,2 and ἑτοιμάσατε in 1,3 represent the same Hebrew verb *pnh*. The latter word would have served for 1,2 also[32], if the text quoted in that verse had stood on its own; but its use in the combined quotation would have been repetitious, and in any case there is a subtle difference between what the forerunner is to do in 1,2 and what the prophet exhorts his audience to do in 1,3, which is better conveyed by the use of a different verb. The implication of this is that behind Matthew's (and therefore Luke's) version there lies the full form of Mark's; while non-access to Mark's source for the combined quotation cannot be proved, access to Mark is still the more economical solution.

In adopting Mark's *testimonium* for the figure of John the Baptist Matthew has taken over with it the subordinate role for him that it implies. This makes it the more likely that ὁ μικρότερος in Matt 11,11b is after all to be referred not to disciples, with whose situation the text is not concerned, but, following Franz Dibelius and others[33], to Jesus himself. While it is certainly true that Matthew uses μικρός to designate disciples, his preferred superlative for this connotation is ἐλάχιστος[34]. The wording of Luke 9,48c suggests that Luke may have been the first to misconstrue him[35].

b. Matt 11,14 anticipates, in typical Matthaean fashion, 17,10-13, where the more allusive identification of John the Baptist with Elijah in Mark 9,11-13 is spelled out explicitly, as is the prospect that he is to be the Messiah's forerunner in death as in life[36]. This too modifies, though

31. R. CAMERON's citation of Wis 7,27 (*Characterizations*, p. 57) is far-fetched. What Wisdom there does to men to make prophets of them is hardly comparable with what the forerunner is to do (to whom?) in preparing the way of the Lord.

32. Theodotion later adopted it for Mal 3,1; cf. E. HATCH – H.A. REDPATH, *A Concordance to the Septuagint*, Oxford, Clarendon Press, 1897, p. 564.

33. F. DIBELIUS, *Zwei Worte Jesu*, in *ZNW* 11 (1910) 188-192; cf. O. MICHEL, μικρός, in *TDNT* 4 (1967) 648-659, pp. 653-654; O. CULLMANN, *The Early Church*, London, SCM, 1956, p. 180; HOFFMANN, *Studien*, pp. 220-224; CATCHPOLE, *Beginning*, pp. 212-213.

34. See Matt 25,40.45; cf. 10,42, and (possibly) 5,19.

35. Luke's choice of wording at 9,48c (LukeR of Mark, but parallel in content to Matt 18,4) suggests that he was the first to read μικρότερος as a reference to disciples.

36. So TRILLING, *Täufertradition*, pp. 272-274, citing especially Matthew's redaction of Mark at 14,3-12; WINK, *Baptist*, pp. 27-28.

in a different way, John's claim to be the prophet *par excellence*. If the deaths of both figures are to be regarded as instances of Israel's murder of its prophets (cf. Matt 23,29-36[37]), then the category of prophet must include Jesus. Whereas in the original form of the saying we have examined John and Jesus are peers, but only John is seen as prophet, in the redaction John is subordinate, but both are prophets. Hence the addition of καὶ ὁ νόμος in 11,13; what has ended with the appearance of John is now not prophecy as such, but the production of scriptures to be fulfilled. Luke was not mistaken in making the connection with Matt 5,17[38].

Finally, 11,12 is introduced by the expression "from the days of John the Baptist until now". "The days of" with a named figure always denotes a past time in Matthew[39]; in the schematic arrangement of the gospel "the days of John the Baptist" corresponds to the section 3,1–4,16, as distinguished from that which begins at 4,17. The meaning of 11,12 in its context must then be that the violence offered to the kingdom covers both stages of its proclamation: another way of putting what has been argued above of the shared passion of John and Jesus[40]. But this is Matthew's *Heilsgeschichte*, addressed to his own implied readership. Whether the saying could have originated, without its present time scheme, in another *Sitz im Leben*[41], or whether, rather, the whole unfinished quest for this[42] has been the pursuit of a chimera, is a question that I must leave to others.

Community of the Resurrection   H. Benedict GREEN
Mirfield West Yorkshire WF14 OBN
England

---

37. TRILLING, *Täufertradition*, p. 274; WINK, *loc. cit.*

38. Cf. the exegesis of Matt 5,17 in J.P. MEIER, *Law and History in the Gospel of Matthew* (AnBib, 71), Rome, Biblical Institute, 1976, pp. 85-87.

39. Cf. Matt 2,1; 23,30; 24,37.

40. D. DAUBE, *The New Testament and Rabbinic Judaism*, Cambridge, University Press, 1956, p. 288, sees this as a possible interpretation of βιάζεται and ἁρπάζουσιν in the light of later rabbinic usage; cf. CHILTON, *Strength*, pp. 222-226. But familiarity with this linguistic background is as credible of Matthew himself as of a source.

41. CHILTON's proposal (*Strength*, p. 229) too readily accepts the priority of the Lucan version.

42. For the history of past interpretation see P.S. CAMERON, *Violence* (n. 1).

DER ANFANG DES SPRUCHBUCHS

Nicht nur mit sieben Siegeln verschlossene Bücher haben ihre Rätsel. Auch und sogar ein Spruchbuch hat es in sich. Dabei sollte man meinen, daß gerade ein solches Werk der Form nach kein Problem aufgibt. Was könnte einfacher als eine Folge von Sprüchen sein! Zum Spruchschrifttum gibt es ein reiches Vergleichsmaterial aus Aegypten, Babylon, dem griechisch-römischen Westen und Israel. Dazu ist viel geschrieben und zuletzt von J.S. Kloppenborg eine Teilzusammenstellung, die allerdings durchweg aus zweiter Hand erstellt worden ist, vorgenommen worden[1]. Darüber hinaus sind das Orakelschrifttum (die λόγια des Hystaspes[2] und der Sibyllinen), die Testimonien[3] (gehörten auch die λόγια des Papias zu dieser Gattung?), die Worte des Moses von Qumran, die Pirque Aboth, die Aboth des Rabbi Nathan u.ä. heranzuziehen. Zur Terminologie ist wichtig 2. Ap. Jak.: die Worte (Mehrzahl) des Jakobus wurden in einem λόγος aufgeschrieben[4]. Zur Verbreitung solcher Zusammenstellungen vgl. Philo, De Vit. Cont. 25; Lk 3,4 (Qumran-Ausdrucksweise!); 4,22; R 8,2; 16,26; Ag 7,18. Für eine Unterscheidung von echtem und zugewachsenem Gut sind die Formgesetze der Entwicklung, die sich aus dem Vergleich mit Jesus Sirach, den Worten Manis, dem chinesischen Jesustext[5], den arabischen Jesusworten[6], dem λόγος des Orpheus, des Bakis, des Epimenides und dem Thomasevangelium ergeben, heranzuziehen.

Es ergibt sich: es gibt Zusammenstellungen verschiedener Weiser – sie beginnen mit den Worten der sieben Weisen –, insbesondere solche, die nach Themen gruppiert sind. Ganz vorherrschend aber ist die Verbindung des im Text angebotenen Spruchguts mit nur einem Namen. Die Bezeichnung von zwei Personen gibt es m. W. nicht. Eine freilich sehr kurze Charakterisierung des Sprechers kommt gelegentlich vor, eine lebensgeschichtliche Einbegleitung, wie sie bei Achikar vorliegt, ist ungewöhnlich. Eine szenische Einführung ist selten, jedoch nicht ausgeschlossen; sie liegt etwa im Apokryphon des Johannes[7] vor. Ganz gelegentlich – so bei Musaios – werden auch Stücke verschiedener

---

1. J.S. KLOPPENBORG, *The Formation of Q*, Philadelphia, PA, 1987.
2. H. WINDISCH, *Die Orakel des Hystapes*, Amsterdam, 1929.
3. R. HARRIS, *Testimonies* I/II, Cambridge, 1916-1920.
4. *Ibid.*, p. 63, l. 30-32.
5. P.Y. SAEKI, *The Nestorian Documents and Relics in China*, Tokio, ²1951, pp. 206ff. (vv. 1-62) enthält nur Worte Jesu, worauf ein Nachtrag (vv. 63-65) über seine Wirksamkeit und seinen Tod folgt.
6. M.A. PAPACION, *Logia et Agrapha Domini Jesu* (PO, XIII,3), Paris, 1919ff.
7. S. GIVERSEN (ed.), *Apokryphon des Johannes*, Kopenhagen, 1963, p. 46.

Art (Theogonie, Sphaira, Hymnus) zusammengestellt[8]. Die einfache Form einer Abfolge von Sentenzen – vielleicht unterbrochen durch Fragen – ist durchaus vorherrschend. Freilich gibt es nicht nur diese sondern auch kompliziertere Strukturen[9]. In dem uns näher liegenden Bereich ist es das Thomasevangelium, das, obschon mit dem modisch gewordenen Titel Evangelium ausgestattet, die Gattung des Spruchbuchs in reinster Form zur Darstellung bringt.

In Q selbst herrscht die einfache Form weithin, aber nicht durchgehend vor[10]. Insbesondere der Anfang gibt Fragen auf. Es mag angemessen sein, auf sie hinzuweisen, indem zwei Stimmen der klassischen Zeit der Bemühung um Q[11] vorgeführt werden. Kein Geringerer als C.H. Weisse hatte vor fünf Generationen die These vertreten, daß Lk 3,7ff. ursprünglich als Jesusworte im Spruchbuch gestanden haben müßten und erst nachträglich auf den Täufer umgemünzt worden seien: nur dies entspräche der Einheitlichkeit des Dokuments, die doch zu fordern sei[12] – ob er gewußt hat, daß schon Origenes die Worte Jesus, dem dominus/σωτήρ zuschrieb[13]? Und A. von Harnack, der konservativste aller Q-Kritiker, hat vermutet, daß zwischen der Täuferperikope und der Versuchungsgeschichte eine Erzählung über Taufe und Berufung Jesu gestanden habe, freilich nicht ohne zu mutmassen, daß beides, Taufe und Versuchung, ja auch die Täuferperikope nicht zum ältesten Q-Gut gehört habe[14]. Wenn auch der Sache nach in die älteste Zeit des Christentums zurückweisend mögen sie nicht sogleich ein integraler Teil des Spruchbuchs gewesen[15] sondern als ein Einsprengsel

8. H. DIELS, *Die Fragmente der Vorsokratiker* I, Berlin, 1912, pp. 20-27.

9. Etwa in den allerdings späten Pirque R. Elieser: den Worten Eliesers sind oft am Ende des jeweiligen Kapitels Worte anderer Rabbinen angehängt. Das Ganze ist durch zwei anscheinend später hinzugekommene (s. G. FRIEDLANDER, *Pirkê de Rabbi Eliezer*, London, 1916, p. 9, n. 1.) Kapitel eingeleitet, in denen verschiedene Wechselgespräche biographischen Inhalts wiedergegeben werden.

10. Schon J. WELLHAUSEN, *Einleitung in die drei ersten Evangelien*, Berlin, ²1911, p. 162, hatte Harnack gegenüber darauf hingewiesen: Q habe »eine kunstmässige und literarische Form«. A. EHRHARDT, *Greek Proverbs in the Gospels*, in *HTR* 46 (1953) 59-77, sah in Q umgebildete griechische Sprichwörter.

11. Zu den Versäumnissen der Beschäftigung mit Q in dieser Generation gehört die unzureichende Verarbeitung dessen, was in dem Jahrhundert zwischen Schleiermacher und Hirsch geleistet worden war. Blässe des Ergebnisses oder bloße Wiederholung dessen, was zuvor gesagt worden war, ist nicht selten die Folge. Der Grund für die zu geringe Beachtung liegt auf der Hand. Es droht ein Kulturabfall, der dem Verlust der Kenntnis der griechischen Sprache seit dem fünften Jahrhundert nicht nachstehen würde.

12. *Die evangelische Geschichte kritisch und philosophisch bearbeitet* II, Leipzig, 1838, pp. 6-9.

13. *Johanneskommentar*, p. 289, l. 9-10. (zu Lk 3,8); *Römerkommentar*, p. 265 (Lommatzsch).

14. *Sprüche und Reden Jesu*, Leipzig, 1907, p. 175. Dadurch unterschied er sich von K.R. KÖSTLIN, *Der Ursprung und die Komposition der synoptischen Evangelien*, Stuttgart, 1853, p. 63, der einen Bericht über Auftreten und Lehre des Täufers als Einleitung zu Q in Anspruch genommen hatte.

15. HARNACK, *Sprüche* (n. 13), p. 170.

hinzugekommen sein. Jede der beiden Thesen, so verschieden sie im Einzelnen auch sind, ist begründet durch den Gesichtspunkt der Einheitlichkeit der Form, die die Einheit des Sprechers in sich schließt. Freilich kommen die von Weisse und Harnack aufgerührten Fragen nicht mit 4,13 zur Ruhe sondern stellen sich bis ins siebte Kapitel hinein, um dann erst durch solche anderer, wenngleich auch literarischer Art abgelöst zu werden.

Sie beginnen auch nicht erst mit der Versuchungsgeschichte, die ja ihrer Form nach nicht in ein Spruchbuch hineingehört. Harnack hatte aus 4,3.9 eine Berufungsgeschichte erschlossen[16], die Möglichkeit einer Wiederherstellung jedoch beiseite geschoben. Muß man sich damit abfinden?

Gemeinhin werden die Taufgeschichten des Mt und Lk als Varianten des Mk-Berichts angesehen[17]. Freilich, die Unterschiede sind nicht gering. Aber die ins Auge springenden Abweichungen sind je verschieden: einerseits Mt 3,14-15 und andererseits Lk 3,22 (in der durch it D angeführten Textform); sie erlauben daher die These, daß hier Einflüße verschiedener Herkunft, des mt Sonderguts[18] wie einer primär oder sekundär sich in das Lukasevangelium einschiebenden judenchristlichen Überlieferung[19] vorliegen.

Aber damit sind die Abweichungen von Mk noch nicht erschöpfend bezeichnet. Die Öffnung des Himmels – hier durch ἀνεωχθῆναι statt σχιζομένους ausgedrückt – ist in Mt/Lk für jedermann sichtbar, der Vorgang der Begnadung mit dem Geist durch ἐπ᾽ αὐτόν angezeigt. Da Lk die Geschichte in einen Satz zusammenpreßt[20], wie er auch sonst Wechselgespräche abkürzt[21], wird man auch einzelne nur bei Mt sich zeigende Unterschiede gegenüber Mk einzubeziehen haben. Hierzu gehören καὶ ἐρχόμενον (3,16) und vielleicht auch εἶδεν[22] und ἰδού (3,16.17)[23]. Dürfte somit das die Taufe selbst beschreibende Stück von

---

16. *Ibid.*, p. 128.

17. So E. KLOSTERMANN, *Das Lukasevangelium*, Tübingen, ²1929, p. 54.

18. W. BUSSMANN, *Synoptische Studien* II, Halle, 1929, p. 199.

19. Vgl. K.A. CREDNER, *Beiträge zur Einleitung in die biblischen Schriften* I, Halle, 1832.

20. J. LEIPOLDT, *Die urchristliche Taufe im Lichte der Religionsgeschichte*, 1928, p. 29: »Bei Lk wird der Taufakt ... sozusagen in einem Partizipium versteckt«.

21. H. CADBURY, *The Style and Literary Method of Luke* I, Cambridge, MA, 1919.

22. Im lukanischen Bericht ist das ganze Geschehen in allen seinen drei Teilen ein objektives, während Mt aus Mk, der die ersten beiden Teile als subjektives Geschehen auffaßt (in der Vorlage auch der dritte Teil; s. J. WELLHAUSEN, *Markus*, p. 6), das εἶδεν einschleppte. Anders E. HIRSCH, *Frühgeschichte des Evangeliums* II, Tübingen, 1941, p. 36.

23. Auf der Seite des Lk finden sich zwei Besonderheiten. Καὶ προσευχομένου ist Vorzugswort in seinem Evangelium und könnte so als Zusatz angesehen werden, wie es 5,16; 6,12; 9,18.28-29; 11,1; 18,28-29 der Fall ist. Lk fügt jedoch, wo er selbst gestaltet, das Wort am Anfang einer Szene ein. So liegt es näher, daß er hier mit προσευχομένου ein anderes Wort ersetzt hat. Damit dürfte es wahrscheinlich sein, daß auch ἀνέβη ἀπό (Mt 3,16) in der Quelle gestanden hat. Σωματικῷ εἴδει ist anderseits Lk fremd (9,29 nur

Mk unabhängig sein, so legt sich nahe, Mt 3,14-15 auf dieselbe Quelle zurückzuführen[24].

Dagegen könnte die starke christologische Stilisierung der Verse sprechen. Müssen sie aber vom Evangelisten herrühren? Inhaltlich dieselbe Aussage findet sich im Ebonitenevangelium, dessen Bericht von Epiphanius im Auszug wiedergegeben ist: die Taufbitte des Johannes, die Weigerung Jesu mit dem Hinweis auf πρέπον πληρωθῆναι πάντα. Die Stellung des Zwiegesprächs ist freilich eine andere. Es folgt auf die Proklamation der himmlischen Stimme. Das πρέπον gilt damit nicht der Taufe Jesu sondern dem Täufer, dem nicht die Taufe durch Jesus zuteil wird. Das ist eine sinnvolle Anordnung. Mt wird aus christologischen Gründen umgestellt haben; er dürfte dabei das Johannes und Jesus zusammenschließende ἡμῖν – sicherlich ein Ergebnis theologischer Reflexion – eingeschoben und vielleicht auch das πληρόω-Motiv durch δικαιοσύνη ergänzt und grammatisch umgeformt haben[25]. Da eine direkte Übernahme aus dem Ebionitenevangelium unmöglich ist[26], wird man an eine beiden Evangelien gemeinsame Quelle zu denken haben.

Die Quelle deutet das Taufgeschehen als Proklamation: die Taube setzt sich ἐπ' αὐτόν, um ihn so zu bezeichnen. Der Geist nimmt dagegen bei Mk Eingang in Jesus (εἰς αὐτόν) ihn solchermassen erneuernd[27]. Handelt es sich in Q um die Feststellung eines status (und dienen die Angaben über die Sichtbarkeit des Ereignisses der Sicherstellung des Vorgangs), so ist in Mk eher an eine durch die Einsenkung des Geistes gewirkte Neuwerdung zu denken. Vor allem aber hat die

εἶδος) und könnte darum auf Q zurückgehen. Ein ähnlicher Ausdruck (ἐν ὁμοιώματι περιστερᾶς) findet sich in sy^{sin} der Mt-Stelle und wird von A. Merx, *Das Evangelium Matthäus*, Berlin, 1902, pp. 46f. als ursprünglicher Text des Mt angesehen. Ist die Lesart von D ὡς περιστεράν verkürzende Wiedergabe derselben und somit Beispiel eines für D. bezeichnenden Verfahrens?

24. Anders G. Strecker, *Der Weg der Gerechtigkeit*, Göttingen, 1962, der an mündliche Weiterbildung der Markusüberlieferung denkt.

25. Matthäisch (*ibid.*, p. 150).

26. Auch der Bericht des Ebionitenevangeliums liegt in einer angereicherten Form vor. Die Verdreifachung der Taufstimme ist sicher nicht ursprünglich. Die Einsenkung des Geistes ist ein Zusatz. Προσπεσών dürfte Ausmalung sein. Gegenüber dem rein persönlichen δέομαι σοῦ κτλ ist das ἐγὼ χρείαν ἔχω, zumal die Wendung das für Q typische ἐγὼ enthält (vgl. Lk 7,8; 10,3 var. lect.; 11,20), vorzuziehen. Ἄφες ist – wie in Mt 3,15 – in einer abgewandelten Weise verwendet. Ist das Wort von dem Kirchenvater, der ἄφες in Mt 3,15 mißverstanden hat, hinzugesetzt worden? Worte, die zur Liturgie der Proselytentaufe gehörten, sind hier verwendet. Der Taufbewerber hat, so scheint es, gesagt: χρείαν ἔχω· τί κωλύει (für letzteres s. Ag 8,36). Worauf der Taufassistent entweder hinderte (κωλύειν) oder gestattete (ἀφιέναι). Χρείαν ἔχω ist dann durch οὐ γὰρ ἱκανός εἰμι (Jeb 47a; vgl. Lk 7,6) ersetzt worden. Κωλύειν – ἀφιέναι entsprechen δέειν und λύειν, Worten, die in Jadaim IV.4 verwendet werden.

27. Demgemäß liegt bei Mk viel eher eine »adoptianische« Auffassung vor als in Q. Wie die Taufstimme in Q gelautet hat, läßt sich nicht mit Sicherheit sagen, da der Einfluß mündlicher Überlieferung wie der Liturgie an einer solche Stelle nicht abzuweisen ist.

Geschichte in Q einen anderen Zielpunkt gehabt. Es ist die Beschreibung des Verhältnisses, in seiner Nähe (ἐγὼ χρείαν ἔχω κτλ.) und Verschiedenheit (ἄφες ἄρτι κτλ.) zwischen Johannes und Jesus, auf die die Erzählung zueilt. Die dem Täufer zugemutete Entsagung ist Gehorsam gegenüber dem an ihn ergangenen Ruf. Zugleich aber wird es eingeschärft, daß er selbst nach Jesu Taufe verlangt hatte; damit ist die christliche Taufe empfohlen. Mt hat daraus eine Szene gemacht, deren Absicht es ist, Jesus dafür zu rechtfertigen, daß er sich einem Ritus des alten Bundes unterwarf[28]. Das ist das für seine Gemeinde kennzeichnende Problem. Es ist darum nicht zufällig, daß man vv. 14-15 als Erzeugnis des Evangelisten angesehen hat[29]. Aber solche Erklärung wird dem Text nur zu einem geringen Teil gerecht. Es handelt sich in dem Stück um die Bestimmung des Verhältnisses zwischen Johannes und Jesus. Das Taufbegehren, wie es in dem Text geschildert ist, streitet gegen die Vorstellung von der Überlegenheit des Täufers. Die Antwort Jesu weist Johannes ein πληροῦν[30] zu, von dem sich sein eigenes Tun abhebt[31].

Das Ergebnis ermöglicht es, den Anfang von Q zu erörtern. Da die Taufe Jesu den Bericht über eine allgemeine Tauftätigkeit des Johannes voraussetzt, stellt sich die Frage, ob dieser oder Reste von ihm noch auffindbar sind. Es ergibt sich, daß Lk 3,2 Schluß 3a; Mt 3,2 als von Mk unabhängiges Gut anzusehen sind[32]. Aller Wahrscheinlichkeit nach stammen die Stücke aus Q und bilden den Anfang der Quelle, die in Lk 3,7ff. eine unbestrittene Fortsetzung findet.

Was die Rede des Täufers anbelangt, so ist stärker, als es in den Zeiten Weisses geschehen ist, der Unterscheid zwischen vv. 7-9 und 10-

---

28. Daß der Täufer Jesus sogleich erkennt (vgl. auch Joh 1,29), ist für ihn kein Problem, da die Leser doch bereits über Jesus Bescheid wissen.

29. So noch H. THYEN, Studien zur Sündenvergebung, Göttingen, 1970, p. 139.

30. Das Wort begegnet 5,17 (Doppelformel in matthäischer Prägung); 23,32 vielleicht Übernahme aus Q. Das spricht, zumal das Wort auch in Ev. Eb. vorkommt, für Herkunft aus Q. Damit wird ein an Mt 5,17 orientiertes Verständnis, wie es G. STRECKER, Weg (n. 23), p. 179, vorschlägt, unwahrscheinlich. Des Johannes Auftreten ist in Q zwar von dem der alttestamentlichen Männer abgehoben (Lk 16,16), aber doch auch als von Jesus verschieden angesehen (Lk 7,28.33ff.).

31. Anders G. STRECKER, Weg (n. 23), pp. 179f., (nach dem Vorgang von G. Bornkamm). Indes zeigt das schon von J.H. LJUNGMAN (Das Gesetz erfüllen. Mt 5,17ff und 3,15 untersucht, Lund, 1953) vorgelegte Material, daß das Wort sich auf das Vollmachen von bereits im Kurs Befindlichem beziehen muß. Die Verwendung in Mt 5,17 ist somit eine sekundäre und erst recht die vom Evangelisten durch ἡμῖν angestrebte in 3,15.

32. Diese Textbasis hat D. CATCHPOLE (The Beginning of Q: A Proposal, in NTS 38 [1992] 205-221) zu erweitern gesucht, indem er den Anfang des Markusevangeliums als von Q beeinflußt ansah. Ähnliches hat J.M. ROBINSON, The Sayings Gospel Q, in The Four Gospels 1992. FS F. Neirynck (BETL, 100), Leuven, 1992, pp. 361-388, nach dem Vorgang von H. SCHÜRMANN (Zur Traditionsgeschichte der Nazareth-Perikope Lk 4,16-30, in A. DESCAMPS – A. DE HALLEUX [ed.], Mélanges bibliques en hommage au R.P. Béda Rigaux, Gembloux, 1970, pp. 185ff.) für Lk 4,16 unternommen.

14 herauszustellen. Was dort steht, hebt sich so sehr von den vorangehenden Versen ab, daß sie Hirsch zu der geradezu spöttischen Bemerkung veranlaßt haben, sie zeigten, was bei »nachträglicher Erfindung
bestenfalls zustande gebracht wird«[33]. In der Tat, sie entsprechen so
sehr der Ethik des Ausgleichs, wie sie Lukas selber bevorzugt[34], daß sie
mit der Täuferbotschaft nicht verquickt werden können[35]. Warum aber
hat Lk sie nicht in den Mund Jesu gelegt, wie er es doch an zahlreichen
Stellen getan hat? Wenn – entgegen der Regel, daß das Werk eines
Größeren eine Anziehungskraft ausübt, sosehr, daß Sprüche und Taten
eines Geringeren in seinen Überlieferungsstrom einbezogen werden[36] –
Ansichten, die Lukas doch gerne mit Jesus verbindet, hier dem Täufer
zugewiesen werden, so muß das einen besonderen Grund haben. Er
kann nur darin liegen, daß Lk in der ihm zuhandenen Überlieferung
bereits sozialethische Aussagen des Täufers vorgefunden hatte, die zu
übernehmen er Anstand nahm. Weil aber ein *rubrum* (in einer Folge
von Abschnitten) vorhanden war, sah er sich veranlaßt, statt dessen
Materialien, an denen ihm lag, bereits an dieser Stelle einzufügen. Die
Verse werden damit zum indirekten Hinweis auf einen weiteren Q-
Zusammenhang, der als solcher untergegangen ist.

Der Versuchungsgeschichte und der Feldrede – letztere ein für ein
Spruchbuch typisches Stück – folgt die Perikope von Hauptmann vom
Kapernaum. Dies Wunder in Q zu finden – es ist das einzige ausge-
führte Stück dieser Art im Spruchbuch – ist so ungewöhnlich, daß M.
Dibelius dem Wort Jesu den Vorrang gibt und nur die Wahl zuläßt
zwischen den Möglichkeiten: entweder »kaum ein« oder gar kein
erzählerischer Rahmen in Q oder aber dieser wurde von den Referenten
als unverbindlich angesehen[37]. Dies wurde von T.W. Manson aufgenommen[38]. Ein Fingerzeig für eine andere Erklärung ergibt sich jedoch
aus der Stellung des Stücks in Q: unmittelbar nach der Feldrede[39]. Ein

---

33. E. Hirsch, *Frühgeschichte* (n. 22), p. 35.

34. S. *TWNT*, VI, pp. 904ff.

35. Der Versuch von R. Eisler (*The Sadoqite Book of the New Covenant*, in *Orient et
Occident. FS M. Gaster*, London, 1936, pp. 130f.), in den Versen eine Kriegsregel für die
Soldaten des messianischen Kriegs zu finden ist eine willkürliche Eintragung, deren
Verfehltheit jedoch die Einsicht in den radikalen Charakter der Täuferbotschaft nicht
behindern sollte.

36. Man findet dies auf allen Gebieten der Dichtung (vgl. die Spuria im Werk
Shakespeares), und erst recht der Musik (so wurde so manches Musikwerk Haydn und
Pergolesi fälschlich zugeschrieben oder die Trompetenouvertüre des Cambridger Clark
unter dem Namen von Purcell herausgegeben). In einem anderen Kulturkreis wurden
christliche Sentenzen in den Mund Mohammeds gelegt (s. I. Goldziher, *Muhamme-
danische Studien* II, Halle, 1890, pp. 384-393).

37. *Die Formgeschichte des Evangeliums*, Tübingen, 1933, pp. 53, 130, und besonders
p. 245.

38. *The Sayings of Jesus*, London, 1937, p. 63.

39. Die *consecutio* zu bestreiten, wie dies P. Haupt (*Worte Jesu und Gemeindeüberliefe-
rung*, Leipzig, 1913) tut, besteht kein Anlaß.

Zusammenhang zwischen Rede und Wunder findet sich schon im jüdischen Prophetismus[40]. Die prophetische Rede ist nicht selten dergestalt mit dem Bericht von einer Tat verbunden, daß ihr ein beglaubigendes Wunder vorangeht oder nachfolgt. Die Rabbinen haben daraus eine Theorie gemacht[41]. Erkennt man diesen Hintergrund, so ist das eine Wunder die notwendige Ergänzung der Verkündigung Jesu. Wird auch oft genug in Q auf die Wundertätigkeit Jesu hingewiesen, so genügt doch der Bericht über eine Großtat Jesu. Zugleich ergibt sich eine Beziehung zur Versuchungsgeschichte. Während Jesus in dieser dem Satan selbst widersteht, erweist er sich in der letzteren als der Herr über die Dämonen[42]. Selbst Mk, der doch eine Dämonenbekämpfung nach der anderen schildert, sondert einen entscheidenden Kampf heraus und läßt diesen auf die Verklärung, d.h. auf eine Mt 4,11 parallele Szene folgen[43]. Dies spricht eher dafür, daß die Szenenfolge in Q eine geordnete ist als daß sie sich zufällig ergeben hätte[44]. Hatte man die Versuchungsgeschichte bereits aus Q herauskatapultiert, während dies bei der Geschichte vom Hauptmann von Kapernaum – man ist versucht zu sagen: seltsamerweise – noch nicht versucht worden ist, so spricht dies Ergebnis eher für als gegen Zusammengehörigkeit in einer noch zu beschreibenden Einheit.

Q setzt in der Anfrage des Täufers und der Rede Jesu über Johannes fort – beides sind Stücke, die szenische Elemente enthalten und in solcher Häufigkeit auf geschichtliche Gegebenheiten Bezug nehmen, daß sie zumindest an der Grenze dessen stehen, was zu einem Spruchbuch gehört. Es ist deutlich, daß die Antwort Jesu auf die Täufergesandtschaft und die Täuferrede nur in einem lockeren, durch das Stichwort Johannes bezeichneten Verhältnis zu einander stehen, während sie tatsächlich verschiedene Situationen, die Antwort die Nach-

---

40. 1 Kg 17,17-24; 2 Kg 4,32-37; vgl. Jos. Ant. VIII,230. – Der Einfluß dieser Vorstellung (und des unter ihrem Einfluß ausgebildeten schriftstellerischen Schemas) ist auch im N.T. erkennbar: auf Mk 1,27 (διδαχὴ καινή) folgt 1,44 (δεῖξον τῷ ἱερεῖ), Mk 2,5 (ἀφίενται) wird durch 2,9 (ἔγειρε) bestätigt. Vgl auch Elieser b. Hyrkanos' Angebot an seine Kollegen, die Zuverlässigkeit seiner Lehre durch ein Wunder beweisen zu wollen – diese weisen freilich die Probe zurück (BMez 59b). In der Auseinandersetzung drückt sich ein Wechsel der Einstellung aus.

41. Sifre Dt 18,19. Zur Erklärung s. E. BAMMEL, *John did no Miracle*, in C.F.D. MOULE (ed.), *Miracles. Cambridge Studies in their Philosophy and History*, London, 1965, pp. 181-202, bes. pp. 189-193.

42. Lk 7,8 schließt ein, daß, wie der Hauptmann seinen Soldaten Befehle erteilt, so Jesus den Krankheitsgeistern ein Paroli bieten kann. Der Vers dürfte zu Q gehören; so auch P. VASSILIADIS, *The Nature and Extent of the Q-Document*, in *NT* 20 (1978) 49-73, p. 69.

43. Mk 9,14ff. Die besondere Schwierigkeit des Falles wird in mehreren Wendungen (Höhepunkt v. 28) unterstrichen. Danach treten die Dämonen in der Erzählung des Evangelisten zurück.

44. D. LÜHRMANN, *Die Redaktion der Logienquelle* (WMANT, 33), Neukirchen, 1969, p. 56.

richt an den lebenden Täufer, die Rede den völligen Abschluß von dessen Wirksamkeit und den Eintritt einer neuen Aera anzeigen.

Die Speisungsgeschichte weist eine Reihe von Gemeinsamkeiten zwischen Mt und Lk gegenüber Mk auf, die, wie aufgezeigt wurde[45], nur durch den Einschlag einer gemeinsamen Quelle erklärt werden können. Es ist dies eine Quelle, die schon im mt Bericht über den Tod des Johannes erkennbar und dort im zweiten Teil vorherrschend ist, die gleichzeitig die Brücke von dort zur Speisungsgeschichte schlägt, indem sie die Jünger des Johannes über den Tod ihres Meisters an Jesus berichten läßt und somit die Bewegung zu dessen Wüstenzug und dem Nachfolgen der Volksmassen in Gang setzt. Dieser Q-Bericht ist als die punktierte Verbindung zwischen der Antwort Jesu und seiner Täuferrede anzusehen. Diese letztere ist eine Sammlung von Zeugnissen *post eventum*; so sehr, daß sie vv. 31ff. sogar Jesu eigenes Wirken einschließen.

Findet die Täuferrede ihren Höhepunkt in der vergleichenden Betrachtung der beiden Gottesgesandten[46], so konzentrieren sich die beiden darauf folgenden Q-Abschnitte ganz auf Jesus: der Weheruf nimmt eine andere Seite dessen, was in v. 34 über die Aufnahme Jesu gesagt wurde, auf, der Jubelruf steht in Beziehung zu 7,34 (φίλος κτλ.), um doch ganz unabhängig das Geheimnis Jesu zu verkünden.

Bis dahin reicht ein Zusammenhang, der wesentlich durch das Miteinander und Gegenüber zum Täufer bestimmt ist. Danach verschwindet er vollständig. Es sind jetzt Sprüche – ganz gelegentlich in der Form einer Chrie[47] – und nichts als solche Sätze, die in diesen Abschnitten auf einander folgen. Zugleich aber treten bisher nicht gebrauchte theologische Begriffe in den Vordergrund[48]. Bis zum Schluß geht es um die Eschatologie, die zuvor nur angeklungen war. Jetzt wird sie vom Gesichtswinkel der Gemeinde aus, als Vorbereitung derselben auf die kommenden Ereignisse abgehandelt. Und zwar geschieht dies in zwei weitgehend parallelen Zusammenhängen, was vermuten läßt, daß sie in einem früheren Stadium unabhängig von einander in Umlauf getreten waren, um dann erst in der Sammlung des Spruchbuchs zusammengebunden worden zu sein[49].

45. H. HELMBOLD, *Vorsynoptische Evangelien*, Stuttgart, 1953, pp. 33ff.; E. BAMMEL, *The Feeding of the Multitude*, in DERS. – C.F.D. MOULE (ed.), *Jesus and the Politics of his Day*, Cambridge, 1984, pp. 211-240, bes. pp. 213ff.

46. Lk 7,33f. Zur Erklärung s. E. BAMMEL, *The Baptist in Early Christian Tradition*, in NTS 18 (1971) 95-128, bes. pp. 124, 126f.

47. Lk 11,37-38 hat einen szenischen Anfang, ohne daß doch am Schluß eine Rahmung erfolgt wäre.

48. E. BAMMEL, *Das Ende von Q*, in O. BÖCHER (ed.), *Verborum Veritas. FS G. Stählin*, Wuppertal, 1970, pp. 39-50.

49. E. HIRSCH, *Frühgeschichte* II (n. 22), p. 35, der bedeutendste Q-Forscher seit Harnack und Wellhausen, hatte aus den Besonderheiten des Anfangs von Q geschlossen, daß das Spruchbuch ein »vollständiges Evangelium« gewesen sei. Diese Beschreibung trifft auf die späteren Teile von Q nicht zu, wird aber auch dem Anfang nicht gerecht.

Vergleicht man damit den Anfang, so wird erst recht deutlich, daß er seiner schriftstellerischen Gattung, seinem Inhalt, seiner Ausdrucksform und seinem theologischen Gehalt nach anderer Art ist. Hier geht es um die Orts- und Verhältnisbestimmung der beiden Gottesmänner, etwas, was für die Gemeinde, die hinter diesen Abschnitten steht, offenbar von größter Bedeutung war. Sie wird durchgeführt im Zwiegespräch, in Beispielgeschichten und in Reden. Es geschieht unter ganz sparsamer Verwendung theologischer Begriffe. Es ist ein eigenständiges Werk, das sich hier vorfindet. Man mag es der Einfachheit halber als Q^1 bezeichnen, sollte darüber aber den Unterschied zu den nachfolgenden Reden (Q^2 und Q^3) nicht in den Hintergrund treten lassen. Die Aufdeckung desselben ist durch die Beobachtungen Weisses und Harnacks gefördert worden, mag auch das, was hier vorgeschlagen wird, in seinem Endergebnis von den großen Meistern abweichen.

The Divinity School   Ernst BAMMEL
St John's Street
Cambridge CB2 1TW
England

DIE VERWÜNSCHUNG DER KÜSTENORTE Q 10,13-15
ZUR FUNKTION DER KONKRETEN ORTSANGABEN
UND ZUR LOKALISIERUNG VON Q

I. TEXTPRAGMATIK: DER WEHE-SPRUCH

Der Totenklageruf *hoj* ('*dahin!*') + Nominativ der Person (bzw.
Präposition 'wegen') ist ein von Amos 5,18-20 geprägtes, rhetorisches
Stilmerkmal, das er aus dem Trauerzeremoniell der üblichen Totenklage (1Kön 13,30; Jer 32,18; 34,5) übernahm, um zu dokumentieren,
daß einem bestimmten menschlichen Verhalten bereits der Keim des
Todes innewohnt[1]. Schon Micha und Jesaja haben diese metaphorisch
rhetorische Verwendung übernommen (Jes 1,4-9 wie Am 5,18-20 typischerweise ohne explizite Unheilsankündigung)[2]. Diese in der Hebräischen
Bibel 51mal verwendete Stilform, wobei »man im Trauerzeremoniell
einem Toten das Wehe« ja »nicht androht«[3], ist zunächst streng von
dem 22maligen Angst- und Schmerzensruf '*oj*, der mit Dativ + Begründung steht (nur Num 24,23 aphrastisch verwendet; mit 2. Person nur
Singular Num 21,29 = Jer 48,48 Moab; Jer 13,27 wie Ez 16,23.23
Jerusalem; Qoh 10,16 eine fiktive Nation), zu unterscheiden, was bei
den AT-Verweisen im Zusammenhang der Q-Wehe[4] selten präzis geschieht.

Die LXX hat dann allerdings beide mit οὐαί transkripiert[5], 32mal für

---

1. K. KOCH u.a., *Amos II* (AOAT 30/2), Neukirchen, 1976, pp. 109f.; J. ZOBEL, *hoj*, in
TWAT II (1977) 382-388; K. BERGER, *Formgeschichte des Neuen Testaments*, Heidelberg,
1984, pp. 191f., 195f., 199f., 202-207; M. SATO, *Q und Prophetie* (WUNT, 2/29),
Tübingen, 1988, pp. 183ff. und grundlegend: C. HARDMEIER, *Texttheorie und biblische
Exegese: Zur rhetorischen Funktion der Trauermetaphorik in der Prophetie* (BEvT, 79),
München, 1978, pp. 16f., 154f.; vgl. *ibid.*, pp. 156-162, gegen die Ableitung aus der
Sippenweisheit und eine pädagogische Funktion, wie E. GERSTENBERGER, *The Woe-
Oracles of the Prophets*, in *JBL* 81 (1962) 249-263, und mit ihm H.W. WOLFF, *Amos'
geistige Heimat* (WMANT, 18), Neukirchen, 1964, p. 14; DERS., *Dodekapropheton II* (BK,
14/2), Neukirchen, 1975, pp. 284ff., sie geben wollten eine Ableitung von
Fluchsprüchen Dt 27 mit einer Drohfunktion, wie C. WESTERMANN, *Grundformen prophe-
tischer Rede* (BEvT, 31), München, ⁴1971, pp. 137ff. und in seinem Gefolge O.H. STECK,
Israel und das gewaltsame Geschick der Propheten (WMANT, 23), Neukirchen, 1967,
pp. 52, 288 und S. SCHULZ, *Q. Die Spruchquelle der Evangelisten*, Zürich, 1972, pp. 61f.,
361 sie geben wollten
2. HARDMEIER, *Texttheorie* (Anm. 1), pp. 21, 381.
3. *Ibid.*, p. 198.
4. Vgl. etwa SCHULZ, *Q* (Anm. 1); W. BAUER, *Wörterbuch*, ⁵1958, p. 1171; H. BALZ,
οὐαί, in *EWNT* II (1981) 1320-1322, bes. pp. 1320f.
5. BLASS-DEBRUNNER-REHKOPF, *Grammatik*, 1976, § 4, 2a Anm. 6; § 5 Anm. 7;
daneben analog Epiktet 3,19,1; 3,22,32 (μοι) für lateinisches *vae*, was als Indiz auf einen

hoj (+ 12mal mit ὦ) und 14mal für 'oj (+ 3mal ὦ). Schwerer wiegt, daß LXX auch im Falle des Totenklagerufs Am 6,1; Jes 10,1.5; 28,1 den Dativ statt des Nominativs eingeführt und damit dem Fluch angeglichen und somit daraus ein Drohwort gemacht hat, während sie bei Am 5,18; Jes 1,4; 5,8ff. den Nominativ der Totenklage beibehalten hat[6]. Sie ist aber hinsichtlich der Vermischung nicht als Verursacher zu sehen. Während der Totenklageruf nur einen expressiven, nicht aber appellativen Charakter hatte, begann im Exil (Ez 13,3.18) mit direkter Anrede eine Uminterpretation und Umfunktionierung zum expliziten Drohruf, wie er über LXX bis in die Q-Belege (mit Dativ!: kollektiv auch 11,39.42-44.46-48.52; individuell 3. Person 17,1, wo ein τούτῳ im δι' οὗ semantisch impliziert ist) hinein dominierend wurde[7]. Seit die Propheten deuteronomistisch als Umkehrprediger verstanden wurden (2Kön 17,7ff.)[8] und das deuteronomistische Geschichtswerk »deshalb gegen die unbedingten Unheilsankündigungen der vorexilischen Propheten Vorbehalte hegte«[9], dominierte somit ein neuer Bezugsrahmen (Jes 30,15; Jer 9,4.15; Hos 7,10; 11,5; Am 4,6-12).

Eine Brücke zu Q[10] bilden die ebenfalls schon deuteronomistisch geprägten 32 Weherufe der Henochepistel (1Hen 92-105), die 94,5.6 in der dritten Person einsetzen und dann ab 94,8 zur anredenden zweiten Person übergehen[11]. Den Höhepunkt und Abschluß bildet die letzte Disputation mit den Toten im Totengericht (103,5 »Wehe euch, ihr toten Sünder...« unter Rückgriff auf 97,6-10). »The Woe juxtaposes in its two major components the paradox of historical injustice and belief in divine judgement. The first line describes the sinners misdeeds, and the second line announces the coming judgement which is the cause for the lament 'Woe' which introduces the form«[12]. Dabei sind die Betroffenen als fiktive Adressaten nur ein 'Zweitpublikum'[13], während

Zusammenhang mit dem römischen Centurio weisen kann. BAUER-ALAND, *Wörterbuch*, [6]1988, p. 1196, verweist weiter auf Vita Aesopi W c.37; P.Oxy 413,184-185 (neben weiteren frühjüdischen Belegen bei TestAbr B 113,16; TestJob 22,2; 53,2; ParJer 9,8; ApkEsr).

6. HARDMEIER, *Texttheorie* (Anm. 1), pp. 170-172.

7. *Ibid.*, pp. 221f.

8. STECK, *Israel* (Anm. 1); HARDMEIER, *Texttheorie* (Anm. 1), p. 384.

9. K. KOCH, *Das Profetenschweigen des deuteronomistischen Geschichtswerkes*, in J. JEREMIAS (Hg.), *Die Botschaft und die Boten. FS H.W. Wolff*, Neukirchen, 1981, pp. 115-128, bes. p. 128; vgl. DERS., *Die Profeten II*, Stuttgart, 1980, pp. 9-21.

10. STECK, *Israel* (Anm. 1), p. 157; SCHULZ, *Q* (Anm. 1), p. 62.

11. G.W.E. NICKELSBURG, *The Apocalyptic Message of 1 Enoch 92-105*, in *CBQ* 39 (1977) 309-328, bes. pp. 310f.; R.A. COUGHENOUR, *The Woe-Oracles in the Ethiopic Enoch*, in *JSJ* 9 (1978) 192-197; SATO, *Q* (Anm. 1), pp. 349-354; M. REISER, *Die Gerichtspredigt Jesu* (NTA, 23), Münster, 1990, pp. 49f.

12. G.W.E. NICKELSBURG, *Riches, the Rich, and God's Judgement in 1 Enoch 92-105 and the Gospel according to Luke*, in *NTS* 25 (1979) 324-344, bes. p. 327.

13. Vgl. zum Gebrauch des rhetorischen Mittels H. LAUSBERG, *Handbuch der literarischen Rhetorik*, München, [2]1973, § 762. In diese Richtung weist auch die generalisie-

primäre Adressaten des Briefes die zur tröstenden toratreuen Gerechten/Weisen (98,9; 99,2.14) und von den Falschlehrern (98,15) Unterdrückten sind (vorausgesetzt ist ein innerjüdischer Gegensatz, wobei in den Unterdrückern die siegreichen Hasmonäer gesehen werden müssen)[14]. »Within this context, the Woes are rhetorical rather than directly addressed to the sinner«[15].

Dasselbe gilt textpragmatisch auch für Q 10,13-14, wo die Städte gegenüber den angeredeten Boten 10,2-12.16 deutlich ein Zweitpublikum darstellen, da »ὑμεῖς in VV. 12.16 die Jünger, in 13-15 ganz andere Leute sind«[16]. Diese rhetorische Funktion ist Sache der Komposition und berechtigt als solche noch nicht unbedingt dazu, daraus literarkritische Konsequenzen auf eine »ursprünglich isoliert überlieferte« Einheit hin zu ziehen[17]: Da diese Weherufe im Unterschied zu den älteren von Q 11,39ff. nicht gegen Pharisäer (Red-Mt 23,13ff. sind diese gegenüber VV. 1-2 ebenfalls nur rhetorisch angeredetes Zweitpublikum, während Red-Lk 11,37-39 sie zu Direktadressaten machte; die doppelte Anrede an Pharisäer einerseits und Gesetzeslehrer andererseits spricht auch hier eher für ein Zweitpublikum als indirekte Adressaten, zumal die den Sprüchen durchgehend fehlende Unheilsansage erst Q 11,49-51 in der dritten Person als Rede der Weisheit nachgetragen ist), sondern gegen Ortschaften gerichtet sind, liegt hier »Ausweitung der Polemik« vor, die Lührmann[18] sonst als Kennzeichen der Q-Redaktion bestimmte. Dennoch sperrt man sich gegen eine Zuordnung zur Q-Redaktion. Man hat aber bisher 'jüngere Q-Schicht' und Q-Redaktion kaum

---

rende Typisierung der Adressaten: »Da der Mensch, dem das 'selig' gilt, in erster Linie 'Typ' ist, wird der 'Gegentyp' ebenfalls häufiger genannt und auch schon mit dem 'Wehe' bedacht. Cf. BERGER, *Formgeschichte* (Anm. 1), p. 191.

14. G.W.E. NICKELSBURG, *Resurrection, Immortality, and Eternal Life in Intertestamental Judaism* (HTS, 26), Cambridge, MA, 1972, p.113; vgl *ibid.*, pp. 129f.: die Hofhistoriographie 1 Makk erscheint als »Book written by 'the Sinners'« (gegen REISER, *Jesu* [Anm. 11], pp. 47-52, der hier Juden als unterdrückte Minderheit in hellenistischen Städten annehmen will, entsprechend seiner Gesamttendenz, immer Nichtjuden als Gerichtsobjekte zu identifizieren).

15. NICKELSBURG, *Riches* (Anm. 12), p. 332; DERS., *Resurrection* (Anm. 14), p. 127.

16. D. LÜHRMANN, *Die Redaktion der Logienquelle* (WMANT, 33), Neukirchen-Vluyn, 1969, p. 62, mit E. KLOSTERMANN, *Das Lukasevangelium* (HNT, 5), Tübingen, ²1929, p. 116; fraglich ist aber die sofort daraus gezogene Folgerung: »denn daß erklärt sich daraus, daß zwei verschiedene Traditionen zusammengefügt sind«. Wenn synchron die rhetorische Funktion im Q-Text ernst genommen wird, so ist ein automatisch diachroner Rückschluß auf »verschiedene Traditionen« so noch nicht möglich.

17. So wie LÜHRMANN, *Logienquelle* (Anm. 16), p. 63; SCHULZ, *Q* (Anm. 1), pp. 361ff.

18. LÜHRMANN, *Logienquelle* (Anm. 16), p. 93; F. NEIRYNCK, *Evangelica* II (BETL, 99), Leuven, 1991, pp. 453f., hat mit Recht auf die sachlich-literarischen Gründe hingewiesen, daß bei Lührmann und Schulz im Anschluß an R. BULTMANN (*Die Geschichte der synoptischen Tradition*, ²1931, p. 352), zwar versucht wird, zwischen 'Sammlung' und 'Redaktion' zu unterscheiden, doch »the title 'Die Redaktion des Redenstoffes' (p. 348) includes 'Sammlung des Redenstoffes' and 'Redekomposition'« (*ibid.*, Anm. 240), so daß beide unscheidbar ineinander übergehen.

sicher und überzeugend durch Kriterien voneinander unterscheiden können.

Neben diesem ersten Indiz ist auch den weiteren, von Schulz für eine Spätdatierung aufgelisteten[19], zuzustimmen: LXX-Abhängigkeit (in dem politisch-satirischen Leichenklagelied über Babel LXX–Jes 14,13. 15)[20], Anspielungen auf ganze AT-Geschichten (wie Jona Q 11,29-30.32, Südkönigin 11,31, Sodom 10,12, Sintflut 17,26-27)[21], Rückblick auf abgeschlossene Wirksamkeit (πάλαι 'längst' »enthält einen Hinweis auf die abgelaufene Zeit der Entscheidung«)[22], Gerichtsterminologie (κρίσις Q nur noch 11,31-32), die bei den älteren Weherufen Q 11,39ff. typischerweise noch gänzlich fehlt[23]. Gerade, daß in dem dort Q 11,39ff. kritisierten Verhalten soziales Handeln im Blick ist, hier aber »die Verbindung von Umkehr und Wundertaten«, die »in Q sonst nicht mehr zu finden« ist[24], dürfte für Q-Redaktion sprechen, wenn man

19. SCHULZ, *Q* (Anm. 1), pp. 362f.

20. REISER, *Jesu* (Anm. 11), p. 209 plädiert zu Unrecht für Unabhängigkleit von LXX, wobei er mit A. HUCK – H. GREEVEN (*Synopse der drei ersten Evangelien*, Tübingen, [13]1981, p. 63) für das Passiv καταβιβασθήσῃ p[45] 01 A C L Θ als ursprüngliche Lesart und die Auslassung des Artikels eintritt; dagegen B.M. METZGER, *A Textual Commentary on the Greek New Testament*, Stuttgart, 1971, pp. 151f.

21. LÜHRMANN, *Logienquelle* (Anm. 16), p. 98 gegen REISER, *Jesu* (Anm. 11), p. 215 der hier mit P. HOFFMANN, *Studien zur Theologie der Logienquelle* (NTAbh, 8), Münster, 1972, p. 303; I.H. MARSHALL, *The Gospel of Luke*, Exeter, 1978, p. 424; J.A. FITZMYER, *The Gospel according to Luke* (AB, 28A), Garden City, 1985, p. 852; J. GNILKA, *Das Matthäusevangelium* (HTKNT, 1/1), Freiburg, 1986, p. 430 für Jesuanizität plädiert.

22. A. POLAG, *Die Christologie der Logienquelle* (WMANT, 45), Neukirchen, 1977, p. 89 – daher späte Bildung mit J. WELLHAUSEN, *Das Evangelium Matthaei*, Berlin, [2]1914, p. 56; BULTMANN, *Die Geschichte* (Anm. 18), p. 118; H. BRAUN, *Spätjüdisch-häretischer und frühchristlicher Radikalismus* II (BHT, 24/2), Tübingen, 1957, p. 49; E. KÄSEMANN, *Exegetische Versuche und Besinnungen* I, Göttingen, 1964, p. 98; E. HAENCHEN, *Der Weg Jesu*, Berlin, [2]1968, p. 226; LÜHRMANN, *Logienquelle* (Anm. 16), p. 64; L. OBERLINNER, *Todeserwartung und Todesgewißheit Jesu* (SBB, 10), Stuttgart, 1980, pp. 90-93; SATO, *Q* (Anm. 1), pp. 199f. – dagegen wiegt nicht das globale e silentio Argument, das REISER, *Jesu* (Anm. 11), p. 214 mit M. HENGEL, *Jesus als messianischer Lehrer der Weisheit und die Anfänge der Christologie* in E. JACOB, u.a. (Hg.), *Sagesse et religion*, Paris, 1979, pp. 147-188, bes. p. 151 für Jesuanizität aufbietet: »Die spätere Gemeinde besaß an diesen... ganz unbedeutenden galiläischen Dörfern kein Interesse mehr«. Mit welcher längeren Dauer einer Wirksamkeit Jesu (über einen Winter hinaus) meint man dabei eigentlich rechnen zu können (vgl. dagegen W. SCHENK, *Gefangenschaft und Tod des Täufers: Erwägungen zur Chronologie und ihren Konsequenzen*, in NTS 29 [1983] 453-483)?

23. SATO, *Q* (Anm. 1), pp. 198f. – und nicht mit SCHULZ, *Q* (Anm. 1), p. 62, Anm. 29, der kühnerweise einfach postuliert: »sie ist aber nichtsdestoweniger vorausgesetzt, wie der gesamte Kontext der ältesten Q-Stoffe beweist«. Bei J.S. KLOPPENBORG, *The Formation of Q: Trajectories in Ancient Wisdom Collections*, Philadelphia, PA, 1987, u.a. erfolgt eine genau umgekehrte Zuordnung: weisheitliche Grundschicht und eschatologisierte Spätschicht.

24. SCHULZ, *Q* (Anm. 1), p. 363; OBERLINNER, *Todeserwartung* (Anm. 22), p. 91; wenn dagegen REISER, *Jesu* (Anm. 11), p. 214: »die Wertung der Wunder als eschatologischer Erweiszeichen« für Jesuanizität beanspruchen will, so kann er sich nicht auf Q 11,20 berufen, da die dortige Wertung ja auch ebenso für die analogen Taten der jüdischen

auch noch den speziellen Sachzusammenhang hier mit der Fernheilung in der Centurio-Geschichte 7,1ff. nicht übersieht.

Innerhalb der rhetorischen Kultur des Hellenismus wird man weniger schnell eine Untereinheit als »mündliches Traditionsstück« veranschlagen als vielmehr primär eine Komposition zum Zwecke der Rezitation ansetzten dürfen: »To posit an 'oral source' ... is wrong, because it merges the literary-historical approach associated with text and source criticism with oral transmission without bringing into view the kind of culture in which oral and written speech interact closely with one another. In other words, those who posit oral sources ... are presupposing a 'copying culture' linked directly to an 'oral culture'. The evidence we have in the 'Progymnasmata' and other documents suggest that this approach bypasses a pervasive culture in Mediterranean society in which oral and written speech interact closely with one another«[25].

II. Textsemantik: Die Ortsnamen

Es ist zu beachten, daß »die allein Matthäus und Lukas gemeinsamen Stücke keine palästinischen 'Landschaftsbezeichnungen' aufweisen«[26]. Außer der verstärkenden Doppelanrede an Jerusalem Q 13,34 (in Rahmung zur erzählten Verwendung Q 4,9, wo Mt umschreibt) haben wir nur die ebenfalls als absagende Anreden hier vorkommenden Ortsnamen (in Relation zu der erzählenden Vorgabe von Kafarnaum in Q 7,1).

Exorzisten gilt und kein Beleg für eine »Reich-Gottes-Verkündigung Jesu« ist. Q 7,22-23 andererseits muß als junges Apophtegma in Q gelten. 'Umkehr' erscheint außer im Täufermund Q 3,8 nur noch im Ninevitenwort 11,32; vgl. Polag, *Christologie* (Anm. 22), p 74: »Im Q-Material erscheint keine ausgesprochene Umkehr-Forderung als Aussage Jesu, weil Jesus nicht als Bußprediger gesehen wird. Das μετανοεῖν muß also Ausdruck für den Akt der Anerkennung überhaupt verstanden werden«.

25. V.K. Robbins, *Writing as a Rhetorical Art in Plutarch and the Gospels*, in D.F. Watson (Hg.), *Persuasive Artistry. FS G.A. Kennedy* (JSNT SS, 50), Sheffield, 1991, pp. 142-168, bes. p. 149.

26. M. Bachmann, *Jerusalem und der Tempel. Die geographisch-theologischen Elemente in der lukanischen Sicht des jüdischen Kultzentrums* (BWANT, 109), Stuttgart, 1980, p. 77, Anm. 30. In der Redaktionsschicht Q 4,1 erscheint ἡ ἔρημος in der narrativen Chrie-Einleitung wie auch Q 3,3a (Mt 3,5) πᾶσα περίχωρος τοῦ Ἰορδάνου die narrative Eröffnung und Chrie-Einleitung von Q 3,7 (ein noch umfänglicheres Segment mit vv. 2b.3b veranschlagen hier A. Polag, *Fragmenta Q*, Neukirchen, 1979, ²1981, pp. 28f.; J. Lambrecht, *John the Baptist and Jesus in Mark 1,1-15: Markan Redaction of Q?*, in *NTS* 38 [1992] 357-384, bes. pp. 363f.). Viel zu oft aber wird der Sachverhalt übersehen, daß gerade 'Galiläa' in Q niemals genannt ist (W. Schenk, *Die Sprache des Matthäus*, Göttingen, 1987, p. 107), ohne daß man diese Nichterwähnung als argumentum e silentio abtun dürfte.

1. Βηθσαΐδα

»The Greek name represents the Aramaic *bet ṣaidā*, 'house of hunting' (or possibly, 'fishing')«[27]. Vor 10,13 aus Q hat Lk 9,10 red. es aus Mk 6,45; 8,22[28], dem Anfang und Ende seiner 'großen Auslassung' eines Mk-Blocks, zur Vorbereitung der Q-Stelle[29] übernommen (zumal dort seine erste Sendungsrede nach Mk voransteht) und zum Schauplatz der Speisung gemacht. Die Angleichung beider Stellen aneinander wird auch daraus deutlich, daß Lk 9,10 wie Q 10,13 die Q-Form des Ortsnamens ohne die »in Galiläa beliebte Nunation« mit Schluß-'n' verwendet[30] und den Ort außerdem als πόλις (von Q 10,11.12 in Verbindung zu 10,13) bezeichnet (Joh 1,44 ist ihm darin gefolgt). Mk 6,45 wie 8,22 gab die Nunationsform Βηθσαϊδάν vor (womit Mk sich diesbezüglich wohl als älter erweist) und kennzeichnete es 8,23.26 als 'Dorf'. »Sicherlich hätte Mk den Ausdruck κώμη nicht angewandt, wenn ihm eine Hauptstadt des Philippus im Sinn gelegen hätte«[31].

Der Tetrarch der halbjüdischen Gaulanitis, Herodes Philippus, hatte

---

27. J.A. FITZMYER, *The Gospel according to Luke* (AB, 28), Garden City, 1985, p. 756; G. DALMAN, *Orte und Wege Jesu* (BFCT, 2/1), Gütersloh, ³1924 = Darmstadt, 1967, pp. 173-180; C. KOPP, *Die Stätten der heiligen Evangelien*, Regensburg, 1959, pp. 230-243: 'Fischfangort'. JosBell 3,58 setzt Mischbevölkerung (Ituräer) voraus; A. KASHER, *Jews and Hellenistic Cities in Eretz-Israël* (TSAJ, 21), Tübingen, 1990, pp. 220f.; E. SCHÜRER, *The History of the Jewish People in the Age of Jesus Christ* II, Edinburgh, ²1979, pp. 171f.

28. FITZMYER, *The Gospel* (Anm. 27), p. 756 gegen A. FUCHS, *Betsaida*, in *EWNT* 1 (1980) 515-516, bes. p. 516.

29. FUCHS, *Betsaida* (Anm. 28), ohne das sich beide Aspekte gegenseitig ausschließen müßten.

30. DALMAN, *Orte* (Anm. 27), p. 175. Zur Topographie der Seegeschichten in der schon als vor-mk angenommene Rahmung vgl. H. HEGERMANN, *Bethsaida und Gennesar: Eine traditions- und redaktionsgeschichtliche Studie zu Mc 4-8*, in W. ELTESTER (Hg.), *Judentum, Urchristentum, Kirche. FS J. Jeremias* (BZNW, 26), Berlin, (1960) ²1964, pp. 130-140.

31. DALMAN, *Orte* (Anm. 27), p. 176: »Die Stätte von Julias vermutet man in *et-tell*, östlich der Nordspitze des Sees, die Reste des ehemaligen Fischerdorfes B. dürften durch die Anschwemmung des Jordan bei seiner Einmündung in den See zugedeckt worden sein« (A. VAN DEN BORN, *Bethsaida*, in *Bibel-Lexikon* [²1968], pp. 204f.). Eine streng verwaltungsrechtliche Differenzierung, B. »was not a city: it was merely the capital of the toparchy of Gaulanitis« (A.H.M. JONES, *The Cities of the Eastern Roman provinces*, Oxford, [1937] ²1971, pp. 282ff. und mit ihm A.N. SHERWIN-WHITE, *Roman Society and Roman Law in the New Testament*, Oxford, 1963, p.131; G. THEISSEN, *Urchristliche Wundergeschichten* [StNT, 8], Gütersloh, [1974] ⁴1980, pp. 130f; R. PESCH, *Das Markusevangelium* I [HTKNT, 2/1], Freiburg, ²1977, p. 417; J. GNILKA, *Das Evangelium nach Markus* I [EKK, 2/1], Zürich-Neukirchen, [1978] ²1986, p. 313) dürfte dem nicht präzis juristischen Charakter unserer Texte nicht gerecht werden. Man hat hier auch zu berücksichtigen, daß Q zwar 4 Belege für πόλις hat, während κώμη in Q völlig fehlt (vgl. SCHENK, *Die Sprache* [Anm. 26], pp. 415ff.): für bloße Dörfer (als der wichtigsten ökonomischen Einheit, da 80-90 % der Bevölkerung von der Landwirtschaft lebten; P. BRIANT, *Dörfer und Dorfgemeinschaften im achämenidischen und hellenitischen Asien*, in *Jahrbuch für Wirtschaftsgeschichte* 4 [1975] 115-133) interessierte sich Q (zumindest in der vorliegenden Redaktionsschicht) nicht sonderlich.

gleich nach seinem Regierungsantritt 4-2 v. Chr. das nordöstlich der Jordanmündung gelegene »Dorf Bethsaida am Ginnesarsee zur Stadt erhoben, mit einer Menge von Einwohnern und anderer Macht versehen und nach der Tochter des Kaisers Julias genannt« (Jos Ant 18,28; vgl. Bell 2,167-168; 3,506-516). Im Palast seiner hier erbauten Burg ist er 34 n. Chr. (kinderlos) gestorben und in dem von ihm vorbereiteten Grabmal bestattet (Jos Ant 18,106-108). Nachdem seine Tetrarchie zunächst der römischen Provinz 'Syria' zugeschlagen worden war, wurde sie 37 n. Chr. (zusammen mit Abilene) von Kaiser Caligula an Agrippa I. gegeben, der 41-44 n. Chr. das ganze herodianische Reich wieder in einer Hand vereinigte. Sein volljährig gewordener Sohn König Agrippa II. wurde 53 n. Chr. von Kaiser Claudius mit der Tetrarchie des Philippus (und Abilene) betraut. Wenn Nero ihm u.a. Gebieten ein 'Julias' zuteilte (Jos Ant 20,158-159; Bell 2,252), so dürfte es sich wohl um das von Antipas in Peräa gegründete 'Julias' handeln[32].

Während die Frage 'Stadt' (Q) oder 'Dorf' (Mk) umstritten scheint, jedoch durch die Unterschiedenheit des alten Fischerdorfes mit der neuen Residenz unterscheidbar ist, so ist aber aus der genannten Ortsgeschichte die heute meist vollzogene Zurechnung zu 'Galiläa' (erst nach Red-Joh 12,21 als Herkunftsort des joh Philippus)[33] noch fraglicher. Ob man sich zur Rechtfertigung darauf berufen kann[34], daß auch Josephus (Ant 18,4) selbst den Gaulaniten Judas später (Ant 18,23) als 'Galiläer' bezeichnete[35], ist nicht minder fraglich. Auch daß Mt die beiden Mk-Belege der Ortsbezeichnung nicht übernahm, spricht gegen eine Zurechnung zu 'Galiläa'. Die Oppositionsbestimmung in Q 10,13 zu Sidon/Tyrus wird wohl nicht auf die Antithese 'kleiner Ort' vs. 'Weltstädte', sondern auf die von 'Juden' vs. 'Nichtjuden' zielen. »Ein reger Verkehr bestand gewiß trotz der Zollgrenze mit der über den See

---

32. Mit O. MICHEL – O. BAUERNFEIND, F. Josephus, De Bello Judaico I, München, (1959) ³1982, p. 444, Anm. 143 (vgl. SCHÜRER, The History [Anm. 27], pp. 176-178) gegen die Heranziehung bei FUCHS, Betsaida (Anm. 28), p. 516.

33. Vgl DALMAN, Orte (Anm. 27), p. 177: »Wer in Bethsaida aufgewachsen war, wird nicht nur Griechisch verstanden haben, sondern auch durch den Verkehr mit Fremden abgeschliffen und an griechische Kultur gewöhnt sein«. Die Antithese lebt dennoch von der Gegenüberstellung Juden vs. Nichtjuden: Wenngleich die Zusammennennung der phönikischen Welthandelsmetropolen 'Tyrus und Sidon' auch rein geographisch erscheinen kann (Philostr Her 1,1; Esr 3,7; 1 Chron 22,4; Jdt 2,28; 1 Makk 5,15; 4 Sib 90; Mk 3,8; 7,31; JosAnt 8,320; 15,95; vgl. BAUER-ALAND, Wörterbuch, pp. 1499f., so ist doch die gemeinsame Nennung in den Völkerorakeln deutlich polemische Drohrede (Jes 23; Jer 47,4; Ez 26-28) LXX-Joel 4,4 werden sie metonymisch zum Prototyp der Feinde Israels überhaupt (LÜHRMANN, Logienquelle [Anm. 16], pp. 63f.; SCHULZ, Q (Anm. 1), p. 215, Anm. 273 vgl. die Kommentare z. St.). Die Argumentation beruht auf dem argumentum a minore ad maius: »Wer das größere Heil abweist, wird schwerer bestraft werden« (BERGER, Formgeschichte [Anm. 1], p. 160).

34. FITZMYER, The Gospel (Anm. 27), p. 765 »some popular confusion«; das gilt erst recht, wenn nach 150 n. Chr. Ptolem Geograph 5,16,4 Betsaida 'Galiläa' zurechnet. Diesen unbedachten Sprachgebrauch hatte ich auch früher noch übernommen (W. SCHENK, Synopse zur Redenquelle der Evangelien, Düsseldorf, 1981, pp. 55f.)

35. DALMAN, Orte (Anm. 27), p. 177 u.a.

nur 4 km entfernten Nachbarstadt Kapernaum«[36]. Dennoch ergibt sich daraus noch nicht die Kennzeichnung des Ortes als 'galiläischer Stadt', wie es die generelle Überschrift über das Segment Wehe über die 'galiläischen Städte' suggeriert. Was den dabei angespielten Wunderbezug betrifft, so ist weiter zu bedenken, daß auch die Mk 8,22-26 dort topographisch angesiedelte Blindenheilung letztlich außerhalb dieses Dorfes situiert ist.

2. Καφαρναούμ

Der im AT noch nicht erwähnte Name »probably means 'village of Nahum' (kepar Naḥum)«[37]. Als »einzige Ortschaft am Nordufer« wurde »das Fischerdorf zum Marktflecken«[38]. »It is usually identified with Tell Ḥum[39], but Josephus (Bell 3,519 Καφαρναούμ) speaks of its 'highly fertilizing spring', which has suggested to some that it might rather have been at Khan Minyeh«[40]. Andererseits argumentiert man: »Dies Kapernaum war auch deshalb tell ḥum, weil der bei Julias verletzte Josephus sich nach dem Dorf der 'Kepharnoker' bringen ließ (Vita 403 Κεφαρνωμόν), offenbar, weil dies die erste Ortschaft diesseits des Jordans war, die ihm Sicherheit bot«[41]. Die ältesten Belege des gräzisierten Namens bieten Q (7,1; 10,15) und Mk (1,21; 2,1; 9,33) immer in der einleitenden Übergangswendung »gehen εἰς K.«, was von

---

36. *Ibid*, p. 174.

37. FITZMYER, *The Gospel* (Anm. 27), p. 535; DALMAN, *Orte* (Anm. 27), pp. 142-163, bes. p. 159 »gräzisiert«; KOPP, *Die Stätten* (Anm. 27), pp. 214-230; S. LOFFREDA, *Cafarnaum: Die Stadt Jesu*, Jerusalem, ²1981; vgl. zur Form καπεναούμ B/D/R 39,2; Ptolem Geogr 5,16,14 hat καπαρναούμ. Der Personenname kommt in der Hebräischen Bibel nur für den Propheten Nah 1,1 vor, ist aber auch sonst durch Funde belegt, und »die Lebenssituation, die diese Namengebung voraussetzte, war sicher häufig genug«, daß nämlich »der Tod eines Angehörigen vorausging, über dessen Verlust die Eltern durch die Geburt dieses Kindes 'getröstet' wurden«. Daß aber jener Nahum, nach dem das 'Nahumsdorf' benannt sei, »der Prophet gewesen sei, ist ein voreiliger Schluß«, da dessen Wirkungsstätte das Südreich war und seine Näherbezeichnung 'Elkoschit' (Nah 1,1) eher an die judäische Südgrenze weist; »auch hätte sich Hieronymus den Hinweis auf eine entsprechende Tradition sicher nicht entgehen lassen, wenn eine solche zu seiner Zeit existiert hätte« (W. RUDOLPH, *Micha-Nahum-Habakuk-Zephanja* [KAT], Gütersloh, 1975, pp. 148ff.).

38. DALMAN, *Orte* (Anm. 27), p. 158.

39. DALMAN, *Orte* (Anm. 27), pp. 149-159; H. BALZ, *Kafarnaum*, in *EWNT* II (1981) 690-691, bes. p. 690 und Kommentare.

40. FITZMYER, *The Gospel* (Anm. 27), p. 535 mit Verweis auf F.M. ABEL, *Le nom de Capernaum*, in *JPOS* 8 (1928) 24-34; E.F.F. BISHOP, *Jesus and Capernaum*, in *CBQ* 15 (1953) 427-437; J. FINEGAN, *The Archeology of the New Testament*, Princeton, 1969, pp. 48-56; vgl. BAUER-ALAND, *Wörterbuch*, p. 867.

41. DALMAN, *Orte* (Anm. 27), p. 159, vgl p. 158, Anm. 1 gegen die Annahme von Khan Minyeh, »weil gerade dort eine Zollstätte an der Via Maris gelegen haben werde. Aber 20 km. von der Grenze an der Jordanfurt bei der Jakobsbrücke lag gewiß kein Zollamt«.

dort erst von Red-Q 7,1 inspiriert sein dürfte, so daß auch die mk zugeordneten Heilungen nicht sicher dort verortet werden können[42]. Nach der Rezeption in den Evangelien Mt 4mal (4,13; 8,5; 11,23; 17,24), Lk 4+0mal (4,23.31; 7,1; 10,15), Joh 5mal (2,12; 4,46; 6,17.24.59) und EvEb (Nr. 34 Zl. 59) ist es zunächst frühchristlich nicht belegt. Während Mk 1,21ff. dort eine Synagoge lokalisiert sowie 1,29ff. pronominalisiert auch das Haus des Simon und Andreas, hatte Q 7,1-2 dort die Person des Truppführeres (ἑκατόνταρχος für 'centurio' als höchstem römischem Mannschaftsrang, daher nicht 'Hauptmann') angesiedelt – auch als Vorbereitung zur Drohrede Q 10,15 (primär als Rückweiser κύριε 7,6 → 6,46 und λόγος 7,7 → 6,47 zur Verstärkung des Schlusses der Grundsatzrede).

Q 10,15 erscheint als Steigerung und gezielter Höhepunkt (Anrede im vokativischen Nominativ καὶ σύ, K. – ähnlich auch in der täuferischen 4Sib 99.105)[43], auf den hin die ersten beiden Orte von VV. 13-14 im wesentlichen als vorbereitende Nennung fungieren. Der Vorwurf ist in der Verfehlungstat (Ruhmrede) wie der daraus sich ergebenden Folge (»der apokalyptische Abstieg in den Hades«)[44] im Anklang an das satirische Trauerlied auf Babel Jes 14,13.15 formuliert, »wegen καταβήσῃ und des Fehlens des Artikels vor ᾅδου« ist »am ehesten Abhängigkeit von der Septuaginta anzunehmen«[45]. Dieser Untergangsspott gegen Kafarnaum »sieht so nicht aus, als sei« dieses »in alter Zeit ein Christenort gewesen«[46].

Die Ruhmrede Kafarnaums sieht man meist auf das Wirken Jesu als des Endzeitpropheten dort bezogen und von da verursacht an[47]. Dies

42. Gegen Reiser, *Jesu* (Anm. 11), p. 210, n. 16, der dazu noch erweitert: »wahrscheinlich auch Mk 5,21-43«. Die archäologischen Synagogenreste dort sind sehr viel später zu datieren, vgl. L.I. Levine (Hg.), *Ancient Synagogues Revealed*, Jerusalem, 1981, pp. 6f., 10, 13-15, 42f., 52-62.

43. Vgl. *ibid.*, pp. 86-89, 210.

44. Schulz, *Q* (Anm. 1), p. 366; Reiser, *Jesu* (Anm. 11), p. 213, Anm. 30 mit Recht gegen die seit J. Jeremias, *ᾅδης*, in *TWNT* I, p. 148, immer noch wiederholte Bestreitung der Identifikation von Hades und Hölle (zuletzt Gnilka, *Das Matthaüsevangelium* [Anm. 21], p. 429), wie sie seit 1 Hen 22 geläufig ist (vgl. auch bei JosBell 2,165).

45. Schulz, *Q* (Anm. 1), p. 363; wenn er aber ebd. Anm. 271 argumentiert, daß »hier in Q eine Umkehrung der atl. Gattung des Völkerorakels« stattfinde – nun gegen Israel gerichtet – so wird man einschränkend darauf verweisen, daß etwa auch Jes 22 Jerusalem als Adressat zwischen Babel Jes 13-14; 21 und Tyrus/Sidon Jes 23 eingeschlossen ist. Man wird auch daran erinnern, daß schon »auch Jerusalem Jes 29,1; Zeph 3,1 oder Israel als ganzes Jes 1,4 Adressat des Totenklagerufes ʾhoj sein« konnte (Zobel, *Hoj* [Anm. 1], p. 287).

46. Dalman, *Orte* (Anm. 27), p. 160, vgl pp. 160f.: »Weder Christen noch Samaritaner noch Heiden haben die Juden dort im 4. Jhdt. zugelassen... Am Anfang des 4. Jhdt. war Kapernaum noch ausschließlicher Judenort (Epiphan Haer 30)«.

47. So Schulz, *Q* (Anm. 1), pp. 365f. mit W. Bousset, *Die Synoptiker* (SNT, I), Göttingen, ³1917, pp. 308f.; J. Schniewind, *Das Evangelium nach Matthäus* (NTD, 2), Göttingen, ⁷1954, p. 148; E. Percy, *Die Botschaft Jesu,* Lund, 1953, p. 113; E. Neuhäusler, *Anspruch und Antwort Gottes,* Düsseldorf, 1962, p. 201; W. Grundmann,

aber hat erst in der red. Umplazierung und der Neueinleitung Mt 11,20 und nur für diese red. Rezeption seine ausdrückliche Begründung. Daher hat man vom red. Q-Zusammenhang der Botenrede her darauf verwiesen, daß in der dortigen, früheren Redaktion eher eine spätere, christliche Mission in Kafarnaum und deren Mißlingen im Blick sei[48]. Auch Q 7,1-10 wird ja vorbereitend zu 10,15 der dortige Centurio ausdrücklich in einer Antithese zum globalen ἐν τῷ Ἰσραήλ (Q 10,9) eingebracht.

Innerhalb der beiden Sprüche selbst gibt es also keinen expliziten Verweis auf Jesus. Auch für eine Zeit der Sprüche vor der Einordnung der Q-Redaktion weisen die 'Machttaten' von VV. 13-14 nicht unbedingt auf einen Jesus-Bezug als Handlungssubjekt, und man kann schon gar nicht den Bezug auf die Machttaten als solche auch noch automatisch von VV. 13-14 her in den Untergangsspott über Kafarnaum V. 15 übertragen und so dort eintragen. Aus dieser mehrfachen Verlegenheit kann man sich auch nicht dadurch befreien, daß man einen Jesusbezug von dem in der Textsequenz erst nachgeordneten Gerichtswort Q 13,26 her schon hier annimmt und von dorther begründet[49], denn jener Spruch ist eher eine steigernde Überbietung der abgewiesenen Berufung auf Abrahamkindschaft durch den Täufer Q 3,8. Da dies aber mit der Zwei-Wege-Rede in Q nicht voransteht, sondern in der Textabfolge erst viel später nachfolgt, kann es nicht in Q 10,15 erinnert werden. Außerdem würde überhaupt mit jedem Rückblick der Zukunftsform, wie sie schon in der von vornherein negierten rhetorischen Frage V. 15b vorliegt, nicht Rechnung getragen (weshalb auch Q 3,8 als sachlicher Bezugspunkt nicht im Blick ist).

Der Selbstruhm setzt also primär eine absolut gewisse Zukunftshoffnung voraus. Da weiterhin zwischen VV. 13-14 und V. 15 eine Steigerung anzunehmen ist, so wird dem nur Rechnung getragen, wenn man den Selbstruhm Kafarnaums in einem dezidiert jüdischen Selbstverständnis der Bewohner (und der Abweisung der Christen) begründet sieht. Das setzt auch die Einschaltung in die Botenrede nach den Abweisungsvorhersagen VV. 10-11 als Sachzusammenhang voraus. Das kafarnaitische Selbstbewußtsein dürfte eher dem Buch-Höhepunkt der

---

Das Evangelium nach Matthäus (THK, I), Berlin, 1968, pp.313f; DERS., *Das Evangelium Lukas* (THK, 3), Berlin, ²1963, p. 211 u.a.

48. So mit Recht WELLHAUSEN, *Das Evangelium Matthaei* (Anm. 22), pp. 54f.; E. KLOSTERMANN, *Das Matthäusevangelium* (HNT, 4), Tübingen, ²1927, p. 100; BULTMANN, *Die Geschichte* (Anm. 18), p. 118. Man beachte, daß auch der Spruch von der unvergebbaren 'Sünde wider den Geist' Q 12,10 das Wirken der späteren Geistträger gegenüber dem Wirken Jesu überordnet (vgl. SCHENK, *Redenquelle* [Anm. 34], was die mk Q-Rezeption dann im Widerspruch zur Q-Redaktion konsequent jesuanisierend umpolt (vgl. W. SCHENK, *Der Einfluß der Logienquelle auf das Markusevangelium*, in *ZNW* 70 [1979] 141-165, bes. pp. 147f., 149f. 162).

49. REISER, *Jesu* (Anm. 11), pp. 213-215 mit MARSHALL, *Luke* (Anm. 21), p. 425.

nachherodianischen AssMose in ihrer Gerichtstheophanie (Kap. 10) entsprechen[50]: Israel wird über die Römer »glücklich sein« (10,8): »(9) Und Gott wird dich erhöhen, und er wird dir festen Sitz am Sternenhimmel verschaffen, am Ort ihrer Wohnung. (10) Und du wirst von oben herabblicken und deine Feinde auf Erden sehen und sie erkennen und dich freuen, und du wirst Dank sagen und dich zu deinem Schöpfer bekennen«[51]. Gerade die Zukunftsformen[52] wie die negierte rhetorische Frage Q 10,15 legen einen solchen Sachzusammenhang und Hintergrund nahe. Q kritisiert an Kafarnaum dann primär den mit (oder wie) AssMose antirömischen Affekt der Erwählungsgewißheit im Gegenüber zum Centurio und auf der Linie der bucheinleitenden Täuferkritik einer Erwählungsgewißheit gegenüber den Fremdvölkern.

3. Χοραζίν

Dieser nur hier erwähnte Ort mit dem indeklinablen Namen ist schwer zu identifizieren:»Its site is not known with certainty. It has often been identified with modern Khirbet Keraze, ruins about two and a half miles northwest of Tell Ḥum. The remains of a third-fourth century synagogue have been found there«[53]. Die herrschende Ansicht zur Lokalisierung geht auf Euseb Onomastikon 303,174 zurück (»ein Dorf in Galiläa, gegen das Christus ein Wehe sprach, nachdem er zu ihm gepredigt hatte. Jetzt ist es verödet, zwei Meilen von Kafarnaum«), der dies deutlich vom mt Text und der anschließenden Nennung von Kafarnaum her so erschloß. Nun ist aber die Nennung dieser beiden Namen hier durch 'Betsaida' voneinander getrennt. Hieronymus (Komm. Jes 3; PL 24,127) lokalisierte im Unterschied zu Euseb die Wüstung am Seeufer (mit Kafarnaum, Tiberias, Betsaida) – also nicht 3 km oberhalb des Tell Ḥum und 270 m über dem Seespiegel. Wenn dieses sehr wohl

---

50. M.-J. LAGRANGE, Évangile selon saint Luc (ETB), Paris, ⁵1941, p. 300.

51. Übers. E. BRANDENBURGER, Himmelfahrt Moses (JSHRZ, 5), Gütersloh, 1976, pp. 57-84, bes. p. 77.

52. REISER, Jesu (Anm. 11), p. 209 mit Recht gegen eine semitisierende Annahme von Konjunktiven bei WELLHAUSEN, Das Evangelium Matthaei (Anm. 22), p. 56 dem KLOSTERMANN, Das Matthäusevangelium (Anm. 48), p. 101; und GNILKA, Das Matthaüsevangelium (Anm. 21), pp. 429ff.: »Und du K., daß du nur nicht – zum Himmel erhoben – zur Hölle herabgestürzt werdest!«.

53. FITZMYER, The Gospel (Anm. 21); vgl H. KOHL – C. WATZINGER, Antike Synagogen in Galiläa I, Leipzig, 1916, pp. 41-58; DALMAN, Orte (Anm. 27), pp. 163-166; KOPP, Die Stätten (Anm. 27), pp. 243-246; FINEGAN, Archeology (Anm. 40), pp. 57f.; gegen H. BALZ, Chorazin, in EWNT III (1983) 1127 u.a. ist die Datierung der aus dem hier vorhandenen schwarzen Basalt errichteten Synagoge »2./3. Jh.« zu früh; vgl. Inschriften bei J. NAVEH, 'I psyps w'bn: On Stone and Mosaic. The Aramaic and Hebrew Inscriptions from Ancient Synagogues, Jerusalem, 1978, pp. 36-38; J.A. FITZMYER – D.J. HARRINGTON, A Manual of Palestinian Aramaic Texts (BibOr, 34), Roma, 1979, § A 19; LEVINE, Synagogues (Anm. 42), pp. 26, 29, 42, 52, 55, 60f., 112f., 122, 134f., 138f., 155, 162f., 166, 170, 185.

das *Krzyym/Karzayim* von b.Men 85a (t.Men 9,2) sein kann (dem Ort, dessen nach Süden geneigte Felder gutes Getreide brachte, so daß es die Omergarbe zum Tempel hätte liefern können, wenn es nur nicht so weit von Jerusalem entfernt gelegen hätte), so besagt das nichts für die Identifizierung des Q Ortes mit diesem *krzjm*. Während hier aber die Endung mit 'Mem' konstant ist, setzt der Name bei Q 10,13 ein 'Nun' am Ende voraus. Das erinnert stark an eine 'Nunation', wie sie beim mk 'Betsaidan' im Unterschied zur Q-Form 'Betsaida' vorlag. Gäbe es einen lokalen Kandidaten für *kwrzj*?

Die Doppelheit von Chorazin/Bethsaida mit der gleichen Verfluchungsanrede + σοι im gleichen Satz und die Antithese zur Doppelheit Tyrus/Sidon spricht eher für einen lokalen Zusammenhang der Nachbarschaft dieser beiden Orte, aber nicht für einen lokal durch Kafarnaum von Betsaida getrennten Ort. Einen Kandidaten für einen Seeort, der wie Betsaida-Julias ebenfalls auf der Ostseite des Sees lag, gäbe es in der Tat mit *Kursi (kwrsj)*. Eine Verwechslung der Konsonanten 'Samek' und 'Zajin' bei der Transkription kann nicht ausgeschlossen werden. Beispielsweise stellt auch die Josephus-Überlieferung vor das Problem des »beispiellos verwahrlosten Zustandes handschriftlicher Überlieferung besonders der Orts- und Personennamen«[54]. Das Problem des Konsonantenwechsels bei Übersetzungen beschäftigt auch die Septuaginta-Forschung ständig: »The change between different consonants must, to a great extent, have seen hapharzed to the ancient translators. The deficiency caused no trouble when the translator came across familiar words, but with unusual terms and grammatical forms, the extension of analogy could lead to the acceptance of great looseless in the sequence of elements«[55]. Gerade bezüglich der Namen gilt: »All transliterations were corrupted during the textual transmission«[56].

Wenn man eine Nunation veranschlagen darf, so fällt der Blick auf die Lokalisierung des Besessenen von Mk 5,1 am Ostufer des Sees χώρα τῶν Γερασηνῶν. »Origenes (zu Joh 6,41) kannte am See von Tiberias eine alte Stadt Gergesa, bei welcher am See ein Absturz liegt, nach Euseb (Onom 74) wurde ein Dorf dieses Namens dort 'auf dem Berge' gezeigt... Nun haftet der Name *kurse* jetzt an einer kleinen Ortslage am Strande südlich von der Mündung des *wadi es-samak*, und mit *gurze*

---

54. A. SCHALIT, *Der Schauplatz des letzten Kampfes zwischen den aufständischen Pharisäern und Alexander Jannäus*, in O. BETZ u.a. (Hg.), *Josephus-Studien. FS O. Michel*, Göttingen, 1974, pp. 300-317, bes. p. 301.

55. S. OLOFSSON, *The LXX Version* (ConBOT, 30), Stockholm, 1990, p. 32 mit J. BARR, *Vocalization and the Analysis of Hebrew among Ancient Translators*, in *Hebräische Wortforschung. FS zum 80. Geburtstag von W. Baumgartner* (VTSuppl, 16), Leiden, 1967, 1-11, bes. pp. 9f.; DERS., *Comparative Philology and the Text of the Old Testament*, Oxford, 1968, pp. 61-65, 209f.

56. OLOFSSON, *The LXX* (Anm. 55), p. 57, Anm. 5 mit S. JELLICOE, *The Septuagint in Modern Study*, Oxford, 1978, p. 20; E. TOV, *Loan-words, Homophony, and Translations in the Septuagint*, in *Bib* 69 (1979) 216-236, bes. p. 228 und Beispiele pp. 235f.

wird in ihrer Nähe am Abhang eines Bergvorsprungs eine Turmruine bezeichnet... Der Name *kurse* oder *gurze* scheint aber schon lange in dieser Gegend beheimatet zu sein: Theoderich (1172) legt hierher, 4 Meilen von Betsaida..., Chorazin, ebenso eine Karte aus dem 12. Jh.«[57]. Die Q-Transskription *kwrsjn* wird also der Mk-Transskription *grsn* entsprechen, die beide auf *kursi/gurzi* zurückweisen. Wie die Heilung des Blinden Mk 8,22-26 außerhalb des Küstendorfes Bethsaida lokalisiert ist, so übrigens auch die Dämonenaustreibung Mk 5,1ff. außerhalb des Küstenortes *k(g)wrz(s)j*.

III. Zur Lokalisierung der Q-Redaktion

Kafarnaum ist der einzig doppelt genannte, konkrete geographische Ort in Q 7,1; 10,15. In 10,15 ist er Ziel- und Höhepunkt der Unheilsansage, auf den hin die beiden Orte von 10,13 vorbereitend stehen. Es ist schwer vorstellbar, daß dabei zuerst ein Ort nordwestlich oberhalb von Kafarnaum genannt, dann einer östlich davon in der Gaulanitis, um dann zur Mitte Kafarnaum als Zentrum zu kommen. Näher liegt es, wenn die Seeorte in der Reihenfolge genannt werden in Richtung von Osten nach Norden: (1) Ostufer *kwrzj*, (2) Nordostufer Bethsaida, (3) Nordufer Kafarnaum. Geht der Blickpunkt gegen die Angeredeten über den See, dann ist der Standort des Redenden gewissermaßen der Brennpunkt oder die Achse dieser Speichen ein Ort am Westufer. Dies weist nach Tiberias (ca. 20 km südlich von Kafarnaum, wie 8 km westlich über dem See gegenüber *kwrzj*), »der von Herodes Antipas 26/27 n. Chr. zu Ehren des Kaisers Tiberius (Jos Ant 18,36ff.) an der Westküste des Sees Gennesaret erbauten Stadt (als Hauptstadt seines Gebietes statt Sephoris)«[58]. Die Stadt hatte eine größtenteils heidnische Bevölkerung und es scheint, daß Jesus sie nie betreten hat«; erst im 2. Jh. wurde sie »zur Metropole des rabbinischen Judentums«[59].

Da nun andererseits der ehemals kafarnaitische Centurio die einzig konkrete Gestalt neben Jesus (und dem Täufer) in Q ist (nicht einmal der Terminus μαθηταί erscheint schon konkret in Bezug auf Jesus-

---

57. DALMAN, *Orte* (Anm. 27), pp. 190f., der damit aber eher belastend das Argument einbringt:»Origenes (zu Joh 6,41) kannte am See von Tiberias eine alte Stadt Gergesa, bei welcher am See ein Absturz liegt, nach Euseb (Onom 74) wurde ein Dorf dieses Namens dort ʿauf dem Bergeʾ gezeigt« wie »auch pSchebi 36c« ein ʿGergesaʾ hier lokalisiert, was GNILKA, *Markus* (Anm. 31), p. 201 aber zu der kaum haltbaren texkritischen Entscheidung ʿGergesenerʾ veranlaßt.

58. H. BALZ, *Tiberias*, in *EWNT* III (1983) 851-852, bes. p. 851; vgl. KOPP, *Die Stätten* (Anm. 27), pp. 278-282; SCHÜRER, *The History* (Anm. 27), pp. 178-182; KASHER, *Jews* (Anm. 27), pp. 221-224; JosAnt 18,36-38 setzt gemischte Bevölkerung voraus; vgl. ausführlich H. DUDMAN – E. BALLHORN, *Tiberias*, Jerusalem, 1988 (Rez. N.A. SIBERMAN, in *BAR* 15/4 [1989] 11-56).

59. H. KÖSTER, *Einführung in das Neue Testament*, Berlin, 1980, pp. 406f.

Anhänger!), so dürften Orts- und Personenbetonung koinzidieren und er als direkt oder indirekt (pseudonym) hinter der Redaktion von Q stehende Gestalt benannt werden. Die Anordnung von Q 10,13-15 nach der Botenrede spricht eher für eine Verfluchung der Seeorte durch die Q Redaktion als durch Jesus selbst. Als Ort des Ausgangspunktes der Handlung wird man sich darum am besten Tiberias vorzustellen haben. Dies ist das Ergebnis meiner Überlegungen, als wir bei der SNTS-Exkursion nach Israel 1981 von Tiberias aus immer wieder den See überquerten und umrundeten.

Die Namen der Küstenorte stehen metonymisch für die Bewohner. Die kommunikationstheoretische Kategorie der 'Proxemik' macht deutlich, daß Distanzen dazu dienen, um bestimmte Relationen auszudrücken, für die solche Distanzen faktisch oder rhetorisch geschaffen werden. Wir haben hier einen Selbstidentifizierungstext des Senders in Relation zu den Adressaten vor uns. Die drei Adressaten als Zielpunkte weisen auf einen gemeinsamen Ausgangspunkt der akustischen Strahlen. Gab es dort, also in Tiberias, so etwas wie eine Versammlung, bei der die Vertreter dieser Küstenorte anwesend waren? Der Kontext wie geprägte Muster kultureller Codes weisen eher auf eine nicht unmittelbar adressaten-bezogene, sondern rein expressive Sprachfunktion.

Rhetorisch kann man sich das als demonstrative 'Hypotypose' (»sub oculos subiectio« Cicero Orat 3,53,202; Quintilian 9,2,20-44; Herennium 4,55,68)[60] vorstellen: »Wir werden diese Wortverkündigung wie bei Ezechiel (35,2 wie 6,2 u.ö.) mit einer Ausdruckshandlung verbunden zu denken haben, in der der Prophet sein Gesicht wie in einer angedeuteten Zeichenhandlung dem Wohngebiet der Bedrohten zuwendet (wie es uns sonst von der Gebetsrichtung der Exulanten aus 1Kön 8,44.48; Dan 6,11 bekannt ist)«[61]. Der ehemalige kafarnaitische Centurio (bzw. als Pseudonym dessen Substitut) wendete sich in Tiberias nach den drei Richtungen über den See, um seine Absage zu formulieren, die sich steigernd in ihrer Spitze gegen Kafarnaum als einer Hochburg israelitischer Erwählungsgewißheit richtete.

Mittelstrasse 3   W. SCHENK
D-6602 Dudweiler

---

60. R. GRAMS, *The Temple Conflict Scene: A Rhetorical Analysis of Matthew 21–23*, in WATSON (Hg.), *Persuasive* (Anm. 25), pp. 41-65, bes. p. 63, setzt eine solche auch für das Ende der Weherede Mt 23,35-36 mindestens in Sinne der mt Komposition voraus.

61. H.W. WOLFF, *Dodekapropheton* III (BK, 14/3), Neukirchen, 1977, p. 25; vgl. *ibid.*, p. 5 zur Anrede Obd 2.14.15b nach v. 1b mit W. ZIMMERLI, *Ezechiel* I (BK, 13/1), Neukirchen, 1969, pp. 142-144. Schon in Mari redete ein Kultprophet in einem Fremdvölkerorakel Babylon drohend an.

MARK AND THE HISTORICAL-CRITICAL METHOD
The Challenge of Recent Literary Approaches to the Gospel [1]

I. Mark and the Historical-Critical Method

1. *The Traditio-critical Tools and their Aims, Methods and Results*

Throughout the twentieth century, literary-critical approaches have dominated Biblical Studies in general and the Gospel of Mark in particular. These approaches in broad terms take the text seriously both as a literary phenomenon and as the end-product of a complex process in which traditions about Jesus, initially transmitted orally and influenced by the religious communities which revered him, came eventually in the course of a generation to written expression at the hands of the gifted writer now unknown to us. While a considerable body of scholarship in more recent times has concentrated on the text in its final form and has asked questions relating, for example, to the work's literary type or the author's style, point of view or rhetorical technique, for the major part of the century the emphasis has focused on the text's component parts and on the complex traditio-historical process which brought it into being.

Chief among the now established literary-critical approaches which have remained historical-critical in orientation are the interrelated methods of source, form and redaction criticism. These methods start with the recognition that, archaeological evidence aside, written texts like the Gospel of Mark are our major route to historical knowledge about Jesus, the early Christian communities and the world of early Christianity. As major champions of what R. Alter has pejoratively termed an 'excavative' approach, source, form and redaction criticism have taught us to start with the evidence before us and to work back from the text (or behind it) to uncover the historical information it is capable of revealing. All three methods attempt to explain, for example, the discrepancies, ambiguities and awkwardnesses apparent on a close reading of the text in terms of the sources, forms and redaction of the literary or oral material drawn upon by the evangelist. Source criticism

---

1. This article was first presented as a paper given (in various forms) at the Conference on 'New Directions for Biblical Studies?' at King's College London (March 30 – April 2, 1992) and at the Colloquium Biblicum Lovaniense XLI at Louvain (August 18-20, 1992) It develops part of a much more extensive treatment of Markan Studies in the last decade, *The Pre-Markan Tradition in Recent Research (1980-1990)*, in *The Four Gospels 1992. FS F. Neirynck* (BETL, 100), Leuven, 1992, pp. 693-723.

has explored the evidence for the use of written sources in the Gospel. Form criticism has investigated the structured form taken by the traditional material, a form taken to be related to its function within the life and worship of the communities which transmitted it. Redaction criticism has analysed the use made by the evangelist of such sources, whether written or oral, and sought to ascertain his literary and theological contribution to the developing Jesus tradition.

2. *The Traditio-historical Method in Decline?*

Throughout the eighties, however, there has been a prevailing impression that the traditio-historical method as practised on the Gospel, using these interrelated tools, has been on the defensive, indeed has been even on the decline. This view was noted in my article in the Neirynck Festschrift and a number of factors cited which might be invoked in support of it[2]. These can be summarised as follows:

a) The advent of new methods and approaches

On the one hand, secular literary criticism and the synchronic approaches (rhetorical criticism, narrative criticism, reader-response criticism, structuralism etc.) have encouraged a more holistic approach to the text and with it a greater emphasis on textually-integrative rather than textually-disintegrative features. At the opposite end of the scale, advocates of a 'Third Quest for the Historical Jesus' have argued, on their part, for more holistic constructions and have decried what they see as the excessive atomisation of the Gospel tradition practised by source, form and redaction critics.

b) The criticisms under criticism

The advent of new methods and approaches in Gospel criticism has also brought with it then a related factor – a direct challenge to the more established methods. Criticisms have been directed increasingly against the three principal methods (source criticism, form criticism and redaction criticism) with respect to the tensions which actually exist between them, to their own intrinsic weaknesses or limitations, to the high degree of speculation involved in their putative diachronic reconstructions and to the lack of consensus in their results.

c) The pre-history of the text in doubt

A third factor is the confusion within the traditio-historical approach itself concerning our understanding of, approach to and definition of 'pre-Markan tradition' (PMT). What is meant by 'tradition' and what is meant by 'pre-Markan'? For some strongly form-critical approaches, the PMT comprises a *Grundschrift*, (an *Ur-Markus*, a primitive or proto-Mark, perhaps even our Gospel of Matthew) or *Grundschriften*, written sources which Mark employed and edited to varying degrees.

2. *Op. cit.*, pp. 693-694.

For classical form criticism, the PMT comprises oral forms taken over by Mark in isolated or clustered pericopae. For a strict redaction (or 'emendation') criticism, it is the immediately preceding text or *Vorlage* recovered when the Markan editorial work is removed. It can be understood as a combination of both written and oral sources behind the Gospel. Some approach the PMT by reference not so much to the text as to the social and religious context which generated the text (or the 'texts within the text'). The PMT is the 'stream of tradition' in which Mark stood or against which he reacted.

Allied with these questions of definition and approach is the question of the *Traditionsprozess* itself and how it is to be understood. There is a lack of certainty regarding the process(es) that brought the Gospels into their present form. A key issue here is whether the process that led from oral tradition to Gospel composition was an inevitable, collective and evolutionary one or whether the non-linear and multi-directional nature of the tradition requires us to posit Gospel composition as the consequence of individual authorial intention adopting a specific genre. Was the Gospel of Mark, in other words, an 'evolutionary' or 'revolutionary' document (to quote the title of L.W. Hurtado's recent article on this subject[3])? Given this diversity of opinion and apparent lack of agreement it is not surprising, therefore, that doubts have been expressed as to the very possibility of reconstructing the pre-history of the text, and voices raised in support of synchronic approaches.

3. *From Redaction Criticism to Literary Criticism*

a) Developments in redaction criticism

Nowhere has the conflict between holistic and atomistic perspectives been more apparent than in the exercise and development of redaction criticism itself. It was the application of the redaction-critical method in particular which contributed to the 'new look' on the Gospel which emerged in Markan Studies from the nineteen sixties onwards[4]. From this period, the history of scholarship on Mark has tended to de-emphasize the evangelist as historian and to draw increasing attention to his creative role as a theologian. While redaction criticism is now regarded as a holistic method with multiple concerns (historical, theological, literary, sociological) it is important to remind ourselves that its primary goal was and is a tradition-critical one viz, to expose the editorial process conducted upon the sources as a means of determining the extent of the evangelist's literary and theological contribution to the developing tradition. The attempt to establish a redactional text of

---

3. L.W. HURTADO, *The Gospel of Mark: Evolutionary or Revolutionary Document?*, in *JSNT* 40 (1990) 15-32.

4. See W.R. TELFORD (ed.), *The Interpretation of Mark* (Issues in Religion and Theology, 7), London - Philadelphia, PA, 1985, pp. 1-41.

Mark[5] has been frustrated not only by problems in methodology[6] but also by an increasing recognition of the linguistic homogeneity of the Gospel[7]. The inability of scholars to make a precise delineation of the sources as well as the increasing conviction that summary passages, seams, insertions or modifications of pericopae are an inadequate base for developing a full picture of Mark's style or theology have led to the widening of the criteria for determining his religious outlook. For this reason, a source-editing approach has come to be amplified, if not eclipsed, by analysis of recurrent motifs, themes or interests in the Gospel overall.

b) The end of redaction criticism?

It is this broadening of the redaction-critical method, however, which has brought it into the field of general literary criticism and hence within range of dehistoricising methods and approaches which undermine its validity as a literary-historical method. In this respect, it could be argued, the method has sown the seeds of its own destruction. Mark's theology is to be reached, it is now commonly argued, not by seeking to document his modifications of tradition but by studying the Gospel in its entirety. As a result the borderline between redaction criticism as a tradition-critical method (with a diachronic perspective) and redaction criticism as a literary-aesthetic discipline (with a synchronic perspective) has become increasingly blurred. Much that passes for redaction criticism, some critics claim, is actually literary criticism.

As remarked in my Neirynck Festschrift article[8], redaction criticism is a discipline in tension with itself, therefore, seeking to remain an historical method but struggling to come to terms with the literary aspects of its source material. It has tried to reconcile both dimensions and this is its strength as well as its weakness. It has come under increasing criticism, however, especially from those who would pull it radically in either direction. J. Muddiman[9] has drawn attention to six recently published works[10] whose holistic approaches have in various

---

5. Cf., e.g., E.J. PRYKE, *Redactional Style in the Markan Gospel* (SNTS MS, 33), Cambridge-Leiden, 1978; F. NEIRYNCK, *The Redactional Text of Mark*, in *ETL* 57 (1981) 144-162; = *Evangelica* (BETL, 60), Leuven, 1982, pp. 618-636; *Words Characteristic of Mark. A New List*, in *ETL* 63 (1987) 367-374; = *Evangelica II* (BETL, 99), Leuven, 1991, pp. 339-346.

6. Cf. D.B. PEABODY, *Mark as Composer* (New Gospel Studies, 1), Mercer, GA, 1987.

7. See F. NEIRYNCK, *Duality in Mark* (BETL, 31), rev. ed., Leuven, 1988.

8. *Op. cit.* (n. 1), p. 708.

9. J.B. MUDDIMAN, *The End of Markan Redaction Criticism?*, in *ExpT* 101 (1990) 307-309. For a further review of recent holistic studies on Mark, see C. BREYTENBACH, *Gesamtdarstellungen zum Markusevangelium*, in *VF* 36 (1991) 50-55.

10. C.C. BLACK, *The Disciples according to Mark* (JSNT SS, 27), Sheffield, 1989; J.D. KINGSBURY, *Conflict in Mark*, Minneapolis, MN, 1989; H.C. WAETJEN, *A Reordering of Power*, Minneapolis, MN, 1989; C.D. MARSHALL, *Faith as a Theme in Mark's Narrative* (SNTS MS, 64), Cambridge, 1989; M.R. THOMPSON, *The Role of Disbelief in Mark*, New York - Mahwah, NJ, 1989; J. SERGEANT, *Lion let Loose*, Exeter, 1988.

ways signalled the demise of redaction criticism. Of these, C.C. Black[11] has taken it to task for, among other things, the lack of consensus in its results, its 'methodological imperialism' and its misplacement of the author (and not the text) at the centre of textual interpretation. This judgment is premature but it highlights the problems of a traditio-critical method being drawn more and more into the domain of literary studies, to which I shall now turn.

II. The Challenge of Recent Literary Approaches to the Gospel

1. A Review of some Recent Literary Studies and Methods

It is difficult to classify far less review current literary approaches to the Gospel given their many overlapping as well as divergent interests and concerns. What I shall venture to do, however, is to select five literary methodologies and then briefly review some studies done recently on Mark in respect of their approaches. Thereafter I shall make some comments on the significance of their results for the historical-critical method.

a) Composition Criticism

One particular trend in the last decade, as we have noted, is that a strict redaction criticism has been giving way to a broader composition criticism in its search for the Markan fingerprints. A prime concern of composition criticism has been to establish the compositional structure of the Gospel. An increasing number of scholars have been proposing chiasmus, or concentric arrangement, as the key, a pervasive rhetorical device in antiquity used and appreciated both in oral teaching and in written discourse as a structuring device[12]. A concentric or 'sandwich' pattern has been detected not only in individual sections of the narrative[13] but also in the Gospel as a whole, though as yet without unanimity[14]. R. Zwick[15] has recently proposed montage (as in cinema-

11. Cf. also C.C. Black, *The Quest of Mark the Redactor: Why has it been pursued and what has it taught us?*, in *JSNT* 33 (1988) 19-39.
12. See A. Stock, *Chiastic Awareness and Education in Antiquity*, in *BTB* 14 (1984) 23-27.
13. On 2,1–3,6, for example, see J. Dewey, *Markan Public Debate* (SBL DS, 48), Chico, CA, 1980; on 4,1-34, G. Fay, *Introduction to Incomprehension: the Literary Structure of Mark 4:1-34*, in *CBQ* 51 (1989) 65-81; on 4,1–8,26, N.R. Petersen, *The Composition of Mark 4:1–8:26*, in *HTR* 73 (1980) 125-217; on 14,1-52, J.P. Heil, *Mark 14,1-52: Narrative Structure and Reader Response*, in *Bib* 71 (1990) 305-332.
14. Contrast, for example, M.P. Scott, *Chiastic Structure: a Key to the Interpretation of Mark's Gospel*, in *BTB* 15 (1985) 17-26, with W. Stenger, *Die Grundlegung des Evangeliums von Jesus Christus. Zur kompositionellen Struktur des Markusevangeliums*, in *LingBib* 61 (1988) 7-56.
15. R. Zwick, *Montage im Markusevangelium* (SBB, 18), Stuttgart, 1989.

tic narration – the production of a rapid succession of images to illustrate an association of ideas) as a clue to uncovering the literary and theological unity of Mark.

A further issue faced by composition criticism is whether Mark himself composed entire pericopae. In his numerous publications, E. Best has rejected this possibility[16] but others, noting the striking continuity of form and language between pre-Markan traditions and the evangelist's own redaction and composition, have been arguing for tradition-inspired composition[17]. Rau[18], following Theissen's compositional analysis, also sees in the Gospel the hand of a more active redactor who has created an intentional and thematic representation of the beginnings of the Christian mission initiated by Jesus. A landmark study in this respect was R. Fowler's *Loaves and Fishes*[19] which, as well as arguing that Mark composed the first feedingstory of 6,34-44 on the basis of 8,1-12, also pressed for a methodological shift in Gospel Studies towards a literary-critical perspective, in this case reader-response.

b) Reader-Response Criticism

The appeal that literary criticism (as practised by contemporary literary critics) should be taken seriously by New Testament scholars is one that has been frequently voiced[20]. Reader-response criticism has brought much to the study of Mark although it has also engendered a vigorous debate concerning the identification of the "reader" whose reception of the text is in view. Some forms of reader-response criticism are only interested in the 'ideal' reader or the (implied) reader 'in' the text, while other approaches emphasize the reception of the text by its ancient readership, and hence retain an historical interest[21]. A useful introduction to the discipline, ed. E.V. McKnight (*Reader Perspectives, Semeia* 48)[22], was also published in 1989, with articles by B.C. Late-

16. Cf., e.g., E. BEST, *Mark: Some Problems*, in *IrBS* 1 (1979) 77-98; *Mark: The Gospel as Story* (Studies of the New Testament and its World), Edinburgh, 1983; *Disciples and Discipleship*, Edinburgh, 1986; *Mark's Narrative Technique*, in *JSNT* 37 (1989) 43-58.

17. Cf., e.g., P. SELLEW, *Composition of Didactic Scenes in Mark's Gospel*, in *JBL* 108 (1989) 613-634 (on 4,3-20 and 7,14-23 as models for the evangelist's composition of 8,14-21; 9,14-29 and 10,1-12); H. FLEDDERMANN, *The Discipleship Discourse (Mark 9:33-50)*, in *CBQ* 43 (1981) 57-75, and J. SAUER, *Die ursprüngliche "Sitz im Leben" von Mk 10:13-16*, in *ZNW* 72 (1981) 27-50 (on 10,13-16 as a model for 9,36-37).

18. G. RAU, *Das Markus-Evangelium. Komposition und Intention der ersten Darstellung christlicher Mission*, in *ANRW* II.25.2 (1983) 2036-2257.

19. R.M. FOWLER, *Loaves and Fishes* (SBL DS, 54), Chico, CA, 1981.

20. Cf., e.g., N.R. PETERSEN, *Literary Criticism for New Testament Critics* (Guides to Biblical Scholarship: New Testament Series), Philadelphia, PA, 1978; R.A. SPENCER (ed.), *Orientation by Disorientation. FS W.A. Beardslee* (Pittsburgh Theological Monograph Series, 35), Pittsburgh, 1980; J.D. McCAUGHEY, *Literary Criticism and the Gospels – a Rumination*, in *AusBR* 29 (1981) 16-25.

21. Cf., e.g., M.A. BEAVIS, *Mark's Audience* (JSNT SS, 33), Sheffield, 1989.

22. E.V. McKNIGHT (ed.), *Reader Perspectives on the New Testament* (Semeia, 48), Atlanta, GA, 1989.

gan, B.M.F. van Iersel, R.M. Fowler, among others, and a post-structuralist response by T.F. Berg which concluded: "The reader is not in the text, and she is not one; the reader is legion, and she can be anywhere"[23].

c) Structuralism

Of various structuralist approaches to Mark, the series of Lévi-Straussian studies by E.S. Malbon[24] should be mentioned. Irrespective of the question of historicity, Mark is revealed as a religious text with mythic structure and meaning[25]. Malbon has had some illuminating things to say about the mythic significance of Mark's spatial references whether geopolitical (Galilee/Jerusalem), topographical (land/sea) or architectural (the house etc.). In common with a number of literary approaches, structuralism is opposed to the fragmentation of the text, although its analysis seeks to uncover the deep structures rather than the surface rhetoric or discourse.

d) (Socio-)Rhetorical Criticism

In respect of the latter, both rhetorical criticism and narrative criticism have played a significant role in Markan Studies. Following on from form criticism, rhetorical criticism has illuminated the structural patterns, rhetorical devices and literary idioms used by the original author and has thereby reinforced a growing appreciation of his literary activity. Dewey's *Markan Public Debate* (1980) was a landmark study in this field highlighting evidence of Markan rhetorical technique in 2,1–3,6 and hence casting doubt on his use of a pre-Markan collection[26]. The work of V.K. Robbins[27] should also be cited. Robbins has suggested a wider categorisation of forms (progressive, repetitive, conventional and minor), drawn attention to the *chreia* form and its development and illuminated the patterns of persuasion used by an ancient writer like Mark in his text. He has also contributed to rhetorical criticism as a discipline which, while literary in its thrust, seeks to maintain the historical perspective of classical form criticism.

---

23. *Ibid.*, p. 187.

24. E.S. MALBON, *Mythic Structure and Meaning in Mark,* in *Semeia* 16 (1979) 97-132; *Galilee and Jerusalem: History and Literature in Markan Interpretation,* in *CBQ* 44 (1982) 242-255; *The Jesus of Mark and the Sea of Galilee,* in *JBL* 103 (1984) 363-377; *Narrative Space and Mythic Meaning in Mark* (New Voices in Biblical Studies), San Francisco, CA, 1986.

25. See also J. DRURY, *Mark 1.1-15: an Interpretation,* in A.E. HARVEY (ed.), *Alternative Approaches to New Testament Study,* London, 1985, pp. 25-36.

26. See J. DEWEY, *Markan Public Debate* (n. 13).

27. V.K. ROBBINS, *Mark 1.14-20: an Interpretation at the Intersection of Jewish and Graeco-Roman Traditions,* in *NTS* 28 (1982) 220-236; *Pronouncement Stories and Jesus' Blessing of the Children: A Rhetorical Approach,* in *Semeia* 29 (1983) 43-74; *Jesus the Teacher. A Socio-Rhetorical Interpretation of Mark,* Philadelphia, PA, 1984; cf. also B.L. MACK – V.K. ROBBINS, *Patterns of Persuasion in the Gospels* (Foundations and Facets: Literary Facets), Sonoma, CA, 1989.

More recently, M.A. Tolbert[28] has also applied the method but in this case has approached the Gospel as fiction and as a self-consciously crafted narrative.

e) Narrative Criticism

Narrative criticism with its emphasis on Mark as 'story' and on the conceptual autonomy of the narrative world created by Mark, has generated a number of insights and an increasing number of productive studies[29]. All have laid stress on the unity of the narrative Mark created and the importance of reading it as a narrative whole. Some have taken the radical view that to approach Mark as narrative is to approach the Gospel as fiction, since there are no textual proofs for history, only metatextual referents[30]. Others[31], while accepting that Mark used narrative techniques, assert that he was also constrained by the traditional material employed. Seeing Mark as an author/narrator with a consistent point of view[32], narrative critics have analysed Mark in terms of its rhetoric, structure, plot, settings and characters[33]. Others have explored single motifs[34], major themes[35] or particular sections or aspects of the narrative[36]. Narrative structure has been seen as a clue to the Gospel by van Iersel[37].

28. M.A. Tolbert, *Sowing the Gospel*, Minneapolis, MN, 1989.

29. Cf. F. Hahn (ed.), *Der Erzähler des Evangeliums* (SBS, 118-119), Stuttgart, 1985; see also D. Rhoads, *Narrative Criticism and the Gospel of Mark*, in *JAAR* 50 (1982) 411-434.

30. Cf. F. Kermode, *The Genesis of Secrecy. On the Interpretation of Narrative*, Cambridge, MA - London, 1979; see H.D. Betz, *Is Hermes the Hierophant, or is Christ?* (Review of F. Kermode, *The Genesis of Secrecy*), in *JR* 62 (1982) 178-185.

31. Cf. E. Best, *Mark's Narrative Technique*, in *JSNT* 37 (1989) 43-58.

32. Cf., e.g., N.R Petersen, *"Point of View" in Mark's Narrative*, in *Semeia* 12 (1978) 97-121; W.S. Vorster, *Mark: Collector, Redactor, Author, Narrator?*, in *JournTheol SAfrica* 31 (1980) 46-61.

33. Cf. e.g. W.H. Kelber, *Mark's Story of Jesus*, Philadelphia, PA, 1979; D. Rhoads – D. Michie, *Mark as Story*, Philadelphia, PA, 1982; see also R. Smith, *Thy Kingdom Come: Some Recent Work on Mark's Gospel*, in *Currents in Theology and Mission* 8 (1981) 371-376.

34. E.g., R.A. Culpepper, *Mark 10.50: why mention the Garment?*, in *JBL* 101 (1982) 131-132.

35. Cf. C.D. Marshall, *Faith* (n. 10): on faith; M.R. Thompson, *Disbelief* (n. 10): on disbelief; J.D. Kingsbury, *The Christology of Mark's Gospel*, Philadelphia, PA, 1983: on christology; *Conflict* (n. 10): on conflict; H.J. Klauck, *Der erzählerische Rolle der Jünger im Markusevangelium*, in *NT* 24 (1982) 1-26: on the disciples; C. Breytenbach, *Nachfolge und Zukunftserwartung nach Markus* (ATANT, 71), Zürich, 1984, and T.J. Geddert, *Watchwords* (JSNT SS, 26), Sheffield, 1989: on discipleship/eschatology.

36. Cf. F.J. Matera, *Passion Narratives and Gospel Theologies*, New York - Mahwah, NJ, 1986: the passion narrative; *The Prologue as the Interpretative Key to Mark's Gospel*, in *JSNT* 34 (1988) 3-20: the prologue; C.W. Hedrick, *The Role of 'Summary Statements' in the Composition of the Gospel of Mark*, in *NT* 26 (1984) 289-311: the *hermeneiai* or parenthetical comments.

37. B. van Iersel, *Reading Mark*, Edinburgh, 1988; cf. A. Stock, *Hinge Transitions in Mark's Gospel*, in *BTB* 15 (1985) 27-31; *The Structure of Mark*, in *Bible Today* 23 (1985) 291-296.

2. The Challenge Posed by Recent Literary Studies

a) The Strengths of Literary-critical Approaches

The literary-critical perspective has been a valuable one in the field of Gospel criticism. It has reminded us that communication is an act involving not only the author but also the text and its reader. It has made us sensitive to the integrity of the text and attuned to questions regarding its reception and its effects as well as its antecedents. It has made us aware of how texts operate as texts, of the distinctiveness of textuality and of the restraints imposed upon a writer by virtue of literary factors (such as genre, composition, rhetoric) as well as historical ones (such as sources or traditions). It has highlighted the textually-integrative features (such as structure, compositional technique or rhetoric) which have operated on the Markan units and stressed the importance of their literary context rather than their prior sociological function. It has allowed Markan Studies to make progress despite the problems encountered in traditio-historical research and has even offered ways to overcome some of the micro-structural problems in the text by reference to its macro-structure. It has opened up new research on the literary-historical environment of the Gospel (especially the Graeco-Roman world and its literature), as well as on its own narrative world. It has led to a greater appreciation of the literary coherence of the Gospel at a global level, if not at the micro-level, and has broadened the canvas for determining the evangelist's literary skill and theological achievement. As a result, new models have been suggested for its interpretation. In place of the Gospel as scrapbook or necklace, we have the Gospel as 'story'[38], 'fiction'[39], 'historical novel'[40], or as 'mythic narrative'[41], 'oral narrative'[42] or 'episodic narrative'[43]. In place of Mark as collector, redactor or even as 'an artist creating a

---

38. Cf. W.H. KELBER, *Mark's Story* (n. 33); D. RHOADS – D. MICHIE, *Mark as Story* (n. 33); J.D. KINGSBURY, *Conflict* (n. 10).

39. Cf. F. KERMODE, *Genesis* (n. 30); M.A. TOLBERT, *Sowing* (n. 28).

40. Cf. T.R. WRIGHT, *Regenerating Narrative: the Gospels as Fiction*, in *Religious Studies* 20 (1984) 389-400.

41. Cf. J. DRURY (n. 25); E.S. MALBON, *Narrative Space* (n. 24); B.L. MACK, *A Myth of Innocence*, Philadelphia, PA, 1988.

42. Cf. T.E. BOOMERSHINE, *Peter's Denial as Polemic or Confession: the Implications of Media Criticism for Biblical Hermeneutics*, in *Semeia* 39 (1987) 47-68; E. BEST, *Mark's Narrative Technique* (n. 16); J. DEWEY, *Oral Methods of Structuring Narrative in Mark*, in *Interpr* 43 (1989) 32-44.

43. Cf. C. BREYTENBACH, *The Gospel of Mark as Episodical Narrative*, in *Scriptura* (special issue 4, 1989) 1-26.

collage'[44], we have Mark the 'story-teller'[45], Mark the 'author/narrator'[46], Mark the 'theologian'[47] and even Mark the 'film director'[48].
b) The Relation of Literary-critical and Historical-critical Methodologies

Despite its value, however, literary criticism has also posed a challenge to the historical-critical method, though not, of course uniformly or even inevitably. Some literary-critical methodologies have developed within the established disciplines and are in many respects in continuity with them (e.g., composition criticism, rhetorical criticism). Socio-rhetorical criticism (cf. V.K. Robbins) preserves a concern for social context while at the same time treating the whole text as the product of compositional activity by an author using ancient rhetorical devices. Some forms of reader-response are concerned with the ancient reader, as we have noted, and hence are historical in orientation. Literary-aesthetic approaches usually remain within the literary world of the text itself and do not normally venture into making judgments on its alleged historical content. Some literary approaches to Mark, such as structuralism, are committedly synchronic and ahistorical, their methods opposed to fragmentation but their purpose to explore how meaning is achieved in a received text without reference to its antecedents or prehistory. They are not theoretically in opposition to tradition-critical methods, therefore[49].

c) Holistic Studies and their Assumptions

Nevertheless, certain assumptions are made in a number of the recent holistic studies on Mark which have implications for the historical-critical method as traditionally practised. The assumption is made that the Gospel is a unified narrative with a single coherent story and that it has a consistent point of view, ideology or theology. The meaning of the text is not given by the author's intention, as methods such as redaction criticism have assumed. Structure is often taken to be the clue to the meaning. The interpretation of the text lies in the interrelationship of its parts and not in the relationship of these parts to their (extra-)textual antecedents. Single scenes, in other words, receive significance from their place in the totality of Mark's story rather than from the modifications the evangelist has made on them. There has been a notable tendency, therefore, to treat passages or even motifs which have

44. Cf. E. Best, in W.R. Telford (ed.), *Interpretation* (n. 4), p. 128.
45. Cf. J.C. Meagher, *Clumsy Construction in Mark's Gospel* (Toronto Studies in Theology, 3), New York - Toronto, 1979; D. Rhoads – D. Michie, *Mark as Story* (n. 33).
46. Cf. N.R. Petersen, *'Point of View'* (n. 32); W.S. Vorster, *Mark* (n. 32).
47. Cf. Dewey (n. 13), Geddert (n. 35), Kelber (n. 33), Kingsbury, Marshall, Thompson (n. 10), Matera (n. 36), et al.
48. Cf. Zwick (n. 15).
49. As G. Sellin, *Textlinguistische und semiotische Erwägungen zu Mk 4.1-34*, in *NTS* 29 (1983) 508-530 and T.R. Wright, *Regenerating Narrative* (n. 40) point out.

hitherto been regarded as tradition-critically discrete as coherent elements within the narrative[50]. Extrinsic factors (e.g., the 'real-world' concerns of the historical author) are often taken to be irrelevant for the Gospel's interpretation since narrative details contribute by and large to the 'story-world' of the text and not to transparent history. Breaks, gaps in the narrative, inconsistencies, ambiguities, duplications are taken as natural literary (or psychological) devices or strategies (opacity, intra-textual allusion, irony, etc.) rather than as source-critical indicators. 'Accumulated redactional additions', grist for the tradition critic's mill, are taken to be within the narrator's own literary horizon or range[51]. Micro-structural problems, in other words, can often be overcome by reference to macro-structure.

3. A Critique of Literary-Critical Approaches

Literary-critical approaches also have their problems, however, and these should be acknowledged if synchronic and diachronic methods are to work in harmony with one another. While there is a problem when extra-textual referents are invoked, there is also a problem of subjectivity when the text itself is its own objective referent. Literary parallels are capable of being multiplied irresponsibly and "the interpreter of the final structures is tempted to create more interrelationships than were intended by the author"[52]. A number of the recent holistic studies have had a tendency to over-estimate Mark's achievement, to skip over evidence of textual incoherence and to harmonize excessively the discrepancies and contradictions. There is a danger of seeking too easy solutions to problems at pericope level by appeal to the macro-structure.

Even literary critics acknowledge that "textual compositeness has been proven to be a fundamental condition of biblical literary art"[53] and that traditio-historical study has simply responded to textual evidence that demanded explanation. This holds for Mark according to most scholars. Mark's 'story-world' also interpenetrates with his 'real-world' and it is the task of historical criticism to press the text at those points where it does. Extrinsic factors are thrust upon the historical critic by virtue of the multiple attestation of traditions. There may indeed be confusion within the historical-critical camp but the sheer variety of literary approaches (rhetorical criticism, composition criti-

50. Cf., e.g., M.A. BEAVIS, Mark's Audience (n. 21): on 4,11-12; T.J. GEDDERT, Watchwords (n. 35): on Mark 13; R.A. CULPEPPER, Mark 10:50 (n. 34): on the garment references.

51. Cf. R.M. FRYE, Literary Criticism and Gospel Criticism, in Theology Today 36 (1979) 207-219.

52. H. RÄISÄNEN, The "Messianic" Secret in Mark (Studies of the New Testament and its World), transl. C. TUCKETT, Edinburgh, 1990, p. 27.

53. N.R. PETERSEN, in R.A. SPENCER (ed.), Orientation (n. 20), p. 30.

cism, narrative criticism, structuralism, etc.) and the tensions existing
between them (structuralism versus poststructuralism, the debate over
the reader, etc.) has led to a similar lack of consensus among them in
their methods and results. Structuralism's 'mythic base' for the Markan
Gospel may be as undifferentiated, after all, as the 'pre-Markan tradition'.

The lack of consensus among the traditio-historical disciplines opera-
ting on Mark may also, however, be exaggerated. There is a striking
and often unacknowledged consensus on the minimal units in Mark
and a widespread acceptance still that the Gospel incorporates pre-
Markan traditions with divergence only over their precise nature and
extent. Mark is a composite text which displays considerable awkward-
ness at pericope level but considerable sophistication when viewed
holistically. That is one of its puzzles. The challenge will be to develop
our methodology in the future so that it can successfully accommodate
both micro- and macroscopic procedures.

University of Newcastle   William R. TELFORD
Department of Religious Studies
Newcastle upon Tyne NE1 7RU
Great Britain

ZUR METHODE DER ERFORSCHUNG VORMARKINISCHER QUELLEN

Die Rückfrage hinter Markus zu seinen Quellen oder zu den ipsissima verba bzw. facta Jesu zurück beschäftigt die Forschung seit der Begründung der Zweiquellentheorie, die Markus als eine der Vorlagen der Evangelisten Mt und Lk ansieht. Viel Akribie und Scharfsinn ist angewendet worden, die Sprache und die theologische Eigenart dieses Evangelisten herauszustellen und von hier aus auf seine Quellen zu schließen. Die Ergebnisse sind sehr unterschiedlich. Einige Forscher rechnen bei Mk mit großer Zuverlässigkeit und Treue in der Wiedergabe[1], andere mit einem hohen Anteil an der Gestaltung der Texte[2]. Einige sehen in Mk den Bearbeiter von schriftlichen Vorlagen[3], andere den Gestalter mündlicher Überlieferung[4].

Erstaunlicherweise ist, soweit ich es übersehe, noch nicht der Versuch unternommen worden, die Methode, sachgemäß hinter Mk zurückzukommen, dort aufzubauen, wo wir auf einigermaßen sicherem Boden

1. In der zweiten Hälfte des 19. Jahrhunderts galt das Markusevangelium weithin als Grundlage für eine Leben-Jesu-Darstellung. Dementsprechend wurde der Quellenwert dieses Evangelium hoch eingeschätzt. In der deutschsprachigen Exegese ist dieser Gesichtspunkt weithin aufgegeben. Für die positive Einschätzung der markinischen Überlieferung vgl. H. RIESENFELD, *Tradition und Redaktion im Markusevangelium*, in *Neutestamentliche Studien für R. Bultmann zu seinem 70. Geburtstag* (BZNW, 21), [2]1957, pp. 157-164; E. BEST, *Mark's Preservation of the Tradition*, in W. TELFORD (ed.), *The Interpretation of Mark*, Philadelphia, PA, - London, 1985, pp. 119-133, sowie J. ROLOFF, *Das Markusevangelium als Geschichtsdarstellung*, in *EvTh* 29 (1969) 73-93.

2. Seit W. WREDE, *Das Messiasgeheimnis in den Evangelien. Zugleich ein Beitrag zum Verständnis des Markusevangeliums*, Göttingen, 1901, sieht man besonders durch die Analysen der Formgeschichtler K.L. Schmidt, M. Dibelius und R. Bultmann verstärkt und durch die Redaktionsgeschichte seit W. MARXSEN, *Der Evangelist Markus. Studien zur Redaktionsgeschichte des Evangeliums* (FRLANT, 67), Göttingen, 1956, zur Methode erhoben, in Markus einen Theologen, der das Evangelium als Kerygma durchgestaltet hat. Besonders instruktiv dazu P. DSCHULNIGG, *Sprache, Redaktion und Intention des Markusevangeliums. Eigentümlichkeiten der Sprache des Markusevangeliums und ihre Bedeutung für die Redaktionskritik* (SBB, 11), Stuttgart, 1984.

3. R. PESCH, *Das Markusevangelium I*, [2]1977; *II*, [3]1984, rechnet besonders in Mk 8,27ff. mit einer schriftlichen Vorlage, die Mk übernommen habe. W. SCHMITHALS, *Das Evangelium nach Markus* (ÖTK, 2) Gütersloh, 1979, sieht im Mk den Bearbeiter eines Ur-Markus.

4. Vgl. dazu bes. W.S. VORSTER, *Markus - Sammler, Redaktor, Autor oder Erzähler?*, in F. HAHN (Hg.), *Der Erzähler des Evangeliums. Methodische Neuansätze in der Markusforschung* (SBS, 118/119), Stuttgart, 1985, pp. 11-36, sowie C. BREYTENBACH, *Das Problem des Übergangs von mündlicher zu schriftlicher Überlieferung*, in *Neotestamentica* 20 (1986) 47-58. Zum Problem von Mündlichkeit und Schriftlichkeit vgl. G. THEIBEN, *Urchristliche Wundergeschichten. Ein Beitrag zur formgeschichtlichen Erforschung der synoptischen Evangelien* (StNT, 8), Gütersloh, 1974, pp. 189-196.

stehen, nämlich bei der Beobachtung, wie Mt und Lk mit dem Mk-Stoff umgegangen sind. Denn sie standen zeitlich und gedanklich dem zweiten Evangelisten wahrscheinlich sehr viel näher als wir. Gerade für jene, die mit einer Bearbeitung von schriftlichen Vorlagen durch Mk rechnen, müßte die Art, wie die beiden Seitenreferenten diese Vorlage umgeschrieben haben, von großer Bedeutung sein. Jene aber, die mündliche Überlieferung als vormarkinische Tradition annehmen, könnten zeigen, daß die Redaktionsarbeit des Mk anders gewesen ist,als wir sie bei Mt und Lk registrieren, natürlich vorausgesetzt, daß sich so etwas zeigen läßt. Gewöhnlich wird bei der Rückfrage nach den Quellen des Mk so vorgegangen, daß man auf Unebenheiten im Text achtet und durch Ausscheidung von Sätzen oder Satzteilen einen neuen Text konstruiert, der Mk vorgelegen haben soll[5]. So wird weithin auch bei der Rekonstruktion des matthäischen[6] und lukanischen Sondergutes[7] verfahren, insofern diese Texte nicht in ihrer Gesamtheit den Evangelisten zugeschrieben werden[8].

Mein Vorschlag geht dahin, dieses Verfahren der Subtraktion, das durchaus sinnvoll und gerechtfertigt sein kann, dadurch zu verifizieren, daß darauf geachtet wird, wie die beiden Großevangelien Mk rezipiert haben. Eine gewisse Schwierigkeit bleibt natürlich bestehen. Sie meldet sich nicht nur da zu Wort, wo wir bedenken, daß Mt und Lk eigenständige Persönlichkeiten waren und darum ganz anders verfahren sein können als es Mk tat, sondern auch da, wo wir den minor agreements Bedeutung zuerkennen und damit rechnen, daß Mt und Lk neben Mk auch andere Traditionen des Mk-Stoffes kannten[9]. Indes geht es uns

5. »Bedenken gegen die(se) klassischen Verfahrensweisen der Literarkritik, durch Subtraktion redaktioneller Textbestandteile den exakten Wortlaut Mk vorgegebener Quellen zu rekonstruieren« stellt D. Lührmann, *Das Markusevangelium* (HNT, 3), Tübingen, 1987, p. 14 fest.

6. Vgl. dazu U. Luz, *Das Evangelium nach Matthäus* (EKK, I/1), ²1989 und (EKK, II/2), 1990, Neukirchen, passim. Dort auch die entsprechende Literatur.

7. H. Klein, *Barmherzigkeit gegenüber den Elenden und Geächteten. Studien zur Botschaft des lukanischen Sondergutes* (BTSt, 10), Neukirchen, 1987, passim; F.W. Horn, *Glaube und Handeln in der Theologie des Lukas* (GTA, 26), Göttingen, 1983, passim. Dort weitere Literatur.

8. G. Sellin, *Studien zu den großen Gleichniserzählungen des Lukas-Sonderguts. Die ἄνθρωπός-τις-Erzählungen des Lukas-Sonderguts, besonders am Beispiel von Lk 10,25-37 und 16,19-31 untersucht*, Diss theol. Münster, 1974 sowie W. Schmithals, *Das Evangelium nach Lukas* (Zürcher Bibelkommentar, 3/1), Zürich, 1980, sehen im lk Sondergut weithin lk redaktionelle Texte.

9. Neirynck, *The Minor Agreements of Matthew and Luke against Mark with a Cumulative List* (BETL, 37), Leuven, 1974; *The Minor Agreements in a Horizontal-line Synopsis* (SNTA, 15), Leuven, 1991; *Evangelica II. Collected Essays* (BETL, 99), 1991, pp. 3-138 sieht in den Minor Agreements redaktionelle Elemente des Mt bzw. Lk. A. Ennulat, *Die Minor Agreements. Ein Diskussionsbeitrag zur Erklärung einer offenen Frage des synoptischen Problems*, Diss. Bern, 1990 rechnet mit begleitender mündlicher Tradition. A. Fuchs, *Die Entwicklung der Beelzebulkontroverse bei den Synoptikern*

hier nicht um eine vollständige Methodenbeschreibung, sondern nur um
den Hinweis, daß eine Verifikation unserer bisherigen Methode innerhalb der angezeigten Grenzen möglich ist. Darum sollen im folgenden
zunächst zwei Markustexte in der Überlieferung des Mt und des Lk so
analysiert werden, als wären sie ein Teil ihres Sondergutes. Das Ergebnis der Analyse wird dann mit dem Mk-Text verglichen, wobei sich
zeigen wird, inwieweit unsere Rekonstruktion festen Boden hat (I).
Daraufhin sollen einige Beobachtungen aufgezeigt werden, wie Mt und
Lk Mk verarbeitet haben. Ein gesamtes Inventar der Möglichkeiten der
Bearbeitung kann hier nicht geboten werden (II). In einem nächsten
Abschnitt werden dann die Erkenntnisse aus den ersten beiden Teilen
zusammengestellt (III). Es folgt die Diskussion der Analyse eines Mk-
Textes, d.h. die Überprüfung unserer Einsicht an einem konkreten
Beispiel (IV). Am Ende wird das Ergebnis zusammengefaßt und die
Tragweite der Methode ausgelotet.

I

Wir analysieren zunächst zwei Abschnitte der Evangelisten Mt und
Lk, nämlich die Erzählung von der Auferweckung der Tochter des
Jairus und von der blutflüssigen Frau (Mt 9,18-26 und Lk 8,40-56),
sowie jene von der Kindersegnung (Mt 19,13-15; Lk 18,15-17). Diese
Analysen, die eigentlich ein Spiel sind, weil wir die Vorlagen bereits
kennen, gebrauchen die üblichen Methoden. Auf große Präzision und
Akribie wird bewußt verzichtet. Die gängigen Methoden werden ange-
wendet, aber das Ganze geschieht eher schemenhaft.

1a. *Mt 9,18-26*

VV. 18-19 und 23-26 gehören zusammen. V. 19 hat keinerlei Funktion in dem Bericht, außer der Feststellung, daß die Jünger Jesus folgen.
In der Erzählung ist aber nur an dieser Stelle von ihnen die Rede. Da
der Vers matthäischer Theologie entspricht, wonach die Jünger Jesus
nachfolgen (vgl. 8,22), ist er als mt anzusehen. V. 18 war einmal mit

(SNTU, B5), Linz, 1980; F. KOGLER, *Das Doppelgleichnis vom Senfkorn und vom Sauerteig in seiner tradititionsgeschichtlichen Entwicklung* (FzB, 59), Würzburg, 1988, und
C. NIEMAND, *Studien zu den Minor Agreements der synoptischen Verklärungsperikopen*
(Europäische Hochschulschriften, XXIII/352), Frankfurt/M - Bern - New York, 1988,
rechnen mit Deutero-Markus als Quelle für Mt und Lk. Bei der Annahme dieser
Quellenlage wird unsere Analyse in I teilweise fragwürdig, weil wir durch Rückfrage zu
den Quellen der beiden Großevangelien dann allenfalls auf Dt-Mk und nicht auf Mk
stoßen. Wir hätten also nur bedingte Möglichkeit der Verifikation. Andererseits erhalten
wir durch Ausklammerung redaktioneller Texte immer einen kürzeren Text als ihn Mk
bietet. Es zeigt sich auch in solchem Falle, daß Abschreiber nicht nur ergänzt, sondern
auch gekürzt haben.

VV. 23ff. verbunden, bevor 8,20-22 eingeschoben wurde. Aber auch V. 18 ist mt überarbeitet. Das zeigt das Wort προσκυνέω[10]. Dasselbe gilt für V. 24, da ἀναχωρέω mt ist[11]. Die Austreibung der Menge in V. 24 ist zudem unnötig. Sie steht zu V. 26 im Widerspruch, der von der Ausbreitung der Kunde berichtet. Aber auch V. 26 ist redaktionell gestaltet, wie 4,24 zeigt.

VV. 20-22 ist eine in sich geschlossene Einheit. Die Massierung der theologischen Sprache σώζω + πιστεύω in VV. 21b.22b fällt auf[12]. Die Betonung des Glaubens entspricht 15,28. Auch dort handelt es sich um eine Frau. Da Mt eine Vorliebe für Dialoge hat[13], ist denkbar, daß der Bericht seiner Tradition stärker erzählerisch geprägt war. Da nirgends eine Verzahnung der beiden Berichte miteinander sichtbar wird, kann diese Mt vorgegeben gewesen sein.

Es ergibt sich: Aus Mt läßt sich erschließen, daß seine Vorlage die Verzahnung der beiden Erzählungen deutlicher ausgesprochen haben kann, daß vielleicht mehr erzählt und weniger im Dialog gesprochen wurde, daß der Abschluß anders ausgesehen haben mag. Aber man würde aufgrund der Darstellung des Mt nicht ahnen, daß die mk Erzählung ein Schweigegebot hat, daß das Hinaustreiben der Menge bei Mk also begründet ist und daß die beiden Geschichten bei Mk zusammengehören müssen, weil Mk berichtet, daß die Tochter stirbt, während Jesus verzieht. Auch sahen wir V. 19 als einen Einschub des Mt an und nicht als eine Umprägung der Tradition, die davon sprach, daß viel Volk mit ihm ging (Mk 5,24), die Jünger mit ihm diskutierten (Mk 5,31), und er nur drei von ihnen mit ins Haus nahm (Mk 5,37). Sosehr die beiden Erzählungen bei Mt und Mk ähnlich sind, aufgrund von Mt kann man nicht Mk rekonstruieren, manches Detail bei Mk ist durch die Überarbeitung des Mt verlorengegangen und kann nicht erahnt werden.

1b. *Lk 8,40-56*

Die Verse 8,40-42 sind lukanisch geprägt. Daß Jesus von der Menge erwartet wird und einer aus dem Volk ihn wegen seines einzigen Kindes[14] anspricht, begegnet so noch Lk 9,37-38[15]. Ebenso ist 9,28 wie 8,51 von Petrus, Jakobus und Johannes die Rede. Die Angabe des

---

10. U. Luz, *Matthäus* (s. Anm. 6), I,49: 7 mal redaktionell.

11. *Ibid.*, I,37: 8 mal redaktionell.

12. H.J. Held, *Matthäus als Interpret der Wundergeschichten*, in G. Bornkamm – G. Barth – H.J. Held, *Überlieferung und Auslegung im Matthäusevangelium* (WMANT, 1), Neukirchen, ⁶1970, p. 169.

13. Vgl. bes. die Einfügungen in Mt 3,14-15; 14,28-31 und 15,12-14.

14. Μονογενής ist lk vgl. J. Jeremias, *Die Sprache des Lukasevangeliums* (KEK), Göttingen, 1980, p. 157.

15. Vgl. auch F. Bovon, *Das Evangelium nach Lukas* (EKK, III/1), Neukirchen, 1989, p. 443, Anm. 6.

Alters des Mädchens, 12 Jahre (V. 42), die keine Begründung hat, könnte aus V. 43 stammen. Da die Einleitung in V. 49a als lk angesehen werden kann[16], könnte die Verzahnung der beiden Berichte auf das Konto des Lk gehen, der den ursprünglichen Anfang der Erzählung von VV. 40ff. nach V. 49 zog. Dafür dürfte man das eigentümliche ἀπέθνῃσκεν in Anspruch nehmen, das V. 42 wie Jos ant 5,4 die Bedeutung von »ist im Begriff zu sterben« haben soll[17]. V. 49c wäre dann als lk Bildung anzusehen, in der 7,6 mit seinem κύριε μὴ σκύλλου aufgenommen ist.

Die Erzählung von der Frau 8,43-48 arbeitet mit dem Motiv von V. 42b: Jesus wird bedrängt. Der Leser empfindet die doppelte Rede Jesu, einmal als Frage (V. 45) und einmal als Feststellung (V. 46) als unnötig. V. 45 ist voll entbehrlich. Da er mit V. 42b zusammenhängt, möchte man ihn Lk zuschreiben. Aber es ist ebenso denkbar, daß Lk an dieser Stelle bloß dramatisiert hat, und das Motiv vom V. 42 aus der lk Vorlage stammt[18].

Παραχρῆμα in VV. 44.47.55 dürfte auf Lk zurückgehen[19]. Die Formel: »Dein Glaube hat dich gerettet; gehe hin in Frieden« in 8,48 stimmt mit der in 7,50 wörtlich überein und steht der in 17,19 sehr nahe. Der Verdacht, daß sie lk ist, liegt nahe. Die Beschreibung des Vorfalls im Hause VV. 51-52 ist unanschaulich. Jesus tritt ein und läßt niemanden nachkommen, redet aber mit der Menge und vollzieht das Wunder. Man wird sich die Sache so denken müssen: VV. 52-53 trägt nach, was vorher ausgelassen wurde. Dann hätte man sich den Vorgang so vorzustellen: Jesus tritt in das Haus ein und erlaubt nicht, daß die Klagenden mitkommen, mit denen er zuvor im Vorraum bzw. im Hof einen Wortwechsel hatte. Hier liegt demnach ein Bruch in der Erzählungsweise vor. Es wäre denkbar, daß VV. 52-53 eine lk Einfügung darstellt, die mit dem Schweigegebot V. 56b zusammenhängt. In V. 56 hat die Erzählung einen guten Abschluß.

Es ergibt sich somit, daß Lk diese beiden Erzählungen überarbeitet und miteinander verzahnt hat. Vergleichen wir allerdings das Ergebnis der Analyse mit Mk, dann stellen wir fest, daß wir neben treffenden Beobachtungen auch sehr weit von der Realität der Vorlage befindliche Schlüsse gezogen haben. Richtig erkannt wurde, daß παραχρῆμα und μονογενής lk Zusatzwörter sind. Ebenso wurde richtig gesehen, daß Lk VV. 45-46 von Lk zu einem doppelten Dialog ausgestaltet worden ist.

---

16. Ἔτι αὐτοῦ λαλοῦντος noch Apg. 10,44. Die Einleitung begegnet allerdings auch bei den anderen Evangelisten, sodaß sich lukanische Herkunft nicht nachweisen läßt; Mk 5,35; 14,43; Mt 12,46; 17,5. Vgl. noch ταῦτα αὐτοῦ λαλοῦντος Mt 9,18; Joh 8,30, sowie ταῦτα αὐτοῦ λέγοντος Lk 9,34.

17. W. BAUER, Wörterbuch zum Neuen Testament s.v.

18. Lk umgeht oft die direkte Rede. Bildung neuer Dialoge: 11,45; 20,16b.

19. J. JEREMIAS, Sprache (s. Anm. 14), p. 70.

Falsch war aber die Annahme, daß die Formel: »Dein Glaube hat dir
geholfen; gehe hin in Frieden« (8,48) in diesem Falle auf Lk zurückgeht. Lk hat hier, wie Mk 5,34 zeigt, nur ein einziges Wort geändert,
aus dem ὕπαγε wurde ein πορεύου. Falsch ist ebenso die Annahme, daß
erst Lk die beiden Geschichten miteinander verzahnt hat und daß er für
das Schweigegebot verantwortlich zeichnet. Der Bruch in der Erzähl-
weise, den wir in VV. 51-54 erkannten, geht auch nicht auf eine
Einfügung in VV. 52-53 durch Lk zurück, sondern auf eine Kürzung
der Vorlage, wie Mk zeigt.

2a. *Mt 19,13-15*

Der Bericht von der Kindersegnung ist in sich geschlossen. Über-
schießend ist in V. 13 neben der Handauflegung das Beten genannt, das
V. 15 fehlt. V. 15 leitet schon zum nächsten Abschnitt über. Der Bericht
dürfte mit der Segnung der Kinder geschlossen haben, möglicherweise
war in der Vorlage auch vom Gebet am Ende die Rede. Andernfalls ist
es in V. 13 Zusatz des Mt. Von Mt her würde man nicht ahnen, daß
Mk in 10,15 eine zweite Begründung der Kindersegnung neben 10,14 =
Mt 19,14 bringt. Man kann nur erkennen, daß in V. 13 das Beten
hinzugesetzt, oder in V. 15 ausgelassen ist. Wir registrieren aber hier
schon, daß Mt genau dort verkürzend eingreift, wo die Forschung für
Mk einen Zusatz annimmt[20].

2b. *Lk 18,15-17*

Der Abschnitt kulminiert in dem zweiten, mit ἀμήν eingeleiteten
Wort. Ἔρχομαι ist im Verhältnis zu den βρέφη von V. 15 schwierig:
Säuglinge können selbst nicht kommen. Darum wird man fragen, ob
Lk nicht seine Quelle abänderte, die von παιδία wie V. 16 sprach, von
Kindern, die man rufen kann, und die dem Rufe Folge leisten können.
Hat man auf diese Weise bei einem Vergleich mit Mk die Vorlage
richtig erschlossen, so ahnt man aufgrund des Lk-Textes nicht, daß die
Vorlage = Mk die Segnung berichtet hat (Mk 10,16). Zum Vergleich:
Mir ist niemand bekannt, der angenommen hätte, Mk 3,23ff., die
Perikope vom Ährenausraufen, habe in einem Stadium der Tradition
mit dem Vermerk geschlossen: »Und er (sc. Jesus) nahm selbst von den
Ähren und aß vor ihnen«. Ich möchte damit nicht sagen, daß ein
solcher Vorschlag zur Rekonstruktion von Mk 3,23ff. sinnvoll wäre,
wiewohl 3,26 von dem Essen Davids und seiner Freunde, nicht nur der
Freunde allein die Rede ist. Aber es wird an dieser Stelle deutlich, daß
Auslassungen durch die Evangelisten kaum oder nicht erschlossen
werden können.

---

20. Vgl. die Analysen von R. PESCH, *Markusevangelium* (s. Anm. 3), p. 133 sowie
J. GNILKA, *Das Evangelium nach Markus* (EKK, II/2), Neukirchen, 1979, p. 180.

Aus diesen Analysen glaube ich folgendes schließen zu müssen:
- Durch Subtraktion, d.h. durch Eliminierung von Zusätzen, kann man die Vorlagen der Evangelisten nur bedingt erschließen. Was die Evangelisten selbst eliminierten, kann kaum nachempfunden werden.
- Wendungen, die ganz nach Prägungen des jeweiligen Evangelisten aussehen, können durchaus Ahhalt am Text der Vorlage haben. Beispielhaft ist das an der Formel: »Dein Glaube hat dir geholfen; gehe hin in Frieden« deutlich geworden.
- Die Feststellung, daß an einer bestimmten Stelle Stil und Sprache eines Evangelisten auftreten, erlaubt noch nicht ein Urteil darüber, ob diese Stelle eine Neuschöpfung oder bloße Umformulierung ist.
- Wir können allerdings mithilfe unserer Analysen ein einigermaßen festes Minimum, ein Erzählgerüst »herausdestilieren«. Die Frage bleibt, wie dieses Minimum ausgestaltet war.
- Mt hat Mk 10,15, Lk Mk 10,16 ausgelassen. Beide Evangelisten haben die Erzählung von Jairus' Tochter und der blutflüssigen Frau gekürzt. Beides zusammengenommen zeigt, daß unsere Suche nach einem festen Kern durch Reduktion, durch Eliminierung von Zusätzen, eine späte Tugend ist, eine Erscheinung, die die Tendenzen des Umgangs mit schriftlichen Vorlagen, wie sie Mt und Lk in Mk fanden, fortführt. Durch unsere Analysen kommen wir also den Grundlagen der Evangelisten nicht näher, wir entfernen uns von ihnen, indem wir wie Mt und Lk reduzieren.

II

Vergleichen wir nun Mk mit den beiden Seitenreferenten und achten auf die vielen und verschiedenartigen Veränderungen derselben am Mk-Text, die wir hier nur sehr summarisch wiedergeben können, dann ergibt sich:
- Beide Evangelisten haben relativ oft gekürzt. Sie reduzieren die berichtenden Texte auf das ihnen Wesentliche. Bei Mt ist das weit häufiger als bei Lk geschehen[21].
- Beide Evangelisten haben Umstellungen von Perikopen und von Versen vorgenommen. Bei Mt ist dies schon durch die Bildung der beiden großen Komplexe Mt 5-7 und 8-9 deutlich. Lk ist sehr viel sorgfältiger mit dem Mk-Stoff verfahren, aber es gibt auch bei ihm Beispiele von Textversetzungen[22].
- Beide Evangelisten nehmen formelhafte Wendungen ihrer Tradition auf und wiederholen sie[23].

21. Zu den Kürzungen des Mt vgl. H.J. HELD, *Matthäus* (s. Anm. 12), pp. 158-182.
22. Vorgezogen wurden: 3,19-20; (4,22-24); 5,10-11; 10,25-28. Nachgestellt wurden: 6,17-19; 8,19-21.
23. Wiederholungen bei Mt: 8,13 15,28; 10,6 15,24; u.ö.; s. dazu meine Studie,

- Beide Evangelisten formulieren Einleitungen zu Abschnitten mit eigenen Worten. Oftmals setzen sie aber entsprechende Einleitungen bei Mk voraus[24].
- Beide Evangelisten können neue Abschlüsse von Perikopen bilden, auch dadurch, daß feststehende Traditionen anschließen[25].
- Beide Evangelisten kombinieren verwandte Texte[26].

Übertragen wir diese Erkenntnisse auf Mk, so müßten wir – vorausgesetzt, er habe schriftliche Vorlagen gehabt – annehmen, daß er Erzählungen raffte, auf jeden Fall aber sprachlich neu gestaltete, Perikopen umstellte bzw. neu ordnete, Wendungen seiner Tradition wiederholte, Einleitungen und Abschlüsse selbst gestaltete, wobei er sich aber der Tradition bediente, Verwandte Texte oder Varianten miteinander verband. Die Frage, ob Mk aber nicht stärker als Mt und Lk von der mündlichen Überlieferung geprägt war, muß uns noch beschäftigen. Sie hängt damit zusammen, ob sich entsprechende Indizien aufzeigen lassen, die gegen eine Annahme schriftlicher Vorlagen sprechen.

III

Für die Rückfrage nach den Quellen des Mk läßt sich aus dem bisher Gesagten folgendes schließen:
1. Die Möglichkeit, daß Mk Erzählungen kürzte oder raffte ist von Fall zu Fall neu zu prüfen. Läßt sich mk Stil oder mk Kompositionstechnik herausstellen, ist dies ein Merkmal dafür, daß Mk an dieser Stelle selbst gestaltet hat. Das haben die beiden Seitenreferenten ebenso getan. Raffung oder Kürzung von Texten kann freilich nur dort angenommen werden, wo Brüche im Text registriert werden. Sie sollten behutsam diskutiert werden. Nicht überall, wo sich Unebenheiten finden lassen, ist mit Interpolationen zu rechnen, es kommen auch Neuformulierungen und Neuakzentuierungen durch Kürzung oder Umschreibung in Frage.
2. Wie Mt und Lk hat auch Mk Einleitungen selbst gestaltet. Es ist aber damit zu rechnen, daß er dabei wie Mt und Lk auf Wendungen

---

Bewährung im Glauben. Studien zum Sondergut des Evangelisten Matthäus (BTSt, 20), Neukirchen, 1992, II,4. Wiederholungen bei Lk: 5,30 15,2 19,7; 7,50 8,48 17.19; 5,31 15,7.10; 10,25 18,17 u.ö. Lk bevorzugt bei Wiederholungen die Variation, während die bei Mt öfter stereotyp sind.

24. Einleitungen mit Anhalt am Mk-Text s. Anm. 31; ohne Anhalt an der Parallele im Mk-Stoff s. Anm. 32.

25. Lk 5,39; 12,18 (Zitat); Mt 19,11-12.

26. Mt 4,1-11; 12,22-30; 13,31-32; Lk 4,1-13; 5,1-11. Die Art der Kombination ist verschieden.

der Tradition zurückgreift. Die seit K.L. Schmidt[27] nahezu selbstverständliche Annahme, daß der Rahmen der Perikopen sekundär sei, ist sehr problematisch. Gerade dort wo etwa Ortsangaben theologisch nichts austragen, muß mit einer bestimmten Tradition gerechnet werden. Im Bereich mündlicher Erzählungen werden Berichte gerne mit Ortsangaben begonnen, die mit dem Ereignis selbst innerlich nicht zusammenhängen. So wird man sich z.B. fragen, ob die Angabe, daß Jesus am Meer predigt (Mk 4,1-2), die mit dem folgenden Gleichnis nichts gemein hat, aber in 2,13 eine Vorbereitung findet, nicht Mk vorgegeben war, ganz unabhängig, ob sie mit dem Gleichnis verbunden war oder nicht. Hier hätten wir auch ein Indiz nachwirkender mündlicher Überlieferung, auch für den Fall, daß Mk 4 dem Evangelisten bereits schriftlich vorgelegen haben sollte.

3. Wiederholungen wie die Notiz, daß Jesus am See predigt, die Leidensweissagungen oder die Aussage, daß Gott alle Dinge möglich sind (Mk 10,27; 14,36 vgl. 9,23) können auf Mk zurückgehen, wobei man vermuten wird, daß sie an einer Stelle in der Tradition verankert waren.

4. Die von E. Lohmeyer[28] vertretene These, daß Mk Varianten derselben Perikope zusammengearbeitet hat, ist angesichts der Tatsache, daß sich diese Methode bei Mt und Lk nachweisen läßt, neu zu bedenken.

5. Da Mt und Lk ihre schriftliche Vorlage, d.h. Mk, oftmals kürzen, muß damit gerechnet werden, daß Mk der mündlichen Überlieferung näher stand als diese. Texte wie Mk 5,1-20.21-43; 11,1-10; 12,1-9 tragen Merkmale von Erzählfreude. Umgekehrt scheint ein Text wie Mk 2,1-12 dadurch, daß er in VV. 6-10 eine Einfügung besitzt, oder einer wie Mk 2,23-28, der am Ende zwei Logien hat, die einen Abschluß bilden können, schon schriftlich bearbeitet.

6. Von den Beobachtungen über den Umgang des Mt und des Lk mit Mk läßt sich allenfalls dort von Mk auf seine Quellen zurückschließen, wo wir schriftliche Vorlagen annehmen. Dort, wo man mündliche Überlieferung annehmen muß, ist diese Methode kaum zu gebrauchen.

An einem konkreten Beispiel soll nun gezeigt werden, inwiefern diese Methode anwendbar ist.

IV

Wir wählen als Beispiel zur Verifikation der obigen grundsätzlichen Erwägungen zur Methode der Rückfrage nach den Quellen des Mk den

27. K.L. SCHMIDT, *Der Rahmen der Geschichte Jesu. Literarkritische Untersuchungen zur ältesten Jesusüberlieferung*, Berlin, 1919.
28. E. LOHMEYER, *Das Evangelium des Markus* (KEK), Göttingen, [14]1959, pp. 44, 130-131, übernommen von W. GRUNDMANN, *Das Evangelium nach Markus* (THK, 2), Berlin, [5]1971, p. 50.

Text Mk 2,13-17 und referieren zunächst die m.E in dem Umgang mit den Methoden vorbildliche und repräsentative Analyse von D.-A. Koch[29], die nicht nur literarische, sondern auch theologische Argumente zur Begründung der Quellenrekonstruktion heranzieht. Koch stellt heraus: Mk 2,13 ist mk Einleitung; Mk 2,14 stellt eine eigenständige Tradition dar; Mk 2,15-17a ist ebenfalls eine selbständige Überlieferung, die aber einen Prozeß der Ausgestaltung erfahren hat; Mk 2,17b finden wir ein an 2,15-17a angehängtes eigenständiges Logion, das von Mk, möglicherweise aber schon auf einer Vorstufe, als V. 14 hinzukam, mit diesem VV. 15-17b kranzformartig umschloß.

In Mk 2,15-17a gehen auf Mk zurück:
- die etwas merkwürdige Ortsbestimmung ἐν τῇ οἰκίᾳ αὐτοῦ, die offen läßt, ob es sich um das Haus des Levi oder das Jesu handelt. Levi kann schwerlich in sein eigenes Haus »nachfolgen«.
- der Nachtrag in 15c ἦσαν γὰρ πολλοί κτλ., der die Verbindung von V. 14 mit VV. 15-17 vertieft, besonders durch das hier und dort auftretende Verb ἀκολουθέω.
- die im Hinblick auf V. 16b redundierende Aussage in V. 16a ἰδόντες κτλ.

Folgende dieser Elemente von Traditionsveränderung lassen sich bei Mt und Lk im Verhältnis zu Mk belegen:
1. Sowohl Mt als auch Lk bilden im Mk-Stoff neue Einleitungen mit Ortsangaben[30]. Beide bilden aber auch neue Einleitungen, wobei sie Material von Mk-Einleitungen verwenden, das sie an der entsprechenden Stelle auslassen[31]. Das bedeutet für Mk 2,13, daß diese Einleitung, die mk Stileigentümlichkeiten enthält, sowohl von Mk gebildet, als auch nur von ihm gestaltet worden sein kann. Eine entsprechende Angabe kann vor Mk auch mit einer anderen Tradition verbunden gewesen sein, wie Mt 5,1-2 und Lk 5,1-3 zeigen, die ihr Material Mk entlehnen, aber an anderer Stelle anbringen. Mk 4,1-2 zeigt neben 2,13, daß es für Mk selbstverständlich ist, daß Jesus am See lehrt.
2. Eine Mk 2,13-17 vergleichbare Tradition, in der eine eigene Einleitung einer Tradition vorangestellt wird, die ihrerseits eine selbständige Überlieferung in sich birgt, finden wir noch Mt 4,12-17. Dort haben wir eine Mk entlehnte Einleitung 4,12, eine eigene Ortsbestimmung in

---

29. D.-A. KOCH, *Jesu Tischgemeinschaft mit den Zöllnern und Sündern. Erwägungen zur Entstehung von Mk 2,13-17*, in D.-A. KOCH – G. SELLIN – A. LINDEMANN (Hg.), *Jesu Rede von Gott und ihre Nachgeschichte im frühen Christentum. Beiträge zur Verkündigung Jesu und zum Kerygma der Kirche. FS W. Marxsen*, Gütersloh, 1989, pp. 57-83.

30. Vgl. Mt 8,2 mit Mk 1,40; Lk 3,1 mit Mk 1,1-2; Lk 3,15 mit Mk 1,7; Lk 19,28 mit Mk 11,1.

31. Vgl. Mt 5,1 mit Mk 3,13; Lk 5,1-3 mit Mk 4,1-2 an beiden Parallelabschnitten des Mk wird die entsprechende Notiz nicht gebracht.

Galiläa wie Mk 2,13b, gefolgt von einem Zitat aus dem AT (Mt 4,13-16 – an sich eine selbständige Tradition) und anschließendem Mk-Text mit neuer Überleitung (ἀπὸ τότε V. 17 vgl. Mk 2,15 καὶ γίνεται). Das hieße: Mt 4,12 ist Mk 2,13 vergleichbar; 4,13-16 Mk 2,14 und 4,17 Mk 2,15ff. Schon viel weiter liegen die beiden noch vergleichbaren Texte Lk 5,1ff. und 4,16ff. Lk 5,1-3 enthält eine lk Einleitung, es folgt eine selbständige Tradition (5,4-9) mit einem Nachtrag aus Mk (5,10-11). Lk 4,16ff. wird nach einer Einleitung mit Ortsangabe (4,16-17) ein Zitat eingebracht (selbständige Tradition) und im Anschluß daran Mk 6,1-6 verwertet, wobei aber die Mk-Tradition völlig verbraucht ist, da sich nur noch Anklänge daran finden (Vv. 22.24). Eine Kombination von zwei geschlossenen selbständigen Traditionen, wie wir sie Mk 2,14 und 2,15-17 vorfinden, gibt es bei Mt und Lk im Mk-Stoff nicht (mehr?). Kombinierte Traditionen bei Mt einerseits und bei Lk andererseits schauen sehr anders aus[32]. Von Mt und Lk her läßt sich also eine mk Bildung wie sie 2,13-17 anzutreffen ist, nicht belegen, wodurch an eine mk Einleitung eine selbständige Tradition (V. 14) angeschlossen wird, gefolgt von einer nächsten[33]. Aber das hatte D.-A. Koch auch nicht vermutet. Er meinte, daß V. 14 mit V. 17b schon vor Mk an die Tradition 2,15-17a angeschlossen wurden. An dieser Stelle wird man also Koch Recht geben müssen. V. 14 wird schon vor Mk mit 2,15ff. zusammengeschlossen gewesen sein.

3. Abschlüsse mit festgeprägten selbständigen Logien lassen sich nur selten im Mk-Stoff der beiden Seitenreferenten nachweisen[34]. Die These, daß Mk 2,17b schon auf vorliterarischer Stufe zu 2,15-17a stieß, trägt dieser Beobachtung Rechnung. Dasselbe gilt für die Annahme Mk 2,14 und 2,17b seien kranzförmig hinzugekommen. Solches läßt sich im Sondergut des Lk 12,13-21 und 18,9-14 mit Vorbehalt aufzeigen.

Nicht belegen von der Bearbeitung des Mk durch Mt und Lk lassen sich die drei von Koch als mk betrachteten Einfügungen. Sie müssen nun durchgesprochen werden:

1. Sosehr sich Einfügungen durch Mt (12,5-7.11-12; 13,12) und Lk (8,16b; 20,18) aufzeigen lassen, haben sie nie redundierenden Charakter wie Mk 2,16a ἰδόντες κτλ. Zwar gibt es auch bei Mt (5,17; 10,34) und bei Lk (7,19-20) Wiederholungen von Aussagen, aber sie sind anders geartet. Allenfalls kann man auf Mt 4,13 hinweisen, wo der Text auf das folgende Zitat hin gestaltet ist. Fallen somit die Belege bei den Seitenreferenten aus, so läßt sich umso klarer zeigen, daß Mk selbst diese Art der Darstellung pflegt. Noch an weiteren drei Stellen be-

---

32. Vgl. Mt 22,1-14; Lk 12,13-21.
33. Dies spricht gegen die Annahme R. PESCH, *Markusevangelium* (s. Anm. 3), I, p. 162, Mk 2,14 sei eine redaktionelle Szene.
34. S. Anm. 25.

schreibt er erzählend einen Sachverhalt, der anschließend in direkter Rede aufgenommen wird (2,18a; 10,32; 14,35b). Es handelt sich also um ein mk Stilmerkmal. Bedenkt man, daß Redundanz ein Stilmittel mündlicher Rede ist, verwundert es nicht zu sehen, daß Mt und Lk an allen vier Stellen diese Redundanz gestrichen haben. Damit wird deutlich, daß Mk der mündlichen Tradition zumindest hierin näher gestanden hat als seine beiden Seitenreferenten.

2. Auch für den Nachtrag ἦσαν γὰρ πολλοί κτλ. gibt es keine wirklichen Parallelen. Man kann zwar auf Lk 8,40 hinweisen, wo ein Nachtrag auch mit ἦσαν γάρ beginnt, aber ἦσαν ist Teil einer umschreibenden Konjugation, es folgt kein Zahlwort. Hingegen läßt sich die Wendung ἦσαν γὰρ … πολλοί noch Mk 6,31 belegen, ἦσαν γάρ mit Zahlwort noch 6,44 und 8,9, mit Substantiv noch 1,16 vgl 5,42. Ohne diese Wendung erfolgen Nachträge noch 4,38a und 11,32b. Bedenkt man die Tatsache, daß die meisten dieser Nachträge von Mt und Lk übergangen oder in den Text neu eingebaut wurden, dann wird man auch an dieser Stelle Mk der mündlichen Überlieferung näher sehen, der seinen Text noch nicht ganz durchgestaltet und darum mit Nachträgen arbeiten muß[35].

3. Auch betreffend die kurze Angabe ἐν τῇ οἰκίᾳ αὐτοῦ läßt sich keine vergleichbare Spezifizierung bei Mt und Lk im Mk-Stoff finden. Mt und Lk verzichten des Öfteren auf Ortsangaben des Mk oder versetzen sie[36]. Diese Ortsangabe ist aber notwendig, weil ein Gastmahl in einem Haus stattfindet. Man wird darum an dieser Stelle auch nicht Redaktion, sondern Tradition vermuten. Dann muß aber der Widerspruch zwischen »Nachfolge« (V. 14) und »seinem Haus« (V. 15), in dem Sinne, daß man nicht in sein eigenes Haus »nachfolgen« kann, anders gelöst werden. Bevor wir eine Lösung suchen, muß kurz ein Blick auf die Bearbeitung unserer Perikope durch Mt und Lk geworfen werden, da sich von hier aus einiges klären läßt.

Vergleicht man, wie Mt und Lk jeweils verschieden Mk 2,13-17 aufgenommen haben, so zeigt sich, daß Mt und Lk je einen Teil, zusammen aber alle Besonderheiten unseres Textes, die D.-A. Koch zu einer Rekonstruktion veranlaßten, gesehen haben. Wir gehen die Stellen durch: Mk 2,13 wird von Mt ganz weggelassen, Lk reduziert die Einleitung auf vier Worte, von denen nur zwei aus Mk stammen[37]. Mk

---

35. Vgl. den Nachtrag des Paulus 1Kor 1,16, der offensichtlich einem Diktat zu verdanken ist.

36. Vgl. bes. die ausgelassene Wendung betreffend das »Haus« in Mk 2,1 parr. und Mk 3,20 par. Sprechend ist auch der Umgang mit der Erwähnung von Bethsaida in Mk 6,45: bei Mt ist sie ausgelassen, bei Lk nach 9,10 versetzt. Mit der Ortsangabe Mk 9,33 verhält es sich umgekehrt: Lk hat sie ausgelassen und Mt nach 17,25-26 versetzt.

37. Καὶ ἐξῆλθον. Aber 5,17 ist ἦν διδάσκων aus Mk 2,13 vorgezogen.

2,15a wird die Wendung ἐν τῇ οἰκίᾳ αὐτοῦ in Mt 9,10 zu ἐν τῇ οἰκίᾳ verkürzt, gemeint ist jetzt wohl das Haus Jesu[38], bei Lk ist es das Haus des Levi. Was bei Mk unklar war, haben die beiden Seitenreferenten zu klären versucht. Mk 2,15c wird von Mt und Lk gestrichen. Mk 2,16a fehlt bei Mt und Lk. Mk 2,17b wird durch Mt von 2,17a durch einen Einschub (Mt 9,13a) getrennt. Mt erkennt also, daß die beiden Halbverse nicht genau aufeinander abgestimmt sind.

Es zeigt sich somit an der Art, wie die beiden Evangelisten Mk bearbeitet haben, daß sie die Brüche im Text auch empfanden, die D.-A. Kochs Analyse prägt. Zwar sah nicht jeder der Evangelisten alle Schwierigkeiten, beide zusammen aber haben alle erkannt. Daraus läßt sich aber noch nicht mit Sicherheit schließen, daß Kochs Analyse zutrifft. Man wird zumindest aus der Tatsache, daß Mt und Lk dieselben Schwierigkeiten mit dem Mk-Text hatten, folgern dürfen, daß Koch in der Reihe derer steht, die einen schriftlichen Text betrachten, wo Mk zumindest auch noch von mündlicher Überlieferung geprägt ist, wie die redundierende Erklärung V. 16a* zeigt. Dies schließt ein, daß wir durch Streichung keinen älteren Text, sondern einen gegenüber Mt und Lk noch jüngeren erhalten.

Die Schwierigkeit des Textes scheint mir mit dem Wort ἀκολουθέω verbunden zu sein. Einerseits ergibt es wenig Sinn, wenn Levi »in das Haus« V. 15 nachfolgt, andererseits klappt die Bemerkung V. 15c: »und sie folgten ihm nach« sichtlich nach. So kann man an dieser Stelle das theologische Interesse des Mk entdecken, der betonen will, daß Jesus mit »nachfolgenden« Zöllnern und Sündern (2,15) zusammensitzt. Ist dies richtig erkannt, dann ließe sich fragen, ob Mk 2,14 nicht nach 1,17-18, im Sinne einer Wiederholung neu formuliert hat. Solche Arbeitsweise läßt sich bei Mt und Lk belegen[39]. Dann wäre zu vermuten, daß der Bruch zwischen V. 14 und V. 15 nicht durch eine Kombination zweier selbständiger Traditionen entstanden ist, eine Technik, die wir so bei Mt und Lk nicht belegen konnten[40], sondern daß er durch eine Umformulierung von V. 14 als Angleichung an 1,17-18 im Sinne einer Wiederholung entstand. Dann hätte Mk aber das Erzählgerüst verän-

---

38. Mt hat αὐτοῦ gestrichen. Damit ist die Frage offen, ob es sich um das Haus des Levi, des Simon oder des Jesu handelt. So W. GRUNDMANN, *Das Evangelium nach Matthäus* (THK, 1), Berlin, 1968, p. 270. Sinnvoll erscheint mir die Streichung allerdings nur, wenn Mt vermeiden wollte, daß das Haus des Levi gemeint ist. Das Haus des Simon ist nicht im Blick. Dort hat sich Jesus nach Mt nur kurz ausgehalten. Bleibt also nur die Annahme, daß Mt auf 4,13 sieht, wonach Jesus nach Kapernaum übersiedelt. 17,24 ist vorausgesetzt, daß er dort ein Haus hat, weil die Tempelsteuer am Wohnort abverlangt wurde. Vgl. A. SCHLATTER, *Der Evangelist Matthäus. Seine Sprache, sein Ziel und seine Selbständigkeit. Ein Kommentar zum ersten Evangelium*, Stuttgart, 1929, p. 538.

39. Vgl. Anm. 23 sowie die Übernahme von Mt 8,22 in 9,19, die I,1a begegnet war pp. 505-506.

40. S.o. IV,2 sowie Anm. 33.

dert, indem er 2,14 zur selbständigen Tradition umprägte. An dieser Stelle wird die Grenze unserer Frage nach den Vorlagen des Mk besonders deutlich[41].

V

Der Versuch, die Methode zu verifizieren, mit der wir hinter Mk nach seinen Quellen zurückfragen, hat nur teilweise zu einem befriedigenden Ergebnis geführt.

Es konnte zwar gezeigt werden, daß die Rekonstruktion der Quellen der Großevangelien durch Eliminierung von Zusätzen der Evangelisten nicht die Quelle selbst, sondern allenfalls feste Bausteine derselben oder das Erzählgerüst[42] »herausdestillieren« kann, daß aber das, was die Evangelisten selber übergangen oder gestrichen haben, kaum erahnt, geschweige denn mit einiger Wahrscheinlichkeit ausgesagt werden kann. Diese kritische Verifikation ist durchaus brauchbar. Darum wird es sinnvoll sein, wenn man genauer hinsieht, wie Mt und Lk mit dem Mk-Stoff umgegangen sind, um ermessen zu können, wie Mk seinerseits seinen Stoff behandelt hat[43].

Es wurde aber auch deutlich, daß Mk noch von der mündlichen Überlieferung geprägt ist. Dafür spricht nicht nur die Erzählfreude, die

41. Weitere Aussagen über die Vorlage des Mk sind darum ganz hypothetisch. Will man allerdings in dieser Richtung weitergehen, dann kann man davon ausgehen, was nach der Streichung von ἀκολουθέω in V. 14 bleibt: Jesus spricht Levi an, und dieser reagiert. Er nimmt ihn in sein (!) Haus zusammen mit Zöllnern und Sündern (gemeint sind seine Bekannten) auf (V. 15). Eine entsprechende Rekonstruktion der Vorlage nähert freilich 2,13-17 der Zachäusgeschichte Lk 19,1-10 an.

42. Lk 4,42-43 übernimmt das Erzählgerüst von Mk 1,35-38. Aber der Abschnitt wird sosehr umformuliert, daß nur vier Worte aus Mk erhalten bleiben. Das ist ein krasses Beispiel von Vorlagen-Veränderung.

43. Dies gilt in erhöhtem Maße für die Rekonstruktion der Vorlage des Mt und des Lk, weil wir deren Arbeitsweise an ihrem Umgang mit Mk studieren können. Daraus lassen sich relativ sichere Urteile über die Wahrscheinlichkeit unserer Rekonstruktionen treffen. Ich möchte das an einem Beispiel illustrieren: Die kontroverse Frage, ob Lk 16,16 seinen ursprünglichen Platz in Q bewahrt hat oder Mt in 11,12-13, läßt sich entscheiden: Lk hat niemals einen Text entfernt, um ihn anderswo einzubringen, wie gleichzeitigem Ersatz desselben durch einen anderen, wie er Lk 7,29-30 zu finden ist. Wenn er einen Text wegläßt, bleibt dort gewöhnlich eine Lücke. Am nächsten käme unsere Prüfstelle Mk 13,10. Der Text wird in Apg 1,7-8 verwendet. Lk 21,13-14 ist die Lücke geblieben. Im Zitat Lk 4,18-19 entfernt er Jes 61,1d LXX und setzt die diesem Stichon sehr nahe stehende Aussage aus 58,6 ein, aber nicht an jene Stelle, sondern an eine später folgende. Lk 20,18 hat er zwar an die Stelle des zweiten Teiles des Zitates = Mk 12,11 eine Sentenz, aber erstens wird das Zitat nicht anderswohin versetzt, wie für Lk 16,16 angenommen und zweitens hat die Sentenz überhaupt keine Beziehung zum Zitat. Umgekehrt hat Mt bei Eliminierung von Mk 2,27 die Einfügung Mt 12,5-7 eingebracht, dasselbe gilt wohl auch für den Ersatz von Mk 4,26-29 durch Mt 13,24-30. Die Wahrscheinlichkeit also, daß Mt den Vers nach 11,12-13 zog, ist groß. Fazit: Die Versetzung von Lk 16,16 nach Mt 11,12-13 ist wahrscheinlich zu machen, der umgekehrte Weg nicht.

an einigen Stellen begegnet, sondern ebenso das Festhalten an theologisch wertlosen Ortsangaben und der Gebrauch des Stilmittels der Redundanz, das Mt und Lk gleicherweise eliminieren. Da Mk also allenfalls an einigen Stellen schriftliche Vorlagen hatte und in der Tradition mündlicher Überlieferung lebt, wo auch Nachträge üblich sind, kann man schwerlich durch Beobachtungen am Umgang des Mt und des Lk mit dem Mk-Stoff direkt auf die Arbeitsweise des zweiten Evangelisten rückschließen.

Dies bedeutet, daß die Hoffnung, wir könnten sichere Aussagen über mk Vorlagen machen, geringer geworden ist. Man wird darum gut tun, auf den vorhandenen Mk-Text genauer zu achten, und nur dort Rückfragen anbringen, wo man mit dem vorliegenden Text nicht zurechkommt[44]. Aber auch in diesem Falle sollte man sich des hypothetischen Charakters einer Rekonstruktion bewußt bleiben. Die Sicherheit darüber wächst nicht damit, daß viele Theologen eine Hypothese mittragen, ein solches Phänomen zeigt nur an, daß heutige Menschen ähnlich denken und in ähnlicher Weise an den Text herangehen. Darum wird die Frage nach den Quellen des Mk nie aufhören, einmal weil die Ergebnisse der Forscher, die hypothetisch bleiben, immer neu hinterfragt werden müssen, und dann, weil die Texte selber eine Rückfrage nahelegen, zumindest dort, wo Unebenheiten festgestellt werden, aber ebenso dort, wo nach dem Jesus gefragt wird, von dem die Evangelien berichten.

Str. Magheru 4   Hans KLEIN
RO-2400 Subiu
Romania

---

44. Dies hat C. Breytenbach in seinem Seminar-Beitrag zu Mk 9,9-13 vorbildlich getan.

THE PUBLICATION OF MARK'S GOSPEL

In this paper, as originally delivered at the Colloquium, I described the significance of E. Randolph Richards' discovery that a professional standard of Greek Shorthand was a regular facility of the public life of government circles in the Rome of Peter and Paul[1]; and I concluded that the Gospel according to Mark shows every sign of being the transcript of Discourses of Peter taken down in Greek shorthand while being delivered. As it was a summary of a fuller presentation that appeared in the Neirynck Festschrift[2], I now beg the indulgence of the reader if I refer him to this article, so that I may have time and space to record here the third essential element of my argument, namely the informations provided by Irenaeus, Clement Alex. and Eusebius that support my hypothesis[3]. This argument may be summed up in the following propositions[4]:

1. The Fathers are unanimous that Peter's disciple Mark was the agent for its publication and not its author. He is always referred to as the ἑρμηνευτής, the go-between, the recorder, for he himself was never a witness of the events described in the Gospel (cf. the Presbyter's assertion, Eus., *EH*, III.39.15).

2. Justin Martyr, writing before A.D. 160, describes the Gospel of Mark as the ἀπομνημονεύματα of Peter (*Dial. Tryph.*, 106,9-10).

3. As Chapman pointed out long ago, and Harnack confirmed[5], Irenaeus is not concerned with the dating of the Gospels in the well-known passage in *Adv. Haer.*, III,1.1, but only with their authenticity. Hence Irenaeus first points out that Mt was written in the Jewish homeland "while Peter and Paul were in Rome evangelizing and founding the Church". Secondly, Irenaeus points out that although Mark was only Peter's disciple and ἑρμηνευτής (and so not an eye

---

1. E.R. RICHARDS, *The Secretary in the Letters of Paul* (WUNT, 2/42), Tübingen, 1991, pp. 26-43.
2. B. ORCHARD, *Mark and the Fusion of Traditions*, in *The Four Gospels 1992. Festschrift Frans Neirynck* (BETL, 100), Leuven, 1992, pp. 779-800.
3. The reader is referred to the Tables of Patristic witnesses (original text and English translation) in my *Mark and the Fusion of Traditions* (n. 2), pp. 789-794.
4. In this Paper "Mk" refers to the Gospel itself and "Mark" to the disciple of Peter. The reader should note that I allow for a pre-70 date for all three Synoptic Gospels despite the current consensus against it, because if my thesis about the use of shorthand is correct then Mk must have been composed before A.D. 64, and Mt and Lk must also have been in existence.
5. J. CHAPMAN, *St Irenaeus and the Dates of the Gospels*, in *JTS* 6 (1904-05), pp. 563-569; A. VON HARNACK, *The Date of Acts and the Synoptic Gospels*, ET, London, 1911, p. 130.

witness) the Gospel according to Mark faithfully presents the teaching that Peter uttered during his lifetime (see also 4. below). And thirdly, he points out that the Gospel according to Luke is equally authentic because it represents the teaching of Paul when he was in Rome evangelizing and founding the Church along with Peter.

4. Eusebius quotes Clement Alex. as authoritative in explaining that in order to save Peter's spoken Discourses from being forgotten and lost for ever, his audience, which included rich *Equites* from the Praetorium (Clem. in 1 Pet. 5), repeatedly demanded to be allowed access to the text, "the actual record of what Peter had delivered orally"; and that Peter after much persuasion agreed to let them have it; and that "to Mark fell the responsibility of making the written Gospel" available (*EH*, II.15).

5. The three reports of Eusebius on the origins of Mk (*EH*, II.15; III.39.15; VI.14.5-7) only make complete sense on the assumption that Peter's audience knew that a shorthand recording had been made. Mark's handing over of the text in its original state (*EH*, II.15.2) could only have happened because Mark, in fulfilment of his role as ἑρμηνευτής, had actually arranged for the Discourses to be recorded, a fact known to the audience through seeing the shorthand writers seated near the rostrum. This knowledge was the grounds for their persistence in demanding to be given "the text as delivered". On the other hand, Peter's reluctance to hand it over was due to the fact of it being the *spoken* text just as he had delivered it, and so unfit to be published in book form without careful editing to remove redundancies, repetitions etc.

6. In the next excerpt (*EH*, III.39.15) Eusebius adds certain circumstantial details about Mk which both confirm its authenticity and accuracy and at the same time explain and defend its non-literary style.

7. In the final extract (*EH*, VI.14.5-7) Eusebius offers a partial explanation of Mk's origin. That is to say, he quotes Clement Alex. that "the two Gospels having the genealogies" were written beforehand and that it resulted from a series of Discourses delivered by Peter which were then handed over to his audience at their request. Clement also adds (S.7) that Peter was in fact quite indifferent to their publication, a statement which is best understood if, as Clement asserts, the Gospels of Mt and Lk were already in existence[6].

8. Finally, what neither Eusebius nor any other ancient writer has told us is what the precise relationship was between Mk on the one hand and Mt and Lk on the other – but at least Eusebius allows us to

---

6. For the controversy over the interpretation of this passage, cf. D.L. DUNGAN (ed.), *The Interrelations of the Gospels* (BETL, 95), Leuven, 1990; H. MERKEL, *Die Überlieferungen der Alten Kirche über das Verhältnis der Evangelien*, ibid., pp. 566-590, esp. 579-580; cf. B. ORCHARD, *Response to H. Merkel*, ibid., pp. 591-604, esp. 603-604.

assume that Peter must have known of the existence and content of Mt and Lk, so that the possibility exists that he could have had the texts of both before him when he delivered his Discourses. Nevertheless this silence does not mean that Peter and Mark did not have a perfectly good reason for their joint action, a reason, furthermore, that must also have been obvious to Eusebius and his contemporaries. Their silence need signify no more than that the reason was too obvious to the ecclesiastical writers to require explicit mention in the context in which they were writing and recording. One good reason could be that Paul required Peter's authentication of the new Gospel of his disciple Luke, since neither he nor Luke had been eye-witnesses of the Lord's Public Ministry. Paul needed somebody of Peter's standing in the Church to vouch for the authenticity of Luke's work before releasing it to his converts in Greece and Asia Minor[7].

In conclusion, the argument outlined above gives support to the increasing number of scholars who recognise that the Synoptic Problem is once more an open question and that further investigation along the lines of the above thesis may open a new and exciting prospect that brings us nearer to Jerome's conviction that: "Petrus habebit ... interpretem Marcum, cuius evangelium Petro narrante et illo scribente conpositum est"[8]. Finally, the instinct of modern scholars regarding the over-all importance of Mk would find further justification now by understanding it as Peter's personal fusion of the traditions of Mt and Lk, i.e. of the Jerusalem and the Pauline traditions.

Ealing Abbey   Dom Bernard ORCHARD
Charlbury Grove
London W5 2DY

---

7. B. ORCHARD – H. RILEY, *The Order of the Synoptics*, Macon, GA, 1987, pp. 263-277.

8. *Epistula* 120,11, ed. Hilberg (CSEL, 55).

CONCENTRIC STRUCTURES IN MARK 2,1–3,6 AND 3,7–4,1
A CASE STUDY

The studies by F. Neirynck about duality in Mk[1] have without doubt contributed considerably to the recognition of concentric structures in Mk. This holds particularly for the list of inclusions, the survey of cases of sandwich arrangement, and the typographic markings of repetitions and duplications. Yet it is striking that, although these surveys have led to a certain consensus on the presence of concentric structures, they have not resulted in any substantial agreement on the segmentation and division of concrete structures. Here consensus is the exception rather than the rule. A case study will enable us to look at the criteria applied and weigh their relative value, and thereby provide insight into the nature and cause of this divergency of opinion. Working at a narrative commentary on Mark I take an example from the opening chapters, whose known difficulty in this respect is attested by the various proposals referred to below. The case study concerns two sequences from the first half of Mk. As the departure point for the analysis of these sequences I use the concentric structures proposed by some of my predecessors: one by J. Lambrecht[2], another by P. Mourlon Beernaert, Joanna Dewey, D. Rhoads and D. Michie[3], and a more extensive one by the late W. Stenger, published as part of a concentric analysis of the whole of Mk[4]. To this I add a partly differing proposal for 3,7–4,1 (see Survey). I will first illustrate these proposals with a view to the differences between them, then defend my own proposal, and, on the basis of this and the function of concentric structures in antiquity, finally put some criteria before you.

1. F. NEIRYNCK, *Duality in Mark. Contributions to the Study of the Marcan Redaction.* *Revised Edition with Supplementary Notes* (BETL, 31), Leuven, 1988.

2. J. LAMBRECHT, *Marcus Interpretator. Stijl en Boodschap in Mc. 3,20–4,34*, Brugge-Utrecht 1969, pp. 74-85; *The Relatives of Jesus in Mark*, in *NT* 16 (1974) 241-258.

3. P. MOURLON BEERNAERT, *Jésus controversé: Structure et théologie de Marc 2,1–3,6*, in *NRT* 95 (1973) 129-149; J. DEWEY, *Markan Public Debate. Literary Technique, Concentric Structure and Theology in Mark 2,1–3,6* (SBL DS, 48), Chico, CA, 1977; D. RHOADS – D. MICHIE, *Mark as Story: An Introduction to the Narrative of a Gospel*, Philadelphia, PA, 1982, pp. 51-53.

4. W. STENGER, *"Die Grundlegung des Evangeliums von Jesus Christus". Zur kompositionellen Struktur des Markusevangeliums*, in *Linguistica Biblica* 61 (1988) 7-56.

I. SIMILARITIES AND DIFFERENCES

The proposed structures presented show similarities and differences.
The segment containing 2,1–3,6 is delimited and divided in the same
way by the four analysts I have consulted. I agree with their suggestions, although I think the first and last sequence had better be
characterized otherwise[5]. So much for the similarities. When seg-
menting the next part of the text the ways of Lambrecht and Stenger, as
well as the one proposed by myself, diverge considerably. For this
reason the three different analyses offer a good opportunity for raising
the question whether there is a criterion on which the choice for one
particular division and arrangement may be based.

Let us first look at the one by Lambrecht. The concentric structure
that he proposes is certainly clarifying, with regard both to the delimitation of the chosen segment – 3,20-35 – and the arrangement effected
within it. This delimitation comes as no surprise in a thematic study
entitled "Ware verwantschap en eeuwige zonde" (True Kinship and
Eternal Sin) from 1969 and "The Relatives of Jesus in Mark" in the
article from 1974. But just because of this the question arises whether
Lambrecht was not guided by his thematic preoccupation when seg-
menting the text. Anyone who tries to arrange these chapters of Mk in
their entirety in concentric structures is faced with the necessity to
weigh this segmentation against another. This necessity has to do with
the way in which Mk 3,9 and 4,1 are interrelated. Impelled by the large
numbers of people gathering to him on the shore of the lake, Jesus
orders his disciples in 3,9 – itself the centre of a concentric sequence
consisting of 3,7-12 – to have a boat ready for him in case the crowd
pushes closer. In 4,1 he then makes use of this or another boat waiting
for him. He embarks, and from the boat addresses the multitude. In
case one opts – as I do – for this delimitation of the – now longer –
segment, the central element and hence the content remain the same,
namely, Jesus' discussion with the scribes about the source of his
unique authority (3,20-30 or 3,23-29). In my segmentation this main
incident is flanked by the formation of the circle of Jesus' twelve closest
helpers and the creation of a larger circle of followers who, in contrast
to his physical relatives, gather round Jesus in true kinship. Why I
think this segmentation is preferable will be argued in the next section.

---

5. After all, both sequences relate to a physical handicap, a handicap, moreover, which
in either case frustrates the use of one or two of the limbs serving to bridge the distance
between one person and another or a thing, the lower – the legs and feet – to move
towards something or someone, the upper – the arms and hands – to reach out to things
or persons, to feel and hold them. Hand/arm and foot/leg being one another's counterparts within a semantic paradigm, the two cures are well suited to be one another's
counterparts also in a narrative structure. In bringing this to expression my characterization of the first and last sequence differs from that of the other four analysts.

Let us now look at the segmentation by Stenger[6]. It is clear that the segment distinguished by Lambrecht fits perfectly in Stenger's division, of which it is one of the sequences. But the very extensive and highly complicated segment proposed by Stenger is incompatible with my division. At first glance the two summaries[7] framing Stenger's segment show a strong affinity. Both of them contain fairly elaborate descriptions of Jesus' healing activities (3,10-11 and 6,53-56). But they differ in other important respects. The boat left by Jesus in 6,54 was not embarked by him in 3,9 but only ordered to be made ready. Another difference concerns the size and origin of the crowd. Vv. 3,7-8 speak of great numbers who have come from far and wide – from Idumaea, Transjordan, Tyre and Sidon, and other places – whereas 6,55 mentions only the inhabitants of the region round Gennesaret. Finally, a third difference between Stenger's two summaries is due to the fact that 3,9, the centre of his first summary, deals with a unique incident, which actually makes it rather difficult to characterize and treat 3,7-12 as a summary[8]. Apart from the choice of another framework, however, the most important difference between Stenger's and my segmentation is that I regard the parable section from verse 4,2 onwards as a separate segment, which, in my view, also constitutes the centre of the part of the book set in Galilee[9].

II. MOTIVES FOR TAKING 3,7–4,1 AND 4,2-34 AS SEGMENTS

What are the motives for preferring a segment which comprises 3,7–4,1 to the segment suggested by Lambrecht, which consists of 3,20-35? It is certainly not the global contents of the segment, for in either segmentation the centre is constituted by the same passage, which is concerned with the nature and source of the authority with which Jesus acts and speaks. No, the motive behind the difference in choice is due to the fact that Lambrecht and I have different views on how the passage

---

6. *Grundlegung* (n. 4), pp. 33-40.

7. For the summaries in Mk, see G. VAN OYEN, *De Summaria in Marcus en de Compositie van Mc 1,14–8,26* (SNTA, 12), Leuven, 1987.

8. G. VAN OYEN, *Summaria* (n. 7), pp. 116, 213-216 is of the opinion that the summary should be confined to 3,10-12. It seems highly questionable to me whether in that case one can still speak of a real summary. Van Oyen himself points out that 10-12 is a subordinate clause which gives the reason why Jesus orders that a boat be made ready. Because of this the emphasis in 7-12 is on the unique occurrence related in v. 9. The relation between the three components is then as follows: vv. 7-8 describe the concourse of people which is so large as to cause danger; vv. 10-12 give the reason why there is such an onrush; v. 9 indicates how to escape from it. If the punctuation of Nestle[26] is correct, it would be more obvious to regard vv. 11-12 (instead of 10-12) as a summary. When 7-10 is read as a unity the emphasis is on v. 9.

9. See B. VAN IERSEL, *Reading Mark*, Edinburgh, 1989, pp. 24-25.

in question should be framed. The two frameworks express two different oppositions. In 3,20-21 + 3,31-35 it is the opposition between Jesus and his relatives. In 3,9 and 4,1 it is the opposition between Jesus and the crowd, in 3,9 specified as an opposition between the pushing crowd and an individual threatened by it, in 4,1 as one between the teacher and the crowd listening to him. In the two different segments the oppositions just mentioned are supported by different spatial categories, Lambrecht's by the categories "inside" and "outside" mine by "on the shore of the lake" and "in a boat on the water". Both oppositions are, narratively speaking, of comparative importance so that a choice cannot be based on them.

Things become different, however, when we consider the recognizability of the repetitions on which the relation between the outer members of either frame is based. The interdependence of 3,7-12 – of 3,9 in particular – and 4,1 is considerably more recognizable than that of 3,20-21 and 3,31-35. A case in point is 3,21. The verse is so vague about the persons meant by οἱ παρ' αὐτοῦ that it does not become clear before 3,31 that they are Jesus' relatives[10]. Incidentally, a similarity in content and form, unnoticed by Lambrecht, is to be found in the judgement of the relatives ὅτι ἐξέστη and its curious counterpart characterizing them in their turn as ἔξω στήκοντες (3,21 and 3,31). Also the contrast between the crowd collecting round Jesus in the house and the relatives intending to fetch him from it, in 3,20-21, may be understood as a counterpart of what is said in 31-35: the relatives have to remain outside, while in the house Jesus creates a new family from other people. But in spite of this there can be no doubt that the similarities in content and form between 3,7-12, where for fear of the pushing crowd a boat is made ready, and 4,1, where Jesus gets into the boat, are at least equally direct and recognizable.

So the issue can be decided only by the syntagms and keywords which 3,20-21 and 3,31-35, on the one hand, and 3,7-9 and 4,1, on the other, have in common.

3,20-21	3,31-35	3,7-9	4,1
καὶ ἔρχεται	καὶ ἔρχεται	πρὸς τὴν θάλασσαν	παρὰ τὴν θάλασσαν
ὄχλος	ὄχλος		πρὸς τὴν θάλασσαν
ἐξῆλθον	ἔξω	πολὺ πλῆθος	ὄχλος πλεῖστον
ἐξέστη	ἔξω στήκοντες	πλῆθος πολὺ	
		τὸν ὄχλον	πᾶς ὁ ὄχλος
		πλοιάριον	πλοῖον

10. For this reason οἱ παρ' αὐτοῦ in 3,21 and its counterpart, which occurs four times in 3,31-34, ἡ μητὴρ αὐτοῦ/μου καὶ οἱ ἀδελφοὶ αὐτοῦ/μου, are not included in the scheme represented in the next paragraph. 3,21 keeps the reader in suspense with regard to the identity of the "associates", which is resolved surprisingly in 3,31. See R.M. FOWLER, *Let the Reader Understand. Reader-Response Criticism and the Gospel of Mark*, Minneapolis, MN, 1991, pp. 200-201.

It appears that the only similarities between 3,20-21 and 3,31-35 are very general terms like καὶ ἔρχεται and ὄχλος, and only two relatively specific terms like ἐξῆλθον and ἔξω, ἐξέστη and ἔξω στήκοντες, which show semantic as well as sound affinity. On the other hand, the members of frame 3,7-9 and 4,1 have in common a number of specific terms (παρὰ/πρὸς τὴν θάλασσαν) and synonyms (πολὺ πλῆθος - ὄχλος πλεῖστος and πλοιάριον - πλοῖον) which clearly bear more directly to the situation than the terms of 3,20-21 and 3,31-35. Here, too, semantic affinity goes together with sound affinity. On account of the more specific character of the terms and therefore the greater recognizability of the two passages, in one of which a boat is made ready and in the other Jesus enters the boat, I prefer to define 3,7–4,1 as a segment, and regard 3,21 only as a preparation for 3,31-35, and not as a framing verse of a segment. The passages in between, which deal with the formation of the twelve and the creation of a spiritual family, are similar enough to be one another's counterparts, and stand at the same time in opposition to the sequence which, inserted between them, describes the true character of Jesus' adversaries. In this way the three sequences, together with the thematically united verses 3,7-12 and 4,1 framing them, can very well constitute a coherent segment.

The segmentation proposed by Stenger raises several objections, too. The concentric structure of his segment is indeed so complicated that, although perceptible to an analyst, it can hardly have been perceived by someone reading the text by himself or reciting it to an audience. But there are two other and more important objections of a different kind. The first is that this particular segmentation violates the unity of a much more clearly visible coherent whole. I am referring to the part of the text which opens with the first and closes with the third crossing of the lake, and in which the stories about the mass feedings have a central function. It is for these and other reasons that this part should be regarded as a segment, which would then consist of 4,35–8,21, as I have explained elsewhere[11].

The second objection is that in Stenger's division the parable section 4,2-34, which is strikingly unlike both in kind of text used and in size to the surrounding text, is merely treated as a sequence. Actually, it is the only speech of such length by Jesus in the first half of the book, and the only speech in the whole book consisting of a collection of parables. This is stated explicitly at the beginning and end of the section. Moreover, the combination of διδάσκω/λάλεω τὸν λόγον with πολλαῖς/πολλά, which occurs in 4,2 and 4,33 but nowhere else, as well as the information found only in 4,34 that Jesus does not address the crowd except in parables but explains everything to his disciples in

11. B. van Iersel, Reading Mark (n. 9), pp. 24-25; 85-86; 95-99.

private, are clearly designed to frame the central position which is occupied by the parable discourse, itself concentric in structure[12].

All this seems to me to be enough evidence for taking 4,2-34 as a segment in its own right, or even as a chapter, which, together with the preceding (1,14-4,1) and the following chapter (4,35-8,21), constitutes one of the main parts of the book. In other words, my objections to Stenger's proposal really come down to the fact that he fails to pay due attention to the macrostructural elements. That is all the more remarkable in the light of the fact that he analyses the book in its entirety. This he does, however, by keeping rigidly to the method of analysing primarily the smallest units or sequences, which he then interconnects and brings together in segments organized according to the concentric principle.

III. CRITERIA FOR CONCENTRIC STRUCTURES

Some of the above authors have tackled the important question of the criteria. As such Stenger mentions indicators of place and time, as well as the constellation of the story-characters. Dewey names content, form, and word repetition, and classes indications of time and place as well as character roles under content. By form she understands also the different text types such as narration and discourse, but these hardly play a part in her book.

These criteria are without doubt effective in helping analysts segment the text and recognize the presence of concentric structures within segments. But they are not much help to analysts who at some point have to choose between one proposed segmentation and another. Clark may be right to write, "Different patterns, each perceived in the same section of a text by a different Gestalt, may all be right"[13]. But that does not mean, of course, that they are all equally good. However, it so happens that by distinguishing between various degrees of similarity Clark himself has unwittingly been of some help with respect to word repetition when he writes: "Rarer words are more significant than commoner words. Identical forms are more significant than similar forms. The same word class is more significant than different word classes formed from the same root. Identical roots are more significant than suppletive roots"[14]. It was precisely on the ground of such considerations that I preferred the segmentation of 3,7-4,1 advanced

---

12. J. LAMBRECHT, Marcus Interpretator (n. 2), pp. 121-124; G. FAY, Introduction to Incomprehension. The Literary Structure of Mark 4,1-34, in CBQ 51 (1989) 65-81.

13. D.J. CLARK, Criteria for Identifying Chiasm, in Linguistica Biblica 35 (1975) 63-72, p. 69.

14. Ibid., p. 65.

above, to Lambrecht's segmentation of 3,20-35 and Stenger's of 3,7-6,56.

But with this I have not argued the validity of the criterion by which I, in contrast to Stenger, judge 4,2-34 to be a separate segment. Before that it is necessary to make explicit the presupposition on which that criterion is based. The majority of authors who recognize concentric structures of different complexity in Mk or other biblical texts seldom or never ask themselves any specific questions about the function of these structures. Those who do regard them as a literary or rhetorical device, that is to say, either as a technique used to achieve a good composition of the book and its parts or as a literary ornament, an aesthetic element serving to embellish the text[15].

Still, the question must be asked if concentric structures should not be assumed to have had a much more basic function[16]. In this context it is essential to realize that ancient Greek manuscripts were written in *scriptio continua*, which means that neither words nor sentences nor larger units were separated from each other, as opposed to our modern printed texts which visually distinguish between words and sentences, and are even divided into paragraphs and chapters. In antiquity readers had to do without these graphic indications. Yet, reciting the gospel to an audience from a manuscript thus written the reciter could not help

15. See N.W. LUND, *Chiasmus in the New Testament*, Chapel Hill, 1942; C.H. LOHR, *Oral Techniques in the Gospel of Matthew*, in *CBQ* 23 (1961) 403-435; D.J. CLARK, *Criteria* (n. 13), pp. 63-72; J. DEWEY, *Debate* (n. 3), pp. 29-39, 131-180; S. BAR-EFRAT, *Some Observations on the Analysis of Structure and Biblical Narrative*, in *VT* 30 (1980) 154-173; A. DI MARCO, *Der Chiasmus in der Bibel*, in *Linguistica Biblica* 36 (1975) 21-97; 37 (1976) 49-68; 39 (1976) 37-85; 44 (1979) 3-70; RHOADS-MICHIE, *Mark* (n. 3), pp. 51-55; R.M. FOWLER, *Loaves and Fishes* (SBL DS, 54), Chico, CA, 1978, pp. 47-49, 69-71, 164-165; *Let the Reader Understand* (n. 10), pp. 140-152. In response to Fowler who remarks in *Let the Reader Understand*, p. 152, that "nowhere in the ancient handbooks of rhetoric or poetics chiasm as such is ever discussed", I suggest that the very absence of such a discussion might be seen precisely as an indication that chiasm was not regarded primarily as a literary device. Just as E. BEST, *Mark. The Gospel as Story*, Edinburgh, 1983, pp. 105-106, he thinks too easily and without any evidence that the recognition of chiasm presupposes a printed and preferably a diagrammed version of a text. Moreover, J.B. WELCH, in the introduction to J.B. WELCH (ed.), *Chiasmus in Antiquity. Structures, Analyses, Exegesis*, Hildesheim, 1981, p. 14, has shown that inverted parallelism was expressly observed in antiquity under the names of *hysteron proton, prohysteron* and *hysterologia* for example by Cicero, Atticus 1,16,1, the Roman commentators Servius and Donatus and by the Scholiast Aristarchus, Scholia A on Odyssey 56, and the Scholia Euripides Orestes 702, and by the Scholia Euripides Phoenissae 887.

16. The only suggestions I have come across that point in the same direction are to be found in C.H. LOHR, *Oral Techniques* (n. 15), p. 404: "These devices of continuity and interconnection seem to have grown up with the tradition and out of the experience of the reciter in handling large masses of material" and in the introduction to J.B. WELCH, *Chiasmus* (n. 15), p. 12: "chiasmus afforded a seriously needed element of internal organization of ancient writing, which of course did not make use of paragraphs, punctuation, capitalization and other synthetic devices...".

structuring the text, if only to make a sensible use of the inevitable shorter or longer breathing pauses. The many forms of concentric structures which are present in the text provided the help the reciter needed. The efficiency of this help is, of course, proportionate to the recognizability of the concentric structures in question, and since all concentric structures are based on the principle of duality and recurrence, or, in other words, on the repetition of elements used before, it must have been easy enough for trained readers to recognize them[17].

If the hypothesis is correct that concentric structures are designed to structure the reading and hearing process by distinguishing between segments, it follows that easily recognizable repetitions take priority over those less identifiable. Consequently, to the criteria for determining concentric segmentations we may add another, namely, the criterion of easy recognizability, by which different segmentations of the text can be weighed against each other on the basis of their functionality. The various degrees of similarity named by Clark can be seen as particularizations of this criterion.

Also the problem how to attune macro- and micro-structural signals to each other comes under the heading of the criterion of easy recognizability. On account of the massive character of their presence, macro-structural signals have a greater recognizability than many micro-structural signals. In my opinion, this goes both for the interdependence of the three crossings of the lake and their being interwoven with the two stories of feeding. It is equally true – be it in another way – of the two chapters that consist almost entirely of spoken text, the parable chapter 4,2-34 and the eschatological discourse in 13.

A third aspect connected with the recognizability of a concentric structure is its simplicity. Not the interesting discoveries produced by the analyst who subjects the text to a full and close scrutiny, but the need of the reciter for structuring determines which concentric structures should be given preference. Therefore, a relatively simple concentric structure takes priority over an intricate one, just as a conventional and expected structure takes priority over the original and unexpected find[18].

---

17. Certainly when seen against the background of the system of education that prevailed at the time. See H.I. Marrou, *Histoire de l'éducation dans l'Antiquité*, Paris, ⁶1965, pp. 229-234, 251-252, 400-415.

18. English translation by W.H. Bisscheroux.

SURVEY OF CONCENTRIC STRUCTURES IN MK 2,1–4,1

2,1–3,6

P. MOURLON BEERNAERT (n. 3)   A 2,1-12   healing of paralysed legs
J. DEWEY (n. 3), p. 110   B 2,13-17 eating with law-breakers
D. RHOADS – D. MICHIE (n. 3), p. 52 C 2,18-22 discussion on non fasting
W. STENGER (n. 4), p. 43   B' 2,23-28 gathering food on sabbath
                                    A' 3,1-6   healing of a withered hand

3,20-35	3,7–6,56	3,7–4,1
J. LAMBRECHT (n. 2), p. 80 cp. *NT* 16 (1974) 252	W. STENGER, p. 33	B. VAN IERSEL
	A 3,7-12 Summarium *See/Boot*	A 3,7-12 preparing a boat
	B 3,12-19 Auswahl der Zwölf *Berg*	B 3,13-19 creating the twelve
A 3,20-21 action of relatives		
B 3,22 accusation by scribes		
C 3,23-29 defense of Jesus	C 3,20-35 Urteil über Jesus *Haus*	C 3,20-30 discussing with scribes
B' 3,30 accusation by scribes		
A' 3,31-35 true kinship		B' 3,31-35 creating a new family
		A' 4,1 getting into the boat
		A 4,2 introducing the parables
	D 4,1-34 Gleichnisrede *Seeufer*	B 4,3-32 parables
		A' 4,33-34 concluding the parables
	B' 4,35-41 Seesturm *Seeboot*	
	A' 5,1-20 Legion *Land der Gerase-ner, Ufer, Dekapolis*	
	A'' 5,21-43 zwei Frauen genesen *Seeufer (Jüdisch), Haus des Jairus*	
	A' 6 1-6 das ungläubige Nazareth *Vaterstadt, Synagoge*	
	B'' 6,7-13	

> Aussendung 12
> *umliegende Dörfer*
> C' 6,14-29
> Urteil über Jesus
> *(Herodes impliziert Ortsangabe)*
> D' 6,30-44
> Speisung 5000
> *einsamer Ort (jüdisch)*
> B''' 6,45-52
> Seewandel *Berg, See, Boot*
> A 6,53-56
> Summarium *Seeufer*

Mgr. Suyslaan 4   Bas van Iersel
NL-6564 BV H. Landstichting

SIGNIFICATION D'UN RÉCIT
ET COMPARAISON SYNOPTIQUE
(MARC 9,14-29 ET PARALLÈLES)

Divers usages de la comparaison synoptique

Expliquer l'origine et la genèse d'un texte et l'interpréter dans l'état où il se présente au lecteur sont deux tâches qu'il importe de ne pas confondre. Pour les textes évangéliques, la comparaison synoptique peut être mise au service de l'un et de l'autre objectif. Elle est couramment pratiquée au service du premier. Et le récit que l'on désigne ordinairement comme «guérison d'un enfant épileptique» n'a pas fini de provoquer des études de ce type[1]. Outre les trois versions de Mt 17,14-21, Mc 9,14-29 et Lc 9,37-43, nous disposons des diverses propositions qui ont été faites pour restaurer, sous les remaniements et les adjonctions que l'on y repère, les formes successives que ce récit aurait connues au cours de son évolution. Chacune de ces formes est (ou par hypothèse devrait être) capable de se faire lire, donc de signifier, en elle-même, indépendamment des autres. Chacune peut être considérée comme un texte à part entière, qui fait sens de tous ses éléments tels qu'ils s'articulent entre eux dans son sein. Pourquoi ne pas les soumettre à comparaison synoptique entre elles et avec les versions canoniques pour apprécier les différences d'orientation qu'elles impriment au travail de la signification du récit tel que chacune le raconte?

Parler de signification comme d'un travail, c'est avoir en lisant une autre ambition que d'assigner au texte considéré un (ou plusieurs) sens, qui, en quelque sorte, en fixerait sous une forme plus ramassée le «contenu» ou le message. S'il fallait en rester à cette conception statique du sens, on ne comprendrait pas qu'il faille constamment relire des textes comme les évangiles, qu'on n'est jamais sûr d'avoir bien compris. La nécessité de relire et, notamment pour le récit qui va nous occuper, la multitude des études qu'il continue de provoquer, témoignent d'un dynamisme de la signification. La signification (au sens actif du mot) d'un texte reste endormie s'il n'est pas lu. Elle se manifeste par la quête de sens qu'elle entretient chez le lecteur, et d'abord par le travail qu'elle lui demande. Si l'on admet que la lecture d'une unité textuelle doit compter avec tous ses éléments et que ceux-ci deviennent signifiants par les relations qui s'établissent entre eux (par leur articula-

---

1. Pour une revue panoramique des opinions critiques, cf. J. DELORME, *Dualité, dissection critique et signification: Marc 9,14-29*, in *The Four Gospels 1992. FS Frans Neirynck* (BETL, 100), Leuven, 1992, pp. 1095-1104.

tion), chaque version (canonique ou non) d'un récit offre des conditions différentes au travail de la signification et de la lecture. La comparaison synoptique peut alors confronter, non seulement des éléments qui diffèrent d'une version à une autre, mais des unités globales de signification. Ce qui, du point de vue rédactionnel, peut être identifié comme relevant d'une retouche ou d'un ajout, n'intervient pas dans la signification d'un texte au titre de retouche ou d'ajout mais à celui d'élément intégré dans une organisation qui le fait signifier autrement qu'à l'état isolé ou intégré dans un autre ensemble.

Complexité d'un récit

Dans les limites de cette étude, la version de Mc sera privilégiée. La comparaison avec les versions plus courtes de Mt et de Lc, éventuellement avec celles que des critiques proposent, permettra d'examiner comment des éléments du récit de Mc, absents ou différemment représentés ailleurs, obligent à reconsidérer la lecture que l'on ferait sans eux ou en ne leur accordant qu'un statut auxiliaire. Il est remarquable en effet que ces autres versions se passent très bien de parcours d'acteurs qui semblent alourdir et compliquer le récit de Mc.

Un récit focalisé sur la transformation d'un enfant présenté par son père à Jésus pourrait exister et se faire lire ou entendre sans les quatre descriptions des effets du mal selon Mc (il n'y en a que deux en Lc et une seule en Mt). Et ce récit pourrait prendre des formes différentes selon qu'il s'agirait d'un enfant malade (épileptique), ou possédé par un mauvais esprit, ou les deux[2]. Ce serait de toute façon un récit à trois acteurs (le père, l'enfant et Jésus) ou quatre (avec «l'esprit»). La répétition des «crises» de l'enfant, comme il est convenu de les appeler, vient-elle simplement accentuer le côté pittoresque ou dramatique de l'histoire mise en scène? Autrement dit, ne relève-t-elle que de la rhétorique? Ou influe-t-elle sur la signification? En d'autres termes, a-t-elle une portée sémiotique?

Ce questionnement peut être poursuivi pour d'autres parcours d'acteurs. Qu'advient-il de la signification quand le père ne se borne pas à informer Jésus comme en Mt et en Lc, mais qu'un dialogue s'établit entre eux comme en Mc? Ou encore quand on compte avec la plainte de Jésus à l'adresse de la «génération sans foi» qu'il ne peut supporter? Cette donnée des trois versions canoniques est considérée par beaucoup comme un ajout sans lequel une forme antérieure du récit est tout à fait

---

2. R. BULTMANN distinguait deux récits primitifs de miracles (*L'histoire de la tradition synoptique*, Paris, 1973, pp. 261-262; = *Die Geschichte der synoptischen Tradition*, Göttingen, ³1957, pp. 225-226). M.-É. BOISMARD distingue un récit d'exorcisme et un de guérison (*Synopse des quatre évangiles*, II, Paris, 1972, p. 258). P.J. ACHTEMEIER restaure tout autrement que Bultmann deux récits de miracles: *Miracles and the Historical Jesus*, in *CBQ* 37 (1975) 471-491. La plupart des critiques admettent un récit primitif de guérison-exorcisme qu'ils reconstruisent de diverses manières.

concevable. Et qu'est-ce qui change, pour la signification, selon que l'on néglige ou non la donnée qui concerne l'échec des disciples (donnée des trois versions, mais absente de certaines reconstitutions critiques), et surtout le débat final entre eux et Jésus à ce sujet (il est absent en Lc et presqu'unanimement considéré comme une dernière couche rédactionnelle en Mc)?

La complexité du récit de Mc tient surtout à la multiplicité des acteurs et à la transformation des rôles de certains au cours de l'action racontée. Il est tentant de simplifier en réduisant le nombre des personnages ou de leurs rôles et d'expliquer la complexité par une série de couches rédactionnelles successives. Chacune relèverait d'intentions particulières. Quelle que soit la valeur explicative des hypothèses engendrées par cette problématique, en rester là serait témoigner d'une conception mentaliste du texte. Un texte se réduirait aux traces laissées de leurs intentions par des rédacteurs qui maîtrisaient leur langage et le sens qu'ils voulaient communiquer. On se ferait une idée purement véhiculaire du langage, simple medium d'une pensée préalable, et une représentation statique de la signification, comme si elle pouvait se stratifier en couches de sens voulus et bien repérables.

I. Jésus, le père et l'enfant

Avec ces trois personnages, et «l'esprit» qui possède l'un d'entre eux, diverses formes du récit sont attestées ou peuvent être imaginées. Nous nous limiterons à la question posée par deux particularités de Mc: les conditions de la signification sont-elles modifiées par la répétition des «crises» de l'enfant et par le dialogue entre Jésus et le père?

1. *Les crises de l'enfant et sa transformation*[3]

Mt fait rapporter par le père à Jésus, comme explication du «mal» de l'enfant «lunatique»: «Car souvent il tombe dans le feu et souvent dans l'eau» (v. 15). En Lc, le père évoque les manifestations du mal en d'autres termes, puis le narrateur raconte brièvement la crise qui se produit au moment de l'approche entre Jésus et l'enfant (vv. 39 et 42). Mc y revient quatre fois, alternant les descriptions par le père et par le narrateur (vv. 18 et 22, 20 et 26). Ces descriptions ne se répètent pas, même si elles se recoupent sur plusieurs détails. Elles se prêtent à un diagnostic médical d'épilepsie. Mais quand on porte ce diagnostic, on caractérise le mal tel qu'il pourrait être défini dans la réalité, en dehors du texte. Or celui-ci ne se soucie pas de médecine. Et la variété des données fournies par le texte doit être analysée, car elle contribue à la

---

3. Pour plus de détails, cf. l'article cité note 1.

signification de l'ensemble du récit. Celui-ci ne se laisse pas réduire à un canevas narratif de guérison et/ou d'exorcisme, habillé de notations réalistes pour en corser la difficulté. Il présente un tableau insistant d'un être aliéné, en ce sens qu'il est totalement dépendant d'un autre, qui le traite comme une chose et le prive des conditions de son développement humain.

Si l'on rapproche toutes les manifestations du mal, il apparaît qu'il atteint l'enfant sous les deux aspects fondamentaux de la vie et de la communication humaines:

a) la station debout et le mouvement dans l'espace (seul élément en Lc) et plus précisément dans l'espace naturel de la vie humaine (seul élément en Mt où l'enfant «souvent tombe dans le feu et souvent dans l'eau»);

b) la parole, qui se trouve empêchée par le dysfonctionnement de la bouche (grincement des dents et écume), à quoi s'ajoute la surdité («esprit muet et sourd», v. 25). Lc ne parle que de l'écume, pas du grincement des dents, et chez lui l'esprit n'est ni sourd ni muet, mais seulement «impur», et il crie (v. 39; en Mc, il ne le fait qu'au moment où il est vaincu, v. 26).

On peut se demander ce qui reste d'humain en ce corps désarticulé et qui est amené passivement à Jésus. À cette insistance sur l'étendue et la gravité du mal, correspond (et cela en Mc seul) une double intervention de Jésus. Il y a d'abord sa parole impérative et aggressive (ἐπιτιμάω comme en Mt et Lc) contre l'esprit (et en Mc, le cri de l'«esprit» qui sort n'est pas simplement un trait conventionel d'un exorcisme réussi, cf. 1,26, mais le premier signal de la défaite de l'«esprit muet»). L'enfant abandonné par l'occupant est laissé «comme mort de sorte que la multitude disait qu'il est mort» (v. 26). Une seconde intervention de Jésus ne vient pas seulement démentir ce jugement. En prenant l'enfant par la main, Jésus pose le premier geste qui, dans ce récit, s'adresse à l'enfant lui-même et pour lui-même. En le mettant debout, il le tire de l'état de non-vie qui était le sien depuis le début et de la position infra-humaine où il se trouve après sa délivrance. Il l'aide à prendre sa place, comme un être capable de se mouvoir, dans l'espace qui convient aux hommes. Le récit pourrait s'arrêter là et cela suffirait déjà pour indiquer qu'il porte bien au-delà des enjeux d'un récit d'acte de puissance à la gloire d'un thaumaturge. Il travaille dans le sens d'une restauration de l'humain dans un être exclu de la promesse de croissance et de vie que représente un enfant. Les versions de Mt et de Lc n'orientent pas dans cette direction.

2. *Le dialogue entre Jésus et le père*

Ce dialogue est propre à Mc (vv. 21-24). Il est considéré comme un ajout «secondaire» par de nombreux critiques[4], Mt ne présente qu'une donnée de ce dialogue, celle qui concerne les chutes répétées de l'enfant dans le feu et dans l'eau, et qu'il situe dans la première (et unique chez lui comme chez Lc) information fournie par le père (v. 15). Le rôle du père se limite alors à celui d'un informateur et d'un simple auxiliaire pour «amener» l'enfant (ou l'«apporter», φέρω: Mt v. 16; Mc vv. 17.20; en Lc comparer προσάγαγε et προσερχομένου αὐτοῦ, vv. 41 et 42). Il en va tout autrement en Mc. La conversation entre Jésus et le père modifie leurs rôles et cela affecte le déroulement du récit, donc aussi son investissement sémantique. C'est l'unique véritable dialogue de ce récit. La séquence question-réponse des vv. 16-17 (propre à Mc) et des vv. 28-29 (parallèle en Mt) et l'échange de paroles en vv. 19-20 (parallèle en Mt et en Lc) ne constituent pas des dialogues. L'instauration d'un dialogue prend d'autant plus d'importance en Mc qu'il (et lui seul) précise que l'enfant «a un esprit muet» (v. 17). Or on sait que chez lui la relation de parole est souvent décisive pour l'orientation prise par un récit[5].

On peut distinguer deux parties ou deux thèmes dans ce dialogue: informations supplémentaires sur la durée et la nature du mal de l'enfant (21-22a) et problème du pouvoir et de la foi (22b-24). La position du père par rapport à Jésus et à son enfant se transforme. Pour la première fois dans le déroulement de ce petit drame, le père se fait suppliant. Auparavant, il déclarait à Jésus qu'il s'était adressé à ses disciples, mais la formule employée ne portait pas la marque d'une supplication: «J'ai dit (εἶπα) à tes disciples de le [l'esprit] chasser et ils n'ont pas eu la force». Les disciples étaient considérés comme détenteurs d'une force (ἰσχύω) et le père recourait à eux comme s'il suffisait de leur demander d'intervenir. Maintenant, il parle tout autrement: «Viens au secours de nous, étant pris aux entrailles pour nous (βοήθησον ἡμῖν σπλαγχνισθεὶς ἐφ' ἡμᾶς)» (v. 22). Puis il dira: «Viens au secours de ma non-foi (βοήθει μου τῇ ἀπιστίᾳ)» (v. 24). De la demande aux disciples d'intervenir contre l'«esprit» à la supplication adressée à Jésus pour «nous», puis pour «moi», le parcours doit être analysé.

1. Le père au début du récit

Il s'adressait aux disciples comme s'ils pouvaient tenir lieu de Jésus et suppléer à son absence: «Maître, j'ai amené mon fils vers toi ... et j'ai

---

4. Par exemple J. ROLOFF, *Das Kerygma und der irdische Jesus*, Göttingen, 1970, pp. 143-152, 205-207; G. PETZKE, *Die historische Frage nach den Wundertaten Jesu. Dargestellt am Beispiel des Exorzismus Mark. ix.14-29 par.*, in *NTS* 22 (1975-76) 180-204, spéc. pp. 188-189, 192-196. J. GNILKA reconnaît des ajouts en 23-24 (*Das Evangelium nach Markus*, II, Zürich - Neukirchen-Vluyn, 1979, p. 45). Pour W. SCHENK, ces vv. 23-24 sont un ajout: *Tradition und Redaktion in der Epileptiker-Perikope Mk 9,14-29*, in *ZNW* 63 (1972) 76-94, pp. 78-79.

5. Cf. J. DELORME, *Au risque de la parole. Lire les évangiles*, Paris, 1991.

dit à tes disciples...» (vv. 17-18). D'autre part, la relation entre le père et le fils se réduisait au fait que le père avait toute l'initiative et faisait à la place de son fils ce qu'il ne pouvait faire lui-même: se déplacer tout seul et parler. Enfin le désir du père, exprimé par sa démarche, concernait la délivrance de l'enfant et se concentrait sur la recherche d'un pouvoir capable d'opérer cette délivrance.

Laissons de côté pour l'instant l'échec des disciples et la plainte de Jésus à l'adresse de la «génération sans foi» (v. 19ab). «Amenez-le-moi» (v. 19c) marque un changement dans la position des acteurs entre eux: les disciples passent à l'arrière-plan, le corps de Jésus devient le centre de l'espace, les autres sont situés par rapport à lui. «L'esprit» réagit le premier, dès qu'il «voit» Jésus (v. 20). Ensuite Jésus fait réagir le père en l'interrogeant (vv. 21-22), puis en contestant sa manière de parler (vv. 23-24).

La réaction de «l'esprit» telle qu'elle est décrite pourrait n'apparaître que comme la confirmation «de visu» pour Jésus de ce qu'il vient d'apprendre par la bouche du père (v. 18). Les deux descriptions se renforcent sans se répéter[6] et l'insistance sur la déstabilisation de l'enfant et le dérèglement de ses mouvements dans l'espace prépare ce que le père va encore ajouter en réponse à la question de Jésus: il arrive souvent que l'enfant soit jeté dans le feu et dans l'eau (v. 22). Or cette précision prend de l'importance dans le dialogue que Jésus provoque en posant sa question.

2. L'épiphanie du père

La question posée par Jésus: «Combien de temps y a-t-il que cela lui arrive?», et la réponse donnée: «Depuis l'enfance», ne peuvent se ramener à un trait conventionnel des récits de miracle où il est de bon ton d'aggraver le mal par sa durée en vue de magnifier la puissance du thaumaturge[7]. Comme l'âge de «l'enfant» reste indéterminé[8], on ne peut savoir depuis combien d'années cela dure et la réponse du père se

---

6. Cf. article cité note 1. Ὅπου ἐὰν αὐτὸν καταλάβῃ de la première crise n'a pas à être repris dans les autres, puisque c'est l'acte de «saisie» qui est supposé inaugurer toutes les crises; à ῥήσσει αὐτόν correspond πεσὼν ἐπὶ τῆς γῆς; «écumer», ἀφρίζω, revient les deux fois; mais tandis que la première fois ce dysfonctionnement de la bouche est complété par le grincement des dents, la deuxième insiste plutôt sur le dysfonctionnement moteur de l'enfant qui «tombant à terre se roulait», ἐκυλίετο; quant au dernier élément de la première description, καὶ ξηραίνεται, «et il devient sec» ou «raide», qui semble marquer l'état final de la crise, il aura son équivalent dans la quatrième et dernière description de l'enfant qui, après la sortie de «l'esprit», «devint comme mort», v. 26.

7. Cf. R. Pesch, *Das Markusevangelium*, II, Freiburg, 1977, p. 91; Gnilka (n. 4), p. 47. Comparer Mc 5,25, où les douze ans de maladie n'ont pas seulement la fonction d'un élément conventionnel, puisqu'ils correspondent à l'âge de la fille de Jaïre que Jésus ranime à 12 ans.

8. On admet communément qu'un enfant est παιδίον jusqu'à 7 ans, παῖς jusqu'à 14 ans. Cf. A. Oepke, *TWNT* V, p. 637.

lit moins en termes de quantité (malgré πόσος χρόνος) que de qualité: «l'enfant» (παιδίον, v. 24) n'a pas connu d'«enfance» (ἐκ παιδιόθεν) préservée des agressions de «l'esprit» qu'il «a». La question de Jésus s'adressait au «père», comme le narrateur le précise (v. 21; comparer v. 17: «quelqu'un de la foule»). Et ce n'est pas seulement parce que cet homme est le mieux placé pour fournir l'information que Jésus veut connaître. Sa qualité de père est intéressée, comme l'indique ce qu'il ajoute sans qu'on le lui ait demandé sur les chutes répétées de l'enfant dans l'eau et dans le feu. Ce n'est pas une simple description de plus, comparables aux deux précédentes, des manifestations du mal, pour ajouter un trait qui aggrave ce que l'on savait déjà, notamment sous l'aspect de la déstabilisation. L'enfant n'est pas jeté à terre, mais hors de l'espace vital humain, «afin de le perdre». Sa vie est menacée et cela concerne le père par qui la vie a été donnée et à qui il revient d'en assurer la croissance. C'est en tant que père qu'il devient suppliant et désormais il se solidarise avec son fils en implorant pour «nous». Le père est atteint par le mal du fils.

Cette première transformation contribue à constituer un couple père-enfant en face du couple «esprit»-enfant, avec des propriétés sémantiques opposées. Le contraste est complet entre l'«esprit», qui est «muet» et qui tend à «perdre» l'enfant, et le père, donateur de vie et qui parle. Face au couple qui déshumanise l'enfant, la relation père-fils représente la seule réserve de vie humaine et d'accès à la parole pour l'enfant. On comprend dès lors que le dialogue avec Jésus passe au premier plan, en pleine opposition au mode d'intervention de «l'esprit». La manière dont celui-ci déstructure le corps de l'enfant se donne à voir, et les descriptions répétées des crises accentuent ce côté spectaculaire du mal. Avec le dialogue au contraire, le drame devient intérieur. La parole échangée appelle écoute et tend à susciter des sujets responsables. Dans le couple père-enfant, tel qu'il est déstructuré par le couple enfant-«esprit muet», c'est au père que revient la responsabilité de la parole. Il ne parle plus pour son fils comme pour un tiers, mais pour «nous».

3. Le suppliant

«Viens au secours de nous». Avec cette demande, le rapport du père à Jésus se précise. Il y a là plus que l'expression d'un désir qui cherche à être réalisé. La demande vaut comme aveu d'un manque, d'une impuissance, et comme appel à l'autre. Celui-ci est plus que le détenteur d'un pouvoir, il est interpellé comme un sujet libre de vouloir ou non. Le père s'en remet à Jésus, à son acceptation. à son point de vue sur l'objet de sa demande, tout en le pressant d'intervenir. Ce qu'il dit mérite d'être examiné. Il recourt à Jésus sous deux aspects très différents, celui du pouvoir et celui de la compassion.

«Si tu peux quelque chose»: le pouvoir n'est pas mis en doute (εἴ τι δύνῃ à l'indicatif), il n'est pas affirmé non plus, et cette incertitude affecte toute la phrase. Le pouvoir conditionne tout le reste. Sans lui, la compassion resterait stérile. Mais alors pourquoi la demander: «viens au secours de nous, étant pris aux entrailles pour nous (σπλαγχνισ-θείς)»? Cette phrase ne relève pas d'une logique abstraite. Elle témoigne d'un homme dans l'impasse, affronté à l'impossible. La contradiction entre l'incertitude du pouvoir et l'appel aux entrailles de Jésus dit à la fois l'intensité de la détresse et celle de l'appel au secours. Elle témoigne d'un être divisé entre son impuissance et son désir qui ne se résigne pas. Sans défense dans le malheur, il refuse l'inexorable et cherche la seule issue, le chemin vers les entrailles de l'autre, vers ce qui en lui peut s'émouvoir et répondre à sa souffrance. La contradiction n'est pas résolue, mais elle est emportée dans le mouvement vers l'autre.

4. Le pouvoir et le croire

Jésus reprend les mots de son interlocuteur: «Si tu peux», et affirme: «Tout est possible à celui qui croit». Deux figures du pouvoir s'opposent: celle qui est placée par le père en Jésus et celle que Jésus situe dans «celui qui croit». On a cherché à réduire ce qu'il y a de paradoxal dans ce dialogue, soit en faisant de Jésus «celui qui croit» et dont la foi est efficace[9], soit en traduisant: «Tout est possible pour (en faveur de) celui qui croit»[10]. Cette traduction est démentie par la construction semblable de la prière de Jésus à son Père à Gethsémani: «Tout est possible à toi, πάντα δυνατά σοι» (14,36), où le datif indique bien le sujet d'un pouvoir, non le bénéficiaire. Quant à penser que Jésus fait allusion à sa foi et à la confiance que l'on peut mettre en elle, ce n'est pas ce qu'indique la suite du dialogue. L'affirmation est générale et «celui qui croit» peut être n'importe quel acteur, donc aussi Jésus. Mais à cause de sa généralité justement, le pouvoir du «croire» n'est le privilège de personne. Et le suppliant comprend bien qu'il est personnellement mis en cause: «aussitôt», il «crie»: «Je crois, viens en aide à ma non-foi».

Le texte précise que c'est «le père de l'enfant» qui crie (v. 24). Nous sommes ici à un moment décisif du récit, non seulement parce que le moment où se pose le problème du pouvoir nécessaire à l'action est toujours important dans un récit, mais surtout parce que le «père» est touché au plus profond. Son cri le manifeste. Il crie avant le cri par lequel la délivrance de l'enfant va commencer (v. 24). C'est le moment

---

9. Selon PESCH (n. 7), Jésus rappelle la puissance de la foi à laquelle la puissance de Dieu obéit, et c'est aussi implicitement une affirmation de la foi de Jésus qui peut accomplir le miracle (p. 92). GNILKA (n. 4) refuse de choisir entre un rappel de la puissance de la foi que Jésus adresse au père et une référence qu'il fait à sa propre foi: c'est lui, non le père, qui est modèle de foi (p. 48). S'il n'y a pas à exclure la foi de Jésus, ce n'est pas sur elle que le texte attire l'attention (comparer la parole «Ta foi t'a sauvé[e]» en 5,34 et 10,52).

10. Par exemple, la *Traduction œcuménique de la Bible* (1re édition, *in loco* avec la note), heureusement corrigée dans la nouvelle édition de 1988.

de la transformation la plus radicale du père, avant celle de son fils. Dans les deux cas, c'est la réaction d'un être qui se déchire.

Le père n'est plus demandeur pour son fils, ni pour «nous», mais pour lui-même. Il devient sujet personnel. Et c'est un sujet divisé. À la contradiction entre l'incertitude du pouvoir et l'appel aux entrailles de Jésus s'ajoute maintenant la contradiction où s'opposent le «croire», subjectivement assumé («Je crois»), et la non-foi reconnue et avouée. Le second verbe n'apporte pas simplement une restriction au premier, comme s'il était écrit: «Je crois, mais je manque de foi». C'est d'un même mouvement qu'il affirme sa foi (πιστεύω) et supplie pour son absence de foi (ἀπιστία, comparer Mt qui parlera de la «petite foi», ὀλιγοπιστία, des disciples. v. 20). Jésus tendait à substituer à la question sur le pouvoir à chercher dans un autre l'appel à un sujet croyant. Le père ne peut pas se présenter comme un tel sujet. Il est révélé à lui-même dans sa division intime. Les deux termes se contestent l'un l'autre, mais ils tiennent ensemble dans la parole d'un «Je» à un «Tu». Entre eux, c'est la minute de vérité. Parce qu'il y a «Tu», le «Je» partagé peut se dire en vérité en implorant l'écoute et l'aide de l'autre.

Qu'est-ce donc que ce «croire» qui rend «tout possible»? Le verbe est sans aucune détermination. Ce n'est pas un «croire que», mesuré par l'énoncé d'un contenu explicite, ni un croire au pouvoir de quelqu'un. Ce n'est même pas un croire en Jésus, du moins au sens où il en sera question dans le quatrième évangile. Jésus ne dit pas: «Celui qui croit en moi», et l'homme ne répond pas: «Je crois en toi». Il recourt à Jésus comme à celui à qui il peut se dire tel qu'il est et demander secours pour croire vraiment. Le croire dont parle Jésus ne peut être que personnel et plus profond que toute détermination ajoutée au verbe par un complément. Il faut penser au «croire» radical qui marque l'avènement d'un sujet croyant. La situation de ce père peut aider à préciser. Il est en quête d'un pouvoir qui les tire, lui et son fils, d'un malheur sans issue et le voilà renvoyé à un pouvoir qui est à chercher en lui-même et qui ne contredit pas sa totale impuissance. En quoi peut-il consister sinon dans le mouvement par lequel un sujet, qui ne peut en rien s'appuyer sur lui-même, s'ouvre en direction d'un autre?

Le cas du père est particulièrement parlant. À la détresse qui le fait se tourner vers Jésus pour «nous», s'ajoute la conscience d'une autre déficience qui le fait prier pour lui. Au moment où il s'ouvre par le croire, il découvre ce qui contredit cette ouverture. Il touche le fond d'incapacité où ne peut naître qu'un croyant lui-même déficient, qui ne peut s'appuyer sur rien, pas même sur sa foi. Ce serait encore une impasse, si cela n'avait pas lieu dans un dialogue. C'est en se parlant l'un à l'autre Jésus et son interlocuteur sont amenés à parler d'un «croire» absolu, dont personne ne dit en direction de qui il s'ouvre. Le père se trouve en quelque sorte acculé à sortir de soi sans aucun recours en soi. Sortir vers qui? ni le père ni Jésus ne le nomment.

Il peut paraître surprenant que Dieu ne soit pas mentionné en ce récit. Mais tout y ménage une sorte de vide, en direction d'un tiers absent. Jésus s'efface devant lui quand il affirme: «Tout est possible à celui qui croit». Comment l'aveu d'impuissance que la foi implique serait-il un pouvoir qui rend tout possible? Sans le Tiers, cet axiome ne serait qu'un paradoxe creux, un jeu de mots sur l'absurde. Par cette parole, Jésus se donne comme celui qui en répond. Il n'est pas le substitut de l'Absent, mais celui qui en témoigne. Il fait que le mouvement par lequel cet homme se tourne vers lui porte plus loin. Il transforme la relation qui se noue entre eux en faisant qu'elle soit traversée par la relation qui les rapporte tous les deux à l'Autre (comment l'appeler autrement?).

5. Le dialogue dans l'ensemble du récit

On voit que le dialogue entre Jésus et le père change l'orientation de tout le récit. Si l'on en tient compte, on ne peut donner à la version de Mc le titre (qui pourrait à la rigueur convenir à celles de Mt et de Lc) de «guérison» ou «délivrance d'un enfant». Le dialogue pourtant ne semble-t-il pas se rattacher au récit de façon artificielle? Il suit l'ordre donné par Jésus de lui amener l'enfant et la crise provoquée en sa présence par «l'esprit» (vv. 19c-20), et il prend fin quand, voyant «que la foule accourt ensemble vers» lui (ἐπι-συν-τρέχει), Jésus passe à l'action contre «l'esprit impur»[11].

En Mt, l'ordre d'amener l'enfant est immédiatement suivi de l'intervention contre «le démon» (vv. 17c-18): cela n'est-il pas plus logique? En Lc, la crise de l'enfant se place entre les deux (vv. 41c-42), mais cela ne brise pas le lien qui paraît naturel entre le fait que Jésus fasse approcher l'enfant et la décision de prendre lui-même les choses en mains après ce que le père lui a dit (en Mt, Mc et Lc) de l'échec des disciples? Une logique de ce genre inspire les critiques qui attribuent le dialogue à une opération rédactionnelle secondaire[12]. Ce faisant, on ne

---

11. L'afflux de la foule au v. 25 embarrasse les critiques. Selon G. THEISSEN, elle a sa place originelle après la chute de l'enfant décrite au v. 20 et cela appuie le caractère secondaire des vv. 21-24 (*Urchristliche Wundergeschichten*, Gütersloh, 1974, pp. 139-140). PETZKE (n. 4) accepte la proposition de Theissen et note que la foule, qui apparaît ordinairement au début et à la fin d'un récit, n'intervient en cours de récit que si elle a une fonction à remplir (cf. 2,4; 5,24.30). Ce point de vue fonctionnel et le souci de retrouver un schéma conventionnel de récit empêchent d'interroger le texte sous toutes ses dimensions syntaxiques (notamment le rapport entre l'action et le savoir des personnages) et sémantiques (notamment le rapport à la vie et à la mort).

12. Par exemple, ROLOFF (n. 4), p. 148. Rappelons l'opinion de H. AICHINGER qui reconstitue un récit bien unifié sans les vv. 21-24 (sauf 22a) ni les doublets de Mc et qui l'attribue à un Deutero-Mc qui serait à la source des accords Mt-Lc contre Mc: *Zur Traditionsgeschichte der Epileptiker-Perikope Mk 9,14-29 par Lk 9,37-43a*, in A. FUCHS (ed.), *Probleme der Forschung* (SNTU, A/3), Wien-München, 1978, pp. 114-143 (sur le récit Dmk pp. 126-129).

rend pas compte d'une autre logique, qui se construit par l'articulation du texte dans son ensemble.

Tel qu'il est situé dans le déroulement de l'action, le dialogue avec le père intervient dans une séquence où l'intérêt de Jésus se porte sur l'enfant, qui est en sa présence pendant tout ce qui va suivre. Son mal n'est pas perdu de vue quand Jésus s'occupe du père, puisque celui-ci va devenir solidaire de son fils. Le mal les atteint tous les deux et il doit être traité chez l'un et chez l'autre. C'est ce que nous avons remarqué en voyant comment, au cours du dialogue, le couple père-enfant se constituait en face du couple «esprit»-enfant. Le dialogue va plus loin encore quand le père dépasse la relation qui le lie à son fils et devient un sujet conscient de sa propre détresse devant Jésus. Alors, on peut parler d'un couple Jésus-père construit par la parole qu'ils échangent en vérité. Et cela importe à la transformation de l'enfant dont Jésus va maintenant s'occuper.

Il le fait en voyant venir la foule. Cette indication ne fournit pas le motif qui pousse Jésus à précipiter le dénouement. Elle marque la différence entre deux temps, celui où la foule est censée être à l'écart et celui où l'action se déroule en sa présence. Il ne faut pas en conclure que cette nouvelle phase de l'intervention de Jésus est pour la foule. On ne sait pas ce qu'elle cherche en affluant. Et la relation entre lui et elle est de l'ordre du «voir», non de la parole comme avec le père. Précisément, dans la scène qui suit, il y aura de nouveau quelque chose à voir, et «beaucoup» (τοὺς πολλούς, «la multitude») se fieront aux apparences. Ils diront de l'enfant abandonné à terre par «l'esprit»: «Il est mort». Mais ce sera démenti par le geste de Jésus qui relèvera l'enfant. La venue de la foule permet de passer d'une scène privée où la relation s'établit entre deux sujets par la parole, à une scène publique où il y a du visible à interpréter, et cela ne va pas sans risque d'erreur. La narration de l'intervention de Jésus en deux temps séparés par l'afflux de la multitude correspond à la distinction de deux niveaux de savoir sur ce qui se passe. Ce que la foule voit, elle échoue à le saisir, tandis que le lecteur peut le relier à ce que le dialogue entre Jésus et le père lui a appris. Aucun acteur du récit ne formule d'autre interprétation que celle, erronée, de la multitude. C'est au lecteur qu'il revient de ne pas se méprendre. Ce dispositif de la narration permet de relancer le travail de la signification et la quête de sens chez le lecteur.

Il faut donc relire dans cette perspective l'ensemble du récit. Pour que le couple «esprit»-enfant soit défait, il faut non seulement que le couple père-enfant s'affirme par contraste, mais que lui-même soit transformé par l'établissement du couple Jésus-père. À partir de là, Jésus dissocie le couple «esprit»-enfant et entre en relation personnelle avec l'enfant. Dans cette perspective, le passage de l'enfant par une mort apparente et son relèvement prennent les traits d'une nouvelle naissance à la vie. Et

l'on s'étonne moins que le couple père-enfant ne soit pas reconstitué. Il
n'en est pas de même en Lc, où Jésus «guérit l'enfant et le rendit à son
père» (v. 42). Il n'y a pas en Mc de retour à une situation première qui,
après avoir été dérangée par l'«esprit», réapparaîtrait à la fin au sein
d'une famille «normale». De même que le père a été amené à se dire
comme sujet personnel, indépendamment de son fils, le fils est rendu à
lui-même et à ses capacités d'occuper sa place, debout, dans l'espace et
la communication des hommes.

Notons enfin que la «sortie» de l'«esprit muet» n'est pas suivie d'une
prise de parole de l'enfant, comme le voudrait la logique d'un récit de
guérison. C'est bien le signe que le récit n'est pas focalisé sur le retour
de l'enfant à une situation saine. L'aventure du père n'en prend que
plus de relief. Nous avons remarqué qu'il lui revient de faire antithèse à
l'«esprit muet». C'est lui qui représente la possibilité pour l'enfant
d'accéder à la parole. Et la parole lui sert à aspirer au «croire» qui lui
manque. Sous cet aspect aussi la relation entre père et fils se trouve
redéfinie. Et le récit, malgré sa fin apparemment brusquée, en dit assez
pour que le lecteur lui demande autre chose qu'un miracle réussi.

II. Génération sans foi

Dans ce contexte, la plainte et l'impatience de Jésus telles qu'elles
s'expriment au v. 19, importent à la signification de l'ensemble du récit.
La critique est tentée d'y voir un ajout à un état du récit qui pourrait
très bien s'en passer[13]. Quelle qu'en soit l'origine, cette donnée
commune aux trois synoptiques représente la réaction de Jésus à ce
qu'il apprend du mal de l'enfant, de la démarche du père auprès des
disciples et de leur échec. Le destinataire de cette parole reste indéterminé en Mt et Lc, tandis qu'en Mc (αὐτοῖς, v. 19), ce peut être les
disciples dont il vient d'être question, et aussi l'homme (le père) qui

---

13. L'apostrophe du v. 19b est largement considérée comme un ajout (J. Sundwall,
Die Zusammensetzung des Markusevangeliums, Åbo, 1934, pp. 58-60; G. Minette de
Tillesse, *Le secret messianique dans l'évangile de Marc* [LD, 47], Paris, 1968, pp. 89-99;
Schenk [n. 4] exclut du récit primitif le motif de la foi: l'ajout de ce motif, étranger à un
récit d'exorcisme mais bien en place dans un récit de guérison, indiquerait que Mc assimile
cet exorcisme aux guérisons, p. 89). Le rapport de l'apostrophe au motif de l'impuissance
des disciples est diversement apprécié. Les deux sont ajoutés selon Boismard (n. 2). Selon
Achtemeier (n. 2), l'apostrophe est un ajout qui amplifie le trait de l'échec des disciples
qui était présent dans un des deux récits primitifs sans y être appuyé. Roloff (n. 4)
n'exclut pas que l'apostrophe «Génération sans foi» au moins ait appartenu au récit
primitif parce qu'on ne retrouve rien de pareil en direction des disciples en Mc (pp. 147-
148); ce sont bien les disciples qui sont interpellés conformément à l'orientation du récit
où l'ordre: «Amenez-le-moi» s'adresse à eux (v. 19c; cp. v. 20 avec 7,32 et 8,22); le motif
de l'impuissance des disciples est primitif et aurait été interprété en deux directions
différentes par les deux ajouts de 21-24 et de 28-29.

vient de parler. De toute façon, le «vous» auquel Jésus s'adresse est représenté dans son entourage immédiat et interpellé comme «génération sans foi (ἄπιστος)». Cette définition est plus importante que de savoir de qui il s'agit.

L'accent porte sur l'incompatibilité entre cette «génération» et Jésus: «Jusques à quand serai-je avec [Mt-Lc: auprès de] vous? Jusques à quand (omis en Lc qui lie les deux verbes par: et] vous supporterai-je?» C'est dans le texte la première apparition (et la seule en Mc et Lc) du futur et d'un «je» de Jésus (cf. Mt v. 20): le temps lui dure et il aspire à être délivré du poids insupportable de cette «génération». Il y a conflit entre son désir et la réalité qui lui est imposée tant qu'elle dure. Cependant, au lieu de fuir ou de prendre de la distance, il affronte la contradiction: il fait approcher l'enfant à propos duquel la «génération sans foi» l'entoure et l'exaspère. C'est donc que l'enfant représente en quelque sorte le lieu du conflit, non plus entre le père et les disciples d'une part et l'«esprit» d'autre part, mais entre Jésus et cette «génération».

Quel est l'enjeu de ce conflit? Cette question doit être résolue dans le contexte du récit de Mc. Il ne suffit pas d'y détecter une réminiscence d'une expression biblique et une allusion à la «génération» pécheresse du temps de l'exode. L'allusion est plus nette en Mt et Lc (et en quelques manuscrits anciens de Mc, dont P⁴⁵) où l'expression compte un qualificatif de plus: «génération sans foi et pervertie, γενεὰ ἄπιστος καὶ διεστραμμένη». Cela rend plus reconnaissable la référence à Dt 32,5LXX: γενεὰ σχολιὰ καὶ διεστραμμένη (cité en Ph 2,15). Il est surprenant de constater que si l'expression semble renvoyer plus clairement à l'AT, elle paraît en même temps moins enracinée dans le récit qu'en Mc. Mt lui donnera une contrepartie en centrant le débat final entre Jésus et les disciples sur l'ὀλιγοπιστία de ceux-ci. Mais à cause de l'absence du dialogue entre Jésus et le père, on ne voit apparaître en Mt et Lc aucune figure antithétique par rapport à la «génération sans foi». En Mc, c'est le père, transformé par le dialogue, qui tient ce rôle. Et l'intervention de Jésus apparaît nettement comme un combat contre la «génération sans foi», en commençant par le père.

Le père fait contraste avec cette «génération» sous deux aspects: d'abord parce qu'il s'en sépare en croyant et appelant Jésus au secours de sa non-foi, et aussi parce que la «génération» trouve en lui une ouverture à autre chose. En effet la figure de la «génération» ne doit pas être privée des résonnances qu'elle reçoit dans ce contexte. La relation père-fils appartient à l'ordre de la «génération». On se contente ordinairement de prendre γενεά pour une désignation conventionnelle d'un groupe dont les membres ont à peu près le même âge ou appartiennent à la même période de l'histoire [14], en oubliant que le

---

14. Il ne faut pas confondre ce que désigne le mot γενεά (ordinairement les contemporains, cf. F. Büchsel, *TWNT* I, p. 661) et ce qu'il signifie (sous quel aspect ou quelle

terme utilisé n'est pas neutre. Il renvoie à l'ordre biologique des naissances et engendrements. La «génération sans foi» apparaît comme une collectivité réduite à cette dimension. C'est un ensemble d'hommes pris dans la successivité du temps, enfermés dans le cycle de la naissance et de la mort, sans être marqués par ce qui s'atteste dans le «croire».

La foi ouvre l'issue qui permet de sortir du cercle en témoignant du manque profond qui creuse en l'homme l'appel à l'Autre. Quand Jésus dit son impatience, le père vient de lui raconter comment il s'est adressé aux disciples en vain. Il y avait bien là de son côté un manque à combler, une ouverture à d'autres, qui étaient censés capables de réaliser un désir. Le diagnostic de Jésus et le dialogue qui suit font apparaître que ce manque et ce désir ne tirent pas l'homme au-dessus de sa condition biologique. Le «croire» révèle un autre manque et un autre désir, qui ne sont pas à combler, mais qui se creusent au contraire et s'avouent. C'est par là que la génération humaine reçoit une autre dimension. Et c'est ce qui arrive en cet homme que Jésus amène à dépasser sa recherche d'un pouvoir extérieur au service de son désir et du lien trop étroit qui attache l'un à l'autre le père et le fils.

Quand, après son apostrophe, Jésus fait amener l'enfant près de lui, son combat commence. Il ne s'attaque pas d'abord à «l'esprit», mais à la «génération sans foi». Sa plainte a dit le désir qui l'inspire et qui éclaire la suite du récit: un homme est conduit au delà de son rôle d'engendreur, et la fécondité d'une génération nouvelle se manifeste dans la délivrance d'un enfant, libéré de ce qui le réduit à l'état infra-humain, et mis debout pour une vie authentiquement humaine. Jésus n'apparaît pas ici simplement comme le thaumaturge plus puissant que les disciples, ou comme un être divin égaré parmi les hommes. Il révèle et rend possible une autre dimension, une autre qualité de génération pour l'homme. On peut se demander s'il faut attribuer au hasard (ou alors le hasard fait bien les choses) le fait qu'un tel récit se place après la révélation secrète du «Fils bien-aimé» par la voix sortie de la nuée sur la montagne de la Transfiguration (9,7).

III. LE DÉBAT AVEC LES DISCIPLES

Les vv. 28-29 sont attribués par l'immense majorité des critiques à une dernière couche rédactionnelle[15]. Dans le texte actuel, ils se relient

---

figure le référent est nommé). La référence au Dt, dans la mesure ou elle est perçue, produit un effet de connotation qui n'abolit pas la signification induite par l'articulation du texte.

15. Pour le rapport entre l'ajout des vv. 29-30 et le motif de l'impuissance des disciples selon les critiques, voir n. 13. Même sans cet ajout, réduire ce motif à la fonction de souligner la gravité du mal (comme l'échec des médecins en 5,26, cf. PETZKE, n. 4, p. 187), c'est faire peu de cas du contraste sémantique (et non simplement fonctionnel) entre Jésus

(comme en Mt) à la déclaration du père sur l'impuissance des disciples contre «l'esprit» (v. 18) et (en Mc seulement) à la discussion initiale entre les scribes et les disciples (v. 14). On revient donc à la fin sur la question du pouvoir telle qu'elle était posée avant que Jésus prenne les choses en mains. Mais la réponse de Jésus à la question des disciples paraît peu cohérente avec le récit: «Cette sorte [d'«esprit»] ne peut sortir par rien sinon par la prière», alors que Jésus n'a pas prié et qu'il a affirmé que «tout est possible à celui qui croit», non à celui qui prie. Ce défaut de cohérence n'empêche pas l'ensemble du récit de constituer une unité de signification, au sens où il provoque au travail de la lecture par l'articulation de tous ses éléments et le jeu de leurs différences. Or, ici, les différences ne manquent pas.

La relation des disciples avec Jésus, par exemple, fait contraste avec leur rapport, au début, avec les scribes (v. 14). La scène avec les scribes[16] se passait dehors, en présence de la foule, sans Jésus. Elle se déroulait au niveau du savoir: en effet, la mention des scribes, sans autre précision, n'est pas anodine. Elle investit dans le débat les valeurs de la «lettre» (γραμματεύς, γράμμα), de la «grammaire», du discours régulier, qu'ils représentent. C'est avec des «savants» que l'on discutait du pouvoir d'expulser l'«esprit» dans le cas particulier de l'enfant amené par son père. À la fin, cette question revient avec le même objet précis: «Pourquoi n'avons-nous pas pu expulser cet [esprit]» bien précis (αὐτό) Mais, seuls avec Jésus dans une maison, les disciples ne discutent plus comme entre experts. Ils se mettent en question eux-mêmes («nous») et assument leur échec devant celui qui leur avait donné une «autorité sur les esprits impurs», qu'ils ont exercée avec succès en d'autres circonstances (6,7.13). Il y a donc un problème avec «cet» esprit-là. Or Jésus répond en parlant, non de celui-là, mais de «cette espèce».

Autre différence encore: au père, Jésus parle de croire, et aux disciples de prière, mais la position du père et celle des disciples ne se ressemblent pas. Le père est demandeur d'un bienfait, les disciples étaient sollicités comme agents d'un pouvoir et c'est à propos de ce rôle qu'ils interrogent Jésus. On ne peut donc comparer les deux affirmations sur la puissance de la foi et sur celle de la prière sans compter avec la différence des destinataires: un homme qui cherchait à utiliser un

---

et les disciples ou les médecins: ces acteurs sont porteurs de valeurs sémantiques différentiées.

16. Selon SCHENK (n. 4), le v. 18b garde des éléments traditionnels (p. ex. ἰσχύω), alors que Mc emploie plus volontiers δύναμαι et comme c'est le seul cas de miracle lié à un débat sur l'impuissance des disciples, le soupçon vient que «les disciples» ont été ajoutés au v. 14, tandis qu'il est invraisemblable qu'on ait ajouté «les scribes» (p. 79; cf. aussi PESCH, n. 9, p. 87). Quoi que l'on pense de ce type de raisonnement, il contribue à voiler la question sémantique posée par l'intervention de tels acteurs dans le récit.

pouvoir extérieur à lui, d'une part, et les agents du combat contre «cette sorte» d'esprits, d'autre part.

Le passage de «cet esprit» à «cette sorte» d'esprits indique que le sens du récit déborde le cas particulier qui vient de faire difficulté. «Cette sorte» n'englobe pas n'importe quel «esprit impur» (selon la dénomination du narrateur, v. 25) et n'est pas forcément celle de tous (et seulement) les «esprits muets» (selon la dénomination du père, v. 17). Mais elle peut être caractérisée à partir de celui-là tel qu'il est défini narrativement par ses méfaits sur l'enfant déshumanisé. En face, l'homme réduit à la «génération sans foi» est totalement démuni et cherche vainement un pouvoir extérieur. Pour celui qui, comme le père, est victime du mal, le traitement passe par la parole vraie qui le fait sortir de soi et l'ouvre par le croire. Pour ceux qui, comme les disciples, entreprennent de combattre le mal, il n'y a d'autre pouvoir que la prière (προσ-ευχή). Celle-ci est à la fois expression d'un vœu, d'un désir (εὔχομαι) et adresse à quelqu'un (προσ-εύχομαι). Dans la prière comme dans le croire, la question du pouvoir est subvertie. Le pouvoir ne réside ni hors de soi, ni dans quelque capacité de soi. Dans l'impuissance, dans l'affrontement avec la limite et l'impossible, c'est, du plus profond de soi, l'appel à l'Autre qui devient puissance.

Il reste remarquable que Jésus n'est pas montré dans ce récit comme modèle de foi ou de prière. Ce n'est pas dans cette direction que son rôle ici peut être caractérisé. Il n'est pas donné en exemple. Il est le révélateur et, en quelque sorte, le catalyseur d'une transformation qui fait émerger un homme nouveau, au sein même de ce qui menace son humanité, jusque dans la relation père-fils où elle prend naissance et à laquelle aucun humain n'échappe.

CONCLUSION

J'ai privilégié le récit de Mc, le plus complexe par comparaison avec ceux de Mt et de Lc, plus courts et apparemment moins chargés d'éléments adventices. Quand on parle d'éléments «secondaires», ce peut être au nom d'observations littéraires. C'est surtout au nom d'une logique qui, seule, permet de distinguer entre données nécessaires et données accessoires pour la réalisation d'un programme. Encore faut-il avoir défini le programme, son enjeu et le type de logique que la représentation des acteurs et des circonstances de temps et de lieux met en œuvre. Il arrive qu'on impose à un texte le schéma d'une organisation qui ne lui convient pas et cela donne un autre récit. On s'interdit d'être dérangé par la complexité d'un texte qui paraît éclater en plusieurs directions alors qu'il oriente vers un point nodal qui ne peut être montré dans le texte, mais que ses divers chemins de sens impliquent.

Il aurait fallu traiter les versions de Mt et de Lc de la même façon que celle de Mc pour comparer leurs structurations respectives. Chacune se fait lire indépendamment des autres, à partir de son articulation interne, et non de ses différences avec les autres. Celles-ci peuvent aider à mieux situer les éléments de chacune dans l'ensemble qui lui est propre. Nous avons vu que la présence ou l'absence de crises répétées chez l'enfant ou de dialogue entre Jésus et le père ne se ramène pas à une addition ou soustraction d'éléments contingents sur le fond d'un canevas commun. Même si des éléments se recoupent d'une variante à l'autre, ils s'articulent différemment et composent des récits différents. On ne peut dire, par exemple, que l'enjeu anthropologique du récit est le même chez Mc et chez les deux autres. La signification, c'est-à-dire l'orientation que le texte donne à la quête de sens du lecteur, n'est pas la même.

Pour être juste, il aurait fallu tenir compte aussi de la place que Mt, Mc et Lc font à leur récit dans l'ensemble de leur livre. Les versions de Mt et de Lc cesseraient alors de paraître appauvries par comparaison avec celle de Mc. L'impression qu'elles donnent de présenter une narration plus serrée, plus unifiée, doit être équilibrée par la mise en lumière des articulations de plus grande envergure qui les prennent en charge. C'est à ce niveau que l'on retrouverait peut-être, sous d'autres formes, quelque chose de l'intérêt pour l'homme et sa transformation qui sous-tend le récit de Mc. Il semble en effet que les enjeux du drame de Jésus ont besoin, chez Mt et Lc, d'un développement linéaire longuement poursuivi, tandis qu'il arrive en Mc qu'ils se concentrent en des récits complexes et puissamment noués, où l'on trouve comme des modèles réduits (ou des diagrammes) de l'articulation de tout le livre.

31, rue J.J. Rousseau   Jean DELORME
F-7400 Annecy

LA «FINALE LONGUE DE MARC»
Un épilogue des quatre évangiles

1. Les études littéraires des évangiles ont pris l'habitude de ne pas considérer les deux épisodes dont l'existence est contestée dans une partie de la tradition manuscrite: la «femme adultère», d'une part (= Jn 7,53–8,11), et la «finale longue de Marc», d'autre part (= Mc 16,9-20). D'un côté, on a raison: manifestement, l'un et l'autre vont mal avec l'évangile auquel ils sont rattachés; ils n'en ont pas le style, ils s'articulent difficilement avec le contexte où ils sont placés. D'un autre côté, leur existence reste insuffisamment expliquée: pourquoi ont-ils été placés là où ils sont? Quand et par qui?

2. Selon leur toute première attestation, l'un et l'autre existaient déjà, en Asie mineure, au début du IIe siècle: pour la «femme adultère», nous avons un témoignage de Papias[1]; et la «finale longue» est associée au nom de l'un des maîtres de celui-ci, Ariston ou Aristion[2]. À cette époque, où en est la rédaction des évangiles? C'est une question qui n'est pas réglée. Aucune attestation aussi ancienne ne vient, en effet, garantir qu'elle soit déjà réalisée; et les *Lettres* d'Ignace, pour autant qu'on accepte la date traditionnelle de vers 110[3], permettent seulement

---

1. Eusèbe, *H. e.* 3,39,17. L'allusion est intéressante pour deux raisons: d'abord, l'épisode appartient à un «Évangile selon les Hébreux» qui ne correspond pas à Jn; ensuite il est appelé «au sujet de la femme accusée de nombreux péchés devant le Seigneur», autrement dit, la femme est dite pécheresse, non adultère. Le premier argument va dans le sens d'une indépendance, à l'origine, d'avec Jn; le second permet d'établir une affinité particulière avec le texte du codex de Bèze, qui parle d'une «femme surprise à pécher» (ἐπὶ ἁμαρτίᾳ γυναῖκα κατειλημμένην, 8,3) et non en délit d'adultère (ἐπὶ μοιχείᾳ), comme le reste de la tradition.

2. Voir J. Hug, *La finale de Marc* (EB, 74), Paris, 1978, pp. 15-16. L'attribution à Ariston de Mc 16,9-20 figure dans un ms copié en 989 et édité: voir *L'évangile arménien*, éd. *phototypique du ms 229 de la bibliothèque d'Etchmiadzin*, Paris, 1920, pp. 18-19. Or, Ariston est le nom de l'évêque de Smyrne qui précède Polycarpe (*Constitutions apostoliques* 7,46,8), contemporain de Jean le Presbytre, successeur à Éphèse de l'Apôtre Jean (*C. ap.* 7,46,7) et maître de Papias; faut-il envisager que l'autre maître de Papias, Aristion, auteur de «récits des paroles du Seigneur» (selon le témoignage de son disciple), soit distinct de l'évêque de Smyrne et de l'auteur présumé de la «finale longue»? Cela nous paraît beaucoup moins probable que la solution contraire.

3. Voir R. Joly, *Le dossier d'Ignace d'Antioche*, Bruxelles, 1979. Ce livre stimulant nous convainc qu'une partie au moins des *Lettres* d'Ignace est largement antidatée; en particulier, tout ce qui concerne la question de l'épiscopat monarchique. Une autre partie, cependant, celle qui contient des allusions parfois très précises aux évangiles, et que Joly passe trop vite en revue, nous semble plus ancienne et la date de 110 nous semble crédible. Voir C.B. Amphoux, *Lc 24 et l'origine de la tradition textuelle du codex de Bèze (D.05 du NT)*, dans *Filología Neotestamentaria* 7 (1991) 21-49, pp. 42-44.

de penser que des écrits évangéliques existent bien déjà, sans qu'on puisse fonder qu'ils ont alors la rédaction que nous leur connaissons. En somme, nos deux épisodes pourraient bien être aussi anciens que la rédaction des évangiles elle-même.

3. Or il existe, avant 200, deux traditions textuelles principales des évangiles, dont les rapports ont été longuement étudiés[4], mais sans qu'une conclusion claire ayant l'assentiment de tous ait été établie: d'un côté, une tradition dont le principal représentant est le codex B (*Vaticanus*, IVe s.), qui atteste les évangiles sans la «femme adultère» ni la «finale longue de *Marc*»; de l'autre, le manuscrit D (*codex de Bèze*, vers 400), seul témoin constant de sa tradition, qui présente les évangiles dans l'ordre *Matthieu – Jean – Luc – Marc*, avec ces deux épisodes en place – le second étant, cependant, amputé à partir du v. 15, à cause d'une lacune du manuscrit, qui a fait l'objet d'un remplacement, au IXe siècle.

4. On ne sait pas d'où vient l'ordre des évangiles que présente D et que l'on retrouve dans quelques autres manuscrits, tous témoins d'anciennes traditions: W.032 (*codex de Freer*, Ve s.), it[abe] (*codex Vercellensis, Veronensis* et *Palatinus*, IVe-Ve s.), got (*codex Argenteus*, VIe s.). On doit seulement noter qu'il existe d'autres ordres, mais chacun n'a qu'un seul témoin, mis à part, bien entendu, l'ordre courant. Aussi, la disposition particulière des évangiles dans le codex de Bèze mérite-t-elle toute notre attention. Et parmi les questions que l'on peut se poser, se trouve celle-ci: existe-t-il un lien entre l'ordre des évangiles et la présence ou l'absence de nos deux épisodes?

Dans le cas de la «femme adultère», on peut montrer qu'il existe une correspondance thématique entre Jean et la partie commune des Synoptiques[5]; et le centre de Jn coïncide alors avec les épisodes qui entourent

---

4. Voir, en particulier J. DUPLACY, *P*[75] *et les formes les plus anciennes du texte de Luc*, dans F. NEIRYNCK (éd.), *L'Évangile de Luc* (BETL, 32), Gembloux, 1973, pp. 111-128; Leuven, [2]1989, pp. 21-38; = J. DUPLACY, *Études de critique textuelle du Nouveau Testament*, éd. J. Delobel (BETL, 78), Leuven, 1987, pp. 151-168.

5. La partie commune des Synoptiques comprend ici seulement les épisodes qui se suivent dans le même ordre. Voici le schéma de cet ensemble:
- thèmes de l'eau et de la semence: le **Baptême** + 4 épisodes / 4 épisodes + la **Multiplication des pains**; la *Tentation*, après le Baptême, annonce les thèmes suivants;
- annonces de la Passion: 1e annonce entre 2 épisodes / 2e + 3e annonce entre 2 + 2 épisodes; la *Transfiguration*, après le premier groupe, marque le centre;
- thème du double messianisme sacerdotal et royal de Jésus: l'**Entrée à Jérusalem** + 8 épisodes / 6 épisodes + le **Procès et la mort** + 2; le *Discours eschatologique*, entre ces groupes, reprend les thèmes.
On notera que, dans cet ensemble, les épisodes sont disposés dans la proportion de 1 pour 2, de part et d'autre d'un centre occupé par la Transfiguration: 4 épisodes développent les premiers récits thématiques (en gras), 8 développent les derniers; et à la première annonce de la Passion répondent les deux autres. De plus, chaque partie est organisée en chiasme, les épisodes de développement étant disposés entre les deux récits thématiques – exception

la «femme adultère», soit d'une part, la montée à Jérusalem pour la Fête des Tentes (chap. 7), et d'autre part, la révélation de Jésus sur lui-même comme étant la Lumière du monde (8,12-29). Dans ce centre, les mots de *Tentes* et de *Lumière* établissent une correspondance avec la Transfiguration, qui est justement au centre de la partie commune des Synoptiques. Or, ce centre n'est pas le milieu; de part et d'autre, les symétries se font dans un rapport du simple au double; si bien que le centre se trouve, en définitive, à la fin du premier tiers de chaque ensemble. Considérons, à présent, les quatre évangiles réunis dans l'ordre de D: la «femme adultère» apparaît alors comme étant, à l'intérieur de Jn, le centre des quatre évangiles à la fois, puisque Jn est précédé de l'un d'eux (Mt) et suivi de deux autres (Lc Mc). Cette manière d'écrire nous paraît un peu déroutante; elle l'était sans doute moins, pour les lecteurs du début du IIe siècle[6].

La «finale longue de *Marc*» trouve, dans cette analyse, une explication toute nouvelle: il s'agirait non pas d'une conclusion de *Marc*, destinée à atténuer la fin abrupte de celui-ci, mais d'un épilogue des quatre évangiles réunis dans l'ordre Mt-Jn-Lc-Mc. Il faut donc voir, à présent, si le contenu de cet épisode se prête à une telle fonction.

Dans le cadre de cette brève communication, je vous propose d'examiner trois arguments: les affinités de la «finale longue» avec la tradition textuelle particulière de D, ceci afin de confirmer le rapport envisagé entre la présence de cet épisode et la tradition de D; l'aptitude du récit de la résurrection, dans cette «finale longue», à conclure globalement les quatre évangiles réunis; la qualité des «signes» que Jésus laisse à ses disciples à représenter les fonctions complémentaires que chaque évangile est destiné à jouer.

---

faite de la conclusion de l'ensemble qui comprend la «mise au tombeau» et la «révélation du tombeau vide», après le Procès et la mort, pour des raisons de chronologie évidente. On retrouve dans une grande partie de Jn une composition analogue, mais reposant sur un seul grand chiasme au lieu de deux:
- thèmes d'eau et de semence: le **Baptême** + épisodes narratifs / la **Multiplication des pains** + Pain de vie;
- partie centrale: Confession des disciples / les Enfants d'Abraham; l'Aveugle-né guéri (les sujets se retrouvent aux mêmes places dans les Synoptiques); les *Tentes* et la *Lumière* correspondent par l'image et la place à la Transfiguration;
- thème du messianisme sacerdotal et royal de Jésus: Bon berger-Lazare + **Entrée à Jérusalem** / 6 épisodes + **Procès et mort** + 2.
Les développements suivent les récits thématiques, en première partie, ils les précèdent en dernière partie, avec la même exception des épisodes finaux que dans les Synoptiques.
   6. En réalité, les analogies de composition sont si frappantes que l'indépendance totale des rédactions a quelque chose d'invraisemblable. À partir d'écrits primitifs distincts, il nous paraît préférable d'envisager que la composition finale et la rédaction de chaque livre s'est faite dans le cadre d'un projet commun, que nous situons à Smyrne, au temps de Polycarpe et de Papias, soit vers 120.

I. La «finale longue» et la tradition de D

C'est dans *Luc* que le *codex de Bèze* présente la tradition textuelle de la résurrection la plus éloignée du texte courant[7]. Or, parmi les quelque 35 variantes significatives de ce manuscrit, pour Lc 24, deux au moins présentent avec la «finale longue» une correspondance remarquable.

1. Mc 16,11: ἀκούσαντες ὅτι ζῇ

Si l'on suit le texte courant du récit du tombeau vide de Lc (24,1-12), le mot essentiel prononcé par les anges est évidemment: ἠγέρθη, «Il est ressuscité» (v. 6). On s'attendrait donc à trouver ce verbe dans la bouche des disciples d'Emmaüs, quand ils font à Jésus un résumé du premier épisode (24,22-24); or, leur résumé emploie un autre mot: λέγουσιν αὐτὸν ζῆν, «(les anges) disent (aux femmes) qu'Il est vivant» (v. 23). Pourquoi ce changement de mot? En réalité, il n'y a pas changement. Le verbe ἠγέρθη manque dans D et une partie de la vieille latine, avec toute sa phrase; cette variante est l'une de celles que l'on nomme «western non-interpolations», depuis Westcott et Hort[8], déjà reconnues par eux comme des formes plus anciennes du texte de Lc. Et dans cette tradition ancienne, la correspondance entre l'épisode et son résumé est tout à fait satisfaisante: les anges posent simplement la question: «pourquoi cherchez-vous celui qui est vivant parmi les morts?» (v. 5); et les femmes en retiennent l'essentiel: «ils ont dit qu'il était vivant» (v. 23). Par ailleurs, ni Mt, ni Jn, ni Mc n'emploient ce verbe à propos de la résurrection. On voit donc, sur ce point, que les vv. 9-11 de la «finale longue» ont un trait qui les lie non seulement à Lc, mais plus précisément à la tradition textuelle D-it qui n'a pas ἠγέρθη, au v. 6.

2. Mc 16,13: ἀπήγγειλαν τοῖς λοποῖς

Dans le texte courant de Lc, ce sont les Onze qui parlent aux disciples d'Emmaüs: ὑπέστρεψαν ... καὶ εὗρον τοὺς ἕνδεκα ... λέγοντας ὅτι ὄντως ἠγέρθη ὁ κύριος, «ils revinrent ... et trouvèrent les Onze ... qui leur disent que le Seigneur était réellement ressuscité» (24,33-34); dans D, en revanche, le participe est au nominatif: εὗρον τοὺς ἕνδεκα..., λέγοντες κτλ., «ils trouvèrent les Onze ... et leur disent etc.»; ce sont les disciples de retour qui parlent. Le latin est ici ambigu: *dicentes* peut traduire les deux leçons. Quant à la «finale longue», elle a ici un accord indéniable avec la tradition D de Lc: ce sont bien les disciples de retour qui parlent.

7. Cf. C.B. Amphoux, *art. cit.* (n. 3).

8. *The New Testament in the Original Greek*, 2 vol., Cambridge-London, 1881-82, I, pp. 294-295.

Ainsi, la «finale longue» présente deux accords significatifs avec la tradition textuelle de D, dans Lc: cela ne peut s'expliquer que si cette «finale longue» a bien un rapport avec cette tradition-là.

II. Une conclusion commune aux quatre évangiles

Les vv. 9 à 16 de la «finale longue» reprennent la structure en trois épisodes de Lc 24: apparition du Vivant à Marie (vv. 9-11); apparition à deux disciples et leur retour (vv. 12-13); apparition aux Onze et appel à la prédication universelle (vv. 14-16). Mais les détails ne viennent pas tous de Lc.

1. Mc 16,11: ἐθεάθη ὑπ᾽ αὐτῆς

L'apparition de Jésus, dans la première scène, est commune à Mt (28,9) et Jn (20,14-18); cette apparition est distincte de la scène du tombeau vide, où les femmes voient un ange (Mt, Mc) ou deux (Lc, Jn); mais si l'on tient compte de la seule présence de Marie Madeleine, c'est le verbe θεωρεῖ de Jn (20,14) qui est repris, dans ἐθεάθη, à côté de ζῆ, ce dernier venant de Lc, comme nous l'avons dit. Le premier épisode associe donc plus particulièrement Jn et Lc.

2. Mc 16,12: δυσὶν ἐξ αὐτῶν

La deuxième scène vient entièrement de Lc (24,13-35).

3. Mc 16,14: ὠνείδισεν τὴν ἀπιστίαν αὐτῶν καὶ τὴν σκληροκαρδίαν

La troisième scène associe d'abord des éléments de Jn et Lc: Jésus apparaît aux Onze réunis plutôt dans une pièce (ἀνακειμένοις, «installés à table», cf. Jn et Lc) que sur une montagne (Mt); il leur reproche leur attitude: ἀπιστία, «manque de foi», fait penser au reproche à Thomas μὴ γίνου ἄπιστος «ne sois pas incrédule» (Jn 20,27), tandis que σκληροκαρδία, «dureté de cœur» et le ton de reproche reprend la critique adressée aux disciples en chemin ὦ ἀνόητοι καὶ βραδεῖς τῇ καρδίᾳ «ô esprits sans intelligence et lents de cœur» (Lc 24,25).

4. Mc 16,15: πορευθέντες ... κηρύξατε...

Puis Jésus donne aux Onze une mission universelle: πορευθέντες εἰς τὸν κόσμον ἄπαντα κηρύξατε τὸ εὐαγγέλιον πάσῃ τῇ κτίσει· ὁ πιστεύσας καὶ βαπτισθεὶς σωθήσεται, «allez dans le monde entier prêcher l'Évangile à toute la création; celui qui croira et se fera baptiser sera sauvé». Les mots sont loin de Jn (20,21) et Lc (24,47-48), tandis qu'ils reprennent fidèlement ceux de Mt: πορευθέντες μαθητεύσατε πάντα τὰ ἔθνη, βαπτίσαντες... «allez, enseignez toutes les nations, baptisant...» (Mt 28,19).

Ainsi, sans qu'aucun détail nouveau n'intervienne, les trois scènes brèves d'apparition du ressuscité reprennent l'essentiel de ce que disent chacun des trois premiers évangiles, selon l'ordre de D: Mt, Jn et Lc; Mc, dans une moindre mesure, puisque celui-ci aborde à peine la question de la résurrection. On peut donc conclure que la «finale longue», dans sa partie qui comprend les vv. 9 à 16, rassemble les leçons finales des différents récits de la résurrection; elle est habilitée à servir d'épilogue commun aux quatre évangiles.

III. La fonction complémentaire des évangiles

Avant la disparition au ciel de Jésus, pour siéger à la droite de Dieu, et le départ des disciples pour la prédication universelle (vv. 19-20), une phrase étonnante s'intercale dans la «finale longue»; s'enchaînant à la précédente par un simple δέ, elle place dans la bouche de Jésus quatre «signes» que celui-ci donne aux disciples (vv. 17-18): σημεῖα δὲ τοῖς πιστεύσασιν ταῦτα παρακολουθήσει, ἐν τῷ ὀνόματί μου δαιμόνια ἐκβαλοῦσιν, γλώσσαις λαλήσουσιν καιναῖς, ὄφεις ἀροῦσιν κἂν θανάσιμόν τι πίωσιν οὐ μὴ αὐτοὺς βλάψῃ, ἐπὶ ἀρρώστους χεῖρας ἐπιθήσουσιν καὶ καλῶς ἕξουσιν.

Manifestement, ces «signes» forment un ensemble; mais lequel? Comment mettre sur le même plan «chasser les démons», «parler en langues», «élever les serpents» et «imposer les mains»? À la rigueur, on peut être tenté de rapprocher le premier et le dernier de ces signes, comme actes de guérison; mais justement, pourquoi ne sont-ils pas groupés? Et quel rapport ont-ils avec les deux autres?

1. Le témoignage d'Ignace d'Antioche

Il est assez inattendu d'aller chercher dans les *Lettres* d'Ignace un élément de comparaison avec ces «signes»; mais c'est leur ordre qui va nous guider, plus que les mots employés.
a. Dans *Éphésiens*, on lit une mise en garde insistante contre les porteurs d'une «mauvaise doctrine» (κακὴ διδαχή, 9,1) : «ce sont des chiens enragés... Il faut vous en garder» (7,1); «que personne ne vous trompe» (8,1); «ne vous y trompez pas, mes frères: ceux qui corrompent... par une mauvaise doctrine (κακὴ διδασκαλία)... n'hériteront pas du royaume de Dieu» (16,1-2).
b. Dans *Magnésiens*, au contraire, l'accent se déplace vers le bon enseignement: «rejetez donc le mauvais levain ... et transformez-vous en un levain nouveau» (10,2).
Rien de nouveau, sur ce thème, dans les trois lettres suivantes, sinon, en

Philadelphiens, une association du mauvais enseignement au risque de division: «fuyez la division et les mauvaises doctrines» (2,1).

c. Dans *Smyrniotes*, le thème de la division est repris avec plus de force: «attachez-vous aux prophètes, tout spécialement à l'Évangile ... et fuyez les divisions comme le premier des maux» (6,2).

d. Dans *Polycarpe* enfin, Ignace se choisit un continuateur: «je n'ai pu écrire à toutes les communautés; tu écriras donc aux communautés les plus en vue, comme détenteur de la connaissance de Dieu» (8,1).

On peut lire, dans cette association rapide de quelques passages, un schéma d'Évangile: rupture avec le passé / formation nouvelle / tension vers l'unité / délégation pour la transmission de la parole; quatre étapes que l'on retrouve dans cet ordre, à travers les images du baptême (rupture), de la multiplication des pains (apprentissage), de la marche vers la croix (union à la volonté du Père), enfin de la mission que donne le ressuscité à ses disciples: transmettre la parole. Et tel est le premier sens que l'on peut donner à nos quatre «signes»:
- «chasser les démons» = rompre avec un (autre) enseignement;
- «parler en langues» = apprendre une (nouvelle) théologie;
- «élever les serpents» = atteindre une unité;
- «imposer les mains» = transmettre la parole à la foule.

2. *L'examen des évangiles*

Mais on ne voit pas bien, dans cette acception, pourquoi il s'agirait de «signes», ni ce que ces parties d'Évangile feraient à la fin de quatre livres réunis. Regardons, à présent, chacun des livres, dans l'ordre où ils se succèdent, dans la tradition de D:

a. *Matthieu* vient en tête: c'est le livre dont l'accent porte sur la personne de Pierre, mais aussi sur la réfutation de l'enseignement pharisien. S'il y a un évangile qui représente l'appel à se tenir à l'écart d'un mauvais enseignement, c'est bien celui-ci.

b. *Jean* vient ensuite: s'il est un évangile dont l'accent porte sur l'enseignement nouveau de Jésus, sans plus s'attarder sur le précédent, c'est bien celui-ci.

c. *Luc* est, en troisième position, l'évangile qui approfondit la théologie, reprenant pour une part le langage de Matthieu, mais avec un certain nombre de contacts avec Jean. Il ne s'agit plus seulement d'entrer dans une démarche théologique nouvelle, mais de mener à terme les conséquences de cet engagement. Des quatre évangiles, Luc est celui qui mène le débat le plus loin.

d. *Marc* enfin ressemble à double titre à la quatrième phase que nous avons repérée, dans la *Lettre à Polycarpe*: d'une part l'évangile est simplifié, en ce qu'il n'aborde ni la question de la naissance, ni celle de la résurrection et de la mission, et qu'il ne donne pas en même proportion que les autres la parole à Jésus; d'autre part, Marc est à Pierre ce que Polycarpe est à Ignace, si l'on suit, sur ce point, le témoignage de Papias, contemporain et ami de Polycarpe.

En d'autres termes, les quatre «signes» nous paraissent devoir être mis en rapport avec la fonction des quatre livres réunis pour recevoir comme centre commun la «femme adultère» et comme épilogue commun la «finale longue».

CONCLUSION

1. Les épisodes particuliers de la «femme adultère» et de la «finale longue dite de *Marc*» doivent être considérés comme formant des lieux variants liés entre eux et associés à l'ordre particulier des évangiles que présente le *codex de Bèze* et quelques autres manuscrits.

2. La «finale longue» est écrite dans un langage imagé, non seulement pour servir de conclusion commune aux quatre évangiles, en reprenant à chacun quelque chose du récit de la résurrection, mais aussi pour en être une clé de lecture qui rende compte du rôle spécifique de chaque livre dans l'ensemble qu'ils forment.

3. Ces deux épisodes appartiennent à la tradition de D, la plus ancienne des évangiles qui nous soit parvenue: leur lien avec les quatre livres est essentiel, ce ne sont ni des interpolations, ni des parties de ces livres, mais des pièces supplémentaires faites pour les associer. Ensuite, dans B, ils ont été retirés, parce que les évangiles ne sont plus articulés entre eux; par la suite, enfin, ils seront parfois réintroduits, sans que l'on sache trop pourquoi et sembleront, alors seulement, des interpolations reconnaissables à leur style, dont la présence devient difficilement explicable et dont on préfère admettre, à partir des éditions du XIXe siècle, le caractère secondaire.

4. Si l'on admet ces conclusions, on accorde à ces deux épisodes une importance toute différente. Et c'est peut-être, en l'état actuel des choses, le plus difficile à accepter: les conclusions nouvelles de la critique textuelle, en matière d'histoire du texte, peuvent-elles ébranler les dogmes les mieux établis de la critique littéraire, en matière d'histoire de la rédaction? Si c'est le cas, le dialogue s'annonce prometteur en résultats et riche en surprises.

Rue Louis Perrier 13   Christian B. AMPHOUX
F-34000 Montpellier   CNRS

ANGELOPHANIE - CHRISTOPHANIE
IN DEN SYNOPTISCHEN GRABESGESCHICHTEN
MK 16,1-8 PAR.
(UNTER BERÜCKSICHTIGUNG VON JOH 20,11-18)

Obwohl R. Bultmann es für »irreführend« hielt, die Geschichte vom leeren Grab »als 'Angelophanie' den Christophanien gegenüberzustellen, weil die ἐπιφάνεια hier und dort einen völlig verschiedenen Sinn hat«[1], sei solches dennoch versucht. Das Problem bleibt ja bestehen. Joh 20,11-18 ist dabei mitzubedenken: zum einen wegen der Entsprechung zu Mk 16,1-8 und Mt 28,9-10, zum anderen wegen der verschiedenen überlieferungs- und redaktionskritischen Lösungsversuche, die auch die Joh-Parallele als Argumentationsbasis verwenden. In eine umfassende Präsentation und Diskussion der verschiedenen Hypothesen, die oft mit recht komplizierten Quellenrekonstruktionen oder redaktionskritischen Argumenten verknüpft sind, kann jedoch nicht eingestiegen werden. Sie sollen nur überblicksartig skizziert werden

I. BEFUND UND PROBLEMSTELLUNG

Der Befund ist bekannt: Bei den Geschichten, die von der Entdeckung des leeren Grabes durch Frauen am Ostermorgen, von den Ereignissen dort bzw. auf dem Weg von dort erzählen, lassen sich zwei Typen feststellen: 1. Geschichten, die nur von einer Angelophanie am Grab berichten (Mk 16,5-7: ein νεανίσκος; Lk 24,4-7: ἄνδρες δύο), und 2. Geschichten, die auf eine Angelophanie noch eine Erscheinung des Auferstandenen selbst (Christophanie) folgen lassen (Mt 28,2-3.5-7.9-10: ἄγγελος κυρίου - 'Ιησοῦς; Joh 20,12-13.14-17: δύο ἄγγελοι - 'Ιησοῦς; vgl. auch den sekundären Schluß Mk 16,9). Bei diesen Christophanien fällt sodann ein doppeltes auf: (a) Der Auferstandene *wiederholt* zum einen die Worte des/der Engel(s) (vgl. den Auftrag in Mt 28,7 und 10 sowie die Frage in Joh 20,13 und 15); zum anderen bedeutet seine Erscheinung eine deutliche *Steigerung* gegenüber der Angelophanie. Obwohl bei Mt nämlich schon der Engel seine Worte hoheitsvoll mit ἰδοὺ εἶπον ὑμῖν (Mt 28,8 diff. Mk 16,7) beschließt, liegt darin, daß nun der Auferstandene selbst begegnet und spricht, ebenso

---

1. R. BULTMANN, *Die Geschichte der synoptischen Tradition* (FRLANT, 29), Göttingen, ²1931, p. 314.

eine Überbietung wie darin, daß Christus die Engelsvorhersage des Voraufgehens und Sehens in Galiläa (V. 7) zu einem ausdrücklichen Befehl an die »Brüder« (= Jünger) steigert: »*damit sie* nach Galiläa gehen; dort werden sie mich sehen« (V. 10)[2]. Bei Joh bekommt man überhaupt den Eindruck, als sei das Auftreten der beiden Engel »gänzlich überflüssig«[3] (v. a. im Vergleich mit Mk 16,5-7) und als komme das Eigentliche erst in der Begegnung Marias mit dem Auferstandenen und in dessen Auftragswort (V. 17) zur Sprache[4]. – (b) Eine Christophanie vor Frauen bzw. vor Maria von Magdala am frühen Ostermorgen scheint in Widerspruch zu stehen zu ältesten Aussagen des Kerygmas, wonach Simon/Kephas die erste Erscheinung (Protophanie) des Auferstandenen erhielt (1 Kor 15,5; Lk 24,34) und Frauen keinerlei Erwähnung finden.

Wie erklärt sich dieser eigentümliche Befund? Hat es tatsächlich eine Proto-Christophanie vor Frauen bzw. vor Maria von Magdala neben einer Angelophanie gegeben? Haben Mk und Lk eine solche unterdrückt bzw. zu einer Engelerscheinung »degradiert«? Handelt es sich bei der Christophanie um eine traditionsgeschichtlich oder redaktionell bedingte Steigerung der von Mk erzählten Angelophanie? Oder liegen zwei in verschiedenen Tradentenkreisen entwickelte Überlieferungen von ersten Ostererfahrungen vor, die später – im Zuge der Überlieferung oder Redaktion – kombiniert wurden? Diese Fragen haben auch deshalb Bedeutung, weil viele neuere feministisch-exegetische Arbeiten (vgl. II.5. und 6.) wie selbstverständlich voraussetzen, daß Frauen bzw. Maria von Magdala die erste Erscheinung des Auferstandenen zuteil wurde und sie als erste zu seinen Zeugen und missionarischen Boten bestellt wurden, ein Faktum, das eine androzentrisch orientierte Kirche alsbald zu unterdrücken suchte.

II. LÖSUNGSVORSCHLÄGE

1. Die konsequent redaktionskritische Deutung von F. Neirynck[5] geht davon aus, daß die Christophanie Mt 28,9-10 eine redaktionelle Bildung des Mt auf der Basis allein des Mk-Textes darstelle und daß die Erscheinung vor Maria von Magdala Joh 20,14-18 von der redaktionel-

---

2. Cf. auch F. NEIRYNCK, *Les femmes au tombeau. Étude de la rédaction matthéenne (Matt. xxviii.1-10)* (1969), in *Evangelica. Collected Essays* (BETL, 60), Leuven, 1982, pp. 273-295, bes. 287.

3. R. BULTMANN, *Das Evangelium des Johannes* (KEK, 2), Göttingen, [13]1953, p. 529.

4. Cf. F. NEIRYNCK, *John and the Synoptics* (1977), in *Evangelica* (n. 2), pp. 365-400, bes. p. 398: »the vision of the angels is toned down and 'truncated' in favor of the christophany«.

5. F. NEIRYNCK, *Femmes* (n. 2), bes. pp. 281-295; *John* (n. 4), bes. pp. 387-390, 396-400; *John and the Synoptics. The Empty Tomb Stories* (1984), in *Evangelica II. 1982-1991. Collected Essays* (BETL, 99), Leuven, 1991, pp. 571-600, bes. 579-588, 595-600.

len Bildung des Mt abhänge (bes. in V. 17). Die eigentümliche joh Kombination von »verstümmelter« Angelophanie (VV. 11-13) und Christophanie (VV. 14-18) sei bloß die konsequent fortgeführte Ersetzung des Engels durch Jesus selbst, die schon Mt 28,5-7.9-10 beginne[6]. Neirynck folgert daher, »that the so-called protophany of Mary Magdalene has no traditional basis«[7].

2. Ein zweiter Lösungstyp nimmt die Weiterentwicklung der Angelophanie zu einer Christophanie schon in vor-mt bzw. vor-joh Tradition an – die Gemeinsamkeiten von Mt 28,9-10 und Joh 20,14-18 gingen darauf zurück –, hält diese Tradition allerdings kaum für alt oder historisch zuverlässig (R. Schnackenburg, D. Zeller, vgl. J. Kremer, E. Haenchen, J. Becker)[8].

3. Eine dritte Hypothese rechnet zwar durchaus mit einer Entwicklung und Ausgestaltung der Ostertradition, erkennt aber hinter der Christophanie vor Frauen oder Maria von Magdala alte Tradition (R.E. Brown, C.K. Barrett) bzw. die sekundär mit der Grabesgeschichte verbundene Erinnerung an eine später stattgefundene Erscheinung vor

6. Cf. F. Neirynck, *Empty Tomb* (n. 5), pp. 581-588, bes. 586-588.

7. *Ibid.*, p. 588. – Eng verwandt mit Neiryncks Lösung ist die Bultmanns: Er hält Mt 28,9-10 für einen redaktionellen Anhang zur mk Grabesgeschichte (*Geschichte* [n. 1], pp. 312, 315, n. 1) und Joh 20,14-18 für eine vom Evangelisten selbst – unter Benutzung des Auftragsmotivs – gestaltete Weiterbildung der Engelerscheinung, die freilich (diff. Neirynck) nicht von Mt abhänge (*Johannes* [n. 3], p. 529). – Neuere Befürworter seiner redaktionellen Lösung für Mt 28,9-10 listet Neirynck selbst auf: *John* (n. 4), p. 388, n. 100; *Empty Tomb* (n. 5), p. 580, n. 49. – Kritik an Neirynck üben u.a. R.E. Brown, *The Gospel According to John (XIII–XXI). Introduction, Translation and Notes* (AB, 29A), Garden City, NY, 1970, pp. 1002, 1003; B. Lindars, *The Gospel of John* (NCB), London, 1972, pp. 596, 604; R. Schnackenburg, *Das Johannesevangelium. III. Teil. Kommentar zu Kap. 13–21* (HTKNT, 4/3), Freiburg, 1975, p. 380; Ders., *Matthäusevangelium 16,21-28,20* (Neue Echter Bibel NT, 1/2), Würzburg, 1987, p. 287; J. Gnilka, *Das Matthäusevangelium. II. Teil. Kommentar zu Kap. 14,1–28,20 und Einleitungsfragen* (HTKNT, 1/2), Freiburg, 1988, p. 493; T.A. Mohr, *Markus- und Johannespassion. Redaktions- und traditionsgeschichtliche Untersuchung der Markinischen und Johanneischen Passionstradition* (ATANT, 70), Zürich, 1982, pp. 398-399; D. Zeller, *Der Ostermorgen im 4. Evangelium (Joh 20,1-18)*, in L. Oberlinner (ed.), *Auferstehung Jesu – Auferstehung der Christen. Deutungen des Osterglaubens* (QD, 105), Freiburg, 1986, pp. 145-161, bes. 149-150 (cf. auch die Replik von F. Neirynck, *John and the Synoptics: 1975-1990*, in A. Denaux [ed.], *John and the Synoptics* [BETL, 101], Leuven, 1992, pp. 3-62, bes. 34-35); J. Kremer, *Die Osterevangelien – Geschichten um Geschichte*, Stuttgart, ²1981, p. 179 (pp. 74, 76 dagegen offen für Neiryncks Auffassung zu Mt 28,9-10).

8. R. Schnackenburg, *Johannesevangelium* (n. 7), pp. 379, 380; D. Zeller, *Ostermorgen* (n. 7), pp. 152-153. Ähnliches dürften auch E. Haenchen, *Das Johannesevangelium. Ein Kommentar* (ed. U. Busse), Tübingen, 1980, pp. 567-569, 579-580, und J. Becker, *Das Evangelium nach Johannes. Kapitel 11–21* (ÖTK, 4/2), Gütersloh, 1981, pp. 608-611, 615, voraussetzen. J. Kremer, *Osterevangelien* (n. 7), meint, »daß Mt 28,9-10 entweder auf eine Matthäus und Johannes gemeinsame freie Wiedergabe von Mk 16,7 zurückgeht oder ganz matthäische Redaktion von Mk 16,7 ist« (p. 76), rechnet für Joh 20,14b-17 aber mit einer »Quelle, die auch Mt 28,8-10 ihre Spuren hinterlassen hat« (p. 179).

Frauen (J. Kremer); sie will zumindest nicht ausschließen, daß »Jesus auch seinen Jüngerinnen – und nicht bloß seinen Jüngern – erschienen ist« (J. Gnilka)[9].

4. Der bereits ältere Lösungsvorschlag von M. Albertz und C. Masson geht davon aus, daß Mk oder schon die ihm vorgegebene Tradition eine ursprünglich im Zusammenhang mit dem Grabbesuch erzählte Christophanie vor Frauen zu einer bloßen Angelophanie degradierte bzw. durch eine solche ersetzte, um die Erscheinungen des Auferstandenen aus apologetischen Gründen für die Apostel bzw. Petrus (vgl. 1 Kor 15,3-7; Lk 24,34) zu reservieren[10].

5. Angesichts der sonstigen urkirchlichen Tendenz, eine Christophanie vor Frauen bzw. Maria von Magdala zu relativieren oder zu verschweigen (vgl. Mk 16,8; 1 Kor 15,3-7; Lk 24,34), erachtet es ein verwandter Lösungsversuch als besonderen Glücksfall, daß Nachrichten darüber – unabhängig voneinander – in Mt wie Joh (vgl. Mk 16,9) erhalten blieben; die Berichte besäßen daher größte historische Glaubwürdigkeit. Diese Auffassung findet sich in älterer wie neuerer Literatur (E. Stauffer, P. Benoit, E. Ruckstuhl, J. Jeremias, S. Schulz, T.A. Mohr)[11], besonders auch in Arbeiten, die sich feministischer Exegese

9. R.E. BROWN, *John* (n. 7), pp. 1002-1004; C.K. BARRETT, *The Gospel According to St. John*, London, ²1978, pp. 560-566; J. KREMER, *Die Osterbotschaft der vier Evangelien. Versuch einer Auslegung der Berichte über das leere Grab und die Erscheinungen des Auferstandenen*, Stuttgart, ³1969, pp. 43-44; J. GNILKA, *Matthäusevangelium* (n. 7), p. 496. Vorsichtiger R. SCHNACKENBURG, *Matthäusevangelium* (n. 7), p. 287. Cf. auch M.-É BOISMARD – A. LAMOUILLE, *L'Évangile de Jean* (Synopse des quatre Évangiles en français, 3), Paris, 1977, pp. 459-466, die eine alte Notiz über eine Christophanie vor »Maria« (= Joh 20,14b) schon für »Document C« voraussetzen.

10. M. ALBERTZ, *Zur Formgeschichte der Auferstehungsberichte*, in *ZNW* 21 (1922) 259-269, p. 268: »Auch der Hauptstock der Tradition, der die Christuserlebnisse der Frauen zu Engelerscheinungen degradiert und damit bewußt hinter die kirchengründenden Erscheinungen zurückstellt, läßt erkennen, daß diese Frauenerlebnisse die ältesten sind«. – C. MASSON, *Le tombeau vide. Essai sur la formation d'une tradition*, in *RTP* 32 (1944) 161-174, p. 170: »La tradition primitive racontait, selon nous, une apparition du Ressuscité aux femmes, près de son tombeau, le premier jour de la semaine, et dans l'évangile de Marc cette tradition est remplacée, pour la première fois à notre connaissance, par le récit d'une apparition d'ange dans le tombeau vide«. – Zur Kritik daran cf. schon R. BULTMANN, *Geschichte* (n. 1), p. 315, n. 1: »Daß *Albertz* ... die Geschichten (in Wahrheit ist es nur *eine* Geschichte) von der Christophanie vor den Frauen für gute alte Überlieferung hält, verstehe ich nicht. Seine Behauptung, daß die Überlieferung in der Hauptsache die Christus-Erlebnisse der Frauen zu Engelerscheinungen degradiert habe, widerspricht der Tatsache, daß Mt 28,9f. und Joh 20,14-17 Fortbildungen von Mk 16,1-8 sind; es liegt also umgekehrt«. Weiters: F. NEIRYNCK, *Femmes* (n. 2), p. 295; P. BENOIT, *Marie-Madeleine et les disciples au tombeau selon Joh 20,1-18*, in W. ELTESTER (ed.), *Judentum - Urchristentum - Kirche. FS J. Jeremias* (BZNW, 26), Berlin, 1960, pp. 141-152, bes. 151; S. HEINE, *Eine Person von Rang und Namen. Historische Konturen der Magdalenerin*, in D.-A. KOCH – G. SELLIN – A. LINDEMANN (ed.), *Jesu Rede von Gott und ihre Nachgeschichte im frühen Christentum. FS W. Marxsen*, Gütersloh, 1989, pp. 179-194, bes. 192-193.

11. E. STAUFFER, *Jesus. Gestalt und Geschichte* (Dalp-Taschenbücher, 332), Bern, 1957, bes. pp. 113-114; P. BENOIT, *Marie-Madeleine* (n. 10), bes. pp. 144-145, 150-152; E. RUCKSTUHL, *Das Heilsereignis der Auferstehung Jesu und die Erscheinungen des*

verpflichtet wissen (E. Moltmann-Wendel, E. Schüssler-Fiorenza, E.M. Wainwright, z. T. F. Bovon)[12]. Über das Verhältnis der angenommenen Christophanie zur Angelophanie wird dabei meist nicht reflektiert; P. Benoit nimmt einen zur theologischen Ausgestaltung des leeren Grabes konträren Verzicht des Mk auf eine Christophanieerzählung sowie eine Interpolation der jüngeren Engelszene Joh 20,11b-13 in eine alte Christophaniegeschichte (VV. 11a.14b-18) an; J. Jeremias rekonstruiert eine historisch-chronologische Abfolge Angelophanie – Christophanie; T.A. Mohr vermutet, daß eine auf Mk 16,8 ursprünglich folgende Christophanie vor Maria Magdalena von Mk unterdrückt wurde[13].

6. Unter Voraussetzung einer Protophanie des Auferstandenen vor Maria von Magdala (cf. II.5.) versuchen M. Hengel und S. Heine auch der Grabesgeschichte (mit Engel) deutlicher gerecht zu werden[14]. Beide erkennen zwei traditionsgeschichtlich bzw. vorstellungsmäßig gesonderte Überlieferungen. Die Christophanie vor Maria von Magdala sei dabei von der Entdeckung des leeren Grabes zurückgedrängt worden, weil sie »unter den Juden und in gewissen Gemeindekreisen Anstoß erregte« und »zunächst nicht geglaubt wurde« (Hengel[15]). Heine ver-

Auferstandenen, in DERS. – J. PFAMMATER, Die Auferstehung Jesu Christi. Heilsgeschichtliche Tatsache und Brennpunkt des Glaubens, Luzern, 1968, pp. 61-131, bes. 95-96; J. JEREMIAS, Neutestamentliche Theologie. I. Die Verkündigung Jesu, Gütersloh, 1971, pp. 289-291, bes. 290; S. SCHULZ, Das Evangelium nach Johannes (NTD, 4), Göttingen, [3]1978, p. 244; T.A. MOHR, Markus- und Johannespassion (n. 7), bes. pp. 381-382, 388, 400-401.

12. E. MOLTMANN-WENDEL, Ein eigener Mensch werden. Frauen um Jesus (Gütersloher Taschenbücher, 1006), Gütersloh, [5]1985, bes. p. 76; E. SCHÜSSLER-FIORENZA, Zu ihrem Gedächtnis... Eine feministisch-theologische Rekonstruktion der christlichen Ursprünge (transl. C. Schaumberger), München, 1988, bes. pp. 404-405; F. BOVON, Le privilège pascal de Marie-Madeleine, in NTS 30 (1984) 50-62, bes. pp. 50-52. E.M. WAINWRIGHT, Towards a Feminist Critical Reading of the Gospel according to Matthew (BZNW, 60), Berlin, 1991, bes. pp. 309-313, läßt es zunächst (p. 313) offen, ob die Christophanie Mt 28,9-10 redaktionell kreiert sei oder auf alter Tradition fuße, setzt in ihrer folgenden Argumentation (pp. 313-314) indes die Historizität der Erscheinung des Auferstandenen vor Frauen voraus. – Im Gegensatz dazu rekonstruiert L. SCHOTTROFF, Frauen in der Nachfolge Jesu in neutestamentlicher Zeit, in W. SCHOTTROFF – W. STEGEMANN (ed.), Traditionen der Befreiung. Sozialgeschichtliche Bibelauslegung. II. Frauen in der Bibel, München, 1980, pp. 91-133, bes. 110-112, hinter der Angelophanie Mk 16,1-8 eine Berufungsepiphanie der Maria von Magdala und einiger anderer Frauen und folgert aus der »inklusiven« Redeweise von Mk 16,7, daß bei der Erscheinung des Auferstandenen in Galiläa auch Frauen dabei waren (vgl. DIES., Maria Magdalena und die Frauen am Grabe Jesu, in EvTh 42 [1982] 3-25, bes. pp. 19-20, 24).

13. Cf. P. BENOIT, Marie-Madeleine (n. 10), pp. 146-148, 149-150; J. JEREMIAS, Theologie (n. 11), p. 290; T.A. MOHR, Markus- und Johannespassion (n. 7), pp. 381-382, 388, 401. – Zur Kritik an Benoit cf. etwa F. NEIRYNCK, Femmes (n. 2), pp. 294-295.

14. M. HENGEL, Maria Magdalena und die Frauen als Zeugen, in O. BETZ – M. HENGEL – P. SCHMIDT (ed.), Abraham unser Vater. Juden und Christen im Gespräch über die Bibel. FS O. Michel (AGSU, 5), Leiden, 1963, pp. 243-256; S. HEINE, Person (n. 10), pp. 179-194. – Zur Kritik an Hengel cf. etwa F. NEIRYNCK, Empty Tomb (n. 5), p. 588, n. 95.

15. M. HENGEL, Maria Magdalena (n. 14), p. 255.

mutet darüber hinaus, daß die alte Tradition vom leeren Grab in Kreisen von Frauen Gestalt gewonnen habe, die mit dem Grab Jesu in Verbindung standen. Umgekehrt könne Maria Magdalena, die primär »als Empfängerin einer Christuserscheinung Autorität hatte, nachträglich in diesen Kreis hineingestellt« worden sein. Jedenfalls müssen Grabestradition und Christophanie, da verschiedenen Tradentenkreisen zugehörig, nicht unbedingt nacheinander, »sondern können ... auch relativ parallel entstanden sein«[16].

Da die Vorschläge einander z. T. diamentral entgegenstehen, kommt man um eine Stellungnahme nicht herum.

III. Wertung und Integration

1. *Anfragen an die rein redaktionskritische Deutung*

Bei aller Wertschätzung der scharfsinnigen Analysen F. Neiryncks, bei vielfacher Anerkennung des darin nachgewiesenen redaktionellen Textanteils bleibt doch die Frage bestehen, ob die Christophanie vor den Frauen (bzw. Maria von Magdala) einfach als redaktionelle »Erfindung« des Mt gelten kann, die sich Joh dann »geborgt« habe[17]. Sind die Differenzen im Vokabular, in Erzähldetails, in der literarischen Gattung zwischen Mt und Joh bei aller Ähnlichkeit (Nähe zum Grab, Abfolge Angelophanie – Christophanie, Struktur der Szene, Auftragsmotiv, Term »Brüder«, eventueller Zusammenhang von ἐκράτησαν und μὴ μου ἅπτου) nicht doch so beträchtlich, daß sich eher die Verbindung über eine gemeinsame Tradition nahelegt? Fehlen in Joh 20,14-18 nicht gerade Übernahmen eindeutig matthäischer Spracheigentümlichkeiten[18]? Und ist die Christophanie Mt 28,9-10 wirklich die spezifisch »matthäische Alternative« zur Engelerscheinung bei Mk[19]? Natürlich läßt sie viel Matthäisches in Sprache und Konzeption erkennen[20]. Aber reicht das aus, um eine redaktionelle Bildung der ganzen Episode zu fordern? Erklärt es sich – im Blick auf den ähnlichen und doch verschiedenen Joh-Text – nicht besser als redaktionelle Gestaltung älterer Tradition? Macht die Christophanie nicht doch (bei Mt wie Joh) »einen recht heimatlosen Eindruck«, so daß die Annahme einer alten

---

16. S. Heine, *Person* (n. 10), p. 193. Nach Heine könnten sich so auch die Variationen in den verschiedenen Frauenlisten erklären: »Man wußte später nicht mehr, welche in welchen Überlieferungskreis gehörten, und ordnete sie nicht ihrer historischen Nähe zu den Ereignissen entsprechend, sondern gemäß ihrer Bekanntheit und Bedeutung in den Gemeinden. Daher findet sich Maria Magdalena in beiden Kreisen« (*ibid.*).

17. So bringt es R.E. Brown, *John* (n. 7), p. 1003, auf den Punkt.

18. Cf. auch D. Zeller, *Ostermorgen* (n. 7), p. 149.

19. So F. Neirynck, *John* (n. 4), p. 389.

20. Dazu cf. bes. F. Neirynck, *Femmes* (n. 2), pp. 287-288.

Einzeltradition vieles für sich hat[21]? Steckt also dahinter nicht doch, trotz aller redaktionellen Formung, ein altes und – wie man unter Wahrung aller Vorsicht mit vielen Auslegern vermuten darf – in der Historie verankertes Traditionswissen um eine besondere österliche Erfahrung der Magdalenerin (und vielleicht auch anderer Frauen), die als Begegnung mit dem Auferstandenen gewertet werden konnte?

Noch grundsätzlicher wird man fragen dürfen: Aus welchen Gründen hätte Mt eine Protophanie vor *Frauen*, die nach jüdischem Recht nicht als zeugnisfähig galten, gebildet? Wäre das im Sinn der Apologetik, wie sie v. a. die Wächtergeschichte verdeutlicht, nicht geradezu kontraproduktiv gewesen[22]? Und hätte man in der Urkirche wirklich eine Erscheinung vor Frauen »erfunden«, wo doch die Tradition sonst ihren Einfluß eher zurückzudrängen sucht[23]? Spricht nicht der Umstand, daß die Christophanie vor Frauen bzw. Maria von Magdala die Tradition von der Protophanie vor Petrus (1 Kor 15,5; Lk 24,34) bzw. die Stellung der Apostel als Osterzeugen relativiert, gerade für das Alter und wohl auch die Authentie dieser Überlieferung[24]? Läßt sich der einzigartige – nur Petrus vergleichbare – Rang der Magdalenerin, den sie in den Frauenlisten des Neuen Testaments (Lk 8,2-3; Mk 15,40-41.47; 16,1parr) einnimmt und der sich in der Väterliteratur sowie in apokryphen Schriften noch verstärkt[25], nicht doch am besten durch ihre »Priorität in der Reihenfolge der Epiphanien und der Geschichte der apostolischen Osterbotschaft«[26] erklären?

Die Frageform will zeigen, daß hier keine absolute Sicherheit zu

---

21. S. HEINE, *Person* (n. 10), p. 186. Cf. auch B. LINDARS, *John* (n. 7), p. 604.

22. Cf. die verächtliche Frage des Celsus: »Wer hat dies gesehen? Ein verrücktes Weib, wie ihr behauptet...« (ORIGENES, *Cels.* 2,55). – Dazu M. HENGEL, *Maria Magdalena* (n. 14), p. 252.

23. Beide zuletzt genannten Argumente werden seit langem zugunsten einer alten, historisch fundierten Tradition ins Treffen geführt: cf. M. ALBERTZ, *Formgeschichte* (n. 10), p. 264; C. MASSON, *Le tombeau* (n. 10), pp. 166, 168; E. STAUFFER, *Jesus* (n. 11), p. 114; P. BENOIT, *Marie-Madeleine* (n. 10), p. 151; M. HENGEL, *Maria Magdalena* (n. 14), pp. 252, 254; E. RUCKSTUHL, *Heilsereignis* (n. 11), p. 96; J. JEREMIAS, *Theologie* (n. 11), p. 290; S. HEINE, *Person* (n. 10), pp. 186-187.

24. Cf. dazu auch P. BENOIT, *Marie-Madeleine* (n. 10), p. 151; E. SCHÜSSLER-FIORENZA, *Gedächtnis* (n. 12), p. 405. – In diesem Zusammenhang ist darauf zu verweisen, daß die Erscheinung vor Petrus im NT nirgendwo ausdrücklich als die »erste« bezeichnet wird. Auch 1 Kor 15,5 setzt Petrus nur an die Spitze der für die Legitimation der urkirchlichen Verkündigung entscheidenden Zeugen.

25. Cf. besonders M. HENGEL, *Maria Magdalena* (n. 14), bes. pp. 248-251; S. HEINE, *Person* (n. 10), pp. 185, 188-189; DIES., *Frauen der frühen Christenheit. Zur historischen Kritik einer feministischen Theologie*, Göttingen, ²1987, pp. 137-142; F. BOVON, *Marie-Madeleine* (n. 12), pp. 52-58; E. SCHÜSSLER-FIORENZA, *Gedächtnis* (n. 12), pp. 370-372. Cf. auch schon K.H. SCHELKLE, *Der Geist und die Braut. Frauen in der Bibel*, Düsseldorf, 1977, pp. 151-152.

26. E. STAUFFER, *Jesus* (n. 11), p. 114; cf. M. HENGEL, *Maria Magdalena* (n. 14), p. 251; R.E. BROWN, *John* (n. 7), p. 1003, und das Resümee bei S. HEINE, *Person* (n. 10), p. 194.

gewinnen ist. Doch wird klar, daß die Annahme einer alten Tradition von einer Christophanie vor Frauen (bzw. Maria Magdalena) gewichtige Gründe auf ihrer Seite hat. Wie wäre aber dann das Verhältnis dieser Christophanie zur Angelophanie am bzw. im leeren Grab zu sehen?

2. Versuch einer Integration

Ist die Christophanie-Tradition bereits alt und die Grabesgeschichte mit Angelophanie – wie ich hier voraussetze – keine bloß legendäre, späte Bildung, so wird man am besten zwei frühe, ursprünglich nebeneinander bestehende Ostertraditionen annehmen[27], die beide mit dem leeren Grab verbunden waren. Da sie im Lauf des Überlieferungs- bzw. Redaktionsprozesses miteinander verknüpft wurden[28], konnte sich einer kritischen Betrachtung der Eindruck ergeben, als sei die eine aus der anderen sekundär erwachsen. Über die zeitliche Priorität einer der Traditionen lohnt es wohl nicht zu streiten. Auch dürfte für das Bewußtsein der betroffenen Frauen, der ersten Empfänger ihrer Botschaft und auch der ersten Tradenten (selbst noch der Evangelisten) die Frage, ob es sich bei der österlichen Ursprungserfahrung um eine Engel- oder um eine Christuserscheinung handelte, nebensächlich gewesen sein[29].

Diese Relativierung läßt sich aus den Ostergeschichten selbst, aber auch aus der offenen biblischen (atl. wie ntl.) Sprechweise und aus bibeltheologischen Einsichten rechtfertigen: Nicht nur stimmen die Verheißungs- bzw. Auftragsworte Mt 28,7.10 sowie die Fragen Joh 20,13.15 weithin überein, sondern auch die Aufwertung des ἄγγελος κυρίου bei Mt, der umfassendes Wissen (V. 5: »*ich weiß*, ihr sucht Jesus...«) und überragende Autorität (V. 7: »seht, *ich* habe es euch gesagt«) bekundet, nähert ihn bereits dem vollmächtigen Reden des Auferstandenen (V. 10) an. Man wird dabei deutlich an die Austauschbarkeit des Erscheinens und Sprechens Gottes mit dem des »Engels Gottes« im AT (vgl. Gen 16,7ff.; 21,17ff.; 22,11ff.; 31,11ff.; Ex 3.2ff.;

27. Cf. auch M. HENGEL, *Maria Magdalena* (n. 14), pp. 253, 255; S. HEINE, *Person* (n. 10), p. 193. – Die ohnehin nicht beweisbare These von M. ALBERTZ, *Formgeschichte* (n. 10), p. 268, und C. MASSON, *Le tombeau* (n. 10), p. 170, ist damit natürlich abgelehnt.

28. Cf. etwa H. GRASS, *Ostergeschehen und Osterberichte*, Göttingen, ²1962, p. 121: »Gerade die Tradition vom leeren Grab ... scheint es gewesen zu sein, welche die Erscheinungen unwiderstehlich an sich zog«, sowie die Rekonstruktion der Traditionsentwicklung bei R.E. BROWN, *John* (n. 7), pp. 998-999.

29. Cf. L. SCHOTTROFF, *Frauen* (n. 12), p. 110. – Der jetzige Textbestand vermag – zusammengeschaut – diese Auffassung zu stützen: Auch als dem gängigen apokalyptischen pattern entsprechender angelus interpres (cf. bes. Mk) steht der Engel keineswegs in exklusivem Gegensatz zum erscheinenden Christus; gegenüber dem Suchen der Frauen bezeugt er ja neben dem leeren Grab auch den Auferstandenen selbst (Mk 16,5-6); andererseits geht dieser bei seiner Epiphanie ausdrücklich auf das vom leeren Grab provozierte Suchen der Maria ein (Joh 20,15).

Ri 2,1ff.) erinnert[30]. – Ferner ist zu beachten, daß schon Paulus unterschiedliche Ausdrucksweisen verwendet, um seine Ostererfahrung vor Damaskus zu beschreiben: Er kann sie ein »Sehen« (1 Kor 9,1), eine »Erscheinung« (1 Kor 15,8), eine ihm von Christus bzw. Gott geschenkte »Offenbarung« (Gal 1,12.15-16), eine innere »Erleuchtung zur Erkenntnis« (2 Kor 4,6) und auch einfach eine »Erkenntnis« (Phil 3,8) nennen[31]. Finden diese alternativen Bezeichnungen für ein und dasselbe Ereignis nicht ihre Analogie in den unterschiedlichen Vorstellungen von Angelophanie und Christophanie, wie sie andere Überlieferungskreise ausprägten? – Man darf daher wohl B. Lindars rechtgeben, der meinte, die Ähnlichkeiten zwischen Angelophanie und Christophanie machten es wahrscheinlich, »that they are alternative versions of the same experience«[32]. Diese alternativen Versionen stammen vermutlich aus verschiedenen Tradentenkreisen, deren nähere Bestimmung allerdings schwerfällt[33], und wurden im Zug der Überlieferung bzw. Redaktion kombiniert.

Schließlich darf man auch allgemein anerkannte bibeltheologische Einsichten zur Rechtfertigung heranziehen: Die Osterbotschaft betrifft kein innerweltliches Geschehen, sondern spricht von der schlechthin außergewöhnlichen Erhöhung des Gekreuzigten zur bleibenden Teilhabe am göttlichen Leben und an der Machtfülle Gottes (vgl. Mt 28,18; Phil 2,9-11 u. ö.). Es handelt sich dabei um eine Wirklichkeit, die nur in bildhaft-metaphorischen Begriffen (wie »Auferstehung/Auferweckung« u. ä.) zum Ausdruck gebracht werden kann, weil sie innerweltliche Bedingungen und damit auch menschliche Vorstellungskraft transzendiert. Was für diese Wirklichkeit selbst zutrifft, gilt aber auch für ihre Kundgabe an die Menschen. Die Vorstellungs- bzw. Artikulationsweisen als »Angelophanie« oder »Christophanie« können daher nur tastende Versuche sein, um die im Glauben erfahrene Wirklichkeit ins Wort zu bringen. Also: Die Erzählungen der Evangelien über die Kundgabe der Osterbotschaft durch einen oder zwei Engel bzw. durch den Auferstandenen selbst sind letztlich Versuche, die österliche Glaubenserfahrung der Frauen (!), die alle menschliche Vorstellungs- und

---

30. Cf. I. Broer, ἄγγελος, in *EWNT* 1 (1980) 32-36, p. 36, sowie J. Kremer, *Osterbotschaft* (n. 9), pp. 25-26, 41 mit n. 24.

31. Cf. auch die unterschiedlichen Schilderungen der Berufung Pauli in Apg 9,3-6; 22,6-8; 26,13-18, die wie Bilder bzw. erzählerisch variierte Veranschaulichungen derselben Erfahrung zu verstehen sind.

32. B. Lindars, *John* (n. 7), p. 596.

33. Man könnte an eher jüdisch bzw. hellenistisch geprägte Tradenten denken. Cf. auch S. Heine, *Person* (n. 10), p. 193, die die Angelophanie in Frauenkreisen beheimatet sieht, die mit dem Grab Jesu in Verbindung standen. Daß Maria von Magdala als Empfängerin einer Christuserscheinung erst sekundär in diese Tradition eingerückt sein soll (*ibid.*), läßt sich aber nicht beweisen.

Artikulationskraft übersteigt, als einzigartige, von Gott (der Engel ist sein Repräsentant) bzw. dem Auferstandenen selbst geschenkte Offenbarung zu beschreiben[34].

Institut für Ntl. Bibelwissenschaft   Roman KÜHSCHELM
Schottenring 21
A-1010 Wien

---

34. Ähnlich jüngst auch J. KREMER, »Nimm deine Hand und lege sie in meine Seite!« Exegetische, hermeneutische und bibeltheologische Überlegungen zu Joh 20,24-29, in The Four Gospels 1992. FS F. Neirynck (BETL, 100), Leuven, 1992, pp. 2153-2181, bes. 2174-2175.

ÉVOLUTION DU MOTIF DE LA FOI
DANS LES MIRACLES SYNOPTIQUES, JOHANNIQUES
ET APOCRYPHES

I. Foi et miracle synoptique

Dans les miracles synoptiques, la foi est une condition du miracle; elle est un préalable nécessaire. Cette foi a un caractère personnel qui relie le thaumaturge et le bénéficiaire du miracle. Elle établit entre eux une relation transformante et efficace; elle est l'opérateur du miracle. La foi en la personne de Jésus est une des caractéristiques les plus fondamentales des miracles synoptiques, mais l'une des plus difficilement définissables, si on les compare par exemple aux miracles d'Épidaure et d'Apollonius de Tyane. Ce qui est exigé du dévôt d'Asclépios ou d'Apollonius, c'est la confiance dans leur puissance de guérison, dans leur pouvoir de délivrance et de salut[1]. Cet élément n'est certes pas absent des miracles synoptiques, comme on le voit, par exemple, dans l'attitude des quatre assistants du paralytique qui n'hésitent pas à défaire le toit et à y creuser un trou, – attitude que Jésus qualifie de foi (Mc 2,5). Mais il y a quelque chose de plus dans le miracle synoptique, qui s'exprime dans la parole du père de l'enfant épileptique: «Je crois! Viens en aide à mon incrédulité!» (Mc 9,24). La protestation impuissante de l'homme devant la souffrance ne peut pas franchir la frontière du possible et du légitime sans faire une confiance absolue à la personne toute-puissante de Jésus. En Jésus, l'impossible devient possible (Mc 9,23: «Tout est possible à celui qui croit»), parce qu'en Jésus l'*eschaton*, la fin, le salut de Dieu est déjà présent et agissant dans le temps et la misère humaine d'une manière exceptionnelle. La seule condition exigée (mais condition efficace puisqu'elle est, en quelque sorte, le producteur du miracle de la part de l'homme), c'est la foi en sa personne: πάντα δυνατὰ τῷ πιστεύοντι (Mc 9,23, déjà cité).

L'expression typique ἡ πίστις σου σέσωκέν σε («Ta foi t'a sauvé») revient à 7 reprises dans le Nouveau Testament, dont 6 fois dans 3 miracles synoptiques et 1 fois dans l'épisode de la pécheresse pardonnée (Lc 7,50), – texte propre à Luc, qui montre que le salut obtenu par la

---

1. G. Theissen, *Miracle Stories of the Early Christian Tradition* (Studies of the New Testament and its World, 3), Edinburgh, 1983, pp. 137-140; E. Lohse, *Die Vielfalt des Neuen Testaments*, Göttingen, 1982, pp. 29-44 (article intitulé: *Glaube und Wunder*); J.-M. van Cangh, *Santé et salut dans les miracles d'Épidaure, d'Apollonius de Tyane et du Nouveau Testament*, dans J. Ries (ed.), *Gnosticisme et monde hellénistique* (Publications de l'Institut Orientaliste de Louvain, 27) Louvain-la-Neuve, 1982, pp. 263-277.

foi en Jésus ne concerne pas la guérison d'un membre particulier du corps, mais de l'homme tout entier[2].

Disons un mot des trois miracles, où se rencontre l'expression: «ta foi t'a sauvé».

1. L'hémorroïsse (Mt 9,22; Mc 5,34; Lc 8,48)

La situation du récit de miracle est décrite avec force détails, dont certains sont proches des descriptions d'Épidaure. Ce fait a amené certains commentateurs à contester l'historicité de notre miracle[3], – ce qui nous paraît loin d'être démontré. Des traits communs se rencontrent dans les récits d'un même genre littéraire, mais ne permettent en aucune manière d'émettre un jugement de dépendance ou a fortiori d'authenticité. Dans le cas présent, on indique la durée de la maladie et les vains efforts tentés par les médecins (Mc 5,25-26: «Il y avait une femme atteinte d'un flux de sang depuis douze années, qui avait beaucoup souffert de beaucoup de médecins et avait dépensé tout son avoir sans le moindre profit; bien au contraire, son état n'avait fait qu'empirer»).

La femme croit que Jésus seul peut la libérer de sa maladie incurable. Mais sa foi doit triompher d'une épreuve supplémentaire. Le flux de sang la rend impure aux yeux de la loi juive (Lv 12,4; 15,25-31; 17,11). Son geste de «toucher» est interdit, puisqu'elle pourrait transmettre son impureté légale à Jésus. Cependant, la femme touche le manteau de Jésus et dépasse l'interdit. D'autre part, le contact avec la personne du thaumaturge produit automatiquement son effet, même sans son consentement. On comprend pourquoi dans ces conditions, Mt 9,22 supprime la mention de cet influx qui pourrait sembler «magique» et situe la guérison après l'intervention volontaire de Jésus. Mais Marc déjà a écarté l'accusation de magie en attribuant la guérison à la foi de la femme: «Ma fille, ta foi t'a sauvée; va en paix» (Mc 5,34)[4].

---

2. W. FOERSTER, σωτηρία, in TWNT VII, p. 990.

3. R. BULTMANN, Die Geschichte der synoptischen Tradition (FRLANT, 29), Göttingen, [7]1967, pp. 228-229; E. LOHSE, Vielfalt (n. 1), pp. 30-31.

4. F. BOVON, L'Évangile selon saint Luc (CNT, 3a), Genève, 1991, pp. 436-437. L'A. souligne bien la portée de la formule «Ta foi t'a sauvé» dans la communauté primitive. Il ne semble pas exclure cependant qu'elle ait pu être prononcée déjà par Jésus. Cf. p. 437: «La femme impure est l'image de celles et de ceux qui désiraient être accueillis dans l'Église. Avec cette formule et la narration de miracles de ce genre, la communauté primitive, convaincue que Dieu ne repoussera pas ces gens, se justifie fièrement face à la Synagogue. Jésus, représentant de Dieu, ne constitue pas, à la différence du sanctuaire de Lv 15,31, une menace de mort pour de tels gens impurs. Au contraire, une force guérissante jaillit de lui, et restaure la vie. La soudaineté de la guérison..., confirme le oui de Dieu à la nouvelle conception de la foi».

2. *L'aveugle Bartimée (Mc 10,52; Lc 18,42)*

Le miracle lui-même n'est pas décrit. À Jésus qui demande à l'aveugle: «Que veux-tu que je fasse pour toi?», celui-ci répond: «Rabbouni, que je voie!» (Mc 10,51). Jésus ne pose aucun geste, ne prononce aucune parole, mais constate simplement: «Ta foi t'a sauvé!». Le véritable opérateur du miracle apparaît être la foi de l'aveugle. C'est sa foi qui prend, en quelque sorte, la place de l'action thaumaturgique de Jésus. L'état initial de l'homme «assis, au bord du chemin» (Mc 10,46) a subi une transformation radicale: «il le suivait sur le chemin» (Mc 10,52)[5]. Bartimée est le seul miraculé qui ait eu la permission de suivre Jésus (en sens contraire, le possédé de Gérasa est envoyé vers les siens, en Décapole, Mc 5,19). Il s'agit là d'une initiative de Bartimée, puisqu'il avait reçu l'ordre de s'en aller: «Va; ta foi t'a sauvé» (v. 52a). D'autre part, Mc 10,49 emploie trois fois le verbe appeler (φωνέω) qui a un sens banal, et non pas le verbe καλέω qui peut avoir le sens technique d' «appeler à la suite de», comme c'est le cas dans l'appel des fils de Zébédée (Mc 1,20). Jésus ne demande aucune récompense en échange du miracle, comme ce sera le cas des apôtres dans les Actes apocryphes (cf. le troc spirituel).

3. *Le lépreux samaritain (Lc 17,19)*

Les dix lépreux implorent Jésus: «Jésus, maître, aie pitié de nous» (Lc 17,13)[6]. Ils font confiance à l'ordre de Jésus: «Allez vous montrer aux prêtres» (Lc 17,14). Le miracle n'est aucunement décrit; seul le résultat est évoqué succinctement: «Et il arriva, comme ils s'en allaient, qu'ils furent purifiés» (v. 14b). Seul parmi les dix lépreux, un Samaritain s'en retourne auprès de Jésus pour rendre gloire à Dieu (v. 18). Le seul lieu valable désormais pour rendre gloire à Dieu n'est plus le Temple de Jérusalem, c'est de se tourner vers Jésus.

Les dix lépreux avaient une foi suffisante, puisque tous les dix furent guéris. Jésus refuse, en effet, d'opérer des miracles lorsqu'il ne rencontre

---

5. J. DUPONT, *L'aveugle de Jéricho recouvre la vue et suit Jésus (Marc 10,46-52)*, in *Études sur les Évangiles synoptiques* (BETL, 70), Leuven, 1988, t. 1, pp. 350-367. L'A. écrit p. 359: «Quelque chose s'est donc passé dans l'intervalle, grâce à quoi l'aveugle est devenu un voyant, l'homme assis est devenu un suiveur, celui qui était marginal a été incorporé au groupe des compagnons de Jésus».

6. L'apostrophe «Jésus», employée au vocatif, ne se trouve jamais chez Mt et Jn et seulement 3 fois chez Mc (Mc 1,24; 5,7: deux fois dans la bouche des démons; Mc 10,47: l'aveugle Bartimée, que nous venons de voir). On la rencontre 5 fois chez Lc: dans les trois textes parallèles à Mc, c'est-à-dire Lc 4,34; 8,28; 18,38 et, en plus, dans les deux textes qui lui sont propres, le texte des dix lépreux de Lc 19,13 et du bon larron de Lc 23,42. Ces deux derniers emplois ont en commun d'être adressés à Jésus par des pécheurs qui demandent et obtiennent la guérison ou le salut (deux réalités qui se correspondent chez Lc comme le signe et le signifié). Cf. E. CHARPENTIER, *L'étranger appelé au salut (Lc 17,11-19)*, in *AssSeign* 59 (1974) 68-79.

pas de foi, comme ce fut le cas à Nazareth (Mc 6,5-6: «Et il ne pouvait faire là aucun miracle ... et il s'étonna à cause de leur manque de foi»). Encore une fois, le pouvoir de Jésus semble lié et comme dépendant de la foi du bénéficiaire! Le Samaritain accède à une foi plus profonde; il témoigne d'un accroissement de foi par rapport aux neuf autres miraculés. Pour Luc, la foi des dix lépreux leur a obtenu la guérison, tandis que la foi plus parfaite (parce qu'elle rend grâce à Jésus et gloire à Dieu) du Samaritain lui a obtenu le salut au sens fort. C'est à lui seul, en effet, que Lc 17,19 adresse l'affirmation typique: «T'étant levé, pars, ta foi t'a sauvé». Cette foi du Samaritain fait de lui un vrai disciple, – ce qui semble répondre avec une pointe polémique à la demande des apôtres quelques versets plus hauts: «Augmente en nous la foi» (Lc 17,5, texte propre à Luc)[7]. Dans les autres miracles synoptiques également, la foi est un préalable et une condition du miracle:

1. *Le paralytique* (Mc 2,5 par. Mt 9,2; Lc 5,20: «Et Jésus, voyant leur foi, dit au paralytique...»). Ici, c'est la foi des accompagnateurs qui est mise en évidence.

2. *Le centurion* (Mt 8,10 par. Lc 7,9: «Jésus admira et dit à ceux qui le suivaient: En vérité, je vous le dis, chez personne je n'ai trouvé pareille foi en Israël». Autre texte propre à Matthieu, en Mt 8,13: «Va, qu'il t'advienne comme tu as cru»). Mise en valeur de la foi de l'étranger, comme dans le cas de la guérison du lépreux samaritain (Lc 17,19).

3. *La tempête apaisée* (Mc 4,40 par. Lc 8,25: «Pourquoi êtes-vous peureux ainsi? Comment n'avez-vous pas de foi?». Texte un peu différent chez Mt 8,26: «Pourquoi êtes-vous peureux, hommes de peu de foi?», – thème propre à Matthieu de l'ὀλιγοπιστία)[8].

4. *Résurrection de la fille de Jaïre* (Mc 5,36 par. Lc 8,50: «N'aie pas peur, crois seulement»). La foi est victorieuse de la peur et même de la mort.

5. *Guérison de deux aveugles*: (Texte propre à Mt 9,28-29: «Croyez-vous que je puisse faire cela?... Qu'il vous arrive selon votre foi»). La mesure du miracle, c'est la foi.

6. *La Cananéenne*: (Texte propre à Mt 15,28: «O femme, grande est ta foi. Qu'il t'arrive comme tu veux»). Deuxième miracle qui récompense la foi d'une personne étrangère.

Il faudrait citer la sentence quadruple de Jésus sur la victoire de la foi qui déplace les montagnes et transplante les arbres. Ce texte contient une double tradition:

---

7. E. CHARPENTIER, *L'étranger* (n. 6), p. 77.
8. L'ὀλιγόπιστος caractérise une situation d'incroyance à l'intérieur même de la foi du disciple. Cf. H.J. HELD, *Matthäus als Interpret der Wundergeschichten*, in G. BORNKAMM – G. BARTH – H.J. HELD, *Überlieferung und Auslegung im Matthäusevangelium* (WMANT, 1), Neukirchen, 1960, pp. 281-283.

1. Mc 11,22-23 et Mt 21,21, d'une part, qui ont le même contexte (figuier desséché) et les mêmes éléments majeurs (que nous soulignons):

Si vous avez de *la foi,* et si vous n'*hésitez* pas dans votre cœur, vous *direz* à cette *montagne*: Enlève-toi et *jette-toi dans la mer* et cela vous sera accordé.

2. Mt 17,20 et Lc 17,6, d'autre part, qui ont des contextes différents, mais les éléments communs suivants:

Si vous avez de la *foi comme un grain de sénevé,*
Vous direz à cette montagne (Mt).   à ce sycomore (Lc).
Passe d'ici à là-bas (Mt).   Plante-toi dans la mer (Lc).
Et elle passera (Mt).   Et il vous obéirait (Lc).
Et rien ne vous sera impossible (Mt).

Plusieurs auteurs pensent que la sentence de Lc 17,6 est primitive et que Mt 17,20 est rédactionnel[9]. Le sens de Lc 17,6 se base sur la foi déposée dans le cœur de l'homme par Dieu, et non comme le résultat d'un effort de l'homme. Il faut d'abord recevoir le germe de Dieu en nous, comme un ensemencement, avant de penser à augmenter la foi (Lc 17,5). Cela signifierait également que Dieu accordera la foi à l'homme après le retour de Jésus au Père[10]. Ce dernier point ne respecte pas le sens obvie du texte, comme celui d'ailleurs de tous les parallèles cités plus haut[11].

Il semble plutôt que nous ayons affaire ici à deux types de *logia* authentiques de Jésus adressés aux disciples, dans le cadre de la mission (Lc 9,1-2 par.) Le genre littéraire est celui de l'avertissement prophé-

9. Par exemple, X. Léon-Dufour, *L'épisode de l'enfant épileptique,* dans *Études d'Évangile* (Parole de Dieu, 2), Paris, pp. 183-227; cf. surtout pp. 199-201. L'A. suit ici l'analyse de E. Lohmeyer, *Das Evangelium des Matthäus* (KEK), Göttingen, 1956, pp. 271-274.

10. X. Léon-Dufour, *L'enfant épileptique* (n. 9), p. 201.

11. La critique a proposé de multiples hypothèses concernant l'interprétation de ces *logia.* Cf. J.D.M. Derrett, *Moving Mountains and Uprooting Trees (Mk 11:22; Mt 17:20; 21:21; Lk 17:6),* in *Bibbia e Oriente* 30 (1988) 231-244. Selon l'A., les deux types de *logia* peuvent être authentiques, puisqu'ils décrivent deux actions attendues pour la fin des temps selon la «parole exécutive» (*executive words*) de Jr 1,10. Le Ps 148,9 («Montagnes et toutes les collines, arbres fruitiers et tous les cèdres») nous dit que les montagnes et les arbres participent à la louange du Créateur (cf. aussi Is 44,23 et 55,12). D'après Is 40,4 et Jr 45,4 (ou 24,6), l'abaissement des montagnes et le déracinement des arbres et leur nouvelle plantation sont le symbole de la fin des temps (originairement, de la fin de l'exil). En Lc 17,6, il s'agirait de replanter les arbres *près* de la mer et non dans la mer (double sens de la préposition *b* ᵉ en hébreu). Le sens du logion serait qu'avec une foi suffisante, les disciples peuvent commander au «nouvel âge» de faire irruption (cf. p. 243). J.A. Fitzmyer, *The Gospel according to Luke* (AB, 28A), New York, 1985, vol. 2, p. 1142, pense que Lc 17,6 a préservé la forme originale de Q mieux que Mt 17,20 qui emprunte l'image de la montagne à Mt 21,21. On ne comprendrait pas pourquoi Lc aurait changé la montagne de Mt en sycomore ou en mûrier. Pour J. Jeremias, *Théologie du Nouveau Testament* (LD, 76), Paris, 1973, p. 209: «Mc 11,23 par. Mt 21,21 présente une forme mêlée», c'est-à-dire composite et Mt 17,20 et Lc 17,6 présenteraient la forme originale qui circulait sous la double image de la montagne et du mûrier.

tique (énoncé d'une condition, suivie d'une promesse ou d'une menace). La foi demandée est la confiance absolue du disciple en la personne de Jésus qui l'envoie et lui donne pouvoir absolu sur Satan (Lc 10,18) et sur ses œuvres (les maladies physiques et psychiques, Lc 13,16). Le sens du *logion* est clair: «arracher ou déraciner les montagnes», «transplanter des arbres» (tel le sycomore) sont des expressions rabbiniques qui signifient réaliser l'impossible[12]. Mais nulle part dans le judaïsme, on ne rencontre l'association de la foi et du doute (ou de l'hésitation) surmontés comme c'est le cas dans la première tradition du *logion* (Mc 11,22-23 par. Mt 21,21). On pourrait avoir ici un *logion* à la fois concret et paradoxal de Jésus lui-même[13].

Mais l'indice d'authenticité le plus important dans le cas du double *logion* sur le déplacement des montagnes (Mt 17,20 et 21,21 par.) est le fait que cette expression n'est jamais appliquée à la puissance de la foi dans le judaïsme. Cette application ne se trouve que dans les *logia* cités et dans I Co 13,2 («Quand j'aurais la foi la plus totale, celle qui transporte les montagnes...») et cela, de manière indépendante, sans que l'un des textes ne fasse référence à l'autre[14].

II. Foi et miracle johannique

On trouve dans l'évangile de Jean, une conception de la foi comme préalable au miracle, très proche des synoptiques. Prenons nos exemples dans les deux cas de miracles-guérisons de son évangile: la guérison du fils du fonctionnaire royal et la réanimation de Lazare. Les autres exemples dont il sera question ensuite pour développer la seconde conception de la foi dans le miracle johannique appartiennent à d'au-

---

12. STRACK-BILLERBECK, I, 759. L'expression «déraciner les montagnes» se dit ʿôqar *harîm* et est appliquée à un rabbin qui accomplit ce qui semble impossible, tel Resch Laqish (vers 250) qui parvient à répondre à toutes les difficultés de la *halakah* qu'on lui oppose (*T.B. Sanh* 24a). En revanche, on appelle «Sinaï», un rabbin, qui sans être un bon disputeur, connaît par cœur tout le matériel de la *halakah*. *T.B. Sota* 9b applique l'expression à Samson dans Jug 13,25 qui a réellement déraciné deux montagnes. Pour le déracinement d'un sycomore, chose particulièrement difficile, puisque les racines de cet arbre s'enfoncent profondément, peuvent percer un rocher et tenir plus de 600 ans dans la terre, cf. STRACK-BILLERBECK, II, 234 qui cite *T.J. Berakot* 9,14a, 23; *T.J. Taʿanit* 1,64b,26; *Gen. Rabba* 12 (9b).

13. *À la rencontre de Dieu. Mémorial Albert Gelin* (en collab.), Le Puy, 1961, cf. l'étude de J. DUPLACY, *La foi qui déplace les montagnes* (*Mt XVII,20; XXI,21 et par.*), pp. 273-287. L'A. écrit p. 279: «Dans la littérature juive, qu'elle soit apocryphe, rabbinique ou qumranienne, la foi tient une place qui n'est pas négligeable; nulle part cependant nous n'y rencontrons l'idée majeure de la parole qui nous occupe: l'efficacité extraordinaire conférée par la foi à celui qui croit et menacée en lui par le doute». Ceci plaiderait en faveur de l'authenticité de Mc 11,23 par. Mt 21,21.

14. J. JEREMIAS, *Théologie* (n. 11), p. 204.

tres types de récits, comme le miracle-don (Cana et la multiplication des pains) et le miracle-légitimation (l'aveugle-né). Or, nous avons montré ailleurs à la suite de G. Theissen[15] que la foi du bénéficiaire était centrale dans les guérisons, tandis que c'était plutôt l'initiative du thaumaturge qui était mise en évidence dans les miracles-don et les miracles-légitimation.

Étudions d'abord le niveau de Jean II-B (3e niveau d'après M.-É. Boismard) qui est proche de la position des synoptiques[16].

1. Dans la guérison du fils du fonctionnaire royal, la foi du quémandeur est mise en valeur: «L'homme crut à la parole que Jésus lui avait dite et il partit... L'homme crut, lui et toute sa famille» (Jn 4,50b.53b). La foi n'a pas besoin du miracle pour s'épanouir. On comprend alors pourquoi Jn 4,48 adresse un reproche, non au père de l'enfant, mais au lecteur de l'évangile qui réclame des miracles pour croire: «Si vous ne voyez signes et prodiges, vous ne croirez pas!» Ce texte est proche du reproche de Jésus à Thomas: «Parce que tu me vois, tu crois. Heureux ceux qui croiront sans avoir vu» (Jn 20,29).

2. Dans la réanimation de Lazare, Jésus s'adresse à Marthe: «Quiconque vit et croit en moi ne mourra jamais. Le crois-tu? Elle lui dit: Oui, Seigneur, je crois...» (Jn 11,26-27) et plus loin: «Ne t'ai-je pas dit que si tu croyais, tu verrais la gloire de Dieu» (Jn 11,40). La réanimation de Lazare est accordée à la foi de Marthe qui précède le miracle.

Le message est très différent dans les autres types de miracles cités (et également à un autre niveau rédactionnel de la guérison du fils du fonctionnaire royal et du miracle de Lazare). Ces niveaux 1 et 2 de Jn sont identifiés au Document C et à Jean II-A par M.-É. Boismard[17].

1. À Cana, les disciples croient parce qu'ils ont assisté au miracle de l'eau changée en vin. «Tel est le début des signes (σημεῖα) que Jésus fit,

---

15. G. THEISSEN, *Miracle Stories* (n. 1), pp. 112-118; J.M. VAN CANGH, *Miracle*, dans *Dictionnaire Encyclopédique de la Bible*, Maredsous, pp. 833-846; voir p. 845.

16. M.-É. BOISMARD, *Rapports entre foi et miracles dans l'Évangile de Jean*, in *ETL* 58 (1982) 357-364, voir pp. 360-361.

17. M.-É. BOISMARD, *Rapports* (n. 16), pp. 358-360; M.-É. BOISMARD – A. LAMOUILLE, *Synopse des quatre Évangiles en français, Tome III, L'Évangile de Jean*, Paris, 1977, pp. 48-50; 149-152. Dans le Doc. C et Jean II-A, Jésus est présenté comme le prophète semblable à Moïse selon Dt 18,18 (cf. Jn 1,45 et 7,40). Ses trois premiers miracles en Galilée (Cana, le fils du fonctionnaire royal et la pêche miraculeuse) sont des «signes» qui correspondent aux trois signes accomplis par Moïse pour authentifier sa mission selon Ex 4,1-9. De part et d'autre, les signes ont valeur apologétique. En revanche, Jean II-B se préoccupe du problème de la deuxième génération chrétienne, des hommes qui n'ont pas été témoins des miracles de Jésus. Il va montrer que la foi fondée sur les miracles est une foi fragile et que la Parole de Jésus est supérieure aux signes (Jn 4,41-42). Jean II-B rejoint la tradition synoptique de la foi qui précède le miracle. Enfin Jean III (4e niveau) accomplit une série de retouches judaïsantes, mais il n'aurait pas joué de rôle significatif dans la relation foi-miracles.

à Cana de Galilée. Et il manifesta sa gloire et ses disciples crurent en lui» (Jn 2,11).

2. Après la multiplication des pains, la foule considère Jésus comme le prophète semblable à Moïse qui nourrit son peuple au désert, et veut le faire roi. C'est donc le signe accompli par Jésus (Jn 6,14) qui déclenche la foi du peuple en lui.

3. Le miracle de l'aveugle-né a pour but de «manifester les œuvres de Dieu en lui» (Jn 9,3). Le signe accompli par Jésus doit conduire les hommes à avoir foi en sa mission. «On n'a jamais entendu que quelqu'un ait ouvert les yeux d'un aveugle-né. Si celui-ci n'était pas de Dieu, il ne pourrait rien faire» (Jn 9,32-33).

4. À un niveau plus ancien de la tradition sur Lazare (Jean II-A), le miracle a pour fonction de susciter la foi en Jésus et dans son envoi par le Père: «Père, je te rends grâce de m'avoir exaucé. Pour moi, je sais que tu m'exauces toujours; mais j'ai parlé à cause de la foule qui se tient à l'entour, afin qu'ils croient que tu m'as envoyé» (Jn 11,41-42).

5. On pourrait y ajouter un stade plus ancien du miracle de la guérison de l'officier royal, du moins si l'on se réfère à un niveau plus ancien, non pas nécessairement de Jn 4,46-54, mais du texte de M.-É. Boismard[18]. En 1965, ce dernier distinguait trois stades du miracle:

a. l'homme croit à la parole de Jésus sans avoir vu le miracle (Jn 4,46b-47.50). C'est la perspective synoptique.

b. au second stade rédactionnel (celui qui nous préoccupe ici), c'est-à-dire aux vv. 51-53, l'homme croit après avoir constaté le miracle. C'est la perspective johannique.

c. le troisième stade (v. 48), qui critique la demande de signes et prodiges, déprécie le miracle et en fait une concession de Dieu à la dureté du cœur des hommes. On retrouvera cette critique du miracle dans l'évangile de l'enfance de Luc, qui oppose l'attitude de Zacharie à celle de Marie[19].

Quoi qu'il en soit de l'évolution de la pensée de M.-É. Boismard (qui, dans ses études plus récentes, fusionne les stades 1 et 2 pour l'attribuer à Jean II-B), nous pensons que celui-ci a bien mis en évidence la différence essentielle entre la perspective synoptique et la perspective habituelle de Jean. Dans la première, la foi joue le rôle de préalable et de condition nécessaire au miracle, tandis que dans la seconde (celle du Doc. C et de Jean II-A), la foi apparaît comme la conséquence du miracle, puisque le signe johannique a pour but de la susciter, en authentifiant les «œuvres» de Jésus comme étant celles de Dieu. Nous croyons d'ailleurs que, par des méthodes différentes, les vues de G. Theissen coïncident avec celles de M.-É. Boismard et les confirment.

18. M.-É. BOISMARD, *Guérison du fils d'un fonctionnaire royal*, in *AssSeign* 75 (1965) 26-37.

19. *Ibid.*, pp. 34-36.

III. FOI ET MIRACLE DANS LES ACTES APOCRYPHES DES APÔTRES

Dans les Actes Apocryphes des Apôtres les plus anciens (Actes de Jean (AJ), Actes d'André (AA), Actes de Paul (AP), Actes de Pierre (APet) et Actes de Thomas (ATh)), nous avons pu établir le bilan suivant: on y compte 23 guérisons, 28 résurrections, 13 exorcismes, 37 épiphanies ou manifestations spéciales, 19 sauvetages miraculeux, 10 miracles de châtiment[20]. En revanche, nous n'y trouvons pas de miracles-don qui ressembleraient à la pêche miraculeuse, aux deux multiplications des pains ou aux noces de Cana des Évangiles. La raison est probablement à chercher dans le mépris qu'ils manifestent pour les biens matériels et dans leur doctrine encratite[21]. Mais nous y trouvons, par contre, deux types de miracles totalement absents des Évangiles et des Actes canoniques: 16 miracles d'animaux et 27 cas de polymorphie (Jésus apparaît soit sous une forme symbolique pour venir en aide aux croyants, soit sous des formes antithétiques pour marquer son unité fondamentale dans la diversité des apparences).

Par rapport aux Évangiles et aux Actes canoniques, nous constatons un renversement des proportions entre les guérisons proprement dites et les résurrections. Les premières sont au nombre de 14 dans les Évangiles et Actes canoniques et les secondes au nombre de 5[22], tandis que, dans les Actes Apocryphes, on compte 23 guérisons et 28 résurrections. La raison de ce fait est claire: les résurrections sont plus spectaculaires et plus indiscutables, et elles sont donc plus aptes à susciter la foi des incroyants[23]. Mais comme l'affirme les *AJ* 47,2-3: «Ce n'est pas une chose difficile pour un homme qui maîtrise de grands mystères que de se dépenser encore dans des petits». Autrement dit, la résurrection du prêtre d'Artémis est pour Jean une activité mineure en regard des grands mystères, c'est-à-dire de la conversion spirituelle. Jean s'adresse d'ailleurs en ces termes au prêtre païen ressuscité: «Veux-tu appartenir

---

20. J.M. VAN CANGH, *Miracles évangéliques - Miracles apocryphes*, in *The Four Gospels 1992. FS F. Neirynck* (BETL, 100), Leuven, pp. 2277-2319.

21. Y. TISSOT, *Encratisme et Actes Apocryphes*, in F. BOVON, et al., *Les Actes Apocryphes des Apôtres. Christianisme et monde païen* (Publications de la Fac. de Théologie de l'Univ. de Genève, 4), Genève, 1981, pp. 109-119.

22. J.M. VAN CANGH, in *Miracle* (n. 15), p. 842.

23. G. POUPON, *L'accusation de magie dans les Actes Apocryphes*, in F. BOVON, et al., *Les Actes Apocryphes* (n. 21), pp. 71-85. L'A. écrit très judicieusement p. 85: «Ayant à rivaliser avec les prétentions des magiciens, les apôtres se devaient d'accomplir sans difficulté ce qui représentait l'exploit suprême, la limite des pouvoirs de la magie, et échappait dès lors à tout soupçon». Simon le magicien s'incline par trois fois vers la tête du cadavre du fils d'une matrone et réussit à lui faire mouvoir la tête et les yeux. Pierre de son côté, prononce une brève prière et touche l'épaule du mort en disant «Lève-toi!». Nicostrate se lève, marche et parle pour prouver la réalité de la résurrection opérée par l'Apôtre (*APet* 28).

à celui au nom et par la puissance duquel tu es ressuscité? Eh bien, crois maintenant, et tu vivras pour l'éternité» (*AJ* 47,11-14)[24].

Un certain nombre de traits distinguent le vrai thaumaturge du magicien. En voici les principaux:

1. Les procédés employés par le vrai thaumaturge sont d'une sobriété parfaite. Il renonce aux formules magiques compliquées et aux moyens techniques (gesticulations et pharmacopée bizarre) utilisés par ses adversaires. Sa parole, simple et impérative, n'a rien à voir avec le charabia et les noms secrets des magiciens. On notera, par exemple, que le stratège Andronicus demande à l'apôtre Jean de rentrer nu au théâtre d'Éphèse pour y guérir les femmes âgées atteintes de diverses maladies incurables et de ne pas y prononcer de nom magique (*AJ* 31,9-12).

2. À l'exception de quelques miracles d'animaux[25], les signes accomplis par les Apôtres ont tous un caractère utile et bienfaisant pour l'homme, à la différence des prodiges des magiciens comme Simon[26].

3. L'Apôtre n'accomplit pas de miracles par sa puissance propre, mais c'est Dieu qui les accomplit à la prière de l'apôtre (et jamais au nom de l'apôtre). Dieu seul est l'auteur du miracle et l'apôtre n'a d'autre puissance que celle de Dieu. Dans *AA Grég* 24,13-17, Philopater décrit André «accomplissant des signes, des prodiges et de grandes guérisons» et il conclut: «Je n'avais qu'une pensée: c'était Dieu lui-même qui accomplissait de telles actions»[27].

4. L'Apôtre est entièrement détaché des biens de ce monde et, en particulier, de l'argent. Il est comme le vrai médecin des âmes, le Christ, qui guérit gratuitement. L'expression ἰώμενος δωρεάν revient comme un *leitmotiv* dans *AJ* 22,6; 56,19; 108,5[28]. On connaît, en revanche, l'anecdote de Simon qui rend ses deux complices invisibles pour s'emparer des bijoux de sa protectrice, Eubula (*APet* 17). L'Apôtre véritable refuse tout don matériel mais il accepte, en échange du miracle, l'âme

---

24. Traduction de E. Junod – J.D. Kaestli, *Acta Iohannis* (Corpus Christianorum. Series Apocryphorum, 1 et 2), Turnhout, 1983, pp. 228-230; cf. aussi le commentaire, p. 513.

25. On pense ici à la résurrection par Pierre d'un hareng saur (*APet* 13). Mais le but des miracles d'animaux est de monter la force surnaturelle de l'Apôtre sur la nature entière, qui participe en quelque sorte à sa tâche d'évangélisation, en lui facilitant sa mission. Cf. l'ânon qui parle et sert de monture à Thomas (*ATh* 41) ou les 4 onagres qui font la révérence et remplacent l'attelage défaillant du général Siphor (*ATh* 70). Un des onagres apostrophe les démons et sermonne l'apôtre à la foi défaillante (*ATh* 73-74 et 78-79).

26. *Homélies Clémentines* II, 34: «Les miracles accomplis par Simon sont inutiles ... Les miracles accomplis par le Christ sont des miracles accomplis par un homme devenu l'instrument d'un Esprit ami des hommes» (trad. de A. Siouville) Paris, 1933, p. 120.

27. Traduction de J.M. Prieur, *Acta Andreae* (Corpus Christianorum. Series Apocryphorum, 5 et 6), Turnhout, 1989, pp. 628-629.

28. Cf. le commentaire de E. Junod – J.D. Kaestli, *Acta Iohannis* (n. 24), pp. 68 et 525-526.

du bénéficiaire qui se convertit à la foi. C'est ce qu'on appelle le *troc spirituel*.

Pour bien comprendre cette notion de *troc spirituel* qui revient surtout dans les Actes de Jean et d'André, mais qui n'est pas absente des autres Actes anciens[29], nous allons citer les principaux textes qui la mentionnent, – ce qui nous permettra de saisir le rapport spécifique que les Actes Apocryphes établissent entre le miracle et la foi.

1. *AJ* 56,18-22: Antipatros, notable de Smyrne, s'apprête à offrir cent mille pièces d'or à l'Apôtre Jean pour obtenir la guérison de ses deux fils jumeaux possédés par un démon. Jean répond:

> Mon médecin ne reçoit pas de salaire d'argent; mais il guérit gratuitement et, en échange (κατάλλαγμα) des maladies, il recueille les âmes de ceux qui ont été guéris. Qu'es-tu donc prêt à donner, Antipatros, en échange de tes enfants? Offre ton âme à Dieu, et tu les retrouveras en bonne santé par la puissance du Christ[30].

2. *AA Grég* 7,18-21: André ressuscite un enfant à Nicomédie, qui avait été tué par sept chiens possédés par le démon. Remarquons qu'ici, contrairement au récit précédent (*AJ* 57,10-11) où Jean congédie le père et ses fils guéris[31], le *troc spirituel* s'effectue de manière explicite: les témoins du miracle se convertissent et l'enfant accompagne l'Apôtre en Macédoine, en qualité de disciple.

> André dit au père: Que me donneras-tu si je rends ton fils à la vie? Il répondit: Comme je n'ai rien de plus précieux que lui, je te le donnerai si, sur ton ordre, il revient à la vie[32].

3. *AA Grég* 16,5-13: Pour obtenir la guérison de sa fille, Nicolas, citoyen de Philippes, veut offrir à André quatre mules et quatre chevaux d'un blanc éclatant. L'Apôtre refuse, mais demande en contrepartie l'âme de Nicolas convertie au vrai Dieu. Son discours est un exemplaire

29. Voir les remarques de E. JUNOD – J.D. KAESTLI, *Acta Iohannis* (n. 24), p. 526 (note 1) et de J.M. PRIEUR, *Acta Andreae* (n. 27), p. 580 (note 9) et p. 585 (note 3). En ce qui concerne *ATh* 62, la foi du général Siphor précède le miracle d'exorcisme. En effet, *ATh* 62 affirme le détachement de l'Apôtre: «J'ai entendu dire de toi que tu ne prends de salaire de personne ...», qui est suivi de la profession de foi du général: «Je crois en toi, Jésus, et je te demande et je te supplie, porte secours à la faible foi que j'ai en toi» (*ATh* 65). La guérison n'est rapportée qu'en *ATh* 77-81, et sans l'exigence explicite de la conversion des âmes des bénéficiaires. En revanche, *ATh* 104 est un bon exemple de troc spirituel. Le général Siphor rapporte au roi Misdée l'exorcisme miraculeux de sa femme et de sa fille opéré par Thomas: «Il ne m'a pas pris de salaire, mais il demande la foi et la pureté, afin que l'on devienne participant avec lui dans les choses qu'il fait». Pour la traduction, cf. A.J. FESTUGIÈRE, *Les Actes Apocryphes de Jean et de Thomas* (Cahiers d'Orientalisme, 6), Genève, 1983, pp. 76-77 et p. 91.

30. JUNOD-KAESTLI, *Acta Iohannis* (n. 24), pp. 240-241; et les remarques pp. 687-689.

31. Mais il faut tenir compte de la lacune entre les chap. 57 et 58 du texte de *AJ*, qui ne permet pas de tirer une conclusion certaine.

32. PRIEUR, *Acta Andreae* (n. 27), pp. 584-585.

typique de la prédication missionnaire des Actes Apocryphes: nécessité de trouver son être intérieur par la contemplation et le détachement de ce qui est terrestre pour accéder à l'éternel.

> Le bienheureux apôtre lui sourit et dit: Je veux bien accepter des présents de toi, Nicolas, mais pas ceux-ci qui sont visibles. Car si tu offres ce que tu as de plus précieux dans ta maison pour ta fille, combien plus ne dois-tu pas pour ton âme? Voici ce que je désire recevoir de toi: que ton homme intérieur connaisse le vrai Dieu, son auteur et le créateur de toutes choses, qu'il repousse ce qui est de la terre et désire les choses éternelles, qu'il néglige ce qui est éphémère et aime ce qui est durable, qu'il refuse ce qui se voit et qu'il tourne, par la contemplation, son attention spirituelle vers ce qui ne se voit pas![33].

Le résultat du miracle est noté par *AA Grég* 16,16-17: «Il persuada tout le monde d'abandonner les idoles et de croire au vrai Dieu».

4. *AA Grég* 26,16-22: André avait ressuscité Philopater, le fils de Sostratus (24,5-7). Ce dernier voulait récompenser l'Apôtre, qui refuse. Il exige, en revanche, le don total du père et du fils au Dieu qui assurera leur salut.

> Le père apporta à l'apôtre de nombreux présents. Mais le saint de Dieu lui dit: Je n'ai rien à recevoir de vous; mon profit, ce sera vous-mêmes, lorsque vous croirez en Jésus, qui m'a envoyé évangéliser en ce lieu. Si je voulais de l'argent, je trouverais en Lesbios un homme opulent, qui pourrait me combler de richesses. Vous donc, apportez-moi comme tribut ce qui est utile pour votre salut[34].

Nous comprenons mieux, après ces citations, le mécanisme du *troc spirituel*. L'Apôtre refuse tout don matériel, mais il exige l'offrande spirituelle du bénéficiaire du miracle. En d'autres mots, les Actes Apocryphes accentuent la tendance que nous avions décelée dans plusieurs miracles de l'Évangile de Jean: le miracle est destiné à susciter la foi et la conversion de l'être intérieur de celui qui le reçoit, ou encore, la guérison du corps doit conduire nécessairement au salut de l'âme. Il est probable, cependant, que cette offrande spirituelle de l'âme exigée *avant* l'accomplissement du miracle ait quelque chose à voir avec la foi exigée du malade dans les miracles synoptiques. Mais ce qui diffère ici, c'est cette notion d'échange, de *troc,* nécessaire à l'obtention du miracle, qui n'a pas grand chose en commun avec la gratuité des guérisons de Jésus dans l'Évangile et la simple constatation du thaumaturge heureux qui s'exclame devant la personne rétablie dans son intégrité: «Ta foi t'a sauvé».

Notons, enfin, que le miracle a aussi une fonction apologétique

---

33. *Ibid.*, pp. 602-603.
34. *Ibid.*, pp. 634-635.

importante dans les Actes Apocryphes par rapport aux spectateurs et assistants, et donc au lecteur. Il doit poser question et semer le trouble dans les esprits païens, qui sont amenés à se demander quel est l'auteur véritable du prodige. Le miracle est donc un signe sensible qui permet à l'homme de s'élever au-dessus du sensible pour se diriger vers l'invisible et le spirituel. C'est ce qu'exprime l'Apôtre André lors de l'exorcisme d'Alcmanès, le jeune serviteur de Stratoclès et de Maximilla. S'adressant d'abord à cette dernière, André dit: «Mon enfant, ce qui trouble le plus ceux qui, échappant à une grande tourmente et erreur, se tournent vers la foi en Dieu, c'est de voir guérir ces maux qui semblent désespérés à la plupart des gens» (*AAgr* 4,8-11)[35]. Puis, s'adressant à Stratoclès, André continue: «L'embarras, le doute et la stupeur qui sont en toi me disposent favorablement. Mets donc au monde l'enfant que tu portes, et ne te contente pas de te livrer aux douleurs de l'enfantement. Je ne suis pas inexpert en matière d'accouchement, pas plus qu'en matière de divination. Ce que tu enfantes, moi je l'aime; ce que tu tais, moi j'en suis épris; ce qui est à l'intérieur, moi je le ferai grandir» (*AAgr* 7,5-10)[36]. On ne peut mieux exprimer le trouble qui envahit le témoin du miracle et l'origine du déclic qui le conduira à la foi.

Avenue du Ciseau 8/202   Jean-Marie van Cangh
B-1348 Louvain-la-Neuve

---

35. *Ibid.,* pp. 446-447.

36. *Ibid.,* pp. 450-451, et pour le commentaire p. 177. On pourrait songer aussi à un rapprochement avec le *logion* 2 de l'*Évangile selon Thomas*: «Jésus a dit: Que celui qui cherche ne cesse de chercher jusqu'à ce qu'il trouve, et quand il trouvera, il sera troublé, et, ayant été troublé, il sera émerveillé, et il dominera le Tout» (trad. J. Ménard [NHS, 5], Leiden, 1975, p. 55).

EIN NEUES FRAGMENT DES PETRUSEVANGELIUMS

1. Die Existenz eines Petrusevangeliums (EvPetr) ist bekannt durch Origenes, Euseb, Didymos u.a. Das wichtigste Zeugnis, Serapion bei Euseb, zeigt, daß es im 2. Jhdt. entstanden sein muß. Seit Harnack u.a. wird ihm PCair 10759 aus dem 8./9. Jhdt. zugeordnet, der sog. »Akhmim-Text«. Wo in der neueren Literatur vom Petrusevangelium gesprochen wird, ist dieses Fragment gemeint. Es enthält die Geschichte Jesu vom Händewaschen des Pilatus über Kreuzigung, Tod und Auferstehung bis zur Versammlung der Jünger am See, ebenso unvermittelt abbrechend, wie es mitten in einem Satz begonnen hatte. POx 2949 läßt sich als eine Fassung von EvPetr 3-5 identifizieren. Er wird »2./3. Jhdt.« datiert und sichert damit die Rückführung des Akhmim-Textes auf das 2. Jhdt.

2. Ich kann einen neuen, bisher noch nicht edierten Papyrus aus Oxyrhynchus (POx 4009) vorstellen, den ich ebenfalls dem Petrusevangelium zuordnen will. Es handelt sich um ein beidseitig beschriebenes Stückchen von 2,9 × 9 cm Größe mit 21 erhaltenen Zeilen im »Recto«, 20 im »Verso«. Die Abkürzung von κύριος als nomen sacrum erweist ihn als christlichen Ursprungs, und dem entspricht sein Inhalt. In der Frage der Datierung sind die Experten noch nicht zu einem abschließenden Urteil gekommen: 3. oder gar 2. Jhdt. Die Erstedition durch P.J. Parsons und mich erfolgt in *The Oxyrhynchus Papyri*; ich bereite einen längeren Aufsatz vor.

Die Rekonstruktion des Wortlauts stellt vor erhebliche Schwierigkeiten, denn erhalten ist jeweils weniger als die Hälfte der Zeilen. Doch bieten die Zeilen 7-12 des »Recto« einen Schlüssel zum Verständnis:

```
 7            ]εσεσθε ως
 8    αρνια ανα μεσ]ον λυκων.
 9    ειπον προς αυ]τον· εαν ου(ν)
10    διασπαραχθω]μεν;
11    ο δε αποκριθεις]λεγει μοι· οι
12    λυκοι διασπαρα]ξαντες το
```

Zeile 11 enthält mit λέγει μοι und anschließendem Kolon eine neue Redeeinleitung, und die vorausgehende Zeile 10 ist nicht bis zum Ende ausgeschrieben. Der Schreiber wollte offenbar einen Sinnabschnitt markieren. Das μοι in Zeile 11 verweist also auf einen Ich-Erzähler.

Das Stichwort λύκων in Zeile 8 führt zunächst zu Mt 10,16a, zumal die vorausgehenden Zeilen 5 und 6 Anklänge an Mt 10,16b zeigen. Das ἔσεσθε ὡς in Zeile 7 in Verbindung mit λύκων verweist aber auf 2Klem 5,2, und das ermöglicht die vorgelegte Rekonstruktion von Zeile 8. Sie ergibt ca 11 auf der linken Seite zu ergänzende Buchstaben.

Es kann dann kein Zufall sein, daß in Zeile 9 ἐὰν οὖ(ν) folgt, da dies in 2Klem 5,3 den Einwand des Petrus einleitet. Dementsprechend ist der erste Teil von Zeile 9 als Redeeinleitung zu rekonstruieren; nach]τον hat der Schreiber zudem freien Raum gelassen. Da Zeile 11 auf einen Ich-Erzähler deutet, ist dieser hier einzuführen, z.B.: εἶπον πρὸς αὐ]τόν. Gesichert wird dies durch die Buchstaben]μεν in Zeile 10, die sich zu einer Verbform in der 1. pluralis ergänzen lassen, z.B. διασπαράχθω]μεν nach 2Klem 5,3.

Die Rekonstruktion der Antwort Jesu in den Zeilen 11ff. nach 2Klem 5,4 ist komplizierter, führt aber durchaus zu einem befriedigenden Ergebnis. Insgesamt ergibt sich, daß es sich in beiden Fassungen um den gleichen Text handelt, wenn auch nicht im selben Wortlaut.

3. Der Textabschnitt 2Klem 5,2-4 ist vom Autor nicht als Zitat gekennzeichnet. Zusammen mit vergleichbaren anderen Einheiten wird er jedoch mit Recht auf ein apokryphes Evangelium zurückgeführt, das literarisch abhängig ist von (den) kanonisch gewordenen. Auch in Helmut Koesters Entwurf der Geschichte der frühchristlichen Evangelien bildet der Zweite Klemensbrief in dieser Hinsicht eine, wenn nicht *die* Ausnahme (*Ancient Christian Gospels*, 1990, 349-360).

Die Gegenüberstellung von 2Klem 5,2-4 und POx 4009 erlaubt nun den Schluß, daß wir mit POx 4009 ein Fragment des Petrusevangeliums vor uns haben. In 2Klem 5,4 heißt es »Jesus sagte zu *Petrus*«, an der entsprechenden Stelle in POx 4009 aber »er sagte zu *mir*«. Daß wir PCair 10759 als *Petrus*evangelium bezeichnen, beruht einzig und allein darauf, daß sich dort der Erzähler in 60 als »*ich* aber, Simon *Petrus*« identifiziert (vgl. »wir« in 26 und 59). Die Logik ist in beiden Fällen dieselbe: der Ich-Erzähler Petrus führt zum Petrusevangelium. In POx 4009 ist diese Identifikation zwar nicht explizit vorgenommen. Es gibt aber keinen anderen Text außer diesen beiden, in dem die Jesusworte Mt 10,16a / Lk 10,3 und Mt 10,28 / Lk 12,4-5 in dieser Weise miteinander verbunden sind, obwohl sie je für sich Parallelen in frühchristlicher Literatur haben. Leicht erklärbar ist die Umsetzung des Ich-Erzählers in die dritte Person Petrus in 2Klem 5,2-4; ihm lag an den Herrenworten, nicht an der Autorität des Erzählers.

4. Ich kann hier nicht auf die Detailprobleme der Textrekonstruktion eingehen, möchte jedoch drei der Fragen zur Diskussion stellen, die sich mir aus der Arbeit an diesem Papyrus ergeben haben:
a. Ist das im Zweiten Klemensbrief benutzte εὐαγγέλιον (8,5) vielleicht das Petrusevangelium? Auch für das Petrusevangelium läßt sich m.E.

feststellen, daß es Besonderheiten der kanonisch gewordenen Evangelien voraussetzt, also deren Endgestalt, nicht nur in ihnen verarbeitete Überlieferungen. Das ist für den Zweiten Klemensbrief unbestritten. Leider gibt es dort aber keine Beziehungen zu den Passionsgeschichten, und die beiden Textfassungen 2Klem 5,2-4 und POx 4009 sind auch nicht einfach identisch. So muß diese Frage offen bleiben.

b. Lassen sich andere Petrustraditionen außerhalb der kanonisch gewordenen Evangelien dem Petrusevangelium zuordnen? Es gibt dafür m.E. mindestens einen Kandidaten: das sog. »Fajum-Fragment« (PVindob G 2325), die Variante zu Mk 14,27-30 parr., der Ankündigung der Verleugnung des Petrus. Der allgemein akzeptierte *genitivus absolutus* εἰπόντος το]ῦ Πέτ(ρου) beruht auf der Ergänzung einer Lücke. Warum aber nicht εἰπόντος ἐμο]ῦ Πέτ(ρου)? Dann wäre das lang gesuchte apokryphe Evangelium gefunden, dem dieser Papyrus zugeordnet werden kann.

c. Ist POx 4009 vor oder nach dem Akhmim-Fragment einzuordnen? Die Paralleltexte lassen zunächst an eine Stellung vergleichbar den Aussendungsreden der Synoptiker denken. Zu erwägen ist jedoch auch eine Situation wie in Joh 21, die sich ja häufig in nicht kanonisch gewordener Jesusüberlieferung findet: Gespräche des Auferstandenen mit Jüngern und Jüngerinnen.

Im Hainbach 9   Dieter LÜHRMANN
D-3550 Marburg-Cyriaxweimar

CLEMENT OF ALEXANDRIA AND THE PARABLE
OF THE FISHERMAN
MATTHEW 13,47-48 OR INDEPENDENT TRADITION?

This short study is the last in a series of four articles investigating whether we have in the 8th Logion of "The Gospel of Thomas" – the Parable of the Fisherman – an early and independent tradition, which might have been even more original than the text of Mt 13, 47-48, the Parable of the Fishnet[1]. The Gospel of Thomas may indeed have preserved early material that might bring us back to the early stages of tradition. However, one has to prove that this is really the case in each of the logia or, at least, to make the archaic character of a logion plausible. The only real attempt to prove this in the case of Thomas 8 has been made by my Utrecht colleague Prof. Dr. Gilles Quispel in his many studies on the "Gospel of Thomas". One of his crown witnesses is Clement of Alexandria.

The eighth logion in Thomas presents the parable in the following way: "Man is like a wise (or: skilled) fisherman, who cast his net into the sea; he drew it up from the sea, full of small fish. Among them he found a large, good fish, that wise fisherman. He cast all the small fish down into the sea. He chose the large fish without difficulty..."[2]. This characteristic form of the parable seems to have some elements in common with the few references which – as we will see – Clement made in some of his writings. First: Clement also refers to one person who cast his net (*versus* Matthew). Second, he seems to contrast the one big fish with the small ones (*versus* Matthew). And third, he speaks of making a choice instead of collecting (*versus* Matthew). These are quite surprising deviations from the form of the text preserved in Matthew. Does this mean that Clement knew the form of the text in Thomas or did he have in mind an extra-canonical tradition that has also influenced the wording of the Gospel of Thomas?

---

1. Cf. *"Philoxenus and the Parable of the Fisherman"*, Concerning the Diatessaron Text of Mt 13,47-50, in The Four Gospels 1992. Festschrift Frans Neirynck (BETL, 100), Leuven, 1992, pp. 1403-1423; *"Chose" or "Collected": Concerning an Aramaism in Logion 8 of the Gospel of Thomas and the Question of Independence*, in HTR 84 (1991) 373-397 (published in 1992); *The Parable of the Fisherman in the Heliand, The Old Saxon Version of Matthew 13:47-50*, in Amsterdamer Beiträge zur älteren Germanistik 36 (1992), 39-58.

2. A. GUILLAUMONT – H.-C. PUECH – G. QUISPEL – W. TILL – YASSAH 'ABD AL-MASIH, *The Gospel according to Thomas*, Leiden - New York, 1959, 4(5)-6(7).

I. THE FISHER OF MEN

Hymn to Christ the Saviour

First of all, I wish to mention a passage which has not played a role in the argumentation so far. In the hymn at the ending of the third book of the Paedagogue[3], Christ is addressed by various names and titles. There are a few lines that may be useful to note as possible references of Clement[4] to the parable of the fishnet (Mt 13,47-48) or that of the fisherman (Thomas 8):

ἁλιεῦ μερόπων	Fisher of men,
τῶν σῳζομένων	that are being saved
πελάγους κακίας,	from the evil sea,
ἰχθῦς ἁγνοὺς	attracting holy fish
κύματος ἐχθροῦ	from the hostile waves
γλυκερῇ ζωῇ δελεάζων.	by the bait of sweet life[5].

The Fisherman

Christ has been addressed in hymnic style as the "Fisherman" who saves men, a Fisher of men, a name given to the discipeles in Mk 1,17 par[6]. One might think of a fisherman that entices the fish with an angle[7] or with bait on the hook[8], but not necessarily, I would think. If a reminiscence of Mk 1,17 is in the mind of the poet of the hymn, he

---

3. Clemens Alexandrinus, *Paed.* III,12.101.3; O. STÄHLIN, *Clemens Alexandrinus* I (GCS), Leipzig, 1905, 291-292; C. MONDÉSERT – C. MATRAY – H.-I. MARROU, *Clément d'Alexandrie, Le Pédagogue* III (SC, 158), Paris, 1970, p. 196:23-28. Cf. F.J. DÖLGER, *Sol Salutis*, Münster, 1925, p. 399, n. 3.

4. I am not able to decide, whether Clement himself is the poet here, or whether he quotes an existing song, or whether the hymn has been added at a later stage of textual tradition. So I take it for granted that Clement wrote these verses.

5. The verb occurs in Clement's *Protrepticus* I, 1.1, O. STÄHLIN (– U. TREU), *Clemens Alexandrinus* I, Berlin, ³1972, p. 3:5 (speaking of Arion of Methymna, cf. Herodotus, *Historiae* I,24; τέχνῃ τῇ μουσικῇ, ὃ μὲν ἰχθὺν δελεάσας, ὃ δὲ κτλ.), cf. the gloss, *ibid.*, p. 296: τὸν δελφῖνα ὁ Ἀρίων. The idea of a bait for a fish also occurs at the end of *Strom.* VII, where Clement writes πολλὰ γὰρ τὰ δελέατα καὶ ποικίλα διὰ τὰς τῶν ἰχθύων διαφοράς, to indicate the way in which he tries to convince all kinds of readers, VII,18.11,3, STÄHLIN, *Clemens Alexandrinus* III, Leipzig 1909, p. 79:7-8.

6. The motive of fishing of men is found with respect to Peter, *Paed.* III,10.52,2 (STÄHLIN, *Clemens Alexandrinus* I (n. 3), p. 266:22-24, αὕτη δὲ βελτίων ἡ ἄγρα, ἣν ἐχαρίσατο ὁ κύριος τῷ μαθητῇ καθάπερ ἰχθῦς δι' ὕδατος ἀνθρώπους ἁλιεύειν διδάξας.

7. Cf. *Paed.* III,12.99,3; STÄHLIN, *Clemens Alexandrinus* I (n. 3), p. 290:12-14, where the Logos is compared, among others, with an angle, οὗτος ὡς ἀληθῶς τεχνάζεται ἵππῳ χαλινόν, ταύρῳ ζυγόν, θηρίῳ βρόχον, κάλαμον ἰχθύι, πάγην ὀρνέῳ...

8. Note MARROU, *op. cit.* (n. 3), p. 197, n. 34: "Clément file sa métaphore: il s'agit d'une pêche à l'hameçon". He may have thought of Lucian, *The Dead Come to Life, or the Fisherman*, pp. 47ff. (A.M. HARMON, *Lucian* III, London - Cambridge, MA, 1921, pp. 70, 72), where mention is of a κάλαμος, a ὁρμία and an ἄγκιστρον.

may have thought of a net as well. He could have thought also of the passage of Mt 13,47-48, the Parable of the Seine[9], or some other tradition – the Parable of the Fisherman – as we now read in the Coptic "Gospel of Thomas", logion 8. One cannot, however, totally exclude the possibility that he has developed the series of names and titles all by himself. The imagery of the fisherman, current as it is in the Mediterranean world of his time, would easily suggest itself to him, when he listed all kind of names such as Shepherd, Guide, Logos, Light, Fountain, Saviour, Plower, King, Wing, Bridle-bit, and other epithets.

On the other hand, since several of these titles are found in the Gospels, one cannot deny his possible use of this metaphor on the basis of some biblical or non-canonical tradition known among Christians of his days. The passage does not, however, give us any clue with respect to the tradition which Clement was dependent upon. Moreover, the imagery of the poem differs from that of both the Gospel of Thomas and Matthew in so far as it depicts the catch of fish as the final saving act, whereas in both Gospels the catch is only a first step after which a final selection or election follows.

II. The Unique Pearl and the Beauty-Fish

Strom. I, 1.16,3

In his introductory chapter of the first book of the *Stromateis* Clement develops the plan of the work that he intends to write. In the latter part of it, he writes that he will not hesitate to use the existing Greek philosophy and the propaedeutical study, at least their most beautiful contributions (τοῖς καλλίστοις). He defends that position with a reference to Paul's words of 1 Cor 9,20ff. and Col 1,28, in which the apostle has made it clear that, just as one has to be a Jew to the Jews, one has *to become a Greek* in order to win the Greeks; and that one has to instruct every man in *all* wisdom in order to make everyone perfect in Christ. One has to speak to one's audience the words with which they are familiar and which they can understand, and by which they could therefore be attracted more easily. In that connection, Clement writes[10]:

9. The Parable of the Fishnet could easily be changed into the Parable of the Fisherman by early exegetes, as I have shown in my study on *Philoxenus* (n. 1), even when it is clear that they read the Parable in the form of Matthew and nothing else.

10. STÄHLIN, *Clemens Alexandrinus* II, Leipzig, 1906, p. 12:9-12 (3rd ed. L. FRÜCHTEL, Berlin, ³1960); C. MONDÉSERT – M. CASTER, *Clément d'Alexandrie, Les Stromates* (SC, 30), Paris, 1951, p. 55. Both mention only Mt 13,46 as the source, as do also most translators, cf. e.g. H.U. MEYBOOM, *Clemens Alexandrinus* V, Leiden, 1914, p. 24 n. 4. M. MEES, *Die Zitate aus dem Neuen Testament bei Clemens von Alexandrien*, Bari, 1970, II, p. 35, no. 126, registrates the parenthesis as Mt 13,46-47. P.M. BARNARD, *Clement of*

1. καὶ δὴ συνελόντι φάναι
2. – ἐν πολλοῖς γὰρ τοῖς μαργαρίταις τοῖς μικροῖς ὁ εἷς,
3. ἐν δὲ πολλῇ τῇ τῶν ἰχθύων ἄγρᾳ ὁ κάλλιχθυς -
4. χρόνῳ τε καὶ πόνῳ τἀληθὲς ἐκλάμψει ἀγαθοῦ παρατυχόντος βοηθοῦ.

Two Connected Parables?

If lines 2f. are to be taken as a parenthesis, the meaning of the phrase may be the following: "And then, to say it in one word, in the long run and with toil the truth will light up, if there is a good helper (the Logos?) nearby, for among the many small pearls there is that unique one, and in the big catch (or: in many a catch?) of fish there is the beauty-fish".

What is striking in this sentence is the parenthesis which reminds us of two parables which in the Gospel of Matthew are closely connected, namely the parable of the pearl merchant, Mt 13,45-46, and that of the fishnet, Mt 13,47ff. If Clement really had in mind these two parables, one must conclude that he read them in the order of Matthew, *not* in that of Thomas, where they are found in different places (resp. *logia* 76 and 8). This latter observation is not unimportant, since it has been the conviction of several scholars that this reference of Clement could not have been to Matthew's text[11], but had its source in some extra-canonical tradition or in Thomas. If Clement referred to the text of Thomas, did he himself connect in this parenthesis these two parables which were separated in that Gospel[12]? Or was there an early tradition[13] that had already connected both parables before they were taken over by Matthew? Or did he merely refer to Matthew?

Alexandria's Biblical Text, Cambridge, 1899, p. 19, mentions this passage for v. 46, although he thinks it not necessary to quote its text, because it does not shed any light on Clement's form of the text in this verse; he also refers to *Paed.* II,118.5 (for the text cf. MEES, *op. cit.*, II, p. 35), where Clement discusses the question of wearing gems; as to the pearl, he observes that one should rather stick to the Word of God, ὃν μαργαρίτην ἡ γραφὴ κέκληκέν που, namely Jesus; the passage has been introduced by the words ὁ δὲ πολυτίμητος μαργαρίτης (cf. πολύτιμον in Matthew), cf. C. MONDÉSERT – H.-I. MARROU, *Clément d'Alexandrie, Le Pédagogue* II (SC, 108), Paris, 1965, p. 224.

11. Cf. e.g. C.-H. HUNZINGER, *Unbekannte Gleichnisse Jesu aus dem Thomas-Evangelium*, in *Judentum, Urchristentum, Kirche. FS J. Jeremias*, Berlin, 1960, pp. 209-220, esp. 217, n. 37: "Dass letzteres eine Anspielung auf das Gleichnis vom Fischnetz ... sein sollte, ist doch kaum denkbar". Hunzinger thinks of extra-canonical tradition as the source for Clement here.

12. HUNZINGER, *Unbekannte Gleichnisse*, p. 217, n. 37: "Dagegen hat schon Clemens ... die beiden Gleichnisse von der Perle und vom grossen Fisch zueinander in Parallele gesetzt".

The Unique Pearl

With respect to the reference to the pearl in the first clause no certainty can be reached. The phrase "for among the many small pearls there is the *one*" reminds us of Matthew's εὑρὼν δὲ ἕνα πολύτιμον μαργαρίτην (omission of ἕνα in Mt 13,46 D Θ *788 pc* it sy°). In the version of Thomas, Logion 76, where the merchant found *a* pearl (ⲉⲁϥϩⲉ ⲁⲩⲙⲁⲣⲅⲁⲣⲓⲧⲏⲥ), sold his merchandise, and bought *that one* pearl (ⲁϥⲧⲟⲟⲩ ⲛⲁϥ ⲙ̄ⲡⲓⲙⲁⲣⲅⲁⲣⲓⲧⲏⲥ ⲟⲩⲱⲧ), it is only in the second phrase that emphasis is laid upon the one pearl.

The contrast between the one and the *many small* ones reminds us of the parable of the Fisherman in Thomas 8[14]. However, the possibility that this contrast might have been suggested to Clement by the wording of Mt 13,45-46 cannot be ruled out. The merchant in Matthew was, in contrast to the merchant in Thomas 76, a *pearl* merchant who sought for good or beautiful pearls (ἀνθρώπῳ ἐμπόρῳ ζητοῦντι καλοὺς μαργαρίτας). There seems to me no real necessity to find in the phrase of Clement a reference to the Gospel of Thomas or to extra-canonical tradition prior to the stage of our Matthaean text[15].

The Beauty-Fish

More problematic is the second phrase "and in the abundant catch of fish(es) – or: in many a catch, that is after a longer period of fishing – there is the beauty-fish". An agreement with Thomas 8 is obvious in so far as the words of Clement seem to focus on *one* fish, cf. Thomas: "Among them the wise fisherman found *a large, good fish*....he chose *the large fish*"[16]. This has given rise to the conviction that Clement was

13. HUNZINGER, *Aussersynoptisches Traditionsgut im Thomas-Evangelium*, in *TLZ* 85 (1960) 843-846, p. 843, found in the Gospel of Thomas a collection of sayings of the Q-type that represented a pre-synoptic stage ("hinsichtlich der literarischen Gattung ... eine ältere Phase der Überlieferungsbildung") with a different order of the logia. One might conclude from this thesis that Hunzinger does not think of Thomas as Clement's source. Or did he consider the possibility that Clement found the two parables in Thomas at different places and still combined them here to suit his purpose, and by chance in the same order as Matthew? It is not quite clear to me.

14. Clement does not speak of a *great* one, but of a *unique* pearl (as in Thomas 8), but the mentioning of the *small* ones suggests that this unique pearl was great.

15. MEES, *Zitate* (n. 10), I, p. 197, interprets Thomas 76 as an *Uminterpretation* of Mt 13,45-46 applied to the "Einzelseele", and suggests that the allusion of Clement is not dependent on Thomas, but on Matthew. However, he suggests that Clement's use of that text was "der gleichen Auslegungsinterpretation verplichtet". This implies that Clement like Thomas thought of the own self soul of man. This is, however, not true. Clement's interpretation was that the many philosophical and propaedeutical contributions of the Greeks should not be a priori rejected; they might contain most valuable knowledge also for Christians as the work of God's providence, cf. *Strom.* I,1.18,4.

16. Cf. GUILLAUMONT, a.o. (ed.), *The Gospel*, 4 (ⲁⲩⲛⲟϭ ⲛ̄ⲧⲃ̄ⲧ1), 6 (ⲙ̄ⲡⲛⲟϭ ⲧⲃ̄ⲧ).

indebted here to the Gospel of Thomas, or rather had made use of the same pre-canonical tradition that was used in Thomas[17]. One should, however, notice the fact that in Thomas emphasis is laid not only upon the *many* and the *one* (in agreement with Clement), but also upon the *small* and the *great* (instead of τὰ καλά and τὰ σαπρά). Clement, however, does not mention here the fact that the catch was one of *small* fishes. By using the word κάλλιχθυς he suggests to us that he had in his source at least the notion of καλός instead of μακρός.

When G. Quispel refered to both *Stromateis* VI,11.95,3 and I,1.16,3 for his evaluation of the *fisherman* parable in Clement as an important testimony for the author's use of a pre-canonical tradition, he concluded that these references show how Clement understood the parable: just as one has to sell everything in order to acquire that *one* pearl, likewise one has to cast away all small fish and keep that one beauty-fish[18]. Apart from the fact that Quispel does not enter into a discussion of the differences between the two allusions (see below, § III), he interprets the first allusion on the basis of the second one. So he finds in Clement not only the *one* fisherman (*Strom.* VI,11.95,3), but also the *one* good or beautiful fish (*Strom.* I,1.16,3). However, in neither of the two allusions does Clement speak of selling or casting away everything in order to choose either the one precious pearl or the one large fish.

Propaedeusis and Philosophy

Clement does not say that one should do away with the other pearls or fish, since his use of the imagery of the pearl and the fish serves another goal: they are symbolizing Greek *propaedeusis* and philosophy, which also Christians should not neglect. For it is *Truth* that in the long run (χρόνῳ), but not without toil (πόνῳ), will lighten up (ἐκλάμψει) among them. You need a special eye to observe what you are looking for, and you need the help of a guide. The essential truth is mixed with, hidden among, philosophical teachings. The ignorant people think that Greek philosophy is unnecessary, superfluous, or even evil, but Clement

17. Cf. G. QUISPEL, *Some Remarks on the Gospel of Thomas*, in *NTS* 5 (1958-59) 276-290, p. 289; ID., *Der Heliand und das Thomas-Evangelium*, in *VC* 16 (1962) 121-153, pp. 149-150 [= *Gnostic Studies* II, Istanbul, Nederlands Historisch-Archeologisch Instituut, 1975, pp. 95-96]; ID., *Het Evangelie van Thomas en de Nederlanden*, Amsterdam-Brussel, Elsevier, 1971, pp. 118-119 (rev. edition: Baarn, 1991, pp. 151-152); ID., *Tatian and the Gospel of Thomas*, Leiden, Brill, 1975, pp. 104-105, esp. p. 105; ID., *The Gospel of Thomas and the Western Text, A Reappraisal*, in *Gnostic Studies* II, pp. 58-59; ID., *Gnosis and the New Sayings of Jesus*, in *Eranos Jahrbuch* 38 (1969), Zürich, 1971, pp. 261-296, 191-192 (*Gnostic Studies* II, pp. 274-275).

18. QUISPEL, *Thomas en de Nederlanden*, pp. 118-119 (rev. ed., pp. 151-152), "Dat toont hoe Clemens ... de gelijkenis van de visser verstond. Zoals men alles moet verkopen om de ene paarl te verwerven, zo moet men alle kleine vissen weggooien en de éne prachtvis houden".

wants to emphasize that even that often neglected philosophy is in a way the work of divine providence or, in other words, the fish and the small pearls are really important because it is possible that one finds in them the truth, the one pearl or the beauty-fish. If one knows what Clement is hinting at in the two parenthetical phrases of this allusion, one can understand why the motif of selling everything or casting away of fish, which belongs to the versions of both Thomas and Matthew in the parables of the pearl and of the fisherman or fish net, is absent here. Clement wishes to preserve Greek *propaedeusis* and philosophy, the work of divine providence, because by way of disclosure one may find in them the truth.

With Toil – Without Toil

There is one real difference here between the Gospel of Thomas and Clement: in Thomas the fisherman casts away the small fishes, and picks then up the great and beautiful fish *without toil* (χωρὶς πόνου)[19]. Clement, however, emphasizes the fact that the discovery of "truth" in Greek philosophy requires time and toil[20] and a good helper, God, Christ or the Logos, who can give guidance in one's search. This implies that Clement's mention of the *one* beauty-fish did *not* go back to the version of Thomas. If Clement, as Quispel suggests, really had in mind some early Judaic-Christian tradition, one has to consider the possibility that "without toil", which is now preserved in Thomas, was not part of that hypothetical original tradition, but rather a redactorial addition on the part of the collector.

A Proverb?

Now it must be asked whether Clement indeed alluded to the two parables here. F.J. Dölger suggested that the parenthetical sentence – which he chose as a device for one of the chapters in his famous ΙΧΘΥΣ – was not so much an allusion to the biblical text as a proverbial saying[21]. He refers to the fact that in Greek sources the κάλλιχθυς was sometimes identified as ἀνθίας, which in turn was

---

19. Reconstruction of the Greek text of Thomas in G. QUISPEL, *Tatian and the Gospel of Thomas*, p. 105.

20. Cf. already J.-B. BAUER, *Zum koptischen Thomasevangelium*, in *BZ* NF 6 (1962) 283-288, esp. p. 284; ID., *Synoptic Tradition in the Gospel of Thomas*, in *Studia Evangelica* III (TU, 88), Berlin, 1984, pp. 314-317, 315-316.

21. F.J. DÖLGER, ΙΧΘΥΣ, II. Band (Textband), *Der heilige Fisch in den antiken Religionen und im Christentum*, Münster, 1922, in § 28 (Der Fisch als Sinnbild der Eucharistie nach der literarischen Bezeugung [pp. 448-453]), spec. p. 448: "Dies aus der Lebenserfahrung der Fischer entnommene Sprichwort".

named ἱερὸς ἰχθύς[22]. Dölger was followed by Bauer, who even supposed that the author of the logion in Thomas knew that proverb[23]. I am inclined to disagree. It is true that the parenthesis has the air of a proverb, but it may have been coined by Clement himself on the basis of the two parables that he knew.

The Source

It is obvious that the term κάλλιχθυς was a technical term in the fishing branch[24]. However, the possibility is not excluded that this term was coined here by Clement himself, having in mind the adjective καλός (cf. Mt: τὰ καλά) of a textual source, either Matthew or another text or tradition[25]. The order *pearl-fish* suggests that the text of Matthew, or a source with the same order of the two parables, was in Clement's mind. The argument that the truth will lighten from among Greek philosophical teaching suggested to him the parable of the pearl, which in his source was connected with that of the fishing net or fisherman. Due to his argument – the one truth becoming visible in Greek philosophy – he might have assimilated the second parable to the first. Although certainty cannot be achieved here, there are no cogent reasons to assume that only a tradition different from Matthew's text could have been in his mind. He may have used the latter and adjusted the form of the parable of the fish net to that of the pearl, emphasizing his own argument that the overwhelming riches of Greek philosophy could contain in themselves the one thing that Christians must look for, *the truth*.

22. Cf. Athenaeus VII, 282AB (C.B. GULICK, *Athenaeus, The Deipnosophists* III, London - Cambridge, MA, (repr.), 1957, p. 266). The Anthias is best of all fish when eaten in the winter. The author refers (282C) to Aristotle (*Hist. An.* 620 B 33) to explain why sponge-divers call it a *holy* fish, since there is no other fish in the neighbourhood when it is there. The identification of the Anthias as "beauty-fish" is not common, as appears from Dorion quoted also by Athenaeus (282CD). The identification, however, guided Dölger, when he lays emphasis on the aspect of holiness: "wir müssten also, um für die Gegenwart voll verständlich zu sein, das Sprichwort so ausprägen: 'Unter vielen kleinen Perlen findet sich *eine* grosse, bei einem reichen Fang gewöhnlicher Fische *ein* heiliger'".

23. BAUER, *Zum koptischen Thomasevangelium*, pp. 283-284, esp. p. 284; ID., *Synoptic Tradition*, pp. 315-316.

24. One might compare the שפרנתא in Talmudic texts (J. LEVY, *Hebräisches und Chaldäisches Wörterbuch über die Talmudim und Midraschim* III, Leipzig, 1883, p. 300; IV, Leipzig, 1889, p. 600), and the discussion whether this fish is according to dietary laws edible or unedible; cf. DÖLGER, *op. cit.* (n. 21), pp. 250-251, on the similarity of Hebrew or Aramaic *and* Greek names of fishes in this connection.

25. Although Thomas contrasts *small* and *great* in logion 8, he still has preserved an element of the tradition that was used in Matthew, when he speaks of a great, *good* fish.

III. THE PARABLE OF THE FISHERMAN

Strom. VI, 11.95,3

There is a second passage[26] that has been mentioned in connection with Mt 13,47-48 and Thomas 8. If Clement had in mind either of these logia he must have quoted it in a very loose way, although he suggests that he quotes it more or less litterally:

1 σιωπῶ τὰ νῦν τὴν ἐν τῷ εὐαγγελίῳ παραβολὴν λέγουσαν·
2 ὁμοία ἐστὶν ἡ βασιλεία τῶν οὐρανῶν
3 ἀνθρώπῳ σαγήνην εἰς θάλασσαν βεβληκότι
4 κἀκ τοῦ πλήθους τῶν ἑαλωκότων ἰχθύων
5 τὴν ἐκλογὴν τῶν ἀμεινόνων ποιουμένῳ.

"For the moment I pass in silence the parable in the Gospel which reads as follows: | The kingdom of heaven | is like unto a man who has cast a trail net into the sea, | and out of the multitude of fishes that were caught | made the choice of the better ones"[27.]

Clement's Interpretation of the Parable

Clement seems to apply here the figure of *apophasis*, suggesting to pass in silence a text which he actually quotes. However, his intention may have been a different one, namely to mention the text without an exposition that would suit his characteristic understanding that Christians should not neglect Greek wisdom. In his reference to the miraculous multiplication of the bread he had explained the barley bread as the propaedeutical studies (αἰνισσόμενος τὴν προπαιδείαν Ἑλλήνων τε καὶ ᾽Ιουδαίων) and the two fishes as the higher realm of Greek philosophy (φιλοσοφίαν Ἑλληνικήν), both of which received the blessing of our Lord. Or the one fish represents the general education (τὴν ἐγκύκλιον, sc. παιδείαν), the other one philosophy[28]. When he then goes to tell his readers that he will pass the text which he quotes in silence "for the moment" (did he intend to deal with it at a later stage

26. O. STÄHLIN, *Clemens Alexandrinus* II, Leipzig, 1906, p. 479:23-26; cf. A. RESCH, *Aussercanonische Paralleltexte zu den Evangelien* I, Leipzig, 1893-1894, pp. 159-160; ID., *Die Logia Jesu, nach dem griechischen und hebräischen Text wiederhergestellt, Ein Versuch*, Leipzig, 1898, pp. 40-41; BARNARD, *Clement of Alexandria's Biblical Text*, 19 (presents lines 1-5); MEES, *Zitate* (n. 10), II, p. 35; I, pp. 197-198 (presents lines 2-5). The apparatus of Mees is faulty and defective.

27. QUISPEL, *Tatian* (n. 17), rightly renders σαγήνην with "a net" (in *Some Remarks* [n. 17], p. 289, "his net"; *Thomas en de Nederlanden* [n. 17], p. 118 [rev. ed., p. 151], "het net").

28. STÄHLIN, *Clemens Alexandrinus* II (n. 10), p. 479:1-16 (*Strom.* VI, 94.2-5), where he refers to a word of Sophocles (Fragm. inc. 695) χορὸς δὲ ἀναύδων ἰχθύων ἐπερρόθει, as analogous to the word of the Lord.

of his *Stromateis*?), he apparently leaves it to his readers to apply the parable of the man who cast his net to the merits of Greek philosophy from which Christians should choose the better elements.

The Differences from Matthew

Clement himself declares that he quotes[29] the passage from "the Gospel". Did he mean by it one of the so-called "canonical" Gospels? In that case it must have been Mt 13,47-48. that was in his mind, a text which, as a matter of fact, has the *incipit* ὁμοία ἐστὶν ἡ βασιλεία τῶν οὐρανῶν.[30] If he really alluded to this text, he must have done so in a very loose way or by using a deviating text of the passage: ἀνθρώπῳ instead of σαγήνῃ, and consequently βεβληκότι for βληθείσῃ, θάλασσαν without an article, τῶν ἑαλωκότων ἰχθύων instead of καὶ ἐκ παντὸς γένους συναγαγούσῃ, τὸ πλῆθος for ὅτε ἐπληρώθη[31], the *omission* of the activity of bringing the net ashore, τὴν ἐκλογὴν...ποιουμένῳ instead of συνέλεξαν, the mentioning of the "better" fishes (τῶν ἀμεινόνων)[32] instead of the *good* ones, τὰ καλά, the *omission* of the use of vessels and of the casting away of the weak ones, τὰ σαπρά. Quispel concluded from these differences that one can no longer argue that the version in the parable in Clement and "Thomas" was based upon the text of Matthew, even not upon a distorted, a so-called wild "Western" text of Matthew. For such a view would be only naive.[33] This seems to be a strong argument, but one should also compare Clement's reference with the text of Thomas or with the hypothetical tradition that one wishes to find behind the text of Thomas. Clement does not speak of a fisherman (ἁλιεύς), nor does he label him as wise; he does not mention the fact that the net was full nor does he speak of the activity of drawing the net out of sea; Clement does not speak of small fish, nor of the throwing away of these small fish; Clement does not focus here on the one "large, good fish", but rather suggests that the person in question selected the better fish (plural!) from those that were less good, which suggests a contrast between good and bad rather than great and small. So it is true that Clement greatly deviates from the precise text of Matthew, but then it should be admitted that he also deviates considerably from the precise text of Thomas. If one would suggest that he loosely quoted logion 8 of Thomas or a pre-canonical tradition now still visible in the text of logion 8, one should leave open the possibility

29. QUISPEL, *Thomas en de Nederlanden*, p. 118, rightly says that Clement does not quote, but makes only an allusion.

30. Mt 13,47, cf. 13,31.33.44.45; 20,1; in that case πάλιν was, of course, absent, since it does not make any sense outside its context.

31. Cf. the two versions of the miraculous draught, Lk 5,6 πλῆθος ἰχθύων πολύ, Jn 21,6 ἀπὸ τοῦ πλήθους τῶν ἰχθύων.

32. Cf. *meliora* in Old Latin *d*.

33. QUISPEL, *Thomas en de Nederlanden*, p. 118 (rev. ed., pp. 151-152).

that he might have given an equally free paraphrase here of the Matthaean text.

The Approach of D. Plooij: the Diatessaron

Before the discovery of "Thomas" the reading of the introduction ὁμοία ... ἀνθρώπῳ attracted less attention than the reading τὴν ἐκλογήν...ποιουμένῳ. This reading replaced *collecting* by *selecting*. In itself, ἐκλογή could mean *collection*, esp. of tribute or taxes[34]. However, since the text of Clement speaks of better fishes, a comparative, the idea of selection presents itself as the natural one. It was pointed out by D. Plooij that this reading ("they selected") was attested in several versions[35]. He also registered the agreement between τῶν ἀμεινόνων and *meliora* in the Old Latin text of Codex Bezae (*d*)[36]. Plooij concluded that Clement could have referred to a version of the parable that differed from the ordinary text of Matthew. Plooij attempted to show that these and other variants had their background in the Diatessaron: "The variants are due to Tatian"[37]. Clement, however, quoted from memory the text of the early harmony either in its *Syriac* form or rather, as Plooij is inclined to think, in its *Old-Latin* form, certainly not a Greek text: the Diatessaron, apparently, was read at a very early stage in Egypt both in a Syriac and in a Latin form. In his view, it is a fact "that a man like Clement of Alexandria when reproducing the Gospel from memory, should do so in the form of the Diatessaron". And the passage in question demonstrates "how deeply that form had fixed itself in his mind"[38].

It seems surprising that Clement would have known the Diatessaron, but the idea could easily suggest itself, if one understands ὁ μὲν τῆς τῶν Ἀσσυρίων who was among those whose lectures Clement had attended was, indeed, Tatian[39]. Clement knew Tatian's *Oratio adversus Graecos* and some of his other works[40]. He might have known, therefore, also

---

34. See for ἐκλογὴν ποιεῖσθαι e.g. Plato, *Leg.* 802B; cf. for ἐκλέγω in the sense of levying tax or toll H.G. LIDDEL – R. SCOTT – H.S. JONES – R. McKENZIE, *A Greek-English Lexicon*, Oxford, ⁹1940, p. 511b (ἐκλέγω).

35. D. PLOOIJ, *Matthew XIII.48b in the Textual Tradition*, in *Meededeelingen der koninklijke Akademie van Wetenschappen* 71:A.1, Amsterdam, 1931, pp. 5, 8.

36. Cf. F.H.A. SCRIVENER, *Bezae Codex Cantabrigiensis*, Cambridge, 1864, p. 36 (fol.44ab), where D has κάλλιστα (= *700*) and *d meliora*. Cf. A. JÜLICHER – W. MATZKOW – K. ALAND, *Matthäus-Evangelium* (Itala I), Berlin, ²1972, p. 93 (*optimos: a b g¹ ff² h*; *quae optima* (*-mae e*) *sunt: e k*); cf. BARNARD, *op. cit.* (n. 10), p. 19 nota.

37. PLOOIJ, *Matthew XIII.48b*, p. 6.

38. PLOOIJ, *Matthew XIII.48b*, resp. pp. 8, 10 and 9-10.

39. STÄHLIN, *Clemens Alexandrinus* II (n. 10), p. 8:22-23 (Strom. I,11.2), cf. A. HARNACK, *Geschichte der altchristlichen Literatur bis Eusebius* I,1, Leipzig, 1893, pp. 488-489.

40. HARNACK, *Geschichte*, II,1 (*Die Chronologie der Litteratur bis Irenäus*), Leipzig, 1897, pp. 284-289, 289.

his *Diatessaron*. This is the thesis defended by Hermann von Soden[41] who refers to ἀμεινόνων as a possible Tatianism[42]. If this were the case, one might ask in what form the parable of the fishing-net was presented by Tatian[43] or – if at all – known to Clement. There is reason to believe that the Diatessaron text did not have a text that was much different from the canonical text of Matthew. The Diatessaron text may have had some specific elements in agreement with Clement's reference: τὴν ἐκλογὴν ποιουμένῳ, cf. ܐܚܒ "they chose"; τῶν ἀμεινόνων might suggest a contrast as found in the Diatessaron tradition between ܛܒ ܛܒ.ܐ, "the best" (or "the good with the good") and ܒܝܫܐ.ܐ, "the inferior", although one cannot rule out that it was merely Clement's own paraphrase of the contrast between τὰ καλά and τὰ σαπρά[44]. In conclusion, it cannot be proven that the Diatessaron was used here by Clement.

The View of M. Mees

A different view has been defended by M. Mees[45]. However, his view is not so clearly expressed as one would wish. It seems that he took a half-way position between the view that Clement merely memorized the Matthaean text and the other approach that Clement was depended on an extra-canonical source of some kind. He defines the form of Clement's reference as an allusion to the Matthaean text which had been transformed by non-canonical influences still preserved in the Gospel of Thomas and in "Western" texts. He writes, "Clemens dagegen sucht unter direktem Bezug auf ausserkanonische Tradition innerhalb des ekklesiologischen Sinnes der Parabel dessen Bedeutung für die Einzelseele besser herauszuarbeiten". This interpretation is absolutely inconceivable, if one reads the reference of Clement in its context. Clement does not speak at all of the individual soul, but merely wants to emphasize that the message of the Gospel enables Christians to choose the better elements of Greek propaedeusis and philosophy. Nothing else he has in mind. In fact, Mees does not interpret the text of Clement here. After having isolated the allusion of Clement from its context, he explains it as if it was the parable in the Gospel of Thomas. This is, as a matter of fact, also done by Quispel[46], when he writes that the *one*

41. H. VON SODEN, *Die Schriften des Neuen Testaments in ihrer ältesten erreichbaren Textgestalt*, I.IIA, Göttingen, ²1911, pp. 1597ff.

42. *Ibid.*, p. 1599.

43. Quispel has defended the thesis that the Diatessaron text was more or less similar to the text of Thomas 8, a view that cannot be sustained by the facts, cf. my article on *Philoxenus* (cf. n. 1).

44. Cf. for a reconstruction my *Philoxenus*, pp. 1410ff. (cf. n. 1).

45. MEES, *Zitate* (n. 10), I, pp. 197-198.

46. QUISPEL, *Some Remarks* (n. 17), p. 289.

fisherman of Clement is God himself, who now gathers candidates to citizenship in his Kingdom. One should interpret Clement *e mente Clementis*. One should not explain what the gist of the parable might have been in some hypothetical source text that Clement could have used, since we have no idea in what specific context it might have had its place in such a document.

The View of A. Resch

One can understand why scholars, assuming that Clement *literally* quoted elements from the text "in the Gospel", have looked for an extra-canonical or pre-canonical source. A. Resch[47] concluded from the introduction ὁμοία ἐστὶν ἡ βασιλεία τῶν οὐρανῶν ἀνθρώπῳ that Clement quoted from a text that must impress us as being original, that is, a text of the pre-canonical *Hebrew* Gospel whose existence he assumed. He refers to the introductions of Mt 20,1 ἀνθρώπῳ οἰκοδεσπότῃ, 22,1 ἀνθρώπῳ βασιλεῖ, 13,24 ἀνθρώπῳ σπείραντι, cf. 18,23, all of them Matthaean passages[48] which have introductions that resemble the one found in Clement (ἀνθρώπῳ)[49]. It was only in Mt 13,47 that Matthew altered the pre-canonical form[50]. However, Resch does not compare other parables in Mt 13, such as v. 31: κόκκῳ σινάπεως (= Mk, Lk?), v. 33: ζύμη (= Lk, Q?), v. 44: θησαυρῷ κεκρυμμένῳ ἐν τῷ ἀγρῷ ("Sondergut"); the last of these has a form that is similar to 13,47. There seems to be no reason to assume that Matthew altered his source text in the case of Matth 13,47.

The Reconstruction of A. Resch and G. Quispel

In spite of the methodological shortcomings of the approach of Resch, one has to consider the possibility that the reference of Clement was prompted by a text of the parable which was different from Matthew's version and which based on a Semitic model.

47. RESCH, *Aussercanonische Paralleltexte* I (n. 26), pp. 159-160; ID., *Die Logia Jesu*, p. 40.

48. One should observe that Mt 13,24; 18,23; 20,1 are Matthaean Sondergut, whereas Mt 22,1 is the specific Matthaean form of a possible Q-text. This may imply that the formula was present in a specific source of Matthew or was his own terminology.

49. Clement does not have the wording ἀνθρώπῳ ἁλιεῖ which QUISPEL, *Der Heliand* (n. 17), p. 149; ID., *Some Remarks on the Gospel of Thomas*, in *NTS* 5 (1959) 276-290, p. 289; ID., *The Gospel of Thomas Revisited*, in B. BARC (ed.), *Colloque international sur les textes de Nag Hammadi*, Québec-Louvain, 1981, pp. 218-266, esp. p. 229, assumes to have been in the text of the Diatessaron; however, although this may have been the text underlying the Coptic text of Thomas 8, it certainly was not the text of the Diatessaron, cf. my *Philoxenus*, pp. 1413-1414 (cf. n. 1).

50. One might ask in this case what could have been the reason for such an alteration, because he could have kept the suggested pre-canonical form without doing harm to his peculiar understanding of the parable.

In the view of Resch, the reconstruction of the original Hebrew saying reads as follows[51]:

עוד דומה מלכות השמים   πάλιν ὁμοία ἐστὶν ἡ βασιλεία τῶν οὐρανῶν
לאיש אשר השליך מכמרת בים   ἀνθρώπῳ, ὃς ἔβαλεν σαγήνην εἰς θάλασσαν,
ויאסף מכל מין דגים   καὶ συνέλαβεν ἀπὸ παντὸς γένους ἰχθύων,
וכאשר נמלאה המכמרת   καὶ ὅτε ἐπληρώθη ἡ σαγήνη,
העלו אתה אל שפת הים וישבו   ἀναβιβάσαντες ἐπὶ τὸν αἰγιαλον καὶ καθίσαντες
ויבחרו את־הטובים אל הכלים   συνέλεξαν τὰ καλὰ εἰς τὰ ἄγγη,
ואת־הרעים השליכו חוצה: τὰ δὲ σαπρὰ ἔξω ἔβαλον.

Apart from the variations in the first three lines, the text of this reconstruction does not differ much from that of the Greek Matthew.

Although Quispel does not present us with a reconstruction of the text in the Aramaic tradition which he presupposes as the source of Clement and Thomas[52], he more or less follows the line of reasoning of Resch. The wording of the parable in the allusion of Clement was, in his view, not caused by a personal application of the text which resulted in the readings different from the Matthaean form (in this regard Quispel deviates from the view of Mees); rather, it reflects an extra-canonical tradition borrowed from a Judaeo-Christian source, in fact the same source from which Thomas had drawn its wording and which, at a later stage, was also the source of the Diatessaron. In his perception the fisherman becomes the subject of all activities in the parable, which means that Clement was in agreement with Thomas in the reading of the singular form in the second part of the parable as well. Quispel disagrees with Resch at this point. Moreover, he differed from Resch by maintaining that the idea of *choosing* (Aramaic גבא) was found in Clement, Thomas and Tatian, whereas Resch had expressed this idea only in the Hebrew part of his reconstruction (בחר)[53]. Quispel rejects the idea that Clement could have been dependent on a "wild" Western text of Matthew. He does not assume that Clement was dependent on Tatian's harmony, *versus* Plooij. Nor does he find the source of Clement in the Gospel of Thomas. For him, Thomas, Tatian and Clement are independent witnesses to an early tradition that was altered in the version of Matthew.

51. RESCH, *Logia* (n. 26), p. 40. His basis is, besides Mt 13,47 and Clement, *Strom.* VI,11.95, also Eusebius, *In Isa.* 19,7-8 (καὶ συλλαβούσῃ ἀπὸ παντὸς γένους ἰχθύων).

52. Cf. QUISPEL, *Some Remarks* (n. 17), 289; *The Gospel of Thomas Revisited* (n. 49), p. 239; *Heliand* (n. 17), p. 150; *Thomas en de Nederlanden* (n. 17), pp. 118-119 (rev. ed., pp. 151-152); *Gnosis and New Sayings* (n. 17), p. 274; *Tatian* (n. 17), pp. 104-105 (ref. to Mees).

53. See for the question of the verb my discussion of the problem in *"Chose" or "Collected"* (cf. n. 1); on the question of the Tatianic form of the text *Philoxenus*, pp. 1417-1418 (cf. n. 1).

Following Mees, Quispel proposes the view that the text of Matthew that Clement knew and had normally used was nothing else than the ordinary Alexandrian text of the first Gospel. If he had used that form of the text here, he would have presented the canonical form of the Parable that is found in Matthew. Consequently, the deviations in his allusion to our parable can only be explained as originating in an extra-canonical or pre-canonical source with which he was also acquainted, a source that must be labelled as Judaeo-Christian and be dated to a time at which the gospel was brought to Egypt by Jewish-Christian mission-aries, that is, before the later gentile-Christian stage of Christianity. This early source explains the deviations which he registered for Cle-ment. As I have demonstrated elsewhere[54], the Aramaism גבא that Quispel detected and used as a decisive proof to postulate an Aramaic source for Thomas, Clement and the Diatessaron is far from convin-cing; if there was an Aramaism here that meant "choose" it would have been בחר, just as in Hebrew (cf. Resch). If one postulates a Semitic verb גבא that could explain both "to choose" and "to collect", one can only denote it as a Syriacism (ܓܒܐ). Moreover, the reference of Clement is free and apparently abbreviated, which precludes any speculation about the exact form of a pre-canonical source, provided that we have to assume that there was such an archaic source in Clement's mind, which I strongly doubt.

The Gospel

Clement tells his readers that he found this parable "in the Gospel". This suggests that he quotes from a canonical Gospel, since in all the instances where he quotes a text that he found "in the Gospel" it is a text taken from one of the four Gospels[55]. If a text is taken from another Gospel such as the Gospel of the Egyptians[56] or from the Gospel to the Hebrews[57] he explicitly says so. Only once, in his quotation of the saying μυστήριον ἐμὸν ἐμοὶ καὶ τοῖς υἱοῖς τοῦ οἴκου μου, he does not mention a name of the Gospel, but differentiates this source from the canonical Gospels when he says ἔν τινι εὐαγγελίῳ, "in some Gospel"[58]. On this basis there is reason to assume that Clement, in spite of the textual differences from the Matthaean parable, wished

54. Cf. "Chose" or "Collected" (n. 1), pp. 383-387.
55. Cf. in STÄHLIN, Clemens Alexandrinus I (n. 3), pp. 96:29; 97:18; 131:23; 134:14; 136:21; 139:32; 160:1; 222:27; 232:13; II, 144:28; 151:22; 222:8; 230:3; 255:18; 479:23; 489:12; III, 151:7; 154:4.
56. Cf. STÄHLIN, Clemens Alexandrinus II (n. 10), pp. 225:3; 238:28.
57. Ibid., p. 137:4.
58. Ibid., p. 368:27.

to refer to Mt 13,47-48, *not* to any other Gospel or tradition[59]. He used it to make his point that the Christian confronted with the wealth of Greek philosophy has to choose its better elements.

IV. CONCLUSION

This short study was devoted to the question of whether Clement knew an independent tradition of the Parable that we have now in its canonical form in Mt 13,47-48. In itself this question cannot be answered. For what he may have known can only be concluded from what he has written, but he will have known a lot more than he revealed in his works. The first passage (I) that we dealt with was the poem attached to the *Paedagogue*, but apart form the question whether it is Clement's own text one cannot conclude from his mention of the ἁλιεύς that he knew a text different from Mt 13,47.

The parenthesis with the motifs of the one pearl and the beauty-fish in the first book of the *Stromateis* (II) is not necessarily borrowed from extra-canonical tradition: the order of the sayings is that of Matthew, the reference to the *one* pearl agrees with the text of Matthew, the mentioning of the beauty-fish (κάλλιχθυς) reminds us of the Matthaean emphasis on the *good* fish (τὰ καλά). The emphasis on the one fish may have been an assimilation to the reference to the one pearl on the part of Clement. With all fairness one cannot say that this could only have been a reference to another, extra- or pre-canonical tradition.

The free quotation in the sixth book of the *Stromateis* (III) is most probably a reference to the text of Matthew. Even if Clement was acquainted with the Alexandrian text of the Gospel, one has to admit that several of his quotations betray traces of a type of text that is usually labeled as Western. This might explain some of the elements in Clement's wording of the strongly abbreviated reference to Mt 13,47-48. Since Clement's interpretation of this text suited his view that the Christian should not neglect Greek philosophy but choose from it the better elements, his wording may have been influenced by his interpretation.

Finally, there is a difference between the allusion (I) and the "quotation" (II) that should not be overlooked. Quispel has chosen from both these references what suited him to claim an extra-canonical provenance. The first text speaks of one fish, the second one of many fish. If one claims that the first reference of Clement has preserved a different tradition ("one fish", with Thomas), then the second reference (more

---

59. HUNZINGER, *Unbekannte Gleichnisse* (n. 11), p. 217, n.37, implicitly admits this.

than one fish) must necessarily be prompted by Matthew. However, both texts presented by Clement preserve the idea of good (κάλλιχθυς I) or better (ἀμεινόνων II) that is closer to Matthew ('good' and "bad") than to Thomas ("great" and "small").

The conclusion must be that there is no convincing argument in these references of Clement for the conclusion that he *must* have been dependent on a Jewish-Christian *extra*- or *pre*-canonical tradition as suggested by Hunzinger and Quispel.

Troskerslaan 27   Tjitze BAARDA
NL-1185 BV Amstelveen

GOSPEL SYNOPSES FROM THE 16TH
TO THE 18TH CENTURIES
AND THE RISE OF LITERARY CRITICISM OF THE GOSPELS

The phenomenon of modern literary criticism of the Gospels found its genesis in the last three decades of the 18th century. The rise of this literary critical method is inseparably associated with the names Gotthold Ephraim Lessing and Johann Jakob Griesbach. The question for which these scholars were searching for an answer was this: how can the similarities as well as the discrepancies between the Gospels be satisfactorily explained in one hypothesis? The solution for Lessing was to assert that the synoptic Gospels all derived from one and the same Aramaic Gospel[1]. Today, this theory is no longer adhered to and therefore plays no role in the critical investigation of the Gospels. Griesbach's hypothesis was of a different nature. He suggested that the similarities and differences between the synoptic Gospels could best be explained by the supposition that the Gospels themselves had a genealogical relationship with each other. Thus, Matthew would have been the source of Luke, and both Matthew and Luke would have been the source of Mark[2]. Although Griesbach's hypothesis in its specific form has only a few advocates today, his type of solution to the so-called "synoptic problem", the so-called "utilization hypothesis", continues to receive general recognition. Practically every researcher of the synoptic Gospels assumes that, in one way or another, there is a relationship of direct dependence between the three synoptic Gospels.

Griesbach launched his theory in 1783 in a book about the stories of Jesus' resurrection in the Gospels. Some six years later, in 1789-1790, he developed his theory more fully. In his research, Griesbach made extensive use of his own edition of a Greek synopsis of the Gospels. Griesbach had first published this synopsis in 1774, in a New Testament

---

1. G.E. LESSING, *Theses aus der Kirchengeschichte*, in ID., *Werke* 7 (ed. H.G. GÖPFERT), München, 1976, pp. 603-613; G.E. LESSING, *Neue Hypothese über die Evangelisten als bloss menschliche Geschichtsschreiber betrachtet*, in ID., *Werke* 7, 1976, pp. 614-636.

2. J.J. GRIESBACH, *Inquiritur in fontes, unde evangelistae suas de resurrectione Domini narrationes hauserint*, Jena, 1783; reprinted in J.J. GRIESBACH, *Opuscula academica* 2 (ed. J.P. GABLER), Jena, 1825, pp. 241-256; J.J. GRIESBACH, *Commentatio qua Marci evangelium totum e Matthaei et Lucae commentariis decerptum esse monstratur*, 1789-1790. A second edition was published in J.C. VELTHUSEN – C.T. KUINOEL – G.A. RUPERTI (ed.), *Commentationes theologicae* 1, Leipzig, 1794, pp. 360-434; this edition was reprinted in J.J. GRIESBACH, *Opuscula academica* 2, 1825, pp. 358-425.

text edition[3]. This synopsis made it possible for him to compare each Gospel with the others, pericope for pericope, and even word for word. With the aid of his synopsis Griesbach came upon two innovative insights which have remained valid even to the present day. These two insights were: 1) that it is not possible to reconstruct the life of Jesus on the basis of the Gospels[4], and 2) that the similarities and discrepancies between the Gospels would have to be explained in terms of each Gospel's formation history, and this could only be done with the aid of a literary-critical hypothesis.

Considering the fact that Griesbach attained these vitally important results with the aid of his synopsis, it seemed to us that one important question deserved attention: namely, whether the historical and literary criticism which Griesbach formulated can already be discerned in a rudimentary form in the synopses earlier than Griesbach's own synopsis. Thus, our question is this: is it possible to find the rudimentary beginnings of Griesbach's method of historical and literary criticism in the various synopses originating between the 16th and the 18th centuries?

From the 16th century until the time of Griesbach, no less than 24 synopses of the Gospels and works of a synopsis-like structure appeared[5]. The new genre of the synopsis rose up in the 16th century beside the much older and more popular genre of the harmony[6]. In the harmonies of the Gospels, the texts of the four Gospels were integrated into one continuous text so that a single flowing overview of the works of Jesus was achieved. At this point, the harmonies become irrelevant for our study due to the fact that the Gospels as individual writings are completely lost in the harmonies. Moreover, the harmony prevents the

---

3. J.J. GRIESBACH, *Libri historici Novi Testamenti Graece. Pars prior, sistens synopsin evangeliorum Matthaei, Marci et Lucae*, Halle, 1774. In 1776 Griesbach published his synopsis separately: *Synopsis evangeliorum Matthaei, Marci et Lucae*, Halle, 1776. A second edition was published in 1797, a third in 1809.

4. GRIESBACH, *Synopsis*, Halle, 1776, p. VIII: "... sed valde etiam dubito, an ex evangelistarum libellis harmonica componi possit narratio, veritati satis consentanea et firmis fundamentis superstructa. Quid? si nullus evangelistarum ordinem temporis accurate ubique secutus est? et si sufficientia non adsunt indicia, e quibus constare possit, quisnam et quibusnam in locis chronologico ordine recesserit? Atque in hac me esse haeresi fateor". Also quoted by W.G. KÜMMEL, *Das Neue Testament. Geschichte der Erforschung seiner Probleme*, Freiburg-München, ²1970, p. 89.

5. J. Calvin (1555); P. Crellius (1566); C. Molinaeus (1572); J. Rubus (1571); A. Copus (1572); Th. Beauxamis (1583-1590); G. Mercator (1592); M. Chemnitz, P. Leyser, J. Gerhard (1593-1626); S. Barradius (1599-1611); J. de la Haye (1607); J. Roberti (1615); C. Becillus (1621); G. Calixtus (1624); Th. Cartwright (1627); J. Lightfoot (1644-1650); A. Arnauld (1653); S. Cradock (1668); F. de Bruin (1690); B. Lamy (1699); J. Clericus (1699); S. le Roux (1699); W. Whiston (1702); N. Toinard (1707); J.A. Bengel (1742).

6. D. WÜNSCH, *Evangelienharmonien im Reformationszeitalter. Ein Beitrag zur Geschichte der Leben-Jesu-Darstellungen* (Arbeiten zur Kirchengeschichte, 52), Berlin - New York, 1983.

reader from confronting the problem of the discrepancies and the similarities between the Gospels, a problem which motivates and encourages the reader to further investigate the formation of the Gospels. Because of these factors, the harmonies have played no significant role in the development of the historical and literary criticism of the Gospels.

From the very beginning, two works have had a profound influence upon the way synopses were arranged: 1) Augustine's treatise *De consensu evangelistarum*, which appeared around the year 400; and 2) the *Harmonia evangelica* published by the German Lutheran Andreas Osiander in the year 1537.

De consensu evangelistarum is a treatise in which the Church Father Augustine strives to prove that the Gospels do not contradict each other[7]. This work was written around the year 400 A.D. with the purpose of countering the criticism of the Manichaeans, who pointed out the discrepancies which appear in the various accounts of the Gospels[8]. Augustine argued that the differences in the sequential order of the pericopae, and the variations within parallel passages of two or more Gospels existed only from a literary perspective of the Gospels, but that these variations provided no substantial problem for the reconstruction of the underlying historical events. The Holy Spirit had given each evangelist the freedom of expression within the literary context. Thus, variations on the literary plane do not signal a contradiction[9]; for, according to Augustine, all kinds of harmonizations could be applied in order to eliminate the discrepancies on the underlying historical plane. An accurate reconstruction of the actual historical events remained, for the most part, possible. Moreover, he maintained that many parallel stories occurring in two or more Gospels, in spite of the differences these stories show in different Gospels, were the accounts of identical historical events. In other words, Augustine "synchronized" these stories. Because of this method of synchronizing the parallel accounts, it became necessary for Augustine to explain the variations between the parallel stories by means of harmonization. But by indicating whether or not certain pericopae should be synchronized, Augustine also designed the plan for the composition of synopses in which the parallel accounts would appear side by side. Only in this way could these parallel accounts become the subject for thorough compari-

---

7. AUGUSTINUS, *De consensu evangelistarum* (ed. F. WEIHRICH; CSEL, 43), Wien-Leipzig, 1904. On Augustine's *De consensu evangelistarum*: H.J. VOGELS, *St Augustins Schrift De consensu evangelistarum unter vornehmlicher Berücksichtigung ihrer harmonistischen Anschauungen* (BibS(F), 13), Freiburg/Br, 1908; H. MERKEL, *Widersprüche zwischen den Evangelien* (WUNT, 13), Tübingen, 1971, pp. 218-261.

8. H. MERKEL, *Widersprüche zwischen den Evangelien* (n. 7), pp. 226-227.

9. AUGUSTINUS, *De consensu evangelistarum*, II 12,27-29, pp. 127-130; II 24,55, p. 157; II 62,120-121, pp. 222-224; II 66,127-128, pp. 229-231.

son. Synopses such as these first appeared in the middle of the 16th century.

Alongside Augustine's approach to the Gospels emerged another approach in the 16th century within the work of the German Lutheran Andreas Osiander. In the harmony which he first published in 1537, *Harmonia evangelica*, Osiander radically rejected Augustine's relatively liberal method of downgrading the significance of the discrepancies between the Gospels, regardless of whether these differences pertained to the sequential order of the pericopae or to disagreements in the details of parallel accounts in two or more Gospels[10]. Augustine had declared that two kinds of differences were unimportant: the differences in the sequence of the pericopae, and those in the contents of parallel accounts from more than one Gospel. Osiander refused to find these differences unimportant. From the basis of a rigid doctrine of inspiration, he argued that each evangelist had preserved the exact historical sequence of the historical events. In each instance that one of the Gospels placed a certain story in a different sequence than one or more of the other Gospels, Osiander proclaimed that a separate historical event was being described. He also used the slightest variation between parallel accounts from two or more Gospels as evidence that these stories went back to different historical events. In contrast to Augustine's synchronizing procedure, Osiander de-synchronized many of the biblical accounts with the result that the history of Jesus' life acquired many absurd repetitions.

The first work in which similar pericopae from two or three Gospels were placed in parallel columns alongside each other was Calvin's commentary on the synoptic Gospels, which appeared in 1555[11]. In contrast to what had been done with the harmonies before his time, Calvin did not attempt to offer a reconstruction of Jesus' life. Rather, he concentrated his commentary mainly upon an explanation of the contents of the first three Gospels. Thus, each of the three Gospels was examined pericope by pericope. But in the case of parallel passages which appeared in two or all three Gospels, he discussed these passages together. The positive effects of this method were two-fold. First, it allowed him to lay the Gospel of John outside the scope of his study. In this way the Fourth Gospel no longer dictated the pattern for the reconstruction of Jesus' activities, a factor which had always been the

---

10. A. OSIANDER, *Harmoniae evangelicae libri quatuor Graece et Latine*, Basel, 1537. See D. WÜNSCH, *Evangelienharmonien im Reformationszeitalter* (n. 6), pp. 86-105 and 122-152.

11. J. CALVIN, *Harmonia ex tribus evangelistis composita, Matthaeo, Marco et Luca*, Geneva, 1555; references will be made to *Ioannis Calvini in harmoniam ex Matthaeo, Marco et Luca compositam commentarii* (ed. A. THOLUCK), Berlin, 1838. On the *Harmonia* of Calvin, see D. SCHELLONG, *Calvins Auslegung der synoptischen Evangelien* (Forschungen zur Geschichte und Lehre des Protestantismus, 10ᵉ Reihe, 38), München, 1969.

case in all the previous harmonies. Calvin was no longer obliged to superimpose the chronology of John upon the synoptics. Thus, he restored to the synoptics their own unique character. The second advantage of Calvin's method of arranging the synoptic Gospels in parallel columns was that this method gave him greater freedom. Calvin did not claim that his arrangement of the pericopae was a restoration of the exact historical succession of events. In his presentation of the synoptic Gospels, Calvin abandoned all pretences that he was delivering a chronological reconstruction[12]. This had never been possible in the composition of harmonies.

Calvin's unpretentiousness about the chronology of Jesus' life, however, proved to be unique. In all the synopses which arose in the latter half of the 16th century subsequent to Calvin's commentary, there appeared a renewed intensified effort to compose an accurate arrangement of Jesus' activities. The Gospel of John was subsequently restored to the scope of each study because it always provided the framework and the guidance for such a reconstruction. Moreover, from this time on, the keenest efforts were exerted to ascertain as nearly as possible the exact historical placement of every event in Jesus' life. As a result, the only passages which were placed together were those particular passages which appeared in two or more of the Gospels and which the author perceived as recounting one historical event. The inconsistencies between these juxtaposed pericopae were then resolved by means of the methods and the reasoning of harmonization. All the synopses published after Calvin's synopsis were actually harmonies in the form of a synopsis. It is therefore not surprising that most of the synopses which appeared between the time of Calvin and Griesbach carried titles such as *Harmonia evangelica* or *Harmonia evangelistarum*.

In several of the synopses, a great number of passages were synchronized, while in other synopses, very few passages were synchronized. Every one of the 24 synopses which was published before the synopsis of Griesbach can be distinctly pinpointed upon a scale ranging from purely Augustinian, to purely Osiandrian, to various grades of compromises in between[13].

12. J. CALVIN, *Harmonia* (n. 11), ad Mt 5,1 (41), p. 135: "Sed in tenendo ordine temporis, quem videbam a Spiritu Dei neglectum, nolui esse nimium curiosus"; *ibid.*, ad Mt 8,23-27 (81), p. 227: "Nunc de tempore restat videndum, quod neque ex Matthaeo, neque ex Luca potest colligi: solus Marcus vesperam notat eius diei, ... Unde apparet, non servatum fuisse ab illis temporis ordinem, quod etiam clare exprimit Lucas, quum dicit, factum esse quadam die: quibus verbis ostendit, se anxie non laborare, quid prius vel posterius fuerit"; *ibid.*, ad Mt 4,5 (32), p. 111: "Non magni interest, quod Lucas secundo loco tentationem recitat, quae in postremum locum a Matthaeo reiicitur: neque enim propositum evangelistis fuit historiae filum sic contexere, ut temporis rationem semper exacte servarent, ...".

13. Most Augustinian synopses were based on the harmony of C. JANSENIUS, *Concordia evangelica*, Louvain, 1549; for instance J. RUBUS, *Historia ac harmonia evangelica*,

It is obvious that the Augustinian understanding of the Gospels contributed more to the development of the historical and literary critical study of these writings than did the Osiandrian understanding. From the Augustinian approach, more of the parallel passages from the different Gospels could be synchronized and arranged beside each other, instead of being de-synchronized and held separate. The obvious benefit of the Augustinian approach was that the pericopae could become the subject for comparison in regard to mutual differences and similarities.

Nonetheless, such a serious analysis remained unexplored: the method of harmonization predominated the field until late in the 18th century. The idea that similarities and differences could be the result of the way the Gospels depended on each other or on older sources never occurred to the makers of the synopses. They persisted in considering the Gospels as trustworthy historical documents from which, with the help of the process of harmonization, one unbroken historical narrative could be established.

The optimistic idea that it was possible to reconstruct an accurate account of Jesus' historical activities on the basis of the four Gospels was reinforced toward the end of the 16th century by the emergence of the science of chronology[14]. This branch of science exercised a negative influence upon the development of a critical investigation of the Gospels. From this time on, many researchers of the Gospels speculated that it was not only possible to regain the correct sequence of events in Jesus' life, but they also advocated that, with the aid of the science of chronology, they could even establish the precise date of these events[15]. The science of chronology bestowed the investigators of the Gospels with the assurance that it was possible to compile an account of Jesus' life that was trustworthy down to the smallest detail. The influence of the science of chronology endured until late into the

Douai, 1571; A. Copus, *Syntaxis historiae evangelicae*, Louvain, 1572; Th. Beauxamis, *Commentaria in evangelicam historiam*, Paris, ¹1583, ²1610; J. de la Haye, *Evangelistarum quaternio*, Douai, 1607. A purely Osiandrian synopsis is the work of C. Molinaeus, *Collatio et unio quatuor evangelistarum*, Paris, 1565. Synopses which are neither purely Augustinian nor purely Osiandrian are for instance: M. Chemnitz – P. Leyser – J. Gerhard, *Harmonia quatuor evangelistarum*, Frankfurt, 1593-1626; Th. Cartwright, *Harmonia evangelica*, Amsterdam, 1627; F. de Bruin, *Overeenstemminge der Evangelien*, Dordrecht, 1690; W. Whiston, *A Short View of the Chronology of the Old Testament, and the Harmony of the Evangelists*, Cambridge, 1702.

14. The first synopsis composed with the aid of chronological data was G. Mercator, *Evangelicae historiae quadripartita monas, sive Harmonia quatuor evangelistarum*, Duisburg, 1592.

15. For instance F. de Bruin, *Overeenstemminge der Evangelien*, Dordrecht, 1690; J. Clericus, *Harmonia evangelica cui subjecta est historia Christi ex quatuor evangeliis concinnata*, Amsterdam, 1699; W. Whiston, *A Short View* (n. 13); N. Toinard, *Evangeliorum harmonia Graeco-Latina*, Paris, 1707.

18th century. Because of the counterproductive influence of both Osiander and the science of chronology, the favorable effect which Augustine's and Calvin's approach could have had upon the study of Jesus' life was decimated.

After evaluating all the synopses prior to approximately 1775, we must conclude that, with the exception of the work of Calvin, not one of the synopses which was published before the time of Griesbach approximated the profound critical insights which Griesbach attained in his synopsis. The answer to our question, then, as to how Griesbach was able to arrive at the conclusion that the life of Jesus cannot be reconstructed, and that the discrepancies and similarities between the Gospels must be explained on the basis of the history of each Gospel's formation, cannot be successfully discovered in the synopses which were published between 1555 and the time of Griesbach.

Rather, the answer should be sought after in the historical criticism of the Bible which took place in the philosophical and religious movement known as deism. At the end of the 17th century and in the first half of the 18th century, the Old and the New Testaments were subjected to a radical historical criticism by English deism. In Germany, deism found a strong representative in the Hamburgian Oriental scholar, Hermann Samuel Reimarus. Reimarus died in 1768. But in the period between 1774-1778, Gotthold Ephraim Lessing published excerpts of the *Apologie*, a previously unpublished document of Reimarus, under the title "Fragmente eines Ungenannten" ("Anonymous Fragments")[16]. In this document, Reimarus alleged that, although it was true that Jesus had been a teacher of pure piety and ethics, the apostles had intentionally changed his teaching. As a result, the Gospels as a whole, according to Reimarus, were the expression of a new theological system which the apostles had deceitfully invented after

---

16. Lessing published the "Fragments" in *Zur Geschichte und Litteratur. Aus den Schätzen der Herzoglichen Bibliothek zu Wolfenbüttel*. The first complete edition of the *Apologie* was published in 1972: H.S. REIMARUS, *Apologie oder Schutzschrift für die vernünftigen Verehrer Gottes* (ed. G. ALEXANDER), 2 vols., Frankfurt/M, 1972. On Reimarus, see H. SIEVEKING, *Hermann Samuel Reimarus (1694-1768)*, in *Zeitschrift des Vereins für Hamburgische Geschichte* 38 (1939) 145-182; G. GAWLICK, *et alii* (ed.), *Hermann Samuel Reimarus (1694-1768): ein "bekannter Unbekannter" der Aufklärung in Hamburg. Vorträge gehalten auf der Tagung der Joachim Jungius-Gesellschaft der Wissenschaften Hamburg am 12. und 13. Oktober 1972*, Göttingen, 1973; G. GAWLICK, *Hermann Samuel Reimarus*, in M. GRESCHAT (ed.), *Gestalten der Kirchengeschichte. 8. Die Aufklärung*, Stuttgart-Berlin-Cologne-Mainz, 1983, pp. 299-311; W. SCHMIDT-BIGGEMANN, *Die destruktive Potenz philosophischer Apologetik oder der Verlust des biblischen Kredits bei Hermann Samuel Reimarus*, in H. Graf REVENTLOW, *et alii* (ed.), *Historische Kritik und biblischer Kanon in der deutschen Aufklärung* (Wolfenbütteler Forschungen, 41), Wiesbaden, 1988, pp. 193-204: H.J. DE JONGE, *Van Erasmus tot Reimarus*, Leiden, 1991; H.J. DE JONGE, *The Loss of Faith in the Historicity of the Gospels: H.S. Reimarus (ca. 1750) on John and the Synoptics*, in A. DENAUX (ed.), *John and the Synoptics*, (BETL, 101), Louvain, 1992, pp. 409-422.

Jesus' eschatological preaching appeared to be without foundation because of his death. Reimarus utilized the discrepancies between the Gospels to demonstrate the unreliability of the Gospel writings.

For many people, however, Reimarus' conclusion that the discrepancies between the Gospels pointed out the fact that the Gospels were the result of the deceitfulness of the apostles and the evangelists was a conclusion that simply went too far. Griesbach, as well as other scholars, admitted that there were differences between the Gospels. But they emphasized that these discrepancies could not be used as evidence of the unreliability of the historical information contained in the Gospels[17]. What was necessary, then, was a theory in which the discrepancies would be taken seriously, but which, at the same time, would safely preserve the authenticity of Jesus' words and the historicity of the recorded events. In order to achieve this goal, Lessing and Griesbach began to explicate the differences and similarities between the Gospels on the basis of the formation of these writings. They did this by assuming one or two older, common sources as well as a secondary, divergent development within the Gospel tradition. The common element, or the similarities, between the Gospels could have arisen from the shared use of a primitive Proto-Gospel ("Urevangelium") in Aramaic, thus Lessing, but it could also be accounted for by the use which one evangelist may have made of the work of one or two other evangelists, thus Griesbach. Regardless of which solution one chose, the new literary criticism was primarily conceived as an apologetic with the specific purpose of refuting the hyper-criticism of Reimarus and keeping his influence under control.

In summary, we can conclude that Lessing's and Griesbach's critical insights originated as a reaction to the hyper-criticism of the deists. The historical events, such as they are narrated in the Gospels, first had to be subjected to radical historical criticism before the discrepancies and the similarities between the Gospels would become the subject of serious literary-critical investigation. However, in order to safely preserve the historical reliability of the Gospels, a plausible explanation of the contradictions and the agreements had to be given. This explanation was found in the history of the formation of the Gospels. Thus, the

---

17. In the *Fontes* Griesbach speaks highly of contemporaries who contest the denial of the historicity of the resurrection of Jesus, see J.J. GRIESBACH, *Fontes*, in ID., *Opuscula academica* (ed. J.P. GABLER), p. 242: "Laudandum profecto est doctorum virorum studium, quo cum in asserenda universae historiae veritate, tum in firmandis et ab obiectionibus liberandis evangelistarum de resurrectione narrationibus, nostra praesertim aetate, elaborarunt". In all probability Griesbach refers to the "Fragments". G.E. LESSING, *Eine Duplik*, in ID., *Werke* 8 (ed. H.G. GÖPFERT), München, 1979, p. 31: "Ich erwidere: die Auferstehung Christi kann ihre Richtigkeit haben, *ob* sich *schon* die Nachrichten der Evangelisten widersprechen".

method of literary criticism which appeared at the end of the 18th century in Germany originated as an apologetic: it was an answer to the hyper-criticism of the deists[18].

Faculteit der Godgeleerdheid
Rijksuniversiteit te Leiden
Postbus 9515
NL-2300 RA Leiden

Marijke H. DE LANG

---

18. For a fuller discussion of the topic of the present contribution, see M.H. DE LANG, *De opkomst van de historische en literaire kritiek in de synoptische beschouwing van de evangeliën van Calvijn (1555) tot Griesbach (1774)* (Diss.), Leiden, 1993.

INDEXES

ABBREVIATIONS

AB	Anchor Bible
AGSU	Arbeiten zur Geschichte des Spätjudentums und Urchristentums
AnBib	Analecta Biblica
ANRW	Aufstieg und Niedergang der römischen Welt
ANTI	Arbeiten zum Neuen Testament und zum Judentum
AOAT	Alter Orient und Altes Testament
ARW	Archiv für Religionswissenschaft
AssSeign	Assemblées du Seigneur
ATANT	Abhandlungen zur Theologie des Alten und Neuen Testament
AusBR	Australian Biblical Review
BAR	Biblical Archaeological Review
BBB	Bonner biblische Beiträge
BDF	Blass-Debrunner-Funk, A Greek Grammar of the New Testament
BETL	Bibliotheca Ephemeridum Theologicarum Lovaniensium
BEvT	Beiträge zur evangelischen Theologie
BFCT	Beiträge zur Förderung christlicher Theologie
BHT	Beiträge zur historischen Theologie
Bib	Biblica
BibLeb	Bibel und Leben
BibS(F)	Biblische Studien (Freiburg, 1895-)
BibS(N)	Biblische Studien (Neukirchen, 1951-)
BJRL	Bulletin of the John Rylands University Library of Manchester
BK	Bibel und Kirche
BN	Biblische Notizen
BNTC	Black's New Testament Commentary
BSt	Biblische Studien
BTB	Biblical Theology Bulletin
BTSt	Biblisch-theologische Studien
BVC	Bible et vie chrétienne
BWANT	Beiträge zur Wissenschaft vom Alten und Neuen Testament
BZ	Biblische Zeitschrift
BZNW	Beihefte zur ZNW
CahThéol	Cahiers théologiques
CB	Cultura bíblica
CBFV	Cahiers bibliques. Foi et Vie
CBQ	Catholic Biblical Quarterly
CNRS	Centre national de recherche scientifique
CNT	Coniectanea Neotestamentica
ConBNT	Coniectanea biblica. New Testament
ConBOT	Coniectanea biblica. Old Testament
CSEL	Corpus Scriptorum Ecclesiasticorum Latinorum
DBS	Dictionnaire de la Bible. Supplément
DEB	Dictionnaire encyclopédique de la Bible
DownR	Downside Review

EB	Études Bibliques
EdF	Erträge der Forschung
EHS	Europäische Hochschulschriften
EKK	Evangelisch-katholischer Kommentar zum Neuen Testament
ErfTS	Erfurter theologische Studien
ETL	Ephemerides Theologicae Lovanienses
ETR	Études théologiques et religieuses
EvTh	Evangelische Theologie
EWNT	Exegetisches Wörterbuch zum Neuen Testament
ExpT	Expository Times
FB	Forschung zur Bibel
FRLANT	Forschungen zur Religion und Literatur des Alten und Neuen Testaments
FS	Festschrift
FzB	Forschung zur Bibel
FZPT	Freiburger Zeitschrift für Philosophie und Theologie
GCS	Die griechischen christlichen Schriftsteller der ersten drei Jahrhunderte
GTA	Göttinger theologische Arbeiten
GTB	Gütersloher Taschenbücher
HNT	Handbuch zum Neuen Testament
HTKNT	Herders Theologischer Kommentar zum Neuen Testament
HTR	Harvard Theological Review
HTS	Harvard Theological Studies
HUCA	Hebrew Union College Annual
ICC	International Critical Commentary
IEJ	Israel Exploration Journal
Interpr	Interpretation
IrBS	Irish Biblical Studies
ITQ	Irish Theological Quarterly
JAAR	Journal of the American Academy of Religion
JBL	Journal of Biblical Literature
JETS	Journal of the Evangelical Theological Society
JJS	Journal of Jewish Studies
JPOS	Journal of the Palestine Oriental Society
JR	Journal of Religion
JRS	Journal of Roman Studies
JSHRZ	Jüdische Schriften aus hellenistisch-römischer Zeit
JSNT	Journal for the Study of the New Testament
JSNT SS	Journal for the Study of the New Testament. Supplement Series
JSOT	Journal for the Study of the Old Testament
JSOT SS	Journal for the Study of the Old Testament. Supplement Series
JTS	Journal of Theological Studies
KAT	E. Sellin (ed.), Kommentar zum A.T.
KEK	Kritisch-exegetischer Kommentar über das Neuen Testament
LCL	Loeb Classical Library
LD	Lectio Divina
LingBib	Linguistica Biblica (LB)
LSJM	H.G. Liddel - R. Scott - H.S. Jones - R. McKenzie, A Greek-English Lexikon

LTK	Lexikon für Theologie und Kirche
LTP	Laval théologique et philosophique
LUÅ	Lunds universitets årsskrift
MGH	Monumenta Germaniae Historica
MTS	Münchener theologische Studien
NCB	New Century Bible
NHS	Nag Hammadi Studies
NICNT	New International Commentary on the New Testament
NovTSup	Novum Testamentum. Supplements
NRT	Nouvelle revue théologique
NT	Novum Testamentum
NTA	New Testament Abstracts
NTAbh	Neutestamentliche Abhandlungen
NTD	Das Neue Testament Deutsch
NTOA	Novum Testamentum et Orbis Antiquus
NTS	New Testament Studies
NTSuppl	Supplements to Novum Testamentum
OBO	Orbis Biblicus et Orientalis
ÖBS	Österreichische biblische Studien
ÖTK	Ökumenisch-theologischer Kommentar zum Neuen Testament
OTS	Oudtestamentische Studiën
PerspRelStud	Perspectives in Religious Studies
PG	Patrologia Graeca
PO	Patrologia Orientalis
QD	Quaestiones Disputatae
RB	Revue biblique
RechBib	Recherches bibliques
RevExp	Review and Expositor
RevistB	Revista bíblica
RHPR	Revue d'histoire et de philosophie religieuses
RivBib	Rivista biblica
RNT	Regensburger Neues Testament
RSR	Recherches de science religieuse
RThom	Revue thomiste
RTL	Revue théologique de Louvain
RTP	Revue de théologie et de philosophie
SANT	Studien zum Alten und Neuen Testament
SBB	Stuttgarter biblische Beiträge
SBFLA	Studii biblici franciscani liber annuus
SBL	Society of Biblical Literature
SBL DS	Society of Biblical Literature. Dissertation Series
SBS	Stuttgarter Bibelstudien
SBT	Studia Biblica et Theologica
SC	Sources chrétiennes
ScEs	Science et esprit
SCM	Students Christian Movement
SEÅ	Svensk exegetisk Årsbok
SFEG	Studien der finnischen exegetischen Gesellschaft
SJT	Scottish Journal of Theology

SKK NT	Stuttgarter Klein Kommentar. Neues Testament
SNT	Die Schriften des Neuen Testaments
SNTA	Studiorum Novi Testamenti Auxilia
SNTS	Studiorum Novi Testamenti Societas
SNTS MS	Studiorum Novi Testamenti Societas. Monograph Series
SNTU	Studien zum Neuen Testament und seiner Umwelt
SPCK	Society for Promoting Christian Knowledge
STANT	Studien zum Alten und Neuen Testament
Str-B	H. Strack - P. Billerbeck, Kommentar zum Neuen Testament
StNT	Studien zum Neuen Testament
TB	Theologische Bücherei
TCGNT	B.M. Metzger, A Textual Commentary on the Greek New Testament
TDNT	Theological Dictionary of the New Testament — TWNT
TF	Theologische Forschung
TGl	Theologie und Glaube
THKNT	Theologischer Handkommentar zum Neuen Testament
TLZ	Theologische Literaturzeitung
TQ	Theologische Quartalschrift
TR	Theologische Rundschau
TRE	Theologische Realenzyklopädie
TSAJ	Texte und Studien zum antiken Judentum
TSK	Theologische Studien und Kritiken
TT	Tijdschrift voor theologie (TvT)
TU	Texte und Untersuchungen
TWAT	Theologisches Wörterbuch zum Alten Testament
TWNT	Theologisches Wörterbuch zum Neuen Testament
TZ	Theologische Zeitschrift
UTB	Uni-Taschenbücher
VC	Vigiliae christianae
VF	Verkündigung und Forschung
VT	Vetus Testamentum
WBC	Word Biblical Commentary
WdF	Wege der Forschung
WMANT	Wissenschaftliche Monographien zum Alten und Neuen Testament
ZBKNT	Zürcher Bibelkommentar zum Neuen Testament
ZNW	Zeitschrift für die neutestamentliche Wissenschaft und die Kunde der älteren Kirche
ZKT	Zeitschrift für katholische Theologie
ZTK	Zeitschrift für Theologie und Kirche
ZWT	Zeitschrift für wissenschaftliche Theologie

INDEX OF AUTHORS

References to the notes are added in superscript to the page numbers.
The asterisk indicates a first full bibliographical reference in this volume.

BIBLICAL REFERENCES

5,5	28
5,6	296
5,7-9	28
5,10	296
5,11-12	303
5,13	95[104]
5,14	142
5,15	95[103] 141 142
5,17-20	259 296 297
5,17	297[50] 461 466 471[30.31] 513
5,18	292 461
5,19	28[80] **294-295** 465
5,20	261 296
5,21-48	259 260 281 **295-297**
5,21-26	260[61]
5,22	295
5,28	295
5,32	295 462
5,34	295
5,39	295
5,41	27[77]
5,44	295 414[60]
5,48	261
6,1	296
6,9-13	432[23]
6,9-10	463
6,9	292
6,10	**292-293** 296
6,13	463
6,23-27	59[96]
6,24	29[84]
6,28	446
6,30	452
6,33	296 297
6,34	28
7,2	27[77] 28
7,6	28
7,12	259 296
7,13-14	192
7,15-27	294
7,17	446
7,18	446
7,19	446
7,21-22	294
7,21	192 292 296
7,22-23	192

7,28	293
8–17	28[79] 54[69]
8–9	299[55] 509
8,1	246[21]
8,2	512[31]
8,5-13	40 44[21] 45 46 96[111]
8,5	246[21] 485
8,10-13	301
8,10-12	59
8,10	569
8,11-12	41 60[98]
8,11	192 301[66] 432[23]
8,12	432[23]
8,13	40[5] 58 452 509[23] 569
8,14-17	247[23]
8,14	246[21]
8,17	297[51]
8,18-22	249[32]
8,19-22	30[88,96,112]
8,19-21	432[23]
8,20-22	506
8,22	505 515[40]
8,23-27	603[12]
8,23	246[21]
8,24	40
8,26	452 569
8,27	446[77]
8,28-34	41
8,28	40[3] 246[21]
9	265 267 269
9,1-8	265 266
9,1	246[21]
9,2	569
9,3	267
9,7	246[21]
9,8	446[77]
9,9-13	265 266
9,9	246[21] 249[32]
9,10	246[21] 515
9,11	266
9,13	288 515
9,14-17	265 266
9,14	266
9,16	535
9,18-26	**505-506**
9,18	505 506 507[16]
9,19	246[21] 505 506 515[40]

MARK

1,1–9,41	361
1,1–8,26	248[28]
1	246
1,1-20	14
1,1-15	30 115[16] 150[6] 231[31] 481[26] 497[25]
1,1-13	231
1,1-8	151[10] 220 231 232
1,1-3	301
1,1-2	512[30]
1,1	5 262 300 301 303 305
1,2-5	151[8]
1,2-3	465
1,2	4 **162-168** 464 465
1,3-4	168[66]
1,3	305 465
1,4	167
1,5	246
1,6	246
1,7-8	4 **168-172** 430[15]
1,7	512[30]
1,9-11	430[15]
1,9	109 218 219 231[31] 246
1,10	73
1,11	33[110]
1,12-13	17[26] 73 430[15]
1,12	246
1,14–4,1	426
1,14-20	497[27]
1,14-15	33[110] 231[31]
1,14	15[15] 246
1,15	457
1,16-20	33[110] 255 361[13]
1,16	221[21] 246 514
1,17-18	515
1,17	583
1,20	568
1,21–6,13	14
1,21-34	247[24]
1,21-28	72 73 96[109]109 246
1,21-22	108
1,21	108 246 484 485
1,24-25	251 252
1,24	109 217 568[6]
1,25-27	251
1,25	217 250
1,26	534
1,27	108 217 455 473[40]
1,29-32	246
1,29-31	96[109]
1,29-30	221[21]
1,29	246 485
1,31	458
1,32-34	72 246
1,33	246[20]
1,34	224 247 250
1,35-38	247 252 516[42]
1,35	213[5] 246[20] 247
1,36	221[21]
1,37-38	247
1,37	247
1,38	248
1,39	72 246[20] 247[23.24]
1,40-45	17[27] 73[137] 96[109]
1,40	512[30]
1,41	378
1,44-45	224 250[35]
1,44	250 329 473[40]
1,45	246[20] 458
2,1–8,26	46[30]
2,1–3,6	7 259 497 **521-530**
2,1-12	96[109] 511 529
2,1-4	17[26] 529
2,1-3	495[13]
2,1-2	370 512
2,1	246[20] 378 480 514[36]
2,2	370 458
2,4	540[11]
2,5	473[40] 566 569
2,6-10	511
2,6-7	259
2,6	370
2,7	162
2,8	162
2,9	473[40]
2,12	217
2,13-17	512[29] **512-516** 529
2,13	246[20] 370 511 512 513 514
2,14	246[20] 512 513 514 515 516
2,15-17	45 512 513
2,15	246[20] 512 513 514 515 516[41]
2,16-17	37[134] 94

OLD TESTAMENT

31,1	293
31,9	300
31,24	293 300
32,5	456 543
32,44-45	293

JUDGES

2,1	564
13,25	571[12]

I SAMUEL (1 REG)

5,3-4	379[70]
14,45	337
18,26	375[57]

II SAMUEL (2 REG)

3,6	379[70]

I KINGS (3 REG)

1,52	337
8,44	490
8,48	490
13,30	477
17,17-24	473[40]
19,2	104
19,10	104
19,11	250
19,14	104

II KINGS (4 REG)

2,8-9	379[70]
2,9-11	373[53]
2,11	274
4,32-37	473[40]
5,3-4	379[70]
7,12	375[57]
17,7	478

I CHRONICLES

17,11	375
22,4	483[33]

II CHRONICLES

13,15	379[70]
15,6	323
36,23	290

EZRA

3,7	483[33]

TOBIT

1,1	303
8,20	375[57]
10,1	375
14,5	375[57]

JUDITH

2,28	483[33]

I MACCABEES

2,58	373[53]
3,60	292[37]
5,15	483[31]

JOB

13,16	328

PSALMS

22	114[10] 275
22,2-3	275[24]
22,4-6	275[24]
22,19	402
69,21	274
91,11	291[35]
95,7	286[16]
117,22	437 438[46]
118,22	102[132] 104
129,8	305
148,9	570[11]

PROVERBS

2,1	446[77]

APOCRYPHAL WRITINGS

OTHER ANCIENT WRITINGS

Christian Authors

Jewish Authors

Other Ancient Writings

LIST OF CONTRIBUTORS

BIBLIOTHECA EPHEMERIDUM THEOLOGICARUM LOVANIENSIUM

LEUVEN UNIVERSITY PRESS / UITGEVERIJ PEETERS LEUVEN

SERIES I

* = Out of print

*1. *Miscellanea dogmatica in honorem Eximii Domini J. Bittremieux*, 1947.

*2-3. *Miscellanea moralia in honorem Eximii Domini A. Janssen*, 1948.

*4. G. PHILIPS, *La grâce des justes de l'Ancien Testament*, 1948.

*5. G. PHILIPS, *De ratione instituendi tractatum de gratia nostrae sanctificationis*, 1953.

6-7. *Recueil Lucien Cerfaux. Études d'exégèse et d'histoire religieuse*, 1954. 504 et 577 p. FB 1000 par tome. Cf. *infra*, nos 18 et 71 (t. III).

8. G. THILS, *Histoire doctrinale du mouvement œcuménique*, 1955. Nouvelle édition, 1963. 338 p. FB 135.

*9. *Études sur l'Immaculée Conception*, 1955.

*10. J.A. O'DONOHOE, *Tridentine Seminary Legislation*, 1957.

*11. G. THILS, *Orientations de la théologie*, 1958.

*12-13. J. COPPENS, A. DESCAMPS, É. MASSAUX (ed.), *Sacra Pagina. Miscellanea Biblica Congressus Internationalis Catholici de Re Biblica*, 1959.

*14. *Adrien VI, le premier Pape de la contre-réforme*, 1959.

*15. F. CLAEYS BOUUAERT, *Les déclarations et serments imposés par la loi civile aux membres du clergé belge sous le Directoire (1795-1801)*, 1960.

*16. G. THILS, *La «Théologie œcuménique». Notion-Formes-Démarches*, 1960.

17. G. THILS, *Primauté pontificale et prérogatives épiscopales. «Potestas ordinaria» au Concile du Vatican*, 1961. 103 p. FB 50.

*18. *Recueil Lucien Cerfaux*, t. III, 1962. Cf. *infra*, n° 71.

*19. *Foi et réflexion philosophique. Mélanges F. Grégoire*, 1961.

*20. *Mélanges G. Ryckmans*, 1963.

21. G. THILS, *L'infaillibilité du peuple chrétien «in credendo»*, 1963. 67 p. FB 50.

*22. J. FÉRIN & L. JANSSENS, *Progestogènes et morale conjugale*, 1963.

*23. *Collectanea Moralia in honorem Eximii Domini A. Janssen*, 1964.

24. H. CAZELLES (ed.), *De Mari à Qumrân. L'Ancien Testament. Son milieu. Ses Écrits. Ses relectures juives* (Hommage J. Coppens, I), 1969. 158*-370 p. FB 900.

*25. I. DE LA POTTERIE (ed.), *De Jésus aux évangiles. Tradition et rédaction dans les évangiles synoptiques* (Hommage J. Coppens, II), 1967.

26. G. THILS & R.E. BROWN (ed.), *Exégèse et théologie* (Hommage J. Coppens, III), 1968. 328 p. FB 700.

27. J. COPPENS (ed.), *Ecclesia a Spiritu sancto edocta. Hommage à Mgr G. Philips*, 1970. 640 p. FB 1000.

28. J. COPPENS (ed.), *Sacerdoce et célibat. Études historiques et théologiques*, 1971. 740 p. FB 700.

29. M. DIDIER (ed.), *L'évangile selon Matthieu. Rédaction et théologie*, 1972. 432 p. FB 1000.
*30. J. KEMPENEERS, *Le Cardinal van Roey en son temps*, 1971.

SERIES II

31. F. NEIRYNCK, *Duality in Mark. Contributions to the Study of the Markan Redaction*, 1972. Revised edition with Supplementary Notes, 1988. 252 p. FB 1200.
32. F. NEIRYNCK (ed.), *L'évangile de Luc. Problèmes littéraires et théologiques*, 1973. *L'évangile de Luc – The Gospel of Luke*. Revised and enlarged edition, 1989. x-590 p. FB 2200.
33. C. BREKELMANS (ed.), *Questions disputées d'Ancien Testament. Méthode et théologie*, 1974. *Continuing Questions in Old Testament Method and Theology*. Revised and enlarged edition by M. VERVENNE, 1989. 245 p. FB 1200.
34. M. SABBE (ed.), *L'évangile selon Marc. Tradition et rédaction*, 1974. Nouvelle édition augmentée, 1988. 601 p. FB 2400.
35. B. WILLAERT (ed.), *Philosophie de la religion – Godsdienstfilosofie. Miscellanea Albert Dondeyne*, 1974. Nouvelle édition, 1987. 458 p. FB 1600.
36. G. PHILIPS, *L'union personnelle avec le Dieu vivant. Essai sur l'origine et le sens de la grâce créée*, 1974. Édition révisée, 1989. 299 p. FB 1000.
37. F. NEIRYNCK, in collaboration with T. HANSEN and F. VAN SEGBROECK, *The Minor Agreements of Matthew and Luke against Mark with a Cumulative List*, 1974. 330 p. FB 900.
38. J. COPPENS, *Le messianisme et sa relève prophétique. Les anticipations vétérotestamentaires. Leur accomplissement en Jésus*, 1974. Édition révisée, 1989. XIII-265 p. FB 1000.
39. D. SENIOR, *The Passion Narrative according to Matthew. A Redactional Study*, 1975. New impression, 1982. 440 p. FB 1000.
40. J. DUPONT (ed.), *Jésus aux origines de la christologie*, 1975. Nouvelle édition augmentée, 1989. 458 p. FB 1500.
41. J. COPPENS (ed.), *La notion biblique de Dieu*, 1976. Réimpression, 1985. 519 p. FB 1600.
42. J. LINDEMANS & H. DEMEESTER (ed.), *Liber Amicorum Monseigneur W. Onclin*, 1976. XXII-396 p. FB 1000.
43. R.E. HOECKMAN (ed.), *Pluralisme et œcuménisme en recherches théologiques. Mélanges offerts au R.P. Dockx, O.P.*, 1976. 316 p. FB 1000.
44. M. DE JONGE (ed.), *L'Évangile de Jean. Sources, rédaction, théologie*, 1977. Réimpression, 1987. 416 p. FB 1500.
45. E.J.M. VAN EIJL (ed.), *Facultas S. Theologiae Lovaniensis 1432-1797. Bijdragen tot haar geschiedenis. Contributions to its History. Contributions à son histoire*, 1977. 570 p. FB 1700.
46. M. DELCOR (ed.), *Qumrân. Sa piété, sa théologie et son milieu*, 1978. 432 p. FB 1700.
47. M. CAUDRON (ed.), *Faith and Society. Foi et Société. Geloof en maatschappij. Acta Congressus Internationalis Theologici Lovaniensis 1976*, 1978. 304 p. FB 1150.

48. J. KREMER (ed.), *Les Actes des Apôtres. Traditions, rédaction, théologie*, 1979. 590 p. FB 1700.
49. F. NEIRYNCK, avec la collaboration de J. DELOBEL, T. SNOY, G. VAN BELLE, F. VAN SEGBROECK, *Jean et les Synoptiques. Examen critique de l'exégèse de M.-É. Boismard*, 1979. XII-428 p. FB 1400.
50. J. COPPENS , *La relève apocalyptique du messianisme royal*. I. *La royauté – Le règne – Le royaume de Dieu. Cadre de la relève apocalyptique*, 1979. 325 p. FB 1000.
51. M. GILBERT (ed.), *La Sagesse de l'Ancien Testament*, 1979. Nouvelle édition mise à jour, 1990. 455 p. FB 1500.
52. B. DEHANDSCHUTTER, *Martyrium Polycarpi. Een literair-kritische studie*, 1979. 296 p. FB 1000.
53. J. LAMBRECHT (ed.), *L'Apocalypse johannique et l'Apocalyptique dans le Nouveau Testament*, 1980. 458 p. FB 1400.
54. P.-M. BOGAERT (ed.), *Le Livre de Jérémie. Le prophète et son milieu. Les oracles et leur transmission*, 1981. 408 p. FB 1500.
55. J. COPPENS, *La relève apocalyptique du messianisme royal*. III. *Le Fils de l'homme néotestamentaire*, 1981. XIV-192 p. FB 800.
56. J. VAN BAVEL & M. SCHRAMA (ed.), *Jansénius et le Jansénisme dans les Pays-Bas. Mélanges Lucien Ceyssens*, 1982. 247 p. FB 1000.
57. J.H. WALGRAVE, *Selected Writings – Thematische geschriften. Thomas Aquinas, J.H. Newman, Theologia Fundamentalis*. Edited by G. DE SCHRIJVER & J.J. KELLY, 1982. XLIII-425 p. FB 1400.
58. F. NEIRYNCK & F. VAN SEGBROECK, avec la collaboration de E. MANNING, *Ephemerides Theologicae Lovanienses 1924-1981. Tables générales. (Bibliotheca Ephemeridum Theologicarum Lovaniensium 1947-1981)*, 1982. 400 p. FB 1600.
59. J. DELOBEL (ed.), *Logia. Les paroles de Jésus – The Sayings of Jesus. Mémorial Joseph Coppens*, 1982. 647 p. FB 2000.
60. F. NEIRYNCK, *Evangelica. Gospel Studies – Études d'évangile. Collected Essays*. Edited by F. VAN SEGBROECK, 1982. XIX-1036 p. FB 2000.
61. J. COPPENS, *La relève apocalyptique du messianisme royal*. II. *Le Fils d'homme vétéro- et intertestamentaire*. Édition posthume par J. LUST, 1983. XVII-272 p. FB 1000.
62. J.J. KELLY, *Baron Friedrich von Hügel's Philosophy of Religion*, 1983. 232 p. FB 1500.
63. G. DE SCHRIJVER, *Le merveilleux accord de l'homme et de Dieu. Étude de l'analogie de l'être chez Hans Urs von Balthasar*, 1983. 344 p. FB 1500.
64. J. GROOTAERS & J.A. SELLING, *The 1980 Synod of Bishops: «On the Role of the Family». An Exposition of the Event and an Analysis of its Texts*. Preface by Prof. emeritus L. JANSSENS, 1983. 375 p. FB 1500.
65. F. NEIRYNCK & F. VAN SEGBROECK, *New Testament Vocabulary. A Companion Volume to the Concordance*, 1984. XVI-494 p. FB 2000.
66. R.F. COLLINS, *Studies on the First Letter to the Thessalonians*, 1984. XI-415 p. FB 1500.
67. A. PLUMMER, *Conversations with Dr. Döllinger 1870-1890*. Edited with Introduction and Notes by R. BOUDENS, with the collaboration of L. KENIS, 1985. LIV-360 p. FB 1800.

68. N. LOHFINK (ed.), *Das Deuteronomium. Entstehung, Gestalt und Botschaft / Deuteronomy: Origin, Form and Message*, 1985. XI-382 p. FB 2000.

69. P.F. FRANSEN, *Hermeneutics of the Councils and Other Studies*. Collected by H.E. MERTENS & F. DE GRAEVE, 1985. 543 p. FB 1800.

70. J. DUPONT, *Études sur les Évangiles synoptiques*. Présentées par F. NEIRYNCK, 1985. 2 tomes, XXI-IX-1210 p. FB 2800.

71. *Recueil Lucien Cerfaux*, t. III, 1962. Nouvelle édition revue et complétée, 1985. LXXX-458 p. FB 1600.

72. J. GROOTAERS, *Primauté et collégialité. Le dossier de Gérard Philips sur la Nota Explicativa Praevia (Lumen gentium, Chap. III)*. Présenté avec introduction historique, annotations et annexes. Préface de G. THILS, 1986. 222 p. FB 1000.

73. A. VANHOYE (ed.), *L'apôtre Paul. Personnalité, style et conception du ministère*, 1986. XIII-470 p. FB 2600.

74. J. LUST (ed.), *Ezekiel and His Book. Textual and Literary Criticism and their Interrelation*, 1986. X-387 p. FB 2700.

75. É. MASSAUX, *Influence de l'Évangile de saint Matthieu sur la littérature chrétienne avant saint Irénée*. Réimpression anastatique présentée par F. NEIRYNCK. *Supplément: Bibliographie 1950-1985*, par B. DEHAND-SCHUTTER, 1986. XXVII-850 p. FB 2500.

76. L. CEYSSENS & J.A.G. TANS, *Autour de l'Unigenitus. Recherches sur la genèse de la Constitution*, 1987. XXVI-845 p. FB 2500.

77. A. DESCAMPS, *Jésus et l'Église. Études d'exégèse et de théologie*. Préface de Mgr A. HOUSSIAU, 1987. XLV-641 p. FB 2500.

78. J. DUPLACY, *Études de critique textuelle du Nouveau Testament*. Présentées par J. DELOBEL, 1987. xxvii-431 p. FB 1800.

79. E.J.M. VAN EIJL (ed.), *L'image de C. Jansénius jusqu'à la fin du XVIIIᵉ siècle*, 1987. 258 p. FB 1250.

80. E. BRITO, *La Création selon Schelling. Universum*, 1987. XXXV-646 p. FB 2980.

81. J. VERMEYLEN (ed.), *The Book of Isaiah – Le Livre d'Isaïe. Les oracles et leurs relectures. Unité et complexité de l'ouvrage*, 1989. X-472 p. FB 2700.

82. G. VAN BELLE, *Johannine Bibliography 1966-1985. A Cumulative Bibliography on the Fourth Gospel*, 1988. XVII-563 p. FB 2700.

83. J.A. SELLING (ed.), *Personalist Morals. Essays in Honor of Professor Louis Janssens*, 1988. VIII-344 p. FB 1200.

84. M.-É. BOISMARD, *Moïse ou Jésus. Essai de christologie johannique*, 1988. XVI-241 p. FB 1000.

85. J.A. DICK, *The Malines Conversations Revisited*, 1989. 278 p. FB 1500.

86. J.-M. SEVRIN (ed.), *The New Testament in Early Christianity – La réception des écrits néotestamentaires dans le christianisme primitif*, 1989. XVI-406 p. FB 2500.

87. R.F. COLLINS (ed.), *The Thessalonian Correspondence*, 1990. XV-546 p. FB 3000.

88. F. VAN SEGBROECK, *The Gospel of Luke. A Cumulative Bibliography 1973-1988*, 1989. 241 p. FB 1200.

89. G. THILS, *Primauté et infaillibilité du Pontife Romain à Vatican I et autres études d'ecclésiologie*, 1989. XI-422 p. FB 1850.

90. A. Vergote, *Explorations de l'espace théologique. Études de théologie et de philosophie de la religion*, 1990. XVI-709 p. FB 2000.
91. J.C. de Moor, *The Rise of Yahwism: The Roots of Israelite Monotheism*, 1990. XII-315 p. FB 1250.
92. B. Bruning, M. Lamberigts & J. Van Houtem (eds.), *Collectanea Augustiniana. Mélanges T.J. van Bavel*, 1990. 2 tomes, XXXVIII-VIII-1074 p. FB 3000.
93. A. de Halleux, *Patrologie et œcuménisme. Recueil d'études*, 1990. XVI-887 p. FB 3000.
94. C. Brekelmans & J. Lust (eds.), *Pentateuchal and Deuteronomistic Studies: Papers Read at the XIIIth IOSOT Congress Leuven 1989*, 1990. 307 p. FB 1500.
95. D.L. Dungan (ed.), *The Interrelations of the Gospels. A Symposium Led by M.-É. Boismard – W.R. Farmer – F. Neirynck, Jerusalem 1984*, 1990. XXXI-672 p. FB 3000.
96. G.D. Kilpatrick, *The Principles and Practice of New Testament Textual Criticism. Collected Essays.* Edited by J.K. Elliott, 1990. XXXVIII-489 p. FB 3000.
97. G. Alberigo (ed.), *Christian Unity. The Council of Ferrara-Florence: 1438/39 – 1989*, 1991. X-681 p. FB 3000.
98. M. Sabbe, *Studia Neotestamentica. Collected Essays*, 1991. XVI-573 p. FB 2000.
99. F. Neirynck, *Evangelica II: 1982-1991. Collected Essays.* Edited by F. Van Segbroeck, 1991. XIX-874 p. FB 2800.
100. F. Van Segbroeck, C.M. Tuckett, G. Van Belle & J. Verheyden (eds.), *The Four Gospels 1992. Festschrift Frans Neirynck*, 1992. 3 volumes, XVII-X-X-2668 p. FB 5000.

Series III

101. A. Denaux (ed.), *John and the Synoptics*, 1992. XXII-696 p. FB 3000.
102. F. Neirynck, J. Verheyden, F. Van Segbroeck, G. Van Oyen & R. Corstjens, *The Gospel of Mark. A Cumulative Bibliography: 1950-1990*, 1992. XII-717 p. FB 2700.
103. M. Simon, *Un catéchisme universel pour l'Église catholique. Du Concile de Trente à nos jours*, 1992. XIV-461 p. FB 2200.
104. L. Ceyssens, *Le sort de la bulle Unigenitus. Recueil d'études offert à Lucien Ceyssens à l'occasion de son 90e anniversaire.* Présenté par M. Lamberigts, 1992. XXVI-641 p. FB 2000.
105. R.J. Daly (ed.), *Origeniana Quinta. Papers of the 5th International Origen Congress, Boston College, 14-18 August 1989*, 1992. XVII-635 p. FB 2700.
106. A.S. van der Woude (ed.), *The Book of Daniel in the Light of New Findings*, 1993. XVIII-574 p. FB 3000.
107. J. Famerée, *L'ecclésiologie d'Yves Congar avant Vatican II: Histoire et Église. Analyse et reprise critique*, 1992. 497 p. FB 2600.
108. C. Begg, *Josephus' Account of the Early Divided Monarchy (AJ 8, 212-420). Rewriting the Bible*, 1993. IX-386 p. FB 2400.

109. J. BULCKENS & H. LOMBAERTS (eds.), *L'enseignement de la religion catholique à l'école secondaire. Enjeux pour la nouvelle Europe*, 1993. XII-260 p. FB 1250
110. C. FOCANT (ed.), *The Synoptic Gospels. Source Criticism and the New Literary Criticism*, 1993. XXXIX-670 p. FB 3000.